Studies in Logic
Volume 95

Transparent Intensional Logic
Selected Recent Essays

Volume 85
Reason to Dissent. Proceedings of the 3rd European Conference on Argumentation. Volume I
Catarina Dutilh Novaes, Henrike Jansen, Jan Albert van Laar and Bart Verheij, eds.

Volume 86
Reason to Dissent. Proceedings of the 3rd European Conference on Argumentation. Volume II
Catarina Dutilh Novaes, Henrike Jansen, Jan Albert van Laar and Bart Verheij, eds.

Volume 87
Reason to Dissent. Proceedings of the 3rd European Conference on Argumentation. Volume III
Catarina Dutilh Novaes, Henrike Jansen, Jan Albert van Laar and Bart Verheij, eds.

Volume 88
Belief Attitudes, Fine-Grained Hyperintensionality and Type-Theoretic Logic
Jiří Raclavský

Volume 89
Essays on Set Theory
Akihiro Kanamori

Volume 90
Model Theory for Beginners. 15 Lectures
Roman Kossak

Volume 91
A View of Connexive Logics
Nissim Francez

Volume 92
Aristotle's Syllogistic Underlying Logic: His Model with his Proofs of Soundness and Completeness
George Boger

Volume 93
Truth and Knowledge
Karl Schlechta

Volume 94
A Lambda Calculus Satellite
Henk Barendregt and Guilio Manzonetto

Volume 95
Transparent Intensional Logic. Selected Recent Essays
Marie Duží, Bjørn Jespersen, Miloš Kosterec and Daniela Vacek, eds.

Studies in Logic Series Editor
Dov Gabbay   dov.gabbay@kcl.ac.uk

Transparent Intensional Logic
Selected Recent Essays

Edited by

Marie Duží

Bjørn Jespersen

Miloš Kosterec

Daniela Vacek

© Individual author and College Publications, 2023
All rights reserved.

ISBN 978-1-84890-412-5

College Publications
Scientific Director: Dov Gabbay
Managing Director: Jane Spurr

http://www.collegepublications.co.uk

All rights reserved. No part of this publication may be reproduced, stored in a retrieval system or transmitted in any form, or by any means, electronic, mechanical, photocopying, recording or otherwise without prior permission, in writing, from the publisher.

PREFACE

This tome includes a selection of twenty-seven papers published between 2010 and 2022. It is intended to provide a survey of some major developments within the theory of Transparent Intensional Logic and its applications over the last decade. In this capacity the tome also serves as a successor to the book *Procedural Semantics for Hyperintensional Logic*, authored by Marie Duží, Bjørn Jespersen and Pavel Materna, and published by Springer-Verlag in 2010. The present selection of papers is divided into six thematically organized chapters. An extensive introduction, written specifically for this book, provides a summary of the results obtained within these six different areas.

Transparent Intensional Logic has strong roots in the former Czechoslovakia, and many important papers are still being written in Czech and Slovak, as well as Polish. We would like to give a nod to several of those whose work is not included in this volume. Some of these researchers are no longer working on Transparent Intensional Logic, while others have contributed by way of constructive criticism. They include Pavel Cmorej, Pavel Materna, František Gahér, Marián Zouhar, Vladimír Svoboda, Jiří Raclavský, Lukáš Bielik, Aleš Horák, Adam Olszewski, František Krejčí, Tomáš Chrz, Tomáš Vlk, Jitka Koukolíková, Petr Kuchyňka, Ivo Pezlar, Marek Menšík, Petr Gajdoš, Jaroslav Müller, Nikola Ciprich, Jakub Macek, Ondřej Kohut, Dominik Sadloň, and several others.

This research was supported by the University of Oxford project *New Horizons for Science and Religion in Central and Eastern Europe*, funded by the John Templeton Foundation (*Pavel Tichý on Individuals, Roles, and God* subgrant; Marie Duží, Miloš Kosterec, and Daniela Vacek). The opinions expressed in these publications are those of the authors and do not necessarily reflect the view of the John Templeton Foundation. This work was also supported by the SGS grant *Application of Formal Methods in Knowledge Modelling and Software Engineering V*, No. SP2022/123, VŠB-Technical University of Ostrava, Czech Republic (Marie Duží and Bjørn Jespersen).

We wish to thank Jane Spurr and Michael Gabbay at College Publications for the extensive and thorough editorial work that went into producing this volume of around eight hundred pages.

March 2023
Marie Duží
Bjørn Jespersen
Miloš Kosterec
Daniela Vacek (née Glavaničová)

CONTENTS

Introduction 1
   Marie Duží, Bjørn Jespersen, Miloš Kosterec and Daniela Vacek

Hyperintensional Logic

Transparent quantification into hyperpropositional attitudes *de dicto* 27
   Bjørn Jespersen and Marie Duží

Transparent quantification into hyperintensional objectual attitudes 73
   Marie Duží and Bjørn Jespersen

Transparent quantification into hyperpropositional contexts *de re* 117
   Marie Duží and Bjørn Jespersen

Qualifying quantifying-in 159
   Bjørn Jespersen

The paradox of inference and the non-triviality of analytic information . . . 193
   Marie Duží

Co-Hyperintensionality, Synonymy and Propositional Unity

First among equals: co-hyperintensionality for structured propositions . . . 233
Bjørn Jespersen

Anatomy of a proposition 249
Bjørn Jespersen

If structured propositions are logical procedures then how are procedures
   individuated? 289
Marie Duží

Procedural isomorphism, analytic information and β-conversion by value . 325
Marie Duží and Bjørn Jespersen

Deduction and Substitution

Substitution inconsistencies in Transparent Intensional Logic 345
Miloš Kosterec

Substitution contradiction, its resolution and the Church-Rosser Theorem
   in TIL 363
Miloš Kosterec

A hyperintensional theory of intelligent question answering in TIL 377
Marie Duží and Michal Fait

Logic of Intensions

(a) presuppositions, requisites and prerequisites

Negation and presupposition, truth and falsity 415
Marie Duží

Presuppositions and two kinds of negation 447
Marie Duží

How to unify Russellian and Strawsonian definite descriptions 467
Marie Duží

An intensional solution to the bike puzzle of intentional identity 485
Bjørn Jespersen

(b) property modifiers

Limiting cases of modal modification: reply to Kosterec 497
  Bjørn Jespersen

Iterated privation and positive predication 503
  Bjørn Jespersen, Massimiliano Carrara and Marie Duží

Left subsectivity: how to infer that a round peg is round 527
  Bjørn Jespersen

Structured lexical concepts, property modifiers, and Transparent Intensional
  Logic 541
  Bjørn Jespersen

A new logic of technical malfunction 567
  Bjørn Jespersen and Massimiliano Carrara

Questions, Answers, Obligations and Norms

Modelling dynamic behaviour of agents in a multiagent world: logical
  analysis of wh-questions and answers 603
  Martina Číhalová and Marie Duží

Δ-TIL and normative systems 635
  Daniela Glavaničová

Fiction and Religion

Rethinking role realism 655
  Daniela Glavaničová

Impossible individuals as necessarily empty individual concepts 671
  Marie Duží, Bjørn Jespersen and Daniela Glavaničová

St. Anselm's ontological arguments 697
  Marie Duží

Ambiguities in natural language and ontological proofs 721
  Marie Duží

Introduction

Marie Duží
Bjørn Jespersen
Miloš Kosterec
Daniela Vacek (née Glavaničová)

Transparent Intensional Logic has been quite lively since the publication of the 550-page tome *Procedural Semantics for Hyperintensional Logic* by Springer in 2010. In fact, the preface stated, in a confident tone, that if TIL 'keeps evolving at its current pace, another update will be called for within the next 5-10 years'. Meanwhile, thirteen years have gone by, and TIL has covered a lot of ground since we last took stock. The areas that have been covered over the last decade include not least the following topics: existential quantification into various kinds of hyperintensional contexts, property modification, topic and focus articulation, inferences with hyperpropositions, varying degrees of hyperintensional individuation, various rules of the lambda calculus, fictional and religious discourse, and impossibility.

So, another update was indeed called for. One way of going about this was to revise the 2010 book extensively. Another was to simply write a new book from scratch with the same broad compass. Both would have been gargantuan enterprises, however, and the book might likely never have made the delicate transition from the purely possible to the contingently actual. A third option, however, was to compile the central papers published in 2010 or later into one volume. And that is what we ended up doing. At around 750 pages, the resulting volume is indeed voluminous, almost voluptuous, but having all of them in one place makes it easy to access, compare and cross-reference these 27 papers that were originally published across a wide range of venues. We have organised the papers under the following six headings: hyperintensional logic; co-hyperintensionality, synonymy and propositional unity; deduction and substitution; logic of intensions: (a) presuppositions, requisites and prerequisites, (b) property modifiers; questions, answers, obligations and norms; fiction, religion, and impossibility. These sections are not exhaustive, though. TIL has also been applied to, for instance, knowledge paradoxes, concepts of truth, connections with the proof theory and intuitionistic logic, and topics from computer science. What we have gathered in this volume are papers that cover the themes that TIL has been applied to more extensively over the last decade.

This volume stands alongside other milestones in the development of TIL, such as Pavel Tichý's 1988 book *The Foundations of Frege's Logic*, Pavel Materna's 1998 monograph *Concepts and Objects*, the 900-page collection *Tichý's Collected Papers in Logic and Philosophy*, published in 2004, as well as the 2010 book. Fortunately, whereas TIL used to be a little-known, ill-understood and underappreciated theory on the fringes of philosophical logic, it has now entered the mainstream and is regularly mentioned in discussions of fine-grained intensionality. At the same time, we are well aware that TIL is not likely to become the default theory, the way Montague's intensional logic used to be the default among linguists, philosophers of language and philosophical logicians. First and foremost, TIL does not subscribe to model-theoretic semantics (except for its first-order fragment, which is the least interesting) but to an interpreted realist version of procedural (or computational or operational) semantics. TIL also comes with some ontological assumptions that not everyone is prepared to take on board, not least objective ('Platonic') computations and an ever-ascending type hierarchy. Yet these features are the reason that TIL is not just a one-trick pony designed to deal with a particular cluster of problems within a particular field.[1] Rather, it is a framework for a systematic, non-reductionist semantic and logical analysis of representational systems of (natural) language. A framework with considerable expressive power is required to make this project viable.

---

[1] As Tichý put it: "[Transparent Intensional Logic is] not only a useful tool for diagnosing the flaws and ambiguities in Frege's logic but also the right medium for modelling our whole conceptual scheme." (1988, ix).

Below follows a summary of each of the six chapters.

Chapter 1 Hyperintensional logic

It is a fundamental tenet of TIL that transparency is pervasive. This means that there are no opaque contexts that would either call for some bespoke non-standard logic and semantics, in which the terms acquire a different meaning and their logical behaviour becomes another, or simply obstruct the application of any non-trivial logic and semantics.[2] Opaque contexts are standardly presented as those in which the rules of basic extensional logic do not hold; in particular, they seem to block the substitution of identicals *salva veritate* and the introduction of existential generalisation ('quantifying-in'). If the intensional contexts of modal logic were opaque, then hyperintensional contexts would be no less so.

Nowadays, hardly any logician or philosopher of language doubts the existence of hyperintensional contexts. It is, however, usually quite a different story when one is challenged to offer a positive delineation or specification of these contexts. Current hyperintensional logics usually view hyperintensions as atomic entities and define axioms and rules that operate on them.[3] TIL follows a different path in virtue of its conception of fine-grained meanings as abstract, algorith-

---

[2] Arguable exceptions are contexts of direct quotation and poetry. See E. Lepore (2009), 'The heresy of paraphrase: when the medium really is the message', *Midwest Studies in Philosophy*, 33, 177-197, and P. Lamarque (2009), 'The elusiveness of poetic meaning', *Ratio*, 22(4), 398-420.

[3] For a representative example, see, for instance, H. Leitgeb, 'HYPE: A system of hyperintensional logic (with an application to semantic paradoxes)', *Journal of Philosophical Logic*, 48(2): 305–405 (2019). For a summary of current approaches to hyperintensionality, see F. Berto and D. Nolan, 'Hyperintensionality', *The Stanford Encyclopedia of Philosophy* (Summer 2021 Edition), Edward N. Zalta (ed.), https://plato.stanford.edu/archives/sum2021/entries/hyperintensionality/ . Note that what this entry says about how TIL handles substitution of pairs like {'is a groundhog', 'is a woodchuck'} and {'Robin Hood', 'Robin of Locksley'}, which are not on an equal footing, anyway, is incorrect. The TIL analysis of the latter sort of pair can be found in Duží et al. (2010, 298-99). The TIL analysis of the former sort of pair can be found in Jespersen (ms.), 'A misdiagnosed conundrum about *woodchuck* and 'groundhog'.'

mically structured procedures that produce (or, in rigorously defined cases, fail to produce) an entity denoted by a given term or phrase. These procedures can occur in one of two distinct modes, either *executed* or *displayed*. In the parlance of TIL, hyperintensional contexts are those in which procedures occur in the displayed mode. It means that the very procedure, and not its product (if any), occurs as a functional argument and as such, lends itself to logical manipulation. For instance, it can now occur as the complement of an attitude, or it can have parts of it operated on, as is the case with existential quantification.

One benefit of being able to display procedures is that fundamental logical laws remain valid also for hyperintensional contexts. This explains why we describe TIL as an extensional logic of hyperintensions. The publications under this heading prove and exemplify the validity of laws of extensional logic also in non-extensional contexts. The general point is that laws such as the substitution of identicals and existential generalisation are valid — *provided they are applied properly*. The bar goes up for what qualifies as identicals and what types of entities can be quantified over. Note that the criteria of identity are the same, both outside and inside non-extensional contexts. The same exacting criteria that apply to the latter also apply to the former. Thus, for instance, it is not so that Hesperus and Phosphorus would be identical in extensional contexts and not identical in non-extensional contexts. Another noteworthy feature is that operations such as substitution and generalisation are not syntactic. Instead, they operate directly on meanings (procedures serving in the role of linguistic meanings), which are abstract, extra-linguistic entities.[4] Likewise, variables are not terms but procedures. A variable that occurs within a hyperintensional context is not free for substitution because it occurs displayed. Hence, the so-called substitution method was developed in order to operate on displayed variables. The substitution method is a technical specification of how to replace the

---

[4]This, of course, does not imply that TIL does not include substitution understood as syntactic replacement as well. Linguistic substitution is, however, not the sort of substitution used in logical investigations.

occurrences of a variable within a procedure with another procedure. One replaces all the occurrences of a variable x within a procedure A with a procedure B. The result is another adjusted procedure C. The method also makes it possible to apply existential generalisation within hyperintensional contexts. One is able to present the occurrence of a variable as free for lambda-binding and, consequently, for the application of an existential quantifier.

The first four papers describe in great detail how to quantify into three different kinds of hyperintensional attitude contexts: (i) propositional *de dicto* (e.g., *believing that whatever does not kill you makes you stronger without believing that whatever does not make you stronger kills you*), (ii) objectual, i.e., non-propositional (e.g., *calculating the sum of five and seven; seeking an abominable snowman without seeking a yeti*), and (iii) propositional *de re* (e.g., *believing of the pope that he is not the pope; the pope being such that he is believed not to be the pope*). The first paper included in this chapter, Jespersen and Duží (2022), 'Transparent quantification into hyperpropositional contexts *de dicto*' focuses on (i). The second paper, Duží and Jespersen (2015), 'Transparent quantification into hyperintensional objectual attitudes' in turn focuses on (ii). The third paper, Duží and Jespersen (2012), 'Transparent quantification into hyperintensional contexts *de re*' is concerned with (iii). The fourth paper in this chapter is Jespersen (2015), 'Qualifying quantifying-in'. Quantifying-in is philosophically interesting because it challenges a theory to be explicit about what entities it is willing and able to quantify over. It is also technically interesting because it forces a theory to spell out exactly how a quantifier outside the hyperintensional context succeeds in binding occurrences of its variable inside the context, how substitution works for hyperintensional contexts, and which positions the theory is willing and able to quantify into.[5] Thus, quantifying-in serves methodologically as a stress test for hyperintensional frameworks.

---

[5] We are speaking loosely, as in a λ-calculus all variable-binding is λ-binding (apart from Trivialization-binding, which is unique to TIL). The set (characteristic function) formed by abstracting over a truth-value is the argument for the quantifier, which is a function from sets to truth-values.

The fifth and final paper, Duží (2010), 'The paradox of inference and the non-triviality of analytic information', exploits TIL procedures to solve the *paradox of inference*.[6] The problem gives rise to the question of how deductive logic can serve as a useful epistemological tool. As many fellow logicians and mathematicians will no doubt agree, the conclusion of a valid argument is often very useful and can often be surprising, too (yes, there are surprises in logic). It seems evident that there is *something* that we *learn* when deducing the conclusion of a valid argument. The paper shows that the paradox of inference arises if only the *propositions*, or *truth-values* (in the case of mathematical arguments), denoted by the premises and conclusion, are considered and evaporates if considering instead the *procedures* encoded by the premises and the conclusion. While the proposition (in the empirical case) or the truth-value (in the mathematical case) denoted by the conclusion is informationally contained in the premises, the *procedure* itself need *not* be (namely, whenever the argument is non-circular). Provided it is not so contained, then what is learnt when drawing the conclusion is a new procedure producing the relevant proposition/truth-value. There is a broader problem connected with the paradox, though. This is the question of why and how analytically true sentences are informative and why and how analytically equivalent sentences can yield different information. The paper differentiates between analytic and empirical information, and shows that while analytically true sentences convey no empirical information on the state of the empirical world, they provide analytic information about a way how to obtain the truths denoted by such sentences.

---

[6] As Cohen and Nagel famously formulated it, "If in an inference the conclusion is not contained in the premises, it cannot be valid; and if the conclusion is not different from the premises, it is useless; but the conclusion cannot be contained in the premises and also possess novelty; hence inferences cannot be both valid and useful." (*An Introduction to Logic and Scientific Method*, London: Routledge and Kegan Paul (1934), p. 173.)

Chapter 2 Co-hyperintensionality, synonymy and propositional unity

In hyperintensional contexts, a procedure is itself an object of predication (thanks to occurring as a functional argument), on which one or more functions produced by the embedding procedure operate. Hence, in such a context, all that can be substituted for this procedure is the procedure itself. On the linguistic level, this means that in a hyperintensional context, we can substitute only strictly synonymous terms. Hence, 'strictly synonymous' is a technical term here understood differently from 'weak dictionary synonymy'. This broaches the question of synonymy, or *identity of meaning*. In TIL, synonymous terms are said to encode one and the same procedure. So, if p_1 and p_2 are procedures, when are p_1 and p_2 co-hyperintensional? Such questions take centre stage in this chapter.

Co-hyperintensionality is about getting the calibration of fine-graining right for a particular sort of context.[7] It is the topic of the first paper in this chapter, namely Jespersen (2021), 'First among equals: co-hyperintensionality for structured propositions'. Too much fine-graining, and we are drawing distinctions without a difference. Too little fine-graining, and the whole point of turning to hyperintensional logic is defied. In TIL, the problem of co-hyperintensionality translates into the problem of picking the right measure of *procedural isomorphism*. It is the topic of the fourth paper, Duží and Jespersen (2013), 'Procedural isomorphism, analytic information, and β-conversion by value'. Roughly, any two procedurally isomorphic constructions are such that they do not differ in any procedurally relevant matter. Thus, if p_1 and p_2 are procedurally isomorphic, then they are one and the same procedure, even though in the non-trivial cases, p_1 and p_2 are two distinct structures. The thing is, of course, that there is not just one universal criterion of procedural isomorphism for any discourse. It is little wonder that Alonzo Church spent many years on his quest for the proper specification of 'intensional identity';

---
[7] See, e.g., F.L.G. Faroldi, (2017), 'Co-hyperintensionality', *Ratio* 30 (3):270-287.

he specified several so-called Alternatives in the process. The versions of procedural isomorphism usually differ as for the *conversions* they invoke.[8]

TIL welcomes the plurality of candidates for procedural isomorphism. The third paper, Duží (2019), charts the relations among the various versions of procedural isomorphism. It demonstrates that the individuation of procedures assigned to expressions as their structured meaning cannot be determined in virtue of some universal criterion applicable to every language. Yet, the positive result is the specification of a set of rigorously defined criteria of fine-grained procedural individuation, partially ordered according to the degree of their being permissive with respect to synonymy. The same problem confronts any formalisation that makes use of λ-bound variables because they have no counterparts in the vernacular. For this reason, the criterion that is the most suitable for an ordinary, non-professional language is arguably one that revolves around α-conversion. This rather minimalist criterion states that procedural isomorphism obtains whenever the differences between procedures consist just in technical manipulations with λ-bound variables. All in all, while the various additional Church-style Alternatives TIL has proposed are logically rigorous, it requires philosophical argument to pair a particular Alternative off with a particular fragment or kind of context from a given language. And any such pairing is likely to be provisional, because there can be no adequacy proof that a given Alternative is fit for purpose.

The hyperintensions of TIL are structured procedures and as such complex or composite, in contrast to 'flat' set-theoretic, entities. When invoking structure and complexity, age-old mereological questions rear their heads, not least how the disparate parts of a whole interact so as to form a whole which may have (emergent) properties none of its parts has. The problem of propositional unity is the subject of the second and the third paper in this chapter, namely Jespersen (2019), 'Anatomy of a proposition' and Duží (2019), 'If structured propositions are logical procedures, then how are proce-

---

[8]The standard conversions of TIL are α, β, η-conversions which are analogues to these standard conversions in the lambda-calculi.

dures individuated?'. The answer that our procedural semantics affords is that a given procedure specifies, in and by itself, how the entities which its constituent sub-procedures produce interact as functions and arguments. This function/argument approach is broadly Fregean, of course, but without the mystery of saturation. Nor is any sub-procedure the unifier (as is characteristic of Bradley-style regress). Rather the entire procedure is its own unifier, because it exhibits how the functions and arguments it produces interact.

Chapter 3 Substitution and deduction

The important role of substitution was presented above. But how can one know that an instance of substitution is *correct*? In TIL, the notion of correct substitution is cashed out in terms of *collisionless substitution*. This notion belongs among several basic definitions within the wider core of the TIL deduction system. Tichý defined correct substitution in (1988). In short, Tichý's definition is correct, as he was careful not to substitute into hyperintensional contexts. For Tichý, as soon as a variable occurs within the scope of a Trivialization, it is displayed and thus not free for substitution. In accordance with this principle, the basic theorem covering the correctness of the definition of substitution and its coherence with other parts of the system (the *Compensation Principle*) was proved. Yet, Tichý did not account for the fact that the procedure of Double Execution cancels the effect of the procedure of Trivialization. For this reason, Duží et al. (2010) extended the definition of a free variable in such a way that it also considered those occurrences of variables that allegedly become free due to the duality of Double Execution and Trivialization. As Double Execution cancels the effect of Trivialization, the variable can become free for substitution. Since that book came out, the task of defining substitution, as well as its correctness, appeared to have been completed.

However, the first two papers in this chapter, Kosterec (2020), 'Substitution contradiction, its resolution and the Church-Rosser Theorem in TIL', and (2021), 'Substitution inconsistencies in Transparent Intensional Logic', discovered inconsistencies in TIL due to too permissive a definition of a variable that is free for substitution. He also proved that this careless extension renders the proposed proof of the Compensation Principle invalid. Hence, Duží et al. (2010) went too far in extending the substitution rules. The correct substitution rule is fundamental, as it is applied in all the basic conversions. Moreover, the validity of some of these conversions is a necessary condition for properly using the substitution method. He proposed an adjusted version of the definitions. However, in (2021) it turned out that new inconsistencies cropped up.

In our opinion, the essence of the problem is this. TIL, as a hyperintensional logical system of partial functions, has much in common with higher-order functional programming languages. In such languages, the syntactic definition of the language must be strictly distinguished from the evaluation strategies for computing the result. Ideally, there should not be cases where different evaluation strategies applied to the same specification yield different results. However, in a complex, intricate higher-order language, it may happen that different evaluation strategies yield different results.

The third paper, Duží and Fait (2021), 'A hyperintensional theory of intelligent question answering in TIL', proposes an interim solution. Compared with Tichý's original definition of variables free for substitution, the only extension is the application of the so-called $^{2}0$-elimination rule, i.e., $^{2}0C = C$.[9] In practical, simple cases, this solution to the problem seems to be harmless. Yet, from a theoretical point of view, the problem of defining a consistent system of TIL in its full complexity, or at least delimiting a consistent subsystem of TIL, remains a great task to be solved. Consequently, a new proof of consistency is still outstanding.

Besides these results, the third paper deals with intelligent question-answering in TIL. The authors are proposing an adjusted system of natural deduction that makes it possible to answer not only

---

[9] A slightly improved proposal can be found in the PhD dissertation recently defended by Duží's student Michal Fait, '*Reprezentace Komputačních Znalostí a Návrh Inferenčního Stroje pro TIL*' ('Representation of Computable Knowledge and Design of an Inference Machine for TIL').

Yes-No questions but also *Wh*-questions. The analysis of empirical *Wh*-questions yields a procedure producing an α-intension, α not the type of a truth-value. The lambda-bound variable ranging over the type α corresponds to the asked-about value of the intension. To derive the value, the authors apply the method of lambda-term unification, which is similar to the method applied in the general resolution method. The authors have also had to adjust Gentzen's system of natural deduction to TIL for the purposes of natural-language processing. The adjustments consist in extending the proof calculus by the special rules rooted in the rich semantics of natural language and by some technical TIL rules for processing procedures. The resulting system answers questions in an 'intelligent' way. This means that the system derives logical consequences entailed by the input data rather than merely searching for answers by keywords.

Chapter 4 Logic of intensions

(a) **presuppositions, requisites and prerequisites.** In this first part of the fourth chapter, Duží (2018), 'Negation and presupposition, truth and falsity', the author introduces our theory of *intensional essentialism*. The idea is that there are analytically necessary relations between intensions that we call *requisites* and *prerequisites*. For instance, the property of being a mammal is a requisite of the property of being a whale. If an individual a happens to be a whale then, as a matter of analytic necessity, a is a mammal. And, if a is not a mammal, then, as a matter of analytic necessity, a is not a whale. The set of all the requisites of a given intension then characterises the intension completely; therefore, this set is the *essence* of the intension. In contrast, we reject individual essentialism; no bare individual has any non-trivial property necessarily. Hence, we adhere to individual anti-essentialism. Prerequisites form a stronger relation between intensions. As an example, the property of being an ex-smoker is a prerequisite of the property of having stopped smoking. If a stopped smoking, then a previously smoked. And not only that; if a did not stop smoking, then a used to smoke and still does. Hence, if a never smoked, then a could neither stop smoking nor not stop smoking. The respective propositions that *a* stopped smoking/did not stop smoking have a *truth-value gap*. To analyse these issues properly, we need a logic of partial functions, such as TIL.

Similar necessary relations can also be seen to obtain between propositions. The relation of a mere entailment between the premises and the conclusion of a valid argument is truth-preserving, i.e., whenever the premises are true, the conclusion must be true as well. If the premises are not true, nothing can be deduced about the truth-value of the conclusion. The relation of presupposition obtains between propositions P and Q whenever P is entailed both by Q and not-Q. Hence, if a presupposition P of Q is not true, then neither Q nor not-Q is true; Q does not have any truth value, and there is a truth-value gap. Again, to deal with presuppositions properly, we need a logic of partial functions, such as TIL.

A special kind of presupposition is the *existential presupposition* that is triggered by sentences of the form "The F is a G", where a definite description 'the F' occurs with supposition *de re*; the property of being a G is ascribed to the referent (if any) of 'the F'. However, Russell in (1905) proposed an analysis of such sentences that does not respect existential presupposition. His famous example is the sentence "The King of France is bald". Russell says that the logical form of the sentence is hidden and must be brought out by analysis. He proposes an analysis of the form "There is a unique individual with the property of being the King of France, and this individual is bald". Though Russell's quantificational theory remains to this day a strong rival of referential theories, it has received its fair amount of criticism, too. One objection is that he simply gets the truth-conditions wrong in important cases of using descriptions when there is no such thing as the unique King of France. This criticism was put forward by Strawson in (1950). Russell has this sentence come out false when there is no unique King of France. Strawson, by contrast, maintains that the sentence is neither true nor false. Obviously, in such a state-of-affairs, the sentence is not true. However, if the sentence were false (rather than without a truth-value), then its negation, "The King of France is not bald", would have to be true, which entails that there is a unique King of France, contrary to the assumption that there is none. Strawson holds that sentences like these *not only entail* but also *presuppose* the existence of a unique King of France. If 'the present King of France' lacks a referent, then the presupposition is not satisfied, and the sentence fails to take a truth-value altogether.

Strawson's criticism launched a long-term dispute about the character of Russellian versus Strawsonian definite descriptions. In the first three papers in this chapter, Duží deals with this issue and proposes a solution: 'How to unify Russellian and Strawsonian definite descriptions' (2014), 'Presuppositions and two kinds of negation' (2017), and 'Negation and presupposition, truth and falsity' (2018). The point of departure is that sentences of the form "The F is a G" are systematically ambiguous. Their ambiguity is rooted in different topic-focus articulations of such sentences. Whereas articulating the topic of a sentence activates a presupposition, articulating the focus frequently yields merely an entailment. The point is this. If 'the F' is the topic phrase, then this description occurs with *de re supposition*, and Strawson's analysis appears to be what is wanted. On this reading, which roughly corresponds to Donnellan's referential use of 'the F', the sentence presupposes the existence of a unique descriptum of 'the F'. The other option is 'G' occurring as the topic and 'the F' as the focus. This reading corresponds to Donnellan's attributive use of 'the F', and the description occurs with *de dicto supposition*. On this reading, the Russellian analysis gets the truth-conditions of the sentence right. The existence of a unique F is merely entailed. The received view still tends to be that there is room for at most one of the two positions, since they are deemed incompatible. But there is no incompatibility between Strawson's and Russell's positions, because they simply do not talk about one and the same meaning of the sentence "The King of France is bald". Russell argued for the attributive use of 'the King of France', Strawson for its referential use.

Another ambiguity concerns two kinds of negation, namely *wide-scope* and *narrow-scope* negation. In the logic of partial functions, it can be easily proved that these two kinds of negation are not equivalent. They differ just in those cases where there is no unique F. While Russell's wide-scope negation, "It is not true that the F is a G", is applied to the whole proposition that the F is a G, Strawson's narrow-scope negation, "The F is not a G", is applied to the property G. As a result, if there is no unique F, Russell's negated proposition gets the value *false*, as indeed it is not true because it is gappy, while Strawson's negation results in a *truth-value gap*, as there is no individual around of which to predicate the property of not being a G.

The final paper, Jespersen (2011), 'An intensional solution to the bike puzzle of intentional identity', solves the following puzzle. The little girl Lotta wants most of all a bicycle for her birthday, but she gets none. Distracted by the gifts she does receive, she at first does not think about the bike. But when seeing her tricycle, she is reminded of the bike. The puzzle is how to analyse these two occurrences of 'the bike' in the absence of a unique bike that Lotta wants. The analysis points out that the shift from "...a bike ..." to "...the bike ..." is parallel to the shift from "...a witch ..." to "...she (the same witch) ..." in Geach's Hob/Nob puzzle and one of Edelberg's Arsky/Barsky puzzles, in which there is a transition from "...someone murdered Smith ..." to "...he [the murderer] ...". The most important feature the puzzles have in common is how to preserve intentional (as opposed to so-called actual, or objective) identity in the apparent absence of a common focus. In Lotta's case, the problem is how to preserve the intentional identity between what she first wants most of all, later forgets about and is even later reminded of, when there is no particular bicycle she wants most of all, forgets about and is reminded of. On all three occasions Lotta is intentionally related to something; only what would that be? Geach's puzzle is simpler, though, because while it is synchronic it involves two agents, while the bike puzzle is diachronic and involves just one agent. This is the difference between intersubjective and intrasubjective intentional identity. The analysis we offer is this. (i) In the state-of-affairs S, the property of being a bike is the extension of the property concept (a property office, whose range are properties of individuals) *the individual-property such that Lotta wants an instance of it more than any other*; (ii) in S, Lotta does not think about/is reminded of the individual-property that she wants an instance of more than any other; (iii), therefore, in S Lotta does not think about/is reminded of the property of being a bike. The puzzle arises because the attributer's usage of 'the bike' blurs the distinction between a second-degree and a first-degree intension (a property concept and an individual-property, respectively). Individual material bikes are immaterial to this solution. Three type-theoretic layers are distinguished in this solution – individuals, first-degree intensions, second-degree intensions – just as in Tichý's analysis of Anselm's attempted proof of the existence of God, discussed in chapter 6.

(b) property modifiers The five papers in this portion of the chapter all deal with property modification. A property modifier is a property-to-property function. TIL has investigated the logic of four kinds of modifiers, namely: pure subsectives, those subsectives that are also intersective, modals, and privatives.

Pure subsectives are straightforward: from a being a round peg, infer that a is a peg. The rule whereby the modifier, *round*, is dropped and the surviving property, *being a peg*, is predicated of a is a rule of so-called right subsectivity. Intersectives call for a rule that trades a modifier for a property. If round is intersective with respect to being a peg, then we can infer from a being a round peg that a is round and a is a peg. The rule being invoked is one of *left subsectivity*, which TIL developed to validate this inference. Left subsectivity is examined in the third paper in this chapter, Jespersen (2016), 'Left subsectivity: how to infer that a round peg is round'.

Privatives form negated properties from properties. They are arguably a special kind of subsectives, because the extension of a negated property is a subset of the complement of the extension of the property that got negated. Thus, fake banknotes form a subset within the set of non-banknotes. Boolean negation yields the right result when privation is not iterated: if a is a fake banknote, then it is not the case that a is a banknote. However, Boolean negation does not work for iterated privation, as in 'being an imaginary burned fake banknote' or 'being a former heir apparent.' Boolean negation together with double negation elimination gets some, but far from all, of the instances of iterated privation right. Instead, where F is the input property that undergoes iterated privation, TIL puts forward a trifurcation of logically possible conclusions between a being an F, a failing to be an F, and it being semantically indeterminate whether a is an F. This trifurcation is a reflection of the fact that privation is about a property that something is *deprived* of. Jespersen, Carrara, and Duží focus on iterated privation in the second paper, 'Iterated privation and positive predication' (2017).

Modal modifiers are explored in the first paper in this chapter, Jespersen (2020), 'Limiting cases of modal modification: reply to Kosterec'. Modals barely have a logic, because if a is, say, an alleged terrorist, then maybe a is a terrorist and maybe a is not a terrorist. Still, when contingent properties are modified by a modal modifier, this bifurcation is the conclusion characteristic of the predication of modally modified properties. However, when the argument property does not admit of bifurcation, as in 'discovering the highest prime number', this bifurcation does not apply. There is no highest prime number, hence nobody can instantiate the property of discovering the highest prime number, hence the left-hand conjunct is false, hence the conjunction is false, hence the inference is invalid. Instead, we draw the conclusion that it is not true for anyone that they have the property F (here, 'being a discoverer of the highest prime') that was modified by *alleged*. Still, this does not turn modals modifying impossible properties into privatives. The reason is that the source of privation is not the modifier (*alleged* versus *fake*) but the argument property itself.

TIL has also developed a general rule of left subsectivity, which applies to all four kinds of modifiers. For instance, if a is an alleged terrorist, then there is a property f such that a is an (alleged f); and if b is a fake banknote, then there is a property g such that b is a (fake g).

The distinction between subsective and privative modification provides a formal handle on the popular distinction between two different views of malfunction in artefacts such as hammers. The final paper in this chapter, Jespersen and Carrara (2013), 'A new logic of technical malfunction', explores this topic. One view maintains that a malfunctioning hammer is still a hammer, because although it fails at hammering, it was designed and produced as a hammer. The other view maintains that a malfunctioning hammer is no longer a hammer, because it now fails at hammering. TIL came to the insight that 'malfunctioning' does not denote a property but a property modifier. The first view construes *malfunctioning* as a subsective modifier and the second view as a privative modifier. If malfunctioning was a property, then a malfunctioning hammer would be an artefact with two properties, unqualified malfunctioning and being a hammer. This result leaves room for the first view only, and it saddles the view with the peculiar property of unqualified malfunctioning, without relativisation to a technical function such a hammering.

The fourth paper, Jespersen (2015), 'Structured lexical concepts, property modifiers, and Transparent Intensional Logic', studies the logical relationship between pairs of simple and modified predicates, as captured by the dual notion of simplification and refinement of property-producing procedures.

Chapter 5 Questions, answers, obligations and norms

The first paper of this chapter, Číhalová and Duží (2022), 'Modelling dynamic behaviour of agents in a multi-agent system: logical analysis of *Wh*-questions and answers', addresses how to analyse agents' activities and questions and answers about such activities. These activities are specified in different tenses with reference to the time when this or that happened or will happen. Dynamic activities are actions that are characterised by an agent who executes the action and by other participants involved in the action. *Wh*-questions about the participants of the actions pose a particular challenge, because the variability of the types of possible answers to such questions is huge. To deal with the problem, the paper proposes a classification of *Wh*-questions apt for communication in a multi-agent system. Though the linguistic classification of *Wh*-questions is helpful, it is not always suitable for communication and reasoning. The paper proposes a classification based on a logical analysis of questions, such that the agents can deductively infer possible answers rather than only extracting answers literally occurring in the input data. We concentrate, in particular, on questions concerning the participants in agents' activities. Our proposal for such a system consists of agents who communicate with their fellow agents by messaging, so that each autonomous agent, despite being resource-bounded, can make more-or-less rational decisions to meet both their own and collective goals. We make a general proposal for a system, such that the 'envelope' of agents' messages can be formalised in any multi-agent system standard, be it FIPA ACL or KQML.[10] Yet, the *content* of messages is encoded in a formalised *natural language*, i.e., in the form of TIL procedures. We concentrate on analysing the content of query messages, particularly the content of those that encode *Wh*-questions and the answers to them. The TIL deduction system that makes it possible to answer such questions in an intelligent way is summarised and applied in order to derive answers. The application of these results to the analysis of *processes* and *events* based on verb valency frames is another novelty of the paper.

The second paper in this chapter, Glavaničová (2016), '∆-TIL and normative systems', focuses on a hyperintensional analysis of deontic modalities within the system of TIL, following an earlier paper, Glavaničová (2015),[11] which argued for such an analysis and proposed a simple variant. The included paper argues that deontic modalities are relative to normative systems. The motivation for this claim ranges from mundane facts to problems and paradoxes of deontic logic: different legal systems impose different obligations and prohibitions, and grant different permissions. Normative conflicts usually arise from the fact that one person can be subject to different normative systems (as

---

[10] These technical terms are used in computer science and explained in the paper.

[11] D. Glavaničová (2015), 'K analýze deontických modalít v transparentnej intenzionálnej logike' *Organon* F, 22(2), 211-228 ('Towards an analysis of deontic modals in TIL').

is the case of Antigone, perhaps the most famous example of a normative conflict). Finally, some problems in deontic logic could be overcome if deontic modalities are relativised. Perhaps the best illustration is contrary-to-duty reasoning, which is beset by difficulties due to the fact that ideal norms are intermixed with contrary-to-duty norms (which are of restorative nature and apply only after the ideal, or first-order, norms have been violated). Subsequently, the paper improves on an earlier analysis by accounting for such a relativisation via two possible analyses that are considered in the paper.

Chapter 6 Fiction, religion and impossibility

The final chapter deals with how to analyse and reason about impossibilia, as well as with applications of TIL to fictional and religious discourse. The fine-grained structure of impossibilia is captured in TIL by means of structured hyperintensions, and thus without the need for impossible worlds or (neo-)Meinongian non-existents. A similar approach is taken in a recent analysis of fiction in terms of TIL, which departs from Tichý's analysis in (1988). A contemporary account of religious discourse by means of TIL is rooted in Tichý (1979), but offers a more rigorous and technical analysis.

The first paper in this chapter, Glavaničová (2021), 'Rethinking role realism', focuses on the semantics of fictional names and the metaphysics of fictional characters. The purpose of the paper is three-fold. First, to overcome some of the pressing difficulties and limitations of role realism, which the author perceives as a promising account of fictional characters that nevertheless has not explored and exploited its full potential yet. Second, to surpass the realist-antirealist dichotomy in the metaphysics of fictional characters, which is standardly being drawn, yet not always in a helpful manner, given that fictional names are being used in different ways, and neither realism nor antirealism alone can fully capture this richness of usage. Third, to sort out some of the core difficulties besetting descriptivism about fictional names. These goals are achieved in terms of hyperintensionally understood roles (individuals-in-hyperintension), in the paper called *individual concepts*.[12] These do exist according to TIL, which might give the impression that the account belongs firmly in the realist camp. However, the paper steers a middle course between realism and antirealism. By distinguishing between the sense and reference of fictional names one is in a position to hold that the sense of a fictional name is a structured hyperintension of the above kind, while the reference is lacking: there is no extensional DCI Tom Barnaby, but there is a hyperintension corresponding to the fictional name of 'Tom Barnaby', and that is what we can think of, co-identify, admire, and so forth. Finally, the third aim is realised by opting for an impossibilist, rather than possibilist, variety of descriptivism about fictional names. This way, the account deals with two arguments against possibilism of fictional characters formulated by Kripke. Note also that descriptivism about fictional names does not commit one to being a descriptivist about proper names such as 'London', unless one is wedded to the claim that fictional names are genuine proper names.

The second paper is Duží, Jespersen, and Glavaničová (2021), 'Impossible individuals as necessarily empty concepts'. Its aim is to propose a general hyperintensional account of a special case of so-called impossible objects, namely, 'impossible individuals'. We begin with what the intensional logic of individuals-in-intension is custom-built to model, and go on to point out where it runs out of steam; the main problem of the intensional account is that there is just one impossible individual-in-intension, which is the necessarily vacant office, i.e., the single office that goes vacant in all possible worlds and at all times. Hence, on the intensional account, we cannot distinguish between, e.g., 'the man without properties' and 'the wooden horse that is a horse'. Then we proceed to put forward a hyperintensional logic of individuals-in-hyperintension, i.e., hyperoffices. We propose identifying 'impossible individuals' with necessarily empty individual concepts. Hence, 'impossible individuals' are explicated as inconsistent hyperoffices, which are different ways of presenting the impossible

---

[12] Note that this understanding of individual concepts is different from that of Stokke (2021), 'Fictional names and individual concepts', *Synthese*, 198(8), 7829-7859.

office. The novelty of this paper consists in developing a method that enables us to discover inconsistencies in the specifications of individual concepts/hyperoffices and thus prove that such concepts could not possibly be matched by an extension (such as an individual or a number). Furthermore, this approach makes possible a fine-grained individuation of impossible individuals. The logic is developed by means of the existing resources available to TIL, and while not requiring the introduction of novel entities, it does require the formulation of several new definitions. The core results are these. We define the novel notions of hyperoffice and hyperrequisite, the former being a hyperintensional counterpart of offices and the latter a hyperintensional counterpart of requisites. Moreover, we propose a method of how to derive hyperrequisites of a hyperoffice and how to prove some of the hyperoffices impossible, because their hyperrequisites are mutually inconsistent. This method is demonstrated by means of some concrete examples like proving that the concept of 'Achilles, the quickest runner, who never overtakes the tortoise, the slowest runner, if he gives the tortoise a head-start and both run at a constant speed' is inconsistent.

The last two papers deal with ontological arguments for the existence of God, namely Duží (2011), 'St Anselm's ontological arguments', and Duží (2013), 'Ambiguities in natural language and ontological proofs'. Duží (2011) provides a detailed analysis of Anselm's argument in favour of the existence of God that can be found in his *Proslogion III*. Duží (2013) summarises these results, together with the previous research on topic-focus ambiguities, and demonstrates them on examples of ambiguity in natural language. Our starting point is that 'God' is a name of an office. For, if 'God' were a *proper* proper name of an individual, then He would trivially exist, which would make it uninteresting to prove and to know that God exists. Tichý (1979) convincingly shows that non-trivial existence is not a property of bare individuals.[13] But if non-trivial existence is not a property of bare individuals, one can ask, *what is non-trivial existence?* Some philosophers, most famously Kant, are inclined to con-

---

[13] Tichý, P. (1979), 'Existence and God', *Journal of Philosophy* 76: 403-420.

clude that existence is simply not a property ascribable to things.[14] Yet, we do characterise non-trivial existence as a property, though not of bare individuals; existence is a property of functions returning a value at a given argument. In the case of offices, it is the property of the office being occupied in a given state-of-affairs.

The majority of ontological proofs of God's existence are flawed.[15] First, there is a conflict of contexts. The line of reasoning can be summarised like this. God possesses all perfections. Since existence is a positive property, God exists. Hence, *existence* is conceived as a positive property of *individuals*, i.e., at the same extensional level as the other properties of individuals, like, for instance, the property of having blue eyes, or even divine properties like being holy, just, omnibenevolent, and omnipresent. Thus, if any being is able to occupy the office of God, this being must have all perfections. But existence cannot be a requisite property of the office of God, which is typed to be occupiable by individuals, because existence is not a property of individuals. Hence, existence is a second-degree intension that is ascribable on the intensional level to the office itself, meaning that the office is occupied. The second, and perhaps even more serious, flaw is the application of an invalid inference rule that can be formulated as follows: Property F is a requisite of office O; therefore, the O is an F. What went wrong here? Again, there is a fallacious confusion about the level of abstraction. While in the premise the O occurs intensionally, i.e., with *de dicto* supposition, in the conclusion O occurs extensionally, i.e., *de re*. For sure, a *requisite* is a necessary relation between intensions, in this case a property and an office. Yet, in the conclusion F is predicated of the *occupant* of O. While the premise is necessarily true, independently of the occupancy of office O, the conclusion is neither true nor false, in case the office goes vacant; there

---

[14]For instance, Aristotle in *Analytica Posteriora*, II, 7, 92b13, says "being is not a genus", Kant, in the *Critique of Pure Reason*: "Being is...not a real predicate", and according to Russell (*Principia Mathematica*, 2nd ed., p. 175) "there is no reason to suppose that a meaning of existence could be found which would be applicable to immediately given subjects".

[15]Not all ontological proofs are incorrect; the authors show that at least St. Anselm's argument in *Proslogion III* is valid, though not sound.

is no individual around of which to predicate F. To obtain a valid argument, an additional premise is called for, namely that O is occupied. But the snag is that such an argument is of no value, because it is circular.

Anselm's argument in favour of God's existence in his *Proslogion III* is not fallacious in the above sense, as Tichý convincingly shows in (1979). The formal apparatus of TIL makes it possible to clarify Tichý's ingenious analysis, which is spelt out in the paper by Duží. The ontological arguments devised by Descartes and others are objectionable from a theological point of view. They assume that God's essence is known. Anselm steers clear of the rationalist arrogance of proclaiming to know God's essence. He describes God with a modest 'That, than which nothing greater can be conceived'. All that Anselm here presumes to know is *something* about God's essence, namely that nothing can conceivably surpass it in greatness. The key to Anselm's argument is the analysis of the label that Anselm uses for his God-like office, namely 'That, than which nothing greater can be conceived'. This term denotes an office one degree higher up than the office of God. Anselm's argument does not suffer from any of the above flaws and is, indeed, *valid*. Hence, did Anselm prove the existence of God? The answer depends on whether his premises are true. The premise that we doubt is the assumption that an office with necessary existence understood as occupancy in *all* possible worlds at *all* times is *eo ipso* greater than any other office that does not have necessary existence as a requisite. Tichý shows that the essence of a necessarily occupied office is minimal, because necessary analytical existence works *against* greatness. The greater (more important) the office, the more difficult for an individual it is to occupy it. Greatness demands exclusivity, not inclusivity. An office that is occupied in all worlds and at all times must have a poor essence containing only trivial requisites. Take, for instance, omniscience. Since any human being is possibly ignorant of this or that fact, omniscience cannot be a requisite of an office occupied in all worlds and times. What makes the holder of the divine office of God so noteworthy is that the *office* He occupies requires so much of its potential occupants. But it is this very same fact that makes it conceivable that the office is actually vacant.

In order to avoid misunderstanding, note that this is not to say that the existence of such a perfect divine being would not be *desirable*. And for a believer, any such being undeniably enjoys necessary existence. Only that God's necessary existence cannot be of a *logico-analytical* character. If 'metaphysical' has any sense, then we might perhaps say that the existence of God is metaphysically necessary.

March 2023, the Editors

Hyperintensional Logic

Transparent quantification into hyperpropositional attitudes de dicto

Bjørn Jespersen   Marie Duží

Abstract We prove how to validly quantify into hyperpropositional contexts de dicto in Transparent Intensional Logic. Hyperpropositions are sentential meanings and attitude complements individuated more finely than up to logical equivalence. A hyperpropositional context de dicto is a context in which only co-hyperintensional propositions can be validly substituted. A de dicto attitude ascription is one that preserves the attributee's perspective when one complement is substituted for another. Being an extensional logic of hyperintensions, Transparent Intensional Logic validates all the rules of extensional logic, including existential quantification. Yet the rules become more exacting when applied to hyperintensional contexts. The rules apply to only some types of entities, because the existence of only some types of entities is entailed by a hyperpropositional attitude de dicto. The insight that the paper offers is how a particular logic of hyperintensions is capable of validating quantifying-in in a principled and rigorous manner. This result advances the community-wide understanding of how to logically manipulate hyperintensions.

1 Introduction

A logic of quantifying-in comes at the end of a long story. The ability to validly perform existential quantification into hyperintensional attitude contexts is the sweet fruits a logic reaps for being properly designed and having a number of attractive meta-theoretical features. We will demonstrate how one particular broadly Fregean theory pulls off quantifying-in.

We adopt Cresswell's negative definition of a *hyperintensional context* as a context in which the substitution of necessarily equivalent terms fails. We share the received conception of *hyperpropositions* as sentential meanings and attitude complements individuated more finely than up to analytic equivalence. For instance, an agent can believe that no bachelor is married without logic forcing the agent to believe that the arithmetic of natural numbers is not recursively axiomatizable, despite both complements being necessary truths. Note that in our theory the substitution of terms (linguistic objects) is a reflection of an underlying substitution of one hyperintension for another (logical objects).

To frame the problem, let χ be a hyperintensional operator that represents a binary relation between an agent b and a hyperproposition A to which agent b has adopted an attitude, whether factive or non-factive. The question we raise and answer in this paper can be schematised preliminarily as follows: is the following inferential schema valid ('*QI*' for 'quantifying-in')?

$$\frac{\chi[b, A(a)]}{\exists y \chi[b, A(y)]} QI$$

Our view is this. In general, which positions within A can be quantified into depends on two factors. The first one is what can be quantified over, something which depends on the *ontology* of the logic being deployed. The second one is whether $\exists y$ is capable of reaching across χ so as to bind occurrences of y within the scope of χ. The feasibility of doing so depends on the *syntax* of the logic.[1] For instance, if b believes that 5 is the sum of 2 and 4 (where $a = 5$), then *QI* can be validly applied to infer that there exists some number y such that b believes that y is the sum of 2 and 4, as this conclusion is entailed by the premise. On the other hand, if b believes that $tg(\pi/2) = 0$ (where $a = tg(\pi/2)$), then *QI* cannot be applied to infer that there is a number y such that b believes that y is equal to 0, because there is no such number. Yet *QI* can be validly applied to infer that there is a *function* y (where $a = tg$) such that b believes that y takes the number $\pi/2$ to 0.

Our answer to the question about validity is a *qualified yes*. Answering in the affirmative is predicated on providing satisfactory solutions to both the ontological and the syntactic problem. As for the first problem, it is key that *QI* be qualified so as not to conjure entities into existence. For instance, if the premise is that b believes that Vulcan causes Mercury to have an erratic orbit, then the conclusion must not be that there is a physical object y such that b believes that y causes Mercury's orbit to be erratic. But this restriction still does not preclude quantifying over non-

---

[1] See Bealer (1982, 26) for discussion of externally quantifiable variables.

extensional entities, i.e., intensions or hyperintensions, something which, however, requires that the framework being deployed must come with a sufficiently rich ontology. For instance, in the above example, the conclusion we would recommend is that there is an *individual concept* such that b believes that the physical object falling under this concept causes Mercury to have an erratic orbit.[2]

As for the second problem, our answer to the question of whether $\exists y$ is capable of reaching across χ and binding occurrences of y within the scope of χ is also a *qualified yes*. The qualifications are due to the fact that a hyperintensional context, and anything located within it, is not immediately amenable to logical manipulation. Intensional contexts, by contrast, do immediately lend themselves to logical manipulation. The operation that 'raises' a context to a hyperintensional one shields it from manipulation from the outside. Therefore, further operations are required in order to, nonetheless, reach into positions located within a hyperintensional context.

The bulk of this paper is devoted to demonstrating, in full detail, how a particular theory is capable of quantifying into hyperpropositional attitude contexts de dicto. The theory in question is Transparent Intensional Logic (TIL), which has two features that enable it to validate *QI*:

- *A fully transparent semantics.* Opacity and shift of semantic value are eschewed in favour of terms and expressions having the same meaning and the same semantic value in all contexts. The same uniform semantics applies to all the different kinds of context.[3]
- *An extensional logic of hyperintensions.* The laws of extensional logic, including existential generalisation, also apply to hyperintensional contexts. However, stronger requirements are placed on the operands than in the case of an extensional logic of intensions and of extensions. What varies with the context is not the validity of the rules themselves, but the types of objects these rules are applicable to.

Transparency and extensionality are two necessary conditions for our strictly compositional theory of quantifying-in. More specifically, what connects the transparent semantics with the extensional logic of hyperintensions is that the combination contributes to making it technically feasible to, first, denote, or present, a hyperintension as an entity in its own right and, next, to manipulate either the entire hyperintension or parts of it. The way we achieve this is by making it feasible for a hyperintension to occur as a functional argument. When a hyperintension occurs as an argument, we shall say that it occurs in the *displayed* mode, i.e., the hyperintension occurs *presented as an argument*. Occurring in the displayed mode contrasts with occurring in the *executed* mode, which involves descending to a lower-type entity. Once a hyperintension is able to occur as an argument, it can

---

[2] Here we use the term 'individual concept' in an intuitive sense. Below we are going to distinguish and rigorously define *individual role* or *office*, i.e., *individual-in-intension*, in opposition to *individual hyperoffice*, which is a hyperintension presenting an office.

[3] A fully transparent semantics qualifies as 'semantically innocent' according to the letter (if not spirit) of Davidson's characterisation, but we arrive at semantic innocence via the opposite route than Davidson's. He attempts to make each context extensional; we generalise from hyperintensional contexts to all other contexts. See Duží et al. (2010, 12).

figure as the complement of an attitude (thus making hyperintensional attitude contexts possible), it can be quantified *over*, it can be quantified *into*, and a part within it can be replaced by another so as to generate a new hyperintensional complex.

Quantifying-in is, above all, *technically* demanding and nowhere close to being trivial. Attempting to quantify into hyperintensions puts pressure on any theory's account of nested contexts, its variables and quantifiers. Therefore, the demonstrated ability of a logic of hyperintensions that comes with an elaborate technical machinery to successfully perform quantifying-in is evidence that the logic is justified in adopting this machinery. Furthermore, we have a theory-internal reason to demonstrate exactly how to quantify-in. TIL makes the strong claim for itself that it is an extensional logic of hyperintensions, and this is one reason why we must be able to preserve the validity of the extensional rule of existential generalisation also when applied to hyperintensional contexts.[4]

On top of that, it is also *philosophically* challenging, hence enlightening, to figure out the nature of the so-called intentional objects that are at the receiving end of an intentional act such as maintaining an attitude. For instance, if the premise is that b believes that the last decimal of the expansion of π is an even number, then what would be a suitable quantificational range? The premise may well be true but, necessarily, the complement of the attitude fails to be true for want of a last decimal of the expansion. Or if the premise is that b believes that the King of Denmark is balding, then what would be a suitable quantificational range? As a matter of contingent fact, the premise may well be true, but the complement is not, for it so happens that nobody is presently the King of Denmark (writing in 2021). Since we cannot quantify over individuals here, then what can we quantify over? Answering this question reveals which kinds of objects one is prepared to embrace in one's ontology. We will show how the ontology of TIL makes it possible to infer the existence of such entities as are logically presupposed, hence also entailed, by the premises. For instance, if b believes that the King of Denmark is balding then there is an individual concept such that b believes that its occupant is balding. Or, if b believes that the last decimal of the expansion of π is an even number then there is the concept of a number such that b believes that the number falling under this concept is even.

---

[4] Morton (1969, 163) says, "treatments of non-truth-functional contexts have assimilated them to intensional contexts, either to shade them with the same dark incorrigibility [i.e., the fact that it is obscure how to calculate the truth-value of an intensional context, thus understood. *The authors*] or to honor them with all the mathematical and philosophical sophistication that the intensional requires." Our conception of intensionality (actually, hyperintensionality) is the latter, which Bealer sums up thus: "[T]here is no genuinely intensional language; when *prima facie* intensional language is properly analysed, it turns out to be extensional language concerning intensional entities." (Bealer 1982, 148) See also Copi (1968, 244) and Klement (2002, 99–100). When these authors speak of 'intensionality' they intend intensionality as understood in mathematics, which is hyperintensionality. The coarse-grained intensionality of possible-world semantics equates co-intensionality with necessary co-extensionality, thus yielding (in a logic of total functions) but one necessary proposition, but one impossible proposition, failure to distinguish between inverse relations, etc., etc.

This paper is continuous with previously published research, starting with Tichý (1986), Materna (1997) and followed by Duží and Jespersen (2015, 2012) and Jespersen (2015a, 2015b), which cover quantifying into hyperpropositional attitudes de re (e.g., *believing of* π that *it* has an infinite decimal expansion, or π being such that *it is believed* to have an infinite decimal expansion) and hyperintensional objectual (i.e., non-propositional) attitudes (e.g., *calculating* the ninety-ninth decimal in the expansion of π, or *seeking* a yeti without seeking an abominable snowman). In this paper we concentrate on hyperpropositional attitudes de dicto.[5] To fix ideas, here are some examples of hyperpropositional attitudes de dicto:

- Tilman knows that 1+1=2, but he does not know that arithmetic is not recursively axiomatizable.[6]
- Tilman is trying to prove that the last decimal of the expansion of π is an even number.
- Tilman knows that Francis is the Pope, but not that he is the Head of the Catholic Church.[7]
- Tilman believes that whatever does not kill him makes him stronger, but not that whatever does not make him stronger kills him.[8]
- Tilman believes that no bachelor is married, but he does not believe that whales are mammals.[9]

Each of these attitudes relates an attributee to a hyperproposition, which offers an idiosyncratic perspective on an empirical or analytical state-of-affairs. An attitude de dicto reproduces exclusively the attributee's own perspective, whereas an attitude de re blends the attributer's and the attributee's respective perspectives. This explains why the content of an attitude de dicto is fully specified and the content of an attitude de re is only partially specified. Linguistically, the difference

---

[5] Yalcin (2015, 207) asks, "what should the semantic analysis of attitudes de re look like from a Fregean perspective—a perspective according to which attitude states are generally relations to structured Fregean thoughts, themselves composed of senses?". Yalcin (2015, 208) claims that "the Fregean position is underdeveloped" and left with a 'lacuna', because no Fregean position has so far specified how to compositionally derive truth-conditions for attitudes de re. We beg to disagree. Both Duží et al. (2010, §5.1.2.2) and Duži and Jespersen (2012) answer Yalcin's question and address his complaint. The Quinian problem of 'double vision' (i.e., the Ralph/Ortcutt case; see Sect. 2.2 below) which Yalcin brings up in (2015, § 4) is solved in Jespersen (2015a, 2015b).

[6] Since all true mathematical sentences denote the truth-value **T**, on an intensional reading the sentence would be a contradiction. On an intensional reading, any true mathematical sentence can be substituted for the complement, and we end up with the paradox of mathematical omniscience.

[7] Since, by definition, the Pope and the Head of the Catholic Church are one and the same office, the sentence would be contradictionary on an intensional reading. Yet, since the sentence can be true, the attitude must be hyperintensional.

[8] Again, on an intensional reading, the sentence would be contradictory; hence, the attitude must be a hyperintensional one.

[9] The attitude must be hyperintensional, because on an intensional reading the sentence is contradictory. If Tilman believes that no bachelor is married then on an intensional reading he must believe any necessarily true proposition, like, e.g., that whales are mammals, and we end up with the paradox of analytical omniscience. The other undesirable extreme is the paradox of analytical idiocy, so to speak. If one believes a necessarily false proposition (e.g., that a forged banknote is a valid banknote) then one would have to believe any necessarily false proposition.

is that a report of an attitude de re includes an anaphor that points outside the embedded context, as in "that *it* is a planet". A report de dicto would have "that *Pluto* is a planet". Moreover, a hyperpropositional attitude de dicto is impervious to the (contingent or necessary) inexistence of, e.g., Vulcan or the last digit of the expansion of π, in that its truth-value depends merely on whether or not it is true that the attributee believes that such-and-such is true. By contrast, attitudes de re come with existential presuppositions already at the extensional level of individuals, numbers, etc.: no *res*, no attitude de re.

The rest of the paper is organised as follows. Part 2 provides systematic background to the problem of quantifying-in, comparing TIL with other positions. Part 3 presents the relevant fragments of TIL. Part 4 presents and proves our rules for quantifying into hyperpropositional contexts de dicto.

2 Background to transparency and quantifying-in

2.1 Quine

Quantifying-in mixes modality with quantification.[10] Quine was squarely opposed to existential quantification into alethic modal contexts, such as $\exists x F x$. His general objection was that it generates 'Aristotelian essentialism', i.e., essentialism de re, which he deemed incoherent.[11] Quine would later, in (1956), adopt a more nuanced stance on existential quantification into a different sort of modal contexts, namely those attributing attitudinal modalities, such as wishing to find a unicorn lair, or believing that the tall handsome stranger spotted on the beach is a spy. In Quine (1956), he distinguishes between *notional* and *relational* attitudes. The sentence "Ralph believes that someone is a spy" lends itself to both readings. The notional reading is that Ralph believes that there are spies. The relational reading is that there is someone of whom Ralph believes that he or she is a spy. Only in the relational case does it make sense to quiz Ralph about who it is he suspects of being a spy.[12] Or for a standard example: "The princess wants to marry a prince". The formalisation of the relational reading in first-order logic (which at least gets the scope distribution right) would be this (χ, a generic attitude operator; M, the binary relation of marrying):

---

[10] So far, so good. But beyond that, exactly what problem, or cluster of problems, is being discussed in Quine (1956), or his previous work on quantifying into modal contexts, is still not entirely clear. See, for instance, Crawford (2008). Bear in mind that we are not engaged in Quine scholarship as such, but rather in charting the systematic roots of the problem of quantifying-in in the light of how we find it most fruitful to frame it.

[11] One argument against quantified modal logic is his example of the 'mathematical cyclist', which is intended to show that it is both necessary and also not necessary that an individual who is a biking mathematician is rational and bipedal. See Duží et al. (2010, §4.2.1) on how to debunk this argument along the same lines as in Stalnaker and Barcan Marcus.

[12] See Kaplan (1986, App. B) on 'the syntactically de re', which is supposed to capture Quine's relational readings. The technique consists in forming a predicate in the passive voice in the vein of 'is believed by *a* to be an *F*'. This yields "The tall handsome stranger spotted on the beach is believed by Ralph to be a spy".

$$\exists x\,(Fx \wedge \chi a\,(Max))$$

The notional reading goes into:

$$\chi a\,(\exists x\,(Fx \wedge Max))$$

Quine dismisses quantifying into notional attitudes. Doing so would validate inferring *from a* believing that there is a planet orbiting between Earth and the Sun that causes Mercury's orbit to be erratic *to* there being a planet between Earth and the Sun such that *a* believes that it causes Mercury's orbit to be erratic. Thus, it is made a necessary condition for Le Verrier's hypothesis about Mercury's orbit that Vulcan exists, which goes far too far by turning believing into a factive attitude. The quantification would also misconstrue what notional attitudes are all about. When Quine wants, on a notional interpretation, a sloop then it should exactly not follow that there is a sloop such that Quine wants it. But, as Kaplan (1986, 230) is right to stress, Quine does want to quantify into relational attitudes. Quine's problem then becomes how exactly to go about that. Quine himself offers his three-place analysis as an attempt to formulate what is, by his lights, a non-opacity-inducing formalisation that makes co-referential terms substitutable. Kaplan (1968) also puts forward some inconclusive proposals, which, however, tie relational attitudes tightly together with the particular terms chosen.

Still, the general problem of variable-binding remains. There is an incongruity between the notional and the relational reading. On both readings, the ∃-bound occurrence of x is located within the scope of χ. But on the notional reading, also ∃ is within the scope of χ. For sure, the entire context induced by χ may be 'opaque' or 'intensional', but the two occurrences of x in $\exists x\,(\ldots x \ldots)$ are on the same level. Not so on the relational reading. While $\exists x$ is in a transparent or extensional position, the occurrence of x within the scope of χ is in an opaque or intensional position. And whereas the quantificational range of x is restricted, due to Quine's extensionalist predilections, to extensional entities, the occurrence of x in an opaque context demands a shift in quantificational range, most likely so as to include individuals-in-intension as well as other extensions-in-intension. However, apart from such entities being beyond the pale for Quine, the formal predicament becomes obvious if we rename the second variable:

$$\exists x\,(\ldots \chi a \ldots y \ldots)$$

The above formula is *open*, because y occurs free, and there is no semblance of contact between $\exists x$ and y. On the other hand, there is a semblance of contact between $\exists x$ and x here:

$$\exists x\,(\ldots \chi a \ldots x \ldots)$$

However, the contact between $\exists x$ and x has been severed, appearances notwithstanding. Thus, the formula exemplifies vacuous quantification, again making '$\exists x$' a dummy.

2.2 Substitutability

In the rest of this section, we will describe and critique some contemporary positions regarding transparency, opacity and substitution, all of which affect the prospects of quantifying-in. The form in which the problem of quantifying-in has been handed down is that it challenges us to make relational attitudes transparent—and the hallmark of transparency is the validity of quantifying-in.[13] Transparency would seem to validate an inference such as this:

$$\frac{b \text{ is such that } a \text{ believes that she is an } F}{c \text{ is such that } a \text{ believes that she is an } F}$$

This seems like a straightforward application of Leibniz's Law, and so ought to be uncontroversial, also because it aligns with the tenet of 'no opacity de re'. Yet Pickel (2015), Cumming (2008) and Caie et al. (2019) think otherwise. Pickel (2015, 345) says,

> What is wanted is a theory that is sensitive to both the state of the world that the agent believes to obtain [...] and the peculiar take she [i.e., the agent] has concerning 'who is who' in this state of the world [so as to make room] for the possibility that sentences differing only by the substitution of co-referential names [...] differ in truth-value.

The point about 'who is who' in a given context is to be captured by

> [...] the fact that variable x_l associated with the name 'Lindsay' may designate different individuals relative to different assignment functions as representing the fact that Lindsay *may* be each of these individuals, where this '*may*' reflects epistemic possibility. (Pickel, 2015, 339.)

On our interpretation, the effect of adding a so-called assignment-unsaturated meaning for the sentence "... Lindsay ..." is similar to the effect sententialists and inscriptionalists obtain when they make the very syntax in which an attitude is

---

[13] Quine states that "*no variable inside an opaque construction is bound by an operator outside*. You cannot quantify into an opaque construction." (Quine, 1960, 166) It is the right move, of course, for Quine to resist quantifying into opaque contexts. In Quine (1960) and elsewhere, he likens trying to quantify into opaque contexts to trying to quantify into quotation contexts. In Quine (1956) he gives an additional reason. In the famous Ralph/Ortcutt case, it is true that a is believed by Ralph to be a spy, that b is not believed by Ralph to be a spy, and that $a = b$. What happens is that quantification 'quantifies away' the two different guises under which Ralph has encountered a/b. There can be no individual such that it is believed, and also not believed, by someone to be a spy. So, quantifying-in would yield a paradox. See also Kaplan (1986, 269–70). But, or so we think, the fact that opacity appears to be the root cause should have given Quine pause. He ought to have reconsidered the assumptions and tenets that landed him in an (ostensibly) opaque context that suspends quantifying-in on pain of paradox. The conclusion should not have been that opacity is a fact of linguistic life, or 'intensional', i.e., anti-extensional, logic a fact of logical life, thus turning some contexts into no-go areas. In fact, the strategy pursued by TIL is to design a formal semantics that cannot generate opacity, again with provisos for quotational contexts. (We note that the line of reasoning found in the Ralph/Ortcutt example resembles that of the reasoning behind the 'mathematical cyclist'; see fn. 12; see fn. 11.)

reported part of the reported attitude. Of course, substitution of co-referential, or even synonymous, terms and expressions will not go through; but that is because the substitution context is a quotational one. The respective attitude contexts of Pickel and Cumming are not quotational. Whereas the sententialist/inscriptionalist makes it matter that their agents may know one name for an individual, but not another, Pickel and Cumming make it matter that an agent may fail to identify *a* as *b*, even though *a* is identical to *b*. This is captured by including assignments relative to which x_a, x_b take different values, although $a = b$.[14] TIL, however, does not want to model "that [the agent] is unsure of whether *Lindsay* and *Nellie* are the same person" (Pickel, 2015, 339), for there is no such thing to model. Not to put too fine a point on it, Lindsay and Nellie not being the same person is not a matter of epistemic (or doxastic) possibility, but a case of the agent being conceptually confused. TIL assumes that its agents are aware of the identity of the individuals toward which they adopt an attitude. Of course, it makes perfect sense for us that agents may be unsure of whether the sun that sets in the evening is the same sun that rises in the morning. But this should be analysed as being unsure about whether two different individual offices are co-occupied.[15] When a pair of semantically proper names are synonyms (and assume 'Lindsay' and 'Nellie' to be such a pair), no Fregean puzzle arises, and 'Millian' substitution is valid. There is no semantic or logical difference between the two names, which are merely notational variants of one another. The initial inference is valid, by the lights of TIL, and the single problem is to safeguard the anaphoric reference from 'she' to '*b*', '*c*'.[16] A transparent semantics is characterised by being able to do so. The substitution is subsequently validated by Leibniz's Law.

Still, we are not entirely on board with framing the problem of quantifying-in in terms of making contexts reporting relational attitudes transparent. We do agree that Quine's distinction between notional and relational readings is intuitively persuasive. In fact, anyone who has absorbed the implications of Russell's example of "I thought your yacht was longer that it is" will probably be fine with Quine's distinction. We also agree that attitude reports de re are logically distinct from

---

[14] The main difference between Pickel and Cumming is that Pickel assigns a more elaborate semantics to his variables. Cumming has, as it were, got only the first half right. Pickel provides an argument to the effect that Cumming is unable to distinguish between true and false beliefs. Assume that *a* believes, (B_a), that the value of x_b is an *F*. This is formalised thus: "$B_a F x_b$". This is a closed formula, because operator *B* binds the variable. Assume that $\sigma(x_b)$ = Dublin. The formula being closed, it retains its truth-value independently of any assignment functions other than the original σ. Now let an arbitrary assignment function, τ, assign a different value: $\tau(x_b)$ = Lublin. It is true, therefore, that *a* believes that Lublin is an *F*. Except, of course, it is not. Pickel's remedy is to assign a *dual* semantics to variables. Whether $B_a F x_b$ "is true on assignment σ depends not just on the value of x_b relative to σ, but also on whether every world-assignment pair [$\langle w, \tau \rangle$], in the agent's belief set makes true [the 'quasi-open proposition' Fx_b]. The assignments in [believer *a*'s] belief set may assign different values to *x* and *y*, even though *x* and *y* co-refer on the input assignment [σ]." (Pickel, 2015, 347). TIL goes in the opposite direction. We do not want the option to change horses in midstream, so to speak, by bringing in an alternative to the 'input assignment' in a static context. TIL does not capture an agent's idiosyncratic perspective by means of 'shiftable' assignment functions, but by means of fine-grained, structure-sensitive hyperpropositions as attitude complements.

[15] See Duží et al. (2010, §3.3.1).

[16] See Duží et al. (2010, §3.5) on anaphoric reference.

attitude reports de dicto.[17] But we do not agree with the residual distinction between *opacity* and *transparency*. First and foremost, all of our contexts are transparent. Put bluntly, if a theory ends up with a category of what it calls opaque contexts then there is something wrong with the theory. The context-*in*variant semantics of TIL is obtained by universalising Frege's denotation-shifting semantics custom-made for 'indirect' contexts. Whereas Frege's semantics for attitude contexts was located on the margins of his overall semantic theory, we locate it right in the centre of ours. The upshot is that it becomes trivially true that all contexts are transparent. All singular-term positions are 'purely referential' (to use Quine's phrase), in the sense that pairs of terms that are co-denoting outside an attitude context remain co-denoting inside an attitude context, and pairs of terms that are not co-denoting inside an attitude context do not become co-denoting outside an attitude context. Thus, although Quine's 'the man in the brown hat' and 'the man on the beach' contingently share the same extension (Bernard J. Ortcutt, as it happens) they never co-denote him. Rather they denote, in every context/independently of context, two distinct individual offices. One comes with the uniqueness condition that its occupant must be the man in the brown hat (relative to some unspecified empirical context), and the other comes with the uniqueness condition that its occupant must be the man on the beach (again relative to some unspecified empirical context).

Second, we do not agree with the (by now obsolete?) dismissive understanding of 'intensional' as 'failing to validate rules of extensional logic and invoking creatures of darkness'. 'Intensional', as we use the term, means only 'involves intensional entities identified with functions from possible worlds'.

Third, and relatedly, when discussing quantifying into non-extensional contexts, we distinguish between *intensional* and *hyperintensional* contexts. Quantifying into intensional contexts is smooth sailing.[18] Quantifying into hyperintensional contexts is technically complicated and ontologically more exacting. The problem is less to do with the fine-graining of such contexts and more to do with having to operate on logical structures, or parts of structures, as opposed to merely operating on functions or their arguments. Quine's original problem with reaching an x inside an attitude context is, thus, also ours. But labelling the problematic context as 'opaque' explains nothing and just relabels the problem. The actual problem is that this x occurs in a different fashion inside a hyperintensional context than in either an intensional or extensional context.[19]

---

[17] Whether *notional/relational* must map onto *de dicto/de re* is far from a foregone conclusion, though, as different theories will have different conceptions of the dicto/re distinction. For instance, should some form or other of *acquaintance* play a role in attitudes de re? [For the record: no, not in TIL. See Duží et al. (2010, 435)].

[18] See Duží and Jespersen (2015, 2012) and Duží et al. (2010, 497–99).

[19] Quine's original objection to quantified modal logic is that (what appears to be) the same variable will have both used and mentioned occurrences within the same context. See also Kaplan (1986, 262–63). On a similar note, Pickel (2015, 340) objects to Cumming (2008), "There is no coordination between the occurrences of x outside of the belief ascription and the x occurring within the belief ascription". Our distinction between *displayed* and *executed* modes of occurrence of procedures, including variables, is sort of parallel to the distinction between words occurring mentioned or used, and quantifying into a displayed procedure is sort of parallel to quantifying into a quotation context. But we do not wish to push the parallel too far. Attempting to quantify into a quotation context is a no-starter, whereas the main

Fourth, the ability or inability to quantify-in is not what sets attitudes de re apart from attitudes de dicto. In TIL, both kinds are equally susceptible to quantifying-in. Nor should their difference be captured by means of scope differences between ∃ and χ. Quantified formulas (or rather their semantic counterparts) are a logical *consequence* of both kinds of attitudes, and not definitional of either of them. Rather their difference is anchored in a difference in logical structure (see Sect. 4.1). Their logical structure reveals that attitudes de re come with an existential presupposition on the level of extensional *res*, and if the presupposition is not satisfied then the quantified sentence is neither true nor false. This is as it should be, for attitudes de re are object-dependent. For instance, in the absence of Le Verrier's intermercurial planet, the appropriate *res* is not around to instantiate properties and fail to instantiate other properties, so predications de re about Vulcan cannot acquire a truth-value. By contrast, attitudes de dicto allow flights of fancy, so to speak, because they are not restrained by existential presuppositions. Still, attitudes are inten*t*ional relations that are invariably *about* something, so also attitudes de dicto qualify as object-dependent, provided objects other than extensional ones are allowed into one's ontology. What quantifying-in brings out is exactly what type of object a given attitude de dicto is dependent upon in the sense of having it as its complement. Logic and semantics intersect with metaphysics here, because the validity of existential quantification into hyperintensional contexts presupposes both suitable quantificational ranges, a transparent semantics and an extensional logic of hyperintensions.

2.3 Transparency versus opacity

To locate TIL in the wider landscape, we are aware of four diverse avenues one might pursue when attempting to validate quantifying-in. One is contextualism as made presentable by Frege and later formally encoded by luminaries such as Church and Montague. Our problem with this is that it allows some contexts to be opaque.[20] Another invokes 'flat' (hyper-) intensions as urged by, e.g., Bealer and Turner.[21] Our problem with this is that it foregoes any notion of objectual (hence, extrasyntactic) logical structures within which to operate on constituents. We are left with manipulating symbols, which sheds no light on hyperpropositions themselves. Yet another approach turns to various variants of sententialism, which relates agents directly to inscribed or uttered tokens (of types) of sentences.[22] Our problem with this is not only its excessive fine-graining and the fact that attitude ascriptions are held hostage to a particular symbolism or spoken language, but also the absurdity of quantifying into quotation contexts. The final one would be top-down, highly expressive, context-invariant theories, which enable objectual quantification into

---

Footnote 19 continued
technical point we are making here is that it is both feasible and sensible to quantify into a displayed context.

[20] For further critical comments on contextualism, see Duží et al. (2010, 110–112).

[21] See Turner (1992, 165) for a 'flat version of Montague's intensional logic' developed within the untyped λ-calculus.

[22] See Berto and Nolan (2021, §2.2) for examples and discussion.

hyperintensional contexts. TIL is, to the best of our knowledge, the only theory of this very kind. It is a defining feature of this sort of position that hyperintensional contexts are continuous with the semantics for intensional and extensional contexts. This marks a departure from Frege's contextualist semantics, of course, as does the introduction of a typed universe. But we still wish to characterise TIL as a broadly Fregean semantics. One reason is that we draw liberally on senses. Another is that the notion of *function* has been chosen as a theoretical primitive in TIL. This second point explains why our general logical framework is provided by the (typed) λ-calculus and its two key operations of application and abstraction, together with its rules of conversion. When a function is a mapping, *sets* and *relations* are rendered particular species of functions, namely such as are identified with their respective characteristic functions.[23]

Interestingly, there is another theory which also employs the typed λ-calculus (except in the vein of Montague Grammar), though with a view to developing a logic of opacity. Caie et al. (2019) sets out to develop such a logic compatible with higher-order classical logic.[24] Classical opacitists (as they call themselves) and TIL ('classical transparentists', presumably) agree on the semantics for the connectives and the identity predicate, but part company over the unconditional validity of Leibniz's Law. This 'law' being unconditionally valid is a necessary condition for Substitution being unconditionally valid. This is the schema of Substitution:

Substitution. $\qquad a = b \rightarrow (\varphi \leftrightarrow \varphi[b/a])$

Opacity is defined as a false instance of Substitution:

Opacity. $\qquad a = b \wedge \neg(\varphi \leftrightarrow \varphi[b/a])$

The metaphysics that goes together with opacity is this:

> We take it to be obvious that Hesperus and Phosphorus are identical, though we are exploring views on which Hesperus and Phosphorus have different properties. (Caie et al., 2019, 12, fn. 31.)

---

[23] 'Function' is historically ambiguous between Frege's *Funktion* (generation of mapping) and *Wertverlauf* (mapping). Church (1956, 16) is clear on this: "If the way in which a function-in-extension yields or produces its values for its arguments is altered without causing any change either in the range of the function or in the value of the function for any argument, then the function remains the same; but the associated *function concept*, or concept determining the function ..., is thereby changed." In modern-day parlance, function concepts qualify as hyperintensions. Our notion of hyperintensions is rooted in Church's *function-in-intension* or *functional concept*, Frege's *Funktion* and *Sinn*, as well as *Turing machine*. *Application* and *abstraction* are theoretical primitives, which are central to the definition of two of our hyperintensions. See Definition 1 (iii), (iv), in Sect. 3.4.

[24] Caie et al. (2019) is an exceptionally rich paper, which we would have liked to engage with at length. For now, we are just scratching the surface and confining ourselves to the core question of the validity of Leibniz's Law, hence of Substitution. Thus, this comparison of 'classical opacity/transparency' is about substitution specifically rather than quantification. We want to stress that we find it commendable that someone should try to develop a *logic* of opacity, which will distinguish between true and false instances of Substitution. Opacity has typically been understood purely negatively as the failure to preserve transparency, but Caie et al. (2019) helps clarify what the logical implications are of adopting opacity. Still, we disagree with treating opacity as a datum (even in the explorative spirit of Caie et al. (2019)), rather than as a symptom of a wrongheaded formal semantics.

This is anathema to TIL. If the second clause is true then we reject the first clause (or *vice versa*). We are quite happy to do so, in fact, because many standard cases of "… is …", such as "Hesperus is Phosphorus" and "Water is H$_2$O", should not go into "… = …", as in "Hesperus = Phosphorus" or "Water = H$_2$O".[25] The welcome upshot is that Leibniz's Law is rendered inapplicable instead of invalid. If one, nonetheless, pushes ahead with "$a = b$" followed by substitution, one ends up with an inference that is valid, for sure, but also unsound. This schema summarises the position TIL assumes as regards substitutability within hyperpropositional attitude contexts, whether de re or de dicto:

Transparency. $\quad a = b \rightarrow \chi\varphi a = \chi\varphi b$

Substitutability within the scope of χ is a necessary condition for the identity, or at least hyperintensional isomorphism, of a and b.[26] This schema is perfectly trivial in TIL, which is because the threshold for being a correct instance of "$a = b$" is high. The constraint is that the substituends for 'a' and 'b' must be pairs of synonymous terms. TIL has a catalogue of identity, congruence and equivalence relations, and depending on whether the context within which one intends to perform substitution is extensional, intensional or hyperintensional, one or the other relation is required for valid substitution (see, e.g. Duží et al., 2010, §2.7.1). Obviously, self-identity guarantees substitutability even in hyperintensional contexts. As soon as transparency is adopted, one steers clear of a tangle such as the following, which opacity seems to be tasked with disentangling:

> […] although for Hesperus to be visible at night just is for Phosphorus to be visible at night, the ancients knew that Hesperus is visible at night, but did not know that Phosphorus is visible at night. (Caie et al., 2019, 15)[27]

Formally:

$$\varphi a = \varphi b \land (\chi\varphi a \land \neg\chi\varphi b)$$

We agree about what the ancients knew and did not know; we disagree that Hesperus being visible at night is the same as Phosphorus being visible at night. In TIL, Hesperus is the office of being the brightest non-lunar object in the evening/night sky, and Phosphorus is the office of being the brightest non-lunar object in the morning sky. These two offices are contingently vacant or occupied, and when occupied, then contingently co-occupied. Hence, "(the occupant of the office of) Hesperus is visible at night" and "(the occupant of the office of) Phosphorus is visible at night" denote two *different* possible-world propositions that just happen to be both true (perhaps since the origin of our Solar system). If "$\varphi a = \varphi b$" is read de dicto or intensionally (meaning that φa, φb are one and the same possible-world

---

[25] "Water = H$_2$O" has never sat well with us. How can a liquid be identified with a molecular structure? This smacks of category mistake, or type-theoretic incongruity. "Water = H$_2$O" feels like a throwback to the long-gone days of materialist reductionism. We would rather say that (pure) water *has* H$_2$O (namely, as its molecular structure).

[26] See Sect. 4.1.1 on procedural isomorphism, which defines co-hyperintensionality.

[27] See also Duží et al. (2010, 3): *Propositional Hesperus/Phosphorus.*

proposition), then it is false. If "$\varphi a = \varphi b$" is read de re or extensionally (meaning that φa, φb are both true), then the second conjunct, "$(\chi\varphi a \wedge \neg\chi\varphi b)$", is improper, hence without truth-value, because χ is not an attitude to a truth-value. The de dicto reading is more consonant with the quote above. The opacitist needs their semantics to accommodate a case of this form: "Something is the same, but the ancients did not know it was the same". The transparentist needs their semantics to accommodate a case of this form: "Something and something are not the same, and the ancients did not know that they were the same."

Opacity helps the opacitist to a true conjunction and the preservation of the Frege puzzles of cognitive significance. The opacitist has recourse to opacity to save the conjunction above from coming out false: it cannot be true that the ancients knew, and also did not know, that the same celestial body was visible at night. The complications that opacity incurs—developing two logics, one for transparency and one for opacity, and maintaining a system of double bookkeeping, one book for transparent contexts and another book for opaque contexts—serve the purpose of maintaining a fairly simple semantics for "a is b", "φa" and "φb".

Transparentists will have to discard the first conjunct in order to preserve the Frege puzzles. To see this, if the conjunction were instead "$a = b \wedge (\chi\varphi a \wedge \neg\chi\varphi b)$" then the conjunction would be necessarily false. If the conjunction were "$a = b \wedge (\chi\varphi a \wedge \chi\varphi b)$" then the conjunction would be necessarily true, with the conjuncts of "$\chi\varphi a \wedge \chi\varphi b$" being mere notational variants. In order to preserve both transparency and the non-triviality of both conjuncts, the transparentist develops a more elaborate semantics for "$a = b$", "φa" and "$\varphi a = \varphi b$" that remains the same whether occurring within the scope of χ or not. Let the first conjunct be "$a = b$". In prose, the result becomes: the office of Hesperus and the office of Phosphorus happen to share the same occupant, and the ancients knew that the occupant of the office of Hesperus was visible at night, but the ancients did not know that the occupant of the office of Phosphorus was visible at night. This is a true conjunction. Let the first conjunct now be as above: "$\varphi a = \varphi b$". In prose, the result becomes: the occupant of the office of Hesperus being visible at night is identical to the occupant of the office of Phosphorus being visible at night, and the ancients knew that the occupant of the office of Hesperus was visible at night, but the ancients did not know that the occupant of the office of Phosphorus was visible at night. As we have argued, "(the occupant of the office of) Phosphorus is visible at night" is a different proposition than "(the occupant of the office of) Hesperus is visible at night"; therefore, "$\varphi a = \varphi b \wedge (\chi\varphi a \wedge \neg\chi\varphi b)$" comes out false. This outcome is in keeping with Transparency; if one maintains that "$\neg(\chi\varphi a = \chi\varphi b)$" then it is no option to maintain, nonetheless, that "$\varphi a = \varphi b$".

For a general characterisation of classical transparentism, we would not hesitate to characterise TIL as a *transparent higher-order logic*, although TIL would not entirely fit the opacitists' description of such a logic in Caie et al., (2019, 8). We are only hesitant about one element in their description, though. This is their list of what characterises a transparent higher-order logic (ignoring the logical relationships

between the various principles, as some entail others), together with further
principles from their catalogue that also suit TIL (we follow their formalisation):

- *Equivalence.* $\quad a = a \land (a = b \land a = c \rightarrow b = c)$
- *Material Equivalence.* $\quad p = q \rightarrow p \leftrightarrow q$
- *Beta-Eta Equivalence.* $\quad \varphi \leftrightarrow \psi$, provided φ and ψ are $\beta\eta$-equivalent
- *Lift Congruence.* $\quad a = b \rightarrow (\lambda X.Xa) = (\lambda X.Xb)$
- *Application Congruence.* $\quad F = G \rightarrow Fa = Ga$
- *Substitution.* $\quad a = b \rightarrow (\varphi \leftrightarrow \varphi\,[b/a])$
- *Universal Instantiation.* $\quad \forall x\varphi \rightarrow \varphi[a/x]$, where a is free for x in φ
- *Leibniz's Law.* $\quad a = b \rightarrow \forall X\,(Xa \leftrightarrow Xb)$

Our proviso remains intact: (the substituends of) 'a', 'b', 'c' must be constants denoting individuals and not offices or anything else, unless we wish to express the self-identity of an office (etc.) bearing more than one name, which is the exception rather than the rule. Our only reservation is with the constraint *Beta-Eta Equivalence*, in case it is recruited for the purposes of hyperintensional individuation or for a logic of *partial* functions. If $\beta\eta$-equivalence is instead only applied to conversion of terms denoting *total* functions occurring in non-hyperintensional contexts, then *Beta-Eta Equivalence* applies to TIL.[28]

3 Transparent Intensional Logic

This part describes and defines the foundations of TIL, together with the particular devices required to operate on hyperintensions.

3.1 Function and procedure

The most fundamental distinction in TIL is between *procedures* and *functions*. Procedures are structured, higher-order entities, and on a given occasion a procedure occurs either in the *displayed* or *executed* mode within another procedure. The default is that procedures occur in executed mode. Functions are modern-day mappings from a domain to a range, $f: x \mapsto f(x)$, with the important proviso that TIL allows also functions that are only *partially* defined. Functions are set-theoretic (hence, unstructured) and first-order entities, unless the elements of a domain or range of a given function are higher-order objects, in which case the function also becomes a higher-order object in the type hierarchy. Sets and relations are defined as particular kinds of functions; a set is identified with its characteristic function, and an *n*-ary relation is identified with a function from *n* number of arguments to a truth-value. Intensional entities (as per possible-world semantics) are identified with functions from a logical space of possible worlds, and necessary co-extensionality equals co-intensionality. Extensional entities such as individuals and truth-values

---

[28] See Jespersen (2021) regarding β-conversion and η-conversion with regard to hyperintensional individuation. See Duží and Kosterec (2017) or Duží and Jespersen (2013) for discussion of β-conversion and η-conversion with regard to a hyperintensional logic of partial functions.

are typed as medadic, or nullary, functions, i.e., as constant values. One important thing to bear in mind is that *execution* applies to procedures while *evaluation* applies to functions.

The *syntax* of TIL is that of a typed λ-calculus enriched with the tools to operate on hyperintensions, i.e., either to execute them or to present them as arguments. Its *semantics* is a procedural one that conceives of meanings as abstract *procedures*.[29] This means that TIL λ-terms denote procedures producing functions rather than denoting the functions themselves. A procedure is structured in a manner that details which logical operations of which types apply to which operands of which types. Typically, the output of one operation will serve as input for another operation. Given the types of the operations and the operands, it can be calculated which type of object the procedure is structured to produce. A simple example: if the procedure specifies the application of a function taking two numbers to a truth-value then the procedure is typed to produce a truth-value. A truth-value is obtained by picking two numbers and applying the function to them. The fact that there may be no object of a particular type as output does not detract from there being a procedure typed to produce an object of this type. Our procedures specify what *types* of entities to manipulate in what ways in order to produce some particular *type* of entity. The *atomic* procedures are of one step and provide their products (i.e., the entities they are typed to produce) as input objects on which molecular procedures operate. The *molecular* procedures are of two steps or more and detail how to proceed from input to output (or in the direction of output, if there is none). Of the procedures we define below, two of them may fail to yield a product.

The connection between procedures and hyperpropositions is that hyperpropositions are identified with particular procedures.[30] Those of the procedures that are hyperpropositions are either those that are typed to produce truth-values or are typed to produce truth-conditions, where truth-conditions are typed as functions from possible worlds to a partial function from times to truth-values.

We account for propositional structure in terms of procedural structure. We must explain how finely individuated procedurally structured propositions are. Otherwise, we cannot know which prospective input operands are admissible in an extensional logic of hyperintensions, for we would not know which substitutions would be valid. Our principle of granularity is quite strict, contributing to an exact calibration of the entities that can be quantified over. The principle is called *procedural isomorphism* and is an obvious nod to its predecessors, Carnap's intensional isomorphism and Church's synonymous isomorphism. Procedural isomorphism will be presented formally in Sect. 4.1.1.

---

[29] Moschovakis (2006) characterises meanings as generalised algorithms. Our procedures likewise qualify as *generalised* algorithms, because they are procedures that need not be *effectively* computable (thereby perhaps straining the idea of an algorithm a bit).

[30] This qualifies TIL as a *reductionist* theory of hyperpropositions, because hyperpropositions are 'reduced' to instances of a more general sort of entity instead of being *sui generis*. TIL is also a reductionist theory of propositions, i.e., the truth-conditions of empirical sentences, because TIL identifies them with functions from possible worlds to functions from times to truth-values.

3.2 Invariance and transparency

The title of the paper promises that quantifying-in is *transparent*, and it is because quantifying-in does not trigger shift of denotation and, thus, does not induce opacity. What *contextualist* semantic theories have got right is that another entity than the one being salient in extensional contexts needs to be picked out. What contextualism is wrong about is its tenet that each term or expression must have a bespoke semantics to suit each different sort of context. Thus, we are not erecting a tower of increasingly indirect senses and denotations. In our context-invariant semantics, a term or expression retains its fixed sense and denotation. This explains why we need devices that can insert a term's or expression's meaning rather than its denotation into argument position so as to make the displayed parts themselves amenable to logical manipulation.

This is the semantic schema of TIL:

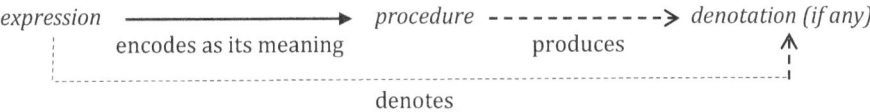

The relation of *encoding*, or *expressing*, between an expression and the procedure assigned to it as its meaning is semantically primary. Once we have the meaning procedure, we are in a position to examine which object the procedure produces, prove what is entailed by the procedure, examine its structure, etc. The semantic relation of denoting between an expression and a denotation (if any) piggybacks on the logical relation of producing between a procedure and its product (if any).

The semantics of definite descriptions, predicates and all other terms must be *top-down* for full referential transparency. This is to say that the above semantic schema that illustrates the relation between a term, the procedure that is its meaning, and its denotation (if any) in a hyperintensional context is the same schema that applies to intensional and extensional contexts. A term or expression expresses a (privileged) procedure as its meaning and denotes the entity (if any) that the procedure is typed to produce.[31] The denoted entity (if any) can be an object of one of the two basic kinds already sketched at the beginning of this part:

(i) a *non-procedural* entity, i.e., an object of a type of order 1 (see below), which comprises all partial *functions*, neither the domain nor range of which contains any procedures;
(ii) a *procedure* of a lower order in the type hierarchy (see below) than that of the relevant meaning procedure, in which case the produced (hence, denoted) procedure occurs as a functional argument.

Abstract procedures cannot be sets, tuples or aggregates of instructions, because sets, tuples or aggregates cannot be *executed*. Rather, they are structured wholes that

---

[31] *Indexicals* being the only exception: while the sense of an indexical remains constant (i.e., as a free variable with a type assignment), its denotation varies in keeping with its contextual embedding. See Duží et al. (2010, §3.4).

themselves can be executed.[32] Importantly, empirical terms, such as the definite description 'the Bishop of Rome' or the predicate 'is a planet', never denote their extension at any world/time pair, a fortiori not the extension in the actual world at the present time. The world/time-relative extensions (if any) fall outside the purview of the semantics. Empirical terms invariably denote the condition that an individual, a set, etc., must satisfy in order to be (in) its extension at the world/time pair of evaluation. We model these conditions as possible-world intensions.[33]

In TIL we reserve the terms 'refer' and 'reference' for the factual and extra-semantic relation between an empirical term and the value of the denoted intension at a given $\langle w, t \rangle$ pair. Thus, 'the man in the brown hat' and 'the man on the beach' co-*refer* to Mr Orcutt, as a matter of extra-semantic *fact*.[34]

3.3 Variables and Trivialisation

The two atomic 'feeder' procedures are:

- *Variable*
- *Trivialisation*

TIL deviates in four relevant respects from the version of λ-calculus made popular by Montague's Intensional Logic. First, *meanings* are not identified with (or modelled as) mappings from world/time pairs. Instead Montague-like meanings (i.e., mappings) are the products of our meaning procedures.

Second, *variables* are not linguistic items. The term 'y' expresses an atomic procedure as its meaning and picks out the entity that an assignment function has assigned to y as its value. Thus, three entities are involved: a term, a variable (a procedure), a value. We are adopting an objectual version of Tarski's conception of variables. Our objectual variables are procedures that produce entities dependently on *valuations*, i.e. assignment functions; we say that variables v-produce. Countably many variables are assigned to each type (see below). Moreover, entities of each type can be organised into sequences of countably many elements. Valuation v picks up one such sequence, and the ith variable v-produces the ith element of the sequence.

Third, the analysis of a piece of language, and this includes "b believes hyperproposition A", does not amount to translating it from some natural language into an artificial language (say, the λ-calculus), which in turn receives an interpretation, which is transferred back to the natural-language sentence. Instead our λ-calculus is an inherently interpreted formal language, which serves as a device to directly denote meaning procedures. Our λ-terms denote procedures. Meanings are studied by studying their structure and constituents as encoded in the λ-calculus of TIL in virtue of the stipulated isomorphism between formulae and meanings. It

---

[32] For more details on the character of these structured wholes and their mereology, see Duží (2019) and Jespersen (2019).

[33] This program of anti-actualist semantics is described in Duží et al. (2010, §2.4.1).

[34] For further details, see Duží et al. (2010, 301–11).

should be stressed again that our hyperpropositional procedures are not linguistic entities; they are higher-order abstract entities.

Fourth, TIL comes with *explicit intensionalisation and temporalisation*. See Sect. 3.5.1 below.

The ideography of TIL also comes with *constants*, which are vehicles of reference that pick out a specific entity in one go without the assistance of other terms and without invoking anything descriptive. We can potentially develop constants for any entity of any type, including hyperpropositions. The semantic counterpart of a constant is a *Trivialisation*. A Trivialisation is a procedure that picks out a specific entity in one go. Where 'Pluto' denotes Pluto (typed as an individual), the Trivialisation of Pluto, ^0Pluto, is a one-step procedure for identifying Pluto. The procedure, just like a non-descriptive proper name, does not specify how to identify the object in question. Trivialisation embodies merely the procedure of 'reaching' into a particular type (here, the type of individuals) and 'extracting' a particular object (here, Pluto) from there. A variable, by contrast, embodies the procedure of 'reaching' into a particular type and 'extracting' an arbitrary object from there.

3.4 Composition, Closure, Double Execution

The two complex, or multi-step, procedures are:

- *Composition*
- *Closure*

Composition is the procedure of functional application, rather than the functional value (if any) resulting from the application. Closure is the procedure of functional abstraction, rather than the resulting function.

TIL contains a duo of explicit Execution procedures, which include these two:

- *Single Execution*
- *Double Execution*

Single Execution, ^1X, is part of Tichý's inductive definition of procedures (called *constructions*) in (1988, §15), but has been left out of the definition below. It is not needed for present purposes because, importantly, the default mode in which procedures occur is as executed. ^1X is the same procedure (though of a higher order in the type hierarchy) as X, provided X is a procedure at all.

Double Execution, ^2X, encodes the transitivity of descending from procedure to product (if any). Double Execution is complex, provided X is a procedure at all. Double Execution will appear in some type specifications in the interest of clarification.

Here is the inductive definition of *procedure*.

Definition 1 (*procedure*)

(i) *Variables* x, y, ... are *procedures* that *produce* objects (elements of their respective ranges) dependently on a valuation v; they *v-produce*.

(ii) Where X is an object whatsoever (an extension, an intension or a *proce-*

dure), ^0X is the *procedure Trivialisation*. ^0X produces (displays) X without any change of X.

(iii) Let $X, Y_1, ..., Y_n$ be arbitrary *procedures*. Then *Composition* $[X\ Y_1...Y_n]$ is the following *procedure*. For any valuation v, the *Composition* $[X\ Y_1...Y_n]$ is *v-improper* if at least one of the *procedures* $X, Y_1, ..., Y_n$ is *v*-improper by failing to *v*-produce anything, or if X does not *v*-produce a function that is defined at the *n*-tuple of objects *v*-produced by $Y_1,...,Y_n$. If X does *v*-produce such a function, then $[X\ Y_1...Y_n]$ *v*-produces the value of this function at the *n*-tuple.

(iv) The (λ-) *Closure* $[\lambda x_1...x_m\ Y]$ is the following *procedure*. Let $x_1, x_2, ..., x_m$ be pair-wise distinct variables and Y a *procedure*. Then $[\lambda x_1...x_m\ Y]$ *v*-produces the function f that takes any members $B_1, ..., B_m$ of the respective ranges of the variables $x_1, ..., x_m$ into the object (if any) that is $v(B_1/x_1,...,B_m/x_m)$-*produced* by Y, where $v(B_1/x_1, ..., B_m/x_m)$ is like v except for assigning B_1 to $x_1, ..., B_m$ to x_m.

(v) The *Double Execution* ^2X is the following *procedure*. Where X is any entity, the *Double Execution* ^2X is *v*-improper if X is not itself a *procedure*, or if X does not *v*-produce a *procedure*, or if X *v*-produces a *v*-improper *procedure*. Otherwise, let X *v*-produce a *procedure* Y and Y *v*-produce an entity Z; then ^2X *v*-produces Z.

(vi) Nothing is a *procedure*, unless it so follows from (i) through (v). □

3.5 Typed universe

TIL comes with a thoroughly typed universe. The ground floor is populated by first-order, non-procedural entities. First-order entities are functions, whether 'typical' functions such as mathematical functions, or characteristic functions and the functions of possible-world semantics, or nullary functions such as individuals and truth-values. Note that intensions—functions from possible worlds—are typed as *first*-order entities, unless they are functions that contain in their range or domain a procedure such as a hyperpropositional attitude, which is typed as a relation-in-intension of an individual to a procedure.[35]

Definition 2 (*simple type*) Let B be a *base*, where a base is a collection of pair-wise disjoint, non-empty sets. Then:

(i) Every member of B is an elementary *type of order 1 over B*.
(ii) Let $\alpha, \beta_1, ..., \beta_m$ ($m > 0$) be types of order 1 over B. Then the collection ($\alpha\ \beta_1\ ...\ \beta_m$) of all *m*-ary partial mappings from $\beta_1 \times ... \times \beta_m$ into α is a functional *type of order 1 over B*.
(iii) Nothing is a *type of order 1 over B* unless it so follows from (i) and (ii). □

---

[35] First-*order*, higher-*degree* intensions are defined as functions from intensions to functions that contain an intension in their domain or range.

For the purposes of natural-language analysis, we are currently assuming the following base of ground types, which form part of the ontological commitments of TIL:

o: the set of truth-values {**T**, **F**}
ι: the set of individuals (the universe of discourse)
τ: the set of real numbers (doubling as times)
ω: the set of logically possible worlds (the logical space)

Hence, we are able to type both extensional and intensional entities. *Intensions* are polymorphous functions of type $(\beta\omega)$, where β is frequently a *chronology* of α-objects of type $(\alpha\tau)$; thus α-intensions are frequently of type $((\alpha\tau)\omega)$, which will be abbreviated as '$\alpha_{\tau\omega}$'. An object of type $\alpha_{\tau\omega}$ is a function from worlds to a function from times to α-typed objects.[36]

Some important extensional and intensional entities include:

- Characteristic function (here, *set of individuals*)/(οι)
- Set-in-intension (here, *property of individuals*)/(οι)$_{\tau\omega}$
- Individual-in-intension (*individual office* or *role*)/ι$_{\tau\omega}$
- Truth-value-in-intension (*truth-condition* or *PWS proposition*)/o$_{\tau\omega}$
- Binary relation-in-intension (here, *attitude*)/(οια)$_{\tau\omega}$

Note that if the complement of the attitude is a truth-condition, as per standard possible-world semantics, then the type of the attitude is (οιο$_{\tau\omega}$)$_{\tau\omega}$, because α = o$_{\tau\omega}$. If the complement of the attitude is a hyperproposition, as in this paper, then α = $*_n$, hence (οι$*_n$)$_{\tau\omega}$ is the type of the attitude. The higher-order types $*_n$ fall outside the purview of Definition 2 and are the province of the ramified type hierarchy, as per Definition 3 below.

3.5.1 Explicit intensionalisation and temporalisation

One of the key features of how TIL analyses natural-language discourse is what we call explicit intensionalisation and temporalisation. It is developed in opposition to Montague's intensional logic. Montague's IL comes with the 'half-hearted' type *s*, where *s* is the type of world/time pairs. *s* is neither a ground type nor a functional type, but only occurs as a fragment of functional types, as in $(s \to t)$. TIL, by contrast, contains a full-fledged type ω for worlds and a full-fledged type τ for instants of time. This enables formulas like "λw [... w ...]", "λt [... t ...]", "λwt [... w ... t ...]", and "$\lambda w \lambda t$ [... w ... t ...]", where it is explicit from the syntax that the evaluation takes place at empirical indices.[37] These indices are not relegated to a meta-language, as is common in other formal-semantic frameworks for natural-language discourse. The non-vacuous occurrence of at least one '*w*' or '*t*', denoting

---

[36] See Duží et al. (2010, §2.5).

[37] For critical comments on Montague's IL and a comparison with TIL, see Duží et al. (2010, §2.4.3).

Transparent quantification into hyperpropositional attitudes *de dicto*

a modal or temporal variable, in the syntax is what marks the difference between empirical and non-empirical language.

Empirical languages incorporate an element of *contingency*, because they denote *empirical conditions* that may or may not be satisfied at some world/time pair of evaluation. For instance, it is only at some world/time pairs that a given individual entertains a given attitude. Our explicit intensionalisation and temporalisation enables us to encode procedures producing possible-world intensions directly in the logical syntax in virtue of terms for world and time variables. Where variable w ranges over possible worlds (type ω) and t over times (type τ), the following logical form essentially characterises the logical syntax of empirical language:

$$\lambda w \lambda t \, [\ldots w \ldots t \ldots]$$

The above schematic Closure is typed to produce a condition satisfiable by world/time pairs.[38] Here is the (privileged or canonical) form of the hyperproposition that Pluto is a planet:[39]

$$\lambda w \lambda t \, [^0 Planet_{wt} \, {}^0 Pluto]$$

The above Closure is a hyperproposition that produces a truth-condition/$o_{\tau\omega}$. The Closure does what it does by abstracting over the respective values of the variables w, t. The purpose is to isolate exactly those worlds and times at which it is true that Pluto is an element of the respective (i.e., world-and-time-relative) set of planets (assuming that a crisp definition of planethood is in place). The general flow of the procedure is to break down and then build up again. An analysis will spell out what is going on.[40] The above procedure contains three occurrences of Composition ('breaking down'):

[1] [$^0 Planet \, w$]: the application of $Planet/(o\iota)_{\tau\omega}$ to a possible world v-produced by $w \to \omega$ to obtain a function of type $((o\iota)\tau)$, a chronology which inputs instants of time and outputs the respective sets of planets at those particular times.

[2] [[$^0 Planet \, w$]t], or $^0 Planet_{wt}$, for short: the application of the chronology obtained at [1] to a time v-produced by $t \to \tau$ to obtain a set of individuals/($o\iota$).

[3] [[[$^0 Planet \, w$]t] $^0 Pluto$], or [$^0 Planet_{wt} \, {}^0 Pluto$], for short: the application of the set obtained at [2] to Pluto/ι to obtain a truth-value/o.

The truth-value obtained is relativised to worlds and times by means of two instances of Closure ('building up') to obtain a truth-condition.

---

[38] When speaking of 'world/time pairs', we are allowing ourselves to pretend that a function from worlds to a function from times to entities is equivalent to a binary function from world/time pairs to entities. This pretence is innocuous in this essay, because here we are not considering the modal and the temporal dimension separately. See Duží et al. (2010, §2.5). Moreover, in a logic of partial functions, such as TIL, *schönfinkelisation* fails to always preserve equivalence: see Duží et al. (2010, 204–05).

[39] By 'privileged' or 'canonical' form we intend the *literal* analysis of a sentence, where syntactically simple terms like 'Pluto' and 'planet' are paired off with a Trivialisation of the denoted object, here $^0 Pluto$, $^0 Planet$. For the notion of literal analyses, see Duží et al. (2010, 105, Defs. 1.10, 1.11).

[40] This exposition relies on Duží et al. (2010, §2.4.2).

3.5.2 Ramified type hierarchy

The relevant logical feature of our ramified hierarchy of types is that we are guaranteed to always have a hyperintension of a higher order at our disposal that will present a hyperintension of a lower order. Without this possibility, we would be falling short of the expressive power required to pull off quantifying-in, once hyperintensions are construed as higher-order entities rather than primitive first-order entities.

The definition of the ramified hierarchy of types decomposes into three parts: firstly, simple types of order 1; secondly, procedures of order n; thirdly, types of order $n+1$.

Definition 3 (*ramified hierarchy of types*)
T_1 (*types of order 1*). See Definition 2.
C_n (*procedures of order n*)

(i) Let x be a variable ranging over a type of order n. Then x is a *procedure of order n over B*.
(ii) Let X be a member of a type of order n. Then ^0X, ^2X are *procedures of order n over B*.
(iii) Let $X, X_1, ..., X_m$ ($m > 0$) be *procedures* of order n over B. Then $[X X_1... X_m]$ is a *procedure of order n over B*.
(iv) Let $x_1, ..., x_m, X$ ($m > 0$) be *procedures* of order n over B. Then $[\lambda x_1...x_m X]$ is a *procedure of order n over B*.
(v) Nothing is a *procedure of order n over B* unless it so follows from C_n (i–iv).

T_{n+1} (*types of order n+1*). Let $*_n$ be the collection of all procedures of order n over B. Then:

(i) $*_n$ and every type of order n are *types of order n + 1*.
(ii) If $m > 0$ and $\alpha_1, ..., \alpha_m$ are types of order $n + 1$ over B, then $(\alpha_1 ... \alpha_m)$ (see T_1 (ii)) is a *type of order n + 1 over B*.
(iii) Nothing is a *type of order n + 1 over B* unless it so follows from T_{n+1} (i) and (ii). □

Notational conventions. '$y \to \alpha$' means that variable y ranges over the type α. If C is a procedure, then '$C \to \alpha$' means that C is typed to produce an entity of type α. That an object a is of a type α is denoted 'a/α'. Thus, for instance, '$C/*_n \to \iota$' means that the procedure C is of order n (i.e. belongs to type $*_n$) and is typed to produce an individual. Throughout this paper we use variables $w \to \omega$ and $t \to \tau$. If $C \to \alpha_{\tau\omega}$ then the frequently used Composition $[[C w] t] \to \alpha$ will be written as 'C_{wt}' for short.

Definition 4 (*existential and universal quantifiers*). The *existential quantifier* $\exists^\alpha/$ $(o(o\alpha))$ is a total polymorphic function that takes a set of α-typed elements to the truth-value **T** if the set is non-empty and otherwise to **F**. The *general quantifier* $\forall^\alpha/$ $(o(o\alpha))$ is a total polymorphic function that takes a set S of α-typed elements to the truth-value **T** if S contains all the elements of type α and otherwise to **F**. □

'∃', '∀' are categorematic terms in TIL, namely functors that denote functions of the above type. Once a set produced by, e.g., λy [… y …] is inputted as an argument to ∃ or ∀, the quantifier returns a truth-value as value. The strings '∃y', '∀y' count as ill-formed in TIL, because all binding is λ-binding or ^{0}-binding (see below for the definition). The proper notation is '[$^0\exists\lambda y$ [… y …]]', '[$^0\forall\lambda y$ [… y …]]'. Anyway, for the sake of simplicity, we may sometimes stick to '∃y [… y …]', '∀y [… y …]', when no confusion can arise.[41]

3.6 Displayed versus executed; free versus bound; valid substitution

We define here what it means for procedures to occur in the *displayed* mode and to occur in the *executed* mode, and we explain what it means for variables to have *free* and to have *bound* occurrences.

When a procedure occurs in the displayed mode, the *procedure* itself becomes an object on which other procedures can operate. We also say that the context of its occurrence is *hyperintensional*, because all the sub-procedures of a displayed procedure occur neither intensionally nor extensionally; they are displayed as well. When a procedure occurs in the executed mode, the *product* (if any) of the procedure is susceptible to being operated on. In this case, the executed procedure is a *constituent* of its super-procedure, and an additional distinction crops up at this level. A constituent producing a function may occur either *intensionally* (de dicto) or *extensionally* (de re). If intensionally, then the produced *function* is the object of predication; if extensionally, then the *value* (if any) of the produced function is the object of predication. The pair of distinctions between displayed/executed and intensional/extensional occurrences enables us to distinguish between three kinds of *context*. The rigorous definitions of the three kinds of contexts can be found in Duží et al. (2010, §2.6). Though the basic ideas are fairly simple, the exact details are rather complicated. For this reason, we only explain intuitively the main ideas here.

- *Hyperintensional context*. A procedure occurs in the *displayed* mode (though another procedure at least one order higher needs to be *executed* in order to produce the displayed procedure).

---

[41] It may be instructive to consider how TIL formalises the *Barcan Formula*: $\Diamond\exists xFx \supset \exists x \Diamond Fx$. There are two ways to go about this. Either we stick to $\Diamond$ or we turn to existential quantification over worlds (ignoring times). S5-possibility is typed as a property of propositions, of type (o(oω)), which is not indexed to worlds, because the S5-modalities are analytic, being valid on equivalence frames. Sub-S5-modalities are not, so properties of propositions are indexed to worlds, and for this reason such properties are of type ((o(oω))ω): see Materna (2005).

(i) [[$^0\exists\lambda w$ [$^0\exists\lambda x$ [$^0F_w\,x$]]] ⊃ [$^0\exists\lambda x$ [$^0\exists\lambda w$ [$^0F_w\,x$]]]]
(ii) [[$^0\Diamond\,\lambda w$ [$^0\exists\lambda x$ [$^0F_w\,x$]]] ⊃ [$^0\exists\lambda x$ [$^0\Diamond\,\lambda w$ [$^0F_w\,x$]]]]

Both formulas, on their intended interpretation, express that if some world has some individual with property F then some individual at some world has property F. It is obvious why the Barcan Formula (and its Converse) requires S5-possibility and that the domain function be constant: for all $w, w' \in W$, $D(w) = D(w')$. It is also obvious (as proved by running a type check) why neither of (i), (ii) engenders the problem that a λ-bound variable has an 'opaque' occurrence.

Transparent quantification into hyperpropositional attitudes *de dicto*

- *Intensional context*. A procedure occurs in the *executed* mode in order to produce a function rather than one of its values (moreover, the executed procedure does not occur within another hyperintensional context).
- *Extensional context*. A procedure occurs in the *executed* mode in order to produce a particular value of a function at a given argument (moreover, the executed procedure does not occur within another intensional or hyperintensional context).

We next turn to a definition of *sub-procedure*.

Definition 5 (*sub-procedure*). Let C be a procedure. Then:

(i) C is a *sub-procedure of* C.
(ii) If C is ^0X or ^2X and X is a procedure, then X is a *sub-procedure of* C.
(iii) If C is [X X_1...X_n] then X, X_1, ..., X_n are *sub-procedures of* C.
(iv) If C is [λx_1...x_n Y] then Y is a *sub-procedure of* C.
(v) If A is a *sub-procedure of* B and B is a *sub-procedure of* C then A is a *sub-procedure of* C.
(vi) A procedure is a *sub-procedure of* C only if it so follows from (i–v). □

In particular, the constituent parts of a procedure are not the particular material, or otherwise non-procedural abstract, objects the procedure operates on. Correspondingly, Mont Blanc cannot be a constituent of a procedure; ^{0}Mont_Blanc can. Instead, *the constituents of a procedure are exclusively those sub-procedures that occur in executed mode*. (See the 10-part decomposition below for illustration.) To define the distinction between displayed and executed mode, we must take the following factors into account. A procedure C can occur in displayed mode only as a sub-procedure within another procedure D that operates on C. Therefore, C itself must be produced by another sub-procedure C' in D. And it is necessary to define this distinction for *occurrences* of procedures, because one and the same procedure C can occur in executed mode in D and at the same time serve as an input/output object for another sub-procedure C' of D that operates on C. The distinction between displayed and execution mode of a procedure can be characterised like this. Let C be a sub-procedure of a procedure D. Then an occurrence of C *occurs in displayed mode in* D if the execution of D does not involve the execution of this occurrence of C. Otherwise, C occurs in *executed mode within* D, i.e., C occurs as a constituent of the procedure D.

To see how this works, consider this sentence:

"Tilman solves the equation $Sin(x) = 0$"

When solving the problem of seeking the numbers x such that the value of the function *Sine* at x equals zero, Tilman is not related to the set of multiples of the number π, i.e., to an object of type (οτ). If he were, Tilman would have already solved the problem, thus pre-empting the search for suitable values of x. Rather Tilman wishes to find the product of the procedure [λx [^{0}= [$^0Sin\ x$] ^{0}0]]. In other words, the sentence expresses Tilman's relation-in-intension to this very procedure, *Solve* emerging as an object of type (οι$*_1$)$_{τω}$. Therefore, the whole sentence encodes this procedure:

Transparent quantification into hyperpropositional attitudes *de dicto*

$$\lambda w \lambda t\ [^0 Solve_{wt}\ ^0 Tilman\ ^0[\lambda x\ [^0= [^0 Sin\ x]\ ^0 0]]]$$

Types and type checking: $^0Solve \rightarrow (o\iota *_1)_{\tau\omega}$; $^0Solve_{wt} \rightarrow (o\iota *_1)$; $^0Tilman \rightarrow \iota$; $^0Sin \rightarrow (\tau\tau)$; $^0= \rightarrow (o\tau\tau)$; $^0 0 \rightarrow \tau$; $x \rightarrow \tau$; $[^0Sin\ x] \rightarrow \tau$; $[^0= [^0Sin\ x]\ ^0 0] \rightarrow o$; $[\lambda x\ [^0= [^0Sin\ x]\ ^0 0]] \rightarrow (o\tau)$; $^0[\lambda x\ [^0= [^0Sin\ x]\ ^0 0]] \rightarrow *_1$; $[^0Solve_{wt}\ ^0Tilman\ ^0[\lambda x\ [^0= [^0Sin\ x]\ ^0 0]]] \rightarrow o$; $\lambda w \lambda t\ [^0Solve_{wt}\ ^0Tilman\ ^0[\lambda x\ [^0= [^0Sin\ x]\ ^0 0]]] \rightarrow o_{\tau\omega}$.

The *procedure* $[\lambda x\ [^0= [^0Sin\ x]\ ^0 0]]$, which is the meaning of the term "The equation $Sin(x)$ equals 0", is *displayed* (by means of *Trivialisation*) as the second argument of the relation $Solve_{wt}$. The evaluation of the truth-conditions expressed by the sentence consists in checking, for any possible world w and for any time t, whether Tilman and this procedure occur in the extensionalised relation-in-intension of *solving* as its first and second argument, respectively. Hence the execution of the hyperproposition expressed by the sentence does not involve the execution of the procedure of solving the equation; this is something Tilman is tasked with.

The *execution* steps specified by the above Closure, i.e., its *constituents*, are as follows. Each procedure is an executed part of itself, hence the Closure (1) is a constituent of itself.

(1) $\lambda w \lambda t\ [^0Solve_{wt}\ ^0Tilman\ ^0[\lambda x\ [^0= [^0Sin\ x]\ ^0 0]]]$
(2) $\lambda t\ [^0Solve_{wt}\ ^0Tilman\ ^0[\lambda x\ [^0= [^0Sin\ x]\ ^0 0]]]$
(3) $[^0Solve_{wt}\ ^0Tilman\ ^0[\lambda x\ [^0= [^0Sin\ x]\ ^0 0]]]$
(4) $^0Solve_{wt}$
(5) $[^0Solve\ w]$
(6) ^0Solve
(7) w
(8) t
(9) ^0Tilman
(10) $^0[\lambda x\ [^0= [^0Sin\ x]\ ^0 0]]$

It might seem that in order to define rigorously the distinction between displayed and executed occurrence it would suffice to say that a procedure occurs displayed within another procedure if it occurs within the scope of a Trivialisation. Yet it is not that simple. The complicating factor is that Trivialisation has a *dual* procedure, namely Double Execution. It follows from Definition 1 that while Trivialisation of a procedure raises the context to the hyperintensional level, Double Execution cancels the effect of Trivialisation, thus lowering the level of the context. The reason is this law of ^{20}-elimination:

$$^{20}C = C$$

for any procedure C.

Note, however, that ^{02}C is *not* equivalent to C, because ^{02}C produces ^2C for any valuation v. The procedure ^2C, and thus also the procedure C, occurs displayed in ^{02}C because they occur within the scope of Trivialisation. Another complicating factor is iteration of Double Execution and Trivialisation. For instance, in ^{2200}C procedure C occurs in executed mode while in ^{2002}C procedure C occurs in displayed mode. The reason is that by applying the above law twice, we get $^{2200}C=C$, but the law can be applied only once to ^{2002}C, thus obtaining $^{2002}C = {^{02}C}$.

For the purposes of this paper, we shall say that a procedure occurs displayed exactly when it occurs within the scope of a Trivialisation, whose effect is not cancelled by Double Execution. To simplify the definition of displayed versus executed mode, we first define ^{20}-*normal form of a procedure*.

Definition 6 (^{20}-*elimination*, ^{20}-*normal form*).
Let X be a procedure and let ^{20}X occur as a sub-procedure of a procedure C. Then the replacement of an occurrence of ^{20}X by the procedure X, the result of which is a procedure C', is called ^{20}-*elimination*, $C \to_{20} C'$. If a procedure C can be transformed into a procedure D by a finite (or empty) sequence of ^{20}-eliminations, so that D does not contain any occurrence of a sub-procedure ^{20}X, then D is the ^{20}-*normal form of C*. □

Definition 7 (*occurrence of a procedure in displayed vs. executed mode*).
Let C and D be procedures in ^{20}-normal form and let D be a sub-procedure of C. Then:

(i) If C is identical to D then D *occurs in C in executed mode*.
(ii) If C is identical to ^0X, and D is a sub-procedure of X, then D *occurs in C in displayed mode*.
(iii) If C is identical to $[X_1 X_2 \ldots X_m]$ and D is a sub-procedure of the X_i, for some i, $1 \leq i \leq m$, then the *occurrence of D in C* is the same as the occurrence of D in X_i.
(iv) If C is identical to $[\lambda x_1 \ldots x_m X]$ and D is a sub-procedure of X, then the *occurrence of D in C* is the same as the occurrence of D in X.
(v) If C is identical to ^1X or ^2X and D is a sub-procedure of X, then the *occurrence of D in C* is the same as the occurrence of D in X.
(vi) The *occurrence of D* in C is in *displayed* or *executed mode* only due to (i–v). □

Remark For the sake of simplicity, we define the occurrence in displayed or executed mode only for procedures in their ^{20}-normal form. This means that we first eliminate those pairs of Double Execution and Trivialisation (in this order) that can be validly eliminated, and then the occurrence of a procedure D in C is in displayed mode if D occurs within the scope of Trivialisation (see Definition 7 (ii)). Thanks to this simplification, Definition 7 leaves undefined the occurrences of, for instance, ^{200}X in ^{2200}X, ^{00}X in ^{2200}X, or ^0X in ^{2200}X. All of these sub-procedures of ^{2200}X occur in executed mode, as does the procedure X in ^{2200}X (according to Definition 6 (i)). Yet, for the purpose of this paper, this simplification is harmless. □

Definition 8 (*constituent of a procedure*). Let C be a procedure and D a sub-procedure of C. The executed occurrences of D are *constituents* of C. □

Corollary *Each procedure C is a constituent of itself, namely its improper constituent. All the other constituents of C are its proper constituents. (The notions of being proper or improper constituents should not be confused with the notions of being v-proper or v-improper procedures.)*

Analogously to formal languages, variables can occur free or bound within a procedure. Importantly, though, it is *occurrences* of variables that occur free or bound. This is because the same variable can have both free and bound occurrences within the same context. An occurrence can also be doubly bound, as when a λ-bound occurrence is also ^{0}-bound. Yet in the case of doubly-bound variables, we say that the variable is simply ^{0}-bound, because if a procedure C is displayed then all its sub-procedures, including its variables, are displayed as well and therefore ^{0}-bound. The general rule is that a higher context is dominant over a lower one. Thus, we define:

Definition 9 (*free variable, bound variable, open/closed procedure*).
Let C be a procedure with at least one occurrence of a variable x. Then:

(i) If the occurrence of x in C is in the displayed mode, then this *occurrence of x is ^{0}-bound in C*.
(ii) Let the occurence of x in C be in the executed mode and let the Closure $[\lambda x_1...x_m X]$ be a sub-procedure of C. If this occurrence of x is a sub-procedure of X and x is identical to one of the variables x_i, $1 \leq i \leq m$, then this *occurrence of x is λ-bound in C*.
(iii) If the occurrence of x is neither ^{0}-bound nor λ-bound in C, then this *occurrence of x is free in C*.
(iv) An *occurrence* of x is *free*, λ-*bound*, ^{0}-*bound* in C only due to (i–iii).

A procedure with at least one occurrence of a free variable is an *open procedure*. A procedure without any occurrences of free variables is a *closed procedure*. □

Corollary *If a procedure D occurs in the displayed mode in C, then all the variables occurring in D are ^{0}-bound in C.*

Definition 10 (*correct substitution*).
Let x be a variable and C, D procedures in ^{20}-normal form. If the variable x is not free in C, then the result of the substitution of D for x in C is C. Let now the variable x be free in C. Then:

(i) If C is identical to x, then the *result of the substitution of D for x in C* is D.
(ii) If C is identical to $[X\ X_1\ ...\ X_n]$, then the *result of the substitution of D for x in C* is $[Y\ Y_1\ ...\ Y_n]$, where $Y, Y_1, ..., Y_n$ are the results of the substitution of D for x in $X, X_1, ..., X_n$, respectively.
(iii) If C is identical to $[\lambda x_1 ... x_m Y]$, then for $1 \leq i \leq m$ let y_i be x_i if x_i is not free in D, otherwise let y_i be the first variable v-producing entities of the same type as x_i such that y_i does not occur in C or D and distinct from $y_1 ... y_{i-1}$. Then the *result of the substitution of D for x in C* is $[\lambda y_1 ... y_m Z]$, where Z is

the result of the substitution of D for x in the result of the substitution of y_i for x_i ($1 \leq i \leq m$) in Y.

(iv) If C is identical to ^2X, where X is a procedure, then the *result of the substitution of D for x in C* is ^2Y, where Y is the result of the substitution of D for x in X. □

Remark The procedure that is the result of the substitution of D for x in C will be denoted '$C(D/x)$'.

We proceed to define two functions already adumbrated above, namely *Sub* and *Tr*, which are needed to address the technical difficulties of quantifying into hyperintensional contexts. These difficulties stem from the fact that all the variables occurring within the hyperintensional context of a displayed procedure are ^{0}-bound. Hence, the objects v-produced by such variables are irrelevant, and so is their λ-binding. Yet, in order to quantify *into* a hyperintensional context, we need a mechanism that makes it possible to operate on displayed procedures; in particular, we need to substitute for a displayed variable. To this end, we have developed a substitution method that makes use of *Sub* and *Tr*.

The polymorphous function $Sub/(*_n*_n*_n*_n)$ operates on procedures: one procedure is substituted for another within a third procedure, thus yielding a fourth procedure. Formally:

Definition 11 (Sub^n). Let $Q_1/*_{n+1} \to *_n$, $Q_2/*_{n+1} \to *_n$, $Q_3/*_{n+1} \to *_n$ v-produce procedures P_1, P_2, P_3, resp., where P_2 is a variable. Then the Composition $[^0Sub^n \, Q_1 \, Q_2 \, Q_3]$ v-produces the procedure P_4 that is the result of a simultaneous correct substitution of P_1 for all occurrences of P_2 in P_3. □

In what follows we will omit the superscript n whenever no confusion can arise.

Definition 12 (Tr). The polymorphic function $Tr^\alpha/(*_n \, \alpha)$ returns as its value the Trivialisation of its α-typed argument. □

In what follows we will omit the superscript α whenever no confusion can arise.

Examples Tr takes Pluto/ι to its Trivialisation of type $*_1$. Thus, the product of the Composition $[^0Tr \, ^0Pluto]$ is ^0Pluto. The Composition $[^0Tr \, y]$ $v(Pluto/y)$-produces ^0Pluto. Where $Planet/(o\iota)_{\tau\omega}$, the Composition $[^0Sub \, [^0Tr \, y] \, ^0x \, ^0[^0Planet_{wt} \, x]]$ $v(Pluto/y)$-produces the Composition $[^0Planet_{wt} \, ^0Pluto]$, which produces a truth-value (which one depends on the particular values chosen for w, t).

Notice the substantial difference between *Trivialisation*, which is a procedure, and *Tr*, which is a function. ^0y produces the variable y regardless of valuation: ^0y just displays y without executing the procedure y. Thus, the variable y is *bound* by Trivialisation in ^0y. On the other hand, $[^0Tr \, y]$ v-produces the Trivialisation of the object v-produced by y. Hence, y occurs *free* in $[^0Tr \, y]$ and can be λ-bound.

Example Let variable $y \to \tau$. Then $[^0Tr \, y]$ $v(\pi/y)$-produces $^0\pi$. The Composition $[^0Sub \, [^0Tr \, y] \, ^0x \, ^0[^0Cot \, x]]$ $v(\pi/y)$-produces the Composition $[^0Cot \, ^0\pi]$. Hence, the Composition $[^0Sub \, [^0Tr \, y] \, ^0x \, ^0[^0Cot \, x]]$ is $v(\pi/y)$-congruent with $[^0Cot \, ^0\pi]$. Importantly, the variable y is *free* for λ-binding in the former, unlike the variable x that is ^{0}-bound.

Definition 11 of the substitution function is also helpful in explaining why our objectual manner of addressing quantifying-into hyperintensional contexts does not inherit the problems of attempting to quantify into *quotational contexts*. Objectual quantifying-in contrasts with quantifying into quotations. Since our hyperintensional λ-calculus tracks syntactic structure closely (though not slavishly, with procedural isomorphism serving to soak up semantically redundant differences; see Sect. 4.1.1), why are we immune to the notorious problems of quantifying into quotation contexts? In an objectual hyperintensional context an expression E is *used* to express the procedure that is its meaning, and this procedure is, furthermore, *displayed* as an argument susceptible to logical manipulation. In a quotational context, E is just *mentioned*, which renders E semantically inert, whereby its meaning plays no role at all and so is neither displayed nor used. Whereas in our logic we can operate on displayed procedures, we never get around to operating on mentioned expressions. However, when we do operate on displayed hyperpropositional procedures, we need a technique to work around the fact that the constituent sub-procedures we want to manipulate also occur displayed. The substitution method (see Definition 11) makes it possible to enter displayed hyperpropositions, extract parts and insert other parts in their place.

3.7 Inference and entailment

Attitudinal sentences being empirical, we need to define analytical entailment between empirical hyperpropositions, i.e., procedures that produce truth-conditions of type $o_{\tau\omega}$. We first characterise entailment in prose followed by a definition. A hyperproposition P is entailed by the hyperpropositions $Q_1, \ldots, Q_n$, iff necessarily, i.e., in all possible worlds and at all times where all the assumptions $Q_1, \ldots, Q_n$ produce true propositions (i.e., satisfied truth-conditions), the hyperproposition P produces a true proposition/satisfied truth-condition as well.

TIL being a logic of *partial* functions, it is apt for dealing with presuppositions, truth-value gaps, non-referring terms and other phenomena of natural language. Yet partiality, as we all know all too well, brings about technical complications. In particular, propositions can take the truth-value **T** at some worlds and times, **F** at others, and at yet other worlds and times have truth-value gaps. Hence, if not all the assumptions of an argument are true, some may be false and others gappy. Consequently, entailment in a logic of partial functions is truth-preserving from premises to conclusion, but not falsity-preserving from conclusion to premises. To manage partiality properly, we need the empirical propositional property of *True*. For completeness, we also define two other properties, namely *False* and *Undefined*, all of type $(oo_{\tau\omega})_{\tau\omega}$. They are defined as follows ($P \rightarrow o_{\tau\omega}$):

$[^0 True_{wt} P]$ v-produces **T** if P_{wt}, otherwise **F**;
$[^0 False_{wt} P]$ v-produces **T** if $\neg P_{wt}$, otherwise **F**;
$[^0 Undefined_{wt} P] = \neg [^0 True_{wt} P] \wedge \neg [^0 False_{wt} P]$.

Definition 13 (*Analytical entailment*).
Let $P, Q_1, \ldots, Q_n \to o_{\tau\omega}$ be hyperpropositions. Then P is *entailed* by $Q_1, \ldots, Q_n$, denoted $Q_1, \ldots, Q_n \models P$, iff $\forall w \forall t \, [[[^0True_{wt} \, Q_1] \wedge \ldots \wedge [^0True_{wt} \, Q_n]] \supset [^0True_{wt} \, P]]$. □

Note that if in Definition 13 we had not applied the property *True*, and instead used simply the Composition $[[Q_{1wt} \wedge \ldots \wedge Q_{nwt}] \supset P_{wt}]$, the whole Composition $\forall w \forall t \, [[Q_{1wt} \wedge \ldots \wedge Q_{nwt}] \supset P_{wt}]$ would produce **F**. The reason is that at those $\langle w, t \rangle$-pairs where at least one of the Q_{iwt} is *v*-improper, the whole Composition is *v*-improper, due to partiality being propagated up.

The last technical devices that we need are λ-introduction and elimination of the left-most $\lambda w \lambda t$. These are applied when dealing with empirical hyperpropositions. If the assumptions are empirical hyperpropositions, our task is then to infer the hyperproposition that is logically entailed by the hyperpropositions in the premises. Entailment means that at any world w_0 and time t_0 of evaluation, the derivation sequence must be truth-preserving from premises to the conclusion. Thus, the typical sequence of derivation steps is this. We have assumptions of the form $\lambda w \lambda t \, [\ldots w \ldots t \ldots]$ producing entities of type $o_{\tau\omega}$, and we assume that the propositions produced by these procedures are true at the world w_0 and time t_0 of evaluation. Using the detailed notation, we obtain the Composition

$$[[[\lambda w \, [\lambda t \, [\ldots w \ldots t \ldots]]] w_0] t_0]$$

which produces an o-object, i.e., a truth-value. By applying restricted β-reduction twice, we eliminate the leftmost $\lambda w \lambda t$, thus obtaining $[\ldots w_0 \ldots t_0 \ldots] \to o$.[42] Now we proceed with derivation steps, until the conclusion of the form $[\ldots w_0 \ldots t_0 \ldots]$, producing a truth-value/o, is derived. Since we are to derive a hyperproposition, we finally abstract over the values of the variables w_0, t_0, thus reintroducing the leftmost $\lambda w \lambda t$ to produce a proposition: $\lambda w \lambda t \, [\ldots w \ldots t \ldots] \to o_{\tau\omega}$. In order to simplify the derivations occurring in proofs and rules, in what follows we omit the initial and final steps of λ-elimination and λ-introduction, respectively.

The proof calculus we usually apply is Gentzen's system of natural deduction adjusted to TIL.[43] We follow Church and Genzten in the classical style of a proof calculus as it is applied in, for instance, HOL languages.[44] The standard rules of a proof calculus are, in TIL, applicable to the *constituents* of procedures that are typed to produce a truth-value. The rules follow the general pattern of I/E pairs. The rules handling the truth-functions are standard, as in classical propositional logic. Since the quantifiers of TIL are functions applicable to classes of objects, the rules for quantifiers are introduced in the way similar to standard λ-calculi. For instance, the rule for universal quantifier eliminiation ($\forall$E) in TIL comes in this form. Let $x \to \alpha, B(x) \to o$: the variable x is free in B; $[\lambda x \, B] \to (o\alpha), \forall/ (o(o\alpha)), C \to \alpha$: a procedure that is *not v-improper*. Then:

---

[42] Restricted β-reduction consists merely in the substitution of variables for variables.

[43] For details, see Duží and Menšík (2020), Duží and Fait (2021) or Duží (2012).

[44] The reason is that TIL is a typed λ-calculus with a Church-style semantics, in which every λ-term comes with a unique type and types are organised into disjoint layers. On the other hand, Curry systems are essentially treated as untyped λ-calculi, in which a term is associated with a set (which may be empty) of potential types. See Gordon and Melham (1993) on HOL.

$$[^0\forall \lambda x\, B]\quad \emptyset$$
$$[[\lambda x\, B]\, C]\quad \forall E$$
$$B(C/x)\quad \beta\text{-reduction}$$

where $B(C/x)$ arises from B by a valid (hence, correct or collision-free) substitution of the procedure C for all occurrences of the variable x in B. That C is not v-improper is a crucial condition for the applicability of this rule. Otherwise, the rule would not be truth-preserving.

For the sake of simplicity, we usually write this rule in the ordinary abbreviated form:

$$\frac{X \vdash [^0\forall \lambda x\, B]}{X \vdash B(C/x)}\,(\forall E)$$

The dual rule ($\forall$I) receives this form (y being a fresh, free variable, i.e., one local to this part of the derivation):

$$\frac{X \vdash B(y/x)}{X \vdash [^0\forall \lambda x\, B]}\,(\forall I)$$

In this paper, we will, however, need the rule of ∃-introduction, (∃I). In classical extensional logics and λ-calculi of *total* functions, the rule is unproblematic. Yet, since TIL is a hyperintensional logic of *partial* functions, we must be careful not to derive that there is a value of a function at an argument when there is none.

(∃I) is valid in its classical form, provided it is applied to a *constituent* of an assumption B. Recall that a *constituent* of B is a procedure that in B occurs in executed mode. Hence, let $D \to \alpha$ be a procedure that occurs as a constituent of the procedure B, the other types as above. Since, by assumption, B produces the truth-value **T** and D is a constituent of B, procedure B is of the form of a Composition: [... D ...]. Then, as per the definition of Composition, procedure D cannot be v-improper, and so the Composition [[$\lambda x\, B$] D] v-produces **T** as well. Thus, the set of α-elements produced by [$\lambda x\, B$] is non-empty, and the application of the quantifier ∃ is truth-preserving. As a result, we arrive at the classical rule:

$$\frac{X \vdash B(D/x)}{X \vdash [^0\exists \lambda x\, B]}\,(\exists I)$$

The crucial condition for the validity of (∃I) is that D must occur as a constituent of B. Hence, this rule quantifies *over constituents*; it does not quantify *into* a hyperintensional context. If it did, we might risk deriving the existence of a non-existent object, thus crossing the line between logic and magic.

Still, any hyperintensional logic worthy of the name is obliged to also explain how to quantify *into* a hyperintensional context. In TIL, this task assumes the form of explaining how to logically operate on a displayed procedure. To this end, we make use of the two functions *Sub* and *Tr* defined above (Definitions 11, 12).

Consider the sentence "There is an object such that Tilman believes (hyperintensionally) that it is a planet". To analyse the sentence, we encounter the problem of the need to λ-bind a ^{0}-bound variable, which does not work as we would like it to $(Believe*/(o\iota*_n)_{\tau\omega}; Planet(o\iota)_{\tau\omega}; y \to \iota)$:

$$\lambda w \lambda t \,[^0\exists \lambda y \,[^0Believe*_{wt}\,^0Tilman\,^0[\lambda w \lambda t \,[^0Planet_{wt}y]]]]$$

The problem is this. The Closure $\lambda y \,[^0Believe*_{wt}\,^0Tilman\,^0[\lambda w \lambda t \,[^0Planet_{wt}\,y]]]$ produces either the whole universe of discourse or an empty class of individuals, according as Tilman believes that the incomplete procedure $[\lambda w \lambda t \,[^0Planet_{wt}\,y]]$ produces a truth-condition satisfied in the world and at the time of evaluation, and independently of the objects assigned to the variable y by valuation v. To obtain a plausible analysis, we must extract the variable y out of the hyperintensional context to make it free for λ-binding. Here is how:

$$\lambda w \lambda t \,[^0\exists \lambda y \,[^0Believe*_{wt}\,^0Tilman \,[^0Sub \,[^0Tr \, y]\,^0x\,^0[\lambda w \lambda t \,[^0Planet_{wt}x]]]]]$$

Now everything runs like clockwork. The Composition $[^0Sub \,[^0Tr \, y]\,^0x\,^0[\lambda w \lambda t \,[^0Planet_{wt}\, x]]]$ v-produces a hyperproposition that some object y is a planet. Assume, e.g., that Tilman believes that Venus is a planet. Then this Composition $v(Venus/y)$-produces the hyperproposition $[\lambda w \lambda t \,[^0Planet_{wt}\,^0Venus]]$, and the class of objects produced by the Closure $\lambda y \,[^0Believe*_{wt}\,^0Tilman \,[^0Sub \,[^0Tr \, y]\,^0x\,^0[\lambda w \lambda t \,[^0Planet_{wt}\, x]]]]$ is non-empty, as it contains at least the object Venus.

Still, there is more to the story of quantifying into hyperintensional contexts. As stated above, in hyperintensional attitudinal sentences we must fully respect the attributee's perspective when one complement is substituted for another. For this reason, we can substitute only procedurally isomorphic complements. To illustrate the problem, consider this argument:

> Tilman believes that the ninth celestial body
> moving in an elliptical orbit around the Earth is a planet
> ──────────────────────────
> There is an object such that Tilman believes that it is a planet

Abbreviate 'the ninth celestial body moving in an elliptical orbit around' as '9-body-moving-around', and analyse the term 'the ninth celestial body moving in an elliptical orbit around the Earth' simply as $\lambda w \lambda t \,[^09\text{-}body\text{-}move\text{-}around_{wt}\,^0Earth] \to \iota_{\tau\omega}$: the individual role of the ninth celestial body moving around the Earth. *Types*: $Earth/\iota$; $9\text{-}body\text{-}move\text{-}around/(\iota\iota)_{\tau\omega}$.

Then the analysis applying the same technique as above results in an *invalid* argument:

$$\frac{\lambda w \lambda t \,[^0Believe*_{wt}\,^0Tilman\,^0[\lambda w \lambda t \,[^0Planet_{wt}\,[^09\text{-}body\text{-}move\text{-}around_{wt}\,^0Earth]]]]}{\lambda w \lambda t \,[^0\exists \lambda y \,[^0Believe*_{wt}\,^0Tilman \,[^0Sub \,[^0Tr \, y]\,^0x\,^0[\lambda w \lambda t \,[^0Planet_{wt}\, x]]]]]}$$

As the ninth celestial body moving in an elliptical orbit around the Earth is Pluto (in the actual world at the present time), consider the valuation $v(Pluto/y)$. The Composition

$[^0Sub\,[^0Tr\,y]\,^0x\,^0[\lambda w\lambda t\,[^0Planet_{wt}\,x]]]$

then $v(Pluto/y)$-produces $[\lambda w\lambda t\,[^0Planet_{wt}\,^0Pluto]]$, which, however, is not the procedure to which Tilman is related in the premise, nor is this procedure procedurally isomorphic to that procedure:

$[\lambda w\lambda t\,[^0Planet_{wt}\,[^09\text{-}body\text{-}move\text{-}around_{wt}\,^0Earth]]]$

4 Quantifying-in

In this part, we describe, prove and apply two rules for quantifying into hyperpropositional attitudes de dicto. The two rules validate quantifying *into* hyperpropositions. One rule quantifies over a constituent procedure; the other rule quantifies over an object produced by a constituent Trivialisation.

4.1 Hyperpropositional attitude contexts de dicto

We study first how to analyse two sample sentences, one expressing an attitude to an empirical and the other to a mathematical hyperproposition:

(E) "Tilman believes that Pluto is a planet"
(M) "Tilman believes that the cotangent of π equals zero"

The first sentence expresses that a doxastic relation-in-intension obtains between Tilman and the hyperproposition that Pluto is a planet. The analysandum does not necessitate hyperpropositional treatment per se, for a standard intensional analysis would suffice, provided we are analysing implicit (i.e., logically closed) beliefs that the agent need not be aware of having and which the agent is not going to manipulate logically, e.g., by drawing inferences. As soon as Tilman is related to a hyperproposition, his attitude is an explicit one. Matters get a good deal more complicated when Tilman believes that Vulcan is not (defined as) a planet, despite Vulcan having been defined to be a planet, and so has an attitude toward Vulcan that flies in the face of its definition. This sort of attitude demands that the complement be a hyperproposition on pain of relating the agent to a blatant contradiction.

Sentence (M) does necessitate hyperintensional treatment, as does any other mathematical attitude. Neither the necessary proposition (the one true at all worlds), nor the impossible proposition (the one true at no worlds) is a suitable complement, because there could be but two mathematical attitudes then. More specifically to the example embedded in (M), since the function *Cotg* is not defined at the argument π, no number is produced, and so there is nothing to be compared to the number zero. The procedure encoded by "*Cotg* (π) = 0" is improper in the sense of producing no truth-value.[45] What Tilman believes (wrongly) is that the very *procedure* encoded by the term "*Cotg* (π) = 0" produces **T**.

The analysis of the two sentences issues in these two Closures:

(E*) $\lambda w \lambda t$ [$^0Believe_{wt}$ ^0Tilman $^0[\lambda w' \lambda t'$ [$^0Planet_{w't'}$ ^0Pluto]]]
(M*) $\lambda w \lambda t$ [$^0Believe_{wt}$ ^0Tilman $^0[^0= [^0Cotg$ $^0\pi$] ^{00}]]

Types: *Believe*/($o\iota *_1)_{\tau\omega}$; *Tilman*/ι; *Planet*/($o\iota)_{\tau\omega}$; *Pluto*/ι; $w, w' \to \omega$; $t, t' \to \tau$; [$^0Planet_{w't'}$ ^0Pluto] $\to$ o; [$\lambda w' \lambda t'$ [$^0Planet_{w't'}$ ^0Pluto]] $\to o_{\tau\omega}$; $^0[\lambda w' \lambda t'$ [$^0Planet_{w't'}$ ^0Pluto]] $\to *_1$; =/($o\tau\tau$); *Cotg*/($\tau\tau$); π, $0/\tau$; [^0Cotg $^0\pi$]$\to \tau$; [$^0= [^0Cotg$ $^0\pi$] ^{00}] $\to$ o; the other types are obvious.

The single most important bit is the Trivialisation of the Closure [$\lambda w' \lambda t'$ [$^0Planet_{w't'}$ ^0Pluto]] and of the Composition [$^0= [^0Cotg$ $^0\pi$] ^{00}], thereby generating a *hyperintensional* context by displaying the Closure and the Composition, respectively. In both analyses the context becomes, furthermore, an *attitude* context thanks to the binary relation *Believe*, which we stipulate to be a relation between doxastic agents and the hyperpropositions they believe to be true.[46] Finally, the attitudes are *de dicto* in virtue of the form of the attitude complement. In the first case, the agent is related to the hyperproposition that Pluto is a planet, and in the second case to the hyperproposition that *Cotg* takes π to 0. (E*) and (M*) are instances of the schema of the logical forms that characterise hyperpropositional attitudes de dicto:

$$\lambda w \lambda t \; [\chi_{wt} \; a\; ^0[\lambda w' \lambda t' [\varphi_{w't'} b]]]$$

$$\lambda w \lambda t \; [\chi_{wt} \; a\; ^0[F \; c]]$$

Types: $\chi \to (o\iota *_1)_{\tau\omega}$; $a, b \to \iota$; $\varphi \to (o\iota)_{\tau\omega}$; $F \to (o\tau)$; $c \to \tau$.

By contrast, hyperpropositional attitudes de re are characterised by either of these two schemas:

$$\lambda w \lambda t \; [\chi_{wt} \; a\; [^0Sub\; [^0Tr \; b]\; ^0it\; ^0[\lambda w' \lambda t' [\varphi_{w't'} \; it]]]]$$

$$\lambda w \lambda t \; [\chi_{wt} \; a\; [^0Sub\; [^0Tr \; c]\; ^0it'\; ^0[F \; it']]]$$

The first schema should be read as "*a* χ's of *b* that it is a φ". In the mathematical case, the second schema should be read as "*a* χ's of *c* that it is an *F*."

Note that the occurrences of the anaphoric pronoun 'it' are analysed as the ^{0}-bound variables $it \to \iota$, $it' \to \tau$. The anaphoric references 'of *b* that it is a φ' and 'of

---

[45] Actually, the sentence "*Cotg* of π equals 0" comes with the *presupposition* that the value of the function *Cotg* exists at π, because this is entailed both by the sentence and its narrow-scope negation, "*Cotg* of π is *not* equal to zero". See Duží (2017, 2018a, 2018b) for more on presupposition and negation.

[46] We are glossing over a slight complication here. Our hyperpropositions are not truth-bearers, so they cannot, strictly and literally, be believed to be *true* (or *false*). Rather it is truth-conditions, i.e., the propositions of possible-world semantics, that are truth-bearers: a truth-condition is true when it is satisfied. So to believe an empirical hyperproposition is to believe that the truth-condition it produces is satisfied at the given world and time of evaluation; and to believe a mathematical hyperproposition amounts to believing that the procedure produces the truth-value **T**. This technical detail is solved in Duží et al. (2010, §5.1.6).

c that it is an F" are then resolved by the Compositions [^0Sub [^0Tr b] ^0it $^0[\lambda w' \lambda t'$ [$\varphi_{w't'}$ it]]] and [^0Sub [^0Tr c] $^0it'$ $^0[F$ it']], respectively.[47]

The question now arises what can be validly deduced from (E) and from (M). Since in both cases Tilman is related to a procedure, we can obviously validly infer that there is a procedure (a *hyperproposition*, in this case) to which Tilman is related by a doxastic attitude:

(EA)
$$\frac{\lambda w \lambda t \ [^0Believe_{wt} \ ^0Tilman \ ^0[\lambda w' \lambda t' \ [^0Planet_{w't'} \ ^0Pluto]]]}{\lambda w \lambda t \ [^0\exists \ \lambda c \ [^0Believe_{wt} \ ^0Tilman \ c]]}$$

(MA)
$$\frac{\lambda w \lambda t \ [^0Believe_{wt} \ ^0Tilman \ ^0[^0= [^0Cotg \ ^0\pi] \ ^00]]}{\lambda w \lambda t \ [^0\exists \ \lambda d \ [^0Believe_{wt} \ ^0Tilman \ d]]}$$

Types: $c/*_2 \rightarrow *_1$; $^2c \rightarrow o_{\tau\omega}$; $d/*_2 \rightarrow *_1$; $^2d \rightarrow o$; the other types as above. The inclusion of ^2c, ^2d spells out the fact that c, d v-produce procedures typed to produce empirical truth-conditions and truth-values, respectively.

In both cases the complements of the attitude, i.e. the procedures $^0[\lambda w' \lambda t'$ [$^0Planet_{w't'}$ ^0Pluto]] and $^0[^0= [^0Cotg \ ^0\pi] \ ^00]$ are *constituents* of the premise; hence, we simply applied the ($\exists$I)-rule proved above. This is a simple matter, because we just quantified *over* a believed hyperproposition, i.e., over an entire hyperintensional context. Still, our main goal and the main novelty of this paper is quantifying *into* hyperintensional contexts.

First, we are going to tackle a simpler case, which is to quantify over a *procedure* that is a constituent of an attitude complement. Then we are going to show that in some special, rigorously defined cases we can also quantify over a *product* of such a procedure. For instance, (M) entails that there is a *procedure* such that Tilman believes that its product equals zero. Indeed, there is such a procedure, namely the improper Composition [$^0Cotg \ ^0\pi$], such that Tilman believes (wrongly) that this procedure produces 0.

As explained above, quantifying into displayed contexts is not a straightforward thing to do. Carelessly quantifying-in is *not* truth-preserving ($c \rightarrow *_1$; $^2c \rightarrow \tau$, i.e., c v-produces a procedure that is typed to produce a number):

$$\frac{\lambda w \lambda t \ [^0Believe_{wt} ^0Tilman \ ^0[^0= [^0Cotg^0\pi] ^00]]}{\lambda w \lambda t \ [^0\exists\lambda c \ [^0Believe_{wt} ^0Tilman ^0 \ [^0=\ ^2c \ ^00]]]}$$

Its invalidity is due to the Trivialisation of the attitude complement, which displays the believed hyperproposition $[^0= [^0Cotg \ ^0\pi] \ ^00]$, but does not execute it. As defined above (see Defs. 6, 7), all the sub-procedures of a displayed procedure are displayed as well. The Trivialisation $^0[^0= \ ^2c \ ^00]$ produces the Composition $[^0= \ ^2c \ ^00]$ regardless of any valuation of the variable c. In particular, a displayed occurrence of a variable does not descend to the value of the variable. For this reason, the truth of

---

[47] For details on how TIL analyses anaphoric resolution, see Duží (2018a).

the premise does not warrant the non-emptiness of the class of procedures v-produced by the Closure

$$\lambda c \ [^0Believe_{wt} \ ^0Tilman \ ^0[^0= \ ^2c \ ^00]]$$

This class is either the whole type $*_1$ or the empty set of first-order procedures, depending on whether or not Tilman is related to the Composition $[^0= \ ^2c \ ^00]$ and independently of the truth of the premise, i.e. independently of whether or not Tilman is related to the Composition in the premise, $[^0= [^0Cotg \ ^0\pi] \ ^00]$.

Fortunately, we have a way out, or rather a way *in*. It is our substitution method that makes it possible to operate on displayed procedures. This inference is valid:

$$\text{(MA}_0\text{)} \quad \frac{\lambda w \lambda t \ [^0Believe_{wt} \ ^0Tilman \ ^0[^0= [^0Cotg \ ^0\pi] \ ^00]]}{\lambda w \lambda t \ [^0\exists^* \ \lambda c \ [^0Believe_{wt} \ ^0Tilman \ [^0Sub \ c \ ^0d \ ^0[^0= d \ ^00]]]]}$$

Additional types: $\exists^*/(o(o*_n))$; $c/*_2 \rightarrow *_1$; $^2c \rightarrow \tau$; $d/*_1 \rightarrow \tau$. The inclusion of ^2c makes it explicit that c v-produces a procedure that is typed to produce numbers.

The variable c occurs free in the Composition $[^0Sub \ c \ ^0d \ ^0[^0= d \ ^00]]$, and the Composition $v([^0Cotg \ ^0\pi]/c)$-produces exactly what it should produce, namely the procedure $[^0= [^0Cotg \ ^0\pi] \ ^00]$, which Tilman is related to as per the premise above. Recall that $v([^0Cotg \ ^0\pi]/c)$ is a valuation just like v, except for assigning the Composition $[^0Cotg \ ^0\pi]$ to c.

One might wonder whether in the case of (E) we could actually infer more than that there is a *procedure* believed by Tilman to produce a condition that is satisfied, as stipulated by (EA). No Closure is v-improper for any v.[48] A Closure of the form $[\lambda x_1...x_m \ X]$ v-produces a function for any v, even when the produced function is degenerate, i.e., one that is undefined at each of its arguments, namely when X is a v-improper procedure for every v. Thus, it might seem that we could validly infer from (E) not only that there is a hyperproposition but also that there is a *truth-condition* $r/o_{\tau\omega}$, such that Tilman believes that r is true in the world w and at the time t of evaluation. Yet this *cannot* be inferred. According to the premise, Tilman is related to the hyperproposition

$$^0[\lambda w' \lambda t' [^0Planet_{w't'} \ ^0Pluto]]$$

rather than the truth-condition produced by this very hyperproposition. Tilman might, of course, be in some relation to the state-of-affairs that Pluto is a planet, and if we inferred that he *is* in a coarse-grained belief relation to this state-of-affairs, i.e. r, we would face the same problem as many attitude logics do, namely one or more variants of the problem of omniscience. Furthermore, no less importantly, we would not be respecting Tilman's doxastic perspective, and so the ascription would not be of a de dicto attitude.

Yet we would still want to draw further conclusions. We want to infer that in some special cases there is some *product* of the procedure which is the constituent

---

[48] We are dealing here with the standard Closure as defined by Definition 1. We do not take into account λ^x-Closure, which can be v-improper under specific conditions. For details, see Duží and Kosterec (2017).

of attitude complement. In the empirical case, we would want to derive, for instance, that there is an individual x such that Tilman believes that x is a planet. And indeed, there is such an individual x, namely Pluto. Or, additionally, that there is a property p such that Tilman believes that Pluto has property p. And indeed, there is such a property, namely the property of being a planet. Similarly, in the mathematical case, we would like to infer, for instance, that there is a number y such that Tilman believes that the value of *Cotg* equals zero at y. And indeed, there is such a number, namely π. Furthermore, we can validly infer that there is a function f such that Tilman believes that the value of f at π is zero.

But again, this inference is *invalid* ($x \to \tau$):

$$\frac{\lambda w \lambda t \,[^0Believe_{wt}{}^0Tilman\,^0[^0 = [^0Cotg\,^0\pi]\,^00]]}{\lambda w \lambda t \,[^0\exists \lambda x\,[^0Believe_{wt}{}^0Tilman\,^0[^0 = [^0Cotg\,^0x]]\,^00]]}$$

because the variable x is ^{0}-bound (see Definition 9). To obtain a *valid* inference, we must apply the substitution method:

(MA$_1$) $\dfrac{\lambda w \lambda t \,[^0Believe_{wt}\,^0Tilman\,^0[^0 = [^0Cotg\,^0\pi]\,^00]]}{\lambda w \lambda t \,[^0\exists\, \lambda x\,[^0Believe_{wt}\,^0Tilman\,[^0Sub\,[^0Tr^\tau\,x]\,^0y\,^0[^0 = [^0Cotg\,y]\,^00]]]]}$

Gloss: "There is a number x such that Tilman believes that the value of *Cotg* at x is 0." *Additional types*: $\exists/(o(o\tau))$, $x, y \to \tau$.

We are substituting the Trivialisation of a number being quantified over, using the functions *Sub*, *Tr* (see Defs. 11, 12). Similarly, we can derive that there is a function $f \to (\tau\tau)$ such that Tilman believes that the value of f at π is zero:

(MA$_2$) $\dfrac{\lambda w \lambda t \,[^0Believe_{wt}\,^0Tilman\,^0[^0 = [^0Cotg\,^0\pi]\,^00]]}{\lambda w \lambda t \,[^0\exists'\, \lambda f\,[^0Believe_{wt}\,^0Tilman\,[^0Sub\,[^0Tr^{(\tau\tau)}\,f]\,^0g\,^0[^0 = [g\,\pi]\,^00]]]]}$

Additional types: $\exists'/(o(o(\tau\tau)))$, $g \to (\tau\tau)$.

Now everything is as it should be. The variables x, f occur *free* in

$$[^0Sub\,[^0Tr^\tau x]\,^0y\,^0[^0 = [^0Cotg\,y]\,^00]]$$
$$[^0Sub\,[^0Tr^{(\tau\tau)} f]\,^0g\,^0[^0 = [g\,\pi]\,^00]]$$

respectively, and the first Composition $v(\pi/x)$-produces $[^0 = [^0Cotg\,^0\pi]\,^00]$, while the second Composition $v(Cotg/f)$-produces the same procedure, namely the one believed by Tilman.

Hence, concerning (MA$_1$), provided the Composition

$$[^0Believe_{wt}{}^0Tilman\,^0[^0 = [^0Cotg\,^0\pi]\,^00]]$$

v-produces the truth-value **T**, the class of numbers v-produced by

$$\lambda x [^0Believe_{wt}{}^0Tilman\,[^0Sub\,[^0Tr^\tau\,x]\,^0y\,^0[^0 = [^0Cotg\,y]\,^00]]]$$

is non-empty (as it contains at least the element π) and the application of $\exists/(o(o\tau))$ is truth-preserving.

Similarly, concerning (MA$_2$), provided the Composition

$$[^0Believe_{wt}\ ^0Tilman\ ^0[^0= [^0Cotg\ ^0\pi]\ ^00]]$$

v-produces the truth-value **T**, the class of functions of type ($\tau\tau$) v-produced by

$$\lambda f[^0Believe_{wt}\ ^0Tilman\ [^0Sub\ [^0Tr^{\tau\tau}\ f]\ ^0g\ ^0[^0= [g\ \pi]\ ^00]]]$$

is non-empty (as it contains at least the function *Cotg*), and the application of $\exists'/$ $(o(o(\tau\tau)))$ is truth-preserving.

Still, from (M) we *cannot* validly infer that there is a *number n* such that Tilman believes that this number equals 0. The reason is that the function *Cotg* is not defined at the argument π; hence the Composition [$^0Cotg\ ^0\pi$] is improper by failing to produce anything. Deriving that there is such a number *n* would, again, cross the line from logic into magic.

Turning now to the empirical case, valid inferences that involve quantifying *into* a hyperpropositional context are, for instance, these ($x, y \to \iota$; $p, q \to (o\iota)_{\tau\omega}$):

(EA$_1$) $\dfrac{\lambda w \lambda t\ [^0Believe_{wt}\ ^0Tilman\ ^0[\lambda w'\lambda t'\ [^0Planet_{w't'}\ ^0Pluto]]]}{\lambda w \lambda t\ [^0\exists\ \lambda x\ [^0Believe_{wt}\ ^0Tilman\ [^0Sub\ [^0Tr^\iota\ x]\ ^0y\ ^0[\lambda w'\lambda t'\ [^0Planet_{w't'}\ y]]]]]}$

Gloss: "There is an individual x such that Tilman believes that x is a planet."

(EA$_2$) $\dfrac{\lambda w \lambda t\ [^0Believe_{wt}\ ^0Tilman\ ^0[\lambda w'\lambda t'\ [^0Planet_{w't'}\ ^0Pluto]]]}{\lambda w \lambda t\ [^0\exists\ \lambda p\ [^0Believe_{wt}\ ^0Tilman\ [^0Sub\ [^0Tr^{(((o\iota)\tau)\omega)}\ p]\ ^0q\ ^0[\lambda w'\lambda t'\ [q_{w't'}\ ^0Pluto]]]]]}$

Gloss: "There is a property p such that Tilman believes that Pluto has p."

The arguments (MA$_1$), (MA$_2$), (EA$_1$) and (EA$_2$) are *valid*, because we are quantifying over objects produced by Trivialisation, namely $^0\pi$, ^0Cotg, ^0Pluto, ^0Planet, and these procedures are not v-improper for any valuation v. Trivialisation just displays the object which we go on to quantify over, and when applied to this object (v-produced by a variable) the function *Tr* returns as its value the Trivialisation of the object. Moreover, we are fully respecting Tilman's perspective here, because our analyses are *literal* ones. This means that semantically simple terms like 'planet', 'Pluto', 'cotangent' and 'π' are analysed by their Trivialisations. Indeed, the sentences do not convey any more information about the meaning of these terms, as a definition or meaning postulate would.[49]

On the other hand, if a constituent of the attitude complement can be v-improper, then we cannot validly infer the existence of the respective object. Assume that instead of a Trivialisation displaying Pluto we were to conceptualise Pluto by means

---

[49] For *literal analysis*, see fn. 39.

of the individual role denoted by the definite description 'the first Kuiper Belt object to be discovered'. Abbreviate this description as '*FKBO*'. The analysis of '*FKBO*' amounts to this procedure:

$\lambda w \lambda t \, [^0First \, \lambda x \, [[^0KuiperBeltObj_{wt} \, x] \wedge [^0Discovered_{wt} \, x]]] \to \iota_{\tau\omega}$

Types: *First*/$(\iota(o\iota))$: the function that picks out at most one individual from a set of individuals (namely the first one to be discovered); *KuiperBeltObj, Discovered*/$(o\iota)_{\tau\omega}$, $x \to \iota$; $[^0KuiperBeltObj_{wt} \, x]$, $[^0Discovered_{wt} \, x] \to o$; $\lambda x \, [[^0KuiperBeltObj_{wt} \, x] \wedge [^0Discovered_{wt} \, x]] \to (o\iota)$; $[^0First \, \lambda x \, [[^0KuiperBeltObj_{wt} \, x] \wedge [^0Discovered_{wt} \, x]]] \to \iota$.

Since the office can possibly go vacant, the following argument similar to (EA₁) is *invalid*:

$$\frac{\lambda w \lambda t \, [^0Believe_{wt} \, {}^0Tilman \, {}^0[\lambda w' \lambda t' \, [^0Planet_{w't'}}{\lambda w \lambda t \, [^0First \, \lambda x \, [[^0KuiperBeltObj_{wt} \, x] \wedge [^0Discovered_{wt} \, x]]]_{w't'}]]]}{\lambda w \lambda t \, [^0\exists \lambda x \, [^0Believe_{wt} \, {}^0Tilman \, [^0Sub \, [^0Tr^\iota x] \, {}^0y \, {}^0[\lambda w' \lambda t' \, [^0Planet_{w't'} \, y]]]]]}$$

The conclusion that there is an *individual* x such that Tilman believes that x is a planet is *not entailed* by the premise, because the Composition (note the rightmost subscripted w't')

$[\lambda w \lambda t \, [^0First \, \lambda x \, [[^0KuiperBeltObj_{wt} \, x] \wedge [^0Discovered_{wt} \, x]]]_{w't'}]$

may be *v*-improper. Thus, though $[^0Sub \, [^0Tr^\iota \, x] \, {}^0y \, {}^0[\lambda w' \lambda t' \, [^0Planet_{w't'} \, y]]]$ $v(a/x)$-produces the procedure $[\lambda w' \lambda t' \, [^0Planet_{w't'} \, {}^0a]]$ for some individual *a*, it is not excluded that *a* fails to be an element of the class of individuals which Tilman believes to be a planet. In other words, the class produced by the Closure

$\lambda x \, [^0Believe_{wt} \, {}^0Tilman \, [^0Sub_1 \, [^0Tr^\iota \, x] \, {}^0y \, {}^0[\lambda w' \lambda t' \, [^0Planet_{w't'} \, y]]]]$

can be empty, and when it is, applying $\exists$ to this class will yield **F**.

Since the Closure $\lambda w \lambda t \, [^0First \, \lambda x \, [[^0KuiperBeltObj_{wt} \, x] \wedge [^0Discovered_{wt} \, x]]]$ cannot be *v*-improper for any *v*, it might seem that we could validly infer that there is an *individual office* $f \to \iota_{\tau\omega}$ such that Tilman believes that the occupant of the office is a planet (though the office may be vacant or, if occupied, its occupant may fail to be a planet). Yet, again, an argument to this effect would be *invalid*:

$$\frac{\lambda w \lambda t \, [^0Believe_{wt} \, {}^0Tilman \, {}^0[\lambda w' \lambda t' \, [^0Planet_{w't'}}{\lambda w \lambda t \, [^0First \, \lambda x \, [[^0KuiperBeltObj_{wt} \, x] \wedge [^0Discovered_{wt} \, x]]]_{w't'}]]]}{\lambda w \lambda t \, [^0\exists \lambda x \, [^0Believe_{wt} \, {}^0Tilman \, [^0Sub \, [^0Tr^{((\tau\tau)\omega)} f] \, {}^0y \, {}^0[\lambda w' \lambda t' \, [^0Planet_{w't'} \, g_{w't'}]]]]]}$$

Gloss: "There is an individual office *f* such that Tilman believes the hyperproposition that the occupant of *f* is a planet." *Additional types*: $f, g \to \iota_{\tau\omega}$.

The argument is invalid, because the office in the premise is conceptualised by means of the Closure $\lambda w \lambda t \, [^0First \, \lambda x \, [[^0KuiperBeltObj_{wt} \, x] \wedge [^0Discovered_{wt} \, x]]]$ rather than by its Trivialisation.

4.1.1 Procedural isomorphism

The main reason these last two arguments are not valid is this. When deriving something from a *hyperintensional* attitude *de dicto*, we must strictly respect the agent's perspective. Hence, there must be a valuation v such that the procedure resulting from the substitution is exactly the same procedure as the one to which the agent was originally related. More precisely, the so v-produced procedure must be *procedurally isomorphic* to the procedure to which Tilman is related as per the premise.[50] In other words, the derived procedure must be encoded by a sentence *synonymous* with Tilman's original attitude complement. In Duží (2019) a series of *criteria* for procedural isomorphism—hence co-hyperintensionality, hence synonymy—has been defined. These criteria are partially ordered from the strongest (most restrictive) to the weakest (most liberal) with respect to synonymy. Here we opt for the almost-strongest criterion C_1. Let us pause to reflect on why we are going for C_1 rather than C_7, which we have elsewhere labelled (A1″) to incorporate it into Church's hierarchy of Alternatives.[51]

C_1. α-conversion
C_7. α-conversion + β-reduction by value

C_7 is applicable to hyperintensional contexts, but only if a slightly contentious assumption is granted. The assumption is that $[[\lambda x_1 ... x_n\ Y]\ D_1 ... D_n]$ is the same procedure as

$$^2[^0Sub\ [^0Tr\ D_1]\ ^0x_1 ... \ [^0Sub\ [^0Tr\ D_n]\ ^0x_n\ ^0Y]]$$

Is the assumption reasonable? That depends. Our hypothesis is that C_7 is applicable to natural-language discourse, including attributions of hyperpropositional attitudes de dicto. But the problem is that C_7 does not extend to attributions of mathematical and logical attitudes de dicto. To see this, consider this example:

Tilman believes that $[^0= [\lambda x\ [^0+\ [log_2\ ^016]\ x]\ [^0Cos\ ^00]]\ ^05]$

Then by C_7 this should follow:

Tilman believes that $[^0=\ ^2[^0Sub\ [^0Tr\ [^0Cos\ ^00]]\ ^0x\ ^0[^0+\ [log_2\ ^016]\ x]]\ ^05]$

But what if Tilman's idiosyncratic perspective is quite another so that he would compute the equation in another way than predicted? The second equation specifies that Tilman first computes $Cos(0)$ to obtain the number 1 and afterwards substitutes 1 for x in $log_2(16)+x$, which gives $log_2(16)+1$. Then he computes $log_2(16)$ to obtain 4, and finally the number 5. Yet, a different computation would be to first compute $log_2(16)$ to obtain 4, and then substitute the result of computing $Cos(0)$, hence number 1, for x into $4+x$, and finally obtain the result 5. If we instead restrict

---

[50] See Jespersen (2021) for arguments in favour of procedural isomorphism, together with a concrete application.

[51] See Anderson (1998).

ourselves to C_1 then if the original attitude is the same as above, what follows is only this:

Tilman believes that $[^0 = [\lambda y [^0 + [log_2 \ ^0 16] \ y] \ [^0 Cos \ ^0 0]] \ ^0 5]$

as only α-conversion is admitted.[52] Here is the formal definition:

Definition 13 (*α-conversion*). Let a procedure Y contain at most $x_1, ..., x_n$ as free variables. Then:

$$[\lambda x_1...x_n Y] \Rightarrow_\alpha [\lambda y_1...y_n Y(y_1/x_1...y_n/x_n)]$$

where $Y(y_1/x_1... y_n/x_n)$ is the procedure that arises from Y by correct substitution of y_1 for all the occurrences of $x_1, ...,$ and y_n for all the occurrences of x_n, is *α-conversion*. □

Thus, our bifurcation of attitude complements into those hyperpropositions that produce empirical truth-conditions and those hyperpropositions that produce truth-values is accompanied by a bifurcation of what procedural isomorphism amounts to. Our current stance is that C_1 is suitable for the former and C_7 for the latter when the relevant context is a hyperpropositional attitude de dicto.

Back to the Kuiper Belt. If *FKBO* is the office produced by the Closure

$$\lambda w \lambda t \ [^0 First \ \lambda x \ [[^0 KuiperBeltObj_{wt} \ x] \wedge [^0 Discovered_{wt} \ x]]],$$

then the Composition

$$[^0 Sub \ [^0 Tr^{((\iota\tau)\omega)} f] \ ^0 g \ ^0 [\lambda w' \lambda t' [^0 Planet_{w't'} \ g_{w't'}]]]$$

$v(FKBO/f)$-produces the Closure $[\lambda w' \lambda t' \ [^0 Planet_{w't'} \ ^0 FKBO_{w't'}]]$, and this procedure differs significantly from the one Tilman was originally related to, namely the Closure

$$[\lambda w' \lambda t' \ [^0 Planet_{w't'} \ \lambda w \lambda t \ [^0 First \ \lambda x \ [[^0 KuiperBeltObj_{wt} \ x] \wedge$$

$$[^0 Discovered_{wt} \ x]]]_{w't'}]]$$

Hence, we can only derive that there is a *procedure* producing the office of *FKBO* such that Tilman believes that whichever the produced office may be, its occupant is a planet:

(EA₃) $$\frac{\lambda w \lambda t \ [^0 Believe_{wt} \ ^0 Tilman \ ^0 [\lambda w' \lambda t' \ [^0 Planet_{w't'} \ \lambda w \lambda t \ [^0 First \ \lambda x \ [[^0 KuiperBeltObj_{wt} \ x] \wedge [^0 Discovered_{wt} \ x]]]_{w't'}]]]}{\lambda w \lambda t \ [^0 \exists \ \lambda c \ [^0 Believe_{wt} \ ^0 Tilman \ [^0 Sub \ c \ ^0 d \ ^0 [\lambda w' \lambda t' \ [^0 Planet_{w't'} \ d_{w't'}]]]]]}$$

Additional types: $c/*_2 \rightarrow *_1$; $^2 c/*_3 \rightarrow \iota_{\tau\omega}$; $d/*_1 \rightarrow \iota_{\tau\omega}$.

---

[52] See Salmon (2010) on arguments for considering β-conversion invalid. See Jespersen (2015a) for (favourable) discussion of Salmon's examples.

A further variation is this. Suppose we type Vulcan as an office rather than an individual (as we must, since TIL has no category of inexistent or merely possible individuals) and that the office of Vulcan comes with the constraint that its respective occupants must each be a planet (as we should in order to align with Le Verrier's specification of Vulcan).[53] Suppose also that it is a datum that Tilman believes that Vulcan is not (defined as) a planet. Then what Tilman believes is necessarily (in this case, analytically) false, because his belief about Vulcan runs afoul of the stipulated definition of Vulcan. What can be derived from his attitude is that there exists an office such that Tilman believes that this office comes without the analytic property of being a planet. This attitude must be construed as a hyperpropositional one, in order to distinguish it from other analytically impossible complements.[54]

The moral to be drawn from the above examples is this. We can quantify over and *into* hyperpropositional contexts, even though the procedure occurring as attitude complement is just *displayed* in such contexts. We can quantify over *procedural complements* of attitudes and over their *procedural constituents*. And we can also quantify over those *objects* that are produced by the constituents of an attitudinal complement, but only if the respective object is displayed by Trivialisation. In the following section, we formulate two rules for quantifying into hyperpropositional contexts de dicto.

4.2 Rules for quantifying into hyperpropositional contexts

As we both warned and promised at the outset, a logic of quantifying-in comes at the end of a long story. We have now obtained everything required to introduce and prove our *general rules for quantifying into hyperpropositional attitudes de dicto*. These are the hardest cases of quantifying-in, and they constitute the core of our novel contribution. Rule (1) quantifies over a *procedure* that is a constituent of an attitude complement, and rule (2) quantifies over an *object* presented by a Trivialisation that is a constituent of an attitude complement.

RULE 1. *Quantifying over a constituent of an attitude complement.*

$$\frac{[B_{wt}\, a\, {}^0P(X/d)]}{[{}^0\exists\, \lambda c\, [B_{wt}\, a\, [{}^0Sub\, c\, {}^0d\, {}^0P(d)]]]}$$

Types: $P(X/d)/*_n$: a procedure with a constituent $X/*_n \to \alpha$ that has been substituted for the variable $d/*_n \to \alpha$; $c/*_{n+1} \to *_n$; ${}^2c \to \alpha$.

Proof

(1) $[B_{wt}\, a\, {}^0P(X/d)]$ $\varnothing$
(2) $[B_{wt}\, a\, [{}^0Sub\, {}^0X\, {}^0d\, {}^0P(d)]] = [B_{wt}\, a\, {}^0P(X/d)]$ Definition 11
(3) $[\lambda c\, [B_{wt}\, a\, [{}^0Sub\, c\, {}^0d\, {}^0P(d)]]\, {}^0X]$ 2, β-expansion
(4) $[{}^0\exists\, \lambda c\, [B_{wt}\, a\, [{}^0Sub\, c\, {}^0d\, {}^0P(d)]]]$ 3, Definition 4

---

[53] Such a constraint is known as a *requisite* in TIL. See Duží et al. (2010, §4.1).
[54] See Duží et al. (2021) for our logic of analytically impossible *hyperoffices*.

Remark Step (4) is truth-preserving, because the class of procedures produced by $\lambda c\ [B_{wt}\ a\ [^0Sub\ c\ ^0d\ ^0P(d)]]$ is non-empty, as it contains at least the procedure X. Actually, since ^0X is a proper constituent of $[B_{wt}\ a\ [^0Sub\ ^0X\ ^0d\ ^0P(d)]]$, we could have just applied the ($\exists$I)-rule on the left-hand side of step (2), omitting step (3). Yet, for the sake of clarity, we proceeded from (2) to (4) via (3).

Finally, we have the rule for quantifying over an object such that its Trivialisation is a constituent of a procedure that occurs as attitude complement.

RULE 2. *Quantifying over a Trivialised object.*

$$\frac{[B_{wt}\ a\ ^0P(^0b/y)]}{[^0\exists\ \lambda x\ [B_{wt}\ a\ [^0Sub\ [^0Tr^\alpha\ x]\ ^0y\ ^0P(y)]]]}$$

Types: $P(^0b/y)/*_n$: a procedure with a proper constituent $^0b/*_n \to \alpha$ that has been substituted for the variable $y/*_n \to \alpha$; $x/*_n \to \alpha$.

Proof

(1) $[B_{wt}\ a\ ^0P(^0b/y)]$ $\emptyset$
(2) $[B_{wt}\ a\ [^0Sub\ [^0Tr^\alpha\ ^0b]\ ^0y\ ^0P(y)]] = [B_{wt}\ a\ ^0P(^0b/y)]$ Definition 11
(3) $[\lambda x\ [B_{wt}\ a\ [^0Sub\ [^0Tr^\alpha\ x]\ ^0y\ ^0P(y)]]\ ^0b]$ 2, β-expansion
(4) $[^0\exists\ \lambda x\ [B_{wt}\ a\ [^0Sub\ [^0Tr^\alpha\ x]\ ^0y\ ^0P(y)]]]$ 3, Definition 4

Step (4) is justified, because the class of α-objects produced by the Closure $\lambda x\ [B_{wt}\ a\ [^0Sub\ [^0Tr^\alpha\ x]\ ^0y\ ^0P(y)]]$ is non-empty, as it contains at least the object b.

Note that, in Rule 2, x occurs *free* in the Composition $[^0Sub\ [^0Tr^\alpha\ x]\ ^0y\ ^0P(y)]$, whereby it lends itself to being λ-bound.

5 Conclusion

The above rules are *almost* trivial, as indeed they should be. After all, quantifying over and into hyperintensional contexts should, *in principle*, if not technically, be as trivial as quantifying into extensional contexts, *as soon as we have availed ourselves of a fully transparent semantics and an extensional logic of hyperintensions* that is strictly compositional. However, the near-triviality of the rules can be obtained only by means of a theory possessing great expressive power (hence the qualification 'almost trivial'). We obtain a sufficient measure of expressive power by means of ramification of procedures so that we can *display* any given procedure by going one level higher. The *Sub* function would become inoperative if it were not for procedures occurring displayed, i.e., presented as functional arguments. The technical finesse the conclusion exhibits resides in the fact that the λ-bound variables over whose values we quantify occur *outside* the hyperintensional context of the displayed procedures.

It is critical for a theory such as Transparent Intensional Logic to demonstrate exactly how it makes quantifying-in come out valid also with respect to hyperpropositional attitudes de dicto. The theory claims to have an extensional logic of hyperintensions, so the extensional rule of existential quantification had better be valid for hyperintensional contexts too. But the impact of the results above extends beyond our particular theory. First, it is good news for the community-wide project devoted to developing and substantiating theories of hyperintensionality that quantifying-in is not unattainable. And second, the demonstrated feasibility of quantifying-in provides the hyperintensional community with a touchstone: does a theory of hyperintensionality succeed in rendering quantifying-in valid? The theory scores a point if it does.

Acknowledgements We are much indebted to two anonymous referees for *Linguistics and Philosophy* whose careful remarks helped improve the quality of this paper. The paper rounds out the quantifying-in trilogy whose other two instalments are our (2012) and (2015). This research has been supported by the University of Oxford project *New Horizons for Science and Religion in Central and Eastern Europe* funded by the John Templeton Foundation, as well as by Grant No. SP2021/87, VSB-Technical University of Ostrava, Czech Republic, *Application of Formal Methods in Knowledge Modelling and Software Engineering IV*.

References

Anderson, C. A. (1998). Alonzo Church's contributions to philosophy and intensional logic. *The Bulletin of Symbolic Logic, 4*, 129–171.
Bealer, G. (1982). *Quality and concept*. Oxford: Clarendon Press.
Berto, F., & Nolan, D. (2021). Hyperintensionality. In E. N. Zalda (Ed.), *The Stanford Encyclopedia of Philosophy* (Summer 2021 edition). https://plato.stanford.edu/archives/sum2021/entries/hyperintensionality/.
Caie, M., Goodman, J., & Lederman, H. (2019). Classical opacity. *Philosophy and Phenomenological Research*. https://doi.org/10.1111/phpr.12587.
Church, A. (1956). *Introduction to mathematical logic*. Princeton, NJ: Princeton University Press.
Copi, I. (1968). *Introduction to logic*. New York: MacMillan.
Crawford, S. (2008). Quantifiers and propositional attitudes: Quine revisited. *Synthese, 160*, 75–96.
Cumming, S. (2008). Variabilism. *Philosophical Review, 117*, 525–554.
Duží, M. (2019). If structured propositions are logical procedures then how are procedures individuated? *Synthese, 196*, 1249–1283.
Duží, M. (2018a). Negation and presupposition, truth and falsity. *Studies in Logic, Grammar and Rhetoric, 54*, 15–46.
Duží, M. (2018b). Logic of dynamic discourse and anaphora resolution. In V. Sornlertlamvanich, P. Chawakitchareon, A. Hansuebsai et al. (Eds.), *Information modelling and knowledge bases XXIX* (pp. 263–279). Amsterdam: IOS Press.
Duží, M. (2017). Presuppositions and two kinds of negation. *Logique et Analyse, 239*, 245–263.
Duží, M. (2012). Towards an extensional calculus of hyperintensions. *Organon F, 19* (supplementary issue 1), 20–45.
Duží, M., & Menšík, M. (2020). Inferring knowledge from textual data by natural deduction. *Computación y Sistemas, 24*, 29–48.
Duží, M., & Jespersen, B. (2012). Transparent quantification into hyperpropositional contexts de re. *Logique et Analyse, 220*, 513–554.
Duží, M., & Jespersen, B. (2013). Procedural isomorphism, analytic information, and β-conversion by value. *Logic Journal of the IGPL, 21*, 291–308.
Duží, M., & Jespersen, B. (2015). Transparent quantification into hyperintensional objectual attitudes. *Synthese, 192*, 635–677.
Duží, M., Jespersen, B., & Materna, P. (2010). *Procedural semantics for hyperintensional logic: Foundations and applications of Transparent Intensional Logic*. Dordrecht: Springer.
Duží, M., Glavaničová, D., & Jespersen, B. (2021). Impossible individuals as necessarily empty individual concepts. In A. Giordani & J. Malinowski (Eds.), *Logic in high definition: Trends in logic*, (pp. 177–202). Cham: Springer.

Duží, M., & Fait, M.(2021). A hyperintensional theory of intelligent question answering in TIL. In R. Loukanova (Ed.), *Natural Language Processing in Artificial Intelligence. NLPinAI 2020*, (pp. 69–104). Cham: Springer.

Duží, M., & Kosterec, M. (2017). A valid rule of β-conversion for the logic of partial functions. *Organon F, 24*, 10–36.

Gordon, M. J. C., & Melham, T. F. (1993). *Introduction to HOL*. Cambridge: Cambridge University Press.

Jespersen, B. (2021). First among equals: Co-hyperintensionality for structured propositions. *Synthese, 199*, 4483–4497. https://doi.org/10.1007/s11229-020-02987-4.

Jespersen, B. (2019). Anatomy of a proposition. *Synthese, 196*, 1285–1324.

Jespersen, B. (2015a). Qualifying quantifying-in. In A. Torza (Ed.), *Quantifiers, quantifiers, and quantifiers: Themes in logic, metaphysics and language* (pp. 241–269). Cham: Springer.

Jespersen, B. (2015b). Should propositions proliferate? *Thought, 4*, 243–251.

Kaplan, D. (1968). Quantifying-in. *Synthese, 19*, 178–214.

Kaplan, D. (1986), Opacity. In L. E. Hahn & P. A. Schilpp (Eds.), *The philosophy of W.V. Quine* (pp. 229–289). La Salle, IL: Open Court.

Klement, K. C. (2002). *Frege and the logic of sense and reference*. New York: Routledge.

Materna, P. (2005). Ordinary modalities. *Logique et Analyse, 189–192*, 57–70.

Materna, P. (1997). Rules of existential quantification into 'intensional contexts'. *Studia Logica, 57*, 331–343.

Morton, A. (1969). Extensional and non-truth-functional contexts. *Journal of Philosophy, 66*, 159–164.

Moschovakis, Y. N. (2006). A logical calculus of meaning and synonymy. *Linguistics and Philosophy, 29*, 27–89.

Pickel, B. (2015). Variables and attitudes. *Noûs, 49*, 333–356.

Quine, W.v.O. (1956). Quantifiers and propositional attitudes. *Journal of Philosophy, 53*, 177–187.

Quine, W. v. O. (1960). *Word and object*. Cambridge, MA: MIT Press.

Salmon, N. (2010). Lambda in sentences with designators: An ode to complex predication. *Journal of Philosophy, 107*, 445–468.

Tichý, P. (1986). Indiscernibility of identicals. *Studia Logica*, 45, 251–273. Reprinted in V. Svoboda, B. Jespersen & C. Cheyne (Eds.), *Pavel Tichý's collected papers in logic and philosophy*. Prague/Dunedin: Filosophia,Czech Academy of Sciences/University of Otago Press, 2004.

Tichý, P. (1988). *The foundations of Frege's logic*. Berlin: De Gruyter.

Turner, R. (1992). Properties, propositions and semantics theory. In M. Rosner & R. Johnson (Eds.), *Computational linguistics and formal semantics* (pp. 159–180). Cambridge: Cambridge University Press.

Yalcin, S. (2015). Quantifying in from a Fregean perspective. *Philosophical Review, 124*, 207–253.

Transparent quantification into hyperintensional objectual attitudes

Marie Duží   Bjørn Jespersen

Abstract We demonstrate how to validly quantify into hyperintensional contexts involving non-propositional attitudes like *seeking, solving, calculating, worshipping*, and *wanting to become*. We describe and apply a typed extensional logic of hyperintensions that preserves compositionality of meaning, referential transparency and substitutivity of identicals also in hyperintensional attitude contexts. We specify and prove rules for quantifying into hyperintensional contexts. These rules presuppose a rigorous method for substituting variables into hyperintensional contexts, and the method will be described. We prove the following. First, it is always valid to quantify *into* hyperintensional attitude contexts and *over* hyperintensional entities. Second, factive empirical attitudes (e.g. *finding the site of Troy*) validate, furthermore, quantifying *over* intensions and extensions, and so do non-factive attitudes, both empirical and non-empirical (e.g. *calculating the last decimal of the expansion of* π), provided the entity to be quantified over exists. We focus mainly on mathematical attitudes, because they are uncontroversially hyperintensional.

1 Introduction

The topic of this paper is quantifying-in. Quantifying-in is existential quantification into modal or attitudinal contexts, mixing quantification with modalities or attitudes.[1] Technically, one or more existential quantifiers need to bind one or more occurrences of one or more variables inside the scope of one or more modal or attitudinal operators. The key problem which quantifying-in poses is whether, and if so just how, in full technical detail, the existential quantifier succeeds in reaching across any such operator in order to bind one or more variables occurring within the scope of the operator. The standard way of phrasing the problem of quantifying-in is that the same variable has occurrences in two different kinds of context. When bound by the quantifier, the occurrence is extensional; when inside the scope of the operator, the occurrence is non-extensional. So the worry is that the quantificational domain of the variable slides from extensional to non-extensional entities, such that the quantifier cannot get a grip on the non-extensional occurrence of the variable.[2]

A subsequent logical problem to the problem of variable-binding is to hone in on just those inferential schemas that are valid. A subsequent philosophical problem is to make good intuitive sense of those valid inferences.

Where Op is an arbitrary modal or attitudinal operator, φ^n an n-ary predicate, a_n n number of constants, and α_n n number of variables, the validity of quantifying-in (QI) presupposes that the instances of this schema be valid:

$$\frac{\ldots Op \ldots (\ldots \varphi^n \ldots a_n \ldots)}{\ldots \exists \alpha_n \ldots Op \ldots (\ldots \varphi^n \ldots \alpha_n \ldots) \ldots} \text{ QI}$$

The schema displays the phenomenon of *exportation*: whereas in the premise the reference to the semantic values of a_n occurs inside the scope of Op, in the conclusion the reference, α_n, occurs outside the scope of Op, thanks to existential quantification over α_n.

Here are two examples, one modal, the other attitudinal, to make matters more concrete, where a may be an entity of any sort (not just an individual):

(*modality*) contingently, a has property F; therefore, there is an x such that, contingently, x has property F

(*attitude*) agent b believes that a has property F; therefore, there is an x such that b believes that x has property F

We delimit our scope in this paper to *attitudes*, as opposed to modalities, that are *hyperintensional*, as opposed to intensional, and *objectual*, as opposed to propositional.

---

[1] The first well-known modern example of quantifying into *modal* contexts may be the *Barcan Formula*: $\Diamond \exists x \varphi \rightarrow \exists x \Diamond \varphi$. Where $\Diamond$ represents logical possibility, *BF* states that if it is logically possible that something be a φ then something has the logical potential to be a φ. The $\exists$-bound occurrence of x in the consequent falls within the scope of $\Diamond$ (hence exemplifying Quine-style 'third-degree modal involvement'), and the question arises how $\exists$ succeeds in binding this occurrence.

[2] See Quine (1960, in particular pp. 147–148).

Transparent quantification into hyperintensional objectual attitudes

A typical example of a hyperintensional objectual attitude would be:

a calculates the square root of 125

First, the complement of *a*'s computational attitude cannot be an intensional entity, where an intensional entity is defined as per possible-world semantics, a mapping defined on a logical space of possible worlds.[3] Intensions fall notoriously short of modelling mathematical attitudes; the lesson is that mathematical complements must be hyperintensionally individuated.

Second, the complement cannot be propositional. If *a* calculates *X*, then *X* is not the sort of entity that can be either true or false (the hallmark of the propositional). *a*'s attitude does not consist in, e.g., calculating whether the square root of 125 is an integer, which *is* a propositional attitude. When calculating the (principal) square root of 125, *a* is involved in the appetitional, as opposed to contemplative, attitude of attempting to arrive at the outcome of a computational procedure, with no guarantee of obtaining it. The outcome is not a truth-value or a truth-condition, but an irrational number, and *a* wishes to know which it is, with no guarantee that there even exists a number that is the square root of 125. For instance, if *a* is calculating the square root of 125 divided by 0, then there is no number that will roll out as the result of the computational effort. Some may even consider the computation illegitimate, because they consider dividing by 0 an illegitimate application of the division function. Still, despite the possible illegitimacy of dividing by zero and despite the necessary absence of a result, it remains an option for *a* to be engaged in the activity of calculating the result of an arithmetic operation.

In this paper we are going to show how variable-binding is technically compatible with quantifying-in; we are going to describe one particular semantic theory capable of sustaining it; and we will provide suitable domains of quantification. The fact that we are quantifying into *hyperintensional* contexts is importantly different from quantifying into intensional contexts, because it is just much more technically challenging to do so. Quantifying into the latter, as we show below, is straightforward. Quantifying into the former is problematic because a hyperintensional context, hence any of its constituents, is 'sealed off' from immediate logical manipulation. Therefore the challenge becomes how to 'open up' a hyperintensional context so as to manipulate one or more of its constituents. The so-called *substitution method* we describe below is our tool to do just that.

More specifically, we *prove* the following. First, it is always valid to quantify *into* hyperintensional attitude contexts and *over* hyperintensional entities. Any entity is hyperintensional as soon as it obeys a principle of individuation finer than logical equivalence. Any attitude context is hyperintensional as soon as the complement of the attitude is a hyperintensional entity. Second, factive empirical attitudes (e.g. *finding the site of Troy*) validate, furthermore, quantifying *over* intensions and extensions, and

---

[3] Co-intensionality for possible-world intensions is necessary co-extensionality: where p, q are mappings, if $p(w) = q(w)$ for all worlds w then $p = q$, i.e. logical equivalence entails identity, which amounts to an extensional principle of individuation for intensions. For a survey of the ascent from intensions to hyperintensions as meanings and attitude complements, see Jespersen (2010, 2012).

so do non-factive attitudes, both empirical and non-empirical (e.g. *calculating the last decimal of the expansion of* π), provided the entity to be quantified over exists. Thus, if *per impossibile* the expansion of π would have a unique last decimal then there is a number x such that x is the product of some computational procedure applied to π. (Soundness, of course, is another matter.) Similarly for non-factive, empirical attitudes, like worshipping a particular deity, who exists at at least all the world/time couples at which someone worships the deity in question.[4]

The *novelties* this paper presents are the following. (1) We present an updated and improved definition of hyperintensional individuation, which amounts to a modification of Church's Alternative (A1).[5] (2) We present a detailed study of the mathematical attitude of calculating. (3) We present updated rules for quantifying into hyperintensional contexts *de dicto*, which are an adjustment and generalization of the rules presented in Duží et al. (2010). (4) We present an analysis of ostensibly logically impossible empirical attitudes like seeking a yeti without seeking an abominable snowman, which revolve around two different hyperintensions presenting one and the same intension. (5) We present, finally, rules for quantifying into hyperintensional attitudes *de re* that correct the rules presented in Duží et al. (2010, § 5.3).

Arguably, valid rules for quantifying-in are indispensable also from a semi-practical point of view, for instance, in order to design the behaviour of software agents in a multi-agent system. Such a system is composed of autonomous and intelligent, but also resource-bounded agents. The agents act in order to achieve their individual as well as collective goals. There is no central dispatcher to control the behaviour of the system. Instead, the agents' behaviour and reasoning is governed by messaging among the agents. The autonomous agents communicate with each other by exchanging messages formulated in a quasi-natural language. In order to behave in a reasonable and intelligent way, the agents must be equipped with an ontology and a knowledge base defined over that ontology. While the latter typically contains factual empirical knowledge, the former is a stable part of the system consisting of conceptual knowledge including inference rules. These rules enable the agents to derive or compute inferable knowledge from the basic pool of explicit knowledge. Here is a simple example, to make matters more concrete. Imagine agent a receives the message that agents b and c are *calculating* the distance from their position to the gas station closest to a's position. In such a situation a cannot infer that there is a gas station close to his position. Instead, a can only infer that b and c share a property, namely the property of being related to the hyperintensional activity of calculating a particular distance. In case a also needs to fill up his car, it is reasonable to send a message to b and c asking to tell him whether they did succeed in calculating the distance. The situation is different if a receives the message that, for instance, *b has calculated* the distance. For now a can draw the conclusion that b has identified a particular number as the distance measured in kilometres between two points; hence a can also draw the conclusion that there is one gas station nearer to his position than any other gas station. a can go on to, for

---

[4] We follow Tichý in holding that it is an analytic truth that deities, including the God of medieval scholasticism, exist contingently. See his (1979) for the argument that necessary existence would detract from the greatness of a deity.

[5] See Church (1993).

instance, request the exact location of the station. This paper, however, is devoted to the theoretical aspects of quantifying-in.

The rest of this paper is organized as follows. Section 2 provides philosophical background to the logical problem of quantifying-in and motivates our choice of background theory. Section 3 sets out the philosophical foundations of our background theory. Section 4 sets out its logical foundations, leading up to the general rules of quantification into hyperintensional objectual attitudes. Section 5 presents the various rules of quantifying-in and proves their validity, exemplifying them by way of philosophical applications.

2 Background and overview

Quantifying-in would, naïvely, seem to pose no problem at all. The rule of existential generalization simply serves to make explicit an ontological commitment incurred in the premise. Thus nobody will bat an eyelid if somebody draws this inference:

$$\frac{\varphi^1 a_1}{\exists x_1 (\varphi^1 x_1)} \quad \text{(EG)}$$

For instance, if the individual Tilman lives in Tilburg then there is at least one element x in the domain of individuals who lives in Tilburg. If the premise is true then the conclusion is the truth that the *quantity* of objects with a particular *quality* (*in casu* living in Tilburg) amounts to at least one.

However, things are not that simple once attitudes or modalities are thrown into the mix, as was mentioned in the Introduction. The main formal problem quantifying-in poses has a syntactic and a semantic, a logical and an ontological aspect. The syntactic aspect is whether the formalism in which quantifying-in is to be carried out sustains variable-binding across modal/attitudinal operators. The semantic aspect is what sort of semantics is required to validate such variable-binding. The logical aspect is which inferences bearing on quantifying-in are valid. The ontological or metaphysical aspect is what sorts of entities one's theory is geared to quantify over. This ontological issue is, of course, well-known independently of quantifying-in. Where variable f ranges over properties of individuals, this inference remains controversial:

$$\frac{\varphi^1 a_1}{\exists f^1 \left(f^1 a_1 \right)} \quad \text{(EG')}$$

That is, if Tilman lives in Tilburg then there is at least one property f that Tilman has. Those who oppose this instance of EG will agree that Tilman lives in Tilburg, but disagree that he has the *property* of living in Tilburg, or they will agree that he does have this property, but shy away from quantifying over intensional entities such as properties. We have no such ontological qualms, so we do not think twice about validating this second inference as well.

We investigate quantifying-in by investigating the logic of instances of two inferential schemas that share the same premise but have two different conclusions.

The first schema is this one:

$$\frac{a \text{ has an objectual attitude } Att \text{ whose complement is } X}{\exists x \, (a \text{ has } Att \text{ toward } x)} \quad (1)$$

Schema (1) exemplifies *quantification over X*, the conclusion making explicit an ontological commitment implicit in the premise. If X belonging to domain *Dom* occurs as the complement of a's attitude then there is an element x in *Dom* that occurs as the complement of a's attitude.

But we need to be careful with *Dom* in order not to draw illicit inferences. For instance, if the premise is that a is seeking an abominable snowman then the conclusion ought *not* be that there is an *individual* (an extensional entity) x such that a is seeking x. For if there are no abominable snowmen, the inference will have crossed the line from logic into magic, conjuring up an individual out of thin air. For a non-empirical example, if the premise is that a is calculating the sum of seven and five the conclusion ought *not* to be that there is a *number* (an extensional entity) y such that a is calculating y. For it is nonsense to calculate a number, numbers themselves being computationally inert. To calculate is to apply an arithmetic operation to a suitable supply of numbers as operands with the purpose of obtaining a number as output value. There may be no output value, of course: five divided by zero has no quotient. Still a may be calculating the quotient of five and zero; a's computational effort is futile, for sure, but no less of an effort for it. Again we do not want the conclusion to conjure up a number (of any category) out of thin air by existential quantification over a domain of numbers (of any category).

Examples such as these suggest to us that the respective quantificational ranges of x, y cannot in all cases be those of extensional entities such as individuals or numbers. But what would a suitable quantificational range be? The validity of (1) requires a reasoned answer. This answer will also spell out what ontological category a given instance of X belongs to. Hence (1) turns out to be instrumental in putting out in the open the ontology underneath assorted objectual attitudes.

The second schema is this one:

$$\frac{a \text{ has an objectual attitude } Att \text{ whose complement is } X(b)}{\exists z \, (a \text{ has } Att \text{ toward } X(z/b))} \quad (2)$$

Schema (2) exemplifies *quantification into X*. The conclusion extracts a component z from X and quantifies over it. Again the inference appears straightforward. If we can quantify over X then surely it must be equally possible to quantify into any position within X. For instance, if a is seeking an abominable snowman then there is a z such that z is abominable and a is seeking z (i.e. a is seeking something abominable). Or if a is calculating the sum of seven and five then there is a z' such that z' is a number and a is calculating the sum of z' and five. However, the same caveats we issued with respect to (1) apply to (2).

The *framework* within which we discuss and solve the problem of quantifying-in is Transparent Intensional Logic. Formally, TIL is a partial, typed, hyperintensional λ-calculus. Its λ-terms are interpreted by way of a *procedural*, as opposed to denotational, semantics. A procedural semantics construes linguistic meaning as a procedure for converting input objects into output objects; a denotational semantics construes meaning as an output object. For instance, the procedural meaning of '5!' is the very procedure of applying the factorial function to 5, whereas the denotational meaning of '5!' is the number 120. Furthermore, TIL is a partial logic in the specific sense that TIL embraces partially defined functions. Partiality is important in the case of such functors as '÷' (division) and 'the Archbishop of Rome' when their respective denotation is applied to an argument that fails to return a value. Finally, TIL comes with a ramified type hierarchy, as known from Russell, encompassing a simple type theory, as known from Montague and Church. Pulling off quantifying-in is taxing for the expressive power of any semantic theory, and what recommends TIL for the task of validating quantifying-in is not least TIL's impressive expressive power. The ramified types enable us to always go one up, as it were, as required by quantification that exceeds the sphere of first-order objects.

Another feature that makes TIL suitable as a background theory for quantifying-in is its top-down approach to logic and semantics. TIL is a context-*in*variant semantics that is generated by generalizing from the hardest case. The hardest case is a hyperintensional context, which is sensitive to hyperintensional distinctions that do not register in an intensional, let alone extensional context. TIL starts out by devising a semantic theory for hyperintensional contexts and goes on to generalize the same semantics to intensional and extensional contexts. Whichever sort of context a term or expression is embedded within, its meaning will remain the same across contextual embedding. Moreover, its denotational relation will also remain fixed. This is because the denotational relation is a function exclusively of the entity the procedural meaning is typed to produce, and not also of the embedding context. The only class of exceptions are indexical terms such as pronouns, whose meaning remains context-invariant, though. The overarching meta-semantic requirement TIL is designed to satisfy is that a logically manageable semantic theory must respect the laws of extensional logic, the compositionality of meaning, the substitutivity of identicals, and referential transparency (which outlaws reference shift).

The sweet fruit we reap from our top-down approach is that TIL is an extensional logic of hyperintensions and of intensions. Therefore, EG must apply also in hyperintensional and intensional contexts. In fact, from an instrumental point of view, testing whether EG comes out valid provides a clear method for testing various theories of non-extensional contexts.[6] Does the theory validate quantifying-in in a transparent and principled manner; or does the theory validate quantifying-in by means of all sorts of adhockery, obscure opacity and contextualist epicycles; or does the theory fail to validate quantifying-in altogether? The second path is likely to be followed by those theories of hyperintensionality that work bottom-up, from extensional through intensional to hyperintensional contexts. This methodology is liable to treat non-extensional contexts as semantic and logical anomalies, rather than as what they are, contexts located smack in the heart of colloquial discourse. As language-users we routinely and confidently speak about what might be true, what ought to be true, what somebody hopes to be or become true, what they are searching for, are afraid of, etc. The

---

[6] Kaplan (1990, p. 14) and Bealer (1982, p. 13) mention quantifying-in as a challenge and a 'classical puzzle' (Bealer) which 'pure semantics' and (hyper-) intensional logic must address adequately.

third path marks either the deplorable failure of a theory to accommodate what its designers set out to accommodate, or it marks the intended failure to do so, on the ground that quantifying-in is considered illogical. Its adherents are not prepared to square off an extensional rule such as EG with non-extensional contexts. As adherents of the first path, we see no problem in principle with applying EG to non-extensional contexts. We do see a string of logical and semantic challenges that call for formally worked-out, principled solutions. This paper is devoted to providing the solutions required.

As it happens, this paper can be seen as a substantiation of a remark made by Montague (2007, p. 517, n. 32). She hints at the fact that TIL is able to develop a theory of non-propositional attitudes:

> An intensional logic based on objects called 'constructions' developed by Pavel Tichý (1988) can capture entailments involving propositional and non-propositional objects. If it can be shown that constructions are also involved in intentional attitudes, the theory of constructions would satisfy important motivations for propositionalism without committing to propositionalism.

Propositionalism is the thesis that, in the final analysis, all attitudes, without exception, take propositions as complements.[7] The present paper is part three of a trilogy devoted to quantifying into hyperintensional contexts. The first two parts address hyperpropositional contexts *de re* and *de dicto*, respectively, presenting and proving logical rules for quantifying-in. The present paper does the same for objectual attitudes. Our trilogy on quantifying-in builds upon a handful of previous TIL studies on quantifying-in, namely: Tichý (1986), which quantifies into intensional contexts and over intensions; Materna (1997), which quantifies into hyperintensional contexts and over hyperintensions; and Duží et al. (2010, § 5.3), which quantifies into intensional and hyperintensional contexts and over hyperintensions, intensions and extensions. Furthermore, Tichý (1988, § 43) studies briefly hyperintensional (or *constructional*) attitudes; Duží et al. (2010, Chap. 5) explores them in great length; (ibid., § 5.2) is devoted to objectual attitudes, and (ibid., § 5.3) is devoted in part to quantifying into objectual attitudes. The rules for quantifying-in have been revised over the years; the present trilogy contains their latest statement.

3 Philosophical foundations

3.1 Which attitudes, if any, are objectual?

The analysanda of this paper pose two problems their propositional brethren do not. First, we simply lack a good name for the non-propositional of the attitudes. Calling them 'non-propositional' offers only a negative description. Calling them 'objectual' seems also quite inclusive, for propositions are reasonably characterized as objects as

---

[7] Crawford (2014) employs a different notion of propositionalism. Crawford's notion of propositionalism is the thesis that the complement of an attitude phrased as a 'that' clause is a proposition and not anything else, like a sentence or, as Crawford would prefer, a plurality of entities like properties and individuals in the vein of Russell's multiple-relation theory of judgement.

well, as is pretty much everything else in a typed universe such as that of TIL. Nor will a linguistic-syntactic criterion do. It might be tempting to characterize, or even define, the analysanda as those attitudes that are denoted by intensional transitive verbs, like 'to seek'. But doing so will ultimately hold a logical category hostage to a linguistic quirk that is not intrinsic to the analysanda.[8] So what, if any, is the unifying feature of non-propositional attitudes? We have not come across one. Therefore, we settle for 'objectual' for the time being in keeping with the practice introduced by Forbes (2000).[9]

Second, if propositionalism is true there are ultimately no analysanda, for all non-propositional attitudes will reduce to propositional ones. For instance, to seek the fountain of youth will be to strive to make the proposition true that the seeker find the fountain of youth. But there are cogent reasons for resisting propositionalism, at the very least with respect to contemplative attitudes like *admiring*, *considering* and, well, *contemplating*.[10] We continue to take objectual attitudes at face value, as irreducible attitudes in their own right, rather than attempting to provide synonymy-preserving translation rules from non-propositional to propositional attitudes.[11] Should a strong philosophical argument emerge to the effect that some attitudes are irreducibly non-propositional, we shall thus already have a detailed theory to account for them.

What we can do is describe by example the sort of attitudes whose behaviour when quantified into we are interested in studying:

- *a* seeks an abominable snowman
- *a* finds an abominable snowman
- *a* admires kindness to strangers
- *a* wants to become a millionaire
- *a* wants a colourless green shirt
- *a* attempts to sing notes beyond reach

---

[8] Likewise it would not do to characterize, let alone define propositional attitudes as all and only those attitudes whose complement is denoted by a 'that'-clause. Just think of how Latin phrases propositional complements, as in Cato's famous "Praeterea censeo Carthaginem delendam esse". Some languages allow both a 'that'-clause variant and a Latin-style accusative-with-infinitive variant, but Latin does not (*"Praeterea censeo ut Carthago delenda sit" is neither here nor there). For instance, in Dutch we have the choice between "Tilman vindt dit niet kunnen" and "Tilman vindt dat dit niet kan" ("Tilman doesn't think that this is appropriate") and in Italian between "Tilman la trova contenta" and "Tilman trova che lei sia contenta" ("Tilman thinks that she is happy"). There are no semantic or logical differences, but competent speakers may well detect an extra-semantic difference. For instance, the subjunctive 'sia' signals a slightly more guarded attribution, leaving more wiggle room to qualify or even retract the attribution.

[9] In Duží et al. (2010) we use 'notional' after inspiration by the Czech phrase 'pojmové postoje' ('conceptual attitudes'). 'Notional' is the English term we would have preferred, for the attitudes under scrutiny confront an agent with a concept or notion of an object, rather than with the conceptualized object directly. But 'notional' does not fit the bill entirely, either: also propositions are notional (because conceptual) in character, and Quine (1956) already reserves 'notional' for a particular sort of attitudes, to be contrasted with those he calls 'relational' (see Sect. 1.3 below).

[10] See Crawford (2008, p. 86, n. 20), Montague (2007), Neale (1990, p. 155, n. 6), and Church (1951).

[11] In fact, there are cases, in English and other languages, where a logical analysis will translate a non-propositional locution into a propositional one. For instance, "I believe you" is short for "I believe what you are claiming". "You stand refuted" is another example of the agent putting forward a proposition being identified, at least linguistically ('you'), with the proposition itself. We are not concerned with such cases in this paper.

- *a* prevents an accident
- *a* attempts to prevent an accident
- *a* worships Baal
- *a* wants to become the Archbishop of Rome
- *a* wants to become the Archbishop of Rome, but not the Head of State of the Vatican
- *a* calculates the square root of (5! + 5)
- *a* calculates the probability of winning the Spanish state lottery
- *a* proves Fermat's Last Theorem (FLT)
- *a* is puzzled by the proof of FLT

A propositional attitude, on our construal, takes invariably either a possible-world proposition (an intensional entity) or a structured hyperproposition as its complement. Thus propositional attitudes can be defined exhaustively by means of the logical type of their respective complements. Not so with objectual attitudes. The list above sports various complements, including *properties* (i.e. sets-in-intension), *events* (typed as possible-world propositions, i.e. truth-values-in-intension), individual *offices* (i.e. individuals-in-intension), *mathematical operations*, *logical operations*, etc. There is little to no reason to assume the above list of complements to be exhaustive. Excluded from our present analysis are cases like "Hitler admires Stalin" in case Stalin is typed as an individual, which in our typed universe is an atomic extensional entity. Relations-in-intension between individuals are not interesting with respect to existential quantification: from $R(a, b)$ it readily follows that there is an x and there is a y such that $R(x, y)$. To make the analysis of "Hitler admires Stalin" logically interesting, 'Stalin' needs to be construed as a name of an individual office, such that Hitler's admiration is aimed at an intensional entity.[12] Only then will Hitler's relation to Stalin qualify as an *attitude*.

What we do in Sect. 5 is to demonstrate, for various particular types of complement, how quantifying-in works with respect to factive and non-factive attitudes. These applications will be instances of the particular rules explained and justified in the first part of Sect. 5.

3.2 De re versus de dicto

Following in the footsteps of Frege's semantic contextualism, Church (1956, p. 8, n. 20) says:

> [I]n "Schliemann sought the site of Troy" the names 'Troy' and 'the site of Troy' occur obliquely. For to seek the site of some other city, determined by a different concept, is not the same as to seek the site of Troy, not even if the two cities should happen as a matter of fact (perhaps unknown to the seeker) to have had the same site.

---

[12] This construal is quite reasonable on independent grounds, for 'Stalin' (or 'Сталин') was Ioseb Jugashvili's *nom de guerre* denoting a particular political persona that was marked by particular properties likely to stir enthusiasm in a fellow dictator. It is this persona Hitler admired, rather than Jugashvili without any qualification of any of his capacities.

According to this sort of contextualist semantics, in a context like "The site of Troy is located in Asia Minor" the definite description (or name, in Church's permissive Fregean sense of 'name') 'the site of Troy' denotes a particular spot in Asia Minor, provided 'the site of Troy' has a unique descriptum, whereas in a context like Church's above 'the site of Troy' denotes a concept of the site of Troy. Church argues that it is a concept of a location, not the location itself, that guides Schliemann's and every other seeker's search for the site of Troy.[13] While we agree with Church's view on what the object of Schliemann's search is, we want no truck with his contextualism.

What might a context-*in*variant semantics for an empirical definite description like 'the site of Troy' look like? What TIL can offer is this. Let 'the site of Troy' be a functor denoting a function from empirical indices to at most one individual, modelling physical locations as logical individuals (i.e. particulars individuated *solo numero*).[14] More specifically, let 'the site of Troy' denote a function from possible worlds to a partial function from times to individuals; we call such a possible-world intension an *individual office*. The functor denotes an empirical condition, namely the condition of being a world/time pair such that it has a unique location that is the site of Troy. The definite description nowhere and never denotes the satisfier, if any, of this condition at the world/time pair of evaluation, i.e. 'the site of Troy' nowhere and never names a particular location. Nor is the function the meaning of the definite description. Rather its meaning is a procedure whose product is the function. (This claim will be qualified below: the meaning is the privileged member of an equivalence class of procedures, a *primus inter pares*).

So what is the semantic status of the location, if any, that is the satisfier of the condition at the world/time pair of evaluation? None. It is semantically inconsequential which particular object, if any, happens to satisfy the condition. What does matter is whether there is a satisfier rather than none and whether the satisfier in question is also at the receiving end of other empirical conditions also requiring uniqueness, such that the *F* is also the *G*.

'The site of Troy' always has, by way of semantic fiat, a *denotation*, namely the function that its meaning produces. 'The site of Troy' has sometimes also a *reference*, namely the value, whenever there is one, of the function *the site of Troy* at the world/time pair of evaluation. The bearer of a property such as *being located in Asia Minor* is a value of the function and not the function itself. Yet 'the site of Troy' is not linked semantically to its reference. This is the point where TIL's distinction between de re and de dicto enters. We say that the meaning presenting a function occurs de re when the function descends to its value, if any, at the argument(s) chosen, and occurs de dicto when the function itself is the subject of predication. Hence in "The site of Troy is located in Asia Minor" the meaning of 'the site of Troy' occurs de re, whereas it occurs de dicto in "Schliemann seeks the site of Troy". That is, 'the site of Troy' invariably denotes a function, and the logical form in which the meaning of 'the site of Troy' occurs determines whether its meaning occurs de re or de dicto. This implemen-

---

[13] Church (1951, n. 15) offers various examples of non-propositional attitudes, including the famous example of Ponce de León searching the fountain of youth.

[14] The type of the functional values can be refined from individuals to the more complex one of locations. For details, see Duží et al. (2010, § 5.2.2).

tation of the de re/de dicto distinction is what enables TIL to maintain that a definite description is a functor denoting a function without being stuck with the surreal view that a function may be located in Asia Minor.

3.3 Relational versus notional

Central to Quine (1956) is his distinction between notional and relational attitudes.[15] If Quine wants a sloop then, if his attitude is notional, any sloop will do to relieve him of sloopnessness, and if his attitude is relational then only a particular sloop will satisfy his wish. The latter is arguably ambiguous: Quine wants a particular object, which happens to be a sloop; or Quine has his mind set on one particular sloop, to the exclusion of all other sloops. Be that as it may, Quine phrases relational attitudes by means of existential locutions: "There is an x such that x is a sloop and Quine wants x". It is this phrasing of relational attitudes that pushes quantifying-in to the fore. Relational attitudes have eluded philosophical conceptualization and logical formalization to a much higher degree than notional attitudes have. The two classical hermeneutic efforts are Kaplan (1968, 1986), followed by Crawford (2008).

Crawford (2008, p. 84) makes a point of distinguishing relational attitudes from de re attitudes, due to the strong conception of the latter he subscribes to:

> The assumption is that triadic or *de re* belief implies that the believer knows who, or which object, his belief is about in the sense that he can in some salient sense identify or recognize it.

We do not share Crawford's exclusive conception of de re attitudes.[16] In fact, ours is a highly inclusive conception of de re attitudes, because an attribution of a de re attitude reflects the attributer's perspective and not the attributee's. This is not to say that we identify notional with de dicto attitudes and relational with de re attitudes. Rather we disregard Quine's pair. The main reason is the murkiness of the notion of relational attitude, including the attempt to conceptualize and distinguish it from that of notional attitude in terms of quantifying-in. A relational attitude, if we have Quine and his commentators right, is all about having a *particular* object with a certain property in mind. Yet existential quantification abstracts from who or what has that property, merely recording the fact that the property has an instance. So it seems that relational attitudes are too strong, and quantification too weak, for them to match up.

---

[15] Quine (1956, p. 177) points out, correctly, that "[a]ppreciation of the difference is evinced in Latin and Romance languages by a distinction of mood in subordinate clauses; thus "Procuro un perro que habl*a*" has the relational sense [...] as against the notional "Procuro un perro que habl*e*...". " (*Italics inserted.*). Italian would have "Cerco un cane che parl*a*" and "Cerco un cane che parl*i*", resp. In the first case (using indicative) I am looking for a particular dog, which by the way also speaks; in the second case (using subjunctive) I am looking for a talking dog, and any talking dog, or canine talker, will do, although there may be none. A rough English approximation might be 'a dog, who talks' and 'a dog that talks'. However, the problem as we see it is how to convert this grammatical distinction found in Romance languages into a logical distinction.

[16] See Duží et al. (2010, p. 435) for the exclusive and the inclusive conception of de re attitudes.

Quine's relational/notional pair is historically at the root of the problem of quantifying-in, but not necessarily conceptually at its root. Quantifying-in rears its head, as soon as an existential quantifier needs to reach across a modal or attitudinal operator. It is not intrinsically the case that the attitudinal variant of quantifying-in must be conceptualized philosophically in terms of relational attitudes. It may be that exportation of terms in subject position is valid only for relational attitudes, but since we allow exportation also of terms in predicate position, the very validity of quantifying-in cannot serve, for us, as a criterion of the specifically relational. Put crudely, we are not comfortable with the relational/notional pair and are not sure what exactly to make of it. Whatever relational attitudes may eventually turn out to be, the philosophical challenge quantifying-in poses is, strictly speaking, to make good sense of the notion that the quantity of entities x_i that are such that somebody entertains a certain attitude toward x_i amounts to at least one.

3.4 Three kinds of context: display versus execution

The dichotomy between de dicto and de re described in Sect. 3.2 is a special case of the three tiers TIL operates with. At the highest level of abstraction, the formal ontology of TIL operates with a fundamental dichotomy between hyperintensions (procedures) and their products, i.e. functions.[17] This dichotomy corresponds to two basic ways in which a procedure (meaning) can occur, to wit, *displayed* or *executed*.[18] If the procedure is displayed then the procedure itself is an object of predication; we say that it occurs *hyperintensionally*. If the procedure is executed, then it is a *constituent* of another procedure, and an additional distinction can be found at this level. The constituent presenting a function may occur either *intensionally* (de dicto) or *extensionally* (de re). If intensionally, then the whole function is an object of predication; if extensionally, then a functional value is an object of predication. Both distinctions are instrumental in selecting a procedure or else what the meaning produces, which is either a function or a functional value, as the functional argument of a function.

For an example of the contrast between displayed and executed procedures, consider the mathematical equation $sin(x) = 0$. If a is solving this equation then a is related to the very meaning of "$sin(x) = 0$" rather than the set of multiples of the number π. a wants to execute the procedure expressed by "$sin(x) = 0$" in order to find out which set of real numbers matches the equation. Hence in "a is solving the equation $sin(x) = 0$" the meaning of "$sin(x) = 0$" is displayed. On the other hand, if we claim that the solution of the equation $sin(x) = 0$ is the set $\{\ldots, -2\pi, -\pi, 0, \pi, 2\pi, \ldots\}$ the meaning of "$sin(x) = 0$" is executed to produce the set which is claimed to be identical to $\{\ldots, -2\pi, -\pi, 0, \pi, 2\pi, \ldots\}$. Yet the constituent meaning of "$sin(x) = 0$" occurs intensionally in the meaning of "The solution of the equation $sin(x) = 0$ is the set $\{\ldots, -2\pi, -\pi, 0, \pi, 2\pi, \ldots\}$".

---

[17] Formally speaking, extensional entities like individuals, numbers and truth-values are extreme forms of 0-ary functions, whereas sets are identified with their characteristic functions.

[18] The vocabulary of 'displayed' and 'executed' replaces the previous vocabulary of 'mentioned' and 'used' employed in Duží et al. (2010), Duží and Jespersen (2012) and elsewhere.

The whole set (a characteristic function) is the object of predication. An example of an extensional occurrence of the meaning of '*sin*' would be provided by the meaning of the simple sentence "$sin(\pi) = 0$". Here the value of the function *sine* at the argument π is the object of which it is predicated that it is equal to zero.

The same differentiation applies also to the meanings of terms stemming from empirical language. For an example of the contrast between intensional and extensional occurrence, consider predication. Predication, in TIL, is an instance of functional application: a characteristic function is applied to a suitable argument in order to obtain a truth-value, according as the argument is an element of the set. In the case of predication of empirical properties, the relevant set is obtained by extensionalizing a property. In the context "The site of Troy is located in Asia Minor" we want the functional value of the office *the site of Troy* to occur either as an argument for the set of entities located in Asia Minor or as an argument for the binary relation (-in-intension) *located in* whose second argument is Asia Minor. Hence the meaning of 'the site of Troy' occurs extensionally here. On the other hand, when Schliemann sought the site of Troy, he was not related to any value of the denoted function. Rather he was related to the whole office aiming to determine its value, if any. As a result, the meaning of 'the site of Troy' occurs intensionally in "Schliemann sought the site of Troy". Similarly, the term 'the temperature in Prague' occurs extensionally in "The temperature in Prague is 13 °C", while in "The temperature in Prague is rising" *the same meaning* of this definite description occurs intensionally. To be rising is a property of the whole function rather than of any value. Finally, in "*a* knows (hyperintensionally) that the temperature in Prague is 13 °C" the same meaning occurs hyperintensionally. When knowing something hyperintensionally, we are related to the very meaning of the embedded clause rather than the produced function (a possible-world proposition in this case).

The two distinctions, between displayed/executed and intensional/extensional, allow us to distinguish between three sorts of *context*. This paper zooms in on hyperintensional contexts. What uniquely characterizes a hyperintensional context is the fact that in it a hyperintension occurs displayed rather than executed. The hyperintension is not executed in order to obtain an object beyond it, namely the object it is typed to present (either a lower-order hyperintension or a function). Instead the hyperintension itself occurs as a functional argument.

Here is a summary of the three kinds of context:

- *hyperintensional context*: one or more hyperintensions occur *displayed* (though one or more hyperintensions at least one order higher need to be executed in order to produce the displayed hyperintensions)
- *intensional context*: one or more hyperintensions are *executed* in order to produce one or more functions (moreover, the executed hyperintensions do not occur within another hyperintensional context)
- *extensional context*: one or more hyperintensions are *executed* in order to produce one or more particular values of one or more functions at one or more given arguments (moreover, the executed hyperintensions do not occur within another intensional or hyperintensional context).

The basic idea underlying the above trifurcation is that the same set of logical rules apply to all three kinds of context, but they operate on different complements: hyperintensions, functions, and functional values, respectively. Consider the rule of substitution of identicals. For a puzzle from the standard repertoire, consider how Partee's puzzle is generated[19]:

$$\frac{\text{the temperature is } 90°\text{F};\quad \text{the temperature is rising}}{90° \text{ F is rising}}$$

Where 'the temperature' is a functor denoting a function, the first premise predicates a property of a *value* of the function whereas the second premise predicates a property of the entire *function*. A necessary requirement of valid substitution in the position denoted by 'the temperature' inside the intensional context denoted by "The temperature is rising" requires swapping one intension (a function) for another; swapping an intension for a mere extension (a functional value) will not do. The morale is that the rule of substitution of identicals has been misapplied, because the substituend is of the wrong kind. The morale is not that the rule 'breaks down' when applied to non-extensional contexts.[20]

Nor will swapping a hyperintension for an intension preserve validity in this argument:

$$\frac{\text{Tilman knows that the glass before him is half-full;}\quad \text{necessarily, whatever is half-full is half-empty, and whatever is half-empty is half-full}}{\text{Tilman knows that the glass before him is half-empty}}$$

The argument is valid if Tilman's two epistemic attitudes take possible-world propositions as complements. It is not valid if, as we are assuming, Tilman's complements are hyperpropositions, for then only hyperpropositions are the proper kind of substituends.

Needless to say, nor will swapping a hyperintension for an extension preserve validity:

$$\frac{\text{Tilman computes 5!}\quad 5! = 120}{\text{Tilman computes 120}}$$

The complements of Tilman's hyperpropositional knowledge and his computational efforts are hyperintensional contexts, in which hyperintensions must be substituted for hyperintensions.

---

[19] See also Duží et al. (2010, pp. 124–125).

[20] Of course, the rule 'breaks down' when applied to *opaque/oblique* contexts. But then, every rule presumably does, for there is no knowing what the logic is of such contexts, if indeed they have one. The notion of opacity/obliqueness is misplaced in a logical semantics, because its task is to enable us to draw inferences we know to be valid.

The technical ability to shift between executing and displaying hyperintensions is what helps TIL to a notion of hyperintensional attitudes in the first place. Displayed hyperintensions figure as the complements of hyperintensional attitudes by being the second argument of functions taking agents to the hyperintensions they take an attitude towards. Displayed hyperintensions pose far greater technical challenges than do executed hyperintensions, not least when quantifying into them. These technical challenges take centre stage in the remainder of this paper.

4 Logical foundations

4.1 Constructions as hyperintensions

Above we referred to hyperintensions interchangeably as 'hyperintensions', 'procedures' and 'meanings'. These three labels capture three different aspects of one and the same underlying notion. The notion in question is that of *construction*; cf. Chap. 1. Constructions are *the* key entities of TIL. They are hyperintensionally individuated procedures, of one or multiple steps, and they serve both as linguistic meanings and as the complements of hyperintensional attitudes. When we talk about hyperintensional attitudes, we intend constructional attitudes. Just to be clear, constructions are not functions, nor are they formulae or otherwise linguistic entities. They are kindred to Platonic forms, Bolzano-style ideas-in-themselves (*Vorstellungen an sich*) and Frege-style *Sinn*. Their inductive definition below enumerates six different constructions.

Three remarks straightaway. The first is that *variables* are constructions. Technically, variables behave as defined by Tarski, in virtue of total functions assigning values to variables according to a valuation function v. But x is not a piece of language; 'x' is: 'x' designates the construction x, which constructs its value in one step simply by having it as its v-assigned value. The second remark is that the construction *Composition*, which is the procedure of applying a function to an argument, is impervious to whether it is ever executed by an agent, and whether the procedure produces a product. The same Platonic traits are featured by *Closure*, which is the procedure of forming a function, except that a Closure always produces a product, to wit a function, however degenerate the function may be. The third remark is that *Trivialization* has the effect, when applied to an object, that the Trivialization displays that object. This is absolutely critical in helping us to a theory of hyperintensional attitudes. Thus, if 'X' denotes some construction, the notation '^0X' (read: 'the Trivialization of the construction X') means that we are to 'look at' X itself, whereas the notation 'X' means that we are to 'look at' what X constructs (if anything).

Tichý, in (1988, Chap. 5), introduces the logical core of TIL in the shape of two fundamental definitions. He first defines *constructions* and afterwards the *ramified hierarchy of types*. He then goes on to explain how the products of particular constructions are typed. In the interest of simplicity we first define *simple types of order 1*, then constructions together with the types of their products, and finally the ramified hierarchy of types.

Transparent quantification into hyperintensional objectual attitudes

Definition 1 (*types of order 1*) Let B be a *base*, where a base is a collection of pair-wise disjoint, non-empty sets. Then:

(i) Every member of B is an elementary *type of order 1 over B*.
(ii) Let $\alpha, \beta_1, \ldots, \beta_m (m > 0)$ be types of order 1 over B. Then the collection $(\alpha \beta_1 \ldots \beta_m)$ of all m-ary partial mappings from $\beta_1 \times .. \times \beta_m$ into α is a functional *type of order 1 over B*.
(iii) Nothing else is a *type of order 1 over B*. □

Remark 1 For the purposes of natural-language analysis, we are currently assuming the following base of *elementary types*, each of which is part of the ontological commitments of TIL:

ο: the set of truth-values {**T, F**};
ι: the set of individuals (constant universe of discourse);
τ: the set of real numbers (doubling as temporal continuum);
ω: the set of logically possible worlds (logical space).

Definition 2 (*construction*)

(i) (*Variable*) Let valuation v assign object o to variable x. Then x is a *construction* that v-constructs o.
(ii) (*Trivialization*) Let X be any object whatsoever (i.e. an extension, an intension, or a *construction*). Then ^0X is the *Trivialization* of X, which constructs X without any change of X.
(iii) (*Composition*) Let X v-construct a function f of type $(\alpha \beta_1 \ldots \beta_m)$, and let $Y_1, \ldots, Y_m$ v-construct entities $B_1, \ldots, B_m$ of types $\beta_1, \ldots, \beta_m$, respectively. Then the *Composition* $[X Y_1 \ldots Y_m]$ v-constructs the value (an entity, if any, of type α) of f on the tuple argument $\langle B_1, \ldots, B_m \rangle$. Otherwise the *Composition* $[X Y_1 \ldots Y_m]$ does not v-construct anything and so is v-*improper*.
(iv) (*Closure*) Let $x_1, \ldots, x_m$ be pair-wise distinct variables and Y a construction. Then $[\lambda x_1 \ldots x_m Y]$ is the *construction* λ-*Closure* (or *Closure*). It v-constructs the following function f of type $(\alpha \beta_1 \ldots \beta_m)$. Let variables $x_1, \ldots, x_m$ v-construct entities of types $\beta_1, \ldots, \beta_m$, and let Y v-construct an α-entity. Let $v(B_1/x_1, \ldots, B_m/x_m)$ be a valuation identical with v at least up to assigning objects $B_1/\beta_1, \ldots, B_m/\beta_m$ to variables $x_1, \ldots, x_m$. If Y is $v(B_1/x_1, \ldots, B_m/x_m)$-improper (see iii), then f is undefined on $\langle B_1, \ldots, B_m \rangle$. Otherwise the value of f on $\langle B_1, \ldots, B_m \rangle$ is the α-entity $v(B_1/x_1, \ldots, B_m/x_m)$-*constructed* by Y.
(v) (*Single Execution*) Let X v-construct object o. Then the *Single Execution* ^1X v-constructs o. Let X be either a non-*construction* or a v-improper *construction*. Then ^1X is v-*improper*.
(vi) (*Double Execution*) Let X v-construct a construction Y and let Y v-construct object Z (possibly itself a *construction*). Then the *Double Execution* ^2X v-constructs Z. Let X be a non-*construction* or a *construction* not constructing another *construction*, or a *construction* constructing a v-improper *construction*. Then ^2X is v-*improper*.
(vii) Nothing else is a *construction*.

The overarching idea behind the notion of construction is that, given some input objects, we can apply operations or procedures or *constructions* to obtain some output objects (or none, in some instances of Composition, Single and Double Execution). As already mentioned, a *variable* constructs an object by having that object as its value dependent on a valuation function v arranging variables and objects in a sequence. *Trivialization* is our objectual counterpart of a non-descriptive constant term, which simply harpoons a particular object. In programming jargon, Trivialization *calls* an object: no object can be operated on without first having been called, i.e. retrieved from a pool of objects. *Composition* is the procedure of functional application, rather than the functional value (if any) resulting from application.[21] *Closure* is the procedure of functional abstraction, rather than the resulting function. The *Single Execution* ^1X is the same construction as X, provided X is a construction at all: the default mode in which constructions occur is Single Execution. Single Execution serves basically to differentiate between v-proper constructions, which are the 'successful' constructions, and everything else, which are either v-improper ('failing') constructions or non-constructions, which cannot be executed at all. *Double Execution* encodes the transitivity of construction.[22]

Variables and Trivializations, as well as those instances of Single Execution where X is an atomic construction, are the one-step or primitive or *atomic* constructions of TIL, and none of them can be improper. In particular, what does not exist cannot be Trivialized. (Similarly, what does not exist cannot be named; but it can be described, as per 'the largest prime' or 'is a winged unicorn' or 'the planet between Mercury and the Sun'.) Composition, Closure, and Double Execution, as well as those instances of Single Execution where X is composite, are the multiple-step or *composite* procedures. An *atomic* construction is a structured whole with but one constituent part, namely the construction itself. Importantly, the constituent part of ^0X is ^0X and not X, which is located beyond ^0X: the product of a procedure is no part of the procedure. A *composite* construction is a structured whole with more constituent parts than just itself.

α-*intensions* are functions of type $(\alpha\omega)$, i.e. mappings with domain in possible worlds ω and range in the arbitrary type α. The frequently occurring type of α-intensions is $((\alpha\tau)\omega)$, i.e. mappings from possible worlds to chronologies of objects of type α, abbreviated as '$\alpha_{\tau\omega}$', where a chronology is a mapping from times τ to α.

Examples of frequently occurring *intensions* are:

- *propositions* (i.e. empirical truth-conditions) of type $o_{\tau\omega}$ (e.g. *that the sky is blue*)
- *properties of individuals* of type $(o\iota)_{\tau\omega}$ (e.g. *being blue*)
- *individual roles/offices* of type $\iota_{\tau\omega}$ (e.g. *the first dog in space*)
- *attributes* of type $(\iota\iota)_{\tau\omega}$ (e.g. *the king of*)
- *binary relations-in-intension between individuals* of type $(o\iota\iota)_{\tau\omega}$ (e.g. *kicking*)
- *propositional attitudes* of type $(o\iota o_{\tau\omega})_{\tau\omega}$ (e.g. *knowing that a certain proposition is true*)

---

[21] Cf. Soames (2010, p. 114).

[22] Triple (Quadruple, …) Execution is a theoretical possibility, though one we have so far never had any use for. The informal explications of constructions above draw on material from Jespersen (2014).

– *hyperpropositional attitudes* of type $(o\iota *_n)_{\tau\omega}$ (e.g. *knowing* that a certain propositional construction constructs a proposition that is true*).

The definition of the ramified hierarchy of types divides into three parts: firstly, simple types of order 1, which were already defined by Definition 1; secondly, constructions of order n; thirdly, types of order $n + 1$.

Definition 3 (*ramified hierarchy of types*)
  $\mathbf{T_1}$ (*types of order 1*). See Definition 1.
  $\mathbf{C_n}$ (*constructions of order n*)

  (i) Let x be a variable ranging over a type of order n. Then x is a *construction of order n over B*.
  (ii) Let X be a member of a type of order n. Then ^0X, ^1X, ^2X are *constructions of order n over B*.
  (iii) Let $X, X_1, \ldots, X_m$ $(m > 0)$ be constructions of order n over B. Then $[X \, X_1 \ldots X_m]$ is a *construction of order n over B*.
  (iv) Let $x_1, \ldots, x_m, X$ $(m > 0)$ be constructions of order n over B. Then $[\lambda x_1 \ldots x_m X]$ is a *construction of order n over B*.
  (v) Nothing is a *construction of order n over B* unless it so follows from $\mathbf{C_n}$ (i)–(iv).

  $\mathbf{T_{n+1}}$ (*types of order n + 1*)
  Let $*_n$ be the collection of all constructions of order n over B. Then

  (i) $*_n$ and every type of order n are *types of order n + 1*.
  (ii) If $m > 0$ and $\alpha, \beta_1, \ldots, \beta_m$ are types of order $n + 1$ over B, then $(\alpha \beta_1 \ldots \beta_m)$ (see $\mathbf{T_1}$ (ii)) is a *type of order n + 1 over B*.
  (iii) Nothing else is a *type of order n + 1 over B*.

Example 1 The number 1 and the function + are objects belonging to types τ and $(\tau\tau\tau)$, respectively, which are types of order 1. The Trivializations ^{01}, $^0+$ are thus constructions of order 1 belonging to type $*_1$, the type of order 2. If a variable x v-constructs numbers then x is a construction of order 1 belonging to $*_1$, the type of order 2. The Composition $[^0+ \, x \, ^01]$ v-constructs the successor of the number v-constructed by x. The Closure $\lambda x \, [^0+ \, x \, ^01]$ constructs the successor function of type $(\tau\tau)$, a type of order 1. Hence this Composition and this Closure are also constructions of order 1 belonging to $*_1$, the type of order 2. The Trivializations of these constructions, i.e. ^0x, $^0[^0+ \, x \, ^01]$, $^0[\lambda x \, [^0+ \, x \, ^01]]$, are constructions of order 2 belonging to $*_2$, the type of order 3. The Trivialization $^0[^0[\lambda x \, [^0+ \, x \, ^01]]]$, or '$^{00}[\lambda x \, [^0+ \, x \, ^01]]$' for short, is a construction of order 3, i.e. a member of $*_3$, the type of order 4. This Trivialization constructs a member of the type of order 3, namely the Trivialization $^0[\lambda x \, [^0+ \, x \, ^01]]$. The Double Execution $^2[^0[\lambda x \, [^0+ \, x \, ^01]]]$, or '$^{20}[\lambda x \, [^0+ \, x \, ^01]]$' for short, is also a construction of order 3, i.e. a member of $*_3$, which is the type of order 4. It constructs what is constructed by what is constructed by the Trivialization $^0[\lambda x \, [^0+ \, x \, ^01]]$, which is the successor function, a member of the type of order 1. In general, ^{20}C v-constructs the same object as C v-constructs, if any; only that if C is a construction of order n then ^0C is a construction of order $n + 1$ and ^{20}C is a construction of order $n + 2$.

Definition 4 (*quantifiers*) The *quantifiers* $\forall^\alpha, \exists^\alpha$ are total, type-theoretically polymorphous functions of type $(o(o\alpha))$, for an arbitrary type α, defined as follows. The *universal quantifier* $\forall^\alpha$ is the function that associates a class S of α elements with **T** if S contains all the elements of type α, otherwise with **F**. The *existential quantifier* $\exists^\alpha$ is the function that associates a class S of α elements with **T** if S is a non-empty class, otherwise with **F**. □

Remark 2 Since the topic of this paper is existential quantification, we will examine below various arguments whose conclusion is an existentially quantified construction. One should keep in mind, though, that quantifiers are not 'special symbols' as in first-order predicate logic. Rather they are classes of classes of α-objects. Thus existential quantification translates into the procedure of applying the existential quantifier $\exists^\alpha$ to a class of α-objects. For instance, if *Transcendental*, of type $(o\tau)$, is the class of transcendental numbers, then to claim that there are transcendental numbers amounts to claiming that *Transcendental* is a non-empty class: $[^0\exists^\tau \, ^0Transcendental]$. Moreover, since we work with properly partial functions, before applying an existential quantifier we must first prove that the argument class is non-empty. For instance, if : is the division function of type $(\tau\tau\tau)$, this would be an invalid derivation: $[^0 = [^0: {}^05 \, ^00] \, ^00] \vdash [^0\exists^\tau \, \lambda x \, [^0 = [^0: {}^05 \, ^00] \, x]$, because the class constructed by the Closure $\lambda x \, [^0 = [^0: {}^05 \, ^00] \, x]$ is not non-empty. It is a degenerate class whose characteristic function is undefined at all its arguments, because the Composition $[^0: {}^05 \, ^00]$ is v-improper, and so is the Composition $[^0 = [^0: {}^05 \, ^00] \, x]$ for every valuation v.

Notational conventions Some logical objects, like *truth-functions* and *quantifiers* (cf. Definition 4), are extensional entities: $\wedge$ (conjunction), $\vee$ (disjunction) and $\supset$ (implication) are of type (ooo), and $\neg$ (negation) of type (oo). When using constructions of truth-functions, we will omit Trivialization and use infix notation to conform to standard notation in the interest of better readability. Also when using constructions of identities of α-entities, $=_\alpha /(o\alpha\alpha)$, we omit Trivialization, the type subscript, and use infix notation when no confusion can arise. Instead of '$[^0\exists^\alpha \, \lambda x \ldots]$', '$[^0\forall^\alpha \, \lambda x \ldots]$' we will write '$\exists x \ldots$', '$\forall x \ldots$' when no confusion arises. Below all type indications will be provided outside the formulae in order not to clutter the notation. Furthermore, 'X/α' means that an object X is (a member) of type α; '$X \to_v \alpha$' means that the type of the object *valuation*-constructed by X is α. We write '$X \to \alpha$' if what is v-constructed does not depend on a valuation v. This holds throughout: the variables $w \to_v \omega$ and $t \to_v \tau$. If $C \to_v \alpha_{\tau\omega}$ then the frequently used Composition $[[Cw]t]$, which is the intensional descent (a.k.a. extensionalization) of the α-intension v-constructed by C, will be encoded as 'C_{wt}'.

Example 2 Let $Cot, Sin/(\tau\tau)$ be the trigonometric functions *Cotangent, Sine*, respectively, π/τ, $Improper/(o*_1)$ the class of constructions of order 1 that are v-improper for every valuation v. Then

$^0Cot/*_1 \to (\tau\tau)$; $^0\pi/*_1 \to \tau$; $[^0Cot \, ^0\pi]/*_1 \to \tau$; $^0Improper/*_2 \to (o*_1)$;
$^0[^0Cot \, ^0\pi]/*_2 \to *_1$; $[^0Improper \, ^0[^0Cot \, ^0\pi]]/*_2 \to o$;
$[^0=_{(\tau\tau)} [^0Sin \, ^0\pi] \, ^00]/*_1 \to o$, or '$[[^0Sin \, ^0\pi] = {}^00]$' for short;

$[^0 \wedge [^0Improper\ ^0[^0Cot\ ^0\pi]]\ [^0=_{(\tau\tau)}\ [^0Sin\ ^0\pi]\ ^0 0]]/*_2 \to$ o, or

'$[[^0Improper\ ^0[^0Cot\ ^0\pi]] \wedge [[^0Sin\ ^0\pi] = {}^0 0]]$', for short

Example 3 Let $Happy/(o\iota)_{\tau\omega}$ be a property of individuals, $Tilman/\iota$ an individual. Then $[[^0Happy\ w]t]/*_1 \to (o\iota)$, or '$^0Happy_{wt}$' for short, v-constructs the population of the property of being happy in a given w and t; $[^0Happy_{wt}\ ^0Tilman]/*_1 \to$ o v-constructs **T** or **F** according as Tilman is happy in a given world w and time t of evaluation, and $\lambda w \lambda t\ [^0Happy_{wt}\ ^0Tilman]/*_1 \to o_{\tau\omega}$ constructs the proposition that Tilman is happy. If $Know/(o\iota*_n)_{\tau\omega}$ is a hyperpropositional attitude, then the Closure $\lambda w \lambda t\ [^0Know_{wt}\ ^0Tom\ ^0[\lambda w \lambda t\ [^0Happy_{wt}\ ^0Tilman]]]/*_2 \to o_{\tau\omega}$ constructs the proposition that Tom (hyperintensionally, i.e. explicitly) knows that Tilman is happy.

4.2 Displayed versus executed constructions

In Sect. 3.4 we sketched the difference between the two modes in which a construction can occur, to wit, *displayed* and *executed*. The Trivialization ^0C of a construction C displays the construction C *and* all the subconstructions of C. Hence C is not executed, and so does not obtain an object beyond C. Instead C occurs itself as a functional argument. Thus we have this contrast:

- (*executed Composition*) $[^0Cot\ ^0\pi]$: its constituent parts are the Composition itself, ^0Cot, $^0\pi$. Since the cotangent function is not defined at π, the Composition is v-improper for any valuation v
- (*displayed Composition*) $^0[^0Cot\ ^0\pi]$: this time the only constituent part of this construction is the Trivialization itself, $^0[^0Cot\ ^0\pi]$. The Composition $[^0Cot\ ^0\pi]$ is *not* a constituent part. Instead it is displayed, in virtue of being constructed by its Trivialization. In $[^0Improper\ ^0[^0Cot\ ^0\pi]]$ the Composition $[^0Cot\ ^0\pi]$ is also displayed rather than executed, and the Composition $[^0Improper\ ^0[^0Cot\ ^0\pi]]$ constructs **T**, for it is true that the construction $[^0Cot\ ^0\pi]$ is v-improper for every valuation v. "$[^0Improper\ [^0Cot\ ^0\pi]]$" would mean that what $[^0Cot\ ^0\pi]$ constructs is improper, which is literally nonsensical.

To further demonstrate the difference between displayed and executed constructions, consider this hyperintensional objectual attitude:

a calculates the cotangent of π

Types: $a \to_v \iota$: a construction of an individual; $Cot/(\tau\tau)$: the trigonometric cotangent function; $Calculate/(o\iota*_n)_{\tau\omega}$: a relation-in-intension of an individual to a construction.

If an agent is related to what $[^0Cot\ ^0\pi]$ constructs then the agent will be related to nothing. But though the agent's computational efforts are bound to be futile, the agent is still engaged in a computational activity in which the agent is related intentionally to something rather than nothing. By relating a mathematician to a construction, of type $*_n$, we are not relating the mathematician to a piece of mathematical syntax. For sure, apart from simple so-called mental maths, computational acts are aided by syntactic manipulation; but to calculate is not tantamount to manipulating syntax. As Brown

(1999, pp. 92–93) rightly says, '2' and 'two' have the same sense; similarly '2 + 5' and 'two plus five' share the same sense. In TIL we say that the last two terms encode one and the same Composition: $[^0+\ ^02\ ^05]$. It is also irrelevant which name for an object is used when the object is Trivialized. Thus, for instance, ^{02} and ^0Two are one and the same construction, and so are $[^0+\ ^02\ ^05]$ and $[^0Plus\ ^0Two\ ^0Five]$. Hence from our point of view, *calculating 2 + 5* and *calculating two plus five* are one and the same attitude.[23] To calculate is, rather, tantamount to manipulating abstract, extra-mental, extra-notational procedures. Different (sorts of) agents may well manipulate those procedures in somewhat different ways. Humans, computers, and extraterrestrials (should they exist) encode the procedures in different ways, and already the history of human mathematics has seen many notational systems and different ways of encoding mathematical computations, but the mathematical procedures transcend these differences.[24]

The analysis of the attitude mentioned above is this construction:

$$\lambda w \lambda t\ [^0Calculate_{wt}\ a\ ^0[^0Cot\ ^0\pi]] \tag{1}$$

In (1) the Composition $[^0Cot\ ^0\pi]$ is *displayed* (by means of Trivialization) as the second argument of the extensionalized relation-in-intension *Calculate*; and so are all the sub-constructions within this Composition. They are *not* constituents of the Closure (1). The Closure (1) decomposes into these constituent parts:

– $\lambda w \lambda t\ [^0Calculate_{wt}\ a\ ^0[^0Cot\ ^0\pi]]$
– $\lambda t\ [^0Calculate_{wt}\ a\ ^0[^0Cot\ ^0\pi]]$
– $[^0Calculate_{wt}\ a\ ^0[^0Cot\ ^0\pi]]$
– $[[^0Calculate\ w]\ t]$
– $[^0Calculate\ w]$
– $^0Calculate$
– w
– t
– a
– $^0[^0Cot\ ^0\pi]$

But *not* also:

– $[^0Cot\ ^0\pi]$
– ^0Cot
– $^0\pi$

At any $\langle w, t \rangle$, whoever evaluates whether the truth-condition constructed by (1) is satisfied at $\langle w, t \rangle$ is not ipso facto calculating the Composition $[^0Cot\ ^0\pi]$. They are only checking whether a is in the process of executing this Composition, assigning

---

[23] For sure, the empirical *execution* of a procedure can be more effective or easier using one notational system rather than another. Brown (ibid.) calls this aspect the *computational role* of a particular notation. We agree on this point. Yet this is a pragmatic aspect; the semantic role of particular notations remains the same.

[24] See Duží (2014a).

the truth-value **T** or **F**, according as a is engaged in this futile activity. Hence (1) constructs a proposition that returns **T** or **F** at $\langle w, t \rangle$, regardless of the fact that $[^0Cot\ ^0\pi]$ constructs nothing.

Recall the three kinds of context in which a construction can occur, namely *hyperintensional, intensional* and *extensional*. (1) is an example of a construction in which the Composition $[^0Cot\ ^0\pi]$ occurs hyperintensionally. Hence its parts ^0Cot and $^0\pi$ also occur hyperintensionally, i.e. in displayed mode.

On the other hand, in the Composition

$$[[^0Cot\ ^0\pi] = ^0 0] \qquad (2)$$

the Composition $[^0Cot\ ^0\pi]$ occurs executed. (2) decomposes into these constituents:
- $[[^0Cot\ ^0\pi] = ^0 0]$
- $[^0Cot\ ^0\pi]$
- ^0Cot
- $^0\pi$
- $^0 0$
- $^0 =$

$[^0Cot\ ^0\pi]$ being improper, the whole Composition (2) is improper as well: the function =, typed to take a pair of numbers to a truth-value, does not obtain the required left-hand argument to operate on.

If a construction C occurs executed as a constituent of a construction D, then C can occur in D either *intensionally* or *extensionally*.[25] Since in (2) the Composition $[^0Cot\ ^0\pi]$ occurs executed, its part ^0Cot occurs executed as well, namely extensionally. The first argument of the function = is typed to be the *value* of the cotangent function at the argument π. And since there is no such value, (2) comes out improper.

To adduce an example of an intensional occurrence of an executed construction, consider "The cotangent function is trigonometric". Where $Trigonometric/(o(\tau\tau))$ is the class of trigonometric functions, the sentence receives the analysis

$$[^0Trigonometric\ ^0Cot] \qquad (3)$$

The construction ^0Cot is a constituent that occurs intensionally. The entire cotangent function, rather than any particular value, is the argument of the function *Trigonometric*.

A context in which constructions occur only *executed*, whether the context be intensional or extensional, is easy to logically operate on. For one thing, existential generalization into such contexts goes smoothly, as expected. For instance, if it is true that the cotangent is a trigonometric function then there is a trigonometric function $(f \rightarrow_v (\tau\tau))$:

$$\frac{[^0Trigonometric\ ^0Cot]}{\exists f[^0Trigonometric\ f]}$$

---

[25] Here we use the terms 'intensionally' and 'extensionally' in the sense of occurring in an intensional or extensional context, respectively, rather than in the sense of possible-world semantics. See Duží et al. (2010, § 2.6).

If it is true that the sine of π equals zero then there is a function whose value at π is zero, and there is a number at which the value of sine equals zero:

$$\frac{[[^0Sin\ ^0\pi] = {}^0 0]}{\exists f[[f\ ^0\pi] = {}^0 0]} \quad \frac{[[^0Sin\ ^0\pi] = {}^0 0]}{\exists x[[^0Sin\ x] = {}^0 0]}$$

To revisit an empirical example from Sect. 3.4, from the premise that the temperature in Barcelona is rising we can deduce that there is an intension m (*in casu* a magnitude of type $\tau_{\tau\omega}$) such that m is rising. But we cannot deduce that there is a particular *value* that is rising, for the construction of the magnitude occurs intensionally. Let the type assignments be as follows: $Rising/(o\ \tau_{\tau\omega})_{\tau\omega}$: a property of a magnitude; $Temperature\_in/(\tau\iota)_{\tau\omega}$; $Barcelona/\iota$; $\lambda w \lambda t\ [^0Temperature\_in_{wt}\ ^0Barcelona]$ $\rightarrow \tau_{\tau\omega}$: magnitude; $m \rightarrow_v \tau_{\tau\omega}$. Then we have the valid argument

$$\frac{\lambda w \lambda t\ [^0Rising_{wt}\ \lambda w \lambda t\ [^0Temperature\_in_{wt}\ ^0Barcelona]]}{\lambda w \lambda t\ \exists m[^0Rising_{wt}\ m]}$$

while this argument is invalid:

$$\frac{\lambda w \lambda t\ [^0Rising_{wt}\ \lambda w \lambda t\ [^0Temperature\_in_{wt}\ ^0Barcelona]]}{\lambda w \lambda t\ [^0= \lambda w \lambda t\ [^0Temperature\_in_{wt}\ ^0Barcelona]_{wt}\ ^090]}{\lambda w \lambda t\ [^0Rising_{wt}\ ^090]}$$

In the first premise the Closure $\lambda w \lambda t\ [^0Temperature\_in_{wt}\ ^0Barcelona]$ occurs intensionally while in the second, extensionally. Hence only an equivalent construction of the same function can be substituted for this Closure; a merely v-congruent construction will not suffice.

4.3 Substitution method

Applying logical operations to hyperintensional contexts is far from being an open-and-shut matter. The technical complications we are confronted with are rooted in *displayed* constructions. For instance, a variable occurring in a hyperintensional context is displayed, i.e. Trivialization-bound, which means being bound in a manner that overrides λ-binding. In particular, since a displayed construction cannot at the same time be executed, valuation does not play any role in such a context. Yet an argument of the form

$$\frac{a \text{ calculates the cotangent of } \pi}{a \text{ calculates the cotangent of something}}$$

is obviously valid. But careless existential generalization into a hyperintensional context similar to generalization into an intensional or extensional context is *not* valid:

$$\frac{\lambda w \lambda t\ [^0Calculate_{wt}\ a\ ^0[^0Cot\ ^0\pi]]}{\lambda w \lambda t\ [^0\exists \lambda x\ [^0Calculate_{wt}\ a\ ^0[^0Cot\ x]]]}$$

Transparent quantification into hyperintensional objectual attitudes

The reason is this. The Trivialization $^0[^0Cot\ x]$ constructs the Composition $[^0Cot\ x]$ independently of any valuation v. Thus from the fact that at $\langle w, t \rangle$ it is true that a calculates $[^0Cot\ ^0\pi]$, we can *not* validly infer that a calculates $[^0Cot\ x]$, because a calculates the cotangent of π rather than of x. Put differently, the class of numbers constructed by $\lambda x[^0Calculate_{wt}\ a\ ^0[^0Cot\ x]]$ will be non-empty, according as a calculates $[^0Cot\ x]$ and regardless of a's calculating $[^0Cot\ ^0\pi]$. The problem just described of λx being unable to catch the occurrence of x inside the Trivialized construction is TIL's way of phrasing the standard objection to quantifying-in. Yet in TIL we have a way out (or perhaps rather, a way in). In order to validly infer the conclusion, we need to *pre-process* the Composition $[^0Cot\ x]$ and substitute the Trivialization of π for x. Only then can the conclusion be inferred. To this end we deploy the polymorphic functions $Sub^n/(*_n*_n*_n*_n)$ and $Tr^\alpha/(*_n\ \alpha)$ that operate on constructions in the manner stipulated by the following dual definition.

Definition 5 (Sub^n, Tr^α) Let C_1, C_2, $C_3/*_{n+1} \to *_n$ v-construct constructions D_1, D_2, D_3, respectively. Then the Composition $[^0Sub^n\ C_1C_2C_3]$ v-constructs the construction D that results from D_3 by collisionless substitution of D_1 for all occurrences of D_2 in D_3. The function $Tr^\alpha/(*_n\alpha)$ returns as its value the Trivialization of its α-argument. □

Example 4 Let variable $y \to_v \tau$. Then $[^0Tr^\tau\ y]\ v(\pi/y)$-constructs $^0\pi$. The Composition $[^0Sub^1\ [^0Tr^\tau\ y]\ ^0x\ ^0[^0Cot\ x]]\ v(\pi/y)$-constructs the Composition $[^0Cot\ ^0\pi]$.

Remark 3 Note that there is a substantial difference between the *construction* Trivialization and the *function* Tr^α. Whereas ^0y constructs just the variable y regardless of valuation, y being ^{0}-bound in ^0y, $[^0Tr^\tau\ y]$ v-constructs the Trivialization of the object v-constructed by y. Hence y occurs free in $[^0Tr^\tau\ y]$.

Below we will omit the superscripts n and α and write simply 'Sub' and 'Tr' whenever no confusion can arise.

It should be clear now how to validly derive that a calculates the cotangent of something if a calculates the cotangent of π. The valid argument, in full TIL notation, is this:

$$\frac{\lambda w \lambda t\ [^0Calculate_{wt}\ a\ ^0[^0Cot\ ^0\pi]]}{\lambda w \lambda t\ [^0\exists \lambda y\ [^0Calculate_{wt}\ a\ [^0Sub\ [^0Tr\ y]\ ^0x\ ^0[^0Cot\ x]]]]}$$

Proof. Let $Empty/(o\tau)$ be an empty set of real numbers. Then for any world-time pair $\langle w, t \rangle$ the following steps are truth-preserving:

(1) $[^0Calculate_{wt}\ a\ ^0[^0Cot\ ^0\pi]]$ $\quad\quad\quad\quad\quad\quad\quad\quad\quad\quad\quad\quad\quad\quad\quad$ ∅
(2) $[^0=_{v(\pi/y)}\ [^0Sub\ [^0Tr\ y[\ ^0x\ ^0[^0Cot\ x]]\ ^0[^0Cot\ ^0\pi]]$ $\quad\quad$ 1, Definition 5
(3) $[^0Calculate_{wt}\ a\ [^0Sub\ [^0Tr\ y]\ ^0x\ ^0[^0Cot\ x]]]$ $\quad\quad\quad\quad$ 1, 2, Leibniz
(4) $[\lambda y\ [^0Calculate_{wt}\ a\ [^0Sub\ [^0Tr\ y]\ ^0x\ ^0[^0Cot\ x]]]\ ^0\pi]$ $\quad$ 3, λ-abstraction
(5) $\neg[^0Empty\ \lambda y\ [^0Calculate_{wt}\ a\ [^0Sub\ [^0Tr\ y]\ ^0x\ ^0[^0Cot\ x]]]]$ $\quad$ 4, Definition 2 (iii)
(6) $[^0\exists \lambda y\ [^0Calculate_{wt}\ a\ [^0Sub\ [^0Tr\ y]\ ^0x\ ^0[^0Cot\ x]]]]$ $\quad\quad$ 5, EG

4.4 Hyperintensional individuation in terms of procedural isomorphism

Another issue we need to deal with is this. We must specify the rules for valid *substitution*, because our logic is an extensional logic of hyperintensions where the extensional rules of existential generalization and Leibniz's substitution of identicals are valid in all contexts, whether extensional, intensional or hyperintensional. Again, in an extensional or intensional context there is no problem. We can substitute equivalent constructions according to these rules of substitution:[26]

Rules of substitution into extensional and intensional contexts Let C, D be constructions that v-construct the same object for a given valuation v. Then C, D are *v-congruent* and can be validly substituted in *extensional contexts*. Let C, D be constructions that v-construct the same object for every valuation v. Then C, D are *logically equivalent* and can be validly substituted in *intensional contexts*.

Logically equivalent constructions are v-congruent, while the converse obviously does not hold. Yet the substitution of merely logically equivalent hyperintensions is not valid in hyperintensional contexts, as already Carnap (1947, §§13ff) in effect pointed out. From the linguistic point of view, in a hyperintensional context only synonymous expressions can be substituted. The reason, phrased in TIL terminology, is that the very meaning is displayed. Our thesis is that synonymous expressions have structurally isomorphic meanings.[27] And since meaning is a procedure, we need to define the relation of *procedural isomorphism* between constructions, constructions being a bit too fine-grained from the procedural point of view. The main issue is this. Constructions that differ at most by using different λ-bound variables of the same type differ so slightly that we wish to say that such constructions are one and the same procedure. For instance, the Closures $\lambda x\ [^0+\ x\ ^01]$, $\lambda y\ [^0+\ y\ ^01]$, $\lambda z\ [^0+\ z\ ^01]$, and so on, are by Definition 2 different constructions of the successor function. Yet from the procedural point of view they are isomorphic. They consist of the same steps:

- take the function *plus*
- take *any* number that is the value of x (or y, or z, or ...)
- take the number 1
- apply the function *plus* to the chosen number x (or y, or z, or ...) and 1
- abstract over the chosen number x (or y, or z, or ...)

Thus if a calculates $[\lambda x\ [^0+\ x\ ^01]\ ^05]$ and b calculates $[\lambda y\ [^0+\ y\ ^01]\ ^05]$, we would like to infer that a and b are related to one and the same procedure, although two different constructions figure as complements. In both cases a and b are calculating the successor of 5. But mathematical language introduces a distinction that is absent from natural language. Thus we want something like the following sort of argument to come out valid:

$$\frac{a \text{ calculates } [\lambda x\ [^0+\ x\ ^01]\ ^05]}{b \text{ calculates } [\lambda y\ [^0+\ y\ ^01]\ ^05]}$$
There is a procedure c such that a and b calculate c

---

[26] For details and proofs, see Duží et al. (2010, § 2.6, § 2.7).
[27] See also Duží (2014b).

Transparent quantification into hyperintensional objectual attitudes

The conclusion must actually be stated more precisely, because when quantifying over procedures we are quantifying over constructions:

$$\frac{a \text{ calculates } [\lambda x\ [^0+\ x\ ^01]\ ^05]}{b \text{ calculates } [\lambda y\ [^0+\ y\ ^01]\ ^05]}$$

There are constructions c, c' such that a calculates c and b calculates c', and c, c' are procedurally isomorphic

The notion of procedural isomorphism is a nod to Carnap's intensional isomorphism and Church's synonymous isomorphism. Any two terms or expressions whose respective meanings are procedurally isomorphic are deemed semantically indistinguishable, hence synonymous. Thus procedurally isomorphic constructions can be mutually substituted in any context, including hyperintensional ones. Nothing in this particular paper hinges critically on this or that particular calibration of procedural isomorphism. But it is critical to have available to us such an exact calibration. Without it our definition of hyperintensional context would lack one of its cornerstones, namely an exact criterion of valid substitution inside such contexts. Without it, we would fall short of providing a full theory of the sort of context we are explaining how to quantify into.

Church proposed several alternatives in order to specify a criterion of synonymy. The weakest, or most permissive, one is Alternative (A2), which is logical equivalence. (A1) includes α- and β-conversion, while the strongest, or most restrictive, one, (A0), includes α-conversion and meaning postulates for atomic constants such as 'bachelor' and 'fortnight'. Church's (A0) and (A1) leave room for additional Alternatives. One such would be (A½), another (A¾). The former includes α- and η-conversion while the latter adds to these two *restricted* β-conversion *by name*. In Duží et al. (2010) we advocate (A½) whereas in Duží and Jespersen (2012) we prefer (A¾) to soak up those differences between β-transformations that concern only λ-bound variables and thus (at least appear to) lack natural-language counterparts. The *restricted* version of *equivalent* β-reduction by name consists in substituting free variables for λ-bound variables of the same type. For instance, the Composition $[\lambda x\ [^0+x\ ^01]\ y]$ can be simplified to the Composition $[^0+\ y\ ^01]$. Thus this transformation is just a manipulation with λ-bound variables that has much in common with η- and less with β-reduction. The latter is the operation of applying a function f to its argument a in order to obtain the value of f at a (leaving it open whether a value emerges). No such features can be found in restricted β-reduction. It is just a formal simplification of the original construction.

Recently, however, we have grown discontent both with (A½) and (A¾). Hence we wish to suggest a new definition of procedural isomorphism, (A1″), which is one of the novel contributions of this paper. This variant is very close to Church's (A1). (A1″) includes α- and β-conversion *by value*. Thus we exclude η-conversion, and introduce a new version of β-conversion.[28]

---

[28] We are grateful to Jakub Macek for the proposal to include β-conversion by value.

There are two reasons for not including η-conversion. The first reason is that it is actually rather peculiar to claim that two procedures are isomorphic if they do not have the same number of constituents. Yet the η-expanded construction of the form $\lambda x \ [Fx]$ has two more constituents than the equivalent η-reduced construction F, because the former adds the steps of applying the function v-constructed by F to the variable x followed by abstraction over the values of x. The second and more important reason is the fact that η-conversion does *not preserve logical equivalence* in a logic of *partial functions* such as TIL. To see this, consider the following example. Let F v-construct a function of type $((\alpha \beta)\gamma)$ that is not defined at the argument v-constructed by $A \to_v \gamma$. Then the Composition $[F \ A] \to_v (\alpha\beta)$ is v-improper. However, the η-expanded construction $\lambda x \ [[F \ A] \ x] \to_v (\alpha\beta)$, $x \to \beta$, v-constructs a *degenerate function*, which is a function undefined at all its arguments. To be sure, due to the v-improperness of $[F \ A]$ the Composition $[[F \ A] \ x]$ is also v-improper. But λ-abstraction raises the context to an intensional one, hence the Closure $\lambda x \ [[F \ A] \ x]$ v-constructs a degenerate function, which *is* an object, if a bizarre one. Hence the constructions $[F \ A]$ and $\lambda x \ [[F \ A] \ x]$ are not logically equivalent.[29]

In practice the exclusion of η-conversion from the definition of procedural isomorphism is going to be harmless. When analyzing expressions in TIL we apply our method of *literal analysis*, which consists of three steps: (i) assigning types to the objects mentioned by the sub-terms of the analyzed expression E; (ii) combining the Trivializations of the objects mentioned by the semantically simple sub-terms of E in order to obtain the construction of the object (if any) denoted by E; (iii) checking whether the resulting construction is type-theoretically coherent. Due to step (ii) the application of this method yields a construction (namely the meaning of E) that does not contain η-expanded subconstructions. For instance, the literal analysis of "Tilman is happy" is the Closure $\lambda w \lambda t \ [^0 Happy_{wt} \ ^0 Tilman]$ rather than $\lambda w \lambda t \ [\lambda w \lambda t \ [\lambda x \ [^0 Happy_{wt} \ x]]_{wt} \ ^0 Tilman]$, because the literal analysis of the predicate 'is happy' is the Trivialization $^0 Happy$ rather than the Closure $\lambda w \lambda t \ [\lambda x \ [^0 Happy_{wt} x]]$. The types are $Happy/(o\iota)_{\tau\omega}$; $Tilman/\iota$; $x \to \iota$.

The reasons for excluding unrestricted β-conversion are these. Though it is the fundamental computational rule of the λ-calculi, it is underspecified by this rule: $[\lambda x \ C(x) \ A] \vdash C(A/x)$. The procedure of applying the function v-constructed by $\lambda x \ C(x)$ to the argument v-constructed by A can be executed in two different ways: *by value* or *by name*. If by name then *procedure A is substituted for all the occurrences of x into C*. In this case there are two problems. First, conversion of this kind is not guaranteed to be a logically equivalent transformation as soon as partial functions are involved. This is due to the fact that A occurs in the extensional context of the left-hand side construction, whereas when dragged into C its occurrence may become intensional. Second, even in those cases where β-reduction is an equivalent transformation, it may yield *loss of analytic information* of which function has been applied to which argument.[30] The idea of conversion by value is simple. Execute the procedure A first, and only if A does not fail to produce an argument value on which

---

[29] We are grateful to Jiří Raclavský for calling our attention to this problem. See also Raclavský (2010).
[30] For details, see Duží (2010), Duží and Jespersen (2013, Sect. 5.4).

C is to operate, substitute this *value* for x. The solution preserves logical equivalence, avoids the problem of loss of analytic information, and moreover, in practice it is more efficient. The efficiency is guaranteed by the fact that procedure A is executed only once, whereas if this procedure is substituted for all the occurrences of the λ-bound variable it can subsequently be executed more than once.

To elucidate the problem, imagine one has a procedure (embodied as a program) $C(x)$ with a 'hole' x (i.e. an unsaturated procedure with a formal parameter x), and a subprogram A that specifies the material (argument value) to be filled into the hole x. There are two ways of going about filling x:

(1) (*by name*) inserting into the hole x the whole subprogram A and then computing $C(A/x)$
(2) (*by value*) computing A first in order to obtain the argument value a, and then inserting a into the hole x and computing $C(a/x)$

Case 1 In this case there may be an undesirable side effect. Imagine that the subprogram A is somehow garbled and as a result the whole procedure C gets garbled as well after the insertion, damage being propagated upwards. Moreover, instead of the hole x one gets A, and A may conflict with C. This is a case of invalid β-reduction that fails to preserve equivalence. Furthermore, even if A does not damage C when computing $C(A)$, after the execution of $C(A)$ one will have lost track of A. The two procedures have been merged together. Suppose one wants to compute another procedure $E(x)$ and to supply the same material for x. Even if the execution of $C(A)$ turns out to be successful, A may have been changed by the execution. There is no guarantee that the same material will be supplied for x into $E(x)$. This is a case of valid β-reduction preserving equivalence but yielding loss of analytic information.

Case 2 Keep $C(x)$, $E(x)$, and A separate. Procedure A is evaluated only if needed, and if so, only once. Everything is as it should be: no loss of analytic information arises and equivalence is preserved.

Remark 4 In programming languages the difference between Cases 1 and 2 revolves around the programmer's choice of *evaluation strategy*. Historically, call-by-value and call-by-name date back to *Algol 60*, a language designed in the late 1950s. The difference between call-by-name and call-by-value is often called *passing by reference* versus *passing by value*, respectively. Only purely functional languages such as *Clean* and *Haskell* use call-by-name. For instance, *Java* manipulates objects by reference. However, *Java* does not pass arguments by reference, but by value. Call-by-value is not a single evaluation strategy, but rather a cluster of evaluation strategies in which a function's argument is evaluated before being passed to the function. In *call-by-reference* evaluation (also referred to as *call-by name* or *pass-by-reference*), a calling procedure receives an implicit reference to the argument sub-procedure. This typically means that the calling procedure can modify the argument sub-procedure. A call-by-reference language makes it more difficult for a programmer to track the effects of a procedure call, and may introduce subtle bugs. The notion of *reduction strategy* in the λ-calculi is similar to the *evaluation strategy* in programming languages, though slightly distinct. Our proposal amounts to a *specification of an evaluation strategy by-value as adapted to TIL*. Similar work has been done since the early 1970s, but merely for simple-typed or untyped λ-calculi. For instance, Plotkin (1975) proved that the two strategies are not operationally equivalent. Moreover, the call-by-name strategy *cannot* be used for a hyperintensional context like *calculating*, or in hyperintensional λ-calculi such as TIL due to operational non-equivalence. Our *substitution method* based around the functions *Sub* and *Tr* is similar to Chang and Felleisen (2012)'s call-by-need reduction by value. But their work is couched in an untyped λ-calculus. TIL, by contrast, is a hyperintensional, typed λ-calculus.

Our definition of β-equivalence is this:

Definition 6 (β-*conversion by value*) Let $Y \to_v \alpha$; $x_1, D_1 \to_v \beta_1, \ldots, x_n, D_n \to_v \beta_n$, $[\lambda x_1 \ldots x_n Y] \to_v (\alpha \beta_1 \ldots \beta_n)$. Then the conversion

$$[[\lambda x_1 \ldots x_n Y] D_1 \ldots D_n] \to_\beta {}^2[{}^0Sub\ [{}^0Tr\ D_1]\ {}^0x_1 \ldots [{}^0Sub\ [{}^0Tr\ D_n]\ {}^0x_n\ {}^0Y]]$$

is β-*reduction by value*. The reverse conversion is β-*expansion by value*. □

Claim 1 *Let C, D be constructions such that C is identical to* $[[\lambda x_1 \ldots x_n Y] D_1 \ldots D_n]$ *and D to* ${}^2[{}^0Sub\ [{}^0Tr\ D_1]\ {}^0x_1 \ldots [{}^0Sub\ [{}^0Tr\ D_n]\ {}^0x_n\ {}^0Y]]$. *Then C, D are strictly equivalent in the sense that for any valuation v they either v-construct one and the same entity or are both v-improper.*

Proof of Claim 1. If one or more of the constructions $D_1, \ldots, D_n$ are v-improper then so are both C and D, according to Definition 2, (iii) and (vi). Otherwise, let $D_1, \ldots, D_n$ all be v-proper, v-constructing the objects $d_1, \ldots, d_n$, respectively. Then by Definition 2, (iv) the Closure $[\lambda x_1 \ldots x_n Y]$ v-constructs the following function f. If Y is $v(d_1/x_1, \ldots, d_n/x_n)$-improper, then f is undefined on $\langle d_1, \ldots, d_n \rangle$ and thus C is $v(d_1/x_1, \ldots, d_n/x_n)$-improper according to Definition 2, (iii). Otherwise the value of f on $\langle d_1, \ldots, d_n \rangle$ is the α-entity $v(d_1/x_1, \ldots, d_n/x_n)$-constructed by Y. Let the entity $v(d_1/x_1, \ldots, d_n/x_n)$-constructed by Y be a. Then by Definition 2, (iii) of Composition, the construction C v-constructs a. We are to show that the construction D also v-constructs a. The first Execution of D constructs $Y(x_1/{}^0d_1, \ldots, x_n/{}^0d_n)$, i.e. the construction Y where according to the definition of the functions *Sub* and *Tr* all the occurrences of the variables $x_1, \ldots, x_n$ are replaced by ${}^0d_1, \ldots, {}^0d_n$, respectively. Since the Trivializations ${}^0d_1, \ldots, {}^0d_n$ construct the entities $d_1, \ldots, d_n$, respectively, the second Execution $v(d_1/x_1, \ldots, d_n/x_n)$-constructs the entity a, or else nothing in case Y is $v(d_1/x_1, \ldots, d_n/x_n)$-improper. Hence C and D come out strictly equivalent.

Remark 5 That constructions C, D are β-equivalent will be denoted '${}^0C \approx_\beta {}^0D$', $\approx_\beta /(o*_n*_n)$. In order to avoid misconceptions, in what follows we will use the term 'λ-conversion' in the same sense as Church's for the conversion that we also call 'β-conversion by name', which is specified by the following rule:

$$[[\lambda x_1 \ldots x_n\ Y] D_1 \ldots D_n] \to Y(D_1/x_1, \ldots, D_n/x_n)$$

where the contracted construction arises from Y by collisionless substitution of $D_1, \ldots, D_n$ for $x_1, \ldots, x_n$, respectively. The term 'β-conversion' will be reserved for β-conversion by value.

Transparent quantification into hyperintensional objectual attitudes

In order to define *procedural isomorphism* on the set of constructions of a particular order, we still need another definition, to wit the definition of α-conversion. The standard definition, which defines α-equivalent constructions as those that differ at most by using different λ-bound variables, is insufficient, because the β-reduced constructions C, D that arise from α-equivalent constructions do not differ at most by using different λ-bound variables. For instance, the constructions

$$[\lambda x\ [^0+\ x\ ^01]\ ^05]\text{ and }[\lambda y\ [^0+\ y\ ^01]\ ^05]$$

are α-equivalent according to the standard definition. Yet their respective β-reduced forms

$$^2[^0Sub\ [^0Tr\ ^05]\ ^0x\ ^0[^0+\ x\ ^01]]\text{ and }^2[^0Sub\ [^0Tr\ ^05]\ ^0y\ ^0[^0+\ y\ ^01]]$$

would not be α-equivalent. Yet they ought to be, because from the procedural point of view it is irrelevant which variables are used as formal parameters of the respective procedure. Thus we define:

Definition 7 (α-*conversion*) Let C, D be constructions. Then C, D are α-*equivalent*, denoted '$^0C \approx_\alpha\ ^0D$', $\approx_\alpha\ /(o*_n*_n)$, if either C, D differ at most by using different λ-bound variables, or their β-expanded forms differ at most by using different λ-bound variables.

Claim 2 α-*equivalent constructions are strictly equivalent by being either v-improper or v-constructing one and the same entity.*

Proof of Claim 2. Thanks to Claim 1 it suffices to prove that Closures of the form $[\lambda x_1 \ldots x_n Y(x_1, \ldots, x_n)]$, $[\lambda y_1 \ldots y_n Y(y_1, \ldots, y_n)]$, where $Y(x_1, \ldots, x_n)$ differs from $Y(y_1, \ldots, y_n)$ only by collisionless substitution of the variables $x_1, \ldots, x_n$ for $y_1, \ldots, y_n$, respectively, v-construct one and the same function. But this immediately follows from Definition 2, (iv).

Definition 8 (*procedural isomorphism*) Let C, D be constructions. Then C, D are *procedurally isomorphic* iff either C and D are identical or there are constructions $C_1, \ldots, C_n (n > 1)$ such that $^0C = {^0C_1}$, $^0D = {^0C_n}$, and for each C_i, $C_{i+1} (1 \leq i < n)$ it holds that $^0C_i \approx_\alpha\ ^0C_{i+1}$ or $^0C_i \approx_\beta\ ^0C_{i+1}$.

Corollary of Definition 8 Procedural isomorphism is an equivalence relation defined on a set of constructions such that procedurally isomorphic constructions are strictly equivalent in the sense that for any valuation v they either v-construct one and the same entity or they are v-improper.

Proof of Corollary Follows immediately from Claims 1 and 2.

Example 5 The above constructions

$$[\lambda x\ [^0+\ x\ ^01]\ ^05],\ ^2[^0Sub\ [^0Tr\ ^05]\ ^0x\ ^0[^0+\ x\ ^01]],$$
$$[\lambda y\ [^0+\ y\ ^01]\ ^05],\ ^2[^0Sub\ [^0Tr\ ^05]\ ^0y\ ^0[^0+\ y\ ^01]]$$

are all procedurally isomorphic, because the following equivalences hold:

$${}^0[\lambda x\ [{}^0+\ x\ {}^0 1]\ {}^0 5] \approx_\alpha {}^0[\lambda y\ [{}^0+\ y\ {}^0 1]\ {}^0 5]$$
$${}^0[\lambda x\ [{}^0+\ x\ {}^0 1]\ {}^0 5] \approx_\beta {}^{02}[{}^0 Sub\ [{}^0 Tr\ {}^0 5]\ {}^0 x\ {}^0[{}^0+\ x\ {}^0 1]]$$
$${}^{02}[{}^0 Sub\ [{}^0 Tr\ {}^0 5]\ {}^0 x\ {}^0[{}^0+\ x\ {}^0 1]] \approx_\alpha {}^0[\lambda y\ [{}^0+\ y\ {}^0 1]\ {}^0 5]$$
$${}^0[\lambda y\ [{}^0+\ y\ {}^0 1]\ {}^0 5] \approx_\beta {}^{02}[{}^0 Sub[{}^0 Tr\ {}^0 5]\ {}^0 y\ {}^0[{}^0+\ y\ {}^0 1]]$$
$${}^{02}[{}^0 Sub\ [{}^0 Tr\ {}^0 5]\ {}^0 x\ {}^0[{}^0+\ x\ {}^0 1]] \approx_\alpha {}^{02}[{}^0 Sub\ [{}^0 Tr\ {}^0 5]\ {}^0 y\ {}^0[{}^0+\ y\ {}^0 1]]$$

This completes the exposition of the logical tools we need. We are now ready to specify the rules of existential generalization into hyperintensional contexts.

5 Rules for quantifying-in with applications

In Duží et al. (2010, § 5.3) we specified what we called rules (7) and (8) for quantifying into hyperintensional objectual attitudes *de dicto* and *de re*. In what follows we adjust those rules, which is another novel contribution of this paper. First, rule (7) for quantifying into hyperintensional attitudes de dicto can be simplified in case we quantify *over* the complement of the attitude. Hence we specify here rule (R_1). Second, rule (7) is generalized to quantify into the attitude complement over a constituent X of this complement. Since in a hyperintensional context we must fully respect the perspective of the agent to whom the attitude is ascribed, we can quantify only over the constituent construction X rather than an object v-constructed by X: see rule R_2 below. Yet on the additional assumption that the constituent X is v-proper we obtain a variant R'_2 of the rule R_2 that quantifies also over the object v-constructed by X. Third, rule (7) makes it possible to quantify over constructions only. Yet we need to quantify over non-constructions as well. Thus we specify a stronger rule R_3 for quantifying *into* hyperintensional contexts that makes it possible to quantify *over* objects of any type. Yet as mentioned above, we must respect the attitude agent's perspective. For this reason the rule R_3 is applicable only if the complement constituent X is a Trivialization, because then we can use the *Tr* function: see rule R_3 below. Furthermore, we add a rule for factive attitudes: see rule R_4 below. Last but not least, the rules that were called (6) and (8) in (ibid.) for quantifying into hyperintensional contexts de re are not correct, because in the respective conclusions we failed to acknowledge the hyperintensional character of the attitude. Here we present two correct active and passive variants of rule R_5 for quantifying into hyperintensional contexts de re.

Remark 6 In Remark 2 we explained that since we work with properly partial functions, prior to applying an existential quantifier we must first prove that the argument class is non-empty. Thus in the proofs that follow below we will use variants of the following steps. Let $F \rightarrow_v (o\alpha\beta); a \rightarrow_v \alpha; b \rightarrow_v \beta$. If $[F\ a\ b]$ v-constructs **T** then according to Definition 2 (iii) all the three constituents of this Composition are v-proper. In particular, if B is a β-object v-constructed by b, then $[F\ a\ x]$ $v(B/x)$-constructs **T** as well. Hence the Composition $[\lambda x\ [F\ a\ x]\ {}^0 B]$ v-constructs **T**, which in turn means that the class of β-objects v-constructed by the Closure

Transparent quantification into hyperintensional objectual attitudes

$\lambda x\ [F\ a\ x]$ is non-empty, and the application of the existential quantifier yields **T** as well: $[^0\exists^\beta \lambda x\ [F\ a\ x]]$.

Let the types be $Att^* \rightarrow (\omicron\iota*_n)_{\tau\omega}$: an arbitrary construction of a hyperintensional objectual attitude relation; $a \rightarrow_v \iota$: a construction of an individual; $\exists^*/(\omicron(\omicron*_n))$; $C/*_n$: a construction of attitude complement; ^0C, $c/*_{n+1} \rightarrow_v *_n$. Then the rule of quantifying *over* hyperintensional objectual contexts is straightforward:

$$\frac{[Att^*_{wt}\ a\ ^0C]}{[^0\exists^*\lambda c\ [Att^*_{wt}\ a\ c]]} \quad (R_1)$$

Proof of R_1. Let $Empty^*/(\omicron*_n)$ be an empty class of constructions. Then the following proof-steps are truth-preserving:

(1) $[Att^*_{wt}\ a\ ^0C]$ ∅
(2) $[\lambda c\ [Att^*_{wt}\ a\ c]\ ^0C]$ 1, λ-abstraction
(3) $\neg[^0Empty^*\ \lambda c\ [Att^*_{wt}\ a\ c]]$ 2, Definition 2 (iii)
(4) $[^0\exists^*\lambda c\ [Att^*_{wt}\ a\ c]]$ 3, EG

The rule for quantifying *into* hyperintensional contexts makes use of the function *Sub*. Let $C(X)$ be a construction of an attitude complement with a constituent $X/*_n \rightarrow_v \alpha$; $c/*_{(n+1)} \rightarrow_v *_n$; $^2c/*_{n+2} \rightarrow_v \alpha$; $y \rightarrow_v \alpha$. Then:

$$\frac{[Att^*_{wt}\ a\ ^0C(X/y)]}{[^0\exists^*\lambda c\ [Att^*_{wt}\ a\ [^0Sub\ c\ ^0y\ ^0C(y)]]]} \quad (R_2)$$

Proof of R_2. According to Definition 5 of the *Sub* function $[^0Sub\ c\ ^0y\ ^0C(y)]$ $v(X/c)$-constructs the construction $C(X/y)$. Let $=_*/(\omicron*_n*_n)$ be the identity of constructions of order n. Then the following proof-steps are truth-preserving:

(1) $[Att^*_{wt}\ a\ ^0C(X/y)]$ ∅
(2) $[^0=_*\ [^0Sub\ c\ ^0y\ ^0C(y)]\ ^0C(X/y)]$ 1, Definition 5
(3) $[Att^*_{wt}\ a\ [^0Sub\ c\ ^0y\ ^0C(y)]]$ 1, 2, Leibniz
(4) $[\lambda c\ [Att^*_{wt}\ a\ [^0Sub\ c\ ^0y\ ^0C(y)]]\ ^0X]$ 3, λ-abstraction
(5) $\neg[^0Empty^*\ \lambda c\ [Att^*_{wt}\ a\ [^0Sub\ c\ ^0y\ ^0C(y)]]]$ 4, Definition 2 (iii)
(6) $[^0\exists^*\lambda c\ [Att^*_{wt}\ a\ [^0Sub\ c\ ^0y\ ^0C(y)]]]$ 5, EG

If the constituent X is v-proper, we can use a variant of the rule R_2 called R'_2. Let the additional types be $x \rightarrow_v \alpha$; $\exists/(\omicron(\omicron\alpha))$. Then:

$$\frac{[Att^*_{wt}\ a\ ^0C(X/y)]}{[^0\exists^*\lambda c\ [[Att^*_{wt}\ a\ [^0Sub\ c\ ^0y\ ^0C(y)]] \wedge {^0\exists}\lambda x\ [x = {^2c}]]]} \quad (R'_2)$$

Proof of R'_2. Let $Proper/(\omicron*_n)$ be the class of constructions that are not v-improper, $=_*/(\omicron*_n*_n)$ the identity of constructions of order n, $=_\alpha/(\omicron\alpha\alpha)$ the identity of α-objects, $Empty/(\omicron\alpha)$ an empty class of α-objects. According to Definition 2 (i) and (vi), the

Double Execution $^2c\, v(X/c)$-constructs what Xv-constructs. Thus if X is v-proper then $[^0=_\alpha {}^2c\, X]$ v-constructs **T**. Hence the following proof-steps are truth-preserving:

(1) $[Att^*_{wt}\, a\, {}^0C(X/y)]$ ∅
(2) $[^0=_* [^0Sub\, c\, {}^0y\, {}^0C(y)]\, {}^0C(X/y)]$ 1, Defintion 5
(3) $[Att^*_{wt}\, a\, [^0Sub\, c\, {}^0y\, {}^0C(y)]]$ 1, 2, Leibniz
(4) $[^0Proper\, {}^0X]$ ∅
(5) $[^0=_\alpha {}^2c\, X]$ 4, Definition 2 (i), (vi)
(6) $[\lambda x\, [^0=_\alpha {}^2c\, x]\, X]$ 5, λ-abstraction
(7) $[[\lambda x [^0=_\alpha {}^2c\, x]\, X] \wedge [Att^*_{wt}\, a\, [^0Sub\, c\, {}^0y\, {}^0C(y)]]]$ 6, 3, ∧I
(8) $\neg[^0Empty^*\, \lambda c\, [\neg[^0Empty\, \lambda x\, [^0=_\alpha {}^2c\, x]]$
$\wedge [Att^*_{wt}\, a\, [^0Sub\, c\, {}^0y\, {}^0C(y)]]]]$ 7, Definition 2 (iii)
(9) $[^0\exists^* \lambda c\, [^0\exists\, \lambda x\, [^0=_\alpha {}^2c\, x]$
$\wedge [Att^*_{wt}\, a\, [^0Sub\, c\, {}^0y\, {}^0C(y)]]]]$ 8, EG

If the constituent X is the *Trivialization* of an α-object b, thus guaranteeing that the construction is proper, then we can access this hyperintensional context to quantify over this α-object. To this end we have another special rule R$_3$ that makes use of the function Tr:

$$\frac{[Att^*_{wt}\, a\, {}^0C(^0b/y)]}{[^0\exists \lambda x [Att^*_{wt}\, a\, [^0Sub\, [^0Tr\, x]\, {}^0y\, {}^0C(y)]]]} \quad (R_3)$$

Proof of R$_3$. According to Definition 5 the Composition $[^0Sub\, [^0Tr\, x]\, {}^0y\, {}^0C(y)]$ $v(b/x)$-constructs the construction $C(^0b/y)$ in which the occurrences of y have been replaced by ^0b. Thus the following proof-steps are truth-preserving:

(1) $[Att^*_{wt}\, a\, {}^0C(^0b/y)]$ ∅
(2) $[^0=_* [^0Sub\, [^0Tr\, x]\, {}^0y\, {}^0C(y)]\, {}^0C(^0b/y)]$ 1, Definition 5
(3) $[Att^*_{wt}\, a\, [^0Sub\, [^0Tr\, x]\, {}^0y\, {}^0C(y)]]$ 1, 2, Leibniz
(4) $[\lambda x [Att^*_{wt}\, a\, [^0Sub\, [^0Tr\, x]\, {}^0y\, {}^0C(y)]]\, {}^0b]$ 3, λ-abstraction
(5) $\neg[^0Empty\, \lambda x [Att^*_{wt}\, a\, [^0Sub\, [^0Tr\, x]\, {}^0y\, {}^0C(y)]]]$ 4, Definition 2 (iii)
(6) $[^0\exists \lambda x [Att^*_{wt}\, a\, [^0Sub\, [^0Tr\, x]\, {}^0y\, {}^0C(y)]]]$ 5, EG

Next we specify a rule for *factive* attitudes like *finding* or *having solved*. Factive attitudes are defined in terms of the notion of *requisite*.[31] A requisite is an analytically necessary relation-in-extension between two intensions such that, necessarily, any object that instantiates one intension also instantiates the other (though not necessarily the other way around). For instance, if the office of Head of State of the Vatican is a requisite of the office of Archbishop of Rome (i.e. the office of Pope) then, necessarily, whoever occupies the papal office must also occupy the requisite office.

Let $Att^{f*}/(o\iota*_n)_{\tau\omega}$ be a factive objectual attitude. The type of *requisite* relevant to factive hyperintensional attitudes is $Req/(o(o\iota\alpha*_n)_{\tau\omega}\, (o\iota*_n)_{\tau\omega})$, which is defined as follows. Let $Ident^\alpha/(o\iota\alpha*_n)_{\tau\omega}$ be a relation between an individual, an α-object

---

[31] See Duží et al. (2010, § 4.1).

Transparent quantification into hyperintensional objectual attitudes

and a construction such that the individual succeeds in identifying the α-object as the product of this construction, $x \to_v \iota, c \to_v *_n, {}^2c \to_v \alpha$, then:

$$[{}^0Req\ {}^0Ident^\alpha\ Att^{f*}] = \forall w \forall t\ \forall x\ c\ [[Att^{f*}_{wt}\ x\ c] \supset [{}^0Ident^\alpha_{wt}\ x\ {}^2c\ c]]$$

$Ident^\alpha$ is a requisite of Att^{f*} iff, necessarily for all individuals x and all constructions c, it holds that if x has an attitude Att^{f*} to c then x has identified the α-product ${}^2c$ of construction c.

Hence we *define* factive hyperintensional attitudes as those for which the above requisite relation holds.

The rule R_4 for factive objectual attitudes is this:

$$\frac{[Att^{f*}_{wt}\ a\ {}^0C]}{[{}^0\exists \lambda x\ [[x = C] \wedge [{}^0Ident_{wt}\ a\ x\ {}^0C]]]} \quad (R_4)$$

Additional type $C/*_n \to_v \alpha$.
Proof of R_4

(1) $[Att^{f*}_{wt}\ a\ {}^0C]$ ∅
(2) $[{}^0Req\ {}^0Ident^\alpha Att^{f*}]$ Definition of factivity
(3) $\forall w \forall t \forall x\ c[[Att^{f*}_{wt} xc] \supset [{}^0Ident^\alpha_{wt}\ x\ {}^2c\ c]]$ 2, Definition of Req.
(4) $[[Att^{f*}_{wt}\ a\ {}^0C] \supset [{}^0Ident^\alpha_{wt}\ a\ {}^{20}C\ {}^0C]]$ 3, ∀E, a/x, ${}^0C/c$
(5) $[{}^0Ident^\alpha_{wt}\ a\ {}^{20}C\ {}^0C]$ 1, 4, MPP
(6) $[{}^0Ident^\alpha_{wt}\ a\ C\ {}^0C]$ 5, Definition 2, (vi): ${}^{20}C = C$
(7) $[{}^0Proper\ {}^0C]$ 6, Definition 2, (iii)
(8) $[{}^0=_\alpha\ x\ C]$ 7, Definition 2
(9) $[{}^0Ident^\alpha_{wt}\ a\ x\ {}^0C]$ 6, 8, Leibniz
(10) $[[{}^0=_\alpha xC] \wedge [{}^0Ident^\alpha_{wt}\ a\ x\ {}^0C]]$ 8, 9, ∧I
(11) $\neg [{}^0Empty\ \lambda x[[x = C] \wedge [{}^0Ident^\alpha_{wt}\ a\ x\ {}^0C]]]$ 10, λ-abstraction
(12) $[{}^0\exists \lambda x[[{}^0=_\alpha\ x\ C] \wedge [{}^0Ident^\alpha_{wt}\ a\ x\ {}^0C]]]$ 11, EG

The steps (6)–(8) above call for elucidation. In the Composition $[{}^0Ident^\alpha_{wt}\ a\ C\ {}^0C]$ the construction C occurs both displayed and executed. The first occurrence of C is executed while the second is displayed. Hence the first occurrence of C is a constituent of $[{}^0Ident^\alpha_{wt}\ a\ C\ {}^0C]$. Since this Composition v-constructs **T**, according to Definition 2, (iii) this constituent must be proper. Thus we have step (7): $[{}^0Proper\ {}^0C]$. And since C is v-proper, it v-constructs an α-object, which in turn justifies step (8): $[{}^0=_\alpha\ x\ C]$.

(R_1)–(R_4) are rules for quantifying into hyperintensional attitudes *de dicto*. Next we define a pair of rules for quantifying into hyperintensional contexts *de re*, both in a passive and an active variant:

Transparent quantification into hyperintensional objectual attitudes

$$\frac{[Att^*_{wt} \ a \ [^0Sub \ [^0Tr \ X] \ ^0y \ ^0C(y)]]}{[^0\exists \lambda x \ [Att^*_{wt} \ a \ [^0Sub \ [^0Tr \ x] \ ^0y \ ^0C(y)]]]} \quad (R_5 \ act)$$

$$\frac{[\lambda x \ [Att^*_{wt} \ a \ [^0Sub \ [^0Tr \ x] \ ^0y \ ^0C(y)] \ X]]}{[^0\exists \lambda x \ [Att^*_{wt} \ a \ [^0Sub \ [^0Tr \ x] \ ^0y \ ^0C(y)]]]} \quad (R_5 \ pas)$$

Types: $X/*_n \to \alpha$; $x, y/*_n \to_v \alpha$; $\exists/(o(o\alpha))$; y free in $C(y)/*_n$.

Proof of R_5 act

(1) $[Att^*_{wt} \ a \ [^0Sub \ [^0Tr \ X] \ ^0y \ ^0C(y)]]$ $\varnothing$
(2) $[\lambda x[Att^*_{wt} \ a \ [^0Sub \ [^0Tr \ x] \ ^0y \ ^0C(y)]] \ X]$ 1, λ-abstraction
(3) $\neg[^0Empty \ \lambda x \ [Att^*_{wt} \ a \ [^0Sub \ [^0Tr \ x] \ ^0y \ ^0C(y)]]]$ 2, Definition 2 (iii)
(4) $[^0\exists \lambda x[Att^*_{wt} \ a \ [^0Sub \ [^0Tr \ x] \ ^0y \ ^0C(y)]]]$ 3, EG

Proof of R_5 pas. Since X occurs extensionally in the assumption, the proof is trivial:

(1) $[\lambda x[Att^*_{wt} \ a \ [^0Sub \ [^0Tr \ x] \ ^0y \ ^0C(y)] \ X]]$ $\varnothing$
(2) $\neg[^0Empty \ \lambda x[Att^*_{wt} \ a \ [^0Sub \ [^0Tr \ x] \ ^0y \ ^0C(y)]]]$ 2, Definition 2 (iii)
(3) $[^0\exists \lambda x \ [Att^*_{wt} \ a \ [^0Sub \ [^0Tr \ x] \ ^0y \ ^0C(y)]]]$ 3, EG

In Duží et al. (2010, § 5.3) we specified what we called rules (2) and (4) for quantifying into intensional contexts, which are contexts of empirical attitudes $Att/(o\iota\alpha_{\tau\omega})_{\tau\omega}$ to *intensions*. In such cases the premise of the active variant has the form $[Att_{wt} \ a \ ^2[^0Sub \ [^0Tr \ X] \ ^0y \ ^0C(y)]]$. The result of the substitution must itself be executed in order to obtain an intension, which explains the use of *Double Execution*. In the case of attitudes to hyperintensions, the result of the substitution is directly the construction to which a is related. For this reason the Compositions $[^0Sub \ [^0Tr \ X] \ ^0y \ ^0C(y)]$ and $[^0Sub \ [^0Tr \ x] \ ^0y \ ^0C(y)]$ require only one execution.

5.1 Mathematical objectual attitudes: applications

As explained above, mathematical attitudes are invariably hyperintensional. For instance, if Tilman is seeking the last decimal of π, then he is seeking something. Yet he is not seeking one particular number, because there is no such number that would be the last decimal of π. And if *per impossible* there were such a number Tilman would still be related to a construction typed to construct such a number rather than the number itself, because otherwise there would be no *process* of seeking the last decimal of π. Tilman would be confronted with the *product* (a particular number) straightaway; the seeker would ipso facto be a finder, because there would be a relation (-in-intension) between Tilman and a number.

Thus we have this valid argument:

> Tilman is seeking the last decimal of π
> ―――――――――――――――――――
> Tilman is seeking something

where *something* is restricted type-theoretically, so that the conclusion states that Tilman is seeking something of one particular type.

In this case we apply (R₁):

$$\frac{\lambda w \lambda t \; [^0 Seek^*_{wt} \; {}^0 Tilman \; {}^0 [^0 Last\_Dec \; {}^0 \pi]]}{\lambda w \lambda t \; [^0 \exists^* \lambda c \; [^0 Seek^*_{wt} \; {}^0 Tilman \; c]]} \quad (R_1)$$

Types: $Seek^*/(o\iota *_n)_{\tau\omega}$; $Tilman/\iota$; $Last\_Dec/(\upsilon\tau)$: the function that associates a number with its last decimal digit; π / τ; $c/*_2 \to_v *_1$.

Another inference based on (R₁) is this:

$$\frac{\text{Tilman is proving Fermat's Last Theorem}}{\text{There is a numerical construction } c \text{ such that Tilman is proving } c}$$

Let FLT be specified as follows:[32]

$$\forall x \; y \; z \; n[[n > {}^0 2] \supset \neg [x^n + y^n = z^n]]$$

Then our argument obtains this analysis:

$$\frac{\lambda w \lambda t \; [^0 Prove_{wt} \; {}^0 Tilman \; {}^0 [\forall x \; y \; z \; n \; [[n > {}^0 2] \supset \neg [x^n + y^n = z^n]]]]}{\lambda w \lambda t \; [^0 \exists^* \lambda c [^0 Prove_{wt} \; {}^0 Tilman \; c]]} \quad (R_1)$$

Types: $Prove/(o\iota *_n)_{\tau\omega}$; the other types are obvious.

Yet another example:[33]

$$\frac{\text{Tilman is solving the equation } (x^2 + x - 2) = 0}{\text{There is something Tilman is solving}}$$

$$\frac{\lambda w \lambda t \; [^0 Solving_{wt} \; {}^0 Tilman \; {}^0 [\lambda x [x^2 + x - 2] = 0]]}{\lambda w \lambda t \; [^0 \exists^* \lambda c \; [^0 Solving_{wt} \; {}^0 Tilman \; c]]} \quad (R_1)$$

Here is an application of (R₂):

$$\frac{\text{Tilman computes the value of } sin(x)/cos(x) \text{ at } \pi}{\text{There is a construction such that Tilman computes its Composition with } \pi}$$

$$\frac{\lambda w \lambda t \; [^0 Compute_{wt} \; {}^0 Tilman \; {}^0 [\lambda x \; [^0 : \; [^0 Sin \; x] \; [^0 Cos \; x]] \; {}^0 \pi]]}{\lambda w \lambda t [^0 \exists^* \lambda c \; [^0 Compute_{wt} \; {}^0 Tilman \; [^0 Sub \; c \; {}^0 g \; {}^0 [g \; {}^0 \pi]]]]} \quad (R_2)$$

---

[32] We are using ordinary infix notation without Trivialization to make the formalization of the construction easier to read. Hence "$[x^n + y^n = z^n]$" is a shorthand notation for a couple of Compositions. If Pn is the function n^{th} *power* then in the full TIL notation we have "$[^0= [^0+[^0 Pn \; x] \; [^0 Pn \; y]][^0 Pn \; z]]$".

[33] Here we are again using a shorthand infix notation without Trivialization.

Types: $c/*_2 \to_v *_1$; $g/*_1 \to_v (\tau\tau)$; $\lambda x\ [^0: [^0Sin\ x]\ [^0Cos\ x]]/*_1 \to_v (\tau\tau)$; the other types are obvious.

Since a Closure is not v-improper for any valuation v, we can apply (R'_2):

$$\frac{\text{Tilman computes the value of } sin(x)/cos(x) \text{ at } \pi}{\text{There is a construction of a function such that Tilman computes its value at } \pi}$$

$$\frac{\lambda w \lambda t\ [^0Compute_{wt}\ ^0Tilman\ ^0[\lambda x\ [^0: [^0Sin\ x][^0Cos\ x]]\ ^0\pi]]}{\lambda w \lambda t\ [^0\exists *\lambda c\ [^0\exists \lambda f[f = {}^2c] \wedge [^0Compute_{wt}\ ^0Tilman\ [^0Sub\ c\ ^0g\ ^0[g\ ^0\pi]]]]]} \quad (R'_2)$$

Additional types: ${}^2c, g \to_v (\tau\tau)$.

From the premise in the first example above we can also derive that there is a number such that Tilman is seeking its last decimal. Thus we have another valid argument:

$$\frac{\text{Tilman is seeking the last decimal of } \pi}{\text{There is a number such that Tilman is seeking its last decimal}}$$

This inference requires (R_3):

$$\frac{\lambda w \lambda t\ [^0Seek^*_{wt}\ ^0Tilman\ ^0[^0Last\_Dec\ ^0\pi]]}{\lambda w \lambda t\ [^0\exists \lambda x\ [^0Seek^*_{wt}\ ^0Tilman\ [^0Sub\ [^0Tr\ x]\ ^0y\ ^0[^0Last\_Dec\ y]]]]} \quad (R_3)$$

Types: $x, y/*_1 \to_v \tau$; $\exists/(o(o\tau))$.

If Tilman is seeking the millionth digit of the decimal expansion of π, he may succeed in his effort and identify that number. Thus we have another argument that illustrates the application of (R_4):

$$\frac{\text{Tilman finds the millionth digit of the decimal expansion of } \pi}{\begin{array}{c}\text{There is a number such that Tilman identifies it} \\ \text{as the millionth digit of the decimal expansion of } \pi\end{array}}$$

$$\frac{\lambda w \lambda t\ [^0Find_{wt}\ ^0Tilman\ ^0[^0Mill\_Dec\ ^0\pi]]}{\lambda w \lambda t\ [^0\exists \lambda x[[x = [^0Mill\_Dec\ ^0\pi]] \wedge [^0Ident_{wt}\ ^0Tilman\ x\ ^0[^0Mill\_Dec\ ^0\pi]]]]} \quad (R_4)$$

Types: $Find/(o\iota*_n)_{\tau\omega}$; ν: the type of naturals; $Mill\_Dec/(\nu\tau)$: the function that associates a real number with its millionth decimal digit; $Ident/(o\iota\nu*_n)_{\tau\omega}$.

Suppose that Tilman is solving the equation $(x^2 + x - 2) = 0$ and that his effort meets with success, in that he finds the solution he was seeking. We can apply rule R_1:

$$\frac{\text{Tilman has solved the equation } (x^2 + x - 2) = 0}{\text{There is something that Tilman has solved}}$$

$$\frac{\lambda w \lambda t \ [^0Solved_{wt} \ ^0Tilman \ ^0[\lambda x \ [x^2 + x - 2] = 0]]}{\lambda w \lambda t \ [^0\exists \lambda c \ [^0Solved_{wt} \ ^0Tilman \ c]]} \quad (R_1)$$

The argument is no doubt valid. Yet in this case we would like to derive more. To this end we apply (R_4). If Tilman has solved the equation $x^2 + x - 2 = 0$ then there is an ($o \tau$)-object (in this case the set $\{1, -2\}$) satisfying the equation, and Tilman has identified this set as the product of the construction $[\lambda x \ [x^2 + x - 2] = 0]$. Thus we have:

$$\frac{\lambda w \lambda t \ [^0Solved_{wt} \ ^0Tilman \ ^0[\lambda x \ [x^2 + x - 2] = 0]]}{\lambda w \lambda t \ [^0\exists \lambda s \ [[s = [\lambda x[x^2+x-2]=0]] \wedge [^0Ident_{wt} \ ^0Tilman \ s \ ^0[\lambda x[x^2 + x - 2] = 0]]]]}$$

Additional types: variable $s \rightarrow_v (o\tau)$, $Ident/(o\iota(o\tau)*_n)_{\tau\omega}$

In Duží et al. (2010, Chap. 2) we defined the distinction between attitudes *de dicto* and *de re* for attitudes to empirical notions. In mathematics a *de re* attitude is characterized by an *extensional* occurrence of a constituent that v-constructs the value of the denoted function. This value is then anaphorically referred to in the attitude complement. Here is an example:

$$\frac{\text{The last decimal of } \pi \text{ is being calculated by Tilman}}{\text{There is a number such that Tilman calculates } \textit{it} \text{ as the last decimal of } \pi}$$

The argument is valid, though drastically unsound: the premise *presupposes* the existence of the last decimal of π. And if *per impossibile* a number n were the last decimal of π then Tilman would be obtaining n as a result of his calculation of the last decimal of π. Hence, existential generalization simply serves to make explicit an implicit ontological presupposition incurred in the premise. In this case it is the presupposed existence of the value of the function denoted by 'the last decimal of' at the argument π.

If we analyzed the premise similarly as above, that is, in terms of the Closure

$$\lambda w \lambda t \ [^0Calculate_{wt} \ ^0Tilman \ ^0[^0Last\_Dec \ ^0\pi]]$$

the existence of a last decimal of π would neither be presupposed, nor would it follow. The Composition $[^0Last\_Dec \ ^0\pi]$ occurs hyperintensionally here, but in the de re case it must occur extensionally. In order for $[^0Last\_Dec \ ^0\pi]$ to be a constituent occurring extensionally, we must again deploy the functions *Sub* and *Tr*:

$$\lambda w \lambda t \ [^0Calculate_{wt} \ ^0Tilman \ [^0Sub \ [^0Tr \ [^0Last\_Dec \ ^0\pi]] \ ^0y \ ^0[[^0Last\_Dec \ ^0\pi] = y]]]$$

Now we can apply (R_5)-act in order to obtain the conclusion:

$$\frac{\lambda w \lambda t \; [{}^0Calculate_{wt} \; {}^0Tilman \; [{}^0Sub \; [{}^0Tr \; [{}^0Last\_Dec \; {}^0\pi]] \; {}^0y \; {}^0[[{}^0Last\_Dec \; {}^0\pi] = y]]]}{\lambda w \lambda t \; [{}^0\exists \lambda x \; [{}^0Calculate_{wt} \; {}^0Tilman \; [{}^0Sub \; [{}^0Tr \; x] \; {}^0y \; {}^0[[{}^0Last\_Dec \; {}^0\pi] = y]]]]}$$

5.2 Empirical objectual attitudes: an application

In Duží et al. (2010, § 5.2, § 5.3) much attention was devoted to objectual attitudes whose complement is an intension like seeking or finding the site of Troy. Hence we analyzed these attitudes as relations-in-intension sharing the polymorphous type $(o \iota \alpha_{\tau\omega})_{\tau\omega}$. We suggested that the default interpretation of objectual attitudes is as intensional attitudes, because these attitudes concern an empirical object where it is irrelevant how the intension is presented to, or conceptualized by, the ascribee.

This may often be true, but there are also cases where the mode of presentation of the intension does matter. This is so with regard to, e.g., Tilman seeking an abominable snowman without him seeking a yeti. In this case an intensional analysis will yield a contradiction, because Tilman would be related, and at the same time not related, to one and the same property by the *seeking* relation. Thus a truthful report of such a situation needs to be hyperintensional. A hyperintensional analysis avails itself of two different hyperintensions presenting the same property. When construed hyperintensionally, Tilman's search is only ostensibly inconsistent.

To get the example of Tilman seeking an abominable snowman and not seeking a yeti off the ground, we are stipulating that 'is a yeti' and 'is an abominable snowman' are a pair not of synonymous but merely equivalent predicates. Their respective meanings are co-intensional, but not procedurally isomorphic (co-hyperintensional). The rationale for this stipulation is that the latter predicate has a molecular structure thanks to the application of the property modifier denoted by 'abominable' to the property denoted by 'snowman', whereas the former predicate is atomic.[34] One could object that it seems reasonable to assume that there is a meaning postulate in place to the effect that 'is a yeti' is shorthand for, or a notational variant of, 'is an abominable snowman', the same way 'lasts a fortnight' is arguably short for 'lasts two weeks'. What speaks against this assumption, at least through the lens of TIL, is that the Trivialization ${}^0Yeti$ and the Composition $[{}^0Abominable \; {}^0Snowman]$ are not procedurally isomorphic, but only equivalent constructions. Furthermore, from a formal point of view at least, it is questionable what semantic and inferential gain may be accrued from introducing a redundant predicate like 'is a yeti', on its construal as a mere notational variant of 'is an abominable snowman'.[35]

What we have on our hands is an empirical hyperintensional attitude, and we can apply (R₁):

> Tilman is seeking an abominable snowman and not seeking a yeti
> ―――
> There is something Tilman is seeking and something (else) he is not seeking

---

[34] For details on property modifiers, see Jespersen (2014, §5).
[35] See Jespersen (2014, §6) for the parallel example of 'is a bachelor', 'is an unmarried man'.

$$\frac{\lambda w \lambda t\ [[^0 Seek^*_{wt}\ {}^0Tilman\ {}^0[{}^0Abominable\ {}^0Snowman]] \wedge \neg[^0Seek^*_{wt}\ {}^0Tilman\ {}^{00}Yeti]]}{\lambda w \lambda t\ [{}^0\exists^*\lambda c\ {}^0\exists^*\lambda d\ [[{}^0Seek^*_{wt}\ {}^0Tilman\ c] \wedge \neg[{}^0Seek^*_{wt}\ {}^0Tilman\ d]]]}$$

Types: $Yeti, Snowman/(o\iota)_{\tau\omega}$; $Abominable/((o\iota)_{\tau\omega}(o\iota)_{\tau\omega})$: a property modifier; $[{}^0Abominable\ {}^0Snowman] \rightarrow (o\iota)_{\tau\omega}$; $c, d/*_2 \rightarrow *_1$; ${}^2c, {}^2d \rightarrow_v (o\iota)_{\tau\omega}$.

In this case by applying (R'_2) we can derive a further conclusion:

$$\frac{\text{Tilman is seeking an abominable snowman and not seeking a yeti}}{\begin{array}{c}\text{There is a property such that Tilman is seeking an instance of it via a construction } c\\ \text{and not seeking an instance of it via another construction } d\end{array}}$$

$$\frac{\lambda w \lambda t\ [[^0 Seek^*_{wt}\ {}^0Tilman\ {}^0[{}^0Abominable\ {}^0Snowman]] \wedge \neg[^0Seek^*_{wt}\ {}^0Tilman\ {}^{00}Yeti]]}{\lambda w \lambda t\ [{}^0\exists^*\lambda c\ {}^0\exists^*\lambda d\ {}^0\exists\lambda p\ [[p = {}^2c] \wedge [p = {}^2d] \wedge [{}^0Seek^*_{wt}\ {}^0Tilman\ c] \wedge \neg[{}^0Seek^*_{wt}\ {}^0Tilman\ d]]]}$$

Note that the premise demands the double Trivialization ${}^{00}Yeti$, because Tilman seeks what ${}^{00}Yeti$ constructs, namely ${}^0Yeti$.

Moreover, by applying R_3 we can derive that Tilman is seeking something abominable (where $p, q \rightarrow (o\iota)_{\tau\omega}$):

$$\frac{\lambda w \lambda t\ [[^0 Seek^*_{wt}\ {}^0Tilman\ {}^0[{}^0Abominable\ {}^0Snowman]] \wedge \neg[^0Seek^*_{wt}\ {}^0Tilman\ {}^{00}Yeti]]}{\lambda w \lambda t\ [{}^0\exists\lambda p\ [{}^0Seek^*_{wt}\ {}^0Tilman\ [{}^0Sub\ [{}^0Tr\ p]\ {}^0q\ {}^0[{}^0Abominable\ q]]]]}$$

6 Conclusion

We demonstrated above how to validly quantify into various sorts of hyperintensional contexts involving objectual (i.e. non-propositional) attitude complements. This cluster of logical results was obtained in virtue of an extensional logic of hyperintensions, namely Transparent Intensional Logic, which comes with a context-invariant, top-down semantic theory that yields universal transparency to the exclusion of opaque contexts. An extensional logic of hyperintensions is permissive or inclusive in the sense of validating all the rules of extensional logic, including substitution of identicals and existential generalization, also in hyperintensional contexts, but must at the same time be restrictive or exclusive with regard to what counts as admissible operands.

The novelties of the paper are the following. The paper offers a formally worked-out, philosophically motivated criterion of hyperintensional individuation, which is defined in terms of a slightly more carefully stated version of α-conversion and β-conversion by value, which amounts to a modification of Church's Alternative (A1). Moreover, we presented a detailed study of the attitude of calculating. We propounded updated rules for quantifying into hyperintensional contexts de dicto, which are an adjustment and generalization of the rules presented in Duží et al. (2010). We presented an analysis of ostensibly logically impossible empirical attitudes, which require at least two different hyperintensional presentations of one and the same empirical property. Finally, we put forward rules for quantifying into hyperintensional attitudes de re, which correct the rules presented in Duží et al. (2010, § 5.3).

Transparent quantification into hyperintensional objectual attitudes

We have proved two major things. First, it is always valid to quantify *into* hyperintensional attitude contexts and *over* hyperintensional entities. Second, factive attitudes (e.g. *finding an abominable snowman* or *having solved an equation*) validate, furthermore, quantifying over the (intensional or extensional) entities presented by the respective constituent of the attitude complement, and so do non-factive attitudes provided the respective constituent of the attitude complement presents the sort of object that is to be quantified over.

Acknowledgments We are grateful to three anonymous referees, two of whom engaged thoroughly with the manuscript and whose comments improved the quality of the paper. This work has been supported by Internal Grant Agency of VSB-Technical University Ostrava Project No. SP2014/157, *Knowledge Modeling, Process Simulation and Design* (Marie Duží and Bjørn Jespersen), and Marie Curie Fellowship No. 628170, *USHP: Unity of Structured Hyperpropositions*, FP7-PEOPLE-2013-IEF (Bjørn Jespersen). A version of this paper was read as an invited lecture by Bjørn Jespersen at Munich Centre for Mathematical Philosophy, October 2013, and by Marie Duží at Logica 2014, Hejnice, Czech Republic, June 2014.

References

Bealer, G. (1982). *Quality and concept*. Oxford: Clarendon Press.
Brown, J. R. (1999). *Philosophy of mathematics*. London: Routledge.
Carnap, R. (1947). *Meaning and necessity*. Chicago: Chicago University Press.
Chang, S., & Felleisen, M. (2012). The call-by-need lambda calculus, revisited. In *Programming languages and systems. Lecture Notes in Computer Science* (Vol. 7211, pp. 128–147).
Church, A. (1951). The need for abstract entities. *American Academy of Arts and Sciences Proceedings*, *80*, 100–113.
Church, A. (1956). *Introduction to mathematical logic*. Princeton: Princeton University Press.
Church, A. (1993). A revised formulation of the logic of sense and denotation. Alternative (1). *Noûs*, *27*, 141–157.
Crawford, S. (2008). Quantifiers and propositional attitudes: Quine revisited. *Synthese*, *160*, 75–96.
Crawford, S. (2014). Propositional or non-propositional attitudes? *Philosophical Studies*, *168*, 179–210.
Duží, M. (2010). The paradox of inference and the non-triviality of analytic information. *Journal of Philosophical Logic*, *39*(5), 473–510.
Duží, M. (2014a). Communication in a multi-cultural world. *Organon F*, *21*(2), 198–218.
Duží, M. (2014b). Structural isomorphism of meaning and synonymy. *Computación y Sistemas, Mexico*, *18*(3), 439–453.
Duží, M., & Jespersen, B. (2012). Transparent quantification into hyperpropositional contexts de re. *Logique & Analyse*, *220*, 513–554.
Duží, M., & Jespersen, B. (2013). Procedural isomorphism, analytic information, and β-conversion by value. *Logic Journal of the IGPL*, *21*, 291–308.
Duží, M., Jespersen, B., & Materna, P. (2010). *Procedural semantics for hyperintensional logic. Foundations and applications of transparent intensional logic*. Berlin: Springer.
Forbes, G. (2000). Objectual attitudes. *Linguistics and Philosophy*, *23*, 141–183.
Jespersen, B. (2010). How hyper are hyperpropositions? *Language and Linguistics Compass*, *4*, 96–106.
Jespersen, B. (2012). Recent work on structured meaning and propositional unity. *Philosophy Compass*, *7*, 620–30.
Jespersen, B. (2014). Structured lexical concepts, property modifiers, and transparent intensional logic. *Philosophical Studies* (forthcoming). doi:10.1007/s11098-014-0305-0.
Kaplan, D. (1968). Quantifying in. *Synthese*, *19*, 178–214.
Kaplan, D. (1986). Opacity. In L. Hahn (Ed.), *W. V. Quine* (pp. 229–289). La Salle: Open Court.
Kaplan, D. (1990). Dthat. In P. Cole (Ed.), *Syntax and semantics* (Vol. 9). New York: Academic Press.
Materna, P. (1997). Rules of existential quantification into 'intensional contexts'. *Studia Logica*, *59*, 331–343.
Montague, M. (2007). Against propositionalism. *Noûs*, *42*, 503–518.
Neale, S. (1990). *Descriptions*. Cambridge: MIT Press.

Plotkin, G. D. (1975). Call-by-name, call-by-value, and the lambda calculus. *Theoretical Computer Science*, *1*, 125–159.
Quine, W. V. (1956). Quantifiers and propositional attitudes. *Journal of Philosophy*, *53*, 177–187.
Quine, W. V. (1960). *Word and object*. Harvard: MIT Press.
Raclavský, J. (2010). On partiality and Tichý's transparent intensional logic. *Hungarian Philosophical Review*, *54*, 120–128.
Soames, S. (2010). *What is meaning?* Princeton: Princeton University Press.
Tichý, P. (1979). Existence and God. *Journal of Philosophy*, *76*, 403–420.
Tichý, P. (1986). The indiscernibility of identicals. *Studia Logica*, *45*, 251–273.
Tichý, P. (1988). *The foundations of Frege's logic*. Berlin: de Gruyter.

TRANSPARENT QUANTIFICATION INTO HYPERPROPOSITIONAL CONTEXTS *DE RE*

MARIE DUŽÍ AND BJØRN JESPERSEN

Abstract
This paper is the twin of (Duží and Jespersen, in submission), which provides a logical rule for transparent quantification into hyperpropositional contexts *de dicto*, as in: Mary believes that the Evening Star is a planet; therefore, there is a concept c such that Mary believes that what c conceptualizes is a planet. Here we provide two logical rules for transparent quantification into hyperpropositional contexts *de re*. (As a by-product, we also offer rules for possible-world propositional contexts.) One rule validates this inference: Mary believes of the Evening Star that it is a planet; therefore, there is an x such that Mary believes of x that it is a planet. The other rule validates this inference: the Evening Star is such that it is believed by Mary to be a planet; therefore, there is an x such that x is believed by Mary to be a planet. Issues unique to the *de re* variant include partiality and existential presupposition, substitutivity of co-referential (as opposed to co-denoting or synonymous) terms, anaphora, and active vs. passive voice. The validity of quantifying-in presupposes an extensional logic of hyperintensions preserving transparency and compositionality in hyperintensional contexts. This requires raising the bar for what qualifies as co-denotation or equivalence in extensional contexts. Our logic is Tichý's Transparent Intensional Logic. The syntax of TIL is the typed lambda calculus; its highly expressive semantics is based on a procedural redefinition of, *inter alia*, functional abstraction and application. The two non-standard features we need are a hyperintension (called *Trivialization*) that presents other hyperintensions and a four-place substitution function (called *Sub*) defined over hyperintensions.

0. Introduction

Quine (1956) and Kaplan (1968), (1986) introduced the topic of quantifying-in — existential quantification into modal and attitudinal contexts — into the repertoire of philosophical logic and continue to shape the discussion of it today. Quine and Kaplan, as well as their commentators, such as Forbes (1996), (2000) and Crawford (2008), remain baffled by quantifying-in for both logical, ontological and hermeneutic reasons.[i] This paper demonstrates, in full logical detail, how to quantify into attitude contexts of the toughest kind, namely hyperintensional ones. Following Cresswell (1975), hyperintensional attitude contexts are those in which the complements of an agent's attitude are more finely individuated than up to necessary equivalence. Quantifying into intensional attitude contexts — in which the complements are individuated up to necessary equivalence, as in possible-world semantics — falls out as a by-product of our solution to the hyperintensional variant.

The cornerstone of our approach is that we avail ourselves of an extensional logic of hyperintensions. Only an extensional logic will validate the rule of existential generalization, hence only an extensional logic of hyperintensions will stand a chance of validating quantifying-in. We assign to terms and expressions occurring in hyperintensional contexts the very same semantics that we assign to those very same terms and expressions when occurring in intensional and extensional contexts. As a result of this top-down approach, the logical rule of existential generalization applies indiscriminately to all contexts. The upside of our top-down approach is that referential transparency and compositionality of meaning are preserved throughout, together with semantic innocence, since we have no recourse to reference shift.[ii] At no point do we invoke contextualist epicycles to somehow create

---

[i] Quine's stance towards quantifying into modal and attitudinal contexts is a convoluted one, though. Both Kaplan (1986), Crawford (2008), and Forbes (1996), (2000) point out that whereas Quine is dismissive of quantifying into modal, especially modal *de re*, contexts (which would yield 'Aristotelian essentialism' sentences of the form, "There is an x such that x is necessarily an F"), he strives to make good sense of what he calls *relational* (roughly, *de re*) attitude ascriptions like, "There is a sloop that I want", which presuppose the validity of quantifying into attitude contexts. That is, whereas Quine *rejects* the argument $\Box Fa \therefore \exists x \Box Fx$, he *embraces* the argument $\delta Gb \therefore \exists y \delta Gy$. See Crawford (2008) and Forbes (1996), (2000) for detailed discussion of Quine's excursions into dyadic versus triadic belief relations, the latter being an attempt of his to recuperate transparency for relational beliefs. For streamlined accounts of Quine's take on quantifying-in, see Hookway (1988, Chs. 5–7) and Kemp (2006, Ch. 6).

[ii] See Duží et al. (2010, p. 12) where we contrast Davidson's 'paratactic' conception of semantic innocence with a 'hypotactic' one. See also Tichý (1975).

a secondary semantics for 'non-extensional' contexts. The perceived downside would be that we revise the prevalent extensionalist semantic theory of terms and expressions, in that we universalize Frege's semantics earmarked for *Sinn*-sensitive contexts to all contexts, including those that are merely *Bedeutung*-sensitive. Be that as it may, it is a strength of our solution that it is emphatically not tailor-made specifically for validating quantifying-in. Instead it is just yet another application of a large-scale background theory. So our solution to quantifying-in is principled and not *ad hoc*.

Laying out the required semantics requires a fair amount of footwork. Once this is in place, however, all that remains is filling in the nitty-gritty details of quantifying-in. The devil is in the detail, as ever, and quantifying into hyperintensional contexts is far from being technically trivial. But it is feasible. Showing one way of how to exactly go about this is the task of this paper. Our solution marks an advance for philosophical logic in general and hyperintensional logic in particular. Kaplan (1990, p. 14) lists quantifying-in as one of the challenges facing the program of pure semantics. So does Bealer (1982, p. 13), who lists quantifying-in as one of ten 'classical puzzles' any (hyper-) intensional logic worth its name must be capable of addressing adequately. And the community-wide project of establishing a general hyperintensional logic gains in credibility from cracking a hard nut.[iii]

The rest of the paper is organized as follows. Section 1 details the three aspects of quantifying-in: the logical, the ontological, and the hermeneutic one. This paper is devoted to the first aspect. Section 2 presents the relevant theoretical foundations of our extensional logic of hyperintensions. Section 3 sets out our theory of hyperpropositional and intensional attitudes *de dicto* and *de re*. Section 4 provides the respective rules of quantifying into hyperpropositional and possible-world propositional attitude contexts *de re*.

1. *The Three Aspects of Quantifying-in*

Quantifying-in spans three issues. The first is the logical one whether it is formally possible to quantify *into* so-called non-extensional contexts. This is, narrowly speaking, a question of the technical resources of a logical symbolism. The second is the philosophical one whether it is ontologically acceptable to quantify *over* non-extensional entities. This is, in essence, a question of the ontological commitments of a given logical theory. The third is the likewise philosophical, or hermeneutic, question of to what extent it

---

[iii] See Bealer (1982, §7 and §11).

makes sense to say, for instance, that there is somebody that somebody believes to be happy; that there is somebody such that they are believed by somebody to be happy; or that there is somebody of whom somebody believes that they are happy. This question concerns the link between philosophy and logic: if some logical symbolism enables quantifying-in then what philosophical notion has been symbolized? Or conversely, exactly what philosophical notion are we supposed to adequately interpret logically?

Let δ be a generic attitude operator.[iv] Then the first question broached above translates into whether these two argument schemata (in the notation of predicate logic) are valid:

$$\frac{\delta F a}{\exists x \delta F x}$$

where the individual a is being quantified away, and

$$\frac{\delta F a}{\exists f \delta f a}$$

where the property F is being quantified away.

Both schemata are valid without qualification — *provided* the principle of existential generalization is untrammelled by considerations of which sort of position in which sort of context one is attempting to quantify into. But riding roughshod over contextual embedding is no option, of course. The logical problem is that δ generates a context that seals f and x off from $\exists$, which needs to reach across δ to catch f and x. (Definition 4 in Section 2 defines *hyperintensional*, *intensional* and *extensional context* by defining what it means for a hyperintension to occur either *mentioned* or *used*.) This is one reason why it would be naïve to assume that if, e.g., b believes that a is an F then it logically follows that there is somebody that b believes to be an F, or that there is a property that b believes a to have. Another reason is that the truth of an ascription of a non-factive attitude such as *believing* need not discharge existential presuppositions, as does *knowing*.[v]

[iv] For ease of exposition, we shall contrast existential *quantifiers* with attitude *operators* in our informal discussion. However, formally speaking, TIL does not have attitude operators. Instead TIL has binary *relations*-in-intension between agents and either propositions or hyperpropositions (propositional constructions). These relations are partial functions, such that it is either true or false or neither, at some world/time pair of evaluation, that the relevant agent entertains the relevant attitude to the relevant (hyper-)proposition.

[v] To know that Pegasus is a horse is not to know something factual. It is to know something *conceptual*. To understand the concept of Pegasus is to know, *inter alia*, that Pegasus is a horse. Such knowledge does not presuppose the existence of an individual that is the horse Pegasus. It does presuppose the existence of a set of properties jointly defining the individual

It may be true that the attributee b believes that a is an F while it is at the same time false that a exists.[vi] But, if b knows that a is an F then it needs to be true already that a exists. The set of worlds at which Fa is known is a (proper) subset of the set of worlds at which Fa is true. The set of worlds at which Fa is believed is the union of the set of worlds at which Fa is true and the set of worlds at which Fa is not true (because either false or without truth-value). This is how room is created for believing falsehoods, whether contingent or necessary (as with inconsistent beliefs), and believing propositions without truth-value.[vii]

---

concept of Pegasus. The property of being a horse will be in that set, so will the property of being winged. See Duží et al. (2010, pp. 286–88) on 'Sherlock Holmes' and (ibid., §4.1 'Requisites defined') on necessary relations-in-extension between intensions.

[vi] TIL pursues a Fregean tack in questions of attribution of existence: saying of an individual that it exists is trivially true. See Duží et al. (2010, §§2.3.1–2.3.2 'Existence and extensions', 'Existence and intensions'). In the main text we are pretending, for ease of exposition, that it be conceivable for a not to exist.

[vii] There is an interesting direct parallelism between factive attitude operators and subsective modifiers and between non-factive attitude operators and modal modifiers. Both the rule of factivity and the rule of subsection are, syntactically, elimination rules:

$$\textit{Known } A \therefore A$$

and

$$[\textit{Modifier Property}](x) \therefore \textit{Property}(x)$$

For instance, since the modifier *Skillful* is subsective, it follows that a skillful musician is a musician. Set-theoretically, any set of skillful logicians must be a subset of a set of logicians. Modal modifiers are somewhat elusive, oscillating as they do between being subsective and being privative. (See Jespersen and Primiero (2012) on the logic of modal modification.) The disjunction of A and $\neg A$ is a classical tautology and so is too weak to capture what is characteristic of non-factive operators and modal modifiers (that they are hit-or-miss). But the conjunction of two mutually exclusive possibilities (matching the limiting case of union where the intersection is empty) sums up the little that can be inferred (other than various instances of existential generalization):

$$\textit{Believed } A \therefore \textit{Possibly, } A \wedge \textit{possibly, } \neg A$$

and

$$[\textit{Modifier}' \textit{ Property}](x) \therefore \textit{Possibly, Property}(x) \wedge \textit{possibly, } \neg \textit{Property}(x)$$

For instance, if x is an alleged terrorist then x is a terrorist or x is not a terrorist: there is a world/time pair at which x is a terrorist and there is another world/time pair at which x is not a terrorist. Both non-factive attitude operators and modal modifiers leave it open which side truth comes down on.

The second, ontological, question is exemplified by the second schema. Whereas it is uncontroversial to quantify over individuals, it is controversial, in some quarters, to quantify over so-called intensional entities such as properties, propositions, relations-in-intension, and individual concepts. Besides, if we do not assume that a is an individual but an individual concept or role or office, such that b believes that the incumbent of that office is an F, then the first schema involves quantification over individual concepts. We are not going to argue independently for the acceptability or indispensability of non-extensional entities here. Instead we simply assume them, introducing two kinds of non-extensional entities: possible-world intensions and hyperintensions.[viii] Our notion of hyperintension will be defined in Definition 2 in Section 2. For now, our hyperintensions serve in the capacities as modes of presentation of other entities, linguistic senses, and the complements of hyperintensional attitudes. In particular, hyperpropositions are sentential senses and are modes of presentation of truth-conditions, or possible-world propositions, or empirical states-of-affairs. Our logic contains the resources to quantify over hyperintensions. This is thanks to our ramified type hierarchy, in which our hyperintensions are organized, since there is always going to be a hyperintension presenting another hyperintension located one step down. (Definition 3 in Section 2 defines *ramified type hierarchy*.)

The basic idea informing the rule of existential generalization is simple enough. The conclusion of the rule of existential generalization makes explicit an existential commitment incurred by the premise. If the individual Mary is happy then there is an element in the domain of individuals that is happy:

$$\frac{Fa}{\exists x F x}$$

This much is uncontroversial. Now what if the pope — the incumbent of the papal office — is happy? Then we would not hesitate to infer that there is an

---

[viii] A valid objection, however, is that possible-world intensions are intensions on the cheap, because they are extensionally individuated:

$$\forall f g (\forall w (f(w) = g(w)) \to f = g)$$

Co-intensionality amounts to nothing other than necessary co-extensionality, because f, g are mappings. This explains why TIL ranks possible-world intensions as *first*-order objects and types them in the *simple* type theory (provided they do not have domain or range in hyperintensions, i.e. TIL constructions, in which case they are *higher*-order objects and must be typed in the *ramified* type theory). Outside the idiom of possible-world semantics, 'intensional' tends to equate 'hyperintensional' (unless used in the condescending sense of 'non-extensional'). Just one example: Hindley and Seldin (1986, p. 72).

individual office whose occupant is happy. What if "*as ølglas er halvfuldt*" means that a's glass of beer is half-full, but not that a's glass is half-empty? Then we would not hesitate to infer that there is a hyperproposition presenting an empirical state-of-affairs, such that that hyperproposition is the meaning of that Danish sentence.

Quantifying over hyperintensions yields weaker propositions than does quantifying over intensional or extensional entities, because if we infer that there is a hyperintension we still have not inferred, and so do not yet know, whether this hyperintension presents anything, be it an intension or an extension. Let f be an individual office.[ix] Then if a believes that the occupant of f is an F, it follows that there is a *hyperintension* presenting an intensional entity belonging to the type of individual offices, such that a believes that the occupant of some office is an F. This inference would be a trivial one to draw. A more interesting inference to draw is that there is an *individual office*, such that a believes that its occupant is an F. A still more interesting inference to draw is that there is an *individual*, such that a believes that that individual is an F. Yet this conclusion is not always forthcoming.[x] If Mary believes that the King of Canada is happy, does it follow that there is an x such that

---

[ix] There is a substantial difference between proper names and definite descriptions. This distinction is of crucial importance due to their vastly different logical behaviour. Independently of any particular theory of proper names, it should be granted that a *proper* proper name (as opposed to a definite description grammatically masquerading as a proper name) is a rigid designator of a numerically particular individual. On the other hand, a definite *description* like, for instance, 'the Mayor of Dunedin', 'the King of France', 'the pope', 'the first man to run 100 m in less than 9 seconds', 'the Evening Star', etc., offers an *empirical criterion* that enables us, in principle, to establish which individual, if any, satisfies the criterion in a particular state of affairs. We model such criteria as possible-world intensions, which are functions that for each possible world and each time return at most one individual. Proper names do not come with an empirical criterion for fixing their bearers: it is purely a matter of linguistic *fiat* which name has which bearer (so proper names are no empirical terms for us).

[x] The set of inferences we just considered amounts to what Klement (2002, p. 157) calls 'at least a *minimally* adequate treatment' of quantifying-in. Klement's discussion of quantifying-in is faithful to the historical Frege, such that existential quantification will be over either a 'saturated' *Gegenstand* or an 'unsaturated' *Funktion*. Our *neo*-Fregean setting allows for quantification over extensional or intensional or hyperintensional objects. Frege did not have the intermediate level (on the almost uncontroversial assumption that *Sinn*, which Frege frequently, though not always, argued to be individuated in terms of cognitive significance, is hyperintensional). We agree with Klement that Frege's analysis of quantifying into "Gottlob believes that the Morning Star/Vulcan is a planet" amounts to, "There is some *Sinn* that, when saturated with the incomplete *Sinn* of "ξ is a planet", yields a *Gedanke* believed by Gottlob", with no *Bedeutung* being invoked (i.e. without executing something akin to Church's Δ mapping from a *Sinn* to its *Bedeutung*), so the fact that 'The Morning Star' picks out a *Bedeutung*, and 'Vulcan' does not, is of no logical import. What matters is that the *Eigennamen* (in Frege's inclusive notion of proper name) 'The Morning Star' and 'Vulcan' both have a *Sinn*. (*Ibid.*, pp. 156–57.)

Mary believes that x is happy? Absent the additional premise that the King of Canada exists, the suggested inference will be a fallacy in case x ranges over individuals. However, if *believing* is replaced by a factive attitude like *knowing* then Mary's knowledge that the King is happy presupposes that it be true that Canada has exactly one king. With Mary's factive attitude as a premise, existential generalization over individuals in the conclusion is straightforward — from an ontological, though not logical, point of view; for there remains the problem of how the quantifier is to bind an x inside the scope of an attitude operator.

The third question concerns the hermeneutic comprehensibility of predicating of a random individual the property of being believed (in a hyperintensional manner) by some attributee to be such-and-such. For instance, Kaplan (1969, p. 221) pauses to reflect on the meaningfulness of the quantified *de re* ascription, "Someone is such that Ralph believes that he is a spy" (cf. entry (10), *ibid.*, p. 210). The notion of having an attitude *of* X lends itself to basically two different construals. On one construal, an attitude *de re* requires an exceptionally intimate epistemic relation between agent and X, perhaps in a manner that circumvents, or is prior to, most or all propositional knowledge about X, and may not be easy to come by. On the other construal, an attitude *de re* is parasitic on other attitudes, ultimately with an attitude *de dicto* at the origin, and much easier to come by.[xi] Ours is the second approach, which is devoid of the enigma integral with the first one.

This paper is the twin of another paper setting out the logic of transparent quantification into hyperpropositional contexts *de dicto*. These are the last two so far in a string of papers beginning with Tichý (1986), which quantifies into intensional contexts and over intensions; Materna (1997), which quantifies into hyperintensional contexts and over hyperintensions; Duží (2000), which corrects and simplifies Materna (1997), but has a flaw of its own;[xii] Duží et al. (2010, §5.3 'Quantifying in'), which puts forward a technically correct but philosophically strained solution that is replaced by a technically more elegant and philosophically appealing solution in Duží and Jespersen (submitted). In the twin paper we analyze, in particular, the following argument, for which we consider four analyses, two of which are valid, and one of which is the final analysis:

a believes that the Evening Star is a planet

There is a hyperintension presenting an individual office such that a believes that the occupant of that office is a planet

---

[xi] See Duží et al. (2010, p. 435) for discussion.
[xii] See Duží et al. (2010, p. 500, n. 106).

We also show how to validate the following inference:

$$\frac{a \text{ believes that the Evening Star is a planet}}{\begin{array}{c}\text{There is an individual office such that } a \text{ believes that}\\ \text{the occupant of that office is a planet}\end{array}}$$

We leave out of consideration non-empirical 'that'-clause attitudes, such as "a knows that π is a transcendental number", and notional attitudes, such as "a seeks the fountain of youth" and "a calculates the first one million decimals of π". The logic of quantifying into possible-world propositional attitudes falls directly out of our logic of hyperpropositional attitudes, since the former attitudes are technically less demanding and are obtained by lifting various restrictions. The current paper follows a similar pattern. We also restrict ourselves to hyperpropositional empirical attitudes *de re*, but since intensional attitudes *de re* are a by-product, as it were, thanks to the trickle-down effect of how our theory is set up, we display, for illustration, how to quantify into intensional attitudes *de re*.[xiii]

We will concentrate on quantifying into the singular-reference position of $\delta F a$. Our main focus is on singular terms having the semantics of definite descriptions, because they are logically more intricate, and so more interesting, than singular terms with the semantics of proper names. We assume, in keeping with prevalent theories, that the meaning of a proper name (whatever the details of one's favourite theory of the meaning of proper names) is such that a proper name rigidly refers to one and the same individual whatever the contextual embedding. Hence, the transfer from the attributee's perspective to the attributer's, and vice versa, goes smoothly. On the other hand, the meaning of a definite description may occur either *de dicto* or *de re*, and a definite description does not refer rigidly to a particular individual. Rather it denotes an empirical *condition* that may be satisfied by individuals.

Here we are assuming, rather than arguing, that 'The Evening Star' and 'The Morning Star' are not two different names for the same individual. Instead 'The Evening Star' names one individual office and 'The Morning Star' names another individual office. When we say that the Evening Star is the Morning Star, we mean to say that these two offices are contingently co-occupied by the same individual. That is, "The Evening Star is the Morning Star" does not express the self-identity of an individual bearing two names,

---

[xiii] Also hyperintensional notional ('hypernotional') attitudes are amenable to being quantified into. See Duží et al. (2010, §§5.2–5.3 'Notional attitudes', 'Quantifying in').

but the contingent convergence of two named offices in one anonymous individual.[xiv] We say of 'The Evening Star' and 'The Morning Star' that they are not synonymous and do not co-denote, or are not equivalent (because they do not denote the same office), but co-refer (because their respective denotations happen to be co-extensional). For another standard example, although Quine's 'the man in the brown hat' and 'the man on the beach' happen to co-refer to Bernard J Ortcutt, because their offices happen to co-describe him, they do not co-denote him. Rather they denote, in every context, two distinct individual offices. There are worlds and times at which these two offices are co-occupied, e.g. by Ortcutt, but this empirical fact has no bearing on the semantic properties of these two definite descriptions.[xv] Their semantic properties concern instead whether they are synonymous (hence co-denoting) or merely co-denoting. Our strategy is to raise the bar somewhat for what qualifies as identity and equivalence of senses and synonymy vs. co-denotation of words and apply substitution of identicals and equivalents to those (fewer) pairs of words that do pass muster. The opposite, and common, strategy is to maintain a lower bar, which, however, generates referential opacity and inapplicability of substitution and quantification in various modal and attitudinal contexts.[xvi] Definition 7 in Section 2 defines *synonymy*, *equivalence* (co-denotation) and *co-reference*.

We shall analyze the sentence

"Mary believes of the Evening Star that it is a planet"

and its 'exported' variant, which introduces anaphoric reference:

"The Evening Star is such that Mary believes of *it* that *it* is a planet"

The exported variant can also be transformed from active to passive voice, from

"The Evening Star is believed by Mary to be a planet"

to

[xiv] For justification, see Duží et al. (2010, §3.3.1 'Hesperus is Phosphorus: co-occupation of individual offices').

[xv] For further details, see Duží et al. (2010, pp. 301–11).

[xvi] Duží et al. (2010, Ch. 1, esp. §1.2, §1.4.2.3, §1.5.2 'The top-down vs. bottom-up approach to logical semantics', 'The top-down approach to semantics revisited', 'Supposition *de dicto* and *de re* vs. reference shift') provides details on this project of universal transparency.

"The Evening Star is such that *it* is believed by Mary to be a planet"

The strongest conclusion is that there is an *individual* such that Mary believes that that individual is a planet. This conclusion is forthcoming in two cases. The first case is factive attitudes: you cannot know that the pope is a German unless there is exactly one pope of whom it is true that he is a German. The second case is attitudes *de re*, including *belief*: you cannot believe of the pope that he is a Protestant unless there is exactly one pope of whom to believe that he is a Protestant.

Two other conclusions, one weaker than the other, can be inferred as well. The weaker of the two is that there is a hyperintension presenting an office such that the attributee believes that its occupant is a planet. The stronger of the two is that there is an office such that the attributee believes that its occupant is a planet. While hyperintensional attitudes *de dicto* and *de re* both validate these last two conclusions, the important difference is that attitudes *de re* validate, furthermore, the strongest conclusion that there is an individual of whom an attitude is being entertained. In our logic, if there is no individual of whom or which to have the relevant attitude *de re*, the proposition that the attributee believes, or knows, of the F that he/she/it is an G will be without truth-value (rather than false). Contrast this with the attribution of a belief *de dicto* that the F is a G, which will have a truth-value. When a *partial* function such as a possible-world proposition trades a world for a gap, we say that the hyperintension being used to present the proposition is *improper*. Definition 2 in Section 2 defines *proper* and *improper* hyperintensions.

2. *Theoretical Foundations*

The background theory we have implicitly presupposed so far is Tichý's Transparent Intensional Logic. What makes TIL suitable for the job of quantifying into hyperintensional contexts is that the theory construes the semantic properties of the sense and denotation relations of terms and expressions as remaining invariant across linguistic contexts and that its ramified type theory enables quantification up to any order.[xvii]

[xvii] *Indexicals* being the only exception: while the sense of an indexical remains constant, its denotation trivially varies in keeping with its contextual embedding. See Duží et al. (2010, §3.4 'Pragmatically incomplete meanings').

Formally, TIL is an extensional logic of hyperintensions based on the partial, typed λ-calculus enriched with a ramified type structure to accommodate hyperintensions. The syntax of TIL is the familiar one of the λ-calculus, with the addition of a hyperintension called Trivialization (symbolized by a superscripted nought). The semantics is a *procedural* (as opposed to denotational) one. Thus, functional application, in TIL, is not the result of applying a function to an argument, but instead the very *procedure* of applying function to argument; and functional abstraction, in TIL, is not the result of forming a function, but instead the very *procedure* of sorting two selections of entities into functional arguments and values, respectively. Furthermore, variables are not terms, but hyperintensions: 'x' denotes the atomic hyperproposition x that presents the value that an assignment function has accorded to x (relative to a type assignment and a sequence of variable/value pairs). The TIL concept of procedurally construed hyperintensions is *construction*. Thus, hyperintensional attitudes translate into *constructional attitudes* and hyperintensional contexts into *constructional contexts*. Of the six different kinds of constructions that their inductive definition enumerates, we shall need four altogether in order to quantify into hyperpropositional contexts *de re* and a fifth for the intensional ones.

The first three definitions below constitute the logical heart of TIL. The subsequent five definitions build upon those. Taken together, they make up the logical tools needed to pull off quantifying into hyperpropositional and possible-world propositional contexts *de dicto* and *de re*. These two variants of quantifying-in are importantly different, so we exhibit the former for illustration (the fourth and final analysis alluded to in Section 1). The definitions are as follows.

Definition 1: (types of order 1) *Let B be a* base, *where a base is a collection of pair-wise disjoint, non-empty sets. Then:*
  (i) *Every member of B is an elementary* type of order 1 over B.
  (ii) *Let* $\alpha, \beta_1, \ldots, \beta_m (m > 0)$ *be types of order 1 over B. Then the collection* $(\alpha \ \beta_1 \ldots \beta_m)$ *of all m-ary partial mappings from* $\beta_1 \times \ldots \times \beta_m$ *into* α *is a functional* type of order 1 over B.
  (iii) *Nothing is a* type of order 1 over B *unless it so follows from (i) and (ii)*. □

Remark. For the purposes of natural-language analysis, we are currently assuming the following base of ground types, each of which is part of the ontological commitments of TIL:

o: the set of truth-values $\{\mathsf{T},\mathsf{F}\}$;
ι: the set of individuals (a constant universe of discourse);
τ: the set of real numbers (doubling as temporal continuum);
ω: the set of logically possible worlds (the logical space).

Definition 2: (construction)
  (i) *The* variable x *is a* construction *that constructs an object O of the respective type dependently on a valuation v: x v-constructs O.*
  (ii) Trivialization: *Where X is an object whatsoever (an extension, an intension or a* construction*), ^0X is the construction Trivialization. It constructs X without any change in X.*
  (iii) *The* Composition $[X\ Y_1 \ldots Y_m]$ *is the following* construction. *If X v-constructs a function f of type $(\alpha\beta_1 \ldots \beta_m)$, and $Y_1, \ldots, Y_m$ v-construct entities $B_1, \ldots, B_m$ of types $\beta_1, \ldots, \beta_m$, respectively, then the* Composition $[X\ Y_1 \ldots Y_m]$ v-constructs *the value (an entity, if any, of type α) of f on the tuple argument $\langle B_1, \ldots, B_m \rangle$. Otherwise the* Composition $[X\ Y_1 \ldots Y_m]$ *does not v-construct anything and so is v-improper.*
  (iv) *The* Closure $[\lambda x_1 \ldots x_m\ Y]$ *is the following* construction. *Let $x_1, x_2, \ldots, x_m$ be pair-wise distinct variables v-constructing entities of types $\beta_1, \ldots, \beta_m$ and Y a construction v-constructing an α-entity. Then $[\lambda x_1 \ldots x_m\ Y]$ is the* construction λ-Closure *(or* Closure*). It v-constructs the following function f of the type $(\alpha\beta_1 \ldots \beta_m)$. Let $v(B_1/x_1, \ldots, B_m/x_m)$ be a valuation identical with v at least up to assigning objects $B_1/\beta_1, \ldots, B_m/\beta_m$ to variables $x_1, \ldots, x_m$. If Y is $v(B_1/x_1, \ldots, B_m/x_m)$-improper (see iii), then f is undefined on $\langle B_1, \ldots, B_m \rangle$. Otherwise the value of f on $\langle B_1, \ldots, B_m \rangle$ is the α-entity $v(B_1/x_1, \ldots, B_m/x_m)$-constructed by Y.*
  (v) *The* Single Execution ^1X *is the* construction *that either v-constructs the entity v-constructed by X or, if X v-constructs nothing, is v-improper.*
  (vi) *The* Double Execution ^2X *is the following* construction. *Where X is any entity, the* Double Execution ^2X *is v-improper (yielding nothing relative to v) if X is not itself a construction, or if X does not v-construct a construction, or if X v-constructs a v-improper construction. Otherwise, let X v-construct a construction Y and Y v-construct an entity Z: then ^2X v-constructs Z.*
  (vii) *Nothing is a* construction, *unless it so follows from (i) through (vi).*
  □

The definition of the ramified hierarchy of types decomposes into three parts. Firstly, simple types of order 1, which were already defined by Definition 1. Secondly, constructions of order n, and thirdly, types of order $n + 1$.

Definition 3: (ramified hierarchy of types)
T_1 (types of order 1). *See Definition 1.*
C_n (constructions of order n)
- (i) *Let x be a variable ranging over a type of order n. Then x is a* construction of order n over B.
- (ii) *Let X be a member of a type of order n. Then ^0X, ^1X, ^2X are* constructions of order n over B.
- (iii) *Let $X, X_1, \ldots, X_m (m > 0)$ be constructions of order n over B. Then $[X\ X_1 \ldots X_m]$ is a* construction of order n over B.
- (iv) *Let $x_1, \ldots x_m, X (m > 0)$ be constructions of order n over B. Then $[\lambda x_1 \ldots x_m\ X]$ is a* construction of order n over **B**.
- (v) *Nothing is a* construction of order n over B *unless it so follows from* C_n *(i)–(iv)*.

T_{n+1} (types of order $n + 1$). *Let $*_n$ be the collection of all constructions of order n over B. Then*
- (i) $*_n$ *and every type of order n are* types of order $n + 1$.
- (ii) *If $0 < m$ and $\alpha, \beta_1, \ldots, b_m$ are types of order $n + 1$ over B, then $(\alpha\ \beta_1 \ldots \beta_m)$ (see T_1 ii)) is a* type of order $n + 1$ over B.
- (iii) *Nothing is a* type of order $n + 1$ over B *unless it so follows from (i) and (ii).* □

Empirical languages incorporate an element of *contingency* that non-empirical ones lack. Empirical expressions denote *empirical conditions* that may or may not be satisfied at some empirical index of evaluation. Non-empirical languages have no need for an additional category of expressions for empirical conditions. We model these empirical conditions as *possible-world intensions*. Intensions are entities of type $(\beta\omega)$: mappings from possible worlds to an arbitrary type β. The type β is frequently the type of the *chronology* of α-objects, i.e. a mapping of type $(\alpha\tau)$. Thus α-intensions are frequently functions of type $((\alpha\tau)\omega)$, abbreviated as '$\alpha_{\tau\omega}$'. We shall typically say that an index of evaluation is a world/time pair $\langle w, t \rangle$. *Extensional entities* are entities of some type α where $\alpha \neq (\beta\omega)$ for any type β.

Examples of frequently used intensions are: *propositions* of type $o_{\tau\omega}$, *properties of individuals* of type $(o\iota)_{\tau\omega}$, binary *relations-in-intension between individuals* of type $(o\iota\iota)_{\tau\omega}$, *individual offices* of type $\iota_{\tau\omega}$. As for individual offices, they are simply partial functions which, relative to a world/time pair $\langle w, t \rangle$, return at most one individual as value. The notion of office is broader than, say, social role, though social roles like *the pope* and *the King of France* were the original sources of inspiration. Given a $\langle w, t \rangle$, there is a function from *individual offices* to *individuals*. This function is neither a surjection, nor an injection, but a properly partial function, for some offices will go vacant. Given a $\langle w, t \rangle$, there is no function from *individuals* to *individual offices*, for some individual may occupy more than one office. Conversely, it is not given that each individual occupies at least one office. Importantly, the logical traffic does not flow from attributees (individuals) to individual offices, for not every attributee is guaranteed to occupy an office presenting a particular attributee.

Individual offices may be denoted by definite descriptions, but may just as well be denoted by proper names not reducible to definite descriptions. It depends on the linguistic quirks of a particular natural language in which manner a particular office is denoted. For instance, on our analysis of 'Hesperus', 'Phosphorus' these Latin/English names are better off naming two distinct offices (rather than the same individual), whereas 'Prague' is arguably a proper name for Prague, containing no descriptive material. (See Duží et al. (2010, §3.2 'Proper names'.))

Our *explicit intensionalization and temporalization* enables us to encode constructions of possible-world intensions, by means of terms for possible-world variables and times, directly in the logical syntax.[xviii] Where w ranges over ω and t over τ, the following logical form (to be explained below) essentially characterizes the logical syntax of any empirical language:

$$\lambda w \lambda t\, [\ldots w \ldots t \ldots]$$

Logical objects like *truth-functions* and *quantifiers* are extensional: $\wedge$ (conjunction), $\vee$ (disjunction) and $\supset$ (implication) are of type (ooo), and $\neg$ (negation) of type (oo). *Quantifiers* $\forall^\alpha$, $\exists^\alpha$ are type-theoretically polymorphous, total functions of type $(o(o\alpha))$, for an arbitrary type α, defined as follows. The *universal quantifier* $\forall^\alpha$ is a function that associates a class A of α-elements with T if A contains all elements of the type α, otherwise with F. The *existential quantifier* $\exists^\alpha$ is a function that associates a class A of α-elements with T if A is a non-empty class, otherwise with F. Below all type indications will be provided outside the formulae in order not to clutter the notation. Furthermore, 'X/α' means that an object X is (a member) of type α. '$X \to_v \alpha$' means that the type of the object *valuation*-constructed by X is α. We write '$X \to \alpha$' if what is v-constructed does not depend on a

---

[xviii] See Duží et al. (2010, §2.4 'Explicit intensionalization and temporalization') or Jespersen (2005).

valuation v. Throughout, it holds that the variables $w \to_v \omega$ and $t \to_v \tau$. If $C \to_v \alpha_{\tau\omega}$ then the frequently used Composition $[[C\ w]t]$, which is the intensional descent (a.k.a. extensionalization) of the α-intension v-constructed by C, will be encoded as 'C_{wt}'.

When assigning constructions to expressions as their context-invariant meanings, we use a particular *method of semantic analysis*. The method consists in three steps, which are (a) type-theoretical analysis, (b) synthesis, and (c) type-theoretical checking. For illustration, here is the analysis of the sentence

"Mary believes that the Evening Star is a planet"

(a) The types of the objects that receive mention in the sentence are: *Mary*/ι; *Believe**/$(o\iota *_n)_{\tau\omega}$: a relation-in-intension of an individual (a doxastic agent) to a *propositional construction*; *Evening_Star*/$\iota_{\tau\omega}$: an individual office; *Planet*/$(o\iota)_{\tau\omega}$: a property of individuals. *Hyperpropositional* belief, *Believe** (with asterisk) of type $(o\iota *_n)_{\tau\omega}$, contrasts with *propositional* belief, *Believe* (without asterisk) of type $(o o_{\tau\omega})_{\tau\omega}$, which is how possible-world semantics (perhaps skipping the temporal parameter) types propositional attitudes.[xix]

(b) We combine constructions of the objects *ad* (a) in order to construct the proposition of type $o_{\tau\omega}$ denoted by the sentence. Here is how. First, since a property of individuals is not a type-theoretically proper object to predicate of an individual office, we must first extensionalize both intensions: $[[^0Planet\ w]\ t] \to_v (o\iota)$, $[[^0Evening\_Star\ w]\ t] \to_v \iota$, or '$^0Planet_{wt}$' and '$^0Evening\_Star_{wt}$' for short. Now the Composition

---

[xix] So the type-theoretic difference between *propositional* and *hyperpropositional* attitudes is the difference between $(o o_{\tau\omega})_{\tau\omega}$ and $(o\iota *_n)_{\tau\omega}$. One major philosophical difference is that the former are used to model *implicit* attitudes and the latter to model *explicit* attitudes, which translates into the logical difference between those attitudes that are *deductively closed* and those that are not. If a knows implicitly/propositionally that the Morning Star is a planet then a knows implicitly/explicitly every proposition entailed by the proposition that the Morning Star is a planet. Implicit knowledge notoriously leads to one form or other of logical omniscience (arguably *the* problem plaguing epistemic logic). If a knows*, explicitly/hyperpropositionally, that the Morning Star is a planet then much less is entailed, depending on what sort of logical intelligence in the shape of command of rules of inference has been assigned to a. (See Duží et al. (2010, §5.1.5 'Epistemic closure and inferable knowledge') for the notion of *inferable* knowledge, which charts the amount of explicit knowledge a would be able to harvest if a were to apply his entire logical intelligence maximally to his existing stock of explicit knowledge.) In this paper our concern is not *why* hyperpropositional attitudes *de re* would or could or should be attributed to an agent, but rather how to obtain a particular conclusion from them.

[$^0Planet_{wt}$ $^0Evening\_Star_{wt}$] v-constructs T or F according as the individual that occupies the office of Evening Star at a given $\langle w, t\rangle$-pair of evaluation belongs to the class of planets at the same $\langle w, t\rangle$-pair.[xx] To obtain the proposition that the Evening Star is a planet we must abstract over the values of the variables w, t:

$$\lambda w \lambda t\ [^0Planet_{wt}\ ^0Evening\_Star_{wt}]$$

This is the predication of the property of being a planet of the occupant of the office of Evening Star.

Since an empirical hyperpropositional attitude is always a relation to a construction constructing a possible-world proposition, we model Mary's act of believing as the Composition

$$[^0Believe^*_{wt}\ ^0Mary\ ^0[\lambda w \lambda t\ [^0Planet_{wt}\ ^0Evening\_Star_{wt}]]]$$

In other words, the nested Closure constructing the proposition that the Evening Star is a planet must be Trivialized, as *per* $^0[\lambda w \lambda t [^0Planet_{wt}\ ^0Evening\_Star_{wt}]]$. This Composition constructs T or F, according as Mary believes* at $\langle w, t\rangle$ that the Evening Star is a planet. Yet what is denoted by the sentence does not depend on contingent facts like Mary's being related or not to a particular hyperproposition. Thus we must again abstract over the values of w, t in order to construct the proposition denoted by the sentence (cf. explicit intensionalization and temporalization):

$$\lambda w \lambda t\ [^0Believe^*_{wt}\ ^0Mary\ ^0[\lambda w \lambda t\ [^0Planet_{wt}\ ^0Evening\_Star_{wt}]]]$$

(c) We check whether the particular constituents of the above Closure are combined in compliance with the type-theoretical rules. To this end we draw a type-theoretical tree. In the interest of economy, we omit the steps of checking extensionalizations like $[^0Planet\ w] \to_v ((o\iota)\tau)$ and $[[^0Planet\ w]t] \to_v (o\iota)$. Thus we directly draw $^0Planet_{wt} \to_v (o\iota)$. Moreover, instead of two steps of intensionalization, e.g. $\lambda t\ [^0Planet_{wt}\ ^0Evening\_Star_{wt}] \to_v (o\tau)$ and $\lambda w \lambda t\ [^0Planet_{wt}\ ^0Evening\_Star_{wt}] \to ((o\tau)\omega)$, we will directly draw $\lambda w \lambda t\ [^0Planet_{wt}\ ^0Evening\_Star_{wt}] \to o_{\tau\omega}$. The type-theoretically annotated tree is depicted by Figure 1.

[xx] See Duží et al. (2010, §2.4.2 'Predication as functional application') for details.

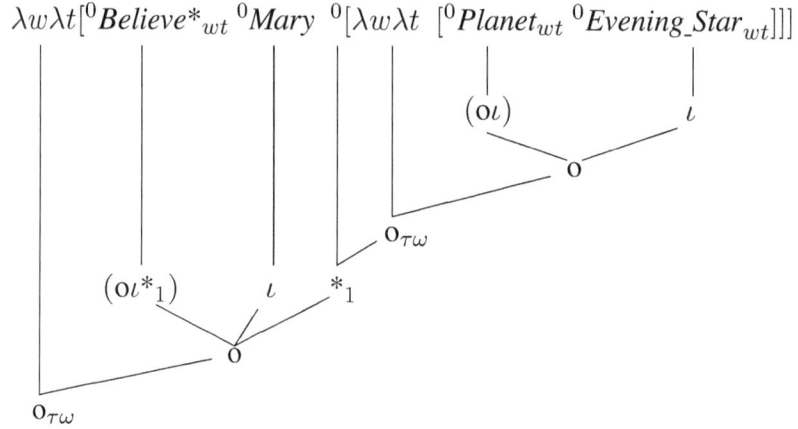

Figure 1. Type-theoretical tree

The above example illustrates also the difference between a *sub-construction simpliciter* and a *constituent sub-construction*, i.e. between a sub-construction which is *mentioned* as a functional argument, thereby displaying itself, and a sub-construction which is *used* to construct an object different from the sub-construction. The former case constitutes a hyperintensional context, the latter an extensional/intensional context. In our example the sub-construction that is mentioned within the whole analysis is the Closure $[\lambda w \lambda t\ [^0Planet_{wt}\ ^0Evening\_Star_{wt}]]$. This is so because this hyperproposition is the second argument of the function $Believe^*_{wt}$, the first argument being *Mary*. The hyperproposition is mentioned by the constituent $^0[\lambda w \lambda t\ [^0Planet_{wt}\ ^0Evening\_Star_{wt}]]$, and thus the mentioned Closure and all its sub-constructions occur hyperintensionally.

Figure 2 illustrates using/mentioning entities at the three different levels.

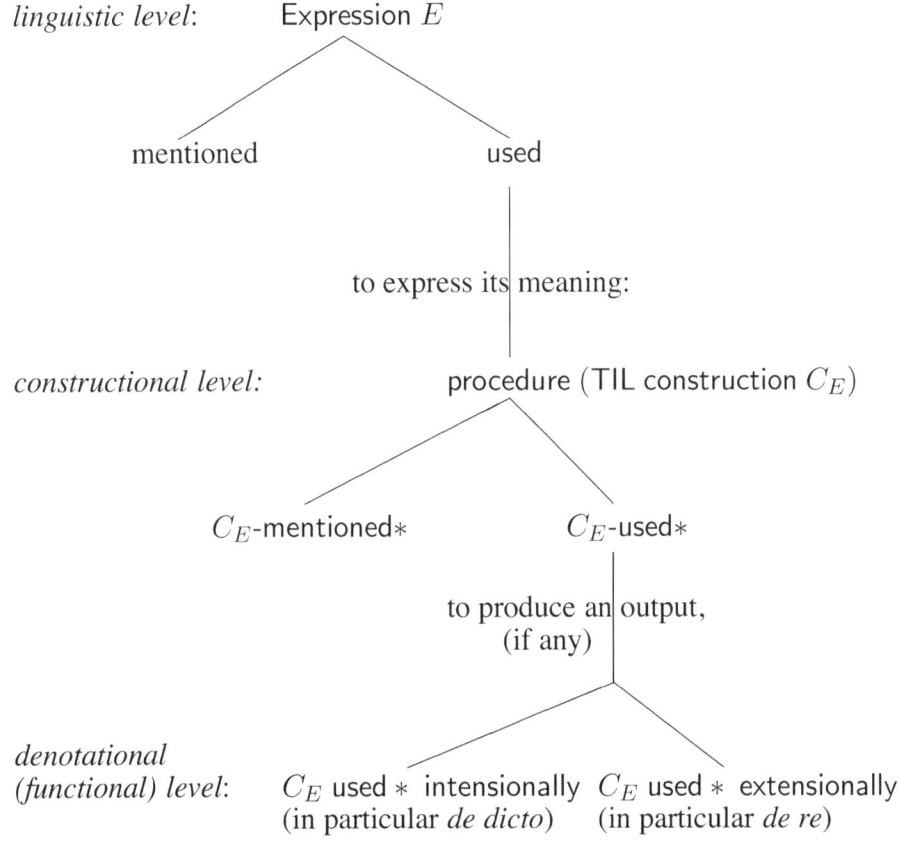

Figure 2. Using/mentioning entities

The three kinds of context are defined in Duží et al. (2010, §2.6). Here we need only the definition of the distinction between using and mentioning constructions:

Definition 4: (construction mentioned vs. used as a constituent) *Let C be a construction and D a sub-construction of C.*
  (i) *If D is identical to C (i.e., $^0C = {}^0D$) then the occurrence of D is* used as a constituent *of C.*
  (ii) *If C is identical to $[X_1\ X_2 \ldots X_m]$ and D is identical to one of the constructions $X_1, X_2, \ldots, X_m$, then the occurrence of D is* used as a constituent *of C.*
  (iii) *If C is identical to $[\lambda x_1 \ldots x_m\ X]$ and D is identical to X, then the occurrence of D is* used as a constituent *of C.*

(iv) *If C is identical to ^1X and D is identical to X, then the occurrence of D is* used *as a constituent of C.*
(v) *If C is identical to ^2X and D is identical to X, or ^0D occurs as a constituent of X and this occurrence of D occurs as a constituent of Y v-constructed by X, then the occurrence of D is* used *as a constituent of C.*
(vi) *If an occurrence of D is* used *as a constituent of an occurrence of C' and this occurrence of C' is* used *as a constituent of C, then the occurrence of D is* used *as a constituent of C.*
(vii) *If an occurrence of a sub-construction D of C is* not *used as a constituent of C then the occurrence of D is* mentioned *in C.*
(viii) *No occurrence of a sub-construction D of C is* used/mentioned *in C unless it so follows from (i)–(vii).* □

Remark. In theory, a construction may be mentioned by another kind of construction than Trivialization; but in this paper we limit ourselves to Trivialization. Thus the Trivialization $^0[\lambda w \lambda t\ [^0Planet_{wt}\ ^0Evening\_Star_{wt}]]$ *mentions* the Closure $[\lambda w \lambda t\ [^0Planet_{wt}\ ^0Evening\_Star_{wt}]]$ and all the constituents of this Closure.[xxi]

Traditionally, the validity of quantifying-in has been fielded as a logical criterion for distinguishing (i) extensional/ transparent/'relational' (Quine) contexts from (ii) non-extensional/opaque/'notional' (Quine) contexts. The idea is that extensional (etc.) contexts are those that validate quantifying-in. And conversely, if a context resists quantifying-in, it is deemed to be in violation of one or more of the laws of extensional logic and as eluding full logical analysis. What we are saying is that also intensional and hyperintensional contexts may be quantified into, but that the feasibility of doing so presupposes that it be done within an extensional logic of hyperintensional contexts. Deploying a non-extensional logic of hyperintensions in order to quantify into hyperintensional contexts would, indeed, be a non-starter, generating opacity and thereby making hyperintensional attitude contexts logically intractable: it would be left logically lawless which terms (or meanings, as we would have it) could be substituted for which ones inside an attitude report. However, whether one accepts quantifying into (hyper-) intensional contexts or wants to restrict quantification to extensional contexts, like "Mary is happy", the logical question still remains which sort of context validates which sort of quantifying-in. Tichý issues in (1986, p. 256; 2004, p. 654) a warning against inter-defining the notion of extensional context and the validity of the rules of substitution of co-referring terms and existential

---

[xxi] The use/mention distinction normally applies only to *words*; in TIL it applies also to the *meanings* of words (i.e., constructions). See Duží et al. (2010, §2.6 'Three kinds of context').

generalization on pain of circularity (where TIL and Quine agree on the use of 'co-referential'):

> Q: When is a context extensional?
> A: A context is extensional if it validates (i) the rule of substitution of co-referential terms and (ii) the rule of existential generalization.
> Q: And when are (i), (ii) valid?
> A: Those two rules are valid when applied to extensional contexts.

We steer clear of the circle by defining extensionality for (i) *hyperintensions* presenting functions, for (ii) *functions* (including possible-world intensions), and for (iii) *functional values*. These three levels are squared off with three kinds of context:

(i′) *hyperintensional contexts*, in which a hyperintension is not *used* to present an object, but is itself *mentioned* as functional argument (though a hyperintension of one order higher needs to be used to mention this lower-order construction);

(ii′) *intensional contexts*, in which a hyperintension is *used* to present a function without presenting a particular value of the function (moreover, the hyperintension does not occur within another hyperintensional context);

(iii′) *extensional contexts*, in which a hyperintension is *used* to produce a particular value of the function at a given argument (moreover, the hyperintension does not occur within another intensional or hyperintensional context).

The leading idea is that transparency in hyperintensional contexts requires identity of senses (hence pairs of synonymous words), while transparency in intensional contexts requires only equivalence of senses (hence pairs of co-denoting words).

If a construction C occurs mentioned in D, then all its sub-constructions (including C) occur *hyperintensionally* in D. Moreover, all the variables occurring within such a *hyperintensional context* are ^{0}bound. Thus in TIL we have two ways of binding variables: λ-binding (as in any λ-calculus) and ^{0}binding (which is unique to TIL). The latter is dominant over the former, because a higher-order context is dominant over a lower-order one. Thus we define:

Definition 5: (free and bound variables) *Let C be a construction with at least one occurrence of a variable ζ.*

(i) *Let C be ζ. Then the occurrence of ζ in C is free.*

(ii) *Let C be ^0X. Then every* occurrence of ζ in C is ^{0}bound *('Trivialization-bound')*.
(iii) *Let C be $[\lambda x_1 \ldots x_n\ Y]$. Any* occurrence of ζ in Y *that is one of $x_i, 1 \leq i \leq n$, is λ-bound in C unless it is ^{0}bound in Y. Any* occurrence of ζ in Y *that is neither ^{0}bound nor λ-bound in Y is* free *in C.*
(iv) *Let C be $[X\ X_1 \ldots X_n]$. Any* occurrence of ζ *that is* free, ^{0}bound, λ-bound *in one of $X, X_1, \ldots, X_n$ is, respectively,* free, ^{0}bound, λ-bound in C.
(v) *Let C be ^1X. Then any* occurrence of ζ *that is* free, ^{0}bound, λ-bound *in X is, respectively,* free, ^{0}bound, λ-bound in C.
(vi) *Let C be ^2X. Then any* occurrence of ζ *that is* free, λ-bound *in a constituent of C is, respectively,* free, λ-bound *in C. If an occurrence of ζ is ^{0}bound in a constituent ^0D of C and this occurrence of D is a constituent of X' v-constructed by X, then if the occurrence of ζ is* free, λ-bound *in D it is* free, λ-bound *in C. Otherwise, any other occurrence of ζ in C is ^{0}bound in C.*
(vii) *An occurrence of ζ is* free, λ-bound, ^{0}bound *in C only due to (i)–(vi).*

A construction with at least one occurrence of a free variable is an open construction. A construction without any free variables is a closed construction.
□

The next notion we need to define is that of *synonymy*. Our notion of synonymy is defined in virtue of *procedural isomorphism*. Only procedurally isomorphic constructions, to the exclusion of merely equivalent ones, are substitutable *salva veritate* in hyperintensional contexts. The term 'procedural isomorphism' is a nod to Carnap's *intensional isomorphism* and Church's *synonymous isomorphism*. Church's Alternatives (0) and (1) leave room for additional Alternatives in between. One would be Alternative (1/2), another Alternative (3/4). The former includes α- and η-conversion while the latter adds a restricted form of β-conversion.[xxii] If we must choose, we would prefer Alternative (3/4) to soak up those differences between β-transformations that lack natural-language counterparts. The exact calibration of procedural isomorphism is less pressing here. What is important is that we should have a formal theory of synonymy and that, since we decide to include some form of β-conversion in the mix, we should have a means to block instances of invalid β-conversion.

One reason for excluding unrestricted β-conversion is the well-known fact that β-conversion is not an equivalent transformation in logics boasting

---

[xxii] For Alternative (1/2), see Jespersen (2010).

partial functions, such as TIL. Another reason is that occasionally even β-equivalent constructions have different natural-language counterparts; witness the difference between attitude reports *de dicto* vs. *de re*. Thus, the difference between "a believes that b is happy" and "b is believed by a to be happy" is just the difference between β-equivalent meanings. The former (*de dicto*) receives the possible-world analysis

$$\lambda w \lambda t \, [^0 Believe_{wt} \, a \, \lambda w \lambda t \, [^0 Happy_{wt} \, b]]$$

while the latter (*de re*) receives the possible-world analysis

$$\lambda w \lambda t \, [\lambda x [^0 Believe_{wt} \, a \, \lambda w \lambda t \, [^0 Happy_{wt} \, x]] b]$$

Types: $Happy/(o\iota)_{\tau\omega}$; $x \to_v \iota$; $a, b \to \iota$.

Note that attitudes *de dicto* and *de re* are in general *not* equivalent. The following two sentences denote different propositions:

"a believes that the pope is happy";
"The pope is believed by a to be happy"

Their propositional analyses are ($Pope/\iota_{\tau\omega}$):

$$\lambda w \lambda t \, [^0 Believe_{wt} \, a \, \lambda w \lambda t \, [^0 Happy_{wt} \, {}^0 Pope_{wt}]];$$

$$\lambda w \lambda t \, [\lambda x [^0 Believe_{wt} \, a \, \lambda w \lambda t \, [^0 Happy_{wt} \, x]] {}^0 Pope_{wt}]$$

While the former Closure constructs a proposition that may well be *true* even when there is no pope (the papal office going vacant), the proposition constructed by the latter Closure will have a truth-value *gap* at such a world/time pair. This is because at such a world/time pair at which the office is vacant the Composition $^0 Pope_{wt}$ is v-improper. Due to compositionality, the whole Composition $[\lambda x [^0 Believe_{wt} \, a \, \lambda w \lambda t \, [^0 Happy_{wt} \, x]] {}^0 Pope_{wt}]$ comes out v-improper and so does not v-construct what it is typed to construct, namely a truth-value.

The *restricted* version of *equivalent* β-conversion we have in mind consists in substituting free variables for λ-bound variables of the same type, and will be called β_r-*conversion*. For instance, we see little reason to differentiate semantically or logically between "b is believed by a to be happy" and "b

has the property of being believed by a to be happy".[xxiii] The latter sentence expresses

$$\lambda w \lambda t \, [\lambda w' \lambda t' \lambda x [^0 Believe_{w't'} \, a \, \lambda w \lambda t \, [^0 Happy_{wt} \, x]]_{wt} \, b]$$

This is merely a β_r-expanded form of

$$\lambda w \lambda t \, [\lambda x [^0 Believe_{wt} \, a \, \lambda w \lambda t \, [^0 Happy_{wt} \, x]] \, b]$$

Thus we define:

Definition 6: (procedurally isomorphic constructions: (A3/4)) *Let C, D be constructions. Then C, D are α-equivalent iff they differ at most by deploying different λ-bound variables. C, D are η-equivalent iff one arises from the other by η-reduction or η-expansion. C, D are β_r-equivalent iff one arises from the other by β_r-reduction or β_r-expansion. C, D are procedurally isomorphic, denoted '$^0 C \approx {}^0 D$', $\approx\!/(o*_n *_n)$, iff there are closed constructions $C_1, \ldots, C_m, m \geq 1$, such that $^0 C = {}^0 C_1, {}^0 D = {}^0 C_m$, and all $C_i, C_{i+1} (1 \leq i < m)$ are either α-, η- or β_r-equivalent.* □

Remark. The four constructions $^0 Prime$, $\lambda x [^0 Prime \, x]$, $\lambda y [^0 Prime \, y]$, $\lambda z [\lambda x [^0 Prime \, x] z]$ are procedurally isomorphic, while $\lambda x [[^0 Card \, \lambda y [^0 Divide \, y \, x]] = {}^0 2]$ is only equivalent to them; it constructs the set of primes, to be sure, but does so in a non-isomorphic manner. (*Types*: $x, y, z \to \nu$, the type of natural numbers; $Card/(\nu(o\nu))$: the number of elements of a final set of natural numbers; $Divide/(o\nu\nu)$: the relation of x being divisible by y.)

Remark. Given a set of procedurally isomorphic constructions, we privilege the element that is in *normal form* to serve as a representative of the set. That element is the simplest one in the set and is defined as the alphabetically first, non-η-reducible construction. Thus, of the four constructions mentioned in

---

[xxiii] This is not to say we see no reason at all not to differentiate. For instance, if the believer is a self-assured nominalist then he may protest that while he does believe that a is happy he does not believe that a has any properties. Or it could be argued that one thing is to believe that a is happy and another is to believe that a has the property of being happy, because the latter at least appears to presuppose that the believer have the additional conceptual resources to master the notion of *property*. Furthermore, Soames (2010, Ch. 2) takes issue with Frege's claim, in 'Über Begriff und Gegenstand', that "das Prädikat 'fallend unter den Begriff *Mensch*' [dasselbe bedeutet wie] 'ein Mensch'". This would namely mean that "Jesus ist ein Mensch" and "Jesus fällt unter den Begriff *Mensch*" would express the same Thought, i.e. be synonymous, i.e. share the same logical structure, which is hardly true of these two sentences. Further research is required. See Duží et al. (2010) and also Duží and Jespersen (2012) for discussion.

the previous Remark, ^0Prime is the one in normal form. See Duží et al. (2010, §2.2.1 'Concepts and synonymy', esp. p. 155). When in this paper we speak of *the* construction of something we intend a construction in normal form.

Since merely co-referential expressions can be substituted *salva veritate* only in extensional contexts, merely co-denotational or equivalent expressions in intensional and extensional contexts, and synonymous expressions in all contexts, we define:

Definition 7: (synonymous, equivalent and co-referential expressions) *Expressions E_1 and E_2 are* synonymous *if their meanings are procedurally isomorphic. Expressions E_1 and E_2 are* equivalent *(or* co-denoting*) if their meanings v-construct one and the same object for every valuation v. Finally, empirical expressions E_1 and E_2 are* co-referential *if their meanings construct intensions whose values are the same at the $\langle w, t \rangle$ of evaluation.*
□

To summarize, the relevant tenets of TIL are these five:

1. (*hyperintensional syntax*) its syntax explicitly mentions hyperintensions;
2. (*anti-contextualism*) a non-indexical term's sense and denotation remain constant for *all* contexts;
3. (*mention versus use*) what is context-sensitive is whether a hyperintension occurs *mentioned* or *used* in a given context: if mentioned, it itself is operated on; if used, what it yields is operated on;
4. (*ramified type hierarchy*) the ramified type hierarchy enables higher-order hyperintensions to present lower-order hyperintensions (which in turn enables quantifying into hyperintensional contexts of any order);
5. (*mode of presentation*) it displays in logical terms how n-order constructions construct n-1-order constructions and first-order objects, by defining the various ways in which various constructions construct objects of various types.

Our neo-Fregean semantic schema, which applies to all contexts, is this:

Transparent quantification into hyperpropositional contexts *de re*

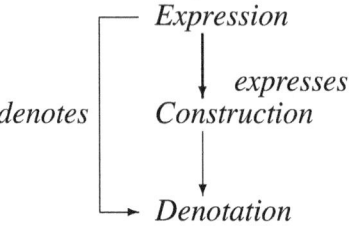

Figure 3. Semantic schema

The most important relation in this schema is between an expression and its meaning (a construction). We can investigate *a priori* what (if anything) a construction constructs and what is entailed by it. Once a construction is explicitly given as a result of logical analysis, the entity (if any) it constructs is already implicitly given, whereas it requires inquiry *a posteriori* to establish the reference of an empirical term at a given world/time pair. As a limiting case, the logical analysis may reveal that the construction fails to construct anything because it is improper. And if the construction is not improper, the denotation can be either a first-order object (i.e. a non-construction) or a lower-order construction. Intensional constructions (constructions of objects of type $(\beta\omega)$) are always proper, since they always construct an intension (including degenerate ones, which return no value at all or always the same value). In linguistic terms, every word whose sense is an intensional construction has a denotation, but will lack a reference at some or all $\langle w, t \rangle$ pairs, in case its denotation (a partial function) fails to return a value. This applies to, *inter alia*, 'The pope', 'The Morning Star' and 'The Evening Star'.

3. *Hyperintensional and Intensional Attitudes* de dicto *and* de re

We begin by explaining how we understand the distinction between attitudes *de dicto* and *de re*. The philosophical difference between attitudes *de dicto* and *de re* is pivoted on an *inversion of perspective*: an attribution *de dicto* reproduces the attributee's perspective; an attribution *de re*, the attributer's. Let $F/\iota_{\tau\omega}$ be an office and $G/(o\iota)_{\tau\omega}$ a property. Consider then the sentence

"*a* believes that the F is a G"

Let a's belief be an intensional attitude; $Believe/(o\iota o_{\tau\omega})_{\tau\omega}$. The meaning of the definite description 'the F' occurs with supposition *de dicto*. The reason is this: a is related to the *whole* proposition that the F is a G. Hence

a's attitude depends not only on the actual and current truth-value of this proposition but on all its values. Consequently, a's attitude concerns also the entire office F and not only its actual and current value. Even if there is no such value, a may well believe that the F is a G. The analysis of the sentence is this Closure:

$$\lambda w \lambda t \, [^0Believe_{wt} \, a \, [\lambda w^* \lambda t^* [^0 G_{w^*t^*} \, {}^0 F_{w^*t^*}]]]$$

Remark. *-superscripted letters for w, t variables represent the attributee's perspective, while those without superscript represent the attributer's. In the interest of full generality, throughout the rest of this paper we will use $a \to \iota$ as an arbitrary construction of an individual agent. Derivatively, 'a' will be an arbitrary name for an arbitrary individual.

In case a's belief is a hyperintensional attitude, $Believe*/(o\iota^*_n)_{\tau\omega}$, then a is related to a hyperproposition, i.e. a propositional construction, and the sentence encodes this construction:

$$\lambda w \lambda t \, [^0Believe^*_{wt} \, a \, {}^0[\lambda w^* \lambda t^* [^0 G_{w^*t^*} \, {}^0 F_{w^*t^*}]]]$$

As before, a's attitude does not concern only the value of 'the F' in the actual world at the present moment. Now the hyperproposition $[\lambda w^* \lambda t^* [^0 G_{w^*t^*} \, {}^0 F_{w^*t^*}]]$ is itself the object of a's belief. Regardless of whether there is a value of the office F, the whole office has a role to play, as it is embedded within the attributee's perspective $\langle w^*, t^* \rangle$.

One worry, though, that one may have concerning attitudes *de dicto*, both intensional and hyperintensional, is the following. Constructions (usually Trivializations) of individual offices occur as part of the hyperpropositions that either construct a possible-world proposition or are themselves constructed to figure as complements of attitudes. Does this demand of the attributees that they possess a notion of individual office? The worry is that this may be asking too much, as it would require attributees to have conceptual resources they may actually, and reasonably, lack. Our position is this. If an attributee lacks any concept of intensions in their personal conceptual repertoire then indeed no attribution of an intension-involving attitude is an option. Such an attribution would fail to respect the attributee's perspective, whatever alternative perspective that might happen to be, as the attribution would 'hyper-intellectualize' the attributee's actual attitude.[xxiv] To have intensions in one's personal conceptual repertoire means comprehending the intensional character of some entity, e.g. the Evening Star. Its intensional character amounts in essence to the fact that it is not the numerically same individual that is the Evening Star in all possible empirical circumstances (all pairs of worlds and times), whenever a celestial body happens to be the Evening Star. But suppose the designated attributee uses 'The Evening Star' as a name for the *individual* Venus, because Venus is the actual Evening Star, while the designated attributer uses 'The Evening Star' as a name for the *individual office* of Evening Star. Then the consequence, relative to our framework, is that attributer and attributee speak at cross purposes, 'The Evening Star' being an instance of homonymy. The designated attributer is, therefore, not in a position to make a faithful attribution of an attitude *de dicto* to the designated attributee. Our framework observes the constraint that attributer and attributee must find themselves within the same *conceptual system* (see Duží et al. (2010, §2.2.3 'Conceptual system'). This involves according the same logical character to the Evening Star, be it as an individual or as an individual office, hence according the same semantic character to 'The Evening Star', as a name for an individual and a name for an individual office, respectively.

The situation is completely different with attitudes *de re*. To explain the nature of the attitude clearly, we use the passive form:

"The F is believed by a to be a G"

Now the attributer uses the office F as a pointer to a particular individual. The attributer might just as well have used any other office also occupied by that individual to single out the individual. For the proposition denoted by the sentence to be true, there must be a specific individual to whom a is related by believing that this individual has the property of being a G. This does not, however, mean that a is aware of the fact that this individual occupies the office F. There are namely two *independent* questions: "*Who* holds the office F" and "*What* does a think of that individual?" The attributer, not the attributee, needs to make the connection between office and occupant.

Now for the analysis of hyperpropositional attitudes *de re*. As above, let *Believe**/$(o\iota^*_n)_{\tau\omega}$ be a relation-in-intension of an individual agent a to a

---

[xxiv] We are indebted to a referee for the apt phrase 'hyper-intellectualize' and for urging us to clarify our stance on the topic under what circumstances attributees must possess a notion of individual office.

hyperproposition. Then the active variant of a hyperpropositional attitude *de re* is this:

"a believes* of the F that *it* is a G"

The embedded clause "*it* is a G" contains the anaphoric reference 'it' to its antecedent 'the F'.[xxv] The meaning of this clause is an *open* construction with a free variable *it* $\rightarrow_v \iota$: $\lambda w \lambda t \ [^0 G_{wt} \ it]$. Recall that our assignment of constructions to expressions as their meaning is context-*in*variant. Hence the meaning of this clause is the same in all contexts, whether extensional, intensional or hyperintensional.

Its meaning is any construction procedurally isomorphic with $\lambda w \lambda t \ [^0 G_{wt} \ it]$, e.g. $\lambda w^* \lambda t^* \ [^0 G_{w^* t^*} \ it]$. The latter is an α-equivalent variant of the former with superscripted variables w^*, t^*, in order to represent the attributee's perspective. The attributer wants to express the fact that the individual who is the value of *it* is the holder of F. If F goes vacant, then there is no such holder and the proposition denoted by the sentence has a truth-value gap. On the other hand, if there is a holder of F, we must *pre-process* the Closure $\lambda w \lambda t \ [^0 G_{wt} \ it]$ in such a way that we substitute a construction of the holder of F (if any) for the variable *it* in the Closure. To this end we apply a *substitution technique* using the function Sub. Sub is of the polymorphous type $(*_n *_n *_n *_n)$ and operates on constructions in the following way. Let X, Y, Z be constructions of order n. Then Sub is a mapping which, when applied to $\langle X, Y, Z \rangle$, returns the construction that is the result of correctly substituting X for Y in Z. A correct substitution is one that does not make any variable occurring free in X bound in the resulting construction (no 'collision'). For illustration, the Composition $[^0 Sub \ ^{00}1 \ ^0 x \ ^0[^0\!> x \ ^0 0]]$ constructs the result of substituting $^0 1$ for x into $[^0\!> x \ ^0 0]$, which is the Composition $[^0\!> \ ^0 1 \ ^0 0]$. Therefore, the Composition $[^0 Sub \ ^{00}1 \ ^0 x \ ^0[^0\!> x \ ^0 0]]$ is equivalent to $^0[^0\!> \ ^0 1 \ ^0 0]$, both constructing the Composition $[^0\!> \ ^0 1 \ ^0 0]$ that constructs T.

Another polymorphous function we need when applying this substitution method is $Tr/(*_n \ \alpha)$ defined as follows.[xxvi] Let α be a type of order n, o an object of type α. Then Tr is a function which, when applied to o, returns the Trivialization of o. There is an essential difference between the *construction* Trivialization and the *function* Tr. For instance, whereas the Trivialization

---

[xxv] For our method of the analysis of sentences with anaphoric references, see Duží et al. (2010, §5.3 'Quantifying in').

[xxvi] Tichý introduces Sub in (1988, p. 75) and Tr in (*ibid.*, p. 68), where Tr is typed to take natural numbers to their respective Trivialization. Tr is easily generalized as a polymorphous function, however.

$^0 3$ constructs the number 3, the Composition $[^0 Tr\ ^0 3]$ constructs the Trivialization $^0 3$. Whereas the Trivialization $^0 x$ ^{0}binds the variable x and constructs just x, the variable x is free in the Composition $[^0 Tr\ x]$, which v-constructs the Trivialization of the number that v assigns to x. Thus, $[^0 Tr\ x]\ v(2/x)$-constructs the construction $^0 2$. To illustrate the application of *Sub* and *Tr*, consider the schematic Composition $[^0 Sub\ [^0 Tr\ ^0 A_{wt}]\ ^0 y\ ^0[\ldots y \ldots]]$, where $A/\iota_{\tau\omega}$; $y \to_v \iota$; b/ι. This Composition either v-constructs the Composition $[\ldots ^0 b \ldots]$, in case $^0 A_{wt}$ v-constructs b, or is v-improper, in case $^0 A_{wt}$ is v-improper, the individual role A going vacant at $\langle w, t \rangle$. In order to obtain the product of the substitution result, if any, we must execute the resulting Composition. To this end we apply *Double Execution*: $^2[^0 Sub\ [^0 Tr\ ^0 A_{wt}]\ ^0 y\ ^0[\ldots y \ldots]]$.

In our case we need to substitute the Trivialization of the individual v-constructed by $^0 F_{wt}$ for the variable *it* into the Closure $\lambda w^* \lambda t^*\ [^0 G_{w^* t^*}\ it]$. Thus we get

$$[^0 Sub\ [^0 Tr\ ^0 F_{wt}]\ ^0 it\ ^0[\lambda w^* \lambda t^*\ [^0 G_{w^* t^*}\ it]]]$$

If $^0 F_{wt}$ is v-improper (i.e., F is vacant at $\langle w, t \rangle$), then due to compositionality (cf. Definition 2. iii), the whole Composition is v-improper. Let $^0 F_{wt}$ v-construct the individual b. Then the result of the substitution is the Closure $[\lambda w^* \lambda t^*\ [^0 G_{w^* t^*}\ ^0 b]]$. Since we analyze *hyper*propositional attitude, the agent a is related to this very Closure. Hence the analysis of "a believes* of the F that *it* is a G" is this Closure:

$$\lambda w \lambda t\ [^0 Believe^*_{wt}\ a\ [^0 Sub\ [^0 Tr\ ^0 F_{wt}]\ ^0 it\ ^0[\lambda w^* \lambda t^*\ [^0 G_{w^* t^*}\ it]]]]$$

The truth-value of this proposition at a given $\langle w, t \rangle$-pair of evaluation depends on the holder of the office at $\langle w, t \rangle$; it is irrelevant who occupies it at worlds/times other than $\langle w, t \rangle$. We say that the meaning of 'the F', i.e. $^0 F$, occurs with *de re* supposition here. In this case *the two de re principles* are valid. They are (i) the principle of *existential presupposition* and (ii) the principle of *substitution of co-referential* expressions. It is not only entailed but also *presupposed* that the F exists, which means that the office F is occupied at a given $\langle w, t \rangle$. For, if the office goes vacant then for the same reason also the negated sentence "a does *not* believe* of the F that *it* is a G" denotes a proposition with a truth-value gap. Hence, in order that the denoted proposition have *any* truth-value, the office F must be occupied.

As for the substitution principle, if the office succeeds in picking out an individual b, then we can validly infer that b is believed* by a to be a G.

And if this individual happens to occupy another office $H/\iota_{\tau\omega}$, then we can validly infer that the H is believed* to be a G. We have got the following *valid* argument, based on the principle of predication *de re*, which is derived from the principle of substitution of co-referential terms:

$$\lambda w \lambda t \, [^0Believe^*_{wt} \, a \, [^0Sub \, [^0Tr \, {}^0F_{wt}] \, {}^0it \, {}^0[\lambda w^* \lambda t^* \, [^0G_{w^*t^*} \, it]]]]$$
$$\lambda w \lambda t \, [^0F_{wt} = {}^0H_{wt}]$$
$$\overline{\lambda w \lambda t \, [^0Believe^*_{wt} \, a \, [^0Sub \, [^0Tr \, {}^0H_{wt}] \, {}^0it \, {}^0[\lambda w^* \lambda t^* \, [^0G_{w^*t^*} \, it]]]]}$$

The rationale informing the principle of predication *de re* is that if two offices are co-occupied at $\langle w, t \rangle$ then what, at $\langle w, t \rangle$, is predicated of the occupant of one office is *eo ipso* what is predicated, at $\langle w, t \rangle$, of the occupant of the other office.[xxvii]

The *passive* variant of the hyperpropositional attitude *de re* is phrased in this manner:

"The F is believed* by a to be a G"

The property of being believed* by a to be a G is ascribed to the holder of F (if any). In order to construct that property, we must again apply the substitution technique. The reason is this. The seemingly straightforward construction of the property — the Closure $\lambda w \lambda t \, \lambda x [^0Believe^*_{wt} \, a \, {}^0[\lambda w^* \lambda t^* \, [^0G_{w^*t^*} \, x]]]$ — is *not* correct. The variable x occurs within the scope of a Trivialization in the Closure $[\lambda w^* \lambda t^* \, [^0G_{w^*t^*} \, x]]$, because a is related to the *construction* of a proposition rather than the proposition so constructed. Hence x occurs ^{0}bound, which amounts to being hyperintensionally mentioned by the Trivialization, and so x is not amenable to a direct logical operation like λ-binding. As already mentioned, ^{0}binding, which raises a context to the hyperintensional level, is dominant over λ-binding, which creates a lower-level intensional context. The substitution technique yields the correct construction of the property:

$$\lambda w \lambda t \, [\lambda x [^0Believe^*_{wt} \, a \, [^0Sub \, [^0Tr \, x] \, {}^0x \, {}^0[\lambda w^* \lambda t^* \, [^0G_{w^*t^*} \, x]]]]]$$

We now need to apply this property to the holder of F. Hence, we extensionalize the property (by β_r-reduction of the above Closure) and Compose the

---

[xxvii] See Duží et al. (2010, p. 123), the *rule of substitution of v-congruent constructions* (*ibid.*, p. 124) and the *extensional rule of substitution* (*ibid.*, p. 274).

result with $^0F_{wt}$. The resulting analysis of the passive *de re* variant becomes

$$\lambda w \lambda t\, [\lambda x [^0Believe*_{wt}\, a\, [^0Sub\, [^0Tr\, x]\, ^0x\, ^0[\lambda w^*\lambda t^*\, [^0G_{w^*t^*}\, x]]]]\, ^0F_{wt}]$$

Next we generalize the results to intensional attitudes *de re*. Let *Believe*/$(o\iota o_{\tau\omega})_{\tau\omega}$ be a propositional attitude, as above. The critical difference between intensional and hyperintensional attitudes *de re* consists in the presence or absence, respectively, of Double Execution. The analysis of the active form "*a* believes of the *F* that *it* is a *G*" is as above, with one difference. Let $^0F_{wt}$ *v-construct* an individual *b*. Then the result of the Composition $[^0Sub\, [^0Tr\, ^0F_{wt}]\, ^0it\, ^0[\lambda w^*\lambda t^*\, [^0G_{w^*t^*}\, it]]]$ is the *Closure* $\lambda w^*\lambda t^*\, [^0G_{w^*t^*}\, ^0b]$. But this time *a* is related to the *proposition* constructed by this Closure. Thus we have to execute the Closure to obtain what it constructs. Enter Double Execution (boldfaced):

$$\lambda w \lambda t\, [^0Believe_{wt}\, a\, {}^{\mathbf{2}}[^0Sub\, [^0Tr\, ^0F_{wt}]\, ^0it\, ^0[\lambda w^*\lambda t^*\, [^0G_{w^*t^*}\, it]]]]$$

The passive variant could be analysed in the same way. Yet there is an easier solution, which does not apply the substitution method. In order to construct the property of being believed by *a* to be a *G*, we use this Closure:

$$\lambda w \lambda t \lambda x\, [^0Believe_{wt}\, a\, [\lambda w^*\lambda t^*\, [^0G_{w^*t^*}\, x]]]$$

We Compose this property construction (extensionalized with respect to the attributer's perspective) with $^0F_{wt}$ and abstract again over the values of w, t in order to obtain a proposition. The resulting analysis is this:

$$\lambda w \lambda t\, [\lambda x\, [^0Believe_{wt}\, a\, [\lambda w^*\lambda t^*\, [^0G_{w^*t^*}\, x]]]\, ^0F_{wt}]$$

When we compile them all, we have a hyperintensional and an intensional variant of attitudes *de dicto*, and a hyperintensional and an intensional variant of attitudes *de re* in their respective active and passive forms:

(*de dicto*)
 "*a* believes/believes* that the *F* is a *G*"
 $\lambda w \lambda t\, [^0Believe_{wt}\, a\, [\lambda w^*\lambda t^*\, [^0G_{w^*t^*}\, ^0F_{w^*t^*}]]]$
 $\lambda w \lambda t\, [^0Believe*_{wt}\, a\, ^0[\lambda w^*\lambda t^*\, [^0G_{w^*t^*}\, ^0F_{w^*t^*}]]]$

(*de re active*)
   "*a* believes/believes* of the *F* that it is a *G*"
   $\lambda w \lambda t\ [^0Believe_{wt}\ a\ ^2[^0Sub\ [^0Tr\ ^0F_{wt}]\ ^0it\ ^0[\lambda w^*\lambda t^*\ [^0G_{w^*t^*}\ it]]]]$
   $\lambda w \lambda t\ [^0Believe^*_{wt}\ a\ [^0Sub\ [^0Tr\ ^0F_{wt}]\ ^0it\ ^0[\lambda w^*\lambda t^*\ [^0G_{w^*t^*}\ it]]]]$

(*de re passive*)
   "The *F* is believed/believed* by *a* to be an *F*"
   $\lambda w \lambda t\ [\lambda x\ [^0Believe_{wt}\ a\ [\lambda w^*\lambda t^*\ [^0G_{w^*t^*}\ x]]]\ ^0F_{wt}]$
   $\lambda w \lambda t\ [\lambda x\ [^0Believe^*_{wt}\ a\ [^0Sub\ [^0Tr\ x]\ ^0x\ ^0[\lambda w^*\lambda t^*\ [^0G_{w^*t^*}\ x]]]]\ ^0F_{wt}]$

Let us take stock. Hyperpropositional attitudes *de re*, as we just described them, have a string of characteristic features that set them apart from their *de dicto* counterparts. First, they are attitudes *of* somebody or something. Second, they are parasitic on preceding attitudes, either another attitude *de re* or ultimately an attitude *de dicto*. Third, they occasion an *inversion of perspective*, from attributee's to attributer's. Fourth, they have an integral tension built into them: *qua* hyperintensional they reproduce the attributee's perspective; qua *de re* the individual objects about whom or which the attitudes are entertained are picked out from the attributer's perspective. Says Quine,

> Spelling dissolves the syntax and lexicon of the content clause and blends it with that of the ascriber's language. So long as we rest with the unanalyzed quotational form, on the other hand, the inverted commas mark an opaque interface between two ontologies, two worlds: that of the man in the attitude, however benighted, and that of our responsible ascriber of the attitude. (1992, pp. 69–70.)

Transpose Quine's language-centric approach into our construction-centric one. Then explicit intensionalization and temporalization is what enables us to keep separate the two 'worlds' or 'ontologies' that Quine alludes to; namely, the perspective of the attributee and that of the attributer. One set of λ-bound w, t variables represents the attributer's perspective and another set the attributee's. The inversion of perspective explains why the following argument, sporting an attitude *de re* in the first premise as well as in the conclusion, is *valid* and its *de dicto* counterpart is invalid:

(1)   The Evening Star is believed by *a* to be a planet
(2)   The Evening Star = the Morning Star
(3)   The Morning Star is believed by *a* to be a planet

The rationale is that the respective meanings of 'The Evening Star' and 'The Morning Star' occur *de re*: the respective occupants of the offices, which are individuals, are picked out rather than the respective offices, which are mappings. The first premise means that, at the index of evaluation, the occupant of the office of Evening Star has the property of being believed by a to be a planet. The second premise means that, at the same index, the two offices of Evening Star and Morning Star are co-occupied. The conclusion means that, at the same index, the occupant of the office of Morning Star has the property of being believed by a to be a planet. (1) and (3) are two different truth-*conditions* (possible-world propositions), for sure, but for any dual index at which (2) is true, (1) and (3) will share the same truth-*value*. It is immaterial to the validity of the argument whether a's belief be intensional or hyperintensional.

By contrast, this argument is *invalid*:

(1′) a believes that the Evening Star is a planet
(2′) The Evening Star = the Morning Star
(3′) a believes that the Morning Star is a planet

The premises are too weak to sustain the conclusion, whether a's belief be intensional or hyperintensional. In (1′) the sense of 'The Morning Star' occurs *de dicto*, in (2) *de re*, and in (3′) *de dicto* again.[xxviii] It is irrelevant that the two offices happen to be co-extensional when what is wanted is that they should be co-intensional. But, on the other hand, if there were but one office and not two then the argument would come out trivially valid, because the conclusion would simply be a rephrasing of the first premise. The invalidity of the existing argument feeds on the classical confusion of function and functional value (or concept and instance, to use another vernacular).

Hence as soon as (1) is true, the two principles unique to contexts *de re* kick in. The validity of substituting terms that co-refer has been illustrated by the first valid argument. The principle of *existential presupposition*, that the

---

[xxviii] There is a structural analogy with *Partee's* puzzle of 90°F rising: the temperature is 90°F; the temperature is rising ∴ 90°F is rising. What just went wrong? A temperature is a magnitude (a number-in-intension, like *the number of the planets*), hence a mapping, while 90°F is one of its values (a number). In the first premise 'the temperature' occurs *de re* because a particular value of the function is identified. In the second premise 'the temperature' occurs *de dicto* because the mapping is the subject of predication. So where the conclusion, with its predicate 'is rising', demands a reference to a mapping, Partee's puzzle has a reference to a functional value. Hence the fallacy. See Duží et al. (2010, pp. 124–125).

relevant office(s) must be occupied, yields this *valid* argument when applied to (1):

(1) <u>The Evening Star is believed by a to be a planet</u>
(4) The Evening Star exists

On the other hand, the following argument is *invalid*:

(1′) <u>a believes that the Evening Star is a planet</u>
(4′) The Evening Star exists

In the *de dicto* case a may well believe that the Evening Star is a planet even if there is no Evening Star, the office going vacant. This is so, because this office now receives mention within a's perspective, in the intensional/hyperintensional context of what is believed by a.

4. *Rules for Quantifying into Hyperpropositional and Propositional Contexts* de re

The technical challenge of untying an x occurring mentioned in the context $\delta[\ldots x \ldots]$ and $\exists$-binding it requires three non-standard devices. The first is *Trivialization*. The second is Sub. The third is Tr. We say that Trivialization is *used* to *mention* other constructions (cf. Definition 4 and the subsequent Remark). The point of mentioning a construction is to make it, rather than what it presents, a functional argument. TIL interprets δ as a binary relation-in-intension between an agent a entertaining an attitude and a construction in its capacity as attitude relatum. Relations, in turn, are construed as functions, such that δ is typed as a function from worlds to a function from times to a function from agents and hyperpropositions to truth-values: given a world/time pair, it is either true or false that a particular agent has a particular attitude to a particular hyperproposition. In order for the relevant construction to figure as the second argument of the relevant attitude relation, it itself needs to be mentioned. If a given (first-order) hyperproposition is not mentioned but used, the resulting relatum is a possible-world proposition, thus reinstalling the logic of attitudes known from modal logic. A hyperpropositional attitude context is one in which the second argument of the attitude relation is a propositional *construction*.

In Duží and Jespersen (submitted) *the rule for quantifying into hyperpropositional attitudes de dicto* is the following. Let the types be: $Att^* \rightarrow$

$(o\iota^*{}_n)_{\tau\omega}$: an arbitrary construction of a hyperpropositional attitude relation; $a \to \iota$; $C(X)/*_n \to_v o_{\tau\omega}$: a propositional construction with a constituent $X/*_n \to_v \alpha$; $c/*_{(n+1)} \to_v *_n$; $^2c/*_{(n+2)} \to_v \alpha$; $\exists^*/(o(o^*{}_n))$. Then the rule is this:

$$\frac{[Att^*{}_{wt}\ a\ {}^0C(X)]}{[{}^0\exists^*\lambda c\ [Att^*{}_{wt}\ a\ [{}^0Sub\ c\ {}^0X\ {}^0C(X)]]]}$$

Proof. The Composition $[{}^0Sub\ c\ {}^0X\ {}^0C(X)]$ $v(X/c)$-constructs the construction $C(X)$. Hence at any $\langle w, t \rangle$ at which $[Att^*{}_{wt}\ a\ {}^0C(X)]$ v-constructs T the class v-constructed by $\lambda c\ [Att^*{}_{wt}\ a\ [{}^0Sub\ c\ {}^0X\ {}^0C(X)]]$ is non-empty and the conclusion $[{}^0\exists^*\lambda c\ [Att^*{}_{wt}\ a\ [{}^0Sub\ c\ {}^0X\ {}^0C(X)]]]$ v-constructs T as well. □

Remark. Contrast $[Att^{*\prime}{}_{wt}\ a\ {}^0[{}^0Sub\ c\ {}^0X\ {}^0C(X)]]$ with $[Att^*{}_{wt}\ a\ [{}^0Sub\ c\ {}^0X\ {}^0C(X)]]$. The latter constructs a truth-value that depends on whether the agent has the attitude Att^* to the *result* of executing a substitution. The former also constructs a truth-value, but this time it depends on whether the agent is related by $Att^{*\prime}$ to the very *procedure* of executing that substitution, i.e. the agent needs to become a practicing logician. $Att^{*\prime}$ would have to change its type to $(o\iota^*{}_{n+1})_{\tau\omega}$, because the result of the Trivialization ${}^0[{}^0Sub\ c\ {}^0X\ {}^0C(X)]$ is the Composition $[{}^0Sub\ c\ {}^0X\ {}^0C(X)]$ that belongs at least to $*_{n+1}$, i.e. a construction of order $n+1$ that v-constructs a construction of order n.

Now the final analysis of the valid argument

$$\frac{a\ \text{believes that the Evening Star is a planet}}{\begin{array}{c}\text{There is a construction of an individual office such that}\\ a\ \text{believes that the occupant of that office is a planet}\end{array}}$$

is as follows. Let $ES \to \iota_{\tau\omega}$ be a construction of the office of Evening Star. Then the resulting analysis is this:

$$\frac{\lambda w \lambda t\ [{}^0Believe^*{}_{wt}\ a\ {}^0[\lambda w \lambda t\ [{}^0Planet_{wt}\ ES_{wt}]]]}{\lambda w \lambda t\ [{}^0\exists \lambda c\ [{}^0Believe^*{}_{wt}\ a\ [{}^0Sub\ c\ {}^0ES\ {}^0[\lambda w \lambda t\ [{}^0Planet_{wt}\ ES_{wt}]]]]]}$$

Quantifying into hyperpropositional attitudes *de dicto* requires but one rule. Not so with quantifying into hyperpropositional attitudes *de re*, which all come in an active and a passive variant. The twin arguments and their twin analyses are as follows.

(*active*)

$$\frac{a \text{ believes* of the } F \text{ that } it \text{ is a } G}{\text{There is an individual of which } a \text{ believes* that it is a } G}$$

$$\frac{\lambda w \lambda t \, [^0Believe^*_{wt} \, a \, [^0Sub \, [^0Tr \, ^0F_{wt}] \, ^0it \, ^0[\lambda w^* \lambda t^* \, [^0G_{w^*t^*} \, it]]]]}{\lambda w \lambda t \, [^0\exists \lambda y \, [^0Believe^*_{wt} \, a \, [^0Sub \, [^0Tr \, y] \, ^0it \, ^0[\lambda w^* \lambda t^* \, [^0G_{w^*t^*} \, it]]]]]}$$

(*passive*)

$$\frac{\text{The } F \text{ is believed* by } a \text{ to be an } F}{\text{There is an individual that is believed* by } a \text{ to be a } G}$$

$$\frac{\lambda w \lambda t \, [\lambda x \, [^0Believe^*_{wt} \, a \, [^0Sub \, [^0Tr \, x] \, ^0x \, ^0[\lambda w^* \lambda t^* \, [^0G_{w^*t^*} \, x]]]] \, ^0F_{wt}]}{\lambda w \lambda t \, [^0\exists \lambda y \, [^0Believe^*_{wt} \, a \, [^0Sub \, [^0Tr \, y] \, ^0x \, ^0[\lambda w^* \lambda t^* \, [^0G_{w^*t^*} \, x]]]]]}$$

We are now in a position to formulate the corresponding *rules for quantifying into hyperpropositional attitudes de re*. Let the types be: $Att^* \to (o\iota^*_n)_{\tau\omega}$; $a \to \iota$; $x, y, it/*_n \to_v \iota$; $\exists/(o(o\iota))$; $X/\iota_{\tau\omega}$ (an individual office); $C(x), C(it) \to o_{\tau\omega}$ propositional constructions with at least one free occurrence of variables x, it, respectively. Then the rules are:

(*active hyperintensional variant*)

$$\frac{[Att^*_{wt} \, a \, [^0Sub \, [^0Tr \, ^0X_{wt}] \, ^0it \, ^0C(it)]]}{[^0\exists \lambda y \, [Att^*_{wt} \, a \, [^0Sub \, [^0Tr \, y] \, ^0it \, ^0C(it)]]]}$$

(*passive hyperintensional variant*)

$$\frac{[\lambda x \, [Att^*_{wt} \, a \, [^0Sub \, [^0Tr \, x] \, ^0x \, ^0C(x)]] \, ^0X_{wt}]}{[^0\exists \lambda y \, [Att^*_{wt} \, a \, [^0Sub \, [^0Tr \, y] \, ^0x \, ^0C(x)]]]}$$

Proof. By the definition of Composition, if the antecedent v-constructs T, then it is v-proper, and so is $^0X_{wt} \to_v \iota$. Hence there is an individual occupying X at $\langle w, t \rangle$. Let this individual be b/ι. Then:

(*active variant*)

1. $[Att^*_{wt}\ a\ [^0Sub\ [^0Tr\ ^0X_{wt}]\ ^0it\ ^0C(it)]]$ ∅
2. $[Att^*_{wt}\ a\ [^0Sub\ [^0Tr\ y]\ ^0it\ ^0C(it)]]$ 1, $v(b/y)$-constructs T
3. $\lambda y\ [Att^*_{wt}\ a\ [^0Sub\ [^0Tr\ y]\ ^0it\ ^0C(it)]]$ v-constructs a non-empty class
4. $[^0\exists \lambda y\ [Att^*_{wt}\ a\ [^0Sub\ [^0Tr\ y]\ ^0it\ ^0C(it)]]]$ 3, EG

(*passive variant*)

1. $[\lambda x[Att^*_{wt}\ a\ [^0Sub\ [^0Tr\ x]\ ^0x\ ^0C(x)]]\ ^0X_{wt}]$ ∅
2. $[Att^*_{wt}\ a\ [^0Sub\ [^0Tr\ ^0X_{wt}]\ ^0x\ ^0C(x)]]$ 1, β-reduction
3. $[Att^*_{wt}\ a\ [^0Sub\ [^0Tr\ y]\ ^0x\ ^0C(x)]]$ 2, $v(b/y)$-constructs T
4. $\lambda y\ [Att^*_{wt}\ a\ [^0Sub\ [^0Tr\ y]\ ^0x\ ^0C(x)]]$ v-constructs a non-empty class
5. $[^0\exists \lambda y\ [Att^*_{wt}\ a\ [^0Sub\ [^0Tr\ y]\ ^0it\ ^0C(it)]]]$ 4, EG

Those are the twin rules for quantifying into *hyperpropositional* contexts *de re*. Notice that whereas in the *de dicto* case quantifying-in is technically complicated and, without auxiliary assumptions, we are guaranteed to infer only that there is a *construction* such that ..., in the *de re* case quantifying-in is straightforward; moreover, we can infer that there is an *individual* such that ...

The corresponding pair of rules for quantifying into *propositional* contexts *de re* can now be easily stated. Let $Att \to (o\iota o_{\tau\omega})_{\tau\omega}$ be a construction of a propositional attitudes *de re*; the other types as above. Then:

(*active intensional variant*)

$$\frac{[Att_{wt}\ a\ ^2[^0Sub\ [^0Tr\ ^0X_{wt}]\ ^0it\ ^0C(it)]]}{[^0\exists \lambda y\ [Att_{wt}\ a\ ^2[^0Sub\ [^0Tr\ y]\ ^0it\ ^0C(it)]]]}$$

(*passive intensional variant*)

$$\frac{[\lambda x\ [Att_{wt}\ a\ C(x)]\ ^0X_{wt}]}{[^0\exists \lambda y\ [Att_{wt}\ a\ C(y)]]}$$

Proof. By the definitions of Composition and Double Execution, if the antecedent v-constructs T, then it is v-proper, and so is $^0X_{wt} \to_v \iota$. Hence there is an individual occupying X at $\langle w,t \rangle$. Let this individual be b/ι. Then:

(*active variant*)

1. $[Att_{wt}\ a\ ^2[^0Sub\ [^0Tr\ ^0X_{wt}]\ ^0it\ ^0C(it)]]$ $\varnothing$
2. $[Att_{wt}\ a\ ^2[^0Sub\ [^0Tr\ y]\ ^0it\ ^0C(it)]]$ $1, v(b/y)$-constructs T
3. $\lambda y\ [Att_{wt}\ a\ ^2[^0Sub\ [^0Tr\ y]\ ^0it\ ^0C(it)]]$ v-constructs a non-empty class
4. $[^0\exists \lambda y\ [Att_{wt}\ a\ ^2[^0Sub\ [^0Tr\ y]\ ^0it\ ^0C(it)]]$ $3, \text{EG}$

(*passive variant*)

1. $[\lambda x\ [Att_{wt}\ a\ C(x)]\ ^0X_{wt}]$ $\varnothing$
2. $[Att_{wt}\ a\ C(^0X_{wt})]$ $1, \beta$-reduction
3. $[Att_{wt}\ a\ C(y)]$ $2, v(b/y)$-constructs T
4. $\lambda y\ [Att_{wt}\ a\ C(y)]$ v-constructs a non-empty class
5. $[^0\exists \lambda y\ [Att_{wt}\ a\ C(y)]]$ $4, \text{EG}$

(*example of active variant*)

$$\frac{\text{Mary believes of the Evening Star that it is a planet}}{\text{There is an individual such that Mary believes that it is a planet}}$$

$$\frac{\lambda w \lambda t\ [^0B_{wt}\ ^0Mary\ ^2[^0Sub\ [^0Tr\ ^0Evening\_Star_{wt}]\ ^0it\ ^0[\lambda w \lambda t\ [^0Planet_{wt}\ it]]]]}{\lambda w \lambda t\ [^0\exists \lambda x\ [[^0B_{wt}\ ^0Mary\ ^2[^0Sub\ [^0Tr\ x]\ ^0it\ ^0[\lambda w \lambda t\ [^0Planet_{wt}\ it]]]]}$$

(*example of passive variant*)

$$\frac{\text{The Evening Star is believed by Mary to be a planet}}{\text{There is an individual such that it is believed by Mary to be a planet}}$$

$$\frac{\lambda w \lambda t\ [\lambda y\ [^0B_{wt}\ ^0Mary\ \lambda w \lambda t\ [^0Planet_{wt}\ y]]\ ^0Evening\_Star_{wt}]}{\lambda w \lambda t\ [^0\exists \lambda z\ [[^0B_{wt}\ ^0Mary\ \lambda w \lambda t\ [^0Planet_{wt}\ z]]]}$$

Types: $B/(o\iota o_{\tau\omega})_{\tau\omega}$; Mary/$\iota$; Planet/$(o\iota)_{\tau\omega}$; Evening_Star/$\iota_{\tau\omega}$.

This completes our exposition of quantifying into hyperpropositional and possible-world propositional contexts *de re*.

Conclusion

Above we presented and proved two rules for quantifying into hyperpropositional attitude contexts *de re* and two rules for quantifying into propositional attitude contexts *de re*. We also presented the rule for quantifying into hyperpropositional contexts *de dicto*, for comparison. Quantifying into hyperintensional contexts requires an extensional logic of hyperintensions in order to be executed in a principled manner. Quantifying into intensional contexts requires an extensional logic of intensions in order to be executed in a principled manner. Transparent Intensional Logic is one such theory. Much non-trivial footwork is required to lay out such a large-scale logical semantics. Once this is done, though, quantifying into hyperintensional and intensional contexts turns out to be as trivially valid as quantifying into non-attitudinal (and non-modal), or extensional, contexts. The difference with extensional contexts is only a matter of logical complexity. In order to relate an agent to a hyperproposition, the hyperproposition needs to occur mentioned in order to present itself rather than what it constructs, namely a proposition. The complication is that, since every constituent of a mentioned construction itself occurs mentioned, the quantifier cannot bind any variable occurring inside the mentioned context. The solution consists in pre-processing the mentioned construction by means of a substitution technique that makes variables amenable to binding. In this manner quantifying into hyperintensional contexts is rendered valid while at the same time observing compositionality and transparency. This marks an advance for philosophical logic in general and for hyperintensional logic in particular.

ACKNOWLEDGEMENTS

This research was funded by Grant Agency of the Czech Republic Project #401/10/0792 *Temporal Aspects of Knowledge and Information*, as well as by Grant Agency of VSB-TU Ostrava Project #SP2011/56 *Knowledge-based Approach to Modelling, Simulation and Visualization of Software Processes*. Versions of the present paper were read by Bjørn Jespersen as invited talks at Seminario di logica e filosofia analitica, Università degli Studi di Padova, 29 June and 2 July 2010, and as a contributed talk at *LRR10*, Ghent, 20–22 September 2010. We are indebted to two anonymous referees for *Logique et Analyse* for helpful advice and to one in particular for insightful questions on individual offices that led us to clarify the notion further.

REFERENCES

Bealer, G. (1982), *Quality and Concept*, Oxford: Clarendon Press.
Crawford, S. (2008), 'Quantifiers and propositional attitudes: Quine revisited', *Synthese*, vol. 160, pp. 75–96.
Cresswell, M.J. (1975), 'Hyperintensional logic', *Studia Logica*, 34:25–38.
Duží, M. (2000), 'Existential quantification into intentional contexts', in: *The Logica Yearbook 1999*, T. Childers (ed.), Prague: FILOSOFIA, Czech Academy of Sciences, pp. 258–72.
Duží, M., Jespersen, B. (2012), 'Procedural isomorphism, analytic information, and β-conversion by value', to appear in *Logic Journal of the IGPL*, doi: 10.1093/jigpal/jzs044.
Duží, M., Jespersen, B. (submitted), 'Transparent quantification into hyperpropositional contexts *de dicto*'.
Duží, M., B. Jespersen and P. Materna (2010), *Procedural Semantics for Hyperintensional Logic. Foundations and Applications of Transparent Intensional Logic*, Berlin: Springer.
Forbes, G. (1996), 'Substitutivity and the coherence of quantifying in', *The Philosophical Review*, 105:337–71.
Forbes, G. (2000), 'Objectual attitudes', *Linguistics and Philosophy*, 23:141–83.
Hindley, J.R. and J.P. Seldin (1986), *Introduction to Combinators and λ-Calculus*, Cambridge: Cambridge University Press.
Hookway, C. (1988), *Quine*, Stanford: Stanford University Press.
Jespersen, B. (2005), 'Explicit intensionalization, anti-actualism, and how Smith's murderer might not have murdered Smith', *Dialectica*, vol. 59, pp. 285–314.
Jespersen, B. (2010), 'Hyperintensions and procedural isomorphism: Alternative (1/2)', in: *The Analytical Way. Proceedings of the 6th European Congress of Analytic Philosophy*. T. Czarnecki, K. Kijania-Placek, O. Poller, J. Woleński (eds.), London: College Publications, pp. 299–320.

Jespersen, B., Primiero G. (2012), Alleged assassins: realist and constructivist semantics for modal modification, accepted for publication in Proceedings of TibLLC, Lecture Notes in Artificial Intelligence, Springer, to appear.

Kaplan, D. (1968), 'Quantifying in', Synthese 19:178–214.

Kaplan, D. (1986), 'Opacity', in: *The Philosophy of W.V. Quine*, L. Hahn (ed.), La Salle: Open Court, pp. 229–89.

Kaplan, D. (1990), 'Dthat', in: *Syntax and Semantics*, vol. 9, P. Cole (ed.), New York: Academic Press.

Kemp, G. (2006), *Quine: A Guide for the Perplexed*, London, New York: Continuum.

Klement, K.C. (2002), *Frege and the Logic of Sense and Reference*, New York, London: Routledge.

Materna, P. (1997), 'Rules of existential quantification into 'intensional contexts'', *Studia Logica*, vol. 57, pp. 331–43.

Quine, W.v.O. (1956), 'Quantifiers and propositional attitudes', *Journal of Philosophy*, vol. 53, pp. 177–86.

Quine (1992), *The Pursuit of Truth*, Cambridge: Harvard University Press.

Soames, S. (2010), *What Is Meaning?*, Princeton: Princeton University Press.

Tichý, P. (1975), 'What do we talk about?', *Philosophy of Science*, vol. 42, pp. 37–58. Reprinted in: *Pavel Tichý's Collected Papers in Logic and Philosophy*, V. Svoboda, B. Jespersen, C. Cheyne (eds.), Dunedin: University of Otago Press; Prague: Filosofia, Czech Academy of Sciences (2004), pp. 207–20.

Tichý, P. (1986), 'Indiscernibility of identicals', *Studia Logica*, vol. 45, pp. 251–73. Reprinted in: *Pavel Tichý's Collected Papers in Logic and Philosophy*, Dunedin: University of Otago Press; Prague: Filosofia, Czech Academy of Sciences (2004), pp. 649–71.

Qualifying quantifying-in

Bjørn Jespersen

ABSTRACT

Quantifying-in is existential quantification into non-extensional contexts headed by a modal or attitudinal operator. The sense and sensibility of quantifying-in has often been challenged. This paper outlines a transparency-preserving semantics as a prerequisite for the logical validity of quantifying-in. The paper demonstrates how to formally validate quantifying into a non-factive, hyperintensional attitude context.

0. INTRODUCTION

The rule of existential generalization is one of the hallmarks of extensional logic. It is also a rule with strong intuitive appeal. Its conclusion makes explicit an ontological commitment implicit in the premise. If the premise states that some specific a has some specific quality F then the conclusion states that there is some x that has F. For instance, if the individual Tilman lives in Tilburg then there is at least one element x in the domain of individuals who lives in Tilburg. If the premise is true then the conclusion is the truth that the *quantity* of objects with the particular *quality* of living in Tilburg amounts to at least one. In set-theoretic terms, the set of individuals living in Tilburg is said to be non-empty. The conclusion is indifferent to whether it is Tilman or some other individual who lives in Tilburg: *any* individual will do as long as *some* individual has the quality in question. The idea underlying quantification, whether existential or universal or generalized (e.g. *at least three*), is abstraction from the particular and specific to the general and arbitrary in order to extract a pure quantity. It would be misconceived to ask *which* particular element of the domain of quantification is the value of the existentially bound variable.

So far, so good. This inference schema is an uncontroversial component of Logic 101:

$$(1) \quad \frac{Fa}{\exists x\,(Fx)} \text{ EG}$$

We may haggle, for sure, over the formal semantics of the schema, e.g. whether to project an objectual versus substitutional, or a constructivist versus realist, etc. interpretation of the quantifier onto the schema. But whatever the details of the logic of the inference and the meaning of the conclusion, the very validity of the schema is beyond dispute. Its validity is a datum that any viable semantics of quantifiers must accommodate. We need stray only a bit from (1), however, before dispute erupts. For with "*Fa*" as our premise, there are two positions to quantify into – the position of the singular term 'a' and the position of the predicate 'F'. If Tilman lives in Tilburg, as before, then he is not someone without properties, for there is at least one property f that Tilman has:

$$(2) \quad \frac{Fa}{\exists f\,(fa)} \text{ EG}$$

The philosophical objection is that quantifying over properties goes too far. Tilman may well live in Tilburg, but this is not to say that he thereby has the property of living in Tilburg, for properties form an ontological category that is better dismissed. This sort of objection tends to feed on a general distrust in intensional entities such as properties, propositions, magnitudes (e.g. *the number of planets*), individual roles (e.g. *the Sultan of Brunei*), etc.[1]

Existential generalization becomes even more contentious, as well as more complicated, than (2) when quantification mixes with modalities or attitudes. When this happens, one or more existential quantifiers need to bind one or more occurrences of one or more variables inside the scope of one or more modal or attitudinal operators (functors). Restricted to one schematic modal or attitudinal operator Op and one quantifier, the characteristic scope distribution is this:[2]

$$\exists x \ldots Op \ldots x$$

Here is a semi-formalized example:

$$(3) \quad \frac{\text{Contingently, } Fa}{\exists x \, (\text{contingently, } Fx)} \quad \text{EG}$$

(3) exemplifies so-called *quantifying-in*. This is so because the $\exists$-bound occurrence of x occurs inside the scope of the modal operator 'contingently'. Similarly for f in (4):

$$(4) \quad \frac{\text{Contingently, } Fa}{\exists f \, (\text{contingently, } fa)} \quad \text{EG}$$

The first at least well-known modern-day example of quantifying into *modalities* is presumably the *Barcan Formula* in one of its formulations:

---

[1] Provided both schemata are valid, it is an option to unify them into a third schema, whose conclusion means that somebody (something) has some property:

$$(1+2) \quad \frac{Fa}{\exists x \, \exists f \, (fx)} \quad \text{EG}$$

[2] The inverse scope distribution, $Op \ldots \exists x \ldots Fx$, would be the schema underlying sentences like "Contingently, there is some x such that x is an F". This scope distribution does not exemplify quantifying-in and, while being of great independent logical and philosophical interest, will not be discussed here.

$$\Diamond \exists x Fx \Rightarrow \exists x \Diamond Fx$$

Where $\Diamond$ represents logical possibility, BF states that if it is logically possible that something be an F then, as a matter of strict (i.e. necessitated) implication, something has the logical potential to be an F. The $\exists$-bound occurrence of x in the consequent falls within the scope of $\Diamond$, so the question arises how $\exists$ succeeds in reaching across $\Diamond$ and binding this occurrence. $\Diamond Fx_i$ is a modal, hence intension-sensitive context, so if $\exists$ binds x_i that range over extensional entities such as individuals, the question arises whether the occurrences of x_i within the context $\Diamond Fx_i$ retains its quantificational range or must range over individuals-in-intension or is maybe deprived of a range altogether.[3]

The earliest discussion of what is in effect quantification into *attitudes* may be one of Buridanus's *insolubilia* from 1350 which Geach (1965, p. 430) represents thus:[4]

> Let us then have our horse-coper arguing again. "If I owe you a horse, then I owe you something. And if I owe you something, then there is something I owe you. And this can only be a thoroughbred of mine: you aren't going to say that in virtue of what I said there's something else I owe you. Very well, then: by your claim, there's one of my thoroughbreds I owe you. Please tell me which one it is.

Of course, there is no one particular horse the coper owes to the man he is trying to befuddle with a fallacy. The coper's trick is the transition from there being a particular property that the coper owes the man an arbitrary instance of to there being a particular instance of that property that the coper owes.

Quine famously challenged quantified modal logic to make quantifying-in comprehensible. He later went on to challenge attitude logic to do the same. The first modern example of mixing existential quantification with attitudes is probably Quine (1956). The topic of quantifying into attitudes arises for Quine due to his notion of *relational attitude*. If Quine wants a sloop then, if his attitude is notional, any sloop will do to relieve him of slooplessness, and if his attitude is relational then only a particular sloop will satisfy his wish. The latter is arguably ambiguous: Quine wants a particular object, which happens to be a sloop; or Quine has his mind set on one particular sloop, to the exclusion of all other sloops.[5] Be that as it may, Quine phrases relational attitudes by means of quantified locutions: "There is an x such that x is a sloop and Quine wants x". It

---
[3] See Williamson (2013, pp. 46ff) on the early reactions to quantifying into BF.
[4] See Zimmermann (2006, p. 715, n. 1).
[5] See Sainsbury (2010).

is this phrasing of relational attitudes that, historically at least, pushes quantifying-in to the fore in attitude logic.

Quine is dismissive of quantifying into modal contexts, for fear of condoning modality de re. Quine is also dismissive of quantifying into attitude contexts exemplifying notional attitudes. He is, as we just saw, sympathetic to quantifying into contexts exemplifying relational attitudes.[6] Quine's problem with this particular category of attitudes is how to make good logical sense of it. This leads him to put forward his well-known three-place analysis, which is intended to preserve referential transparency. Whatever one makes of this analysis, at least part of the appeal of relational attitudes seems to be that there is guaranteed to be an individual at the receiving end of the attitude: there is an individual whom or which the attitude is directed at (hence the qualification 'relational').[7] There, at least, quantification over individuals seems safe.

Quantification over individuals also at least appears to be safe as soon as the modal or attitudinal context being quantified into is a *factive* one. Necessity and contingency are factive modalities: from "Necessarily, A is true" and "Contingently, A is true" we can infer "A is true". From "Possibly, A is true" we cannot infer "A is true", but only "Maybe A is true". Knowledge is a factive attitude: from "a knows that A is true" we can infer "A is true". Belief is not factive: from "a believes that A is true" we cannot even infer "Maybe A is true", for we have not excluded the possibility that A be inconsistent. From "Necessarily, Venus has a moon" we can infer "There is an individual x such that x is a moon of Venus". (Never mind soundness; validity is what we are after.) From "a knows that Venus has a moon" we may likewise infer "There is an individual x such that x is a moon of Venus". Some non-propositional attitudes are also factive. For instance, from "a finds the site of Troy" we may infer "There is an individual x such that x is the site of Troy". But from "a seeks the site of Troy" we may not infer this conclusion, for there may be no unique site of Troy.

In general, two issues bearing on quantifying-in need to be kept separate. One is quantification *over* the domain that b belongs to, where b occurs inside the context $Op... b$ .... . The other is quantification *into* the context $Op ... b ....$. The former makes explicit the ontological commitment mentioned at the outset, specifying the ontological category of b. The latter sort of conclusion extracts a component b from the attitude complement, which is the scope of Op, and quantifies over its domain: $\exists z... Op ... z .... $. One reason

---

[6] See not least Kaplan (1986, pp. 230-31) and Crawford (2008).
[7] Of course, it is not just that there is some individual at whom or which the attitude is directed – there is *one particular* individual at the receiving end of the attitude. It is doubtful whether existential quantification possesses enough expressive power to capture the dimension of particularity, as in "There is a princess that the prince wishes to marry, though not just any princess out there, but one particular princess." Cf. my initial remark about the quantity of instances of a particular quality or property.

for operating with this distinction is that we may, for instance, quantify *into* a *hyperintensional* context and quantify *over* a particular kind of *intensional* or *extensional* entity. Another reason is that we may want to quantify into one, but not all, positions inside a given context. For instance, if *a* is seeking an abominable snowman then there is a *z* such that *z* is abominable and *a* is seeking *z* (i.e. *a* is seeking somebody or something abominable). The salient question is here what the quantificational range of *z* may be. If only extensional entities like individuals are an option then there will be far fewer cases of quantifying-in. The number of cases shoots up if also *intensional* entities, i.e. functions from possible worlds, are declared legitimate quantificational ranges. The number further increases if also *hyperintensional* entities may be quantified over. I will show that when we are quantifying *into* a hyperintensional empirical attitude context, such as believing that the glass before you is half-empty (but not necessarily also that the glass is half-full, or vice versa), then we may always quantify *over* hyperintensions and intensions, but not individuals, due to the non-factivity of doxastic attitudes.[8] That is, when *a* is seeking an abominable snowman, or some other cryptozoid, no instance of the property of being an abominable snowman is being quantified into existence, so to speak.

In this paper I will address three topics. The first two belong together, one being a special case of the other. The first topic concerns quantifying into *non-factive* attitude contexts, as just sketched. The second topic concerns what I dub *doublethink* (borrowing a term from Orwell) to describe inconsistent beliefs, which are inherently non-factive: I have no conceptual space for dialetheia. If quantification is restricted to extensions, in neither case is quantifying-in warranted, which is only reasonable, since Quine seems to have fielded the (im-) possibility of quantifying-in as something like a nonsense-detector: does the application of EG to premises involving attitudes or modalities eventuate in nonsensical or otherwise untoward conclusions? Both of the above cases call for qualification to warrant quantifying-in. I will be describing both topics mainly in prose, referring to existing literature that contains the formal details of my approach. The third topic is technical in nature, bearing on how to quantify into a non-factive, empirical, hyperpropositional attitude context and quantifying over intensional entities.

This paper is the latest installment of a series of papers devoted to quantifying-in. The other papers are Duží and Jespersen (2012), Duží and Jespersen (revised and resubmitted), and Duží and Jespersen (in revision). These papers themselves build primarily on Tichý (1986), Materna (1997), and Duží et al. (2010, §5.3). The present

---

[8] The need for hyperintensions as the complements of at least some attitudes was realized in modern times as early as Carnap (1947, pp. 53-54), thus it was known from its very inception that modal logic was insufficient as an all-encompassing attitude logic. Marcus, in a 1961 paper, also notes that epistemic and doxastic attitudes require 'a stronger equivalence relation...than strict equivalence', mentioning Carnap's *intensional isomorphism* as one attempt to obtain what is in effect a hyperintensional criterion of equivalence (Marcus, 1993, p. 14).

paper offers more by way of philosophical exposition and critique than was possible in the three papers co-authored with Duží, which target mainly the logical and semantic intricacies of quantifying-in.

The rest of the paper is organized as follows. Section 1 clears the semantic ground for the logic of quantifying-in. Section 2 discusses how to qualify non-factive attitudes, including inconsistent beliefs, so as to warrant quantifying-in. Section 3 demonstrates the logical details of quantifying into a hyperintensional context, as described above.

1. TOP-DOWN TRANSPARENCY

It is important to bear in mind that Quine does not reject quantifying-in tout court. Rather he points out that quantifying-in is problematic. But he never unambiguously identifies what the source, as opposed to symptom, of the problem is. Is it perhaps failure of Leibniz's Law? Or maybe the existence of opacity? Or the mix of quantification and modalities or attitudes within the same context? As I suggested above, most likely quantifying-in is fielded as a criterion or stress test for whether modal and attitudinal contexts behave logically, which for Quine means behaving according to the laws of extensional logic. If existential generalization fails for modal or attitudinal contexts then he has constructed an argument with a false or even nonsensical conclusion, hence there must be something illogical about one or more of the premises, and the culprits have no place in an austere, regimented language. What I call the argument from doublethink is modeled on Quine's prior modal arguments designed to derive the absurd conclusion that some individual *x* has, and also lacks, a modal property such as being necessarily larger than five, or that some individual *y* has, and also lacks, a modal property such as being necessarily two-legged.[9] A doublethink *reductio* is pivoted on quantifying into existence an individual that is believed, and also not believed, to be an *F*.

Here is a reconstruction of one way of going about generating such a Quine-style *reductio*. One deploys an extensionalist semantics to contexts that are sensitive to more than just the identity and difference of extensions, and Leibniz's Law, *as defined for extensional contexts*, turns out to be invalid (not surprisingly). One then concludes that non-extensionalist contexts are logically lawless, or at the very least iffy. Quine's general stance is that any sort of context that defies substitution of identicals (i.e. is opaque) must also defy quantifying-in.

---

[9] See Duží et al. (2010, §4.2.1) and Marcus (1993, pp. 18-21). Quine would not phrase his point in terms of properties, but I do, in order to extract a general lesson that applies also beyond the Procrustean bed of Quine's extensionalist semantics.

Kaplan, in reaction to Quine, pursues a different stance. Kaplan (1986, pp. 242ff) maintains that failure of intersubstitutivity does not entail failure of quantifying-in, deploying his theory of arc quotes to get this project off the ground.

Forbes (1996), in turn, sees it as his task to conceive of a device that will bar co-referential names from being substitutable within certain contexts in order to create 'substitution-resistant positions' (*ibid.*, p. 352) without altering their reference relation.[10] Forbes (*ibid.*, pp. 357-62) does sketch a template for 'unproblematic quantifying-in', which is predicated on exportation of, in this case, 'Superman':[11]

(*a*)   Lois believes that Superman is an extraterrestrial
(*b*)   Superman is someone whom Lois believes to be an extraterrestrial

(*c*)   There is someone whom Lois believes to be an extraterrestrial

But the transformation (as Forbes *ibid.*, p. 358 calls it) of (*a*) into (*b*) obliterates the huge differences between de dicto and de re attitudes.[12] So I am not convinced that Forbes has shown how to, indirectly, quantify into (*a*).

Whatever the details, I believe all three approaches are conceptually misguided.[13] The way I see it, the rules of extensional logic, including existential generalization, referential transparency, substitutivity of identicals, and compositionality form one package, such that all of them must be accommodated simultaneously. Cherry-picking is not a viable option. In essence, what is wanted is an extensional logic of non-extensional (including hyperintensional) contexts. A semantics heeding universal transparency must precede such a logic. The philosophical idea is that once universal transparency has been safeguarded we have made a critical step toward availing ourselves of an extensional logic for any and all sorts of contexts, i.e. the extensional, the intensional, and the

---

[10] Forbes's device is *logophors*, so-labeled. 'Superman' and 'Clark Kent' refer to the same individual, but when reporting Lois's attitude toward this individual it affects the truth-value of the report whether 'Superman' or 'Clark Kent' is used to report her attitude. Forbes's logophors appear to be more quotational in character than Forbes would want, being an uneasy halfway house between Quinian and Fregean tenets. See Forbes (2013) for his most recent application of logophors.
[11] Furthermore, from (*b*) together with (*d*) Superman is Clark Kent, we are supposed to infer (*e*) Clark Kent is someone whom Lois believes to be an extraterrestrial.
[12] See Duží and Jespersen (2012).
[13] So is the approach in Priest (2012). Priest argues that substitutivity of identicals fails for both modal and epistemic contexts, and therefore sees it as his task to construct a logic (based around impossible worlds) in which the rule does not hold in order to accommodate arguments such as this: (i) This man [wearing a hood] is your brother; (ii) You do not know who this man is; (iii) Therefore, you do not know who your brother is. In my view, Priest's analysis of (i) is too heavy on the extensions, leaving little or no conceptual space for convergence between intensions. (See also fn. 16 below.)

hyperintensional ones. Any such logic will, qua extensional, validate the rules of extensional logic, including EG. There is no cogent reason to hang on to the idea that a logic for non-extensional contexts must itself be non-extensional.[14]

Sylvan (2003, p. 29) cites an original example of alleged opacity, which none the less replicates a familiar pattern:

> The denominator of 2/4 is 4. But 2/4 = ½. So by transparency [substitution of identicals], the denominator of ½ is 4.

Which, of course, it is not. Sylvan uses this fallacy to argue that not all mathematical contexts are extensional and transparent, some being intensional and opaque. I think Sylvan overstates what goes wrong in the above substitution. He is right that the conclusion does not follow. Only this is not due to opacity; it is due to *wrong substituends*. In this particular sense the fallacy is indeed about non-extensionality, because extensional values cannot be swapped:

(i) *Denominator* (2/4) = 4
(ii) 2/4 = ½
_____
(iii) *Denominator* (½) = 4

When the denominator of a fraction is highlighted, as per (i) and (iii), a sensitivity to computational or algebraic structure is highlighted that is absent when only the result of computing the fraction is highlighted, as per (ii). So where exactly does the argument go wrong? As almost always, an identity or equivalence at a lower level, (ii), is transferred up into a higher-level context, (iii). To be sure, two quarter dollars is the same amount as a half-dollar, but these are two different ways of arriving at the same amount of fifty cents. (i) and (iii) are sensitive to the differences between these two different ways of arriving at fifty cents, whereas (ii) is not. Hence inside the context induced by 'the denominator of' the only sort of appropriate substituends are fractions with the same denominator as in the original premise, (i). This makes for an exceedingly exacting criterion of substitutivity. The proper conclusion requires that the denominator be 4, while leaving room for a numerator different from 2. Whether a different numerator is possible *salva veritate* is a mathematical matter and not a logical one (bearing on preservation of validity) or a semantic one (bearing on preservation of meaning).

---

[14] Davidson's sketch of his so-called paratactic theory of attitude contexts is on the same track. Davidson likewise eschews reference shift in order to heed 'semantic innocence'. For a brief comparison between Davidson's 'paratactic' approach and the 'hypotactic' one I am advocating here, see Duží et al. (2010, p. 12). See also Bealer (1982, p. 148).

The well-known pattern Sylvan's example replicates is this. Already Smullyan (1948) objected to this example of Quine's (adjusted to our post-Plutonic times), stressing the need to distinguish between a condition and the satisfier of the condition:

(i.i)   Necessarily, 8 exceeds 5
(ii.i) The number of planets is 8
_____

(iiii.i) Necessarily, the number of planets exceeds 5

The argument is valid, *provided* 'The number of planets' names 8, just as '8' does. If this is so then (ii.i) states the self-identity of a number co-denoted by a definite description and a constant. So (iii.i) and (i.i) come out denoting one and the same proposition, though phrasing it differently, and the conclusion is identical to one of the premises. If the argument is going to pack any punch, (ii.i) must receive a somewhat different analysis. It is most reasonably construed as stating a logically *contingent* astronomical fact, which may still be grounded in nomological necessity: as the laws of nature would have it, the number of planets is 8, though logically the number of planets might have been another number, including 0. Accordingly, the number of planets is a *magnitude* (an empirical condition) whose values (satisfiers) are natural numbers. (ii.i) means that, contingently, the magnitude denoted by 'The number of planets' takes the value 8. Therefore, 'The number of planets' cannot replace '8' inside the scope of '$\Box$', which requires equivalence of conditions and not just of their satisfiers.[15]

Another example is *Partee's puzzle*:

(i.ii)   The temperature is rising
(ii.ii) The temperature is 90°F
_____

(iii.ii) 90°F is rising

___

[15] This argument is valid, because we remain safely within the same sort of context throughout (and the mathematics checks out): $\Box$(8 exceeds 5); $\Box$($2^3 = 8$) ∴ $\Box$(2^3 exceeds 5). See also Marcus (1993, pp. 36-38) on Smullyan. It is a by now well-established insight that "the equality relation that holds between expressions such as '9' and 'the number of planets' must be distinguished from the equality relation that holds, for example, between the expressions '9' and '7 + 2'. (Marcus, *ibid.*, p. 37.) (I would prefer the equality relations to relate, in the final analysis, not expressions, but their non-linguistic denotations.) In particular, this expresses a falsehood: "$\Box$(9 = the number of planets)", even if pretending that our solar system has exactly 9 planets, for this necessitation is not an option, as soon as "9 = the number of planets" is taken to state a logically contingent astronomical fact.

The first premise ascribes the property of rising to a magnitude (the temperature at some location), whereas the second premise picks out the value of the magnitude (at a particular index that is suppressed). The context '…is rising' requires as a substituend a term for a magnitude rather than just a term for one of its values.[16]

Kaplan's example below buttresses my suspicion that an insufficient analysis of (what appears to be) identity sentences fuels much of the frustration with operating on modal and attitude contexts. Kaplan (1986, p. 264) considers this argument:

(i.iii) It will soon be the case that the President of the United States is a woman
(ii.iii) The President of the United States = Nancy Reagan's spouse
_____
(iii.iii) It will soon be the case that Nancy Reagan's spouse is a woman

The conclusion is open to two readings, at least, on both of which it is peculiar, as intended by Kaplan. Either 'Nancy Reagan's spouse' is taken to have as its semantic value the individual who (in the mid-1980s) is both the President of the United States and the husband of Nancy Reagan, or whatever individual is a woman and Nancy Reagan's spouse in the near future (counting from 1986). The first reading we may call the transsexual one, for it requires of Nancy Reagan's spouse to go ahead and become a woman. The situation on the ground is that Ronald Reagan, as it happens, will be undergoing radical surgery. The second reading we may call the lesbian one, for it requires Nancy Reagan to go ahead and marry a woman. Kaplan's verdict is:

> Thus, substitutivity fails. Contexts of S [the operator 'it will soon be the case'] are opaque. (*Ibid.*)

I agree that substitutivity fails – for the *wrong* sort of substituends, that is. And if opacity is immunity to substitutivity of wrong substituends then opacity is a good thing. What is going on, though, is that Kaplan misdiagnoses why the argument is fallacious. The problem is that (i.iii) and (iii.iii) are explicitly temporal while (ii.iii) is not. The proper temporalization of (ii.iii) would be along the lines of:

(ii.iii′) Currently, the President of the United States = Nancy Reagan's spouse

If we set the current time as t_0, and the near future at t_1 (relative to 1986), then 'The President of the United States at t_0' and 'Nancy Reagan's spouse at t_0' share the same semantic value; Ronald Reagan, given the actual course of events. On the transsexual

---

[16] For further details and discussion, see Duží et al. (2010, pp. 124-25).

reading, (iii.iii) goes into "At t_1, the President of the United States at t_0 is a woman". On the lesbian reading, (iii.iii) goes into "At t_1, Nancy Reagan's spouse at t_1 is a woman".

But we also need to analyze '=' properly.[17] The sign obviously does not state the self-identity of some individual who is both the President of the United States and Nancy Reagan's spouse. So what does it state? "The President of the United States at t_0 = Nancy Reagan's spouse at t_0" comes with temporalization and so is on the right track. But the analysis is an analysis of time-indexed definite descriptions: given a time, a definite description denotes an individual (or nothing at all), on a Kaplan-style extensionalist analysis of definite descriptions. This analysis leaves it obscure what the semantics (esp. the semantic value) is of a definite description in the absence of a time assignment. In a paper published the same year as Kaplan's, Tichý (1986, p. 254) says,

> The sentence ["The man who lives next door is the man who runs the city"] conveys information about two offices, that of the man who lives next door and that of the man who runs the city. It gives us no clue as to who occupies those offices. But it tells us nevertheless something about them that might not have been the case: namely that they are co-occupied, that some individual or other holds them both. We have seen [*ibid.*, p. 253] that an office is a function whose value at a world-time is the occupant (if any) of the office in that world at that time. The assertive content of an identity sentence like the one just considered is simply to the effect that two such functions happen to take the same value in the actual world at the present time.

For starters, then, these two identity statements must be kept separate:

(i) $office_1 =_i office_2$ (*identity between intensions*)
(e) $office_1(wt) =_e office_2(wt)$ (*identity between extensions*)

In Tichý's semantic theory the analysis of (ii.iii) must define the set of world-time pairs at which the two offices named 'The President of the United States' and 'Nancy Reagan's spouse', respectively, share the same occupant. The analysis does not include Ronald Reagan. The set of world-time pairs at which those two offices are co-occupied will have as a proper subset those world-time pairs at which Ronald Reagan is their shared occupant.

---

[17] Sleigh (1967) takes opacity to be a fact of linguistic life, noting the resulting standard issues with substitutivity of identicals and quantifying-in. However, Sleigh offers no analysis of "Cicero = Tully" (*ibid.*, p. 23) or "Dr. Salazar = the dictator of Portugal" (*ibid.*, p. 24), nor does he note their obvious differences.

Tichýs' semantic theory is designed with universal transparency in mind.[18] As far as definite descriptions are concerned, his basic tenet is that they nowhere and never denote their respective unique descriptum (if any) and instead always, in any sort of context, denote one and the same empirical condition (what he calls an 'office'), which is modeled as a function from the logical space of possible worlds to a chronology, which in turn is modeled as a (partial) function from a domain of times to entities such as individuals, numbers, sets, etc. Programmatically stated, Tichý takes Frege's semantics for oblique ('*ungerade*') contexts and universalizes it so as to apply to all contexts. One crucial addition to Frege's semantics is the implementation of empirical indices such as worlds and times to model both modal and temporal variability. Another crucial addition is that it is insufficient to have 'the *F*' denote a *Sinn* or intension without the option to descend from the *Sinn* or intension to what it presents or has as a value at the index pair of evaluation. We want to be spared the embarrassment that a *Sinn* or intension is a celestial body illuminated by the Sun. Simply elevating the semantic value from a planet to a mode of presentation of a planet, as Frege does, is only half the job. Tichý accounts for the extensionalization of an intension by way of the intension being applied to the empirical indices of evaluation: given a world and a time, we are given the entity (if any) who or which occupies the office of the *F* at that dual index. Similarly, predicates do not denote, or have as their semantic value, either a set or a multitude of individuals, but a property; sentences do not denote a truth-value, but a truth-condition, which is what possible-world semantics knows as a 'proposition'.[19]

According to Tichý, 'Nancy Reagan's spouse' never has as its semantic value, or denotation, Ronald Reagan or any other individual. Rather its semantic value is the *condition* of being Nancy Reagan's spouse. Similarly, the semantic value of 'The Morning Star' is not Venus or any other individual, but the condition of being the brightest non-lunar celestial body in the morning sky. Reference shift has been abolished. Consequently and crucially, the reason 'Hesperus', 'Phosphorus' (or rather either their respective denotations or meanings) do not substitute is not because they would be identicals that opacity prevented from being substituted. There is no such thing as opacity in Tichý's

---

[18] See, for instance, Tichý (1986, pp. 251-56), (1978), (1975), and Duží et al. (2010, pp. 1-14). Tichý (1986, p. 253) wrong-foots Frege's reference-shifting semantics with the example, "The man who lives next door is sick and Ali believes that *he* is." What does '*he*' refer back to? Frege cannot offer a satisfactory answer. See also Forbes (1996, p. 344, display (5)). Frege, we might add, would also have trouble with this variant of quantifying-in: $\exists x\ (Fx \wedge Bel\ a\ (\ldots x \ldots))$. The two occurrences of *x* seem not to share the same value, the two values presumably being an extension and an intension, according to reference-shift theories. If they differ, an attempt to quantify-in will bring out this incongruity: there is no value of *x* such that that value is both an *F* and believed by *a* to be such-and-such.

[19] Tichý models a *property* as a function from worlds to a function from times to sets of individuals, identifying a set with its characteristic function, and he models a *proposition* as a function from worlds to a partial function from times to truth-values (i.e. truth-value gaps are an option).

semantics. Instead the reason is because they are not identicals. So the reason why Leibniz's Law 'fails' is because it is being misapplied to the wrong substituends, namely two non-synonymous, indeed not even logically equivalent definite descriptions (or offices/intensions, in the material mode).

So how are those two conditions, of being Nancy Reagan's spouse and being the brightest non-lunar celestial body in the morning sky, to be brought into contact with Reagan and Venus? By means of an additional premise, which states an empirical fact:

| (i.iv) | At $\langle w, t \rangle$ Nancy Reagan's spouse is male |
(ii.iv)	At $\langle w, t \rangle$ Nancy Reagan's spouse is Ronald Reagan
(iii.iv)	At $\langle w, t \rangle$ Ronald Reagan is male

| (i.v) | At $\langle w, t \rangle$ the Morning Star is a planet |
(ii.v)	At $\langle w, t \rangle$ the Morning Star is Venus
(iii.v)	At $\langle w, t \rangle$ Venus is a planet

Premises (i.iv/v) share the general linguistic form "The F is a G". Tichý offers various ways of logically analyzing this form, depending on the degree of semantic structure we wish to make explicit. For instance, (i.iv) obtains an individual (the person married to Nancy Reagan, or else nobody) via another individual (Nancy Reagan), while (ii.iv) obtains an individual (or else nobody) in one go. These differences are less relevant here, for all I want to make a case for at this point is that empirical definite descriptions denote a condition rather than the satisfier (the unique descriptum), if any, at the index or indices of evaluation. Kaplan, like so many before and after him, assumes that the right sort of substituends must be a pair of definite descriptions as soon as they happen to share the same descriptum, the background assumption being that the semantic value of a definite description is its descriptum. This overly extensionalist theory of definite descriptions is bound to run into trouble amidst non-extensional contexts, with referential opacity looming on the horizon.

In Section 3 I will present all the relevant semantic details, including the type-theoretic ones. At this juncture I will present the basic ideas in a semi-formal way to get the philosophy across. In case we construe the definite descriptions 'Nancy Reagan's spouse' and 'The Morning Star' as having identical semantic structure, then (i.iv/v) share this logical form (to be revised in Section 3), which underlies "The Morning Star is a planet":[20]

$$\lambda w \lambda t\, [Planet_{wt}\, MS_{wt}]$$

Let me decompose this complex, structured whole into its constituent parts, followed by type assignments. I am treating, for now, the modal and temporal indices as if they formed one index, thus glossing over subtleties that are irrelevant here.

- *Planet* : property
- $Planet_{wt}$: set
- *MS* : office
- MS_{wt} : individual
- $[Planet_{wt}\, MS_{wt}]$: (a presentation of a) truth-value
- $\lambda w \lambda t\, [Planet_{wt}\, MS_{wt}]$: (a presentation of a) proposition (truth-condition)

$[Planet_{wt}\, MS_{wt}]$ is the application of a set to an individual with a view to obtaining a truth-value. If *MS* is undefined at $\langle w, t \rangle$, the application fails and no truth-value emerges. If *MS* is defined at $\langle w, t \rangle$, the application of $Planet_{wt}$ to MS_{wt} yields a truth-value, according as the individual that is the extension of *MS* at $\langle w, t \rangle$ is a member of the extension of *Planet* at $\langle w, t \rangle$. The emerging truth-value is abstracted over by λt, and the resulting chronology (here, a function from times to truth-values) is abstracted over by λw.[21] An empirical truth-condition is, allowing a slight simplification, the set of world-time pairs at which a given function from worlds and times to truth-values returns the truth-value True. In set-theoretic terms, the truth-condition is this:

$$MS\langle w, t \rangle \in Planet\langle w, t \rangle$$

It is an open empirical question whether the actual world and the present time are members of the satisfaction class of this proposition.[22] Tichý's semantics is opposed to

---

[20] See Tichý (1971), Duží (2010).

[21] Hence it is a slight simplification when I use the notation '$\langle w, t \rangle$' as though intensions were defined on a *pair* of arguments rather than being defined on, first, worlds and, next, on times. The simplification is innocuous enough in this essay, but it is crucial to be technically able to treat the modal and the temporal separately. Tichý (1986) explains why, as does Duží et al. (2010, pp. 205-27), offering more by way of technical and philosophical exposition.

[22] The present time is here both the time *at* which and *about* which it is being asserted that the Morning Star is a planet. Hence the index of assertion and the index of evaluation coincide here.

privileging the actual world and the present time, treating instead all worlds and all times as being equal.[23]

(ii.iv/v) also share the same form, in case we align the former with the latter. Thus the semantic structure of "The Morning Star is Venus" is:

$$\lambda w \lambda t \, [= MS_{wt} \, Venus]$$

The newcomers are these two:

- *Venus* : individual
- = : identity between individuals

Identity relations, according to Tichý, are polymorphous functions which, when type-theoretically well-defined, take a pair of objects of the same type to a truth-value, according as the two functional arguments are one and the same object.[24] The challenge, then, is to capture the contingency of the truth (or falsity or truth-value gap, for that matter) that the Morning Star is Venus without infringing the absolute self-identity of Venus. First and foremost, the Morning Star and Venus are two distinct entities, even of two distinct types (an office and an individual, respectively). So what "The Morning Star is Venus" means is that, at $\langle w, t \rangle$, the office of Morning Star is occupied by Venus. The condition is that whatever individual is the occupant of *MS* at $\langle w, t \rangle$ be identical to Venus; or equivalently, due to the symmetry of identity, that Venus be identical to whatever individual is the occupant of *MS* at $\langle w, t \rangle$.

Notice that Tichý construes "The Morning Star is Venus", "The Morning Star is a planet", and all the other sentences we brought up above, as *modal* contexts. They all have a modal profile, and it is the same for all of them, namely contingency. Thus, a more careful analysis would rephrase, e.g., "The Morning Star is Venus" as "Contingently, the Morning Star is Venus". This is important, for this implies that every empirical sentence is an intensional context. Tichý does not introduce a contingency operator; rather he uses abstraction over at least worlds and often also times to capture contingency.[25] To amplify

---

[23] See Tichý (1971) and Duží et al. (2010, pp. 178-90).

[24] See Duží et al. (2010, pp. 296-300) for a survey of different sorts of identity statements, and (*ibid.*, pp. 301-10) for a detailed analysis of "Hesperus is Phosphorus", predicated on the premise that 'Hesperus', 'Phosphorus' denote two distinct offices. The sentence does not express the necessary self-identity of an individual bearing two names, but the contingent convergence of two distinct, differently named conditions in the same anonymous satisfier.

[25] An obvious exception to the standard pattern of $\lambda w \lambda t \, [...w...t...]$ is the modeling of nomological ('soft') necessity, which is captured thus: $\lambda w \forall t \, [...w...t...]$. Relative to a set of worlds, such-and-such is

the point made above, the more careful analysis is *not* "Actually and presently, the Morning Star is Venus".

In the full, final analysis presented in Section 3, the so-called *Trivialization* $^0MS_{wt}$ is a three-step *procedure* that is *typed* to produce or present an individual. Whether the procedure, if executed, does indeed produce or present an individual — namely the individual that occupies the office of Morning Star at the $\langle w, t \rangle$ of evaluation), and if so, which individual is thus produced — is beyond the procedure. Similarly, the Trivialization $^0Planet_{wt}$ is a three-step procedure that is typed to produce a set of individuals at $\langle w, t \rangle$. There is always going to be a set of planets, although it may be the empty set of individuals. In Section 3 the notation will become slightly, but importantly, more elaborate, because we want to identify the various parts of a whole, each part being a sub-procedure within a complex procedure. This is important because we need to gain access to some of those parts inside a *displayed* (as opposed to *executed*) procedure in order to manipulate them. In Tichý's theory, whenever an agent entertains a hyperpropositional attitude, the agent is related intentionally to a displayed procedure, where the attitude complement is the very procedure rather than what it produces when executed.[26] That is to say, in Fregean parlance, that the agent is related to a mode of presentation of a truth-condition. The twist is that the agent may well be innocent of which truth-condition is so presented.

2. TWO ARGUMENTS AGAINST UNQUALIFIED QUANTIFYING-IN

The general line of objection both to modalities and attitudes consists in arriving at a paradoxical property – like being necessarily, and also not necessarily, two-legged; or being believed, and also not being believed, by *a* to be a spy. In the light of paradox, quantifying-in becomes a spurious undertaking, for how could there be any value of *x* with this or that paradoxical property?

If existential quantification is not an option then, ipso facto, one of the hallmarks of extensional logic is not an option. Hence something somewhere is not quite right. Is the culprit a poor analysis of one or more of the premises, or is it any of the inference rules? Let me spill the beans straightaway. If you ask me, the arguments are flawed because of a

---

always or never true, i.e. laws of nature are necessary and atemporal only relative to an equivalence class of nomologically indistinguishable worlds. The major source of inspiration is the Armstrong-Dretske-Tooley conception of nomological necessity. See Duží et al. (2010, pp. 411-14).

[26] Tichý's original term was 'constructional attitude': see his (1988, pp. 221-24). 'Construction' is the term Tichý coined for his structured hyperintensions: see Section 3 of this essay. Tichý never got around to developing his notion of constructional/hyperintensional attitude to any great degree. The most recent references on hyperintensional attitudes *à la* Tichý are Duží et al. (2010, Ch. 5) and the three papers by Duží and myself.

deficient analysis of singular terms such as definite descriptions, which leads to a deficient analysis of identity sentences flanked by at least one definite description, which leads to wrongful applications of rules of extensional logic. The definite descriptions 'The man on the beach', 'The man in the brown hat' may contingently share the same unique descriptum (an individual). If they do, they still do not denote, or are in any semantically significant way 'about', their shared descriptum. Rather, to restate my position, they denote two distinct empirical conditions. The logical form of "The man on the beach is the man in the brown hat" is to the effect that two distinct conditions, named 'The man on the beach' and 'The man in the brown hat', contingently share the same anonymous satisfier. Hence, despite the contingent convergence of the two conditions, it is one thing to know or believe that the man on the beach is a spy and quite another that the man in the brown hat is a spy. Hence a does not entertain the contradictory belief that an individual both is, and is not, a spy. Hence it does not follow that there is an individual x such that a believes, and does not believe, that x is a spy.

The key move, thus, is to bar Leibniz's Law from applying in the first place, rather than dismissing the Law as invalid. The Law is valid, for sure, also in the most exacting attitude contexts, but it is not always applicable. Its substituends must be chosen carefully. A mere coincidence of two conditions in one satisfier is not good enough for substitution inside an attitude context. What is substitutable are hyperintensions for hyperintensions, intensions (functions) for intensions, and extensions (functional values) for extensions.

It is also important to keep the semantic and the logical issues apart while keeping their interplay in mind. Issues like quantification and substitution of identicals are logical ones; issues like the sense and denotation of definite descriptions and the sense of identity sentences flanked by definite descriptions are semantic ones. The interplay is first and foremost that a proper semantic analysis of 'the F'/'the G' and "The F = the G" must precede the application of Leibniz's Law and EG. Faced with an insufficient semantic analysis, the Law and/or EG are liable to being misapplied.

2.1 THE ARGUMENT FROM NON-FACTIVITY

The idea behind this particular argument is easily stated. An instance of EG will take us from a truth to a falsehood if EG conjures an object — an arbitrary value of an ∃-bound variable — into existence. Here is an example:

$$(5) \quad \frac{\text{Tilman is seeking the fountain of youth}}{\exists x \, (\text{Tilman is seeking } x)} \text{ EG}$$

where *x* ranges over *individuals*, on the assumption that the fountain of youth may be construed metaphysically as an individual. (5) violates the constraint that we may well seek what fails to exist. For a non-empirical example:

$$(6) \quad \frac{\text{Tilman is calculating the quotient of dividing 5 by 0}}{\exists y \,(\text{Tilman is calculating } y)} \quad \text{EG}$$

where *y* ranges over *natural numbers*. EG is not a magic wand we can wave to create a number where previously there was none. What is more, I am not comfortable with having Tilman be computationally related to a number. Calculation, in a nutshell, is all about applying operations to numbers in their capacity as operands in order to obtain a new number. And the computational effort may be futile, either because the agent lacks the sufficient skill to complete the calculation, or because the operation and one or more operands are a mismatch. Tilman's arithmetic predicament is that 0 is not a suitable divisor. The morale I draw is that this arithmetic predicament must not affect the semantics of Tilman's calculating the quotient of $\langle 5, 0 \rangle$. The sentence "Tilman is calculating the quotient of dividing 5 by 0" is perfectly meaningful and an apt vehicle for making an assertion about what Tilman is up to. So what we do is take a step back. Tilman is to be related computationally to a procedure and not the sort of object the procedure is typed to produce. It does affect the logic of Tilman's activity that 0 is a dysfunctional divisor. For his attitude is non-factive, hence quantifying over numbers is not an option, hence quantifying-in seems to be impossible, hence the attitude reported in the premise seems somewhat iffy. But Tilman's attitude is just fine, and quantifying-in *is* valid. We just need to quantify over procedures instead. The analysis of (6) actually proves helpful in unearthing the nature of Tilman's complement: where we might naïvely have expected a number, we realize we need instead a procedure typed to produce numbers. The format of the proper analysis, I submit, is (6'):

$$(6') \quad \frac{\text{Tilman is calculating the quotient of dividing 5 by 0}}{\exists c \,(\text{Tilman is calculating } c)} \quad \text{EG}$$

What is going on in the premise is that Tilman is intentionally related to some arithmetic procedure that he expects to deliver the quotient of dividing 5 by 0. The premise does not presuppose this or that particular procedure, e.g. the procedure of applying the division function to $\langle 5, 0 \rangle$. The conclusion does nothing other than spell out that there is some *procedure* or other that Tilman is deploying to this end.

(5) is a different kettle of fish by opening up the prospect of also quantifying over intensions.[27] Of course, there is also going to be a procedure (multiple, in fact) producing a given intension, so we can quantify over procedures as well, but quantifying over the lower-level entities of intensions makes for a stronger conclusion. What is going on in the premise is that Tilman is in the process of tracking down the occupant of an office. It is the office of the fountain of youth that is guiding Tilman's search and is what he is intentionally related to. The format of the proper analysis, I submit, is (5′):

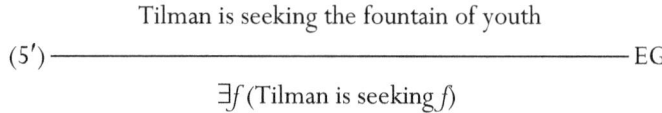

$$(5')\ \dfrac{\text{Tilman is seeking the fountain of youth}}{\exists f\,(\text{Tilman is seeking } f)} \ \text{EG}$$

where f ranges over *offices*. (5′) is a case of quantifying into an intensional context and quantifying over intensions of a particular type (offices, as it happens). It is an additional option to also quantify over hyperintensions producing intensions. (6′) is a case of quantifying into a hyperintensional context and quantifying over hyperintensions of a particular type (those producing natural numbers, as it happens).

In general, the argument from non-factive attitudes against quantifying-in has bite only if, when quantifying into a non-extensional context, we insist on quantifying over extensions such as individuals and numbers. The argument is seen to be barking up the wrong tree as soon as we include intensions and hyperintension (procedures) into our ontology for our variables to quantify over. The retreat, as it were, or ascent to non-extensional entities is not an attempt to dodge the problem. Rather it serves to get clearer about the attitude complement in the premise.

---

[27] Zimmermann (2006, p. 728) brings up this 'unwelcome inference':

$$\dfrac{\text{I owe you nothing [i.e. there is nothing I owe you]}}{\text{I owe you something [i.e. there is something I owe you]}}$$

Unwelcome it is, in case we are quantifying over extensional entities. But suppose we are quantifying over *properties*:

$$\dfrac{\text{There is no property of which I owe you an instance}}{\text{There is at least one property of which I do not owe you an instance}}$$

Then we obtain a valid argument favouring quantifying-in.

2.2 THE ARGUMENT FROM DOUBLETHINK

Quine (1956) has us consider these three assumptions:

(1) Ralph believes that the F is an H
(2) Not (Ralph believes that the G is an H)
(3) The F = the G
_____

(4)   ?

Quine then asks: does Ralph, or does he not, believe that the individual who is both the F and the G is an H? In Quine's example, Ralph believes that the man he has seen in the brown hat is a spy; Ralph does not believe (i.e. abstains from believing) that the man he has seen on the beach is a spy; the man in the brown hat and the man on the beach are one and the same man.

The tricky bit is not that it is inferable that there is an individual x such that Ralph has both seen x wear a brown hat and has seen x on the beach. The tricky bit is rather that it seems we could infer that that there is an individual x such that Ralph both believes, and does not believe, that x is a spy. What quantification does is quantify away the two different aspects under which Ralph has made acquaintance with an individual, retaining only the individual himself, in his capacity as a value of x. Quine's question is unreasonable, in my view, for Ralph does not know that (3) is true. If he did, he would rationally have to update his belief base. Only then would it make sense for Quine to ask his question. The reason, of course, why Quine raises this question is because he wants to challenge the logic underlying (1) and (2). From the above premise set it seems we can extract the contradiction that there is an x such that Ralph believes that x is a spy and Ralph does not believe that x is a spy.

A reductio enjoins us to reconsider the premises and the rules of inference. The solution, as suggested above, is to make the semantics of 'the F'/'the G' the pivotal point. What we can infer from (1) is that there is an office y such that Ralph believes that the occupant of y at $\langle w, t \rangle$, i.e. y_{wt}, is a spy. What we can infer from (2) is that there is an office z such that it is not the case that Ralph believes that z_{wt} is a spy. What we can infer from (3) is that there are two offices z', z'' such that $z'_{wt} = z''_{wt}$, i.e. that z', z'' are co-occupied at $\langle w, t \rangle$. What we *cannot* infer from (1) through (3) is the conjunction that there is an office z''' such that Ralph believes that z'''_{wt} is a spy and it is not the case that Ralph believes that z'''_{wt} is a spy. The reason for this is that z'_{wt}, z''_{wt} are not interchangeable inside (1), (2). These contexts are not extensional, for what matters is not the convergence between

z'_{wt}, z''_{wt} in some anonymous individual, as reported by (3). Instead what matters is whether 'z''', 'z'''' co-denote the same office. And they do not, for $z' \neq z''$. So 'z'_{wt}' and 'z''_{wt}' are not intersubstitutable in the context preceded by 'believes'. The upshot is that (3) becomes irrelevant. With (3) out of the picture, (1) and (2) are too weak to sustain the contradictory conclusion we have been trying to avoid all along.

3. VALIDATING QUANTIFYING-IN

In this section I present the logical details required to pull off quantifying into a non-factive, hyperpropositional attitude context within Tichý's framework called Transparent Intensional Logic. Formally, TIL is a partial, typed, hyperintensional λ-calculus. Its λ-terms are interpreted by way of a procedural (as opposed to denotational or extensionalist) semantics. TIL belongs squarely to the paradigm of theories of hyperintensionally individuated, structured meaning. TIL is arguably the most elaborate procedural semantics for logical analysis of natural language on the market.[28] TIL arguably also offers what are presently the most worked-out criteria of hyperintensional individuation.[29] What is of primary importance here is that TIL has an elaborate theory of hyperintensional attitudes.

Still new theories of hyperintensions are being spawned at present. They divide into at least three different kinds: (i) hyperintensions as primitive black-boxes (e.g. Thomason 1980, Bealer 1982 and later); (ii) Cresswell-style hyperintensions as set-theoretic sequences; and (iii) hyperintensions as procedures (e.g. Hanks 2011, 2013, Soames 2010). My (2012) explains why I have little time for (i) and (ii), and why I much prefer (iii). The basic idea is that hyperintensional individuation is procedural individuation, and that procedures are very apt at accommodating very fine semantic and logical differences. For instance, a theory of procedural semantics worth its name will assign two distinct meanings, i.e. procedures, to '7 + 5' and '5 + 7'. Accordingly, one procedure is to calculate the sum of $\langle 7, 5 \rangle$, and quite another to calculate the sum of $\langle 5, 7 \rangle$, because the respective arguments are organized in two distinct sequences.

---

[28] See Duží et al. (2010, Ch. 1).

[29] Duží and Jespersen (forthcoming, Section 2) motivates and defines TIL's latest criterion, called (A''), which is a variant of Church's Alternative (A1), by containing a slightly more detailed definition of α-conversion and β-conversion-by-value, whereas Church has α-conversion and β-conversion-by-name. The main reason we are leaving out η-conversion is that it fails to guarantee equivalent conversion in a partial logic such as TIL. See also Jespersen (forthcoming, Section 3, Def. 4) for the exact definition of A''.

The example I will be analyzing here is the following sentence:

"Le Verrier believes that Vulcan causes Mercury's perturbations" (*analysandum*)

Le Verrier had discovered Neptune in 1846, his observation of the planet being preceded by mathematical calculations and speculations. He claimed, in 1860, to have established the existence of a planet orbiting between Mercury and the Sun, also on the basis of observation (though somebody else's) preceded by calculation and speculation. The grammatical proper name 'Vulcan' (or 'Vulcanus'), originally used for the Roman god of fire and volcanoes, seemed an apt name for a planet so close to the Sun. Problem is, no planet has so far ever been found between Mercury and the Sun. Must the semanticist draw the conclusion that the astronomer's 'Vulcan' lacks a semantic value? The conclusion seems tempting; but it is a temptation that should not be yielded to. For Le Verrier has a belief *about* something, and his intentional act is one I want to take seriously in the sense of according an abstract object to it. What we can rule out is that his intention was directed at an *individual*, for there is none at the receiving end, unlike what holds for his beliefs about Neptune. So this attempt to quantify-in will be a wheel spinning in the void:[30]

> There is an individual x such that Le Verrier believes that x causes Mercury's perturbations.

But this one latches on to an entity:

> There is an office f such that Le Verrier believes that the occupant of f causes Mercury's perturbations.

So does this one:

> There is a hyperintension h such that Le Verrier believes that the occupant of the office constructed by h causes Mercury's perturbations.

---

[30] One might still wonder why that conclusion does not follow. The reason is that this existential quantification takes place *outside* Le Verrier's doxastic perspective. The actual celestial scheme of things does not include an individual that causes Mercury's perturbations. Hence the conclusion would be false. This becomes especially clear if we phrase the conclusion as a belief *de re*: There is an individual x of which Le Verrier believes that it causes Mercury's perturbations; or: There is an individual x that is believed by Le Verrier to cause Mercury's perturbations (cf. n.35). This sort of attribution would be forthcoming if, for instance, Le Verrier had first identified Venus and then gone on to misidentify Venus as the cause of Mercury's perturbations. The opposite case, with the quantifier inside the scope of the belief operator, would state an uncontroversial truth: Le Verrier believes that there is an individual x such that x causes Mercury's perturbations. (Thanks to Alessandro Torza for raising the initial point.)

I stipulate Le Verrier's doxastic attitude to be a relation-in-intension between an individual and a hyperproposition. Alternatively, his complement might have been an intension, *in casu* a proposition. But my reason for going with the hyperproposition is to demonstrate how to *quantify into a hyperpropositional attitude context* while making the strongest quantification we can make when non-factive empirical attitudes are involved, which is in this case *quantification over offices*.

3.1 BASIC DEFINITIONS

To proceed from the philosophical remarks made above to a logical theory of quantifying-in, we need to introduce the following basic definitions, which also introduce the relevant notation. The notation will be implemented in Section 3.2. Section 3.3 presents and proves the validity of the rule of quantifying-in that our analysandum requires.

Definition 1 (*types of order 1*). Let B be a *base*, where a base is a collection of pair-wise disjoint, non-empty sets. Then:
(i) Every member of B is an elementary *type of order 1 over B*.
(ii) Let $\alpha, \beta_1, ..., \beta_m$ ($m > 0$) be types of order 1 over B. Then the collection $(\alpha \beta_1 ... \beta_m)$ of all m-ary partial mappings from $\beta_1 \times ... \times \beta_m$ into α is a functional *type of order 1 over B*.
(iii) Nothing else is a *type of order 1 over B*. □

For the purposes of natural-language analysis, we are currently assuming the following base of *ground types*, each of which is part of the ontological commitments of TIL:

> ο: the set of truth-values $\{\mathbf{T}, \mathbf{F}\}$;
> ι: the set of individuals (constant universe of discourse);
> τ: the set of real numbers (doubling as temporal continuum);
> ω: the set of logically possible worlds (logical space).

Construction is Tichý's formal notion of structured hyperintension, interpreted philosophically as a procedure.[31]

Definition 2 (*construction*).
(i) (*Variable*) Let valuation v assign object o to variable x. Then x is a v-*construction* of o.

---

[31] I am leaving out two constructions — *Single* and *Double Execution* — which I do not need when quantifying into the particular hyperintensional contexts considered here.

(ii) (*Trivialization*) Let X be any object whatsoever (i.e. an extension, an intension, or a construction). Then ^0X is the *Trivialization* of X, which *constructs* X without any change of X.

(iii) (*Composition*) Let X, $Y_1,\ldots Y_m$ be objects of any type. Let X *v-construct* a function f of type $(\alpha\ \beta_1\ldots\beta_m)$, and let $Y_1, \ldots, Y_m$ *v-construct* entities $B_1, \ldots, B_m$ of types $\beta_1, \ldots, \beta_m$, respectively. Then the *Composition* $[X\ Y_1\ldots Y_m]$ *v-constructs* the value (an entity, if any, of type α) of f on the tuple argument $\langle B_1, \ldots, B_m \rangle$. Otherwise the *Composition* $[X\ Y_1\ldots Y_m]$ does not *v-construct* anything and so is *v-improper*.

(iv) (*Closure*) Let $x_1,\ldots, x_m$, Y be objects of any type. Let $x_1,\ldots, x_m$ be pair-wise distinct variables *v-constructing* entities of types $\beta_1, \ldots, \beta_m$, and let Y be a *construction v-constructing* an α-entity. Then $[\lambda x_1 \ldots x_m\ Y]$ is the *construction* λ-*Closure* (or *Closure*). It *v-constructs* the following function f of type $(\alpha\beta_1\ldots\beta_m)$. Let $v'(B_1/x_1,\ldots,B_m/x_m)$ be a valuation identical with v at least up to assigning objects $B_1/\beta_1, \ldots, B_m/\beta_m$ to variables $x_1, \ldots, x_m$. If Y is $v'(B_1/x_1,\ldots,B_m/x_m)$-improper (see iii), then f is undefined on $\langle B_1, \ldots, B_m \rangle$. Otherwise the value of f on $\langle B_1, \ldots, B_m \rangle$ is the α-entity $v'(B_1/x_1,\ldots,B_m/x_m)$-*constructed* by Y.

(v) Nothing else is a *construction*. □

Here are some informal explications of each kind of construction.[32] Bear in mind that the overarching idea behind the notion of construction is that, given some input objects, we can apply operations or procedures, i.e. constructions, to obtain some output objects (or none, in some instances of Composition). A *variable* constructs an object by having this object as its value dependently on a valuation function *v* arranging variables and objects in a sequence. *Trivialization* is TIL's objectual or material counterpart of a non-descriptive constant term, which simply harpoons a particular object. *Composition* is the procedure of functional application, rather than the functional value (if any) resulting from application. *Closure* is the procedure of functional abstraction, rather than the resulting function.

Variables and Trivializations are the one-step or primitive or *atomic* constructions of TIL. In particular, what does not exist cannot be Trivialized. (Similarly, what does not exist cannot be named; but it can be described, as per 'the largest prime' or 'is a winged unicorn'.) Composition and Closure are the multiple-step or *composite* procedures. An *atomic* construction is a structured whole with but one proper part, namely the construction itself. Importantly, the proper part of ^0X is ^0X and not X, which is located beyond ^0X: the product of a procedure is no part of the procedure. A *composite* construction is a structured whole with more proper parts than just itself.

---

[32] These explications draw on material from Jespersen (forthcoming, Section 3).

The definition of the typed universe of TIL amounts to a definition of the ramified hierarchy of types which divides into three parts; firstly, simple types of order 1, which were already defined by Definition 1; secondly, types belonging to order $*_n$; thirdly, types of order $*_{n+1}$.

Definition 3 (*ramified hierarchy of types*).
T_1 (*types of order 1*). See Def. 1.
C_n (*constructions of order n*)
  i) Let x be a variable ranging over a type of order n. Then x is a *construction of order n over B*.
  ii) Let X be a member of a type of order n. Then ^0X is a *construction of order n over B*.
  iii) Let $X, X_1,..., X_m$ ($m > 0$) be constructions of order n over B. Then $[X\ X_1...\ X_m]$ is a *construction of order n over B*.
  iv) Let $x_1,...x_m$, X ($m > 0$) be constructions of order n over B. Then $[\lambda x_1...x_m\ X]$ is a *construction of order n over B*.
  v) Nothing is a *construction of order n over B* unless it so follows from C_n (i)-(iv).

T_{n+1} (*types of order $*_{n+1}$*) Let $*_n$ be the collection of all constructions of order $*_n$ over B. Then
  i) $*_n$ and every type of order n are *types of order n+1*.
  ii) If $m > 0$ and $\alpha, \beta_1,...,\beta_m$ are types of order $n+1$ over B, then $(\alpha\ \beta_1\ ...\ \beta_m)$ (see T_1 ii)) is a *type of order n + 1 over B*.
  iii) Nothing else is a *type of order n + 1 over B*. □

As a notational convention, 'X/α' means that object X is of type α.

Definition 4 (*existential quantifier*). The *existential quantifier* $\exists^\alpha$ is a type-theoretically polymorphous, total function of type $(o(o\alpha))$, for an arbitrary type α, defined as follows: $\exists^\alpha$ is the function that associates a class S of α-elements with **T** if S is a non-empty class, otherwise with **F**. □

An occurrence of a bound variable is either ^{0}-bound ('Trivialization-bound') or λ-bound or both. Bound occurrences contrast with free occurrences. Hence:

Definition 5 (*free and bound occurrences of variables*). Let C be a construction with at least one occurrence of a variable ξ.

i) Let C be ξ. Then the *occurrence of ξ in C is free*.
ii) Let C be ^0X. Then every *occurrence of ξ in C is ^{0}-bound*.

iii) Let C be $[\lambda x_1...x_n\, Y]$. Any *occurrence of* ξ in Y that is one of x_i, $1 \leq i \leq n$, is λ-*bound* in C unless it is ^{0}-*bound* in Y. Any *occurrence of* ξ in Y that is neither ^{0}-*bound* nor λ-*bound* in Y is *free* in C.

iv) No other *occurrence* of ξ is *free*, λ-*bound*, ^{0}-*bound* in C. □

3.2 EXECUTED VERSUS DISPLAYED OCCURRENCE OF CONSTRUCTIONS, AND TWO ADDITIONAL FUNCTIONS

If our analysandum above were an intensional attitude, as per possible-world semantics, then the analysis would be this, where P is the relational property, of type $(o\iota)_{\tau\omega}$, of causing Mercury's perturbations:

$$\lambda w \lambda t\ [^0B_{wt}\ ^0LeV\ \lambda w \lambda t\ [^0P_{wt}\ ^0V_{wt}]]$$

B is typed as a relation-in-intension between an individual (a doxastic agent) and a proposition (truth-condition): $B/(o\iota o_{\tau\omega})_{\tau\omega}$.

The hyperproposition $\lambda w \lambda t\ [^0P_{wt}\ ^0V_{wt}]$, of type $*_1$, produces a proposition, of type $o_{\tau\omega}$, and Le Verrier believes that this proposition is true. TIL says that $\lambda w \lambda t\ [^0P_{wt}\ ^0V_{wt}]$ occurs *executed* in the context $\lambda w \lambda t\ [^0B_{wt}\ ^0LeV\ \lambda w \lambda t\ [^0P_{wt}\ ^0V_{wt}]]$, because it descends to its product (a proposition). Le Verrier's attitude becomes a hyperintensional one as soon as $\lambda w \lambda t\ [^0P_{wt}\ ^0V_{wt}]$ occurs *displayed*.[33] The hyperintensional analysis is this:

$$\lambda w \lambda t\ [^0B^*_{wt}\ ^0LeV\ ^0[\lambda w \lambda t\ [^0P_{wt}\ ^0V_{wt}]]]$$

B^* is typed as a relation-in-intension between an individual (a doxastic agent) and a hyperproposition: $B^*/(o\iota *_1)_{\tau\omega}$. With Le Verrier as the first argument of B^*, the second argument is the construction $[\lambda w \lambda t\ [^0P_{wt}\ ^0V_{wt}]]$. What Le Verrier believes* is that the hyperproposition presents a proposition that is true.

The advertised qualifications of quantifying-in are the following two. First, B/B^* is a non-factive attitude, so we need to be careful when selecting a quantificational range for the $\exists$-bound variable x occurring in the hyperintensional context

$$^0[\lambda w \lambda t\ [^0P_{wt}\ x]]$$

---

[33] Duží and Jespersen (forthcoming, Sections 2.4 and 3.2) offers a detailed exposition of the twin notion of executed and displayed occurrence of constructions.

The range cannot be ι; I suggest $\iota_{\tau\omega}$, i.e. offices occupiable by individuals. If we go along with this typing, we need to extensionalize the value of x to obtain the right type of object of which to predicate the property of being a P. Hence

$$^0[\lambda w \lambda t\ [^0P_{wt}\ x_{wt}]]$$

Second, x will be *doubly bound*. When saying that x is $\exists$-bound I am being imprecise, for we are inside a λ-calculus, so in principle all variable-binding is λ-binding. Hence $\exists \lambda x$ is what we want: the function $\exists$ is applied to the set produced by λx, yielding a truth-value (just as in Montague). However, TIL has an additional form of variable-binding, introduced in Def. 5 ii), namely Trivialization-binding: ^0x. Thus x is both λ-bound and Trivialization-bound — and the latter trumps the former, for the Trivialization of a context makes each of its constituent parts occur Trivialized as well, as per Def. 4 ii):

$$^0\exists \lambda x \ldots\ ^0[\lambda w \lambda t\ [^0P_{wt}\ x_{wt}]]$$

This means that x occurs displayed in $^0[\lambda w \lambda t\ [^0F_{wt}\ x_{wt}]]$, for each component part of this context occurs displayed, without x descending to any of the values in its quantificational range. The upshot is that the λ of $\exists \lambda x$ cannot bind x. For this λ to bind x, x would have to occur executed in order to descend to a value. This explains why the following will not do:

$$\lambda w \lambda t\ [^0\exists \lambda x\ [^0B*_{wt}\ ^0LeV\ ^0[\lambda w \lambda t\ [^0P_{wt}\ x_{wt}]]]]$$

This simplistic analysis of quantifying-in would be not unlike the futile attempt to quantify into a quoted context, an undertaking Quine would frequently, fervently and correctly warn against. Without suitable qualification, quantifying-in will be rendered illogical. We need a much more subtle way in than forced entry. The logical challenge is to make a Trivialization-bound occurrence of x amenable to λ-binding. Some logical work needs to be performed in the '?'-marked area of

$$^0\exists \lambda x \ldots ? \ldots\ ^0[\lambda w \lambda t\ [^0P_{wt}\ x_{wt}]]$$

TIL makes x amenable to λ-binding by means of the polymorphous functions *Sub* and *Tr*. *Sub* substitutes (all the occurrences of) one construction for (all the occurrences of) another construction inside a third construction to obtain a fourth construction.

Substitution is construed as a primitive operation. *Tr* takes an entity of the arbitrary type α and returns its Trivialization.[34]

Definition 6 (Sub^n). Let $C_1/*_{n+1} \to *_n$, $C_2/*_{n+1} \to *_n$, $C_3/*_{n+1} \to *_n$ v-construct constructions D_1, D_2, D_3, respectively. Then the Composition $[^0Sub^n\ C_1\ C_2\ C_3]$ v-constructs the construction D that results from D_3 by collisionless substitution of D_1 for all occurrences of D_2 in D_3. □

Definition 7 (Tr^α). The function $Tr^\alpha/(*_n\ \alpha)$ returns as its value the Trivialization of its α-argument. □

For instance, let variable y v-construct entities of type ι, such as a. Then $[^0Tr^1\ y]$ $v(a/y)$-constructs ^0a. Therefore, the Composition $[^0Sub^1\ [^0Tr^1\ y]\ ^0x\ ^0[^0F_{wt}\ x]]$ $v(a/y)$-constructs the Composition $[^0F_{wt}\ ^0a]$. Note that there is a substantial difference between the *construction* Trivialization and the *function* Tr^α. Whereas ^0y constructs just the variable y regardless of valuation, as y is ^{0}-bound in ^0y, $[^0Tr^1\ y]$ v-constructs the Trivialization of the object v-constructed by y. Hence y occurs free in $[^0Tr^1\ y]$.

3.3. RULES OF QUANTIFYING-IN

We now have everything we need to introduce two *rules of existential quantification into hyperpropositional attitude contexts*. For the first rule, let the type-theoretic assignments be as follows, where '$C \to_v \alpha$' means that construction C constructs an entity of type α dependently on a valuation v of the variables involved: as above, $B*/(o\iota*_n)_{\tau\omega}$ is a hyperpropositional attitude relation; $\exists/(o(o*_n))$; a an individual of type ι; $C(X)/*_n \to_v o_{\tau\omega}$ a propositional construction with a constituent $X/*_n$ such that X v-constructs entities of type α; $d/*_n \to_v \alpha$; $c/*_{(n+1)} \to_v *_n$. This last type assignment makes it clear that quantifying into hyperintensional contexts requires a fair amount of expressive power, since we need a higher-order construction to construct a lower-order construction.

The *rule* is this:

$$\frac{[B*_{wt}\ ^0a\ ^0C(X/d)]}{[^0\exists\lambda c\ [B*_{wt}\ ^0a\ [^0Sub\ c\ ^0d\ ^0C(d)]]]} \text{(Rule A)}$$

---

[34] Duží and Jespersen (forthcoming, Section 3.3) provides a detailed exposition of *Sub* and *Tr*.

The basic idea behind the proof of the rule is as follows. The Composition $[^0Sub\ c\ ^0d\ ^0C(d)]$ $v(X/c)$-constructs the construction $C(X)$. Hence at any $\langle w, t \rangle$ at which $[B*_{wt}\ ^0a\ ^0C(X/d)]$ v-construct **T**, the set of constructions v-constructed by $\lambda c\ [B*_{wt}\ ^0a\ [^0Sub\ c\ ^0d\ ^0C(d)]]$ is non-empty, and the conclusion $[^0\exists*\lambda c\ [B*_{wt}\ ^0a\ [^0Sub\ c\ ^0d\ ^0C(d)]]]$ v-constructs **T** as well.[35]

The quantification in the conclusion states explicitly that the set of constructions such that they occur displayed inside the context C is non-empty. The rule actually borders on triviality. This fact only speaks in its favour, for quantifying into hyperintensional contexts should, *in principle*, if not technically, be no different from quantifying into extensional contexts. The technical finesse the conclusion exhibits resides in the fact that the variable c occurs *outside* the hyperintensional context of the displayed construction C. Therefore, c occurs *free* in the Composition $[^0Sub\ c\ ^0d\ ^0C(d)]$, making it amenable to λ-binding and subsequently to existential quantification.

The above rule is too weak, however, to yield the conclusion that there is an *office f* such that Le Verrier believes that f_{wt} has property P. To validate the following inference, we need a stronger rule of quantifying-in, which will be presented below:[36]

Le Verrier believes* that Vulcan causes Mercury's perturbations
___
There is an *office f* such that Le Verrier believes* that f_{wt} causes Mercury's perturbations

The stronger *rule* we need is this one:

$$\frac{[^0B*_{wt}\ ^0a\ ^0C(X/g)]}{[^0\exists'\lambda f[^0B*_{wt}\ ^0a\ [^0Sub\ [^0Tr\ f]\ ^0g\ ^0C(g)]]]} \quad (Rule\ B)$$

---

[35] This rule stems from Duží and Jespersen (forthcoming) where it is labeled 'Rule$_4$,' and the full proof, of twelve steps and involving additional notions, is provided. Rule$_4$ applies to *de dicto* attitudes, such as the above analysandum "Le Verrier believes* that Vulcan causes Mercury's perturbations'. There is a different rule for the *de re* variant (R$_5$), which may be phrased in either of two ways: (i) "Le Verrier believes* *of* Vulcan that *it* causes Mercury's perturbations", which uses the active voice and introduces an anaphor, and (ii) "Vulcan is believed by Le Verrier to cause Mercury's perturbations", which uses the passive voice in order to predicate of the occupant of Vulcan the property of being believed* by Le Verrier to be such-and-such. Hyperintensional and intensional propositional attitudes *de re* are studied in great detail in Duží and Jespersen (2012). Non-propositional ('objectual') attitudes like *calculating* are studied in Duží and Jespersen (forthcoming).

[36] This rule is a slightly restricted variant of what is called 'Rule$_3$' in Duží and Jespersen (forthcoming).

The rule, however, applies only if X is already a Trivialization of a $\iota_{\tau\omega}$-object. If the office were constructed in a more complex manner than merely by means of Trivialization, then we would not be in a position to substitute its Trivialization: a's perspective in the premise must be reproduced in the conclusion in order to retain the hyperintensional character of a's attitude. I am presupposing that X is a Trivialization in order to keep the rule manageable. Hence, let X be a Trivialization of a $\iota_{\tau\omega}$-object. Then we can *quantify into* the hyperintensional context Trivialized by $^0C(X/g)$ by means of *Rule A* and *quantify over* this $\iota_{\tau\omega}$-object by means of *Rule B*. The new types are: $f, g \to_v \iota_{\tau\omega}$; $\exists'/(o(o\iota_{\tau\omega}))$.

The idea behind the proof of *Rule B* is this. Let X be the Trivialization of the $\iota_{\tau\omega}$-typed object b, i.e. X is ^0b. Then $[^0Sub\ [^0Tr\ f]\ ^0g\ ^0C(g)]\ v(b/f)$-constructs the construction C in which all the occurrences of g have been replaced by occurrences of ^0b. Thus, if $[^0B*_{wt}\ ^0a\ ^0C(X/g)]$ v-constructs **T** then $[^0B*_{wt}\ ^0a\ [^0Sub\ [^0Tr\ f]\ ^0g\ ^0C(g)]]\ v(b/f)$-constructs **T**. The conclusion, $[^0\exists'\lambda f[^0B*_{wt}\ ^0a\ [^0Sub\ [^0Tr\ f]\ ^0g\ ^0C(g)]]]$, means that there is an office f such that a believes* that such-and-such is true of f_{wt}. It does not follow that a believes* that the same is true of individual g_{wt}, even if f and g are co-occupied, or is true of individual i, even if i occupies f.

The full *proof* of *Rule B* is this. According to Defs. 6 and 7, the Composition $[^0Sub\ [^0Tr\ x]\ ^0y\ ^0C(y)]\ v(b/x)$-constructs the construction $C(^0b/y)$ in which the occurrences of y have been replaced by ^0b. Thus the following proof-steps are truth-preserving, *Att** a hyperintensional attitude:

1) $[Att*_{wt}\ a\ ^0C(^0b/y)]$ ∅
2) $[^0=_* [^0Sub\ [^0Tr\ x]\ ^0y\ ^0C(y)]\ ^0C(^0b/y)]$ 1, Defs. 6, 7
3) $[Att*_{wt}\ a\ [^0Sub\ [^0Tr\ x]\ ^0y\ ^0C(y)]]$ 2, Leibniz
4) $[\lambda x\ [Att*_{wt}\ a\ [^0Sub\ [^0Tr\ x]\ ^0y\ ^0C(y)]]\ ^0b]$ 3, λ-abstraction
5) $\neg[^0Empty\ \lambda x\ [Att*_{wt}\ a\ [^0Sub\ [^0Tr\ x]\ ^0y\ ^0C(y)]]]$ 4, Def. 2 iii)
6) $[^0\exists \lambda x\ [Att*_{wt}\ a\ [^0Sub\ [^0Tr\ x]\ ^0y\ ^0C(y)]]]$ 5, EG

We are able now to formalize the inference stated in prose above.[37] The most significant types are as follows: V (*Vulcan*), an office of type $\iota_{\tau\omega}$; LeV (*Le Verrier*), an individual of type

---

[37] When *analyzing* an argument bearing on a natural-language inference, we encode in symbolic notation the propositional constructions that are the respective meaning of the premise(s) and the conclusion. When *proving* an argument, the first step is λ-elimination, because each step is to be *truth*-preserving (valid) and not meaning-preserving.

ι; B^*, a hyperintensional attitude whose complement (second argument) is a construction of a proposition; and *Sub* of type $(*_1*_1*_1*_1)$.

$$\lambda w \lambda t \, [^0B^*_{wt} \, ^0LeV \, ^0[\lambda w \lambda t \, [^0P_{wt} \, ^0V_{wt}]]]$$

$$\lambda w \lambda t \, [^0\exists' \lambda f [^0B^*_{wt} \, ^0LeV \, [^0Sub \, [^0Tr \, f] \, ^0g \, ^0[\lambda w \lambda t \, [^0P_{wt} \, g_{wt}]]]]]$$

One admissible value of f is the office of Vulcan, regardless of the empirical fact that Vulcan is actually vacant. The Composition $[^0Sub \, [^0Tr \, f] \, ^0g \, ^0[\lambda w \lambda t \, [^0P_{wt} \, g_{wt}]]]$ $v(V/f)$-constructs the Closure $\lambda w \lambda t \, [^0P_{wt} \, ^0V_{wt}]$.

Note that if, in the conclusion, Le Verrier were related to the Trivialization $^0[^0Sub \, c \, ^0V \, ^0[\lambda w \lambda t \, [^0P_{wt} \, ^0V_{wt}]]]$, rather than the Composition $[^0Sub \, c \, ^0V \, ^0[\lambda w \lambda t \, [^0P_{wt} \, ^0V_{wt}]]]$, he would find himself facing the very procedure of executing the substitution, and not just its product or result. Le Verrier would need to be not only an astronomer and mathematician, but also a logician. This is one assumption we should not be making; if we want agents to carry out acts of substitution themselves, we need to add the (empirically unrealistic) premise that agents always execute the substitutions they are confronted with and do so flawlessly. The above analysis relates Le Verrier instead to the result of the substitution.

Also the inference does not require Le Verrier to perform an inferential act to the effect that since he believes* that Vulcan causes Mercury's perturbations then there is an office whose occupant he believes* to have this property. Le Verrier is not availing himself of inferential knowledge. Whoever does draw the above inference learns the logical nature of Vulcan, namely that Vulcan is typed as an office, of type $\iota_{\tau\omega}$, and not as an individual, of type ι, and also that there exists at the pair of evaluation $\langle w, t \rangle$ at least one office such that Le Verrier believes* that its occupant causes Mercury's perturbations.

CONCLUSION

Above I demonstrated how to achieve existential quantification into one sort of hyperintensional attitude context and over intensional entities of a particular type. This achievement helps move hyperintensional logic in particular and philosophical logic and formal semantics in general one step further ahead. The investigation into the validity of quantifying into hyperintensional attitude contexts serves at least two purposes. One is to make explicit an ontological commitment that is implicit in the premise. Reflecting on quantifying-in challenges us to get clear(er) about the nature of the object that is constructed by a particular constituent construction that occurs inside an agent's hyperintensional attitude complement. The other purpose is to field quantifying-in as a touchstone for various theories of hyperintensionality: do they, or do they not, validate quantifying-in, and if they do, how do they achieve this? TIL validates quantifying-in, and it does so in a principled manner. Quantifying-in, in TIL, does not require contextualist epicycles or other ad hoc measures, but flows forth from its semantics, which sports universal transparency.[38]

REFERENCES

Bealer, G. (1982), *Quality and Concept*, Oxford: Clarendon Press.
Duží, M. (2012), 'Extensional logic of hyperintensions', *Lecture Notes in Computer Science*, vol. 7260, pp. 268-90.
Duží, M. and B. Jespersen (forthcoming), 'Transparent quantification into hyperintensional objectual attitudes', *Synthese*, DOI: 10.1007/s11229-014-0578-z.
Duží, M. and B. Jespersen, 'Transparent quantification into hyperpropositional contexts *de dicto*', in revision.
Duží, M. and B. Jespersen (2012), 'Transparent quantification into hyperpropositional contexts *de re*', *Logique et Analyse*, vol. 220, pp. 513-54.
Duží, M., B. Jespersen and P. Materna (2010), *Procedural Semantics for Hyperintensional Logic: Foundations and Applications of Transparent Intensional Logic*, LEUS, vol. 17, Berlin: Springer.
Forbes, G. (2013), 'Marcus and substitutivity', *Theoria* (Spain), vol. 78, pp. 359-74.
Forbes, G. (1996), 'Substitutivity and the coherence of quantifying in', *Philosophical Review*, vol. 105, pp. 337-72.
Geach, P. (1965), 'A medieval discussion of intentionality', in: *Logic, Methodology and Philosophy of Science*, Y. Bar-Hillel (ed.), Amsterdam: North-Holland, pp. 425–33.
Hanks, P.W. (2013), 'First-person propositions', *Philosophy and Phenomenological Research*, vol. 86, pp. 155-82.
Hanks, P.W. (2011), 'Structured propositions as types', *Mind*, vol. 120, pp. 11-52.
Jespersen, B. (2010), 'Recent work on structured meaning and propositional unity', *Philosophy Compass*, vol. 7, pp. 620-30.

---

[38] The research reported herein was funded by *FP7-PEOPLE-2013-IEF* Project No. 628170 *USHP: Unity of Structured Hyperpropositions*, and VŠB-Technical University of Ostrava Project No. SP2014/157: *Knowledge Modeling, Process Simulation and Design*. Versions of this paper were read as an invited lecture at Munich Centre of Mathematical Philosophy, Ludwig Maximilian University, 24 October 2013, and as an invited tutorial at the Eberhard Karls University of Tübingen, 7 February 2013. I am indebted to Marie Duží for precious comments; to Alessandro Torza for his kind invitation to contribute to this volume, and granting much-needed deadline extensions, as well as helpful comments on the penultimate draft; and to Iker for making the writing process so much longer and infinitely more joyful.

Jespersen, B. (forthcoming), 'Structured lexical concepts, property modifiers, and Transparent Intensional Logic', *Philosophical Studies*, DOI: 10.1007/s11098-014-0305-0.

Kaplan, D. (1986), 'Opacity', in: *The Philosophy of W.V. Quine*, L.E. Hahn and P.A. Schilpp (eds.), Open Court. pp. 229-289.

Marcus, R.B. (1993), *Modalities*, New York, Oxford: Oxford University Press.

Materna, P. (1997), 'Rules of existential quantification into 'intensional contexts'', *Studia Logica*, vol. 59, pp. 331-43.

Priest, G. (2002), 'The hooded man', *Journal of Philosophical Logic*, vol. 31, pp. 445-67.

Quine, W.V. (1956), 'Quantifiers and propositional attitudes', *Journal of Philosophy*, vol. 53, pp. 177-87.

Sainsbury, M. (2010), 'Intentionality without exotica', in: *New Essays on Singular Thought*, R. Jeshion (ed.), Oxford University Press, pp. 300-18.

Sleigh, R.C., Jr. (1967), 'On quantifying into epistemic contexts', *Nous*, vol. 1, pp. 23-31.

Soames, S. (2010), *What Is Meaning?*, Princeton University Press.

Smullyan, R. (1948), 'Modality and description', *Journal of Symbolic Logic*, vol. 13, pp. 31-37.

Sylvan, R. (2003), 'The importance of nonexistent objects and of intensionality in mathematics', *Philosophia Mathematica*, vol. 11, pp. 20-52.

Thomason, R. (1980), 'A model theory for propositional attitudes', *Linguistics and Philosophy*, vol. 4, pp. 47–70.

Tichý, P. (1971), 'An approach to intensional analysis', *Nous*, vol. 5, pp. 273-97.

Tichý, P. (1975), 'What do we talk about?', *Philosophy of Science*, vol. 42, pp. 80-93.

Tichý, P. (1978), 'Two kinds of intensional logic', *Epistemologia*, vol. 1, pp. 143-64.

Tichý, P. (1986), 'Indiscernibility of identicals', *Studia Logica*, vol. 45, pp. 251-73.

Tichý, P. (1988), *The Foundations of Frege's Logic*, Berlin: de Gruyter.

Williamson, T. (2013), *Modal Logic as Metaphysics*, Oxford: Oxford University Press.

Zimmermann, T.E. (2006), 'Monotonicity in opaque verbs', *Linguistics and Philosophy*, vol. 29, pp. 715-61.

The Paradox of Inference and the Non-Triviality of Analytic Information

Marie Duží

Abstract The classical theory of semantic information (*ESI*), as formulated by Bar-Hillel and Carnap in 1952, does not give a satisfactory account of the problem of what information, if any, analytically and/or logically true sentences have to offer. According to *ESI*, analytically true sentences lack informational content, and any two analytically equivalent sentences convey the same piece of information. This problem is connected with Cohen and Nagel's paradox of inference: Since the conclusion of a valid argument is contained in the premises, it fails to provide any novel information. Again, *ESI* does not give a satisfactory account of the paradox. In this paper I propose a solution based on the distinction between *empirical information* and *analytic information*. Declarative sentences are informative due to their meanings. I construe meanings as *structured hyperintensions*, modelled in Transparent Intensional Logic as so-called *constructions*. These are abstract, algorithmically structured procedures whose constituents are sub-procedures. My main thesis is that constructions are the vehicles of information. Hence, although analytically true sentences provide no *empirical information* about the state of the world, they convey *analytic information*, in the shape of constructions prescribing how to arrive at the truths in question. Moreover, even though analytically equivalent sentences have equal empirical content, their analytic content may be different. Finally, though the empirical content of the conclusion of a valid argument is contained in the premises, its analytic content may be different from the analytic content of the premises and thus convey a new piece of information.

The paradox of inference and the non-triviality of analytic information

1 Introduction

In 1934 Cohen and Nagel put forward the *paradox of inference*:

> If in an inference the conclusion is not contained in the premises, it cannot be valid; and if the conclusion is not different from the premises, it is useless; but the conclusion cannot be contained in the premises and also possess novelty; hence inferences cannot be both valid and useful. ([9], p. 173.)

This paradox arises because of the tension between (a) the *validity* (legitimacy) of an inference, and (b) the *utility* of an inference. One can reformulate the problem posed by the paradox thus: How can (deductive) logic function as a useful epistemological tool? For an inference to be legitimate, the recognition of the premises as true must already have accomplished what is needed for the recognition of the truth of the conclusion; but if the conclusion is to be useful the recognition of its truth should not take place already when the truth of the premises is ascertained.

For illustration, consider this argument:

Everybody is at home or has gone shopping.
If Charles went shopping, then he bought some milk.
Charles did not buy any milk.
Charles is at home.

If we establish the premises as true thanks to empirical investigation, then we need not empirically investigate the state of the world in order to get to know whether Charles is at home. Pure reasoning is sufficient to conclude that he is.

For a mathematical example, consider the following argument:

All numbers divisible by 4 or 6 are even.
Some numbers which are divisible by 6 are also divisible by 4.
It is not true that no even number is divisible by 4.

This time we do not examine the state of the world in order to establish whether the premises are true. However, no matter how we establish their truth-value (be it by running a proof or consulting a textbook on mathematics), once they have been established, no further investigation is called for. Pure reasoning suffices to determine that it is not true that no even number is divisible by 4.

As many fellow logicians and mathematicians will no doubt agree, the conclusion of a valid argument is often very useful, and can often be surprising too. It seems evident that there is *something* that we *learn* when deducing the conclusion of a sound argument. So it won't do to claim that we learn nothing. I show in this paper what it is that we learn when drawing valid inferences from premises known to be true. Deductive logic is as useful an epistemic tool as we always knew it to be; but the nature of what a sound argument teaches us is liable to come as a surprise.

The paradox of inference is an instance of the broader problem of the usefulness of analytically true sentences. There has been a long philosophical dispute concerning the definition of analytic truth and the relation between analytic and synthetic truths, a distinction that goes as far back as to Leibniz, at least. For the purpose of this paper it is sufficient to adopt the explication that an analytically true sentence is true solely in virtue of its meaning. Since we presuppose full linguistic competence in language-users, sentences like "No bachelor is married", "Whales are mammals", and also mathematical sentences like "The problem of logical validity is not decidable in first-order predicate logic" come out analytically true.[1] Provided that we understand the meanings of the predicates 'is a whale' and 'is a mammal' as used in current English, when learning that whales are mammals we do not acquire information bearing on the state of the world. We do learn something bearing on a necessary relation between two properties. If you know that the individual before you is a whale, you need not (empirically) examine the world in order to get to know that the individual is a mammal.

Thus an analytically true sentence is true independently of any possible state of the world. I shall say that an analytically true sentence containing empirical expressions *denotes* a possible-world (PWS) proposition (conceived as a function from possible worlds to a function from times to truth-values) that takes the truth-value **T** in all possible worlds at all times.[2] True mathematical sentences are analytically true and denote not a world- and time-indexed (though constant) proposition but the truth-value **T**.[3]

Every deductively valid argument with premises $P_1,...,P_n$ and conclusion P corresponds to an analytically true conditional sentence of the form, "If P_1 and ... and P_n, then P". Of course, if the argument is deductively valid, then it cannot be the case that all the premises $P_1,...,P_n$ are true and the conclusion P is not true. So the conditional sentence must be analytically true. Let me emphasize that by 'argument' I do not mean a judgement, if a judgement is the *act* of inferring conclusion from premises, a judgement involving the *execution* of some cognitive procedures. Rather, by 'argument' I understand a set of declarative sentences (premises) along with another declarative sentence (a conclusion). These two concepts of argument are discussed in [40], where Sundholm warns against conflating sentences and judgements: "The relata in logical consequence are propositions, whereas an inference affects a passage from known judgements to a

---

[1] P. Tichý put the point succinctly in a [41] paper: "We assume, of course, a normal linguistic situation, in which communication proceeds between two people, both of whom understand the language. Logical semantics does not deal with other linguistic situations." ([43], p. 55, n.1.) Likewise, C.A. Anderson says about Church's Alternative (0): "Sense is what is known when the language is understood. In accordance with this, the intensional semantical rules should state essential facts about the semantics, the mastery of which constitutes (ideal) competence with the language. These may include the rules of synonymy [.]" ([3], p. 163.)

[2] 'PWS' abbreviates 'possible-world semantics'.

[3] I am not going to deal with Kant's distinction between synthetic and analytic judgements *a priori*. This problem has been tackled in [15]. Roughly, an analytic judgement *a priori* is defined there as an effectively executable procedure whose product is a recursive function (conceived as a set-theoretical mapping); a synthetic judgement *a priori* is an ineffective procedure, either because its product is a non-recursive function or because the product is a recursive function specified by the procedure in a non-effective way. By *effectively executable procedure* I mean the notion as introduced by Alonzo Church, that is an algorithm that computes λ-computable functions (that is, partial recursive functions).

novel judgement that becomes known in virtue of the inference in question" ([40], p. 27).

According to the procedural semantics I shall set out below, an argument encodes a *procedure*, which may or may not be executed by an epistemic agent, rather than the *process* of actually executing the procedure. To avoid misconception, I want to stress that the procedure encoded by an analytically true sentence does not have to be effectively executable. Accordingly, a passage from known premises to a novel conclusion of a valid argument does not have to be effectively executable. An analytically true sentence need not be logically true. If a sentence is logically true then it is also analytically true, but not *vice versa*. This is because analytical validity conceived as truth in all possible worlds at all times is independent of a logical system in which its meaning happens to be regimented. A logically true sentence is provable in some sufficiently expressive logical calculus, though discovering such a calculus is obviously a non-trivial task. Similarly, an analytically valid argument need not be logically valid. If an argument is logically valid then it is analytically valid, but not *vice versa*. So below I am going to define the difference between logically and analytically true sentences, and between logically and analytically valid arguments, in order to compare them as for analytic information they convey.

My starting-point is the characterisation of information as being objective and semantic, as found in [19, 20]. I am going to investigate information that encapsulates its *truthfulness*, and is independent of any informee. Thus I adopt a *realist* view of meaning and information, as defended in [20]. In particular, I am not going to deal with the counterpart of the 'scandal of deduction' put forward in [23], which is Bar-Hillel-Carnap's paradox of contradictory sentences. Since a contradictory sentence denotes a proposition that excludes *all* possible worlds (and all times), it should be the most informative one possible. Yet, since knowledge presupposes truth, I presume that the sentence has to be true in order to provide useful information.

If we put things in terms of possible-world semantics, sentences are informative due to the propositions they are associated with by either denoting or expressing them. As I said above, sentences *denote* PWS propositions, where PWS propositions are functions mapping possible worlds to truth-values or to functions from times to truth-values. Indexing truth-values both to worlds and times serves to capture both modal and temporal variability. Empirical sentences denote contingent propositions, which are true at some world/time pairs, and false at others. Empirical sentences are informative because the propositions they denote are *contingently* true (false). Sentences have *empirical content*, which is the set of world/time pairs excluded by the propositions denoted by them. The more world/time pairs a sentence excludes, the greater empirical content it has, and thus the more informative it is. And the more we know, the more 'powerful' propositions we are competent to assert, where a proposition is more powerful the fewer possible worlds and times it is true at. If we were empirically omniscient, we would be competent to assert the most informative proposition true in a singleton set consisting only of the actual world and the present moment.

It is, however, readily seen that PWS does not solve the problem of the informativeness of *analytically* true sentences. Analytically true sentences denote the necessary proposition *TRUE*, which takes the truth-value **T** in all possible worlds at all times, and so these sentences are uninformative from the point of view of PWS.[4]

The conclusion of a valid argument is true in a superset of the set of world/time pairs in which all the premises are true. Equivalently, the set of world/time pairs excluded by the conclusion is a subset of the set of world/time pairs excluded by the premises. In this sense it is true that the empirical semantic content of the conclusion of a valid argument *is contained* in the premises, which explains why we do not gain any *novel* piece of *empirical information* by validly inferring the conclusion of a sound argument.

Moreover, mathematical sentences are true or false in all possible worlds and at all times, so possible worlds and times are, strictly speaking, out of place here. Rather we ought to say that mathematical sentences are true or false independently of worlds and times. Frege touched upon the topic of the informational value of mathematical sentences in [21] when he considered the case of a triangle's medians: the mathematical sentence that the point of intersection of two pairs of a triangle's medians is one and the same point is informative, unlike the sentence that the point is self-identical.[5] Yet both sentences are equivalent by denoting the truth-value **T**. From this point of view, mathematics turns out to be just about the so-called *great fact*.[6] For another example, we readily grant that

i) "12 = 12"

is not at all informative, whereas we no less readily grant that

ii) "7+5 = 9+3"

is informative. But why?

A similar problem arising along the same line of reasoning is the question whether analytically equivalent sentences yield equal semantic information. Analytically equivalent sentences denote the same PWS proposition and thus exclude the same set of world/time pairs. Does this mean that they are equally informative? PWS predicts them to be. However, wouldn't we say that, for instance, the sentence "Prague is the capital of the Czech Republic" is less informative than the sentence "Prague is the capital of the Czech Republic and no bachelor is married"? Surely we would (and should). Yet, since the proposition denoted by the second clause is the proposition *TRUE*, which excludes no world/time pairs, the two sentences exclude exactly the same set of such pairs. Thus PWS predicts them to share the same empirical content. So much the worse for PWS as a general theory of information, as many others have pointed out; see, e.g., [2, 38] for recent statements of this objection to the crude individuation of informational content.

In this paper I begin and end with the paradox of inference, since the paradox is what provoked me to probe into the principles underlying semantic information.

---

[4] The other extreme would be analytically untrue sentences, which exclude all worlds/times. They denote impossible propositions or, in the mathematical case, they either do not denote anything or denote the truth-value **F**. However, as stated above, I am not going to deal with them.

[5] This example is the first that Frege gives in [21], prior to setting out his heralded Hesperus/Phosphorus example. While the latter may lend itself to a solution within PWS, the former does not. This is already reason enough not to explicate Frege's intuitive notion of *Sinn* in terms of PWS intensions.

[6] See, e.g., [45].

Thus the narrow aim of this paper is to offer a principled solution to this paradox. The challenge is to explain how the validity and the utility of a deductive argument do not cancel one another out. The main goal of this paper is to present a solution based on a distinction between two kinds of information: *empirical (factual)* and *analytic*. The broad scope of this paper, however, is to offer a no less principled account of why analytic information is far from being trivial. This is to say that the semantic framework within which the paradox of inference is solved is not tailored to that paradox only: the framework is of a much wider scope than that. The scope extends to proposing criteria for comparing the yield of analytic information of analytically true sentences and of equivalent sentences involving empirical expressions.

The rest of the paper is organized as follows. Section 2 presents the background of classical theories of semantic information. In Section 3 the semantic framework of my background theory, TIL, is introduced. In order to examine the analytic content of analytically true sentences, the literal logical form (*LLF*) of an expression is defined in Section 4. Based on the notion of *LLF*, analytically and logically true sentences are then distinguished and their analytic content investigated. In Section 5 the paradox of inference is examined along the same lines. The concepts of analytically and logically valid arguments are defined, and finally some factors bearing on the epistemic utility of a valid argument are spelt out.

2 State of the Art

2.1 ESI and 'The Scandal of Deduction'

The questions concerning the amount of information yield of sentences are squarely *semantic* in kind. The classical attempt at answering them is [4], in which a theory of (*empirical*) *semantic information (ESI)* is presented. The guiding intuition is the same as outlined above; the more possibilities a proposition excludes, the more informative it is.[7] For instance, the conjunction $P \wedge Q$ excludes more possibilities than does the disjunction $P \vee Q$; therefore, a conjunction is more informative than a disjunction. Bar-Hillel and Carnap built *ESI* around a monadic predicate language. They conceived of possibilities as a set of so-called state descriptions, which is the set of atomic sentences that can be formulated in the language by applying primitive monadic predicates to individual constants.

Let W be a set of state descriptions, S a sentence. Then the semantic *content* of S is defined as the set of $w \in W$ that make S false: $Cont(S) =_{df} \{w \in W : w \models \neg S\}$. Obviously, for any logically/analytically true sentence T it holds that $Cont(T) = \emptyset$.

ESI is concerned not only with the individuation of empirical information content (*Cont*), but also with its *measure*. Since the set of individual constants and primitive monadic predicates of their language is finite, the set of state descriptions is finite as well. Thus the measure of the informativeness of a sentence can be based on the probability of the states it describes as being the case. *ESI* defines two distinct methods of measuring, a *content measure (cont)* and an *information measure (inf)*.

---

[7] For a summary of Bar-Hillel and Carnap's theory, see also [12] and [38].

Yet both the content measure and the information measure of an analytically true sentence amount to zero. Moreover, *ESI* predicts that analytically equivalent sentences convey the same information, and that the informational content of the conclusion of a valid argument is contained in the informational content of the premises. In sum, these are all the wrong answers to the questions posed by the paradox of inference.

Hintikka in [23] characterises the failure of *ESI* to provide an account of the information yield of deductive inferences as the *scandal of deduction*. He makes an attempt to obtain a measure of the information yield by distinguishing between what he calls *depth information* and *surface information*. However, Sequoiah-Grayson shows in [39] that Hintikka's attempt fails. It fails primarily because his method, based on the concept of distributive normal form, applies only to a restricted set of deductions in the polyadic predicate calculus, and so fails to apply at all to the deductions in the monadic predicate calculus and the propositional calculus. Sequoiah-Grayson says:

> The consequence is that the problem of obtaining a measure of the information yield of deductive inferences remains an open one. The failure of Hintikka's proposal will suggest that a purely syntactic approach to the problem be abandoned in favour of an intrinsically semantic one. ([39], p. 67.)

Another attempt to solve the problem is [38]. There Sequoiah-Grayson investigates the measure of information along the lines of *ESI*, where particular doxastic states of agents (or, *situations*) rather than state descriptions or possible worlds are used. He specifies the basis of a theory of *psychological information* (*PI*) in which the frame semantics of substructural logic is invoked. By weakening the axioms of linear and relevant logics he specifies his theory of *PI* and provides it with a Kripke-style frame semantics. *Situations* serve the same purpose as do possible worlds, with the augmentation that they may be incomplete and/or inconsistent, because resource-bounded rational agents may entertain inconsistent beliefs. Impossible situations are logically impossible situations and correspond to confused epistemic states of agents. In such a model each agent is allowed to be confused in each their own way, without all such confused states being identified with each other.

The result is a theory with a relevance semantics specified in terms of the information flow between the doxastic states of agents. The idea of plugging the basis of a semantic theory into doxastic states is not new, as Sequoiah-Grayson admits. For instance, [22] comes with belief sets, where these are sets of sentences closed under logical consequence. Gärdenfors thus presents a theory of idealized, logically omniscient agents. What is novel about Sequoiah-Grayson's theory is that it takes into account resource-bounded and fallible agents. The theory is still work in progress, though. On this point Sequoiah-Grayson says:

> [So] there exists a tension between the frame conditions it would appear that we would like, given a putative theory of *PI*, and those that we may get, given the constraints imposed by a theory of information flow. This remains an open problem. ([38], p. 394.)

However, in my opinion, a theory such as Sequoiah-Grayson's will meet with similar problems as Bar-Hillel and Carnap's did. Within Sequoiah-Grayson's theory we can hardly explain *what* an agent learns when inferring the conclusion of a sound argument, and *why* equivalent sentences need not be equally informative. Moreover, the theory does not explain *why* classically valid and relevantly invalid inferences may come out informative. True, if P and Q are equivalent, a may believe that P without believing that Q. In this sense *PI* can distinguish equivalent sentences. And having executed a valid inference, a finds himself in a new state, which may exclude previously an impossible situation that was initially (and mistakenly) considered possible. However, unless we admit that what the agent learns is just a new piece of syntax (which we won't since sententialism is not a satisfactory solution) such a theory does not provide an answer to the question *what* the agent learns, and thus fails to provide a satisfactory solution to the paradox of inference.

Thus I am not going to follow the path outlined above. My goal is rather to investigate the objective notion of analytic information conveyed by sentences, independently of whether a sentence is contained in the doxastic state of an agent. As we have seen above, the basic principle of informational content adopted by Bar-Hillel and Carnap, in its most general formulation, is given by the inverse relationship principle: "Whenever there is an increase in available information, there is a decrease in possibilities, and *vice versa*." ([2], p. 662.)

This formulation gives rise to questions concerning the character of the excluded 'possibilities'. If we limit ourselves to Tarskian models, world-like entities or situations, we won't be in a position to answer the basic question posed by the paradox of inference: "*What* do we learn when inferring the conclusion of a sound argument?" I am going to show that we learn a new *procedure* the product of which is the proposition (or truth-value, in the case of mathematics) denoted by the conclusion. To put it in another way, we must primarily investigate the *procedure* yielding the proposition/truth-value as its *product*, and only secondarily the product itself. For this reason we need a *procedural* semantic framework.

2.2 Procedural Semantics and Analytic Information

Procedural semantics contrasts with set-theoretical denotational semantics.[8] The prevailing denotational approach to semantics conceives of the meaning of an expression E as the extra-linguistic entity denoted (or referred to) by E. Since the pioneering paper [21] the advocates of denotational semantics have striven to define so-called *structured meanings*.[9] Various adjustments of Frege's semantic schema have been proposed, shifting the entity named by an expression from the extensional level to the intensional level. Yet natural language is rich enough to generate expressions that talk about neither extensional nor intensional objects. It has become increasingly clear since the 1970s that we need to individuate meanings more finely than in terms of what PWS intensions afford, and the need for *hyperintensional* semantics is now broadly recognised. My position is a plea for a hyperintensional semantics that takes expressions as encoding *algorithmically structured procedures* producing either extensional or intensional entities or lower-order procedures as their products. This approach—which could be characterized as being informed by an

---

[8] For discussion, see [28], and also [27].
[9] See, for instance, [11].

algorithmic or *computational turn*—has been advocated by, for instance, Moschovakis in [36]. Yet much earlier, in the early 1970s, Tichý introduced his notion of *construction* as the centrepiece of TIL.[10]

Constructions are based on a robust concept of semantic structure as an extra-linguistic, abstract procedure (a generalized algorithm). Because procedures are inherently structured, they consist of one or multiple constituent subprocedures that are to be executed in order to arrive at the product (if any) produced by the respective procedure. TIL agrees with Moschovakis's conception of Frege's sense as "an (abstract, idealized, not necessarily implementable) algorithm which computes the denotation of [a term]" ([37], p. 27).

To anticipate a common misapprehension, I wish to emphasize that the procedures I have in mind are not syntactic objects. Just like one and the same algorithm can be encoded by different programs possibly written in different programming languages, so one and the same procedure can be encoded by different pieces of syntactic items belonging to different languages. Moreover, the linguists' annotated trees depicting syntactic structure, though being illustrative diagrams, fall short of capturing *semantic* structure. These syntactic trees are ordered n-tuples, and such set-theoretic objects are not suitable candidates as structured meanings.[11] Though having elements, an *instruction* to glue them together into a coherent structure is bound to be missing. My procedural conception of hyperintensionality is not a syntactic conception, and TIL constructions are not syntactic structures. They are objectual procedures consisting of sub-procedures. Thus an answer to Russell's question, "What binds the constituents of propositions together?" can be offered.[12] Propositional unity is established by the very procedure that generates a compound whole from its individual constituents. The meaning of an expression E is not a *list* of the meanings of the sub-expressions of E. Rather, it is the *procedure* detailing in what particular ways its sub-procedures are combined.

A most important feature of my procedural semantics is that to exercise linguistic competence with respect to an expression is to know its sense, i.e. the procedure encoded by the expression, rather than the entity that this procedure produces. For instance, to master the mathematical constant 'π' is not to know what real number it denotes. Obviously, no finitely limited agent, such as a human being, can know the infinite sequence of digits 3.14159… Rather, being linguistically competent with respect to 'π' is tantamount to knowing a procedure for, e.g., computing *the ratio of the circumference of a circle to its diameter.* Similarly, to master the empirical predicate 'is a bachelor' is neither to know what individuals or set of individuals it refers to, nor is it to know the property it denotes. (Empirical properties of individuals are construed as functions from logical space to chronologies of sets of individuals.) Rather it is to know a procedure which for any state of affairs enables the language-user to determine whether a given individual is a bachelor.[13] Moreover,

---

[10] See Tichý ([42], in particular Ch. Five) and ([43], pp. 873–885).
[11] See [24].
[12] See also [30, 31].
[13] Fuzziness and vagueness aside.

The paradox of inference and the non-triviality of analytic information

some expressions do not denote anything, yet are anything but meaningless. For instance, mathematicians needed to understand the meaning of 'the greatest prime' prior to proving that there is no greatest prime. They had to master the procedure expressed by this expression in order to show that the procedure fails to produce a product.

To adduce an example, the expressions '$3^2 - 2^2$' and '$(3 + 2) \times (3 - 2)$' do not have the same sense. They encode two different ways of constructing the number 5 in terms of two other numbers. The sense of '$3^2 - 2^2$' is the procedure that consists in the application of the square function to the number 3, application of the square function to the number 2, and subtraction of the result of the latter from the result of the former. Thus though the sentences "$3^2 - 2^2 = 5$" and "$(3 + 2) \times (3 - 2) = 5$" do not exclude any possible world or time and thus do not convey any factual information, they convey two distinct pools of analytic information by picking out two distinct constructions of the truth-value **T** out of the infinitely many possible constructions of this truth-value.

I turn now to solving the paradox of inference and the related problem of the information value of analytically true sentences. The paradox of inference can be summarized thus:

(1.1) Valid arguments are uninformative,
      because their conclusion is contained in the premises.
(1.2) Uninformative arguments are epistemically useless.
(1.3) Valid arguments are epistemically useless.

Since we intuitively reject the conclusion as invalid, the truth of at least one of the premises seems doubtful. While the second premise is trivially true, I am going to show that the first premise is false. The procedural semantics of TIL allows us to distinguish between *empirical* and *analytic* information. By the *empirical information* conveyed by a sentence *S* I mean the factual content of *S*, which is the set of world/time pairs excluded by *S*. By the *analytic content* of *S* I mean the set of procedural constituents of the meaning (construction) expressed by *S*. So we can reformulate the above argument thus:

(2.1) Valid arguments are *factually uninformative*,
      because the empirical information conveyed by the conclusion is contained in the empirical information conveyed by the premises.
(2.2) Factually *and analytically* uninformative arguments are epistemically useless.
(2.3) Valid arguments are epistemically useless.

This argument is invalid, thus blocking the derivation of the conclusion that valid arguments are epistemically useless. In what follows I show that some valid arguments are analytically informative and, therefore, epistemically useful.

A related problem that I am going to address as well is the problem of the *great fact* broached above. Since all true mathematical sentences converge in the truth-value **T**, mathematics is only about **T**, 'the great fact', which is obviously an unhappy outcome. Moreover, all analytically true sentences, even those containing empirical expressions, are factually uninformative. So an argument parallel to the one above summarizing the paradox of inference would be:

The paradox of inference and the non-triviality of analytic information

(3.1) Analytically true sentences are uninformative,
because they do not exclude any possible world or time.
(3.2) Uninformative sentences are epistemically useless.
(3.3) Analytically true sentences are epistemically useless.

Again, we can reformulate the argument to bring out its invalidity:

(4.1) Analytically true sentences are *factually* uninformative,
because they do not exclude any possible world or time.
(4.2) Factually *and analytically* uninformative sentences are useless.
(4.3) Analytically true sentences are useless.

In what follows I am going to show that analytically true sentences are useful because they have analytic content. In general, a (mathematical, analytical or empirical) sentence S reveals analytic information about the constituent steps to be executed in order to arrive at the entity (if any) that the meaning of S, i.e., a particular construction, constructs. It might seem, naïvely, that the analytic informativeness of a sentence would depend on the number of steps involved in the respective construction. However, since a shorter procedure may still be more informative than a longer one, we need some qualitatively better criteria. I am not going to propose an *absolute measure* of analytic information. Instead, I am going to examine some criteria for *comparing* the information yield of equivalent sentences.

3 TIL in Brief

TIL constructions are uniquely assigned to expressions as their algorithmically structured meanings.[14] When claiming that constructions are algorithmically structured, I mean the following. The objects a construction operates on are not constituents of the construction. Just like the constituents of a computer program are its sub-programs, so the constituents of a construction are its sub-constructions. Thus on the lowest level of non-constructions, the objects that constructions work on have to be supplied by other (albeit trivial) constructions. This is in principle achieved by using atomic constructions. A construction C is atomic if it does not contain any other constituent but C. There are two atomic constructions: *Variables* and *Trivializations*. They supply objects (of any type, including constructions) on which compound constructions operate. The constructions themselves may occur not only as constituents to be executed in order to arrive at the object, if any, they construct, but also as objects that still other constructions operate on. Thus when a construction C is Trivialized, it is not a constituent to be executed; rather, C itself is an object of predication. *Compound* constructions, which consist of other constituents than just themselves, are *Composition* and *Closure*. Composition is the procedure of applying a function f to an argument A to obtain the value (if any) of f at A. It is *improper* (i.e., does not construct anything) if f is not defined at A. Closure is the procedure

---

[14] Portions of this section draw on material presented by the author as 'Topic-focus articulation from the semantic point of view' at the conference CICLing 2009 in Mexico City see [14], and by the author as 'Concepts are structured meanings' at the conference ECAP VI in Krakow, co-authored with P. Materna, and on Duží et al. [17].

of constructing a function by abstracting over variables in the ordinary manner of the λ-calculi.[15]

The fundamental primitive objects of the ontology of TIL are functions rather than relations or sets. Thus the formal language in which TIL constructions are encoded is inspired by the (typed) λ-calculi. Yet *a function is not a procedure*. We view functions as set-theoretical mappings, and one and the same mapping can be produced by infinitely many procedures. The terms of the language in which TIL constructions are encoded are viewed procedurally. Abstraction ('Closure' in TIL) is the very procedure of forming a function (and not the resulting function), and application ('Composition' in TIL) is the very procedure of applying a function to an argument (and not the resulting value). The functional dependencies underlying compositionality are technically accommodated by means of the interplay between abstraction and application. Note that we strictly distinguish between procedures and their products, and between functions and their values.[16]

Constructions, as well as the entities they construct, all receive a type. The ontology of TIL is organized in an infinite, bi-dimensional hierarchy of types. One dimension is made up of non-constructions, i.e., entities unstructured from the algorithmic point of view. The other dimension of the type hierarchy is made up of constructions, which are structured, higher-order entities constructing lower-order entities. The definitions are inductive, and they proceed in three stages. First, I define the simple types of order 1 comprising non-constructions; then I define constructions; finally, I define the ramified hierarchy of types.

Definition 1 (*types of order 1*) Let B be a *base*, i.e., a collection of non-empty sets. Then

i) Every member of B is a *type of order 1*.
ii) Let $\alpha, \beta_1,...,\beta_m$ be arbitrary *types of order 1*. Then the set $(\alpha\beta_1...\beta_m)$ of partial functions with values in α and arguments in $\beta_1,...,\beta_m$, respectively, is a *type of order 1*.
iii) *Nothing is a type of order 1* unless it so follows from i) and ii). □

Definition 2 (*construction*)

i) *Variables x, y, z, ...* are *constructions* that construct objects of the respective types dependently on valuations v. Let a total valuation function v be given that associates variables $x_1, x_2, ..., x_n, ...$ with a sequence *Seq* of objects $a_0, a_1, ..., a_n, ...$ of a type α. Then the *variable x_n v(aluation)-constructs* the nth object a_n of *Seq* relative to v.

---

[15] There are two other compound constructions, (single) *Execution* and *Double Execution. Execution*, ^1C, is the procedure of executing C in order to obtain the product, if any, of C. Thus, ^1C is the same procedure as C, because the default mode in which a construction occurs is its Execution. Higher-order constructions can be executed twice over, which is achieved by *Double Execution*, ^2C. However, in this paper we will not need Execution and Double Execution, and thus I omit these two constructions in the definitions below.

[16] The contrast between functions and constructions of functions is not unlike the contrast between functions-in-extension and functions-in-intension. But I am hesitant to push the parallel, since function-in-intension remains a poorly-understood notion. See [7].

ii) *Trivialization*: Where X is an object whatsoever (even a *construction*), ^0X is a *construction* called *Trivialization*. It constructs X without the mediation of other constructions and leaves X unchanged.

iii) The *Composition* $[X\ Y_1\ \ldots\ Y_m]$ is this *construction*: If X *v-constructs* a function f of a type $(\alpha\ \beta_1\ldots\beta_m)$, and $Y_1,\ldots,Y_m$ *v-construct* entities $b_1,\ldots,b_m$ of types $\beta_1,\ldots,\beta_m$, respectively, then the *Composition* $[X\ Y_1\ \ldots\ Y_m]$ *v-constructs* the value (an entity, if any, of type α) of the function f at the tuple argument $\langle b_1,\ldots, b_m\rangle$. Otherwise the *Composition* $[X\ Y_1\ \ldots\ Y_m]$ does not *v-construct* anything: it is *v-improper*.

iv) *Closure*: Let $x_1, x_2, \ldots, x_m$ be pairwise distinct variables and Y a construction. Then $[\lambda x_1\ldots x_m\ Y]$ is a *construction* called λ-*Closure* (or simply *Closure*). It *v-constructs* the following function f. Let $v(b_1/x_1,\ldots,b_m/x_m)$ be a valuation identical with v at least up to assigning objects $b_1,\ldots,b_m$ to variables $x_1,\ldots,x_m$, respectively. If Y is $v(b_1/x_1,\ldots,b_m/x_m)$-improper (see iii), then f is undefined at $\langle b_1,\ldots,b_m\rangle$. Otherwise the value of f at $\langle b_1,\ldots,b_m\rangle$ is the object $v(b_1/x_1,\ldots,b_m/x_m)$-constructed by Y.

v) Nothing is a *construction*, unless it so follows from (i) through (iv). □

Comments The *Trivialisation* ^0X of an object X simply constructs X without any change.[17] One may wonder whether this construction is indispensable. Can't an object X construct itself? No, it cannot. First, as stated above, we strictly distinguish between procedures and their products, i.e., constructions and what they construct. Thus an object and its construction are different entities. TIL opts for homogeneity within constructions: the only possible constituents of a construction are constructions. Mont Blanc is as little a constituent of a construction as of a Fregean *Sinn*. What may be a constituent is a construction of Mont Blanc, for instance $^0Mont\_Blanc$, the simplest *v*-independent construction of this object. Second, the lower-order objects that higher-order constructions operate on may in turn be constructions supplied by a Trivialization. In this way Trivialization makes it possible to distinguish between using constructions as constituents of compound constructions and mentioning constructions as input/output objects.

As mentioned above, there is an important difference between the formal λ-calculi and the TIL language of constructions, which is the formalism in which we notationally manipulate constructions, which are extra-linguistic logical objects. Whereas in the formal λ-calculi a λ-term is interpreted as the *result* of the procedure encoded by the term, a term of the TIL language of constructions is interpreted as this very *procedure*. For instance, the λ-term '(+ 3, 2)' is usually interpreted as denoting the number 5, but the TIL term '$[^0+\ ^03\ ^02]$' is interpreted as denoting the *construction* $[^0+\ ^03\ ^02]$, which is the procedure consisting of the following constituents:

i) $^0+$: take the function *addition*;
ii) ^{03}: take the number 3;

---

[17] A comparison with programming languages might be helpful: The Trivialisation ^0X and its use may be compared to the mechanism of a *(fixed) pointer* to an entity X and its *dereference*, respectively.

iii) $^0 2$: take the number 2;
iv) $[^0+\ ^0 3\ ^0 2]$: apply the result of step (i) to the objects obtained at (ii) and (iii) to obtain a number.

Similarly, the term '$\lambda x\ (x+1)$' is interpreted as denoting the *function (mapping)* Successor, while the TIL term '$[\lambda x\ [^0+\ x\ ^0 1]]$' (where $x \to \nu$, the type of natural numbers) is interpreted as the compound *procedure* whose *product* is the Successor function.

This is so because TIL constructions are objects *sui generis* assigned to expressions as their meanings. For instance, in a formal λ-calculus, non-denoting terms are meaningless, whereas in TIL they have a meaning, which is an improper construction. Thus, whereas 'dividing 5 by 0' is normally a meaningless term, in TIL it has a meaning, *viz.* the Composition $[^0:\ ^0 5\ ^0 0]$. This very Composition can be an object of predication, like in the sentence "Dividing five by zero is improper". The meaning of this sentence is the Composition $[^0 Improper\ ^0[^0:\ ^0 5\ ^0 0]]$, where *Improper* is the class of improper constructions, which fail to construct anything. What is improper is the Composition $[^0:\ ^0 5\ ^0 0]$ itself, and it must be supplied as an argument of *Improper*, here by its Trivialization, $^0[^0:\ ^0 5\ ^0 0]$.

However, within the simple theory of types, as defined by Definition 1, we cannot assign a type to a construction like $[^0:\ ^0 5\ ^0 0]$, or to a set of constructions like *Improper*. This is so because a construction cannot be of the same type as the object it constructs. It must be of a higher-order type. Thus we proceed inductively. Constructions that construct entities of order 1 are *constructions of order 1*. They themselves belong to a *type of order 2*, denoted by '$*_1$'. All of the above constructions are of type $*_1$. The type $*_1$, together with atomic types of order 1, serves as the base for the following induction rule: any collection of partial mappings, of type $(\alpha\ \beta_1...\beta_m)$, involving $*_1$ in their domain or range is a *type of order 2*. Type $*_2$ is the collection of constructions which construct entities of order 1 or 2; $*_2$ and partial mappings involving such constructions, belong to a *type of order 3*. This induction may in principle continue *ad infinitum*, which is why this type hierarchy is ramified.

The definition of the ramified hierarchy of types decomposes into three parts. First, simple types of order 1 were already defined by Definition 1. Second, I define constructions of order n, and third, types of order $n + 1$.

Definition 3 (*ramified hierarchy of types*)
T_1 *(types of order 1)*. See Definition 1.
C_n *(constructions of order n)*

i) Let x be a variable ranging over a type of order n. Then x is a *construction of order n over B*.
ii) Let X be a member of a type of order n. Then $^0 X$ is a *construction of order n over B*.
iii) Let $X, X_1,..., X_m$ ($m > 0$) be constructions of order n over B. Then $[X X_1... X_m]$ is a *construction of order n over B*.
iv) Let $x_1,... x_m, X$ ($m > 0$) be constructions of order n over B. Then $[\lambda x_1...x_m\ X]$ is a *construction of order n over B*.

The paradox of inference and the non-triviality of analytic information

v) Nothing is a *construction of order n over B* unless it so follows from $\mathbf{C}_n$ (i)-(iv).

$\mathbf{T}_{n+1}$ *(types of order n + 1)* Let $*_n$ be the collection of all constructions of order n over B. Then

i) $*_n$ and every type of order n are *types of order n + 1*.
ii) If $0 < m$ and $\alpha, \beta_1,...,\beta_m$ are types of order $n + 1$ over B, then $(\alpha \beta_1 ... \beta_m)$ (see T_1 ii)) is a *type of order n + 1 over B*.
iii) Nothing is a *type of order n + 1 over B* unless it so follows from (i) and (ii).

To sum up, our neo-Fregean semantic schema is an adjusted version of Frege's semantic schema as visualized by the following figure.

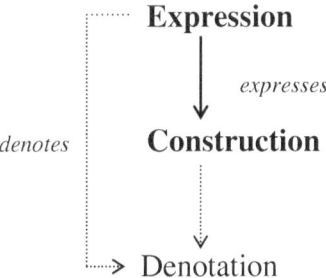

The most important relation in this schema is between an expression and its meaning, i.e., a construction. Once we have exactly defined *construction*, we can logically examine it; we can investigate what (if anything) the construction constructs, what is entailed by it, what is its analytic content, etc. Thus constructions are semantically primary, denotations secondary. Once a construction is explicitly given as a result of logical analysis, the entity (if any) it constructs is already implicitly given. As a limiting case, the logical analysis may reveal that the construction fails to construct anything by being improper. And if the construction is not improper, the denotation can be an object of any type of the TIL ontology, either a non-construction or a construction of a lower-order.

The ontology of objects we can talk about within TIL is determined by the base of the ramified type hierarchy. TIL is an open-ended system, with no one base being given once and for all. The choice of base depends on the domain(s) and language we happen to be investigating. When investigating purely mathematical language, the base could consist of, e.g., two atomic types: o, the type of truth-values, and ν, the type of natural numbers. When analyzing (fragments of) an ordinary natural language, we use the *epistemic base* {o, ι, τ, ω}. It is the collection of four atomic, or ground, types:

o   {**T, F**} (members: *truth-values*)
ι   the universe of discourse (members: *individuals*)
τ   the set of *real numbers* (doubling as *instants of time*)
ω   the logical space (members: *possible worlds*).

Since *function* is a primitive notion, we model *sets* and *relations* by their characteristic functions. Thus, for example, the set of prime numbers is a function of type (oτ) that associates any number with **T** or **F**, according as the given number is a prime. The binary relation > defined on numbers is a function of type (oττ) that

207

associates any couple of numbers with **T** or **F**, according as the first number is greater than the second. The type of binary arithmetic functions is $(\tau\tau\tau)$. The set of such functions is an object of type $(o(\tau\tau\tau))$.

TIL operates with a single *procedural semantics*, as explained above. But within this one semantics TIL observes a strict demarcation between two kinds of subsidiary semantics: one for logical and mathematical languages and another for empirical languages, whether colloquial or scientific. The demarcation hinges not on formal vs. natural, but on empirical vs. non-empirical. The defining difference is that empirical languages incorporate an element of *contingency* that the non-empirical ones lack. Empirical expressions denote *empirical conditions* that may or may not be satisfied. Non-empirical languages have no need for an additional category of expressions for empirical conditions.

For instance, the predicate 'is a student' does not denote each individual that happens to be a student, nor a class of individuals which happen to be students. Rather, it denotes a *property* of individuals, the 'populations' of which are particular sets of individuals depending on particular states-of-affairs. To master 'is a student' is not to know a particular set of individuals; rather, it is to know how, for any state-of-affairs, to determine whether a given individual satisfies the condition for being a student. We model these empirical conditions as possible-world *intensions*.

PWS intensions are entities of type $(\beta\omega)$: mappings from possible worlds to the arbitrary type β. The type β is frequently the type of the *chronology* of α-objects, i.e., a mapping of type $(\alpha\tau)$. Thus α-intensions are frequently functions of type $((\alpha\tau)\omega)$, abbreviated as '$\alpha_{\tau\omega}$'. *Extensions* are entities of a type α where $\alpha \neq (\beta\omega)$ for any type β.

Thus we distinguish between the *hyperintension* (i.e., a construction of an intension *I*) assigned to an empirical expression *E* as its *meaning*, and the possible-world *intension I denoted by E*. However, as soon as we introduce an *epistemic base* for a given empirical language, the procedural semantics of the language operates in the same way as in the case of mathematical language. This is so because we apply *explicit intensionalization* and *temporalization*, that is, we insert terms for possible-world variables and times directly into the logical syntax. We can thus directly construct possible-world intensions. Where a variable *w* ranges over possible worlds, type ω, and *t* over times, type τ, the following form essentially characterizes the syntax of explicit intensionalization and temporalization:

$$\lambda w \lambda t [\ldots w \ldots t \ldots].$$

In the parlance of TIL, this Closure is a construction constructing a possible-world intension. Alternative characterizations would be that the Closure is a hyperintensionally individuated, algorithmically structured mode of presentation of a function from logical space to a function from times to entities, or that it is a procedure whose product is a condition to be satisfied by world/time pairs. For instance, in terms of the condition/satisfier jargon, a possible-world proposition is a condition that a $\langle w, t \rangle$ pair satisfies if and only if the pair makes the proposition true.[18]

---

[18] For details see [25].

The paradox of inference and the non-triviality of analytic information

Examples of frequently used intensions are:

Propositions (denoted by declarative sentences) are of type $((o\tau)\omega)$, or '$o_{\tau\omega}$' for short. For instance the proposition that the highest mountain is in Asia is currently true, but it might have been otherwise (hence the modal parameter ω), and it has not always been and presumably will not always be so (hence the temporal parameter τ).

Properties of individuals (usually denoted by nouns or intransitive verbs like 'is a student', 'walks') are of type $(((o\iota)\tau)\omega)$, '$(o\iota)_{\tau\omega}$' for short; dependently on worlds ω and times τ they pick out the set of individuals that happen to have the property.

Binary *relations-in-intension* between individuals are of type $(((o\iota\iota)\tau)\omega)$, '$(o\iota\iota)_{\tau\omega}$' for short. For instance 'loves', 'is taller than' denote such relations-in-intension. That an individual a is taller than another individual b is only contingently so (modal parameter ω); and has not always been and will not always be so (temporal parameter τ).

Individual offices/roles (cf. Church's individual concepts) are of type $((\iota\tau)\omega)$, '$\iota_{\tau\omega}$' for short. For instance, 'the highest mountain', 'the Queen of Canada' denote individual offices. Again, that an individual a (currently Mt Everest) happens to be the highest mountain is only contingently so.

Quantifiers $\forall^\alpha$, $\exists^\alpha$ are extensions, *viz.* type-theoretically polymorphous functions of type $(o(o\alpha))$, for the arbitrary type α, defined as follows. The *universal quantifier* $\forall^\alpha$ is a function that associates a class A of α-elements with **T** if A contains all elements of the type α, otherwise with **F**. The *existential quantifier* $\exists^\alpha$ is a function that associates a class A of α-elements with **T** if A is a non-empty class, otherwise with **F**.

Notation and abbreviations
- 'X/α' means that the object X is (a member) of type α;
- '$X \to_v \alpha$' means that the type of the object v-constructed by X is α. We use '$X \to \alpha$' if what is v-constructed does not depend on a valuation v.
- I will standardly use the variables $w \to_v \omega$ and $t \to_v \tau$.
- If $C \to_v ((\alpha\tau)\omega)$, i.e. $\alpha_{\tau\omega}$ for short, then the frequently used Composition $[[C\ w]\ t]$, which is the intensional descent (a.k.a. extensionalization) of the α-intension v-constructed by C, will be written as 'C_{wt}'.
- When using constructions of truth-value functions, namely $\wedge$ (conjunction), $\vee$ (disjunction) and $\supset$ (implication) of type (ooo), and $\neg$ (negation) of type (oo), I often omit Trivialisation and use infix notion to conform to standard notation in the interest of better readability. Also when using constructions of identities of α-entities, $=_\alpha/(o\alpha\alpha)$, I omit Trivialization, the type subscript, and use infix notion when no confusion arises. For instance, instead of '$[^0\supset\ [^0=_\iota a\ b]\ [^0=_{(o\tau)\omega} \lambda w\lambda t[P_{wt}a]\lambda w\lambda t[P_{wt}b]]]$', where $=_\iota/(o\iota\iota)$ is the identity of individuals and $=_{((o\tau)\omega)}/(oo_{\tau\omega}o_{\tau\omega})$ the identity of propositions; $a, b \to \iota$, $P \to (o\iota)_{\tau\omega}$, I will write '$[[a = b] \supset [\lambda w\lambda t[P_{wt}a] = \lambda w\lambda t[P_{wt}b]]]$'.
- I will use '$\forall x\ A$' and '$\exists x\ A$' instead of '$[^0\forall^\alpha\ \lambda x\ A]$' and '$[^0\exists^\alpha\ \lambda x\ A]$', respectively, when no confusion can arise.

Examples
- $Positive\_number/(o\tau)$; $^0Positive\_number \to (o\tau)$; $x, y \to_v \tau$; $\lambda x\ [^0> x\ ^0 0] \to (o\tau)$, the class of positive numbers. The Closure $\lambda x\ [^0> x\ ^0 0]$ is a construction of

order 1; it constructs the (characteristic function of the) class of positive numbers, an entity belonging to a type of order 1, *viz.* (oτ). Thus the Closure itself belongs to a type of order 2, *viz.* $*_1$. We write $\lambda x\ [^0{>}\ x\ ^0 0]/*_1 \rightarrow$ (oτ). The Trivialisation of this Closure, $^0[\lambda x\ [^0{>}\ x\ ^0 0]]/*_2 \rightarrow *_1$, belongs to a type of order 3, *viz.* $*_2$, and constructs the Closure $[\lambda x\ [^0{>}\ x\ ^0 0]]$, an entity belonging to a type of order 2, $*_1$.

- The Composition $[^0{:}\ x\ ^0 0]/*_1 \rightarrow_v \tau$ is *v*-improper for every valuation *v*. It is a construction of order 1 (belonging to $*_1$, the type of order 2), because its constituents $^0{:}, x, ^0 0$ are constructions of order 1 *v*-constructing, respectively, the division function, a number, and the number zero. The Trivialisation $^0[^0{:}\ x\ ^0 0]/*_2 \rightarrow *_1$ is a construction of order 2 (belonging to $*_2$, the type of order 3), *v*-proper for every valuation *v*. It constructs the Composition $[^0{:}\ x\ ^0 0]$.
- If *Improper*/(o$*_1$) is the class of constructions of order 1 that are *v*-improper for every valuation *v*, then the Composition $[^0 \textit{Improper}\ ^0[^0{:}\ x\ ^0 0]]/*_2 \rightarrow$ o is a construction of order 2 belonging to $*_2$, the type of order 3. If somebody knows that dividing any number *x* by zero is improper by failing to yield any number, what they know is not the truth-value **T**. Instead what they know is that this Composition constructs the truth-value **T**. Therefore, *Know(ing)* is here a relation-in-intension of an individual (of type ι) to a construction (of type $*_2$), and so receives the type (oι$*_2$)$_{\tau\omega}$.
- The sentence "Tom knows that dividing any number *x* by zero is improper" receives thus the analysis $\lambda w \lambda t\ [^0 \textit{Know}_{wt}\ ^0\textit{Tom}\ ^0[^0 \textit{Improper}\ ^0[^0{:}\ x\ ^0 0]]]$, *Tom*/ι. Note that the Composition $[^0 \textit{Improper}\ ^0[^0{:}\ x\ ^0 0]]$ must be Trivialized here, because this very Composition is the object of predication, *viz.* that Tom knows that this Composition constructs the truth-value **T**. The context of its occurrence is hyperintensional.

When assigning constructions to expressions as their meanings as part of my semantic analysis, I use the following *method of semantic analysis*. The method consists in three steps which are (a) type-theoretical analysis, (b) synthesis and (c) type-theoretical checking.[19] For illustration, here is an analysis of the sentence "No bachelor is married".

(a) *Type-theoretical analysis*, i.e., assigning types to all the objects mentioned by various atoms and molecules of the analysed sentence. In our case we have:

Bachelor, *Married*/(oι)$_{\tau\omega}$—properties of individuals; *No*/((o(oι))(oι))—the function that assigns to a given set *M* the set of those sets of individuals which have an empty intersection with *M*.

(b) *Synthesis*, i.e., using the *constructions* of the objects *ad* (a) in order to construct the proposition (of type o$_{\tau\omega}$) denoted by the whole sentence. Now we have to take into account the fact that the sentence does not talk about any particular bachelor or any particular married person. It talks about the properties of being a bachelor and being married. If we understand 'bachelor' and 'married' as

---
[19] For details see also [34]; Duží et al. [17].

The paradox of inference and the non-triviality of analytic information

used in current English, we are in a position to know *a priori* that these two properties cannot share instances. Consequently, the respective extensions of these two properties at any given $\langle w, t \rangle$ have an empty intersection. The extension of a ι-property at a given $\langle w, t \rangle$ is a set of individuals, an (oι)-object. In order to obtain its extension at a $\langle w, t \rangle$ of evaluation, we have to extensionalize the property by applying it to a world w and a time t.[20] In our case we have $[[^0Bachelor\ w]\ t]$ and $[[^0Married\ w]\ t]$, abbreviated as '$^0Bachelor_{wt}$', '$^0Married_{wt}$', respectively. Now by applying the function *No* to the extension of *Bachelor* (by means of the Composition $[^0No\ ^0Bachelor_{wt}]$), we obtain the set of those sets of individuals which are disjoint with the extension of *Bachelor* at $\langle w, t \rangle$. The application of this set to the extension of *Married* by means of the Composition

$$[[^0No\ ^0Bachelor_{wt}]\ ^0Married_{wt}]$$

yields a truth-value **T** or **F**, depending on whether at the given world and time the set of married people belongs to the set of those sets which are disjoint with the set of bachelors.

By abstracting over the values of w and t, we obtain this analysis of the sentence:

$$\lambda w \lambda t [[^0No\ ^0Bachelor_{wt}]\ ^0Married_{wt}].$$

(c) Type-theoretical checking:

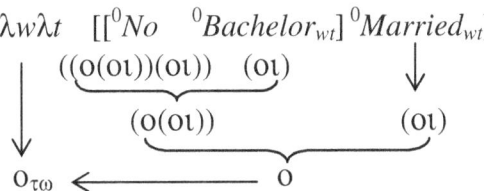

The type of the constructed object is $o_{\tau\omega}$. So the sample sentence expresses as its meaning a construction constructing a proposition, which explains why the sentence denotes a proposition. Put differently, its meaning is a hyperproposition, which is a procedure producing a proposition. Notice that the semantic analysis does not terminate in a truth-value, even though "No bachelor is married" expresses an analytic truth.

Note also that we analyse the sentence using the restricted quantifier *No*. If we used the non-restricted existential quantifier ($\exists$) together with negation ($\neg$) and conjunction ($\wedge$), we would obtain the analysis of an equivalent, though not synonymous, sentence, "There is no individual such that it is a bachelor and it is married" expressing the Closure $\lambda w \lambda t\ \neg \exists x\ [[^0Bachelor_{wt}\ x] \wedge [^0Married_{wt}\ x]]$. See, however, Section 4.2.

---

[20] For details on predication of properties see [26].

The paradox of inference and the non-triviality of analytic information

By way of examples I illustrated how TIL operates smoothly for all kinds of logical-semantic context, whether extensional, intensional or hyper-intensional, while adhering to the compositionality principle throughout. Due to the rich ontology of entities organized in the ramified hierarchy of types, TIL flouts none of the principles of extensional logic and is, insofar, an *extensional* logic. This will do as an outline of the philosophy of TIL, together with its basic definitions. Now I am going to apply the TIL apparatus to an investigation of the information conveyed by sentences.

4 Analytic Information

4.1 Empirical Content of Sentences

As stated in Section 2, sentences are factually informative thanks to their empirical content.[21] We characterized the empirical content of a sentence S as the set of possible worlds and times excluded by S. Now we can put this characterisation on a more solid ground. Let $P/o_{\tau\omega}$ be the proposition denoted by a sentence S. Then the *empirical content of S, $EC(S)$*, is the set of $\langle w, t \rangle$-pairs at which P does not take the truth-value **T**, because the proposition P either takes value **F** or is undefined at $\langle w, t \rangle$.

Let T be an analytically true sentence. Then T denotes the proposition *TRUE*, which takes the value **T** at all $\langle w, t \rangle$-pairs, and $EC(T) = \emptyset$. Let T' be a contradictory sentence denoting an impossible proposition, i.e. a proposition that does not take the value **T** at any $\langle w, t \rangle$.[22] Then $EC(T')$ is the set W of all $\langle w, t \rangle$-pairs. Thus neither T nor T' conveys any useful empirical information about the state of the world.

On the other hand, an empirical sentence S conveys non-trivial empirical information, because $EC(S) \subset W$. When we combine analytic and empirical sentences, we can compare the empirical content of the resulting sentences. For example, consider the following atomic sentences:

  S: "Charles is a logician",
  M_1: "1+1=2",
  M_2: "1+1=3"

and the four compound sentences $S_1 - S_4$:

  S_1: "Charles is a logician and 1+1=2",
  S_2: "Charles is a logician and 1+1=3",
  S_3: "Charles is a logician or 1+1=2",
  S_4: "Charles is a logician or 1+1=3".

The sentences M_1 and M_2 are not factually informative, because their empirical content is an empty set and the whole logical space, respectively. The empirical

---

[21] Portions of this section draw on material presented in [13].
[22] I say '*a* proposition', not '*the* proposition', because due to partiality there are many impossible propositions, which differ by taking **F** or no value at different $\langle w, t \rangle$-pairs.

content of the compound sentences S_1 through S_4 is obtained by applying the set-theoretic operators of union (∪) and intersection (∩) to the EC of the atomic sentences:

$$EC(S_1) = EC(S) \cup EC(M_1) = EC(S) \cup \emptyset = EC(S)$$
$$EC(S_2) = EC(S) \cup EC(M_2) = EC(S) \cup W = W$$
$$EC(S_3) = EC(S) \cap EC(M_1) = EC(S) \cap \emptyset = \emptyset$$
$$EC(S_4) = EC(S) \cap EC(M_2) = EC(S) \cap W = EC(S).$$

The conjunction of an analytically true sentence with an empirical sentence S does not increase the empirical content of S (the case of S_1). The conjunction of an analytically false sentence with an empirical sentence S voids the empirical content of S by yielding the whole logical space (the case of S_2). The disjunction of an empirical sentence S and an analytically true sentence also voids the empirical content of S by yielding an empty content (the case of S_3). Finally, the disjunction of an empirical sentence S and an analytically false sentence does not change the empirical content of S (the case of S_4).[23]

Nonetheless, in the next section we want to explain that even analytically true sentences convey information, because they have non-empty *analytic*, as opposed to *empirical*, content.

4.2 Analytic Content of Sentences

Analytically true sentences are true exclusively in virtue of their meaning, independently of states-of-affairs.[24] There are two kinds of such sentences, mathematical ones and the ones containing empirical expressions. This gives rise to the following definition:

Definition 4 (*analytically true sentence*) A mathematical *sentence* is *analytically true* iff it expresses a construction constructing the truth-value **T**. A *sentence* involving empirical expressions is *analytically true* iff it expresses a construction constructing the proposition *TRUE*. □

Mathematical sentences are analytical in the above sense: when evaluating their truth-values, possible worlds and times do not matter as points of evaluation. As for sentences involving empirical expressions, "No bachelor is married" contains the empirical predicates 'is a bachelor' and 'is married', yet the sentence is analytical. At no world/time are the properties *being a bachelor* and *being married* co-instantiated by the same individual. However, the analysis of the sentence that we presented in Section 3, i.e. the Closure

(*) $\lambda w \lambda t \left[\left[^0No\ ^0Bachelor_{wt} \right] ^0Married_{wt} \right],$

does not reveal that the proposition so constructed takes **T** at all $\langle w, t \rangle$-pairs. The proposition in question is the necessary proposition *TRUE*; yet the analysis does not

---

[23] A similar conception was advocated by [46].
[24] Recall that we are not analysing a formal, non-interpreted language. Instead, we presuppose full understanding and linguistic competence. Thus from our point of view, 'analytically true' is not synonymous with 'true on all interpretations'; rather, it is synonymous with 'true with respect to all possible worlds and times' or 'true independently of possible worlds and times'.

The paradox of inference and the non-triviality of analytic information make it possible to *prove* it. We need to refine the analysis. To this end we make use of the fact that the property of being a bachelor is *defined* as the property of being an unmarried man, so the sentence is analytically, *ex definitione*, true. As soon as we replace the simple predicate 'is a bachelor' by this definition, the truth of the sentence is obvious: "No unmarried man is married". Still, to prove it we need a finer analysis that makes use of the definition of the restricted quantifier *No*. It is a function that operates on sets of individuals and returns **T** iff the sets are disjoint. By using the variables $m, n/*_1 \rightarrow_v (o\iota), x \rightarrow_v \iota$, we obtain the equivalences

$$^0No = \lambda m \lambda n \neg \exists x[[m\,x] \wedge [n\,x]],$$
$$[[^0No\,m]n] = \neg \exists x[[m\,x] \wedge [n\,x]].$$

The property of being a bachelor can be defined by Composing the constructions of the negation and of the properties *Married* and *Man* as follows:

$$^0Bachelor = \lambda w \lambda t \lambda x \left[\neg [^0Married_{wt}\,x] \wedge [^0Man_{wt}\,x] \right].$$

Now by substituting the respective definitions (and applying β-reductions) we obtain:

$$\left[[^0No\;^0Bachelor_{wt}]\;^0Married_{wt} \right] = \neg \exists x \left[[^0Bachelor_{wt}\,x] \wedge [^0Married_{wt}\,x] \right] = $$
$$\neg \exists x \left[\neg [^0Married_{wt}\,x] \wedge [^0Man_{wt}\,x] \wedge [^0Married_{wt}\,x] \right].$$

Since this last construction obviously and provably *v*-constructs **T** for any valuation *v*, we can generalize to

$$\forall w \forall t \neg \exists x \left[\neg [^0Married_{wt}\,x] \wedge [^0Man_{wt}\,x] \wedge [^0Married_{wt}\,x] \right].$$

Substituting this construction for the Composition $[[^0No\;^0Bachelor_{wt}]\;^0Married_{wt}]$ into (*) we obtain

(**) $\quad \lambda w \lambda t \left[\forall w \forall t \neg \exists x \left[\neg [^0Married_{wt}\,x] \wedge [^0Man_{wt}\,x] \wedge [^0Married_{wt}\,x] \right] \right].$

We have proven that the sentence "No bachelor is married" denotes the proposition *True*.

The above example illustrates the method of *refining* a construction by replacing it by an equivalent one that reveals a provable way to the product. But now, *which* of the equivalent constructions (*), (**) should be assigned to the sentence as its meaning? The method of semantic analysis of an expression *E* outlined in Section 3 heeds Carnap's *principle of subject matter* ([6], §24.2, §26) as translated into TIL: It yields a construction *C* (assigned to *E* as its meaning) such that every closed sub-construction of *C* constructs an object mentioned by *E*, i.e., an object denoted by a sub-expression of *E*. Hence the construction $\lambda w \lambda t\, [[^0No\;^0Bachelor_{wt}]\;^0Married_{wt}]$ is the meaning of the sentence "No bachelor is married", unlike, for instance, the construction

$$\lambda w \lambda t \left[[[^0No\;^0Bachelor_{wt}]^0Married_{wt}] \wedge [^0<\;^02\;^05] \right].$$

Though both constructions construct one and the same proposition *True*, the latter contains sub-constructions constructing objects that do not receive mention in the

The paradox of inference and the non-triviality of analytic information

sentence (viz. the numbers 2, 5 and the relation <). This is also the motivation why I adhere to the principle of subject matter. An adequate analysis of an expression E contains constructions of all and only objects that receive explicit mention in E. This method of semantic analysis does not, however, specify the manner in which the mentioned objects are constructed. The following definition imposes the demand that the extra-logical objects that receive mention by *semantically simple* sub-expressions of E should be constructed by their Trivialisations.

Definition 5 (*literal meaning of an expression*) Let E be an expression whose semantically simple sub-expressions are $S_1,...,S_n$, and let $S_1,...,S_n$ denote the extra-logical objects $X_1,...,X_m$. Let C_E be a construction that is assigned to E as its meaning; i.e., there is no closed subconstruction of C_E constructing an object that is not denoted by a subexpression of E. Then C_E is the *literal meaning of E* iff $^0X_1,...,^0X_m$ are all closed subconstructions of C_E constructing the objects $X_1,...,X_m$, respectively. □

Remark I am aware of the problem of determining which objects are logical and which are extra-logical.[25] For the present purposes, I consider as logical objects only truth-functions, quantifiers, and identity relations.

Following the above method of analysis, the sentence "No bachelor is married" could have had assigned (at least) three constructions as its meaning:

(C$_1$) $\lambda w \lambda t$ [[^{0}No ^{0}Bachelor$_{wt}$] ^{0}Married$_{wt}$]

(C$_2$) $\lambda w \lambda t$ [[^{0}No [^{0}Unmarried ^{0}Man]$_{wt}$] ^{0}Married$_{wt}$]

(C$_3$) $\lambda w \lambda t \; \neg \exists x \; [\neg [^0Married_{wt} \; x] \wedge [^0Man_{wt} \; x] \wedge [^0Married_{wt} \; x]]$.

Remark In (C$_2$) I am using the property modifier $Unmarried/((o\iota)_{\tau\omega}(o\iota)_{\tau\omega})$. It is a function that, when applied to a property (here, *being a man*), gives another property (here, *being an unmarried man*).

Of these, only (C$_1$) is the literal meaning of the sentence "No bachelor is married". In 'logician's English' (C$_2$) is the literal meaning of another (equivalent) sentence, namely "No unmarried man is married", and (C$_3$) of the sentence "It is not so that there is an individual x such that x is not married and x is a man and x is married".

Recalling our problem of the analytic information conveyed by sentences, we ask, "What do we learn when knowing that (C$_1$), (C$_2$) and (C$_3$), respectively"? We do not learn anything about the state of the world, for sure. It is not the proposition T$_{RUE}$ that we get to know, because nobody with finite, human-like capacities can survey all elements of an uncountable infinite set such as this mapping. It would amount to knowing an actual infinity, which is beyond our finite capacities.

---

[25] This problem was tackled as early as in 1837 by Bolzano, who introduced a modern method of variation of (objective) representations ('Vorstellungen an sich') and defined '*generally valid*' sentences *with respect to representations* $r_1,...,r_m$ such that the sentence remains true if these representations are changed or varied. (See ([5], §§147–48.))

215

The paradox of inference and the non-triviality of analytic information

Yet we have the capacity to *potentially* know actual infinities. In *any* world at *any* time, following the instructions presented by (C_1), (C_2) or (C_3) amounts to arriving at the truth-value **T**. Understanding the sentences "No bachelor is married", "No unmarried man is married" and "It is not so that there is an individual x such that x is not married and x is a man and x is married" amounts to knowing three different constructions, (C_1), (C_2) and (C_3), detailing how to arrive, in any world at any time, at **T**. Since (C_3) is a more detailed construction than (C_2) and (C_2) is more detailed than (C_1), I suggest that the information value of these sentences increases from (C_1) to (C_3). The reason is that the degree of the level of information depth, as D'Agostini and Floridi [18] characterizes it, is decreasing from (C_1) to (C_3). To prove the validity of (C_1) we need to add additional information (here the definition of the property *Bachelor* and of the quantifier *No*) that is not explicitly contained in the literal meaning of (C_1). And the more such hidden information is brought up to the surface, the more informative and logically tractable the meaning becomes.

For an analogy, imagine you need to go from place A to place B. You consult a map and figure out an itinerary from A to B via X. Did you learn something? Surely you did. You obtained a piece of information to the effect that the mapping $\{A\} \to \{B\}$ can be realised by Composing the mappings $\{A\} \to \{X\}$ and $\{X\} \to \{B\}$. Now you start from A moving toward X but, alas, the stretch around X is closed due to the area being flooded. You conduct a search on traffic web sites and discover a new itinerary from A to B via Y and Z. As a result, you follow the instruction to go from A to B via Y and Z, realising the mapping $\{A\} \to \{B\}$ by composing the mappings $\{A\} \to \{Y\}$, $\{Y\} \to \{Z\}$ and $\{Z\} \to \{B\}$. Wasn't it again a useful piece of new information you learnt? Surely it was. Yet from the set-theoretical point of view, in all three cases the result is the same, viz. the mapping $\{A\} \to \{B\}$.

TIL constructions are such itineraries, specifying a route to an output given some input entities.[26] In a broader sense, not only a declarative sentence but any meaningful expression conveys some itinerary. For a mathematical example, compare the atomic Trivialisation $^0Successor$ and the compound Closure $\lambda x\ [^0+ x\ ^0 1]$. Though they are equivalent by constructing the same function *Successor* of type ($\tau\tau$), the latter is more informative than the former. $^0Successor$ is the instruction to select the successor function among all the other ($\tau\tau$)-typed functions, and insofar qualifies as a fully-fledged construction, though one with a serious flaw: it fails to specify *how* to select that function.[27] The rival Closure $\lambda x\ [^0+ x\ ^0 1]$ offers a *how*. It conveys an interesting piece of information on how to obtain the mapping. If we decompose the Closure, its individual constituent steps are:

(i) $^0+$ (take the function *plus*);
(ii) x (take *any* natural number);
(iii) $^0 1$ (take the number 1);
(iv) $[^0+ x\ ^0 1]$ (apply the result of step (i) to the pair of outputs *ad* (ii) and (iii), and output the resulting value);

---

[26] Some of these routes are 'roads to nowhere' in the shape of improper constructions, or 'roads with a void destination', which are procedures that fail to deliver a product but are no less procedures for that.

[27] Moreover, the atomic construction $^0Successor$ is a non-executable, ineffective procedure. It is an instruction to take an actual infinity, viz. the mapping *Successor*, and supply it as a result.

(v) $\lambda x\ [^0+\ x\ ^01]$ (abstract from the input *ad* (ii) and output the mapping).

The Closure $\lambda x\ [^0+\ x\ ^01]$ consists of the constituents $^0+$, x, ^{01}, $[^0+\ x\ ^01]$ and itself. $^0Successor$, in contrast, consists only of itself. So there are no further procedures to decompose $^0Successor$ into. $^0Successor$ is a one-step instruction like "Go from *A* to *B*", *vide* the analogy above. The Closure is a compound instruction like "Go from *A* to *B* via *Y* and *Z*".

From the above sentences imbued with the meanings (C_1), (C_2) and (C_3), only the last sentence has the 'literal logical form' that makes it possible to prove the analytical truth of the original sentence. Thus the last sentence is not only analytically but also *logically true*. In order to define the notion of logically true sentence, we need still another definition:

Definition 6 (*literal logical form of an expression*) Let C_E be the literal logical analysis of *E*, the subconstructions of which construct (by Trivialisation) the extra-logical objects $X_1,\ldots,X_n$, X_i/α_i. Let $V_1 \rightarrow_v \alpha_1,\ldots, V_n \rightarrow_v \alpha_n$ be variables not occurring in C_E. Then the *literal logical form* (*LLF*) of *E* is a construction LC_E that differs from C_E only in replacing all occurrences of ^0X_i by V_i ($1 \leq i \leq n$). □

It is important to note that according to Definition 6 only Trivialisations of *extra-logical* objects are replaced by type-theoretically appropriate variables in order to obtain the literal logical form of the relevant expression.[28] Logical objects like truth-functional connectives and quantifiers are left unchanged. Thus the literal logical form of a sentence corresponds to a formula of a formal language. The formulae of a formal language are associated with their models by means of an interpretation of special non-logical symbols. A formula is then logically true if it is true on every interpretation.

As we explained in Section 3, constructions are not syntactic objects. We do not translate sentences of a natural language into a formal language with a view to interpreting this second language. Instead, by means of 'the language of constructions' we directly examine constructions as expressed by natural-language sentences. Yet there is a similarity with the formal approach. If a sentence is logically true, it is true in virtue of its logical form, regardless of any particular extra-logical objects receiving mention in the sentence. For instance, the sentence "No natural number is even and not even" is logically true, unlike the sentence "No natural number is even and odd", which is only analytically true. The literal logical form assigned to the former is

$$\neg \exists x[[Ex] \wedge \neg[Ex]],$$

whereas the literal logical form assigned to the latter is

$$\neg \exists x[[Ex] \wedge [Ox]].$$

Types: $x \rightarrow_v \tau$; $E, O \rightarrow_v (o\tau)$.

The former construction *v*-constructs **T** for *all* valuations of the variable *E*. However, there are valuations of variables *E* and *O* for which the latter construction

---

[28] For the notion of logical form, see also [16].

v-constructs **F**. These are those valuations for which E and O v-construct sets with a non-empty intersection.[29]

Thus definition 6 enables us to easily define *logically true sentence*.

Definition 7 (*logically true sentence*) A mathematical *sentence S* is *logically true* iff the *LLF* of *S* v-constructs the truth-value **T** for every valuation v. A *sentence S* involving empirical expressions is *logically true* iff the *LLF* of *S* v-constructs the proposition *TRUE* for every valuation v. □

Obviously, any logically true sentence is analytically true. It is a well-known fact that the converse does not hold, as indeed the above examples showed.

By *the analytic information conveyed by an expression E* is meant the literal meaning of *E*, i.e. the TIL construction expressed by *E*. The amount of analytic information conveyed by *E* depends on the way particular constituents of the literal meaning of *E* are combined. Thus we define

Definition 8 (*analytic information, analytic content*) The *analytic information conveyed by an expression E* is the literal meaning of *E*. The *analytic content of an expression E* is the set of constituents of the literal meaning of *E*. □

For instance, the analytic information conveyed by the sentence "No bachelor is married" is the Closure $\lambda w \lambda t$ [[^{0}*No* ^{0}*Bachelor*$_{wt}$] ^{0}*Married*$_{wt}$]. The analytic content of this sentence is the set {$\lambda w \lambda t$ [[^{0}*No* ^{0}*Bachelor*$_{wt}$] ^{0}*Married*$_{wt}$], [[^{0}*No* ^{0}*Bachelor*$_{wt}$] ^{0}*Married*$_{wt}$], [^{0}*No* ^{0}*Bachelor*$_{wt}$], ^{0}*No*, ^{0}*Bachelor*, [^{0}*Bachelor w*], [[^{0}*Bachelor w*]t], ^{0}*Married*, [^{0}*Married w*], [[^{0}*Married w*]t], w, t}.

Definitions 4 through 8 provide us with the logical machinery required to compare the degree of informativeness of analytically/logically true sentences, or in general of analytically equivalent sentences. This I am going to do in the next paragraphs.

4.3 Comparing the Information Content of Analytically Equivalent Sentences

We have seen that analytically equivalent sentences denote the same proposition and thus exclude the same set of $\langle w, t \rangle$-pairs. They convey the same empirical information. Yet, as I demonstrated above, analytically equivalent sentences do not necessarily have the same analytic content. Now I am going to formulate some criteria for comparing the informative value of analytically equivalent sentences. First, I want to define exactly how fine-grained my individuation of analytic information is. So I need to lay down when two sentences are informationally indistinguishable. Let the analytic content of a sentence *S* be denoted by '*AC(S)*'. Obviously, the following condition is valid:

---

[29] Similarly, the formula $\neg \exists x[E(x) \wedge \neg E(x)]$ of first-order predicate logic is true on every interpretation assigning a subset of the universe to the symbol '*E*', whereas there are interpretations of '*E*' and '*O*' on which the formula $\neg \exists x[E(x) \wedge O(x)]$ is false, *viz.* those interpretations that assign non-disjoint sets to the symbols '*E*' and '*O*'.

The paradox of inference and the non-triviality of analytic information

If $AC(S_1) = AC(S_2)$ then the sentences S_1 and S_2 are *equally analytically infomative*.

Actually, if the sentences S_1 and S_2 have the same analytic content, then S_1, S_2 have the same meaning. For example, the sentences "5 is a prime", "Five is a prime", and "Fünf ist eine Primzahl" are synonymous; they have the same meaning and thus the same analytic content; hence, they are informationally indistinguishable. The reason is because the literal meaning of all these sentences is [$^0Prime\ ^0 5$]. The Trivialization ^0Prime is identical with the Trivialization $^0Primzahl$, because what is Trivialized is the *set* of primes, independently of the (English or German) name we use to denote this set.[30]

However, having equal analytic content is a sufficient, though not necessary, condition for two expressions to be synonymous. In order to define synonymy, the above condition has to be slightly weakened along the following lines: the expressions E_1, E_2 are *synonymous* iff their literal meanings are *procedurally isomorphic*. Procedural isomorphism is defined as the transitive closure of α- and η-equivalence.[31] Thus we define:

Definition 9 (*procedurally isomorphic constructions*) Let C, D be constructions. Then C, D are α-*equivalent* iff they differ at most by deploying different λ-bound variables. C, D are η-*equivalent* iff one arises from the other by η-reduction or η-expansion. C, D are *procedurally isomorphic*, denoted '$^0C \approx\ ^0D$', $\approx/(o*_n*_n)$, iff there are closed constructions $C_1,\ldots,C_m$, $m \geq 1$, such that $^0C =\ ^0C_1$, $^0D =\ ^0C_m$, and all C_i, C_{i+1} ($1 \leq i < m$) are either α- or η-equivalent. □

For instance, the constructions ^0Prime, $\lambda x\ [^0Prime\ x]$, $\lambda y\ [^0Prime\ y]$, $\lambda z\ [\lambda x\ [^0Prime\ x]\ z]$, are procedurally isomorphic, while $\lambda x\ [[^0Card\ \lambda y\ [^0Divide\ y\ x]] =\ ^0 2]$ is only equivalent to them; it does construct the set of primes, but does so in a non-isomorphic manner.

Types: $x, y, z \rightarrow \nu$, the type of natural numbers; $Card/(\nu(o\nu))$: the number of elements of a set of natural numbers; $Divide/(o\nu\nu)$: the relation of dividing x by y.

---

[30] By claiming that synonyms do not add any analytic content, the proposed solution might seem to be open to other problems, such as, for instance, *Mates' puzzle* (see [35]). Roughly, the idea of the puzzle is that even if 'P_1' and 'P_2' are stipulated to be synonymous predicates, one may know that a is P_1 and still not know that a is P_2, or the other way around. Standard examples are the pairs 'is a woodchuck'/'is a groundhog', or Church's 'lasts a fortnight'/'lasts a period of fourteen days'. I do not attempt to solve this puzzle because syntactic differences in synonymous expressions and other merely notational variants are irrelevant from the logical point of view. Failure of substitutability due to linguistic incompetence is a pragmatic problem. Kripke's Pierre puzzle can be explained away along similar lines. See also [32] and Duží et al. ([17], § 5.1.1). It is a problem of linguistic competence (though across two different languages) rather than a logical problem.

[31] Presumably the first attempt to define synonymy was due to Carnap, in terms of intensional isomorphism, in [6]. The idea was this: expressions are intensionally isomorphic if they are composed from subexpressions with the same intensions in *the same way*. Church criticized Carnap's criterion of the identity of belief in [8]. Roughly, Church's criticism was based on the fact that *syntactically* simple intensionally isomorphic expressions can have assigned different compound meanings. He proposed three alternatives of the criterion of *synonymous isomorphism*, of which the closest to my solution is (A1); expressions are synonymous if they are λ-convertible (see [3], p. 162). But, Church's λ-convertibility includes also β-conversion, which goes too far due to partiality. See also Jespersen [27].

The paradox of inference and the non-triviality of analytic information

Procedural isomorphism gives rise to this principle:

The sentences S_1, S_2 are synonymous, and thus convey the same analytic information, iff their literal meanings are procedurally isomorphic.

Since we want to compare the analytical informational value of sentences that are equivalent but not synonymous (which would be trivial), we might consider comparing the *number* of constituents contained in the respective analytic contents. If the number of constituents of the literal meaning of a sentence S_1 is greater than the number of constituents of a sentence S_2, I will write '$|AC(S_1)| > |AC(S_2)|$'. However, a simple criterion based on the number of steps is impossible. The mere number of steps is insufficient to define the (relative) degree of information, since some steps do not contribute to the informational value of sentences, while others are incomparable. For one thing, how would we compare empirical sentences with mathematical ones?

It might seem that if $AC(S_1) \subset AC(S_2)$—i.e., if $AC(S_1)$ is a proper subset of $AC(S_2)$—then S_1 would be less analytically informative than S_2. Again, a moment's reflection reveals that it is not so. This is due to the fact that the analytic content of a sentence is construed as the *set* of its meaning constituents. As pointed out above, while constructions are procedures and as such structured and complex, sets lack structure. Consider, for instance, sentences of the form "p" and "p or q". Though the analytic content of the former is a (proper) subset of the latter, "p or q" is less or equally empirically informative than "p". If we know that p, then the degree of our uncertainty about the world decreases to a greater extent than when knowing that p or q. Since we now want to compare the degree of information of analytically equivalent sentences, i.e. of sentences that convey the equal amount of empirical information, q must be a contradiction in order that "p or q" and "p" be equivalent. And increasing the analytic content of a sentence by a contradiction certainly does not increase the degree of useful analytic information conveyed by the sentence. In general, we want to examine the increase and decrease of analytic information in harmony with the respective increase and decrease of empirical information. Hence a criterion given by simple set-theoretic inclusion is *not* plausible, either.

The first criterion (*AC*), which I am going to formulate now, is based on the fact that a conjunctive extension of the analytic content of a sentence such that the extended sentence is still equivalent to the original one results in more analytically informative sentence. For instance, "Whales are mammals" is less analytically informative than "Whales are mammals belonging to the order Cetacea", or, "Whales are mammals *and* the problem of logical validity is not decidable within the first-order predicate logic". Thus we formulate the *criterion* (*AC*):

Let sentences S_1, S_2 be analytically equivalent, and let $AC(S_1) \subset AC(S_2)$. If S_2 is of a form equivalent to 'S_1 and T', for some non-contradictory sentence T, then S_2 is analytically more informative than S_1.

This criterion is, however, not applicable in the case of equivalencies obtained by refining the meaning, like the above case of "No bachelor is married". The analytic contents of (C1), (C2) and (C3) are not comparable by set-theoretical inclusion. We need a structurally qualitative criterion. As explained above, the analytic information increases from (C_1) to (C_3). This is because one constituent of (C_1) or (C_2) has been replaced by a more complex, but still equivalent, constituent.

The paradox of inference and the non-triviality of analytic information

For a mathematical example, consider the sentence

T_1 "If 2 < 5 and 5 < 11 then 2 < 11".

It is analytically, but not logically, true. Its literal meaning is

T_1' $[[[^0< {}^02 \ {}^05] \wedge [^0< {}^05 \ {}^011]] \supset [^0< {}^02 \ {}^011]]$

and the LLF of T_1 is ($L \rightarrow_v (o\tau\tau)$, $k, m, n \rightarrow_v \tau$):

T_1" $[[[L\,k\,m] \wedge [L\,m\,n]] \supset [L\,k\,n]]$.

There is a valuation v such that the antecedent v-constructs **T** and the consequent **F**. (For instance, the valuation v that assigns the relation $\neq$ to the variable L, and the numbers 2, 5, 2 to variables k, m, n, respectively.) For the same reason, even the sentence T_2 is not logically true:

T_2 "If 2 < 5 and 5 < 11 and if < is transitive then 2 < 11".

Though T_2 has greater analytic content and specifies a more detailed procedure than T_1, it literally leaves it open what is the definition of the transitive relation. The literal meaning of T_2 and its respective *LLF* are (the variable $T \rightarrow_v (o(o\tau\tau))$ v-constructing a class of binary relations):

T_2' $[[[^0< {}^02 \ {}^05] \wedge [^0< {}^05 \ {}^011] \wedge [^0Transitive \ {}^0<]] \supset [^0< {}^02 \ {}^011]]$

T_2" $[[[L\,k\,m] \wedge [L\,m\,n] \wedge [T\,L]] \supset [L\,k\,n]]$

T_2" is not the form of a logically true sentence. Only when we explicitly define the class of transitive binary relations by (types: $r \rightarrow_v (o\tau\tau)$; $x, y, z \rightarrow_v \tau$)

$\lambda r \ \forall x \forall y \forall z [[r\,x\,y] \supset [[r\,y\,z] \supset [r\,x\,z]]]$

is the logically true sentence T_3 obtained:

T_3 "If 2 < 5 and 5 < 11 and if $\forall x \forall y \forall z (x < y \supset (y < z \supset x < z))$ then 2 < 11".

T_3 expresses this Composition:

T_3' $[[[^0< {}^02 \ {}^05] \wedge [^0< {}^05 \ {}^011] \wedge \forall x \forall y \forall z [[^0< x\,y] \supset [[^0< y\,z] \supset [^0< x\,y]]]] \supset [^0< {}^02 \ {}^011]]$

The logical form of T_3 is the form of a logically true sentence:

T_3" $[[[L\,k\,m] \wedge [L\,m\,n] \wedge \forall x \forall y \forall z [[L\,x\,y] \supset [[L\,y\,z] \supset [L\,x\,z]]]] \supset [L\,k\,n]]$

The analytic information conveyed by these sentences increases from T_1 to T_3. The logically true sentence T_3 provides, thanks to its meaning, such detailed instructions on how to arrive at the produced truth-value that its truth is easily provable; and it is readily seen that it provides the greatest analytic information of the three. Sentences T_1 and T_2 are comparable *via* the criterion (*AC*). The analytic content of T_1 is a proper subset of the analytic content of T_2, and the extension of $AC(T_1)$ to $AC(T_2)$ does not consist in the irrelevant disjunctive extension. Yet (*AC*) is not applicable to T_2 and T_3. Their analytic contents differ only in that the Trivialization $^0Transitive$ occurring as a constituent of T_2 has been replaced by a complex definition of the set of transitive binary relations. I will say that the meaning of T_3 is a *refinement* of the meaning of T_2, and I define:

Definition 10 (*refinement of a construction*) Let a construction C_2 differ from a construction C_1 only by containing a compound constituent that constructs an entity X instead of the Trivialisation ^0X. Then C_2 is a *refinement of* C_1. If a construction C_3 is a refinement of C_2 and C_2 is a refinement of C_1, then C_3 is a *refinement of* C_1. □

Corollaries. If C_2 is a refinement of C_1, then

i) C_1, C_2 are equivalent but *not* procedurally isomorphic
ii) $AC(C_2)$ is not a superset of $AC(C_1)$
iii) $|AC(C_2)| > |AC(C_1)|$.

For example, the Closure $\lambda x\,[^0Card\,\lambda y\,[^0Divide\,y\,x] = {^0}2]$ is a refinement of the atomic construction ^0Prime. However, the Closure $\lambda x\,[^0Prime\,x]$ is not a refinement of ^0Prime, these two constructions being procedurally isomorphic.

There can be more than one refinement of a construction C. For instance, the Trivialization ^0Prime is in fact the least informative procedure for producing the set of primes. Using particular definitions of the set of primes, we can refine ^0Prime in many ways, including:

$$\lambda x[^0Card\,\lambda y[^0Divide\,y\,x] = {^0}2],$$
$$\lambda x[[x \neq {^0}1] \land \forall y[[^0Divide\,y\,x] \supset [[y = {^0}1] \lor [y = x]]]],$$
$$\lambda x[[x > {^0}1] \land \neg\exists y[[y > {^0}1] \land [y < x] \land [^0Divide\,y\,x]]].$$

In order to render the increase in information yield such as that from T_2 to T_3 we are now going to define a *qualitative criterion* based on the notion of meaning *refinement*. Having two analytically equivalent sentences, then if the literal meaning of one is a refinement of the literal meaning of the other, the former is more informative than the latter. Thus we formulate this *criterion (AR)* based on meaning refinement:

Let S_1 and S_2 be sentences with literal meanings CS_1, CS_2, respectively, such that CS_2 is a refinement of CS_1. Then CS_2 *is more analytically informative than* CS_1 ($CS_2 >_{an} CS_1$). If $CS_2 >_{an} CS_1$ then we also say that sentence S_2 *is more informative than* sentence S_1.

If applying (AR) to sentences T_2, T_3, it is easily seen that $T_3' >_{an} T_2'$, hence T_3 is more informative than T_2.

By refining the meaning C_S of a sentence S we uncover a more fine-grained construction C_S' such that C_S and C_S' are equivalent, yet not procedurally isomorphic, and such that the latter is more analytically informative than the former.

Remark. The relation $>_{an}$ defined by (AR) is transitive. But theoretically, we could keep refining one and the same construction *ad infinitum*. For instance, we could still refine the definitions above of the set of primes by refining the Trivialization ^0Divide thus:

$$^0Divide = \lambda yx[\exists z[x = [^0Mult\,yz]]].$$

Types: $x, y, z \to_v \nu$; $Mult/(\nu\nu\nu)$: the function of multiplication defined over the domain of natural numbers ν. Substituting the Closure for the Trivialization yields a more informative refinement:

$$^0Prime <_{an} [\lambda x[^0Card\, \lambda y[^0Divide\, y\, x] = {^0}2]] <_{an}$$
$$[\lambda x[^0Card\, \lambda y[\exists z[x = [^0Mult\, yz]]] = {^0}2]] <_{an} \ldots$$

What counts as the uppermost level of refinement will depend on the *conceptual system* in use. A conceptual system is determined by the set of its *primitive* concepts, which is the set of Trivializations of entities of a type of order 1 (non-constructions). The *derived* concepts of a conceptual system are then the compound closed constructions (i.e., constructions without free variables) which can be obtained by using the set of primitive concepts and variables of appropriate types. It has been proved that the set of refinements of a construction C obtainable within a given conceptual system forms a complete lattice with respect to the partial order defined as follows: $C_1 \leq C_2$ iff $C_1 <_{an} C_2$ or C_1, C_2 are procedurally isomorphic.[32]

This result is in harmony with the results recently published in [18], exploring deductions in propositional logic. By revisiting Hintikka's notions of surface and depth information D'Agostino and Floridi examine different levels of informational depth:

> The deepest possible level coincides with Carnap and Bar-Hillel's semantic information and is a kind of potential information, which is intractable and not increased by deductive inference. By way of contrast, the most basic level, "shallow information", is tractable and is increased by deductive inference. (*Ibid.*, p. 35.)

We can translate this idea into TIL as follows. The more hidden assumptions like the above transitivity of the relation < are needed to prove the sentence, the less analytic information is provided. Thus each refinement of a meaning increases the amount of analytic information. It brings some hidden analytic information to the surface, and makes the meaning more tractable. For this reason a logically true sentence conveys more analytic information than does an analytically, but not logically, true sentence. And if two analytically equivalent sentences S_1 and S_2 are such that the meaning of S_2 is a refinement of the meaning of S_1, then S_2 conveys more analytic information than S_1.

5 The Information Value of a Valid Argument and the Paradox of Inference

Now we are going to apply the above method of exploring analytic information to the case of valid arguments as well. If an argument A is valid then, necessarily, the conclusion excludes a subset of the set of world/time pairs excluded by the set of premises. In other words, the conclusion of a valid argument is *redundant* with respect to the *empirical information* conveyed by the set of premises. It is in this sense that the conclusion may be said to be *contained* in the premises. Thus, by inferring S from $S_1,\ldots,S_n$ we cannot acquire any new empirical information.

However, the informational value of a valid argument is preserved as soon as we consider analytic information. The essential point is the procedure/product bifurcation. A *construction* of the conclusion may not occur in the premises; if it

---

[32] See [34]. The notion of conceptual system employed above is due to Pavel Materna; see his [33].

does not we have to discover it, and the construction we discover is new to us, hence epistemically useful and non-trivial. What happens is that we acquire a novel piece of *analytic information* about a particular *way of constructing* the proposition/truth-value denoted by the conclusion.

Thus we may paraphrase Cohen and Nagel's paradox along these lines:

> If in an argument the *empirical content* of the conclusion is not contained in the *empirical content* of the premises, the argument cannot be valid.
> If the conclusion is not different from any of the premises, it is epistemically useless.
> If the *empirical content* of the conclusion is contained in the *empirical content* of the premises, the conclusion does not possess novelty.
> Arguments cannot be both valid and epistemically useful.

This argument is valid but not sound. The third premise is not true. To restate the point, though the empirical content of the conclusion of a valid argument is contained in the empirical content of its premises, the *analytic content* of the conclusion need not be so contained. And if it is not, the literal meaning of the conclusion is a novelty.

This is to say that useful content is not exhausted by empirical content; analytic content is also a part of what is epistemically useful. Though analytic content does not count as content bearing on the world, it does count as objective and useful content. The question then is whether it is still paradoxical that through inference we do not learn anything about the world. In my opinion, it is not. If it were paradoxical then we should also have to admit that mathematical reasoning is paradoxical, because pure mathematics does not convey any empirical information about the world. However, presumably no rational being denies the epistemic usefulness of mathematics. Similarly, when running a computer program we do not obtain any empirical information in addition to the stock of empirical information that has been already stored in the computer database. Does this mean that executing a computer program is a paradoxical and pointless activity? Surely not; a computer program encodes an objective and useful algorithm whose execution conveys new analytic information. Only if we were logically and mathematically omniscient would we not need to discover new constructions, and as a result mathematics and logic would be epistemically useless disciplines.

However, if the literal meaning of the conclusion does occur among the premises—i.e., if the literal meaning of the conclusion is procedurally isomorphic with the literal meaning of some premise(s)—then the argument is *trivial* in the sense of offering no new analytic information. Such an argument is *circular*.

To adduce a simple example, the argument

$$\frac{\text{Anna wears a sky-blue blouse}}{\text{Anna wears an azure blouse}}$$

is trivial. The literal meaning of the premise and the conclusion is the same, provided 'is sky-blue' and 'is azure' are synonymous predicates.[33]

---

[33] Inferring such a conclusion is like running a program that only prints the text stored in its memory. From this point of view, even if the program translates the text into another language, it does not convey any new analytic information. Yet one would hardly deny that the translation was useful. Yes, it is useful, only not from the logical point of view. We might perhaps say that it conveys new *linguistic* information about the language itself, rather than about what the language conveys to us. But this is another story that I shall not deal with in this paper.

On the other hand, the argument

$$\frac{\text{Charles is a bachelor}}{\text{Charles is an unmarried man}}$$

is not trivial. As we have seen above, the literal meaning of the conclusion is a refinement of the literal meaning of the premise, and so the conclusion is more informative than the premise. Thus, though the conclusion denotes the same proposition as does the premise, it provides a new (and more informative) construction of this proposition. Again, it brought information that was hidden in the premise, *viz.* that being a bachelor involves being unmarried, to the surface and so made this snippet of information explicit.

Now suppose we assert that S and we want to justify our assertion. The most cogent way to do so is to come up with a sound argument whose conclusion is S. Let the premises of the respective argument be $S_1,\ldots,S_n$, and let the argument be sound. We get an analytically true sentence of the form

$$\text{If } (S_1 \text{ and} \ldots \text{and } S_n) \text{ then } S.$$

What novelty did we learn? Originally, we had just the proposition that S; now we have learned one of the ways of *justifying* S. Is this an important new piece of information? The answer depends on whether the argument is non-trivially valid. If the literal meaning of conclusion S is procedurally isomorphic to the literal meaning of some premises, we can learn nothing new. The utility of a non-trivial *sound* argument depends on several factors, the rigorous formulation of which remains an open problem. One of the relevant factors is the analytical vs. logical validity of an argument.

An analytically valid argument is truth-preserving, which is a necessary, though not sufficient, condition for logical validity. As explained in Section 1, every argument can be transformed into a corresponding conditional sentence (*via* the rule of implication introduction). A deductively valid argument is transformed into an analytically true sentence. In the case of a mathematical argument, the resulting implicative sentence denotes the truth-value **T**. In the case of an argument involving empirical expressions, the implicative sentence denotes the proposition TRUE. In both cases the implicative sentence has empty empirical content; however, it has non-empty analytic content. Thus we define:

Definition 11 (*analytically/logically valid argument*) Let $S_1,\ldots,S_n$ be the premises and S the conclusion of an argument A, and let S_A be the respective implicative statement of the form "If S_1 and ... and S_n then S". Then

i) *A is analytically valid* iff S_A is analytically true.
ii) *A is logically valid* iff S_A is logically true. □

Consider the following argument A_1:

$$A_1 \quad \frac{\text{Whales are mammals.}}{\text{No bachelor is married.}}$$

Since both the premise and the conclusion are analytically true sentences, the argument is analytically valid; there is no possible world w and time t at which the premise would be true and the conclusion false. However, A_1 can hardly serve as a useful way of *justifying* the conclusion, because whales have nothing to do with bachelors.

On the other hand, the argument A_2 (a logically valid and sound argument) is valuable also for justifying the conclusion:

$$A_2 \quad \frac{\text{Bachelor is a man who is not married.} \quad \text{Charles is a bachelor.}}{\text{Charles is not married.}}$$

Similarly, the following mathematical argument A_3 is analytically, but not logically, valid, and A_3 does not serve to justify the conclusion:

$$A_3 \quad \frac{\text{No prime number greater than 2 is even.} \quad \text{The number 9 is not prime.}}{\text{The number 9 is not even.}}$$

Note that a logically valid argument can be often obtained from an analytically valid one by refining the meanings of the premises. Recall the example concerning the transitivity of the relation *less than* (<) defined on numbers. The argument

$$A_4 \quad \frac{2 < 5; \; 5 < 11; \; \text{the relation } < \text{ is transitive}}{2 < 11}$$

is analytically, but not logically, valid. As soon as we refine the meaning of the predicate 'is transitive' by using the definition of transitivity, we obtain a logically valid argument:

$$A_5 \quad \frac{2 < 5; \; 5 < 11; \; \forall x \forall y \forall z (x < y \supset (y < z \supset x < z))}{2 < 11.}$$

Since no additional hidden assumptions are needed to prove the validity of A_5, this logically valid argument conveys more analytic information than the corresponding A_4, and so it is also a more useful way of justifying the conclusion.

My procedural semantics made it possible to define the difference between a trivial and a non-trivial argument, and between analytically and logically valid arguments. As a result, logically valid, non-circular and sound arguments are analytically more informative ways of justifying a conclusion than are merely analytically valid arguments.

Another problem connected with the utility of arguments is the problem of the provability (or decidability) of premises. Consider the following argument A_6:

$$A_6 \quad \frac{\text{Every even number greater than 2 is the sum of two primes.} \quad \text{54768787829486598958980688888 is an even number greater than 2.}}{\text{54768787829486598958980688888 is the sum of two primes.}}$$

In order that the conclusion may present a new piece of analytic *knowledge* and be epistemically useful, the conclusion needs to be true, and we must know it to be so. However, we cannot decide it just by means of the premises of A_6, as long as

The paradox of inference and the non-triviality of analytic information

Goldbach's Hypothesis remains unproved. This is due to the fact that the first premise expresses the non-effective procedure[34]

$[^0 \forall \lambda n [[[^0Even\ n] \wedge [^0 > n\ ^02]] \supset [^0 \exists \lambda k\ l[[^0Prime\ k] \wedge [^0Prime\ l] \wedge [^0 = n[^0 + k\ l]]]]]]$.

If this construction constructs **T** (though in a non-effective way), the proof will consist in finding an algorithmically effective construction equivalent to (and probably amounting to a refinement of) the one above.[35]

If an argument is valid, but not sound, its epistemic utility is dubious, unless the conclusion is obviously not true. However, arguing *ad absurdum* requires another contrapositive inference (*modus tollens*) in order to serve as a useful justification for a claim. For instance, an argument of the form "If the problem of logical validity is decidable in first-order predicate logic, then 1+1=3" can serve to justify the claim that the problem of logical validity is not decidable in first-order predicate logic, because 1+1 is obviously not 3. However, the use of *modus tollens* is much more controversial if the falsity of the conclusion is not obvious. Thus, to take a historical example, consider:[36]

> If Special Relativity is true, then the mass of the electron has a specific dependence on velocity.
> Experimentally, the mass of the electron does not have this dependence.
> Special Relativity is false.

Einstein rejected this argument on the ground that the alternative ether theories due to Bucherer and Abraham that appeared to be borne out by the experiment were inherently less plausible than his own. Experiment does not always yield a definite result. Later, Max Planck re-analysed Kaufmann's data, and showed that Kaufmann's experiments were no longer an obstacle to the theory of Special Relativity.

To sum up, a non-circular, valid, but not sound argument can serve to falsify some of its premises, provided its conclusion is obviously false.

6 Conclusion

The paradox of inference arises if only the *propositions*, or *truth-values* (in the case of mathematical arguments), denoted by the premises and conclusion are considered, and evaporates if considering instead the *constructions* expressed by the premises

---

[34] that is a synthetic concept *a priori* of a truth-value, see [15].

[35] A similar problem crops up even in case of arguments formulated within propositional logic. It is a well known fact that though propositional logic is decidable, it is generally conjectured to be computationally intractable (due to its NP-hardness), as follows from Cook's famous [10] theorem. D'Agostini and Floridi investigate this problem in [18], and *contra* Hintikka they show that even deduction in propositional logic is informative. They define different levels of information depth according to the *computational complexity* of the decision procedure. Thus an argument is the more informative the less additional analytic information is needed to prove its validity, and thus the less computationally complex procedure is involved in the proof.

[36] See [29].

and the conclusion. The powerful framework provided by the procedural semantics of Transparent Intensional Logic matches the problems posed by the paradox of inference. I showed *what* one learns when validly inferring a conclusion from true premises. While the *product* of the procedure assigned to the conclusion as its meaning—namely, the proposition (in the empirical case) or the truth-value (in the mathematical case) denoted by the conclusion—*is* informationally contained in the premises, the *procedure* itself need *not* be (namely, whenever the argument is non-circular). Provided it is not so contained, then what learnt when drawing the conclusion is a new procedure producing the relevant proposition/truth-value.

This procedural approach maps out how to solve the broader problems connected with the paradox. These concern why and how analytically true sentences are informative, and why and how analytically equivalent sentences can yield different information. Not only that; based on the notion of (literal) procedural meaning, it was smooth sailing defining the difference between the analytic and the logical validity of sentences and arguments, and specifying the analytic content of sentences.

The direction for future research should be clear. Given the added complexity involved in the fine-grained individuation of analytic information, it is sensible to further investigate the informational aspects of algorithmically structured procedural meanings. In particular, the aspects that affect the epistemic utility of valid arguments were only outlined. We examined a criterion for comparing information yield based on the notion of meaning refinement. We also sketched a criterion based on the set-theoretic inclusion of analytic contents. Yet, other criteria involving analytic content were not investigated. Echoing the example of "p" vs. "p or q" mentioned in Section 4.3, we should investigate the degrees of decrease in uncertainty and thus increase of information when being informed that p, p or q, p and q, and other forms of molecular sentences.

Thus we should investigate in what ways sentential meanings are procedurally structured. The way to go would be to explicate the interplay between information and meaning in a novel way by focusing primarily on the constituent steps of particular constructions and their mutual effect with respect to information increase. Yet the clarity of this direction does not imply its triviality. The complexity of the work going into building such a procedural theory of information is almost certain to guarantee that complications we are currently unaware of will crop up. A sensible approach will be to develop the theory by reconsidering the relevant logic theories of information flow as recently presented by Abramsky [1], van Benthem and Martinez [44], Sequoiah-Grayson, Allo [2], and others, from the procedural point of view. Also, including provability logic and the theory of complexity in investigating the information increase involved in turning an analytically valid argument into a logically valid one, as outlined by D'Agostino and Floridi for propositional logic, seems to be a promising direction for further research.[37] It will be the purpose of a future paper to identify and overcome the obstacles lying ahead in this direction. For

---

[37] A terminological note might be useful. My notion of analytically but not logically valid argument corresponds to D'Agostino and Floridi's synthetic reasoning *a priori*. As mentioned above, constructions used in such an argument are my synthetic concepts *a priori*. A logically valid argument corresponds to D'Agostini and Floridi's analytical deduction. Again, in my terminology, in such an argument only analytical concepts *a priori* are used.

The paradox of inference and the non-triviality of analytic information

now, it has been the purpose of the present paper to solve the paradox of inference and to propose a general framework for a procedural theory of analytic information.

Acknowledgements I am indebted to Bjørn Jespersen, Sebastian Sequoiah-Grayson and Pavel Cmorej for valuable comments. Last but not least, I am grateful to two anonymous reviewers who carefully reviewed the previous versions of this paper and highly contributed to its improvement.

This work has been supported by the Grant Agency of Czech Republic, projects No. GACR 401/07/0451 "Semantisation of pragmatics" and GACR 401/10/0792 "Temporal aspects of knowledge and information".

References

1. Abramsky, S. (2008). Information, processes and games. In P. Adriaans & J. van Benthem (Eds.), *Philosophy of information: Handbook of the philosophy of science* (pp. 483–550). Amsterdam: Elsevier Science.
2. Allo, P. (2007). Logical pluralism and semantic information. *Journal of Philosophical Logic, 36*, 659–694.
3. Anderson, C. A. (1998). Alonzo Church's contributions to philosophy and intensional logic. *The Bulletin of Symbolic Logic, 4*(2), 129–171.
4. Bar-Hillel, Y., & Carnap, R. (1952). An outline of a theory of semantic information, rep. in Bar-Hillel (1964) (ed.), *Language and Information* (pp. 221–274). Addison-Wesley, Reading, MA.
5. Bolzano, B. (1837). *Wissenschaftslehre I, II*. Sulzbach.
6. Carnap, R. (1947). *Meaning and necessity*. Chicago University Press.
7. Church, A. (1941). *The calculi of lambda conversion*. Princeton: Princeton University Press.
8. Church, A. (1954). Intensional isomorphism and identity of belief. *Philosophical Studies, 5*, 65–73.
9. Cohen, M. R., & Nagel, E. (1934). *An introduction to logic and scientific method*. London: Routledge and Kegan Paul.
10. Cook, S. A. (1971). The complexity of theorem-proving procedures. In: *STOC '71: Proceedings of the third annual ACM symposium on Theory of computing* (pp. 151–158). New York: ACM.
11. Cresswell, M. J. (1985). *Structured meanings*. Cambridge, Mass: MIT.
12. Duží, M. (1992). Semantic information connected with data. In J. Biskup & R. Hull (Eds.), *Database theory ICDT'92* (pp. 376–390). Berlin: Springer, Lecture Notes in Computer Science.
13. Duží, M. (2006). Informativnost matematických či analyticky pravdivých tvrzení a paradox inference' (in Czech). *Filosofický časopis, 54*(4), 501–522.
14. Duží, M. (2009). Topic-focus articulation from the semantic point of view, In A. Gelbukh (Ed.), *Computational linguistics and intelligent text processing* (pp. 220–232). Springer, LNCS 5449.
15. Duží, M., & Materna, P. (2004). A procedural theory of concepts and the problem of the synthetic *a priori*. *Korean Journal of Logic, 7*, 1–22.
16. Duží, M., & Materna, P. (2005). Logical form. In G. Sica (Ed.), *Essays on the foundations of mathematics and logic, vol. 1* (pp. 115–153). Monza: Polimetrica International Scientific.
17. Duží, M., Jespersen B., Materna P. (2010). *Procedural semantics for hyperintensional logic; Foundations and applications of transparent intensional logic*. Series Logic, Epistemology and the Unity of Science. Berlin: Springer.
18. D'Agostino, M., & Floridi, L. (2009). The enduring scandal of deduction. Is propositional logic really uninformative? *Synthese, 167*, 271–315.
19. Floridi, L. (2004). Outline of a theory of strongly semantic information. *Minds & Machines, 14*, 197–222.
20. Floridi, L. (2005). 'Is information meaningful data'? *Philosophy and Phenomenological Research, 70*, 351–370.
21. Frege, G. (1892). Über Sinn and Bedeutung. *Zeitschrift für Philosophie und philosophische Kritik, 100*, 25–50.
22. Gärdenfors, P. (1988): *Knowledge in flux: Modelling the dynamics of epistemic states*, A Bradford Book, Cambridge Massachusetts: The MIT.
23. Hintikka, J. (1970). Surface information and depth information. In J. Hintikka & O. Suppes (Eds.), *Information and inference* (pp. 263–297). Reidel: Dordrecht.
24. Jespersen, B. (2003). Why the tuple theory of structured propositions isn't a theory of structured propositions. *Philosophia, 31*, 171–183.

25. Jespersen, B. (2005). Explicit intensionalisation, anti-actualism, and how Smith's murderer might not have murdered Smith. *Dialectica, 59*, 285–314.
26. Jespersen, B. (2008). Predication and extensionalization. *Journal of Philosophical Logic, 37*, 479–499.
27. Jespersen, B. (2010). Hyperintensions and procedural isomorphism: Alternative (½). *In The Analytical Way. Proceedings of the 6th European Congress of Analytic Philosophy.* Tadeusz Czarnecki, K. Kijania-Placek, O. Poller, and J. Woleński (eds.), College Publications, London, pp. 301–322.
28. Johnson-Laird, P. N. (1977). Procedural semantics. *Cognition, 5*, 189–214.
29. Kaufmann, W. (1906). 'Über die Konstitution des Elektrons', *Annalen der Physik, 19*, 487–553, <http://gallica.bnf.fr/ark:/12148/bpt6k15326w/f497.chemindefer>
30. King, J. C. (1995). Structured propositions and complex predicates. *Nous, 29*(4), 516–535.
31. King, J. C. (2001). Structured propositions, http://plato.stanford.edu/entries/propositionsstructured/, version as of 8 August 2001.
32. Materna, P. (1998). Concepts and objects. *Acta Philosophica Fennica, 63*, Helsinki.
33. Materna, P. (2004). *Conceptual systems.* Berlin: Logos Verlag.
34. Materna, P., & Duží, M. (2005). The Parmenides principle. *Philosophia, 32*, 155–180.
35. Mates, B. (1950). 'Synonymity', in: *University of California Publications in Philosophy, 25*, 201–226.
36. Moschovakis, Y. N. (1994). Sense and denotation as algorithm and value. In J. Väänänen & J. Oikkonen (Eds.), *Lecture Notes in Logic* (Vol. 2, pp. 210–249). Berlin: Springer.
37. Moschovakis, Y. N. (2006). A logical calculus of meaning and synonymy. *Linguistics and Philosophy, 29*, 27–89.
38. Sequoiah-Grayson, S. (2006). Information flow and impossible situations. *Logique et Analyse, 196*, 371–398.
39. Sequoiah-Grayson, S. (2008). The scandal of deduction (Hintikka on the information yield of deductive inferences). *Journal of Philosophical Logic, 37*(1), 67–94.
40. Sundholm, G. (1997). Inference vs. consequence. In T. Childers (Ed.), *The logica yearbook 1997* (pp. 26–36). Prague 1998.
41. Tichý, P. (1966). K explikaci pojmu obsah věty. *Filosofický časopis* 14, pp. 364–372. Translation 'On explication of the notion "the content of a sentence", reprinted in: Tichý (2004), pp. 53–68.
42. Tichý, P. (1988). *The foundations of Frege's logic.* Berlin: De Gruyter.
43. Tichý, P. (2004). *Collected papers in logic and philosophy.* In V. Svoboda, B. Jespersen, C. Cheyne (Eds.), Prague: Filosofia, Czech Academy of Sciences, and Dunedin: University of Otago Press.
44. van Benthem, J., & Martinez, M.-C. (2008). The stories of logic and information. In P. Adriaans & J. van Benthem (Eds.), *Philosophy of information: handbook of the philosophy of science* (pp. 217–280). Amsterdam: Elsevier Science.
45. Wagner, S. J. (1986). California semantics meets the Great Fact. *Notre Dame Journal of Formal Logic, 27*(3), 430–455.
46. Wittgenstein, L. (1922). *Tractatus Logico-Philosophicus.* London: Routlege.

Co-Hyperintensionality, Synonymy and Propositional Unity

First among equals: co-hyperintensionality for structured propositions

Bjørn Jespersen

Abstract

Theories of structured meanings are designed to generate fine-grained meanings, but they are also liable to *overgenerate* structures, thus drawing structural distinctions without a semantic difference. I recommend the proliferation of very fine-grained structures, so that we are able to draw any semantic distinctions we think we might need. But, in order to contain overgeneration, I argue we should insert some degree of individuation between logical equivalence and structural identity based on *structural isomorphism*. The idea amounts to forming an equivalence class of different structures according to one or more formal criteria and designating a privileged element as a representative of all the elements, i.e., a *first among equals*. The proposed method helps us to a cluster of notions of *co-hyperintensionality*. As a test case, I consider a recent objection levelled against the act theory of structured propositions. I also respond to an objection against my methodology.

1 Introduction

Mary loves John. Mary is such that she loves John. Mary is one of those (maybe the only one) who love John. John is such that he is one of those (maybe the only one) that Mary loves. Mary and John, in that order, are such that the first one loves the second one.

Did we just say pretty much the same thing, though in different ways? Or does each of these sentences express something importantly different? My immediate reason for asking this question is because a recent paper, Båve (2019), levels an objection against the act-theoretic conception of propositions, arguing that it fails to assign a unique meaning to "Mary loves John". I am convinced, however, that the objection can be rebutted. I am also convinced there is a general lesson in there for friends of structured propositions. This lesson bears on a methodological point that dispenses with a recurring problem for theories embracing structured propositions. The problem, in brief, is how to dial down the excessive fine-graining that afflicts structured propositions when allowed to generate distinctions that are not obviously, or obviously not, of semantic relevance.[1] Here I will be making a case for the general form of the solution to the challenge posed in Båve (*ibid.*). The form of the solution carries over easily to theories of structured propositions other than just the various act-theoretic ones. To profit from the proposed solution, however, it is a requirement that the theory in question has already been developed formally, or else readily lends itself to being formally developed.

Let me be more specific. A common feature of theories of structured meanings is *overgeneration* of structures. Overgeneration is exactly the card Båve plays against the act-theoretic conception. This move makes sense for Båve to make, because he considers just two principles of individuation: (coarse-grained) *logical equivalence* and (very fine-grained) *structural identity*. However, he ought to have considered a third principle of individuation: (not overly fine-grained) *structural isomorphism*.[2] The lesson for friends of all sorts of structured propositions is that there is a method to handle overgeneration. Here is how. First, allow an untrammelled *proliferation* of structured propositions in order to generate all the propositions you think you will ever need. Next, collect them into *equivalence classes* in accordance with one or more carefully selected criteria for membership. Finally, pick one member of each set as a *representative* of all of its fellow elements. This designated member is the structured proposition that is the meaning of the sentence which you originally set out to assign a meaning to.

The rest of the paper is organized as follows. Section 2 explains how the key notions are related. Section 3 presents Båve's objection. Section 4 dismantles this objection and sets out my positive contribution. Section 5 addresses an objection to my methodology.

---

[1] The problem I am addressing in this paper is syntactic distinctions without a semantic difference. But a further issue is that a poorly-designed theory of hyperintensionality allowing too much fine-graining is at risk of engendering *paradoxes*. See Landini (2009), Cocchiarella (2007, 111*ff*). Also see Klement (2002, 112–13) on the violation of Cantor's theorem ('more sets than members') due to the Myhill-Russell paradox. Hyperintensional and set-theoretic paradoxes are topics I will not broach here, though, not least because it would involve us in a thorough discussion of logics/calculi that are either untyped or else developed within a simple type theory or a ramified type hierarchy.

[2] *Cf.* Carnap's *intensional isomorphism*, Church's *synonymous isomorphism*, and the *procedural isomorphism* of Transparent Intensional Logic (see Duží 2019; Duží et al. 2010).

2

The act-theoretic conception of propositions (or *act theory*, for short) holds that a proposition whose satisfaction conditions are truth-conditions is identical to a structured predicative act or event type. The atomic proposition that object a has property F is identical to the act type of predicating F of a; the atomic proposition that objects a, b are related by relation R is the act type of predicating R of (a, b) or $\langle a, b \rangle$, depending on whether R is symmetric; the molecular proposition *Fa and Rab* is the act type of predicating of the propositions *Fa*, *Rab* that they form a conjunctive proposition.[3]

Båve claims to be able to generate a *reductio* of a fragment of act theory. He claims that any sentence containing a *polyadic predicate* such as 'loves' or 'is located between' induces *structural ambiguity*, which results in an unacceptable *multiplication of propositions*. I agree with Båve's observation about structural ambiguity, but I intend to show that the resulting sprawl of propositions need not be a problem for act theory or any other theory of structured propositions.

To begin with a monadic predicate, the sentences "Venus is a planet", "Venus is such that it is a planet", "Venus is something that is a planet" and "Venus is one of the planets" can be made, if one so desires, to come out synonymous, i.e., as notational variants of one another. The last three, to be sure, demand more logical processing or contain more logical steps than the first one. But a well-designed semantic theory of natural language should have the means to blot out such differences, in case it deems them insignificant. This is emphatically not to advocate that meanings should be individuated only up to necessary, or truth-conditional, equivalence; far from it. We definitely want to preserve various hyperintensional distinctions, e.g., in order to preserve various forms of topic and focus articulation so that we may keep track of what exactly is being asserted, or to specify the exact intellectual trajectory a particular agent follows when entertaining a particular attitude with a particular structure. For instance, it is arguably one thing to believe that Mary loves John and another thing to believe that Mary has the property of loving John. The latter attitude complement adds and highlights the notion of a property, and whereas the former can be construed as involving either a relation (*loving* being a relation extending from Mary to John) or a property (*loving John*), the latter rules out the relational reading. In fact, Båve's primary examples of structural ambiguity are examples of hyperintensional distinctions we do want to preserve. But too much fine-graining is too much of a good thing. So, what we are basically looking for is one or more reasonable and operative criteria of *co-hyperintensionality*, such that

---

[3] *Vide* Hanks (2015), Soames (2019). A referee wondered whether the act-theoretic account of conjunctive propositions requires several layers of predicative acts. I myself find the act-theoretic conception of molecular propositions rather problematic, and my (2021) explains why even conjunctive propositions are tricky. Still, the act theorist is not simply nesting assertoric predications within assertoric predications. The official explanation, at least, according to Hanks is that *target-shifted* predication, $\vdash_\uparrow$, serves to mention the act type *Fa* and the act type *Rab* without engaging in two assertoric acts, and **CONJ** is the act type that conjoins those two atomic act types into the molecular act type of asserting both of them in a particular order. The act-theoretic formula looks like this: $\vdash_\uparrow \langle\, (\ \vdash\langle \mathbf{a}, \mathbf{F} \rangle,\ \vdash\langle\langle \mathbf{a}, \mathbf{b}\rangle, \mathbf{R}\rangle),\ \mathbf{CONJ} \rangle$.

any two co-hyperintensional structured propositions become members of an equivalence class sporting a privileged member.[4]

Bear in mind that hyperintensionality was originally negatively defined: any individuation that defies the identification of logical equivalents is hyperintensional. This leaves open the question what is the upper bound to hyperintensional individuation, which translates into the quest for criteria of co-hyperintensionality. Only when we have availed ourselves of a criterion of co-hyperintensionality can we develop a notion of *validity* for hyperintensional contexts. For then we are not only blocking (invalidating) undesired arguments, but also enabling (validating) inferences we do want to go through. At such a point we will have arrived at a hyperintensional *logic*.[5] When hyperintensions are *structured* entities, the task becomes how to formulate a principle of structural isomorphism that defines co-hyperintensionality for structurally diverse, but otherwise relevantly identical, structures. My diagnosis is that Båve's attempted *reductio* is predicated on ignoring structural isomorphism and focusing exclusively on structural diversity.

3

I describe here how Båve puts his attempted *reductio* together. *Asymmetric* polyadic predicates are delicate, because the order of the relata matters, so I will stick to such examples. First, Båve (*ibid.*, 183) claims that

(i) "Mary loves John"

can be analysed in three different ways:

(ii) as the result of saturating "x loves John" with 'Mary'
(iii) as the result of saturating "Mary loves y" with 'John'
(iv) as the result of saturating "x loves y" with 'Mary' and 'John' in the first and second argument place, respectively.

---

[4] For recent surveys of strategies for obtaining fine-graining and various degrees of granularity, see Faroldi (2017), Sedlár (2019), Giordani and Malinowski (2021, 1–11). See Ayhan (2020, esp. §2.2.) on forming equivalence classes (under various conversion rules from the λ-calculus), in this case of *derivations*, so as to define identity criteria for logical *proofs*.

[5] Various theories embracing hyperintensionally individuated entities are keen to include a separate level of intensionally individuated entities, where co-intensionality is tantamount to logical equivalence. Examples would be Bealer's *type 1* and *type 2* PRP's, i.e., propositions, relations, and properties (1982), Cocchiarella's *two levels* (2007), and the *constructional* versus *intensional* level in Transparent Intensional Logic (Duží et al. 2010). All three positions reserve, roughly speaking, the *hyperintensional* level for *attitudes* and *assertions* and the intensional level for *modalities* and *empirical states-of-affairs* (though some modalities, most notably *counterpossibles*, are definitely hyperintensional). These two levels are logically connected. The approach characteristic of such two-tiered theories is that the hyperintensional level is not deductively closed, whereas the truth-conditional/intensional level is: here are located the deductive consequences of, e.g., believed and asserted hyperpropositions.

First among equals: co-hyperintensionality for structured propositions

Each of these three ways of saturating the argument slots corresponds to an *alternative analysis* of "Mary loves John".[6] Next, he introduces the family of functions f_n where f_n takes so-called semantic correlates of terms and expressions to structured propositions and where n indicates the arity of the predicate involved. Båve later replaces f_n by Zalta's *plug*, which he deploys as a device to model the act type of substituting the semantic correlate of a name for the value of a variable. For instance, f_1 takes the semantic correlates $[F(x)]$ and $[a]$ of the monadic predicate "ξ is an F" and the name 'a' to the semantic correlate $[F(a)]$ of the sentence "a is an F". Correspondingly, f_2 takes the semantic correlates of a dyadic predicate and two names to a proposition composed of them (see *ibid.*, 187).

Finally, Båve attempts to set act theory up for a *reductio*. This is the key passage:

> [...] a sentence '*Fa*' must be taken to express a [structured] proposition composed of the semantic correlates of '$F(ξ)$' and 'a', that is, $[F(ξ)]$ and $[a]$. $[F(a)]$ is thus the value of some function f from $[F(ξ)]$ and $[a]$; that is, $[F(a)] = f([F(ξ)], [a])$. But for a sentence like 'Mary loves John', there are two choices for the respective '$[F(ξ)]$' and 'a' [i.e. '$[R(ξ, ζ)]$', 'a', 'b'. BJ.]. Thus, its semantic correlate, [Mary loves John], must be identical to both f([Mary loves ξ], [John]) and f([ξ loves John], [Mary]). And this is just what it means for a proposition to have alternative analyses. (*Ibid.*, 186.)

This may be a bit hard to parse, so I will explain what is going on. Båve's point is that f takes two different arguments, namely ([Mary loves ξ], [John]) and ([ξ loves John], [Mary]), to the same value, [Mary loves John]. So, we have: [Mary loves John] $= f$([Mary loves ξ], [John]) $= f$([ξ loves John], [Mary]).

The problem, as Båve sees it, is that act theory creates room for two equally good contenders to being the proper way of saturating slots such that a slot-free (i.e., saturated) formula (i.e., a sentence) is generated.[7] The sentence "Mary loves John" expresses as its meaning a structured proposition composed of the respective semantic correlates of '[*Love* (ξ, ζ)]','Mary','John'. But, Båve wonders, is that proposition f([Mary loves ξ], [John]) or is it f([ξ loves John], [Mary])? Which of these two structures is *the* structure of [Mary loves John]? This question supposedly places act theory before a dilemma that is entirely of act theory's own making. The intended *reductio* is that the act theorist has no non-arbitrary way of selecting one structure as *the* structure of the act type that is the meaning of "Mary loves John". Absent such a selection procedure, there is an uncalled-for structural ambiguity, hence an uncalled-for proliferation of structures, i.e., act types, i.e., propositions.

To get a handle on how exactly Båve's intended *reductio* goes, I suggest turning to the *lingua franca* of natural-language semantics, namely the λ-calculus, for a

---

[6] Båve ought to have phrased his point in terms of alternative *decompositions* rather than *analyses*. As Levine (2002) stresses, any analysis is a *unique analysis*, with only simple constituents left, whereas no one decomposition is required to terminate in rock-bottom atoms. Båve's point can be made more forcefully in case there is no analysis/decomposition with a unique feature (such as identifying all the simple constituents) to have recourse to.

[7] The passage above leaves out (iv), but the availability of just two different structures already suffices to make his point.

more neutral symbolism that is well-understood.[8] In this calculus, [Mary loves John] emerges as the *contractum* of multiple equivalent *reduxes*. The contractum receives this form:

(i*) Lmj

The three 'alternative analyses' Båve mentioned at the outset match the following λ-abstracts:

(ii*) $(\lambda x\,(Lxj))\,m$
(iii*) $(\lambda y\,(Lmy))\,j$
(iv*) $(\lambda xy\,(Lxy))\,\langle m, j\rangle$

In fact, why stop right here? For now, we are considering only proliferation and not also restriction. Thus, we are free to generate formulas/structures such as these[9]:

(v*) $(\lambda x\,(\lambda y\,(Lxy))\,j)\,m$
(vi*) $(\lambda y\,(\lambda x\,(Lxy))\,m)\,j$

Or, if the logical ideography in question allows λ-binding predicate variables and allows predicates to occur in subject position ("Being wise is wonderful"), we can carry the proliferation even further by generating a formula/structure like this one:

(vii*) $(\lambda xy\,((\lambda r\,(rxy))\,L))\,\langle m, j\rangle$

The formula expresses that L is one of the (binary and asymmetric) relations between individuals x, y such that L applies to m, j; or, equivalently, that L is a (binary and asymmetric) relation between individuals such that it relates x, y and m, j are such that they are values of x, y whereby L relates them. From here, we could carry on generating abstracts by iterating λ-abstraction at our pleasure. Only doing so would be philosophically pointless because these abstracts have no natural natural-language counterparts (we would most likely just have strings of increasingly contorted 'such that' constructions). The reduxes above, however, do have such counterparts as they highlight different topics and foci.[10] For instance, while (i*) is neutral or plain, (ii*) makes m the topic, (iii*) makes j the topic, (iv*) makes the pair $\langle m, j\rangle$ the topic, and (vii*) makes L the topic.

Before moving on, I want to say a bit more about the shift from Frege's to Church's logic and ideography as encapsulated in the λ-calculus. Notice that Båve's argument based on Frege-style complex predicates, with *saturation* of *slots*, is

---

[8] Hanks's act-theoretic notation for "Mary loves John" would be (*cf.* Hanks (2015, 85)): ⊢⟨⟨**Mary, John**⟩, **LOVES**⟩. However, the syntax is not accompanied by a logic, so we would not know how to draw inferences by means of it.

[9] I am indebted to a referee for suggesting (v*), (vi*).

[10] Båve claims, "*A fortiori,*"Mary loves John" does not seem to "say" different things depending on the "parsing"." (*Ibid.*, 195) But it very much does. The truth-conditions are the same, for sure, provided we rule out truth-value gaps, but the seven 'parsings' *do* 'say' different things, namely in virtue of topic/focus articulation.

nothing new. (What is new is the application specifically to act theory.) For instance, Tichý (1986, 519–20) asks which function Frege has '–' denote in '9 – 2': (i) the function of subtracting the second argument from the first, $\xi - \zeta$, or (ii) the function of subtracting the first argument from the second, $\zeta - \xi$. This is important, (i) and (ii) being distinct functions (whether unsaturated Fregean ones or modern-day mappings). If the question is left unanswered, the result is that '–' comes out two-way ambiguous. In fact, we can even generate three-way ambiguity with '2 – 2': $\xi - \zeta$, $\zeta - \xi, \xi - \xi$. This ties in with a passage in Klement (2002, 104–05):

> The possibility of 'alternative analyses' or subject/predicate renderings of the same *Gedanke* […] is a consequence of functional comprehension. Frege, too, is committed to functions existing for each of Church's lambda abstracts. For Church's '$(\lambda x \, x > 7)$', Frege has simply '$\xi > 7$', and for Church's '$(\lambda x \, 9 > x)$', Frege has '$9 > \zeta$'. The difference, however, is that Frege's notation clearly shows the unsaturatedness of these functions, whereas Church's does not [nor did Church intend his ideography to do so, of course. *BJ*]. The notation "$(\lambda x \, x > 7)9$" would seem wholly unnatural to Frege; it would be akin to writing "$(\xi > 7)9$", which would only obscure the fact that the *Sinn* of '9' is thought to *complete* the incomplete *Sinn* of '$\xi > 7$' to form a whole, and, in so doing, it *eliminates* the unsaturatedness marked by 'ξ'. The resulting *Gedanke* is better expressed simply as "$9 > 7$". Note that the same whole is formed when the incomplete *Sinn* of '$9 > \zeta$' is completed by the *Sinn* of '7'.

Klement (*ibid.*) goes on to argue that

> Frege would transcribe *both* Church's "$(\lambda x \, x > 7)9$" and his "$(\lambda x \, 9 > x)7$" simply as "$9 > 7$". This too leads us to the conclusion that Frege would see no difference in the *Sinne* of lambda converts, and thus that we ought to favor Alternative (1) over Alternative (0) as the more Fregean alternative […].

Again, this is so because Frege, on Klement's reading, would have had little time for λ-abstracts in the first place.[11] Note, however, that the (hypothesized) aversion against λ-abstracts rests on the theory-internal reason that Frege wants his ideography to signal the unsaturatedness of his functions. If we are agnostic about unsaturatedness then we are free to translate a predicate like '$\xi > 7$' into '$\lambda x \, (x > 7)$'. We are also free not to agree with Frege's (hypothesized) misgivings about λ-abstracts. Thus, though Båve frames the problem of alternative analyses (or decompositions) explicitly in terms of saturation, his point about structural ambiguity can be made equally well in terms of variables and functional application/abstraction.

---

[11] For a comparison of Church's three alternative interpretations of *synonymous isomorphism* – (A0), based on α-conversion together with meaning postulates for semantically simple terms; (A1), based on β-conversion; and (A2), based on logical equivalence – see Klement (*ibid.*, 101–11) and Anderson (2001), which also considers an intermediate alternative. α-conversion is just uniform renaming of λ-bound variables; e.g., $(\lambda x \, (Lmx)) \, j =_\alpha (\lambda y \, (Lmy)) \, j$. α-conversion is often a prelude to β-conversion in order not to get entangled in collision of variables, and the result of correct conversion is known as αβ-identity.

Båve argues at length that the alternative analyses he puts forward are distinct act types, and I agree. Accordingly, we have, for instance, $f_2([\text{Mary loves } \xi], [\text{John}]) \neq_h f_2([\xi \text{ loves John}], [\text{Mary}])$, where '$=_h$' expresses the *hyperintensional* identity (as opposed to *truth-conditional* equivalence) relation between structures. The differently structured propositions $f_2([\text{Mary loves } \xi], [\text{John}])$ and $f_2([\xi \text{ loves John}], [\text{Mary}])$ are co-intensional (because they converge in the same truth-condition) at those two arguments, despite the respective arguments being distinct. The same function takes two distinct arguments to the same value, because such is the effect of these two instances of saturation (or substitution) as per f_2. When Båve speaks of identity in the quote above, he obviously intends coarser-grained (viz., truth-conditional) identity, as in: $f_2([\text{Mary loves } \xi], [\text{John}]) =_{eq} f_2([\xi \text{ loves John}], [\text{Mary}])$. Otherwise he would be simultaneously arguing for *alternative* (i.e., multiple) analyses and *identity* (i.e., singularity) between them, which would defy his *reductio*.

I think we can now appreciate the point Båve aims to make. When he claims there is *identity* between the *alternative analyses* and (i*), Båve's point is that the contractum can be equivalently and equally well generated, by way of β-conversion, from any of these reduxes and that the act theorist is at a loss as to which formula (hence which corresponding semantic correlate, i.e., structured proposition) to select as *the* meaning of "Mary loves John". Obviously, no semantic theory wants to assign more than one structurally determinate proposition to a lexically and structurally unambiguous sentence as its meaning (or semantic correlate). If this were the end of it, Båve's attempted *reductio* would be successful.

4

But it is not, provided the act theorist is prepared to adopt my proposal. The awkward question is supposed to be this: which of (i*) through (vii*) is *the* meaning of "Mary loves John"? Or as Båve dramatizes the problem:

> But which of the [six] propositions expressed by ["Mary loves John"] do we believe when, as we would naïvely put it, we "believe that [Mary loves John]"? [All six of them?] Could one believe one but not the [rest]? (*Ibid.*, 195. *I stuck with the original rather than Båve's additional example.*)

My answer is: pick the one whose logical form matches the syntactic form of the sentence the closest. If the analysandum is "Mary loves John" then you pick (i*) *Lmj*. If the analysandum is along the lines of "Mary is such that she loves John", "Mary is someone who loves John" or "Mary is among those who love John" then you pick (ii*) $(\lambda x (Lxj)) m$, i.e. $f_2([\xi \text{ loves John}], [\text{Mary}])$.

What the act theorist should not do is join their detractor in treating the various analyses as being on an *equal* footing. The right thing to say is that "Mary loves John" means *Lmj*, and that it is a *further* question which other structures *Lmj* is structurally isomorphic to. That is, the meaning of "Mary loves John" is nowhere close to being structurally ambiguous. (ii*) through (vii*) are the respective meanings of six different sentences, which are mutually truth-conditionally equivalent, but not synonymous, because (ii*) through (vii*) are not hyperintensionally identical. Or to answer Båve's question head-on: no, we do not believe all six of them at the same time, for the doxastic relation combines a believer and one proposition. Of course, if *belief* is coarse-grained and, thus, individuated only up to truth-conditional equivalence then any of (i*) through (vii*) can serve equally well as complement. But if, on the other hand, *belief* is very fine-grained and individuated by dint of structural identity (*cf.* inscriptionalism or sententialism), then only (i*) will do. What we believe, *ex hypothesi*, is that Mary loves John, pure and simple, without any part being highlighted.

If, as I recommend, the act theorist embraces Båve's ambiguity, the two remaining tasks to be completed are (*a*) defining an equivalence class of act-theoretic propositions, and (*b*) designating one member as a *primus inter pares* to serve as the single meaning of a sentence and the complement of a hyperpropositional attitude.

We begin with (*a*), which is to some degree anticipated in Båve (*ibid.*, 199). He rejects identifying propositions with equivalence classes of act types as a viable 'retreat position' for act theory. On this proposal, the various alternative analyses (decompositions) of [Mary loves John] are collected into a set, and [Mary loves John] is then identified with this set. Båve has two objections to this, both of which are legitimate: "this [retreat position] does not take propositions to be (syntactically) structured", and it fails to "[distinguish] logically equivalent propositions without thereby multiplying propositions wherever there are alternative analyses." The remedy he suggests is to make the criterion of equivalence so austere that only structurally identical propositions qualify as equivalent. But, as he in effect says, we then lose many equivalences we would want to maintain.

What stymies this retreat position is that [Mary loves John] is identified with a *set* of (however loosely or austerely) equivalent propositions instead of being a privileged *member* of a set of equivalent propositions. If we go with the latter approach, we select a criterion of co-hyperintensionality that blots out structural differences between pairs of co-hyperintensional propositions when those are theoretically irrelevant. We trim the fat, as it were. If we stick to (ii*), (iii*) for a toy example, they form the equivalence class $\{(\lambda x\ (Lxj))\ m, (\lambda y\ (Lmy))\ j\}$ under β-conversion, assuming, strictly for the sake of exposition, that this conversion rule constitutes the criterion of structural isomorphism for propositions. Such an equivalence class is generated by applying a conversion rule (or a cluster of conversion rules) to the structure underlying an input sentence such as "Mary loves John". The members are structurally isomorphic in the sense that they convert to one another under the chosen conversion rule (or cluster thereof). The different λ-formulas that represent the structured propositions which are members of the equivalence class come with different syntactic structures, but the conversion rule(s) generating the class dictate(s) that these syntactic differences are semantically insignificant.[12] Co-hyperintensionality is now predicated on structurally distinct hyperintensions being structurally isomorphic. Thus, co-hyperintensionality remains fine-grained, as it should, but gets a little coarser, as it also should. Structural isomorphism is the position tucked in between structural identity and logical equivalence that Båve failed to consider. The (right) answer to Båve's question above as to what we believe when we believe that Mary loves John now becomes instead: (i*) or any other proposition structurally isomorphic to it; for any pair of such propositions is freely substitutable within this hyperintensional context.

Since I am making a methodological rather than substantial point in this paper, my only concern is to settle for some particular rule (or set of rules) of conversion in order to arrive at an equivalence class, and not to push for this or that particular rule (or set of rules). However, we still need to pause to ponder the special role β-conversion plays in Båve's argument against act theory. This is β-conversion:

$$(\lambda x_1, \ldots, x_n A(x_1, \ldots, x_n) y_1, \ldots, y_n) \approx_\beta A(y_1, \ldots, y_n)$$

where each y_i is free for each x_i in A. Remember that (ii*) through (vii*) β-reduce to (i*). So in case β-conversion is deemed too coarse as a reasonable criterion of co-hyperintensionality then Båve's identification – i.e., [Mary loves John] = f([Mary loves ξ], [John]) = f([ξ loves John], [Mary]) – cannot be generated and so Båve can no longer place act theory before the dilemma of having to select one of f([Mary loves ξ], [John]), f([ξ loves John], [Mary]) at the expense of the other. Apart from wanting to evade the dilemma, there is independent reason, anyway, for banning β-conversion as a suitable criterion of co-hyperintensionality for structured propositions. Already the three structures of Lmj, $(\lambda x\ (Lxj))\ m$, and $(\lambda y\ (Lmy))\ j$ are arguably so distinct that it seems an open-and-shut question which one must be the structure of the meaning of "Mary loves John", and that is Lmj, as I have been arguing. Lmj has a logical connection with $(\lambda x\ (Lxj))\ m$ and $(\lambda y\ (Lmy))\ j$, for sure, but neither of them enters the picture as a candidate structure for the meaning of "Mary loves John".[13] Pointing out as much could, narrowly speaking, be the right rejoinder to Båve's charge of ambiguity. However, this sort of reply would miss the more profound issue implicit in Båve's challenge. And that is how

---

[12] See Duží (2019), Jespersen (2015), Salmon (2010) for a discussion of whether to include β-conversion (and if so, which particular variant, i.e., by-name or by-value) or other conversion rules of the λ-calculus to get the calibration of co-hyperintensionality right for this or that particular sort of context.

[13] Barendregt (1991, 20) notes an *asymmetry* in β-reduction that is relevant to my line of reasoning: $(\lambda x\ (x^2+1))\ 3 = 10$ can be understood as 10 being the result of computing $(\lambda x\ (x^2+1))\ 3$, but not vice versa. Likewise, I would say, $(\lambda x\ (Lxj))\ m = Lmj$ – or $(\lambda y\ (Lmy))\ j = Lmj$ – can be understood as Lmj being the result of computing $(\lambda x\ (Lxj))\ m$ – or $(\lambda y\ (Lmy))\ j$ – though not vice versa. But note the following. If one considers an equivalence class under β-conversion then the relation between any two β-converts in this class can be described as one of material equivalence. The reason is that the function (provided we remain within a calculus of *total* functions) yielding the various β-converts is one and the same. Yet at the (hyperintensional) level of computation, β-conversion is asymmetric, as Barendregt emphasizes. Once a series of computations has terminated in the normal form – here, Lmj or 10 – then there is no trace of how this form was obtained. For instance, in Duží and Jespersen (2013) we revisit the old verb-ellipsis cases such as "John loves his wife, and so does Peter" and show that the application of *two different properties – loving one's wife* versus *loving John's wife* – to John followed by β-reduction-by-name reduces the first conjunct to "John loves John's wife" in both instances, leaving it indeterminate which of

to allow propositional structures to stray from the grammatical structure of a given sample sentence, i.e., to allow proliferation of propositional structures, without generating structural ambiguity. Enter structural isomorphism.

However, invoking structural isomorphism requires taking a closer look at complex predicates.[14] The particular structure of a proposition will be in part a function of the property or relation being predicated. Therefore, this question arises: must any two co-intensional predicates that exhibit different syntactic structures map onto two structurally distinct (hyper-) properties (ignoring relations for now), which in turn yield the same evaluation function? For instance, should 'is someone who is someone who is such that they love John' denote a property different from what 'loves John' denotes? The worry lurking in the background is that we do not want to be saddled with a bloated ontology populated by (hyper-) properties some of whose differences in structure are without semantic significance. Any such ontological excess among the semantic values of predicates will devolve onto structured propositions once such predicates are used to predicate properties of individuals. One could rightly object that a property whose logical structure matches perfectly (as far as λ-abstracts will allow) the syntactic structure of 'is someone who is someone who is such that they love John' has no business being in the structured proposition that Mary loves John.[15] But, for instance, in a theory such as Transparent Intensional Logic the syntactic differences between two predicates do map onto two different objective logical structures; these in turn yield mappings each of which has a task to fulfill in determining the satisfaction conditions denoted by the predicates in question. (Other theories may opt for syntactic complexes combined with metaphysical simples, as in Bealer.) Still, there is a way to temper this proliferation of objective structures. Those two syntactically distinct predicates will co-denote the same property (i.e., mapping of empirical indices onto sets of individuals), while each also expressing a different conceptualization of it. That is, we are looking at two differently structured itineraries (i.e., hyperintensions) travelling toward the same satisfaction condition (i.e., intension). Those two predicates will come out co-intensional without being co-hyperintensional. Consequently, *being someone who is someone such that they love John* and *loving John* will be one and the same property. But this property cannot be a constituent of a structured proposition, according to, e.g., Transparent Intensional Logic; a particular conceptualization, with a particular logical structure, of it can. This particular structure will affect the overall structure of the proposition, and we already know what the method is for obtaining the desired degree of propositional granularity.

Footnote 13 (continued)

the two properties is to be picked up by 'so does' in the second conjunct. On one reading, both John and Peter are exemplary husbands. On the other reading, there is trouble on the horizon.

[14] I am indebted to a referee for pressing me on this point.

[15] Pursuing this topic more rigorously requires taking a stand on the semantic import of η-conversion: $\lambda x(fx) \approx_\eta f$, provided x is not free in f. But I will leave it at that for now. See, however, Ayhan (2020, fn. 6) for discussion and references

We move on to (*b*). Which of the three members of $\{Lmj, (\lambda x(Lxj))m, (\lambda y (Lmy))j\}$ should be privileged as a first among equals? A natural guideline, which I already applied above, is that we want the best approximation we can get to a match between sentential and propositional structure, because structure serves to specify the sequence in which we process meaning. For instance, the syntactically unadorned "Mary loves John" enjoins us to simply arrange Mary and John in the *loving* relation, with Mary in subject and John in object position, as the *loving* relation extends from Mary to John. And that is all the sentence does, so our pick is *Lmj*. Topic/focus articulation will systematically affect the selection of the privileged member, but the unadorned "Mary loves John" (unaccompanied by pitch emphasis when spoken) is merely concerned with getting the truth-condition right and so is characterized by being insensitive to topic/focus articulation.

My pick of *Lmj* runs counter to Båve's reason for claiming (*ibid.*, 183) that "Mary loves John" is analyzable into multiple act types (or multiple structures, more generally). Of course, "Mary loves John" is so analyzable, but that is irrelevant. In my view, the structures $(\lambda x (Lxj)) m$ and $(\lambda y (Lmy)) j$ are the respective meanings of *other* sentences along the lines of "Mary is someone who loves John" and "John is someone whom Mary loves". In fact, the differences between these three structures are hard to miss. "Mary loves John" expresses the application of the binary *relation* of loving to the ordered pair ⟨Mary, John⟩. "Mary is someone who loves John" expresses the application of the *property* of loving John to Mary. "John is someone whom Mary loves" expresses the application of the *different property* of being loved by Mary to John. To be sure, a formal semanticist who has convinced themselves that β-conversion defines structural isomorphism is going to claim that these three structures are co-hyperintensional. And in this case we are facing one meaning rather than three. But I have been trying to argue why β-conversion is too coarse for the purposes of structural isomorphism.

5

The above policy of proliferation of structured propositions appears vulnerable to the objection that it trivializes the task of assigning meanings to sentences. The policy predicts a more-or-less bijective relationship between sentences and propositions, whereas (so the objection goes) the mapping ought to be surjective, taking multiple sentences to the same proposition. Some differences in sentential structure should not go over into differences in propositional structure. If, on the other hand, propositional structure tracks, by and large, sentential structure, then the semanticist barely gets to make fallible claims about sentence/meaning pairs, because any two distinct sentential structures will have already been mapped into two different propositional structures. Barely any pairs of sentences will, therefore, occur in the synonymy relation. An objection along these lines is put forward in Pickel (2018), which targets not only Jeffrey King's theory, which has proliferation of propositional structures as an accidental by-product, but also a theory such as mine, which actively encourages proliferation. What does commend a pro-proliferation approach, according to Pickel, is this:

[It offers] a maximally flexible framework [...] For instance, [when sentences S, S^* have already been deemed to express different propositions $[\![S]\!]$, $[\![S^*]\!]$] it might be found that there is a construction $\Sigma\,(.)$ such that the observational data support $[\![\Sigma\,(S)]\!] \neq [\![\Sigma\,(S^*)]\!]$. This data will be easier to accommodate if we already have that $[\![S]\!] \neq [\![S^*]\!]$. (*Ibid.*, Sect. 2, fn. 12.)

If instead the (less-profligate) semanticist had ventured forth with the claim that $[\![S]\!] = [\![S^*]\!]$ then the truth of $[\![\Sigma\,(S)]\!] \neq [\![\Sigma\,(S^*)]\!]$ would constitute a *counterexample*. One would learn from this the *non*-trivial truth that $[\![S]\!] \neq [\![S^*]\!]$, which would emphatically not be an artefact of one's semantics.[16]

What to make of Pickel's objection? I think it is spot on. The concept of synonymy is central to any formal semantics worth its name, because it regulates such things as equality of *expressive power* and the *substitutability* of sentences in hyperpropositional attitude reports. Any logically and philosophically interesting mapping from a domain of sentences onto a range of propositions must obviously be a surjective one. But it is exactly for this sort of reason that proliferation is only the first half of my recommended approach. The second half consists namely in tightening the noose by means of equivalence classes and the appointment of representative members.[17]

This reply to the objection is incomplete, however, without a satisfactory answer to this question: *which* formal criterion should we pick? My answer is this. The choice of criterion calls for philosophical discretion. Different sorts of hyperintensional contexts are likely to be different not least by calling for different degrees of fine-graining.[18] Imagine we are confronted with a context which our philosophical considerations have convinced us requires a certain granularity to validate certain inferences and block certain other inferences (often dressed up as puzzles by which to measure the mettle of rivalling theories). Then we consult our abundant supply of structured meanings and superimpose a formal criterion (e.g., again strictly for the purpose of exposition, α-conversion paired with η-conversion), which yields a class

---

[16] Pickel's appeal to counterexamples seems to presuppose that the semanticist cannot have recourse to some form of Frege-Church-Montague-style *contextualism*, which would accommodate $[\![S]\!] = [\![S^*]\!]$ and $[\![\Sigma\,(S)]\!] \neq [\![\Sigma\,(S^*)]\!]$ within the same semantic theory. On the topic of counterexamples, I readily grant that the methodology I am recommending lends itself to the sort of self-immunization Popper famously warned against. A semanticist facing a looming falsification might, for instance, be tempted to deny that the problematic context is actually of the sort governed by the chosen criterion of granularity. But we also know why the temptation should not be yielded to, because the argument from trivialization will eventually kick in.

[17] This second half appears still to be absent from (or, at the very least, underdeveloped in) King's theory, which *is* marred by excessive fine-graining, as Pickel correctly notes in (*ibid.*, fn. 11).

[18] See the catalogue of degrees of granularity in Duží (2019). Likewise, Miller (2017) operates with two tiers of hyperintensional individuation in order to enable bearing different propositional attitudes ('weak hyperintensional distinction') to metaphysically equivalent theories ('strong hyperintensional equivalence'). An alternative path to weak hyperintensional distinction Miller brings up turns on *lexical* differences between, e.g., constants (so that Lois can believe that Superman is amazing without believing that Clark Kent is amazing). However, the relevance to *structurally* diverse propositions is only indirect, and my proposal above does not tamper with the constants and predicates involved, but basically makes do with increasing or decreasing the levels of logical *processing*.

with a privileged element. Our choice of criterion leads us to make fallible predictions, as decreed by Pickel, and after canvassing a series of test cases we may well want to reconsider our initial choice.

There is no one sacrosanct, or absolute, measure of co-hyperintensionality. Structural isomorphism is not one particular measure of granularity, but rather a cluster of such measures. Structural isomorphism is a form whose content is this or that specific criterion given by one or more conversion rules.

6 Conclusion

I have extracted a general lesson from my solution to a specific objection. The objection was that a certain theory of structured propositions is stuck with structurally ambiguous sentences where no such ambiguity is called for. The first step toward a solution was to point out that there is a position tucked in between structural identity and logical equivalence, namely structural isomorphism. The next step was to argue that all theories of structured propositions (or structured meanings, in general) should go for maximal multiplication of their respective structures, but then do the following: (*i*) provide philosophical motivation for the choice of a specific formal criterion of individuation for a particular kind of context, (*ii*) apply this criterion to one's rich supply of structures to extract an equivalence class of structurally isomorphic structures, (*iii*) designate a representative element as a first among equals, which is then the meaning of the sentence (or piece of language, in general) that one set out to assign a meaning to. This general approach to how a theory of structured meanings can profit from proliferation of structures does presuppose that the theory in question is susceptible to formal treatment, which includes one or more formally precise criteria of individuation of structures. A theory of structured meanings that is not yet sufficiently developed so as to rigorously individuate and identify its structures is liable to be embarrassed by the objection from overgeneration.[19]

Funding Grant no. GA18-23891-S of the Grant Agency of the Czech Republic.

Complaince with ethical standards

Conflict of interest The authors declare that they have no conflict of interest.

Open Access This article is licensed under a Creative Commons Attribution 4.0 International License, which permits use, sharing, adaptation, distribution and reproduction in any medium or format, as long as you give appropriate credit to the original author(s) and the source, provide a link to the Creative Commons licence, and indicate if changes were made. The images or other third party material in this article are included in the article's Creative Commons licence, unless indicated otherwise in a credit line to the

---

[19] I am much obliged to Marie Duží, Rachel Boddy and two anonymous referees for *Synthese* for very helpful comments on previous versions. This research was funded by Grant Agency of the Czech Republic project No. GA18-23891S, *Hyperintensional Reasoning over Natural Language Texts*, and Internal Grant Agency of VSB-Technical University of Ostrava project No. SGS No. SP2020/62, *Application of Formal Methods in Knowledge Modelling and Software Engineering III*.

material. If material is not included in the article's Creative Commons licence and your intended use is not permitted by statutory regulation or exceeds the permitted use, you will need to obtain permission directly from the copyright holder. To view a copy of this licence, visit http://creativecommons.org/licenses/by/4.0/.

References

Anderson, C. A. (2001). Alternative (1*): A criterion of identity for intensional entities. In C. A. Anderson & M. Zeleny (Eds.), *Logic, Meaning and Computation* (pp. 393–427). Dordrecht: Kluwer Academic Publishers.
Ayhan, S. (2020). What is the meaning of proofs? *Journal of Philosophical Logic.* https://doi.org/10.1007/s10992-020-09577-2.
Barendregt, H. (1991). *Lambda Calculi With Types.* Retrieved from https://ttic.uchicago.edu/~dreyer/course/papers/barendregt.pdf.
Bealer, G. (1982). *Quality and Concept.* Oxford: Clarendon Press.
Båve, A. (2019). Acts and alternative analyses. *Journal of Philosophy, 116,* 181–205.
Cocchiarella, N. (2007). *Formal Ontology and Conceptual Realism, Synthese Library 339.* Dordrecht: Springer-Verlag.
Duží, M. (2019). If structured propositions are logical procedures then how are procedures individuated? *Synthese, 196,* 1249–1283.
Duží, M., & Jespersen, B. (2013). Procedural isomorphism, analytic information, and β-conversion by value. *Logic Journal of the IGPL, 21,* 291–308.
Duží, M., Jespersen, B., Materna, P. (2010). *Procedural Semantics for Hyperintensional Logic,* Heidelberg *et al.*: Springer-Verlag.
Faroldi, F. L. G. (2017). Co-hyperintensionality. *Ratio, 30,* 270–287.
Giordani, A., & Malinowski, J. (2021). Logic in high definition – trends in logical semantics. In A. Giordani & J. Malinowski (Eds.), *Logic in High Definition, Trends in Logic (Studia Logica Library) 56* (pp. 1–11). Dordrecht: Springer-Verlag.
Hanks, P. (2015). *Propositional Content.* Oxford: Oxford University Press.
Jespersen, B. (2021). 'Two tales of the turnstile', *IfCoLog Journal of Logics and their Applications,* forthcoming.
Jespersen, B. (2015). Should propositions proliferate? *Thought, 4,* 243–251.
Klement, K. C. (2002). *Frege and the Logic of Sense and Reference.* New York, London: Routledge.
Landini, G. (2009). Cocchiarella's formal ontology and the paradoxes of hyperintensionality. *Axiomathes, 119,* 115–142.
Levine, J. (2002). Analysis and decomposition in Frege and Russell. *Philosophical Quarterly, 52,* 195–216.
Miller, K. (2017). A hyperintensional account of metaphysical equivalence. *Philosophical Quarterly, 67,* 772–793.
Pickel, B. (2018). Structured propositions and trivial composition. *Synthese.* https://doi.org/10.1007/s11229-018-1853-1.
Salmon, N. (2010). Lambda in sentences with designators: an ode to complex predication. *Journal of Philosophy, 107,* 445–468.
Sedlár, I. (2019). Hyperintensional logics for everyone. *Synthese.* https://doi.org/10.1007/s11229-018-02076-7.
Soames, S. (2019). Propositions as cognitive acts. *Synthese, 196,* 1453–1473.
Tichý, P. (1986). Constructions. *Philosophy of Science, 53,* 514–534.

Anatomy of a proposition

Bjørn Jespersen

Abstract This paper addresses the mereological problem of the unity of structured propositions. The problem is how to make multiple parts interact such that they form a whole that is ultimately related to truth and falsity. The solution I propose is based on a Platonist variant of procedural semantics. I think of procedures as abstract entities that detail a logical path from input to output. Procedures are modeled on a function/argument logic, but are not functions (mappings). Instead they are higher-order, fine-grained structures. I identify propositions with particular kinds of molecular procedures containing multiple sub-procedures as parts. Procedures are among the basic entities of my ontology, while propositions are derived entities. The core of a structured proposition is the procedure of predication, which is an instance of the procedure of functional application. The main thesis I defend is that procedurally conceived propositions are their own unifiers detailing how their parts interact so as to form a unit. They are not unified by one of their constituents, e.g., a relation or a sub-procedure, on pain of regress. The relevant procedural semantics is Transparent Intensional Logic, a hyperintensional, typed λ-calculus, whose λ-terms express four different kinds of procedures. While demonstrating how the theory works, I place my solution in a wider historical and systematic context.

1 Introduction

This paper addresses the problem of *the unity of structured propositions*. I argue that the problem is a *mereological* one in that we must explain how multiple *parts* make up one *whole*. A propositional *structure* is a path of stepping stones leading up to a destination, where the destination is emphatically not part of the path. A propositional structure forms a *unity* because the stepping stones are arranged systematically such that one stepping stone leads to the next one in a specific manner.

The arc of the paper extends from the mereological problem of the unity of structured propositions (which divides into the problem of how parts interact and how to avoid an infinite regress of intermediaries) through the conception of structured propositions as logical procedures detailing a trajectory from input to output, to the identification of the procedure of functional application as the unifier of atomic non-empirical propositions and the procedure of functional abstraction as an additional unifier of empirical propositions.

My points of departure are that structure is *procedural* structure and that a structured proposition is a molecular or compound or complex or multi-step procedure. More specifically, I identify structured propositions with particular kinds of objective logical (as opposed to, say, psychological or pragmatic) molecular procedures whose parts are sub-procedures (as opposed to entities such as mountains or numbers). The underlying logic is a typed function/argument logic that specifies which functions of which logical types are lined up to be applied to which arguments of which types to obtain values (if any) of which types. When identified with procedures, propositions become logical flow charts detailing how one entity arrived at as a *value* in a particular way becomes the *argument* of another function or what type of entity a *function* that has been produced in a particular way is to be applied to. Though modeled on a function/argument logic, procedures are not functions-in-extension, i.e., mappings. Nor are they set-theoretic sequences, nor, for that matter, the formulae of a symbolic notation. Instead they are Platonic, higher-order, fine-grained structures. Procedures, as I understand them, are neither set-theoretic, nor inscriptional, nor linguistic entities. They are mereological entities, because they are wholes with parts. Furthermore, procedures are governed by a mereology that cannot be fully extensional, because their parts interact with one another. Procedural propositions are individuated not only in terms of their proper parts but also in terms of how their parts interact.

The framework I will be relying on below maintains a distinction between non-empirical propositions—as expressed by, e.g., "1 is odd"—and empirical propositions—as expressed by, e.g., "Miles smiles". My thesis is that the logical procedure of *predication* is always the unifier of non-empirical, atomic structured propositions and one of the unifiers of empirical, atomic structured propositions, and that predication is an instance of the procedure of *functional application*. I argue, furthermore, that a non-empirical atomic proposition is identical to (rather than, say, an outcome of) the procedure of functional application. Therefore, the non-empirical atomic proposition that particular a has property F is tantamount to monadic predication. Probably only a procedural semantics is in a position to hold that a proposition is a propositional unifier; in fact, its own unifier. A procedural semantics is able to claim this because the proposition serves to unify its proper parts and does so by being a specification of how they interact. A fortiori, no *proper* part is the unifier on pain of unleashing a Bradley-style regress.

It is a crucial feature of my theory that procedures can be *displayed without being executed*. A displayed procedure displays its structure of interlocking sub-procedures without proceeding to execution. An executed procedure produces the product (if any) it is typed to produce. Only when a propositional or any other procedure is displayed can it itself be studied and described as an object in its own right, as the procedure it is, in lieu of the entity it is typed to produce. When 'looking at' a structured proposition, what we 'see' is that, in the simple case of monadic predication, a sub-procedure typed to produce a property and another sub-procedure typed to produce an object are lined up such that the property is primed to be predicated of the object.

The procedure that is the sense of an *empirical* sentence like "Miles smiles" is typed to produce a (coarse-grained) truth-condition that is satisfied at all and only empirical indices at which it is true that Miles smiles. The procedure must capture the modal profile of *contingency* that characterizes the truth-condition: whether the truth-condition happens to be satisfied is a matter of contingency. The procedure that is the form of the sense of a *mathematical* sentence like "1 is odd" is identified with a (fine-grained) truth-condition that is typed to produce a truth-value. (Its truth-condition is not the necessary proposition of possible-world semantics.) The procedure must capture the modal profile of *necessity* that characterizes the truth-condition: whether the truth-condition is satisfied is a matter of necessity. This applies equally to non-mathematical necessities like the analytic truth expressed by "Green is a colour".[1]

Propositions-as-procedures cannot be truth-bearers: procedures are not of the right making to be true or false. This might seem like a cogent reason to disqualify propositions-as-procedures, for being a truth-bearer is commonly considered one of the defining features of propositionhood. But I am none too worried about this, because there is an inherent and intimate connection between the proposition that Miles smiles and its truth-condition, and between the proposition that 1 is odd and its truth-value. This connection is forged by the cooperation between procedures and types (see below). In fact, I am still able to accommodate the locution that propositions are truth-bearers in a way that suits procedural semantics. Furthermore, my procedural propositions fill the important propositional roles of, e.g., being sentential meanings and the complements of attitudes expressed by 'that'-clauses.

The idea of propositional structure being procedural structure will be developed within the framework of *Transparent Intensional Logic* (TIL). So will the solution to the one of the two major problems pertaining to propositional unity that I take on in this paper.[2] Tichý started developing TIL simultaneously with the inception of Montague

---

[1] My background theory encompasses three kinds of non-empirical necessity (mathematical, analytic, logical) and one empirical kind, namely nomological necessity ('soft necessity'). See Duží et al. (2010: §4.5). However, the only relevant distinction in this paper bears on whether empirical indices should, or should not, be included in the form of the proposition in question.

[2] Tichý would touch upon the unity problem on a couple of occasions. For instance, in (1988: p. 7) he objects that a notation-based theory has abstract entities hang like 'Christmas decorations from a branch' instead of integrating them into a whole that is beyond the notation. In (1995: p. 182) he sketches the theory I am unfolding below of how functional application and abstraction 'hold complexes together', to use his phrase.

Grammar.[3] TIL has been developing ever since and presented in hundreds of papers as well as the two monographs Tichý (1988) and Duží et al. (2010). I will be relying on the most recent expositions of TIL. Formally, TIL is a hyperintensional, typed λ-calculus. Its different kinds of λ-terms express different kinds of logical procedures. The relevant procedures are the multi-step, operational ones of *functional application* and *functional abstraction* and the one-step 'feeders' that 'feed' the former with input to operate on. Fox and Lappin (2005: p. 45) says about abstraction and application in general, with no particular reference to TIL:

> One reason for desiring abstraction and application is that it enables semantic expressions to be composed. Although it is perhaps not an essential requirement of a theory for computational semantics that the process of composition be conducted within the theory itself, conventionally it is seen as desirable to consider the fragments of semantic interpretation associated with non-sentential phrases as carriers of meaning that can receive an interpretation within a single theory. The λ-calculus (in all its forms) provides a vehicle for expressing functions and function application. By adopting a version of the λ-calculus, a semantic theory gains the possibility of expressing derived functions (by way of abstraction) and the corresponding functional types. The abstraction and application of λ-calculus provide a means of including the derivation of semantic representations within the theory. The reasons provide motivation for exploring intensional theories that embody versions of the λ-calculus.

TIL transposes Church's syntactic computations of functional abstraction and application into an *objectual* key. Computations, accordingly, are Platonic entities which may, or may not, be implemented by an agent in a world at a time. Furthermore, the formalism of TIL is an inherently *interpreted* formalism, which is to say that syntax and semantics are developed in tandem.[4] We retain the feature that "the process of composition [is] conducted within the theory itself". This is in keeping with what Muskens (2005: p. 486) says about computational or operational or procedural semantics:

> We want to explicitly have [the connection between (hyper-) intensions and extensions] at the object level in order to be able to give it a computational interpretation.

The formal object language itself contains the syntactic and semantic resources to both execute and display computational structures such as propositions. They are not being relegated to some meta-level. Instead TIL comes with a completely typed universe that includes both first-order and higher-order types organized in a ramified type hierarchy that includes a simple type theory. The ramified type hierarchy is indispensable, because propositions are objects of a higher-order type.

The rest of this paper is structured as follows. Section 2 provides background to the problem of the unity of structured (hyper-) propositions. Section 3 sets out the relevant

---

[3] Duží et al. (2010: §2.4.3) compares Tichý's thoroughly transparent intensional logic against Montague's opacity-friendly counterpart.

[4] May (2006) explains the Fregean notion of inherently interpreted terms and expressions, a notion alien to modern-day model-theoretic semantics.

foundations of TIL and explains the anatomy of the proposition that 1 is odd. Section 4 further clarifies the foundations and applies them to the anatomy of the proposition that Miles smiles. Atomic empirical propositions have a more elaborate logical structure than atomic mathematical propositions. This is so because they must include empirical parameters such as worlds and times in order to capture their contingency. These propositions embody functional application as well as functional abstraction, both of which are propositional unifiers. A formal appendix containing definitions is found at the end.

2 Philosophical motivation and state of the art

2.1 What is the problem?

There is a gaping hole in the edifice of structured propositions. When we invoke structured propositions as a means to explain a host of semantic phenomena we still have most of our work ahead of us. First and foremost, if propositions are structured then what is propositional *structure*? My view is that any theory of structured propositions is drastically incomplete without an integral account of the unity of such structures.[5] I share the impatience Keller (2013: p. 657) vents:

> Though the friends of structured propositions have been tolerably clear about what the constituents of propositions are, they have been frustratingly evasive about the *relation* of constituency itself. Is a proposition related to its constituents as a set is to its members, or a composite object to its parts? Or are propositional constituents 'parts' in some other, *non*-mereological sense? If so, does this mean that commitment to [structured propositions] entails commitment to different fundamental parthood relations? Or is *constituency* supposed to be taken as a theoretical primitive, not explicable in terms of *membership* or *parthood*? If this is the case, how does invoking this notion explain anything?

We must identify one or more propositional unifiers. It will not suffice to line up target constituents and leave it at that. As card-carrying advocates of structured propositions, we must explain how the parts interact. The scope of the problem was made clear early on in the development of English-speaking analytic philosophy. Russell (1903: pp. 140–141) says:

> [An *aggregate*] is completely specified when all its simple constituents are specified; its parts have no direct connection *inter se*, but only the indirect connection involved in being parts of one and the same whole. (…) But other wholes occur, which contain relations or what may be called predicates, not occurring simply as terms [in Russell's all-inclusive sense of object] in a collection, but as relating or qualifying. *Such wholes are always propositions.* These are not completely specified when their parts are all known. (*Italics added.*)

---

[5] McGrath (2014: §8) notes, "Any theory that construes propositions as structured entities would seem to face the problem of the *unity* of the proposition."

Anatomy of a proposition

Unities, unlike aggregates, are the sort of wholes whose parts have *connection inter se*.[6] The parts must interact for the whole to be unified. To use Russell's notorious example, consider the proposition that *A* and *B* differ. He decomposes the proposition into the three parts *A*, *B*, the difference relation. This enumeration, in whatever permutation, does not exhaust the proposition. There is more to the proposition than its parts, namely whatever the parts' connection inter se amounts to. This is just a restatement of the difference between an aggregate and a unity. Without a chassis, a presumed proposition is bound to splat, being but a sprawl of straggling entities which would not be parts of a whole, as there would be no whole for them to be parts of. Russell's admitted inability to recompose ('reconstitute') the proposition he has just decomposed goes to show that even though he may have had a theory of constituents he did not have a theory of the unity of the *proposition*.[7] What he did have was a theory of the unity of *facts*. Facts are unified because the constituent property or relation is *instantiated* by the constituent object or objects. If facts are identified with true propositions, then Russell can charitably be said to have had a theory of the unity of true propositions. And insofar as he had little time for false propositions as denizens of his post-1900 ontology, there was no reason per se to be bothered by not having a theory of the unity of false propositions. But it is a widely-shared constraint that a theory of propositions must apply uniformly to true propositions and to false propositions (and to gappy and to glutty propositions, if such be taken on board), just like a theory of roses must apply uniformly to red roses and to white roses. Russell has no uniform theory of the unity of both kinds of proposition to pass on to the neo-Russellian.

Any unity problem is a *mereological* problem. The problem is how multiple objects, possibly belonging to different ontological categories, occur as the parts of one whole. The problem of the unity of the proposition is just an instance of the wider problem of the unity of structures. To be structured means to be a *whole* that has *parts* that are organized *systematically*. The parts need to interact in such a way that they as a unit achieve something that they could not have achieved individually or as a mere aggregate. The reason I take the unity problem seriously is that it offers us a window unto the structure of structured propositions. A theory of unity is a touchstone for a theory of structure. If we have a problem with unity that would be an indication of a problem with structure.

The problem of the unity of the proposition has the makings of a riddle wrapped in a mystery inside an enigma.[8] In particular, how can many ones become one one? How can one one encompass a multitude? We cannot approach the unity problem the same way we would *set theory*'s fundamental conceptual problem of how a set is 'a Many that allows itself to be thought of as a One', as Cantor phrased it. The *elements* of a *set* lack direct connection inter se, even when they are lined up in a sequence, $\langle a, b, c \rangle$,

---

[6] Russell's aggregate/unity distinction effectively rehashes a distinction Aristotle draws in *Metaphysics* Z.17 between such wholes as are mere heaps and such wholes as have several parts and are more than just the sum of their parts.

[7] See also the last line of (ibid.: §54).

[8] As Churchill famously characterized Russia (the Soviet Union, actually).

whereas direct connection inter se is exactly what characterizes the *parts* of a *whole*.[9] Such connectedness is a prerequisite for systematicity. Even though the metaphysics of sets may be murky, we at least know exactly how to populate them with elements, whether we do so 'intensionally' by way of a condition to be fulfilled by prospective elements or 'extensionally' by way of enumeration of elements (Russell ibid.: §68). By contrast, we are still looking for an account of how to populate wholes with parts.[10]

The unfortunate fact is that there is (to the best of my knowledge) no well-developed and well-established general *intensional mereology of abstract entities*. When Keller (ibid.) and Merricks (2015: Ch. 4) weigh mereology, and find it too light for the purposes of structured propositions, they are targeting Classical Extensional Mereology. CEM comes with some well-known principles that are no-starters for a viable theory of structured propositions. For instance, the extensionalist principle of *uniqueness of composition* ('same proper parts, same whole') is far too restrictive. It is instructive to spell out exactly why, and I will do so below. Basically, though, more than one whole can be formed from the same stock of proper parts. Likewise, the principle of *unrestricted composition* flies in the face of the constraint that parts must interact to form a whole. Again, it is instructive to say exactly why this is so, and I will expound why the theory I put forward is very picky about what can possibly interact with what. By way of preview, the three items North Korea, your left eyebrow, and $\{-1\}$ do not form a whole (in any sense I would understand) and so they do not qualify as the parts (in any sense I would understand) of any one whole. On the other hand, a mode of presentation of the characteristic function of a set and a mode of presentation of an individual qualify as parts of a whole that is itself a part of a whole that is a proposition. The parts need to be type-theoretically (or categorically) congruent. Thus, with interaction among parts and type-theoretic restrictions, the mereology I am envisioning is bound to deviate from CEM. TIL is imbued with a specific intensional mereology of one particular kind of abstract entities, namely the procedures that are the heart of TIL. In this paper I will be presupposing this mereology rather than arguing for it in detail.[11]

---

[9] Lewis (1993) argues for a close affinity between set theory and mereology, according to which sets can be said to have parts. I cannot discuss his position here, however.

[10] Caplan et al. (2010) accounts for sets in mereological terms, recovering set-theoretic notions and axioms from mereological-hylomorphic ones. The recovery may work formally, but one must accept that sets are wholes that have parts. For instance, $\{a\}$ is said to be a fusion whose material part is a and whose formal part is $\emptyset$, where the empty set is the higher-order attribute *instantiating some attribute* (property or relation) *or other* (cf. ibid.: p. 516). $\emptyset$ is the set that lacks material parts altogether, but still has a part, namely a formal part, which is an attribute that is uninstantiated. The authors' Fine-inspired view of sets keeps sets and membership conditions too close for comfort by the standards of a procedural semantics like mine that keeps procedure and product strictly apart.

[11] I will mention, though, that, albeit *non-extensional*, my mereology is still *well-founded*, obeying the classical definitions of the parthood and proper-parthood relations as partial orders. In particular, it respects *anti-symmetry* (thus excluding mutual parthood), contrary to the non-extensional mereology of Cotnoir (2010) and Cotnoir and Bacon (2012). For a defence of extensionalist mereology, see Varzi (2008). The straitjackets that do not fit TIL are *uniqueness of composition*, which implies *extensionality* (the tenet that the identity of a whole is determined by its proper parts alone), as well as *idempotence* (the tenet that the reiteration of a part does not create a new whole). Note that proposition A and proposition $A \wedge A$, though truth-conditionally idempotent, are not mereologically idempotent in TIL and qualify as two distinct propositions.

So it would seem that before we semanticists are in a position to invoke anything structured, such as propositions, we must complete some preparatory metaphysical work prior to proceeding to semantics proper. Thus, I sympathize with the temptation to embrace some notion of structured propositions and delimit the unity problem to the *semantic* problem of how *truth-conditions* are generated while giving the metaphysical unity problem short shrift. Soames in King et al. (2014: p. 32) is explicit about his priorities:

> The problem we need to solve [...] is *not* to find some relation born by the constituents of a proposition to one another that 'holds them together' as parts of a single complex entity; the problem is to explain the intentionality of propositions. The former, misconceived, problem stems from the idea that for any complex entity there must be some relation in which its parts stand by virtue of which they are all parts of a single thing. [...] since the same questions [of a suitable unifying relation] arise for all complex entities, there is no special 'uniting' problem *of this sort* for propositions. What is special is that propositions must be—*inherently and without further interpretation by us*—capable of being true or false.

Contrast this with Liebesman (2015: p. 520):

> Roughly [...] the challenge is to identify the feature that unifies the constituents of a proposition. Just as some pieces of wood fail to compose a table if improperly arranged or of the wrong character, some entities fail to compose a proposition if they are improperly arranged or of the wrong character.

And Johnston (2006: p. 683):

> The problem of the unity of the proposition is then two-fold: How is it that items like Aristotle [a *topic*] and the property of liking dogs [a *predicable*] make up some third complex item, the proposition that Aristotle liked dogs, and how is it that a complex item like this, unlike the sum or the set or the group or the sequence of the constituents, is a nonarbitrary bearer of truth value?

This passage is in keeping with the general tenor of Johnston (ibid.) that the mereological unity problem is a precursor to the semantic problem of truth-conditions or truth-aptness in general.[12] Soames, on the other hand, is essentially claiming that the mereological unity problem can be safely epochéed, for it is not unique to structured propositions, but extends to sets as well. He mentions both unordered and ordered sets, as well as linguistic trees, without mentioning the fact that trees are just graphic

---

[12] Cf. also Johnston (ibid.: p. 665): "A solution to the unity problem requires a principle that explains not only how such disparate items as Socrates and wisdom can form a complex whole, but also how that whole is non-conventionally [i.e., inherently] a bearer of truth and falsity." Appears to share Johnston's double-barreled understanding of what the unity problem is. King's unity question UQ1 asks in what way a proposition is more than a mere collection or enumeration of its (target) constituents, while UQ2 asks how the truth-condition of a proposition is fixed.

illustrations of ordered sets. I find the argument slightly baffling, for any set-theoretic entity lacks complexity, so sets and structures are not commensurable.[13]

Structured propositions, on the other hand, are not set-theoretic but mereological objects. So they do have a special unity problem of the mereological sort.[14] In fact, what makes their unity problem special is that structured propositions must be the unique sort of complex entities that are linked to truth and falsity in the shape of *truth-conditions* or *truth-values*. Propositional structure must be conducive to truth-aptness or truth-directedness, to put it that way. There is an obvious way to bridge from the mereological unity problem to the semantic problem of truth-conditions: a structured proposition must be unified in such a way as to be or represent or yield a truth-condition. But I see no pressing reason to call the latter problem a *unity* problem.

As I read Soames (ibid.), he appears to want to replace the metaphysical problem of the structure of structured propositions by a pragmatic-cum-cognitive account of how agents carry out predicative and other cognitive acts in thought and speech that will undergird his theory of how propositions succeed in being vehicles of representation which will in turn underpin his account of how truth-conditions are generated. As he says (ibid.), "the key to solving [the semantic unity problem] is to recognize the obvious fact that predication is something that agents do." Now, Soames is in marked opposition to propositions being Platonic entities. So, he does not see himself facing the problem of accounting for the unity of Platonic propositions that Frege and Russell tried to tackle head-on. But even if Soames identifies propositions with particular kinds of intellectual or linguistic acts that human agents may token, he considers his propositions to be structured. He speaks of them as being complex and as having constituents. Therefore, I suppose the question does rear its head as to *how* Soames's non-Platonic, pragmatic-cognitive, structured propositions are structured and unified. In fact, precisely the problem of the unity of structured propositions crops up explicitly in Hanks's kindred act-theoretic conception of propositions.[15] Hanks's answer is that predication is in charge of unity. I agree verbally, though not substantially, as will become obvious below. The act theorists and I essentially differ over whether predication is primarily a pragmatic or a logico-semantic concept.

---

[13] Soames's argument appears to be that *propositional* unity is just an instance of the over-arching problem of the unity of any sort of structured or complex entity, *therefore* the metaphysical (as opposed to semantic) problem of propositional unity should not be singled out as a particular problem. I still fail to see why the problem of unity would be 'misconceived'. In any event, Soames seems a tad too brisk in his dismissal of the mereological problem of propositional unity.

[14] The propositions of (im-)possible-world semantics are well-known examples of propositions conceptualized as set-theoretic entities. This holds whether such a proposition is a satisfaction *class* of (im-)possible worlds or the characteristic *function* of the class, for functions (i.e., mappings) are themselves just sets (or sets are, conversely, just functions, where functions are mere maps between the elements in a domain and the elements in a range). The mereological unity problem does not arise for the model-theoretic intensions of (im-)possible-world semantics.

[15] Textor (2017) highlights some of the obvious, but unacknowledged, common features between act-theoretic propositions and Husserlian judgements. Another historical point of reference would be Kant, who was not content with an empirical object being simply an aggregate of impressions (as Hume would have it) but sought to combine a manifold of impressions into a synthetic unity by means of an intellectual process he called *synthesis*. A manifold of impressions is united in the concept of an object, and only by having this concept can we have experience of objects (see, for instance, *KdRV*, B130-37).

2.2 Aspects of the mereological unity problem

Let me get more specific about the problem of propositional unity by going through a number of points about which we as advocates of structured propositions must make a decision when devising our theories.

Consider the mathematical proposition that 1 is odd. Mathematical propositions do not get much simpler than that. We have a familiar natural number, 1. We have a familiar mathematical property, being an odd number. But on top of that we have a third factor. The number and the property have been made to interact. How, though? The question is not how the numeral '1' and the adjective 'odd' are made to interact syntactically in the English sentence "One is odd". The English copula 'is' takes care of that. The question is rather how two mathematical (hence abstract) entities—a number and a property—hook up. It would seem that the unity of the proposition that 1 is odd is brought about by combining (in a manner still to be explained) 1 and oddness and the third factor, which provides for systematic organization of the parts. Upon combination, the proposition that 1 is odd emerges. Or else, it would seem, the proposition is identified with this very combinatorial procedure. I suggest that an answer along one of these two lines must be the form of any answer to how at least atomic mathematical propositions are unified. Two overlapping questions that immediately crop up are the following ones.

- OBJECT VERSUS CONCEPT. Are the parts the number (e.g., 1) and the property (e.g., being odd) themselves, or conceptualizations of them, or pairs of both concepts and the object they conceptualize?

The concept/object contrast, in modern times, harks back to the Mt Blanc dispute between Russell and Frege. The choice of the nature of propositional parts is important when it comes to the *granularity* of structured propositions.[16] But it also matters when it comes to the inner workings of structured propositions as to what options are open to the theorist. In particular, a concept conceptualizes an object and in so doing points beyond itself, as an object does not, while the conceptualized object is typically that of which something is (held to be) true or false.

- ENTITIES VERSUS OPERATIONS. Which parts of a propositional whole are inert entities that are operated on and which parts are operations or have an operational character? Is one or more operations not a proper part, but the formal structure of the proposition?

This latter distinction maps onto the former, but only if concepts are construed as operations, so the two distinctions should not be run into one. It is tempting to phrase the question about the third factor as a question about the nature of the *relation* that *relates* the number and the property. But this is a pre-emptive way of framing the question, because it excludes non-relations as what brings the property and the number

---

[16] I will ignore here the adjacent question of how *fine-grained* structured propositions ought to be. Of course, a full account of structured propositions must address granularity, for we must lay down when any two structured propositions are isomorphic (semantically indistinguishable while also structurally distinct) and when they are equivalent in various respects (weak vs. strong equivalence, etc.) in order to distinguish between valid and invalid inferences involving structured propositions.

into contact. Therefore, I stick to a neutral phrase like 'hooking up', for the same reason that Sainsbury (1996/2002: p. 17) speaks of 'concatenation'.

It is unavoidable that a third factor is called for, simply because the unadorned *juxtaposition* of a number and a property cannot establish interaction between the two. (This is my basic objection to modeling structures as sequences: see below.) But there are basically two different ways of attempting to obtain the required interaction. One way is that a third entity—be it a relation, a mapping, an operator of functional application, set membership, predication, or whatnot—is added. This third entity will serve as something that works on inert entities. The addition of the third entity must be implemented in such a way that a *regress* is avoided (see below).

The other way is that the two entities are made for one another, the way a lock and a key are made for one another, such that they handle the required interaction themselves and are insofar not inert. I am, of course, alluding to Frege's metaphor of saturation.[17] When an unsaturated entity ('the lock') and a saturated entity ('the key') are juxtaposed, they are drawn to one another like two magnets, and they gel: the key automatically goes into the lock and turns. Still, there is a third factor involved, be it saturation or ascription. This sort of view seems less in danger of unleashing a regress, but it requires some metaphysical footwork to explain the category of unsaturated (or 'gappy') objects to steer clear of obscurantism. Liebesman (ibid.) appears to advocate a theory along those lines:[18]

> The proposition that Frege is wise is composed of Frege and wisdom. Frege and wisdom, in turn, are related by ascription: wisdom is ascribed to Frege. This distinguishes the proposition that Frege is wise from the mere sum of Frege and wisdom: in composing the sum, Frege and wisdom need not be related by ascription. (Ibid.: p. 552.)
>
> The ascription view is *not* a view about predicational acts. Rather, it is a view about the semantics of predicates: expressions with the semantic function of ascribing. (Ibid.: p. 554.)

I am not convinced that this sufficiently explains how predicates can in and by themselves do anything, such as predicate properties. Moreover, predicates can occur mentioned rather than as being busy ascribing properties, in which case Liebesman's theory will go nowhere toward explaining propositional unity.[19]

Furthermore, it is desirable to be able to switch between whether a 'lock' and a 'key' do hook up and when they do not. There is a distinction between (*i*) objects, concepts, operations, etc. being lined up and described individually, together with a description of the interaction they would be capable of, and (*ii*) the actual implementation or application or execution of operations, etc. You can show the lock and the key and

---

[17] Bellucci (2014) describes Peirce's take on unity: both the property and the subject of predication are unsaturated. Cantú (2006) describes Bolzano's *Sätze an sich*, which can reasonably be claimed to remain underinvestigated in analytic philosophy.

[18] For comparison, Liebesman's *ascription view*, that predicates ascribe properties, contrasts with the *entity view*, that predicates denote entities such as properties. TIL belongs to the entity camp: predicates denote properties, and (extensionalized) properties are subsequently predicated (see Sect. 3 of this essay).

[19] I am indebted to a referee for this journal for this observation.

describe how they connect. Or you can insert the key in the lock and turn it. When the lock is turned, there is again a bifurcation of options. Either the result of the insertion and turning of the key is a complex state with a lock and a key in it such that the latter is located inside the former in a turned state, or the result is an altogether new state or object that perhaps does not involve a key or a lock or insertion or turning. Transposed to propositions, what I am referring to as an altogether new state or object would be, for instance, a truth-value, which lacks structure and constituents and which does not reveal the processes by which it was arrived at.

To anticipate terminology which I will explain below, the difference between (*i*) and (*ii*) is this difference:

- DISPLAY VERSUS EXECUTION. A (suitably) structured sequence of interlocking entities and operations occurs displayed when the object of study is this very structure without it being executed. It occurs executed (on condition of being suitably structured) when proceeding to the entity beyond it that the structure is a presentation of or itinerary toward.

I suspect Russell (1903: §54) had a kindred distinction in mind when distinguishing between 'a relation in itself' and 'a relation actually relating'. However, while it makes sense to say that a relation occurs displayed such that it can be talked about as an entity in its own right, it does not make sense to speak of a relation occurring executed, even though the analogue is that a relation is instantiated.

As far as my own theory goes, the gist of it is to identify structures with abstract logical procedures that detail what operations apply to what entities in order to obtain what other entities. One source of inspiration would be a Frege–Church–Montague-style function/argument logic.[20] Therefore the sort of whole that is a proposition is a procedure that specifies which functions apply to which arguments in order to obtain which types of values. Moreover, each part of any such whole is itself a procedure. For this reason, a proposition is a compound procedure that consists of sub-procedures. Mt Blanc cannot figure as part of a propositional procedure, for there is nothing procedural about a mountain. What can figure as a propositional part is a procedure that, when executed, yields Mt Blanc. Finally, a full disintegration of a compound procedure will sort the sub-procedures into those that are *atomic* and those that are *molecular*.[21] I rely on Levine (2002) with respect to the distinction between *analysis* and *decomposition*.

- ANALYSIS. Each propositional content admits of a unique ultimate analysis into simple constituents.
- DECOMPOSITION. Each propositional content admits of distinct decompositions, no one of which is intrinsically privileged over the others.

Levine argues convincingly that analysis is compatible, and decomposition incompatible, with Russell and conversely for Frege. My theory, though generally leaning toward Frege and away from Russell, comes down on the side of analysis, for the

---

[20] See also *Tractatus* (§5.47): "Whenever there is compositeness, argument and function are present."

[21] Cf. Harte (2012: p. 130): "[There are] two (exclusive) ways in which something can be one: by being a unified whole or by being a mereological atom." Cf. Simons (2000: p. 16): a mereological atom has one part, namely itself, so it has no proper parts. A mereological atom, by my lights, qualifies as being structured, though minimally so.

theory comes with atoms. However, and this is important, atoms are susceptible to *refinement*, so being atomic is not an absolute property. An atomic procedure can be refined into a molecular procedure, though not within the same propositional context and, trivially, not with its procedural identity intact.[22]

Zooming further in, the unity problem as adumbrated above turns out to be an open-ended cluster of problems. Here are two pairs of problems, the first of which is this one:

- MATHEMATICAL VERSUS EMPIRICAL. Are *mathematical/logical* and *empirical* propositions unified in the same way? How much of a structural overlap is there?

The proposition that one is odd does not come with complicating factors such as empirical indices like worlds and times. Empirical propositions do need such indices to capture their modal profile as contingent truths or falsehoods. These truths and falsehoods obtain relative to indices. When Miles smiles, he does so contingently. On the other hand, if a mathematical proposition is true (false), then it is necessarily or absolutely true (false). I will show below that non-empirical and empirical propositions share the same procedural core; but also that empirical propositions are bound to have a more elaborate structure. They incorporate functional application and its dual, functional abstraction, because I am incorporating abstraction over worlds and times. So, there is more than one kind of propositional unifier. This ties in with the second point:

- ATOMIC VERSUS MOLECULAR. Are *atomic* and *molecular* propositions unified in the same way?

One difference immediately stands out. Even an atomic proposition must combine *heterogeneous* entities into a novel kind of entity. Even if the parts are all conceptual rather than objectual, the account is not complete without an account of how Miles the individual and the property of smiling are made to interact.[23] The task is then to explain how an individual and a monadic intension (a one-place property) combine into a medadic intension (a proposition).[24]

---

[22] Whether a procedure for producing a particular product is an atomic or a molecular one depends on which particular *conceptual system* is in use. Of two distinct conceptual systems, one may have an atomic and the other a molecular procedure as its parochial manner of conceptualizing a particular object. Whereas it is absolute whether a procedure is either atomic or molecular, it is relative (namely to conceptual systems) whether the procedure a given conceptual system uses to produce a certain entity is an atomic or a molecular one (provided the system has the procedural means to produce the relevant entity in the first place). See Duží et al. (2010: §2.2.3) for a definition and elucidation of *conceptual system*. See my (2015: pp. 340–344) for the converse of *refinement*, which is *simplification*, the replacement of a molecular procedure by an atomic procedure that produces the same entity. An example from the 'disciplinary matrix' of intensional logic would be the procedural difference between the respective meanings of the predicates 'is a bachelor' and 'is an unmarried man'.

[23] Diogenes and his descendants take exception to properties as abstract entities. So be it. I want to make room for a Platonic conception of properties, or in fact just any conception that treats properties as something over and above their instances or tokens or tropes.

[24] Some compound propositions, on the other hand, must combine *homogeneous* entities into a third entity of the same kind. This happens when a disjunctive or a conjunctive or an implicational proposition is formed from two input propositions. But even the ostensibly cut-and-dried case of binary truth-functional connectives is complicated. At least classically, the truth-functions take truth-values to truth-values, not

2.3 Tuples, list, and regress

Zooming out again a bit, we encounter two classical pitfalls that any viable theory of structured propositions must avoid. They are the *list* and the *regress* pitfall. In general, any solution to the list problem must be developed with an eye to the regress problem, for the two issues are interconnected. It is by attempting to solve the list problem that one is liable to generate the regress problem by proliferating intermediaries. So, there is no point in advocating a solution to the former if the solution is known or likely to generate the latter. As I see it, the list problem should be solved by developing a theory of interaction; the regress problem should be (dis-)solved by preventing it from arising.

- LIST. A list or enumeration of entities, operations and whatever else is bound to underdetermine structure. The list lacks interaction among the items, so no unity problem arises for lists. A list amounts to a Russellian aggregate but not to a Russellian unity. A list is necessary, but not sufficient, for being structured.

There is a modern-day theory of propositions that lands in the list pitfall. The *tuple theory* (as I like to call it) identifies propositions with, or models them as, *n-tuples* or set-theoretic *sequences*. My fundamental objection to the tuple theory is that it underdetermines what a structured proposition is all about. Of course, an ordered juxtaposition of entities is necessary. But I would have to be persuaded that juxtaposition would be sufficient for propositionhood. The perhaps most widespread objection is a Benacerraf-style objection. The theory can provide no principled choice between ⟨*property, individual*⟩ and ⟨*individual, property*⟩ as the proposition that the individual has the property. This is because the tuple theory lacks an account of the interaction between its elements. Nor is any of this satisfactory:

- ⟨*operation, individual, property*⟩
- ⟨*operation, property, individual*⟩
- ⟨⟨*operation*, ⟨*property, individual*⟩⟩
- ⟨⟨*operation*, ⟨*individual, property*⟩⟩

Whatever the operation may be, it still just occurs as one item alongside other items. It fails to interact with the other items on the list. This flaw is already sufficient reason for me to discard the tuple theory of structured propositions. To be sure, sequences are indispensable when lining up concepts, objects, operations, etc., in a particular order and specifying ordered sub-sets, as in ⟨⟨x, y⟩, z⟩ or ⟨x, ⟨y, z⟩⟩. But that's it.[25] Anything beyond this information has got to be projected onto the sequence from outside rather

---

Footnote 24 continued
propositions to propositions. Entailment does operate on propositions, but the output value is a truth-value and not a proposition. Still, we are at least confined to the realm of truth-values ('propositions-in-extension') and truth-conditions ('truth-values-in-intension'). Other compound propositions must combine a proposition and a non-proposition into a novel proposition, as when Boolean negation is applied to an input proposition. My (2012a) offers a sketch of how to account for the unity of various compound propositions.

[25] See my (2012: §3) for a set of objections to propositions as sequences. The verdict is that sequences are neither structures, nor propositions. For instance, tuples cannot be truth-bearers. Nor, for that matter, can *sets* of worlds be truth-bearers; but fortunately, their characteristic *functions* can, in the sense that they return truth-values (or truth-value gaps or gluts).

than being present in the sequence 'inherently and without further interpretation by us'. In particular, anything to do with the interaction among the elements ('parts') would reside elsewhere. But interaction is essential to structure. So, what are those exterior structures that are being projected onto sequences, and how are their parts unified into wholes? If such structures exist, then surely *they*, and not sequences, should take centre stage. The sort of answer I would not be interested in would say something like, "Think of $\langle x, \langle y, z \rangle \rangle$ as the proposition that object y has property/falls under concept z, where x is the operation of predication or instantiation or set membership or subsumption, or whatever else, that applies to y, z in that order." By being asked to 'think' that, the most interesting theoretical task of them all is being dumped in my lap, leaving it up to me to do the theoretician's most challenging work for them.

The other pitfall is the *regress* pitfall.

- REGRESS. A regress is launched as soon as the designated unifier is one item among the items it is designated to unify into a whole. Any link between any two items itself requires two further links to hook up with those two items; and so on. A regress offers unity, but only temporarily.

One way to tackle the regress problem would be to allow a regress to get started, and then dogmatically, though not arbitrarily, bring it to a halt.[26] But I would prefer the regress to not get rolling in the first place. What I find attractive about a broadly *hylomorphic* approach is that it comes off to a promising start as regards the nature of the prospective unifier. Says Harte (2012: p. 133):

> [...] in Aristotle, a whole is something whose parts have a certain position or ordered arrangement, in accordance with some principle of structural organization, be it spatial or otherwise. [...] Aristotle identifies the organizational principle of [...] wholes as (Aristotelian) form ($\varepsilon\iota\delta o\varsigma$). [A whole has 'something else' beyond its parts, and this] 'something else' is not a further part of the whole [...], but is rather its nature ($\phi\upsilon\sigma\iota\varsigma$) and principle ($\alpha\rho\chi\eta$)[...], and this, although Aristotle does not here explicitly use the term, is form ($\varepsilon\iota\delta o\varsigma$).

On a hylomorphic approach, there is form, and there is content. When this distinction is applied to propositions, the structure of the proposition is a matter of form, not of content. Unity is provided by something that is on the side of form and not of content. Therefore, it is not obvious that we are headed for a regress. The challenge, however, becomes how to be able to predicate properties of something that is form and not content. Surely it must be possible to predicate of a given form that it is a propositional unifier. And we know that this special kind of predication must not make the form occur as a piece of content in the whole it unifies.[27] But this kind of

---

[26] Kai Wehmeier (in personal communication) has pointed out that (on the assumption that *Gedanken* are function/argument compounds) the Fregean *Gedanke* of $H(a)$ has two parts: $H(\ )$, a. In computational terms, $H(a)$ is the application of the unsaturated property/*Begriff* $H(\ )$ to the saturated object/*Gegenstand* a. Frege prohibits factoring $H(a)$ out into H, $(\ )$, a: neither $(\ )$ nor H is a stand-alone part by Frege's lights. A Bradley-style regress, accordingly, is blocked straightaway in a manner that is dogmatic, because this three-way decomposition is dismissed, but also non-arbitrary, because a decomposition would yield something, viz. $(\ )$ and presumably also H, that is neither a *Begriff* nor a *Gegenstand*.

[27] See McDaniel (2009: p. 260, fn. 27).

predication requires that the form (the propositional unifier) can be treated as an entity in its own right, for otherwise nothing can be predicated of it. The dialectics, in other words, is that the unifier must, on the one hand, be sufficiently 'ephemeral' so as to not start a regress and, on the other hand, sufficiently 'robust' so as to be capable of being a subject of predication. There is a way to strike this balance in my theory, and that is because it comes with a vehicle of stratification, or, more specifically, a vehicle of *ramification*.[28] The unifier—the whole proposition-as-procedure—can be displayed and so shown to be a self-sufficient entity with no need for anything further to prop it up.

3 The procedural semantics of Transparent Intensional Logic

3.1 What is procedural semantics?

Tichý opens his (1988) with the metaphor of travelling from one place via two different routes to a shared destination. The metaphor underpins his conception of linguistic meaning as an objective logical procedure. A procedural conception of meaning conceptualizes meaning as the very path from one or more points to at most one new point. This might sound like meaning could be reduced to a mere mapping between points, but there is substantially more to meaning-as-procedure than a mere correspondence. Whereas a correspondence records the fact *that* something maps onto something, a procedure explains *why* and *how* that correspondence obtains. A procedure describes how to start out at a point of departure, traverse a path, and arrive at a destination whenever there is one.

Consider the identity sentence "$4^2 = 2^4$".[29] According to general procedural semantics, the sentence is ambiguous. Taken one way, it expresses the falsehood that the procedure of raising 4 to the power of 2 is identical to the procedure of raising 2 to the power of 4. Taken another way, it expresses the truth that those two procedures converge in the same result (without specifying which number is the shared result). Additional notation, therefore, is required for disambiguation. For now, this will do to make the point clear: "*Executed* $(4^2) = $ *Executed* (2^4)" versus "*Procedure* $(4^2) ='$ *Procedure* (2^4)". The important thing is to be able to distinguish, both notionally and notationally, between procedure and product. As is seen, from the parts 2, 4, exponentiation (or respective modes of presentation of these three), two distinct wholes can be formed. If we held to uniqueness of composition, we would be barred from drawing the non-extensional distinction between *Procedure* (4^2) and *Procedure* (2^4).

---

[28] Russell arrived at an analogous stance concerning the set-theoretic paradoxes: "Whatever involves *all* of a collection must not be one of the collection [...]." (1908: p. 63). Russell had admittedly vicious circles, not regress, in mind when he stratified his universe into types. But the analogy carries over to wholes jeopardized by regress.

[29] The example of 4^2 and 2^4 has been lifted from Frege (1891).

I am contrasting *procedural* with *denotational semantics*, a distinction well-known from the formal languages of computer science.[30] But the term 'procedural semantics' is used for other theories of meaning (and linguistic processing) as well; see, for instance, Bezuidenhout (2004), Woods (1981) and Johnson-Laird (1977). Fodor (1978) critiques the latter conception, arguing that one of its many vices is that it embraces a verificationist theory of meaning (ibid.: p. 237):

> [...] if 'that's a chair' goes over into instructions, it must be instructions to *do* something. [...] it's closer to the spirit of the movement [i.e., the sort of procedural semantics that has procedures discharge multiple duties as what words and sentences *mean*, what we *understand* when we understand a word or sentence, and what we use to *categorize* objects] to take it to be an instruction to confirm 'that's a chair', viz. by checking whether that [...] has the features in terms of which 'chair' is procedurally defined. Indeed, one just about has to take [this] route if one is going to argue that procedures capture intensions [...]; it's at least *possible* to believe that 'that's a chair' means 'that's something that has the observable features F where 'F' operationally defines 'chair'.

The opening pages of Tichý (1971) do sound like Tichý would subscribe to the above conception of procedures:

> [...] what can my understanding of 'dog' consist in if not a link in my mind between the word and a suitable dog-discriminating procedure? (Ibid.: p. 273.) My suggestion is [...] to look at the basic epistemic situation as a confrontation between a set of objects [the universe of discourse] and a subject equipped with a battery of identification procedures. The executing of the procedures by the subject is then what is usually called experience. (Ibid.: p. 274.)

However, what Tichý understands by 'procedure' in (1971) is 'possible-world intension'. The intension, or discriminating procedure, of 'dog' does nothing other than induce a dichotomy of the universe into dogs and non-dogs. This notion of procedure is *not* the one that underlies the procedures I am deploying here and which will be defined below in the "Appendix". *A fortiori*, the meaning of a sentence is not a procedure for determining whether the sentence expresses a truth. If empirical discriminating procedures were identified with linguistic meanings, then TIL would indeed have been a verificationist semantics. TIL has an operational, but not operationalist, conception of meaning.

Let me briefly compare TIL to another contemporary theory of procedural semantics.[31] Though the act theories of propositions do not label themselves as procedural theories, that is what they are. Hanks (2015) puts forward the following compound

---

[30] See, for instance, Moggi (1989) for the contrast between *procedural* and *denotational* and *logical* (in effect, *model-theoretic*) approaches. See Pezlar (2017) for a very recent exposition of the procedural semantics of Transparent Intensional Logic and a comparison with a constructivist counterpart, Martin-Löf's type theory.

[31] Collins (2017) and Moltmann (2013) operate with a distinction between an action or structure and its outcome, both coming out in favour of the latter as the weightier of the two. Hence, their respective theories do not belong to the camp of procedural semantics.

propositional procedure as the meaning of "1 is odd" (to stick with my original example):

$$\vdash \langle \mathbf{1},\ Odd \rangle$$

The proposition $\vdash \langle \mathbf{1},\ Odd \rangle$ is a predicative act type (as opposed to token). It is the type of act that an agent tokens when predicating being odd of 1. $\vdash \langle \mathbf{1},\ Odd \rangle$ as a unit produces the truth-condition that is satisfied exactly when it is true that 1 is an odd integer. The proposition breaks down into three act types. **1** is the sub-procedure of referring to 1 (a definite integer), Odd the sub-procedure of expressing the property of being an odd integer, and $\vdash$ the sub-procedure of predicating the property of the integer.[32]

TIL disagrees on two accounts. First, predication is not primarily, but only derivatively, an act to be carried out by agents. Instead predication is in and by itself a logical operation.[33] Second, whereas Hanks's propositional unifier, $\vdash$, is a proper part, TIL's is not. On the other hand, we agree that predication—rather than instantiation or some primitive operation, say—is what concatenates the two sub-procedures identifying, respectively, being odd and 1.

Thus procedures, as TIL understands them, are neither epistemic nor pragmatic, nor mental. Rather they are logical. This is how TIL encodes the proposition that 1 is odd:

$$\left[{}^0Odd\ {}^0 1 \right]$$

Everything is typed in TIL, and *Odd* is of type (oν), i.e., ($\nu \to$ o), where ν is the type of natural numbers and o the type of truth-values. The atomic, or one-step, procedure ${}^0Odd$ produces the characteristic function of the set of odd natural numbers. ${}^0Odd$ carries the dual information that the type (oν) is accessed and that the set of odd naturals is extracted from it. The atomic procedure ${}^0 1$ produces the number 1. 1 is of type ν. The procedure ${}^0 1$ carries the dual information that the type ν is accessed and that the particular object 1 is extracted from ν.

---

[32] Hanks (in personal communication) has stressed that, "There cannot be stand-alone acts of predication. It does not make sense to *just* perform an act of predication—you cannot just predicate, without any object or property involved. So, the type of act of predication has to be accompanied or conjoined with other acts of picking out a target for predication and a property to be predicated of that target." I agree, on the strong reading of 'stand-alone act (or: part)' that such an act (part) would presuppose no further acts (parts). Hanks (in personal communication) agrees to the moniker 'procedural semantics'.

[33] The contrast between predication as a pragmatic or mental act and as a logical procedure is explored in my (2017). See also Johnston (ibid.) on the contrast between the *subjectivist* approach pivoted on subjective acts of predication and the *objectivist* approach pivoted on an objective link between objects and properties. At (ibid.: p. 684) he brings the two together in the following manner, with the objectivist approach enjoying conceptual priority: "[…] when I perform the act of predicating *F*-ness of some individual *a*, I thereby relate myself in judgment to an objective entity, the predication of *F*-ness of *a*. […] But this predication of *F*-ness of *a* is just the proposition that *a* has *F*-ness." Collins (2017: §1) claims that my (2017) and Johnston (2006) subscribe to the 'fallacious dichotomy' that the choice is between 'cognitively alienating Platonism' and 'an account that grounds propositions in acts'. This is an overstatement. These two papers explore two different conceptions of predication that can be used to underpin two different conceptions of propositions. Although in favour of the objectivist conception, neither paper fields a *tollendo ponens* to the effect that since one of the alternatives fails, the other alternative prevails.

While ^0Odd is typed to produce a function, $^0 1$ is not typed to produce a functional argument per se. It takes the structure of [^0Odd $^0 1$] to put $^0 1$ into the argument slot. It also takes the structure of [^0Odd $^0 1$] to put ^0Odd into the function slot. ^0Odd might equally well occur in a or the argument slot, as when a property is predicated of *Odd*. Once ^0Odd and $^0 1$ have been put into the function slot and the argument slot, respectively, how are function and argument made to interact? By way of the procedure of functional application. Tichý's own informal explanation goes like this:

> Let $^0Function$ be a procedure producing a mapping and $^0Argument$ a procedure producing an argument of the mapping. $^0Function$ and $^0Argument$ can be combined into a compound procedure which consists in executing $^0Function$, thus obtaining a mapping, then executing $^0Argument$, thus obtaining an argument of the mapping, and then applying the mapping to the argument, thus obtaining the value (if any) of the former at the latter. [...] Note that the compound symbol '[$^0Function$ $^0Argument$]' names the *procedure*, not the object produced by it." (1988: p. 64). (*Formula adapted.*)

Note also that the *definition* in the "Appendix" of the procedure [$^0Function$ $^0Argument$] does not explain how the atomic sub-procedures $^0Function$, $^0Argument$ 'combine into' the molecular one. The definition assumes that they have already been so combined. Note, furthermore, that it is inconsequential in which order $^0Function$, $^0Argument$ are executed, whereas the typing dictates that *Function* is to be applied to *Argument* and not the other way around. Some executions run *in parallel*. Other executions are *serial*, especially when one procedure must be executed to yield a functional value which subsequently becomes the argument of another function. My initial flow-chart metaphor was intended to capture the serial character of executions and the value-to-argument transformations.

By reversing the order of the sub-procedures ^0Odd, $^0 1$ in [^0Odd $^0 1$] we obtain [$^0 1$ ^0Odd]. [$^0 1$ ^0Odd] also counts as a procedure in TIL, albeit an ill-typed one, as it has got the respective procedures producing the argument and the function arranged back to front. Therefore, this procedure does not produce anything and so is *improper*. But am I not facing a Benacerraf-style problem of my own? The intended procedure of applying *Odd* to 1 could equally well (the objection goes) be given by [$^0 1$ ^0Odd].[34] It is surely a matter of notational convention (the objection continues) that '[^0Odd $^0 1$]' counts as well-formed and '[$^0 1$ ^0Odd]' as ill-formed. I agree with these observations, but I do not agree that they give rise to a Benacerraf problem. The notational conventions reflect the fact that the intended procedure is the operation of applying the product of ^0Odd to the product of $^0 1$. The relevant notational convention is that what occurs to the left designates the function-producing procedure and what occurs to the right designates the argument-producing procedure. The Benacerraf problem arises for the tuple theory because it lacks a principled answer as to the correct sequence, which in turn arises because it lacks a theory of interaction among parts. My theory, by contrast, has a theory of interaction among parts in terms of function, argument and application,

---

[34] Thanks to one of the referees for pressing me on this point.

hence can demarcate procedurally correct from procedurally incorrect sequences of parts.

It is also important to appreciate the fact that the procedure of functional application does *not* apply to the procedures ^0Odd, $^0 1$. Instead it applies to the respective products of ^0Odd, $^0 1$. There is, for sure, a matching procedure, namely [$^{00}Odd\ ^{00}1$], but it too is ill-typed: what ^{00}Odd is typed to produce is ^0Odd, which is not a function. What $^{00}1$ is typed to produce (namely $^0 1$) is capable of occurring as a functional argument, but then a function defined on higher-order objects is required for type-theoretic congruence. Such a function would, for instance, be the characteristic function of a set of procedures typed to produce integers.

3.2 Trivialization and variable

The closed procedure [$^0Odd\ ^0 1$] comes with so-called Trivializations. Trivialization is a non-standard addition to the λ-calculus, and it is central to contemporary TIL, so I will explain the notion here.

First, Trivialization can be compared, up to a point, to the constants of a formal language. Both a constant and a Trivialization pick out one specific entity in each their own manner. Kaplan may have lamented that "proper names are a mess and if it weren't for the problem of how to get the kids to come in for dinner, I'd be inclined to just junk them".[35] But, of course, Kaplan, like the rest of us, needs proper names (a unique name for a particular entity) in order to address individuals (in a vocative manner) or to talk about individuals (in an objective manner). The computer scientist would say that we need to *call* or *retrieve* entities as a prelude to operating on them. But whereas the constant '1' denotes this, that or the other object relative to this, that or the other interpretation, $^0 1$ invariably produces 1 (regardless of how the Trivialization of 1 and the integer 1 are encoded syntactically, or if they are encoded at all).[36]

Second, Trivialization is TIL's test of objecthood: whatever is in the ontology of TIL can be Trivialized, and what cannot be Trivialized is not an object. For instance, the largest prime is not an object. Still, there are multiple procedures (all improper) that are typed to produce the largest prime. It is just that Trivialization is not one of them. Every Trivialization is, as we say, a *proper* procedure in that it must produce an entity. (The closest linguistic counterpart would be Russellian names, which must have a bearer.)

Third, a related, basic feature of Trivialization is this:

$$\left[^0\leftrightarrow \left[^0=^0a\ ^0b \right] \left[^0=\ '\ ^{00}a\ ^{00}b \right] \right]$$

The gloss is that a, b are identical exactly when the Trivialization of a is identical to the Trivialization of b. So, the identity and difference of Trivializations is grounded in

---

[35] Kaplan (1990: p. 15).

[36] See Duží et al. (2010: §3.2) on proper names in TIL. The theory amounts to a procedural version of Millianism, so to speak. The meaning of a semantically proper name is a Trivialization, ^0a, which does not describe a, but is also distinct from a.

the identity and difference of individuals (or whatever other objects are Trivialized). The identity criteria of the latter flow upwards to their Trivializations. But if this is so, then why bother to have Trivializations at all? Why the dressed-up $[^0Odd\ ^01]$ rather than the plain $[Odd\ 1]$? The latter simple 'says': "Apply *Odd* to 1 to obtain a truth-value." Which is what that Composition is all about. One can arrive at the same view via an argument from predication: *Odd* is to be predicated of 1, not ^0Odd of ^{01}.[37] So, again, why not cut out the middleman? If TIL had no Trivializations, as per pre-1988 TIL, then we would have a situation analogous to Lagadonian languages. In a Lagadonian language an object is also its own name. In Trivialization-less TIL an object would also be its own representation or mode of presentation. In the publication immediately preceding Tichý (1988), Tichý (1986: p. 514) says:

> Also '7' can be regarded as [expressing a way of arriving at] seven *qua* the result of a particular, albeit trivial, procedure: the procedure consisting in starting with seven and leaving it at that.

(Ibid.: p. 524), ξ an arbitrary type:

> Each object of type ξ is also a ξ-procedure; it v-[produces] itself for any v [i.e., independently of valuation].

Objects would do dual duty both as representation and what is represented.[38] Fourth, therefore, the introduction of the notion of Trivialization helps factor out these two duties, enabling objects to be what is represented without also having to represent themselves.[39] With these two duties factored out, there is no risk of TIL creating space for the absurdity that a mountain, say, would be either a procedure or part of a procedure. *Odd* and 1 are not immediately given, but need to be retrieved first. What *is* immediately given, relative to $[^0Odd\ ^01]$, are those two Trivializations.

Fifth, Trivialization is a vehicle that enables a procedure to occur displayed rather than executed. Just as there is a direct path to rock-bottom entities like integers and individuals, there is the same direct path to procedures. The result is this:

---

[37] Collins (2017: §3) levels an objection against Hanks's theory of sub-acts along just these lines: "a *reference to Bill* [i.e., a sub-act for identifying Bill] cannot be a constituent of the proposition that Bill sneezes, for a reference to Bill doesn't sneeze". But one does not follow from the other. Acts are not known to sneeze, but this does not bar them from being propositional constituents, as long as there is an explicit descent from the act to a product capable of sneezing.

[38] By introducing Trivialization, Tichý spares himself the embarrassment of making a mistake he himself warns against: "Failure to distinguish clearly between entities and different ways of [producing] them is an inexhaustible source of philosophical confusion and doubletalk." (Ibid.: p. 515.). Prior to (1988) in which Tichý introduced his ramified type hierarchy, he made do with a simple type theory, which explains why he had objects represent themselves.

[39] Both Church's and Tichý's respective type theories would be stuck with 'double-typing'—Church: ι_0 and ι_1; Tichý: ι and $*_1$ (if we are typing individuals)—because Mt Blanc, say, would have to be of both types. That something is both representation and what is represented does not sit well with the fundamental Fregean tenet that sense and reference are distinct entities and that to be a sense is to determine or (re-)present something beyond the sense. This explains in part why Tichý needed a notion like Trivialization. To see Trivialization being put to full use, see Duží and Jespersen (2015) where Trivialization is what enables *hyper*intensional attitudes. For a comparison of Church's and Tichý's respective type theories, see Kosterec (forthcoming).

Anatomy of a proposition

$$^0\left[^0Odd\ ^01\right]$$

This move displays the procedure [$^0Odd\ ^01$], thus blocking the transition to what it produces. Therefore, the procedure itself can occur as a functional argument, hence properties can be predicated of *it* in lieu of its product.[40]

Sixth, the basic difference between a Trivialization and a *variable* is this. Whereas a Trivialization reaches into a particular domain, relative to a type assignment, and extracts a *specific* object, a variable reaches into a particular domain, relative to a type assignment, and extracts an *arbitrary* object. Variables in TIL are not letters, but procedures: 'x' is a letter that expresses the procedure x which produces an entity a relative to a valuation function v assigning values to variables as per $v(x) = a$. Variables are said to valuation-produce ('v-produce' for short) entities, because they presuppose a valuation or assignment function.[41] TIL's conception of variables is, roughly, like an objectual variant of Tarski's syntactic conception, not least by presupposing assignment functions. Kaplan, for one, also departs from a Tarskian semantics for variables, but with the twist that variables (as linguistic entities) are said to be paradigmatic vehicles of direct reference. Our variables are equally non-descriptive, but, contra Kaplan, their respective values (when of first order) are not meanings at all; variables themselves are meanings, rudimentary as they are. It is variables, not their values (again when of first order), that are capable of occurring as propositional parts. What our variables do is provide *arbitrary* entities imbued with a *specific* type as input to operate on.

3.3 Open and closed, executed and displayed procedures

Consider [$^0Odd\ ^01$] again. It decomposes into three parts:
- [$^0Odd\ ^01$] itself, which is the improper part of this procedure and its only molecule
- ^0Odd, which is one of the two proper parts and one of the two atoms
- ^{01}, which is the other proper part and the other atom

Hence, an analysis (as opposed to decomposition) of [$^0Odd\ ^01$] yields its two proper parts. From the procedure [$^0Odd\ ^01$] we can form the sequence $\langle ^0Odd, ^01\rangle$. The sequence reproduces the order in which the proper parts occur within the procedure. The procedure of functional application is not one of the proper parts of [$^0Odd\ ^01$]. Instead it is the form of the whole that is the particular proposition [$^0Odd\ ^01$]. The proposition already has unity, and already is a unit, because it is a molecular procedure that makes explicit how the respective entities which its proper parts produce are arranged as function and argument. The distinction between the proper parts and the improper part of a proposition is seen to be of profound importance, because it is tantamount to the distinction between the content and the form of a proposition.

---

[40] For illustration, "Tilman knows that 1 is odd" is formalized thus:
$\lambda w \lambda t [^0Know_{wt}\ ^0Tilman\ ^0[^0Odd\ ^01]]$, where *Know* is a relation-in-intension (type: $(\omicron\iota*_1)_{\tau\omega}$) between an individual (the knower) and a hyperproposition. Section 4 explains λ-abstraction over worlds and times. See also Duží et al. (2010: §5.1.2.2).

[41] See Rabern (2013) on variables and variable binding in Kaplan.

Anatomy of a proposition

The procedure of which [$^0Odd\ ^01$] is an instance is called *Composition*. The dual of Composition is *Closure*.[42] Whereas Composition 'breaks down' a function by being typed to proceed to its value at an argument, Closure goes in the opposite direction by 'building up' a function as a correspondence between the elements of a domain and the elements of a range.

[$^0Odd\ ^01$] is a *closed* procedure. What happens if we have an *open* procedure? An open procedure contains one or more free occurrences of one or more variables. A stand-alone variable is, thus, a limiting case of an open procedure. TIL deviates from Frege's semantics in an important respect as regards formulae like "...x..." in which x occurs free. Tichý (1986: p. 522) says about Frege:

> [...] instead of treating a gappy formula as a name [*Eigenname*, in Frege's inclusive sense of proper name] of the unspecific truth-value [produced] by the incomplete [procedure], he treats it as a name of the [procedure] itself. But he does not treat the result of filling the gap in the formula in the same spirit. He does not regard it as a name of the corresponding complete [procedure], but rather as a name of the truth-value [produced] by it. The complete [i.e., closed] [procedure] thus becomes homeless and Frege finds himself counterintuitively ascribing its structural features to the truth-value itself.

What Tichý is advocating is a *uniform* semantics for

- '[$^0Odd\ ^01$]'
- '[$^0Odd\ x$]'
- '[$f\ ^01$]'
- '[$f\ x$]'

The open procedure [$f\ x$] is the procedure of obtaining one arbitrary object of one specific type and another arbitrary object of another specific type and applying the former to the latter in order to obtain a truth-value. Only no truth-value is forthcoming for want of a specific function and a specific argument. What we can obtain is something conditional: *if* F is the value of f and a the value of x *then* the truth-value is **T** (or **F**, as the case may be).

Each of the four formulae expresses a procedure. A procedural ('intensionalist') semantics pairs off '$7^2 - (6 \times 7)$' or '5!' with a procedure, not the product of the procedure, whereas a denotational ('extensionalist') semantics pairs it off with a number. In particular, the semantic value of '[$^0Odd\ ^01$]' is not a truth-value, nor is the semantic value of, say, '$7^2 - (6 \times 7)$' the number 7, as little as '5!' has the number 120 as its semantic value. A denotational semantics will have an infinite multitude of names for 7 or for 120 (likewise for each truth-value, etc.), which seems like a massive case of semantic redundancy.

On the other hand, according to procedural semantics, '120' and '5!' do not share the same semantic value.[43] They both express a procedure as their seman-

---

[42] The dual of Trivialization is Double Execution. See Remark 2 in the "Appendix".

[43] If procedural semantics has a slogan, it would be "Same procedure, same meaning; different procedure, different meaning". As soon as one has a formally rigorous theory of procedures, one thereby has a formally rigorous theory of identity and individuation of meaning. The salient point is whether the procedures in

271

Anatomy of a proposition

tic value, and their respective procedures are not identical. $^0 120$ is the procedure of identifying 120 in one go. $[^0! \ ^05]$ is the procedure of identifying the result of applying the factorial function to 5, without specifying the number that is the result. Therefore, the sentence "5! = 120" is mathematically informative. It does not express that 120 is identical to itself, but that when 5 is the argument of the factorial function then 120 is the value. The procedure is encoded thus: $[^0= [^0!^05] \ ^0120]$. For a closer look, this structure decomposes into the following proper parts:

- $^0=$
- $[^0! \ ^05]$
- $^0 120$
- $^0!$
- ^{05}

The last two have been obtained in virtue of the transitivity of parthood. There is a hierarchy of mereological composition at play: $^0!, \ ^05$ are not on the same level as $^0=, \ ^0 120$, as indicated by the use of Composition, $[^0! \ ^05]$, so the identity relation does not relate 120 and either 5 or factorial. It relates 120 and the *result* of applying factorial to 5. The identity relation does not 'see' how the resulting number has been calculated; the identity relation simply inputs that number as one of two arguments.[44]
$[^0= \ ^0[^0! \ ^05] \ ^0120]$ decomposes into just three proper parts:

- $^0=$
- $^0[^0! \ ^05]$
- $^0 120$

The Trivializations $^0!, \ ^05$ occur displayed in the Composition $[^0! \ ^05]$ because it occurs displayed, as per being Trivialized: $^0[^0! \ ^05]$. Therefore, neither of $^0!$ and ^{05} is a constituent of $[^0= \ ^0[^0! \ ^05] \ ^0120]$.

In what relevant ways does $[^0= [^0! \ ^05] \ ^0120]$ differ from $[^0= \ ^0120 \ [^0! \ ^05]]$? The latter procedure arranges the two arguments of the binary identity function in the opposite order. So, it should be rather glossed as, "120 is the result of applying the factorial function to 5", or more loosely, "120 can be obtained by computing five factorial", or in standard mathematese, "120 can be described as five factorial". Intuitively, the difference is between whether five factorial or 120 is emphasized. Still,

---

Footnote 43 continued

question track semantically relevant distinctions in their target language. Making a case for adequacy is a distinctly philosophical task.

[44] If we wanted to prevent $[^0! \ ^05]$ from being executed, we could Trivialize it as per $[^0= \ ^0[^0! \ ^05] \ ^0120]$, but this Composition would mean (absurdly) that a number-producing procedure were identical to a number. For illustration, let x, y be of type $*_1$ (see Def. 3 in the "Appendix") and let them range over the arbitrary first-order type α. Then:

- $[^0= xy]$, where $= /(o\alpha\alpha)$: identity between the value of x and the value of y (which is true, provided x, y v-produce the same α-typed object)
- $[^0=' \ ^0x^0y]$, where $=' /(o *_1 *_1)$: identity between the procedures x, y (which cannot be true, x, y being distinct procedures)
- $[^0=" \ ^{00}x^{00}y]$, where $=" /(o *_2 *_2)$: identity between the Trivialization of x and the Trivialization of y (which cannot be true, $^0x, \ ^0y$ being distinct procedures).

these two different procedures are susceptible to being *executed* in identical manners. Thus, to amplify a point made above, the definition of Composition (see Def. 2, iii, in the "Appendix") does not prescribe any particular order of executing particular proper sub-procedures. They can be executed in parallel, or in the order in which they are syntactically encoded, or in reverse order, or by shifting between executing a procedure producing an argument, then executing the procedure producing a function, then executing another procedure producing another argument (whenever the function is of arity 2 or more). The Composition in question is not identical to any particular Composition that would incorporate this or that particular execution as its own structure. Execution is an empirical matter and as such extraneous to the logical structure of a Composition. Nonetheless, it is a valuable feature of TIL that it is in a position to distinguish between the order in which the arguments of the identity function (or any other relation) occur. This is valuable whenever we want to be able to display one of these two Compositions and assign it to an agent as the complement of an arithmetic attitude they have, without thereby also displaying and assigning the other Composition as a complement. An agent may be able to apply the identity function to ⟨120, 5!⟩ without being able to apply it to ⟨5!, 120⟩ if, for instance, the agent is unaware that identity is commutative or, for idiosyncratic reasons, refuses to commute the arguments.

3.4 Procedures without product

What happens when a procedure has no product? Then it becomes extra important that the parts of a procedure operate on *typed* entities. A procedure, whether producing a product or not, is *typed* to produce an entity of a particular type. This explains why we can say of a procedure that it is typed to produce (say) the largest prime. This answer comes, however, with the presupposition of *correct typing*. The types must match up to keep the ball rolling, as it were, until we arrive at a final type. Incorrect typing causes the type processing to grind to a halt. For instance, the Composition [^0Odd $^0Barcelona$] can be displayed (as I just did by mentioning it), but it cannot be executed. *Odd* demands an entity of type ν as argument; Barcelona is of type ι. The procedure that details the application of *Odd* to Barcelona fails to describe a path to a truth-value, although the value of *Odd* is exactly a truth-value. This is as it should be; there is no fact of the matter as to whether Barcelona is an odd number.[45]

With an untyped universe, the answer is likely to be a different one, namely that it is false that Barcelona is an odd number. I find that a theory should make it possible to raise the question whether Barcelona is odd, but also that questions based on a category mistake, such as wrong typing, do not afford an answer. The existence of ill-typed procedures dramatizes the chasm between displayed and executed procedures. Every procedure can be displayed, hence described both as a whole and with respect to its individual parts. Not every procedure can be executed.

---

[45] [^0Odd $^0Barcelona$] exemplifies unrestricted mereological composition, which was objected to in Sect. 2.

3.5 Predication

Predication is an instance of Composition. My (2008) provides the details of the logic of predication, but fails to provide a philosophical answer to the question *why* [$^0Function\ ^0Argument$] is a case of predication rather than something else that would also have Composition as its logical backbone.[46] All that (ibid.: p. 496) says is:

> our grasp of predication is such that we do understand that if we take a property and an entity and feed them into a 'machine of predication' enabling us to say something about something else we retrieve a Yes or else a No, according as the entity has the property or not. Such an input/output 'machine of predication' is what went into symbols as '[$^0Function\ ^0Argument$]'. (*Formula adapted.*)

It is further argued that it is methodologically neater if predication and application are one operation (one being a special case of the other) than both of them being primitives, and that we have enough of a pre-theoretic grasp of application so as to introduce it as a primitive. The latter claim is in keeping with the definition of Composition, which does not explain *how* a function proceeds from its argument(s) to the value (if any): it just does (whenever there is a value to arrive at). Still, even if it be granted that the logic of Composition is intuitively understood, the question remains why [$^0Odd\ ^01$] is the logic of the *predication* of being odd of 1.

The argument I would offer is by way of elimination, namely: what could it possibly be if not predication? In particular, it could not be *instantiation*, as soon as instantiation is understood to be factive. Predication should not pre-empt the question whether the entity of which a property has been predicated instantiates the property. My view is that the logic of predication is exhausted by the juxtaposition of a function and an argument accompanied by the procedure of applying the function to the argument to obtain a truth-value.[47] Whether the function and the argument must be type-theoretically congruent to prevent nonsense (Julius Caesar being a prime, and suchlike) is an additional issue. Which truth-value rolls out depends on whether the argument entity instantiates or lacks the property predicated of it. Saying this much commits me to the view that any such juxtaposition must count as a case of predication, and I am only happy to take on this commitment.[48]

---

[46] Soames (2010: p. 29) voices a similar concern: "What structural features of a proposition *do* show what is predicated of what, and *how*, exactly, do they manage to do that?" and "there is nothing [...] in any abstract structure we might construct, or explicitly specify, which, *by its very nature* [without extraneous conventions], indicates that anything is predicated of anything." (Ibid.:31). Soames uses this as a springboard for his act-theoretic view that *agents* are in charge of predicating something of something.

[47] My (ibid.: pp. 489–491) considers and rejects the idea that the juxtaposition is between an individual and a *propositional function*.

[48] Duží et al. (2010: p. 198) considers an alternative to predication being exhausted by Composition. If we rework our empirical example into a mathematical one, we get: [$^0Pred\ ^0Odd\ ^01$], where *Pred* is a function from a property and a number to a truth-value. Again, Composition is the logical operation involved, but we are now dealing with a binary relation (a two-argument function). This Composition is the meaning of the sentence "Being odd is predicated of 1". This is different from the sentence "1 is odd", which is the analysandum, and which does not mention predication.

3.6 Truth-conditions

It is *immanent* to [^0Odd ^{0}1] what the type of its product is. The Composition is typed to produce a *truth-value* in the light of the types assigned to *Odd* and 1. The relation between the Composition and the truth-value is an internal one because the types have been frontloaded into the theory. The logical link between [^0Odd ^{0}1] and a truth-value is non-arbitrary.

Thus, even though [^{0}= ^{0}120 [^{0}! ^{0}5]], [^{0}= [^{0}! ^{0}5] ^{0}120], [^0Odd ^{0}1] are not the sort of thing that *is* true or false, they still deserve to be called *propositions*. Each of them is typed to produce a truth-value. While [^0Odd ^{0}1] and the rest of them lack the property of being either true or false, they are still inherently related to the type of truth-values. In fact, since I believe we ought to preserve the locution that a proposition is a truth-bearer, I would simply say that [^0Odd ^{0}1], etc., are truth-bearers in virtue of producing a truth-value.[49] (I explore this issue in more detail in Sect. 4.)

How does the notion of *truth-condition* enter the fray? We already have a very coarse-grained truth-value and a fine-grained proposition. It might be tempting to interject a truth-condition of intermediate granularity. An obvious candidate to consider would be the necessary proposition of possible-world semantics, the constant function from possible worlds (and perhaps other empirical parameters) to the truth-value **T**. But, of course, empirical parameters are entirely irrelevant to mathematical propositions. Numbers are not assigned to the domain(s) of worlds, where they would be out of place, and because the necessary proposition is (modelled as) a *constant* function it exactly blots out the dimension of contingency that possible-world intensions are eminent at capturing.

Hence, the necessary proposition, or any other possible-world intension, seems to be but a pointless detour on the path to the truth-value. Furthermore, all mathematical (and logical and analytic) truths would share the same truth-condition, which is hopeless as a tool for discriminating among such truths. Why not instead *identify* the truth-condition of [^0Odd ^{0}1] with the truth-condition of any other procedure that is equivalent with [^0Odd ^{0}1]?[50] If we go along with this, [^{0}= ^{0}120 [^{0}! ^{0}5]] and [^{0}= [^{0}! ^{0}5] ^{0}120], though not identical procedures, will still be linked by the fact that they share the same truth-condition. The truth-condition can be stated thus: "The number that is produced by ^{0}120 is the same number as is produced by [^{0}! ^{0}5], where the order between these two sub-procedures is irrelevant". This proposal still interjects a notion of truth-condition between mathematical propositions and truth-values, but one that is much finer-grained than the constant function above. A mathematical truth-condition is supposed to capture what a particular corner of mathematical reality must be like, and the exact path toward that corner is irrelevant.

---

[49] Duží et al. (2010: §5.1.6) raises and solves the comparable problem of *epistemic shift*, which arises 'for any system of hyperintensional logic within which hyperpropositions are capable of figuring as objects of knowledge but not also as truth-bearers'. The rule of factivity needs to be stated in a technically slightly more sophisticated way.

[50] See Duží et al. (2010: p. 48, Def. 1.5.)

4 What procedural semantics can do for propositional unity

4.1 Propositions as primary or derived entities

The previous section laid out the foundations of a procedural account of structure. This section lays out the foundations of a procedural account of unity. Let us take stock before moving on.

Formally speaking, propositions are the medadic intensions. Because they are of zero arity, they do not reveal much about themselves. By contrast, dyadic relations, for instance, are more informative: we are to imagine two items (or in the limiting case, the same item twice over) standing in some relation to one another (or itself), and the relation comes with various properties, such as being anti-symmetric or serial or Euclidean, and it is either a relation-in-intension or a relation-in-extension. One can start out with different sorts of objects and consequently define a host of relations over them. Propositions demand a different sort of treatment. Roughly, they can be either at the front or at the rear of a theory, but not in the middle. They can be introduced as theoretical primitives, like Thomason's primitive hyperpropositions of type p (1980). Or one may, for instance, introduce individuals as objects belonging to the sub-domain D_{-1} and unary properties as objects belonging to the sub-domain D_1 and subsequently define those propositions in which a property is predicated of an individual as objects belonging to the sub-domain D_0.[51]

The propositions of TIL are *derived* entities, because they presuppose the notions of procedure and type. To understand TIL's theory of propositions, one must already understand TIL's theory of procedures and types. However, TIL propositions are not afterimages of or emanations from categorically distinct entities. For comparison, King starts out with (i) a sentence "Fa", analyzes it by means of (ii) a linguistic tree that consists of 'a', 'F', and the so-called sentential relation R_{sent}, and ends up with (iii) a, F and the so-called propositional relation R_{prop}.[52] King's is a syntax-to-semantics theory that attempts to take linguistic trees and beef them up into propositions thanks to the pragmatic acts of interpretation that language-users perform 'spontaneously and unreflectively', not least when interpreting R_{sent} as *predicating F of a*. R_{sent} is eventually replaced by R_{prop} which inherits the former's status as a relation of predication and which is the unifying backbone of King's propositions.

TIL propositions are procedures among other procedures. Neither sentences, nor language-users, nor their interpretations (which bridge from syntax to semantics in King) are involved. We start out with and also end with procedures. Yet the atomic procedures (Trivializations and variables) are object-dependent. Objects are conceptually prior to atomic procedures. That is to say that the feeder procedures presuppose non-

---

[51] I am alluding to Bealer's formal theory of intensions. For exposition and discussion, see Fox and Lappin (2005: §2.4) and my (2008). In the main text, I am not being entirely faithful to Bealer, for he would never say that a property and an individual are 'inside' a proposition or that a property is predicated of an individual 'in' a proposition. Bealer's intensions are all metaphysically simple. What is structured are formulae.

[52] I am cutting an ever-growing story extremely short for a rough-and-ready comparison. See King (2017, 2013) for recent statements of his position. See Pickel (2015) for a critique.

procedures, and the complex procedures presuppose atomic procedures. The order of explanation, however, proceeds in the opposite direction, from top to bottom.

This order is in keeping with my general top-down methodology. My top-down approach to how unity is engendered starts out with procedures. Anyone who understands functional application and abstraction computationally (as intended by Church, λ-conversion being the logic of computation) ipso facto understands Composition and Closure, as conceived by TIL. Having introduced definitions as per Def. 2 (cf. "Appendix"), the approach goes on to distinguish between molecular and atomic procedures. Afterwards it identifies certain molecular procedures with particular propositions, then makes the types explicit and explains how procedures descend to products: truth-conditions or truth-values, as the case may be.

The bottom-up approach, which I find to be characteristic of Russell, starts out with atoms—a concrete particular like Mt Blanc, an abstract universal like the property of being a mountain—then adds a relation to connect the atoms and afterwards at some point a proposition emerges, somehow.

4.2 How does unity emerge from sub-procedures?

In general, each molecular procedure unifies its proper parts within a procedure that can be *executed* as a unit, as a whole. It is a whole that is typed to produce an entity of a particular type beyond the producing procedure. Its sub-procedures, for sure, produce (at most) an object each, but the point of my theory is exactly that these objects are the stepping-stones toward a final object, which is the product of the molecular procedure.

More specifically, in the procedural semantics of TIL, the very proposition is the unifier. A propositional unifier serves to unify a proposition's proper parts, though not its improper part, which is the proposition itself. Verbally, though not substantially, a part of the proposition is the unifier, but that is because the part in question is the improper part, i.e., the entire proposition. Offering this sort of solution to the unity problem is arguably feasible only because the relevant improper part is a molecular procedure.[53] The propositional procedure, or procedural proposition, has unity because it lines up some procedures as parts and indicates what is to be done to the entities they are typed to produce. Because it has unity, the proposition can occur displayed as a whole, a unit, and have properties predicated of it. When the proposition, this unit, occurs executed, its parts interact in the process of producing the product of the proposition. That the parts, i.e., sub-procedures, interact is to say that by being executed they descend to their products, which the proposition arranges as functions and arguments. This procedural account is a far cry from an account that identifies the unifier with a relation whose relata are lined up like peas in a pod.[54]

---

[53] This is not among the 'several moves one might consider' in McDaniel (2012: p. 260, fn. 27).

[54] In fact, to characterizing a relation as a unifier is not an option, as soon as relations are construed strictly set-theoretically as nothing other than a dichotomy of the Cartesian product of a universe of discourse. For then there is no complex entity and hence no need for a unifier. See Tichý (1995: pp. 176–177) for this objection.

I owe an explanation of how 'application' (and 'abstraction', for that matter) is to be understood more specifically.[55] Def. 2 (iii) defines the logic of application. But a conceptual question remains. Procedures are not agents, so in what way can they be associated with anything like application? Is this particular procedure simply the application of a function? Well, yes and no, for the term 'application' is actually three-way ambiguous. Sundholm (1983: p. 164) claims (correctly, in my view) that the term 'construction' can mean any of these three:

- process of construction (a)
- object obtained as the result of a process of construction (b)
- construction-process as object (rather than as something 'dynamic') (c)

Meanings (a) and (b) exemplify the ubiquitous act/result ambiguity, while (c) is the reification of (a). This three-way ambiguity carries over immediately to 'application' (and 'abstraction'). The reading I intend for 'functional application' ('functional abstraction') is (c). Thus understood, the answer is Yes. Understood as (a) or (b), the answer is No. Agents enter at (a), but not at (c). The act theories I discussed above would appear to have a leg up, since they can account for application (and abstraction) as something that people do. My Platonist retort, of course, is to ask *what* it is that agents do when executing acts of application and abstraction.[56] On the (c) reading, application (and abstraction and other procedures) is primarily a matter of detailing formal relationships between various entities, in this case between functions and arguments. These formal relationships amount to a structure, because they display what entity is in the function slot and what entity is in the argument slot, and what is the type of the resulting value (if any).[57] In the simplest terms, TIL procedures are reified functional dependencies.

However, Sainsbury, for one, is not likely to be persuaded by the gist and the crux of a theory such as mine. He says (ibid.: p. 107):

Perhaps some look to the Fregean notion of functional application. However, there is no solution in this quarter. The question of what makes the difference between a collection consisting of a function and its potential arguments, on the one hand, and the 'insertion' of these arguments into the function, and their insertion in one rather than another order, is of essentially the same kind as our original question. *Argument-function unity is of a piece with propositional unity.* ['Our original question' is this (ibid.: p. 104): given a collection of meanings arranged so as to say just one thing, what cements the meanings together in the required way? What is the nature of the further ingredient or entity involved, here referred to as 'arrangement' [and elsewhere as 'concatenation'], over and above the meanings themselves?] (*Italics added.*)

---

[55] This addresses a concern voiced by one of the referees.

[56] See my (2017). The topic is which of (a) and (c) is conceptually prior.

[57] TIL has a Platonist ontology, because it understands application and the other procedures as per (c). Embracing the ramified type hierarchy (cf. Def. 3 in the "Appendix"), which types the procedures as entities in their own right, amounts to embracing Platonism. Furthermore, TIL is Platonism *ante rem*, because our procedures are conceptually prior to their products, if any.

Being someone who looks to the Fregean notion of functional application, I should explain the logic of the transition from a collection of multiple meanings to one (more complex) meaning. The 'concatenation' Sainsbury is asking for is, I suggest, a compound procedure that prescribes how argument/function unity is to be obtained. Remember that the notion of procedure is conceptually prior to the notions of predication and proposition. Hence, the circularity Sainsbury is hinting at does not obviously arise on my account.

4.3 Atomic empirical propositions

TIL applies an overarching procedural semantics to every kind of language. For instance, predication is invariably Composition. But empirical sentences must be paired off with propositions with a more elaborate logical structure than sentences expressing necessary truths or necessary falsehoods. As was mentioned at the outset, procedures occur already on the object level. This enables the symbolism of TIL to explicitly encode the empirical parameters that are stepping stones in the reified computation of the product of a given procedure. The two empirical parameters that TIL currently operates with are possible worlds and instants of time. Variables w_i ranging over worlds and variables t_i ranging over times are λ-bound in the following manner:

$$\lambda w [\lambda t [\ldots w \ldots t \ldots]]$$

The phenomenon that such variables occur already on the object level is called *explicit intensionalization and temporalization*.[58] To exemplify how this works, here is the proposition that matches "Miles smiles":

$$\left[\lambda w \left[\lambda t \left[\left[\left[^0 Smiles\ w\right] t\right]\ ^0 Miles\right]\right]\right]$$

This Closure is typed to construct a function from worlds to a function from times to the truth-values obtained by applying the relevant characteristic function of particular sets of smiling individuals to the individual Miles. The Closure does what it does by abstracting over the respective values of the variables w, t. The purpose is to isolate all and only those worlds and times at which it is true that Miles is an element of the relevant (i.e., world-and-time-relative) set of smiling people.

The most striking difference between the above proposition and the proposition [$^0 Odd\ ^0 1$] is that the former is a Closure and the latter a Composition. The former is a Closure because it must make the ascent from a truth-value to a (coarse-grained) truth-condition and does so by abstraction over worlds and times. The general flow of the procedure is to break down and then build up again. A decomposition, accompanied by type assignments, spells out what is going on.[59] Empirical properties are of the type

---

[58] See my (2005). Duží et al. (2010: §2.4.–2.5) and Tichý (1980) explain why $\lambda w \lambda t [\ldots w \ldots t \ldots]$ should not be collapsed into $\lambda wt [\ldots w \ldots t \ldots]$.

[59] This exposition relies on my (2008: pp. 491–492) and Duží et al. (2010: §2.4.2).

(*world* → (*time* → (*individual* → *truth-value*))).⁶⁰ That is, an empirical property is (modelled as) a function from worlds to a function from times to sets of individuals, which in turn is identified with a function from individuals to truth-values. The proposition underlying "Miles smiles" contains three occurrences of Composition.

[1] The application of *Smiles*/(*world* → (*time* → (*individual* → *truth-value*))) to *w* ranging over worlds to obtain a function of type (*time* → (*individual* → *truth-value*)), a chronology which inputs instants of time and outputs the respective sets of smiling people at those particular times.
[2] The application of the chronology obtained at [1] to *t* ranging over times to obtain a set of individuals/(*individual* → *truth-value*).
[3] The application of the set obtained at [2] to the individual Miles to obtain a truth-value.

The truth-value obtained at [3] is relativized to worlds and times by means of two instances of Closure to obtain a truth-condition. The third functional application, [3], is the predication of *Smiles* of Miles. The availability of a set for the operation of predication is functionally dependent on a property having already undergone extensionalization in the two preceding steps. The key steps are: first *extensionalization* of the property to obtain the characteristic function of a set, then *predication*. Predication is extensional insofar as a set is applied to an individual, but intensional insofar as the set has been obtained as the extension of a property. When another world and time are the indices of evaluation it is likely that a set with a different population emerges as the extension. This is how contingency is preserved.

It would have been wonderful to be able to make the sweeping claim that all empirical propositions, without exception, are Closures. However, this is not entirely so. Assume that P is a coarse-grained empirical truth-condition. Then the Trivialization ^0P is η-equivalent to the Closure $[\lambda w[\lambda t[[^0P\ w]]t]]]$.⁶¹ The contractum, ^0P, is mereologically atomic, yet an empirical proposition. What speaks against ^0P is that it barely qualifies as an analysis even of a simple subject-verb sentence like "Miles smiles", since it simply black-boxes the logical structure of the analysandum.⁶² Maybe there is still use for a Trivialization like ^0P, but then as the procedural counterpart of a sentence like "It rains", which is in effect a one-word sentence due to the dummy subject 'it'; but I won't explore one-word sentences here. The Closure $[\lambda w[\lambda t[[[^0Smiles\ w]t]\ ^0Miles]]]$, on the other hand, makes explicit each logical step from the predication of an empirical property of Miles to the truth-condition that the proposition produces. Therefore, $[\lambda w[\lambda t[[[^0Smiles\ w]t]\ ^0Miles]]]$ is the privileged or canonical procedure underlying

---

⁶⁰ Formally expressed: $(o\iota)_{\tau\omega}$, short for '$(\omega \to (\tau \to (\iota \to o)))$'. See Remark 1 in the "Appendix".
⁶¹ In standard notation, η-conversion is the conversion between $\lambda x(Ax)$ and A, where x is not free in A. In particular, η-reduction serves to reduce instances of λ-abstraction.
⁶² See Duží et al. (2010: §2.1.3) for a ranking, in terms of 'better and worse', of the admissible analyses of a given sentential meaning. The ranking is based on which desirable inferences can be drawn and which undesirable ones can be blocked.

"Miles smiles".[63] The notation can be abbreviated thus:

$$\lambda w \lambda t \left[{}^0Smiles_{wt} \, {}^0Miles \right]$$

The above Closure breaks down as follows. Its *open atomic sub-procedures* are these two:

- w, t

Its *closed atomic sub-procedures* are these two:

- ${}^0Smiles, {}^0Miles$

Its *open molecular sub-procedures* are these four:

- $\lambda t [{}^0Smiles_{wt} \, {}^0Miles]$, $[{}^0Smiles_{wt} \, {}^0Miles]$, ${}^0Smiles_w$, ${}^0Smiles_{wt}$

Its *closed molecular procedure* is only the Closure itself:

- $\lambda w \lambda t [{}^0Smiles_{wt} \, {}^0Miles]$

As is seen, $\lambda w \lambda t \, [{}^0Smiles_{wt} \, {}^0Miles]$ contains eight proper parts. Its two propositional unifiers are Composition and Closure. The core or body of the proposition is a Composition, because the product of ${}^0Smiles$ is to be predicated of the product of ${}^0Miles$. Two instances of Composition, $[[{}^0Smiles \, w]t]$, are precursors to the application of the function so produced to Miles as per $[{}^0Smiles_{wt} \, {}^0Miles]$. Two instances of Closure are required in order to ascend from a truth-value to a truth-condition indexed to worlds and times.

Just like $[{}^0Odd \, {}^01]$, $\lambda w \lambda t \, [{}^0Smiles_{wt} \, {}^0Miles]$ is not a truth-bearer. So, what justifies the claim that $\lambda w \lambda t \, [{}^0Smiles_{wt} \, {}^0Miles]$ is the sort of procedure that is a proposition? More generally, which procedures are propositions? I offer this type-theoretic answer: any closed procedure is a proposition iff it is typed to produce either a truth-value or a truth-condition. A closed procedure is an empirical proposition if it is typed to produce an object of type (*world* → (*time* → *truth-value*)), i.e., a coarse-grained truth-condition. A closed procedure is a non-empirical proposition if it is typed to produce a truth-value. The motivation for the restriction to closed procedures is to blot out an open procedure like $[{}^0Smiles_{wt} \, {}^0Miles]$, which is typed to produce a truth-value, yet is not a non-empirical proposition. Both kinds of propositions, empirical and non-empirical, are of type $*_1$ (with provisos for type raising, cf. Def. 3 (a) in the "Appendix"). This is the lowest of the higher-order types. Objects of type $*_1$ are invariably procedures, and they belong to the lowest type of procedures because what they produce are non-procedures, namely functions. Truth-values are zero-adic functions, and they belong to the realm of first-order entities. An important link between the metaphysical question of unity and the semantic question of truth-conditions and truth-values is that, given some procedures whose structure and unity have already been settled, the fact whether a given procedure is typed to yield a truth-condition or a truth-value serves as a filter to sort the propositions from the non-propositions.

---

[63] See Duží and Jespersen (2015) on *procedural isomorphism*, which justifies privileging one among multiple isomorphic procedures. η-equivalence is not part of the definition of procedural isomorphism, being too coarse a filter.

5 Conclusion

This paper has explored what sort of solution a realist procedural semantics equipped with a typed universe of first-order and higher-order entities can offer to the problem of the unity of the proposition. I claim to have shown that the theory can, at least, solve one of the two sub-problems of the unity problem and do so in a manner that does not get in the way of solving the other sub-problem.

We have covered quite some ground in this paper, so let me summarize the overall arc. The arc extends

(i) from the mereological problem of the unity of structured propositions, which divides into the list and the regress problem,
(ii) through the conception of such propositions as instances of particular kinds of logical procedures as defined by Transparent Intensional Logic,
(iii) to the procedure of functional application, in its capacity as the logic underlying predication, as the unifier of atomic mathematical and other non-empirical propositions, and the procedure of functional abstraction as the additional unifier of atomic empirical propositions.

Here is a more detailed summary. First, I pointed out that any theory of structured propositions must come with an account of structure, including an account of the unity of such structures. I characterized the problem of unity as a mereological (hence metaphysical rather than semantic) problem that centers on how parts interact so as to form a whole. I mentioned two pitfalls that any viable theory of structured meaning must steer clear of. One is the list pitfall, where a theory lines up target parts while failing to explain how they interact and thus form a whole. The other one is the regress pitfall, which is the excessive proliferation of intermediaries typically triggered by a faulty solution to the list problem. In this paper, I do not claim to have solved the regress problem. I do claim to have solved the list problem, and in my best judgment this solution does not preclude a solution to the regress problem within the procedural semantics of Transparent Intensional Logic.

Next, I argued that predication holds the key to structure and unity. I further argued that predication is an instance of the logical procedure of functional application (Composition). I introduced and described some of the foundations of Transparent Intensional Logic, showing how the theory conceptualizes structure as procedural structure. The single most important thing to understand about how the theory thinks of propositions is that they are identical to particular kinds of procedures. In particular, propositions are not the outcomes of procedures. I explained how a procedure can occur either displayed or executed. A formal vehicle that can draw this distinction is required when we want to predicate properties of a procedure rather than of its product, for instance, when describing the proper parts of a procedure (its sub-procedures) or mentioning its unifier (or unifiers). I also raised the issue that procedural propositions are not themselves truth-bearers, but are still linked inherently, thanks to the type theory, to entities typed as truth-conditions and truth-values.

Finally, I presented and explained the particular structures which Transparent Intensional Logic assigns to the atomic mathematical sentence "1 is odd" and the atomic empirical sentence "Miles smiles". Monadic predication, in the form of functional application, exhausts the structure of the former. The structure of the latter embeds functional application within a wider structure that includes the procedure of functional abstraction (Closure) as well.

Acknowledgements The research reported herein was supported by Marie Curie Fellowship FP-7-PEOPLE-2013-IEF628170, Grant Agency of the Czech Republic Project No. GA15-13277S, and VSB-TU Ostrava Project No. SP2017/133. Versions of this paper were read at the *Barcelona Workshop on Reference 9* (*BW9*): *Unity and Individuation of Structured Propositions*, Barcelona, 22–24 June 2015; Institute of Culture and Society, University of Aarhus, 11 April 2014; ILLC, University of Amsterdam, 18 May 2016; Department of Philosophy, Groningen University, *GroLog*, 12 May 2016; Department of Philosophy, Lingnan University, Hong Kong, 30 September 2015; Department of Philosophy, National University of Singapore, 23 September 2015; Department of Philosophy, Stockholm University, 24 April 2015; Department of Computer Science, TU Ostrava, 27 March 2014; Department of Philosophy, UNAM, Mexico City, 11 March 2015; Department of Logic and Philosophy of Science, UC Irvine, *C-ALPHA*, 6 March 2015; Department of Logic, History and Philosophy of Science, *Logos*, University of Barcelona, 18 February 2015. I wish to thank the following for great comments along the way: Marie Duží, Manuel García-Carpintero, Bryan Pickel the various audiences, and not least two anonymous referees for *Synthese*.

Appendix

This appendix contains four definitions accompanied by remarks for clarification.

Above I have been using the term 'procedure'. Tichý's own term of art was 'construction'. I prefer 'procedure' because the term seems more evocative than 'construction', which furthermore has misleading idealist connotations. Whichever the term, the inductive definition below lays down what TIL procedures are. They are embedded within a typed universe. The following three definitions constitute the core of TIL.

Definition 1 (*types of order 1*). Let B be a *base*, where a base is a collection of pair-wise disjoint, non-empty sets. Then:

(i) Every member of B is an elementary *type of order 1 over B*.
(ii) Let $\alpha, \beta_1, \ldots, \beta_m (m > 0)$ be types of order 1 over B. Then the collection $(\alpha\ \beta_1 \ldots \beta_m)$ of all m-ary partial mappings from $\beta_1 \times \cdots \times \beta_m$ into α is a functional *type of order 1 over B*.
(iii) Nothing is a *type of order 1 over B* unless it so follows from (i) and (ii).

□

Remark 1 For the purposes of natural-language analysis, we are currently assuming the following base of *ground types*, which form part of the ontological commitments of TIL:

ο: the type of truth-values = {**T, F**}
ι: the type of individuals (the universe of discourse)
τ: the type of real numbers (doubling as discrete times)
ω: the type of logically possible worlds (the logical space)

For the purposes of a fairly restricted arithmetic discourse, these may suffice as ground types:

o: the type of truth-values = {**T**, **F**}
v: the type of natural numbers

Definition 2 (*procedure*).

(i) The *variable x* is the *procedure* that produces an object *X* of the respective type dependently on a valuation v; x v-*produces* X.

(ii) Where *X* is an object whatsoever (an extension, an intension or a *procedure*), *Trivialization* is the procedure ^0X. ^0X produces X without any change of X.

(iii) The *Composition* $[XY_1…Y_m]$ is the following *procedure*. If X v-produces a function g of a type $(\alpha\beta_1…\beta_m)$, and $Y_1, …, Y_m$ v-*produce* entities $B_1, …, B_m$ of types $\beta_1, …, \beta_m$, respectively, then the *Composition* $[XY_1…Y_m]$ v-*produces* the value (an entity, if any, of type α) of g on the tuple argument $\langle B_1, …, B_m \rangle$. Otherwise the *Composition* $[XY_1…Y_m]$ does not v-*produce* anything and so is v-*improper*.

(iv) The *Closure* $[\lambda x_1…x_m Y]$ is the following *procedure*. Let $x_1, x_2, …, x_m$ be pair-wise distinct variables v-producing entities of types $\beta_1, …, \beta_m$ and Y a *procedure* v-producing an α-entity. Then $[\lambda x_1…x_m Y]$ is the *procedure* λ-*Closure*. It v-*produces* the following function f of the type $(\alpha\beta_1…\beta_m)$. Let $v(B_1/x_1, …, B_m/x_m)$ be a valuation identical with v at least up to assigning objects $B_1/\beta_1, …, B_m/\beta_m$ to variables $x_1, …, x_m$. If Y is $v(B_1/x_1, …, B_m/x_m)$-improper (see iii), then f is undefined on $\langle B_1, …, B_m \rangle$. Otherwise the value of f on $\langle B_1, …, B_m \rangle$ is the α-entity $v(B_1/x_1, …, B_m/x_m)$-produced by Y.

(v) Nothing is a *procedure*, unless it so follows from (i) through (vi). □

Remark 2 Def. 2 leaves out the procedures *Single* and *Double Execution*, ^1X and ^2X, which we do not need for the present foundational study. I will just note that Double Execution is the dual of Trivialization. Thus, the effect of applying Double Execution to Trivialization is the annihilation of the effect of the latter. Hence ^{20}X is equivalent to X. Trivialization raises the type whereas Double Execution lowers it. See my (2015: pp. 328–329) for definitions and elucidation.

Remark 3 Since ^1X and ^2X are Single and Double Execution, respectively, it would be natural if ^0X was known as *Zero Execution*. In fact, whereas 'Trivialization' gives the wrong idea about Trivialization, which is anything but trivial, 'Zero Execution' sums up what ^0X is all about: ^0X *displays X*. If X is a procedure, then ^0X does not proceed to executing X. This is in fact the gist of Tichý's original definition that ^0X produces *X* without any change of X. In this paper, however, I will stick to the original term 'Trivialization' for continuity.

Remark 4 Our procedural reading of the λ-calculus affects how we count occurrences of variables. Syntactically, 'λx $[^0Odd$ $x]$' contains two occurrences of 'x'. Procedurally, λx $[^0Odd$ $x]$ contains only one occurrence of x, namely in $[^0Odd$ $x]$. λx is the procedure of abstracting over the values assigned to x, but the syntactic occurrence of 'x' serves only to connect to the x in $[^0Odd$ $x]$ in order to specify that the variable over whose values is to be abstracted is x, something which 'λy $[^0Odd$ $x]$' would fail to express.

Definition 3 (*ramified hierarchy of types*).
T_1 (*types of order 1*). See Def. 1.
C_n (*procedures of order n*)

(i) Let x be a variable ranging over a type of order n. Then x is a *procedure of order n over B*.
(ii) Let X be a member of a type of order n. Then ^0X is a *procedure of order n over B*.
(iii) Let $X, X_1, \ldots, X_m$ ($m > 0$) be *procedures* of order n over B. Then $[X X_1 \ldots X_m]$ is a *procedure of order n over B*.
(iv) Let $x_1, \ldots x_m, X$ ($m > 0$) be *procedures* of order n over B. Then $[\lambda x_1 \ldots x_m X]$ is a *procedure of order n over B*.
(v) Nothing is a *procedure of order n over B* unless it so follows from C_n (i)–(iv).
T_{n+1} (*types of order n + 1*). Let $*_n$ be the collection of all procedures of order n over B. Then:
  (a) $*_n$ and every type of order n are *types of order n + 1*.
  (b) If $0 < m$ and $\alpha, \beta_1, \ldots, \beta_m$ are types of order $n+1$ over B, then $(\alpha \beta_1 \ldots \beta_m)$ (see T_1 ii)) is a *type of order n + 1 over B*.
  (c) Nothing is a *type of order n + 1 over B* unless it so follows from T_{n+1} (a) and (b). □

The final definition is of *displayed* and *executed procedures*.

Definition 4 (*displayed vs. executed procedure*). Let C be a *procedure* and D a *sub-procedure* of C. Then:

(i) If D is identical to C then the *occurrence* of D is *executed* in C.
(ii) If C is identical to $[X_1 X_2 \ldots X_m]$ and D is identical to one of the *procedures* $X_1, X_2, \ldots, X_m$, then the *occurrence* of D is *executed* in C.
(iii) If C is identical to $[\lambda x_1 \ldots x_m X]$ and D is identical to X, then the *occurrence* of D is *executed* in C.
(iv) If an *occurrence* of D is *executed* in C' and this *occurrence* of C' is *executed* in C, then the *occurrence* of D is *executed* in C.
(v) If an *occurrence* of a *sub-procedure* D of C is not *executed* in C then the *occurrence* of D is *displayed* in C.
(vi) No *occurrence* of a *sub-procedure* D of C is *executed/displayed* in C unless it so follows from (i)–(vi). □

Remark 5 Words come with the convention that they point to an object beyond themselves. Procedures come with the analogous convention that they point beyond themselves to a product. It is no accident that the default mode is the *executed* one. The primary purpose of a procedure is to be a path to a product so that the latter may be the argument of a function. But there are more 'theoretical' cases where a procedure becomes itself the object of study. One such case is hyperintensional attitude contexts. Another is the theoretical study of our apparatus, like when scrutinizing the unity and structure of propositions.

I have described in the main text two kinds of atomic propositions, while cursorily touching upon a third one. Since propositions are *propositional unifiers* in the particular sense I described above, we can individuate the three kinds of unifiers in terms of the sort of procedures they are.

- Where A is of type $o_{\tau\omega}$, the proposition ^0A is a Trivialization. It is a mereological atom, so it has unity in the minimal, if not vacuous sense that it is a structure whose zero proper parts are unified into a whole. ^0A is not a case of monadic predication; ^0A is a logical black box.
- Where F is of type $(o\alpha)$ and a of α, the non-empirical proposition $[^0F\ ^0a]$ is a Composition. It is a mereological molecule with two proper parts, two sub-procedures, whose products are such that one is to be applied to the other. $[^0F\ ^0a]$ is a fine-grained truth-condition that is typed to produce a truth-value.
- Where G is of type $(o\beta)_{\tau\omega}$ and b of β, the empirical proposition $\lambda w \lambda t\ [^0G_{wt}\ ^0b]$ is a Closure. It is a mereological molecule with eight proper parts, one of which is a Composition that is the predication of G of b. This predication is indexed to worlds and times. The twofold λ-abstraction is the procedure that the relevant characteristic function of G_{wt} is applied to b at *any* world and at *any* time that are selected as points of evaluation.

By *displaying* the last two of these propositions, we are able to express within the theory itself that both of them unify sub-propositional procedures into the procedures that are the propositions in question. (Remember that if they occurred *executed* instead, we would be expressing something about their respective products.) ^0A is excluded because it does not unify one or more proper parts into a whole (nor, of course, does ^0A unify itself).

I will exemplify how this works by means of the minimal proposition $[^0F\ ^0a]$. The type of *Unify* is here $(o *_1 *_1 *_1)$, $*_1$ first-order procedures, where the two right-most types type the two input parts and the left-most higher-order type types the output whole. The result of applying the former to the latter is **T** if they are indeed the proper parts of the whole, and otherwise **F**. The unifier is displayed and can therefore occur as a functional argument. We need ramification to pull this off, the Trivialization $^0[^0Odd\ ^01]$ being of type $*_2$, i.e., a second-order procedure.

$$\left[^0Unify\ ^0\left[^0Odd\ ^01\right]\ ^{00}Odd\ ^{00}1 \right]$$

The gloss is that what the Trivialization $^0[^0Odd\ ^01]$ produces, namely the Composition $[^0Odd\ ^01]$, unifies what ^{00}Odd and $^{00}1$ produce, namely ^0Odd and ^{01} and in that order, into $[^0Odd\ ^01]$: two Trivializations are unified into one Composition. We know what the 'glue' is between the parts, namely the procedure of predicating the product of ^0Odd of the product of ^{01}. Propositional glue, in TIL, is not one item among several items, but instead a molecular procedure that is the form of a content.

References

Bellucci, F. (2014). Peirce and the unity of the proposition. *Transactions of the Charles S. Peirce Society*, 50, 201–219.

Bezuidenhout, A. (2004). Procedural meaning and the semantics/pragmatics divide. In C. Bianchi (Ed.), *The semantics/pragmatics distinction* (pp. 101–131). Stanford: CSLI Publications.

Cantú, P. (2006). Bolzano et les propositions en soi: une théorie objective des vérités. In J. Benoist (Ed.), *Propositions et états de choses* (pp. 51–66). Paris: Vrin, Paris.
Caplan, B., Tillman, C., & Reeder, P. (2010). Parts of singletons. *Journal of Philosophy, 107*, 501–533.
Collins, J. (2017). The redundancy of the act. *Synthese*. doi:10.1007/s11229-017-1382-3.
Cotnoir, A. J. (2010). Anti-symmetry and non-extensional mereology. *Philosophical Quarterly, 60*, 396–405.
Cotnoir, A. J., & Bacon, A. (2012). Non-wellfounded mereology. *Review of Symbolic Logic, 5*, 187–204.
Duží, M., & Jespersen, B. (2015). Transparent quantification into hyperintensional objectual attitudes. *Synthese, 192*, 635–677.
Duží, M., Jespersen, B., & Materna, P. (2010). *Procedural semantics for hyperintensional logic*. Dordrecht: Springer.
Fodor, J. A. (1978). Tom Swift and his procedural grandmother. *Cognition, 6*, 229–247.
Fox, C., & Lappin, S. (2005). *Foundations of intensional semantics*. Oxford: Blackwell.
Frege, G. (1891/1986). Funktion und Begriff. In G. Patzig (Ed.), *Funktion Begriff Bedeutung* (pp. 17–39). Göttingen: Vandenhoeck & Ruprecht.
Hanks, P. (2015). *Propositional content*. Oxford: Oxford University Press.
Harte, V. (2012). *Plato on parts and wholes*. Oxford: Clarendon Press.
Jespersen, B. (2005). Explicit intensionalization, anti-actualism, and how Smith's murderer might not have murdered Smith. *Dialectica, 59*, 285–314.
Jespersen, B. (2008). Predication and extensionalization. *Journal of Philosophical Logic, 37*, 479–499.
Jespersen, B. (2012). Recent work on structured meaning and propositional unity. *Philosophy Compass, 7*, 620–630.
Jespersen, B. (2012a). Post-Fregean thoughts on propositional unity. In J. Maclaurin (Ed.), *Rationis defensor: Essays in honour of Colin Cheyne. Studies in the history and philosophy of science* (Vol. 28, pp. 235–254).
Jespersen, B. (2015). Structured lexical concepts, property modifiers, and Transparent Intensional Logic. *Philosophical Studies, 172*, 321–345.
Jespersen, B. (2017). Is predication an act or an operation? In P. Stalmaszczyk (Ed.), *Philosophy and logic of predication. Studies in philosophy of language and linguistics* (vol. 7, pp. 223–245), Peter Lang GmbH.
Johnston, M. (2006). Hylomorphism. *Journal of Philosophy, 103*, 652–698.
Johnson-Laird, P. (1977). Procedural semantics. *Cognition, 5*, 189–214.
Kaplan, D. (1990/1978). Dthat. In P. Yourgrau (Ed.), *Demonstratives*. Oxford: Oxford University Press. Originally appeared in *Syntax and Semantics*, P. Cole (ed.). New York: Academic Press.
Keller, L. (2013). The metaphysics of propositional constituency. *Canadian Journal of Philosophy, 43*, 655–678.
King, J. C. (2013). Propositional unity: What's the problem, who has it and who solves it? *Philosophical Studies, 165*, 71–93.
King, J. C. (2017). On propositions and fineness of grain (again!). *Synthese*. doi:10.1007/s11229-016-1291-x.
King, J. C., Soames, S., & Speaks, J. (2014). *New thinking about propositions*. Oxford: Oxford University Press.
Kosterec, M. On the number of types. *Synthese*. doi:10.1007/s11229-016-1190-1.
Levine, J. (2002). Analysis and decomposition in Frege and Russell. *Philosophical Quarterly, 52*, 195–216.
Lewis, D. (1993). Mereology is megethology. *Philosophia Mathematica, 3*, 3–23.
Liebesman, D. (2015). Predication as ascription. *Mind, 124*, 517–569.
May, R. (2006). The invariance of sense. *Journal of Philosophy, 103*, 111–144.
McDaniel, K. (2009). Structure-making. *Australasian Journal of Philosophy, 87*, 251–274.
McGrath, M. (2014). Propositions. In E.N. Zalta (Ed.), *The Stanford Encyclopedia of Philosophy (Spring 2014 Edition)*. http://plato.stanford.edu/archives/spr2014/entries/propositions/.
Moggi, E. (1989). Computational lambda-calculus and monads. In *Proceedings of the fourth annual symposium on logic in computer science* (pp. 14–23). Piscataway, NJ: IEEE Press.
Moltmann, F. (2013). Propositions, attitudinal objects, and the distinction between actions and products. *Canadian Journal of Philosophy, 43*, 679–701.
Muskens, R. (2005). Sense and the computation of reference. *Linguistics and Philosophy, 28*, 473–504.
Pezlar, I. (2017). Algorithmic theories of problems. *Logic and Logical Philosophy*. doi:10.12775/LLP.2017.010.

Pickel, B. (2015). Are propositions essentially representational? *Pacific Philosophical Quarterly*. doi:10.1111/papq.12123.
Rabern, B. (2013). Monsters in Kaplan's logic of demonstratives. *Philosophical Studies, 164*, 393–404.
Russell, B. (1903). *Principles of Mathematics*. New York: Norton Library.
Russell, B. (1908/1968). Mathematical logic as based on the theory of types. Reprinted in R. C. Marsh (Ed.), *Logic and Knowledge, fourth impression*. New York: The MacMillan Company.
Sainsbury, M. (1996). How can some thing say something? In R. Monk, A. Palmer (Eds.), *Bertrand Russell and the origins of analytic philosophy* (pp. 137–153). Bristol: Thoemmes. Reprinted in *Departing From Frege*, Oxford: Routledge (2002).
Simons P (2000). *Parts: A study in ontology*. Oxford: Clarendon Press.
Soames, S. (2010). *What is meaning?*. Princeton: Princeton University Press.
Sundholm, B. G. (1983). Constructions, proofs, and the meaning of logical constants. *Journal of Philosophical Logic, 12*, 151–172.
Textor, M. (2017). Judgement, perception, and predication. In M. Textor & F. Moltmann (Eds.), *Act-based conceptions of propositional content*. New York: Oxford University Press.
Thomason, R. (1980). A model theory for attitudes. *Linguistics and Philosophy, 4*, 47–70.
Tichý, P. (1971). An approach to intensional analysis. *Nous, 5*, 273–297. Reprinted in Tichý (2004).
Tichý, P. (1980). Foundations of partial type theory. *Reports on Mathematical Logic, 14*, 59–72. Reprinted in Tichý (2004).
Tichý, P. (1986). Constructions. *Philosophy of Science, 53*, 514–534. Reprinted in Tichý (2004).
Tichý, P. (1988). *The foundations of Frege's logic*. Berlin: deGruyter.
Tichý, P. (1995). Constructions as the subject-matter of mathematics. In W. Depauli-Schimanovich, E. Köhler, F. Stadler (Eds.), *The foundational debate* (pp. 175–85), Dordrecht: Kluwer. Reprinted in Tichý (2004).
Tichý, P. (2004). Collected papers in logic and philosophy. In G. Cheyne, B. Jespersen, & V. Svoboda (Eds.), Prague: Filozofia; Dunedin: University of Otago Press.
Varzi, A. C. (2008). The extensionality of parthood and composition. *Philosophical Quarterly, 58*, 108–133.
Wittgenstein, L. (1922/1984). *Tractatus logico-philosophicus*. Reprinted as Suhrkamp Taschenbuch Wissenschaft (Vol. 501). Frankfurt: Suhrkamp.
Woods, W. A. (1981). Procedural semantics as a theory of meaning. In A. K. Joshi & B. L. Webber (Eds.), *Elements of discourse understanding* (pp. 300–334). Cambridge: Cambridge University Press.

If structured propositions are logical procedures then how are procedures individuated?

Marie Duží

Abstract This paper deals with two issues. First, it identifies structured propositions with logical procedures. Second, it considers various rigorous definitions of the granularity of procedures, hence also of structured propositions, and comes out in favour of one of them. As for the first point, structured propositions are explicated as algorithmically structured *procedures*. I show that these procedures are structured wholes that are assigned to expressions as their meanings, and their constituents are sub-procedures occurring in executed mode (as opposed to displayed mode). Moreover, procedures are not mere aggregates of their parts; rather, procedural constituents mutually interact. As for the second point, there is no universal criterion of the structural isomorphism of meanings, hence of co-hyperintensionality, hence of synonymy for every kind of language. The positive result I present is an ordered set of rigorously defined criteria of fine-grained individuation in terms of the structure of procedures. Hence procedural semantics provides a solution to the problem of the granularity of co-hyperintensionality.

Introduction

It is good and well that we philosophers of language and logicians invoke structured meanings as cornerstones of our respective semantic theories. But, first, what is the *structure* of structured meanings? And, second, how are structured meanings *individuated*? In this paper, I am going to investigate structured *procedures* in the role of structured linguistic meanings. The framework I will use is Tichý's transparent intensional logic (TIL) that comes with a *procedural* semantics, according to which the structured meaning of an expression is explicated as a *procedure* that produces at most one object, which is denoted by the expression.[1] In well-defined cases procedures fail to produce anything, which reflects the fact that there are meaningful terms that do not refer to anything, like 'the greatest prime number'. When an object is produced, the produced object is a possible-world semantic (PWS) intension in the case of empirical expressions, and an extension in the case of logical/mathematical expressions, or a (lower-order 'displayed') procedure, which is especially the case with the complements of hyperintensional attitudes. These procedures are rigorously defined in TIL as so-called *constructions*. The main points I will be arguing for below are these two:

- Structured meanings are *procedurally* structured. TIL constructions are procedurally structured wholes that are assigned to expressions as their meanings, and their constituents are sub-procedures occurring in executed mode (as opposed to displayed mode).
- There is no universal criterion of the structural isomorphism of meanings, hence of co-hyperintensionality, hence of synonymy for every kind of language.[2] Though the individuation of TIL constructions is rigorously defined, the individuation of structured meanings does not coincide seamlessly with the individuation of constructions. The *positive result* of this paper is that we can put forward an ordered set of rigorously defined criteria of fine-grained individuation in terms of procedural structure. Hence procedural semantics offers a principled solution to the problem of the granularity of co-hyperintensionality.

My starting point is provided by King (2014, p. 1).

It is a truism that two speakers can say the same thing by uttering different sentences, whether in the same or different languages. For example, when a German speaker utters the sentence 'Schnee ist weiß' and an English speaker utters the sentence 'Snow is white', they have said the same thing by uttering the sentences they did. Proponents of propositions hold that, speaking strictly, when speakers say the same thing by means of different declarative sentences, there is some (non-linguistic) thing, a *proposition*, that each has said.

The question that many logicians and philosophers have been worried about is what kind of object is this 'same thing', the 'proposition', that sentences can have in common. The two sentences 'Schnee ist weiß' and 'Snow is white' in the quote by King certainly have the same meaning, hence they are synonymous: the same thing they have in common is their *meaning*. Logically or analytically equivalent sentences also have something in common, though they may fail to be synonymous. For instance, sentences of the form "It is not true that if *A* then *B*" and "*A* and not *B*" are logically equivalent, yet I take it to be obvious that they do not have the same meaning.

---

[1] See Duží, Jespersen and Materna (2010, Chapters 1 and 2), and also Tichý (1988).
[2] Faroldi (2016) makes a similar point.

If structured propositions are logical procedures then how are procedures individuated?

Otherwise we would not have to teach students how to negate implicative sentences: linguistic competence would do. These two sentences share the same truth-conditions: whenever one is true, so is the other.[3]

Propositions should arguably perform many other functions in addition to being bearers of truth or falsity and being the things expressed by declarative sentences. They are commonly thought to be:[4]

- the meanings of sentences
- the objects that can be true or false
- the objects that are necessary, possible, or contingent, that is, bearers of modal properties
- the objects that can be true with a certain likelihood or to a certain degree, that is, bearers of probabilities or fuzzy degrees of truth
- the complements of propositional attitudes, that is, objects that can be understood, known, believed, desired, etc.
- the informational content of sentences

Obviously, one and the same 'thing' can hardly play all of these roles. Thus, several conceptions of propositions have been developed. While PWS-propositions modelled as functions from possible worlds and times to truth-values are the objects that can be true or false at this or that world and time, true to a certain degree, and arguably also objects that are necessary, (merely) possible or contingent, they are not the structured meanings of sentences, because as set-theoretical mappings they are not structured. Furthermore, they are too coarse-grained to serve as meanings in the first place, and as the complements of explicit propositional attitudes (which the agents are aware of having and can manipulate logically, as when acquiring inferential knowledge), because they are individuated only up to analytical equivalence.[5] Moreover, in Duží (2010) it has been shown that PWS-propositions cannot be bearers of the so-called analytic information content of sentences, because if they were the paradox of inference would be inevitable and analytically true sentences would convey no information and thus be useless.[6]

---

[3] When I say that the two sentences are logically equivalent I tacitly presuppose here that both A and B have a truth-value. In other words, I disregard the possibility of truth-value gaps. In the logic of partial functions, wide-scope and narrow-scope negation may fail to be equivalent. For details, see Duží (2017b).

[4] See, for instance, Pickel (2017).

[5] Hanks and Soames have recently presented theories of *complex acts* in a series of articles and books, see, for instance, Hanks (2011, 2015) and Soames (2012, 2014). Complex acts with which propositions are identified can differ with respect to different ways of cognizing objects and properties. *Distinct* complex acts can deal with the same objects, which have the same properties and stand in the same relations. In other words, these theories can handle the cases of distinct propositions expressed by analytically equivalent sentences denoting one and the same PWS-proposition.

[6] The paradox of inference was put forward in Cohen and Nagel (1934, p. 173). It goes roughly like this: since the conclusion of a valid argument is contained in the premises, it fails to provide any novel information. Yet Duží (2010) argues that it seems evident that there is *something* that we *learn* when deducing the conclusion of a sound argument. We obtain a new piece of analytic information about the *procedure* the product of which is the proposition (or truth-value, in the case of mathematics) denoted by the conclusion.

If structured propositions are logical procedures then how are procedures individuated?

One straightforward way to accommodate both fine-grained, structured propositions and coarse-grained, flat PWS-propositions within one and the same theory is to operate with two different levels with the former at the top and the latter ones below. This is the way we proceed in TIL. At the top, hyperintensional level, we explicate fine-grained propositions as *algorithmically structured procedures* that are assigned to sentences as their meanings. At the lower, intensional level are the PWS-propositions produced by these procedures as their products.

One might wonder what kind of an object our abstract structured procedure is, and what motivates us to explicate meanings as structured procedures. As for the former, let me say this. Procedures are neither set-theoretical mappings (Church's functions-in-extension), nor properties or types. Rather, they might be compared to functions-in-intension, as suggested by Church in (1941, pp. 2–3). To anticipate a possible misunderstanding, note that in the semantics of mathematics, the terms 'function-in-intension' and 'function-in-extension' are used in this sense: function-in-extension corresponds to the modern notion of a function as a set-theoretical mapping, and function-in-intension could arguably correspond to our notion of *procedure* producing a mapping. Thus function-in-intension is a structured *way* or *rule* laying down how to obtain a function-in-extension. Only I am hesitant to push the parallel, since function-in-intension remains a poorly-understood notion. See also Church (1956, pp. 2–3).

Maybe the best explanation of the character of abstract procedures is provided in Duží et al. (2010, §1.3, pp. 54–56). Briefly, abstract procedures are generalized algorithms, as suggested in Moschovakis (1994, 2006), see also van Lambalgen and Hamm (2004). In Moschovakis (2006) a procedure is an "(abstract, idealized, not necessarily implementable) algorithm" (2006, p. 27). Algorithms are normally understood to be effectively computable.[7] But not every procedure can be evaluated in an effective way. This is in particular the case of procedures that are assigned as meanings to *empirical* expressions. Their evaluation calls for an 'oracle' that supplies empirical facts.[8] For the most recent account of abstract procedures, I agree with Jespersen (2017a) which characterizes procedures in this way:

> [...] I identify structured propositions with particular kinds of objective logical (as opposed to, say, psychological or pragmatic) molecular procedures whose parts are sub-procedures (as opposed to entities such as mountains or numbers). The underlying logic is a typed function/argument logic that specifies which functions of which logical types are lined up to be applied to which arguments of which types to obtain values (if any) of which types. [...] Though modelled on a function/argument logic, procedures are not functions-in-extension, i.e., mappings. Nor are they set-theoretic sequences, nor, for that matter, the formulae of a symbolic notation. Instead they are Platonic, higher-order, fine-grained structures. Procedures, as I understand them, are neither set-theoretic, nor inscriptional, nor linguistic entities. They are mereological entities, because they are wholes with parts. Furthermore, procedures are governed by a mereology that cannot be fully extensional, because their parts interact with one another.

---

[7] See Cleland (2002) for discussion.

[8] For details, see Duží (2014).

If structured propositions are logical procedures then how are procedures individuated?

As for the latter question, i.e. the motivation to explicate the meanings of sentences, or generally of any linguistic terms, *procedurally*, I'd like to refer to Duží (2014a). To summarise the main ideas, there are two main reasons. The first one is obvious. That the structured meaning of a sentence cannot be a possible-world semantics proposition (PWS-proposition) should be obvious. A PWS-proposition is a set of possible worlds (and times); in this set, there is no trace of the structure of the respective sentence. For instance, Westerhoff (2005) criticizes the opinion that possible-world semantics is a proper tool for explaining the semantics of structures:

> Consider the sense in which states of affairs (possible worlds) could be taken to have parts. It is straightforward to argue that the state of affairs that John loves Becca has John as a part. But it is equally straightforward to argue that John's brain is part of the state of affairs that John loves Becca. But the mere parts (John's brain as opposed to John) are just any parts of that particular bit of the world we happen to be talking about, whether they take part in our *conceptualization* or not. (Ibid., p. 609).[9]

The second argument is this. How is it possible that we are able to learn a (new) language? On its standard conception, a language is a (potentially) infinite set of expressions. In order to obtain such an infinity, we need a sequence of instructions detailing which operations to apply to which operands that would make it feasible to get to know any (as opposed to every) element of the infinite set in a finite number of operational steps. I am in favour of the idea that this sort of sequence of instructions is exactly the sort of structured procedure I have been talking about so far.

The procedural character of structured meanings in mathematics should be obvious. For instance, when one is seeking the solution of the equation $sin(x) = 0$ he/she is not related to the infinite set $\{..., -2\pi, -\pi, 0, \pi, 2\pi, ...\}$, because otherwise the seeker would immediately be a finder and there would be nothing to solve. On the other hand, relating the seeker to a particular syntactic term is not general enough. The Ancient Greek or Babylonian mathematicians, for instance, would solve such an equation using a different syntactic system. Rather, the seeker is related to the very *procedure* consisting of these constituents: applying the function sine to a real number x, checking whether the value of the function is zero, and, if so, abstracting over the value of the input number x. When solving the equation, the seeker aims to execute this procedure to potentially produce the infinite set of multiples of π.

For an empirical example, consider the sentence "The Pope is a Pole". The sentence encodes an instruction how, in *any* possible world w at *any* time t, to evaluate its meaning procedure producing the reference of the sentence at the world w and time t of evaluation, i.e., a truth-value. This instruction consists of a few simple steps: take the individual office *Pope*; take the property of being a *native of Poland*; extensionalize the papal office, i.e., find out empirically who (if anybody) is the Pope at the world w and time t of evaluation (if there is no such individual, then finish with no truth-value); and finally, check (empirically) whether the individual occupying the papal office is a native of Poland in the world w and time t of evaluation; if so, produce the truth-value **T**, otherwise **F**.

---

[9] Similar arguments can be found also in Tichý (1995, pp. 179–80).

One might object that procedures cannot be true or false, and thus procedurally structured hyperpropositions cannot be intrinsically connected with truth-conditions.[10] But the same objection would be applicable to sentences themselves. A sentence is a piece of syntax endowed with meaning. Neither a piece of syntax, nor a PWS-proposition understood as a set of worlds and times, is true or false. What then does it mean that, for instance, the sentence "The Pope is a Pole" is true or false, or, as the case may be, has a truth-value gap? There is no mystery, however. It means that the evaluation of its procedural meaning in a given state-of-affairs as described above yields a truth-value or no truth-value. If evaluating the meaning procedure of the sentence "The Pope is a Pole" in the actual world in the period between October 16, 1978 and April 2, 2005, one obtains **T**. If evaluating after April 2 and before April 19, 2005, one obtains a truth-value gap. Later on, one obtains **F**.

Hence hyperpropositions that are typed to produce PWS-propositions, or truth-values in the case of mathematics, unambiguously *produce* truth-conditions, or truth-values, upon being executed, and in this way, they are intrinsically connected with truth-conditions. Hence, this objection serves no purpose.

Thus, I take it for granted that formal semantics demands a notion of hyperintensionality and that meanings of sentences, or generally of any expressions, are structured procedures. The focus of my research below is to put forward a formally precise and philosophically persuasive theory of fine-grained, structured meanings.

My background theory is TIL, as set out in Tichý (1988) and Duží et al. (2010). The formal apparatus of TIL will be fairly familiar to those who are acquainted with typed λ-calculi or Montague's IL system[11], because from the formal point of view TIL is a hyperintensional, partial, typed λ-calculus. It is partial, because we embrace properly partial functions; and hyperintensional, because TIL terms are interpreted procedurally, which is to say that they denote abstract *procedures* (roughly, Church's functions-in-intension) producing set-theoretical functions/mappings (Church's functions-in-extension) rather than the mappings themselves. This is actually in good harmony with the original interpretation of the terms of the λ-calculus, which was indeed procedural. For instance, Barendregt (1997, p. 184) says,

> [I]n this interpretation the notion of a function is taken to be intensional, i.e., as an algorithm.

I would prefer to say, "... is taken to be *hyperintensional*", because the term 'intensional' is currently reserved for mappings from possible worlds (if not among proof-theoretic semanticists, then at least among model-theoretic semanticists).

Thus, λ-Closure, $[\lambda x_1 ... x_n X]$, transforms into the very procedure of producing a function by abstracting over the values of the variables $x_1, ..., x_n$. Similarly, Composi-

---

[10] In order to terminologically distinguish truth-conditions (understood as functions from possible worlds and times to truth-values) from procedures producing truth-conditions, in what follows I will use the term '*PWS-propositions*' for the former, and the term '*hyperproposition*' for structured procedures producing PWS-propositions, or truth-values in the case of mathematics.

[11] Tichý's TIL was developed simultaneously with Montague's IL. For a critical comparison of TIL and IL, see Duží et al. (2010, §2.4.3).

tion, $[XX_1...X_n]$, transforms into the very procedure of applying a function produced by the procedure X to the tuple-argument (if any) produced by the procedures X_1, ..., X_n. The procedural semantics of TIL makes it possible to explicitly deal with those features that are otherwise hidden if dealing only with the products of the procedures, i.e. functions-in-extension. These features concern in particular operations in a hyperintensional context where the very procedure denoted by a term is being operated on. For instance, if Tilman calculates the cotangent of the number π, he is not related to a non-existing number. He is related to the *procedure* of applying the function *cotangent* to the number π, aiming to uncover the product of this procedure. And even if the function *cotangent* were defined at this number, it still makes no sense to compute a number without any procedure specifying how to obtain that number. Hence the procedure of applying the cotangent function at the number π is here the object of predication, making the context of calculating a hyperintensional one. In TIL we strictly distinguish between *procedures* producing set-theoretical functions and the *functions* (-in-extensions) themselves (including sets and atomic objects such as truth-values, numbers and individuals viewed as zero-place functions). Not to lose one's way in this stratified ontology all entities (including procedures) receive a type within a *ramified hierarchy of types*.

The rest of this paper is organised as follows. In Sect. 1 I introduce the relevant basic principles and definitions of TIL. Section 2 introduces the three kinds of context, namely hyperintensional, intensional and extensional ones, in which a TIL construction can occur. Section 3 deals with the mereological structure of TIL constructions. In Sect. 4 I deal with the problem of the individuation of structured procedures and the problem of synonymy. Section 5 contains some concluding remarks.

1 Basic principles of TIL

As mentioned above, the terms of the TIL symbolism denote abstract procedures that produce set-theoretical mappings (functions-in-extension) or lower-order procedures. These procedures are defined as TIL *constructions*.

Definition 1 (*Construction*)

(i) *Variables* x, y, ... are *constructions* that *construct* objects (elements of their respective ranges) dependently on a valuation v; they v-*construct*.
(ii) Where X is an object whatsoever (even a *construction*), ^0X is the *construction Trivialization* that *constructs* X without any change of X.
(iii) Let X, Y_1, ..., Y_n be arbitrary *constructions*. Then *Composition* $[XY_1...Y_n]$ is the following *construction*. For any v, the *Composition* $[XY_1...Y_n]$ is v-*improper* if at least one of the *constructions* X, Y_1, ..., Y_n is v-improper by failing to v-construct anything, or if X does not v-*construct* a function that is defined at the n-tuple of objects v-*constructed* by Y_1,...,Y_n. If X does v-*construct* such a function, then $[XY_1...Y_n]$ v-*constructs* the value of this function at the n-tuple.
(iv) (λ-) *Closure* $[\lambda x_1...x_m Y]$ is the following *construction*. Let $x_1, x_2, ..., x_m$ be pair-wise distinct variables and Y a *construction*. Then $[\lambda x_1...x_m Y]$ v-*constructs* the function f that takes any members $B_1, ..., B_m$ of the respective ranges of

the variables $x_1, \ldots, x_m$ into the object (if any) that is $v(B_1/x_1, \ldots, B_m/x_m)$ constructed by Y, where $v(B_1/x_1, \ldots, B_m/x_m)$ is like v except for assigning B_1 to $x_1, \ldots, B_m$ to x_m.

(v) Where X is an object whatsoever, ^1X is the *construction Single Execution* that v-constructs what X v-constructs. Thus, if X is a v-improper *construction* or not a *construction* as all, ^1X is v-*improper*.

(vi) Where X is an object whatsoever, ^2X is the *construction Double Execution*. If X is not itself a *construction*, or if X does not v-construct a *construction*, or if X v-constructs a v-improper *construction*, then ^2X is v-*improper*. Otherwise ^2X v-constructs what is v-constructed by the *construction* v-constructed by X.

(vii) Nothing is a *construction*, unless it so follows from (i) through (vi). □

Comments Being procedural objects, constructions can be executed in order to operate on input objects (of a lower-order type) and produce the object (if any) they are typed to produce, while non-procedural objects, i.e. non-constructions, cannot be executed. Hence the constituents of constructions cannot be non-procedural objects; non-procedural objects must be presented, or referred to, by atomic constructions. *Trivialization* and *Variables* are the two atomic constructions that present input objects (which can also be lower-order constructions) to be operated on. The operational sense of Trivialization is similar to that of constants in formal languages. A Trivialization presents an object X without the mediation of any other procedures. Using the terminology of programming languages, the Trivialization of X, '^0X' in symbols, is just a *pointer* referring to X. Variables produce objects dependently on valuations; they v-construct. We adopt an objectual variant of the Tarskian conception of variables. To each type (see Def. 2) are assigned countably many variables that range over this particular type. Objects of each type can be arranged into infinitely many sequences. The valuation v selects one such sequence of objects of the respective type, and the first variable v-constructs the first object of the sequence, the second variable v-constructs the second object of the sequence, and so on. Hence the execution of a Trivialization or a variable never fails to produce an object; these constructions are not v-improper for any valuation v. The (λ-) Closure $[\lambda x_1 \ldots x_m Y]$ is also not v-improper for any v, as it always v-constructs a function. Even if the constituent Y is v-improper for every valuation v, the Closure is not v-improper. Yet in such a case the constructed function is a bizarre object; it is a degenerate function that lacks a value at any argument. However, the other molecular constructions, namely Composition, Single and Double Execution, can fail to present an object of the type they are typed to produce, they can be v-*improper*. The main source of improperness is an application of a function to an argument at which the function is not defined.[12]

With constructions of constructions, constructions of functions, functions, and functional values in our stratified ontology, we need to keep track of the traffic between multiple logical strata. The *ramified type hierarchy* does just that. The type of first-order objects includes all non-procedural objects. Therefore, it includes not only the standard objects of individuals, truth-values, sets, functions, etc., but also functions

---

[12] The other source can be a type-theoretically incoherent ('nonsensical') way of composing a construction, for instance, by composing the Sun with being a natural number.

If structured propositions are logical procedures then how are procedures individuated?

defined on possible worlds (i.e., the intensions germane to possible-world semantics). The type of second-order objects includes constructions of first-order objects and functions with such constructions in their domain or range. The type of third-order objects includes constructions of first- and second-order objects and functions with such constructions in their domain or range; and so on, ad infinitum.

Definition 2 (*Ramified hierarchy of types*). Let B be a *base*, where a base is a collection of pair-wise disjoint, non-empty sets. Then:

$\mathbf{T}_1$(*types of order 1*).

(i) Every member of B is an elementary *type of order 1 over B*.
(ii) Let $\alpha, \beta_1, \ldots, \beta_m$ ($m > 0$) be types of order 1 over B. Then the collection $(\alpha \beta_1 \ldots \beta_m)$ of all m-ary partial mappings from $\beta_1 \times \ldots \times \beta_m$ into α is a functional *type of order 1 over B*.
(iii) Nothing is a *type of order 1 over B* unless it so follows from (i) and (ii).

$\mathbf{C}_n$ (*constructions of order n*)

(i) Let x be a variable ranging over a type of order n. Then x is a *construction of order n over B*.
(ii) Let X be a member of a type of order n. Then ^0X, ^1X, ^2X are *constructions of order n over B*.
(iii) Let $X, X_1, \ldots, X_m$ ($m > 0$) be constructions of order n over B. Then $[X X_1 \ldots X_m]$ is a *construction of order n over B*.
(iv) Let $x_1, \ldots, x_m, X$ ($m > 0$) be constructions of order n over B. Then $[\lambda x_1 \ldots x_m X]$ is a *construction of order n over B*.
(v) Nothing is a *construction of order n over B* unless it so follows from $\mathbf{C}_n$ (i)–(iv).

$\mathbf{T}_{n+1}$(*types of order n + 1*)
Let $*_n$ be the collection of all constructions of order n over B. Then

(i) $*_n$ and every type of order n are *types of order n + 1*.
(ii) If $m > 0$ and $\alpha, \beta_1, \ldots, \beta_m$ are types of order $n + 1$ over B, then $(\alpha \beta_1 \ldots \beta_m)$ (see $\mathbf{T}_1$ ii)) is a *type of order n + 1 over B*.
(iii) Nothing is a *type of order n + 1 over B* unless it so follows from (i) and (ii). □

For the purposes of natural language analysis, we are assuming the following base of ground types:

ο: the set of truth-values $\{\mathbf{T}, \mathbf{F}\}$;
ι: the set of individuals (the universe of discourse);
τ: the set of real numbers (doubling as discrete times);
ω: the set of logically possible worlds (the logical space).

We model sets and relations by their characteristic functions. Thus, for instance, (ο ι) is the type of a set of individuals, while (ο ι ι) is the type of a relation-in-extension between individuals. Empirical expressions denote *empirical conditions* that may or may not be satisfied at the particular world/time pair of evaluation. These empirical conditions are modelled as possible-world-semantic *(PWS) intensions*. PWS intensions are entities of type (β ω): mappings from possible worlds to an arbitrary type β. The type β is frequently the type of the *chronology* of α-objects, i.e., a mapping of type (α τ). Thus α-intensions are frequently functions of type ((α τ) ω), abbreviated as '$α_{τω}$'. *Extensional entities* are entities of a type α where α ≠ (β ω) for any type β. Where w ranges over ω and t over τ, the following logical form essentially characterizes the logical syntax of empirical language: $λwλt[...w....t...]$.

Examples of frequently used PWS intensions are: propositions of type $o_{τω}$, properties of individuals of type $(oι)_{τω}$, binary relations-in-intension between individuals of type $(oιι)_{τω}$, individual offices (or roles) of type $ι_{τω}$, attitudes to constructions of type $(oι *_n)_{τω}$.

Logical objects like *truth-functions* are extensional: ∧ (conjunction), ∨ (disjunction) and ⊃ (implication) are of type (o o o), and ¬ (negation) of type (o o). Below all type indications will be provided outside the formulae in order not to clutter the notation. The outermost brackets of the Closure will be omitted whenever no confusion arises. Furthermore, '$X/α$' means that an object X is (a member) of type α . '$X →_v α$' means that X is typed to v-construct an object of type α, if any. We write '$X → α$' if what is v- constructed does not depend on a valuation v. Throughout, it holds that the variables $w →_v ω$ and $t →_v τ$. If $C →_v α_{τω}$ then the frequently used Composition $[[Cw]t]$, which is the intensional descent (a.k.a. extensionalization) of the α-intension v-constructed by C, will be encoded as 'C_{wt}'. Whenever no confusion arises, we use traditional infix notation without Trivialisation for truth-functions and the identity relation, to make the terms denoting constructions easier to read.

2 Displayed versus executed constructions

Here I go through the two modes in which constructions (procedures) can occur, either displayed or executed. This distinction is a crucial ingredient of my account of the constituents of structured propositions, as they themselves are also procedures.

When a construction occurs *displayed*, then the *construction* itself becomes the object on which other constructions can operate; we say that it occurs *hyperintensionally*. When a construction occurs *executed*, then the *product* of the construction is the object to operate on.[13] In this case the executed construction is a *constituent* of its super-construction, and an additional distinction can be found at this level. The constituent presenting a function may occur either *intensionally* (de dicto) or *extensionally* (de re). If intensionally, then the produced *function* is the object of predication; if extensionally, then the *value* of the produced function is the object of predication. The two distinctions, between displayed/executed and intensional/extensional occurrence, enable us to distinguish between three kinds of *context*. The rigorous definitions of the three kinds of contexts can be found in Duží et al. (2010, §2.6). The exact details are rather complicated, though the basic ideas are fairly simple. Thus, here I only explain the main ideas, with the rigorous definition of displayed vs. executed occurrence of a construction coming afterwards.

---

[13] If there is no such product, the construction is v-improper.

If structured propositions are logical procedures then how are procedures individuated?

- *Hyperintensional context* a construction occurs in *displayed* mode (though another construction at least one order higher needs to be executed in order to produce the displayed construction)
- *Intensional context* a construction occurs in *executed* mode in order to produce a function rather than its value (moreover, the executed construction does not occur within another hyperintensional context)
- *Extensional context* a construction occurs in *executed* mode in order to produce a particular value of a function at a given argument (moreover, the executed construction does not occur within another intensional or hyperintensional context).

The basic idea underlying the above trifurcation is that the same set of logical rules applies to all three kinds of context, but these rules operate on different complements: procedures, produced functions, and functional values, respectively. Having defined the three kinds of context, we are thus in a position to build up TIL as an extensional logic of hyperintensions.[14]

The analysis of the meaning of an expression consists in furnishing the expression with the construction encoded by it. The meaning of an empirical sentence is a construction that is typed to produce a PWS-proposition, and the meaning of a mathematical/logical sentence is a construction that is typed to produce a truth-value. If a construction C is typed to produce a truth-value ($C \to_v o$) or a PWS-proposition ($C \to_v o_{\tau\omega}$) then C is a *hyperproposition*.

When assigning a construction to a sentence (or generally to a piece of language), we apply a three-step *method of analysis*. First, we assign types to the objects that receive mention in the sentence. Second, we combine *constructions* of these objects so that to obtain a hyperproposition that constructs the PWS-proposition or a truth-value denoted by the sentence. Finally, we apply type-theoretical control to check whether the resulting hyperproposition is composed in a type-theoretically coherent way. To this end, we often draw a derivation tree; yet the tree is *not* the structure, it is just a graphic representation of the hyperpropositional structure.

Since the distinction between executed and displayed occurrence of a construction plays a significant role in particular in attitudinal sentences, I will use as a paradigmatic example the attitude of calculating. When a calculates something, for instance $2+5$ or cotangent of the number π, a is not related to the number 7 or to a non-existing number, respectively. It makes no sense to calculate a number without any mathematical operation. Rather, a is related to the very *procedure* expressed by the terms '$2+5$' or 'cotangent of π'; a wants to find out what the procedure in question produces. Thus, *Calculate* is of type $(o \iota *_1)_{\tau\omega}$: relation-in-intension of an individual to a construction of a number. Here is the analysis of the sentence "Tom calculates the cotangent of π" followed by its derivation tree accompanied by type assignments.

(i) *Type analysis. Tom*/ι; *Calculate*/$(o \iota *_1)_{\tau\omega}$; *Cot(angent)*/$(\tau\tau)$; π / τ.
(ii) *Synthesis.* In order to apply the relation-in-intension *Calculate* to its two arguments, we have to extensionalize it first: $[[^0Calculate\ w]t]$, or $^0Calculate_{wt}$ for short. Since Tom is related to the very procedure $[^0Cot\ ^0\pi]$ of applying the function *Cotangent* to the number π rather than to its non-existing product,

---

[14] For details see Duží (2012).

the Composition [$^0Cot\ ^0\pi$] must be Trivialized in order to become displayed: $^0[^0Cot\ ^0\pi]$. The agent, Tom, also must be pinpointed by Trivialization, as explained above. Thus, we have [$^0Calculate_{wt}\ ^0Tom\ ^0[^0Cot\ ^0\pi]] \to_v o$. Finally, abstracting over the values of the variables w, t, we construct the PWS-proposition denoted by the sentence:
$\lambda w \lambda t [^0Calculate_{wt}\ ^0Tom\ ^0[^0Cot\ ^0\pi]] \to_v o_{\tau\omega}$

(iii) *Derivation tree.*

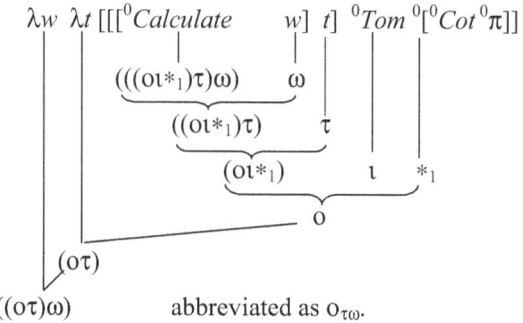

abbreviated as $o_{\tau\omega}$.

The resulting type is the type of a PWS-proposition.

Note that the types of the objects that the constructions $^0\pi, ^0Cot$ and [$^0Cot\ ^0\pi$] are typed to produce (i.e., τ, ($\tau\tau$) and τ, respectively) are irrelevant here. This is since Composition [$^0Cot\ ^0\pi$] occurs here only displayed as an argument of the relation $^0Calculate_{wt}$. In any world w and time t, the evaluation of the truth-conditions of the analysed sentence amounts just to checking whether Tom does calculate Cotangent of π, i.e. the execution of the Composition

[$^0Calculate_{wt}\ ^0Tom\ ^0[^0Cot\ ^0\pi]]$;

yet execution of this Composition does not involve the execution of the procedure [$^0Cot\ ^0\pi$]; this is the futile activity Tom is trying to do.

To put these ideas on more solid grounds, we define:

Definition 3 (*Subconstruction*). Let C be a construction. Then

(i) C is a *subconstruction of C*.
(ii) If C is $^0X, ^1X$ or ^2X and X is a construction, then X is a *subconstruction of C*.
(iii) If C is [$X X_1 \ldots X_n$] then $X, X_1, \ldots, X_n$ are *subconstructions of C*.
(iv) If C is [$\lambda x_1 \ldots x_n Y$] then Y is a *subconstruction of C*.
(v) If A is a *subconstruction of B* and B is a *subconstruction of C* then A is a *subconstruction of C*.
(vi) A construction is a *subconstruction of C* only if it so follows from (i)–(v). □

As mentioned above, it is important for our theory of procedurally structured constructions that a construction can be not only executed as a procedural whole to produce an object (if any) but can itself figure as an argument or value of a function produced by another construction of a higher order. Yet the constituents of a construction are *not* the particular material or abstract objects that the construction operates on. Rather, *the*

If structured propositions are logical procedures then how are procedures individuated? *constituents are only those sub-constructions that occur in executed mode*; those that occur as objects to be operated on are *displayed* as arguments or values. To define the distinction between displayed and executed mode, we must take the following into account:

- a construction C can occur in displayed mode only as a subconstruction of another construction D that operates on C;
- C itself has, therefore, to be constructed by another subconstruction C' of D; and
- it is necessary to define this distinction for *occurrences* of constructions, because one and the same construction C can occur executed in D and at the same time serve as an input/output object for another subconstruction C' of D that operates on C.

The distinction between displayed and execution mode of a construction is characterised as follows, with a rigorous definition following afterwards.

Displayed versus executed subconstruction Let C be a subconstruction of a construction D. Then an occurrence of C is displayed in D if the execution of D does not involve the execution of this occurrence of C. Otherwise, an occurrence of C is executed in D and C occurs as a constituent of D.

A simple example to illustrate the situation. Consider this argument.

(Calc)
$$\frac{\text{Tilman calculates } 2+5}{\text{Tilman calculates } 7.}$$
$$2+5 = 7$$

The conclusion is obviously unreasonable, and probably even nonsensical, for how could anybody be calculating anything in the absence of an arithmetical operation? The reason why the substitution within the first premise based on the identity specified by the second premise is invalid is this. There is a substantial difference between using the term '2 + 5' in the first and the second premise. The first premise expresses Tilman's relation(-in-intension) to the very procedure of applying the function plus to the arguments 2 and 5. Tilman is trying to execute this procedure, and the *procedure*, which is the meaning of '2 + 5', is *displayed* as an argument of calculating in the first premise. The evaluation of the truth-conditions expressed by the first premise consists in any possible world w at any time t in checking whether Tilman is in the extensionalized relation of calculating to the procedure of adding 2 and 5. Hence the execution of the hyperproposition expressed by the first premise does not involve the execution of the procedure of adding 2 and 5; this is something Tilman is responsible for. On the other hand, in the second premise the *procedure* of adding 2 and 5 is *executed* to identify the result with the number 7.

The analyses of premises P_1, P_2 are:

P_1: $\lambda w \lambda t [^0 Calculate_{wt} {}^0Tilman\ {}^0[^0+\ {}^02\ {}^05]]$ /∗2, → $o_{\tau\omega}$

P_2: $[^0 = [^0+\ {}^02\ {}^05]\ {}^07]$ /∗1, → o.

Types: $Tilman/\iota$; $Calculate/(\text{o}\iota *_1)_{\tau\omega}$; $+/(\tau\tau\tau)$; 2, 5, 7/τ; $=/(\text{o}\tau\tau)$.

If structured propositions are logical procedures then how are procedures individuated?

It should be obvious that the identity specified by P_2, namely the identity of the number presented by the Trivialization $^0 7$ and by the Composition $[^0+ {}^0 2\, {}^0 5]$, does not make the substitution of $^0 7$ for the Trivialization $^0[^0+ {}^0 2\, {}^0 5]$ in P_1 possible. Such a substitution would constitute a type-theoretical category mistake, attempting as it would to substitute an entity of one type for an entity of another type, because $^0 7$ constructs the number 7 while $^0[^0+ {}^0 2\, {}^0 5]$ constructs the Composition $[^0+ {}^0 2\, {}^0 5]$. This goes to show that the occurrence of $[^0+ {}^0 2\, {}^0 5]$ is *displayed* in the P_1 premise by another constituent of P_1, namely the Trivialization $^0[^0+ {}^0 2\, {}^0 5]$, whereas it is *executed* in P_2. This particular occurrence of $^0[^0+ {}^0 2\, {}^0 5]$, in turn, occurs executed in P_1.

The *execution* steps specified by P_1, i.e., the *constituent parts* of P_1, are as follows.

(1) $\lambda w \lambda t [^0 Calculate_{wt}\, {}^0 Tilman\, {}^0[^0+ {}^0 2\, {}^0 5]]$
(2) $\lambda t [^0 Calculate_{wt}\, {}^0 Tilman\, {}^0[^0+ {}^0 2\, {}^0 5]]$
(3) $[^0 Calculate_{wt}\, {}^0 Charles\, {}^0[^0+ {}^0 2\, {}^0 5]]$
(4) $^0 Calculate_{wt}$
(5) $[^0 Calculate\, w]$
(6) $^0 Calculate$
(7) w
(8) t
(9) $^0 Tilman$
(10) $^0[^0+ {}^0 2\, {}^0 5]$

Note that each construction is a part of itself, hence the Closure (1) is a constituent of itself. The other constituents are *proper parts* of (1). The Composition $[^0+ {}^0 2\, {}^0 5]$ is not a part of (1), it occurs displayed in (1) as an object on which the other constituent parts operate.

Constructions are displayed by Trivialization. As the above examples illustrate, all the subconstructions of a displayed construction occur displayed as well. A context in which a construction occurs displayed is a hyperintensional context. It might seem that in order to define rigorously the distinction between displayed and executed occurrence it would suffice to say that a construction occurs displayed if it occurs within the scope of a Trivialization. Alas, matters are more complex than that. The complicating factor is this. Trivialization has a dual operation, namely Double Execution. It follows from Definition 2, (vi) that while Trivialization raises the context to the hyperintensional level, Double execution cancels the effect of Trivialization, because this law is valid: $^{20}C = C$. Therefore, the effect of Trivialization is voided by Double Execution.

Thus, we define:

Definition 4 (*Displayed vs. executed occurrence of a construction*) Let C be a construction and D a subconstruction of C.

(i) If D is identical to C then the *occurrence of D is executed in C*.
(ii) If C is identical to $[X_1 X_2 ... X_m]$ and D is identical to one of the constructions $X_1, X_2, ..., X_m$, then the *occurrence of D is executed in C*.
(iii) If C is identical to $[\lambda x_1 ... x_m X]$ and D is identical to X, then the *occurrence of D is executed in C*.
(iv) If C is identical to $^1 X$ and D is identical to X, then the *occurrence of D is executed in C*.

If structured propositions are logical procedures then how are procedures individuated?

(v) If C is identical to ^2X and D is identical to X, or ^0D occurs executed in X and this occurrence of D occurs executed in Y v-constructed by X, then the *occurrence of D is executed in C*.

(vi) If an occurrence of D is executed in C' and this occurrence of C' is executed in C, then the *occurrence of D is executed in C*.

(vii) If an occurrence of a subconstruction D of C is not executed in C then the *occurrence of D is displayed in C*.

(viii) No occurrence of a subconstruction D of C is executed/displayed in C unless it so follows from (i)–(vii).

Remark If a construction D is displayed in C then all the variables occurring in D are Trivialization-bound in C, i.e. bound by Trivialization. *Proof* follows from Definition 4; if D is displayed in C then there is a construction D' such that $^0D'$ is, and D' is not, executed as a constituent of C, and D is a subconstruction of D'.

Definition 5 (*Constituent part of a construction*) Let C be a construction and D a subconstruction of C. Then any occurrence of D is a *constituent part* of C if the occurrence is executed in C.

Corollary *Since a construction C occurs executed in itself (as per Def. 4, i), C is a constituent part of C. Other subconstructions of C occurring in the execution mode (as per Def. 4, ii, iii, iv, v) are proper constituent parts of the construction C.*

Claim 1 The relation of being a constituent part of a construction is a partial order on the collection of constructions.

Proof

(a) *Reflexivity* follows immediately from Def. 4, (i)
(b) *Transitivity* follows immediately from Def. 4, (vi)
(c) *Antisymmetry* Suppose that C_1 is a part of C_2 and C_2 is a part of C_1, and C_1 is not identical with C_2. Then Def. 4, i) is not applicable. Hence C_1 is a *proper* part of C_2 and C_2 is a *proper* part of C_1. This contradicts the corollary of Def. 5, because none of the items (ii), (iii), (iv) and (v) of Def. 4 is applicable. Hence C_1 is identical to C_2.

Definition 6 (*Atomic and molecular constructions*). A *construction* is *atomic* if it does not contain any other constituents but itself. If a construction has at least one proper constituent part, then the *construction* is *molecular.*

Corollary *A construction C is atomic if C is*

- *a variable, or*
- *a Trivialization ^0X, where X is an object of any type, even a construction*
- *a Single execution ^1X where X is an object of a type of order 1, that is, X is not a construction*
- *a Double execution ^2X where X is an object of a type of order 1, that is, X is not a construction.*

3 On the mereological structure of constructions

Above we saw that each construction is a structured whole with unambiguously determined constituent parts. Moreover, each construction can be executed as a whole to yield at most one object, and each construction can itself figure as a whole object on which other constructions operate. That an atomic construction is a whole is trivially true, because an atomic construction is a constituent part of itself (Def. 4, i). Now the question arises what *unifies* the *proper* parts of a molecular construction. The proper constituents of a molecular construction *interact* by producing functions and their values. The product of one or more constituents becomes an argument of the function produced by another constituent. If one or more constituents fail to produce an object (that is, if they are v-improper) the whole construction which is typed to operate on this object fails as well (that is, the whole construction comes out v-improper), because the process of producing an output object has been interrupted. Hence, constructions (or procedures in general) are not mere aggregates of their proper parts. The elements of an aggregate lack '*direct connection inter se*' even when they are organised in an ordered sequence or list. And direct connection inter se is exactly what makes something *parts* of a whole.[15]

A simple example to illustrate the interaction in question. The Composition $[^0+\ ^02\ ^05]$ is the procedure of applying the function + to the couple of numbers 2 and 5 (in this order) to produce the value of + at this couple. Using programming-language jargon, the execution of this procedure can be described as follows. Since the constituent part $^0+$ is composed with ^{02} and ^{05}, it *calls* the other two constituent parts, ^{02}, ^{05}, to yield their respective products, namely the numbers 2 and 5, so that the couple (2, 5) can serve as the argument of the function + produced by $^0+$. In this way, the execution of the whole Composition produces the value of the function + at the argument (2, 5), to wit, the number 7.[16]

Similarly, the Closure $\lambda x[^0+\ x\ ^01]$, when executed, produces the successor function. Again, using programming jargon, it is a procedure with the formal parameter x. Whenever the actual argument n is substituted for x into the procedural 'body' $[^0+\ x\ ^01]$, the body produces n's successor, the number $n + 1$. Since this process can be executed for *any* number n, by abstracting over the values of n the mapping from naturals to their successors is produced.

Now we can compare the structure of abstract procedures (TIL constructions) with Classical Extensional Mereology (CEM). Cotnoir (2013) recapitulates the three main principles of CEM as follows.

Extensionality If x and y have the same mereological make-up, then x and y are identical.
Antisymmetry If x is part of y and y part of x, then x and y are identical.
Idempotency If x is a proper part of y, then the sum of x and y is identical to y.

---

[15] See Russell (1996: §136). For more on interaction between parts, see Jespersen (2017b).

[16] The fact that 7 is the number produced is a piece of mathematical knowledge external to the above Composition; 7 is not mentioned above. If we wanted to indicate that this particular number is produced, we would specify the identity $[[^0+\ ^02\ ^05] = ^07]$.

If structured propositions are logical procedures then how are procedures individuated?

The principle of antisymmetry has been proved in Claim 1.

The principle of idempotency can be formulated like this. It is not possible to add a further occurrence of a proper part x to y, because any such 'addition' would be 'swallowed up' by the existing occurrence of x. In other words, one thing cannot be part of the same whole twice or more times over. This seems to be a valid principle for material entities, but obviously does not hold for abstract entities such as structured procedures. One and the same constituent sub-construction can occur twice or more times in a whole construction. A simple example: the Composition $[^0+\ {}^02\ {}^02]$ of applying the addition function + to the couple (2, 2) has two occurrences of the part ^{02}.[17] Moreover, we *cannot* simply *add* another proper part to an unambiguously determined structured whole. If we wish to iterate a part (i.e. add another instance of a part already found in the whole), we must also determine the *way* this additional part is composed with the other parts; this addition makes for *another* construction. For a simple example, consider the constructions $A, B \to $ o that are typed to produce a truth-value. Then the constructions $[A \supset B]$, $[[A \land A] \supset B]$ are *not identical*, though they are equivalent by producing the same truth-value. These two Compositions are two distinct procedures, because the latter instructs us to process a conjunction whereas the former contains just one of the conjuncts. The truth-conditional idempotency between A and $[A \land A]$ is irrelevant to the absence of mereological idempotency between them.

Extensionality, as expressed by "Same parts = same whole", is in classical mereology of material objects a subject of much dispute.[18] In this paper I am disregarding the mereology of concrete entities, such as bronze statues and the chunks of bronze they are made of, and focusing on the mereology of *abstract* logical procedures. In the mereology of abstract procedures (TIL constructions, in my case), the principle of extensionality is trivially valid if it is applied both to proper and improper parts, because it is tantamount to reflexivity, as has been proved above. The stronger principle

"The same *proper* parts = the same whole"

is, however, *not valid*. The failure of the stronger extensionality axiom was obvious already to Bernard Bolzano. In his (1837) Bolzano shows that the mere sum of the components of the content of a concept does not define the concept.[19] We have to take into account the *way of composing* these components.[20] Bolzano worked out a systematic realist theory of concepts (*Vorstellungen an sich*), construing concepts as

---

[17] In this respect, the structure of constructions is similar to the formal mereology introduced in Bennet (2013).

[18] For instance, Cotnoir illustrates this problem in (ibid., p. 835): "The classic counterexample to extensionality involves objects (e.g., a statue) and the matter which constitutes them (e.g., a lump of clay). They presumably have different properties: e.g., the clay can survive squashing whereas the statue cannot. They must, therefore, be different objects. Yet every part of one appears to be part of the other. Their structure (insofar as mereology is concerned, anyway) is exactly the same. Another example involves the construction of two objects by a rearrangement of the same parts. Suppose my son builds a house out of some Lego bricks. He then destroys the house (as he often does) and proceeds to build a boat from the same Lego bricks. Is the house identical to the boat? Or are they distinct? Extensionality would seem to force us to identify the two."

[19] A theory of concepts has been worked out in TIL by Materna in (1998, 2004). We explicate concepts as closed constructions in their normal form. For details, see also Duží et al. (2010, §2.2).

[20] "die *Art,wie* diese Theile untereinander verbunden sind" (1837, §244).

If structured propositions are logical procedures then how are procedures individuated?

objective entities endowed with *structure*. Our theory is continuous with this conception. Traditional theories of concepts built on the Port Royal school define a concept as a couple consisting of an *extension* (*Umfang*) and an *intension* (*Inhalt*, or content). The intension of a concept C is the sum of features or sub-concepts $C_1,...,C_n$, while the extension of C is the intersection of the sets of objects having these features by falling under the sub-concepts $C_1,...,C_n$. Thus, the so-called *Law of inverse proportion of extension and intension* (the more components in the intension, the fewer elements in the extension, and vice versa) is valid within the framework of Port Royal logic. For instance, the extension of the concept *Prague inhabitants* is greater than that of *Prague inhabitants speaking German*. Bolzano criticizes this Law in (1837: §120). He adduces an example of a pair of concepts for which the Law is not valid.

1. A man who understands all European languages
2. A man who understands all *living* European languages

The first concept contains *fewer components* than the second one but (contra the Law) its extension is *smaller* than the extension of the second concept. This is due to the fact that the actual-world set of all European languages that ever existed, currently exist or once will exist is greater than the set of all living (i.e. currently spoken) European languages, hence there are *fewer* people falling under this more exacting concept. By this example, Bolzano wants to show that the *way* of composing particular components is important. The classical Port Royal theory of concepts presupposes only a *conjunctive* method of composition.[21] The 'sum' of the components of an intension is meant as their conjunctive connection. Then, of course, the Law is an elementary consequence of set theory. However, if the way of composing is not conjunctive, the Law does not hold. For instance, the Law holds for the concepts expressed by '*Prague citizens speaking Czech*' and '*Prague citizens speaking Czech and German*'. However, it obviously does not hold for the concepts expressed by '*Prague citizens speaking Czech*' and '*Prague citizens speaking Czech or German*'.

Not only that; Bolzano also shows that a concept is not the same thing as its intension/content. As an example, Bolzano considers two mathematical concepts, 3^5 and 5^3. These concepts have exactly the same proper parts, namely the respective concepts of the numbers 3 and 5, and the concept of the power function. Yet 3^5 and 5^3 are different concepts. This is due to the fact that the procedure of raising 3 to the power of 5 is different from the procedure of raising 5 to the power of 3.

$$^0[^0Power\ ^03\ ^05] \neq {}^0[^0Power\ ^05\ ^03]$$

Types $Power/(\tau\,\tau\,\tau)$; $3,5/\tau$; $[^0Power\ ^03\ ^05], [^0Power\ ^05\ ^03]/*_1 \to \tau$; $^0[^0Power\ ^03\ ^05]/*_2 \to *_1$; $^0[^0Power\ ^05\ ^03]/*_2 \to *_1$; $\neq/(o*_1*_1)$: the relation of not being identical between constructions of order 1.

Even if constructions C_1 and C_2 produce the same object and have the same proper parts, they can be non-identical. For instance, according to Def. 1, Compositions

---

[21] By these critical remarks, I do not want to imply that the classical concept theory is not useful. There are many useful applications of this theory. So-called Formal Concept Analysis has been successfully applied in computer science. For details, see, e.g., Ganter and Wille (1999).

If structured propositions are logical procedures then how are procedures individuated? $[^0+\ ^02\ ^05]$ and $[^0+\ ^05\ ^02]$ are not identical, though they consist of the same proper parts and produce the same number:

$$[^0+\ ^02\ ^05] = [^0+\ ^05\ ^02]$$

but

$$^0[^0+\ ^02\ ^05] \neq\ ^0[^0+\ ^05\ ^02]$$

Types $+/(\tau\tau\tau);\ 2,5/\tau;\ [^0+\ ^02\ ^05],\ [^0+\ ^05\ ^02]/*_1\ \to\ \tau;\ =/(o\tau\tau);\ ^0[^0+\ ^02\ ^05],\ ^0[^0+\ ^05\ ^02]/*_2 \to *_1;\ \neq /(o*_1*_1)$.

Again, this is as it should be. The respective meanings of the terms '2 + 5' and '5 + 2' are insufficient in order to prove that they are equivalent. It must, furthermore, be *proved* that the addition function is commutative, using, for instance, the axioms of Peano arithmetic.

4 Hyperintensionality and inferences

As mentioned above, the basic idea underlying our distinction between the three kinds of context in which a construction can occur is that the same set of logical rules applies to all three kinds of context, but these rules are properly applicable to objects of different types. In an extensional context, the relevant objects are the values of the constructed functions; in an intensional context, the produced functions themselves; and in a hyperintensional context, the constructions themselves.

The rules that operate in an extensional or intensional context are easy to specify, for instance, in the standard manner of the λ-calculi, because in an intensional context equivalent constructions are substitutable, that is, constructions v-constructing the same object for every valuation v.[22] However, applying logical rules into a hyperintensional context is far from being straightforward. The technical complications we are confronted with are rooted in *displayed* constructions, because a displayed construction cannot at the same time be executed. The original motivation for hyperintensionality was a negative one. Whenever substitution of logically/analytically equivalent terms fails, the context was declared hyperintensional. Thus, the main reason for introducing hyperintensionality was originally to block various inferences that were argued on philosophical grounds to be invalid. Naturally, the converse question arises as to which arguments involving hyperintensional contexts are valid. I am going to deal with these two issues now.

4.1 Invalid inferences

Consider this argument:[23]

$$\frac{\text{Tilman is seeking his brother}}{\text{Tilman is seeking his male sibling}}$$

---

[22] For the rules of substitution see Duží, Materna (2017), and for the rules of existential quantification see Duží and Jespersen (2015).

[23] Church (1951, n. 15) offers various examples of non-propositional attitudes, including the famous example of Ponce de León searching the fountain of youth.

If structured propositions are logical procedures then how are procedures individuated?

Is this argument valid? In my opinion, it is not. Tilman can be seeking his brother without him seeking his male sibling, though both 'male sibling of' and 'brother of' denote one and the same attribute.[24] To get the example of Tilman seeking his brother and not seeking his male sibling off the ground, I am stipulating that 'is a brother of' and 'is a male sibling of' are a pair not of synonymous but merely equivalent predicates. Their respective meanings are co-intensional, but not co-hyperintensional. The rationale for this stipulation is that the latter predicate has a molecular structure thanks to the application of the modifier denoted by 'male' to the attribute denoted by 'sibling', whereas the former predicate is atomic.[25] Hence this is a case where the mode of presentation of one and the same intension matters.[26] In this case an intensional analysis will yield a contradiction, because Tilman would be related, and at the same time not related, to one and the same property by the *seeking* relation.[27]

Here is the proof of the contradiction. First, the property to which Tilman is related is constructed by this Closure: $\lambda w \lambda t [^0 Brother\_of_{wt}\ ^0 Tilman]$. Thus, the analysis of the premise is this construction:[28]

$$\lambda w \lambda t [^0 Seek_{wt}\ ^0 Tilman\ \lambda w \lambda t [^0 Brother\_of_{wt}\ ^0 Tilman]]$$

Types: Seek/$(\omicron\iota(\omicron\iota)_{\tau\omega})_{\tau\omega}$: the relation-in-intension of an individual to a property the instance of which the seeker wants to find; *Tilman*/ι; *Brother_of*/$((\omicron\iota)\iota)_{\tau\omega}$: attribute, i.e., an empirical function associating an individual with a set of individuals, his or her brothers.

The proof of the contradiction is this:

(1) $\lambda w \lambda t\ [^0 Seek_{wt}\ ^0 Tilman\ \lambda w \lambda t [^0 Brother\_of_{wt}\ ^0 Tilman]]$ Ø
(2) $\lambda w \lambda t \neg [^0 Seek_{wt}\ ^0 Tilman\ \lambda w \lambda t [[^0 Male\ ^0 Sibling\_of]_{wt}\ ^0 Tilman]]$ Ø
(3) $[^0 Seek_{wt}\ ^0 Tilman\ \lambda w \lambda t [^0 Brother\_of_{wt}\ ^0 Tilman]]$ λ-elimination, 1)
(4) $\neg [^0 Seek_{wt}\ ^0 Tilman\ \lambda w \lambda t [[^0 Male\ ^0 Sibling\_of]_{wt}\ ^0 Tilman]]$ λ-elimination, 2)
(5) $[\lambda w \lambda t [[^0 Brother\_of]_{wt}\ ^0 Tilman] = \lambda w \lambda t [[^0 Male\ ^0 Sibling\_of]_{wt}\ ^0 Tilman]]$ Ø

---

[24] It might be debatable whether the argument is invalid, and whether 'brother of' and 'male sibling of' are not synonymous. As for the latter, the two terms are equivalent rather than strictly synonymous, as I explain above. As for the former, true, on its intensional reading the argument would be valid. In such a case Tilman would be related to the property of being Tilman's brother or Tilman's male sibling, regardless of the way in which this property is conceptualised. Yet, from a strictly logical point of view, if it is just *possible* that the premise was true without the conclusion being true as well, the argument should not be considered valid. For this reason, I opt for the hyperintensional reading and analysis of the above argument.

[25] For details on property modifiers, see Jespersen (2015b, §4). Here we deal with a subsective attribute modifier that assigns to an attribute *sibling of (somebody)* a new attribute *male sibling of (somebody)*.

[26] I agree with Church's view, see his (1956, p. 8, n. 20). Church argues that in "Schliemann sought the site of Troy" it is a concept of a location, not the location itself, that guides Schliemann's and every other seeker's search for the site of Troy.

[27] Here I analyse *de dicto* seeking; Tilman wants to find out *who* his brother is. It can be the case, for instance, in such a situation where Tilman receives information that his parents might have had another son of whom he had no idea before. For more details on the difference between *de dicto* and *de re* seeking, see Duží (2003), or Duží et al. (2010, § 5.2.2).

[28] For simplicity, I am ignoring the anaphoric reference 'his' and stick to the result of resolving this reference by substituting $^0 Tilman$ for the anaphoric variable denoted by 'his'. More on the logic of dynamic discourse and anaphora resolution, see Duží (2017a).

If structured propositions are logical procedures then how are procedures individuated?

(6) [$^0Seek_{wt}$ ^0Tilman $\lambda w \lambda t$[[^0Male $^0Sibling\_of$]$_{wt}$ ^0Tilman]]   Leibniz's Law, 3, 5
(7) Contradiction!   4, 6, $\wedge$I

Additional types. Sibling_of/$((o\iota)\iota)_{\tau\omega}$; *Male*/$(((o\iota)\iota)_{\tau\omega}((o\iota)\iota)_{\tau\omega})$: an attribute modifier.

To block the above invalid inference, a hyperintensional analysis must be applied. Here is how.

(1) $\lambda w \lambda t$ [$^0Seek*_{wt}$ ^0Tilman $^0[\lambda w \lambda t[^0Brother\_of_{wt}$ $^0Tilman]]]$ $\varnothing$
(2) $\lambda w \lambda t \neg [^0Seek*_{wt}$ ^0Tilman $^0[\lambda w \lambda t[[^0Male$ $^0Sibling\_of]_{wt}$ $^0Tilman]]]$ $\varnothing$
(3) $\neg[^0=*$ $^0[\lambda w \lambda t[^0Brother\_of_{wt}$ $^0Tilman]]$ $^0[\lambda w \lambda t[[^0Male$ $^0Sibling\_of]_{wt}$ $^0Tilman]]]$
    $\varnothing$

*Additional types Seek**/$(o\iota*_n)_{\tau\omega}$: the relation-in-intension of an individual to a *construction* of a property; =*/$(o*_n*_n)$: the identity of constructions.

No contradiction arises. When construed hyperintensionally, Tilman's search is only ostensibly inconsistent. One could object that it seems reasonable to assume that there is a meaning postulate in place to the effect that 'is a brother of' is shorthand for, or a notational variant of, 'is a male sibling of', the same way 'lasts a fortnight' is arguably short for 'lasts two weeks'. Yet it is questionable what semantic and inferential gain may be accrued from introducing a redundant predicate as a mere notational variant of another predicate.[29] What speaks against this assumption, at least through the lens of TIL, is that the Trivialization $^0Brother\_of$ and the Composition [^0Male $^0Sibling\_of$] are not co-hyperintensional but only equivalent constructions. Furthermore, the latter is a refinement of the former providing more analytic information than just the Trivialization of the attribute.[30]

4.2 Valid inferences in hyperintensional contexts

Above I illustrated how invalid inferences can be blocked in hyperintensional contexts. But there is the other side of the coin, which is the *positive* topic of which inferences *should be validated*.

For instance, an argument like this:

$$\frac{\textit{Tilman calculates the cotangent of } \pi}{\text{There is a number } x \text{ such that Tilman calculates the cotangent of } x}$$

is obviously valid. Surely, if Tilman calculates the cotangent of π, then there is such a number, namely the number π, the cotangent of which Tilman calculates. But careless existential generalization into a hyperintensional context is *not* valid:

$$\frac{\lambda w \lambda t[^0Calculate_{wt}\,^0Tilman\,^0[^0Cot\,^0\pi]]}{\lambda w \lambda t[^0\exists \lambda x[^0Calculate_{wt}\,^0Tilman\,^0[^0Cot\,x]]]}$$

---

[29] See Jespersen (2015b, §5) for the parallel example of 'is a bachelor', 'is an unmarried man'.
[30] For details on analytic information see Duží (2010).

If structured propositions are logical procedures then how are procedures individuated?

The reason is this. The Trivialisation $^0[^0Cot\ x]$ constructs the Composition $[^0Cot\ x]$ *independently* of any valuation v. Thus, from the fact that at $\langle w,\ t\rangle$ it is true that Tilman calculates $[^0Cot\ ^0\pi]$, we can *not* validly infer that Tilman calculates $[^0Cot\ x]$, because Tilman calculates the cotangent of π rather than of an arbitrary value of x. Put differently, the variable x occurring displayed in a hyperintensional context is not amenable to the logical operation of λ-binding, because it is bound by Trivialization ('^{0}-bound'). In other words, the Composition $[^0Cot\ x]$ is not a constituent of the whole construction. The problem just described of λx being unable to catch the occurrence of x inside the displayed construction is TIL's way of phrasing the standard objection to quantifying-in (i.e. the impossibility of reaching across an attitude operator). Yet in TIL we are able to overcome this obstacle. To validly infer the conclusion, we need to apply our *substitution method* that pre-processes the Composition $[^0Cot\ x]$ and substitutes the Trivialization of π for x. Only then can the conclusion be inferred. To this end we deploy the polymorphic functions $Sub/(*_n*_n*_n*_n)$ and $Tr/(*_n\ \alpha)$ defined as follows.

The function Sub of type $(*_n*_n*_n*_n)$ operates on constructions in this way. When applied to constructions C_1, C_2, C_3, Sub returns as its value the construction D that is the result of substituting C_1 for C_2 in C_3. The likewise polymorphic function Tr returns as its value the Trivialization of its argument.

For instance, if the variable x ranges over ι, the Composition $[^0Tr\ x]$ $v(John/x)$-constructs ^0John. Note one essential difference between the function Tr and the construction Trivialization. Whereas the variable x is *free* in $[^0Tr\ x]$, the Trivialization ^0x *displays* the variable x by constructing just x independently of valuation. Thus, for instance, the Composition

$$[^0Sub\ [^0Tr\ x]\ ^0him\ ^0[^0Wife\_of_{wt}\ him]]$$

$v(John/x)$-constructs the Composition $[^0Wife\_of_{wt}\ ^0John]$, while the Composition

$$[^0Sub\ ^0x\ ^0him\ ^0[^0Wife\_of_{wt}\ him]]$$

constructs the Composition $[^0Wife\_of_{wt}\ x]$ independently of valuation. Consequently, the following inference comes out valid:[31]

$$\frac{\lambda w\lambda t[^0Calculate_{wt}\ ^0Tilman\ ^0[^0Cot\ ^0\pi]]}{\lambda w\lambda t[^0\exists\lambda x[^0Calculate_{wt}\ ^0Tilman\ [^0Sub[^0Tr\ x]\ ^0y\ ^0[^0Cot\ y]]]]}$$

Gloss. Since the variable x occurs free as a *constituent* of $[^0Tr\ x]$, it v-constructs the Trivialization of the number v-constructed by x. Hence $[^0Sub\ [^0Tr\ x]\ ^0y\ ^0[^0Cot\ y]]$ $v(\pi/x)$-constructs the Composition $[^0Cot\ ^0\pi]$, to which Tilman is related according to the premise. For this reason, it follows from the premise that the class of numbers v-constructed by $\lambda x[^0Calculate_{wt}\ ^0Tilman\ [^0Sub\ [^0Tr\ x]^0y\ ^0[^0Cot\ y]]]$ is non-empty; the function $\exists$ can be validly applied.

Hence existential generalization into a hyperintensional context is just a technical issue that is easily solvable by our substitution method. Another fundamental rule that

---

[31] Valid rules for existential quantification into hyperintensional context have been specified in Duží and Jespersen (2015).

If structured propositions are logical procedures then how are procedures individuated?

is universally valid and should thus be applicable even in hyperintensional contexts is Leibniz's Law of *indiscernibility of identicals*, which translates into a rule of substitution of identicals. However, there is a philosophical rather than technical problem here. At the linguistic level, a hyperintensional context is such a context where the very meaning is the object of predication, and the problematic issue is the individuation of procedures. That is, how hyper are hyperintensionally individuated structured meanings? If there is one central question permeating hyperintensional logic and semantics then it is arguably this one.

There is a simple answer, which, unfortunately, also happens to be simplistic. Since we assign constructions to expressions as their meaning, then if a construction C occurs displayed in a hyperintensional context, then, trivially, an *identical* (not merely equivalent) construction is substitutable.[32] So the answer is simplistic because trivial because self-substitution is trivially valid.

Example. Suppose that 'cerulean' and 'azure' are synonymous terms. Since synonymous terms have the same meaning, they express the same construction; thus, the Trivializations $^0Cerulean/*_1 \to (\text{οι})_{\tau\omega}$ and $^0Azure/*_1 \to (\text{οι})_{\tau\omega}$ are *identical*. One and the same property has been Trivialized, regardless of the name we use for that property.[33] Let now $Believe*/(\text{οι}*_n)_{\tau\omega}$ be a hyperintensional relation-in-intension of an individual to a hyperproposition (i.e., to a construction of the proposition). Then the following argument is valid:

Tilman believes* that the Italian national football team wear azure shirts; Cerulean is azure

Tilman believes* that the Italian national football team wear cerulean shirts

---

The standard objection would be that the argument is not valid, because it can be true that Tilman believes that the shirts are azure without him believing them to be cerulean. But no, this is not possible. For sure, Tilman can assent to a *sentence* and fail to assent to another sentence, though the two sentences that report his attitude are synonymous but deploy two different predicates. But then the problem has to do with Tilman's linguistic incompetence (be it a restricted vocabulary or failure to recognize a pair of synonyms). Richard's principle of Transparency bears directly on this objection:

> ... It is impossible for a (normal, rational) person to understand expressions which have identical senses but not be aware that they have identical senses. (Richard 2001, pp. 546–7)

Hence the paradox of analysis is *not* a problem of hyperintensionality. Rather, it is a matter of linguistic incompetence and *not of logical incompetence*.

---

[32] Constructions C, D are analytically *equivalent* if and only if for any valuation v C and D v-construct the same object or are both v-improper.

[33] See Duží et al. (2010, § 5.1.1) for discussion of Mates's (1952) puzzle. The authors argue here that if 'is a woodchuck' and 'is a groundhog' are synonymous predicates then there is no room for even the slightest hyperintensional distinction. The Trivializations $^0Woodchuck$ and $^0Groundhog$ are not two constructions, but one and the same construction.

If structured propositions are logical procedures then how are procedures individuated?

On the other hand, this example is from the logical point of view too trivial. It is obvious that *identical* constructions are always mutually substitutable, because there is nothing to substitute; there is just one construction.[34]

At the linguistic level, strictly *synonymous* expressions (expressions encoding one and the same *procedure*) are substitutable in any hyperintensional context. Synonymy of semantically simple expressions is a matter of linguistics. Now we are, however, interested in the synonymy of *complex* expressions.[35] Since semantically complex expressions encode molecular procedures, the issue of synonymy of complex expressions transforms into the problem of the identity of their composed meanings, i.e., the problem of the identity of molecular procedures. To this end we introduce the relation of *procedural isomorphism*.

4.3 Procedural isomorphism and synonymy

For a simple example, consider the analysis of the sentence

"Tilman is solving the equation *Sin(x)=0*"

As explained at the outset, when solving this equation, Tilman is not related to the infinite set of multiples of the number π, because then there would be nothing to solve: Tilman would have the solution straightaway. In his effort to solve the equation he is related to the very procedure

$$\lambda x[^0= [^0Sin\ x]\ ^00];$$

he wants to find out what the procedure produces. Hence, *Solving* is of the type $(o\iota *_n)_{\tau\omega}$. The analysis amounts to this construction:

$$\lambda w \lambda t [^0Solving_{wt}\ ^0Tilman\ ^0[\lambda x[^0= [^0Sin\ x]\ ^00]]]$$

But couldn't we equally well assign to the above sentence as its meaning the following construction?

$$\lambda w \lambda t [^0Solving_{wt}\ ^0Tilman\ ^0[\lambda y[^0= [^0Sin\ y]\ ^00]]]$$

Both constructions $\lambda x[^0= [^0Sin\ x]\ ^00]$ and $\lambda y[^0= [^0Sin\ y]\ ^00]$ seem to play the same procedural role in this hyperintensional context, because they are α-equivalent. When aiming to find the solution Tilman must perform these procedural steps:

- Take the function sine (^0Sin)
- Take *any* real number (*x*, or *y*, …)
- Apply the sine function to this number to obtain its value ($[^0Sin\ x]$; or $[^0Sin\ y]$; …)
- Compare the value with the number 0 ($[^0= [^0Sin\ x]\ ^00]$; or $[^0= [^0Sin\ y]\ ^00]$; …)

---

[34] This holds also for terms of different languages. Recall the example from the outset of this paper. The sentences 'Schnee ist weiß' and 'Snow is white' are synonymous, because the terms 'Schnee' and 'Snow' are atomic references to the same property; the same holds for the terms 'weiß' and 'white'. Hence, the respective Trivializations ^0Schnee, ^0Snow and $^0Weiß$, ^0White are *identical* constructions, and the respective Closures $\lambda w \lambda t\ [^0Weiß_{wt}\ ^0Schnee]$, $\lambda w \lambda t\ [^0White_{wt}\ ^0Snow]$ are also identical.

[35] For the discussion on the issue of synonymy of complex expressions see also Duží (2014b).

If structured propositions are logical procedures then how are procedures individuated?

- If the value is equal to zero, assign the number $(x, y, \ldots)$ to the resulting set. In other words, abstract over the value of the variable $(\lambda x, \lambda y, \ldots)$

Any difference there might be between x, y, or any other variable ranging over the reals, does not translate into a procedural difference. This amounts to a distinction without a difference.[36]

We furnish non-synonymous terms with different constructions, i.e., different procedures. Hence, two terms are *synonymous* if they express one and the same *procedure*. This is trivial, but the deep issue is this. From the semantic point of view constructions are in some cases too fine-grained so that their difference cannot be expressed in a given language. This is usually the case with λ-bound variables that are not used in an ordinary vernacular. We need a slightly less fine-grained criterion of synonymy in order to weed out certain distinctions without a semantic difference. My thesis is that *synonymous expressions share structurally isomorphic meanings*. Meaning being a procedure, we need to define the relation of *procedural isomorphism* holding between constructions.

The problem of how fine-grained hyperintensional entities, hence meanings, should be was important already for Carnap who introduced in (1947: §§13*ff*) the relation of *intensional isomorphism*. However, Church (1954) found a counterexample of two terms that are obviously not synonymous, yet intensionally isomorphic. Church himself considered several so-called Alternatives of how to constrain these entities so as to develop a notion of *synonymous isomorphism*.[37] Senses are identical if the respective expressions are (A0) 'synonymously isomorphic', (A1) mutually λ-convertible, (A2) logically equivalent. (A2), the weakest criterion, was refuted already by Carnap, and was not acceptable to Church, either. (A1) was considered to be the right criterion of synonymy. Yet it has been subjected to a fair amount of criticism, in particular due to the inclusion of unrestricted β-reduction ('by name'). For instance, Salmon (2010) adduces examples of expressions that should intuitively not be taken to be synonymous, yet their meanings are mutually β-convertible.[38] Moreover, *partiality* throws a spanner in the works; β-conversion by name is not guaranteed to be an equivalent transformation as soon as partial functions are involved.[39] Church also considered Alternative (A1′), which is (A1) plus η-convertibility. Yet η-convertibility is plagued by similar defects as those of β-convertibility by name. The alternative (A0) arose from Church's criticism of intensional isomorphism, and it is synonymy resting on α-equivalence and meaning postulates for semantically simple terms. Of course, we need meaning postulates to fix synonymy for pairs of semantically simple terms (possibly even of different languages). Now we are, however, interested in the synonymy of molecular terms, which depends on structural isomorphism.[40]

---

[36] By this I do not want to suggest that variables x and y (or any other different variables) are one and the same procedure and substitutable in all contexts in any language. They are *different* constructions, and in a logical or programming language this difference may turn out to be significant. See also Pickel and Rabern (2016) on 'the antinomy of the variable'.

[37] For details see Anderson (1998) and Church (1993).

[38] For discussion of Salmon's arguments, see Jespersen (2015a).

[39] For details see Duží (2017b).

[40] See Duží (2014b).

If structured propositions are logical procedures then how are procedures individuated?

In TIL similar work has been done by Materna (1998, §5.3) and (2004, §1.4.2.2) where the relation of *quasi-identity* of closed constructions is defined. It includes α- and η- conversion. This criterion has been later coined *procedural isomorphism* and incorporated into Duží (2010) as Alternative (A 1/2). Duží and Jespersen (2013) and Duží (2014b) put forward a new definition of the criterion of structured synonymy called (A 3/4). It includes α-equivalence, η-equivalence, and so-called restricted $β_r$-conversion. Finally, in Duží and Jespersen (2015) and Duží (2014) alternative (A1″) is introduced. Close to Church's (A1), it includes an adjusted version of α-conversion and β-conversion *by value*, while η-conversion is excluded. (A1″) arguably counts at present as the right calibration of procedural isomorphism, hence of co-hyperintensionality, from the point of view of TIL. However, there can be no such thing as a transcendental argument for the necessity and sufficiency of (A1″). It is perfectly conceivable, indeed likely that (A1″) is going to face cogent counterexamples.

It should be obvious now that the problem of co-hyperintensionality is not simple, and the question arises whether there is a unique universal solution. I am going to formulate several conditions that should be met by constructions C and D in order for them to qualify as procedurally isomorphic, hence substitutable in hyperintensional contexts. Yet before doing so, let me summarize the definitions of particular conversions; α-conversion, β-conversion by name, and η-conversion are defined in the ordinary manner of the λ-calculi. In the TIL formalism they are as follows.[41]

α-conversion. Constructions C and D are α-equivalent if they differ at most by using different λ-bound variables. Formally, let a construction Y contain at most $x_1, \ldots, x_n$ as free variables. Then:

$$[\lambda x_1 \ldots x_n \ Y] \Rightarrow_\alpha [\lambda y_1 \ldots y_n \ Y(y_1/x_1 \ldots y_n/x_n)]$$

where $Y(y_1/x_1 \ldots y_n/x_n)$ is the construction that arises from Y by collision-less substitution of y_1 for all the occurrences of $x_1, \ldots, y_n$ for all the occurrences of x_n, is α-*conversion*.

β-conversion by name. Let $Y \to_v \alpha$; $x_1, D_1 \to_v \beta_1, \ldots, x_n, D_n \to_v \beta_n$; $[\lambda x_1 \ldots x_n \ Y] \to_v (\alpha \beta_1 \ldots \beta_n)$. Then:

$$[[\lambda x_1 \ldots x_n \ Y]D_1 \ldots D_n] \Rightarrow_{\beta n} Y(D_1/x_1 \ldots D_n/x_n),$$

where $Y(D_1/x_1 \ldots D_n/x_n)$ is the construction that arises from Y by collision-less substitution of D_1 for all the occurrences of $x_1, \ldots, D_n$ for all the occurrences of x_n, is β-*conversion by name*.

As a special case of β-conversion by name we define *restricted $β_r$-conversion*. Let $Y \to_v \alpha$; $x_1, y_1 \to_v \beta_1, \ldots, x_n, y_n \to_v \beta_n$; $[\lambda x_1 \ldots x_n \ Y] \to_v (\alpha \beta_1 \ldots \beta_n)$. Then:

$$[[\lambda x_1 \ldots x_n \ Y]y_1 \ldots y_n] \Rightarrow_{\beta r} Y(y_1/x_1 \ldots y_n/x_n),$$

where $Y(y_1/x_1 \ldots y_n/x_n)$ is the construction that arises from Y by collision-less substitution of y_1 for all the occurrences of $x_1, \ldots, y_n$ for all the occurrences of x_n, is *restricted β-conversion by name*.

---

[41] For details on β-conversion in λ-calculi see Duží and Kosterec (2017).

If structured propositions are logical procedures then how are procedures individuated?

Using the functions *Sub* and *Tr* introduced above, β-*conversion by value* is defined as follows.

β-conversion by value.
Let $Y \to_v \alpha; x_1, D_1 \to_v \beta_1, \ldots, x_n, D_n \to_v \beta_n, [\lambda x_1 \ldots x_n Y] \to_v (\alpha \beta_1 \ldots \beta_n)$.
Then

$$[[\lambda x_1 \ldots x_n Y] D_1 \ldots D_n] \Rightarrow_{\beta v} {}^2[{}^0 Sub \, [{}^0 Tr \, D_1] \, {}^0 x_1 \ldots [{}^0 Sub \, [{}^0 Tr \, D_n] \, {}^0 x_n \, {}^0 Y]]$$

is β-*conversion by value*.

Duží and Jespersen (2015) proves that this conversion is strictly equivalent in the sense that for any valuation v the left-hand and right-hand side constructions v- construct the same object or both are v-improper, unlike unrestricted β-conversion by name.[42]

η-conversion. Let $Y \to_v (\alpha \beta_1 \ldots \beta_n); x_1 \to_v \beta_1, \ldots, x_n \to_v \beta_n$. Then:

$$[\lambda x_1 \ldots x_n [Y \, x_1 \ldots x_n]] \Rightarrow_\eta Y$$

is η-*conversion*.

Next, I put forward and assess several conditions to be met by constructions C and D in order to qualify as procedurally isomorphic, hence substitutable in hyperintensional contexts.

(a) S*trict equivalence*; for any valuation v constructions C and D v-construct the same object or are both v-improper.
(b) Constructions C and D have the same number of constituents.

Both conditions are met only by α-conversion and by meaning postulates. Condition (a) is met by β_r-conversion (i.e. the restricted β-conversion by name that only substitutes variables for λ-bound variables of the same type) and by β_v-conversion by value. However, both β_r-conversion and β_v-conversion by value do not meet condition (b). Finally, η-conversion fails to meet either of them.[43]

It is a well-known fact that β-conversion by name does not preserve equivalence in a logic of partial functions. Yet the fact that η-conversion also does not preserve logical equivalence in a logic of *partial functions* such as TIL might be surprising. To see why, consider the following example. Let F v-construct a function of type $((\alpha \beta)\gamma)$ that is not defined at the argument v-constructed by $A \to_v \gamma$. Then the Composition $[F \, A] \to_v (\alpha \beta)$ is v-improper. However, the η-expanded construction

---

[42] In programming languages, the difference between conversion by name and by value revolves around the programmer's choice of *evaluation strategy*. Historically, call-by-value and call-by-name date back to *Algol 60*, a language designed in the late 1950s. The difference between call-by-name and call-by-value is often called *passing by reference* versus *passing by value*, respectively. Call-by-value is not a single evaluation strategy, but rather a cluster of evaluation strategies in which a function's argument is evaluated before being passed to the procedure. In *call by-reference* evaluation (also referred to as *call-by name* or *pass-by-reference*), a calling procedure receives an implicit reference to the argument sub-procedure. This typically means that the calling procedure can modify the argument sub-procedure. A call-by-reference language makes it more difficult for a programmer to track the effects of a procedure call, and may introduce subtle bugs. The notion of *conversion strategy* in the λ-calculi is similar to the *evaluation strategy* in programming languages.

[43] For the proofs see, for instance, Duží and Jespersen (2015) or Duží and Kosterec (2017).

If structured propositions are logical procedures then how are procedures individuated?

$\lambda x \, [[F \, A] \, x] \to_v (\alpha \beta), x \to \beta$, v-constructs a *degenerate function*, which is a function undefined at all its arguments. To be sure, due to the v-improperness of $[F \, A]$ the Composition $[[F \, A] \, x]$ is also v-improper. But λ-abstraction raises the context to an intensional one, hence the Closure $\lambda x \, [[F \, A] \, x]$ v-constructs a degenerate function, which *is* an object, if a bizarre one. Hence the constructions $[F \, A]$ and $\lambda x \, [[F \, A] \, x]$ are not strictly equivalent.

We might formulate weaker requirements like the following two.

(c) *Weak equivalence*; for any valuation v constructions C and D v-construct the same object, *provided* neither of them is v-improper.
(d) Constructions C and D have the same number of *closed constituents*.

Both of these requirements are met by η-conversion, while β-conversion by name meets only (c). β-conversion by value meets, of course, (c) because it satisfies (a), but it does not meet (d).

However, if we postulated that the term '$[[\lambda x_1 \ldots x_n \, Y] D_1 \ldots D_n]$' is just a notational shorthand for '$^2[^0Sub \, [^0Tr \, D_1] \, ^0x_1 \ldots [^0Sub \, [^0Tr \, D_n] \, ^0x_n \, ^0Y]]$', then β-conversion by value would trivially meet also the condition (d).[44] Such a notational convention is well justified, because conversion by value specifies the correct and proper way of executing the procedure of applying a function to its argument, unlike the β-conversion by name.

But then an adjusted version of α-conversion is called for. Consider, for instance, the constructions

$$[\lambda x \, [^0+ \, x \, ^01] \, ^05] \text{ and } [\lambda y \, [^0+ \, y \, ^01] \, ^05]$$

They are α-equivalent according to the standard definition. Yet their respective β_v-reduced forms

$$^2[^0Sub \, [^0Tr \, ^05] \, ^0x \, ^0[^0+ \, x \, ^01]] \text{ and } ^2[^0Sub \, [^0Tr \, ^05] \, ^0y \, ^0[^0+ \, y \, ^01]]$$

would not be α-equivalent. Yet they ought to be, because from the procedural point of view it is irrelevant which bound variables are used as formal parameters of the respective procedure.

Thus, the adjusted version of α-**conversion** is defined as follows. Let C, D be constructions. Then C, D are α-*equivalent*, if either C, D differ at most by using different λ-bound variables, or their β_v-expanded forms differ at most by using different λ-bound variables.

Let us next reflect on meaning postulates. Above we wondered what semantic and inferential gain can be obtained from introducing a redundant predicate like 'is a brother of', on its construal as a mere notational variant of 'is a male sibling of', and we did not stipulate those terms to be synonymous. In my opinion, we can accept only very few meaning postulates for semantically simple terms as assigning to these simple terms complex synonymous terms. It is usually just the case of introducing a shorthand for something frequently used, like 'fortnight' for 'a period of fourteen days'. In mathematics, it can be the case of introducing a new term as a shorthand for a long definition; for instance, 'group' for an 'algebraic system consisting of a set, an

---

[44] This proposal can be found in Duží (2014).

identity element, one binary operation and its inverse operation'. Once we introduce such a shorthand into a language, the two terms become automatically synonymous. Yet a problem can arise that for one and the same mathematical object there are more non-synonymous definitions. For instance, 'lattice' can be defined either as a partially ordered set L such that every two-element subset of L has an infimum and supremum in L, or as an algebra with two binary operations *meet* and *join* satisfying the axioms of commutativity, associativity and absorption. Then we must decide which of them is the primary definition of 'lattice' and prove that the other one is just equivalent.[45]

Now I am in the position to specify a series of *criteria* for procedural isomorphism partially ordered from the strongest (most restrictive) to the weakest (most liberal). Of course, there is no warranty that the list as specified below is exhaustive. Nonetheless, I provide good reasons for each of these criteria and specify conditions under which this or that criterion is applicable. Hence, when one needs to pick this or that criterion, he/she knows the conditions under which the criterion can be safely applied.

Where 'MP' abbreviates 'meaning postulates', the proposed criteria are as follows. First, I adduce the criteria that apply none or only one kind of conversion. Afterwards, I consider variants of applying more than one conversion.

C0 MP (and nothing else)

This is the most restrictive criterion that would be applicable in *any language*, provided the above specified conditions are met. Recall Mates's puzzle and the paradox of analysis. As mentioned above, it is not a problem of hyperintensionality and synonymy; rather, it is a problem of linguistic competence.

C1 MP, α-conversion

This criterion is applicable in any non-professional, ordinary language where *λ-bound variables are not explicitly used*.

Yet, for instance, it cannot be carelessly applied in a *functional programming language* where a λ-bound variable plays the role of a formal parameter of a procedure for which an actual argument should be substituted when calling the procedure.

Consider, for instance, the easy procedure $\lambda x\,[^0+x\,^0 1]$, $x \rightarrow_v \tau$, computing the successor function. Whenever we call this procedure to compute the successor of a number n we must substitute this number n for the formal parameter x. If we applied α-conversion to this procedure, for instance, $\lambda y\,[^0+y\,^0 1]$, $y \rightarrow_v \tau$, every calling procedure deployed to obtain the successor of the number n would have to be adjusted. Thus, in such a language $\lambda x\,[^0+x\,^0 1]$ is not procedurally isomorphic with $\lambda y\,[^0+y\,^0 1]$.

C2 MP, β_r-conversion

This criterion is applicable in any non-professional, ordinary language *where λ-bound variables are not explicitly used*.

---

[45] An important role of non-synonymous definitions of the number π is examined in Duží et al. (2009).

If structured propositions are logical procedures then how are procedures individuated?

Yet, for instance, in a slightly more technical jargon β_r-conversion is not applicable as a criterion of procedural isomorphism. For instance, is there any semantic difference between the following sentences?

(1) "The president of the USA is a Republican"
(2) "The holder of the office of President of the USA is a Republican"
(3) "The president of the USA has the property of being a Republican"
(4) "The holder of the office of President of the USA has the property of being a Republican"

In my opinion, there is. These sentences do not have, strictly speaking, the same meaning, though their respective analyses reveal that they express constructions that are just β_r-equivalent. For instance, (1*) is a β_r-reduced form of (2*):

(1*) $\lambda w \lambda t [^0 Republican_{wt} [^0 President\_of_{wt} \, ^0 USA]]$

(2*) $\lambda w \lambda t [^0 Republican_{wt} \lambda w_1 \lambda t_1 [^0 President\_of_{w1t1} \, ^0 USA]_{wt}]$

Types. $Republican/(o\iota)_{\tau\omega}$; $President\_of/(\iota\iota)_{\tau\omega}$; USA/ι; $[^0 President\_of_{wt} \, ^0 USA] \to_v \iota$; $\lambda w_1 \lambda t_1 [^0 President\_of_{w1t1} \, ^0 USA] \to \iota_{\tau\omega}$.

C3 MP, β_v-conversion

This criterion is applicable in any language, *provided we postulate*, as proposed above, that the term '$[[\lambda x_1 \ldots x_n Y] D_1 \ldots D_n]$' is just a *notational shorthand* for

'$^2[^0 Sub\,[^0 Tr\, D_1]\, ^0 x_1 \ldots [^0 Sub\,[^0 Tr\, D_n]\, ^0 x_n^0 Y]]$'.

C4 MP, η-conversion

This criterion is not applicable in any logic of partial functions, because it does not preserve strict equivalence. In an ordinary language, the exclusion of η-conversion from the definition of procedural isomorphism might seem to be harmless. When analysing expressions in TIL we apply our method of *literal analysis* according to which semantically simple terms are furnished with the Trivialisation of the denoted object as their meaning. For instance, the literal analysis of "The Pope is wise" (when understood de re) is the Closure

$\lambda w \lambda t [^0 Wise_{wt} \, ^0 Pope_{wt}]$

rather than the Closure

$\lambda w \lambda t [\lambda w \lambda t [\lambda x [^0 Wise_{wt} x]]_{wt} \, ^0 Pope_{wt}]$,

because the literal analysis of the predicate 'is wise' is the Trivialization $^0 Wise$ rather than the Closure $\lambda w \lambda t [\lambda x [^0 Wise_{wt} x]]$, which should be glossed as 'is someone who is wise' or 'is one of the wise ones'. The types are $Wise/(o\iota)_{\tau\omega}$; $Pope/\iota_{\tau\omega}$; $x \to \iota$. Yet the sentences "The Pope is wise" and "The Pope is one of the wise ones" can hardly be taken as strictly speaking synonymous, as the latter makes a detour via the population of wise individuals at the indices of evaluation.

If structured propositions are logical procedures then how are procedures individuated?

C5 MP, β_n-conversion

This criterion is in general not applicable in any logic of partial functions, because it does not preserve strict equivalence; nor is it applicable in an ordinary language, because we do use non-referring terms like 'the King of France'. Moreover, as Duží and Jespersen (2013) shows, β_n-conversion by name has other serious defects which include the loss of analytic information and non-effectiveness.

C6 MP, α-conversion, β_r-conversion

The applicability rests on the assumptions as those of **C1** and **C2**

C7 MP, adjusted α-conversion, β_v-conversion

The applicability rests on the same assumptions as those of **C1** and **C3**

C8 MP, adjusted α-conversion, β_r-conversion, β_v-conversion

The applicability rests on the same assumptions as those of **C1**, **C2** and **C3**

C9 MP, adjusted α-conversion, β_r-conversion, β_v-conversion, η-conversion

The applicability rests on the same assumptions as those of **C1**, **C2** and **C3**, provided semantically simple terms are analysed as mere references to the denoted object (i.e., Trivialization of the denoted object)

C10 MP, α-conversion, β_r-conversion, β_v-conversion, β_n-conversion, η-conversion

The applicability rests on the same assumptions as those of **C1, C2, C3, C9**, provided properly partial functions are not involved

To illustrate mutual dependences and ordering of these criteria, here is a graph (in the form of a Hasse diagram).

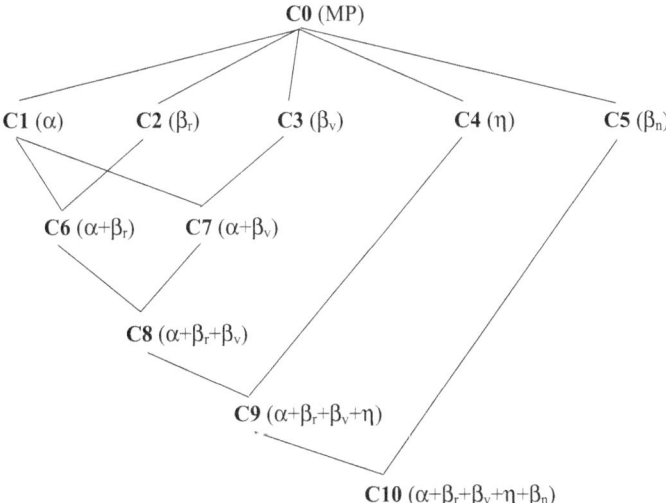

To sum up, in an ordinary language without explicitly used λ-bound variables, the most liberal criterion for procedural isomorphism includes meaning postulates for

semantically simple terms, adjusted α-conversion, $β_r$-conversion, and $β_v$-conversion, which is the criterion **C8**. The more technical the language, the less liberal a criterion can be applied, so that, at the other extreme, the most restrictive criterion includes just meaning postulates defining semantically simple terms (criterion **C0**). Criterion **C9** is applicable, provided one strictly applies the method of *literal* analysis, i.e., provided semantically simple terms are conceived as mere references to the objects denoted by the terms. The most liberal criterion **C10** is applicable only in a logic of total functions. Other variants combining particular conversions are thinkable, of course, yet, for an ordinary vernacular we recommend as the most suitable the criterion **C8**.

As a result, the **rule of substitution of co-hyperintensional terms in hyperintensional contexts** can be formulated only conditionally:

If constructions C, D are procedurally isomorphic per one of the existing criteria of procedural isomorphism *then* C, D can be validly substituted within a hyperintensional context, *provided* the discourse has been so defined as to obey that particular calibration of procedural isomorphism.

The methodological take-home is that it is a philosophical and linguistic decision—not one based on pure logic—which sorts of discourse obey which calibrations of procedural isomorphism.

5 Conclusion

In this paper, I have discussed structured propositions explicated as algorithmically structured logical procedures. I have put forward a number of reasons in favour of a procedural semantics that furnishes expressions with meaning procedures encoded by those expressions. There are two issues I dealt with in this paper. The first one concerns the mereological structure of procedures, while the second one concerns the granularity of structured meaning procedures.

Concerning the former, I explicated the fundamental distinction between the occurrence of a procedure in the executed mode and the displayed mode. If a procedure occurs in the executed mode, then the procedure is a constituent part of another procedure (and of itself), while if a procedure occurs in the displayed mode, then the procedure itself figures as an object on which other procedures operate. Yet the input object(s) on which a procedure operates and the output object (if any) that a procedure produces are not constituent parts of the procedure. The constituent parts of a procedure are defined as those sub-procedures that occur in the executed mode. Thus, I have also demonstrated that procedures are structured wholes consisting of unambiguously determined parts, which are those sub-procedures each of which must be individually executed whenever the whole procedure is to be executed to produce at most one object. Moreover, I have proposed a solution to the problem of what unifies the proper parts of a molecular procedure. The proper constituents of a molecular procedure *interact* in the process of producing an object. The product of one or more constituents becomes an argument of the function produced by another constituent. If one or more constituents fail to produce an object, the whole procedure, which is typed to operate on an object of an already specified type, fails as well, because the process of producing an output object has been interrupted. Hence, procedures are not mere set-theoretical aggregates of their proper parts. The elements of an aggregate lack *direct connection inter se*, even when they are organised in an ordered sequence or list. And direct connection inter se is exactly what makes some things *parts* of a whole. As another novel result, I proved that this part-whole relation is a partial order. On the other hand, the mereology of structured procedures is non-classical, because the principles of extensionality and idempotence do not hold; and it is desirable that they should not, as already Bolzano demonstrated.

In the second part of the paper I dealt with the problem of co-hyperintensionality, and in general with the problem of valid inferences in a hyperintensional context, where such a context is defined in terms of a procedure occurring in the displayed mode. I demonstrated that the problem of validly applying extensional rules of inference (such as the rule of existential generalization and substitution of identicals) in a hyperintensional context is closely connected with the problem of the structural isomorphism of meanings, hence of co-hyperintensionality, hence of synonymy. I demonstrated that the individuation of procedures assigned to expressions as their structured meaning cannot be decided in virtue of a universal criterion applicable to every language. Yet, the positive result of this paper is that I have specified a set of rigorously defined criteria of fine-grained procedural individuation, partially ordered according to the degree of their being permissive with respect to synonymy. It turned out that the formalization of procedures in my background theory Transparent Intensional Logic (TIL) may become a bit too fine-grained from the point of view of the semantics of natural language. Yet the same problem must be met in any formalization that makes use of λ-bound variables, i.e. in any λ-calculus, because in an ordinary vernacular we do not use λ-bound variables. For this reason, I proposed a criterion that is the most suitable for an ordinary, non-professional language. It is the criterion that declares that procedural isomorphism of TIL constructions obtains whenever the differences between constructions consist just in technical manipulations with λ-bound variables. Thus, the rule of co-hyperintensionality (i.e. the rule for substitution of synonymous terms in hyperintensional contexts) has been formulated only conditionally.

Acknowledgements The research reported here in was supported by the Grant Agency of the Czech Republic, Project No. GA15-13277S, *Hyperintensional logic for natural language analysis*, and by the internal grant agency of VSB-TU Ostrava, Project SGS No. SP2017/133, "Knowledge modelling and its applications in software engineering III". Versions of this paper were read at the *Barcelona Workshop on Reference 9 (BW9): Unity and Individuation of Structured Propositions*, Barcelona, 22–24 June 2015. I want to thank Bjørn Jespersen for great comments along the way, and not least two anonymous referees for *Synthese*.

References

Anderson, C. A. (1998). Alonzo Church's contributions to philosophy and intensional logic. *Bulletin of Symbolic Logic*, *4*, 129–171.
Barendregt, H. P. (1997). The impact of the lambda calculus. *Bulletin of Symbolic Logic*, *3*(2), 181–215.
Bennet, K. (2013). Having a part twice over. *Australian Journal of Philosophy*, *91*(1), 83–103.
Bolzano, B. (1837). *Wissenschaftslehre*. Sulzbach: von Seidel.
Carnap, R. (1947). *Meaning and necessity*. Chicago: Chicago University Press.
Church, A. (1941). *The calculi of lambda conversion*. Princeton: Princeton University Press.

Church, A. (1951). The need for abstract entities. *American Academy of Arts and Sciences Proceedings, 80*, 100–113.
Church, A. (1954). Intensional isomorphism and identity of belief. *Philosophical Studies, 5*, 65–73.
Church, A. (1956). *Introduction to mathematical logic*. Princeton: Princeton University Press.
Church, A. (1993). A revised formulation of the logic of sense and denotation. Alternative (1). *Noûs, 27*, 141–157.
Cleland, C. E. (2002). On effective procedures. *Minds and Machines, 12*, 159–179.
Cohen, M. R., & Nagel, E. (1934). *An introduction to logic and scientific method*. London: Routledge and Kegan Paul.
Cotnoir, A. J. (2013). Strange parts: The metaphysics of non-classical mereologies. *Philosophy Compass, 8*(9), 834–845.
Duží, M. (2014). A procedural interpretation of the Church-Turing Thesis. In A. Olszewski, B. Brożek, P. Urbańczyk (Eds.), *Church's Thesis: Logic, mind and nature*. Copernicus Center Press, Krakow 2013.
Duží, M. (2017a). Logic of dynamic discourse; anaphora resolution. In *Proceedings of the 27th international conference on information modelling and knowledge bases-EJC 2017*, Thailand.
Duží, M. (2017b). Presuppositions and two kinds of negation. *Logique & Analyse*, the special issue on *How to Say 'Yes' and 'No'* (Vol. 239, pp. 245–263).
Duží, M. (2003). Notional attitudes (on wishing, seeking and finding). *ORGANON F, 10*(3), 237–260.
Duží, M. (2010). The paradox of inference and the non-triviality of analytic information. *Journal of Philosophical Logic, 39*(5), 473–510.
Duží, M. (2012). Extensional logic of hyperintensions. *Lecture Notes in Computer Science, 7260*, 268–290.
Duží, M. (2014a). Communication in a multi-cultural world. *ORGANON F, 21*(2), 198–218.
Duží, M. (2014b). Structural isomorphism of meaning and synonymy. *Computación y Sistemas, 18*(3), 439–453.
Duží, M., & Jespersen, B. (2013). Procedural isomorphism, analytic information, and β-conversion by value. *Logic Journal of the IGPL, 21*(2), 291–308.
Duží, M., & Jespersen, B. (2015). Transparent quantification into hyperintensional objectual attitudes. *Synthese, 192*(3), 635–677.
Duží, M., Jespersen, B., & Materna, P. (2009). 'π' in the sky. In G. Primiero & S. Rahman (Eds.), *Acts of knowledge: History, philosophy and logic*. Essays dedicated to Göran Sundholm. London: College Publications Tribute Series 1.
Duží, M., Jespersen, B., & Materna, P. (2010). *Procedural semantics for hyperintensional logic. Foundations and applications of transparent intensional logic*. Berlin: Springer.
Duží, M., & Kosterec, M. (2017). A valid rule of β-conversion for the logic of partial functions. *ORGANON F, 24*(1), 10–36.
Duží, M., Macek, J., & Vích, L. (2014). Procedural isomorphism and synonymy. In M. Dančák & V. Punčochář (Eds.), *Logica yearbook 2013* (pp. 15–33). London: College Publications.
Duží, M., & Materna, P. (2017). Validity and applicability of Leibniz's law of substitution of identicals. In P. Arazim & T. Lavička (Eds.), *The logica yearbook 2016* (pp. 17–35). London: College Publications.
Faroldi, F. L. G. (2016). Co-hyperintensionality. *Ratio*,. https://doi.org/10.1111/rati.12143.
Ganter, B., & Wille, R. (1999). *Formal concept analysis, mathematical foundations*. New York: Springer.
Hanks, P. (2011). Structured propositions as types. *Mind, 120*(477), 11–52.
Hanks, P. (2015). *Propositional content*. Oxford: Oxford University Press.
Jespersen, B. (2015a). Structured lexical concepts, property modifiers, and transparent intensional logic. *Philosophical Studies, 172*(2), 321–345.
Jespersen, B. (2015b). Should propositions proliferate? *Thought, 4*, 243–251.
Jespersen, B. (2017a). Anatomy of a proposition. *Synthese*, S.I. Unity of structured propositions, published online August 2017. https://doi.org/10.1007/s11229-017-1512-y.
Jespersen, B. (2017b). Is predication an act or an operation? In P. Stalmaszczyk (Ed.), *Philosophy and logic of predication, studies in philosophy of language and linguistics* (Vol. 7, pp. 223–245). Peter Lang GmbH: Frankfurt/Main.
King, J. C. (2014). Structured propositions. In E. N. Zalta (ed.) *The Stanford encyclopedia of philosophy* (Spring 2014 Edition). http://plato.stanford.edu/archives/spr2014/entries/propositions-structured/.
Materna, P. (1998). *Concepts and objects* (Vol. 63). Helsinki: Acta Philosophica Fennica.
Materna, P. (2004). *Conceptual systems*. Berlin: Logos.

Mates, B. (1952). Synonymity. In L. Linsky (Ed.), *Semantics and the philosophy of language* (pp. 111–138). Urbana, IL: University of Illinois Press.

Moschovakis, Y. N. (1994). Sense and denotation as algorithm and value. In J. Väänänen & J. Oikkonen (Eds.), *Lecture notes in logic* (Vol. 2, pp. 210–249). Berlin: Springer.

Moschovakis, Y. N. (2006). A logical calculus of meaning and synonymy. *Linguistics and Philosophy, 29*, 27–89.

Pickel, B. (2017). Are propositions essentially representational? *Pacific Philosophical Quartelly,*. https://doi.org/10.1111/papq.12123.

Pickel, B., & Rabern, B. (2016). The antinomy of the variable: A Tarskian resolution. *Journal of Philosophy, 113*(3), 137–170.

Richard, M. (2001). Analysis, synonymy and sense. In: A. Anderson, M. Zelëny (Eds.), *Logic, meaning and computation, essays in memory of Alonzo Church*. Synthese Library 305 (vol. III, pp. 545–572).

Russell, B. (1903). *The principles of mathematics*. New York: Norton paperback edition 1996. Norton & Company.

Salmon, N. (2010). Lambda in sentences with designators: An ode to complex predication. *Journal of Philosophy, 107*, 445–468.

Soames, S. (2012). *What is meaning?*. Princeton: Princeton University Press.

Soames, S. (2014). A cognitive theory of propositions. In J. C. King, S. Soames, & J. Speaks (Eds.), *New thinking about propositions* (6th ed., pp. 91–125). Oxford: Oxford University Press.

Tichý, P. (2004). Collected papers in logic and philosophy. In V. Svoboda, B. Jespersen, C. Cheyne (Eds.), Prague: Filosofia, Czech Academy of Sciences and Dunedin: University of Otago Press.

Tichý, P. (1988). *The foundations of Frege's logic*. Berlin: De Gruyter.

Tichý, P. (1995). Constructions as the subject matter of mathematics. In W. De Pauli-Schimanovich, et al. (Eds.), *The foundational debate* (pp. 175–185). Amsterdam: Kluwer Academic Publisher. (Reprinted in Tichý (2004), pp. 873–885).

van Lambalgen, M., & Hamm, F. (2004). Moschovakis' notion of meaning as applied to linguistics. In M. Baaz, S. Friedman, J. Krajicek (Eds.), *Logic Colloquium'01. Digital Academic Repository*. Amsterdam: University of Amsterdam. http://dare.uva.nl/record/123675/. Accessed 13 September 2017.

Westerhoff, J. (2005). Logical relations between pictures. *Journal of Philosophy, 102*, 603–623.

Procedural isomorphism, analytic information and β-conversion by value

MARIE DUZÍ and BJØRN JESPERSEN

Abstract

This article solves, in a logically rigorous manner, a problem originally advanced as a counterexample to Chomsky's theory of binding and recently discussed in a 2004 paper by Stephen Neale. The example is this. John loves his wife, and so does Peter. Hence John and Peter share a property. But which one? (i) Loving John's wife: then John and Peter love the same woman. (ii) Loving one's own wife: then, unless they are married to the same woman, John loves one woman and Peter loves another woman. Since 'John loves his wife' is ambiguous between attributing (i) or (ii) to John, 'So does Peter' is also ambiguous between attributing (i) or (ii) to Peter. With unrestricted β-reduction, the lambda-term counterparts of the attributions of (i) and (ii) to John both β-reduce to (ii). Which, intuitively, they should not. With suitably *restricted* β-conversion, the two redexes do not reduce to the same contractum and can be reconstructed from their respective contracta. This article details how to apply this restricted rule of β-conversion to contexts containing anaphora such as 'his' and 'so does'. The logical contribution of the article is a generally valid form of β-conversion 'by value' rather than 'by name'. The philosophical application of β-conversion 'by value' to a context containing anaphora is another contribution of this article.

1 Introduction

The dialectics of this article is to move from linguistics through logic to semantics. An issue originally bearing on binding in linguistics is used to make a point about β-conversion in the typed λ-calculus. This point, in turn, is used to help us to a definition of hyperintensional individuation.

Our working hypothesis is that hyperintensional individuation is procedural individuation and that the relevant procedures are isomorphic modulo α- or η- or restricted β-convertibility 'by name'. Any two terms or expressions whose respective meanings are procedurally isomorphic are deemed semantically indistinguishable, hence synonymous. *Procedural isomorphism* is a nod to Carnap's *intensional isomorphism* and Church's *synonymous isomorphism*. Our resulting definition of procedural isomorphism slots in between Church's Alternatives (A0) and (A1) and will be called (A3/4).

Sag ([24], §2.2) attributes to Ross [23] the insight that the sentence 'John scratched his arm, and Mary did too' is ambiguous between what Ross calls a 'strict' and a 'sloppy' reading. Sag himself ([24], p. 127) offers the example 'Betsy$_i$ loves her$_i$ dog, and Sandy$_j$ does ϕ, too'. Sentences exemplifying this sort of ambiguity (to be spelt out below) exhibit two flaws in Chomsky's theory of binding as set out in [3]. First, Chomsky cannot accommodate the ambiguity, thus erroneously predicting sentences in this vein to be unambiguous. Second, the single reading Chomsky does offer is the less natural one, which is the strict one. The strict reading has Mary scratching John's arm and Sandy loving Betsy's dog. In formal terms, the problem for Chomsky is that for node α to bind node β, they must, inter alia, be co-indexed. Yet the phenomenon of verb–phrase (VP) ellipsis allows for sloppy identity, in violation of co-indexing, hence preventing α from binding β.

Our own engagement with VP ellipsis originally grew out of a critique of Neale [20], which we presented in Duží et al. ([9], pp. 333–336). The present article greatly expands on and also amends what we thought at the time.

The example we will focus on is the following. John loves his wife. So does Peter. Therefore, John and Peter share a property. Only which one? There are two options. (i) Loving John's wife. Then John and Peter love the same woman (and there is trouble on the horizon). (ii) Loving one's own wife. Then, unless they are married to the same woman, John loves one woman and Peter loves another woman (and both men are in both cases exemplary husbands).[1]

The property predicated of Peter in 'So does Peter' is a function of the property predicated of John in 'John loves his wife'. Since the latter sentence (the source clause) is ambiguous between attributing (i) or (ii) to John, the former (the target clause) is also ambiguous between attributing (i) or (ii) to Peter. The ambiguity of the anaphoric expression 'his wife' as applied to John is visited upon the likewise anaphoric expression 'so does'. On the *strict* reading of 'John loves his wife, and so does Peter' property (i) is the one they share. On the *sloppy* reading, property (ii) is the one they share.[2]

What is special about 'John loves his wife, and so does Peter' is that it essentially involves *anaphoric* expressions, in this case 'his' and 'so does'. It might seem tempting, though, to attempt to forestall the ambiguity by analysing 'John loves his wife' as though it were synonymous with 'John loves John's wife'. Then 'So does Peter' would unequivocally attribute to Peter the property of loving John's wife, i.e. (i). But this analysis would be an overly crude one, entirely annihilating the particularly *anaphoric* character of 'his'. This indexical attributes to John a first-person perspective on a particular woman that is lost in 'John's wife', which comes with a non-privileged perspective on the same woman that is equally available to Peter and the rest of us.[3] Instead the form of the solution must be in terms of resolution of verb–phrase ellipsis.[4] It needs to be spelt out which of two properties applies to John in 'John loves his wife' and so applies to Peter in 'So does Peter'.[5]

---

[1] It is interesting to note that the ambiguity of 'John loves his wife, and so does Peter' is an artefact of a language such as English (or German '*seine* Frau' and Dutch '*zijn* vrouw') where 'his' lends itself both to reflexive and non-reflexive meanings. Languages such as Czech and Danish (the respective mother tongues of the two authors) cannot reproduce this ambiguity. Consider 'John loves his wife'. The occurrence of 'his' is the source of a three-way ambiguity. The property ascribed to John is one of these three. (i) John loving *his own* wife. This is the interpretation one must opt for, if 'John loves his wife' is analysed in isolation: 'his' must be reflexive. Czech would have 'Jan miluje svou ženu' and Danish, 'Johannes elsker sin kone'. (ii) John loving *John's* wife. This interpretation marks a shift from the first-person perspective of (i) to a third-person perspective, whereby John's privileged perspective is lost. The truth-condition may be the same, but there is a loss of semantic subtlety. (iii) John loving *another man's* wife. The second man must be identified deictically. This interpretation is an option only if 'his' in 'John loves his wife' is allowed to draw in material (in this case, a male individual) from the surrounding context. If Peter is identified deictically by means of 'his' then (iii) will entail that John loves Peter's wife. In spoken discourse, the intonation of 'his' would be emphasized to distinguish (iii) from (i). Czech would have 'Jan miluje *jeho* ženu' and Danish, 'Johannes elsker *hans* kone'.
[2] For 'sloppy' and 'strict', see Ross [23], Sag [24], Salmon [25], Van Eijck and Francez [11] and Neale ([20], pp. 140ff).
[3] Cf. Castañeda's advocacy of 'he*'. For discussion, see Duží et al. ([9], pp. 317–318, esp. n. 47). See also Salmon [25].
[4] See Van Eijck and Francez [11].
[5] The referee wondered, quite reasonably, whether our solution to 'John loves his wife, and so does Peter' readily extends to other cases, or whether it is *ad hoc*. The referee brought up this example: 'John loves his wife, and so do his children'. Here is our take on this example. The property denoted by 'so do' is one of (i), (ii). (i) is the property *loving the woman/individual* (the property of being a wife remaining suppressed) *who is John's wife*. This interpretation has a strong *de re* flavour, for the children do not conceptualize the woman in question as a *wife*. Rather *John's wife* is used to pick out an individual about

Since the properties *loving John's wife* and *loving one's own wife* as attributed to John are distinct, there is room for oscillation between the sloppy and the strict reading. But once we feed the formal renditions of attribution of these two properties to John into the widespread λ-calculus for logical analysis, a problem arises. The problem is this. Their respective β-*redexes* are distinct, for sure, but they share the same β-*contractum*. This contractum corresponds to the strict reading. So β-conversion predicts, erroneously, that two properties applied to John β-reduce to one. The result is that the sloppy reading gets squeezed out. β-reduction blots out the anaphoric character of 'his wife', while the resulting contractum is itself β-expandable back into both the strict and the sloppy reading. Information is lost in transformation. The information lost when performing β-reduction on the formal counterparts of 'John loves his wife' is whether the property that was applied was (i) or (ii), since both can be reconstructed from the contractum, though neither in particular. The sentence 'John loves his wife, and so does Peter' ostensibly shows that the λ-calculus is too crude an analytical tool for at least one kind of perfectly natural use of indexicals.

This article demonstrates that, and how, the λ-calculus is up for the challenge—*provided* a form of β-conversion by value is adopted. The *logical contribution* of the article is a generally valid form of β-reduction *by value* rather than *by name*. The *philosophical application* of β-reduction by value to a context containing anaphora is another contribution of this article. The standard approach to VP ellipsis based on λ-abstracts and variable binding can, thus, be safely upheld.

Other theories kindred to ours tackling ellipsis resolution as exemplified by sentences in the vein of 'John loves his wife, and so does Peter' would include Van Eijck and Francez [11] and Loukanova [17], both of which are based on a procedural, or computational, semantics of function-based programming languages. However, their procedural semantics is of the *imperative* variant and ours of the *declarative* variant. The advantage of the declarative variant is that it gives us a logical specification of the procedures in terms of *rules* (*what to do*), rather than just an imperative program for the execution of procedures in terms of *instructions* (*how to do it*). Declarative semantics is prior to imperative semantics, because it makes it possible to validate the declared procedure prior to execution. Our declarative procedural semantics also makes it straightforward to infer that there is a property that John and Peter share. Furthermore, Loukanova ([17], §3) is alert, as we are, to the need to constrain β-conversion. However, Loukanova's restricted β-reduction corresponds to what in our theory would be restricted β-reduction *by name*.

The rest of this article is organized as follows. Section 2 sets out the relevant foundations of the framework of λ-calculus within which we raise and solve the problem. Section 3 formalizes the relevant English sentences within the symbolism of that formal framework. Section 4 presents and justifies our solution to the problem.

2 Foundations of TIL

The problematic reduction and its solution will both be discussed within the framework of Tichý's Transparent Intensional Logic. Tichý's TIL was developed simultaneously with Montague's Intensional Logic.[6] The technical tools of the two disambiguations of the analysandum will be familiar from Montague's intensional logic, with two important exceptions.

---

whom to subsequently predicate a property; hence the way how she is picked out is immaterial. (ii) is the property *being a child of John's and loving one's own wife*. If this is the property that 'so do' picks out then the sample sentence comes out a poorly phrased English sentence. A better phrasing would be, '…, and his children also love their wives'. In this case the two anaphoric expressions are 'his', 'their', with no room for ambiguity. The drama that 'so' otherwise creates will have evaporated.

[6]For a critique of Montague's intensional logic, see Duží et al. ([9], §2.4.3).

One exception is that we λ-bind separate variables $w_1...w_n$ ranging over possible worlds and $t_1...t_n$ ranging over times. This dual binding is tantamount to *explicit intensionalization and temporalization*.[7] The other exception is that *functional application* is the logic both of extensionalization of intensions (functions from possible worlds) and of predication. Application is symbolized by square brackets, '[...]'. Intensions are extensionalized by applying them to worlds and times, as in [[*Intension w*]*t*], abbreviated by subscripted terms for world and time variables: *Intension*$_{wt}$ is the extension of the generic intension *Intension* at $\langle w, t \rangle$. Thus, for instance, the extensionalization of a property yields a set, and the extensionalization of a proposition yields a truth-value (or no value at all).[8] The *predication* of the property F of John is, logically, a matter of applying the extensionalized property F (i.e. the characteristic function of a set) to John in order to obtain a truth-value, according as John is a member of the set of Fs at $\langle w, t \rangle$.[9]

Formally, a *property* of individuals is a function from worlds to a function from times to a partial function from individuals to truth-values (characteristic functions of sets). A *proposition* is a function from worlds to a partial function from times to truth-values. An *attribute* like *the wife_of* is a function from worlds to a function from times to a partial function from an individual to an individual: relative to $\langle w, t \rangle$, given one individual *x/John*, the attribute yields either the individual that is the wife of *x/John* or no individual, in case *x/John* is single or polygamous. An *individual role* or *office* like *John's wife* (assuming a cultural background of monogamy) is a function from worlds to a partial function from times to individuals: relative to $\langle w, t \rangle$, the role yields either the individual that is John's wife at $\langle w, t \rangle$ or no individual, in case John is single or polygamous. Finally, an *n-place relation-in-intension* is a function from worlds to a function from times to a partial function from *n*-tuples to truth-values.

A main feature of the λ-calculus is its ability to systematically distinguish between functions and functional values. An additional feature of TIL is its ability to systematically distinguish between functions and modes of presentation of functions and modes of presentation of functional values. The TIL operation known as *Closure* is the very procedure of presenting or forming or obtaining or *constructing* a function; the TIL operation known as *Composition* is the very procedure of *constructing* the value (if any) of a function at an argument. Compositions and Closures are both multiple-step procedures, or *constructions*, that operate on input provided by two one-step constructions, which figure as sub-procedures of Compositions and Closures, namely *variables* and so-called *Trivializations*. Characters such as '*x*', '*y*' '*z*' are words denoting variables, which construct the respective values that an assignment function has accorded to them.[10] The linguistic counterpart of a Trivialization is a constant term always picking out the same object. An analogy from programming languages might be helpful. The Trivialization of an object X (whatever X may be) and its use are comparable to a *fixed pointer* to X and the *dereference* of the pointer. In order to operate on X, X needs to be grabbed, or 'called', first. Trivialization is one such one-step grabbing mechanism. Similarly, in order to talk about China (in non-demonstrative and non-indexical English discourse), we need to name China, most simply by using the constant 'China'. Trivialization is important in what follows, because in order to substitute one sub-construction for another inside a construction it is crucial to be able to grab those three individual constructions.

---

[7] See Duží *et al.* ([9], §2.4) and Jespersen [14]. We note that Van Eijck and Francez [11] and Loukanova [17] both lack explicit intensionalization and temporalization, even though the latter builds on Moschovakis' extension of Montague's IL, whereby TY$_2$ (in which *s* is a regular type) becomes available.

[8] For details, see Duží *et al.* ([9], §2.4).

[9] For details, see Duží *et al.* ([9], §2.4.2) and Jespersen [15].

[10] See Tichý ([26], §14) on this objectual notion of variables.

Procedural isomorphism, analytic information and β-conversion by value

The logical core of TIL is its notion of *construction* and its *type hierarchy*, which divides into a ramified type theory and a simple type theory. The ramified type hierarchy organizes all higher order objects, which are all constructions, as well as all functions with domain or range in constructions. The simple type hierarchy organizes first-order objects, which are non-constructions like extensions (individuals, numbers, sets, etc.), possible-world intensions (functions from possible worlds) and their arguments and values, including those values whose values are themselves intensions (like *China's most adorable property*). The relevant *definitions* are as follows.

DEFINITION 2.1 (*types of order 1*)
Let B be a *base*, where a base is a collection of pair-wise disjoint, non-empty sets. Then:

(i) Every member of B is an elementary *type of order 1* over B.
(ii) Let $\alpha, \beta_1, \ldots, \beta_m$ ($m > 0$) be types of order 1 over B. Then the collection $(\alpha\beta_1\ldots\beta_m)$ of all m-ary partial mappings from $\beta_1 \times \ldots \times \beta_m$ into α is a functional *type of order 1* over B.
(iii) Nothing is a *type of order 1* over B unless it so follows from (i) and (ii). ∎

REMARK
For the purposes of natural-language analysis, we are currently assuming the following base of ground types, which are part of the ontological commitments of TIL:

o: the set of truth-values $\{\mathbf{T}, \mathbf{F}\}$;
ι: the set of individuals (constant universe of discourse);
τ: the set of real numbers (doubling as temporal continuum);
ω: the set of logically possible worlds (logical space).

DEFINITION 2.2 (*construction*)
(i) The *variable x* is a *construction* that constructs an object O of the respective type dependently on a valuation v: x v-constructs O.
(ii) *Trivialization*: where X is an object whatsoever (an extension, an intension or a *construction*), ^0X is the *construction Trivialization*. It constructs X without any change.
(iii) The *Composition* $[XY_1\ldots Y_m]$ is the following *construction*. If X v-constructs a function f of type $(\alpha\beta_1\ldots\beta_m)$, and $Y_1, \ldots, Y_m$ v-construct entities $B_1, \ldots, B_m$ of types $\beta_1, \ldots, \beta_m$, respectively, then the *Composition* $[XY_1\ldots Y_m]$ v-constructs the value (an entity, if any, of type α) of f on the tuple argument $\langle B_1, \ldots, B_m \rangle$. Otherwise the *Composition* $[XY_1\ldots Y_m]$ does not v-construct anything and so is v-improper.
(iv) The *Closure* $[\lambda x_1\ldots x_m Y]$ is the following *construction*. Let $x_1, \ldots, x_m$ be pair-wise distinct variables v-constructing entities of types $\beta_1, \ldots, \beta_m$ and Y a construction v-constructing an α-entity. Then $[\lambda x_1\ldots x_m Y]$ is the *construction* λ-*Closure* (or *Closure*). It v-constructs the following function f of the type $(\alpha\beta_1\ldots\beta_m)$. Let $v(B_1/x_1, \ldots, B_m/x_m)$ be a valuation identical with v at least up to assigning objects $B_1/\beta_1, \ldots, B_m/\beta_m$ to variables $x_1, \ldots, x_m$. If Y is $v(B_1/x_1, \ldots, B_m/x_m)$-improper (see iii), then f is undefined on $\langle B_1, \ldots, B_m \rangle$. Otherwise the value of f on $\langle B_1, \ldots, B_m \rangle$ is the α-entity $v(B_1/x_1, \ldots, B_m/x_m)$-constructed by Y.
(v) The *Single Execution* ^1X is the *construction* that either v-constructs the entity v-constructed by X or, if X is not itself a construction or X is v-improper, ^1X is v-improper.
(vi) The *Double Execution* ^2X is the following *construction*. Where X is any entity, the *Double Execution* ^2X is v-*improper* (yielding nothing relative to v) if X is not itself a construction, or if X does not v-construct a construction, or if X v-constructs a v-improper construction. Otherwise, let X v-construct a construction Y and Y v-construct an entity Z: then ^2X v-constructs Z.

(vii) Nothing is a *construction*, unless it so follows from (i) through (vi). ∎

The definition of the ramified hierarchy of types decomposes into three parts. First, simple types of order 1, which were already defined by Definition 2.1. Secondly, constructions of order n, and thirdly, types of order $n+1$.

DEFINITION 2.3 (*ramified hierarchy of types*)
$\mathbf{T}_1$ *(types of order 1)*. See Definition 2.1.
$\mathbf{C}_n$ *(constructions of order n)*

(i) Let x be a variable ranging over a type of order n. Then x is a *construction of order n over B*.
(ii) Let X be a member of a type of order n. Then ^0X, ^1X, ^2X are *constructions of order n over B*.
(iii) Let $X, X_1, ..., X_m$ ($m > 0$) be constructions of order n over B. Then $[XX_1...X_m]$ is a *construction of order n over B*.
(iv) Let $x_1, ... x_m, X$ ($m > 0$) be constructions of order n over B. Then $[\lambda x_1...x_m X]$ is a *construction of order n over B*.
(v) Nothing is a *construction of order n over B* unless it so follows from $\mathbf{C}_n$ (i)–(iv).

$\mathbf{T}_{n+1}$ *(types of order n + 1)* Let $*_n$ be the collection of all constructions of order n over B. Then

(i) $*_n$ and every type of order n are *types of order n + 1*.
(ii) If $m > 0$ and $\alpha, \beta_1, ..., \beta_m$ are types of order $n + 1$ over B, then $(\alpha\beta_1...\beta_m)$ (see $\mathbf{T}_1$ (ii)) is a *type of order n + 1 over B*.
(iii) Nothing is a *type of order n + 1 over B* unless it so follows from (i) and (ii). ∎

Empirical languages incorporate an element of *contingency* that non-empirical ones lack. Empirical expressions denote *empirical conditions* that may, or may not, be satisfied at some empirical index of evaluation. Non-empirical languages have no need for an additional category of expressions for empirical conditions. We model these empirical conditions as *possible-world intensions*. Intensions are entities of type $(\beta\omega)$: mappings from possible worlds to an arbitrary type β. The type β is frequently the type of a *chronology* of α-objects, i.e. a mapping of type $(\alpha\tau)$. Thus α-intensions are frequently functions of type $((\alpha\tau)\omega)$, abbreviated as '$\alpha_{\tau\omega}$'. We shall typically say that an index of evaluation is a world/time pair $\langle w, t \rangle$. *Extensional entities* are entities of a type α where $\alpha \neq (\beta\omega)$ for any type β.

Examples of frequently used intensions are: *propositions* of type $o_{\tau\omega}$, *properties of individuals* of type $(o\iota)_{\tau\omega}$, binary *relations-in-intension between individuals* of type $(o\iota\iota)_{\tau\omega}$, *individual offices* of type $\iota_{\tau\omega}$ and *attributes* of type $(\iota\iota)_{\tau\omega}$. The method of explicit intensionalization and temporalization encodes constructions of possible-world intensions directly in the logical syntax. Where w ranges over ω and t over τ, the following logical form essentially characterizes the logical syntax of empirical language:

$$\lambda w \lambda t\ [...w...t...]$$

For instance, let ^0Happy construct the property of being happy, and let ^0Pope construct the office of Pope. Then $\lambda w \lambda t\ [^0Happy_{wt}\ ^0Pope_{wt}]$ is a Closure constructing the possible-world proposition that returns $\mathbf{T}$ at all and only those $\langle w, t \rangle$-pairs whose incumbent of the office of Pope and whose set of happy individuals are such that the former is an element of the latter. That is, the Closure $\lambda w \lambda t\ [^0Happy_{wt}\ ^0Pope_{wt}]$ constructs this empirical truth-condition P: $\langle w, t \rangle \in P =_{df} Pope_{wt} \in' Happy_{wt}$. Whether the pair consisting of the actual world and the present moment is a member of P is beyond logic and semantics, and must be established empirically.

Logical objects like *truth-functions* and *quantifiers* are extensional: ∧ (conjunction), ∨ (disjunction) and ⊃ (implication) are of type (ooo), and ¬ (negation) of type (oo). *Quantifiers* $\forall^\alpha$, $\exists^\alpha$ are type-theoretically polymorphous total functions of type ($o(o\alpha)$), for an arbitrary type α, defined as follows. The *universal quantifier* $\forall^\alpha$ is a function that associates a class A of α-elements with **T** if A contains all elements of the type α, otherwise with **F**. The *existential quantifier* $\exists^\alpha$ is a function that associates a class A of α-elements with **T** if A is a non-empty class, otherwise with **F**. Below all type indications will be provided outside the formulae in order not to clutter the notation. Furthermore, 'X/α' means that an object X is (a member) of type α. '$X \to_v \alpha$' means that the type of the object v-constructed by X is α. Throughout, it holds that the variables $w \to_v \omega$ and $t \to_v \tau$. If $C \to_v \alpha_{\tau\omega}$ then the frequently used Composition [[Cw]t], which is the extensionalization of the α-intension v-constructed by C, will be encoded as 'C_{wt}'.

DEFINITION 2.4 (*free and bound variables*)
Let C be a construction with at least one occurrence of a variable ξ.

(i) Let C be ξ. Then the *occurrence of ξ in C is free*.
(ii) Let C be ^0X. Then every *occurrence of ξ in C is ^0bound* ('Trivialization-bound').
(iii) Let C be [$\lambda x_1...x_n Y$]. Any *occurrence of ξ in Y* that is one of x_i, $1 \leqslant i \leqslant n$, is λ-*bound* in C unless it is ^0bound in Y. Any *occurrence of ξ in Y* that is neither ^0bound nor λ-*bound* in Y is *free* in C.
(iv) Let C be [$XX_1...X_n$]. Any *occurrence of ξ* that is *free*, ^0bound, λ-*bound* in one of $X, X_1, ..., X_n$ is, respectively, *free*, ^0bound, λ-*bound in C*.
(v) Let C be ^1X. Then any *occurrence of ξ* that is *free*, ^0bound, λ-*bound* in X is, respectively, *free*, ^0bound, λ-*bound in C*.
(vi) Let C be ^2X. Then any *occurrence of ξ* that is *free*, λ-*bound* in a constituent of C is, respectively, *free*, λ-*bound in C*. If an occurrence of ξ is ^0bound in a constituent ^0D of C and this occurrence of D is a constituent of X' v-constructed by$X$, then if the occurrence of ξ is free, λ-bound in D it is *free*, λ-*bound in C*. Otherwise, any other occurrence of ξ in C is ^0bound in C.
(vii) An *occurrence* of ξ is *free*, λ-*bound*, ^0bound in C only due to (i)–(vi).

A construction with at least one occurrence of a free variable is an *open construction*. A construction without any free variables is a *closed construction*. ∎

The next notion we need to define is that of *synonymy*. Our notion of synonymy is defined in terms of *procedural isomorphism*. Procedural isomorphism shares similarities with Loukanova's Moschovakis-based *referential synonymy*: 'Terms are *referentially synonymous* if *the same algorithm computes* their common denotation' ([17], p. 499).

Church's Alternatives (0) and (1) leave room for additional Alternatives.[11] One such would be Alternative (½), another Alternative (¾). The former includes α- and η-conversion while the latter adds a restricted β-conversion by name.[12] If we must choose, we would prefer Alternative (¾) to soak up those differences between β-transformations that concern only λ-bound variables and thus (at least appear to) lack natural-language counterparts.

One reason for excluding unrestricted β-conversion is the well-known fact that β-conversion is not an equivalent transformation in logics boasting *partial functions*, such as TIL. Another reason

---
[11](A0) is α-conversion and synonymies resting on meaning postulates; (A1) is α- and β-conversion; (A1') is α-, β- and η-conversion; (A2) is logical equivalence. See Church [4]. Anderson [1] adds (A1*) as a generalization of (A0), in which identity is the only permissible permutation. (A1*) is an automorphism defined on a set of λ-terms.
[12]For (A½), see Jespersen [16].

is that occasionally even β-equivalent constructions have different natural-language counterparts; witness the difference between attitude reports *de dicto* versus *de re*. Thus the difference between '*a* believes that *b* is happy' and '*b* is believed by *a* to be happy' is just the difference between β-equivalent meanings. Where attitudes are construed as in possible-world semantics, as relations to intensions (rather than hyperintensions), the attitude *de dicto* receives the analysis

$$\lambda w \lambda t \left[{}^0 Believe_{wt} \; {}^0 a \; \lambda w \lambda t \left[{}^0 Happy_{wt} \; {}^0 b \right] \right]$$

while the attitude *de re* receives the analysis

$$\lambda w \lambda t \left[\lambda x \left[{}^0 Believe_{wt} \; {}^0 a \; \lambda w \lambda t \left[{}^0 Happy_{wt} \; x \right] \right] \; {}^0 b \right]$$

Types: $Happy/(o\iota)_{\tau\omega}$; $x \to_v \iota$; $a, b/\iota$; $Believe/(o\iota o_{\tau\omega})_{\tau\omega}$.

The *de dicto* variant is the β-equivalent contractum of the *de re* variant. The variants are equivalent because they construct one and the same proposition, the two sentences denoting the same truth-condition. Yet they denote this proposition in *different ways*, hence they are not synonymous. The equivalent β-reduction leads here to a *loss of analytic information*, namely loss of information about *which* of the two ways, or *constructions*, has been used to construct this proposition.[13] In this particular case the loss seems to be harmless, though, because there is only one, hence unambiguous, way to β-expand the *de dicto* version into its equivalent *de re* variant.[14]

However, unrestricted equivalent β-reduction sometimes yields a loss of analytic information that cannot be restored by β-expansion. In Section 3 we show how.

The *restricted* version of *equivalent* β-conversion we have in mind consists in substituting free variables for λ-bound variables of the same type, and will be called β_r-*conversion*.

Restricted β-conversion is just a formal manipulation with λ-bound variables that has much in common with η-conversion and less with β-reduction. The latter is the operation of applying a function $f/(\beta\alpha)$ to its argument value a/α in order to obtain the value of f at a (leaving it open whether a value emerges). It is the fundamental computational rule of functional programming languages. Thus if f is constructed by the Closure C

$$C = \lambda x [\ldots x \ldots]$$

then β-reduction is here the operation of calling the procedure C with a formal parameter x at the actual parameter a: $[\lambda x[\ldots x \ldots] \; {}^0 a]$. Now a construction of the value a is substituted for x and the 'body' of the procedure C is computed, which means that the Composition $[\ldots \; {}^0 a \ldots]$ is evaluated in order to obtain the value of the function f at a.

No such features can be found in β_r-reduction. If a variable $y \to_v \alpha$ is not free in C then the β_r-contractum of $[\lambda x[\ldots x \ldots] y]$ is $[\ldots y \ldots]$. Now the evaluation of the Composition $[\ldots y \ldots]$ does not yield a value of f. As a result we just obtain a formal simplification of $[\lambda x[\ldots x \ldots] y]$.

For instance, we see little reason to differentiate semantically or logically between '*b* is believed by *a* to be happy' and '*b* has the property of being believed by *a* to be happy'.[15] The latter sentence

---

[13] For the notion of analytic information, see Duží [6] and Duží et al. ([9], §5.4).

[14] In general, *de dicto* and *de re* attitudes are not equivalent, but logically independent. Consider '*a* believes that the Pope is not the Pope' and '*a* believes *of* the Pope that *he* is not the Pope'. The former, *de dicto*, variant makes *a* deeply irrational and most likely is not a true attribution, while the latter, *de re*, attribution is perfectly reasonable and most likely the right one to make. In TIL the *de dicto* variant is *not* an equivalent β-contractum of the *de re* variant due to the partiality of the role $Pope/\iota_{\tau\omega}$.

[15] This is not to say we see no reason at all not to differentiate. For instance, it could be argued that one thing is to believe that *a* is happy and another is to believe that *a* has the property of being happy, because the latter at least appears to

expresses

$$\lambda w \lambda t \big[[\lambda w' \lambda t' [\lambda x\ [^0 Believe_{w't'}\ {}^0 a\ \lambda w \lambda t [^0 Happy_{wt}\ x]]]]_{wt}\ {}^0 b\big]$$

This is merely a β_r-expanded form of

$$\lambda w \lambda t \big[\lambda x\ [^0 Believe_{wt}\ {}^0 a\ \lambda w \lambda t [^0 Happy_{wt}\ x]]\ {}^0 b\big]$$

Thus we define:

DEFINITION 2.5 (*procedurally isomorphic constructions: Alternative* (³/₄))
Let C, D be constructions. Then C, D are α-*equivalent* iff they differ at most by deploying different λ-bound variables. C, D are η-*equivalent* iff one arises from the other by η-reduction or η-expansion. C, D are β_r-*equivalent* iff one arises from the other by β_r-reduction or β_r-expansion. C, D are *procedurally isomorphic*, denoted '$^0 C \approx {}^0 D$', $\approx / (o *_n *_n)$, iff there are closed constructions $C_1, ..., C_m$, $m \geqslant 1$, such that $^0 C = {}^0 C_1$, $^0 D = {}^0 C_m$, and all C_i, C_{i+1} ($1 \leqslant i < m$) are either α-, η- or β_r-equivalent. ∎

To summarize, our neo-Fregean semantic schema, which applies to all contexts, without exception, is this:

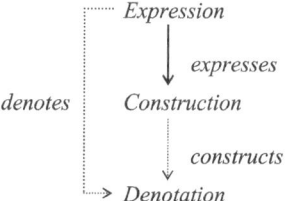

The most important relation in this schema is between an expression and its meaning (a construction). We can investigate *a priori* what (if anything) a construction constructs and what is entailed by it. Once a construction has been explicitly given as a result of logical analysis, the entity (if any) it constructs is already implicitly given, whereas it requires inquiry *a posteriori* to establish the reference (as opposed to denotation) of an empirical term at a given world/time pair. As a limiting case, the logical analysis may reveal that the construction fails to construct anything because it is improper. Whenever the construction is not improper, the denotation can be either a first-order object (i.e. a non-construction) or a lower-order construction. Intensional constructions (constructions of objects of type $(\beta\omega)$) are always proper, since they always construct an intension (including degenerate ones, which return no values at all or always the same value). In linguistic terms, every word whose sense is an intensional construction has a denotation, but will lack a reference at some or all $\langle w, t \rangle$ pairs, in case its denotation (a partial function) fails to return a value. This applies to, *inter alia*, 'The Pope', 'The Morning Star', 'The Evening Star' and 'John's wife'.[16]

---

presuppose that the believer have the additional conceptual resources to master the notion of *property*. Or if the believer is a self-assured nominalist then he may protest that while he does believe that a is happy he does not believe that a has any properties. Further research is required to decide one way or the other.

[16] For the semantics of 'The Evening Star' and 'The Morning Star', and an analysis of 'The Evening Star is the Morning Star', see Duží *et al.* ([9], §3.3.1).

Procedural isomorphism, analytic information and β-conversion by value

3 Translations into TIL

The semantic counterpart of 'so does' is the free variable $p \to (o\iota)_{\tau\omega}$ ranging over properties. The reason is because the logical form of the analysandum translates into English as 'John has a property, and Peter has that property too'. The analysis of 'So does Peter' is the *open* Closure

$$\lambda w \lambda t [p_{wt} \; {}^0Peter]$$

which takes a truth-value dependently on the valuation of p: 'p_{wt}' represents the result of extensionalizing the value of p to obtain a set. For comparison, the predication of the determinate property F of Peter is this *closed* Closure:

$$\lambda w \lambda t [{}^0F_{wt} \; {}^0Peter]$$

Further, $Love/(o\iota\iota)_{\tau\omega}$ is a binary relation-in-intension, John and Peter are individuals, and x ranges over individuals. The two properties, (i) loving John's wife and (ii) loving one's own wife, are analysed as follows:

(1') $\lambda w \lambda t \; [\lambda x \; [{}^0Love_{wt} \; x \; [{}^0Wife\_of_{wt} \; {}^0John]]]$
(2') $\lambda w \lambda t \; [\lambda x \; [{}^0Love_{wt} \; x \; [{}^0Wife\_of_{wt} \; x]]]$

The *strict* analysis of 'John loves his wife' is obtained by applying (1') to John:

(1") $\lambda w \lambda t \; [\lambda x \; [{}^0Love_{wt} \; x \; [{}^0Wife\_of_{wt} \; {}^0John]] \; {}^0John]$

The *sloppy* analysis of 'John loves his wife' is obtained by applying (2') to John:

(2") $\lambda w \lambda t \; [\lambda x \; [{}^0Love_{wt} \; x \; [{}^0Wife\_of_{wt} \; x]] \; {}^0John]$

By Composing (1") and (2") with the semantic counterpart of 'So does Peter', we obtain:

(1''') $\lambda w \lambda t \; [[\lambda x \; [{}^0Love_{wt} \; x \; [{}^0Wife\_of_{wt} \; {}^0John]] \; {}^0John] \wedge [p_{wt} \; {}^0Peter]]$
(2''') $\lambda w \lambda t \; [[\lambda x \; [{}^0Love_{wt} \; x \; [{}^0Wife\_of_{wt} \; x]] \; {}^0John] \wedge [q_{wt} \; {}^0Peter]]$

However, (1''') and (2''') are *incomplete* analyses of 'John loves his wife, and so does Peter' both on its strict and its sloppy reading. The respective constructions contain *free* occurrences of p, q and thus do not construct a proposition, until and unless a valuation of these variables is provided. Yet the two senses of the (ambiguous) sentence are *not incomplete*. The reason is because the respective properties constructed by (1') and (2') are the appropriate valuations of p, q. The valuation of p in (1''') yields the closed Closure

(1'''') $\lambda w \lambda t \; [[\lambda x \; [{}^0Love_{wt} \; x \; [{}^0Wife\_of_{wt} \; {}^0John]] \; {}^0John] \wedge$
$\qquad [\lambda x \; [{}^0Love_{wt} \; x \; [{}^0Wife\_of_{wt} \; {}^0John]] \; {}^0Peter]]$

Hence, by existential generalization, there is a property p (namely (1')) that John and Peter share:

$$\lambda w \lambda t \; [{}^0\exists \lambda p \; [[p_{wt} \; {}^0John] \wedge [p_{wt} \; {}^0Peter]]]$$

The valuation of q in (2''') yields the closed Closure

(2'''') $\lambda w \lambda t \; [[\lambda w \lambda t \; [\lambda x \; [{}^0Love_{wt} \; x \; [{}^0Wife\_of_{wt} \; x]]]_{wt} \; {}^0John] \wedge$
$\qquad [\lambda w \lambda t \; [\lambda x \; [{}^0Love_{wt} \; x \; [{}^0Wife\_of_{wt} \; x]]]_{wt} \; {}^0Peter]]$

Hence, by existential generalization, there is a property q (namely (2')) that John and Peter share:

$$\lambda w\lambda t\,[^0\exists\lambda q\,[[q_{wt}\,^0John] \wedge [q_{wt}\,^0Peter]]]$$

So far, so good. But at this juncture two problems emerge. First, TIL is strictly compositional and anti-contextualist in the following sense: constructions are assigned to disambiguated expressions as their context-invariant meanings, and the meaning of a molecular expression depends exclusively on how the meanings of its constituents are put together. Accordingly, the open constructions $\lambda w\lambda t$ $[p_{wt}\,^0Peter]$, $\lambda w\lambda t\,[q_{wt}\,^0Peter]$ should be constituents of the resulting analyses, because they are the meanings of the ambiguous clause 'So does Peter'. *Yet these meanings are incomplete*; only after a valuation of the variables p, q has been supplied do these constructions construct a proposition. If the sentence 'So does Peter' is uttered in a situation where the speaker succeeds, in whatever manner, in identifying a property (say, the property of singing) then the pragmatically identified meaning associated with the sentence *in this situation* is the construction $\lambda w\lambda t\,[^0Sing_{wt}\,^0Peter]$. This construction is $v(Sing/p)$-congruent with the construction $\lambda w\lambda t\,[p_{wt}\,^0Peter]$, but it is not equivalent to it. In another situation we may well obtain a different construction, because the variable p will v-construct a different property, e.g. the property of loving one's own wife. Hence the pragmatically identified meaning associated with the sentence *in the given situation of utterance* is a closed construction, whereas the context-insensitive meaning of the sentence is the open construction.[17]

If the sentence 'So does Peter' occurs embedded in a *linguistic context*, does it also have a pragmatically incomplete meaning? Since we are advocating an anti-contextualist approach, the answer must be Yes. The sentence has the same meaning in every context, which is to say that it expresses, always and in every context, one and the same *open* construction. Hence the closed constructions (1'''') and (2'''') are merely equivalent, and not procedurally isomorphic (i.e. synonymous), with the meanings of 'John loves his wife, and so does Peter' on its sloppy and its strict reading, respectively.

At the same time, when the clause 'So does Peter' occurs embedded in a linguistic context as in the sentence 'John loves his wife, and so does Peter' then we, as readers or hearers, are actually able to identify the antecedent which the anaphoric reference 'so does' refers to. In this way, *after disambiguating* the source clause, we get to know the construction of *which* of the two candidate properties must be substituted for 'so does' in order to complete the meaning of the target clause. Thus the whole sentence has a *complete* meaning. The solution to the apparent dilemma between according an incomplete or a complete meaning to 'So does Peter' consists in the application of the *substitution method* that we are going to deploy in Section 4. The substitution method *pre-processes* the meaning of 'So does Peter' by substituting the construction of the respective property to which 'so does' anaphorically refers for the meaning of 'so does', i.e. for the variable p or q, respectively. This substitution method is the *declarative* counterpart of the dynamic resolution of anaphoric reference as applied in Loukasova [17] or Van Eijck and Francez[11] in an imperative fashion.[18]

This is not to say that we completely avoid the imperative method for computing the complete meaning of sentences with anaphoric sentences. The method for implementing the substitution of an appropriate antecedent to accompany an anaphoric reference is introduced in Duží et al. ([9], § 3.5.3). But we prefer to specify the 'what to do' first, which is the declaration of the substitution that is introduced in Section 4.

---

[17] For the notion of *pragmatic meaning* being invoked here, see Duží et al. ([9], §3.4).

[18] Interestingly, Van Eijck and Francez ([11], p. 2) says, 'A procedure is a one definition-multiple use construct. 'We say that the meaning of a pragmatically incomplete phrase is a case of 'one-definition', i.e. a context-invariant open procedure (with free variables as formal parameters) coupled with 'multiple uses' (filling the free variable gaps by actual values relative to context).

The *substitution method* comes with two special functions.[19] The polymorphous function *Sub* of type $(*_n *_n *_n *_n)$ operates on constructions as follows. When applied to constructions C_1, C_2, C_3, *Sub* returns as its value the construction D that is the result of the correct (i.e. collision-less) substitution of C_1 for C_2 in C_3. For instance, the result of the Composition [^{0}*Sub* ^{00}*John* ^{0}*him* ^{0}[^{0}*Wife_of*$_{wt}$ *him*]] is the Composition [^{0}*Wife_of*$_{wt}$ ^{0}*John*]. The logical operation of substitution is treated as a primitive one.

The likewise polymorphous function *Tr* returns as its value the Trivialization of its argument. Thus the result of [^{0}*Tr* ^{0}*John*] is ^{0}*John*. If the variable x ranges over ι, the Composition [^{0}*Tr* x] $v(John/x)$-constructs ^{0}*John*. Note one essential difference between the function *Tr* and the construction Trivialization. Whereas the variable x is *free* in [^{0}*Tr* x], the Trivialization ^0x *binds* the variable x by constructing just x independently of valuation.[20]

The second and more alarming problem of the above analysis was broached above and concerns β-conversion. β-reduction on (1") and (2") uniformly and *equivalently* yields the contractum

(1/2") $\lambda w \lambda t$ [^{0}*Love*$_{wt}$ ^{0}*John* [^{0}*Wife_of*$_{wt}$ ^{0}*John*]]

Hence, $p = q$, in case the contractum (1/2") is deemed the correct analysis both of 'John loves John's wife' and 'John loves his own wife'. But loving John's wife and loving one's own wife are *two different properties* even when one and the same woman happens to be at the receiving end of John's loving.

It is uncontroversial that the contractum (1/2") can be equivalently expanded back both to (1") and (2"). The problem is, of course, that there is no way to reconstruct *which* of (1"), (2") would be the correct redex:

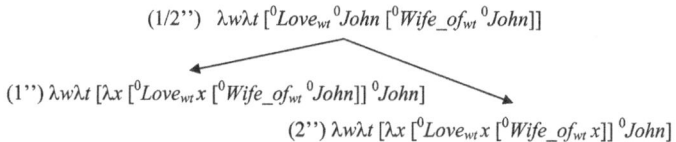

(1/2") $\lambda w \lambda t$ [^{0}*Love*$_{wt}$ ^{0}*John* [^{0}*Wife_of*$_{wt}$ ^{0}*John*]]

(1") $\lambda w \lambda t$ [λx [^{0}*Love*$_{wt}$ x [^{0}*Wife_of*$_{wt}$ ^{0}*John*]] ^{0}*John*]

(2") $\lambda w \lambda t$ [λx [^{0}*Love*$_{wt}$ x [^{0}*Wife_of*$_{wt}$ x]] ^{0}*John*]

The fact that 'John loves his wife, and so does Peter' is ambiguous is reflected by the fact that the Closure (1/2") is compatible with two merely equivalent, rather than procedurally isomorphic, λ-expansions: (1") and (2"). Consequently, there is no way to know whether to substitute (1') or (2') for the semantic counterpart of 'so does' in the meaning of 'So does Peter'.

The diagnosis of the source of the problem is that unrestricted β-reduction leads to a loss of *analytic information* about *which construction* constructs the property that was predicated of John, hence of Peter, when a token of 'John loves his wife, and so does Peter' was originally put forward in discourse. We are operating on the (not unreasonable) pragmatic assumption that the speaker intended to predicate one particular property of John and Peter rather than two properties or remain indifferent as to which of the two got predicated.

---

[19] *Sub* is introduced in Tichý ([26], p. 75) and *Tr* at ([26], p. 68).
[20] Since TIL is a λ-calculus, all variable binding is λ-binding—except for Trivialization-binding. One area where Trivialization-binding plays a key role is *existential quantification into hyperintensional contexts*, where a quantifier is introduced with a view to binding a variable that occurs bound by Trivialization, because the variable occurs inside a Trivialized context. For discussion, see Duží et al. ([9], §5.3). For amended solutions, see Duží and Jespersen [10], B. Jespersen and M. Duží (submitted for publication).

4 Solution by means of TIL

By way of preview, our solution has the following features. First, as explained above, unambiguous terms and expressions with an incomplete meaning, like 'his wife' or 'So does Peter', are analysed in *all* contexts as expressing an open construction containing at least one free variable with a fixed domain of quantification. Second, the solution uses β-conversion *by value*, as in the substitution method, rather than conversion *by name*. Third, the substitution method is applied to sentences containing anaphora, like 'so does' and 'his', in order to pre-process the meaning of the incomplete clause.

β-conversion is *the* key rule of the λ-calculus. Translated into TIL, β-conversion is the fundamental rule for computing the value of the function v-constructed by $[\lambda x\, Y]$ at an argument v-constructed by a construction C. Its version 'by name' is this, where $Y(C/x)$ is the result of correct substitution of a construction C for x in Y:

$$[[\lambda x Y]C] \vdash Y(C/x)$$

It is a well-known fact that β-conversion is not generally valid in the logic of *partial* functions.[21] If C is v-improper the Composition $[[\lambda x Y]\ C]$ is v-improper as well. But if Y is itself a Closure then it is never v-improper. Thus it may happen that the right-hand side is not equivalent to the left-hand side. For this reason the rule is usually restricted to (what TIL would construe as) C not being v-improper for any valuation v. But such a restriction to non-recursively defined cases of v-properness would be a serious shortcoming of TIL or indeed any other formal semantics based on the λ-calculus.

Fortunately, it turns out to be feasible to formulate a *generally valid computational rule*. The invalid rule above is moulded on the programming technique of calling a sub-procedure C by name: the sub-procedure itself is substituted for the 'local variable' x in the 'procedure body' Y. Programmers are well aware of the fact that this technique can have undesirable side-effects, unlike the technique of calling a sub-procedure by value.[22] The idea is simple: execute the sub-procedure C first, and then—*provided this execution does not fail*—substitute the construction of the result ('pass by the value') for x.[23] If C fails then abort the execution of the substitution procedure.

For simplicity's sake, we introduce the TIL translation of *the rule of β-conversion by value* in its simplified version for unary functions (generalization to n-ary functions is obvious):

$$[[\lambda x\ Y]C] \vdash {}^2[{}^0Sub\ [{}^0Tr\ C]\ {}^0x\ {}^0Y]$$

Note that the Composition on the right-hand side must undergo Double Execution. This Double Execution may be improper, in which case the attempt to substitute fails. Provided C is v-proper, it v-constructs an entity, say e. Then the result of the first step (the substitution $[{}^0Sub\ [{}^0Tr\ C]\ {}^0x\ {}^0Y]$)

---

[21] Moggi [18] would appear to have been the first to advance a definition of a *partial* λ-calculus. He investigates various formal systems for reasoning about partial functions with a particular emphasis on the lambda calculi. Fefermann [12] introduces axioms (λ_p) for *Partial Lambda Calculus (LPT)*, though with limitations on the instantiation of the term to which a λ-conversion is applied. Beeson [2] introduces a partial λ-calculus in which application is not necessarily total, but which lacks strictness for application. See also Duží et al. ([9], §2.7).

[22] A recent reference to the distinction between 'call by name' and 'call by value' is Pierce ([21], pp. 56–57). See also, for instance, Hyde ([13], Ch. 11) or Plotkin [22].

[23] For conversion by name, see Claim 2.5 and the subsequent proof in Duží et al. ([9], pp. 267–268); for conversion by value, see Claim 2.6 and the subsequent proof in ([9], pp. 269–270). For the general strategy (inspired by programming languages) of distinguishing between *succeeding, failing* and *aborting with error*, see also Van Eijck and Francez [11].

is the *construction* $Y(^0e/x)$. The resulting construction must then be executed in order to obtain the value of the function v-constructed by $[\lambda x Y]$ at the argument e: hence *Double* Execution. Otherwise, if C is v-improper, the substitution fails to construct anything, because due to the compositionality constraint the whole Composition $[^0Sub\ [^0Tr\ C]\ ^0x\ ^0Y]$ is v-improper and so is $^2[^0Sub\ [^0Tr\ C]\ ^0x\ ^0Y]$ (cf. Definition 2.2, (iii) and (vi)). In this manner compositionality is preserved and the above rule of β-conversion by value is always valid even when C is v-improper. In such a case, the function constructed by $[\lambda x Y]$ does not obtain an argument and so the operation of application cannot proceed to produce a value.

As mentioned above, we also introduce an imperative variant of the declaration of this substitution procedure.[24] We deploy discourse referents that are free variables serving a dual purpose. First, just like the variables of an imperative programming language, discourse referents function as memory cells where a program stores objects in order to temporarily remember them. Thus each closed constituent of the meaning of an expression occurring in a given discourse becomes a temporal value of a type-theoretically appropriate discourse-referent variable. The substitution method substitutes these values for anaphoric variables to complete the meanings of anaphoric clauses. Here our substitution method is applied in such a manner that discourse-referent variables serve their second purpose, namely as ordinary constituents of the Composition $[^0Sub\ ...]$. The completed, hence closed construction becomes in turn a new value of a discourse-referent variable of an appropriate type. In this way the discourse variables are gradually updated.

At this point we have lined up everything we need in order to analyse the particular constituents of 'John loves his wife'. The analysis of an anaphor is in terms of a free variable ranging over the same type as the type of the relevant antecedent.[25] We will analyse 'his wife' as being synonymous with (the ungainly but clear) 'the wife of himself'. Thus the semantic counterpart of 'himself' is a free variable $him \rightarrow_v \iota$, and the analysis of the description 'the wife of himself' is $\lambda w \lambda t\ [^0Wife\_of_{wt}\ him]$ $\rightarrow_v \iota_{\tau\omega}$. This open Closure v-constructs the *individual office* of somebody's only wife dependently on the valuation of *him*. That is the sense in which the meaning of 'the wife of himself' is *pragmatically incomplete*. Valuation of the free variable *him* can be provided either by the situation of utterance (e.g. deictically) or by a linguistic discourse in which the expression is used. The latter case is the case of anaphoric reference, which is what we are interested in for now.

The property of loving John's wife is constructed as above:

(1*) $\lambda w \lambda t\ \lambda x\ [^0Love_{wt}\ x\ [^0Wife\_of_{wt}\ ^0John]]$

In order to construct the property of loving one's own wife we Compose the meaning of 'the wife of himself' (namely the open Composition $\lambda w \lambda t [^0Wife\_of_{wt}\ him]$) with the Trivialization of the relation $Love/(o\iota\iota)_{\tau\omega}$. To this end we again apply the substitution technique:

(2*) $\lambda w \lambda t\ \lambda x\ [^0Love_{wt}\ x\ ^2[^0Sub\ [^0Tr\ x]\ ^0him\ ^0[^0Wife\_of_{wt}\ him]]]$

The Double Execution $^2[^0Sub...]$ v-constructs the individual who is the wife of the value of *him*. Note that the variable *him* is Trivialization-bound in (2*). Its valuation depends on the valuation of the variable x. The meaning of 'the wife of himself' remains the same: $\lambda w \lambda t\ [^0Wife\_of_{wt}\ him]$. It is a construction of an indexical individual office that must be extensionalized here in order to v-construct an individual: $[\lambda w \lambda t\ [^0Wife\_of_{wt}\ him]]_{wt}$. The substitution constituent $^2[^0Sub\ [^0Tr\ x]\ ^0him\ ^0[\lambda w \lambda t$ $[^0Wife\_of_{wt}\ him]_{wt}]]$, or its β_r-reduced form $^2[^0Sub\ [^0Tr\ x]\ ^0him\ ^0[^0Wife\_of_{wt}\ him]]$, pre-processes

---

[24] For details, see Duží et al. ([9], § 3.5.3).
[25] This idea was first worked out within TIL in Duží [5].

the meaning of 'the wife of himself' (or 'his own wife') by substituting the Trivialization of the respective first person v-constructed by x for *him*.

The constructions that are the meanings of 'John loves John's wife' and 'John loves his own wife' are, respectively:

(1**) $\lambda w \lambda t\ [\lambda w \lambda t\ \lambda x\ [^0Love_{wt}\ x\ [^0Wife\_of_{wt}\ {}^0John]]_{wt}\ {}^0John]$
(2**) $\lambda w \lambda t\ [\lambda w \lambda t\ \lambda x\ [^0Love_{wt}\ x\ {}^2[^0Sub\ [^0Tr\ x]\ {}^0him\ {}^0[^0Wife\_of_{wt}\ him]]]_{wt}\ {}^0John]$

Notice that due to the substitution technique, which preserves the meaning of 'his wife' as context-invariant, no information is lost now, because (2**) makes it explicit that the property that has been applied to John is the property of loving the wife of *himself*. Thus (1**) and (2**) do not reduce to one and the same construction, (1**β) and (2**β) being two distinct constructions:

$\lambda w \lambda t\ [\lambda w \lambda t\ \lambda x\ [^0Love_{wt}\ x\ [^0Wife\_of_{wt}\ {}^0John]]_{wt}\ {}^0John] \to_{\beta r}$
$\lambda w \lambda t\ [\lambda x\ [^0Love_{wt}\ x\ [^0Wife\_of_{wt}\ {}^0John]]\ {}^0John] \to_{\beta}$

(1**$^\beta$) $\lambda w \lambda t\ [^0Love_{wt}\ {}^0John\ [^0Wife\_of_{wt}\ {}^0John]]$;

$\lambda w \lambda t\ [\lambda w \lambda t\ \lambda x\ [^0Love_{wt}\ x\ {}^2[^0Sub\ [^0Tr\ x]\ {}^0him\ {}^0[^0Wife\_of_{wt}\ him]]]_{wt}\ {}^0John] \to_{\beta r}$
$\lambda w \lambda t\ [\lambda x\ [^0Love_{wt}\ x\ {}^2[^0Sub\ [^0Tr\ x]\ {}^0him\ {}^0[^0Wife\_of_{wt}\ him]]]\ {}^0John] \to_{\beta}$

(2**$^\beta$) $\lambda w \lambda t\ [^0Love_{wt}\ {}^0John\ {}^2[^0Sub\ [^0Tr\ {}^0John]\ {}^0him\ {}^0[^0Wife\_of_{wt}\ him]]]$

To be sure, the constituent $^2[^0Sub\ [^0Tr\ {}^0John]\ {}^0him\ {}^0[^0Wife\_of_{wt}\ him]]$ of (2**β) is *equivalent* to the constituent $[^0Wife\_of_{wt}\ {}^0John]$ of (1**β). This is only as it should be, though: (1**) and (2**) are *equivalent* by constructing one and the same proposition, but they do so in two *different ways*. Thus no analytic information is lost, because (1**β) and (2**β) are not procedurally isomorphic. Those are two different constructions, conveying two different pieces of analytic information about two different ways of constructing one and the same proposition. Let us dwell on this important point for a moment. The *result* of the substitution in (2**β) is:

$\lambda w \lambda t\ [^0Love_{wt}\ {}^0John\ {}^2[^0Sub\ [^0Tr\ {}^0John]\ {}^0him\ {}^0[^0Wife\_of_{wt}\ him]]] \to_{\beta}$

$\lambda w \lambda t\ [^0Love_{wt}\ {}^0John\ [^0Wife\_of_{wt}\ {}^0John]]$

But, crucially, in (2**β) we are not losing the analytic information that the property *loving his wife* is applied to John, unlike in (1**β). In other words, (1**β) is the meaning of 'John loves John's wife', whereas (2**β) is the meaning of 'John loves his wife'. Those two formulae are logically equivalent, because John is the value of *his*. But they do not display procedurally isomorphic constructions; hence they are not synonymous formulae. The basic point is not to lose analytic information about *which* of the two properties has been predicated of John. Only by always being able to keep track of which property gets predicated can we analyse 'John loves his wife, and so does Peter' in such a way that the sloppy reading does not reduce to the strict reading.

In order to Compose (1**) and (2**) with the meaning of 'So does Peter', namely $\lambda w \lambda t\ [p_{wt}\ {}^0Peter]$, we again need to pre-process this open Closure by means of the substitution technique. In other words, we must substitute the antecedent meaning that constructs the property which 'so does' refers to for the variable $p \to (o\iota)_{\tau\omega}$. In order to achieve better readability of the resulting analyses, let us denote the construction of the property of loving John's wife by 'P^{John}' and the construction of the property of loving one's own wife by 'P^{own}':

(strict) $P^{John's} = \lambda w \lambda t\ \lambda x\ [^0Love_{wt}\ x\ [^0Wife\_of_{wt}\ {}^0John]]$
(sloppy) $P^{own} = \lambda w \lambda t\ \lambda x\ [^0Love_{wt}\ x\ {}^2[^0Sub\ [^0Tr\ x]\ {}^0him\ {}^0[^0Wife\_of_{wt}\ him]]]$

Thus we have:

(1***) $\lambda w \lambda t\ [[P^{John's}{}_{wt}\ {}^0John] \wedge {}^2[{}^0Sub\ {}^0P^{John's}\ {}^0p\ {}^0[p_{wt}\ {}^0Peter]]]$
(2***) $\lambda w \lambda t\ [[P^{own}{}_{wt}\ {}^0John] \wedge {}^2[{}^0Sub\ {}^0P^{own}\ {}^0q\ {}^0[q_{wt}\ {}^0Peter]]]$

The procedure of pre-processing shows why β-conversion by value makes for a superior analysis when compared to conversion by name. If $P^{John's}$ is substituted for p in (1***), the result is that Peter loves John's wife. If P^{own} is substituted for q in (2***), the result is that Peter loves his own wife. If conversion by name is deployed, the result is inevitably that Peter loves John's wife. Only conversion by value can deliver those two different results. Only by adopting the substitution technique, based on pre-processing of variables and conversion by value, can we obtain two distinct contracta for the two original redexes. The announced restriction of β-conversion consists in the restriction to deploying only conversion by value when analysing anaphoric reference to properties.

Both (1***) and (2***) entail that John and Peter share a common property, though not the same in both cases. Here are the two (structurally identical) proofs. For any $\langle w, t \rangle$-pair the following proof steps are truth-preserving:

(1) $[[P^{John's}{}_{wt}\ {}^0John] \wedge {}^2[{}^0Sub\ {}^0P^{John's}\ {}^0p\ {}^0[p_{wt}\ {}^0Peter]]]$ ∅
(2) $[[P^{John's}{}_{wt}\ {}^0John] \wedge [P^{John's}{}_{wt}\ {}^0Peter]]$ Sub, 1
(3) $\exists p\ [[p_{wt}\ {}^0John] \wedge [p_{wt}\ {}^0Peter]]$ EG, 2

(1') $[[P^{own}{}_{wt}\ {}^0John] \wedge {}^2[{}^0Sub\ {}^0P^{own}\ {}^0p\ {}^0[p_{wt}\ {}^0Peter]]]$ ∅
(2') $[[P^{own}{}_{wt}\ {}^0John] \wedge [P^{own}{}_{wt}\ {}^0Peter]]$ Sub, 1'
(3') $\exists q\ [[q_{wt}\ {}^0John] \wedge [q_{wt}\ {}^0Peter]]$ EG, 2'

On the strict reading of 'John loves his wife, and so does Peter' the shared property p is $P^{John's}$, i.e. the property of loving John's wife, because the Composition $[[p_{wt}\ {}^0John] \wedge [p_{wt}\ {}^0Peter]]$ is $v(P^{John's}/p)$-congruent with the Composition $[[P^{John's}{}_{wt}\ {}^0John] \wedge [P^{John's}{}_{wt}\ {}^0Peter]]$. The sloppy reading, which we prefer, entails that the shared property is P^{own}, i.e. the property of loving one's own wife, because the Composition $[[q_{wt}\ {}^0John] \wedge [q_{wt}\ {}^0Peter]]$ is $v(P^{own}/q)$-congruent with the Composition $[[P^{own}{}_{wt}\ {}^0John] \wedge [P^{own}{}_{wt}\ {}^0Peter]]$.

5 Conclusion

We offered a logical analysis of resolution of VP ellipsis as exemplified by 'John loves his wife, and so does Peter'. On the *strict* interpretation, John loves John's wife, therefore Peter loves *John's wife*. On the *sloppy* interpretation, John loves his own wife, therefore Peter loves *his own wife*. (Whether Peter's wife is the same woman as John's wife is semantically and logically immaterial.)

The critical part of this particular sample sentence is the anaphoric expression 'his', which is ambiguous between 'his own' and 'John's' in this context. The ambiguity is visited upon the anaphoric expression 'so does': the property predicated of Peter in the target clause is a function of the property predicated of John in the source clause.

The *logical* problem is that, on too coarse an analysis, the respective redexes of the sloppy and the strict reading reduce to the same contractum, which corresponds to the strict reading. The unpleasant consequences are that the anaphoric character of 'his wife' is lost in conversion and that two properties—*loving John's wife* and *loving one's own wife*—are predicted, wrongly, to be equivalent. This erroneous prediction would detract from the value of the λ-calculus as a means of transparent logical analysis of anaphora in the form of the so-called variable-binding analysis based on λ-abstracts.

The solution to this predicament consists in using a generally valid rule of *β-reduction by value* (that exploits our substitution method) whenever there is a clause hosting a pragmatically incomplete meaning.[26] We assign one and the same *open construction* to such a clause in every context. The substitution method makes it possible to dynamically pre-process the open construction by supplying values for the free anaphoric variables. Thus no analytic information is lost.[27]

We are able to distinguish between two constructions that are *equivalent*, yet not *procedurally isomorphic*. Our concept of procedural isomorphism is at present defined as $(A^3/_3)$, which is cast in terms of α-, η- and β_r-conversion. The concept of β_r-conversion is itself defined by means of β-reduction *by name*.

The substitution mechanism based on pre-processing is a declarative variant of the imperative solution proposed by Van Eijck and Francez [11]. Both field one procedural definition with multiple uses.

Moreover, thanks to our declarative procedural semantics the conclusion that John and Peter share a common property is but a simple inference away.

Acknowledgements

The research reported herein was funded by Grant Agency of the Czech Republic Project 401/10/0792, *Temporal Aspects of Knowledge and Information* and by the internal grant agency of VSB-Technical University Ostrava, Project SP2012/26, *An Utilization of Artificial Intelligence in Knowledge Mining from Software Processes*. We wish to thank Margot Colinet for helpful advice on linguistics, and an anonymous referee for *Logic Journal of the IGPL* for raising questions that led to clarification and improvement of various points. Versions of the present article were read as invited lectures by Bjørn Jespersen at Department of Philosophy, Bristol University, and School of Computer Science, University of Birmingham, October 2012. Thanks to Giulia Terzian and Mihaela Popa for the kind invitations, and the audiences for lively discussions.

References

[1] C. A. Anderson. Alonzo Church's contributions to philosophy and intensional logic. *Bulletin of Symbolic Logic*, **4**, 129–171, 1998.
[2] M. J. Beeson. Lambda logic. In *Automated Reasoning: IJCAR 2004*, D. Basin and M. Rusinowitch, eds, pp. 460–474. Vol. 3097 of *Lecture Notes in Artificial Intelligence*, 2004.
[3] N. Chomsky. *Studies on Semantics in Generative Grammar*. Mouton, 1972.
[4] A. Church. A revised formulation of the logic of sense and denotation. Alternative (1). *Noûs*, **27**, 141–157, 1993.

---

[26] In general, all β-reductions can be restricted to 'call by value'. Duží and her research team have been developing a computational variant of TIL, namely the functional programming language *TIL-Script* (see [7, 8]). In this interpreted formalism only β-reduction by value is used. This strategy is simple and safe. For instance, also Moschovakis uses a call-by-value interpretation of β-reduction in Moschovakis [19]. There are also good, 'algorithmic' reasons for the call-by-value interpretation of composition in general, even in first-order languages without types; see Plotkin [22].

[27] The substitution technique was originally developed by Duží in order to properly analyse sentences containing anaphoric reference. Later the technique turned out to be very useful in cracking many other hard nuts in formal semantics, e.g. substitution inside hyperpropositional attitudes, attitudes *de re*, and quantifying into hyperintensional contexts. For details, see Duží *et al.* ([9], Ch. 5), Duží and Jespersen [10], B. Jespersen and M. Duží (submitted for publication).

[5] M. Duží. Semantic pre-processing of anaphoric references. In *RASLAN 2007*, P. Sojka, A. Horák, eds, pp. 43–56. Masaryk University, 2007.
[6] M. Duží. The paradox of inference and the non-triviality of analytic information. *Journal of Philosophical Logic*, **39**, 473–510, 2010.
[7] M. Duží, N. Ciprich, and M. Košinár. TIL-Script language. In *Information Modeling and Knowledge Bases XX*. Y. Kiyoki, T. Tokuda, H. Jaakola, X. Chen, and N. Yoshida, eds, pp. 166–179. IOS Press, 2008.
[8] M. Duží, M. Čihalová, N. Ciprich, and M. Menšik. Agents' reasoning using TIL-Script and Prolog. In *Information Modeling and Knowledge Bases XXI*, T. Weltzer Družovec, H. Jaakkola, Y. Kiyoki, T. Tokuda, and N. Yoshida, eds, pp. 135–154. IOS Press, 2009.
[9] M. Duží, B. Jespersen, and P. Materna. *Procedural Semantics for Hyperintensional Logic: Foundations and Applications of Transparent Intensional Logic. Logic, Epistemology, and the Unity of Science*, vol. 17. Springer, 2010.
[10] M. Duží and B. Jespersen. Transparent quantification into hyperpropositional contexts de re. *Logique et Analyse*, **220**, forthcoming.
[11] J. van Eijck and N. Francez. Verb-phrase ellipsis in dynamic semantics. In *Applied Logic: How, What and Why?*, M. Masuch and L. Polos, eds, pp. 29–60. Kluwer, 1995.
[12] S. Feferman. Definedness. *Erkenntnis*, **43**, 295–320, 1995.
[13] R. Hyde. *The Art of Assembly Language Programming*, 1996. Available at http://www.arl.wustl.edu/~lockwood/class/cs306/books/artofasm/toc.html.
[14] B. Jespersen. Explicit intensionalization, anti-actualism, and how Smith's murderer might not have murdered Smith. *Dialectica*, **59**, 285–314, 2005.
[15] B. Jespersen. Predication and extensionalization. *Journal of Philosophical Logic*, **37**, 479–499, 2008.
[16] B. Jespersen. Hyperintensions and procedural isomorphism: Alternative ($^1/_2$). In *The Analytical Way. Proceedings of ECAP VI*, T. Czarnecki, K. Kijania-Placek, O. Poller, and J. Wolenski, eds, pp. 299–320. College Publications, 2010.
[17] R. Loukanova. β-reduction and antecedent-anaphora relations in the language of acyclic recursion. In: *IWANN 2009, Part I*, J. Cabestany et al., eds, pp. 496–503, vol. 5517 of *Lecture Notes in Computer Science*, 2009.
[18] E. Moggi. *The Partial Lambda-Calculus*. PhD Thesis, University of Edinburg, 1988. Available as a *LFCS report* at http://www.lfcs.inf.ed.ac.uk/reports/88/ECS-LFCS-88-63/ (Accessed 7 September 2009).
[19] Y. N. Moschovakis. A logical calculus of meaning and synonymy. *Linguistics and Philosophy*, **29**, 27–89, 2006.
[20] S. Neale. This, that, and the other. In *Descriptions and Beyond*, A. Bezuidenhout and M. Reimer, eds, pp. 68–182. Oxford University Press, 2004.
[21] C. B. Pierce. *Types and Programming Languages*. MIT Press, 2002.
[22] G. D. Plotkin. Call-by-name, call-by-value and the λ-calculus. *Theoretical Computer Science*, **1**, 125–159, 1975.
[23] J. Ross. *Constraints on Variables in Syntax*. PhD Thesis, MIT, 1967.
[24] I. Sag. *Deletion and Logical Form*. PhD Thesis, MIT, 1976.
[25] N. Salmon. Reflections on reflexivity. *Linguistics and Philosophy*, **15**, 53–63, 1992.
[26] P. Tichý. *The Foundations of Frege's Logic*. deGruyter, 1988.

Deduction and Substitution

Substitution inconsistencies in Transparent Intensional Logic

Miloš Kosterec

ABSTRACT
This paper presents several important results for Transparent Intensional Logic (TIL). The conversions that are standardly taken to be valid – namely restricted β-conversion by name and β-reduction by value – are shown to be invalid. The core principle on which their validity is based – the so-called Compensation Principle – is also shown to be invalid. Further, the paper demonstrates the flaws of the proof of the Compensation Principle.

Introduction

The failure of substitution of intensionally equivalent terms in many philosophically relevant contexts (*knowing, believing, thinking about, claiming, ...*) led to the postulation of hyperintensional contexts and hyperintensional entities (e.g. structured propositions). A plethora of systems have been developed to investigate hyperintensional phenomena. These can be roughly divided into structuralist and non-structuralist accounts. Structuralists usually posit some hyperintensional entity to stand for the meaning of a language term. Although non-structuralists accept the existence of hyperintensional phenomena, they deal with the problems they present by using weaker logics with semantics that are often specified using the notion of impossible worlds.[1]

Transparent Intensional Logic (TIL) is a structuralist approach. It is a partial lambda calculus interpreted over the inductively defined hierarchy of entities and containing positively defined hyperintensions called *constructions*. According to the procedure-like properties of these hyperintensions, the semantics used within TIL is often called procedural. A good first step toward understanding TIL is to grasp the difference between a procedure and the result of that procedure. The notion of construction grasps this basic idea technically. In TIL, constructions are sharply distinct from any entity they may produce.[2]

TIL is now a well-established system within the field of philosophical logic and semantics. Its supporters have already provided interesting models of various philosophical topics such as the paradox of inference (see Duží, 2010; Duží & Jespersen,

2013), logics for hyperintensions (see Duží, 2012; Duží & Jespersen, 2015), the modification of properties (see Jespersen & Carrara, 2013), and paradoxes (see Raclavský, 2011). The core of this paper deals with the validity of different notions of β-reduction from a procedural perspective (see Duží & Jespersen, 2013; Duží & Kosterec, 2017; Pezlar, 2018), as analysed (and for particular kinds of reduction, also proven) within the framework of TIL.

The main claims of this paper are as follows. The notions of the free occurrence of a variable and of collisionless substitution, as specified in Duží et al. (2010) and Kosterec (2020), are inconsistent with the validity of β-reduction by value (BV), *restricted β-reduction by name* (RBN), and, most importantly, the validity of the so-called *Compensation Principle* (CP), which is a theorem that really ought to be fulfilled by any correct notion of substitution. As a result, the proofs of validity provided for each of the reductions, as well as the proof of the validity of the Compensation Principle, are invalid.[3] This paper presents counterexamples to the theorems and investigates the roots of the failure of the relevant proofs.

The theorems invalidated by the counterexamples in the paper present the *core principles* on which many of the investigations within classical TIL in the last 10+ years have been based. The validity of the so-called *substitution method* (which is really the validity of β-reduction by value) depends on the validity of the Compensation Principle. This method was used in several different areas in classical TIL: in presenting the extensional logic of hyperintensions (Duží et al. (2010), Duží and Jespersen (2015)), in investigations into the logic of propositional and notional attitudes (see e.g. Duží and Jespersen (2012)), when discussing the problems of co-hyperintensionality (see e.g. Duží (2019), Jespersen (2020)), and when considering the loss of analytic information by β-reduction by name (Duží and Jespersen (2013)), to name just a few.

TIL is also used beyond the field of analytic philosophy. For example, the substitution method is used in applications of TIL in the field of informatics: in the analysis of inferring knowledge from textual information (Duží and Menšík (2020)) and in hyperintensional reasoning over knowledge bases in natural languages (Duží and Horák (2020)). The results achieved within these investigations via the assumption of the validity of the investigated theorems are therefore put into doubt by the results of my paper.

In addition, the principles investigated in this paper (e.g. β-reduction by value) could be interesting when considering whether TIL is a case of a system with explicit substitution (see Abadi et al. (1991), Raclavský (2020, chapter 3.4.3)). Following Raclavský, however, it is important to note that TIL is a typed system, and it is unclear whether the restrictions on substitution posed by this are present in the lambda calculi with explicit substitution.

The following consists of six sections. The first presents the standard foundational definitions of TIL, as well as further definitions that are necessary for sustaining the paper's arguments. Throughout the paper, I use the term *classical TIL* for the system as it has standardly been presented after Duží et al. (2010). I investigate the proofs of the validity of restricted β-reduction by name (RBN) and β-reduction by value (BV) in the second section. The third section is the core section of the paper. I demonstrate the existence of several inconsistencies in classical TIL connected to the assumed (and allegedly proven) validity of RBN, BV and CP. These inconsistencies are demonstrated via counterexamples. The fourth section contains the investigation of the proof of the validity of CP. In the fifth section, I elaborate on the roots of the problems and discuss possible ways to solve the issues. The paper ends with a brief conclusion.

1. TIL in brief

The main notion specified within TIL is the inductively defined universe of entities called *constructions*. These stand for hyperintensional entities. The constructions are connected to other entities within the type hierarchy, which are to be considered the object they produce. This relation is specified recursively using the notion of *v*-construction (or constructing according to the valuation *v*). Just as many different hyperintensions can stand for (denote) the same intension, so many different constructions can construct the same entity. No wonder some supporters of TIL take constructions to *be* hyperintensions. One further similarity between procedures and constructions is the possibility of failure. Just as a procedure can fail to provide an outcome, so there is a possibility of failure when it comes to constructing constructions.

TIL recognises six kinds of constructions.[4] *Trivialisation* is the simplest construction that provides an entity. The Trivialisation of an entity simply provides that entity as is; in short, if *a* is an entity, then ^0a is a construction that constructs that entity. *Variables* are considered to be meaningful parts of TIL.[5] Variables are standalone constructions in TIL, not just syntactic placeholders.[6] They are the second simple construction kind. A variable constructs an entity with respect to a valuation. *Execution* is another (although rarely used) kind of construction; in short, if *X* is a construction, then ^1X is a construction that constructs the same entity as *X*. Another kind of construction – one that is not equivalent to *Execution* – is called *Double Execution*: if *X* is a construction that constructs another construction *Y*, then ^2X constructs the same entity as *Y*. *Composition* is perhaps the most commonly used kind of construction. This is no surprise insofar as the compositions constitute the procedure of application of a function on arguments. *Closure* is a kind of construction that produces a function by definition. Such constructions abstract over a given type of entity (which presents a domain of constructed functions) and specify the process of acquiring the value of the function that uses the construction that was abstracted over. This is all grasped by the following main definition:

Definition 1 (*construction*):

(i) *Variables x, y, …* are *constructions* that construct objects (elements of their respective ranges) dependent on a valuation *v*; they *v*-construct.
(ii) Where *X* is any object whatsoever (even a construction), ^0X is the *construction Trivialisation* that constructs *X* without any change.
(iii) Let $X, Y_1, \ldots, Y_n$ be arbitrary constructions. Then *Composition* $[X Y_1 \ldots Y_n]$ is the following *construction*. For any *v*, the Composition $[X Y_1 \ldots Y_n]$ is *v-improper* if at least one of the constructions $X, Y_1, \ldots, Y_n$ is *v*-improper or if *X* does not *v*-construct a function that is defined at the *n*-tuple of objects *v*-constructed by

$Y_1, \ldots, Y_n$. If X does v-construct such a function, then $[X\, Y_1 \ldots Y_n]$ v-constructs the value of that function at the n-tuple.

(iv) (λ-)*Closure* $[\lambda x_1 \ldots x_m\, Y]$ is the following *construction*. Let $x_1, x_2, \ldots, x_m$ be pair-wise distinct variables and Y a construction. Then $[\lambda x_1 \ldots x_m\, Y]$ v-*constructs* the function f that takes any members $B_1, \ldots, B_m$ of the respective ranges of the variables $x_1, \ldots, x_m$ into the object (if there is one) that is $v(B_1/x_1, \ldots, B_m/x_m)$-constructed by Y, where $v(B_1/x_1, \ldots, B_m/x_m)$ is like v except that it assigns B_1 to $x_1, \ldots, B_m$ to x_m.

(v) Where X is any object whatsoever, ^1X is the *construction Execution* that v-constructs what X v-constructs. Thus, if X is a v-improper construction or not a construction at all, ^1X is v-improper.

(vi) Where X is any object whatsoever, ^2X is the *construction Double Execution*. If X is not itself a construction, or if X does not v-construct a construction, or if X v-constructs a v-improper construction, then ^2X is v-improper. Otherwise, ^2X v-constructs what is v-constructed by the construction v-constructed by X.

(vii) Nothing is a *construction* unless it so follows from (i) through (vi).

The relation between a construction and the object (if any) that it constructs with respect to a valuation is defined recursively. The relation (which is really a partial function) is said to v-construct, as in 'a construction C v-constructs an object $c\ldots$'. This point is not usually highlighted, as the specification of the relation is usually part of the definition of construction (as above).[7] The v-construction (or rather v-constructing) relation holds between constructions (as they are the objects that are supposed to construct something) and other objects within the ramified type hierarchy (possibly other constructions). It is specified for each kind of construction. The relation is specified for simple constructions like Trivialisations and Variables. Then, the relation is specified for complex constructions (possibly containing other constructions as their subconstructions) recursively (e.g. the object related by this relation to a Composition is specified by the use of objects related by this relation to its subconstructions).

We can also have constructions that do not construct anything. For example, Composition $[X_1\, X_2 \ldots X_n]$ can be v-improper for several reasons: some of X_i could be improper, or the function produced by X_1 could fail to be defined on arguments provided by other constructions, or X_1 could fail to v-construct a function.

The universe of entities considered in TIL is a ramified typed hierarchy of entities that contains both procedural entities (constructions) and non-procedural entities (individuals, functions, etc.). The vicious circle is avoided due to the use of type theory, which uniquely assigns a type to any entity within the theory. The hierarchy contains simple entities besides constructions, collections of constructions, functions among these collections, and so on.[8] Although a definition of the type theory of TIL is not needed to understand the analysis of the proofs, I have decided to include one here for the sake of completeness.

Definition 2 (*ramified hierarchy of types*): Let B be a *base*, where a base is a collection of pair-wise disjoint, non-empty sets. Then:

T₁ (types of order 1)

(i) Every member of B is an elementary *type of order 1 over B*.
(ii) Let $\alpha, \beta_1, \ldots, \beta_m$ ($m > 0$) be types of order 1 over B. Then the collection ($\alpha\ \beta_1 \ldots \beta_m$) of all m-ary partial mappings from $\beta_1 \times \ldots \times \beta_m$ into α is a functional *type of order 1 over B*.
(iii) Nothing is a *type of order 1 over B* unless it so follows from (i) and (ii).

Cₙ (constructions of order n)

(i) Let x be a variable ranging over a type of order n. Then x is a *construction of order n over B*.
(ii) Let X be a member of a type of order n. Then $^0X, ^1X, ^2X$ are *constructions of order n over B*.
(iii) Let $X, X_1, \ldots, X_m$ ($m > 0$) be constructions of order n over B. Then $[X X_1 \ldots X_m]$ is a *construction of order n over B*.
(iv) Let $x_1, \ldots, x_m, X$ ($m > 0$) be constructions of order n over B. Then $[\lambda x_1 \ldots x_m X]$ is a *construction of order n over B*.
(v) Nothing is a *construction of order n over B* unless it so follows from **Cₙ** (i) through (iv).

Tₙ₊₁ (types of order n + 1)
Let $*_n$ be the collection of all constructions of order n over B. Then

(i) $*_n$ and every type of order n are *types of order n + 1*.
(ii) If $m > 0$ and $\alpha, \beta_1, \ldots, \beta_m$ are types of order n + 1 over B, then ($\alpha\ \beta_1 \ldots \beta_m$) (see T₁ ii) is a *type of order n + 1 over B*.
(iii) Nothing is a *type of order n + 1 over B* unless it so follows from (i) and (ii).

For the purposes of natural language analysis, the following base of types is usually assumed:

ο: the set of truth-values **T, F**;

ι: the set of individuals (the universe of discourse);

τ: the set of real numbers (doubling as discrete times);

ω: the set of logically possible worlds (the logical space).

Definitions 1 and 2 are the foundation of TIL. Many further definitions were provided within the system of TIL. These are used in the investigation of logical relations among constructions. They are all dependent on these foundational definitions and as such should be consistent with them. I will further provide the definitions needed for the argumentation in the paper.

The notion of a *subconstruction* enables us to analyse a relation between construction and its building blocks and among constructions in general.

Definition 3 (*Subconstruction*): Let C be a construction. Then

(i) C is a *subconstruction of C*.
(ii) If C is ^0X, ^1X or ^2X and X is a construction, then X is a *subconstruction of C*.
(iii) If C is $[X X_1 \ldots X_n]$, then $X, X_1, \ldots, X_n$ are *subconstructions of C*.
(iv) If C is $[\lambda x_1 \ldots x_n Y]$, then Y is a *subconstruction of C*.
(v) If A is a *subconstruction* of B and B is a *subconstruction* of C, then A is a *subconstruction of C*.
(vi) A construction is a *subconstruction of C* only if it so follows from (i) to (v).

(Duží, 2019, p. 1260)

We must, however, be careful not to conflate the notion of construction with the notion of the occurrence of a construction. A complex construction can contain other constructions as its subparts more than once, in different places. The notion of a subconstruction does not enable us to differentiate between different uses of the same construction within more complex constructions. For that reason, TIL specifies the notion of the occurrence of a construction. Any construction is either executed or not during the process of constructing the result of the (complex) construction. This can be grasped via the notions of executed and displayed occurrences of construction:

Definition 4 (*Displayed vs. executed occurrence of a construction*): Let C be a construction and D a subconstruction of C.

(i) If D is identical to C then the *occurrence of D is executed in C*.
(ii) If C is identical to $[X X_1 \ldots X_m]$ and D is identical to one of the constructions $X, X_1, \ldots, X_m$, then the *occurrence of D is executed in C*.
(iii) If C is identical to $[\lambda x_1 \ldots x_n X]$ and D is identical to X, then the *occurrence of D is executed in C*.
(iv) If C is identical to ^1X and D is identical to X, then the *occurrence of D is executed in C*.
(v) If C is identical to ^2X and D is identical to X, or ^0D occurs executed in X and this occurrence of D occurs executed in Y v-constructed by X, then the *occurrence of D is executed in C*.
(vi) If an occurrence of a subconstruction D is executed in C' and this occurrence of C' is executed in C, then the *occurrence of D is executed in C*.
(vii) If an occurrence of a subconstruction D of C is not executed in C, then the *occurrence of D is displayed in C*.
(viii) No occurrence of a subconstruction D of C is executed/displayed in C unless it so follows from (i) to (vii).

Duží (2019, pp. 1262–1263)

Definitions 3 and 4 serve the investigation of the structure of constructions and the place (or terms of use) of constructions used within other constructions. Subconstructions with executed occurrences are called *constituents*.

Because TIL contains variables, it should specify the basic property of a variable – whether free or bound. TIL, however, contains not one but two binders (binding operators, if you will). Variables can be bound either by lambda in Closures or by Trivialisation. Trivialisation has a binding precedence over Closure:[9]

Definition 5 (*free variable, bound variable, open/closed construction*): Let C be a construction with at least one occurrence of a variable ξ.

(i) Let C be ξ. Then the *occurrence of ξ in C is free*.
(ii) Let C be ^0X. Then every *occurrence of ξ in C* is ^{0}*bound* ('Trivialisation-bound').
(iii) Let C be $[\lambda x_1 \ldots x_n \, Y]$. Any *occurrence of ξ* in Y that is one of x_i, $1 \leq i \leq n$, is λ-*bound* in C unless it is ^{0}*bound* in Y. Any *occurrence of ξ* in Y that is neither ^{0}*bound* nor λ-*bound* in Y is *free* in C.
(iv) Let C be $[X X_1 \ldots X_n]$. Any *occurrence of ξ* that is *free*, ^{0}*bound*, λ-*bound* in one of $X, X_1, \ldots, X_n$ is, respectively, *free*, ^{0}*bound*, λ-*bound in C*.
(v) Let C be ^1X. Then any *occurrence of ξ* that is *free*, ^{0}*bound*, λ-*bound* in X is, respectively, *free*, ^{0}*bound*, λ-*bound in C*.
(vi) Let C be ^2X. Then any *occurrence of ξ* that is *free*, λ-*bound* in a constituent of C is, respectively, *free*, λ-*bound in C*. If an occurrence of ξ is ^{0}*bound* in a constituent ^0D of C and this occurrence of D is a constituent of X' v-constructed by X, then if the occurrence of ξ is free, λ-bound in D it is *free*, λ-*bound in C*. Otherwise, any other occurrence of ξ in C is ^{0}*bound in C*.
(vii) An *occurrence of ξ* is *free*, ^{0}*bound*, λ-*bound in C* only due to (i) through (vi).

A construction with at least one occurrence of a free variable is an *open construction*. A construction without any free variables is a *closed construction* (Duží et al. (2010, p. 47)).

The careful reader will surely see that this makes the notions of the *freeness/boundedness* of occurrences of construction dependent on valuations (i.e. they are not only structurally based). The definition of a free occurrence of a variable provides a means of specifying the correct substitution of a variable in a construction:

Definition 6 (*collisionless substitution*): Let x be a variable and C, D any kinds of construction. If x is not free in C, then *the result of substituting D for x in C is C*. Assume that x is free in C. Then:

(a) If C is x, then *the result of substituting D for x in C is D*. If C is ^1X or ^2X, then *the result of substituting D for x in C is ^1Y, ^2Y*, where if C is ^2X and X contains a ^{0}*bound* occurrence of x in a constituent of the form ^0Z, and this occurrence of x is a constituent of X' that is v-constructed by X, then Y is ^0W, where W is the result of substituting D for x in Z. Otherwise, Y is the result of substituting D for x in X.
(b) If C is $[X X_1 \ldots X_m]$, then *the result of substituting D for x in C is $[Y Y_1 \ldots Y_m]$*, where $Y, Y_1, \ldots, Y_m$ are the results of substituting D for x in $X, X_1, \ldots, X_m$, respectively.
(c) Let C be of the form $[\lambda x_1 \ldots x_m \, Y]$; for $1 \leq i \leq m$, let $y_i = x_i$ if x_i is not free in D, and otherwise the first variable v-constructing entities of the same type as x_i, not occurring in C, not free in D, and distinct from $y_1, \ldots, y_{i-1}$. Then *the result of*

substituting *D* for *x* in *C* is [λy_1 ... y_m *Z*], where *Z* is the result of substituting *D* for *x* in the result of substituting y_i for x_i ($1 \leq i \leq m$) in *Y*.

Kosterec (2020, p. 12)

The careful reader will again notice that this definition makes the notion of the result of the substitution dependent on valuations. Note that definition 6 is not stipulated in such a way that *x* must be a subconstruction of *C*. This concludes my presentation of the relevant definitions.[10,11]

2. Proofs of validity for RBN and BV

This section contains an investigation of the proofs of validity for RBN and BV (i.e. the equivalence of both sides of the conversion) that have been presented within classical TIL. This section enables us to appreciate the importance of the validity of CP for the proofs of the validity of the β-conversions.

2.1. RBN in classical TIL

Let us start with the following claim:

> 'Claim 2.5 (β-reduction 'by name') Let x_i ($1 \leq i \leq m$) occur in α-generic context of *Y*, and let D_i occur in a non-generic extensional context of the Composition [[λx_1 ... x_m *Y*] D_1 ... D_m]. Then if, for some *i* and *v*, D_i is *v*-improper then the β-reduction 'by name' [[λx_1 ... x_m *Y*] D_1 ... D_m] ⊢ *Y*(D_i/x_i) is *not a valid rule*. Otherwise, β-reduction 'by name' is a valid rule.'
> Duží et al. (2010, p. 267)
>
> Remark: *Y*(D_i/x_i) stands for the result of the collisionless substitution of D_i for x_i in *Y*.

RBN is covered by the 'otherwise' clause of this claim. The constructions of the arguments in the case of RBN, i.e. variables, are proper for all valuations by the definition of construction and the specification of valuation. What is the proof of claim 2.5?

> 'Proof. If D_i is *v*-proper for all *i* and *v*. the proof of 'otherwise' clause follows from Compensation Principle. ... ' Duží et al. (2010, p. 267)

In order to substantiate the proof of the validity of RBN, we must therefore show that it is a consequence of the Compensation Principle. Let us present the principle:

> 'Claim 2.4 (*Compensation Principle*) Let *C* be a construction. Then for any valuation *v* and a construction *D*, if *D* *v*-constructs an entity *d* then *C*(*D*/*x*) *v*-constructs an entity *c* iff *C* *v*(*d*/*x*)-constructs *c*.' Duží et al. (2010, p. 265)

Remarks: *C*(*D*/*x*) stands for the result of the collisionless substitution of *D* for *x* in *C*. *v*(*d*/*x*) is a valuation that differs from the valuation *v* at most in that it assigns the entity *d* to the variable *x*.

Less formally, the Compensation Principle states that if we properly substitute a construction constructing some entity for all of the free occurrences of a variable in some construction, then the resulting construction is equivalent to the original construction provided the relevant variable is assigned the respective entity. In other words, if we substitute properly for a variable, then we can assume that the variable is replaced by a construction to be substituted.

Let us now turn to the proof of the validity of RBN:

Proof: We have two constructions:

$$[[\lambda x_1 \ldots x_m Y] y_1 \ldots y_m] \vdash Y(y_i/x_i)$$

The left-hand construction $[[\lambda x_1 \ldots x_m Y] y_1 \ldots y_m]$ is a composition which, for any valuation v, v-constructs the result (if any) of the application of the function f which is v-constructed by the Closure $[\lambda x_1 \ldots x_m Y]$ on the m-tuple of arguments $< b_1, \ldots, b_m >$ v-constructed by variables $y_1, \ldots, y_m$. By the definition of Closure, the value (if any) of the function f on the m-tuple of arguments v-constructed by variables $y_1, \ldots, y_m$ is given as the object (if any) that is $v(b_1/x_1, \ldots, b_m/x_m)$ constructed by the construction Y. According to the Compensation Principle, $Y v(b_m/x_m, \ldots, b_m/x_m)$-constructs an object c iff $Y(y_1/x_1, \ldots, y_m/x_m)$ v-constructs the object c. $Y(y_1/x_1, \ldots, y_m/x_m)$ is the right-hand side of RBN. Therefore, the validity of RBN really is proven by the use of the Compensation Principle. ∎

This proof presupposes the validity of the Compensation Principle for any number of substitutions for any number of variables.

2.2. BV in classical TIL

Let us now turn to the claim and the proof of the validity of BV:

> 'Claim 1 Let C, D be constructions such that C is identical to $[[\lambda x_1 \ldots x_n Y] D_1 \ldots D_n]$ and D to $^2[^0Sub\ [^0Tr\ D_1]\ ^0x_1\ \ldots\ [^0Sub\ [^0Tr\ D_n]\ ^0x_n\ ^0Y]]$. Then C, D are strictly equivalent in the sense that for any valuation v they either v-construct one and the same entity or are both v-improper.

Proof of Claim 1. If one or more of the constructions $D_1, \ldots, D_n$ are v-improper then so are both C and D according to Definition 2 (iii) and (vi) [author: i.e. definition of Construction]. Otherwise, let $D_1, \ldots, D_n$ all be v-proper, v-constructing the objects $d_1, \ldots, d_n$, respectively. Then by Definition 2, (iv) the Closure $[\lambda x_1 \ldots x_n Y]$ v-constructs the following function f. If Y is $v(d_1/x_1, \ldots, d_n/x_n)$-improper, then f is undefined on $< d_1, \ldots, d_n >$ and thus C is $v(d_1/x_1, \ldots, d_n/x_n)$-improper according to Definition 2, (iii). Otherwise the value of f on $< d_1, \ldots, d_n >$ is the α-entity $v(d_1/x_1, \ldots, d_n/x_n)$-constructed by Y. Let the entity $v(d_1/x_1, \ldots, d_n/x_n)$-constructed by Y be a. Then by Definition 2, (iii) of Composition, the construction C v-constructs a. We are to show that the construction D also v-constructs a. The first execution of D constructs $Y(x_1/^0d_1, \ldots, x_n/^0d_n)$, i.e. the construction Y where according to the definition of functions Sub and Tr all the occurrences of the variables $x_1, \ldots, x_n$ are replaced by $^0d_1, \ldots, ^0d_n$, respectively. Since the Trivialisations $^0d_1, \ldots, ^0d_n$ construct the entities $d_1, \ldots, d_n$, respectively, the second execution $v(d_1/x_1, \ldots, d_n/x_n)$-constructs the entity a, or else nothing in case Y is $v(d_1/x_1, \ldots, d_n/x_n)$-improper. Hence C and D come out strictly equivalent.' Duží and Jespersen (2015, p. 664) (compare with Duží et al. (2010, pp. 269–270) and Duží and Kosterec (2017, pp. 26–27)).

Remark: $Y(x_1/^0d_1, \ldots, x_n/^0d_n)$ stands for the result of the collisionless substitution of $^0d_1$ for $x_1, \ldots, ^0d_n$ for x_n in Y.

This proof also presupposes the validity of the CP. The first part is simple – it only investigates what is v-constructed by $[[\lambda x_1 \ldots x_n\ Y]\ D_1 \ldots D_n]$ according to the basic definition of construction. The investigation into what is v-constructed by $^2[^0Sub\ [^0Tr\ D_1]\ ^0x_1 \ldots [^0Sub\ [^0Tr\ D_n]\ ^0x_n\ ^0Y]]$ presupposes the validity of the Compensation Principle in claims about what is v-constructed by $Y(x_1/^0d_1, \ldots, x_n/^0d_n)$. It follows from the Compensation Principle that $Y(x_1/^0d_1, \ldots, x_n/^0d_n)$ v-constructs the same object that is $v(d_1/x_1, \ldots, d_n/x_n)$-constructed by Y for any v.

Thus, we have demonstrated that the proofs of the validity of RBN and BV both presuppose the validity of the Compensation Principle.

3. Inconsistencies

I will now present several intricate inconsistencies that are connected to the supposedly valid and proven theorems in TIL. In the next three subsections, I provide counterexamples to the validity of RBN and BV. Most importantly, I will demonstrate that CP is not valid in classical TIL.

3.1. RBN is not valid in classical TIL

Let us now investigate the following conversion. Let y be a variable. Let z be a variable of the same type as x. Let us consider a valuation v which assigns variables as follows: y v-constructs x, x v-constructs k and z v-constructs j such that $k \neq j$. Then

$$[[\lambda x^2 y]z] \to\ ^2y(z/x)$$

is a case of RBN. Also, $^2y(z/x)$ stands for the result of the collisionless substitution of the variable z for the free occurrences of the variable x in the construction ^2y. But (!) with respect to the definitions of classical TIL, ^2y does not contain any occurrences of variable x. Therefore, $^2y(z/x) =\ ^2y$. $[[\lambda x^2 y]\ z]$ is a Composition that v-constructs the value of function f v-constructed by $[\lambda x^2 y]$ on the argument v-constructed by z (i.e. j). The value of function f in this case (following the definition of Closure) is the entity (if any) that is $v(j/x)$-constructed by ^2y. y $v(j/x)$-constructs the construction x (according to the assumption). Therefore, $^2y\ v(j/x)$-constructs j and, consequently, $[[\lambda x^2 y]\ z]$ v-constructs j. Let us now investigate the right-hand side of the conversion. y v-constructs x (by the assumption), and x v-constructs k (again, by the assumption). Therefore, ^2y v-constructs k. It was previously established that $^2y(z/x) =\ ^2y$. Therefore, $^2y(z/x)$ also v-constructs k. But $k \neq j$ (by assumption). Therefore, we have found a counterexample to the validity of RBN in classical TIL.

3.2. BV is not valid in classical TIL

Let us investigate the following conversion. Let y be a variable. Let z be a variable of the same type as x. Let v be a valuation that assigns variables as follows: y v-constructs x, x v-constructs k and z v-constructs j such that $k \neq j$. Then

$$[[\lambda x^2 y]z] \not\to [^0Sub\ [^0Tr\ z]\ ^0x\ ^{02}y]$$

is a case of BV, and it should be valid. Let us investigate what is v-constructed by both sides of the conversion. Nothing changes in our analysis of what is constructed by the left-hand side of the conversion from the case of RBN. With respect to the assumptions, $[[\lambda x\, ^2y]\, z]$ v-constructs j. Let us investigate the right-hand side of the conversion. $^2[^0Sub\ [^0Tr\, z]\ ^0x\ ^{02}y]$ is a Double Execution. It v-constructs what is v-constructed by the construction (if any) that is v-constructed by $[^0Sub\ [^0Tr\, z]\ ^0x\ ^{02}y]$. This is a Composition that constructs the value of the Sub function on the arguments ^0j (the entity v-constructed by $[^0Tr\, z]$), x and ^2y. In other words, the Composition v-constructs the result of the collisionless substitution of construction ^0j for the free occurrences of construction x in construction ^2y. But (!) according to the definitions of classical TIL (and also Kosterec, 2020), ^2y does not contain any occurrences of x, and thus $Sub(^0j, x, ^2y) = {}^2y$. Therefore, the right-hand side v-constructs what is v-constructed by ^2y. By assumption, y v-constructs x and x v-constructs k; therefore, the right-hand side v-constructs k. But $k \neq j$ (by assumption). Therefore, we have found a counterexample to the validity of BV in classical TIL.

3.3. The Compensation Principle is not valid in classical TIL

The existence of counterexamples to the validity of RBN and BV implies that the proofs of their validity must be flawed. RBN is a rather straightforward consequence of the Compensation Principle, which is also presupposed as the main building block of the proof of the validity of BV. I claim that the Compensation Principle is not valid in classical TIL or in TIL as presented in Kosterec (2020). Let us investigate the following:

Claim: The Compensation Principle is invalid.

Proof: Let y be a variable that v-constructs the variable x. Let x v-construct the entity k. Let D v-construct the entity j, and let $j \neq k$. Then, by the Compensation Principle, if D v-constructs an entity j, then $^2y(D/x)$ v-constructs an entity c iff $^2y\, v(j/x)$-constructs c.

Let us investigate this consequence of the Compensation Principle. *According to the definitions of classical TIL*, ^2y does not contain any free occurrence of the variable x. Therefore, $^2y(D/x)$ is equivalent to ^2y. $^2y(D/x)$ therefore v-constructs the same entity as ^2y for any valuation. By the assumptions, y v-constructs x and x v-constructs k. Therefore, ^2y v-constructs k. Now consider the other construction in the equivalence. What is $v(j/x)$-constructed by ^2y? $v(j/x)$ differs from v in that it assigns j to variable x. It does not differ from v in the entity assigned to y. That is, $y\, v(j/x)$-constructs x, and $x\, v(j/x)$-constructs j. Therefore, $^2y\, v(j/x)$-constructs j. But $j \neq k$. Therefore, it is not always the case that if D v-constructs an entity j, then $^2y(D/x)$ v-constructs an entity c iff $^2y\, v(j/x)$-constructs c. This is a counterexample to the validity of the Compensation Principle. ∎

4. Investigation of the problem with the proof of the Compensation Principle

The validity of the Compensation Principle was established by the proof in Duží et al. (2010, pp. 265–266). Therefore, since the principle does not hold, the proof must be

flawed. Let us investigate the proof to locate the problem. The proof takes the form of an induction on the notion of the *rank* of the construction:
'Let C be any construction. Then:

(i) If C is an atomic construction, then the *rank* of C is 1.
(ii) If C is of the form $[X X_1 \ldots X_m]$ then the *rank* of C is $r+1$, where r is the greatest among the *ranks* of $X, X_1, \ldots, X_m$.
(iii) If C is $[\lambda x_1 \ldots x_m Y]$ then the *rank* of C is $r+1$, where r is the *rank* of Y.
(iv) If C is of the form ^1X and X is of *rank* r, then C is of *rank* $r+1$.
(v) If C is of the form ^2X and X is of *rank* r, then C is of rank $r+2$.'

Duží et al. (2010, p. 265)
The proof begins as follows:
Let C be any construction. Let x be a variable, and let D be a construction that is substitutable for x. Then

'If x is *not* free in C then $C(D/x) = C$ and the Claim [author: i.e. the Compensation Principle] is valid. ... ' Duží et al. (2010, p. 265)

I claim that this is not the case according to the definitions of classical TIL (compare also with Kosterec (2020)). The counterexample to the validity of the Compensation Principle provided above is a counterexample to the part of the proof just quoted. x is *not free* in ^2y. Therefore, $^2y(D/x) = {}^2y$, but the claim is not valid: $^2y(D/x)$ v-constructs k, but ^2y v(j/x)-constructs j and $j \neq k$.

The proof also gets the induction wrong in the case of Double Execution. The proof takes the form of an induction on *the rank of construction*. The part of the proof that concerns the Double Execution runs as follows:

'If C is of the form ^2X then by Definition 2.22 $C(D/x)$ is of the form $^2X(D/x)$. By Definition 1.4, x is free in $^2X(D/x)$ if either x is free in $X(D/x)$, or is ^{0}bound in a constituent ^0Y of $^2X(D/x)$ and x is free in Y and Y is a constituent of what is v-constructed by $X(D/x)$. If x is free in $X(D/x)$, then by the induction hypothesis, if $X(D/x)$ v-constructs Z then X v(d/x)-constructs Z, **and again by the induction hypothesis, if Z(D/x) v-constructs c then Z v(d/x) constructs c.** If x is free in a constituent of Z v-constructed by $X(D/x)$, then **by the induction hypothesis, if Z(D/x) v-constructs c then Z v(d/x)-constructs c.**' Duží et al. (2010, p. 266).

The part of the proof in bold wrongly uses the induction hypothesis (that the Compensation Principle is valid for all constructions of ranks lower than the construction investigated at that moment) to cover the case of construction Z constructed by construction X in ^2X. The induction was on the rank of construction. In the case of Double Execution, however, *there is no relation between the rank of X* (or its subconstructions) in ^2X and *the rank of Z* constructed by X. X can construe a construction that has a much higher rank than its own. Therefore, it would not be covered by the induction hypothesis. Therefore, the proof in the case of Double Execution assumes, wrongly, that it can use its induction hypothesis to cover *all* Z constructed by X in ^2X. That is simply incorrect. The proof, for example, does not cover a case such as the following:

Let x be a variable. Its rank is by definition 1. Let it v-construct $^{22222}k$. Then, by definition, the rank of $^{22222}k$ is much higher than 1. Therefore, we cannot apply the induction hypothesis here.[12]

5. Discussion

This section elaborates on the sources of the inconsistencies and generates the motivation to change the relevant definitions. Recall the investigated constructions on the left-hand sides of the first two counterexamples: $[[\lambda x\,^2y]\,z]$. In investigating them, I used only the definitions of the notions of *construction* and *v-constructing*. I did not use the definitions of an *executed occurrence of a construction*, a *free occurrence of a variable* or a *collisionless substitution for a variable* at all when investigating what is v-constructed by the Composition being examined. There was no need. I only needed to use definition 1 (i.e. the definition of a *construction*), since I was investigating the question of what is v-constructed by $[[\lambda x\,^2y]\,z]$ or by ^2y with respect to the conveniently specified valuation v. On the other hand, I always had to use these definitions when investigating Double Executions on the right-hand side of the counterexamples, i.e. $^2y(z/x)$, $^2[^0Sub\,[^0Tr\,z]\,^0x\,^{02}y]$, and $^2y(D/x)$. In all cases, the constructions acquired *after substitution* v-constructed a variable x at some point of the whole procedure, but *without there being any restrictions imposed on the assignment of that variable when investigating what is v-constructed by the result of the substitution*. There is a stark contrast between the analysis of the result of applying the function provided by Closure on arguments provided by further subconstructions of Composition and the analysis of the results of executing constructions specified by β-conversions. There is simply a loss of the conditions specified by the definition of Closure when we follow the definition of collisionless substitution. After the substitution, the resulting constructions should not be investigated with respect to all v. Rather, *following the definition of Closure*, we should include the valuation specifications as they are given in the definition of Closure for the values of the provided function. Nothing like this is specified in the definition of collisionless substitution. This was the source of the inconsistencies investigated in the paper.

If we apply the definition of Closure properly, we should not lose focus of the fact that *any occurrence of a variable that happens to be executed during the execution of the construction that provides the value of the function constructed by that Closure is considered with respect to the valuation assignments presented by the definition of Closure.* Consider the case:

$$\lambda x\,^2y$$

and definition 1. This is a Closure, and it v-constructs function f. What function? By definition 1,

> '... the function f that takes any members $B_1, \ldots, B_m$ of the respective ranges of the variables $x_1, \ldots, x_m$ into the object (if any) that is $v(B_1/x_1, \ldots, B_m/x_m)$-constructed by Y, where $v(B_1/x_1, \ldots, B_m/x_m)$ is like v except for assigning B_1 to $x_1, \ldots, B_m$ to x_m.' [emphasis mine]

We therefore apply the function to an argument which was the object v-constructed by a variable z in the counterexamples (which was an object j). The value of the Composition

$[[\lambda x\,^2y]\,z]$ is given as the value of the function provided by the construction of the function to be applied (i.e. by the Closure $[\lambda x\,^2y]$). Therefore, the object that is

v-constructed by the Composition was given by the object (if any) that is **$v(j/x)$-constructed** by the constructions that are $v(j/x)$-constructed by ^2y. y conveniently v-constructed x, and we had to take the particular assignment in the valuation (i.e. $v(j/x)$) into account. This specification of the assignment of the particular variable to the applied argument *is completely lost in the definition of collisionless substitution*.

Further, consider the case presented in the counterexample to the Compensation Principle. In effect, definition 1 enables cases of variables that can occur during the execution of a construction (and not be present within that construction as its subconstruction). These cases are completely omitted in the definitions of an *executed occurrence of a construction*, a *free occurrence of a variable* and a *collisionless substitution for a variable*. These definitions do not take into consideration these occurrences of a construction, which need not be present *as subconstructions of a construction* but nevertheless play a part in the whole procedure covered by the construction. The definition of Closure, when combined with the definition of Composition, seems to ask for this kind of consideration, however. Consider the following case. Let F be a constant function with variable x as a value. Suppose that P does not contain any occurrences of variable x. Ask yourself: is the object constructed by the construction $^2[^0F\ ^0P]$ *independent of all valuations*? It is clearly not. By the specification, the construction is equivalent to x. But if we follow the definition of *a free occurrence of a variable*, we must consider the construction $^2[^0F\ ^0P]$ to be closed, without any occurrences of free variables. The definition of Closure covers these cases and effectively *binds* the variables executed during *the entire process* of providing the value for the function. But the definition of *a free occurrence of a variable* in the important point discussed here (i.e. *vi*) is based on the notion of a *constituent* (i.e. an executed occurrence of a construction). This leads us to the investigation of those definitions. Here, we can see that the definition of a *displayed vs. an executed occurrence of a construction* does not enable us to consider the 'hidden' relevant occurrence of variable x when considering which object is constructed by $^2[^0F\ ^0P]$. The problems thus begin as early as that definition.

This concludes my investigation into the sources of the contradictions. I have suggested that there are two sources – the definition of collisionless substitution does not take into account *valuation assignments* inherent in the application of the function provided by Closure on arguments. These assignments are explicit in the definition of Closure, but considerations connected to them are absent from the definition of collisionless substitution. The second problem stems from the need also to consider 'hidden' occurrences of constructions when dealing with the *freeness/boundedness* of constructions, and consequently the relevant places available for substitution.

6. Conclusion

In this paper, I have presented inconsistencies within classical TIL. I have also investigated the roots of these inconsistencies based on the (supposedly proved) validity of RBN and BV. The source of the invalidity of these conversions is traced back to the invalidity of the basic principle – CP. This paper presents a strong case for adopting the new versions of several basic definitions for TIL.

Notes

1. Jago (2014, ch. 3) offers a helpful investigation of the differences between (some of) the main proponents of structuralism and non-structuralism.
2. There are constructions that produce *other* constructions within TIL, of course. These constructions are sharply distinct, *in terms of numerical identity*, from the objects they produce. The ramified type hierarchy of TIL serves to avoid vicious circles within the system. A construction is sharply distinct from any object it produces, such that it cannot produce itself or any object that would depend on that construction for its own specification. I think this is best covered on multiple occasions by Raclavský in his discussions about the Vicious Circle Principles (see, e.g., Raclavský (2020, chapter 2.2.5)).
3. Tichý proved the principle for the versions of the system prior to his *Foundations* (i.e. Tichý (1982, 1986)) as well as for his TIL, *but this was restricted to constructions of the first order*. My counterexamples are against the validity of the Compensation Principle for constructions in general. Importantly, the counterexamples use proper Double Executions. Therefore, they necessarily concern constructions of orders higher than one. I do not claim that Tichý's proof is incorrect or that his version of the Compensation Principle is invalid.
4. The use of capitalised terms for names of kinds of constructions in classical TIL (i.e. Trivialisation, Composition, Double Execution, etc.) would seem to be a stylistic decision on Duží et al.'s part. This convention is not presumed by Tichý or used by Raclavský, however. I consistently spell the names with capital letters as another way to focus my investigation on what I introduce as 'classical TIL' in the paper.
5. The main philosophical motivations are presented, e.g., in Tichý (1988, ch. 4).
6. Classical TIL usually does not present a language accompanied by a model-theoretic semantics. Raclavský (2020), however, does present the system this way. Distinguishing between language terms and their denotational values is much more accurate when discussing the system presented therein.
7. Raclavský (2020, chapter 2.6), however, does specify this relation in a standalone definition of model-theoretic semantics for language L_{TTT}.
8. For Tichý (1988, chapter 16), and in classical TIL, *a construction of order n is a type* assigned to a construction, and it is also a *collection* of constructions of the relevant order. Various presentations of Tichý's system dispense with the notion of collection and instead use the term *set* (e.g. Raclavský (2020, chapter 2.4)) in the formulation of a ramified type hierarchy. This does not seem to present a problem, because sets as objects themselves are modelled via their characteristic functions in TIL.
9. Duží et al. (2010, 47) state: 'TIL has two kinds of binding, either by Trivialisation or by lambda. In both cases variables behave in harmony with the general principle that a bound variable is not free for substitution.' Also, following, e.g., Raclavský et al. (2015, chapter 2.6), we can add that the Trivialisations do not need any further information from valuations (concerning the assignment of values to variables) in order to construct their object.
10. The basis of the system of Transparent Hyperintensional Logic (THL) is very similar to the relevant parts of 'classical TIL'. However, THL and TIL present their basic definitions in rather different ways. Raclavský (2020) presents an original form of basic definitions that is more in line with the standard formulations of standard logical systems. In fact, the distinction between syntax and semantics (*constructional* and *denotational*) is respected much more here than in classical TIL. The definitions on which THL is based are presented in several steps, each providing a stronger language emanating from combinations of previously specified languages. These languages are then given their interpretation over models. Again, the defined notions are quite similar (if not the same) as those found in classical TIL.
11. The notion of 'a form of a construction' used in definition 6 is not defined within TIL. This is the definition taken from Kosterec (2020). I agree with an anonymous reviewer that

the word 'form' is redundant and potentially misleading. This part of the definition of collisionless substitution follows the conditions of a free occurrence of a variable within a Double Execution.

12. Raclavský (2020) ends with the original proof of the Compensation Principle. According to my own analysis, the proof is different from that presented in classical TIL. I do not discuss my counterexamples with respect to the system presented by Raclavský (2020) or the validity of the proof presented therein, as this deserves its own paper. I am also not completely sure that the relevant definitions (e.g. *subconstruction* of classical TIL and k^{th} - and $(k - 1)^{st}$ *-order subconstruction* of THL, the definition of *a free (occurrence of a) variable* and the definition *of collisionless substitution* vs. the definition of the *substitution function*) are equivalent. So again, I did not want the investigation into these relations between THL and TIL (or rather the definitions on which they are built) to hinder the presentation of my main point – the invalidity of important theorems in classical TIL.

Funding

This work was supported by VEGA: [Grant Number grant number 2/0117/19 Logic, Epistemology, and Metaphysics of Fiction.].

References

Abadi, M., Cardelli, I., Curien, P.-L., & Levy, J.-J. (1991). Explicit substitutions. *Journal of Functional Programming*, 1(4), 375–416. https://doi.org/10.1017/S0956796800000186

Duží, M. (2010). The paradox of inference and the Non-triviality of analytic information. *Journal of Philosophical Logic*, 39(5), 473–510. https://doi.org/10.1007/s10992-010-9127-5

Duží, M. (2012). Towards an extensional calculus of hyperintensions. *Organon F*, 19(supplementary issue 1), 20–45.

Duží, M. (2019). If structured propositions are logical procedures then how are procedures individuated? *Synthese*, https://doi.org/10.1007/s11229-017-1595-5.

Duží, M., & Horák, A. (2020). Hyperintensional reasoning based on natural language knowledge base. International Journal of uncertainty. *Fuzziness & Knowledge-Based Systems (IJUFKS)*, 28(3), 443–468. https://doi.org/10.1142/S021848852050018X

Duží, M., & Jespersen, B. (2012). Transparent quantification into hyperintensional contexts de re. *Logique et Analyse*, 220, 513–554.

Duží, M., & Jespersen, B. (2013). Procedural isomorphism, analytic information, and β- conversion by value. *Logic Journal of the IGPL*, 21(2), 291–308. https://doi.org/10.1093/jigpal/jzs044

Duží, M., & Jespersen, B. (2015). Transparent quantification into hyperintensional objectual attitudes. *Synthese*, 192(3), 635–677. https://doi.org/10.1007/s11229-014-0578-z

Duží, M., Jespersen, B., & Materna, P. (2010). *Procedural semantics for hyperintensional logic: Foundations and applications of Transparent Intensional logic*. Springer.

Duží, M., & Kosterec, M. (2017). A valid rule of β-conversion for the logic of partial functions. *Organon F*, 24(1), 10–36.

Duží, M., & Menšík, M. (2020). Inferring knowledge from textual data by natural deduction. *Computación y Sistemas*, 24(1), 29–48. https://doi.org/10.13053/CyS-24-1-3345

Jago, M. (2014). *The impossible: An essay on hyperintensionality*. Oxford University Press.

Jespersen, B., & Carrara, M. (2013). A New Logic of technical malfunction. *Studia Logica*, *101*(3), 547–581. https://doi.org/10.1007/s11225-012-9397-8

Jespsersen, B. (2020). First among equals: Co-hyperintensionality for structured propositions. *Synthese*. https://doi.org/10.1007/s11229-020-02987-4

Kosterec, M. (2020). Substitution contradiction, its resolution and the church-rosser theorem in TIL. *Journal of Philosophical Logic*, *49*(1), 121–133. https://doi.org/10.1007/s10992-019-09514-y

Pezlar, I. (2018). On Two notions of computation in Transparent Intensional logic. *Axiomathes*, https://doi.org/10.1007/s10516-018-9401-7.

Raclavský, J. (2011). Semantic paradoxes and Transparent Intensional logic. In M. Peliš, & V. Punčochář (Eds.), *The logica yearbook 2011* (pp. 239–252). College Publications.

Raclavský, J. (2020). *Belief attitudes, fine-grained hyperintensionality and type-theoretic logic*. College Publications. Studies in Logic 88. ISBN 978-1-84890-334-0.

Raclavský, J., Kuchyňka, P., & Pezlar, I. (2015). *Transparentní intenzionální logika jako characteristica universalis a calculus ratiocinator [Transparent Intensional Logic as Characteristica Universalis and Calculus Ratiocinator]*. ISBN 978-80-210-7973-1, Brno: Masarykova univerzita (Munipress).

Tichý, P. (1982). Foundations of partial type theory. *Reports on Mathematical Logic*, *14*, 52–72.

Tichý, P. (1986). Indiscernibility of identicals. *Studia Logica*, *45*(3), 251–273. https://doi.org/10.1007/BF00375897

Tichý, P. (1988). *The Foundations of frege's logic*. Walter de Gruyter & co.

Substitution contradiction, its resolution and the Church-Rosser Theorem in TIL

Miloš Kosterec

Abstract

I present an analysis according to which the current state of the definition of substitution leads to a contradiction in the system of Transparent Intensional Logic (TIL). I entail the contradiction using only the basic definitions of TIL and standard results. I then analyse the roots of the contradiction and motivate the path I take in resolving the contradiction. I provide a new amended definition of collision-less substitution which blocks the contradiction in a non-ad hoc way. I elaborate on the consequences of the amended definition, namely the invalidity of the Church-Rosser theorem (the so-called diamond property). I present a counterexample to the validity of the theorem in TIL with an amended definition of substitution.

1 Introduction

The existence of hyperintensional phenomena is widely accepted. The peculiar properties of hyperintensional contexts (namely the invalidity of substitution of intensionally equivalent terms) has motivated research on the enhancement of possible world semantics based on the notion of possible worlds by posing and modelling hyperintensions as standalone phenomena (either structurally or non-structurally, see e.g. Jago [13], chapter 3). Transparent Intensional Logic (TIL) belongs among the structuralist (semantic) theories that positively define hyperintensions as structured procedure-like objects called *constructions*. At base, the fundamental distinction in TIL is between procedures and their results (to the extent that there are any).

This chapter originally appeared in J. of Phil. Log. (2020), 49, pp. 121–133.

Substitution contradiction, its resolution and the Church-Rosser Theorem in TIL

The system of TIL has recently been used in many different problems, usually connected with the existence of hyperintensional objects, phenomena or contexts. The first established version of TIL was presented by Tichý [23], and its consequences and properties were investigated by Materna ([14],[16]) and Raclavský [21]. Duží et al. [5] presented the now-standard version of TIL with many further definitions and results. It was used to solve problems of analytic information (Duží [4]) and the loss of analytic information of β-reduction by name (Duží, Jespersen [7]), as a means of analysing malfunctions (Jespersen, Carrara [15]) and paradoxes (Raclavský [22]), as a system for formulating logic for hyperintensional contexts (Duží [6]; Duží, Jespersen [8]), as a system for investigating the individuation of structured propositions and co-hyperintensionality (Duží [9]), and more.

TIL is formally specified as a typed partial lambda calculus with procedural semantics based on a ramified hierarchy of types (see Duží et al. [5], chapter 2.7; Barendregt [1]). It is similar to the system developed by Church (see Church [3]).[1] The notion of *substitution* belongs to core concepts in many formal systems, and TIL is no exception. Collision-less substitution is a basis for the specification of β-reduction (a basic rule for any lambda calculus). Informally, correct substitution does not lead to the binding of previously unbound variables. The function (*Sub*), specified with respect to the definition, is a basic building block in recent work in TIL. It is thus rather inconvenient that the actual definition of collision-less substitution leads to contradiction in the system of TIL. The roots of the contradiction are open to analysis, however, and they are relatively easy to remedy in a non-ad hoc way. It is enough to follow the procedural behaviour of constructions and to amend the definition so that it better respects it. The obvious resolution of the contradiction in TIL presented here has an important consequence for TIL from the perspective of meta-theoretical analysis: the Church-Rosser theorem (CRT) is not valid in the amended system.[2] CRT states the so-called diamond property for lambda calculus, according to which the result of the reduction of a lambda term is unique. It does not depend on the order of the reductions of particular subterms.[3] Its (in) validity is considered to be among the basic meta-theoretical properties of any lambda calculus.

The paper is structured as follows. The first section contains the basic, standard principles of TIL. I provide the core definitions that will be used and discussed in the paper in the second section – namely the actual definition of the free/bound occurrence of a variable within a construction, collision-less substitution and (restricted) β-conversion by name. The third section provides the entailment of the contradiction within the system of TIL using only standard definitions and already-proven results. The next chapter elaborates on the reasons for the contradiction and presents the resolution of the roots of the contradiction. I present an amended version of the definition of collision-less substitution which blocks the contradiction in a non-ad hoc way. The fifth section investigates the consequences of the proposed resolution

---

[1] The Church's system is based on the simple theory of types (see Church [2]; Hindley [12]). TIL, on the other hand, includes the ramified cumulative theory of types (see Tichý [23], 66). It contains simple type theory as a part. For a detailed comparison of the type theories of Church's system and TIL, see Kosterec [18].
[2] The *conditional* invalidity of the CRT (based on the *actual* definitions of the system of TIL) is analysed in another paper (see Kosterec [19]).
[3] β-reduction has been investigated in TIL in many works and in several different ways (see e.g. Duží, Jespersen [7]; Duží, Kosterec [10]; Kosterec [19]; Pezlar [20]).

of the contradiction for the validity of the Church-Rosser theorem in TIL. In particular, the invalidity of the theorem is demonstrated by a counterexample. The paper closes with a brief conclusion.

2 The basic principles of TIL

In this section, I will introduce the system of TIL along the lines that have become standard since 2010. I will provide a definition of the concept of *construction*, which presents a positive definition of hyperintension within TIL. TIL is a typed lambda calculus over a ramified type hierarchy, the definition of which will also be presented. Readers who are familiar with these notions can skip this section.

The concept of *construction* is the basic concept of TIL. Constructions are procedure-like objects. Like other procedures, constructions differ from what they construct. Constructions present ways of grasping particular objects. Just as procedures can fail, constructions can fail to construct objects. Likewise, just as there are multiple ways to produce a given object, there are many different (possibly infinite) ways to grasp (construct) a given object, be it an individual, an intension or another concept. The objects (if any) that are produced by constructions therefore do not individuate the constructions. They are individuated according to the definition of construction. TIL recognizes six kinds of construction. The first kind consists in grasping the simple procedure of presenting an object. It trivially presents the object and is called *Trivialization*. If a is an object, then ^0a is a construction that constructs that object. A second particular feature of TIL is that it recognizes variables as standalone procedures. The object constructed by a variable is specified to it by a valuation. Consequently, the object constructed by a construction containing variables can be dependent on valuations. Another kind of construction is *Execution*. The name speaks for itself. If X is a construction, then ^1X is a construction that constructs the same object as X. The fourth kind of construction is called *Double Execution*: if X is a construction that constructs another construction Y, then ^2X constructs the same object as Y. The fifth kind of construction is called *Composition*. This is the procedure of applying a function to a tuple of arguments. The construction contains as a proper part a construction that produces a function and other constructions that provide an n-tuple of arguments. The result of the whole composition is the value (if there is one) of the function for the n-tuple of arguments. The last kind of construction in TIL is *Closure*. Closure is a procedure that explicitly produces a function. It abstracts over some domain (which is specified by the variables positioned after lambda). The values of the function are given by the body of the procedure, which is given by some other construction. With this introduction in hand, let us now provide the definition in full:

Definition 1 (*construction*)

(i) *Variables x, y, …* are *constructions* that construct objects (elements of their respective ranges) dependently on a valuation v; they v-construct.
(ii) Where X is any object whatsoever (even a construction), ^0X is the *construction Trivialization* that constructs X without any change.
(iii) Let $X, Y_1,…,Y_n$ be arbitrary constructions. Then *Composition* $[X\ Y_1…Y_n]$ is the following *construction*. For any v, the Composition $[X\ Y_1…Y_n]$ is v-*improper* if

some of the constructions X, $Y_1,...,Y_n$ is v-improper, or if X does not v-construct a function that is defined at the n-tuple of objects v-constructed by $Y_1,...,Y_n$. If X does v-construct such a function, then $[X\ Y_1...Y_n]$ v-constructs the value of this function at the n-tuple.

(iv) (λ-)*Closure* $[\lambda x_1...x_m\ Y]$ is the following *construction*. Let $x_1, x_2, ..., x_m$ be pair-wise distinct variables and Y a construction. Then $[\lambda x_1...x_m\ Y]$ *v-constructs* the function f that takes any members $B_1, ..., B_m$ of the respective ranges of the variables $x_1, ..., x_m$ into the object (if any) that is $v(B_1/x_1,...,B_m/x_m)$-constructed by Y, where $v(B_1/x_1,...,B_m/x_m)$ is like v except for assigning B_1 to $x_1, ..., B_m$ to x_m.

(v) Where X is any object whatsoever, ^1X is the *construction Execution* that v-constructs what X v-constructs. Thus if X is a v-improper construction or not a construction at all, ^1X is v-improper.

(vi) Where X is any object whatsoever, ^2X is the *construction Double Execution*. If X is not itself a construction, or if X does not v-construct a construction, or if X v-constructs a v-improper construction, then ^2X is v-improper. Otherwise ^2X v-constructs what is v-constructed by the construction v-constructed by X.

(vii) Nothing is a *construction*, unless it so follows from (i) through (vi).

TIL includes procedural (constructions) as well as non-procedural objects (individuals, functions, etc.) within its ontology. The vicious circle is avoided by including the type system in the ontology. The core idea is to avoid a situation where a particular object is specified by itself. TIL introduces any object into its ramified hierarchy by assigning the object a particular type. From the specified base, we have simple non-procedural objects, collections of these, functions among these collections, and so on, generated inductively over this base. Constructions, on the other hand, are considered procedure-like objects which do not really belong among the types specified thus far. TIL thus recognizes a further induction principle, which consists in generating constructions of non-procedural objects, constructions of constructions of non-procedural objects, constructions of those constructions, and so on. Here is the precise formulation:

Definition 2 (*ramified hierarchy of types*). Let B be a *base*, where a base is a collection of pair-wise disjoint, non-empty sets. Then:

$\mathbf{T_1}$ *(types of order 1)*

i) Every member of B is an elementary *type of order 1 over B*.
ii) Let $\alpha, \beta_1,..., \beta_m$ ($m > 0$) be types of order 1 over B. Then the collection $(\alpha\ \beta_1 ... \beta_m)$ of all m-ary partial mappings from $\beta_1 \times ... \times \beta_m$ into α is a functional *type of order 1 over B*.
iii) Nothing is a *type of order 1 over B* unless it so follows from (i) and (ii).

$\mathbf{C_n}$ *(constructions of order n)*

i) Let x be a variable ranging over a type of order n. Then x is a *construction of order n over B*.
ii) Let X be a member of a type of order n. Then $^0X, ^1X, ^2X$ are *constructions of order n over B*.
iii) Let $X, X_1,..., X_m$ ($m > 0$) be constructions of order n over B. Then $[X X_1... X_m]$ is a *construction of order n over B*.

iv) Let $x_1,..., x_m, X$ ($m > 0$) be constructions of order n over B. Then $[\lambda x_1...x_m X]$ is a *construction of order n over B*.
v) Nothing is a *construction of order n over B* unless it so follows from $\mathbf{C}_n$ (i)-(iv).

$\mathbf{T}_{n+1}$ (*types of order $n + 1$*).
Let $*_n$ be the collection of all constructions of order n over B. Then

i) $*_n$ and every type of order n are *types of order $n + 1$*.
ii) If $m > 0$ and $\alpha, \beta_1,..., \beta_m$ are types of order $n + 1$ over B, then $(\alpha\ \beta_1\ ...\ \beta_m)$ (see $\mathbf{T}_1$ ii) is a *type of order $n + 1$ over B*.
iii) Nothing is a *type of order $n + 1$ over B* unless it so follows from (i) and (ii).

For the purposes of natural language analysis, we usually assume the following base of ground types:

    o: the set of truth-values $\{\mathbf{T}, \mathbf{F}\}$;
    ι: the set of individuals (the universe of discourse);
    τ: the set of real numbers (doubling as discrete times);
    ω: the set of logically possible worlds (the logical space).

In its present form, TIL deals with sets via their characteristic functions. These are assigned a type with respect to a particular base. For example, the set of prime numbers is grasped by a function that maps every prime number to Truth (**T**) and all the others to False (**F**). Its type is (oτ) – the type of functions from numbers τ to truth values o. Possible world intensions, familiar from PW semantics, are modelled via functions that are dependent on possible worlds and times – if α is a type, then $((\alpha\tau)\omega)$ is an intension (usually abbreviated as $\alpha_{\tau\omega}$) – a function from possible worlds ω to chronologies of objects of a particular type $(\alpha\tau)$. Propositions – as intensions into the type of truth values – are assigned a type $o_{\tau\omega}$.
    This concludes the presentation of the basic concepts of the system of TIL.

3 Substitution in TIL

This section provides the definitions of notions that are important for the entailment of the contradiction within the actual form of the system of TIL, namely the definition of the *free/bound occurrence* of a variable within a construction, *collision-less substitution* and (restricted) β-conversion by name. I present each of these definitions in turn. Each definition is presented and then illustrated in several examples. Let us start with the definition of a free variable:
    "**Definition 1.4 (*free variable, bound variable, open/closed construction*)** Let C be a construction with at least one occurrence of a variable ξ.

(i) Let C be ξ. Then the *occurrence of ξ in C is free*.
(ii) Let C be ^0X. Then every *occurrence of ξ in C is ^0bound* ('Trivialization-bound').

(iii) Let C be [λx$_1$...x$_n$ Y]. Any *occurrence of* ξ in Y that is one of x$_i$, $1 \leq i \leq n$, is λ-*bound* in C unless it is ^{0}*bound in* Y. Any *occurrence of* ξ *in* Y that is neither ^{0}*bound* nor λ-*bound in* Y is *free* in C.

(iv) Let C be [X X$_1$ ... X$_n$]. Any *occurrence of* ξ that is *free*, ^{0}*bound*, λ-*bound* in one of X, X$_1$,...,X$_n$ is, respectively, *free*, ^{0}*bound*, λ-*bound in* C.

(v) Let C be ^{1}X. Then any *occurrence of* ξ that is *free*, ^{0}*bound*, λ-*bound* in X is, respectively, *free*, ^{0}*bound*, λ-*bound in* C.

(vi) Let C be ^{2}X. Then any *occurrence of* ξ that is *free*, λ-*bound* in a constituent of C is, respectively, *free*, λ-*bound in* C. If an occurrence of ξ is ^{0}*bound* in a constituent ^{0}D of C and this occurrence of D is a constituent of X' v-constructed by X, then if the occurrence of ξ is free, λ-bound in D it is *free*, λ-*bound in* C. Otherwise, any other occurrence of ξ in C is ^{0}*bound* in C.

(vii) An *occurrence* of ξ is *free*, ^{0}*bound*, λ-*bound* in C only due to (i)-(vi).

A construction with at least one occurrence of a free variable is an *open construction*. A construction without any free variables is a *closed construction*." (Duží et al. [5], 47).
  Examples:
  Let x, y be distinct variables. Let F, D stand for any construction. Then

- x is free in x, ^{1}x, ^{2}x, ^{20}x, [^{0}F x], λy[D x y],
- x is bound in ^{0}x, ^{02}x, ^{0}[^{0}F x], λx[D x y]

The definition of the free occurrence of a variable provides a means of specifying the correct substitution for a variable in a construction:

"**Definition 2.22 (collisionless substitution)** Let x be a variable and C, D any kinds of construction. If x is not free in C, then *the result of substituting D for x in C is C*. Assume now, that x is free in C. Then:

(a) If C is x then *the result of substituting D for x in C is D*. If C is ^{1}X or ^{2}X then *the result of substituting D for x in C is ^{1}Y, ^{2}Y*, where Y is the result of substituting D for x in X.

(b) If C is [X X$_1$ ... X$_m$] then *the result of substituting D for x in C is* [Y Y$_1$ ... Y$_m$], where Y, Y$_1$,...,Y$_m$ are the results of substituting D for x in X, X$_1$,...,X$_m$, respectively.

(c) Let C be of the form [λx$_1$...x$_m$ Y]; for $1 \leq i \leq m$, let $y_i = x_i$ if x_i is not free in D, and otherwise the first variable v-constructing entities of the same type as x_i, not occurring in C, not free in D, and distinct from y_1,...,y_{i-1}. Then *the result of substituting D for x in C is* [λy$_1$...y$_m$ Z], where Z is the result of substituting D for x in the result of substituting y_i for x_i ($1 \leq i \leq m$) in Y."
  (Duží et al. [5], 264; see also Tichý [23], 74)

Examples:
  Let x, y be distinct variables. Let F, D stand for any construction. Let -> $_{(C,x)}$ connect any construction with the result of substituting a construction C for variable x in the construction. Then

Substitution contradiction, its resolution and the Church-Rosser Theorem in TIL

- $x \to_{(C,x)} C$
- $^2x \to_{(C,x)} {}^2C$
- $^0x \to_{(C,x)} {}^0x$
- $\lambda y[D\ x\ y] \to_{(C,x)} \lambda y[D\ C\ y]$
- $\lambda x[D\ x\ y] \to_{(C,x)} \lambda x[D\ x\ y]$
- $^0[^0F\ x] \to_{(C,x)} {}^0[^0F\ x]$

The last important notion used in the entailment of the contradiction is β-conversion by name:

"**β-conversion by name.** Let $Y \to_v \alpha$; $x_1, D_1 \to_v \beta_1, \ldots, x_n, D_n \to_v \beta_n$; $[\lambda x_1 \ldots x_n\ Y] \to_v (\alpha\ \beta_1\ \ldots\ \beta_n)$. Then:

$[[\lambda x_1 \ldots x_n\ Y]\ D_1\ \ldots\ D_n] =>_{\beta n} Y(D_1/x_1 \ldots D_n/x_n)$,

where $Y(D_1/x_1 \ldots D_n/x_n)$ is the construction that arises from Y by collision-less substitution of D_1 for all the occurrences of $x_1, \ldots, D_n$ for all the occurrences of x_n, is β-conversion by name." Duží ([9], 26)

$Y \to_v \alpha$ and other similar statements stand for the statement that the construction Y is typed to produce the object of type α with respect to the valuation v.

Examples:

Let x, y be distinct variables. Let F, D stand for any construction (of the appropriate type, so that the conversion rule can be applied). Then:

- $[[\lambda x\ x]\ D] =>_{\beta n} D$
- $[[\lambda x\ ^2x]\ D] =>_{\beta n} {}^2D$
- $[[\lambda x\ ^0x]\ D] =>_{\beta n} {}^0x$
- $[[\lambda x\ [D\ x\ y]]\ F] =>_{\beta n} [D\ F\ y]$
- $[[\lambda y\ [D\ x\ y]]\ F] =>_{\beta n} [D\ x\ F]]$
- $[[\lambda x\ ^0[^0F\ x]]\ D] =>_{\beta n} {}^0[^0F\ x]$

Although the β-conversion by name is not valid as soon as the partial functions are recognized, the restricted version of the conversion is valid. 'Restricted reduction by name' in TIL refers to reduction that only has variables as the constructions that provide the arguments for application of the function. Such reduction is proven to be valid in TIL – i.e. it connects equivalent constructions (see Duží et.al [5], 265-268, especially the proof of claim 2.5).

4 Contradiction in TIL

This section presents the entailment of the contradiction in the actual form of the system of TIL. I will present the entailment in steps:

Let x, y be distinct variables. Then:

1. $^2{}^0x$ is equivalent to x.

   – This follows from the definition of construction. ^0x constructs x, and $^2{}^0x$ v-constructs whatever is v-constructed by x.

2. $[\lambda x\, x]$ is equivalent to $[\lambda x\, {}^{20}x]$.
– This follows from the definition of closure. From 1, we know that the bodies of the closures, i.e. x and ${}^{20}x$, are equivalent. If we also abstract over the same variable – here x – then we get equivalent constructions of the same function.

3. x is free in x.
– By definition 1.4.i.

4. x is free in ${}^{20}x$.
– By definition 1.4.vi.[4]

5. $[[\lambda x\, {}^{20}x]\, y]$ is equivalent to $[[\lambda x\, x]\, y]$.
– Both constructions are compositions. From 2, we know that the constructions constructing the function to be applied are equivalent – they always v-construct the same function. Also, these compositions have the same construction, i.e. y, as the construction constructing the argument for the function. Both compositions thus apply the same function on the same argument. Therefore, they v-construct the same value (if any) for any valuation, i.e. they are equivalent constructions.

6. Both $[[\lambda x\, {}^{20}x]\, y]$ and $[[\lambda x\, x]\, y]$ are examples of constructions, for which restricted β-conversion by name can be provided.
– First, both compositions contain a closure as the construction constructing function to be applied. It is sufficient to assume that both variables are typed to construct entities of the same type. Further, the construction constructing the argument is a variable. Therefore, for both constructions the restricted β-conversion by name is defined.

7. β-conversions by name of both $[[\lambda x\, {}^{20}x]\, y]$ and $[[\lambda x\, x]\, y]$ are valid.
– This follows from the validity of restricted β-conversion by name.

8. The β-conversions by name according to definition:

$$[[\lambda x\, {}^{20}x]\, y] =>_{\beta n} {}^{20}x$$

– Although x is free in ${}^{20}x$ by def. 1.4.vi, we still cannot substitute for it – the definition 2.22.a blocks it. First, ${}^{20}x$ is a case of construction of type${}^2X$. Therefore, we must apply the clause: *If C is ${}^1X$ or ${}^2X$, then the result of substituting D for x in C is ${}^1Y$, ${}^2Y$, where Y is the result of substituting D for x in X*. In this case, the result of substituting y for x in ${}^{20}x$ is ${}^2Y$, where Y is the result of substituting y for x in ${}^0x$.

---

[4] This is not the case, however, by Tichý's definition ([23], 74). This problem was solved by Duží et al. ([5], 47).

Substitution contradiction, its resolution and the Church-Rosser Theorem in TIL

But this is ^0x by def. 2.22, because x is not free in ^0x by def. 1.4.ii. Therefore, the result of substituting y for x in ^{20}x is ^{20}x.

$$[[\lambda x\, x]y] =>_{\beta n} y$$

- By def. 1.4.i, x is free in x. The result of substituting y for x in x is y by def. 2.22.a.

9. ^{20}x is not equivalent to y.
- From 1, ^{20}x is equivalent to x. By assumption, x and y are distinct variables. Therefore, they are not equivalent – there exists at least one valuation according to which they construct different objects.

10. By equivalence among constructions: ^{20}x is equivalent to y.
- The equivalencies ($\leftrightarrow$) demonstrated thus far give us:

$$^{20}x \leftrightarrow [[\lambda x\, ^{20}x]y] \leftrightarrow [[\lambda x\, x]y] \leftrightarrow y.$$
$$^{20}x \leftrightarrow [[\lambda x\, ^{20}x]y]\, \text{from 8.}$$
$$[[\lambda x\, ^{20}x]y] \leftrightarrow [[\lambda x\, x]y]\, \text{from 5.}$$
$$[[\lambda x\, x]y] \leftrightarrow y\, \text{from 8.}$$

Therefore, ^{20}x *is equivalent to* y by the transitivity of the equivalence relation.

11. Statement 10 is in contradiction with statement 9.

The entailment is based only on the standard definitions and proven results. Therefore, there is a contradiction in the system of TIL. This problem can be resolved, however.

5 Analysis and resolution of the contradiction

This section presents the analysis of the roots of the contradiction. It then suggests a proposal for resolving the causes of the contradiction and presents a way to block the contradiction.

The problem is apparent in the following: $[[\lambda x\, ^{20}x]\ y] =>_{\beta n} {^{20}x}$. According to definition 1.4, x is *free* in ^{20}x. Nevertheless, according to definition 2.22, we cannot substitute for it – it is blocked by the first clause of the definition:

If C is x then *the result of substituting D for x in C is D. If C is* ^1X *or* ^2X, *then the result of substituting D for x in C is* ^1Y, ^2Y, *where Y is the result of substituting D for x in X.*

The result of the substitution, according to the definition, is ^2Y, where Y is the result of substituting D for x in X. But in our case, X is ^0x. x is not free in ^0x. Definition 2.22 states:

If x is not free in C, then *the result of substituting D for x in C is C*.

Therefore, the result of substituting y for x in ^0x is ^0x. Thus, the result of substituting y for x in ^{20}x is ^{20}x, *according to definition 2.22*. The core cause of the contradiction is the first clause of definition 2.22. It does not enable us to substitute for free occurrences of variables, which freedom is provided by the voiding effect that a double execution has on trivialization. Although the definition of the free occurrence of a variable covers this effect (see def. 1.4.vi), definition 2.22 does not. This is the root of the problem. Because constructions like x and ^{20}x do depend on the valuations of the variable x, we must amend definition 2.22 so that it respects this behaviour.

The amended version of the definition of collision-less substitution is as follows:

Definition 2.22* (*collision-less substitution*) Let x be a variable and C, D any kinds of construction. If x is not free in C, then *the result of substituting D for x in C is C*. Assume that x is free in C. Then:

(a) If C is x, then *the result of substituting D for x in C is D*. If C is ^1X or ^2X, then *the result of substituting D for x in C is $^1Y, ^2Y$, where **if C is ^2X and X contains a ^{0}bound occurrence of x in a constituent of the form ^0Z, and this occurrence of x is a constituent of X' that is v-constructed by X, then Y is ^0W, where W is the result of substituting D for x in Z.** Otherwise, Y is the result of substituting D for x in X.

(b) If C is $[X\ X_1\ \ldots\ X_m]$, then *the result of substituting D for x in C is $[Y\ Y_1\ \ldots\ Y_m]$*, where $Y, Y_1, \ldots, Y_m$ are the results of substituting D for x in $X, X_1,\ldots,X_m$, respectively.

(c) Let C be of the form $[\lambda x_1\ldots x_m\ Y]$; for $1 \le i \le m$, let $y_i = x_i$ if x_i is not free in D, and otherwise the first variable v-constructing entities of the same type as x_i, not occurring in C, not free in D, and distinct from $y_1,\ldots,y_{i-1}$. Then *the result of substituting D for x in C is $[\lambda y_1\ldots y_m\ Z]$*, where Z is the result of substituting D for x in the result of substituting y_i for x_i ($1 \le i \le m$) in Y.

This blocks the contradiction. Now,

$$[[\lambda x\,^{20}x]y] = >_{\beta n}\,^{20}y,$$

as it should be. First, we have to substitute y for x in ^{20}x. We have to use clause 2.22*.a):

If C is ^1X or ^2X, then *the result of substituting D for x in C is $^1Y, ^2Y$, where **if C is ^2X and X contains a ^{0}bound occurrence of x in a constituent of the form ^0Z, and this occurrence of x is a constituent of X' v-constructed by X, then Y is ^0W, where W is the result of substituting D for x in Z.**

In our case,

i) $C = {^{20}x}$,
ii) $X = {^0x}$,

iii) ^0x contains a ^0bound occurrence of x in a constituent of the form $^0Z - {}^0x$ is its own constituent and contains a ^0bound occurrence of x – here $^0Z = {}^0x$.
iv) This occurrence of x in ^0x is a constituent of X' v-constructed by $X - {}^0x$ v-constructs x, and x is a constituent of x.
   Therefore,
v) Y is ^0W, where W is the result of substituting D for x in Z. In our case, W is the result of substituting y for x in x; therefore, $W = y$. Y is thus ^0y. And the whole result of substituting y for x in ^{20}x is ^{20}y.

In this way, the contradiction is blocked.[5] The definition is also in accordance with the procedural character of constructions. It respects the fact, grasped by def. 1.4.vi, that double execution voids trivialization. Therefore, if we consider such occurrences of variables as free, we will be able to substitute for these occurrences. The function values provided by closure $[\lambda x^{20}x]$ *are given by* what is v-constructed by x. This construction constructs an identity relation for the type of objects v-constructed by x. Therefore, after its application on any argument, we will be given that argument. This feature is provided by the amended definition of substitution. $[[\lambda x^{20}x] y] => _{\beta n} {}^{20}y$, and ^{20}y is equivalent to y. The object constructed by y is constructed by the construction after β-conversion by name employing definition 2.22*.

6 The consequence of the resolution: The invalidity of the Church-Rosser theorem

The important consequence of the proposed amended definition of collision-less substitution is that the Church-Rosser theorem is not valid for β-reduction by name. The counterexample is easy to follow:
   Let x, y and z be distinct variables. The constructions to be reduced are in bold.

i) $[[\lambda x\ [[\lambda y\ {}^2y]\ {}^0x]]\ z] => _{\beta n} [[\lambda y\ {}^2y]\ {}^0x] => _{\beta n} {}^{20}x$
ii) $[[\lambda x\ [[\lambda y\ {}^2y]\ {}^0x]]\ z] => _{\beta n} [[\lambda x^{20}x]\ z] => _{\beta n} {}^{20}z$

$^{20}x \neq {}^{20}z$ in TIL, and neither is further reducible. Therefore, CRT does not hold in TIL (with an amended definition of collision-less substitution) for β-reduction by name.
   Although the validity of CRT providing the diamond property is desirable for any lambda calculus, especially in connection with its possible use in computer science, its invalidity is definitely not a knock-down argument against the system. The system of Intensional Logic familiar from Montague is another case where CRT does not hold (see Friedmann, Warren [11], 323; Muskens [17], 24; Duží et al. [5], 202-203). Some could say that the invalidity is *only* the consequence of the amended definition of collision-less substitution. I claim that the invalidity is based on any definition that enables us to correctly substitute for the free occurrence of x in ^{20}x. If we preclude this, then there is a contradiction in TIL. On the other hand, if we enable it, then the CRT is not valid for β-reduction by name. The counterexample is not based on much more

---
[5] The reader is invited to check the definition for other relevant cases, such as $[[\lambda x^{20}[[\lambda z\ z]\ x]]\ y]$.

than this. It is preferable to accept the invalidity of CRT, which does not block actual work done in philosophical logic, as opposed to accepting a contradiction in the system, which invalidates the use of the system as a whole, no matter the field of use.

7 Conclusion

This paper presents a meta-theoretical analysis of the system of Transparent Intensional Logic. The core third section presents an entailment of the contradiction within the system of TIL using only standard definitions and proven results. The contradiction is based on the incorrect specification of the collision-less substitution for variables, whose $^0boundedness$ is voided by the use of double execution. This fact, although grasped by the definition of the free occurrence of a variable, is not respected in the actual definition of correct collision-less substitution. An amended definition of collision-less substitution that blocks the entailment of the contradiction is presented. Further, the consequent invalidity of the Church-Rosser theorem for β-reduction by name is demonstrated. CRT invalidity in TIL is preferable to the inconsistency of TIL as a whole.

Acknowledgments I thank Marián Zouhar, Martin Vacek, Daniela Glavaničová and Matteo Pascucci for their comments on a previous version of the paper. I would also like to thank Carolyn Benson for correcting my English.

References

1. Barendregt, H. P. (1992). *Lambda Calculi with Types*. ://ttic.uchicago.edu/~dreyer/course/papers/barendregt.pdf. Accessed 11 September 2017.
2. Church, A. (1940). A formulation of the simple theory of types. *The Journal of Symbolic Logic, 5*(2), 56–68.
3. Church, A. (1951). A Formulation of the Logic of Sense and Denotation. In P. Henle, H. M. Kallen, & S. K. Langer (Eds.), *Structure, Method and Meaning: Essays in Honor of Henry M. Sheffer* (pp. 3–24). New York: The Liberal Arts Press.
4. Duží, M. (2010). The Paradox of Inference and the Non-Triviality of Analytic Information. *Journal of Philosophical Logic, 39*(5), 473–510.
5. Duží, M., Jespersen, B., & Materna, P. (2010). *Procedural Semantics for Hyperintensional Logic: Foundations and Applications of Transparent Intensional Logic*. Berlin: Springer.
6. Duží, M. (2012). Towards an extensional calculus of hyperintensions. *Organon F, 19*(supplementary issue 1), 20-45.
7. Duží, M., & Jespersen, B. (2013). Procedural isomorphism, analytic information, and B- conversion by value. *Logic Journal of the IGPL, 21*(2), 291–308.
8. Duží, M., & Jespersen, B. (2015). Transparent Quantification into Hyperintensional objectual attitudes. *Synthese, 192*(3), 635–677.
9. Duží, M. (2017): If structured propositions are logical procedures then how are procedures Individuated?. *Synthese*. https://doi.org/10.1007/s11229-017-1595-5
10. Duží, M., & Kosterec, M. (2017). A valid rule of β-conversion for the logic of partial functions. *Organon F, 24*(1), 10–36.
11. Friedmann, J., & Warren, D. S. (1980). λ-Normal Forms in an Intensional Logic for English. *Studia Logica, 39*, 311–324.
12. Hindley, J. R. (1997). *Basic Simple Type Theory*. Cambridge University Press.
13. Jago, M. (2014). *The Impossible: An Essay on Hyperintensionality*. Oxford: Oxford University Press.

14. Jespersen, B., & Materna, P. (2002). Are Wooden Tables Necessarily Wooden? Intensional Essentialism Versus Metaphysical Modality. *Acta Analytica, 17*(1), 115–150.
15. Jespersen, B., & Carrara, M. (2013). A New Logic of Technical Malfunction. *Studia Logica, 101*(3), 547–581.
16. Materna, P. (1998). *Concepts and Objects*. Helsinki: Acta Philosophica Fennica 63.
17. Muskens, R. (1995): *Meaning and Partiality*. CSLI Leland Stanford Junior University, California: Stanford.
18. Kosterec, M. (2016). On the number of Types. *Synthese*. https://doi.org/10.1007/s11229-016-1190-1.
19. Kosterec, M. (submitted): On the Validity of the Church-Rosser Theorem for β-reductions in Transparent Intensional Logic.
20. Pezlar, I. (2018). On Two Notions of Computation in Transparent Intensional Logic. *Axiomathes*. https://doi.org/10.1007/s10516-018-9401-7.
21. Raclavský, J. (2009). *Jména a deskripce*. Olomouc: Nakladatelství Olomouc.
22. Raclavský, J. (2011). Semantic Paradoxes and Transparent Intensional Logic. In M. Peliš & V. Punčochář (Eds.), *The Logica Yearbook 2011* (pp. 239–252). London: College Publications.
23. Tichý, P. (1988). *The Foundations of Frege's Logic*. Berlin: Walter de Gruyter & co.

A Hyperintensional Theory of Intelligent Question Answering in TIL

Marie Duží and Michal Fait

Abstract The paper deals with natural language processing and question answering over large corpora of formalised natural language texts. Our background theory is the system of Transparent Intensional Logic (TIL) which is a partial, hyperintensional, typed λ-calculus. Having a fine-grained analysis of natural language sentences in the form of TIL constructions, we apply Gentzen's system of natural deduction adjusted for TIL to answer questions in an 'intelligent' way. It means that our system derives logical consequences entailed by the input sentences rather than merely searching answers by keywords. The theory of question answering must involve special rules rooted in the rich semantics of a natural language, and the TIL system makes it possible to formalise all the semantically salient features of natural languages in a fine-grained way. In particular, since TIL is a logic of *partial* functions, it is apt for dealing with non-referring terms and sentences with truth-value gaps. It is important because sentences often come attached with a *presupposition* that must be true so that a given sentence had any truth-value. And since answering is no less important than raising questions, we also propose a method of adequate unambiguous answering questions with presuppositions. In case the presupposition of a question is not true (because either false or 'gappy'), there is no unambiguous direct answer, and an adequate complete answer is instead a negated presupposition. There are two novelties; one is the analysis and answering of Wh-questions that transform into λ-terms referring to α-objects where α is not the type of a truth-value. The second is integration of special rules rooted in the semantics of natural language into Gentzen's system of natural deduction, together with a heuristic method of searching relevant sentences in the labyrinth of input text data that is driven by constituents of a given question.

A hyperintensional theory of intelligent question answering in TIL

1 Introduction

Formal analysis of interrogative sentences and appropriate answers should not be missing from any formal system dealing with natural language processing because questioning and answering plays an essential role in our communication and has many logically relevant features. To this end, many systems of *erotetic logic* have been developed.[1] In general, these logics specify axioms and rules that are special for questioning and answering. The systems of erotetic logics are valuable, as they render many exciting features of Yes-No questions and answers. However, many other important features of questions stem from their *presuppositions*.[2] Everybody who is at least partially acquainted with the methods applied in the social sciences has heard of the importance to consider the presuppositions of a question in *questionnaires*. Yet, to our best knowledge, none of the systems of erotetic logic deals with the presuppositions of questions in a satisfactory way. This is unsatisfactory because they fail to consider *properly partial functions*, which lack a value at some of their arguments. For instance, propositions (in their capacity as truth-bearers) can have *truth-value gaps*. Moreover, we need question-answering systems that would be able to extract pieces of information from natural language texts and answer not only Yes-No questions but also *Wh-questions*, which is beyond the capacities of ordinary erotetic logics.

In the era of information overload, the systems that can answer questions raised over the large corpora of text data in an 'intelligent' way gain more and more interest in the research community. To achieve such a goal, logic and computational linguistics are the disciplines that should work hand in hand in natural language processing and question answering. Moreover, the logical system should make it possible to render all the semantically salient features of natural language in a fine-grained way. We have a suitable system at hand, though. It is Tichý's Transparent Intensional Logic (TIL), which comes with a *procedural* semantics that assigns abstract procedures to the terms and expressions of natural language as their meanings. These procedures are rigorously defined as TIL constructions which produce lower-order objects as their products or in well-defined cases fail to produce an object. In case of *empirical* expressions, the produced entity is a *possible-world semantic (PWS)* α-*intension* viewed as a *partial* function from possible worlds to a function from instants of time to α-typed entities (where α is a placeholder for specific types) such that each world-time pair is taken to *at most one* value of type α.[3]

In this paper, we introduce a system that derives the logical consequences of information recorded in the huge knowledge bases of text data. Thus, the system not only answers the questions by providing explicit knowledge sought by keywords. It answers in an 'intelligent' way and computes *inferable* knowledge [ ] such that rational human agents would produce if only this were not beyond their time and space capacities. To this end, we apply Gentzen's system of natural deduction adjusted to

---

[1] See for instance, [ ], [ ], [ ], [ ], [ ], [ ].
[2] See [ ].
[3] For more details on TIL, see, for instance, [ ] or [ ].

our background theory of Transparent Intensional Logic (TIL). Duží and Horák in [ ] introduce the system that applies the goal-driven, backward-chaining strategy of inferring answers by general resolution method adjusted for TIL. It seems to be a natural choice because by applying the goal-driven strategy, we can easily solve the problem of searching for relevant information resources in the huge labyrinth of input data. Yet, a problem arises here, namely the problem of integrating special rules rooted in the rich natural language semantics into the deduction process because input formulas for the resolution method must come in the Skolem clausal form (see [ ]). These semantic rules include, inter alia, the rules of left and right subsectivity for *property modifiers*, the rules for handling non-referring terms and propositions with truth-value gaps, the rules dealing with *factive verbs* like 'knowing' or 'regretting', *presuppositions* of sentences, *de dicto* vs *de re* attitudes, and many other.

There are two main goals of the paper. The first one is to illustrate how to derive answers deduced from the sentences extracted from natural language texts, and how to integrate the special rules of natural language semantics into the system of Gentzen's natural deduction. This integration has been dealt with in the paper ([ ]) by the authors published in the proceedings of the ICAART 2020 conference. The second main goal and the *novelty* of this paper is the analysis of Wh-questions and deducing answers to them. In English, one can find two main types of questions: open-ended and closed-ended. While open-ended questions have many options, closed-ended questions have simple answers with few options. Here we do not deal with open-ended questions. Rather, we concentrate on closed-ended questions, which are Yes-No questions and simple Wh-questions that are similar to Yes-No questions, but the variety of answers is greater. They are, for instance questions beginning with 'what' asking for a thing, 'when' asking for time, 'who' asking for a person, 'where' asking for a place or location of something, 'why' asking for a reason, and 'how' asking for directions or instructions. The analysis of Wh-questions transforms in our TIL formalism into λ-terms denoting procedures that produce α-intensions where α is not a truth-value. The sought answer should provide an object of type α, which is the value of the α-intension asked for in the world and time of evaluation. The classical system of natural deduction does not make it possible because in such a system we deal only with formulas denoting truth-values. We show how to deal with such λ-terms and how by suitable substitutions obtain the sought values that serve as answers to Wh-questions.

In terms of practical applications, our theoretical results are being implemented as one of the most important components of an intelligent question-answering system over large corpora of natural language texts. To this end we are making use of the Normal Translation Algorithm (NTA) that has been developed in the Centre for Natural Language Processing at the Faculty of Informatics, Masaryk University of Brno [ ]. NTA is a method that integrates logical analysis of sentences with a linguistic approach to semantics. The result of NTA so far is a corpus of more than six thousands of constructions obtained by the analysis of newspaper sentences that serve as an input for our inference machine. Furthermore, our procedural approach makes it possible to implement the extensional logic of hyperintensions so as to provide relevant information from a wide range of natural-language resources.

The rest of the paper is organized as follows. Sect. 2 introduces our background system of Transparent Intensional Logic (TIL). In Sect. 3 we briefly describe the rules of natural deduction adjusted to TIL. In Sect. 4 we introduce the semantic rules and their formalization in TIL. Sect. 5 deals with Wh-questions and answers to them. Sect. 6 illustrates our method of intelligent question answering by two case studies. Finally, Sect. 7 contains some concluding remarks.

2 Foundations of TIL

TIL is a rich and expressive system with *procedural* (as opposed to set-theoretical) semantics that makes it possible to properly analyse in a fine-grained way almost all the semantically salient features of natural language. Referring for details to numerous papers (see, e.g., [ ], [ ], [ ], [ ], [ ], [ ], [ ]) and in particular to the book ([ ]), we just briefly recapitulate. The meaning of a linguistic term is conceived as an abstract algorithmically structured *procedure* encoded by the term, where the structure of the meaning procedure is almost isomorphic with the structure of the term.[4] These procedures can be viewed as instructions how, in any possible world and time, to evaluate or compute the object denoted by the term, if any.[5] Pavel Tichý, the founder of TIL, coined these meaning procedures *constructions*.

The *general semantic schema* involving the *meaning* (i.e., a construction) of an expression E, *denotation* (i.e., the object, if any, denoted by E), and *reference* (i.e., the value of an intension, if the denotation is an intension, in the actual world at the present time), is depicted by Fig. 1.

Fig. 1 General Semantic Schema

The relation of *encoding* (or *expressing*) between expression and construction assigned to it as its meaning is semantically primary. Once we have the meaning construction, we can examine which object (the denotation, if any) the construction produces, prove what is entailed by the construction, examine its structure, etc. Denotation is thus semantically secondary. Moreover, denotation can be missing in case of meaningful, yet *non-denoting* terms like, e.g., 'the greatest prime number' or '$tg(\frac{\pi}{2})$'.

---

[4] See [ ] for the mereology of abstract procedures.
[5] A kindred theory of procedural semantics has been introduced by Moschovakis in [ ] and further developed by Loukanova, see, e.g., [ ]. Moschovakis likened those meaning procedures to 'generalized algorithms'.

Importantly, empirical terms, such as the definite descriptions 'the first player in the WTA singles ranking', 'the president of the Czech Republic' or the predicate 'is a married man', invariably denote the condition that an individual, a set, etc., must satisfy in order to be (in) its extension at the world/time pair of evaluation. We model these conditions as PWS (possible world semantic) intensions, i.e. functions with the domain of possible worlds. However, extensions of these intensions in any possible world at any time, a fortiori extensions in the actual world at the present time are not a semantic issue, they are empirical facts. We say that a term *refers* to its extension in a world/time pair of evaluation. Hence, the world/time-relative extensions (if any) of intensions denoted by empirical linguistic terms fall outside the purview of the semantics.

The semantics of definite descriptions, predicates, and all other linguistic terms is top-down for full referential transparency. This is to say that the above semantic schema that illustrates the relation between a linguistic term, the procedure (construction) that is its meaning, and its denotation (if any) is the same schema in any context, be it a hyperintensional, intensional or extensional context.[6] A term or expression expresses a (privileged) construction as its meaning and denotes the entity (if any) that the construction produces.[7] The *denoted entity* (if any) can be an object of one of three basic kinds:

- a *non-procedural entity*, i.e. an object belonging to a type of order 1 (see below) that comprises all *partial functions* the domain and range of which does not contain any constructions, including nullary functions like numbers and individuals
- a *procedural entity*, i.e. a construction belonging to a type of order $n > 1$ (see below).
- a partial function involving constructions in its domain or range, i.e. an object belonging to a type of order $n > 1$ (see below).

Tichý defined six kinds of constructions, namely *variables*, *Trivialization*, *Composition*, *(λ-)Closure*, *Execution*, and *Double Execution*. While variables and Trivializations are atomic constructions that do not contain any other constituents but themselves, Composition and Closure are molecular constructions that consist of constituents other than just themselves. Abstract or physical objects on which constructions operate are not their constituents; they are beyond constructions and must be 'grabbed' and supplied to be operated on. Atomic constructions serve this grabbing role. *Trivialization* roughly corresponds to a constant of formal languages; where X is an object whatsoever of TIL ontology, Trivialization ^0X produces X. Using terminology of programming languages, Trivialization ^0X is just a pointer to X,

---

[6] The three kinds of context have been defined in [, §2.6]. See also [ ]. Briefly, in a hyperintensional context a construction is an object of predication. In an intensional context, the function produced by a construction is an object of predication, while in an extensional context the value (if any) of the produced function is an object of predication.

[7] *Indexicals* being the only exception: while the sense of an indexical remains constant (a free variable with a type assignment), its denotation varies in keeping with its contextual embedding. See [, §3.4].

a simple grabbing mechanism. *Variables* produce objects of their respective ranges dependently on valuations, they *v-construct*. *Composition* $[FA_1 \ldots A_n]$ is the *procedure* of applying the function f produced by F to its tuple argument $\langle a_1, \ldots, a_n \rangle$ produced by constituents $A_1, \ldots, A_n$ to obtain the value of f, if any; dually, *Closure* $[\lambda x_1 \ldots x_m C]$ is the procedure of declaring or constructing a function by abstracting over the values of λ-bound variables in the ordinary manner of lambda calculi. TIL is a logic of *partial* functions, i.e. functions that can lack a value at some of their arguments. Thus, Composition fails to produce an object, if the function f is not defined at the argument $\langle a_1, \ldots, a_n \rangle$. In such a case we say that the Composition is *v-improper*. While in this paper we do not need and thus do not define Single Execution, Double Execution is an important construction; it executes a given displayed construction twice over, thus decreasing the mode of occurrence of the displayed construction to the executed mode. Thus, we define.

Definition 1 (*construction*)

(i) *Variables* x, y, ... are *constructions* that *construct* objects (elements of their respective ranges) dependently on a valuation v; they *v-construct*.

(ii) Where X is an object whatsoever (even a *construction*), ^0X is the *construction Trivialization* that *constructs* X without any change in X.

(iii) Let X, $Y_1,\ldots,Y_n$ be arbitrary *constructions*. Then *Composition* $[X\, Y_1\ldots Y_n]$ is the following *construction*. For any valuation v, if X does not *v-construct* a function that is defined at the *n*-tuple of objects (if any) v-constructed by $Y_1,\ldots,Y_n$, the *Composition* $[X\, Y_1\ldots Y_n]$ is *v-improper*. If X does *v-construct* such a function, then $[X\, Y_1\ldots Y_n]$ *v-constructs* the value of this function at the *n*-tuple.

(iv) (λ-)*closure* $[\lambda x_1 \ldots x_m Y]$ is the following *construction*. Let x_1, x_2, ..., x_m be pair-wise distinct variables and Y a *construction*. Then Closure $[\lambda x_1 \ldots x_m Y]$ *v-constructs* the function f that takes any members $B_1,\ldots,B_m$ of the respective ranges of the variables $x_1,\ldots,x_m$ into the object (if any) that is $v(B_1/x_1,\ldots,B_m/x_m)$-*constructed* by Y, where $v(B_1/x_1,\ldots,B_m/x_m)$ is like v except for assigning B_1 to $x_1,\ldots,B_m$ to x_m.

(v) Where X is an object whatsoever, ^2X is the *construction Double Execution*. If X is not itself a *construction*, or if X does not *v-construct* a *construction*, or if X *v-constructs* a *v-improper construction*, then ^2X is *v-improper*. Otherwise ^2X *v-constructs* what is *v-constructed* by the *construction v-constructed* by X.

(vi) Nothing is a *construction*, unless it so follows from (i) through (v).

From the formal point of view, TIL is a typed λ-calculus that operates on functions (intensional level) and their values (extensional level), as ordinary λ-calculi do; in addition to this dichotomy, there is however the highest *hyperintensional* level of procedures producing lower-level objects.[8] And since these procedures themselves can serve as objects on which other higher-order procedures operate, there is a fundamental dichotomy between two modes in which constructions can occur, namely *displayed* (as an object to be operated on) and *executed* to v-construct a lower-level object. In principle, constructions are displayed by Trivialization. A dual operation

---

[8] For the introduction on particular theories of hyperintensions, see [ ].

to Trivialization is *Double Execution* that executes constructions twice over. Hence, while ^0X displays X, $^2{}^0X$ voids the effect of Trivialization and is thus equivalent to executed X. Below we refer to this equivalence as to $^2{}^0$-rule. Yet, since the product of a Double Execution of a *free variable* ranging over constructions depends on valuation of the variable and is thus unpredictable, we restrict applicability of this rule to closed constructions of order 1.

To avoid vicious circle problem and keep track of particular logical strata in its stratified ontology, TIL ontology is organized into a *ramified hierarchy of types* built over a base. For natural language processing, we use the epistemic base consisting of four atomic types, namely o (the set of truth-values), ι (individuals), τ (times or real numbers), and ω (possible worlds). The type of constructions is $*_n$, where n is the order of construction.

Definition 2 *(ramified hierarchy of types)*. Let B be a *base*, where a base is a collection of pair-wise disjoint, non-empty sets. Then:

T₁ *(types of order 1)*.
(i) Every member of B is an elementary *type of order 1 over B*.
(ii) Let α, $β_1$, ..., $β_m$ ($m > 0$) be types of order 1 over B. Then (α $β_1$ ... $β_m$), i.e. the collection of all m-ary partial mappings from $β_1 × ... × β_m$ into α, is a functional *type of order 1 over B*.
(iii) Nothing is a *type of order 1 over B* unless it so follows from (i) and (ii).

C_n *(constructions of order n)*
(i) Let x be a variable ranging over a type of order n. Then x is a *construction of order n over B*.
(ii) Let X be a member of a type of order n. Then ^0X, ^2X are *constructions of order n over B*.
(iii) Let X, X_1,..., X_m ($m > 0$) be constructions of order n over B. Then $[X X_1...X_m]$ is a *construction of order n over B*.
(iv) Let x_1, ..., x_m, X ($m > 0$) be constructions of order n over B. Then $[\lambda x_1...x_m X]$ is a *construction of order n over B*.
(v) Nothing is a *construction of order n over B* unless it so follows from **C_n** (i)-(iv).

T_{n+1} *(types of order n + 1)* Let $*_n$ be the collection of all constructions of order n over B. Then
(i) $*_n$ and every type of order n are *types of order n + 1*.
(ii) If α, $β_1$,...,$β_m$ ($m > 0$) are types of order $n + 1$ over B, then (α $β_1$ ... $β_m$) (see **T₁** (ii)) is a *type of order n + 1 over B*.
(iii) Nothing is a *type of order n + 1* over B unless it so follows from (i) and (ii).

Notational conventions. That an object X belongs to a type α is denoted as '$X/α$'. That a construction C v-constructs an α-object (provided not v-improper) is denoted by '$C →_v α$'; we will often say that C is typed to v-construct an α-object, for short. Throughout, variables $w →_v ω$ and $t →_v τ$ (possibly with subscripts) are used as ranging over possible worlds and times, respectively. If $C →_v α_{τω}$ then the frequently used Composition $[[C w] t]$, aka extensionalization of the α-intension v-constructed by C, is abbreviated as C_{wt}. We use classical infix notation without Trivialization for truth-value functions ∧ (conjunction), ∨ (disjunction), ⊃ (implication), and ¬ (negation). Also, identities $=^\alpha$ of α-objects are written in the infix way without Trivialization and the superscript α whenever no confusion arises.

Empirical sentences and terms denote (PWS-)*intensions*, functions with the domain of possible worlds ω; they are frequently mappings from ω to *chronologies* of α-objects, hence functions of types $((\alpha\tau)\omega)$, or $\alpha_{\tau\omega}$, for short. Where variables w, t range over possible worlds ($w \to \omega$) and times ($t \to \tau$), respectively, constructions of intensions are usually Closures of the form

$$\lambda w \lambda t \,[\ldots w \ldots t \ldots].$$

For a simple example of the analysis of an empirical sentence, consider the sentence "John is a student". First, types: *Student*$/(o\iota)_{\tau\omega}$ is a property of individuals and *John*$/\iota$ individual. The sentence "John is a student" encodes as its meaning the hyper-proposition (i.e. construction of a proposition)

$$\lambda w \lambda t \,[^0Student_{wt}\, ^0John].$$

The property *Student* must be extensionalized first, $Student_{wt} \to (o\iota)$ and only then can it be applied to the individual *John*$/\iota$, thus obtaining a truth-value **T**, **F** in accordance with John belonging to the population of students in a given world w and time t of evaluation: $[^0Student_{wt}\, ^0John] \to o$. Abstracting over the values of variables w, t the proposition of type $o_{\tau\omega}$ that John is a student is produced.

We model sets and relations by their characteristic functions. Hence, $(o\iota)$, $(o\iota\iota)$ are types of a set of individuals and of a binary relation-in-extension between individuals, respectively. *Quantifiers* $\forall^\alpha$, $\exists^\alpha$ are type-theoretically polymorphic total functions of types $(o(o\alpha))$ defined as follows. Where B is a construction that v-constructs a set of α-objects, $[^0\forall^\alpha B]$ v-constructs **T** if B v-constructs the set of all α-objects, otherwise **F**; $[^0\exists^\alpha B]$ v-constructs **T** if B v-constructs a non-empty set, otherwise **F**. Instead of $[^0\forall^\alpha \lambda x\, A]$, $[^0\exists^\alpha \lambda x\, A]$ we write '$\forall x A$', '$\exists x A$' whenever no confusion arises.

The above introduced TIL system might be familiar to those who are familiar with Montague style semantics. Yet, TIL deviates in four relevant respects from the version of λ-calculus made popular by Montague's Intensional Logic. First, and most importantly, *meanings* are not identified with (or modelled as) mappings from world/time pairs. Instead Montague-like meanings (i.e. mappings) are the products of our meaning procedures (TIL constructions). Thus, while Montague's system is an *intensional* logic operating on functions and their values, TIL is a *hyperintensional* logic operating on constructions of functions, functions, and their values. Second, *variables* are not linguistic items. The term 'y' expresses an atomic procedure as its meaning and picks out the entity that an assignment function has assigned to y as its value. Thus, three entities are involved: a term, a variable (a procedure), a value. Furthermore, our variables can themselves occur as products of procedures placed higher up. This is essential in what follows, in particular for operations into hyperintensional contexts. Third, the analysis of a piece of language does not amount to translating it from some natural language into an artificial language (say, the λ-calculus), which in turn receives an interpretation, which is transferred back to the natural-language sentence. Instead our λ-calculus is an inherently interpreted formal language, which serves as a device to directly denote (talk about) meanings; our λ-terms denote TIL constructions. Meaning procedures are studied by studying their structure and constituents as encoded in the λ-calculus of TIL in virtue of the isomorphism between formulae and meanings. It should be stressed again that our constructions are not linguistic entities; they are higher-order abstract procedures. Fourth, in TIL we have *explicit intensionalisation* and *temporalisation*. Whereas Montague's IL combines worlds and times, TIL treats worlds and times as two distinct ground types, which enables separate variables ranging over these two separate types.[9]

To complete our brief introduction to the formal apparatus of TIL, we are going to define the substantial distinction between a construction occurring in *executed* vs *displayed mode*. To define the distinction, we must take the following factors into account. A construction C can occur in displayed mode only as a sub-construction within another construction D that operates on C. Therefore, C itself must be produced by another sub-construction E of D. And it is necessary to define this distinction for *occurrences* of constructions because one and the same construction C can occur executed in D and at the same time serve as an input/output object for another sub-construction E of D that operates on C.

The distinction between displayed and executed mode can be characterised like this (with rigorous definition coming below). Let C be a sub-construction of a construction D. Then an occurrence of C is *displayed in D* if the execution of D does not involve the execution of this occurrence of C. Otherwise, C occurs in *executed* mode within D, i.e. C occurs as a *constituent* of the procedure D. Let us illustrate an occurrence of a displayed construction by a simple example. Consider this sentence:

"John is solving the equation $Sin(x) = 0$"

When solving the problem of seeking the numbers x such that the value of the function *Sine* at x equals zero, John is not related to the set of multiples of the number π, i.e. to an object of type $(o\tau)$. If he were, John would have already solved the problem. Rather John wishes to find the product of the construction $\lambda x \, [^0= [^0 Sin \, x] \, ^0 0]$. In other words, the sentence expresses John's relation-in-intension to this very construction and *Solve* is thus an object of type $(o\iota *_1)_{\tau\omega}$. Therefore, the whole sentence encodes this construction:

$$\lambda w \lambda t \, [^0 Solve_{wt} \, ^0 John \, ^0 [\lambda x \, [^0= [^0 Sin \, x] \, ^0 0]]]$$

Types and type checking: $^0 Solve \to (o\iota *_1)_{\tau\omega}$; $^0 Solve_{wt} \to (o\iota *_1)$; $^0 John \to \iota$; $^0 Sin \to (\tau\tau)$; $^0= \to (o\tau\tau)$; $^0 0 \to \tau$; $x \to \tau$; $[^0 Sin \, x] \to \tau$; $[^0= [^0 Sin \, x] \, ^0 0] \to o$; $[\lambda x \, [^0= [^0 Sin \, x] \, ^0 0]] \to (o\tau)$; $^0 [\lambda x \, [^0= [^0 Sin \, x] \, ^0 0]] \to *_1$; $[^0 Solve_{wt} \, ^0 John \, ^0 [\lambda x \, [^0= [^0 Sin \, x] \, ^0 0]]] \to o$; $\lambda w \lambda t \, [^0 Solve_{wt} \, ^0 John \, ^0 [\lambda x \, [^0= [^0 Sin \, x] \, ^0 0]]] \to o_{\tau\omega}$.

---

[9] For critical comments on Montague's IL and a comparison with TIL, see [, §1.5].

A hyperintensional theory of intelligent question answering in TIL

The *construction* $[\lambda x \, [^0= [^0 Sin \, x] \, ^0 0]]$ is *displayed* (using Trivialization) as the second argument of the relation $^0 Solve_{wt}$. The evaluation of the truth-conditions expressed by the sentence consists in checking, for any possible world w and for any time t, whether John and this construction occur in the extensionalized relation-in-intension of solving as its first and second argument, respectively. Hence the execution of the procedure encoded by the sentence does not involve the execution of the equation $\lambda x \, [^0= [^0 Sin \, x] \, ^0 0]$; this is something John is tasked with.

The execution steps specified by the above Closure, i.e. its constituents, are as follows. Each construction is an executed part of itself, hence the Closure (1) is a constituent of itself.

(1) $\lambda w \lambda t \, [^0 Solve_{wt} \, ^0 John \, ^0[\lambda x \, [^0= [^0 Sin \, x] \, ^0 0]]]$
(2) $\lambda t \, [^0 Solve_{wt} \, ^0 John \, ^0[\lambda x \, [^0= [^0 Sin \, x] \, ^0 0]]]$
(3) $[^0 Solve_{wt} \, ^0 John \, ^0[\lambda x \, [^0= [^0 Sin \, x] \, ^0 0]]]$
(4) $^0 Solve_{wt}$
(5) $[^0 Solve \, w]$
(6) $^0 Solve$
(7) w
(8) t
(9) $^0 John$
(10) $^0[\lambda x \, [^0= [^0 Sin \, x] \, ^0 0]]$

Definition 3 (*displayed vs executed mode of occurrence of a construction*). Let C be a construction and D a sub-construction of C. Then:

(i) If C is identical to $^0 X$ and D is identical to X, then the *occurrence of D and of all the sub-constructions of D are displayed in C*.
(ii) If D is *displayed* in C and C is a sub-construction of a construction E such that E is not identical to $^2 F$ for any construction F, then the *occurrence of D and of all the sub-constructions of D are displayed in E*.
(iii) If D is identical to C, then the *occurrence of D is executed in C*.
(iv) If C is identical to $[X_1 \, X_2 \ldots X_m]$ and D is identical to one of the constructions $X_1, X_2, \ldots, X_m$, then the *occurrence of D is executed in C*.
(v) If C is identical to $[\lambda x_1 \ldots x_m \, X]$ and D is identical to X, then the *occurrence of D is executed in C*.
(vi) If C is identical to $^2 X$ and D is identical to X, then the *occurrence of D is executed in C*.
(vii) If C is identical to $^{20} X$ such that X is typed to v-construct an object of a type of order 1, and D is identical to X, then the *occurrence of D is executed in C*.
(viii) If an occurrence of D is executed in a construction E such that this occurrence of E is executed in C, then the *occurrence of D is executed in C*.

Definition 4 (*constituent of a construction*) Let C be a construction. Then *constituents of C are those sub-constructions of C that occur in executed mode in C*.

Corollary. Each construction C is a constituent of itself, namely its *improper constituent*. All the other constituents of C are its *proper constituents*.[10]

Analogously to formal languages, variables can occur free or bound within a construction. In TIL, there are two kinds of binding variables, namely λ-binding and binding by Trivialization, o-binding. Thus, an occurrence of a variable can also be double-bound, as when a λ-bound occurrence is also o-bound. Yet in the case of double-bound variables, we say that the variable is simply o-bound because o-binding is stronger than λ-binding. If a construction C is displayed then all its subconstructions, including its variables, are displayed as well and therefore o-bound, regardless of whether they occur within the scope of a λ-operator. The general rule is that a higher context is dominant over a lower one. Thus, we define:

Definition 5 (*free variable, bound variable, open/closed construction*). Let C be a construction with at least one occurrence of a variable ξ.

(i) Let C be ξ. Then the *occurrence of ξ in C is free*.
(ii) Let C be ^0X. Then *every occurrence of ξ in C is o-bound*.
(iii) Let C be $[\lambda x_1 \ldots x_n Y]$. Any *occurrence of ξ in Y* that is one of x_i, $1 \leq i \leq n$, is λ-*bound in C* unless it is *o-bound in Y*. Any other *occurrence of ξ in Y* that is neither *o-bound* nor λ-*bound in Y* is *free* in C.
(iv) Let C be $[X X_1 \ldots X_m]$. Any *occurrence of ξ* that is *free, o-bound, λ-bound* in one of $X, X_1, \ldots, X_m$ is, respectively, *free, λ-bound, o-bound* in C.
(v) Let C be ^2X. Then any *occurrence of ξ* that is *free, λ-bound* in a constituent of C is, respectively, *free, o-bound, λ-bound* in C.
(vi) An *occurrence* of ξ is *free, λ-bound, o-bound* in C only due to (i)-(v).

A construction with at least one occurrence of a free variable is an *open construction*. A construction without any occurrences of free variables is a *closed construction*.

Corollary. If a construction D is displayed in C, then all the *variables* occurring in D are *o*-bound in C.

Importantly, o-bound variables occur in the displayed mode, and thus, they are not constituents of the super-construction C in which they occur. Therefore, the product of C is invariant of any valuation of o-bound variables occurring in C. In other words, o-bound variables figure just as objects to operate on rather than executed variables v-producing objects dependently on an assignment function.

A few examples: Let $x \to \tau$ be a variable ranging over numbers. Then while x v-constructs numbers, ^0x v-constructs just x for any valuation v (or independently of valuations); therefore, $^0x \to *_1$. The Composition $[^0{>} \, x \, ^00]$ v-constructs **T** if the number v-constructed by x is greater than zero. Trivialization of this Composition, $^0[^0{>} \, x \, ^00]$ produces just the Composition $[^0{>} \, x \, ^00]$ independently of valuations. Hence, the Closure $\lambda x \, [^0{>} \, x \, ^00]$ constructs the set of positive numbers, an (oτ)-object. The variable x is λ-bound here. But the Closure $\lambda x \, ^0[^0{>} \, x \, ^00]$ constructs a

---

[10] The notions of being proper or improper constituents should not be confused with the notions of being v-proper or v-improper constructions.

constant function of type $(*_1\tau)$ that associates any number with the construction $[^0\!\!> x\,{}^0 0]$. This is so because the variable x is now o-bound rather than λ-bound.

3 Natural Deduction in TIL

The standard rules of a proof calculus are in TIL applicable to constituents of those constructions that produce truth-values. To avoid misunderstanding, we follow Church and Gentzen in the classical style of a proof-calculus as it is applied, for instance, in HOL languages. Hence, we do not apply the Curry-Howard correspondence.[11] The rules of the natural deduction system follow its general pattern and are thus introduced in I/E pairs.[12]

The rules dealing with truth-functions, namely conjunction introduction ($\wedge$-I) and elimination ($\wedge$-E), disjunction introduction ($\vee$-I) and elimination ($\vee$-E), implication introduction ($\supset$-I) and elimination ($\supset$-E, known also as modus ponendo ponens MPP) are standard, as in propositional logic. Additionally, there are rules dealing with quantifiers (general $\forall$ and existential $\exists$). Again, these rules are of two kinds, namely introduction and elimination rules. Yet, quantifiers in TIL (see above) are not special symbols; rather, they are *functions* applicable to classes of objects. Hence, our task is to explain how the rules for quantifiers are introduced in the TIL system. Here is how.

Let $x \to \alpha$, $B(x) \to $ o: the variable x is free in B; $[\lambda x\, B] \to (o\alpha)$, $\forall/(o(o\alpha))$, $C \to \alpha$: a construction that is *not v-improper*. Then the general quantifier elimination in full TIL detail consists of these steps:

$$[^0\forall \lambda x\, B] \qquad \varnothing$$
$$[[\lambda x\, B]\, C] \qquad \forall\text{-E}$$
$$B(C/x) \qquad \beta\text{-reduction}$$

where $B(C/x)$ arises from B by a collision-less, valid substitution of the construction C for all occurrences of the variable x in B. For sure, if the condition B is true of all the elements of type α, it must be also true of the object v-constructed by C. Note, however, that in order the rule be truth-preserving, C must not fail to produce such an object. Otherwise, if C were v-improper, the Composition $[[\lambda x\, B]\, C]$ would be v-improper as well though by assumption $[^0\forall \lambda x\, B]$ v-constructs **T**.

For the sake of simplicity, we write this rule in the shortened ordinary form:

$$\frac{X \vdash [^0\forall \lambda x\, B]}{X \vdash B(C/x)} \qquad (\forall\text{-E})$$

The dual rule $\forall$-I then receives this form (y being a 'fresh' free variable, i.e. "local" to this part of the proof):

---

[11] More precisely, Church in [ ] applies Hilbert's deductive system with the rules of lambda conversion and many additional axioms. Gordon and Melham in the HOL system apply natural deduction in the sequent form [, §22.3].

[12] The rules of natural deduction adjusted to TIL have been first briefly introduced in [ ].

$$\frac{X \vdash B(y/x)}{X \vdash [^0\forall \lambda x\, B]} \quad (\forall\text{-I})$$

In classical logic the existential quantifier ∃ is dual to the general quantifier ∀. Thus, it might seem that whereas the rule ∃-I for ∃ introduction is unproblematic, the difficulties would arise with the rule ∃-E for elimination of the existential quantifier. This is true but not the whole truth. Since TIL is a logic of *partial* functions, we must be careful also with the ∃-I rule so as not to derive that there is a value of a function at an argument when there is none.

As in classical logic, the rules for existential quantifier functions, ∃/(o(oα)), are parallel to those for disjunction (∨).

Let $x, y \to \alpha$, $B \to o$, $[\lambda x\, B] \to (o\alpha)$, $\exists/(o(o\alpha))$, $[^0\exists \lambda x\, B] \to o$, $C \to o$. Then the rule of *existential quantifier elimination* (∃-E) is:

$$\frac{\begin{array}{c} X \vdash [^0\exists \lambda x\, B] \\ Y, B(y) \vdash C \end{array}}{X, Y \vdash C} \quad (\exists\text{-E})$$

where the 'fresh' variable y does not occur free in any construction at Y or in C.

Comment. Recall the rule for eliminating disjunction; it is rather complicated.

$$\frac{\begin{array}{c} X \vdash A \vee B \\ Y, A \vdash C \\ Z, B \vdash C \end{array}}{X, Y, Z \vdash C} \quad (\vee\text{-E})$$

Roughly, it says this; consider both the disjuncts A and B, and if you manage to prove another construction C taking first A as an assumption and then B, you proved C from $A \vee B$. The rule is well justified. Proving C from A is equivalent to proving $A \supset C$, and proving C from B is equivalent to proving $B \supset C$. Hence, we have proved $(A \supset C) \wedge (B \supset C)$, which is equivalent to $(A \vee B) \supset C$. By modus ponendo ponens, we have proved C.

This suggests that to eliminate an existential quantification $[^0\exists \lambda x\, B]$ and derive another construction C, we should be able to conclude C starting from B with *any* 'value' substituted for x in B. We do this by substituting a 'fresh' free variable y that does not occur free in C (or anywhere outside the proof sequence).

The rule of existential quantifier introduction is valid in its classical form provided applied to a constituent. Recall that a *constituent* of B is a construction that does not occur displayed in B. Let $D \to \alpha$ be a construction that occurs as a constituent of the construction B, the other types as above. Since, by assumption, B produces a truth-value **T** and D is its constituent, B is of the form of a Composition $[\ldots D \ldots]$. Then, by definition of Composition, the construction D cannot be v-improper and the

Composition $[[\lambda x\ B]\ D]$ v-constructs **T** as well. Thus, the set of α-elements produced by $\lambda x\ B$ is non-empty and the application of $\exists$ quantifier is truth-preserving.

As a result, we obtain the classical *existential quantifier introduction* ($\exists$-I) rule:

$$\frac{X \vdash B(D/x)}{X \vdash [^0\exists\lambda x\ B]} \quad (\exists\text{-I})$$

The crucial condition in this rule is that D occurs as a *constituent* of B. Hence, this rule quantifies over constituents, it does not apply into a hyperintensional context. If it were not so, we might 'magically' derive existence of a non-existent object, which would not be correct, of course. For instance, consider this sentence as an assumption:

"*a* calculates the cotangent of π"

The analysis of the sentence is this construction:

$$\lambda w \lambda t\ [^0Calculate_{wt}\ a\ ^0[^0Cot\ ^0\pi]]$$

Types. $Calculate/(\text{οι}*_n)_{\tau\omega}$; $a \to \iota$; $Cot/(\tau\tau)$; π/τ; $[^0Cot\ ^0\pi] \to \tau$; $^0[^0Cot\ ^0\pi] \to *_1$. Since $^0[^0Cot\ ^0\pi]$ is a *constituent* of the above assumption, we can apply the (E-I) rule to derive that there is a *construction* $c \to *_1$ such that a calculates c:

$$\lambda w \lambda t\ [^0\exists\lambda c\ [^0Calculate_{wt}\ a\ c]]$$

However, if we applied the (E-I) rule to the displayed construction $[^0Cot\ ^0\pi]$, we would attempt to derive that there is a *number* $x \to \tau$ such that a calculates x:

$$\lambda w \lambda t\ [^0\exists\lambda x\ [^0Calculate_{wt}\ a\ ^0x]]$$

Such a derivation is invalid for three reasons. First, there is no such number because the function cotangent is not defined at the number π. Second, even if there were such a number, it makes no sense to compute a number. Third, the variable x is o-bound and thus not amenable to λ-binding as explained above.

Yet, any logic that deserves the claim of being hyperintensional, should also explain how to operate *into* a hyperintensional context, i.e. how to operate with a displayed construction. Thus, besides the classical rule of existential quantifier introduction, in TIL we can also quantify *into* hyperintensional contexts. Referring for details to [ ], where the authors introduce the rules for quantifying into hyperintensional context, we briefly recapitulate. Among those rules there is the rule for quantifying over an object supplied by Trivialization. We can quantify over an object produced by Trivialization inside a displayed construction because Trivialization does not fail to supply such an object for any valuation v.

Consider an argument of the form

$$\frac{a \text{ calculates the cotangent of } \pi}{a \text{ calculates the cotangent of something}}$$

A hyperintensional theory of intelligent question answering in TIL

It is obviously valid. There is 'something', namely the number π, the cotangent of which a calculates. But careless application of the rule ($\exists$-I) is *not valid*:

$$\frac{\lambda w \lambda t \; [^0Calculate_{wt} \; a \; ^0[^0Cot \, ^0\pi]]}{\lambda w \lambda t \; [^0\exists \lambda x \; [^0Calculate_{wt} \; a \; ^0[^0Cot \, x]]]}$$

The reason is this. The Trivialisation $^0[^0Cot\,x]$ constructs the Composition $[^0Cot\,x]$ independently of any valuation v because the variable x is o-bound. Thus from the fact that at $\langle w, t \rangle$ it is true that a calculates $[^0Cot\,^0\pi]$ we *cannot* validly infer that a calculates $[^0Cot\,x]$, because a calculates the cotangent of π rather than of x. Put differently, the class of numbers constructed by $\lambda x \; [^0Calculate_{wt} \; a \; ^0[^0Cot\,x]]$ will be non-empty, according as a calculates $[^0Cot\,x]$ and regardless of a's calculating $[^0Cot\,^0\pi]$. The problem just described of λx being unable to catch the occurrence of x inside the Trivialized construction is TIL's way of phrasing the standard objection to quantifying-in. Yet in TIL we have a way out (or perhaps rather, a way in). In order to validly infer the conclusion, we need to *pre-process* the Composition $[^0Cot\,x]$ and substitute the Trivialization of π v-produced by another free variable y for x. Only then can the conclusion be inferred. To this end we deploy the polymorphic functions $Sub^n/(*_n *_n *_n *_n)$ and $Tr^\alpha/(*_n \alpha)$ that operate on constructions in the manner stipulated by the following dual definition.

Definition 6 (Sub^n, Tr^α)
Let $C_1/*_{n+1} \to *_n$, $C_2/*_{n+1} \to *_n$, $C_3/*_{n+1} \to *_n$ v-construct constructions D_1, D_2, D_3, respectively. Then the Composition $[^0Sub^n \; C_1 \; C_2 \; C_3]$ v-constructs the construction D that results from D_3 by collision-less substitution of D_1 for all occurrences of D_2 in D_3. The function $Tr^\alpha/(*_n \alpha)$ returns as its value the Trivialization of its α-argument.

Example. Let variable $y \to \tau$. Then $[^0Tr^\tau \; y] \; v(\pi/y)$-constructs $^0\pi$. The Composition $[^0Sub^1 \; [^0Tr^\tau \; y] \; ^0x \; ^0[^0Cot\,x]] \; v(\pi/y)$-constructs the Composition $[^0Cot\,^0\pi]$. Hence, the Composition $[^0Sub^1 \; [^0Tr^\tau \; y] \; ^0x \; ^0[^0Cot\,x]]$ is $v(\pi/y)$-congruent with $[^0Cot\,^0\pi]$. Importantly, the variable y is *free* for λ-binding in the former unlike the variable x that is o-bound.

Below we will omit the superscripts n and α and write simply 'Sub' and 'Tr' whenever no confusion can arise.

It should be clear now how to validly derive that a calculates the cotangent of something if a calculates the cotangent of π. The valid argument, in full TIL notation, is this:

$$\frac{\lambda w \lambda t \; [^0Calculate_{wt} \; a \; ^0[^0Cot\,^0\pi]]}{\lambda w \lambda t \; [^0\exists \lambda y [^0Calculate_{wt} \; a \; [^0Sub[^0Tr\,y] \; ^0x \; ^0[^0Cot\,x]]]]}$$

There are two rules for quantifying into a hyperintensional context, one that quantifies over a construction, the other over an object produced by Trivialization, as the above example illustrates. We are not going to introduce these rules here because it would needlessly make our exposition hard to read. Suffice to say that the *substitution method* introduced above must be applied whenever without its application a *conflict of contexts* would arise.

The last technical devices that we need are λ-introduction and elimination of the left-most $\lambda w \lambda t$. They are applied when dealing with empirical propositions. If the assumptions are empirical propositions, as it is often the case when processing natural-language texts, our task is to derive the proposition that is logically entailed by the propositions in premises. Logical entailment between propositions is defined below. In prose, a proposition $P \to o_{\tau\omega}$ is entailed by the propositions $Q_1, \ldots, Q_n$ iff necessarily, i.e. in all possible worlds and times in which all the assumptions $Q_1, \ldots, Q_n$ are true the proposition P is true as well. Hence, in any world w_0 and time t_0 of evaluation the derivation sequence must be truth-preserving from premises to the conclusion. Thus, the typical sequence of derivation steps is this. We have assumptions of the form $\lambda w \lambda t [\ldots w \ldots t \ldots] \to o_{\tau\omega}$, and we assume that the propositions produced by these constructions are true in the world w_0 at time t_0 of evaluation. Using the detailed notation, we obtain the Composition $[[[\lambda w [\lambda t [\ldots w \ldots t \ldots]]] w_0] t_0] \to o$. By applying restricted β-reduction twice, we eliminate the left-most $\lambda w \lambda t$, thus obtaining $[\ldots w_0 \ldots t_0 \ldots] \to o$.[13] Now we proceed with derivation steps until the conclusion of the form $[\ldots w_0 \ldots t_0 \ldots] \to o$ is derived. Since we are to derive a proposition, we finally abstract over the values of the variables w_0, t_0, thus introducing the left-most $\lambda w \lambda t$ to construct a proposition: $\lambda w \lambda t [\ldots w \ldots t \ldots] \to o_{\tau\omega}$.

In order to simplify the derivations, in what follows we omit the initial and final steps of λ-elimination and introduction, respectively.

4 Semantic Rules

There are many features of the rich semantics of natural language that must be formalized by special rules that are not found in the formal logical languages. TIL is a logical system that has been primarily applied to the analysis of natural language because it is a powerful system apt for this task. Since it is out of the scope of this paper to deal with all the natural language semantic peculiarities, we refer for details to [ ]. To illustrate the problems we have to deal with when building up a question answering system over natural language corpora, we are now going to deal with factive verbs and presuppositions triggered by them, property modifiers, and anaphoric references.

---

[13] The restricted β-reduction is just the substitution of variables for variables of the same type. Since variables are not v-improper for any valuation v, it is a strictly equivalent conversion. In the logic of partial functions, such as TIL, β-reduction 'by name' is in general not an equivalent transformation. If the construction that is substituted for λ-bound variables is v-improper, in some cases the redex does not v-construct the same object as the contractum. For this reason, in our applications we use β-reduction by value. For details, see [ ] or [ ].

A hyperintensional theory of intelligent question answering in TIL

4.1 Factive Attitudes and Presuppositions

Factive verbs like to 'know that', 'regret that', 'be sorry', 'be proud', 'be indifferent', 'be glad that', 'be sad that', etc., presuppose that the embedded clause denotes a true proposition. For instance, if one asks, "Does John regret his being late?" and John was not late, there is no direct answer Yes or No. For, both answers entail that John did come late. In such a case an appropriate answer conveys information that the presupposition is not true, like "It is not true that John regrets his coming late, because he was not late". Note that while the direct answer applies *narrow scope* negation, the complete answer denies by *wide scope* negation.[14] Hence, both John regretting and John not regretting his being late entail that John was late. If John was not late, he could neither regret nor not regret it; therefore, the proposition that he regrets it has a truth-value gap. Schematically, if K is a factive verb and X its complement clause, the following rules are valid:

$$K(X) \vdash X, \neg K(X) \vdash X$$

Factive verbs should be distinguished from implicative verbs like 'to manage' or 'to dare'. While sentences applying factive verbs presuppose the truth of the embedded clause, those with implicative verbs only entail it.[15] Schematically, where I is an implicative verb and X the complement clause, we have the following rules.

$$I(X) \vdash X, \neg I(X) \vdash \neg X$$

TIL is a logic of partial functions, and as such is apt for dealing with presuppositions and truth-value gaps. Yet, partiality, as we all know very well, brings about technical complications. To manage them properly, we define properties of propositions *True*, *False* and *Undefined*, all of type $(oo_{\tau\omega})_{\tau\omega}$, as follows ($P \to o_{\tau\omega}$):

$[^0True_{wt} P]$ v-constructs **T** if P_{wt}, otherwise **F**;

$[^0False_{wt} P]$ v-constructs **T** if $\neg P_{wt}$, otherwise **F**;

$[^0Undefined_{wt} P] = \neg[^0True_{wt} P] \wedge \neg[^0False_{wt} P]$.

Now we can rigorously define the difference between presupposition and a mere entailment. Let P, Q be constructions of propositions. Then

Q is entailed by P iff
$\forall w \forall t \, [[^0True_{wt} P] \supset [^0True_{wt} Q]]$;

---

[14] For details on narrow and wide scope negation see [ ], and for answering questions with presuppositions, see [ ].

[15] We are not going to deal with implicative verbs here; yet, see [ ], and also [ ] for detail. Note however, that the notion of presupposition that these authors deal with is pragmatic in nature, while we deal with logical presuppositions the definition of which comes below. It appears the implicative verbs listed above presuppose a weaker version of a presupposition; 'to manage something' presupposes 'to try that something' (and a certain difficulty of the task) and 'to dare' presupposes a sort of 'wanting'. We are grateful to an anonymous referee for this note.

A hyperintensional theory of intelligent question answering in TIL

Q is a presupposition of P iff
$$\forall w \forall t \, [[[^0True_{wt} \, P] \vee [^0False_{wt} \, P]] \supset [^0True_{wt} \, Q]].$$

Hence, we have:

Q is a presupposition of P iff $\forall w \forall t \, [\neg[^0True_{wt} \, Q] \supset [^0Undefined_{wt} \, P]]$.

If a presupposition of a proposition P is not true, then P has no truth value.

Factive verbs being a special case of attitudinal verbs, they thus denote relations-in-intension of an individual to the meaning of the embedded clause, which is a construction of a proposition.[16] Hence, if K is the meaning of a factivum, then $K/(\omicron\iota*_n)_{\tau\omega}$. Furthermore, let $c/*_{n+1} \rightarrow *_n$, $^2c \rightarrow o_{\tau\omega}$, $^2c_{wt} \rightarrow o$ be a variable ranging over constructions of propositions, $a \rightarrow \iota$. Then the rules (FA) dealing with factive propositional attitudes are:

$$\frac{[^0K_{wt} \, a \, c]}{^2c_{wt}} \qquad \frac{\neg[^0K_{wt} \, a \, c]}{^2c_{wt}} \qquad \text{(FA)}$$

Hence, the analysis of the above example together with the proof that John came late comes down to these constructions.

First, types: $Regret/(\omicron\iota*_n)_{\tau\omega}$; $John/\iota$; $Late/((\omicron\iota)_{\tau\omega}(\omicron\iota)_{\tau\omega})$: property modifier (see Sect. 4.2); $Coming/(\omicron\iota)_{\tau\omega}$.

For the sake of simplicity, we now ignore the preprocessing of the anaphoric pronoun 'his', substituting John for 'his' directly. See, however, Sect. 4.3.

1) $[^0Regret_{wt} \, ^0John \, ^0[\lambda w \lambda t \, [[^0Late \, ^0Coming]_{wt} \, ^0John]]]$ ∅
2) $^{20}[\lambda w \lambda t \, [[^0Late \, ^0Coming]_{wt} \, ^0John]]_{wt}$ 1, FA
3) $[\lambda w \lambda t \, [[^0Late \, ^0Coming]_{wt} \, ^0John]]_{wt}$ 2, ^{20}-E
4) $[[^0Late \, ^0Coming]_{wt} \, ^0John]$ 3, β-r

In this proof, we applied also β-reduction of λ-calculi (step 4) and elimination of Trivialization by Double Execution, (^{20}-E) in step 3. This rule is specified as follows:

(^{20}-E) $^{20}C = C$

The (^{20}-E) rule is valid for any closed construction C that is typed to v-construct a non-procedural object of a type of order 1.

In our proof, the application of (^{20}-E) rule is justified because the Trivialized construction is the Closure $[\lambda w \lambda t \, [[^0Late \, ^0Coming]_{wt} \, ^0John]]$ which is a closed construction of order 1.

---

[16] Here we deal with an empirical case of an attitude to a proposition. In case of mathematical attitudes the embedded clause denotes a truth-value. For details and the rules for mathematical factive attitudes, see [, §5.1].

4.2 Property Modifiers

Property modifiers are denoted mostly by adjectives and they are functions in extension that applied to a root property return as a value the modified property. In this subsection we deal with properties of individuals and modifiers of such properties of type $((o\iota)_{\tau\omega}(o\iota)_{\tau\omega})$. There are three basic kinds of modifiers, namely *intersective*, *subsective*, and *privative*. Here are some examples.

a) Intersective. "A yellow elephant is yellow and is an elephant."
b) Subsective. "A skilful surgeon is a surgeon."
c) Privative. "Forged passport is a non-passport."

We are not going to analyse these modifiers in detail here. TIL analysis has been introduced in numerous papers, see, e.g. [ ], [ ], [ ], [ ]. The issue we deal with bellow is the rule of left subsectivity.[17]

The principle of left subsectivity is trivially (by definition) valid for intersective modifiers. If Jumbo is a yellow elephant, then Jumbo is yellow. Yet how about the other modifiers? If Jumbo is a small elephant, is Jumbo small? If you factor out *small* from *small elephant*, the conclusion says that Jumbo is small. Yet this would seem a strange thing to say, for something appears to be missing: Jumbo is a small *what*? Nothing or nobody can be said to be small — or forged, skilful, good, notorious, or whatnot, without any sort of qualification. A complement to provide an answer to the question, 'a ... *what*?' is required. We introduce the rule of left subsectivity that is valid for all kinds of modifiers including subsective and privative ones. The idea is simple. From *a* is an [*MP*] we infer that a is an *M-with respect to something*.

The scheme of defining the left subsectivity rule is this (SI being substitution of identical properties, Leibniz's Law):

1)	*a* is an *MP*	assumption
2)	*a* is an (*M* something)	1, EG
3)	*M** is the property (*M* something)	definition
4)	*a* is an *M**	2,3, SI

To put the rule on more solid grounds of TIL, let $\pi = (o\iota)_{\tau\omega}$ for short, $M \to (\pi\pi)$ be a modifier, $P \to \pi$ an individual property, $[MP] \to \pi$ the property resulting from applying M to P. Further, let $= /(o\pi\pi)$ be the identity relation between properties, and let $p \to_v \pi$ range over properties, $x \to_v \iota$ over individuals. Then the *proof* of the rule is this (additional type: $\exists/(o(o\pi))$):

1)	$[[MP]_{wt}\, a]$	assumption
2)	$\exists p\, [[Mp]_{wt}\, a]$	1, $\exists$I
3)	$[\lambda x\, \exists p\, [[Mp]_{wt}\, x]\, a]$	2, β-expansion
4)	$[\lambda w'\lambda t'\, [\lambda x\, \exists p\, [[Mp]_{w't'}\, x]]_{wt}\, a]$	3, β-expansion
5)	$M^* = \lambda w'\lambda t'\, [\lambda x\, \exists p\, [[Mp]_{w't'}\, x]]$	definition
5)	$[M^*_{wt}\, a]$	4, 5, SI

---
[17] Here we partly draw on material from [, §4.4] and from [ ].

Any valuation of the free occurrences of the variables w, t that makes the first premise true will, together with step five, make the conclusion true. Left subsectivity (LS), dressed up in full TIL notation, is this:

$$\frac{[[MP]_{wt}\, a]\quad [M^* = \lambda w \lambda t\, \lambda x\, \exists p\, [[Mp]_{wt}\, x]]}{[M^*_{wt}\, a]} \quad (LS)$$

This specification of the rule easily dismantles objections raised against the (LS) principle by Gamut [, §6.3.11] and Geach [ ]. Summarising very briefly, there are arguments against (LS) like if Jumbo is a small elephant and a large mammal, then Jumbo is small and large — contradiction! Yet, there is no contradiction, because Jumbo is small as an elephant and large as a mammal. Hence the properties p, q with respect to which Jumbo is a [^{0}Small p] and [^{0}Large q] are distinct.

Of course, nobody and nothing is absolutely small or absolutely large. Everybody is made small by something and made large by something else. And, nobody is absolutely good (except God) or absolutely bad, then everybody has something they do well and something they do poorly. That is, everybody is both good and bad, which here just means being good at something and being bad at something else, without generating paradox (*Good, Bad*/$(\pi\pi)$):

$$\lambda w \lambda t\, \forall x\, [\exists p\, [[^0 Good\, p]_{wt}\, x] \wedge \exists q\, [[^0 Bad\, q]_{wt}\, x]].$$

But nobody can be good at something and bad *at the same thing* simultaneously.

Similarly, if Jumbo is a small elephant and Mickey is a large mouse, then Jumbo is small, and Mickey is large; which does not entail that Jumbo is smaller than Mickey. Again, to derive the conclusion, it would have to be granted that Jumbo is small with respect to the same property as Mickey, which is not so.

4.3 Anaphoric References and Substitution Method

Resolving anaphoric references is a hard nut for every linguist dealing with the semantics of natural languages because there are frequently many ambiguities as for to which part of the foregoing discourse the anaphoric pronoun refers. Logic cannot disambiguate any sentence, of course. Instead, logic can contribute to disambiguation and better communication by making these hidden features explicit and logically tractable. If a sentence or term is ambiguous, we furnish it with multiple constructions as its proposed meanings and leave it to the agent to decide which of these meanings is the intended one.

To deal with anaphoric references, we apply generalized Hans Kamp's Discourse Representation Theory (DRT), see [ ], [ ]. 'DRT' is an umbrella term for a collection of logical and computational linguistic methods developed for a *dynamic interpretation* of natural language, where each sentence is interpreted within a certain discourse. DRT as presented in [ ] is a first-order theory. Thus, only terms denoting individuals (indefinite or definite noun phrases) can introduce so-called discourse referents, which are free variables that are updated when interpreting the discourse.

Since TIL semantics is procedural, hence hyperintensional and higher-order, not only individuals, but entities of any type, like properties of individuals, propositions, relations-in-intension, and even constructions (i.e., meanings of antecedent expressions), can be linked to anaphoric variables. Moreover, the thoroughgoing typing of the universe of TIL makes it possible to determine the respective *type-theoretically appropriate antecedent*, which also contributes to disambiguation.[18]

For instance, the ambiguous anaphoric reference to properties as in Neale's example "John loves his wife and so does Peter" has been analysed in [ ]. The authors prove that the sentence entails that John and Peter share a property. Only that it is ambiguous which one; there are two options, (i) loving John's wife and (ii) loving one's own wife. The property predicated of Peter in 'so does Peter' is a function of the property predicated of John in 'John loves his wife'. Since the source clause is ambiguous between attributing (i) or (ii) to John, the target clause is likewise ambiguous between attributing (i) or (ii) to Peter. The ambiguity of the anaphoric expression 'his wife' as applied to John is visited upon the likewise anaphoric expression 'so does'. The authors propose the analyses of both readings and show that unrestricted β-reduction 'by name' reduces both readings to the strict one on which John and Peter love John's wife, which is undesirable.[19]

The solution consists in the application of β-reduction 'by value' that makes use of the above defined functions *Sub* and *Tr*. To recall, the function *Sub* operates on constructions so that the Composition $[^0 Sub\, C_1\, C_2\, C_3]$ produces a construction D that is the result of the collision-less substitution of the product of C_1 for the product of C_2 into the product of C_3. The function $Tr/(*_n\, \alpha)$ produces the Trivialization of the α-object.

What is also special about "John loves his wife, and so does Peter" is that it involves *two anaphoric* terms, namely 'his' and 'so does'. It might seem tempting, though, to analyse "John loves his wife" as though it were synonymous with "John loves John's wife". Then "So does Peter" would unambiguously attribute to Peter the property of loving John's wife. But this analysis would not be plausible as it would entirely annihilate the *anaphoric* character of 'his'. Instead, the form of the solution must be in terms of resolution of verb-phrase ellipsis. It needs to be spelt out which of two properties applies to John in "John loves his wife" and so applies to Peter in "So does Peter".

The property (i) of loving John's wife is produced by

$$\lambda w \lambda t \lambda x\, [^0 Love_{wt}\, x\, [^0 Wife\text{-}of_{wt}\, ^0 John]]$$

while the property (ii) of loving one's own wife is produced by

$$\lambda w \lambda t \lambda x\, [^0 Love_{wt}\, x\, ^2[^0 Sub\, [^0 Tr\, x]\, ^0 y\, ^0[^0 Wife\text{-}of_{wt}\, y]]]$$

---

[18] The algorithm for dynamic discourse representation within TIL has been specified in [ ] and implemented by Kotová [ ]. It is applied in a multi-agent system to govern the communication of individual agents by messaging.

[19] Loukanova in [ ] also warns against unrestricted β-reduction and its undesirable results.

From the logical point of view, anaphoric pronouns denote variables, valuation of which is supplied by referring to an appropriate antecedent. To this end, we apply the *substitution method* that exploits the functions *Sub* and *Tr*.

To adduce an example of referring to the *meaning* of a term, i.e. to the encoded construction, the sentence "Sin of π equals zero and John knows it" encodes the following construction as its meaning.[20]

$$\lambda w \lambda t \, [[[^0Sin\,^0\pi] = \,^00] \wedge$$
$$^2[^0Sub\,[^0Tr\,^0[[^0Sin\,^0\pi] = \,^00]]\,^0it\,^0[^0Know_{wt}\,^0John\ it]]]$$

Types. $Sin/(\tau\tau); 0, \pi/\tau; [[^0Sin\,^0\pi] = \,^00] \to o; Know/(o\iota*_n)_{\tau\omega}; John/\iota; it \to *_n$.

Note that the result of the substitution (application of the *Sub* function) is an adjusted *construction* $[^0Know_{wt}\,^0John\,^0[[^0Sin\,^0\pi] = \,^00]]]$. But the second argument of conjunction must be a truth-value; hence, the adjusted construction must be executed—therefore Double Execution.

This analysis is fully compositional. The meaning of "John knows it"

$$\lambda w \lambda t \, [^0Know_{wt}\,^0John\ it]$$

contains a *free* variable *it* as its constituent. If the sentence is uttered in isolation, the valuation assignment is a pragmatic matter of a speaker/interpreter. However, if the sentence is embedded in the discourse context, the variable *it* becomes *bound*, and the value assignment is provided by the substitution method.[21]

5 Wh-Questions

Up until now we have considered classical truth-preserving derivations only. In other words, in our proof sequences and rules so far would figure only constructions producing truth values. Such a method makes it possible to answer Yes-No questions. For instance, if the query put forward is "Is *a* going to Brussels?", then we aim at deriving from the input textual sentences the consequence confirming the answer in the affirmative: "*a* is going to Brussels." If we succeed, the answer is 'Yes', otherwise

---

[20] We analyse $Know(ing)/(o\iota*_n)_{\tau\omega}$ as a hyperintensional attitude, i.e. the relation-in-intension of an individual to a *hyperproposition* (construction of a truth value or a PWS proposition). In case of mathematics it is obvious that such attitudes must relate an individual to the very procedure rather than its product; it makes no sense to know a truth value without any mathematical operation producing it. In an empirical case intensional attitudes are also thinkable. Yet, since intensional attitudes inevitably yield a variant of the well-known paradox of logical/mathematical omniscience, we vote for the hyperintensional analysis here.

[21] A similar stance and solution can be found in [ ].

'No'.[22] Yet, one can also ask, "Who is going to Brussels?" and we want the system to provide the answer '*a*'.

Before introducing the method of deriving answers to Wh-questions, we briefly recapitulate the theory of questions and answers as developed within the TIL system.[23] From the logical point of view, interrogative empirical sentences denote α-intensions of a type $((\alpha\tau)\omega)$, or $\alpha_{\tau\omega}$ for short. The direct answer to the question posed by an interrogative sentence is the value, if any, of the denoted α-intension, i.e. an object of type α.

Interrogative empirical sentences can be classified according to many criteria, and various categorisations of questions have been proposed. Questions can be open-ended or close-ended. Open questions give the respondent greater freedom to provide information or opinions on a topic while closed questions call for an answer of a specific type. In this paper, we deal with close questions. These questions can be classified into three basic types, to wit Yes-No questions, Wh-questions and exclusive-or questions.

Yes-No questions like "Does John regret his being late?", "Did the Pope ever visit Prague?" present a proposition whose actual truth-value the inquirer would like to know. In the case of *Wh-questions* like "Who is the Pope?", "When did you stop smoking?", "Who are the members of the European Union?", "Why did John come late?" there is a much greater variety of possible answers because the type of the denoted intension is $\alpha_{\tau\omega}$ for any type α but o. It can be the type of an individual, a set of individuals, time moment, location, property, or whatever else. In case of *exclusive-or questions* like "Are you going by train, or by car?", "Is Tom an assistant, or a professor?" the adequate answer does not provide a truth value; instead, it conveys information on which of the alternatives is the case.

Concerning answers, we distinguish between *direct* and *complete* answers. A direct answer provides directly the α-value of the asked α-intension. A complete answer is that the α-value of the posed α-intension is an α-object. For instance, the direct answer to the Wh-question "Who is the No.1 player in the WTA singles ranking?" is *Ashleigh Barty*, while the complete answer is the proposition that *Ashleigh Barty is the No.1 player in the WTA singles ranking*. Obviously, to each direct answer corresponds the respective complete answer. Possible direct answers to Wh-questions determine the type α of the α-intension in question.

For instance, a possible direct answer to the question

(1)   "Who are the first three players in WTA ranking singles?"

is a set of individuals, currently (writing in July 2020) {*Ashleigh Barty, Simona Halep, Karolina Plíšková*}, which is an object of type (οι). Thus, the analysis of this question consists in a construction of a property of individuals, an object of type $(οι)_{\tau\omega}$:

(1*) $\lambda w \lambda t \lambda x \, [[^0WTA\text{-}Ranking_{wt} \, x] \leq {}^03] \to (οι)_{\tau\omega}$

---

[22] If *a* does not exist, the answer is just that *a* does not exist because there is an existential presupposition on *a*'s existence.

[23] For more details, see, for instance, [ ], [, §3.6], [ ].

Types: $x \to_v \iota$; ^{0}WTA-Ranking/$(\tau\iota)_{\tau\omega}$: attribute of an individual that is an empirical function assigning to individuals their current position (if any) in WTA ranking singles; $3/\tau$, $\leq/(o\tau\tau)$.

On the other hand, the direct answer to the question

(2)   "Who is the No. 1 player in the WTA singles ranking?"

should be a single individual; currently, she is *Ashleigh Barty*. Hence, the analysis of the question must produce an individual office (or role), an object of type $\iota_{\tau\omega}$. Here is how:

(2*) $\lambda w \lambda t \, [^0I \lambda x \, [[^0WTA\text{-}Ranking_{wt} \, x] = \, ^01]] \to \iota_{\tau\omega}$

Additional type. $I/(\iota(o\iota))$: the singularizer, i.e. a function that associates a set S of individuals with the only member of S provided S is a singleton, and otherwise (if S is an empty or a multi-valued set) is undefined.

Note that the question presupposes that the set of individuals to whom the WTA ranking is assigned is non-empty. If it were empty, then there can be no direct answer, and our method provides a complete answer informing that the presupposition is not true. In our case, the answer would be that there is nobody to whom the WTA ranking is assigned.[24]

The problem to solve is now this. Having derived a set of TIL constructions of *propositions* which can provide answers to Yes/No questions, we need a method how to answer also Wh-questions.

Assume, for instance, that we have extracted and formalised the sentence

(3)   "Ashleigh Barty is the first player in the WTA singles ranking."

(3*) $\lambda w \lambda t \, [[^0WTA\text{-}Ranking_{wt} \, ^0Barty] = \, ^01]$

To answer the question (2), we aim at finding a suitable substitution for the variable x occurring in (2*). In other words, using terminology of formal languages, we are looking for a proper construction with which (2*) can be unified. Obviously, in this simple example (3*) can serve the goal. Here is the derivation of the desired answer ^0Barty:

1)	$[^0I \lambda x \, [[^0WTA\text{-}Ranking_{wt} \, x] = \, ^01]]$	Question
2)	$[[^0WTA\text{-}Ranking_{wt} \, x] = \, ^01]$	1, I-E, λ-E
3)	$[[^0WTA\text{-}Ranking_{wt} \, ^0Barty] = \, ^01]$	assumption
4)	$x = \, ^0Barty$	2, 3, Unification

Comments. We derived that on the assumption (3), the direct answer to the question (2) is *Barty*. Of course, the WTA-Ranking is an *empirical* attribute denoting an *intension* of type $(\tau\iota)_{\tau\omega}$. Hence, who is the No.1 in WTA ranking depends crucially on the possible world and time in which we evaluate. The fact that we derived *Barty* as the

---

[24] The general analytic schema for questions with presuppositions applies a rigorously defined, strict function 'If-then-else'. Where P is a presupposition of a question Q, in plain English, the schema is "If P then Q else non-P". For details, see [ ], [ ].

direct answer to the question (2) does not mean that Barty is necessarily the No.1 in the WTA ranking, of course. This answer is only entailed by the proposition denoted by (3). Barty has not been and will not always be No.1; and if the circumstances were different, i.e. in another possible world in which Barty would have lost with, for instance, Svitolina, the latter would be the No.1.[25]

When deriving the answer to a Wh-question, we apply an adjusted Robinson's algorithm of unification as known from the general resolution method. We are looking for a construction with the same constituents as a given question up to the variable the value of which we want to obtain. The adjustment of the algorithm is this. Sometimes the constituents are not strictly identical; it suffices that by applying basic arithmetic, we can conclude that this or that construction is suitable for answering. To illustrate, consider this knowledge base:

$\lambda w \lambda t \, [[^0 WTA\text{-}Ranking_{wt} \, ^0Barty] = ^01]$
$\lambda w \lambda t \, [[^0 WTA\text{-}Ranking_{wt} \, ^0Halep] = ^02]$
$\lambda w \lambda t \, [[^0 WTA\text{-}Ranking_{wt} \, ^0Pliskova] = ^03]$
$\lambda w \lambda t \, [[^0 WTA\text{-}Ranking_{wt} \, ^0Kenin] = ^04]$
$\lambda w \lambda t \, [[^0 WTA\text{-}Ranking_{wt} \, ^0Svitolina] = ^05]$
. . .
$\lambda w \lambda t \, [[^0 WTA\text{-}Ranking_{wt} \, ^0Kvitova] = ^012]$
. . .

To derive the answer to the question (1), i.e. "who are the first three players in WTA ranking singles?", we can use the first three constructions because the question transforms into the construction

$\lambda w \lambda t \, \lambda x \, [[^0 WTA\text{-}Ranking_{wt} \, x] \leq ^03] \to (\iota)_{\tau\omega}$

and the condition that the ranking be less than or equal to 3 is met. Hence, we derive the answer {Barty, Halep, Pliskova}.

Here is another example.

"The US President met the Czech President in the Reduta Jazz Club, Prague, in 1994".

This sentence is multiply ambiguous. This ambiguity concerns the question who met with whom in the Reduta Jazz Club. The ambiguities stem from the interplay between the time reference 1994 and the current/then presidencies.[26] Of course, those who know the history of the relations between the United States and the Czech Republic remember that a memorable moment occurred in 1994 when then US President Bill Clinton visited the Czech Republic and took in the music at the Reduta Jazz Club. The then-president of the Czech Republic Václav Havel presented Clinton with a saxophone and Clinton jammed with the band for a few songs. Under

---

[25] We are grateful to an anonymous referee for this comment.
[26] This example is taken from [ ] where a detailed analysis of various readings is provided together with the analysis of presuppositions with respect to current time and the year 1994.

this reading, the sentence presupposes the existence of the Czech and US Presidents in 1994. Both definite descriptions occur with supposition *de re* with respect to 1994, because both the *de re* principles are valid with respect to the year 1994. In particular, there is an existential *presupposition* that both the presidential offices were occupied in 1994.

Hence, we have the following derivation:

1) $[\mathit{If}\,\forall u\,[[^01994\,u] \supset [[^0\mathit{Exist}_{wu}\,\lambda w \lambda t\,[^0\mathit{Pres}_{wt}\,^0\mathit{USA}]] \wedge [^0\mathit{Exist}_{wu}\,\lambda w \lambda t\,[^0\mathit{Pres}_{wt}\,^0\mathit{CR}]]]]]$
   $\mathit{then}\,\exists v\,[[^01994\,v] \wedge [^0\mathit{Meet}_{wv}\,[^0\mathit{Pres}_{wv}\,^0\mathit{USA}]\,[^0\mathit{Pres}_{wv}\,^0\mathit{CR}]\,^0\mathit{Reduta}]]$
   $\mathit{else\,fail}]$ ∅
2) $\forall u\,[[^01994\,u] \supset [^0\mathit{Clinton} = [^0\mathit{Pres}_{wu}\,^0\mathit{USA}]]]$ ∅
3) $\forall u\,[[^01994\,u] \supset [^0\mathit{Havel} = [^0\mathit{Pres}_{wu}\,^0\mathit{CR}]]]$ ∅
4) $\forall u\,[[^01994\,u] \supset \exists x\,[x = [^0\mathit{Pres}_{wu}\,^0\mathit{USA}]]]$ 2, ∃-I
5) $\forall u\,[[^01994\,u] \supset [^0\mathit{Exist}_{wu}\,\lambda w \lambda t\,[^0\mathit{Pres}_{wt}\,^0\mathit{USA}]]]$ 4, Def. Exist
6) $\forall u\,[[^01994\,u] \supset \exists x\,[x = [^0\mathit{Pres}_{wu}\,^0\mathit{CR}]]]$ 3, ∃-I
7) $\forall u\,[[^01994\,u] \supset [^0\mathit{Exist}_{wu}\,\lambda w \lambda t\,[^0\mathit{Pres}_{wt}\,^0\mathit{CR}]]]$ 6, Def. Exist
8) $[[^01994\,v] \supset [^0\mathit{Exist}_{wv}\,\lambda w \lambda t\,[^0\mathit{Pres}_{wt}\,^0\mathit{USA}]]]$ 5, ∀-E v/u
9) $[[^01994\,v] \supset [^0\mathit{Exist}_{wv}\,\lambda w \lambda t\,[^0\mathit{Pres}_{wt}\,^0\mathit{CR}]]]$ 7, ∀-E v/u
10) $[^01994\,v]$ Assumption
11) $[^0\mathit{Exist}_{wv}\,\lambda w \lambda t\,[^0\mathit{Pres}_{wt}\,^0\mathit{USA}]]$ 8, 10, MPP
12) $[^0\mathit{Exist}_{wv}\,\lambda w \lambda t\,[^0\mathit{Pres}_{wt}\,^0\mathit{CR}]]$ 9, 10, MPP
13) $[[^0\mathit{Exist}_{wv}\,\lambda w \lambda t\,[^0\mathit{Pres}_{wt}\,^0\mathit{USA}]] \wedge [^0\mathit{Exist}_{wv}\,\lambda w \lambda t\,[^0\mathit{Pres}_{wt}\,^0\mathit{CR}]]]$ 11, 12, ∧-I
14) $[[^01994\,v] \supset [[^0\mathit{Exist}_{wv}\,\lambda w \lambda t\,[^0\mathit{Pres}_{wt}\,^0\mathit{USA}]] \wedge [^0\mathit{Exist}_{wv}\,\lambda w \lambda t\,[^0\mathit{Pres}_{wt}\,^0\mathit{CR}]]]]$ 13, ⊃-I
15) $\forall u\,[[^01994\,u] \supset [[^0\mathit{Exist}_{wu}\,\lambda w \lambda t\,[^0\mathit{Pres}_{wt}\,^0\mathit{USA}]] \wedge [^0\mathit{Exist}_{wu}\,\lambda w \lambda t\,[^0\mathit{Pres}_{wt}\,^0\mathit{CR}]]]]$ 14, ∀-I, u/v
16) $\exists v\,[[^01994\,v] \wedge [^0\mathit{Meet}_{wv}\,[^0\mathit{Pres}_{wv}\,^0\mathit{USA}]\,[^0\mathit{Pres}_{wv}\,^0\mathit{CR}]\,^0\mathit{Reduta}]]$
   1, 15, Def. if-then-else
17) $[[^01994\,v] \supset [^0\mathit{Clinton} = [^0\mathit{Pres}_{wv}\,^0\mathit{USA}]]]$ 2, ∀-E, v/u
18) $[[^01994\,v] \supset [^0\mathit{Havel} = [^0\mathit{Pres}_{wv}\,^0\mathit{CR}]]]$ 3, ∀-E, v/u
19) $[[^01994\,v] \wedge [^0\mathit{Meet}_{wv}\,[^0\mathit{Pres}_{wv}\,^0\mathit{USA}]\,[^0\mathit{Pres}_{wv}\,^0\mathit{CR}]\,^0\mathit{Reduta}]]$ 16, ∃-E
20) $[^01994\,v]$ 19, ∧-E
21) $[^0\mathit{Meet}_{wv}\,[^0\mathit{Pres}_{wv}\,^0\mathit{USA}]\,[^0\mathit{Pres}_{wv}\,^0\mathit{CR}]\,^0\mathit{Reduta}]$ 19, ∧-E
22) $[^0\mathit{Clinton} = [^0\mathit{Pres}_{wv}\,^0\mathit{USA}]]$ 17, 20, MPP
23) $[^0\mathit{Havel} = [^0\mathit{Pres}_{wv}\,^0\mathit{CR}]]$ 18, 20, MPP
24) $[^0\mathit{Meet}_{wv}\,^0\mathit{Clinton}\,^0\mathit{Havel}\,^0\mathit{Reduta}]$ 21, 22, 23, SI
26) $[^01994\,v] \wedge [^0\mathit{Meet}_{wv}\,^0\mathit{Clinton}\,^0\mathit{Havel}\,^0\mathit{Reduta}]$ 20, 24, ∧-I
26) $\exists v\,[[^01994\,v] \wedge [^0\mathit{Meet}_{wv}\,^0\mathit{Clinton}\,^0\mathit{Havel}\,^0\mathit{Reduta}]]$ 25, ∃-I

Types. $t, u, v \to \tau$; $1994/(o\tau)$; $\mathit{Exist}/(o\iota_{\tau\omega})_{\tau\omega}$: the property of an individual office of being occupied; $\mathit{Pres}(\mathit{ident\text{-}of})/(\iota\iota)_{\tau\omega}$; $\mathit{USA}, \mathit{CR}/\iota$; Reduta/ι: the Reduta Jazz Club in Prague; $\mathit{Meet}/(o\iota\iota\iota)_{\tau\omega}$: the relation-in-intension, who meets with whom, where.

Remark. For the sake of simplicity, we omitted the presupposition that the whole year 1994 must precede the time of evaluation t, a presupposition which is obviously met.[27] Yet, we take into account the presupposition that both presidents had to exist in 1994. To this end, we apply the *If-then-else-fail* function, which is defined as follows.

$$^2[^0I\lambda c[P_{wt} \wedge c = {}^0Q]]_{wt}$$

Types. $I/(*_n(o*_n))$: the singulariser on constructions; the function that associates a singleton of constructions with the only element of the set, otherwise undefined; the variable $c \rightarrow *_n$; $P \rightarrow o_{\tau\omega}$: the presupposition of Q; $Q \rightarrow \alpha_{\tau\omega}$.

To make the constructions easier to read, instead of '$[^0\textit{If-then-else-fail}\,P_{wt}\,{}^0Q]$', we simply write '*If* P_{wt} *then* Q_{wt} *else fail*'.

We have derived that in some time of 1994 Clinton met with Havel in the Reduta Jazz Club, Prague. By applying the unification algorithm to properly chosen constructions from the above derivation, we can now answer questions like

"Who met with whom in the Reduta Jazz Club in 1994?"
"When did Clinton meet with Havel in the Reduta Jazz Club?"
"Where did the US President meet with the Czech president in 1994?"

For instance, the first question transforms into the construction $(x, y \rightarrow \iota)$

$$\lambda w \lambda t \lambda xy\, [\exists v\, [[^01994\,v] \wedge [^0Meet_{wv}\,x\,y\,{}^0Reduta]]]$$

Having applied (λ-E) rules, unification with (16) yields the answer 'the US President with the Czech President', while by unifying with (26) we obtain the answer 'Clinton with Havel'.

Similarly, the second question amounts to the following construction ($c \rightarrow (o\tau)$: a variable ranging over time intervals).

$$\lambda w \lambda t\, \lambda c\, [\exists v\, [[c\,v] \wedge [^0Meet_{wv}\,{}^0Clinton\,{}^0Havel\,{}^0Reduta]]]$$

By application of λ-E rules and unifying with (26) the answer 'in 1994' is produced.

6 Two Case Studies

In this section, we illustrate the above-introduced methods by two examples of integrating the rules dealing with property modifiers and with factive verbs, respectively.

---

[27] For the analysis of sentences in past and future tenses with time references and their presuppositions, see [ ], [ ].

A hyperintensional theory of intelligent question answering in TIL

6.1 Reasoning with Property Modifiers

Scenario. John is a married man. John's partner is Eve. John is a member of a sports club and a student. All students like holidays. Everybody married believes that his/her partner is fantastic. Frank is a student. Frank thinks that Peter is an actor.

Question. Does John believe that Eve is fantastic?

To formalise our mini knowledge base, we start with assigning *types* to the objects that receive mention in the text: *John, Eve, Peter, Frank, S(port)C(lub)*/ι; *Partner(-of)*/$(\iota)_{\tau\omega}$; *Married^m*/$((o\iota)_{\tau\omega}(o\iota)_{\tau\omega})$; *Married, Actor, Student, Fantastic*/$(o\iota)_{\tau\omega}$; *Member, Like*/$(o\iota\iota)_{\tau\omega}$; *Holidays*/α: for the sake of simplicity, we don't analyse the type of holidays, which is harmless here; *Believe, Think*/$(o\iota*_n)_{\tau\omega}$; $w \to \omega$; $t \to \tau$; $x, y \to \iota$.

Analysis of the sentences of our scenario comes down to these constructions:

A. $\lambda w \lambda t \, [[^0Married^m \, ^0Man]_{wt} \, ^0John]$
B. $\lambda w \lambda t \, [[^0Partner_{wt} \, ^0John] = ^0Eve]$
C. $\lambda w \lambda t \, [[^0Member_{wt} \, ^0John \, ^0SC] \wedge [^0Student_{wt} \, ^0John]]$
D. $\lambda w \lambda t \, \lambda x \, [[^0Student_{wt} \, x] \supset [^0Like_{wt} \, x \, ^0Holidays]]$
E. $\lambda w \lambda t \, \forall x \, [[^0Married_{wt} \, x] \supset$
  $[^0Believe_{wt} \, x \, [^0Sub \, [^0Tr \, [^0Partner_{wt} \, x]] \, ^0y \, ^0[\lambda w \lambda t \, [^0Fantastic_{wt} \, y]]]]]$
F. $\lambda w \lambda t \, [^0Student_{wt} \, ^0Frank]$
G. $\lambda w \lambda t \, [^0Think_{wt} \, ^0Frank \, ^0[\lambda w \lambda t \, [^0Actor_{wt} \, ^0Peter]]]$

Conclusion/question:
Q. $\lambda w \lambda t \, [^0Believe_{wt} \, ^0John \, ^0[\lambda w \lambda t \, [^0Fantastic_{wt} \, ^0Eve]]]$

To derive the answer, we are going to apply the system of Gentzen's natural deduction (ND) adapted to TIL. In addition to the standard rules of the ND system, we need the rule of left subsectivity (LS) for dealing with the property modifier *Married^m*. The rule results in

(LS) $[[^0Married^m \, ^0Man]_{wt} \, x] \vdash [^0Married_{wt} \, x]$

Informally, this rule represents the fact that "A married man is married".

We must also deal with technical rules and functions specific for TIL. For instance, application of the functions *Sub* and *Tr* must be evaluated appropriately, or Leibniz's law of substitution of identicals specified for TIL in [ ] and [ ] must be appropriately applied.

Here is the derivation.

1) $[[^0Married^m\ {}^0Man]_{wt}\ {}^0John]$ ⌀
2) $[[^0Partner_{wt}\ {}^0John] = {}^0Eve]$ ⌀
3) $\forall x\ [[^0Married_{wt}\ x] \supset [^0Believe_{wt}\ x\ [^0Sub\ [^0Tr\ [^0Partner_{wt}\ x]]\ {}^0y$
  $^0[\lambda w \lambda t\ [^0Fantastic_{wt}\ y]]]]]$ ⌀
4) $[[^0Married_{wt}\ {}^0John] \supset [^0Believe_{wt}\ {}^0John\ [^0Sub\ [^0Tr\ [^0Partner_{wt}\ {}^0John]]$
  $^0y\ {}^0[\lambda w \lambda t\ [^0Fantastic_{wt}\ y]]]]]$ 3, ∀-E, $^0John/x$
5) $[[^0Married_{wt}\ {}^0John] \supset [^0Believe_{wt}\ {}^0John\ [^0Sub\ [^0Tr\ {}^0Eve]\ {}^0y$
  $^0[\lambda w \lambda t\ [^0Fantastic_{wt}\ y]]]]$ 2,4, SI (Leibniz)
6) $[^0Married_{wt}\ {}^0John]$ 1, LS
7) $[[^0Believe_{wt}\ {}^0John\ [^0Sub\ [^0Tr\ {}^0Eve]\ {}^0y\ [^0Fantastic_{wt}\ y]]]]$ 5,6, MPP
8) $[[^0Believe_{wt}\ {}^0John\ [^0Fantastic_{wt}\ {}^0Eve]]]$ 7, Sub,Tr

The answer to the question Q is Yes, of course; it follows from our mini knowledge base that John indeed believes that Eve is fantastic.

However, in this proof, we simplified the situation. We took into account only the premises relevant for deriving the conclusion, ignoring the others. For instance, from premises D and F, one can infer (by applying ∀-E and MPP) that "Frank likes holidays". Similarly, by applying ∧-E, ∀-E, and MPP to the premises C and D we can infer that John likes holidays. Yet, these conclusions are pointless when answering the question Q.

In practice, there are a vast number of sentences formalised in the form of TIL constructions so that extracting the relevant ones is not so easy. Moreover, implementation of the method within the interactive question answering system calls for an algorithm of selecting appropriate input sentences so that to reduce inferring consequences that are not needed. To this end, we propose a simple solution that nevertheless restricts the number of input premises and thus also the length of the proofs significantly. We select only those sentences that talk about the objects that receive mention in a given question.

In our example, the following constructions would be selected because they contain the constituents $^0Believe$, ^0John, $^0Fantastic$, and ^0Eve, which they have in common with the question Q.

A. $\lambda w \lambda t\ [[^0Married^m\ {}^0Man]_{wt}\ {}^0John]$
B. $\lambda w \lambda t\ [[^0Partner_{wt}\ {}^0John] = {}^0Eve]$
C. $\lambda w \lambda t\ [[^0Member_{wt}\ {}^0John\ {}^0SC] \land [^0Student_{wt}\ {}^0John]]$
E: $\lambda w \lambda t\ \forall x\ [[^0Married_{wt}\ x] \supset$
  $[^0Believe_{wt}\ x\ [^0Sub\ [^0Tr\ [^0Partner_{wt}\ x]]\ {}^0y\ {}^0[\lambda w \lambda t\ [^0Fantastic_{wt}\ y]]]]]$

The premises D, F, and G are irrelevant because they do not have any constituent in common with the question Q. This heuristic method does not guarantee that all the selected constructions are necessary for deriving the answer (in our case the premise C is spare), nor that the chosen set is sufficient for deriving the answer. It may happen that in the proof process, the heuristic method must be iterated to select additional input sentences. Anyway, it turns out that in most cases, a one-step heuristic is sufficient, and the process of proving is effectively optimised.

A hyperintensional theory of intelligent question answering in TIL

6.2 Reasoning with Factive Propositional Attitudes

Scenario. The Mayor of Ostrava is Tomáš Macura. Prof. Vondrák likes teaching. The Mayor of Ostrava regrets that the President of Technical University of Ostrava (TUO) does not know (yet) that he (the President of TUO) will go to Brussels. The President of TUO is prof. Snášel. Prof. Snášel likes swimming. Prof. Vondrák is a politician.

Question. Will prof. Snášel go to Brussels?

Types: *Snasel, Macura, Vondrak, Brussels*/ι; *President*(*of TUO*); *Like*/(οια)$_{\tau\omega}$; *Mayor*(*of Ostrava*)/ι$_{\tau\omega}$; *Know, Regret*/(οι*$_n$)$_{\tau\omega}$; *Swimming, Teaching*/α;[28] *Politician*/(οι)$_{\tau\omega}$; *Go*/(οιι)$_{\tau\omega}$.

Knowledge base:

    A. λwλt [$^0Mayor_{wt}$ = ^0Macura]
    B. λwλt [$^0Like_{wt}$ $^0Vondrak$ $^0Teaching$]
    C. λwλt [$^0Regret_{wt}$ $^0Mayor_{wt}$ ^{0}[λwλt ¬[$^0Know_{wt}$ $^0President_{wt}$
        [^0Sub [^0Tr $^0President_{wt}$] ^0he ^{0}[λwλt [$^0Go_{wt}$ he $^0Brussels$]]]]
    D. λwλt [$^0President_{wt}$ = ^0Snasel]
    E. λwλt [$^0Like_{wt}$ ^0Snasel $^0Swimming$]
    F. λwλt [$^0Politician_{wt}$ $^0Vondrak$]

Conclusion/question:
Q: λwλt [$^0Go_{wt}$ ^0Snasel $^0Brussels$]

What is interesting about this example is that it makes it possible to demonstrate a *top-down derivation* from hyperintensional level of the complement of Regreting/not knowing that "he will go to Brussels" to the extensional level of Snasel's going to Brussels. It is made possible by application of the rules for factive attitudes defined above, plus resolution of anaphoric references by the substitution method. To recapitulate, here are the rules ($c \rightarrow *_n$, $^2c \rightarrow 0_{\tau\omega}$, $^2c_{wt} \rightarrow 0$).

(FA1)   [$^0Regret_{wt}$ a c] ⊢ $^2c_{wt}$

(FA2)   ¬[$^0Know_{wt}$ a c] ⊢ $^2c_{wt}$

For technical reasons, we also need the rule of ^{20}-Elimination, a simple technical adjustment, which holds for any closed construction C that is typed to v-construct a non-procedural object of a type of order 1.

(^{20}-E) $^{20}C = C$

---

[28] For the sake of simplicity, we assign type α to these activities, because this simplification is harmless to the derivation we are going to demonstrate.

A hyperintensional theory of intelligent question answering in TIL

For the selection of constructions that are relevant for deriving the answer, we now apply the heuristics described above. Constituents of the question Q are ^0Go, ^0Snasel, and $^0Brussels$. These constituents occur as sub-constructions of the sentences C, D, and E.

C. $\lambda w \lambda t\, [^0Regret_{wt}\, ^0Mayor_{wt}\, ^0[\lambda w \lambda t\, \neg [^0Know_{wt}\, ^0President_{wt}$
    $[^0Sub\, [^0Tr\, ^0President_{wt}]\, ^0he\, ^0[\lambda w \lambda t\, [^0Go_{wt}\, he\, ^0Brussels]]]]]$
D. $\lambda w \lambda t\, [^0President_{wt} = {}^0Snasel]$
E. $\lambda w \lambda t\, [^0Like_{wt}\, ^0Snasel\, ^0Swimming]$

In sentence C there is another constituent, namely ^0Mayor, and this same constituent also occurs in the premise A. By iterating the heuristics, we include A among the premises as well:

A. $\lambda w \lambda t\, [^0Mayor_{wt} = {}^0Macura]$

The proof of the argument, i.e. the derivation of the answer to the question Q from premises A, C, D, and E, is as follows:

1) $[^0Regret_{wt}\, ^0Mayor_{wt}\, ^0[\lambda w \lambda t\, \neg [^0Know_{wt}\, ^0President_{wt}$
    $[^0Sub\, [^0Tr\, ^0President_{wt}]\, ^0he\, ^0[\lambda w \lambda t\, [^0Go_{wt}\, he\, ^0Brussels]]]]]$ ∅
2) $[^0President_{wt} = {}^0Snasel]$ ∅
3) $[^0Like_{wt}\, ^0Snasel\, ^0Swimming]$ ∅
4) $[^0Mayor_{wt} = {}^0Macura]$ ∅
5) $^{20}[\lambda w \lambda t\, \neg [^0Know_{wt}\, ^0President_{wt}$
    $[^0Sub\, [^0Tr\, ^0President_{wt}]\, ^0he\, ^0[\lambda w \lambda t\, [^0Go_{wt}\, he\, ^0Brussels]]]]_{wt}$ 1, FA1
6) $[\lambda w \lambda t\, \neg [^0Know_{wt}\, ^0President_{wt}$
    $[^0Sub\, [^0Tr\, ^0President_{wt}]\, ^0he\, ^0[\lambda w \lambda t\, [^0Go_{wt}\, he\, ^0Brussels]]]]_{wt}$ 5, ^{20}-E
7) $\neg [^0Know_{wt}\, ^0President_{wt}$
    $[^0Sub\, [^0Tr\, ^0President_{wt}]\, ^0he\, ^0[\lambda w \lambda t\, [^0Go_{wt}\, he\, ^0Brussels]]]$ 6, β-r
8) $^2[^0Sub\, [^0Tr\, ^0President_{wt}]\, ^0he\, ^0[\lambda w \lambda t\, [^0Go_{wt}\, he\, ^0Brussels]]_{wt}$ 7, FA2
9) $^2[^0Sub\, [^0Tr\, ^0Snasel]\, ^0he\, ^0[\lambda w \lambda t\, [^0Go_{wt}\, he\, ^0Brussels]]_{wt}$ 8,2 SI
10) $^2[^0Sub\, ^{00}Snasel\, ^0he\, ^0[\lambda w \lambda t\, [^0Go_{wt}\, he\, ^0Brussels]]_{wt}$ 9, Tr
11) $^{20}[\lambda w \lambda t\, [^0Go_{wt}\, ^0Snasel\, ^0Brussels]]_{wt}$ 10, Sub
12) $[\lambda w \lambda t\, [^0Go_{wt}\, ^0Snasel\, ^0Brussels]]_{wt}$ 11, ^{20}-E
13) $[^0Go_{wt}\, ^0Snasel\, ^0Brussels]$ 12, β-r

Since we proved that the premises A, C, D, and E entail that Snasel is going to Brussels, the answer to the question Q is Yes.

However, the above scenario makes it possible to answer other questions as well. For instance, we can ask,

Q1. "Who is going to Brusells?" $\lambda w \lambda t\, \lambda x\, [^0Go_{wt}\, x\, ^0Brussels]$
Q2. "Where does Snasel go?" $\lambda w \lambda t\, \lambda y\, [^0Go_{wt}\, ^0Snasel\, y]$
Q3. "Who is the Mayor of Ostrava?" $\lambda w \lambda t\, \lambda z\, [^0Mayor_{wt} = z]$

and many other Wh-questions. The technique of answering consists in applying the unification algorithm to a given question and an appropriate formalised sentence from the scenario, as described above. For instance, the first question is easily unified with the construction (13), thus producing the answer 'Snasel'.

7 Conclusion

In this paper, we introduced the system for 'intelligent' question answering over natural language texts. The system derives answers to the questions as logical consequences of assumptions extracted from given text corpora. When designing such a system, we had to solve several problems. First, natural language sentences must be analysed in a fine-grained way so that all the semantically salient features of a language are captured by an adequate formalisation. To this end, we exploited the system of Transparent Intensional Logic (TIL). Second, there are special rules rooted in the rich semantics of natural language which are not found in standard proof calculi. The problem is how to integrate these rules with a given proof system. We met the problem by natural deduction adapted to TIL. Third, there is the problem of how to extract just those sentences that are needed for deriving the answer from the large corpora of input text data. As a solution, we proposed a heuristic method driven by the constituents of a given question. Last but not least, we dealt with the problem of answering Wh-questions.

There are two novelties of the paper. While in the previous proposals based on TIL it has been tacitly presupposed that it is possible to pre-process the natural language sentences first, and then to apply a standard proof calculus, we gave up this assumption, because it turned up to be unrealistic. Instead, we voted for Gentzen's natural deduction system so that those special semantic rules could be smoothly inserted into the derivation process together with the standard I/E rules of the proof system. Yet, by applying the forward-chaining strategy of the natural deduction system, we faced up the problem of extracting those sentences that are relevant for the derivation of the answer. As a solution, we proposed a heuristic method that selects those sentences that have some constituents in common with the posed question.

The second novel result is the method of answering Wh-questions. The analysis of such questions yields constructions of the form $\lambda x [\ldots]$. A direct answer provides the value of the variable x by the substitution that unifies a given query with an appropriate sentence from an input knowledge base.

Future research will concentrate on the comparison of this approach with the system of deriving answers utilising the backwards-chaining strategy of general resolution method and sequent calculus, and an effective implementation there-of.

Acknowledgements This research was supported by the Grant Agency of the Czech Republic, project no. GA18-23891S, Hyperintensional Reasoning over Natural Language Texts, and by the internal grant agency of VSB-Technical University of Ostrava, project SGS No. SP2020/62, Application of Formal Methods in Knowledge Modelling and Software Engineering III. Michal Fait was also supported by the Moravian-Silesian regional program No. RRC/10/2017 "Support of science and research in Moravian-Silesian region 2017".

A short version of the paper (see [ ]) has been presented at the Special Session on Natural Language Processing in Artificial Intelligence (NLPinAI) of 12th International Conference on Agents and Artificial Intelligence, ICAART 2020, Valletta, Malta. This paper is its major extension. In addition to many touches here and there that have been made to improve the quality, we added a section on logical analysis of Wh-questions and deriving answers to Wh-questions. Moreover, the section dealing with TIL natural deduction has been extended by the rules for existential quantification into hyperintensional contexts. Also, the two case studies in Sect. 6 have been revised, and Wh-questions answered here.

References

1. Baglini, R., Francez, I.: The implications of managing. Journal of Semantics **33**(3), 541–560 (2016). URL https://doi.org/10.1093/jos/ffv007
2. Church, A.: A formulation of the simple theory of types. The Journal of Symbolic Logic **5**(2), 56–68 (1940). URL https://doi.org/10.2307/2266170
3. Číhalová, M., Duží, M.: Questions, answers, and presuppositions. Computacion y Sistemas **19**(4), 647–659 (2015). URL https://doi.org/10.13053/CyS-19-4-2327
4. Duží, M.: Tenses and truth-conditions: a plea for if-then-else. In: M. Peliš (ed.) Logica Yearbook 2009, pp. 63–80. College Publications, London (2010). URL http://collegepublications.co.uk/logica/?00017
5. Duží, M.: Extensional logic of hyperintensions. In: A. Düsterhöft, M. Klettke, K. Schewe (eds.) Conceptual Modelling and Its Theoretical Foundations - Essays Dedicated to Bernhard Thalheim on the Occasion of His 60th Birthday, *Lecture Notes in Computer Science*, vol. 7260, pp. 268–290. Springer (2012). URL https://doi.org/10.1007/978-3-642-28279-9_19
6. Duží, M.: Towards an extensional calculus of hyperintensions. Organon F **19**(supplementary issue 1), 20–45 (2012). URL http://www.klemens.sav.sk/fiusav/organon/?q=en/towards-extensional-calculus-hyperintensions
7. Duží, M.: Property modifiers and intensional essentialism. Computacion y Sistemas **21**(4), 601–613 (2017). URL https://doi.org/10.13053/CyS-21-4-2811
8. Duží, M.: Logic of dynamic discourse; anaphora resolution. In: N. Yoshida, Y. Kiyoki, P. Chawakitchareon, C. Koopipat, A. Hansuebsai, V. Sornlertlamvanich, B. Thalheim, H. Jaakkola (eds.) Information Modelling and Knowledge Bases XXIX, *Frontiers in Artificial Intelligence and Applications*, vol. 301, pp. 263–279. IOS Press, Amsterdam (2018). URL https://doi.org/10.3233/978-1-61499-834-1-263
9. Duží, M.: Negation and presupposition, truth and falsity. Studies in Logic, Grammar and Rhetoric **54**(67), 15 – 46 (2018). URL https://doi.org/10.2478/slgr-2018-0014
10. Duží, M.: Ambiguities in natural language and time references. In: A. Horák, K. Osolsobě, A. Rambousek, P. Rychlý (eds.) Slavonic Natural Language Processing in the 21st Century, pp. 28–50. Tribun EU, Brno, Czech republic (2019)
11. Duží, M.: If structured propositions are logical procedures then how are procedures individuated? Synthese **196**(4), 1249–1283 (2019). URL https://doi.org/10.1007/s11229-017-1595-5
12. Duží, M., Fait, M.: Integrating special rules rooted in natural language semantics into the system of natural deduction. In: A. Rocha, L. Steels, J. van den Herik (eds.) ICAART 2020 - Proceedings of the 12th International Conference on Agents and Artificial Intelligence, vol. 1, pp. 410–421 (2020). URL https://doi.org/10.5220/0009369604100421
13. Duží, M., Fait, M., Menšík, M.: Adjustment of goal-driven resolution for natural language processing in TIL. In: A. Horák, P. Rychlý, A. Rambousek (eds.) Proceedings of t he 13th Workshop on Recent Advances in Slavonic Natural Languages Processing, RASLAN 2019, pp. 71–81. Tribun EU (2019). URL http://nlp.fi.muni.cz/raslan/2019/paper04-duzi.pdf
14. Duží, M., Horák, A.: Hyperintensional reasoning based on natural language knowledge base. International Journal of Uncertainty, Fuzziness and Knowlege-Based Systems **28**(3), 443–468 (2020). URL https://doi.org/10.1142/S021848852050018X

15. Duží, M., Jespersen, B.: Procedural isomorphism, analytic information and β-conversion by value. Logic Journal of the IGPL **21**(2), 291–308 (2013). URL https://doi.org/10.1093/jigpal/jzs044
16. Duží, M., Jespersen, B.: Transparent quantification into hyperintensional objectual attitudes. Synthese **192**(3), 635–677 (2015).
    URL https://doi.org/10.1007/s11229-014-0578-z
17. Duží, M., Jespersen, B.: An intelligent question-answer system over natural-language texts. In: S.B. Kim, I. Zelinka, V. Hoang Duy, T. Trong Dao, P. Brandstetter (eds.) AETA 2018 – Recent Advances in Electrical Engineering and Related Sciences: Theory and Applications, *Lecture Notes in Electrical Engineering*, vol. 554, pp. 162–174. Springer (2020). URL https://doi.org/10.1007/978-3-030-14907-9_17
18. Duží, M., Jespersen, B., Materna, P.: Procedural Semantics for Hyperintensional Logic - Foundations and Applications of Transparent Intensional Logic, *Logic, Epistemology, and the Unity of Science*, vol. 17. Springer, Berlin (2010). URL https://doi.org/10.1007/978-90-481-8812-3
19. Duží, M., Kosterec, M.: A valid rule of β-conversion for the logic of partial functions. Organon F **24**(1), 10–36 (2017). URL http://www.klemens.sav.sk/fiusav/organon/?q=sk/valid-rule-v-conversion-logic-partial-functions
20. Duží, M., Materna, P.: Validity and applicability of leibniz's law of substitution of identicals. In: P. Arazim, T. Lavička (eds.) Logica Yearbook 2016, pp. 17–35. College Publications, London (2017). URL http://collegepublications.co.uk/logica/?00030
21. Duží, M., Menšík, M.: Logic of inferable knowledge. In: H. Jaakkola, B. Thalheim, Y. Kiyoki, N. Yoshida (eds.) Information Modelling and Knowledge Bases XXVIII, *Frontiers in Artificial Intelligence and Applications*, vol. 292, pp. 405–425. IOS Press, Amsterdam (2017). URL https://doi.org/10.3233/978-1-61499-720-7-405
22. Duží, M., Menšík, M.: Inferring knowledge from textual data by natural deduction. Computacion y Sistemas **24**(1), 29–48 (2020). URL https://doi.org/10.13053/CyS-24-1-3345
23. Fait, M., Duží, M.: Substitution rules with respect to a context. In: S.B. Kim, I. Zelinka, V. Hoang Duy, T. Trong Dao, P. Brandstetter (eds.) AETA 2018 – Recent Advances in Electrical Engineering and Related Sciences: Theory and Applications, *Lecture Notes in Electrical Engineering*, vol. 554, pp. 55–66. Springer (2020). URL https://doi.org/10.1007/978-3-030-14907-9_6
24. Gamut, L.T.F.: Logic, Language and Meaning, vol. II - Intensional Logic and Logical Grammar. The University of Chicago Press, London (1991). URL https://press.uchicago.edu/ucp/books/book/chicago/L/bo3628700.html
25. Geach, P.T.: Good and evil. Analysis **17**(2), 32–43 (1956). URL https://doi.org/10.2307/3326442
26. Gordon, M.J.C., Melham, T.F.: Introduction to HOL. Cambridge University Press (1993). URL https://doi.org/10.1017/S0956796800001180
27. Harrah, D.: The logic of questions. In: G.F. Gabbay D.M. (ed.) Handbook of Philosophical Logic, *Handbook of Philosophical Logic*, vol. 8, pp. 1–60. Springer, Dordrecht (2002). URL https://doi.org/10.1007/978-94-010-0387-2_1
28. Higginbotham, J.: Interrogatives. In: K. Hale, S.J. Keyser (eds.) The View from Building 20: Essays in Linguistic in Honor od Sylvain Bromberger, pp. 195–227. The MIT Press, Cambridge, MA, (1993)
29. Horák, A.: The normal translation algorithm in transparent intensional logic for czech. Ph.D. thesis, Masaryk university, Brno (2002). URL https://www.fi.muni.cz/~hales/disert/thesis.pdf
30. Jespersen, B.: Structured lexical concepts, property modifiers, and transparent intensional logic. Philosophical Studies **172**(2), 321–345 (2015). URL https:/doi.org/10.1007/s11098-014-0305-0
31. Jespersen, B.: Left subsectivity: How to infer that a round peg is round. Dialectica **70**(4), 531–547 (2016). URL https://doi.org/10.1111/1746-8361.12159

32. Jespersen, B., Carrara, M., Duží, M.: Iterated privation and positive predication. Journal of Applied Logic **25**(supplement), 548–571 (2017). URL https://doi.org/10.1016/j.jal.2017.12.004
33. Jespersen, B., Duží, M.: Introduction to the special issue on hyperintensionality. Synthese **192**(3), 525–534 (2015). URL https://doi.org/10.1007/s11229-015-0665-9
34. Kamp, H.: A theory of truth and semantic representation. In: J. Groenendijk, T. Janssen, M. Stokhof (eds.) Formal Methods in the Study of Language, Part 1, pp. 227–322. Mathematical Center, Amsterdam (1981)
35. Kamp, H., Reyle, U.: From Discourse to Logic. Introduction to Model-Theoretic Semantics of Natural Language, Formal Logic and Discourse Representation Theory, *Studies in Linguistics and Philosophy*, vol. 42, 1 edn. Springer, Dordrecht (1993). URL https://doi.org/10.1007/978-94-017-1616-1
36. Keenan, E.L., Hull, R.D.: The logical presuppositions of questions and answers. In: J.S. Petöfi, D. Franck (eds.) Präsuppositionen in Philosophie und Linguistik, vol. 7, pp. 441–466. Athenäum, Frankfurt (1973)
37. Kotová, I.: Logika dynamického diskursu. Master's thesis, VSB-Technical University of Ostrava (2018). URL https://dspace.vsb.cz/handle/10084/128520?locale-attribute=cs. In Czech
38. Loukanova, R.: beta-reduction and antecedent-anaphora relations in the language of acyclic recursion. In: J. Cabestany, F.S. Hernández, A. Prieto, J.M. Corchado (eds.) Bio-Inspired Systems: Computational and Ambient Intelligence, 10th International Work-Conference on Artificial Neural Networks, IWANN 2009. Proceedings, Part I, *Lecture Notes in Computer Science*, vol. 5517, pp. 496–503. Springer (2009). URL https://doi.org/10.1007/978-3-642-02478-8_62
39. Loukanova, R.: Algorithmic semantics of ambiguous modifiers with the type theory of acyclic recursion. In: Proceedings of the 2012 IEEE/WIC/ACM International Conference on Web Intelligence and Intelligent Agent Technology Workshops, WI-IAT 2012, pp. 117–121 (2012). URL https://doi.org/10.1109/WI-IAT.2012.246
40. Łupkowski, P.: Erotetic inferences in natural language dialogues. In: Proceedings of the Logic & Cognition conference, pp. 39–48 (2012)
41. Moschovakis, Y.N.: A logical calculus of meaning and synonymy. Linguistics and Philosophy **29**(1), 27–89 (2006). URL https://doi.org/10.1007/s10988-005-6920-7
42. Nadathur, P.: Causal necessity and sufficiency in implicativity. In: Proceedings of SALT, vol. 26, pp. 1002–1021 (2016). URL https://doi.org/10.3765/salt.v26i0.3863
43. Peliš, M.: Consequence relations in inferential erotetic logic. In: M. Bílková (ed.) Consequence, Inference, Structure, Miscellanea Logica VII, pp. 53–88. Charles University of Prague (2008)
44. Peliš, M., Majer, O.: Logic of questions and public announcements. In: N. Bezhanishvili, S. Löbner, K. Schwabe, L. Spada (eds.) Logic, Language, and Computation - 8th International Tbilisi Symposium on Logic, Language, and Computation, TbiLLC 2009, *Lecture Notes in Computer Science*, vol. 6618, pp. 145–157. Springer (2011). URL https://doi.org/10.1007/978-3-642-22303-7_9
45. Tichý, P.: Questions, answers, and logic. American Philosophical Quarterly **15**(4), 275–284 (1978). Reprinted in [, pp. 293-304].
46. Tichý, P.: The logic of temporal discourse. Linguistics and Philosophy **3**(3), 343–369 (1980). URL https://doi.org/10.1007/BF00401690. Reprinted in [, pp. 373–403].
47. Tichý, P.: The Foundations of Frege's Logic. De Gruyter (1988). URL https://doi.org/10.1515/9783110849264
48. Tichý, P.: Collected Papers in Logic and Philosophy. Filosofia, Czech Academy of Science, and University of Otago Press, Prague, Dunedin (2004)
49. Wisniewski, A.: The Posing of Questions: Logical Foundations of Erotetic Inferences, *Synthese Library*, vol. 252. Springer, Dordrecht (1995). URL https://doi.org/10.1007/978-94-015-8406-7

LOGIC OF INTENSIONS

NEGATION AND PRESUPPOSITION, TRUTH AND FALSITY
Marie Duží

Abstract. There are many kinds of negation and denial. Perhaps the most common is the Boolean negation *not* that applies to propositions-in-extension, i.e. *truth-values*. The others are, inter alia, the *property of propositions* of not being true which applies to propositions; the *complement function* which applies to *sets*; *privation* which applies to *properties*; *negation as failure* applied in logic programming; negation as *argumentation ad absurdum*, and many others. The goal of this paper is neither to provide a complete list, nor to analyse all of them. Rather, I am going to deal with negation of propositions that come attached with a presupposition that is entailed by the positive as well as negated form of a given proposition. However, there are two kinds of negation, namely internal and external negation. I am going to prove that while the former is presupposition-preserving, the latter is presupposition-denying. This issue has much in common with the difference between topic and focus articulation within a sentence. Whereas articulating the topic of a sentence activates a presupposition, articulating the focus frequently yields merely an entailment. The main contribution of this paper is the proof that the two kinds of negation are not equivalent. While the Russellian wide-scope (external) negation gets the truth-conditions of a sentence right for a subject occurring as a focus, Strawsonian narrow-scope (internal) negation is validly applicable for a subject occurring as the topic. I also deal with other kinds of presupposition triggers, in particular factive attitudes and prerequisites of a given property. My background theory is Transparent Intensional Logic (TIL).[1] TIL is an expressive logic apt for the analysis of sentences with presuppositions, because in TIL we work with partial functions, in particular with propositions with truth-value gaps. Moreover, the procedural semantics of TIL make it possible to uncover the hidden semantic features of sentences, make them explicit and logically tractable.

Keywords: negation of propositions, presupposition, wide-scope vs. narrow-scope negation, topic-focus articulation, truth-value gaps, requisites and prerequisites, Transparent Intensional Logic, if-then-else-fail function.

1. Introduction

There are many kinds of negation and denial. In this paper, I am not going to deal with the complement function, nor with negation as failure or argumentation ad absurdum. Instead, I am going to deal with negation of propositions, or rather affirmative and denying forms of sentences denoting propositions that come attached with a presupposition.[2] Negation of propositions is often semantically restricted to contradictory opposition between propositions, in which *not A* is to be understood as "it is not the case that A".[3] However, negation of propositions often includes contrariety rather than contradiction:

> As introduced in Aristotle's *Categories* (11b17), the genus of opposition (*apophasis*) is divided into species that include contrariety and contradiction. Contradictory opposites, whether affirmative and negative counterparts of a singular predication (*Socrates is wise/Socrates isn't wise*) or quantified expressions (*All pleasure is good/Some pleasure is not good*), are mutually exhaustive as well as mutually exclusive, while contrary opposites (*Socrates is wise/Socrates is unwise*; *All pleasure is good/No pleasure is good*) do not mutually exhaust their domain. Contraries cannot be simultaneously true, though they may be simultaneously false. Members of a contradictory pair cannot be true **or** false simultaneously; contradictories "divide the true and the false between them". Contrary terms (*enantia*) come in two varieties (*Cat.* 11b38ff.). In immediate or logical contraries (*odd/even*, *sick/well*), a true middle—an entity satisfying the range of the two opposed terms but falling under neither of them—is excluded, e.g., an integer neither odd nor even. But mediate contrary pairs (*black/white*, *good/bad*) allow for a middle—a shirt between black and white, a man or an act neither good nor bad. Neither mediate nor immediate contraries fall under the Law of Excluded Middle [LEM] (*tertium non datur*).
>
> Horn, Wansing (2017, §1.4)

Yet a similar phenomenon arises also in the case of *privative modifiers* of *properties*. The problem of privation of properties has been dealt with by Jespersen, Carrara and Duží (2017) where the authors show that modifiers privative with respect to a property P turn the root property P to the property $[M\ P]$ that is *contrary* rather than contradictory with respect to P. To this end they apply the method of *intensional essentialism*, which operates on properties (intensions) rather than their extensions. The authors argue that each property P is necessarily associated with an essence, which is the set of the so-called *requisites* of P that jointly define P. Privation deprives P of *some but not all* of its requisites, replacing them by their contradictories. Thus, the standard rule of *single privative modification* that replaces privative modifiers by Boolean negation is valid, for sure, but also too simplistic. If an individual a instantiates the privatively modified property $[M\ P]$ then it is true that a is *not* a P, but the rule fails to express the fact that the properties $[M\ P]$ and P have something in common. For instance, a *forged banknote* is not a banknote, yet it still has much in common with banknotes. A forged banknote is not just some object or other that fails to be a banknote, but rather it is an object that must have a host of properties in common with banknotes. Though forged banknotes and, say, horses and lions are not banknotes, there is a sense in which forged banknotes are much 'closer' to banknotes than are horses and lions. As mentioned above, the authors solve the problem by means of requisites assigned to each property P as its *essence* and define privation along these lines.

> A modifier M is *privative* with respect to a property P iff the modified property $[M\ P]$ lacks at least one, but *not all*, of the requisites of the property P. Moreover, the essence of $[M\ P]$ contains at least one other requisite that does not belong to the essence of P, and *contradicts* at least one of the requisites of P. As a result, M is privative with respect to P iff the essence of $[M\ P]$ has a non-empty intersection with the essence of P, and this intersection is a *proper* subset of both the essences of P and of $[M\ P]$. (ibid.)

Thus, there is a difference between seemingly same propositions as "*a* is *not* a banknote" and "*a* is a *non*-banknote", where '*non*' stands for a privative modifier. While the law of excluded middle holds for the former, it fails in the case of the latter. For sure, *a* cannot be both a banknote and a *non*-banknote, but it can be the case that *a* is neither a banknote nor a *non*-banknote.

The law of excluded middle fails also in the case of sentences denoting propositions that come attached with a *presupposition*. A presupposition P of a proposition S is entailed both by the positive form of S and its negated form '*non-S*'. If the presupposition P is not the case, the proposition S is neither true nor false. The problem I am going to deal with is the ambiguity of '*non-S*', to wit the external (wide-scope) and internal (narrow-scope) application of '*non*', and the closely related issue of topic-focus articulation of sentences.

The rest of this paper is organised as follows. Section 2 summarises the issues connected with narrow-scope vs. wide-scope negation, and a long-term dispute on Russellian vs. Strawsonian analysis of sentences with the schematic form "The F is a G". The solution to this dilemma based on different topic-focus articulations of sentences is then proposed in Section 4, coming after Section 3, where the relevant foundations of my background theory TIL are introduced. In Section 4 the difference between narrow-scope and wide-scope negation is rigorously defined by applying TIL analysis. Using the difference between these two kinds of negation, I also differentiate presupposition from mere entailment. In Section 5 I deal with ambiguities stemming from topic-focus articulation of a sentence in general and propose a general analytic schema for such sentences. Finally, in Section 6 I deal with other cases where a presupposition can be generated, for instance, by factive attitudes like 'knowing' or by prerequisites of a given property that is applied to the subject of a sentence. Finally, concluding remarks can be found in Section 7.

2. Negation, presupposition, and the excluded middle

The law of the excluded middle fails in the case of sentences that come attached with a *presupposition*. In his classic paper on sense and reference, Frege (1892) argues that both (a) and its contradictory (b) presuppose that the name *Kepler* has a denotation.[4]

(a)   Kepler died in misery.

(b)   Kepler did not die in misery.

Every affirmative or negative sentence with a singular description '*SD*' presupposes the existence of a unique referent of '*SD*'. According to Frege, if the presupposition fails, no assertion is made, but this presupposition is not a part of the content of the sentence. Hence (a) does not entail existence, or the negation of (a) would not be (b) but *"Kepler did not die in misery or the name 'Kepler' has no reference"*, an outcome Frege seems to have taken as an absurdity. Yet this outcome foreshadows the need to deal with sentences that are neither true nor false due to the fact that their presupposition is not true.

Russell (1905) was not willing to tolerate the truth-value gaps incurred on Frege's analysis, and reconsidered the status of contradictory negation with vacuous subjects:

> By the law of the excluded middle, either "*A* is *B*" or "*A* is not *B*" must be true. Hence either "the present king of France is bald" or "the present king of France is not bald" must be true. Yet if we enumerated the things that are bald and the things that are not bald, we should not find the king of France on either list. Hegelians, who love a synthesis, will probably conclude that he wears a wig. (ibid. 485)

To resolve this ostensible paradox while preserving a classical analysis in which every meaningful sentence is true or false, Russell banishes singular terms like *the king of France* from logical form. He claims that we have to uncover the real logical form of such sentences that is otherwise hidden.

Though it seems that the form of (c) and (d) is the form of subject-predicate sentences, we have to unpack them as existentially quantified sentences.

(c)   The king of France is bald.

(d)   The king of France is not bald.

On Russell's theory of descriptions, the logical form of (c) is

(c') $\exists x(Kx \land \forall y(Ky \supset y = x) \land Bx))$

which is the (false) proposition that there is an entity with the property of being king of France, and this entity is unique, and it is bald.

However, the negated sentence (d) is ambiguous, depending on the scope of negation, which yields two non-equivalent logical forms of (d):

(d') $\exists x(Kx \land \forall y(Ky \supset y = x) \land \neg Bx))$

(d") $\neg \exists x(Kx \land \forall y(Ky \supset y = x) \land Bx))$

The former, (d'), with *narrow-scope* (internal) negation, is the proposition that there is a unique and hairy king of France, which is simply false in the absence (or oversupply) of male French monarchs. Hence, for Russell (d') cannot be the right logical form of the negation of (c), because we would end up with the result that both (c) and its negation are false, which contradicts the principle of the excluded middle.

On the other hand, in (d") the *wide-scope* (external) negation is applied. The description *the king of France* falls within the scope of the external negation and yields a true proposition. Indeed, the non-existence of a king of France guarantees the truth of (d"). Hence Russell in the effort of following the principle of the excluded middle must admit that (d") is the right logical form of the negation of (c). Furthermore, (d"), unlike (d') fails to entail the existence of the king of France. Horn (1989, p. 107) clarifies this reading as

(d_r)   The king of France isn't bald, because there isn't any king of France.

Though Russell's quantificational theory remains to this day a strong rival of referential theories, it has received its fair amount of criticism. Russell's opponents claim that he simply gets the truth-conditions wrong in important cases of using descriptions when there is no such thing as the unique F.[5]

This criticism was launched by Strawson who in (1950) objected that Russell's theory predicts the wrong truth-conditions for sentences like "The present King of France is bald". For Strawson, negation normally or invariably leaves the subject "unimpaired". Strawson tacitly lines up with Frege and against Russell (and Aristotle) in regarding negative statements like (b) and (d) as unambiguous and necessarily *presuppositional*. For, if the sentence (c) were false then its negation, "The King of France is *not* bald", would be true, which entails that there *is* a unique King of France, contrary to the assumption that there is none. Hence someone who utters (d) does not thereby assert (nor does their statement entail) that there is a king of France. Rather, (d)—along with its affirmative counterpart (c)—*presupposes* it. If this presupposition fails, neither (c) nor (d) can be judged true or false. A statement may be made but the question of its truth value fails to arise.[6]

Russell was very upset by Strawson's criticism. In response to this criticism, he argues that, despite Strawson's protests, the sentence is in fact false:[7]

> Suppose, for example, that in some country there was a law that no person could hold public office if he considered it false that the Ruler of the Universe is wise. I think an avowed atheist who took advantage of Mr. Strawson's doctrine to say that he did not hold this proposition false would be regarded as a somewhat shifty character. (Russell, 1957)

Donnellan (1966) observes that there is a sense in which Strawson and Russell are both right, and both wrong, about the proper analysis of definite descriptions, because definite descriptions can be used in two different ways. On a so-called *attributive use*, a sentence of the form "The F is a G" is used to express a proposition equivalent to "Whatever is uniquely F is a G". Alternatively, on a *referential use*, a sentence of the form "The F is a G" is used to pick out a specific individual, a, and to say of a that it is a G. Donnellan suggests that Russell's quantificational account of definite descriptions might capture attributive uses, but that it does not work for referential uses. Ludlow in (2007) interprets Donnellan as arguing that in some cases descriptions are Russellian and in other cases Strawsonian. Kripke (1977) responds to Donnellan by arguing that the Russellian account of definite descriptions can, by itself, account for both referential and attributive uses, and that the difference between the two cases is entirely a matter of pragmatics.

Neale (1990) supports Russell's view by collecting a number of cases in which intuitions about truth conditions clearly do not support Strawson's view. On the other hand, a number of linguists have recently come to Strawson's defence on this matter. See Ludlow (2007) for a detailed survey of the arguments supporting Strawson's view and arguments supporting Russell's. Here it might suffice to point out that Strawson's concerns have not delivered a knock-out blow to Russell's theory of descriptions, and so this topic remains very much alive. For instance, recently Von Fintel (2004) argues that every sentence containing a definite description 'the F' comes with the existential presupposition that there be a unique F.

In this paper I am disregarding Donnellan's troublesome pragmatic notion of having somebody in mind. Instead, I will propose a *logical analysis* of sentences of the form "The F is a G". What I want to show is this. First, definite descriptions are not deprived of a self-contained meaning and they denote one and the same entity in any context. Thus, they are never Russellian. Second, Russell's insight that a definite description 'the F' does not denote a definite individual is spot-on. According to TIL, 'the F' denotes a *condition* to be contingently satisfied by the individual (if any) that happens to be the F. I will explicate such conditions in terms of possible-world intensions, *viz.* as *individual roles* or *offices* to be occupied by at most one individual per world/time pair. Third, I am going to show that Donnellan is right in holding that sentences of the form "The F is a G" are systematically ambiguous. However, their ambiguity does not concern a shift of meaning of the definite description 'the F', as Fregean or other theories maintain. Instead the ambiguity concerns different *topic-focus* articulations of these sentences.

There are two options. The description 'the F' may occur as the topic of a sentence and property G (the focus) is predicated of its referent. This case corresponds to Donnellan's *referential* use. Using medieval terminology, I will say that 'the F' occurs with *de re supposition*. The other option is 'G' occurring as topic and 'the F' as focus. This reading corresponds to Donnellan's *attributive* use of 'the F' and the description occurs with *de dicto* supposition. Consequently, and crucially, such sentences are ambiguous between a *de dicto* and a *de re* reading. On their *de re* reading they *presuppose* the existence of a unique F. Strawson's analysis appears to be adequate for *de re* cases. On their *de dicto* reading they have the truth-conditions as specified by the Russellian analysis. They do not presuppose, but merely entail, the existence of a unique F. However, the Russellian analysis, though being equivalent to the one I am going to propose, is not an adequate *literal* analysis of *de dicto* readings.

Furthermore, I am going to bring out the *semantic* nature of the topic-focus difference by means of a literal logical analysis. As a result, I furnish sentences differing only as for their topic-focus articulation with different structured meanings producing different possible-world propositions.[8] Since our logic is a hyperintensional logic of *partial functions*, I am able to analyse sentences with presuppositions in a both natural and principled manner. It means that I associate them with hyperpropositions, which in TIL are abstract logical procedures that produce partial possible-world propositions, which occasionally yield truth-value gaps.[9]

We need to work with properly partial functions and propositions with truth-value gaps despite technical difficulties connected with this issue. On a Strawsonian reading, the sentence "The King of France is bald" talks about the office of the King of France (topic) ascribing to the individual (if any) that occupies this office the property of being bald (focus). Thus, it is presupposed that the King of France exists, i.e., that the office is occupied. If the office is vacant the proposition denoted by the sentence lacks a truth-value. On our approach this does not mean that the sentence is meaningless. The sentence has a sense, namely an instruction how in any possible world w at any time t to execute the *procedure* (hyperproposition) of evaluating its truth-conditions. Only if we evaluate these conditions in such a state-of-affairs where the office of the King of France goes vacant does the process of evaluation yield a truth-value gap.

This issue has much in common with the difference between topic and focus articulation within a sentence. As many linguists argue, whereas articulating the topic of a sentence activates a presupposition, articulating its focus frequently yields merely an entailment.[10] The point of departure is that sentences of the form "The F is a G" are ambiguous. Their ambiguity stems from the different topic-focus articulations of such sentences. The issue is this. If 'the F' is the topic phrase, then this description occurs extensionally, i.e. with *de re* supposition, and Strawsonian analysis appears to be what is wanted. On this reading the sentence presupposes the existence of the descriptum of 'the F', because the property G is ascribed to the object, if any, referred to by 'the F'. The other option is 'G' occurring as topic and 'the F' as focus. This reading roughly corresponds to Donnellan's attributive use of 'the F' and the description occurs intensionally with *de dicto* supposition. On this reading the Russellian analysis gets the truth-conditions of the sentence right. The existence of a unique F is merely entailed.

Summarising, the two readings differ also in the way their respective negated form is obtained. Whereas the Strawsonian narrow-scope negated form is "The F is not a G", the Russellian wide-scope negated form would be "It is not true that the F is a G". Thus, in the former case the property of not being a G is ascribed to the object, if any, that is referred to by the *topic phrase* 'the F'. On the other hand, in the Russellian case the property of not being true is ascribed to the whole proposition that the F is a G.[11] I am going to prove that these two readings are not equivalent, because they denote different propositions (truth-conditions individuated up to logical equivalence). While "The F is not a G" lacks a truth-value at those states of affairs where the *F* does not exist, the wide-scope negation "It is not true that the *F* is a *G*" is true at such states of affairs where there is no *F*.

3. Foundations of TIL

The terms of the TIL language denote abstract procedures (roughly, Church's functions-in-intension) that produce set-theoretical mappings (functions-in-extension).[12] These procedures are rigorously defined as TIL *constructions*.

Definition 1 (*construction*)

(i) *Variables* $x, y, \ldots$ are *constructions* that *construct* objects (elements of their respective ranges) dependently on a valuation v; they *v-construct*.

(ii) Where *X* is any object whatsoever (even a *construction*), ^0X is the *construction Trivialization* that *constructs* X without any change of X.

(iii) Let $X, Y_1, \ldots, Y_n$ be arbitrary *constructions*. Then *Composition* $[XY_1 \ldots Y_n]$ is the following *construction*. For any v, the *Composition* $[XY_1 \ldots Y_n]$ is *v-improper* if at least one of the *constructions* $X, Y_1, \ldots, Y_n$ is *v*-improper by failing to *v*-construct anything, or if *X* does not *v-construct* a function that is defined at the *n*-tuple of objects *v-constructed* by $Y_1, \ldots, Y_n$. If *X* does *v-construct* such a function, then $[XY_1 \ldots Y_n]$ *v-constructs* the value of this function at the *n*-tuple.

(iv) ($\lambda-$) *Closure* $[\lambda x_1 \ldots x_m Y]$ is the following *construction*. Let $x_1, x_2, \ldots, x_m$ be pair-wise distinct variables and *Y* a *construction*. Then $[\lambda x_1 \ldots x_m Y]$ *v-constructs* the function f that takes any members $B_1, \ldots, B_m$ of the respective ranges of the variables $x_1, \ldots, x_m$ into the object (if any) that is $v(B_1/x_1, \ldots, B_m/x_m)$-*constructed* by *Y*, where $v(B_1/x_1, \ldots, B_m/x_m)$ is like v except for assigning B_1 to $x_1, \ldots, B_m$ to x_m.

(v) Where *X* is any object whatsoever, ^1X is the *construction Single Execution* that *v-constructs* what *X* *v*-constructs. Thus, if *X* is a *v*-improper *construction* or not a *construction* as all, ^1X is *v-improper*.

(vi) Where *X* is any object whatsoever, ^2X is the *construction Double Execution*. If *X* is not itself a *construction*, or if *X* does not *v*-construct a *construction*, or if *X* *v-constructs* a *v*-improper *construction*, then ^2X is *v-improper*. Otherwise ^2X *v-constructs* what is *v-constructed* by the *construction v-constructed* by *X*.

(vii) Nothing is a *construction*, unless it so follows from (i) through (vi). □

Comments. Being procedural objects, constructions can be executed in order to operate on input objects (of a lower-order type) and produce the object (if any) they are typed to produce, while non-procedural objects, i.e. non-constructions, cannot be executed. Hence the constituents of constructions cannot be non-procedural objects; non-procedural objects must be presented, or referred to, by atomic constructions. *Trivialization* and *Variables* are the two atomic constructions that present input objects (which can also be lower-order constructions) to be operated on. The operational sense of Trivialization is similar to that of constants in formal languages. A Trivialization presents an object X without the mediation of any other procedures. Using the terminology of programming languages, the Trivialization of X, '^0X' in symbols, is just a *pointer* referring to X. Variables produce objects dependently on valuations; they v-construct. We adopt an objectual variant of the Tarskian conception of variables. To each type (see Def. 2) are assigned countably many variables that range over this particular type. Objects of each type can be arranged into infinitely many sequences. The valuation v selects one such sequence of objects of the respective type, and the first variable v-constructs the first object of the sequence, the second variable v-constructs the second object of the sequence, and so on. Hence the execution of a Trivialization or a variable never fails to produce an object; these constructions are not v-improper for any valuation v. The (λ–) Closure $[\lambda x_1 \ldots x_m Y]$ is also not v-improper for any v, as it always v-constructs a function. Even if the constituent Y is v-improper for every valuation v, the Closure is not v-improper. Yet in such a case the constructed function is a bizarre object; it is a degenerate function that lacks a value at any argument. However, the other molecular constructions, namely Composition, Single and Double Execution, can fail to present an object of the type they are typed to produce; they can be v-*improper*. The main source of improperness is an application of a function to an argument at which the function is not defined.[13]

With constructions of constructions, constructions of functions, functions, and functional values in our stratified ontology, we need to keep track of the traffic between multiple logical strata. The *ramified type hierarchy* does just that. The type of first-order objects includes all non-procedural objects. Therefore, it includes not only the standard objects of individuals, truth-values, sets, functions, etc., but also functions defined on possible worlds (i.e., the intensions germane to possible-world semantics). The type of second-order objects includes constructions of first-order objects and functions with such constructions in their domain or range. The type of third-order objects includes constructions of first- and second-order objects and functions with such constructions in their domain or range; and so on, ad infinitum.

Definition 2 (*ramified hierarchy of types*).

Let B be a *base*, where a base is a collection of pair-wise disjoint, non-empty sets. Then:

$\mathbf{T}_1$ (*types of order 1*).
i) Every member of B is an elementary *type of order 1 over B*.
ii) Let $\alpha, \beta_1, \ldots, \beta_m$ ($m > 0$) be types of order 1 over B. Then the collection $(\alpha\beta_1 \ldots \beta_m)$ of all m-ary partial mappings from $\beta_1 \times \ldots \times \beta_m$ into α is a functional *type of order 1 over B*.
iii) Nothing is a *type of order 1 over B* unless it so follows from (i) and (ii).

$\mathbf{C}_n$ (*constructions of order n*)
i) Let x be a variable ranging over a type of order n. Then x is a *construction of order n over B*.
ii) Let X be a member of a type of order n. Then ^0X, ^1X, ^2X are *constructions of order n over B*.
iii) Let $X, X_1, \ldots, X_m$ ($m > 0$) be constructions of order n over B. Then $[XX_1 \ldots X_m]$ is a *construction of order n over B*.
iv) Let $x_1, \ldots, x_m, X$ ($m > 0$) be constructions of order n over B. Then $[\lambda x_1 \ldots x_m X]$ is a *construction of order n over B*.
v) Nothing is a *construction of order n over B* unless it so follows from $\mathbf{C}_n$ (i)–(iv).

$\mathbf{T}_{n+1}$ (*types of order n + 1*)
Let $*_n$ be the collection of all constructions of order n over B. Then
i) $*_n$ and every type of order n are *types of order n + 1*.
ii) If $m > 0$ and $\alpha, \beta_1, \ldots, \beta_m$ are types of order $n + 1$ over B, then $(\alpha\beta_1 \ldots \beta_m)$ (see $\mathbf{T}_1$ (ii)) is a *type of order n + 1 over B*.
iii) Nothing is a *type of order n + 1 over B* unless it so follows from (i) and (ii). □

For the purposes of natural language analysis, we are assuming the following base of ground types:
o: the set of truth-values $\{\mathbf{T}, \mathbf{F}\}$;
ι: the set of individuals (the universe of discourse);
τ: the set of real numbers (doubling as times);
ω: the set of logically possible worlds (the logical space).

We model sets and relations by their characteristic functions. Thus, for instance, $(o\iota)$ is the type of a set of individuals, while $(o\iota\iota)$ is the type of a relation-in-extension between individuals. Empirical expressions denote *empirical conditions* that may or may not be satisfied at the particular world/time pair of evaluation. These empirical conditions are modelled as possible-world-semantic *(PWS) intensions*. PWS intensions are entities of type $(\beta\omega)$: mappings from possible worlds to an arbitrary type β. The type β is frequently the type of the *chronology* of α-objects, i.e., a mapping of type $(\alpha\tau)$. Thus α-intensions are frequently functions of type $((\alpha\tau)\omega)$, abbreviated as '$\alpha_{\tau\omega}$'. *Extensional entities* are entities of a type α where $\alpha \neq (\beta\omega)$ for any type β. Where w ranges over ω and t over τ, the following logical form essentially characterizes the logical syntax of empirical language: $\lambda w \lambda t [\ldots w \ldots t \ldots]$.

Examples of frequently used PWS intensions are: *propositions* of type $o_{\tau\omega}$, *properties of individuals* of type $(o\iota)_{\tau\omega}$, *binary relations-in-intension* between individuals of type $(o\iota\iota)_{\tau\omega}$, *individual offices* (or roles) of type $\iota_{\tau\omega}$, *attitudes to constructions* of type $(o\iota *_n)_{\tau\omega}$.

Logical objects like *truth-functions* are extensional: $\wedge$ (conjunction), $\vee$ (disjunction) and $\supset$ (implication) are of type (ooo), and $\neg$ (negation) of type (oo). Below, all type indications will be provided outside the formulae in order not to clutter the notation. The outermost brackets of the Closure will be omitted whenever no confusion arises. Furthermore, 'X/α' means that an object X is (a member) of type α. '$X \rightarrow_v \alpha$' means that X is typed to v-construct an object of type α, if any. We write '$X \rightarrow \alpha$' if what is v-constructed does not depend on a valuation v. Throughout, it holds that the variables $w \rightarrow_v \omega$ and $t \rightarrow_v \tau$. If $C \rightarrow_v \alpha_{\tau\omega}$ then the frequently used Composition $[[Cw]t]$, which is the intensional descent (a.k.a. extensionalization) of the α-intension v-constructed by C, will be encoded as 'C_{wt}'. Whenever no confusion arises, we use traditional infix notation without Trivialisation for truth-functions and the identity relation, to make the terms denoting constructions easier to read.

Definition 3 (*quantifiers, singularizers*)

The *universal quantifier* $\forall^\alpha$ is a total polymorphic function of type $(o(o\alpha))$ that takes a class A of α-elements to **T** if A contains all elements of the type α, otherwise to **F**. The *existential quantifier* $\exists^\alpha$ is a total polymorphic function of type $(o(o\alpha))$ that takes a class A of α-elements to **T** if A is a non-empty class, otherwise to **F**. The *singularizer* $\imath^\alpha$ is a partial polymorphic function of type $(\alpha(o\alpha))$ that takes a class A to its only α-element if A is a singleton, otherwise (if A is an empty or multiple-element class) is the singularizer undefined at A. □

Again, to make the constructions easier to read, as a notational convention I will often write '$\forall x B$', '$\exists x B$' and '$\iota x B$', instead of the full TIL notation '$[^0\forall^\alpha \lambda x B]$', '$[^0\exists^\alpha \lambda x B]$' and '$[^0\iota^\alpha \lambda x B]$', whenever no confusion arises. The additional types are $x \to \alpha$, $B \to o$, $\lambda x B \to (o\alpha)$, $[^0\forall^\alpha \lambda x B] \to o$, $[^0\exists^\alpha \lambda x B] \to o$, $[^0\iota^\alpha \lambda x B] \to \alpha$.

We invariably furnish expressions with procedurally structured meanings, which are explicated as TIL constructions. Thus, TIL constructions are assigned to expressions as their context-invariant meanings, and the analysis of an unambiguous sentence (or generally any term) consists in discovering the logical construction encoded by a given sentence. To this end we have developed the *TIL method of analysis* that consists of three steps:

1) *Type-theoretical analysis*, i.e., assigning types to the objects that receive mention in the analysed expression.
2) *Type-theoretical synthesis*, i.e., combining the constructions of the objects obtained in step (1) in order to construct the object (if any) of the respective type denoted by the whole expression.
3) *Type-theoretical checking*, i.e. checking whether the proposed analysis is type-theoretically coherent.

To illustrate the method, I will use Jespersen's exemplary sentence "Vulcan is a planet". Here 'Vulcan' is not a proper name; rather it stands for the definite description 'the small planet in an orbit between Mercury and the Sun'. Its existence was proposed by Le Verrier in an attempt to explain peculiarities of Mercury's orbit. A number of reputable investigators became involved in the search for Vulcan, but no such planet was ever found, and the peculiarities in Mercury's orbit have now been explained by Albert Einstein's theory of general relativity. I am going to analyse the sentence *à la* Strawson, i.e. with 'Vulcan' as a topic referring to that hypothetical individual to which the property of being a planet is ascribed.

First, type-theoretical analysis. The sentence mentions the following objects. $Vulcan/\iota_{\tau\omega}$ is an individual role; $Planet/(o\iota)_{\tau\omega}$; the whole sentence denotes a proposition, that is, an object of type $o_{\tau\omega}$.

Second, synthesis. Since we intend to arrive at the *literal* analysis of the sentence, the objects denoted by semantically simple expressions are constructed by their Trivializations: ^0Vulcan, ^0Planet. Now we are to apply the property of being a planet to the holder of the Vulcan office. In other words, we want to express the hypothetical fact that the holder (if any) obtained by extensionalisation of the office with respect to world w and time t of evaluation, $^0Vulcan_{wt} \to \iota$, belongs to the population of planets in this world and time, i.e. $^0Planet_{wt} \to (o\iota)$. Since the population is a set modelled as a function of type $(o\iota)$ it suffices to apply this function to that individual. We have

$$[{}^0Planet_{wt}\ {}^0Vulcan_{wt}] \to o$$

Evaluating this Composition in a given $\langle w, t\rangle$-pair we obtain a truth value (**T** or **F**) or nothing, according as Vulcan is a planet, or does not exist in this $\langle w, t\rangle$-pair, respectively.

Abstracting over the values of w and t we obtain the Closure that constructs the proposition denoted by our sentence:

$$\lambda w \lambda t\ [{}^0Planet_{wt}\ {}^0Vulcan_{wt}] \to o_{\tau\omega}.$$

Third, type checking. To this end we usually draw the derivation tree as illustrated by Fig. 1.[14]

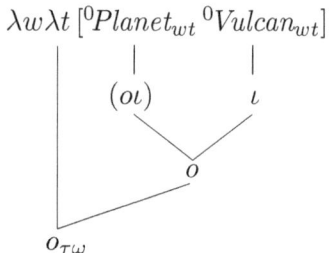

Figure 1. Derivation tree

Now it should be clear that this sentence not only entails, but also presupposes that Vulcan exists. For, if it does not exist in the world w and time t of evaluation, the Composition ${}^0Vulcan_{wt}$ is v-improper by failing to produce any individual holding the *Vulcan office*. By Def. 1 (iii), 'partiality is propagated up', which means that the Composition $[{}^0Planet_{wt}\ {}^0Vulcan_{wt}]$ is v-improper as well; no truth-value is produced. Hence the proposition constructed by the above Closure has a *truth-value gap* in such a state-of-affairs where Vulcan does not exist.

So much for the basic notions of TIL and its method of analysis.

4. Presuppositions and the two kinds of negation

As stated at the outset of this paper, sentences often come attached with a presupposition that is entailed both by the sentence and its negation. The entailment relation is defined as usual. A proposition P is analytically entailed by a proposition S, $S \models P$, if P takes the truth-value **T** at all $\langle w, t\rangle$-pairs at which S takes the value **T**.[15]

To define analytic entailment formally, we need the propositional property $\mathit{True}/(oo_{\tau\omega})_{\tau\omega}$ which is defined as follows. Let P be a propositional construction $(P/*_n \to o_{\tau\omega})$. Then

$[^0\mathit{True}_{wt} P]$ v-constructs $\mathbf{T}$ iff P_{wt} v-constructs $\mathbf{T}$, otherwise $\mathbf{F}$.

For completeness, there are two other properties of the same type, namely *False* and *Undefined*, defined as follows:

$[^0\mathit{False}_{wt} P]$ v-constructs $\mathbf{T}$ iff P_{wt} v-constructs $\mathbf{F}$, otherwise $\mathbf{F}$

$[^0\mathit{Undefined}_{wt} P]$ v-constructs $\mathbf{T}$ iff P_{wt} is v-improper, otherwise $\mathbf{F}$

Note that $[^0\mathit{True}_{wt} P]$ v-constructs $\mathbf{F}$ in two cases, namely if P_{wt} v-constructs $\mathbf{F}$ or if P_{wt} is v-improper. Hence, for instance, if a proposition v-constructed by P is not true at a given $\langle w, t\rangle$-pair, it does not have to be false, because there is the third possibility of being undefined. Formally, we have these relations $(=/(ooo))$:

$$[^0\mathit{True}_{wt} P] = \neg[^0\mathit{False}_{wt} P] \wedge \neg[^0\mathit{Undefined}_{wt} P]$$
$$[^0\mathit{False}_{wt} P] = \neg[^0\mathit{True}_{wt} P] \wedge \neg[^0\mathit{Undefined}_{wt} P]$$
$$[^0\mathit{Undefined}_{wt} P] = \neg[^0\mathit{True}_{wt} P] \wedge \neg[^0\mathit{False}_{wt} P]$$

Analytical entailment is defined as follows $(P, S/*_n \to o_{\tau\omega}, \models / (oo_{\tau\omega}o_{\tau\omega}))$.[16]

$$(S \models P) \text{ iff } \forall w \forall t\, [[^0\mathit{True}_{wt} S] \supset [^0\mathit{True}_{wt} P]]$$

The logical difference between a presupposition and mere entailment is this:

P is a *presupposition* of S iff $(S \models P)$ and $(\mathit{non}\text{-}S \models P)$

P is *merely entailed* by S iff $(S \models P)$ and neither $(\mathit{non}\text{-}S \models P)$ nor $(\mathit{non}\text{-}S \models \mathit{non}\text{-}P)$

Comments. If P is a presupposition of S and P is not true at a given $\langle w, t\rangle$-pair, then *neither S nor non-S is true*. Hence, S has no truth-value at such a $\langle w, t\rangle$-pair at which its presupposition is not true. On the other hand, if P is merely entailed by S, then if S is not true we cannot deduce anything about the truth-value, or lack thereof, of P.

Using the properties of propositions *True* and *False*, we can rigorously define the difference between presupposition and mere entailment.

Definition 4 (*presupposition vs. mere entailment*)

Let P and S be propositional constructions $(P, S/*_n \to o_{\tau\omega})$. Then
P is entailed by S iff $\forall w \forall t\, [[^0\mathit{True}_{wt} S] \supset [^0\mathit{True}_{wt} P]]$
P is a presupposition of S iff $\forall w \forall t\, [[[^0\mathit{True}_{wt} S] \vee [^0\mathit{False}_{wt} S]] \supset [^0\mathit{True}_{wt} P]]$

□

Hence, I agree with Frege and Strawson that survival under negation is the most important test for a presupposition. However, in order to decide whether there is a presupposition of S, we have to take into account the two ways in which the negated form *non-S* can be obtained. To illustrate the situation, consider again the sentence "The King of France is bald". If the royal office is occupied and we want to say that its holder is *not* bald, we would simply use the form "The King of France is *not* bald". This is Strawsonian *narrow-scope negation*. The property of not being bald is ascribed to the holder of the royal office.[17] Thus the analyses of the Strawsonian reading of the sentence and of its negation come down to these constructions:

(S) $\lambda w \lambda t\ [^0Bald_{wt}\ \lambda w \lambda t\ [^0King\_of_{wt}\ ^0France]_{wt}]$

(*non-S*) $\lambda w \lambda t\ \neg [^0Bald_{wt}\ \lambda w \lambda t\ [^0King\_of_{wt}\ ^0France]_{wt}]$

However, if the royal office is not occupied, one would protest, saying, "No, it is not true that the King of France is bald, for the King of France does not exist". This is Russellian *wide-scope negation*. The property of not being true is ascribed to the whole proposition that the King of France is bald.[18] And indeed, *it is not true* that the King of France is bald, because the proposition denoted by the sentence has a truth-value gap.

In order to analyse Russellian wide-scope negation, we apply the above defined propositional property $True/(oo_{\tau\omega})_{\tau\omega}$:

(*non-R*) $\lambda w \lambda t\ \neg [^0True_{wt}\ \lambda w \lambda t\ [^0Bald_{wt}\ \lambda w \lambda t\ [^0King\_of_{wt}\ ^0France]_{wt}]]$

(*non-R*) is the wide-scope negation of the proposition that it is true that the King of France is bald constructed by

(R) $\lambda w \lambda t\ [^0True_{wt}\ \lambda w \lambda t\ [^0Bald_{wt}\ \lambda w \lambda t\ [^0King\_of_{wt}\ ^0France]_{wt}]]$

This is not exactly Russell's analysis. As mentioned above, the Russellian rephrasing of the sentence "The King of France is bald" is "There is a unique individual such that he is the King of France and he is bald". The analysis of this sentence comes down to

(R^*) $\lambda w \lambda t\ [^0\exists \lambda x\ [[x = \lambda w \lambda t\ [^0King\_of_{wt}\ ^0France]_{wt}] \wedge [^0Bald_{wt}x]]]$.

Additional types. $\exists/(o(o\iota));\ =/(o\iota\iota);\ x/*_1 \rightarrow_v \iota$.[19]

Yet (R) gets the truth-conditions of the Russellian reading right, because (R) and (R^*) are equivalent in the sense of constructing the same proposition. This analysis *does not presuppose* the existence of the holder of the royal office, unlike the proposition constructed by (S). The analysis reveals that these two readings are not equivalent. Though (R) and (S) are *co-entailing* they denote *different propositions*, which I am going to prove now.

First, the equivalence of (R) and (R^*).

a) Let the royal office be occupied in a given world w and time t by an individual a. Then if this individual a is bald, the proposition
$$\lambda w \lambda t \, [^0Bald_{wt} \, \lambda w \lambda t \, [^0King\_of_{wt} \, ^0France]_{wt}]$$
takes the value **T** in such a world-time pair, otherwise **F**, and so does (R) according to the definition of the property *True*. By assumption
$$[^0a = [\lambda w \lambda t \, [^0King\_of_{wt} \, ^0France]_{wt}].$$
Hence the Composition
$$[^0a = [\lambda w \lambda t \, [^0King\_of_{wt} \, ^0France]_{wt}] \wedge [^0Bald_{wt} \, ^0a]]$$
v-constructs **T** and so does
$$[\lambda x \, [x = [\lambda w \lambda t \, [^0King\_of_{wt} \, ^0France]_{wt}] \wedge [^0Bald_{wt} \, x]] \, ^0a]$$
if a is bald. It means that the class of individuals
$$\lambda x \, [x = [\lambda w \lambda t \, [^0King\_of_{wt} \, ^0France]_{wt}] \wedge [^0Bald_{wt} \, x]]$$
is non-empty according as the individual a is bald or not. Thus according to the definition of the quantifier $\exists$, the proposition constructed by (R^*) takes the value **T** if a is bald, otherwise **F**, exactly as does the proposition constructed by (R).

b) Let the royal office be vacant in a given world w and time t. Then by Def. 1, iii) the following Compositions are v-improper:
$$[\lambda w \lambda t \, [^0King\_of_{wt} \, ^0France]_{wt}]$$
$$[^0Bald_{wt} \, \lambda w \lambda t \, [^0King\_of_{wt} \, ^0France]_{wt}]$$
$$[x = [\lambda w \lambda t \, [^0King\_of_{wt} \, ^0France]_{wt}]]$$
$$[[x = \lambda w \lambda t \, [^0King\_of_{wt} \, ^0France]_{wt}] \wedge [^0Bald_{wt} \, x]].$$
This in turn means that the proposition constructed by
$$\lambda w \lambda t \, [^0Bald_{wt} \, \lambda w \lambda t \, [^0King\_of_{wt} \, ^0France]_{wt}]$$
is undefined and by the definition of the property *True* the proposition constructed by (R) takes the value **F**. But so does (R^*), because the class constructed by
$$\lambda x \, [[x = \lambda w \lambda t \, [^0King\_of_{wt} \, ^0France]_{wt}] \wedge [^0Bald_{wt} \, x]]$$
is empty and the application of the existential quantifier $\exists$ to an empty class results in **F**.

Note that from (b) it also follows that neither (R) nor (R^*) comes with the existential presupposition that the King of France exists. Non-trivial existence of empirical objects is in TIL explicated as a property of intensions to be instantiated at a given $\langle w,t\rangle$-pair of evaluation.[20] Thus to say that unicorns do not exist is tantamount to saying that at the given world w and time t the property of being a unicorn has an empty class of individuals as its population. Similarly, that the King of France does not exist means that the office of the King of France is vacant at the $\langle w,t\rangle$-pair of evaluation. Hence if there were an existential presupposition, the propositions constructed by (R) and (R^*) would have no truth-value in case of the royal office being vacant. Yet, these propositions take the value **F**. In other words, neither $(non\text{-}R)$ nor $(non\text{-}R^*)$ entails that the royal office is occupied.

Now I am going to prove that (S), and thus also $(non\text{-}S)$, presupposes the existence of the King of France. To this end I must prove that the following arguments are valid (though not sound):

$$\frac{\text{The King of France is (not) bald}}{\text{The King of France exists}}$$

First, the analysis of the conclusion amounts to this construction:

$$\lambda w \lambda t \, [^0Exist_{wt}[\lambda w \lambda t \, [^0King\_of_{wt} \, ^0France]]]$$

where $Exist/(o\iota_{\tau\omega})_{\tau\omega}$ is the property that an office has when it is occupied. This property is defined as follows:

$$^0Exist =_{of} \lambda w \lambda t \lambda c \, [^0\exists \lambda x \, [x = c_{wt}]].$$

Types: $\exists/(o(o\iota))$; $c \to_v \iota_{\tau\omega}$; $x \to_v \iota$; $=_{of}/(o(o\iota_{\tau\omega})_{\tau\omega}(o\iota_{\tau\omega})_{\tau\omega})$: the identity of properties of individual offices; $=/(o\iota\iota)$: the identity of individuals, $x \to_v \iota$.

Now I am ready to prove the validity of the above arguments and thus the validity of the claim that the Strawsonian reading is associated with a presupposition of the royal office being occupied.

At any $\langle w,t\rangle$-pair the following proof steps are truth-preserving:

1) $(\neg)[^0Bald_{wt} \, \lambda w \lambda t \, [^0King\_of_{wt} \, ^0France]_{wt}]$ $\emptyset$
2) $\neg[^0Improper_{wt} \, ^0[\lambda w \lambda t \, [^0King\_of_{wt} \, ^0France]_{wt}]]$ 1), by Def. 1, iii)
3) $\neg[^0Empty \, \lambda x \, [x = [\lambda w \lambda t \, [^0King\_of_{wt} \, ^0France]]_{wt}]]$ 2), by Def. 1, iv)
4) $[^0\exists \lambda x \, [x = [\lambda w \lambda t \, [^0King\_of_{wt} \, ^0France]]_{wt}]]$ 3), EG
5) $[\lambda c \, [^0\exists \lambda x \, [x = c_{wt}]] \, \lambda w \lambda t \, [^0King\_of_{wt} \, ^0France]]$ 4), λ-abstraction
6) $^0Exist_{wt} = \lambda c \, [^0\exists \lambda x \, [x = c_{wt}]]$ Def. of $Exist$
7) $[^0Exist_{wt}[\lambda w \lambda t \, [^0King\_of_{wt} \, ^0France]]]$ 5), 6), substitution of identicals

Remark. At step (2) the property of being *Improper* of type $(o*_1)_{\tau\omega}$ is applied to the *construction* $[\lambda w \lambda t\, [^0King\_of_{wt}\, {}^0France]_{wt}]$ of type $*_1$ that is supplied here by its Trivialisation ${}^0[\lambda w \lambda t\, [^0King\_of_{wt}\, {}^0France]_{wt}]$ belonging to type $*_2$. On the other hand, at step (3) the property of being *Empty* of type $(o(o\iota))$ is applied to the set of individuals constructed by $\lambda x\,[x = [\lambda w \lambda t\, [^0King\_of_{wt}\, {}^0France]]_{wt}]$. These two steps are necessary in order to existentially generalize at step (4). In a logic of partial functions such as TIL we cannot carelessly generalize before having proved that the set to which the existential quantifier is applied is non-empty.

The following Table 1 illustrates the truth conditions of the propositions constructed by (R), (S), (non-R) and (non-S) with respect to the occupancy of the office of the King of France (KF).[21] Indeed, (R) and (S) are co-entailing. Whenever (R) is true (S) is true as well, and vice versa. Yet the propositions (R) and (S) are not identical, because (non-R) and (non-S) are not co-entailing. At those $\langle w,t\rangle$-pairs where the King of France does not exist, both (S) and (non-S) are undefined, the propositions having a truth-value gap, while (R) and (non-R) are false and true, respectively.

Table 1

Russellian vs. Strawsonian analysis

	KF	(R)	(S)	(non-R)	(non-S)	
w_1, t_1	a	T	T	F	F	a is the KF and is bald
w_2, t_2	a	F	F	T	T	a is the KF and isn't bald
w_3, t_3	$\bot$	F	$\bot$	T	$\bot$	The KF does not exist
w_4, t_4	b	F	F	T	T	b is the KF and isn't bald
w_5, t_5	b	T	T	F	F	b is the KF and is bald
w_6, t_6	$\bot$	F	$\bot$	T	$\bot$	The KF does not exist
...						

5. Ambiguities in topic-focus articulation

5.1. Presuppositions generated by a singular term topic

The above analyses provide a solution to the almost hundred-year old dispute over Strawsonian versus Russellian definite descriptions that has been summarised in Section 2. The ambiguity of sentences of the form "The F is a G" is not rooted in a shift of *meaning* of the definite description 'the F'. Rather the ambiguity stems from different *topic-focus articulations* of such sentences. Whereas articulating the topic of a sentence activates a presupposition, articulating the focus frequently yields merely an entailment.[22] If 'the F' is the topic phrase then this description occurs extensionally that is with *de re* supposition and Strawson's analysis appears to be what is wanted. The sentence *presupposes* that the description 'the F' refers to an object of the proper type. The other option is 'G' occurring as topic and 'the F' as focus. On this reading the description 'the F' occurs intensionally that is with *de dicto* supposition, and the Russellian analysis gets the truth-conditions of the sentence right. The existence of a unique F is *merely entailed*.

The received view still tends to be that there is room for at most one of the two positions, since they are deemed incompatible. But there is no incompatibility between Strawson's and Russell's positions, because they simply do not talk about one and the same meaning of the sentence "The King of France is bald". My novel *contribution* is to point out this *ambiguity* which yielded the false dilemma. Russell argued for the attributive use of 'the King of France' and Strawson for its referential use.

It is a matter of *pragmatics*, of course, which reading is the intended one on an occasion of use. Logic cannot decide which among multiple readings happens to be the intended one. Yet, I cannot agree with Kripke (1977) on two accounts. First, it is not *entirely* a matter of pragmatics which reading is the intended one; it is also a matter of semantics. Second, and more importantly, the Russellian analysis of sentences with definite descriptions cannot, by itself, account for both the referential and the attributive uses. Our fine-grained logical method of analysis as presented in this paper demonstrates that these readings are *not equivalent*, and that the Russellian reading does not take into account any presuppositions triggered by the topic of the sentence in question. Thus, though logic itself cannot decide between multiple readings, it can contribute to disambiguation of a sentence by making these different meanings *explicit*. In case the sentence is ambiguous, logic can bring out this ambiguity and, as a result, propose different constructions to be assigned as different meanings to (non-equivalent) readings. Choosing between them becomes also a matter of *semantics*.

5.2. Presuppositions generated by a general term topic

Up until now I have utilized the singularity of an individual office of type $\iota_{\tau\omega}$ when analysing sentences that come attached with the existential presupposition. If the office denoted by 'the F' goes vacant at a given world w and time t of evaluation, the extensionalization F_{wt} is v-improper, and if the description 'the F' occurs as the topic of a sentence (i.e. referentially or *de re*) the so constructed proposition has a truth-value gap. However, the regimentation of a presupposition can be more complicated. In particular, the topic term does not have to be a singular one; it can be also a plural term like 'the popes of Rome and Avignon' or a general one like 'a penguin'. We encounter the phenomenon of topic-focus ambiguity and the associated *de dicto* – *de re* ambivalence also in sentences containing general terms. As an example, consider a seemingly unambiguous sentence

"All the students of my winter-term Logic course passed the exam test"

However, this sentence is ambiguous. If we take into account possible topic-focus articulations, we obtain a pair of non-equivalent sentences differing only in terms of this articulation (for clarity, I will mark the topic phrase in italics):

(1) "All *the students* of my winter-term Logic course passed the exam test"

(2) "All the students of my winter-term Logic course passed *the exam test*"

Now I am going to show that the two versions of the above sentence are not equivalent, because their truth-conditions are different.

Scenario (1).
Q.: What about the students who signed up for the Logic course, how did they do?
A.: Oh well, they all passed the final exam.

On this reading we are talking about the topic that is the students who signed up for the Logic course; hence, the sentence *presupposes* that there are some students enrolled in the Logic course in winter term; *if not* (for instance, because the course runs in summer term), then the proposition denoted by (1) has *no truth-value*. For, if there are no students in the course, the *negated* sentence cannot be true as well:

(neg-1) "Some students of my winter-term Logic course *did not* pass the exam test".

However, the sentence *only entails* that the final exam has taken place. Because, the sentence (1) can be false for two reasons: *Either* some of the students failed, *or* none of the students succeeded because the exam has yet to take place.

Scenario (2).
Q.: What about the final exam in Logic, what are the results?
A.: Oh well, all students passed.

Now the topic is the final exam in the Logic course. On this reading there is a *presupposition* that the final exam has already taken place; if it is *not the case*, then there is a truth-value gap, because the negated sentence cannot be true as well:

(neg-2) "The *final exam* has not been passed by all students of my Logic course"

Needless to say, that in these examples we apply an internal, narrow-scope negation. If we applied the wide-scope external negation, we would have:

"It is not true that all the students of my winter-term Logic course passed the exam test"

Perhaps because some of the students failed, or the exam test is still to take place, or perhaps no students attempted the test. No presupposition would be taken into account, which is not very informative.

Now if we want to analyse properly those readings that take into account the topic-focus articulation and the associated presuppositions, we need a general analytic schema for such sentences, which I am going to introduce now. To illustrate the schema, consider again a sentence S with a presupposition P. It encodes as its meaning the procedure the evaluation of which can be described as follows:

In any $\langle w, t \rangle$-pair of evaluation,

if P_{wt} is true

then evaluate S_{wt} to produce a truth-value,

else fail to produce a truth-value.

To formulate this schema rigorously, we need to define the *if-then-else-fail* function. Here is how. The procedure encoded by "If $P(\to o)$ then $C(\to \alpha)$, else $D(\to \alpha)$" behaves as follows:

a) If P *v*-constructs **T** then execute C (and return the result of type α, that C is typed to produce, provided C is not *v*-improper).
b) If P *v*-constructs **F** then execute D (and return the result of type α, that D is typed to produce, provided D is not *v*-improper).
c) If P is *v*-improper then no result, gap.

Hence, *if-then-else* is seen to be a (strict) function of type $(\alpha\, o\, *_n\, *_n)$, and its definition decomposes into two phases.[23]

First, select a construction to be executed on the basis of a specific condition P. The choice between C and D comes down to this Composition:

$$[^0\iota^* \lambda c[[P \wedge [c = {}^0C]] \vee [\neg P \wedge [c = {}^0D]]]]$$

Negation and presupposition, truth and falsity

Types: $P \to_v o$ v-constructs the condition of the choice between the execution of C or D, $C/*_n$, $D/*_n \to_v \alpha$; $c \to_v *_n$; $\iota^*/(*_n(o*_n))$: the singularizer function that associates a singleton of constructions with the construction that is the only element of this singleton, and is otherwise (i.e. if the set is empty or many-valued) undefined.

If P v-constructs **T** then the variable c v-constructs the *construction C*, and if P v-constructs **F** then the variable c v-constructs the *construction D*. In either case, the set constructed by

$$\lambda c\, [[P \wedge [c = {}^0C]] \vee [\neg P \wedge [c = {}^0D]]]$$

is a singleton and the singularizer ι^* returns as its value either the construction C or the construction D.[24]

Second, the selected construction is executed; therefore, Double Execution must be applied:

$$^2[{}^0\iota^* \lambda c\, [[P \wedge [c = {}^0C]] \vee [\neg P \wedge [c = {}^0D]]]]$$

As a special case of the *if-then-else-fail* function, no construction D is to be selected whenever P is not satisfied. Thus, the definition of the *if-then-else-fail* function of type $(\alpha o *_n)$ is this:

$$^2[{}^0\iota^* \lambda c\, [P \wedge [c = {}^0C]]]$$

Indeed, if P v-constructs **F**, then the class constructed by $\lambda c\,[P \wedge [c = {}^0C]]$ is empty so that the singularizer function does not supply as its value any construction. As a result, according to Def. 1, both the composition $[{}^0\iota^* \lambda c\,[P \wedge [c = {}^0C]]]$ and its Double Execution are v-improper.

Now we are ready to apply this definition to the case of a presupposition. Let $P/*_n \to o_{\tau\omega}$ be a construction of a presupposition of $S/*_n \to o_{\tau\omega}$. Furthermore, let $c/*_{n+1} \to_v *_n$, $^2c \to_v o$. Then the type of the *if-then-else-fail* function is $(oo*_n)$ and its definition comes down to this construction:

$$\lambda w \lambda t\, [{}^0\textit{if-then-else-fail}\, P_{wt}\, {}^0[S_{wt}]] = \lambda w \lambda t\, {}^2[{}^0\iota^* \lambda c\, [P_{wt} \wedge [c = {}^0[S_{wt}]]]]$$

Gloss. In the first phase the construction S_{wt} is selected, provided P_{wt} v-constructs **T**. In the second phase S_{wt} is executed. In case P_{wt} does not v-construct **T**, no construction is selected and executed, hence

$$^2[{}^0\iota^* \lambda c\, [P_{wt} \wedge [c = {}^0[S_{wt}]]]]$$

is v-improper and the so-constructed proposition has a truth-value gap, as it should have.

In what follows, instead of the above definition I will use this abbreviated notation to make the *general analytic schema* easier to read:

$$\lambda w \lambda t\, [\textit{if } P_{wt} \textit{ then } S_{wt} \textit{ else fail}\,].$$

For illustration, let us analyse Strawson's (1952, pp. 173ff) example

All John's children are asleep.

Here the topic of the sentence is 'John's children'. The sentence can be uttered for instance as an answer in the situation when we are talking about John's children (knowing that he has some children) and we just want to know what are they doing. Hence, there is a presupposition to the effect that John has children.[25] Hence the evaluation of truth-conditions of this reading can be formulated like this:

If John has any children
then check whether each and every one of them is asleep
else fail to produce a truth-value.

We have come down to this analysis:

$\lambda w \lambda t$ [<i>if</i> [$^0\exists$ [^{0}Children_of$_{wt}$ ^{0}John] <i>then</i>

$\qquad\qquad\qquad$ [[^{0}All [^{0}Children_of$_{wt}$ ^{0}John]] ^{0}Sleep$_{wt}$] <i>else fail</i>]

Types: <i>Children_of</i>$((\omicron\iota)\iota)_{\tau\omega}$: the empirical function (attribute) that dependently on a state of affairs associates an individual with the set of those individuals who are his or her children; <i>John</i>/ι; <i>Sleep</i>/$(\omicron\iota)_{\tau\omega}$; $\exists/(\omicron(\omicron\iota))$; <i>All</i>/$((\omicron(\omicron\iota))(\omicron\iota))$: a restricted quantifier that associates a set S of individuals with all the supersets of S.

Remark. Here I use the restricted quantifier All, because I want to arrive at the literal analysis of the sentence. Such an analysis follows Frege's principle (1884, p. 60): It is simply not possible to speak about an object without somehow denoting or naming it.[26] If the unrestricted general quantifier were used the resulting construction would be:

$\lambda w \lambda t$ [<i>if</i> [$^0\exists$ [^{0}Children_of$_{wt}$ ^{0}John] <i>then</i>

$\qquad\qquad\qquad$ [$^0\forall \lambda x$ [[[^{0}Children_of$_{wt}$ ^{0}John] x] $\supset$ [^{0}Sleep$_{wt}$ x]]] <i>else fail</i>]

This is an equivalent construction producing the same proposition as the above one, yet it is not the literal analysis of our sentence, because the truth-function of implication is not mentioned in the sentence.[27]

6. Other cases of presuppositions

Other cases of generating a presupposition are, for instance, <i>factive attitudes</i> like 'knowing', 'realizing', 'discovering', etc. For instance, if you say, "I didn't realize that he had left" then the conveyed message <i>presupposes</i>

that *it is true* that he had left. Notice that here we again apply narrow-scope negation. For sure, (using wide-scope negation) it cannot be true that I realized that he had left if he had not left. But it can neither be false, because then the proposition that I didn't realize that he had left could not be true either. In such a situation the proposition has a truth-value gap, and in compliance with Def. 4, the truth of the complement of the factive attitude is a presupposition of the attitude.

Similarly, the sentence

"John knows that arithmetic is recursively axiomatizable"

denotes the proposition with a truth-value gap. If somebody would claim it, you would protest. "No, it cannot be true, because Gödel proved in 1931 the two famous incompleteness theorems!". Indeed, it is neither true nor false, because John can neither know nor not know that arithmetic is recursively axiomatizable. For these reasons we have to introduce special rules for factive attitudes.

Let $K \to (o\iota o_{\tau\omega})_{\tau\omega}$ be a factive attitude to a proposition, $x \to \iota$; $p \to o_{\tau\omega}$; $True/(oo_{\tau\omega})_{\tau\omega}$. Then the rules are as follows:

$$\frac{[^0K_{wt}\, x\, p]}{[^0True_{wt}\, p]} \qquad \frac{\neg[^0K_{wt}\, x\, p]}{[^0True_{wt}\, p]}$$

This is the case of *intensional* attitudes; that is the agent x is related to a *proposition* of type $o_{\tau\omega}$. However, it is a well-known fact that every epistemic logic that takes into account only intensional attitudes faces the problem of *logical-mathematical omniscience* that can be restricted only up to equivalence. Yet, if it is possible that the agent's attitude is sensitive to the *way* in which a given proposition is presented (or constructed in TIL terminology), the more appropriate way of analysing such attitudinal sentences is a *hyperintensional attitude*, that is, a relation-in-intension of an agent to a *hyperproposition* (i.e. the construction of a proposition). For instance, John can know that arithmetic is *not* recursively axiomatizable, but he does not have to know that Peano arithmetic is incomplete.[28]

The rules for hyperintensional factive attitudes are as follows. Let $K^* \to (o\iota *_n)_{\tau\omega}$ be a factive attitude to a construction of a proposition, $x \to_v \iota$; $c/*_n \to_v *_{n-1}$; $^2c \to_v o_{\tau\omega}$; $True/(oo_{\tau\omega})_{\tau\omega}$. Then the rules are as follows:

$$\frac{[^0K^*_{wt}\, x\, c]}{[^0True_{wt}\, {}^2c]} \qquad \frac{\neg[^0K^*_{wt}\, x\, c]}{[^0True_{wt}\, {}^2c]}$$

The frequency of sentences that come attached with a presupposition in natural language is maybe much greater that one would suppose. Another example are sentences with verbs like 'to stop doing something'. One cannot stop doing something if they have never done it. Imagine that somebody asks "Did you stop beating your wife? Answer *yes* or *no*." What would the poor guy answer if he has never beaten his wife, or if he has not been married? Yes? "So, you did beat your wife." No? "So, you still do beat your poor wife."

The reason for this situation is due to what we call *intensional essentialism*. As mentioned at the outset, each intension $P/\alpha_{\tau\omega}$ (e.g. a property, relation-in-intension, etc.) comes with a collection of requisites that jointly define the intension P. We call this collection the *essence of P*. For instance, the property of having stopped smoking comes with a bulk of requisites including, not least, the property of being a former smoker. Thus, the predication of such a property P of a may fail, causing $[^0 P_{wt} a]$ to be v-improper, if a is not a former smoker. And then the proposition $\lambda w \lambda t\, [^0 P_{wt} a]$ comes with a truth-value gap for an a who has never smoked in the world w and time t of evaluation.

The requisite relations *Req* are a family of relations-in-extension between two intensions, so they are of the polymorphous type $(o\alpha_{\tau\omega}\beta_{\tau\omega})$, with the possibility that $\alpha = \beta$.[29] Infinitely many combinations of *Req* are possible, but for our purpose and for illustration it suffices to define this one:

$$Req/(o(o\iota)_{\tau\omega}(o\iota)_{\tau\omega})$$

Req is a relation between two properties of individuals, such that one is a requisite of the other defined as follows.

Definition 5 (*requisite relation*)

Let X, Y be constructions such that $X, Y/*_n \to (o\iota)_{\tau\omega}$; $x \to \iota$. Then $[^0 Req\ Y\ X] = \forall w \forall t\, [\forall x\, [[^0 True_{wt}\, \lambda w \lambda t\, [X_{wt}\, x]] \supset [^0 True_{wt}\, \lambda w \lambda t\, [Y_{wt}\, x]]]]$.

□

Gloss *definiendum* as, "Y is a requisite of X", and *definiens* as, "Necessarily, i.e. at every $\langle w, t \rangle$, any x that instantiates X at $\langle w, t \rangle$ also instantiates Y at $\langle w, t \rangle$."

Note, however, that failing to satisfy some of the requisites does not suffice to generate a presupposition. For instance, the property of being a mammal is a requisite of the property of being a whale. It is a contingent matter whether this or that individual is a whale or say a lion or whatever.

Yet, necessarily, i.e. in all worlds and times, if an individual a happens to be a whale then it must be a mammal. Formally:

$$[^0Req\ ^0Mammal\ ^0Whale] =$$
$$\forall w \forall t\ [\forall x\ [[^0True_{wt}\ \lambda w \lambda t\ [^0Whale_{wt}\ x]] \supset [^0True_{wt}\ \lambda w \lambda t\ [^0Mammal_{wt}\ x]]]]$$

Now assume that the individual a is *not* a mammal. Then the predication of the property of being a whale of a is simply false, $[^0Whale_{wt}\ a] = {}^0\mathbf{F}$, rather than v-improper, and the proposition that a is a whale, $\lambda w \lambda t\ [^0Whale_{wt}\ a]$, *does not presuppose* but *merely entails* that a is a mammal.

Similarly, finding something after a prior search does not presuppose the existence of the sought thing, it merely entails its existence. Recall the tragedy in Dallas on November 22, 1963. When police were seeking the murderer of JFK, the FBI and the Warren Commission finally officially concluded that Oswald was the lone assassin. Though many challenged the findings of the Warren Report and believed that Kennedy was the victim of a conspiracy, assume that their conclusion was right. Yet another scenario is possible. The police may have failed in identifying the only murderer of JFK, because there were more murderers or because the police simply did not work well. Then it would be *true* that they *did not find* the murderer of JFK. If the existence of the lone murderer were a presupposition of identifying the murderer, the proposition that they failed in finding the murderer could not be true; rather, it would have a truth-value gap.[30]

In order to generate a presupposition, we need to define a stronger notion of requisite, to wit the notion of *prerequisite*, $Prereq/(o(o\iota)_{\tau\omega}(o\iota)_{\tau\omega})$ defined as follows.

Definition 6 (*prerequisite relation*)

Let X, Y be constructions such that $X, Y/*_n \to (o\iota)_{\tau\omega}$; $x \to \iota$. Then

$[^0Prereq\ Y\ X] =$
$\forall w \forall t\ [\forall x\ [[[^0True_{wt}\ \lambda w \lambda t\ [X_{wt}\ x]] \vee [^0False_{wt}\ \lambda w \lambda t\ [X_{wt}\ x]]]$
$\supset [^0True_{wt}\ \lambda w \lambda t\ [Y_{wt}\ x]]]]$.

Gloss *definiendum* as, "Y is a prerequisite of X", and *definiens* as, "Necessarily, any x for which it is true or false that x instantiates X at $\langle w, t \rangle$ then x also instantiates Y at $\langle w, t \rangle$."

Corollary. If it is not true that x instantiates the prerequisite Y of the property X then the proposition that x instantiates X is neither true not false, it has no truth-value. Hence, the proposition that x instantiates Y is a *presupposition* of the proposition that x instantiates X.

The property of being a previous smoker is not only a requisite of the property of having stopped smoking, it is a *prerequisite*. As we have seen above, necessarily, if *a* stopped smoking then *a* is an ex-smoker. Yet not only this. If *a did not stop smoking*, then *a* has been a (previous) smoker. Thus, the proposition that *a* stopped smoking has a *presupposition* that *a* used to be a smoker.

7. Conclusion

In this paper I have demonstrated and proved that narrow-scope and wide-scope negation are not equivalent. If a sentence comes with a presupposition, then narrow-scope negation is the relevant one, because wide-scope negation is presupposition-denying. I also dealt with the ambiguities in natural language stemming from different topic-focus articulations within a sentence. First, I dealt with the existential presupposition of sentences with a singular topic term like 'the F'. I demonstrated that both the proponents of Russell's quantificational analysis and of Strawson's referential analysis of definite descriptions are partly right and partly wrong, because sentences of the form "The F is a G" are systematically ambiguous. Their ambivalence stems from different topic-focus articulation, and I brought out the *semantic*, as opposed to pragmatic, character of this ambivalence. I showed that a definite description occurring in the topic of a sentence with *de re* supposition corresponds to the Strawsonian analysis of definite descriptions, while a definite description occurring in the focus with *de dicto* supposition corresponds to the Russellian analysis. While the clause standing in topic position triggers a presupposition, a focus clause usually only entails rather than presupposes another proposition. The procedural semantics of TIL provides rigorous analyses such that sentences differing only in their topic-focus articulation are assigned different constructions producing different propositions (truth-conditions) and having different consequences. These analyses propose a solution to the old dispute about Russelian vs. Strawsonian analysis of the sentence "The King of France is bald". In fact, there is no incompatibility between Strawson's and Russell's positions, because they simply do not talk about one and the same meaning of the sentence. I pointed out this *ambiguity* which yielded the false dilemma. Russell argued for the attributive use of 'the King of France' and Strawson for its referential use. I also generalized the method of analysing topic-focus ambiguities for sentences with a general term occurring in the topic position and provided a general analytic schema for sentences with a presupposition.

It is a matter of *pragmatics*, of course, which reading is the intended one on an occasion of use. Yet, our fine-grained logical method of analysis as presented in this paper demonstrates that sentences differing in point of topic-focus articulation are not equivalent, and thus choosing between particular readings becomes also a matter of *semantics*. Logic can contribute to the disambiguation of a sentence by making these hidden features explicit and logically tractable. In case there are more *non-equivalent* senses of a sentence we furnish the sentence with *different meanings*. Finally, I applied this general analytic schema to other cases of sentences that come attached with a presupposition, in particular presuppositions generated by factive attitudes or presuppositions generated by the prerequisites of a given property.

Acknowledgements

This research was funded by the Grant Agency of the Czech Republic (GACR) project GA18–23891S "Hyperintensional Reasoning over Natural Language Texts", and by the internal grant agency of VSB_TU Ostrava, project No. SP2018/172, "Application of Formal Methods in Knowledge Modelling and Software Engineering".

NOTES

[1] See Tichý (1988), Tichý (2004), Duží, Jespersen and Materna (2010).

[2] In this section I use terms like 'proposition', 'presupposition' and 'property' in their intuitive sense, with rigorous definition coming in Section 3.

[3] In these paragraphs I partly draw on material from Horn (1989).

[4] I refrain here from the analysis of *proper* proper names. In my background theory, which is Transparent Intensional Logic (TIL), proper names coin *something*, and thus if Kepler is the name of an individual, then Kepler trivially exists. TIL is based on a fixed universe of discourse, i.e. the fixed domain of bare individuals. Hence, there are no non-existing individuals.

[5] Besides, many hold against Russell's translation of atomic sentences like "The *F* is a *G*" into the molecular form "There is at least one *F* and at most one thing is an *F* and that thing is a *G*", because Russell disregards the standard constraint that there must be a fair amount of structural similarity between analysandum and analysans.

[6] Nevertheless, for Strawson, *sentences* are meaningful in and of themselves, independently of empirical facts like the contingent non-existence of the King of France.

[7] Here I partly draw on and summarise material from Duží (2009, 2014).

[8] For details on structured meanings, see Jespersen (2012) and Duží (2017).

[9] For an introduction to the notion of hyperproposition, see Jespersen (2010) and Jespersen, Duží (2015).

[10] See, for instance, Hajičová (2008), Gundel (1999), Gundel and Fretheim (2004).

[11] Gahér (2001) makes a similar point on the two kinds of negation. The author talks about wide-scope negation as 'weak' (or 'sentential', 'propositional') negation and about narrow-scope negation as 'strong' negation. However, there is an issue on which our positions are not compatible. While Gahér argues that "[...] all forms of 'strong' (non-sentential) negation are substitutable by equivalent transparent paraphrases containing only sentential negation [...]", I am going to prove below that these two forms are not equivalent.

[12] As an extreme case the produced function/mapping can be a nullary function, that is, an atomic object such as an individual, number, or a truth-value.

[13] The other source can be a type-theoretically incoherent ('nonsensical') way of composing a construction, for instance, by composing the Earth with being a natural number.

[14] To simplify the tree, I apply these rules: if $C \to \alpha_{\tau\omega}$ then $C_{wt} \to \alpha$, and if $D \to \alpha$ then $\lambda w \lambda t D \to \alpha_{\tau\omega}$. Indeed, unpacking the abbreviations '$\alpha_{\tau\omega}$' and 'C_{wt}', we have: $C \to ((\alpha\tau)\omega)$, $[Cw] \to (\alpha\tau)$, $[[Cw]t] \to \alpha$. Similarly the second rule: $D \to \alpha$, $\lambda t D \to (\alpha\tau)$, $\lambda w \lambda t D \to ((\alpha\tau)\omega)$.

[15] For the slight difference between *analytical* and *logical* entailment see Duží (2010).

[16] Again, I use the infix notation '$(S \models P)$' instead of the proper TIL notation '$[^0\models SP]$' to make the formulae easier to read.

[17] As explained at the outset, there is still a difference between being *non-bald* (property negation) and being an x such that *not: x is bald* (boolean negation). Here the latter is applied.

[18] For the difference between narrow-scope and wide-scope negation with respect to a presupposition, see also Hajičová (2008).

[19] Note that in TIL we do not need a construction to specify the uniqueness of the King of France, because it is inherent in the meaning of 'the King of France'. The meaning of definite descriptions like 'the King of France' is a construction of an individual office of type $\iota_{\tau\omega}$ occupied at each $\langle w, t \rangle$-pair by at most one individual.

[20] For details see Duží et al. (2010, § 2.3).

[21] I use the symbol '⊥' to mark a truth-value *gap* rather than the truth-value F.

[22] This assumption is based on Hajičová (2008), and supported by other linguists as well. See, for instance Gundel (1999), Gundel and Fretheim (2004) and Strawson (1952, esp. p. 173ff.).

[23] The definition introduced here is a slightly adjusted version of the definition presented in Duží (2010a).

[24] Note that in this phase C and D are not constituents to be executed; rather they are merely displayed as objects to be selected by the variable c. This is to say that, in TIL, constructions themselves can be objects to be operated on, and without this *hyperintensional* approach we would not be able to define the *strict* function *if-then-else*. For the difference between constructions occurring in the *displayed mode (hyperintensionally)* and *executed mode* (as constituents of a super-construction), see, for instance, Duží (2017).

[25] The other option would be, for instance, the scenario of talking about those who are asleep, and the sentence would be offered as an answer, "Among those who are asleep are all of John's children". On this reading the sentence would only entail that John has children.

[26] The German original goes, "Überhaupt ist es nicht möglich von einem Gegenstand zu sprechen, ohne ihn irgendwie zu bezeichnen oder benennen."

[27] For more details on the method of arriving at the best literal meaning of a sentence, see Duží et al. (2010, §2.1)

[28] For the sake of simplicity, I ignore here the fact that possible worlds and times are irrelevant for mathematical propositions. For details on mathematical attitudes, see Duží et al. (2010, Ch. 5).

[29] For comparison, Jespersen (2006) offers a detailed study of a requisite relation, of type $(o\iota_{\tau\omega}\iota_{\tau\omega})$, where one individual office is a requisite of another individual office, the way the office of Commander-in-Chief is a requisite of the office of President of the United States. The paper analyses "Superman is Clark Kent" as expressing that this particular requisite relation obtains between one office denoted by 'Superman' and another office denoted by 'Clark Kent'. If you occupy the office of Superman you must co-occupy the office of Clark Kent, but you can occupy the Clark Kent office without occupying the Superman office. This goes to show that TIL offers an intensional analysis (based on intensional essentialism) of "Superman is Clark Kent", contrary to the prevalent 'Millian' extensional analyses.

[30] More details on attitudes of seeking and finding can be found in Duží et al. (2010, §5.2.2).

REFERENCES

Donnellan, K. S., (1966). Reference and definite descriptions, *Philosophical Review*, vol. 77, pp. 281–304.

Duží M. (2010). The paradox of inference and the non-triviality of analytic information. *Journal of Philosophical Logic*, vol. 39, No. 5, pp. 473–510.

Duží M. (2010a). Tenses and truth-conditions: a plea for *if-then-else*. In *the Logica Yearbook 2009*, Peliš, M. (ed.), London: College Publications, pp. 63–80.

Duží M., Jespersen B. and Materna P. (2010). *Procedural Semantics for Hyperintensional Logic. Foundations and Applications of Trasnsparent Intensional Logic*. Berlin: Springer, series Logic, Epistemology, and the Unity of Science, vol. 17.

Duží, M. (2009). Strawsonian vs. Russellian definite descriptions. *Organon F*, 2009, vol. XVI, No. 4, pp. 587–614.

Duží, M. (2014). How to Unify Russellian and Strawsonian Definite Descriptions. In *Recent Trends in Philosophical Logic, Studia Logica*, Roberto Ciuni, Heinrich Wansing, Caroline Willcommen (eds.), vol. 41, pp. 85–101.

Duží, M. (2017). If structured propositions are logical procedures, then how are procedures individuated? *Synthese* special issue on the Unity of propositions. DOI: 10.1007/s11229-017-1595-5

Fintel, Kai von (2004). Would you believe it? The King of France is Back! (Presuppositions and Truth-Value Intuitions). In: *Descriptions and Beyond*, Reimer, M., Bezuidenhout, A. (eds.), Oxford: Clarendon Press, pp. 315–341.

Frege, G. (1884). *Die Grundlagen der Arithmetik*, Breslau: W. Koebner.

Frege, G. (1892). Über Sinn und Bedeutung. *Zeitschrift für Philosophie und philosophische Kritik* 100: 25–50.

Gahér, F. (2001). Negation and presupposition. In: *The Logica Yearbook* 2000, Ondrej Majer (ed.), Prague: Filosofia, pp. 133–150.

Gundel, J. K. (1999). Topic, focus and the grammar pragmatics interface. In *Proceedings of the 23rd Annual Penn Linguistics Colloquium. Penn Working Papers in Linguistics*, vol. 6.1, J. Alexander, N. Han and M. Minnick (eds.), pp. 185–200.

Gundel, J. K. and Fretheim, T. (2004). Topic and Focus. In *The Handbook of Pragmatics*. Laurence Horn and Gregory Ward (eds.), Blackwell, pp. 174–196.

Hajičová, E. (2008). What we are talking about and what we are saying about it. In: *Computational Linguistics and Intelligent Text Processing*, A. Gelbukh (Ed.), Berlin, Heidelberg: Springer-Verlag LNCS, vol. 4919, pp. 241–262.

Horn, L.R. (1989). *A Natural History of Negation*, Chicago: University of Chicago Press.

Horn, L.R., Wansing, H. (2017). *Negation. The Stanford Encyclopedia of Philosophy* (Spring 2017 Edition), Edward N. Zalta (ed.), URL = https://plato.stanford.edu/archives/spr2017/entries/negation/.

Jespersen, B. (2006). The phone booth puzzle, *Organon F*, vol. 13, pp. 411–38.

Jespersen, B. (2010). How hyper are hyperpropositions?, *Language and Linguistics Compass*, vol. 4, pp. 96–106.

Jespersen, B. (2012). Recent work on structured meaning and propositional unity, *Philosophy Compass*, vol. 7, pp. 620–30.

Jespersen, B., Carrara, M., Duží, M. (2017). Iterated privation and positive predication, *Journal of Applied Logic*, Vol. 25, Supplement, December 2017, Pages S48–S71.

Jespersen, B., Duží, M. (2015). Introduction to the special issue on Hyperintensionality. *Synthese*, vol. 192, No. 3, pp. 525–534.

Kripke, S. A. (1977). Speaker's reference and semantic reference. In Peter A. French, Theodore E. Uehling Jr & Howard K. Wettstein (eds.), *Studies in the Philosophy of Language*. University of Minnesota Press, pp. 255–296.

Ludlow, P. (2007). *Descriptions*. Available from http://plato.stanford.edu/entries/descriptions/#2.

Neale, S., (1990). *Descriptions*. Cambridge: MIT Press Books.

Russell, B. (1905). On denoting, *Mind*, vol. 14, pp. 479–493.

Russell, B., (1957). Mr. Strawson on referring, *Mind*, vol. 66, pp. 385–389.

Strawson, P. F. (1950). On referring, *Mind*, vol. 59, pp. 320–334.

Strawson, P.F. (1952). *Introduction to Logical Theory*, London: Methuen.

Tichý, P. (1988). *The Foundations of Frege's Logic*, Berlin, New York: De Gruyter.

Tichý, P. (2004). *Collected Papers in Logic and Philosophy*, V. Svoboda, B. Jespersen, C. Cheyne (eds.), Prague: Filosofia, Czech Academy of Sciences, and Dunedin: University of Otago Press.

PRESUPPOSITIONS AND TWO KINDS OF NEGATION

Marie Duzi

Abstract

In this paper I deal with sentences that come with a presupposition that is entailed by the positive as well as negated form of a given sentence. However, there are two kinds of negation, namely narrow-scope and wide-scope negation. I am going to prove that while the former is presupposition-preserving, the latter is presupposition-denying. Thus the main contribution of this paper is the proof that these two kinds of negation are not equivalent. This issue has much in common with the difference between topic and focus articulation within a sentence. Whereas articulating the topic of a sentence activates a presupposition, articulating the focus frequently yields merely an entailment. My background theory is Transparent Intensional Logic (TIL). TIL is an expressive logic apt for the analysis of sentences with presuppositions, because in TIL we work with partial functions, in particular with propositions with truth-value gaps. Moreover, procedural semantics of TIL makes it possible to define a general analytic schema of sentences associated with presuppositions, which is another novel contribution of this paper.

Introduction

Sentences often come attached with a presupposition that is entailed by the positive as well as negated form of a given sentence. Thus if the presupposition of a sentence S is not true, the sentence S can be neither true nor false. I follow Frege and Strawson in treating survival under negation as the most important test for presupposition. However, there are two kinds of negation, namely Strawsonian *narrow-scope* and Russellian *wide-scope negation*. While the former is presupposition-preserving, the latter is presupposition-denying.

This issue has much in common with the difference between topic and focus articulation within a sentence. I find that whereas articulating the topic of a sentence activates a presupposition, articulating its focus frequently yields merely an entailment. The point of departure is that sentences of the form "The F is a G" are ambiguous. Their ambiguity stems from different topic-focus articulations of such sentences. The issue is this. If 'the F' is the topic phrase then this description occurs extensionally, i.e. with *de re* supposition, and the Strawsonian analysis appears to be what is wanted. On this reading the sentence presupposes the existence of the descriptum of 'the F', because the property G is ascribed to the object, if any, referred to by 'the F'. The other option is 'G' occurring as topic and 'the F' as focus. This reading corresponds to Donnellan's attributive use of 'the F' and the description occurs intensionally with *de dicto* supposition. On this reading the Russellian analysis gets the truth-conditions of the sentence right. The existence of a unique F is merely entailed.

From a logical point of view, the two readings differ also in the way their respective negated form is obtained. Whereas the Strawsonian narrow-scope negated form is "The F is not a G", the Russellian wide-scope negated form is "It is not true that the F is a G". Thus in the former case the property of not being a G is ascribed to the object, if any, that is referred to by the topic phrase 'the F'. On the other hand, in the Russellian case the property of not being true is ascribed to the whole proposition that the F is a G. I am going to prove that these two readings are not equivalent, because they denote different propositions (truth-conditions individuated up to logical equivalence). While "The F is not a G" lacks a truth-value at those states of affairs where the F does not exist, the wide-scope negation "It is not true that the F is a G" is true at such states of affairs where there is no F.

To capture this difference, a logic of partial functions is needed. My background theory is Transparent Intensional Logic (TIL).[1] TIL is an expressive logic apt for the analysis of sentences with presuppositions, because in TIL we work with partial functions, in particular with propositions with truth-value gaps.

The rest of this paper is organised as follows. The relevant foundations of TIL are introduced in Section 1. In Section 2 the difference between narrow-scope and wide-scope negation is explained. Using the difference between these two kinds of negation, I also differentiate presupposition from mere entailment. In Section 3 I deal with ambiguities stemming from topic-focus articulation of a sentence. Finally, in Section 4 I generalise these results and propose a general analytic schema for sentences that come attached with a presupposition.

1. Foundations of TIL

The terms of the TIL language denote abstract procedures (roughly, Church's functions-in-intension) that produce set-theoretical mappings (functions-in-extension).[2] These procedures are rigorously defined as TIL *constructions*.

---

[1] See Tichý (1988), Tichý (2004), Duží, Jespersen and Materna (2010).
[2] As an extreme case the produced function/mapping can be a nullary function, that is, an atomic object such as an individual, number, or a truth-value.

Being procedural objects, constructions are designed to be executed in order to operate on input objects (of a lower-order type) and produce the object (if any) they are typed to produce, while non-procedural objects, i.e. non-constructions, cannot be executed. Thus non-procedural objects cannot be constituents of constructions, and there are two simple constructions that present objects to be operated on. They are *Trivialization* and *Variables*.

The operational sense of Trivialization is similar to that of constants in formal languages. It presents an object X without the mediation of any other procedures. Using the terminology of programming languages, the Trivialization of X, in symbols '^0X', is just a pointer to X.

Variables produce objects dependently on valuations: they are said to v-construct. We adopt an objectual variant of the Tarskian conception of variables. For each type (see Definition 2 below), there are countably many variables assigned that range over this type. Objects of each type can be arranged into infinitely many sequences. A valuation v selects such a sequence of objects of the respective type, and the first variable v-constructs the first object of the sequence, the second variable v-constructs the second object of the sequence, and so on. Thus the execution of a Trivialization or of a variable never fails to produce an object.

The execution of some other, compound, constructions can fail to present an object they are typed to produce. In such a case we say that they are v-*improper*. There are two kinds of improperness. Either a construction is compounded in a type-theoretically incoherent way, or it is an application of a function to an argument at which the function is not defined (i.e. it lacks a value at this argument). Here is the definition of *construction*.

Definition 1 (*construction*)

(i) *Variables $x, y, \ldots$ are constructions* that construct objects (elements of their respective ranges) dependently on a valuation v; they v-construct.

(ii) Where X is an object whatsoever (even a *construction*), ^0X is the construction *Trivialization* that constructs X without the mediation of any other constructions.

(iii) Let $X, Y_1, \ldots, Y_n$ be arbitrary constructions. Then the *Composition* $[X Y_1 \ldots Y_n]$ is the following *construction*. For any v, the Composition $[X Y_1 \ldots Y_n]$ is v-*improper* if one or more of the constructions $X, Y_1, \ldots, Y_n$ are v-improper, or if X v-constructs a function that is not defined at the n-tuple of objects v-constructed by $Y_1, \ldots, Y_n$. If X v-constructs a function that is defined at the n-tuple of objects v-constructed by $Y_1, \ldots, Y_n$ then the Composition $[X Y_1 \ldots Y_n]$ v-constructs the value of this function at the n-tuple.

(iv) The (λ-)*Closure* $[\lambda x_1 \ldots x_m Y]$ is the following *construction*. Let $x_1, x_2, \ldots, x_m$ be pair-wise distinct variables and Y a construction. Then $[\lambda x_1 \ldots x_m Y]$ v-*constructs* the function f that takes any members $B_1, \ldots, B_m$

of the respective ranges of the variables $x_1, \ldots, x_m$ into the object (if any) that is $v(B_1/x_1, \ldots, B_m/x_m)$-constructed by Y, where $v(B_1/x_1, \ldots, B_m/x_m)$ is like v except for assigning B_1 to $x_1, \ldots, B_m$ to x_m.

(v) Where X is any object whatsoever, ^1X is the *construction Execution* that v-constructs what X v-constructs. Thus if X is a v-improper construction or not a construction at all, then ^1X is *v-improper*.

(vi) Where X is any object whatsoever, ^2X is the *construction Double Execution*. It v-constructs what is v-constructed by the construction v-constructed by X. Thus if X is not itself a construction, or if X does not v-construct a construction, or if X v-constructs a v-improper construction, then ^2X is *v-improper*.

(vii) Nothing is a *construction*, unless it so follows from (i) through (vi).*

Note that Closure $[\lambda x_1 \ldots x_m\ Y]$ is never v-improper for any valuation v, as it always v-constructs a function. Even if the constituent Y is v-improper for all valuations v, the Closure is not v-improper. Yet in such a case the thus constructed function is a bizarre object; it is a degenerate function that lacks a value at any argument.

With constructions of constructions, constructions of functions, functions, and functional values in our stratified ontology, we need to keep track of the traffic between multiple logical strata. The ramified type hierarchy does just that. The type of first-order objects includes all objects that are not constructions. Therefore, it includes not only the standard objects of individuals, truth-values, sets, etc., but also functions including functions defined on possible worlds (i.e., the intensions germane to possible-world semantics). The type of second-order objects includes constructions of first-order objects, and functions that have such constructions at their domain or range. The type of third-order objects includes constructions of first- and second-order objects, and functions that have such constructions at their domain or range. And so on, ad infinitum.

Definition 2 (*ramified hierarchy of types*). Let B be a *base*, where a base is a collection of pair-wise disjoint, non-empty sets. Then:

T_1 *(types of order 1).*

i) Every member of B is an elementary *type of order 1 over B*.

ii) Let $\alpha, \beta_1, \ldots, \beta_m$ $(m > 0)$ be types of order 1 over B. Then the collection $(\alpha\ \beta_1 \ldots \beta_m)$ of all m-ary partial mappings from $\beta_1 \times \ldots \times \beta_m$ into α is a functional *type of* order 1 *over* the base B.

iii) Nothing is a *type of order 1 over B* unless it so follows from (i) and (ii).

C_n *(constructions of order n)*

i) Let x be a variable ranging over a type of order n. Then x is a *construction of order n over B*.

ii) Let X be a member of a type of order n. Then ^0X, ^1X, ^2X are *constructions of order n over B*.

iii) Let $X, X_1, ..., X_m$ ($m > 0$) be constructions of order n over B. Then $[X X_1 ... X_m]$ is a *construction of order n over B*.

iv) Let $x_1, ...x_m, X$ ($m > 0$) be constructions of order n over B. Then $[\lambda x_1...x_m X]$ is a *construction of order n over B*.

v) Nothing is a *construction of order n over B* unless it so follows from $\mathbf{C}_n$ (i)-(iv).

Tn+1 (types of order $n + 1$)

Let $*_n$ be the collection of all constructions of order n over B. Then

i) $*_n$ and every type of order n are *types of order n + 1*.

ii) If $m > 0$ and $\alpha, \beta_1, ..., \beta_m$ are types of order $n + 1$ over B, then $(\alpha \beta_1 ... \beta_m)$ (see T_1 ii)) is a *type of order n + 1 over B*.

iii) Nothing is a *type of order n + 1 over B* unless it so follows from (i) and (ii).*

We model sets and relations by their characteristic functions. Thus, for instance, (oι) is the type of a set of individuals, while (oιι) is the type of a relation-in-extension between individuals. For the purposes of natural-language analysis, we are assuming the following base of *ground types*:

o: the set of truth-values {**T, F**};

ι: the set of individuals (the universe of discourse);

τ: the set of real numbers (doubling as discrete times);

ω: the set of logically possible worlds (the logical space).

Empirical expressions denote *empirical conditions* that may or may not be satisfied at some world/time pair of evaluation. We model these empirical conditions as possible-world-semantic *(PWS) intensions*. PWS intensions are entities of type (βω): mappings from possible worlds to an arbitrary type β. The type β is frequently the type of a *chronology* of α-objects, i.e., a mapping of type (ατ). Thus α-intensions are frequently functions of type ((ατ)ω), abbreviated as '$\alpha_{\tau\omega}$'. *Extensional entities* are entities of a type α where α ≠ (βω) for any type β. Where w ranges over ω and t over τ, the following logical form essentially characterizes the logical syntax of empirical language: $\lambda w \lambda t$ [...w....t...].

Examples of frequently used PWS intensions are: *propositions* of type $o_{\tau\omega}$, *properties* of individuals of type $(o\iota)_{\tau\omega}$, binary *relations*-in-intension between individuals of type $(o\iota\iota)_{\tau\omega}$, individual *offices* (or roles) of type $\iota_{\tau\omega}$, *magnitudes* of type $\tau_{\tau\omega}$.

Logical objects like *truth-functions* and *quantifiers* are extensional: ∧ (conjunction), ∨ (disjunction) and ⊃ (implication) are of type (ooo), and

¬ (negation) of type (oo). *Quantifiers* ∀^{α}, ∃^{α} are type-theoretically polymorphous, total functions of type (o(oα)), for an arbitrary type α, defined as follows. The *universal quantifier* ∀^{α} is a function that associates a class *A* of α-elements with **T** if *A* contains all elements of the type α, otherwise with **F**. The *existential quantifier* ∃^{α} is a function that associates a class *A* of α-elements with **T** if *A* is a non-empty class, otherwise with **F**.

Notational conventions. Below all type indications will be provided outside the formulae in order not to clutter the notation. The outermost brackets of a Closure will be omitted whenever no confusion arises. We often use infix notation without Trivialization for the application of truth-functions and identities to make the formulae easier to read. Furthermore, '*X*/α' means that an object *X* is (a member) of type α. '*X* →$_v$ α' means that *X* is typed to *v*-construct an object of type α, if any. We write '*X* → α' if what is *v*-constructed does not depend on a valuation *v*. Throughout, it holds that the variables $w →_v ω$ and $t →_v τ$. If $C →_v α_{τω}$ then the frequently used Composition [[*C w*] *t*], which is the intensional descent (a.k.a. extensionalization) of the α-intension *v*-constructed by *C*, will be encoded as 'C_{wt}'.

We invariably furnish expressions with procedurally structured meanings, which are explicated as TIL constructions. Thus TIL constructions are assigned to expressions as their context-invariant meanings, and the analysis of an unambiguous expression consists in discovering the logical construction encoded by a given sentence. To this end we have developed the *TIL method of analysis* that consists of three steps:

1) *Type-theoretical analysis*, i.e., assigning types to the objects that receive mention in the analysed expression.

2) *Type-theoretical synthesis*, i.e., combining the constructions of the objects *ad* (1) in order to construct the object (if any) of the respective type denoted by the whole expression.

3) *Type-theoretical checking*, i.e. checking whether the proposed analysis is type-theoretically coherent.

To illustrate the method, we analyse the stock example "The King of France is bald" *à la* Strawson. *First*, type-theoretical analysis. The sentence mentions the following objects. *King_of*/$(ιι)_{τω}$ is an empirical function that dependently on $\langle w,t \rangle$-pairs assigns to one individual (a country) another individual (its king) or else nothing, depending on whether the country is a monarchy and the monarch is a king rather than a queen; *France*/ι; *King_of_France*/$ι_{τω}$; *Bald*/$(oι)_{τω}$; the whole sentence denotes a proposition, that is, an object of type $o_{τω}$.

Second, synthesis. Now we are to combine the constructions of the objects *King_of* and *France* in order to produce the office *King_of_France* and then ascribe *Baldness* to the holder of the office. Since we intend to arrive at the *literal* analysis of the sentence, the objects denoted by semantically simple expressions are constructed by their Trivializations: $^0King\_of$, ^0France, ^0Bald. In order to construct the office *King_of_France*, we have to combine $^0King\_of$ and ^0France. The function *King_of* must be *extensionalized* first via the Composition $^0King\_of_{wt} \to_v$ (ιι), and the result is then applied to *France*; thus we get $[^0King\_of_{wt}\ ^0France] \to_v ι$. Abstracting over the values of w and t we obtain the Closure that constructs the royal office:

$$\lambda w\lambda t\ [^0King\_of_{wt}\ ^0France] \to ι_{τω}.$$

But the property of being bald cannot be ascribed to an individual office. Instead it is ascribed to the individual (if any) occupying the office. Thus the office has to be extensionalized first: $\lambda w\lambda t\ [^0King\_of_{wt}\ ^0France]_{wt} \to_v ι$. The property itself has to be extensionalized as well: $^0Bald_{wt}$. By composing these two Compositions,

$$[^0Bald_{wt}\ \lambda w\lambda t\ [^0King\_of_{wt}\ ^0France]_{wt}] \to_v o$$

we obtain either a truth-value (**T** or **F**) or nothing, according as the King of France is bald, or does not exist, respectively. Finally, by abstracting over the values of the variables w and t, we construct the proposition:

$$\lambda w\lambda t\ [^0Bald_{wt}\ \lambda w\lambda t\ [^0King\_of_{wt}\ ^0France]_{wt}] \to_v o_{τω}$$

Third, type checking. To this end we usually draw the derivation tree as illustrated by Fig. 1.[3]

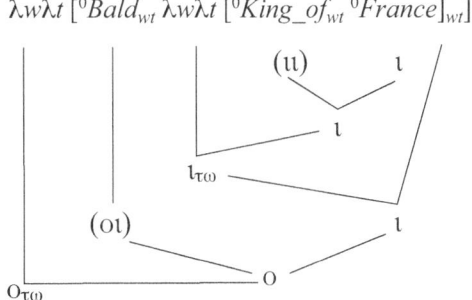

Figure 1. Derivation tree

So much for the basic notions of TIL and its method of analysis.

---

[3] To simplify the tree, I apply these rules: if $C \to_v α_{τω}$ then $C_{wt} \to_v α$, and if $D \to_v α$ then $\lambda w\lambda t\ D \to_v α_{τω}$. Indeed, unpacking the abbreviations '$α_{τω}$' and 'C_{wt}', we have: $C \to_v ((ατ)ω)$, $[Cw] \to_v (ατ)$, $[[Cw]t] \to_v α$. Similarly the second rule: $D \to_v α$, $\lambda t\ D \to_v (ατ)$, $\lambda w\lambda t\ D \to_v ((ατ)ω)$.

2. Presuppositions and the two kinds of negation

As stated at the outset, sentences often come with a presupposition that is entailed both by the sentence and its negation. The entailment relation is defined as usual. A proposition P is analytically entailed by a proposition S, $S \vDash P$, if P takes the truth-value **T** at all $\langle w, t \rangle$-pairs at which S takes the value **T**.[4]

To define analytic entailment formally, we need the propositional property $True/(oo_{\tau\omega})_{\tau\omega}$ which is defined as follows. Let P be a propositional construction $(P/*_n \to o_{\tau\omega})$. Then

$[^0True_{wt}\, P]$ v-constructs **T** iff P_{wt} v-constructs **T**, otherwise **F**.

For completeness, there are two other properties of the same type, namely *False* and *Undefined*, defined as follows:

$[^0False_{wt}\, P]$ v-constructs **T** iff P_{wt} v-constructs **F**, otherwise **F**

$[^0Undefined_{wt}\, P]$ v-constructs **T** iff P_{wt} is v-improper, otherwise **F**

Note that $[^0True_{wt}\, P]$ v-constructs **F** in two cases, namely if P_{wt} v-constructs **F** or if P_{wt} is v-improper. Hence, for instance, if a proposition v-constructed by P is not true at a given $\langle w, t \rangle$-pair, it does not have to be false, because there is the third possibility of being undefined. Formally, we have these relations ($=/(ooo)$):

$[^0True_{wt}\, P] = \neg [^0False_{wt}\, P] \wedge \neg [^0Undefined_{wt}\, P]$

$[^0False_{wt}\, P] = \neg [^0True_{wt}\, P] \wedge \neg [^0Undefined_{wt}\, P]$

$[^0Undefined_{wt}\, P] = \neg [^0True_{wt}\, P] \wedge \neg [^0False_{wt}\, P]$

Analytical entailment is defined as follows (P, $S/*_n \to o_{\tau\omega}$, $\vDash /(oo_{\tau\omega}o_{\tau\omega})$).[5]

$(S \vDash P)$ iff $\forall w\, \forall t\, [[^0True_{wt}\, S] \supset [^0True_{wt}\, P]]$

The logical difference between a presupposition and mere entailment is this:

P is a *presupposition* of S iff $(S \vDash P)$ and $(non\text{-}S \vDash P)$

Thus if P is not true at a given $\langle w, t \rangle$-pair, then *neither S nor non-S* is true. Hence, S has no truth-value at such a $\langle w, t \rangle$-pair at which its presupposition is not true.

On the other hand:

P is *merely entailed* by S if $(S \vDash P)$ and neither $(non\text{-}S \vDash P)$ nor $(non\text{-}S \vDash non\text{-}P)$

---

[4] For the slight difference between *analytical* and *logical* entailment see Duží (2010).
[5] Again, I use the infix notation '$(S \vDash P)$' instead of the proper TIL notation '$[^0 \vDash S\, P]$' to make the formulae easier to read.

Hence if *S* is not true we cannot deduce anything about the truth-value, or lack thereof, of *P*.

However, in order to decide whether there is a presupposition of *S*, we have to take into account two ways in which the negated form *non-S* can be obtained. To illustrate the situation, consider again the sentence "The King of France is bald". If the royal office is occupied and we want to say that its holder is *not* bald, we would simply use the form "The King of France is *not* bald". This is Strawsonian *narrow-scope negation*. The property of not being bald is ascribed to the holder of the royal office.[6] Thus the analyses of the Strawsonian reading of the sentence and of its negation amount to these constructions:

(S) $\quad \lambda w \lambda t \ [^0 Bald_{wt} \ \lambda w \lambda t \ [^0 King\_of_{wt} \ ^0 France]_{wt}]$

(non-S) $\quad \lambda w \lambda t \ \neg [^0 Bald_{wt} \ \lambda w \lambda t \ [^0 King\_of_{wt} \ ^0 France]_{wt}]$

However, if the royal office is not occupied, one would protest, saying, "No, it is not true that the King of France is bald, for the King of France does not exist". This is Russellian *wide-scope negation*. The property of not being true is ascribed to the whole proposition that the King of France is bald.[7]

In order to analyse Russellian wide-scope negation, we apply the above defined propositional property $True/(oo_{\tau\omega})_{\tau\omega}$:

(non-R) $\quad \lambda w \lambda t \ \neg [^0 True_{wt} \ \lambda w \lambda t \ [^0 Bald_{wt} \ \lambda w \lambda t \ [^0 King\_of_{wt} \ ^0 France]_{wt}]]$

(*non-R*) is the wide-scope negation of the proposition that it is true that the King of France is bald constructed by

(R) $\quad \lambda w \lambda t \ [^0 True_{wt} \ \lambda w \lambda t \ [^0 Bald_{wt} \ \lambda w \lambda t \ [^0 King\_of_{wt} \ ^0 France]_{wt}]]$

This is not exactly Russell's analysis. The Russellian rephrasing of the sentence "The King of France is bald" is "There is a unique individual such that he is the King of France and he is bald". The analysis of this sentence comes down to

(R*) $\quad \lambda w \lambda t \ [^0 \exists \lambda x \ [[x = \lambda w \lambda t \ [^0 King\_of_{wt} \ ^0 France]_{wt}] \wedge [^0 Bald_{wt} \ x]]]$.

Additional types. $\exists/(o(o\iota)); =/(o\iota); x/*_1 \rightarrow_v \iota$.[8]

---

[6] There is still a difference between being *non-bald* (property negation) and being an *x* such that *not: x is bald* (boolean negation). However, this issue is out of the scope of this paper.

[7] For the difference between narrow-scope and wide-scope negation with respect to a presupposition, see also Hajičová (2008).

[8] Note that in TIL we do not need a construction to specify the uniqueness of the King of France, because it is inherent in the meaning of 'the King of France'. The meaning of definite descriptions like 'the King of France' is a construction of an individual office of type $\iota_{\tau\omega}$ occupied in each $\langle w, t \rangle$-pair by at most one individual. See also Duží (2009).

Yet (R) gets the truth-conditions of the Russellian reading right, because (R) and (R*) are equivalent in the sense of constructing the same proposition.[9] This proposition does not come with the presupposition that the King of France exists, unlike the proposition constructed by (S). The analysis reveals that these two readings are not equivalent. Though (R) and (S) are *co-entailing* they denote *different propositions*, which I am going to prove now.

First, the equivalence of (R) and (R*).

a) Let the royal office be occupied in a given world w and time t by an individual a. Then if this individual a is bald, the proposition $\lambda w \lambda t$ [$^0Bald_{wt}$ $\lambda w \lambda t$ [$^0King\_of_{wt}$ ^0France]$_{wt}$] takes the value **T** in such a world-time pair, otherwise **F**, and so does (R) according to the definition of the property *True*. By assumption [$^0a = [\lambda w \lambda t$ [$^0King\_of_{wt}$ ^0France]$_{wt}$]. Hence the Composition [$^0a = [\lambda w \lambda t$ [$^0King\_of_{wt}$ ^0France]$_{wt}$] $\wedge$ [$^0Bald_{wt}$ ^0a]] v-constructs **T** and so does [λx [$x = [\lambda w \lambda t$ [$^0King\_of_{wt}$ ^0France]$_{wt}$] $\wedge$ [$^0Bald_{wt}$ x]] ^0a] if a is bald. It means that the class of individuals λx [$x = [\lambda w \lambda t$ [$^0King\_of_{wt}$ ^0France]$_{wt}$] $\wedge$ [$^0Bald_{wt}$ x]] is non-empty according as the individual a is bald or not. Thus according to the definition of the quantifier $\exists$, the proposition constructed by (R*) takes the value **T** if a is bald, otherwise **F**, exactly as does the proposition constructed by (R).

b) Let the royal office be vacant in a given world w and time t. Then by Def. 1, iii) the following Compositions are v-improper:

$$[\lambda w \lambda t\ [^0King\_of_{wt}\ ^0France]_{wt}]$$

$$[^0Bald_{wt}\ \lambda w \lambda t\ [^0King\_of_{wt}\ ^0France]_{wt}]$$

$$[x = \lambda w \lambda t\ [^0King\_of_{wt}\ ^0France]_{wt}]$$

$$[[x = \lambda w \lambda t\ [^0King\_of_{wt}\ ^0France]_{wt}] \wedge [^0Bald_{wt}\ x]].$$

This in turn means that the proposition constructed by

$$\lambda w \lambda t\ [^0Bald_{wt}\ \lambda w \lambda t\ [^0King\_of_{wt}\ ^0France]_{wt}]$$

is undefined and by the definition of the property *True* the proposition constructed by (R) takes the value **F**. But so does (R*), because the class constructed by

$$\lambda x\ [[x = \lambda w \lambda t\ [^0King\_of_{wt}\ ^0France]_{wt}] \wedge [^0Bald_{wt}\ x]]$$

is empty and the application of the existential quantifier $\exists$ to an empty class results in **F**.

---

[9] For more details on Russell's analysis and its comparison with Strawson's analysis see Duží (2014).

Note that from (b) it also follows that neither (R) nor (R*) comes with the existential presupposition that the King of France exists. Non-trivial existence of empirical objects is in TIL explicated as a property of intensions to be instantiated at a given $\langle w, t \rangle$-pair of evaluation.[10] Thus to say that unicorns do not exist is tantamount to saying that at the given world w and time t the property of being a unicorn has the empty class of individuals as its population. Similarly, that the King of France does not exist means that the office of the King of France is vacant at the world and time of evaluation. Hence if there were an existential presupposition, the proposition constructed by (R) or (R*) would have no truth-value in case of the royal office being vacant. Yet, these propositions take the value **F**. In other words, neither (*non-R*) nor (*non-R**) entails that the royal office is occupied.

Now I am going to prove that (S), and thus also (*non-S*), presupposes the existence of the King of France. To this end I must prove that the following arguments are valid (though not sound):

<u>The King of France is (not) bald</u>
The King of France exists

First, the analysis of the conclusion amounts to this construction:

$$\lambda w \lambda t\ [^0Exist_{wt}\ [\lambda w \lambda t\ [^0King\_of_{wt}\ ^0France]]]$$

where $Exist/(o\iota_{\tau\omega})_{\tau\omega}$ is the property that an office has when it is occupied. This property is defined as follows:

$$^0Exist =_{of} \lambda w \lambda t\ \lambda c\ [^0\exists \lambda x\ [x = c_{wt}]].$$

Types: $\exists/(o(o\iota))$; $c \rightarrow_v \iota_{\tau\omega}$; $x \rightarrow_v \iota$; $=_{of}/(o(o\iota_{\tau\omega})_{\tau\omega}(o\iota_{\tau\omega})_{\tau\omega})$: the identity of properties of individual offices; $=/(o\iota\iota)$: the identity of individuals, $x \rightarrow_v \iota$.

Now I am ready to prove the validity of the above arguments and thus the validity of the claim that the Strawsonian reading is associated with a presupposition of the royal office being occupied.

At any $\langle w, t \rangle$-pair the following proof steps are truth-preserving:

1) $(\neg)[^0Bald_{wt}\ \lambda w \lambda t\ [^0King\_of_{wt}\ ^0France]_{wt}]$ ∅
2) $\neg[^0Improper_{wt}\ ^0[\lambda w \lambda t\ [^0King\_of_{wt}\ ^0France]_{wt}]]$ 1), by Def. 1, iii)
3) $\neg[^0Empty\ \lambda x\ [x = [\lambda w \lambda t\ [^0King\_of_{wt}\ ^0France]]_{wt}]]$ 2), by Def. 1, iv)
4) $[^0\exists \lambda x\ [x = [\lambda w \lambda t\ [^0King\_of_{wt}\ ^0France]]_{wt}]]$ 3), EG
5) $[\lambda c\ [^0\exists \lambda x\ [x = c_{wt}]]\ \lambda w \lambda t\ [^0King\_of_{wt}\ ^0France]]$ 4), λ-abstraction
6) $^0Exist_{wt} = \lambda c\ [^0\exists \lambda x\ [x = c_{wt}]]$ Def. of *Exist*
7) $[^0Exist_{wt}\ [\lambda w \lambda t\ [^0King\_of_{wt}\ ^0France]]]$ 5), 6), substitution of identicals

---

[10] For details see Duží *et al.* (2010, § 2.3).

Remark. At step (2) the property of being *Improper* of type $(o*_1)_{\tau\omega}$ is applied to the *construction* [λwλt [^{0}King_of$_{wt}$ ^{0}France]$_{wt}$] of type $*_1$ that is supplied here by its Trivialisation ^{0}[λwλt [^{0}King_of$_{wt}$ ^{0}France]$_{wt}$] belonging to type$*_2$. On the other hand, at step (3) the property of being *Empty* of type $(o(o\iota))$ is applied to the set of individuals λx [x = [λwλt [^{0}King_of$_{wt}$ ^{0}France]]$_{wt}$]. These two steps are necessary in order to existentially generalize at step (4). In a logic of partial functions such as TIL we cannot carelessly generalize before having proved that the set to which the existential quantifier is applied is non-empty.

The following Table 1 illustrates the truth conditions of the propositions constructed by (*R*), (*S*), (*non-R*) and (*non-S*) with respect to the occupancy of the office of the King of France (*KF*).[11]

	KF	(R)	(S)	(non-R)	(non-S)
w_1, t_1	a	T	T	F	F
w_2, t_2	a	F	F	T	T
w_3, t_3	⊥	F	⊥	T	⊥
w_4, t_4	b	F	F	T	T
w_5, t_5	b	T	T	F	F
w_6, t_6	⊥	F	⊥	T	⊥
...					

Table 1. Russellian vs. Strawsonian analysis

Indeed, (*R*) and (*S*) are co-entailing. Whenever (*R*) is true (*S*) is true as well, and vice versa. Yet the propositions (*R*) and (*S*) are not identical, because (*non-R*) and (*non-S*) are not co-entailing. At those ⟨w, t⟩-pairs where the King of France does not exist, both (*S*) and (*non-S*) are undefined, the propositions having a truth-value gap, while (*R*) and (*non-R*) are false and true, respectively.

3. Ambiguities in topic-focus articulation

The above analyses provide a solution to the almost hundred-year old dispute over Strawsonian versus Russellian definite descriptions.[12] The ambiguity of sentences of the form "The *F* is a *G*" is not rooted in a shift of *meaning* of the definite description 'the *F*'. Rather the ambiguity stems from different *topic-focus articulations* of such sentences. Whereas articulating the topic of

---

[11] I use the symbol '⊥' to mark a truth-value *gap* rather than the truth-value F.

[12] See, for instance, Russell (1905, 1957), Strawson (1950, 1964), Donnellan (1966), von Fintel (2004), Neale (1990). A summary of this dispute can be found in Duží (2014).

a sentence activates a presupposition, articulating the focus frequently yields merely an entailment.[13] If 'the *F*' is the topic phrase then this description occurs extensionally that is with *de re* supposition and Strawson's analysis appears to be what is wanted. This reading corresponds to Donnellan's *referential use* of 'the *F*' and the sentence *presupposes* the existence of the descriptum of 'the *F*'. The other option is '*G*' occurring as topic and 'the *F*' as focus. This reading corresponds to Donnellan's *attributive* use of 'the *F*' and the description occurs intensionally that is with *de dicto* supposition. On this reading the Russellian analysis gets the truth-conditions of the sentence right. The existence of a unique *F* is merely entailed.

The received view still tends to be that there is room for at most one of the two positions, since they are deemed incompatible. But there is no incompatibility between Strawson's and Russell's positions, because they simply do not talk about one and the same meaning of the sentence "The King of France is bald". My novel *contribution* is to point out this *ambiguity* which yielded the false dilemma. Russell argued for the attributive use of 'the King of France' and Strawson for its referential use.

For illustration, consider the sentence "The Pope of the Roman Catholic Church visited the Pope of the Coptic Orthodox Church in Egypt in 2010". This sentence demonstrates multiple ambiguities and has at least four non-equivalent readings depending on topic-focus articulation. In what follows I will use 'the Catholic Pope' and 'the Coptic Pope' for short, with *topic* marked in italics.

1) *The Catholic Pope* visited the Coptic Pope in Egypt in 2010.

On this reading the sentence *presupposes* that the Catholic Pope exists now, and *merely entails* that the Coptic Pope existed in 2010 (i.e. diachronic occupation of two different offices). Hence with the additional assumption that the Catholic Pope is Francisco and the Coptic Pope in 2010 was Shenouda III, the sentence entails that Francisco visited Shenouda III in Egypt in 2010.

2) The Catholic Pope visited *the Coptic Pope* in Egypt in 2010. (Or, for clarity, "*The Coptic Pope* was visited by the Catholic Pope in Egypt in 2010")

This reading *presupposes* that the Coptic Pope exists now, and *merely entails* that the Catholic Pope existed in 2010 (i.e. diachronic occupation of two different offices). Hence with the additional assumption that the current

---

[13] This assumption is based on Hajičová (2008), and supported by other linguists as well. See, for instance Gundel (1999), Gundel and Fretheim (2004) and Strawson (1952, esp. p. 173ff.).

Coptic Pope is Tawadros II and the Catholic Pope in 2010 was Benedict XVI, the sentence entails that Tawadros II was visited by Benedict XVI in Egypt in 2010.

3) The Catholic Pope visited the Coptic Pope in Egypt *in 2010*. (Or, for clarity, "*In 2010* the Catholic Pope visited the Coptic Pope in Egypt")

This reading *merely entails* that both the Catholic Pope and the Coptic Pope existed in 2010 (i.e. synchronic occupation of two different offices), because the topic is now the year *2010*. The sentence could have been uttered as an answer to the question "What happened in 2010"? Thus it does not presuppose the occupancy of either of the two offices. If one or both of them were not occupied in 2010, one would protest, for instance like this: "No, it is not true that in 2010 the Catholic Pope visited the Coptic Pope in Egypt, because the Catholic Pope did not exist in 2010". Hence, wide-scope, i.e., presupposition-denying negation, is applied. Thus with the additional assumption that the Catholic Pope in 2010 was Benedict XVI and the Coptic Pope was Shenouda III, the sentence entails that in 2010 Benedict XVI visited Shenouda III in Egypt.

4) The Catholic Pope visited the Coptic Pope in Egypt in 2010.

This is a neutral reading that comes with the *presupposition* that both the Catholic Pope and the Coptic Pope exist now (i.e. synchronic occupation of two different offices).[14] Hence if the Catholic Pope is Francisco and the Coptic Pope is Tawadros II the sentence entails that Francisco visited Tawadros II in Egypt in 2010.

It is a matter of *pragmatics*, of course, which reading is the intended one on an occasion of use. Logic cannot decide which among multiple readings happens to be the intended one. Yet, I cannot agree with Kripke (1977) on two accounts. First, it is not *entirely* a matter of pragmatics which reading is the intended one; it is also a matter of semantics. Second, and more importantly, the Russellian account of definite descriptions cannot, by itself, account for both the referential and the attributive uses. Our fine-grained logical method of analysis as presented in this paper demonstrates that these readings are *not equivalent*, and that the Russellian reading does not take into account any presuppositions triggered by the topic of the sentence in question. Thus though logic itself cannot decide between multiple readings it can contribute to disambiguation of a sentence by making these different

---

[14] Von Fintel (2004) considers in particular such a neutral reading of sentences with definite descriptions. Thus he arrives at the conclusion that using definite descriptions is always connected with an existential presupposition.

meanings explicit. In case the sentence is ambiguous, logic can bring out this ambiguity and, as a result, propose different meanings to be assigned to different (non-equivalent) readings. Thus choosing between them becomes also a matter of *semantics*.

4. General analytic schema for sentences with presuppositions

Up until now I have utilized the singularity of an individual office of type $\iota_{\tau\omega}$ when analysing sentences that have a presupposition. If the office denoted by 'the F' goes vacant at a given world w and time t of evaluation, the extensionalization F_{wt} is v-improper, and if the occurrence of 'the F' is referential (i.e., extensional, or *de re*) the so constructed proposition has a truth-value gap. However, the construction of a presupposition can be more complicated. In particular, the topic term does not have to be a singular one; it can be also a plural term like 'the popes of Rome and Avignon' or a general one like 'a penguin'. Thus we need a general analytic schema for sentences with presuppositions, which I am going to introduce now.

A sentence S that comes with a presupposition P encodes as its meaning this procedure:

> In any $\langle w, t \rangle$-pair of evaluation,
> *if* P_{wt} is true
> *then* evaluate S_{wt} to produce a truth-value,
> *else fail* to produce a truth-value.

To formulate this schema rigorously, we need to define the *if-then-else-fail* function. Here is how. The procedure encoded by "If $P(\to \text{o})$ then $C(\to \alpha)$, else $D (\to \alpha)$" behaves as follows:

a) If P v-constructs **T** then execute C (and return the result of type α, provided C is not v-improper).

b) If P v-constructs **F** then execute D (and return the result of type α, provided D is not v-improper).

c) If P is v-improper then no result.

Hence, *if-then-else* is seen to be a function of type $(\alpha \text{o}*_n *_n)$, and its definition decomposes into two phases.[15]

First, select a construction to be executed on the basis of a specific condition P. The choice between C and D comes down to this Composition:

$$[^0 I^* \lambda c \, [[P \wedge [c = {}^0 C]] \vee [\neg P \wedge [c = {}^0 D]]]]$$

---

[15] The definition introduced here is a slightly adjusted version of the definition presented in Duží (2010a).

Types: $P \to_v o$ v-constructs the condition of the choice between the execution of C or D, $C/*_n$, $D/*_n \to_v \alpha$; $c \to_v *_n$; $I*/(*_n(o*_n))$: the singularizer function that associates a singleton of constructions with the construction that is the element of this singleton, and is otherwise (i.e. if the set is empty or many-valued) undefined.

If P v-constructs **T** then the variable c v-constructs the *construction C*, and if P v-constructs **F** then the variable c v-constructs the *construction D*. In either case, the set constructed by

$$\lambda c\, [[P \wedge [c = {}^0C]] \vee [\neg P \wedge [c = {}^0D]]]$$

is a singleton and the singularizer I* returns as its value either the construction C or the construction D.[16]

Second, the selected construction is executed; therefore, Double Execution must be applied:

$$^2[^0I*\, \lambda c\, [[P \wedge [c = {}^0C]] \vee [\neg P \wedge [c = {}^0D]]]]$$

As a special case of P being a presupposition, *no* construction D is to be selected whenever P is not satisfied. Thus the definition of the *if-then-else-fail* function of type $(\alpha o*_n)$ is this:

$$^2[^0I*\, \lambda c\, [P \wedge [c = {}^0C]]]$$

Now we can apply this definition to the case of a presupposition. Thus let $P/*_n \to o_{\tau\omega}$ be a construction of a presupposition of $S/*_n \to o_{\tau\omega}$. Moreover, let $c/*_{n+1} \to_v *_n$, $^2c \to_v o$. Then the type of the *if-then-else-fail* function is $(oo*_n)$ and its definition is:

$$\lambda w \lambda t\, [{}^0\textit{if-then-else-fail}\, P_{wt}\, {}^0[S_{wt}]] = \lambda w \lambda t\, {}^2[{}^0I*\, \lambda c\, [P_{wt} \wedge [c = {}^0[S_{wt}]]]]$$

Gloss. In the first phase the construction S_{wt} is selected, provided P_{wt} v-constructs **T**. In the second phase S_{wt} is executed. In case P_{wt} does not v-construct **T**, no construction is selected and executed, hence $^2[^0I*\, \lambda c\, [P_{wt} \wedge [c = {}^0[S_{wt}]]]]$ is v-improper and the so constructed proposition has a truth-value gap, as it should have.

In what follows, instead of the above definition I will use this abbreviated notation as the *general analytic schema*:

$$\lambda w \lambda t\, [\textit{if}\, P_{wt}\, \textit{then}\, S_{wt}\, \textit{else fail}].$$

For illustration, let us analyse Strawson's (1952, pp. 173ff) example

All *John's children* are asleep.

---

[16] Note that in this phase C and D are not constituents to be executed; rather they are merely displayed as objects to be selected by the variable c. This is to say that in TIL constructions themselves can be objects to be operated on, and without this *hyperintensional* approach we would not be able to define the *strict* function *if-then-else*.

If the topic of the sentence is 'John's children' then there is a presupposition to the effect that John has children.[17] Hence the truth-conditions of this reading can be formulated like this:

If John has any children
then check whether each and every one of them is asleep
else fail to produce a truth-value.

Thus we have:

$$\lambda w \lambda t \ [if \ [^0\exists \ [^0Children\_of_{wt} \ ^0John] \ then$$
$$[[^0All \ [^0Children\_of_{wt} \ ^0John]] \ ^0Sleep_{wt}] \ else \ fail]$$

Types: $Children\_of/((o\iota)\iota)_{\tau\omega}$: the empirical function (attribute) that dependently on a state of affairs associates an individual with the set of those individuals who are his or her children; $John/\iota$; $Sleep/(o\iota)_{\tau\omega}$; $\exists/(o(o\iota))$; $All/((o(o\iota))(o\iota))$: restricted quantifier that associates a set S of individuals with all the superset of S.

Remark. Here I use the restricted quantifier *All*, because I want to arrive at the *literal* analysis of the sentence. Such an analysis follows Frege's principle (1884, p. 60): It is simply not possible to speak about an object without somehow denoting or naming it.[18] If the unrestricted general quantifier were used the resulting construction would be:

$$\lambda w \lambda t \ [if \ [^0\exists \ [^0Children\_of_{wt} \ ^0John] \ then$$
$$[^0\forall \lambda x \ [[[^0Children\_of_{wt} \ ^0John] \ x] \supset [^0Sleep_{wt} \ x]]] \ else \ fail]$$

This is an equivalent construction producing the same proposition as the above one, yet it is not the literal analysis of our sentence, because the truth-function of implication is not mentioned in the sentence.[19]

5. Conclusion

In this paper I demonstrated and proved that narrow-scope and wide-scope negation are not equivalent. If a sentence comes with a presupposition, then narrow-scope negation is the relevant one, because wide-scope negation is

---

[17] Hence the situation is this. We are talking about John's children, and just want to know what they are doing right now. The other option would be, for instance, the scenario of talking about those who are asleep, and the sentence would be offered as an answer, "Among those who are asleep are all of John's children". On this reading the sentence would only entail that John has children.

[18] The German original goes, "Überhaupt ist es nicht möglich von einem Gegenstand zu sprechen, ohne ihn irgendwie zu bezeichnen oder benennen."

[19] For more details on the method of arriving at the best literal meaning of a sentence, see Duží *et al.* (2010, §2.1).

presupposition-denying. I also dealt with the ambiguities in natural language stemming from different topic-focus articulations within a sentence. While the topic phrase generates a presupposition, the focus phrase usually triggers merely an entailment. It is a matter of *pragmatics*, of course, which reading is the intended one on an occasion of use. Yet, our fine-grained logical method of analysis as presented in this paper demonstrates that sentences differing in point of topic-focus articulation are not equivalent, and thus choosing between particular readings becomes also a matter of *semantics*. Logic can contribute to the disambiguation of a sentence by making these hidden features explicit and logically tractable. In case there are more *non-equivalent* senses of a sentence we furnish the sentence with *different meanings*.

Acknowledgements

This research was funded by the Grant Agency of the Czech Republic (GACR) project GA15-13277S "Hyperintensional logic for natural language analysis", and by the internal grant agency of VSB-TU Ostrava, project SP2015/85 "Knowledge modelling and its applications in software engineering".

References

[1] Donnellan, K. S., (1966). Reference and definite descriptions, *Philosophical Review*, vol. 77, pp. 281-304.
[2] Duží, M. (2009). Strawsonian vs. Russellian definite descriptions. *Organon F*, vol. XVI, No. 4, pp. 587-614.
[3] Duží, M. (2010). The paradox of inference and the non-triviality of analytic information. *Journal of Philosophical Logic*, vol. 39, No. 5, pp. 473-510.
[4] Duží, M. (2010a). Tenses and truth-conditions: a plea for *if-then-else*. In *the Logica Yearbook 2009*, Peliš, M. (ed.), London: College Publications, pp. 63-80.
[5] Duží, M., Jespersen B. and Materna P. (2010). *Procedural Semantics for Hyperintensional Logic. Foundations and Applications of Trasnsparent Intensional Logic*. Berlin: Springer, series Logic, Epistemology, and the Unity of Science, vol. 17.
[6] Duží, M. (2014). How to Unify Russellian and Strawsonian Definite Descriptions. In *Recent Trends in Philosophical Logic, Studia Logica*, Roberto Ciuni, Heinrich Wansing, Caroline Willcommen (eds.), vol. 41, pp. 85-101.
[7] Fintel, Kai von (2004). Would you believe it? The King of France is Back! (Presuppositions and Truth-Value Intuitions). In: *Descriptions and Beyond*, Reimer, M., Bezuidenhout, A. (eds.), Oxford: Clarendon Press, pp. 315-341.
[8] Frege, G. (1884). *Die Grundlagen der Arithmetik*, Breslau: W. Koebner.
[9] Gundel, J. K. (1999). Topic, focus and the grammar pragmatics interface. In *Proceedings of the 23rd Annual Penn Linguistics Colloquium. Penn Working*

Papers in Linguistics, J. Alexander, N. Han and M. Minnick (eds.), vol. 6.1, pp. 185-200.

[10] GUNDEL, J. K. and FRETHEIM, T. (2004). Topic and Focus. In *the Handbook of Pragmatic Theory*. Laurence Horn and Gregory Ward (eds.), Blackwell, pp. 174-196.

[11] HAJIČOVÁ, E. (2008). What we are talking about and what we are saying about it. In: *Computational Linguistics and Intelligent Text Processing*, A. Gelbukh (Ed.), Berlin, Heidelberg: Springer-Verlag LNCS, vol. 4919, pp. 241-262.

[12] KRIPKE, S. A. (1977). Speaker's reference and semantic reference. In Peter A. French, Theodore E. Uehling Jr & Howard K. Wettstein (eds.), *Studies in the Philosophy of Language*. University of Minnesota Press, pp. 255-296.

[13] NEALE, S., (1990). *Descriptions*. Cambridge: MIT Press Books.

[14] RUSSELL, B. (1905). On denoting. *Mind* vol. 14, pp. 479-493.

[15] RUSSELL, B., (1957). Mr. Strawson on referring, *Mind* vol. 66, pp. 385-389.

[16] STRAWSON, P. F. (1950). On referring, *Mind* vol. 59, pp. 320-334.

[17] STRAWSON, P.F., (1964). Identifying reference and truth-values, *Theoria* vol. 3, pp. 96-118.

[18] TICHÝ, P. (1988). *The Foundations of Frege's Logic*. Berlin, New York: De Gruyter.

[19] TICHÝ, P. (2004). *Collected Papers in Logic and Philosophy*. V. Svoboda, B. Jespersen, C. Cheyne (eds.), Prague: Filosofia, Czech Academy of Sciences, and Dunedin: University of Otago Press.

How to unify Russellian and Strawsonian definite descriptions

Abstract

In this paper I will deal with ambiguities in natural language exemplifying the difference between *topic* and *focus articulation* within a sentence. I will show that whereas articulating the topic of a sentence activates a presupposition, articulating the focus frequently yields merely an entailment. Based on analysis of topic-focus articulation, I propose a solution to the almost hundred-year old dispute over Strawsonian versus Russellian definite descriptions. The point of departure is that sentences of the form "The F is a G" are ambiguous. Their ambiguity stems from different topic-focus articulations of such sentences. Russell and Strawson took themselves to be at loggerheads, whereas, in fact, they spoke at cross purposes. My novel contribution advances the research into definite descriptions by pointing out how progress has been hampered by a false dilemma and *how to move beyond that dilemma*. The point is this. If 'the F' is the topic phrase then this description occurs with *de re* supposition and Strawson's analysis appears to be what is wanted. On this reading the sentence *presupposes* the existence of the descriptum of 'the F'. The other option is 'G' occurring as topic and 'the F' as focus. This reading corresponds to Donnellan's *attributive* use of 'the F' and the description occurs with *de dicto* supposition. On this reading the Russellian analysis gets the truth-conditions of the sentence right. The existence of a unique F is merely entailed. This paper demonstrates how to unify these disparate insights into one coherent theory of definite descriptions.

1 Introduction

Natural language has features not found in logically perfect artificial languages. One such feature is *redundancy*; another feature is its converse, namely *ambiguity*. In this paper I will deal with the sort of ambiguity that is pivoted on whether the *topic* or the *focus* of a sentence is highlighted. For instance, "John only introduced Bill to Sue" lends itself to two different kinds of construal: "John did not introduce other people to Sue except for Bill" and "The only person Bill was introduced to by John was Sue".[1] There are two sentences whose semantics, logical properties and logical consequences only partially overlap.

Based on analysis of sentences that differ as for their topic-focus articulation I propose a solution to the almost hundred-year old dispute over Strawsonian versus Russellian definite descriptions.[2] The point of departure is that sentences of the form "The F is a G" are systematically ambiguous.[3] Their ambiguity is, in my

---

[1] See (Hajičová, 2008).
[2] See, for instance, (Russell, 1905, 1957); (Strawson, 1950, 1964); (Donnellan, 1966); (Fintel, 2004); (Neale, 1990).
[3] The sentence that triggered the dispute was "The King of France is bald".

view, not rooted in a shift of meaning of the definite description 'the *F*'. Rather the ambiguity stems from different *topic-focus articulations* of such sentences. My analysis assumes that whereas articulating the topic of a sentence activates a presupposition, articulating the focus frequently yields merely an entailment.[4] The point is this. If 'the *F*' is the topic phrase then this description occurs with *de re* supposition and Strawson's analysis appears to be what is wanted. On this reading that corresponds to Donnellan's *referential use* of 'the *F*' the sentence *presupposes* the existence of the descriptum of 'the *F*'. The other option is '*G*' occurring as topic and 'the *F*' as focus. This reading corresponds to Donnellan's *attributive* use of 'the *F*' and the description occurs with *de dicto* supposition. On this reading the Russellian analysis gets the truth-conditions of the sentence right. The existence of a unique *F* is merely entailed.

The received view still tends to be that there is room for at most one of the two positions, since they are deemed incompatible. But there is no incompatibility between Strawson's and Russell's positions, because they simply do not talk about one and the same meaning of the sentence "The King of France is bald". My novel *contribution* is to point out this *ambiguity* which yielded the false dilemma. Russell argued for attributive use of 'the King of France' whereas Strawson for its referential use. In this paper I will propose a logical analysis of both Russellian and Strawsonian reading of sentences of the form "The *F* is a *G*".

Tichý's Transparent Intensional Logic (TIL) will serve as background theory throughout my exposition.[5] Tichý's TIL was developed simultaneously with Montague's IL (Intensional Logic). The technical tools of disambiguation will be familiar from IL, with two exceptions. One is that we λ-bind separate variables w, $w_1, \ldots, w_n$ ranging over possible worlds and $t, t_1, \ldots, t_n$ ranging over times. This dual binding is tantamount to *explicit intensionalization* and *temporalization*. The other exception is that *functional application* is the logic both of extensionalization of intensions (functions from possible worlds) and of predication.[6] Application is symbolized by square brackets, '[…]'. Intensions are extensionalized by applying them to worlds and times, as in [[*Intension w*] *t*], abbreviated by subscripted terms for world and time variables: $Intension_{wt}$ is the extension of the generic intension *Intension* at $\langle w, t \rangle$. Thus, for instance, the extensionalization of a property yields a set (possibly an empty one), and the extensionalization of a proposition yields a truth-value (or no value at all). A general objection to IL is that it fails to accommodate *hyperintensionality*, as indeed any formal logic interpreted set-theoretically is bound to unless a domain of primitive hyperintensions is added to the frame. Any theory of natural-language analysis needs a hyperintensional semantics in order to crack the hard nuts of natural language semantics. In global terms, divested of its hyperintensional procedural semantics TIL is an anti-contextualist (i.e., transparent), explicitly intensional modification of IL. With its hyperintensional procedural semantics added back on, TIL rises above the model-

---

[4] This assumption is based on (Hajičová, 2008), and supported by other linguists as well. See, for instance (Gundel 1999), (Gundel and Fretheim, in press, http://www.sfu.ca/~hedberg/gundel-fretheim.pdf) and Strawson (1952, esp. p. 173ff.).

[5] For details on TIL, see, in particular, (Duží et al., 2010); (Tichý, 1988, 2004).

[6] For details, see (Jespersen, 2008).

theoretic paradigm and joins instead the paradigm of hyperintensional logic and structured meanings.[7]

The rest of the paper is organized as follows. Section 2 is a brief summary of the bones of contention between Russsellian and Strawsonian conceptions of definite descriptions. The relevant foundations of TIL are introduced in Section 3. Finally, in Section 4 I propose my unification of elements drawn from Strawsonian and Russellian theories of definite descriptions.

2 Russell versus Strawson on definite descriptions

There is a substantial difference between proper names and definite descriptions. This distinction is of crucial importance due to their vastly different logical behaviour. Independently of any particular theory of proper names, it should be granted that a *proper* proper name (as opposed to a definite description grammatically masquerading as a proper name) is a rigid designator of a numerically particular individual. On the other hand, a definite *description* like, for instance, 'the King of France', 'the highest mountain on earth', 'the first man to run 100 m under 9 seconds', etc., offers an *empirical criterion* that enables us to establish which individual, if any, satisfies the criterion in a particular state of affairs.

The contemporary discussion of the distinction between names and descriptions was triggered by Russell (1905). Russell's key idea is the proposal that a sentence like

(1)   "The F is a G"

containing a definite description 'the F' is understood to have, in the final analysis, the logical form

(1') $\exists x \, (Fx \wedge \forall y \, (Fy \supset x{=}y) \wedge Gx)$

rather than the logical form $G(\iota x \, Fx)$.

Though Russell's quantificational theory remains to this day a strong rival of referential theories, it has received its fair share of criticism. Russell's opponents claim that he simply gets the truth-conditions wrong in important cases of using descriptions when there is no such thing as the unique F.[8]

This criticism was launched by Strawson who in (1950) objected that Russell's theory predicts the wrong truth-conditions for sentences like "The present King of France is bald". According to Russell's analysis, this sentence is false. In Strawson's view, the sentence can be neither true nor false whenever there is no unique King of France. Obviously, in such a state of affairs the sentence is not true. However, if the sentence were false then its negation, "The King of France is *not* bald",

---

[7] For a detailed critical comparison of TIL and IL, see (Duží et al., 2010, § 2.4.3).

[8] Besides, many hold against Russell's translation of atomic sentences like "The F is a G" into the molecular form "There is at least one F and at most one thing is an F and that thing is a G", because Russell disregards the standard constraint that there must be a fair amount of structural similarity between analysandum and analysans.

would be true, which entails that there *is* a unique King of France, contrary to the assumption that there is none. Strawson holds that sentences like these *not only entail*, but also *presuppose*, the existence of a unique King of France. If 'the present King of France' fails to refer, then the presupposition is not satisfied and the sentence fails to have a truth value.[9]

Russell (1957), in response to Strawson's criticism, argues that, despite Strawson's protests, the sentence is in fact false:

> Suppose, for example, that in some country there was a law that no person could hold public office if he considered it false that the Ruler of the Universe is wise. I think an avowed atheist who took advantage of Mr. Strawson's doctrine to say that he did not hold this proposition false would be regarded as a somewhat shifty character. (Russell, 1957)

Donnellan (1966) observes that there is a sense in which Strawson and Russell are both right, and both wrong, about the proper analysis of definite descriptions, because definite descriptions can be used in two different ways. On a so-called *attributive use*, a sentence of the form "The F is a G" is used to express a proposition equivalent to "Whatever is uniquely F is a G". Alternatively, on a *referential use*, a sentence of the form "The F is a G" is used to pick out a specific individual, a, and to say of a that a is a G. Donnellan suggests that Russell's quantificational account of definite descriptions might capture attributive uses, but that it does not work for referential uses. Ludlow in (2007) interprets Donnellan as arguing that in some cases descriptions are Russellian and in other cases Strawsonian.

Kripke (1977) responds to Donnellan by arguing that the Russellian account of definite descriptions can, by itself, account for both referential and attributive uses, and that the difference between the two cases is entirely a matter of pragmatics. Neale (1990) supports Russell's view by collecting a number of cases in which intuitions about truth conditions clearly do not support Strawson's view. On the other hand, a number of linguists have recently come to Strawson's defence on this matter. See Ludlow (2007) for a detailed survey of the arguments supporting Strawson's view and arguments supporting Russell's. Here it might suffice to point out that Strawson's concerns have not delivered a knock-out blow to Russell's theory of descriptions, and so this topic remains very much alive. Von Fintel (2004), for instance, argues that every sentence containing a definite description 'the F' comes with the existential presupposition that there be a unique F.

In this paper I am not going to take into account Kripke's pragmatic factors like the intentions of a speaker, for they are irrelevant to a *logical* semantic theory. So I am disregarding Donnellan's troublesome notion of having somebody in mind. Instead, I will propose a *logical analysis* of sentences of the form "The F is a G". What I want to show is this. First, definite descriptions are not deprived of a self-contained meaning and they denote one and the same entity in any context. Thus they are never Russellian. Second, Russell's insight that a definite description 'the F' does not denote a definite individual is spot-on. According to TIL, 'the F' denotes a *condition* to be contingently satisfied by the individual (if any) that happens to be the F. I will explicate such conditions in terms of possible-world inten-

---

[9] Nevertheless, for Strawson, *sentences* are meaningful in and of themselves, independently of empirical facts like the contingent non-existence of the King of France.

sions, *viz.* as individual roles or offices to be occupied by at most one individual per world/time pair. Third, I am going to show that Donnellan is right in holding that sentences of the form "The *F* is a *G*" are systematically ambiguous. However, their ambiguity does not concern a shift of meaning of the definite description 'the *F*', as Fregean or other theories maintain. Instead the ambiguity concerns different *topic-focus* articulations of these sentences.

There are two options. The description 'the *F*' may occur as the topic of a sentence and property *G* (the focus) is predicated of the topic. This case corresponds to Donnellan's *referential* use. Using medieval terminology I will say that 'the *F*' occurs with *de re supposition*. The other option is '*G*' occurring as topic and 'the *F*' as focus. This reading corresponds to Donnellan's *attributive* use of 'the *F*' and the description occurs with *de dicto* supposition. Consequently, and crucially, such sentences are ambiguous between a *de dicto* and a *de re* reading. On their *de re* reading they *presuppose* the existence of a unique *F*. Thus Strawson's analysis appears to be adequate for *de re* cases. On their *de dicto* reading they have the truth-conditions as specified by the Russellian analysis. They do not presuppose, but only entail, the existence of a unique *F*. However, the Russellian analysis, though being equivalent to the one I am going to propose, is not an adequate *literal* analysis of *de dicto* readings.

I am going to bring out the *semantic* nature of the topic-focus difference by means of a literal logical analysis. As a result, I will be furnishing sentences differing only as for their topic-focus articulation with different structured meanings producing different possible-world propositions.[10] Since our logic is a hyperintensional logic of *partial functions*, I am able to analyse sentences with presuppositions in a both natural and principled manner. It means that I associate them with hyperpropositions, which in TIL are abstract logical procedures that produce partial possible-world propositions, which occasionally yield truth-value gaps.[11]

We need to work with properly partial functions and propositions with truth-value gaps. On Strawsonian reading the sentence "The King of France is bald" talks about the office of the King of France (topic) ascribing to the individual (if any) that occupies this office the property of being bald (focus). Thus it is presupposed that the King of France exist, i.e., that the office be occupied. If the office is vacant the proposition denoted by the sentence lacks a truth-value. On our approach this does not mean that the sentence is meaningless. The sentence has a sense, namely an instruction how in any possible world *w* at any time *t* to execute the procedure of evaluating its truth-conditions. Only if we evaluate these conditions in such a state-of-affairs where there is no King of France does the process of evaluation yield a truth-value gap.

---

[10] For details on structured meanings, see (Duží, et al., 2010a) and Jespersen (2012) for a survey.
[11] For an introduction to the notion of hyperproposition, see (Jespersen, 2010).

3 Foundations of TIL

Formally, TIL is an extensional logic of hyperintensions based on the partial, typed λ-calculus enriched with a ramified type structure to accommodate hyperintensions. The syntax of TIL is the familiar one of the λ-calculus, with the addition of a hyperintension called Trivialization (symbolized by a superscripted nought). The semantics is a *procedural* (as opposed to denotational) one. Thus, functional application, in TIL, is not the result of applying a function to an argument, but instead the very *procedure* of applying function to argument; and functional abstraction, in TIL, is not the result of forming a function, but instead the very *procedure* of sorting two domains of entities into functional arguments and values, respectively. The TIL concept of procedurally construed hyperintensions is *construction*. The three definitions below constitute the logical heart of TIL.

Definition 1 (*types of order 1*). Let B be a *base*, where a base is a collection of pair-wise disjoint, non-empty sets. Then:
(i) Every member of B is an elementary *type of order 1 over B*.
(ii) Let $\alpha, \beta_1, ..., \beta_m$ ($m > 0$) be types of order 1 over B. Then the collection $(\alpha\ \beta_1 ... \beta_m)$ of all m-ary partial mappings from $\beta_1 \times ... \times \beta_m$ into α is a functional *type of order 1 over B*.
(iii) Nothing is a *type of order 1 over B* unless it so follows from (i) and (ii). □

Remark. For the purposes of natural-language analysis, we are currently assuming the following base of ground types, each of which is part of the ontological commitments of TIL:

    ο: the set of truth-values {**T, F**};
    ι: the set of individuals (a constant universe of discourse);
    τ: the set of real numbers (doubling as temporal continuum);
    ω: the set of logically possible worlds (the logical space).

Constructions construct objects of appropriate types dependently on *valuation* of variables; they *v-construct*, where v is the parameter of valuation. With the difference that we construe variables as extra-linguistic objects and not as expressions, our theory of variables is otherwise identical to Tarski's. Thus, in TIL variables construct objects of the respective types dependently on valuation in the following way. For each type α there are countably infinitely many variables x_1, x_2, ..., . The members of α (unless α is a singleton) can be organised in infinitely many infinite sequences. Let the sequences be given (as one is allowed to assume in a realist semantics). The valuation v takes a sequence $\langle s_1, s_2, ... \rangle$ and assigns s_1 to the variable x_1, s_2 to the variable x_2; and so on.

When X is an object of any type (including a construction), the Trivialization of X, denoted '^0X', constructs X without the mediation of any other constructions. ^0X is the unique atomic construction of X that does not depend on valuation: it is a primitive, non-perspectival mode of presentation of X. The other constructions are *compound*, as they consist of other constituents apart from themselves. These are *Composition* and *Closure*. Composition is the procedure of applying a function f

How to unify Russellian and Strawsonian definite descriptions

to an argument a to obtain the value (if any) of f at a. Closure is the procedure of constructing a function by abstracting over variables; i.e., the procedure of abstracting, or extracting, a function from a context, as when abstracting $\lambda x(\varphi x)$ from $\varphi(a)$.[12]

Definition 2 (*construction*)
(i) The *variable* x is a *construction* that constructs an object O of the respective type dependently on a valuation v: x v-constructs O.
(ii) *Trivialization*: Where X is an object whatsoever (an extension, an intension or a *construction*), ^0X is the *construction Trivialization*. It constructs X without any change in X.
(iii) The *Composition* $[X\, Y_1...Y_m]$ is the following *construction*. If X v-constructs a function f of type $(\alpha\beta_1...\beta_m)$, and Y_1, ..., Y_m v-construct entities B_1, ..., B_m of types β_1, ..., β_m, respectively, then the *Composition* $[X\, Y_1...Y_m]$ v-constructs the value (an entity, if any, of type α) of f on the tuple argument $\langle B_1, ..., B_m \rangle$. Otherwise the *Composition* $[X\, Y_1...Y_m]$ does not v-construct anything and so is v-*improper*.
(iv) The *Closure* $[\lambda x_1...x_m\, Y]$ is the following *construction*. Let $x_1, x_2, ..., x_m$ be pair-wise distinct variables v-constructing entities of types β_1, ..., β_m and Y a construction v-constructing an α-entity. Then $[\lambda x_1 ... x_m\, Y]$ is the *construction* λ-*Closure* (or *Closure*). It v-constructs the following function f of the type $(\alpha\beta_1...\beta_m)$. Let $v(B_1/x_1,...,B_m/x_m)$ be a valuation identical with v at least up to assigning objects B_1/β_1, ..., B_m/β_m to variables x_1, ..., x_m. If Y is $v(B_1/x_1,...,B_m/x_m)$-improper (see iii), then f is undefined on $\langle B_1, ..., B_m \rangle$. Otherwise the value of f on $\langle B_1, ..., B_m \rangle$ is the α-entity $v(B_1/x_1,...,B_m/x_m)$-constructed by Y.
(v) Nothing is a *construction*, unless it so follows from (i) through (iv). □

The definition of the ramified hierarchy of types decomposes into three parts. Firstly, simple types of order 1, which were already defined by Definition 1. Secondly, constructions of order n, and thirdly, types of order $n + 1$.

Definition 3 (*ramified hierarchy of types*)
T_1 *(types of order 1)*. See Definition 1.
C_n *(constructions of order n)*
i) Let x be a variable ranging over a type of order n. Then x is a *construction of order n over B*.
ii) Let X be a member of a type of order n. Then ^0X, ^1X, ^2X are *constructions of order n over B*.
iii) Let $X, X_1,..., X_m$ ($m > 0$) be constructions of order n over B. Then $[X X_1... X_m]$ is a *construction of order n over B*.
iv) Let $x_1,...x_m, X$ ($m > 0$) be constructions of order n over B. Then $[\lambda x_1...x_m X]$ is a *construction of order n over B*.

---

[12] There are two other compound construction; Execution and Double Execution. Since I do not need them in this paper, they are not incorporated in Definition 2.

v) Nothing is a *construction of order n over B* unless it so follows from C_n (i)-(iv).

T_{n+1} *(types of order n + 1)* Let $*_n$ be the collection of all constructions of order n over B. Then
  i) $*_n$ and every type of order n are *types of order n + 1*.
  ii) If $m > 0$ and $\alpha, \beta_1,...,\beta_m$ are types of order $n + 1$ over B, then $(\alpha \beta_1 ... \beta_m)$ (see T_1 ii)) is a *type of order n + 1 over B*.
  iii) Nothing is a *type of order n + 1 over B* unless it so follows from (i) and (ii). □

Empirical languages incorporate an element of *contingency* that non-empirical ones lack. Empirical expressions denote *empirical conditions* that may or may not be satisfied at some empirical index of evaluation. We model these empirical conditions as *possible-world intensions*. Intensions are entities of type $(\beta\omega)$: mappings from possible worlds to an arbitrary type β. The type β is frequently the type of the *chronology* of α-objects, i.e. a mapping of type $(\alpha\tau)$. Thus α-intensions are frequently functions of type $((\alpha\tau)\omega)$, abbreviated as '$\alpha_{\tau\omega}$'. I shall typically say that an index of evaluation is a world/time pair $\langle w, t \rangle$. *Extensional entities* are entities of some type α where $\alpha \neq (\beta\omega)$ for any type β.

Examples of frequently used intensions are: *propositions* of type $o_{\tau\omega}$, *properties of individuals* of type $(o\iota)_{\tau\omega}$, binary *relations-in-intension between individuals* of type $(o\iota\iota)_{\tau\omega}$, *individual offices* of type $\iota_{\tau\omega}$. Thus individual offices are simply partial functions which, relative to a world/time pair $\langle w, t \rangle$, return at most one individual as value.

Our *explicit intensionalization and temporalization* enables us to encode constructions of possible-world intensions, by means of terms for possible-world variables and times, directly in the logical syntax. Where w ranges over ω and t over τ, the following general logical form characterizes the logical syntax of constructions of intensions: $\lambda w \lambda t [...w....t...]$. For instance, if *King_of* is a function of type $(\iota\iota)_{\tau\omega}$ and *France* an individual of type ι, the office of the King of France is constructed like this: $\lambda w \lambda t [^0King\_of_{wt} {}^0France]$.

Logical objects like *truth-functions* and *quantifiers* are extensional: $\land$ (conjunction), $\lor$ (disjunction) and $\supset$ (implication) are of type (ooo), and $\neg$ (negation) of type (oo). *Quantifiers* $\forall^\alpha, \exists^\alpha$ are type-theoretically polymorphous, total functions of type $(o(o\alpha))$, for an arbitrary type α, defined as follows. The *universal quantifier* $\forall^\alpha$ is a function that associates a class A of α-elements with **T** if A contains all elements of the type α, otherwise with **F**. The *existential quantifier* $\exists^\alpha$ is a function that associates a class A of α-elements with **T** if A is a non-empty class, otherwise with **F**.

Below all type indications will be provided outside the formulae in order not to clutter the notation. Furthermore, 'X/α' means that an object X is (a member) of type α. '$X \to_v \alpha$' means that the type of the object *valuation*-constructed by X is α. Throughout, it holds that the variables $w \to_v \omega$ and $t \to_v \tau$. If $C \to_v \alpha_{\tau\omega}$ then the frequently used Composition $[[C\ w]\ t]$, which is the intensional descent (a.k.a. extensionalization) of the α-intension v-constructed by C, will be encoded as 'C_{wt}'.

When using constructions of truth-functions, we often omit Trivialization and use infix notation to conform to standard notation in the interest of better readability. Also when using constructions of identities of α-entities, $=_\alpha/(o\alpha\alpha)$, we omit Trivialization, the type subscript, and use infix notion when no confusion can arise.

We invariably furnish expressions with procedural structured meanings, which are explicated as TIL constructions. The analysis of an unambiguous empirical sentence thus consists in discovering the logical construction encoded by a given sentence. The *TIL method of analysis* consists of three steps:

1) *Type-theoretical analysis*, i.e., assigning types to the objects that receive mention in the analysed sentence.
2) *Type-theoretical synthesis*, i.e., combining the constructions of the objects ad (1) in order to construct the proposition of type $o_{\tau\omega}$ denoted by the whole sentence.
3) *Type-theoretical checking*, i.e. checking whether the proposed analysans is type-theoretically coherent.

To illustrate the method, we analyse the stock example "The King of France is bald" *à la* Strawson.

First, type-theoretical analysis. The sentence mentions these objects. *King_of*/$(\iota\iota)_{\tau\omega}$ is an empirical function that dependently on $\langle w, t\rangle$-pairs assigns to one individual (a country) another individual (its king); *France*/ι; *King_of_France*/$\iota_{\tau\omega}$; *Bald*/$(o\iota)_{\tau\omega}$.

For the sake of simplicity, I will demonstrate the steps (2) and (3) simultaneously. In the second step we combine the *constructions* of the objects obtained n the first step in order to construct the proposition (of type $o_{\tau\omega}$) denoted by the whole sentence. Since we intend to arrive at the *literal* analysis of the sentence, the objects denoted by the semantically simple expressions are constructed by their Trivializations: $^0King\_of$, ^0France, ^0Bald. In order to construct the office *King_of_France*, we have to combine $^0King\_of$ and ^0France. The function *King_of* must be extensionalized first *via* the Composition $^0King\_of_{wt} \rightarrow_v (\iota\iota)$, and the result is then applied to *France*; we get [$^0King\_of_{wt}\,^0France$] $\rightarrow_v \iota$. Abstracting over the values of w and t we obtain the Closure that constructs the office: $\lambda w \lambda t$ [$^0King\_of_{wt}\,^0France$] $\rightarrow \iota_{\tau\omega}$. But the property of being bald cannot be ascribed to an individual office. Instead it is ascribed to the individual (if any) occupying the office. Thus the office has to be subjected to intensional descent first: $\lambda w \lambda t$ [$^0King\_of_{wt}\,^0France$]$_{wt}$ $\rightarrow_v \iota$. The property itself has to be extensionalized as well: $^0Bald_{wt}$. By Composing these two constructions, we obtain either a truth-value (**T** or **F**) or nothing, according as the King of France is, or is not, bald, or does not exist, respectively. Finally, by abstracting over the values of the variables w and t, we construct the proposition:

$$\lambda w \lambda t\ [^0Bald_{wt}\ \lambda w \lambda t\ [^0King\_of_{wt}\,^0France]_{wt}]$$

This construction is assigned as its meaning to the Strawsonian variant of the sentence "The King of France is bald". So much for the basic notions of TIL and its method of analysis.

4 Definite descriptions: Strawsonian or Russellian?

Now I am going to propose a solution to the Strawson-Russell standoff. In other words, I am going to analyse the phenomena of presupposition and entailment connected with using definite descriptions with supposition *de dicto* or *de re*, and I will show how the topic-focus distinction determines which of the two cases applies.

4.1 Topic-focus ambiguity

When used in a communicative act, an atomic sentence communicates something (the focus *F*) about something (the topic *T*). Thus the schematic structure of an atomic sentence is *F(T)*. The topic *T* of a sentence *S* is often associated with a presupposition *P* of *S* such that *P* is entailed both by *S* and *non-S*. On the other hand, the clause in the focus usually occasions a mere entailment of some *P* by *S*.[13]

To give an example, consider the sentence "Our defeat was caused by John". There are two possible readings of this sentence. Taken one way, the sentence is about our defeat, conveying the snippet of information that it was caused by John. In such a situation the sentence is associated with the presupposition that we were defeated. Indeed, the negated form of the sentence, "Our defeat was not caused by John", also implies that we were defeated. Thus 'our defeat' is the topic and 'was caused by John' the focus clause. Taken the other way, the sentence is about the topic John, ascribing to him the property that he caused our defeat (focus). Now the scenario of truly asserting the negated sentence can be, for instance, the following. Though it is true that John has a reputation for being rather a bad player, Paul was in excellent shape and so we won. Or, another scenario is thinkable. We were defeated, only not because of John but because the whole team performed poorly. Hence, our being defeated is not presupposed by this reading, it is only entailed.

Schematically, if $\models$ is the relation of entailment, then the logical difference between a mere entailment and a presupposition is this:

P is a *presupposition* of *S*:   *(S $\models$ P)* and *(non-S $\models$ P)*
Thus if *P* is not true, then *neither S nor non-S* is true. Hence, *S* has no truth-value.

P is *only entailed* by *S*: *(S $\models$ P)* and neither *(non-S $\models$ P)* nor *(non-S $\models$ non-P)*
Hence if *S* is not true we cannot deduce anything about the truth-value of *P*.

---

[13] See (Hajičová 2008) or (Gundel 1999).

4.2 The King of France revisited

Above we analyzed the sentence "The King of France is bald" on its perhaps most natural reading as predicating the property of being bald (the focus) of the individual (if any) that is the present King of France (the topic). Yet there is another, albeit less natural reading of the sentence. Imagine that the sentence is uttered in a situation where we are talking about baldness, and somebody asks "Who is bald?" The answer might be "Well, among those who are bald there is the present King of France". If you receive such an answer, you most probably protest, "This cannot be true, for there is no King of France now". On such a reading the sentence is about baldness (topic) claiming that this property is instantiated, among others, by the King of France (focus). Since there are no rigorous grammatical rules in English to distinguish between the two variants, the input of our *logical* analysis is the result of a *linguistic* analysis, where the topic and focus of a sentence are made explicit.[14] In this paper I mark the topic clause in italics. The two readings of the above sentence are:

(S) "*The King of France* is bald" (Strawsonian)
(R) "The King of France is *bald*" (Russellian).

The analysis of (S) is as above: $\lambda w \lambda t \, [^0Bald_{wt} \, \lambda w \lambda t \, [^0King\_of_{wt} \, {}^0France]_{wt}]$.

The meaning of 'the King of France', *viz.* $\lambda w \lambda t \, [^0King\_of_{wt} \, {}^0France]$, occurs in (S) with *de re* supposition, because the object of predication is the unique *value* in the chosen $\langle w, t \rangle$-pair of evaluation of the office.[15] To construct this value (if any), the office must be extensionalized. This is achieved in (S) by Composition $\lambda w \lambda t \, [^0King\_of_{wt} \, {}^0France]_{wt}$.

The following *two de re principles* are satisfied: the principle of *existential presupposition* and the principle of *substitution of co-referential* expressions. Thus the following arguments are valid (though not sound):

The King of France is (not) bald
The King of France exists

The King of France is bald
The King of France is Louis XVI
Louis XVI is bald

To prove the validity of the first argument, we need to analyse its conclusion "The King of France exists". In TIL (non-trivial) existence is explicated as a property of intensions to be instantiated in a given $\langle w, t \rangle$-pair of evaluation.[16] Thus to say that unicorns do not exist is tantamount to saying that at the given world w and

---

[14] For instance, in the Prague Dependency Treebank for the Czech language, the tectogrammatical representation contains the semantic structure of sentences with topic-focus annotators. For details, see http://ufal.mff.cuni.cz/pdt2.0/.

[15] For details on the analysis of *de dicto* vs. *de re* supposition within TIL framework, see (Duží *et al.*, 2010), esp. §§ 1.5.2 and 2.6.2, and also (Duží 2004).

[16] For details see (Duží *et al.*, 2010), § 2.3.

How to unify Russellian and Strawsonian definite descriptions

time t the property of being a unicorn has empty class of individuals as its extension. Similarly, that the King of France does not exist means that the office of the King of France is vacant at the world and time of evaluation.

Thus in our case we have $Exist/(o\iota_{\tau\omega})_{\tau\omega}$, the property of an office's being occupied at a given world/time pair that is defined as follows:

$^0Exist =_{of} \lambda w \lambda t \, \lambda c \, [^0\exists \lambda x \, [x =_i c_{wt}]]$.

Types: $\exists/(o(o\iota))$; $c \rightarrow_v \iota_{\tau\omega}$; $x \rightarrow_v \iota$; $=_{of}/(o(o\iota_{\tau\omega})_{\tau\omega}(o\iota_{\tau\omega})_{\tau\omega})$: the identity of properties of individual offices; $=_i/(o\iota\iota)$: the identity of individuals, $x \rightarrow_v \iota$.

We introduce *Louis*/ι, *Empty*/$(o(o\iota))$: the singleton containing the empty set of individuals, and *Improper*/$(o*_1)_{\tau\omega}$: the property of constructions of being v-improper at a given $\langle w, t\rangle$-pair; the other types are as above. Then for any $\langle w, t\rangle$-pair the following proof steps are truth-preserving:

(a) *existence*

1) $(\neg)[^0Bald_{wt} \, \lambda w \lambda t \, [^0King\_of_{wt} \, ^0France]_{wt}]$ Ø
2) $\neg[^0Improper_{wt} \, ^0[\lambda w \lambda t \, [^0King\_of_{wt} \, ^0France]_{wt}]]$ by Def. 2, iii)
3) $\neg[^0Empty \, \lambda x \, [x =_i [\lambda w \lambda t \, [^0King\_of_{wt} \, ^0France]]_{wt}]]$ by Def. 2, iv)
4) $[^0\exists \lambda x \, [x =_i [\lambda w \lambda t \, [^0King\_of_{wt} \, ^0France]]_{wt}]]$ EG
7) $[^0Exist_{wt} \, [\lambda w \lambda t \, [^0King\_of_{wt} \, ^0France]]]$ by def. of *Exist*

Remark. Note that in step (2) the property of being *Improper* of type $(o*_1)_{\tau\omega}$ is applied to the *construction* $[\lambda w \lambda t \, [^0King\_of_{wt} \, ^0France]_{wt}]$ of type $*_1$ that is supplied here by its Trivialisation $^0[\lambda w \lambda t \, [^0King\_of_{wt} \, ^0France]_{wt}]$ belonging to type $*_2$. On the other hand in step (3) *Empty* of type $(o(o\iota))$ is applied to the set of individuals constructed here by $\lambda x \, [x =_i [\lambda w \lambda t \, [^0King\_of_{wt} \, ^0France]]_{wt}]$. These two steps are necessary in order to existentially generalize in step (4). In the logic of partial functions such as TIL we cannot carelessly generalize before proving that the set to which existential quantifier is applied is non-empty.

(b) *substitution*:

1) $[^0Bald_{wt} \, \lambda w \lambda t \, [^0King\_of_{wt} \, ^0France]_{wt}]$ Ø
2) $[^0Louis =_i \lambda w \lambda t \, [^0King\_of_{wt} \, ^0France]_{wt}]$ Ø
3) $[^0Bald_{wt} \, ^0Louis]$ substitution of identicals

As explained above, the sentence (R) is not associated with the presupposition that the present King of France should exist, because 'the King of France' occurs now in the focus clause. The truth and falsity conditions of the Russellian "The King of France is *bald*" are as follows:

- True, if and only if among those who are bald there is the King of France.
- False, if and only if among those who are bald there is no King of France (either because the King's office is not occupied, or its occupant is not bald).

Thus the two readings (S) and (R) have different *truth*-conditions, and they are not equivalent, albeit they are co-entailing. The reason is this. Trivially, by definition a valid argument is *truth-preserving from premises to conclusion*. However, due to partiality, the entailment relation may fail to be *falsity-preserving from conclusion to premises*. As a consequence, if A, B are constructions of propositions such that $A \models B$ and $B \models A$, then A, B are not necessarily equivalent in the sense of constructing the same proposition. Though the propositions take the truth-value **T** at exactly the same world/times, they may differ in such a way that at some $\langle w, t \rangle$-pair(s) one takes the value **F** while the other is undefined. The pair of meanings of (S) and (R) is an example of such co-entailing, yet non-equivalent hyperpropositions.

Next I am going to analyse (R). TIL makes it possible to avoid the other objections against Russell's analysis as well. The Russellian rephrasing of the sentence "The King of France is *bald*" is this: "There is a unique individual such that he is the King of France and he is bald". This sentence expresses the construction[17]

(R*) $\qquad \lambda w \lambda t \, [^0\exists \lambda x \, [x =_i [\lambda w \lambda t \, [^0King\_of_{wt} \, ^0France]_{wt}] \wedge [^0Bald_{wt} \, x]]]$.

TIL analysis of the 'Russellian rephrasing' does not deprive 'the King of France' of its meaning. The meaning is invariably, in all contexts, the Closure $\lambda w \lambda t \, [^0King\_of_{wt} \, ^0France]$. Moreover, even the main objection that Russell simply gets the truth-conditions wrong if there is no King of France is irrelevant, because in (R*) the Closure $\lambda w \lambda t \, [^0King\_of_{wt} \, ^0France]$ occurs intensionally (that is *de dicto*) unlike in the analysis of (S) where it occurs extensionally (*de re*).[18] The existential quantifier ∃ applies to *sets* of individuals rather than a particular individual. The proposition constructed by (R*) is true if the *set* of individuals who are bald contains the individual who occupies the office of King of France, otherwise it is simply false. The truth conditions specified by (R*) are Russellian. Thus we might be content with (R*) as an adequate analysis of the Russellian reading (R). Yet we should not be. The reason is this. Russell's analysis has another defect; it does not comply with *Carnap's principle of subject-matter*, which states, roughly, that only those entities that receive mention in a sentence can become constituents of its meaning.[19] In other words, (R*) is not the literal analysis of the sentence "The King of France is *bald*", because existence and conjunction do not receive mention in the sentence. I am going to propose this literal analysis below. Yet before doing so, I must tackle still another issue in which Russell and Strawson differ, namely the problem of *negation*.

From a logical point of view, the two readings differ in the way their respective *negated* form is obtained. Whereas the Strawsonian negated form is "The *King of France* is *not* bald", which obviously lacks a truth-value at those $\langle w, t \rangle$-pairs where the royal office is not occupied, the Russellian negated form is "It is not true that the King of France is bald", which is true at those $\langle w, t \rangle$-pairs where the office is not occupied. Thus in the Strawsonian case the property of not being bald is ascribed to the individual, if any, that occupies the royal office. On the other hand, in the Russellian case the property of not being true is ascribed to the whole proposition that the King is bald, and thus (the same meaning of) the description

---

[17] Note that in TIL we do not need the construction corresponding to $\forall y \, (Fy \supset x=y)$ specifying the uniqueness of the King of France, because it is inherent in the meaning of 'the King of France'. The meaning of definite descriptions like 'the King of France' is a construction of an individual office of type $\iota_{\tau\omega}$ occupied in each $\langle w, t \rangle$-pair by at most one individual.

[18] For the definition of extensional, intensional and hyperintensional occurrence of a construction, see (Duží et al., 2010, § 2.6).

[19] See (Carnap 1947, §24.2, §26) and (Duží et al, 2010, §2.1.1).

'the King of France' occurs with *de dicto* supposition. In order to ascribe the property of being true to the whole proposition, we apply the propositional property *True*/(oo$_{\tau\omega}$)$_{\tau\omega}$ defined as follows: Let *P* be a propositional construction (*P*/*$_n$ → o$_{\tau\omega}$). Then [^{0}*True*$_{wt}$ *P*] *v*-constructs **T** iff *P*$_{wt}$ *v*-constructs **T**, otherwise **F**.[20] Now the analysis of the sentence (R) is this construction:

(R') $\lambda w \lambda t$ [^{0}*True*$_{wt}$ $\lambda w \lambda t$ [^{0}*Bald*$_{wt}$ $\lambda w \lambda t$ [^{0}*King_of*$_{wt}$ ^{0}*France*]$_{wt}$]]

Neither (R') nor its negation

(R'_neg) $\lambda w \lambda t$ $\neg$[^{0}*True*$_{wt}$ $\lambda w \lambda t$ [^{0}*Bald*$_{wt}$ $\lambda w \lambda t$ [^{0}*King_of*$_{wt}$ ^{0}*France*]$_{wt}$]]

entails that the King of France exists, which is just as it should be. (R'_neg) constructs the proposition *non-P* that takes the truth-value **T** if the proposition that the King of France is bald takes the value **F** (because the King of France is not bald) or is undefined (because the King of France does not exist).

To adduce a more natural example of topic/focus ambiguity, consider another sample sentence:

(1) "*The King of France* visited London yesterday."

The topic phrase of (1) is 'the King of France'. Hence the sentence ascribes to the holder (if any) of the royal office at the world/time pair of evaluation the property of having visited London yesterday (the focus). Thus both (1) and its negation share the presupposition that the King of France actually exist *now* (that is, at the time of evaluation). If this presupposition fails to be satisfied, then neither of the propositions expressed by (1) and its negation "*The King of France* did not visit London yesterday" has a truth-value.

The situation is different in the case of the sentence (2):

(2) "*London* was visited by the King of France yesterday."

Now the property (the focus) of having been visited by the King of France yesterday is predicated of London (the topic). The existence of the King of France at the time of evaluation is presupposed neither by (2) nor by its negation. The sentence can be read as "Among the visitors of London yesterday was the then King of France". The existence of the King of France *yesterday* is only *entailed* by (2) and *not presupposed*.[21] My analyses respect these conditions.

Let *Yesterday*/(($\omicron\tau$)τ) be the function that associates a given time *t* with the time interval that is yesterday with respect to *t*; *Visit*/(o$\iota\iota$)$_{\tau\omega}$; *King_of*/($\iota\iota$)$_{\tau\omega}$; *France*/ι; $\exists$/(o(oτ)).

The analysis of (1) comes down to

---

[20] There are two other propositional properties of the same type, namely *False* and *Undefined*: [^{0}*False*$_{wt}$ *P*] *v*-constructs the truth-value **T** iff [$\neg P_{wt}$] *v*-constructs **T**, otherwise **F**. [^{0}*Undef*$_{wt}$ *P*] *v*-constructs the truth-value **T** iff [$\neg$[^{0}*True*$_{wt}$*P*] $\wedge$ $\neg$[^{0}*False*$_{wt}$*P*]] *v*-constructs **T**, otherwise **F**.

[21] Von Fintel (2004) disregards this reading, saying that any sentence containing 'the King of France' comes with the presupposition that the King of France exist *now*. In my opinion, this is because he considers only the *neutral* reading, thus disregarding topic-focus ambiguities.

(1*) $\lambda w \lambda t$ [λx [$^0\exists \lambda t^*$[[[$^0Yesterday\ t$] t^*] $\wedge$
[$^0Visit_{wt^*}\ x\ ^0London$]]] $\lambda w \lambda t$ [$^0King\_of_{wt}\ ^0France$]$_{wt}$]

In (1*) the royal office is extensionalized with respect to the world w and the time t of evaluation. At such $\langle w, t \rangle$-pairs at which the office is not occupied the proposition constructed by (1*) has no truth-value, because the extensionalization of the office yields no individual, the Composition $\lambda w \lambda t$ [$^0King\_of_{wt}\ ^0France$]$_{wt}$ being v-improper. We have the Strawsonian case of the King's existence being presupposed. On the other hand, the sentence (2) expresses

(2*) $\lambda w \lambda t$ [$^0\exists \lambda t^*$[[[$^0Yesterday\ t$] t^*] $\wedge$
[$^0Visit_{wt^*}\ \lambda w \lambda t$ [$^0King\_of_{wt}\ ^0France$]$_{wt^*}\ ^0London$]]]

In (2*) the royal office is extensionalized with respect to world w and time t^* belonging to the interval [$^0Yesterday\ t$]. If the office goes vacant for all such t^* the Composition $\lambda w \lambda t$ [$^0King\_of_{wt}\ ^0France$]$_{wt^*}$ is v-improper for any t^* belonging to [$^0Yesterday\ t$]. Hence the time interval v-constructed by the Closure λt^*[[[$^0Yesterday\ t$] t^*] $\wedge$ [$^0Visit_{wt^*}\ \lambda w \lambda t$ [$^0King\_of_{wt}\ ^0France$]$_{wt^*}\ ^0London$]] is empty and the existential quantifier takes this interval to **F**. On the other hand, at such a $\langle w, t \rangle$-pair at which the proposition constructed by (2*) is true, the Composition [$^0\exists \lambda t^*$[[[$^0Yesterday\ t$] t^*] $\wedge$ [$^0Visit_{wt^*}\ \lambda w \lambda t$ [$^0King\_of_{wt}\ ^0France$]$_{wt^*}\ ^0London$]]] v-constructs **T**. This means that the second conjunct v-constructs **T** as well and the Composition $\lambda w \lambda t$ [$^0King\_of_{wt}\ ^0France$]$_{wt^*}$ is not v-improper. Thus the royal office is occupied *at some time* t^* belonging to [$^0Yesterday\ t$]. This is as it should be, because (2*) *only entails the existence* of the King of France *yesterday*. We have the Russellian case: the meaning of 'the King of France' occurs with *de dicto* supposition with respect to the temporal parameter t.

5 Conclusion

In this paper I demonstrated that both the proponents of Russell's quantificational analysis and of Strawson's referential analysis of definite descriptions are partly right and partly wrong, because sentences of the form "The F is a G" are systematically ambiguous. Their ambivalence stems from different topic-focus articulation, and I brought out the *semantic*, as opposed to pragmatic, character of this ambivalence. I showed that a definite description occurring in the topic of a sentence with *de re* supposition corresponds to the Strawsonian analysis of definite descriptions, while a definite description occurring in the focus with *de dicto* supposition corresponds to the Russellian analysis. While the clause standing in topic position triggers a presupposition, a focus clause usually only entails rather than presupposes another proposition. The procedural semantics of TIL provides rigorous analyses such that sentences differing only in their topic-focus articulation are assigned different constructions producing different propositions (truth-conditions) and having different consequences.

Moreover, the proposed analysis of the Russellian reading does not deprive definite descriptions of their meaning. Just the opposite; 'the F' receives a context-invariant meaning, which is the construction of an individual office. What is dependent on context is the way this (one and the same) construction is used. Thus I also demonstrated that Donnellan-style referential and attributive uses of an occurrence of 'the *F*' do not bring about a shift of meaning of 'the *F*'. Instead, one and the same context-invariant meaning is a constituent of different procedures that behave in logically different ways.

Acknowledgments. This research was funded by the internal grant agency of VSB-TU of Ostrava, project No. SP2013/207 "Application of artificial intelligence in process-knowledge mining, modelling and management". The present paper is a revised and improved version of a part of the book chapter Duží (2012). I am grateful to an anonymous reviewer for valuable comments that improved to quality of the paper.

References

Carnap, R. (1947). *Meaning and Necessity*, Chicago: Chicago University Press.
Donnellan, K. S., (1966). Reference and definite descriptions, *Philosophical Review*, vol. 77, 281-304.
Duží, M. (2012). Resolving Topic-Focus Ambiguities in Natural Language. In *Semantics in Action – Applications and Scenarios*, Muhammad Tanvir Afzal (ed.), Croatia: InTech Europe, 2012, pp. 239-266.
Duží M. (2004). Intensional Logic and the Irreducible Contrast between *de dicto* and *de re*. *Profil*, vol. 5, No. 1, pp. 1-34, ISSN 1212-9097.
http://profil.muni.cz/01_2004/duzi_de_dicto_de_re.pdf
Duží M., Jespersen B. and Materna P. (2010). *Procedural Semantics for Hyperintensional Logic. Foundations and Applications of Trasnsparent Intensional Logic*. Berlin: Springer, series Logic, Epistemology, and the Unity of Science, vol. 17, 2010.
Duží M., Jespersen B. and Materna P. (2010a). The Logos of Semantic Structure. In: *Philosophy of Language and Linguistics*, vol. 1: The Formal Turn. P. Stalmaszczyk (ed.). Frankfurt: Ontos Verlag, pp. 85-102.
Fintel, Kai von (2004). Would you believe it? The King of France is Back! (Presuppositions and Truth-Value Intuitions). In: *Descriptions and Beyond*, Reimer, M., Bezuidenhout, A. (eds.), Oxford: Clarendon Press, ISBN 0-19-927051-1, pp. 315 – 341.
Gundel, J. K. (1999). Topic, focus and the grammar pragmatics interface. In *Proceedings of the 23rd Annual Penn Linguistics Colloquium. Penn Working Papers in Linguistics*, vol. 6.1, J. Alexander, N.Han and M. Minnick (eds.), pp. 185-200.
Hajičová, E. (2008). What we are talking about and what we are saying about it. In: *Computational Linguistics and Intelligent Text Processing*, A. Gelbukh (Ed.), Berlin, Heidelberg: Springer-Verlag LNCS, vol. 4919, 241-262.
Jespersen, B. (2008). Predication and extensionalization. *Journal of Philosophical Logic*, vol. 37, pp. 479 – 499.
Jespersen, B. (2010). How hyper are hyperpropositions?, *Language and Linguistics Compass*, vol. 4, pp. 96-106.
Jespersen, B. (2012). Recent work on structured meaning and propositional unity, *Philosophy Compass*, vol. 7, pp. 620-30.
Kripke, S., (1977). Speaker's reference and semantic reference. In: *Contemporary Perspectives in the Philosophy of Language*, French, Uehling and Wettstein (eds.), Minneapolis: University of Minnestoa Press, p. 6-27.
Ludlow, P. (2007). Descriptions. Available from http://plato.stanford.edu/entries/descriptions/#2.
Neale, S., (1990). *Descriptions*. Cambridge: MIT Press Books.
Russell, B. (1905). On denoting. *Mind* vol. 14, pp. 479-493.
Russell, B., (1957). Mr. Strawson on referring, *Mind* vol. 66, pp. 385-389.

Strawson, P. F. (1950). On referring, *Mind* vol. 59, pp. 320-334.
Strawson, P.F. (1952). *Introduction to Logical Theory*, London: Methuen.
Strawson, P.F., (1964). Identifying reference and truth-values, *Theoria* vol. 3, pp. 96-118.
Tichý, P. (1988). *The Foundations of Frege's Logic*, Berlin, New York: De Gruyter.
Tichý, P. (2004). *Collected Papers in Logic and Philosophy*, V. Svoboda, B. Jespersen, C. Cheyne (eds.), Prague: Filosofia, Czech Academy of Sciences, and Dunedin: University of Otago Press.

An Intensional Solution to the Bike Puzzle of Intentional Identity

Bjørn Jespersen

Abstract In a 2005 paper Ólafur Páll Jónsson presents a puzzle that turns on intentional identity and definite descriptions. He considers eight solutions and rejects them all, thus leaving the puzzle unsolved. In this paper I put forward a solution. The puzzle is this. Little Lotta wants most of all a bicycle for her birthday, but she gets none. Distracted by the gifts she does receive, she at first does not think about the bike. But when seeing her tricycle, she is reminded of the bike. The question is how we are to analyse these two occurrences of 'the bike' in the absence of a unique bike that Lotta wants. So the semantics of 'the bike' needs to be spelt out, and it must be made explicit what the complements of Lotta's attitudes are. My analysis shows that the attributer's usage of 'the bike' blurs the distinction between a second-order and a first-order intension (a property concept and a property, respectively). My solution can be summed up in this two-premise argument. (*a*) In the state-of-affairs *S*, the property of being a bike is the extension of the property concept *the property such that Lotta wants an instance of it more than any other*; (*b*) in *S*, Lotta does not think about/is reminded of the property that she wants an instance of more than any other; (*c*) therefore, in *S* Lotta does not think about/is reminded of the property of being a bike. This solution requires looking beyond the confines of denotational semantics, which all of Jónsson's eight solution candidates belong to.

This chapter originally appeared in Philosophia (2011), 39, pp. 297–307.

An intensional solution to the bike puzzle of intentional identity

Introduction

In his (2005) Jónsson presents a puzzle that involves intentional identity and definite descriptions. He considers eight solutions and rejects them all, thus leaving the puzzle unsolved. In this paper I put forward a solution. The puzzle is this. Little Lotta wants most of all a bicycle for her birthday, but she gets none. Distracted by the gifts she does receive, she at first does not think about the bike. But when seeing her tricycle, she is reminded of the bike. The question is how we are to understand these two occurrences of 'the bike' in the absence of one particular bike that Lotta wants. We must answer the question what, if anything, these two occurrences of 'the bike' refer to, as well as the question what are the complements of Lotta's notional attitudes of wanting, forgetting about, and being reminded of the bike.

Oddly enough, Jónsson himself does not point out that the shift from "...a bike..." to "...the bike..." is more than reminiscent of Peter Geach's 1967 Hob/Nob puzzle, in which there is a shift from "...a witch..." to "...the witch..." (phrased originally as "...she (the same witch)..."), and one of Walter Edelberg's 1995 Arsky/Barsky puzzles, in which there is a transition from "...someone murdered Smith..." to "...he [the murderer]..." (see 1995, p. 318, for the asymmetry variant). The most important common feature between Geach's puzzle and Jónsson's is how to preserve intentional (as opposed to 'actual') identity in the apparent absence of a common focus. Geach's puzzle is that if there are no witches, how can Hob and Nob possibly be intentionally related to the same witch? In Lotta's case the problem is to preserve the intentional identity between what she first wants most of all, later forgets about and is even later reminded of, when there is no particular bicycle that she wants most of all, forgets about and is reminded of. On all three occasions Lotta is intentionally related to something; only what would that be? Geach would in this case speak of 'one person on different occasions [having] attitudes with a common focus' (1967, p. 627). One noteworthy difference, though, is that Geach's own case is synchronic and involves two agents, while Jónsson's is diachronic and involves one agent. Edelberg (2006) would call Jónsson's a case of *intra*subjective intentional identity, unlike Geach's, which concerns *inter*subjective intentional identity. Because a single-agent variant, Jónsson's is a simpler intentional-identity puzzle than Geach's and can be solved independently of the latter being solved. I leave it open whether the remedies for Jónsson's case carry over to Geach's.

Exposition

Jónsson claims that his puzzle 'doesn't fit any philosophical theory' (*ibid.*, p. 932). I beg to differ. We already do have everything we need in order to present a purely semantic solution to the puzzle. My solution requires more machinery than what Jónsson considers, though. My point of departure is (a) that we may introduce not only first-order intensions (properties of individuals, as it happens), but also higher-order intensions (intensions whose range is properties of individuals, as it happens); (b) that we may bind variables ranging over properties of individuals, possible worlds, and times; (c) that we may bind variables occurring within attitude contexts; and (d) that we need to include into the analysis a third sentence, which figures in

An intensional solution to the bike puzzle of intentional identity

Jónsson's set-up of the puzzle without being part of the puzzle proper as formulated by Jónsson.[1]

My solution is an intensionalist ('neo-Fregean') one in the fashion of, e.g., Alonzo Church, Pavel Tichý, and Graeme Forbes.[2] It can be summed up in this two-premise argument. (*a*) In the state-of-affairs *S*, the property of being a bike is the extension of the property concept *the individual-property such that Lotta wants an instance of it more than any other*; (*b*) in *S*, Lotta does not think about/is reminded of the individual-property that she wants an instance of more than any other; (*c*) therefore, in *S* Lotta does not think about/is reminded of the property of being a bike. The puzzle arises because the attributer's usage of 'the bike' blurs the distinction between a second-order and a first-order intension (a property concept and a property, respectively).[3] This solution squares with none of Jónsson's, all of which belong to the paradigm of denotational semantics, since he assumes that if 'the bike' refers to an extra-linguistic entity then its referent must be a *particular*, a bike in the case at hand. But my analysis borrows elements from his options (III) and (VIII), especially the former. Option (III) says, roughly, that 'the bike' refers anaphorically to some previously introduced expression. Option (VIII) says, roughly, that (1) and (2) below are slapdash descriptions of Lotta's attitudes and must be replaced by more careful ones.

The puzzle is based on a children's story, but I follow Jónsson in pretending that we are not analysing fictional but factual discourse. Here is the puzzle in full.

> In one of her stories, Astrid Lindgren tells us about Lotta, who most of all wanted a bike for her fifth birthday. But she did not get one. Instead she got some lovely gifts: a red purse, a new swing, a picture book and more. And she really liked the gifts and took a walk down the street showing off the red purse. And at that point Astrid Lindgren tells us that:
>
> (1)   Lotta was in a good mood, and did not think about the bike.
>
> But when Lotta returned home she saw the old tricycle which she wanted so much to be replaced by a real bike. And then:
>
> (2)   Lotta was reminded of the bike and got angry.
>
> How shall we understand the definite description 'the bike' in these sentences?

(*Ibid.*, p. 929.)

I abbreviate Jónsson's sentences to get rid of tenses and the conjuncts "Lotta is [was] in a good mood" and "Lotta gets [got] angry", all of which are irrelevant to the puzzle. The pruned sentences are these.

(1)   "Lotta does not think about the bike."
(2)   "Lotta is reminded of the bike."

---

[1] 'Property of individuals' and 'individual-property' are used interchangeably. Properties are intended as universals and not as tropes, such that they may have several instances.
[2] I hasten to add that I am not assuming that the solution to Jónsson's puzzle *must* be in a (neo-) Fregean vein. I merely wish to demonstrate that, and how, such a framework affords a solution, unlike any of those that Jónsson (rightly) rejects.
[3] By 'concept' I intend Church's notion of concept. See, e.g., his (1993).

An intensional solution to the bike puzzle of intentional identity

The main problem disqualifying Jónsson's options is that, as he points out, 'the bike' is not matched by a unique descriptum. There is no one bike such that Lotta wants, thinks about and is reminded of this particular bike and none other. So apparently 'the bike' lacks a reference altogether. Yet Lotta obviously wants, thinks about and is reminded of something. And the function of 'the bike' is evidently to pick out this something, whatever it may be. In fact, unless this much is granted, Jónsson's puzzle simply does not arise.

Jónsson's options fail to include a unique descriptum for failure to encompass a sentence preceding (1) and (2). The sentence in question is this.

(0) "Lotta most of all wants a bike."

Let $X = \{x_1, x_2, \ldots, x_n\}$ be the set of all the sorts of things that Lotta wants for her birthday. Of all the x_i Lotta has a favourite, to wit, the sort of thing she wants more than any other. If her favourite is x_1 then for all x_i different from x_1, Lotta prefers x_1 to x_i. For all the puzzle tells us about Lotta's wishes, any individual vehicle will be just as fine as any other, as long as it is a bicycle and not a tricycle. So we need to abstract from individual bicycles and focus instead on what all bicycles have in common, which is the *property* of being a bicycle. The analysis of (0) is this.

(0.1) "The property of being a bicycle is the unique property f such that for all properties g, $g \neq f$, if Lotta wants an instance of g then Lotta prefers an instance of f to an instance of g."

Lotta's attitude relatum is an *intensional* entity.[4] For instance, someone seeking the fountain of youth is not related to an individual; firstly, because there may be no fountain of youth (in which case the process of seeking could not get off the ground); secondly, because an individual-concept, rather than an individual, is what guides their search by specifying a uniqueness condition; thirdly, in order to block invalid substitutions.[5]

The elements of X are properties, not instances of properties. The shift from individuals to properties holds the key to understanding 'the bike' as it occurs in (1) and (2). What happens is that Astrid Lindgren, the attributer, telescopes 'the sort of thing that Lotta wants most of all, which is an instance of the property of being a bike' into 'the bike'. Linguistic evidence for this claim is provided by this exchange in colloquial English:

A. "Lotta wanted a bike for her birthday."
B. "And did she get the bike?"

Here 'the bike' cannot refer to any individual bike. The only reasonable interpretation seems to be that 'the bike' is used as a shorthand for something like 'the kind of thing you just said she wanted, namely a bike'. Otherwise it is not obvious how the 'the' in 'the bike' might enter the discourse. The occurrence of 'the bike' ties together the discourse, just as Geach says 'the book' does in, "The only man who ever stole a book from Snead made a lot of money by selling the book".

---

[4] Cf. Church (1951, p. 111, n. 14), (1956, p. 8, n. 20).
[5] For instance, on an extensionalist interpretation of notional attitudes, since Oedipus sought the slayer of Laios, and Oedipus was it, Oedipus sought Oedipus [himself].

Geach comments that 'the book' does not fix a particular book in the environment, but points back to the antecedent phrase 'a book' (1972, p. 97). If spelt out, 'the book' is used as a shorthand for something like 'the book that was the only ever to be stolen from Snead'.

This construal of 'the bike' ostensibly suggests analysing (1) and (2) as follows.

(1.1) "Lotta does not think about the sort of thing that she wants most of all, which is an instance of the property of being a bicycle."

(2.1) "Lotta is reminded of the sort of thing that she wants most of all, which is an instance of the property of being a bicycle."

But these analyses overshoot by far what the original sentences (1) and (2) express. So we need to carve (1.1) and (2.1) up into separate sentences. One sentence will express that Lotta is not thinking about/is reminded of the sort of thing she wants most of all. The other sentence will express that the property of being a bicycle is the sort of thing she most of all wants an instance of. But factoring out these sentences reveals that the individual-property of being a bicycle is not sufficient for a full analysis. We need to add a third layer on top of individuals and individual-properties, viz. *properties-in-intension*. The property of being a bicycle just happens to be the unique individual-property such that Lotta prefers an instance of it to an instance of any other individual-property. So the property *being a bicycle* just happens to be the extension of the intension *the individual-property such that Lotta prefers an instance of it to an instance of any other individual-property*. Just as Church-style individual-concepts (i.e., individuals-in-intension) will take individuals as extensions, so concepts of individual-concepts will take individual-concepts as their extensions. Similarly, a concept of individual-properties will take individual-properties as extensions.

In familiar Montague notation, trading linguistic for objectual types, if e is the type of an individual and $<s, <e, t>>$ the type of an individual-property, then a function of type $<s, <s, <e, t>>>$ maps empirical circumstances to individual-properties. Given one set of circumstances, the property that Lotta prefers an instance of is *being a bicycle*. Given another set of circumstances, the property is *being a pony*, say, or none at all. Let Φ be the second-order intension *the individual-property such that Lotta wants an instance of it more than any other*, of type $<s, <s, <e, t>>>$. Then Φ is an individual-property concept, returning for each set of empirical parameters at most one individual-property.

So what is Lotta's attitude relatum in (1) and (2)? It is the extension of Φ at S. And what is the semantics of 'the bike'? Let us distinguish between *expressing* and *referring*, as an intension-involving semantics enables us to.[6] What a term *expresses* is the intension that determines the term's extension relative to a choice of empirical parameters. The so determined extension may well be an intensional entity, though one of a lower order than the determining intension. What a term *refers to* is the intension's extension at a given empirical parameter. The semantics of 'the bike', as it occurs in (1) and (2), is that it expresses Φ and refers to $\Phi(S)$, which turns out to be *being a bicycle*.

---

[6] See Materna (2010) for the most recent statement of this distinction, and Duží (2009) for the most recent account of (empirical) definite descriptions, as elaborated in Transparent Intensional Logic.

This answer cannot be given, unless we drag (0) from the context into the analysandum proper. If we do include (0), together with properties-in-intension, we are not merely analysing free-standing, self-contained sentences, but a *text*, a complex of semantically interlocking sentences.[7] Absent the uniqueness-inducing 'most of all' in (0), the introduction of 'the bike' in (1), (2) would be unjustified, since a uniqueness condition would be presupposed without being specified. Thus, the uniqueness condition involved in the exchange between *A* and *B* above was *the kind of thing you [A] just said she [Lotta] wanted*.

We specify a uniqueness condition in the following manner. (1) and (2) will be the respective conclusions of arguments boasting two premises. The first is premise (0), to establish the identity at *S* between $\Phi(S)$ and the property of being a bike. The second is that Lotta is not thinking about/is reminded of $\Phi(S)$.

The respective arguments, in stilted prose to begin, are as follows.

First argument.

(0.1) The property *being a bicycle* is the unique property f such that for all properties g, $g \neq f$, if Lotta wants an instance of g then Lotta prefers an instance of f to an instance of g.

(1.2) Lotta does not think about the unique f such that for all properties g, $g \neq f$, if Lotta wants an instance of g then Lotta prefers an instance of f to an instance of g.

(1.3) ∴ Lotta does not think about the property *being a bicycle*.

Second argument.

(0.1) The property *being a bicycle* is the unique property f such that for all properties g, $g \neq f$, if Lotta wants an instance of g then Lotta prefers an instance of f to an instance of g.

(2.2) Lotta is reminded of the unique f such that for all properties g, $g \neq f$, if Lotta wants an instance of g then Lotta prefers an instance of f to an instance of g.

(2.3) ∴ Lotta is reminded of the property *being a bicycle*.

It is easily verified that the two arguments are modelled on Leibniz's Law. For present purposes, it is irrelevant whether Leibniz's Law holds for notional-attitude contexts. What is relevant is how to logically analyse these two arguments. The obvious choice of theory is the λ-calculus. It is the logic of functions, and intensions are (modelled as) functions. In particular, we wish to express that one type of function takes another type of function as its values. Montague's Intensional Logic is one such semantics based on the λ-calculus, but I prefer its close rival, Tichý's Transparent Intensional Logic.[8] Tichý construes an intension as a function from possible worlds to a function from times to entities. What is especially helpful about Tichý's logic is that its so-called explicit intensionalization and temporalization consists in explicitly λ-binding variables ranging over possible worlds and instants of time.[9] This way we can introduce and manipulate intensions straightaway. In particular, the extensionalization of intensions takes the form of functional

---

[7] See Ranta (1994, pp. 125ff).
[8] See Duží et al. (2010, §2.4.3).
[9] See Tichý (1971), Jespersen (2005), and Duží et al. (2010, §2.4).

application, as in [*Function Argument*], where square brackets stand for the logical operation of functional application. If 'Φ_{wt}' abbreviates '$[[\Phi w]t]$', the individual-property Φ_{wt} is the result of applying Φ to a world variable w and the result of that application to a time variable t.[10]

We begin by defining Φ. Let ι be a function that takes singletons to their respective elements and is undefined on all other sets. Let $\forall$ be a function from sets of elements of a particular type (individual-properties, in this case) to the truth-value True if the respective sets are the entire respective types and to False if not. Let *Want* be a relation-in-intension between an individual and an individual-property, such that the individual wants to obtain an instance of the property. Let *Want_More_Than* be a relation-in-intension between an individual and an ordered pair of properties <f, g>, such that the individual wants to obtain an instance of the first more than of the second. Then:

$$Def.\ \Phi = \lambda w \lambda t [\iota f [\forall g [f \neq g \wedge Want_{wt}\ Lotta\ g] \supset [Want\_More\_Than_{wt}\ Lotta\ f\ g]]]$$

This definition establishes that the (second-order) property concept Φ is identical to the (second-order) property concept *the unique individual-property such that Lotta wants an instance of it more than she wants an instance of any other individual-property that she also wants an instance of*.

Let *Bike* be the property *being a bike*. That *Bike* is the extension of Φ at some definite world/time pair <W, T> is analysed thus:

$$[Bike = \Phi_{WT}].$$

By abstracting away any particular <W, T> pairs in favour of variables ranging over possible worlds and times, we bind the variables w, t thus:

$$\lambda w \lambda t [Bike = \Phi_{wt}].$$

This yields a *proposition*; namely, the set of world/time pairs at which *Bike* is Φ_{wt}; and S is *ex hypothesi* a member of this set.[11]

That Lotta entertains an attitude *Att* to a particular individual-property F is analysed thus:

$$\lambda w \lambda t [Att_{wt}\ Lotta\ F].$$

And its negation is analysed thus:

$$\lambda w \lambda t \neg [Att_{wt}\ Lotta\ F].$$

Att is a family of relations-in-intension, such as *Thinking_about*, *Seeking*, *Finding*, and *Being_reminded_of*, between individuals (agents such as Lotta) and attitude complements, such as properties or individual-concepts. When extensionalized, Att_{wt} is a world/time-parameterized relation-in-extension, such that the application of Att_w to the elements of, e.g., ⟨*Lotta, F*⟩ yields a truth-value: it is true or

---

[10] See Jespersen (2008).
[11] If we wish to be absolutely correct, we say that $\lambda w \lambda t [Bike = \Phi_{wt}]$ yields a function from the domain of possible worlds to the co-domain of functions from times to individual-properties, such that at those worlds and times *Bike* is the extension of Φ.

An intensional solution to the bike puzzle of intentional identity

false at the given world/time of evaluation that Lotta entertains the attitude *Att* to *F*. If a negation occurs, the function ¬ trades a truth-value for a truth-value in the standard way.

Now we have everything we need to formalize the *first* and *second argument*. In fact, since they are structurally identical except for the occurrence of negation in the former, we need consider only one of them. The only ting we need to keep in mind in formalizing both arguments is that the times of the first argument are prior to those of the second. The notation would need to make this explicit in order to capture the diachronicity of Lotta's changing attitudes to the same property. The *first argument*, when fully analyzed, is this:

(0.2) $\lambda w \lambda t [Bike = \Phi_{wt}]$
(1.4) $\lambda w \lambda t [\neg [Think\_about_{wt}\ Lotta\ \Phi_{wt}]]$
(1.5) ∴ $\lambda w \lambda t [\neg [Think\_about_{wt}\ Lotta\ Bike]]$.

This completes the exposition of the solution to the bike puzzle.

Discussion

The framework within which my solution is couched is neo-*Fregean* because it distinguishes sharply between concept and instance and invariably relates an agent to a concept (*Sinn*) rather than an instance (*Bedeutung*) in attitude contexts, and neo-Fregean because, unlike Frege's own semantics, it extends the semantic schema that Frege reserves for indirect contexts to all contexts.[12] The latter tenet, of context-invariant semantics, is part and parcel of Transparent Intensional Logic, but has no direct bearing on the bike puzzle and so will not be discussed further here. The former twin tenet appears to be open to counterexamples in which my approach predicts that Lotta is related to an abstract entity (a concept) where she ought, in fact, to be related to a concrete entity (an instance).

Let me consider here two variants of this objection. The first variant is this. Suppose that on the morning of her birthday, before her parents are awake, Lotta goes up to the attic to see whether any presents for her are hidden there. We could report this event as follows:

(3) " Lotta searched for the bike."

The associated truth-condition requires that the relation *searching for* obtain between Lotta and a property, i.e. *being a bike*. However, searching in the physical world populated by concrete objects will be in vain if the object of one's search is for something that is inherently abstract. So my construal of the truth-condition of (3) would make it impossible for it ever to be true that Lotta was searching for the bike.

But this objection won't do as a *reductio* of my analysis. For sure, bikes are concrete and the property of being a bike is abstract. But the key point is that what guides Lotta's search for something concrete is something abstract. Lotta is not searching in the physical world for the property of being a bike; what she is searching for is a concrete instance of an abstract universal (*in casu* a property). What

---

[12] See Tichý (1971), (1986), and Duží et al. (2010, Ch. 1).

is going on in the attic is that Lotta is related to *the* property which is such that she wants an instance of that property more than any other property and such that Lotta is searching for *an* instance of it.

Note that if Lotta did in fact receive a bike for her birthday, rode it all day long, tucked it away in the evening, forgot about its whereabouts and went in search of it the next morning, the sentence "Lotta searched for the bike" would have meant something else, namely that she was searching for one particular instance of the property of being a bike. Still, something abstract would have guided her search for something concrete. The relevant abstract entity would have been the (Church-style) individual concept *the unique x such that x is a bike and Lotta received x for her birthday*. Before receiving a bike for her birthday, any bike would have been as good as any. After receiving a bike, this very bike is unique in being the instance of that individual concept. Without having this individual concept 'before her mind' Lotta would not be able to discriminate between the concrete bike that was her birthday present and any other concrete bike that was not.

Note also that *searching* is a non-factive notional attitude, since we may well search for what fails to exist—unlike *finding*, for we can only find what exists (cf. the contrast between *believing* and *knowing*: also falsehoods may be believed, only truths may be known). For instance, to use Church's classical example,[13] Schliemann could have sought the site of Troy even if there had been no such site, but he could not possibly have found it. Likewise, even if her parents had decided not to give her a single present, Lotta might still have searched in the attic for birthday presents. The search would have been in vain, for sure, but searching she was. The point is that the semantic analysis of (3), if embedded in Lindgren's story, needs to avoid making existential presuppositions at the level of concrete objects. The analysis does, however, require the existence of universals, to guide Lotta's search for something particular and concrete.

The second variant of the objection is this. We could describe an event of her daydreaming as follows:

(4) "Lotta wanted to be riding the bike."

Surely, what would make this sentence true is not that Lotta wanted to be riding a certain property. Instead she wanted to be riding something of a concrete nature.

Again, though, this objections fails to sharply distinguish concepts/universals/properties/abstract entities from their instances. Failure to firmly observe this distinction would suggest to me that one was still inclined to hold that 'the bike', if embedded in Lindgren's story, must serve to pick out a concrete bike. Assuming, again, that no bike is the instance of the individual concept *the unique x such that x is a bike and Lotta received x for her birthday*, what (4) means, as *per* Lindgren's story, is that the *wanting-to-ride* relation (-in-intension) relates Lotta to the property of being a bike in such a way that Lotta wants to ride *an* instance of this property more than any other property. Since no bike is the instance of that individual concept, there is no bike such that Lotta is fantasizing about riding *it*. So concrete objects are neither here nor there in a successful analysis of (4). What the analyses of

---

[13] Church (1956, p. 8, n. 20).

(3) and (4) call for are properties and property concepts, just like the analyses of the sentences considered in the previous section.

Conclusion

The answer to Jónsson's question of how we are to understand 'the bike' is that Astrid Lindgren's use of 'the bike' blurs the distinction between Φ and Φ_{wt}, which is the distinction between a concept and an instance of that concept. Once these two levels have been disentangled, the transition in Jónsson's puzzle from "…a bike…" to "…the bike…" no longer poses a semantic puzzle. As in Geach's original case, it seems, on the face of it, that there is a transition from a weaker proposition to a stronger proposition. But there is no such transition, since 'the bike' does not serve to single out some unique bike that Lotta would be intentionally related to in various ways.

Nor is it any longer obscure what the complements of Lotta's attitudes of wanting, forgetting about, being reminded of, wanting to ride, and searching for are. The complements are the same in all five cases; namely, a *property*, which happens to be the one of being a bike.[14]

References

Church, A. (1951). The need for abstract entities in semantic analysis. *American Academy of Arts and Sciences Proceedings, 80*, 100–13.
Church, A. (1956). *Introduction to mathematical logic*. Princeton: Princeton University Press.
Church, A. (1993). A revised formulation of the logic of sense and denotation. Alternative (1). *Noûs, 27*, 141–57.
Duží, M. (2009). Strawsonian vs. Russellian definite descriptions. *Organon F, 16*, 587–614.
Duží, M., Jespersen, B., & Materna, P. (2010). *Procedural semantics for hyperintensional logic: Foundations and applications of Transparent Intensional Logic. Logic, epistemology, and the unity of science* (Vol. 17). Dordrecht: Springer.
Edelberg, W. (1995). A perspectivalist semantics for the attitudes. *Noûs, 29*, 316–42.
Edelberg, W. (2006). Intrasubjective intentional identity. *Journal of Philosophy, 103*, 481–502.
Geach, P. (1967). Intentional identity. *Journal of Philosophy, 64*, 627–32. Reprinted in: *Logic Matters*, Berkely: University of California Press (1972).
Jespersen, B. (2005). Explicit intensionalization, anti-actualism, and how Smith's murderer might not have murdered Smith. *Dialectica, 59*, 285–314.
Jespersen, B. (2008). Predication and extensionalization. *Journal of Philosophical Logic, 37*, 479–99.
Jónsson, Ó. P. (2005). The bike puzzle. *Mind, 114*, 929–32.

---

[14] Versions of this paper were read as invited lectures at *Convegno internazionale LOGICA & METAFISICA*, Department of Philosophy, University of Palermo, 27-29 March 2007, and Department of Analytic Philosophy, Slovak Academy of Sciences, Bratislava, 25 June 2007. The research reported herein was carried out while affiliated with Section of Philosophy, Delft University of Technology. The research was supported by the project *GACR 401/10/0792*. I am indebted to Marie Duží, Tomis Kapitan, Rasa Paulėkaitė, Gabriel Sandu, and an anonymous referee for this journal, for valuable comments and suggestions.

Materna, P. (2010). Denotation and reference. *Organon F, 17*, 3–20.
Ranta, A. (1994). *Type-theoretical grammar*. Oxford: Clarendon.
Tichý, P. (1971). An approach to intensional analysis. *Noûs, 5*, 273–97. Reprinted in: *Collected Papers in Logic and Philosophy*, V. Svoboda, B. Jespersen, C. Cheyne (eds.), Prague: Filosofia, Czech Academy of Sciences; Dunedin: University of Otago Press (2004).
Tichý, P. (1986). Indiscernibility of identicals. *Studia Logica, 45*, 251–73. Reprinted as above.

Limiting Cases of Modal Modification: Reply to Kosterec

Bjørn Jespersen

Kosterec (2019) points out that my current theory of modal modifiers cannot deal satisfactorily with limiting cases. This note solves the problem. The form of the solution is to leave the existing theory as is and instead add a clause handling the limiting case which Kosterec brings up and another clause handling the limiting case at the other end of the spectrum.

My theory of modal modifiers, as set out in (2013), works well, as long as the argument property being modified is either (i) a purely contingent property or (ii) a contingent property with an essential core, provided the resulting modified property (MF) is not applied to an element of the essential core of F.[1] To stick with the original example of mine that Kosterec takes over, we treat this predication as a datum:

"Individual a is an alleged assassin"

Its analysis in Transparent Intensional Logic is this:

$$\lambda w \lambda t \, [[^0Alleged \, ^0Assassin]_{wt} \, ^0a]$$

$Types$: $Alleged/((o\iota)_{\tau\omega}(o\iota)_{\tau\omega})$; $Assassin/(o\iota)_{\tau\omega}$; a/ι; $w/*_1 \to_v \omega$; $t/*_1 \to_v \tau$.

---

[1] See (Duží et al. 2010, §1.4.2.1) for the definitions of *purely contingent property* and *contingent property with an essential core*. See (*ibid.*) for notions and notation.

I claim that two conclusions are forthcoming. The first conclusion is that there is some property f which a is alleged to have:

$$\lambda w \lambda t \; [^0\exists \lambda f \; [[^0Alleged\; f]_{wt}\; {^0}a]]$$

Types: $f/*_1 \to_v (\text{o}\iota)_{\tau\omega}$; $\exists/(\text{o}(\text{o}(\text{o}\iota)_{\tau\omega}))$.

This predication is non-trivial, because not all of us are being alleged to have some property or other.[2] The second conclusion is that maybe a is an assassin and maybe a is not an assassin:

$$\lambda w \lambda t \; [[^0Alleged\; {^0}Assassin]_{wt}\; {^0}a] \supset$$
$$[^0\exists \lambda w' \; [^0\exists \lambda t' \; [^0Assassin_{w't'}\; {^0}a]] \wedge {^0}\exists \lambda w'' \; [^0\exists \lambda t'' \; \neg[^0Assassin_{w''t''}\; {^0}a]]]$$

where $w' \neq w''$, $t' \neq t''$.

A dichotomy is induced over the domain of world/time pairs, such that in one half of the domain it is true that a is one of the assassins and in the other half it is false that a is among the assassins. The open question is which side of the fence a given world/time pair of evaluation comes down on. The logical behaviour that the modal modifier displays is that it oscillates, as it were, between being *subsective* and being *privative*. A subsective modifier has the effect that the modifier is eliminated and the original argument property is predicated of the individual in question. For instance, a skilful surgeon is a surgeon. A privative modifier has the effect that the predication of the privatively modified property is replaced by the boolean negation of the predication of the argument property.[3] For instance, it is not the case that a fake banknote is a banknote.

The counterexample Kosterec levels against my theory is this predicate:

'is an alleged discoverer of the highest prime number'

There is no highest prime number, hence nobody can instantiate the property of discovering the highest prime number, hence the left-hand conjunct

---

[2] See (Jespersen 2016) for the *general rule of left subsectivity*, which in (Duží et al. 2010, §4.4) was introduced under the name of *pseudo-detachment*.

[3] – in the case of *single* privation, that is. In the case of *iterated* privation, privative modifiers are replaced by the general privative modifier *Non*. See (Jespersen et al. 2017).

(from being an alleged assassin to being an assassin) is false, hence the conjunction is false, hence the inference is invalid.

When confronted with impossibilities, the strategy pursued by Transparent Intensional Logic is not to usher in impossible worlds as additional points of evaluation. Instead we introduce constructions of conditions that could not possibly be satisfied (see Duží et al. 2020). What we need here is, first of all, a construction of the impossible property of being a discoverer of the highest prime:

$$\lambda w \lambda t \; [\lambda x \; [^0 Discover_{wt} \; x \; ^0[^0\iota \lambda y \; [[^0 Prime \; y] \wedge \\ {}^0 \forall \lambda z \; [[^0 Prime \; z] \supset [^0\geq y \; z]]]]]]$$

Types: $x/*_1 \to_v \iota$; $y, z/*_1 \to_v \tau$; $Discover/(o\iota*_n)_{\tau\omega}$; $Prime/(o\tau)$; $\iota/(\tau(o\tau))$; $\forall/(o(o\tau))$; $\geq/(o\tau\tau)$.

The analysis of "a is an alleged discoverer of the highest prime" is:

$$\lambda w \lambda t \; [[^0 Alleged \; \lambda w \lambda t \; [\lambda x \; [^0 Discover_{wt} \; x \; ^0[^0\iota \lambda y \; [[^0 Prime \; y] \wedge \\ {}^0 \forall \lambda z \; [[^0 Prime \; z] \supset [^0\geq y \; z]]]]]]]]_{wt} \; ^0 a]$$

How do we eliminate *Alleged*? By invoking the fact that at no world/time pair is a, or anyone else, someone with the property of discovering the highest prime.

We are going to define the property X, which is an analytic property of ι-properties, namely the property of being necessarily uninstantiated ('empty'). Thus, its functional arguments being $F_i \in X$, *Alleged* modifies impossible empirical conditions.[4] First of all, we define $\emptyset^\iota$ as the set of empty ι-sets, whose respective characteristic functions do not return the truth-value 1 for any argument, i.e., they either return 0 or are undefined:

$$^0\emptyset^\iota =_{df} \lambda e \; [^0 \forall \lambda x \; \neg[^0 True* \; ^0[e \; x]]]$$

Types: $e/*_1 \to (o\iota)$; $\emptyset^\iota/(o(o\iota))$; $=/(o(o(o\iota))(o(o\iota)))$; $True*/(o*_n)$: the set of such constructions as v-construct 1 for every valuation v.

---

[4] I should stress that the addition to the theory of modal modifiers I have offered here still does not extend to purely arithmetical cases as expressed by predicates like 'is an alleged proof of the continuum hypothesis'. What is already clear, though, is that, *Proof* being of type $(o*_n)$, namely, a set of hyperpropositions, *Alleged'* as denoted in 'is an alleged proof' must be of type $((o*_n)(o*_n))$.

Now define X as follows:

$$^0X ='_{df} \lambda f\, [^0\forall \lambda w\, [^0\forall \lambda t\, [^0\emptyset^\iota\, f_{wt}]]]$$

Types: $X/(o(o\iota)_{\tau\omega})$; $f/*_1 \to_v (o\iota)_{\tau\omega}$; $='/(o(o(o\iota)_{\tau\omega})(o(o\iota)_{\tau\omega}))$.

A parallel definition of X, to be deployed below, is this one:

$$^0X ='_{df} \lambda f\, [^0\forall \lambda w\, [^0\forall \lambda t\, [^0\forall \lambda x\, \neg[^0True_{wt}\, \lambda w \lambda t\, [f_{wt}\, x]]]]]$$

Type: $True/(oo_{\tau\omega})_{\tau\omega}$: the empirical property of truth-conditions/$o_{\tau\omega}$ of being satisfied (i.e., returning 1) at a given world/time pair of evaluation.

Where $F \in X$, the elimination of *Alleged* proceeds as follows:

$$^0\forall \lambda w\, [^0\forall \lambda t\, [^0\forall \lambda x\, [[[^0Alleged\, ^0F]_{wt}\, x] \supset \neg[^0True_{wt}\, \lambda w \lambda t\, [^0F_{wt}\, x]]]]]$$

This clause is the solution to the problem presented by the first limiting case, which Kosterec has brought up. Of course, X has a mirror-image, Y, which is the analytic property of ι-properties of being necessarily instantiated ('trivial'):

$$^0Y ='_{df} \lambda f\, [^0\forall \lambda w\, [^0\forall \lambda t\, [^0\forall \lambda x\, [f_{wt}\, x]]]]$$

The elimination of *Alleged* now proceeds as follows, for any $G \in Y$:

$$^0\forall \lambda w\, [^0\forall \lambda t\, [^0\forall \lambda x\, [[^0Alleged\, ^0G]_{wt}\, x \supset [^0G_{wt}\, x]]]]$$

The addition of the first clause to my theory of modal modification departs from the observation that nobody and nothing could possibly instantiate any property F when $F \in X$ and F has been modified by *Alleged*. Remember that the definition of modal modifiers applicable to contingent empirical properties (i.e., (*i*), (*ii*)) embodies a bifurcation, and that the way the cookie happens to crumble determines whether the alleged property is true of the individual in question. Modal modifiers applicable to necessarily uninstantiated properties are importantly different, in that the predication can go only one way: the alleged property must fail to be true of the individual in question. Therefore, my account of this second category of modal modifiers aligns them formally with privative modifiers. The difference between the two, though, is that the source of privation is not the modifier (*Alleged* versus *Fake*), but the argument property itself (*being a discoverer of the highest prime, being a married bachelor* versus *being a banknote*). At the other end of the spectrum, when $G \in Y$ and G has been modified by

Alleged, everyone and everything must instantiate G, thus aligning this third category of modal modifiers with (trivial) subsective modifiers. The difference between the two is that the source of triviality is, likewise, not the modifier (though *Genuine*, as in *being a genuine diamond*, adds or detracts nothing), but the argument property itself (e.g., *being as tall as one is*).

Acknowledgments

I am indebted to Marie Duží for valuable comments.

Funding

This research was funded by the Grant Agency of the Czech Republic (GACR) project GA18-23891S *Hyperintensional Reasoning over Natural Language Texts*.

References

Duží, Marie, Glavaničová, Daniela, and Jespersen, Bjørn. 2020. "Impossible Individuals as Necessarily Empty Individual Concepts." In *Logic in High Definition: Developing Fine-Grained Semantics, Trends in Logic*, edited by Alessandro Giordani and Jacek Malinowski, forthcoming.

Duží, Marie, Jespersen, Bjørn, and Materna, Pavel. 2010. *Procedural Semantics for Hyperintensional Logic. Foundations and Applications of Transparent Intensional Logic,* LEUS, vol. 17, Heidelberg et al.: Springer-Verlag. https://doi.org/10.1007/978-90-481-8812-3

Jespersen, Bjørn. 2016. "Left Subsectivity: How to Infer That a Round Peg is Round." *dialectica* 70 (4): 531–47. https://doi.org/10.1111/1746-8361.12159

Jespersen, Bjørn, Carrara, Massimiliano, and Duží, Marie. 2017. "Iterated Privation and Positive Predication." *Journal of Applied Logic* 25 (suppl.): 48–71. https://doi.org/10.1016/j.jal.2017.12.004

Jespersen, Bjørn and Primiero, Giuseppe. 2013. "Alleged Assassins: Realist and Constructivist Semantics for Modal Modifiers." In *Lecture Notes in Computer Science*, vol. 7758, edited by Guram Bezhanishvili, Sebastian Löbner, Vincenzo Marra, and Frank Richter, 94–114. https://doi.org/10.1007/978-3-642-36976-6_8

Kosterec, Miloš. 2019. "Contradiction of Modal Modification. *Organon F* 26 (2): 298–300. https://doi.org/10.31577/orgf.2019.26207

Iterated privation and positive predication

Bjørn Jespersen, Massimiliano Carrara, Marie Duží

ABSTRACT

The standard rule of *single privative modification* replaces privative modifiers by Boolean negation. This rule is valid, for sure, but also simplistic. If an individual a instantiates the privatively modified property (MF) then it is true that a instantiates the property of *not* being an F, but the rule fails to express the fact that the properties (MF) and F have something in common. We replace Boolean negation by property negation, enabling us to operate on *contrary* rather than contradictory properties. To this end, we apply our theory of *intensional essentialism*, which operates on properties (intensions) rather than their extensions. We argue that each property F is necessarily associated with an essence, which is the set of the so-called *requisites* of F that jointly define F. Privation deprives F of *some but not all* of its requisites, replacing them by their contradictories. We show that properties formed from iterated *privatives*, such as being an *imaginary fake banknote*, give rise to a *trifurcation* of cases between returning to the original root property or to a property contrary to it or being semantically undecidable for want of further information. In order to determine which of the three forks the bearers of particular instances of multiply modified properties land upon we must examine the requisites, both of unmodified and modified properties. Requisites underpin our *presuppositional* theory of *positive predication*. Whereas privation is about being deprived of certain properties, the assignment of requisites to properties makes positive predication possible, which is the predication of properties the bearers must have because they have a certain property formed by means of privation.

1. Introduction

There are large amounts of natural-language text data that need to be analyzed and formalized, because we want to build up question-answering systems over these data. We want not only to convey information explicitly recorded in these texts but also to derive implicit information entailed by these explicit data so as to answer questions in an intelligent way. In other words, we want to apply logical *reasoning* to these natural-language corpuses. To this end, we must analyze natural-language sentences in a fine-grained way. Since adjectives that denote property modifiers are part and parcel of our everyday vernaculars as well as artificial languages, we need to logically analyze property modifiers as well. *Privation* being the most complicated kind of property modification, the goal of this paper is a fine-grained analysis of privation accompanied by rules governing reasoning about sentences that contain such modifiers.

Privative modification is an operation that forms negated properties from properties. It is one among three kinds of negation:

- *privation*, which applies to *properties*
- the *complement function*, which applies to *sets*
- the *Boolean not*, which applies to propositions-in-extension, i.e. *truth-values*.

When *propositions* are identified with (or at least modelled as) *sets*, then the complement function subsumes propositional negation as a special case. Nothing in this paper hinges on this. What matters is the contrast between privation, which is property negation and therefore an operation on *intensions*, and set-theoretic negation, which takes a set to its complement and is therefore an operation on *extensions*.

The standard theory of modifiers is Montague Grammar, which is a typed version of model-theoretic intensional logic. This paper provides an extension of this framework such that it is now possible to analyze a particular sort of properties (or predicates, in the formal mode) that would previously fall outside the purview of the framework. The paper also offers reasons for revising one of the existing rules; however, the extension we provide can be incorporated without revising anything. We are building upon the work of not least Coulson and Fauconnier [3], Horn [13–15], Iwańska [16], Jespersen [17], Kamp [22], Montague [25], Partee [27], Primiero and Jespersen [28], while the background theory is based on Duží et al. [6,8].

Montague Grammar comes with a well-entrenched logic for *single privation*. This framework states its logic for the various modifiers in the form of elimination rules. The rule of single privation amounts to replacing the privative modifier by Boolean negation:

$$\frac{a \text{ is a } \textit{fake } \text{banknote}}{a \text{ is } \textit{not} \text{ a banknote}} \; \textit{single privation}$$

This rule is valid, because all that is required for validity is that the property (here, *banknote*) modified by the privative modifier (here, *fake*) not be predicated of a, and the conclusion achieves at least this much. However, the above rule misses the internal link between the property of being a banknote and the property of being a fake banknote. We will probe further into this point below, but the basic idea is that a fake banknote is not just some object or other that fails to be a banknote, but rather it is an object that must have a host of properties in common with banknotes. Though both forged banknotes and, say, weathercocks and zebras are not banknotes, there is an intuitive sense in which forged banknotes are somehow 'closer to' banknotes than are weathercocks and zebras. The challenge before us is to define privation in such a way that it is made explicit what banknotes and forged banknotes have, and must have, in common.

Another problem with the rule of single privation is that it fails to extend to *iterated privation*, as Boolean negation can replace a privative modifier only once. Here are some examples of predicates that express iterated privation:

- 'is an imaginary fake banknote'
- 'is a former heir apparent'
- 'is a former fallen angel'
- 'weighs almost half a kilo'
- 'is anything but a false friend'

- 'is a theory of non-antisymmetric mereology'
- 'is an imaginary, burned fake banknote'

For instance, Horn in [13, pp. 296–308], [14,15] ponders the logic and rhetoric of *double negatives*, e.g. as expressed by 'not un-F' ('not unhappy', 'not impolite', etc.).[1] Is a *not impolite remark* a polite remark, perhaps even a very polite remark, as per litotes (cf. [14, pp. 86ff]; or a remark that is neither polite nor impolite, ending up in the neutral mid-interval? For a further example, consider so-called superdollars, which are not US dollars, but counterfeit 100-dollar bills manufactured in, e.g., North Korea that are materially (though not conceptually) well-nigh indiscernible from their genuine originals.[2] This particular occurrence of 'super' in 'superdollar' has a privative effect, so the predicate 'is a fake superdollar' expresses double privation.[3] A fake superdollar is a fraudulent imitation of what is already a fraudulent imitation. If somebody collects first-degree counterfeit banknotes then they want a superdollar, and not a fake superdollar, which exemplifies second-degree forgery by being a fake.[4] We all know that faking a fake will not return us to the genuine original; but how do we know that? There is also the opposite direction: although you start out with a 100-dollar bill, successfully passing it off as a fake superdollar to a collector of forged banknotes of any degree, your 100-dollar bill has not transmogrified into a fake superdollar, despite being accepted as one. But how do we know that? The answer we will be pursuing is that we know that because we know the meaning of the respective predicates.

But what to replace Boolean negation with in order to develop a logic of iterated privation? We suggest replacing Boolean negation with property negation. First, property negation operates on properties, just as property modifiers do, so the intensional character of modification is carried through to negation. Second, property negation obeys a logic of contraries rather than contradictories, which provides the kind of rule that privative modification requires.

Let us take a closer look at privation. There are two material sources of privation. One is resultative and hence diachronic: individual *a* once was an *F*, but is no longer an *F*.[5] A recaptured fugitive (cf. [11]) once was a fugitive, but is no longer one. Finished meals, burnt (not just charred) pieces of meat, and obsolete banknotes all exemplify resultative privation. Given the actual laws of nature, neither a finished meal, nor a burnt piece of meat can again become a meal or a piece of meat, whereas an obsolete banknote might be restored to its previous glory as a banknote should the social institutions so favour it. The other source is achronic: *a* did not start out as an *F* and might never become an *F*, although it is possible that *a* might in fact become an *F*, as when the relevant social institutions decree that such-and-such fake banknotes shall henceforth acquire the status of valid tender, thus turning them into banknotes. Only this latter property is extraneous to the property of being a fake banknote.

There are two formal sources of privation: either by way of first-degree or higher-degree modification. Either a privative modifier modifies a property that has already been modified by a privative modifier, as when *imaginary* is applied to *fake banknote*. Or a privative modifier modifies another privative modifier, and the resulting modifier is applied to a property, as when *anything but* is applied to *false* and the resulting modifier, *anything but false*, is applied to *friend*.[6] (In this paper we shall consider only first-degree iterated

---

[1] See Horn [13, pp. 38–41] for a historical survey of various takes on contrariety and predicate term negation.
[2] Cf. http://en.wikipedia.org/wiki/Superdollar.
[3] It is not an open-and-shut issue whether some modifiers are absolutely privative while the rest are context-sensitive by being privative only with respect to some argument properties. *Fake* might be an example of the former, though we are issuing no guarantee. Examples of the latter would include *Nordic gold*, which is not gold (but an alloy); *fides punica*, which is not trust (but treachery); a *baker's dozen*, which is not a dozen (but thirteen); and *Rocky Mountain oysters*, which are not oysters. See also [16] on context-sensitive privatives.
[4] We could shift both the real McCoys and the fakes one level up with collectors collecting second-degree fakes and being fooled by third-degree fakes; and so on up.
[5] Other dynamic examples of 'stages of loss in the privative process' and 'incomplete realizations of possible privational histories' (Martin [24, p. 439, 441, resp.]) would include going bald, i.e. progressing (or perhaps regressing) toward being almost or entirely without hair.
[6] *Anything but* is a privative intensifier, just like *very* is a subsective intensifier, as in *very good*.

privation in the interest of brevity.) What we just described is double privation, but the theory readily generalizes to triple, quadruple (etc.) privation, as when *imaginary* is applied to *burned fake banknote*.

In the light of the fact that privative modifiers can be nested, one may wonder: could we avail ourselves of a rule that would calculate, for an arbitrary string of privative modifiers of two or more, whether the root property F is true of a? Our research shows that no such rule is forthcoming. There can be no unique rough-and-ready rule for iterated privation.

Iterated privation issues instead in a *trifurcation* of cases:

(i) a is an F
(ii) a fails to be an F
(iii) it is semantically indeterminate whether a is an F

The fact that this trifurcation emerges reflects the nature of privation. The first of two general points bearing on privation is the negative one that privation is about what something is *not*, or *fails* to be. It is about one or more properties that an object is *deprived of*. In particular, no theory of privatives should predict that fake banknotes are extracted from sets of banknotes: fake banknotes are not banknotes that are fake.[7]

But the second point is the positive one that there is substantially more to privation than deprivation. Let F be a property, M_p a modifier privative with respect to F, and $[M_p F]$ the privatively modified property that results from applying the modifier to the root property. The intuition we wish to capture is that when an object has the property $[M_p F]$ then the object is—in some sense yet to be made clear—'closer' to having F than are many or most other objects that lack the privatively modified property $[M_p F]$.[8] By way of an example, a fake banknote is 'almost' a banknote, definitely barred from being one, yet it has a greater overlap in terms of properties with a banknote than have most other objects. Fake banknotes must share a host of properties with banknotes; otherwise they could not be fake banknotes in the first place, but would be merely, say, colourful slips of paper. For instance, a banknote must mention the issuing authority, a currency and a denomination. Therefore, a fake banknote must also mention an issuing authority, a currency and a denomination. If a fake banknote sports, for instance, the words 'ECB', 'EURO', '100' and is printed on cotton-based paper with the look and feel of garden-variety banknotes then it lends itself to several instances of what we call *positive predication*. Positive predication predicates properties of an object which the object must instantiate and which are not privatively modified.

Positive predication appears to be less complicated vis-à-vis achronic privation than diachronic privation. A burnt piece of meat is ash (inorganic matter) and in this second state not at all close to being meat (organic matter), whereas a fake banknote must be close to being a banknote. However, we are able to put forward a theory of positive predication with regard to objects that exemplify privatively modified properties of either kind, because we offer a *presuppositional* theory of privation. The theory is presuppositional because, for an object to exemplify a privatively modified property, it is presupposed that the object should already exemplify other properties. By way of illustration, the property of being a former smoker comes with the presupposition that, as a matter of analytic necessity, whoever currently instantiates it previously, but no longer, instantiated the property of being a smoker. Or if a has the property of being a Vatican cardinal then has also the property of being fluent in Latin. Beyond the well-rehearsed example of former smokers, the theory extends to not only social artefacts like positions in a hierarchy of institutional power, but also

---

[7] This is to say that we do not stretch the meaning of 'is a banknote' so as to include fake banknotes among the banknotes. Partee [27] suggests using coercion to do just that, such that it becomes meaningful to inquire whether a banknote is a real banknote or a fake banknote. Jespersen [17, p. 544, fn. 14] and Duží et al. [6, p. 400, fn. 52] argue against Partee's suggestion.

[8] Coulson and Fauconnier [3] and Iwańska [16] also think of privation both as the elimination of some, but not all, properties (or concepts, features, etc.) inhering in privatively modified properties, and as the 'blending with' or 'introduction of' additional properties so as to form new, hybrid properties like *stone lion* or *toy elephant*.

technical artefacts like tools and scientific frameworks like taxonomies.[9] The presuppositional theory enables us to infer conclusions about, say, dead whales (a dead whale being a dead mammal), disassembled watches (a disassembled watch not being a timekeeping device) and burnt pieces of meat (a burnt piece of meat having been previously a piece of meat). Importantly, each and every property we countenance has a host of other properties associated with it. Thus, each instance of $[M_p[M_pF]]$ also comes with a host of adjacent properties that their respective bearers must also bear.

We call the adjacent properties *requisites*.[10] Our thesis is that privation is the deprivation of some, but not all, requisites. The surviving requisites, together with some added ones, form the basis of positive predication. The above trifurcation arises because the root property F will be one of the requisites of some multiply privatively modified properties, while *non-F* will be one of the requisites of other multiply privatively modified properties, whereas neither F, nor *non-F* is among the requisites of still other multiply privatively modified properties. In the third and final case, as far as the semantics of such properties goes, there is no semantic fact of the matter as to which side of the fence a comes down on. Extra-semantic, empirical investigation must, in each individual case, determine which side a given individual comes down on. To give a taste of the trifurcation, here is an example of each of its three horns.

- If somebody is *anything but a false friend* then they are a friend (and that to a very high degree) (*i*).
- If something weighs *almost half a kilo* then it weighs less than a kilo and, therefore, does not weigh a kilo (*ii*).[11]
- If someone is a *former heir apparent* then either they are now the incumbent monarch or they are no longer being even considered for the throne (*iii*).

The requisites of a given property enable valid reasoning from assumptions about privatively modified properties. Philosophically speaking, associating requisites with properties amounts, in the case of privation, to laying down at least some of what goes into being a wooden horse, a burnt wooden horse, a burnt fake wooden horse, a fake burnt wooden horse, etc. Achieving the latter, philosophical, objective comes with a fair amount of idealization while still requiring substantial philosophical justification.[12] In this paper we rest content with setting out the formal features of the framework within which we discuss iterated privation and positive predication. Just to be clear, while we will be arguing for a particular *elimination* rule for privatives, we will not attempt to put forward any *introduction* rules for privatives in the vein of:

$$\frac{P_1,\ldots,P_n}{a \text{ is an } [M_pF]}$$

For particular instances of P_i and $[M_pF]$, such a rule would make explicit what the conditions are for being, e.g., a fake banknote, or a wooden horse, or a malfunctioning toothbrush.[13] Philosophy of technology would make a great leap forward if particular instances of P_i could be spelt out with the rigour required

---

[9] For the relevant theory of presuppositions, see [7,9,8].
[10] The notion of requisite was conceived by Tichý and introduced in [30, p. 408]. It has subsequently been turned into a theory of intensional essentialism. See Jespersen and Materna [21], Duží et al. [6, Ch. 3].
[11] We are making the fairly uncontroversial assumption that when something weighs almost half a kilo then it weighs no more than that. We want to blot out the kind of scenario where something that weighs exactly a kilo weighs also 900 grams, almost half a kilo, etc., in virtue of a simple argument of downward monotonicity that also validates the 'countdown' inference that if you have five fingers on your hand then you also have four (three, ..., zero) fingers, which still does not entail that you have fifteen fingers.
[12] See [2].
[13] It is not a matter of course that *malfunctioning* is privative. It is on the causal-role theory of technical function (what cannot hammer cannot be a hammer), whereas it is subsective on the proper-function theory (a malfunctioning hammer was still designed to hammer as its proper function). See Jespersen and Carrara [20]. An interesting study on malfunctioning software has been recently provided by Floridi, Fresco and Primiero [12]. The authors distinguish between two kinds of malfunctioning software, namely in terms of 'negative' dysfunction and 'positive' misfunction. They argue that while dysfunction is the core property of malfunctioning technical artefacts, an executed software token cannot dysfunction, because it will always work in accordance with its design. Yet it can, and often will, misfunction, because the design does not completely live up to the intended specification.

for an introduction rule. But, although the notion of requisite would come in handy, this very ambitious enterprise is beyond the compass of this paper.[14]

The fundamental distinction among modifiers is typically considered to be one between the *subsectives* and the *non-subsectives*.[15] The former group would consist of the *pure subsectives* (that are governed by the upwardly monotonic rule of *right subsectivity*, which amounts to eliminating the modifier and predicating the surviving property) and the *intersectives* (that are governed by the rule of *right subsectivity* and a rule of *left subsectivity*).[16]

Here is a brief comparison in prose of the four standard types of modifiers, where an index is an index of empirical evaluation, such as a possible world or a world/time pair.

- *Pure subsectives.* At every index a skillful surgeon is a surgeon.
- *Intersectives.* At every index a round peg is round and is a peg.
- *Privatives.* At no index is a fake banknote a banknote.
- *Modals.* At some indices an alleged assassin is an assassin, and at some other indices an alleged assassin is not an assassin.

Montague [25, p. 211] seeks to provide a uniform theory of modifiers (strictly speaking, of adjectival phrases). Each modifier, according to Montague, is a property-to-property mapping.[17] We subscribe to this uniform account of the corpus of modifiers. We depart, however, from Montague's contention that these functions are *meaning-to-meaning* functions (ibid.). The contention, of course, makes perfect in Montague's *intensional* framework in which intensions (functions whose domain are the logical space of possible worlds) count as meanings.[18] In our framework, *meaning-to-meaning* functions would be *hyperintension-to-hyperintension* functions. We have such functions, but we do not need them here. We do need hyperintensions, however, when working with modifiers: we need hyperintensions (meanings) when defining a couple of key notions that go into defining modifiers. In a word, we are using hyperintensions in order to operate on intensions.

It is relevant to compare modal and iterated privative modification, for in neither case is only one conclusion possible. The modals require *extra-semantic*, empirical inquiry to establish, for each particular instance, which of two ways the facts happen to go. Only empirical inquiry can decide which allegations of being an assassin are true and which ones are false. The iterated privatives require *intra-semantic* inquiry to establish, for each particular instance, which of the three ways the meanings go. If we land on the third fork, then we need to get out of the armchair and into the field to establish which way the facts happen to go.

Privation is literally radical modification, because the root property is modified away. Subsective modification, by contrast, enriches the root property, whether the modifier be intersective (e.g. *round*) or purely subsective (e.g. *skillful*). A peg, say, is qualified as a round peg, or conversely, something round is qualified as a round peg; and a surgeon as a skillful surgeon. A layer of modification is added on top of the existing requisites of the root property. Privation goes in the opposite direction by purging the root property of some of its requisites. This is the crucial step toward explaining why a fake banknote fails to be a banknote. One property that drops out is that of being valid tender, which comes with requisites of its own. Yet privation

---

[14] See Del Frate [5] for conceptual discussion of a catalogue of engineering conceptions of malfunction.
[15] See, e.g., Makinson [23, pp. 64–65] on the distinction between *qualifiers* and *proper modifiers*.
[16] See Jespersen [17] for two rules of left subsectivity.
[17] A topic we will not be delving further into here is how to decide for a given token of a given adjective whether it denotes a property or a modifier. See, however, Siegel [29], Kamp [22], Montague [25], Beesley [1]. Schematically put, Montague pairs all adjectives off with modifiers, Beesley pairs all adjectives off with properties, and Kamp pairs some adjectives off with modifiers and the rest with properties.
[18] We are glossing over the facts that Montague did not fully commit to s (i.e. combined world/time pairs) as a stand-alone type on an equal footing with e (i.e. 'entity'), t (i.e. truth-value), etc., and that Montague's empirical indices were combined world/time pairs.

not only detracts, but also adds something. One property that gets added is that of being a forgery (i.e. a fraudulent imitation of something or other), which also comes with requisites of its own. The crucial step toward the presuppositional theory required for positive predication is that privation adds new requisites to the purged set of requisites. Moreover, some of these new requisites contradict some of the original purged requisites. This explains why we can predicate several properties of fake banknotes that they must have.

If we did not assign requisites to properties, we would be left with an exceptionally minimalist logic of iterated privation. First of all, the replacement of privatives by Boolean negation can occur only once, as we announced at the outset. Here is why. The standard rule of single privation lays down what to do when it is *true* that a has property $[M_p F]$. The rule fails to state what to do when the premise is the negation that a has property $[M_p F]$. This inference, therefore, is *invalid*:

$$\frac{\neg[[M_p F]\, a]}{\neg\neg[Fa]}$$

If, counterfactually, the rule for privation had specified logical equivalence between $[[M_p F]\, a]$ and $\neg[Fa]$ *then* the above argument would have come out valid. However, the rule of privation does not specify equivalence; rather it specifies that $[[M_p F]\, a]$ entails $\neg[Fa]$. It is also intuitive enough that the above inference must come out invalid. If it did not, all instances of double privation would land on the first fork. Thus, a fake rhinestone diamond would emerge as a diamond. So not only would the inference fail to be truth-preserving by over-generating instances of the first fork, it would also leave no room for the other two forks.

Secondly, therefore, in the interest of setting up a logic of iterated privation, we suggest replacing Boolean negation by property negation, denoted by '*non*'. This replaces contradictories by contraries, which makes for a sufficiently weakened form of negation. Applied to single privation, the result is:

$$\frac{a \text{ is a } \mathit{fake} \text{ banknote}}{a \text{ is a } \mathit{non}\text{-banknote}} \quad single\ privation^*$$

When a is a fake banknote at some index then a is sent to the complement set of the set of banknotes at the same index, though not to just anywhere in the complement, but to its particular subset of fake banknotes. The good news is that we can reiterate *non* so as to form the property *non-non-banknote*. The bad news is that [*non* [*non* F]] would be the final word on iterated privation in the absence of requisites. The above trifurcation would remain, but it would be impossible to decide which particular fork a particular instance of iterated privation landed on. A logic of iterated privation that amounted to replacing privatives by *non* would grind to a halt after having established the general insight that pairs of privatives yield contraries.

The thesis, then, that we are arguing for can be condensed thus. A logic of iterated privation that invokes requisite properties of privatively modified properties enables positive predication and is in a position to land particular instances of multiply privatively modified properties on the right fork.

The rest of the paper is organized as follows. Section 2 sets out the relevant portions of our formal semantic theory. Section 3 compares the logic of subsectives against the logic of privatives, introduces property negation, and offers case studies of each of the forks of the trifurcation.

2. Logical foundations

In this section, we set out the formal framework within which we raise and solve the problem of iterated privation. The framework is a fragment of Tichý's Transparent Intensional Logic (TIL). The relevant fragment is more or less continuous with Montague's intensional logic and its myriad extensions. However, TIL has added a theory of modal modifiers (see Primiero and Jespersen [28]) to the Montagovian corpus, and a spelt-out logic, including an introduction rule, for intersective modifiers (see Jespersen [17]), as well as a general rule of left subsectivity applying to privatives and modals, intersectives and pure subsectives (see Jespersen [17]; Duží et al. [6, §4.4]), which extends to single privation. The present paper is the third and final of a trilogy of papers on how to model various states (especially malfunction) of technical artefacts by means of property modifiers. The two preceding papers are Jespersen and Carrara [19,20].

2.1. Key definitions of transparent intensional logic

We need definitions of the following basic notions:

- *Simple type theory.* We need this definition in order to define both intensional and extensional entities. Properties of individuals are typed as functions from possible worlds to functions from times to sets of individuals, where sets are identified with their characteristic functions. Property modifiers are typed as property-to-property functions. (Modifier modifiers are typed as modifier-to-modifier functions.)
- *Constructions.* We need this definition for the following reasons. Constructions are (fine-grained and structured) *meanings*; we define four of the altogether six constructions that make up the full inductive definition of constructions. Furthermore, the definition introduces the *formalism* of TIL, which is based on λ-abstracts.
- *Requisite.* The requisite relation Req is a relation-in-extension between two properties R and P, such that, necessarily, whatever is (in) the extension of P must, as a matter of analytic necessity, also be (in) the extension of R, though not necessarily conversely. We say that R is a *requisite* of P.
- *Essence.* The essence of a property P is the set of its requisites which together define P.
- *Property negation.* Property negation, *non*, allows *iteration* and obeys a logic of *contraries*.

Note that our theory is based on what we call *intensional essentialism*. The analytically necessary relation of being a requisite of P and being an element of the essence of P obtains between intensional entities such as properties, and not between extensional entities (such as individuals) and intensional entities. Consequently, we subscribe to *individual anti-essentialism*: no individual has any purely contingent property necessarily. By 'purely contingent property' we mean a non-constant property that does not have what we call an essential core; e.g., the property of having exactly as many inhabitants as Prague is necessarily exemplified by Prague, whatever number of inhabitants Prague may happen to have.[19]

We define the essence of a property as a set of its requisites that jointly define the property. For instance, the property of being a mammal is related by the requisite relation to the property of being a whale. Thus, necessarily, if the individual a happens to be a whale at a world/time index of evaluation then a is also a mammal at this world/time. It is an open question (epistemologically and ontologically speaking) whether a is a whale. Establishing whether it is one requires investigation *a posteriori*. On the other hand, establishing whether a must be a mammal in case a happens to be a whale is *a priori*, the requisite relation being in-extension and as such independent of what is true at any particular state of affairs. Comparing the essences of a root property and a modified property enables us to define subsective and privative modifiers in a new way that is an extension of previous definitions.

Definition 1 *(Simple type theory).* Let B be a *base*, where a base is a collection of pair-wise disjoint, non-empty sets. Then:

i) Every member of B is an elementary *type of order 1 over B*.

---

[19] See Duží et al. [6, §1.4.2.1] for a classification of empirical properties and (ibid.: 68) for the notion of essential core.

ii) Let $\alpha, \beta_1, ..., \beta_m$ ($m > 0$) be types of order 1 over B. Then the collection $(\alpha\, \beta_1...\beta_m)$ of all m-ary partial mappings from $\beta_1 \times ... \times \beta_m$ into α is a functional *type of order 1 over B*.
iii) Nothing is a *type of order 1 over B* unless it so follows from (i) and (ii). □

Notation. That an object O is of type α, i.e. belongs to the type α, will be denoted '$O : \alpha$'.

Remark. For the purposes of natural-language analysis TIL uses the following so-called objectual base B consisting of the following atomic types:

- o: the set of truth-values **T, F**;
- ι: the set of individuals (the universe of discourse);
- τ: the set of real numbers (doubling as discrete times);
- ω: the set of logically possible worlds (the logical space).

Definition 2 *(Constructions).*

(i) *Variables* $x, y, ...$ are *constructions* that construct objects (elements of their respective ranges) dependently on a valuation v; they *v-construct*.
(ii) Where X is an object whatsoever (an extension, an intension or a *construction*), ^0X is the *construction Trivialization*. ^0X constructs X without any change in X.
(iii) Let $X, Y_1, ..., Y_n$ be *constructions*. Then *Composition* $[X\, Y_1...Y_m]$ is the following *construction*. If X *v-constructs* a function f of type $(\alpha\beta_1...\beta_m)$, and $Y_1, ..., Y_m$ *v-construct* entities $B_1, ..., B_m$ of types $\beta_1, ..., \beta_m$, respectively, then $[X\, Y_1...Y_m]$ *v-constructs* the value (an entity, if any, of type α) of f on the tuple-argument $\langle B_1, ..., B_m \rangle$. Otherwise $[X\, Y_1...Y_m]$ does not *v-construct* anything and so is *v-improper*.
(iv) The *Closure* $[\lambda x_1...x_m Y]$ is the following *construction*. Let $x_1, x_2, ..., x_m$ be pair-wise distinct variables *v*-constructing entities of types $\beta_1, ..., \beta_m$, respectively, and Y a construction typed to *v*-construct an α-entity. Then $[\lambda x_1...x_m Y]$ is the *construction Closure* (or λ-*Closure*). It *v-constructs* the following function $f : (\alpha\beta_1...\beta_m)$. Let $v(B_1/x_1, ..., B_m/x_m)$ be a valuation identical with v at least up to assigning objects $B_1 : \beta_1, ..., B_m : \beta_m$ to variables $x_1, ..., x_m$. If Y is $v(B_1/x_1, ..., B_m/x_m)$-improper (see iii), then f is undefined on $\langle B_1, ..., B_m \rangle$. Otherwise the value of f on $\langle B_1, ..., B_m \rangle$ is the α-entity $v(B_1/x_1, ..., B_m/x_m)$-constructed by Y.
(v) Nothing is a *construction*, unless it so follows from (i) through (iv). □

Remark. That a variable x *v*-constructs entities of a type α will be referred to as 'ranging over α', denoted by '$x \to_v \alpha$'. We model sets and relations by their characteristic functions. Thus, for instance, $(o\iota)$ is the type of a set of individuals, while $(o\iota\iota)$ is the type of binary relations-in-extension between individuals. Empirical expressions denote *empirical conditions* that may or may not be satisfied at some world/time pair of evaluation. We model these empirical conditions as possible-world-semantic (PWS) *intensions*. PWS intensions are entities of type $(\beta\omega)$: mappings from possible worlds to an arbitrary type β. The type β is frequently the type of the *chronology* of α-objects, i.e., a mapping of type $(\alpha\tau)$. Thus α-intensions are frequently functions of type $(\alpha(\tau\omega))$, abbreviated as '$\alpha_{\tau\omega}$'. *Extensional entities* are entities of the arbitrary type α where $\alpha \neq (\beta\omega)$ for any type β. Where w ranges over ω and t over τ, the following logical form essentially characterizes the logical syntax of empirical language: $\lambda w \lambda t\, [...w...t...]$.

Examples of frequently used PWS intensions are:

- *propositions* of type $o_{\tau\omega}$
- *properties* of individuals of type $(o\iota)_{\tau\omega}$

- *binary relations-in-intension* between individuals of type $(o\iota\iota)_{\tau\omega}$
- *individual offices* (or roles) of type $\iota_{\tau\omega}$

Logical objects like *truth-functions* and *quantifiers* are extensional: ∧ (conjunction), ∨ (disjunction), ⊃ (implication) are of type (ooo), and ¬ (Boolean negation) of type (oo). Since TIL has no syncategorematic symbols, all the symbols in the TIL formalism denote functions, including quantifiers. The *quantifiers* $\forall^\alpha$, $\exists^\alpha$ are type-theoretically polymorphic total functions, just as in Montague Grammar, of type $(o(o\alpha))$, for an arbitrary type α, and are defined as follows.

Definition 3 *(Quantifiers).* The universal quantifier $\forall^\alpha$ is a function of type $(o(o\alpha))$ that takes a class A of α-elements to **T** if A contains all elements of the type α, otherwise to **F**. The existential quantifier $\exists^\alpha$ is a function of type $(o(o\alpha))$ that takes a class A of α-elements to **T** if A is a non-empty class, otherwise to **F**. □

Notational conventions.

- '$\forall x \ldots$' serves as a shorthand for '[$^0\forall \lambda x \ldots$]'; similarly for '$\exists y$': all variable-binding is λ-binding, and universal (existential) quantification is presented by means of Trivialization.
- Below all type indications will be provided outside the formulae in order not to clutter the notation.
- The outermost brackets will be omitted whenever no confusion can arise.
- While '$X : \alpha$' means that an object X is (a member) of type α, '$X \to_v \alpha$' means that X is typed to v-construct an object of type α, if any. We write '$X \to \alpha$' if no confusion concerning valuation arises.
- $w \to_v \omega$ and $t \to_v \tau$.
- If $C \to_v \alpha_{\tau\omega}$ then the frequently used Composition $[[C \ w] \ t]$, which is the intensional descent (a.k.a. extensionalization) of the α-intension v-constructed by C, will be encoded as 'C_{wt}'.

Predication is an instance of Composition.[20] An empirical predicate such as 'is a planet' denotes the property of being a planet; it is subsequently extensionalized in order to obtain the set of planets at the empirical indices of evaluation; the characteristic function of the set is applied, by way of Composition, to the individual of which the property of being a planet is predicated; the result (a truth-value) is finally abstracted over by means of w and t variables in order to construct an empirical truth-condition of type $o_{\tau\omega}$. The form of the predication of being a planet of an individual a is this[21]:

$$\lambda w \lambda t \ [^0Planet_{wt} \ ^0a]$$

The form of the predication of the subsectively modified property of being a gas planet is this:

$$\lambda w \lambda t [[^0Gas \ ^0Planet]_{wt} \ ^0a]$$

To begin, construct, by way of Composition, the property of being a gas planet and then follow the same steps as above.

Types: $Planet : (o\iota)_{\tau\omega}$; $a : \iota$; $Gas : (((o\iota)_{\tau\omega})((o\iota)_{\tau\omega}))$; $[^0Gas \ ^0Planet] \to (o\iota)_{\tau\omega}$; $[[^0Gas \ ^0Planet]_{wt} \ ^0a] \to_v o$; $\lambda w \lambda t \ [[^0Gas \ ^0Planet]_{wt} \ ^0a] \to o_{\tau\omega}$: the proposition that a is a gas planet.

---

[20] See Duží et al. [6, §2.4.2] on predication.
[21] We apply the method of analysis according to which semantically simple predicates like 'is a planet' are associated with the Trivialization of the denoted object; ^0Planet, in this case. See Duží et al. [6, §2.1].

2.2. Requisites

The requisite relations *Req* are a family of relations-in-extension between two intensions, so they are of the polymorphous type $(o\,\alpha_{\tau\omega}\,\beta_{\tau\omega})$, with the possibility that $\alpha = \beta$.[22] Infinitely many combinations of *Req* are possible, but for our purpose we will need just this one:

$$Req: (o\,(o\iota)_{\tau\omega}(o\iota)_{\tau\omega})$$

Req is a relation between two properties of individuals, such that one is a requisite of the other.

TIL embraces *partial functions*.[23] Partiality gives rise to the following complication. The requisite relation obtains necessarily, i.e. for all worlds w and times t, and so the values at this or that $\langle w, t \rangle$ of particular intensions are irrelevant. But the extensions of properties (i.e. sets) are isomorphic to characteristic functions, and these functions are amenable to truth-value gaps. As already mentioned, the property of having stopped smoking comes with a bulk of requisites including not least the property of being a former smoker. Thus, the predication of such a property P of a may also fail, causing $[{}^0P_{wt}\,{}^0a]$ to be v-improper. There is a straightforward remedy, however, namely the propositional property of being true at $\langle w, t \rangle$; *True*: $(o\,o_{\tau\omega})_{\tau\omega}$. Given a proposition *Prop*, $[{}^0True_{wt}\,{}^0Prop]$ v-constructs **T** if *Prop* is true at $\langle w, t \rangle$; otherwise (i.e., if *Prop* is false or else undefined at $\langle w, t \rangle$) it v-constructs **F**.

Definition 4 *(Requisite relation between ι-properties).* Let X, Y be constructions such that X, Y: $*_n \to (o\,\iota)_{\tau\omega}$; $x \to \iota$. Then

$$[{}^0Req\,Y\,X] = \forall w \forall t [\forall x [[{}^0True_{wt}\,\lambda w \lambda t\,[X_{wt}\,x]] \supset [{}^0True_{wt}\,\lambda w \lambda t\,[Y_{wt}\,x]]]].$$

Gloss *definiendum* as, "*Y* is a requisite of *X*", and *definiens* as, "Necessarily, i.e. at every $\langle w, t \rangle$, any x that instantiates X at $\langle w, t \rangle$ also instantiates Y at $\langle w, t \rangle$."

Example. Let the property of being a person be a requisite of the property of being a student. Then the hyperproposition that all students are persons is an analytic truth. It constructs the proposition *TRUE*, which is the necessary proposition, which takes value **T** at all world/time pairs. Wherever and whenever somebody is a student they are also a person. Formally:

$$[{}^0Req\,{}^0Person\,{}^0Student] = \forall w \forall t\,[\forall x\,[[{}^0True_{wt}\,\lambda w \lambda t\,[{}^0Student_{wt}\,x]] \supset [{}^0True_{wt}\,\lambda w \lambda t\,[{}^0Person_{wt}\,x]]]]$$

Claim 1. *Req is a quasi-order on the set of ι-properties.*

Proof. Let X, $Y \to (o\iota)_{\tau\omega}$. Then *Req* belongs to the class $QO:(o(o(o\iota)_{\tau\omega}(o\iota)_{\tau\omega}))$ of quasi-orders over the set of individual properties:

Reflexivity. $[{}^0Req\,X\,X] = \forall w \forall t\,[\forall x\,[[{}^0True_{wt}\,\lambda w \lambda t\,[X_{wt}\,x]] \supset [{}^0True_{wt}\,\lambda w \lambda t\,[X_{wt}\,x]]]].$

Transitivity. We want to prove that $[[[{}^0Req\,Y\,X] \wedge [{}^0Req\,Z\,Y]] \supset [{}^0Req\,Z\,X]]$.

---

[22] For comparison, Jespersen [18] offers a detailed study of a requisite relation, of type $(o\,\iota_{\tau\omega}\,\iota_{\tau\omega})$, where one individual office is a requisite of another individual office, the way the office of Commander-in-Chief is a requisite of the office of President of the United States. The paper analyses "Superman is Clark Kent" as expressing that this particular requisite relation obtains between one office denoted by 'Superman' and another office denoted by 'Clark Kent'. If you occupy the office of Superman you must co-occupy the office of Clark Kent, but you can occupy the Clark Kent office without occupying the Superman office. This goes to show that TIL offers an intensional analysis (based on intensional essentialism) of "Superman is Clark Kent", contrary to the prevalent 'Millian' extensional analyses.

[23] See Duží et al. [6, 276–78] for a philosophical justification of partiality in spite of the associated technical complications.

Iterated privation and positive predication

1. $[[^0Req\,Y\,X] \wedge [^0Req\,Z\,Y]]$ $\emptyset$
2. $[\forall w \forall t\,[\forall x\,[[^0True_{wt}\,\lambda w\lambda t\,[X_{wt}\,x]] \supset [^0True_{wt}\,\lambda w\lambda t\,[Y_{wt}\,x]]]] \wedge \forall w \forall t\,[\forall x\,[[^0True_{wt}\,\lambda w\lambda t\,[Y_{wt}\,x]] \supset [^0True_{wt}\,\lambda w\lambda t\,[Z_{wt}\,x]]]]]$ 1, Definition 4
3. $[[^0True_{wt}\,\lambda w\lambda t\,[X_{wt}\,x]] \supset [^0True_{wt}\,\lambda w\lambda t\,[Y_{wt}\,x]]]$ 2, $\forall E, \wedge E$
4. $[[^0True_{wt}\,\lambda w\lambda t\,[Y_{wt}\,x]] \supset [^0True_{wt}\,\lambda w\lambda t\,[Z_{wt}\,x]]]$ 2, $\forall E, \wedge E$
5. $[[^0True_{wt}\,\lambda w\lambda t\,[X_{wt}\,x]] \supset [^0True_{wt}\,\lambda w\lambda t\,[Z_{wt}\,x]]]$ 3, 4,*
6. $[\forall w \forall t\,[\forall x\,[[^0True_{wt}\,\lambda w\lambda t\,[X_{wt}\,x]] \supset [^0True_{wt}\,\lambda w\lambda t\,[Z_{wt}\,x]]]]]$ 5, $\forall I$
7. $[[^0Req\,Z\,X]]$ 6, Definition 4
8. $[[[^0Req\,Y\,X] \wedge [^0Req\,Z\,Y]] \supset [^0Req\,Z\,X]]$ 7, $\supset I$

Remark. In line (5) '*' denotes the theorem of the transitivity of implication.

In order for a requisite relation to be a weak partial order, it would need to be also anti-symmetric. The *Req* relation is, however, not anti-symmetric. If properties X, Y are mutually in the *Req* relation, i.e. if

$$[[^0Req\,Y\,X] \wedge [^0Req\,X\,Y]]$$

then at every $\langle w, t \rangle$ the two properties are true of exactly the same individuals. This does not entail, however, that X, Y are identical. It may be the case that there is an individual a such that $[X_{wt}\,a]$ v-constructs **F** whereas $[Y_{wt}\,a]$ is v-improper. For instance, the following properties X, Y differ only in truth-value for those individuals who never smoked. Let $StopSmoke{:}(o\iota)_{\tau\omega}$ be the property of having stopped smoking. Whereas X yields truth-value *gaps* on such individuals, Y is *false* of them:

$$X = \lambda w \lambda t \lambda x\,[^0StopSmoke_{wt}\,x]$$
$$Y = \lambda w \lambda t \lambda x\,[^0True_{wt}\,\lambda w\lambda t\,[^0StopSmoke_{wt}\,x]]$$

This makes for a negligible difference that can be abstracted away, so we introduce the equivalence relation $\approx$: $(o\,(o\iota)_{\tau\omega}(o\iota)_{\tau\omega})$ on the set of individual properties; $p, q \to (o\iota)_{\tau\omega}$; $=$: (ooo); $=_{df}$: $(o(o\,(o\iota)_{\tau\omega}(o\iota)_{\tau\omega})(o\,(o\iota)_{\tau\omega}(o\iota)_{\tau\omega}))$, i.e. the identity of binary relations between properties.

$$^0\approx\, = \lambda p q\,[\forall x\,[[^0True_{wt}\,\lambda w\lambda t\,[p_{wt}\,x]] = [^0True_{wt}\,\lambda w\lambda t\,[q_{wt}\,x]]]]$$

Now we can define the *Req'* relation on the factor set of the set of ι-properties as follows.[24] Let $[p]_\approx = \lambda q\,[^0\approx p\,q]$ and $[Req'\,[p]_\approx[q]_\approx] = [Req\,p\,g]$. Then:

Claim 2. *Req' is a partial order on the factor set of the set of ι-properties with respect to the relation $\approx$.*

Proof. It is sufficient to prove that *Req'* is well-defined. Let p, q be ι-properties such that $[^0\approx p\,p']$ and $[^0\approx q\,q']$. Then:

$$[Req'\,[p]_\approx[q]_\approx] = [Req\,p\,g]$$
$$= \forall w \forall t\,[\forall x\,[[^0True_{wt}\,\lambda w\lambda t\,[p_{wt}\,x]] \supset [^0True_{wt}\,\lambda w\lambda t\,[q_{wt}\,x]]]]$$
$$= \forall w \forall t\,[\forall x\,[[^0True_{wt}\,\lambda w\lambda t\,[p'_{wt}\,x]] \supset [^0True_{wt}\,\lambda w\lambda t\,[q'_{wt}\,x]]]] = [Req'\,[p']_\approx[q']_\approx]$$

---

[24] The definition of *Req'* was first introduced in Duží et al. [6, 363–364].

Now, obviously, the relation *Req'* is anti-symmetric:

$$[[^0 Req'\,[p]_\approx\,[q]_\approx] \wedge [^0 Req'\,[q]_\approx\,[p]_\approx]] \supset [[p]_\approx = [q]_\approx]$$

To make the exposition easier to follow, in what follows we will neglect this minor difference between properties $\lambda w \lambda t\, \lambda x [^0 True_{wt}\, \lambda w \lambda t\,[p_{wt}\,x]]$ and p so that instead of the former we will write simply 'p'. □

2.3. Intensional essentialism

Next, we are going to define the essence of a property. Our essentialism is based on the idea that since no purely contingent property can be essential of any individual, essences are borne by intensions rather than by individuals exemplifying intensions. That a property F has an essence means that a relation-in-extension obtains *a priori* between F and a set *Essence* of other properties such that, as a matter of analytic necessity, whenever an individual (an ι-entity) instantiates F at some $\langle w,t \rangle$ then the same individual also instantiates all the properties belonging to *Essence* at the same $\langle w,t \rangle$. Hence our essentialism is based on the requisite relation, couching essentialism in terms of a priori interplay between properties, regardless of who or what exemplifies a given property. The essence of a property F is identical to the set of requisites that jointly define F. The $\langle w,t \rangle$-relative extensions of a given property are irrelevant, as we said; but so are the various equivalent constructions of the property.

Definition 5 *(Essence of a property).* Let $p, q \to (o\iota)_{\tau\omega}$; *Ess*: $((o(o\iota)_{\tau\omega})(o\iota)_{\tau\omega})$, i.e. a function assigning to a given property p the set of its requisites defined as follows:

$$^0 Ess = \lambda p \lambda q\,[^0 Req\,q\,p]$$

Then the essence of a property p is the set of its requisites:

$$[^0 Ess\,p] = \lambda q\,[^0 Req\,q\,p]$$

Each property has many requisites. The question is: how do we know which properties are the requisites of a given property? The answer requires an analytic *definition* of the given property. For instance, consider the property of being a (domestic) cat. A classification according to biological taxonomy can serve as such a definition:

Kingdom: *Animalia*
Phylum: *Chordata*
Clade: *Synapsia*
Class: *Mammalia*
Order: *Carnivora*
Family: *Felidae*
Subfamily: *Felinae*
Genus: *Felis*
Species: *Felis Catus*

Thus, we can define a cat as an animal belonging to all of the above categories.[25] From this definition it follows that, for instance, the sentence "Cats are mammals" comes out analytically true:

$$\forall w \forall t\, [\forall x\, [[^0Cat_{wt}\, x] \supset [^0Mammal_{wt}\, x]]]$$

Hence the property of being a mammal is a requisite of the property of being a cat. All the above properties defined by a given taxonomy belong to the essence of the property of being a cat.

3. Subsectives, privatives, property negation, and case studies

3.1. Subsectives and privatives

With the above definitions in place, we can go on to compare two kinds of subsectives against privatives[26]:

- A modifier M is *non-trivially subsective* with respect to property F iff the modified property $[M\,F]$ has all the requisites of F and at least one additional requisite that is not a requisite of F. In other words, the essence of F is a proper subset of the essence of $[M\,F]$.

For instance, a skillful surgeon is a surgeon because the property of being a skillful surgeon must have all the requisites of the property of being a surgeon, and the additional property of being skillful with respect to the property of being a surgeon.

- A modifier M is *trivially subsective* with respect to F iff the modified property $[M\,F]$ has exactly the same requisites as the property F, i.e. if $[M\,F]$ and F share the same essence, hence are identical properties. The trivial subsectives are trivial in that the modification has no effect on the modified property and so might just as well not have taken place.

For instance, there is no semantic or logical (but perhaps rhetorical) difference between the property of being a diamond and the property of being a *genuine* diamond. Trivial modifiers such as *genuine* and *real* are pure subsectives: genuine diamonds are not located in the intersection of diamonds and objects that are genuine, for there is no such property as being genuine, pure and simple. Genuine diamonds form a subset, though not a proper one, of a given set of diamonds.[27]

- A modifier M is *privative* with respect to F iff the modified property $[M\,F]$ lacks at least one, but not all, of the requisites of the property F. Moreover, the essence of $[M\,F]$ contains at least one other requisite that does not belong to the essence of F, and contradicts at least one of the requisites of F. Hence, M is privative with respect to F iff the essence of $[M\,F]$ has a non-empty intersection with the essence of F, and this intersection is a proper subset of both the essences of F and of $[MF]$.

---

[25] Contra Kripke, it is not a discovery (*a posteriori*, yet 'metaphysically' necessary) that a domestic cat belongs to any of the categories above. The definition of domestic cat in virtue of the conjunction of the above categories is a *stipulative* definition, which is conceptually prior to any empirical discovery of the further properties of various domestic cats (such as weighing seven pounds, basking on a hot tin roof, or having grey stripes). Our stance is at odds with Kripkean essentialism, as we find anyone conducting empirical inquiry in the animal kingdom needs a conceptual steer on what deserves to be called a domestic cat in the first place before they can claim to have had any sort of causal interaction with domestic cats. (These remarks barely scrape the surface of a deep philosophical issue, but they serve at least to indicate where we stand.)

[26] We are disregarding intersective modification in order not to clutter the exposition. However, intersectives are controlled by the same rule of *right subsectivity* that applies to the subsectives, together with the special rule of *left subsectivity* defined in [17].

[27] Iwańska [16, p. 350] refers to 'ideal', 'real', 'true', and 'perfect' as *type-reinforcing* adjectives, which seems to get the pragmatics right of what are semantically pleonastic adjectives. Trivial subsectives should not be confused with subsective intensifiers, as in 'is real pain', when real pain does not contrast with imaginary pain, but with slight pain.

Iterated privation and positive predication

For instance, *forged banknote* has *almost* the same requisites as does *banknote*, but it has also another requisite, namely the property of not being issued by an instance endowed with issuing authority.

To formally define the difference between subsective and privative modification, we need the TIL definition of the relation of being a subset between sets and the operation of the intersection of two sets. The relation of being a *subset* between α-sets, $\subseteq : (o(o\alpha)(o\alpha))$, is defined for any type α as follows. Let $a, b \to_v (o\alpha)$, $x \to_v \alpha$. Then:

$$^0\!\subseteq\, =\, \lambda ab\, [\forall x\, [[a\, x] \supset [b\, x]]]$$

The relation of being a *proper subset*, $\subset : (o(o\alpha)(o\alpha))$, is then defined as usual:

$$^0\!\subset\, =\, \lambda ab\, [[\forall x\, [[a\, x] \supset [b\, x]]] \wedge \neg [^0\!=\, a\, b]]$$

For instance, that the set of primes, *Prime*: $(o\tau)$, is a subset of the naturals, *Natural*: $(o\tau)$, is captured by this construction:

$$[^0\!\subseteq\, ^0Prime\, ^0Natural] = [\forall x\, [^0Prime\, x] \supset [^0Natural\, x]]$$

Similarly, that the set of primes is a proper subset of the naturals is captured by this construction:

$$[^0\!\subset\, ^0Prime\, ^0Natural] = [[\forall x[^0Prime\, x] \supset [^0Natural\, x]] \wedge [^0Prime \neq\, ^0Natural]]$$

The operation of intersection, $\cap : ((o\alpha)(o\alpha)(o\alpha))$, is defined as follows:

$$^0\!\cap\, =\, \lambda ab\, \lambda x\, [[ax] \wedge [bx]]$$

For instance, that the intersection of primes and even numbers, *Even*: $(o\tau)$, is equal to the singleton 2 is captured by this construction:

$$[^0\!\cap\, ^0Prime\, ^0Even] = \lambda x\, [[^0Prime\, x] \wedge [^0Even\, x]] = \lambda x\, [x =\, ^0\!2]$$

In what follows we will use classical (infix) set-theoretical notation for any sets A, B; hence instead of '$[^0\!\subset\, A\, B]$' we will write '$[A \subset B]$', and instead of '$[^0\!\cap\, A\, B]$' we will write '$[A \cap B]$'. Since we will be comparing sets of properties, the type α is here the type of an individual property, $(o\iota)_{\tau\omega}$.

We are now able to provide the following two definitions.

Definition 6 *(Subsective vs. privative modifiers)*. Let $M \to ((o\iota)_{\tau\omega}(o\iota)_{\tau\omega})$; $F, p \to (o\iota)_{\tau\omega}$. Then

- A modifier M is *subsective* with respect to a property F iff

$$[^0Ess\, F] \subseteq [^0Ess\, [M\, F]]$$

- A modifier M is *non-trivially subsective* with respect to a property F iff

$$[^0Ess\, F] \subset [^0Ess\, [M\, F]]$$

- A modifier M is *privative* with respect to a property F iff

$$[[^0Ess\, F] \cap [^0Ess\, [M\, F]]] \neq \emptyset$$
$$\wedge\, \exists p\, [[[^0Ess\, F]\, p] \wedge [[^0Ess\, [M\, F]]\, \lambda w \lambda t\, [\lambda x\, \neg[p_{wt}x]]]]$$

Iterated privation and positive predication

Remark. The second conjunct defining *privative modifier* is to be read as follows: "There is a property p such that it is a requisite of the property F ($[[^0Ess\,F]\,p]$), and among the requisites of the modified property $[M\,F]$ there is a property that *contradicts* p: $[[^0Ess\,[M\,F]]\,\lambda w \lambda t\,[\lambda x\,\neg[p_{wt}x]]]$." This follows from the semantics of privative modification. The privative modifier M not only deprives the property F of one or more of its requisites, it also adds at least one requisite that causes privation.

Remark. The above definition of subsective and privative modifiers is a novel contribution of this paper. It is an improvement over the corresponding definitions in Primiero and Jespersen [28] and Duží et al. [6, §4.4]. As for subsective modifiers, the new definition differentiates between non-trivially and trivially subsective modifiers. As for privatives, the original definition is a logical consequence of this new one, as we are going to prove below. It not only stipulates that among the requisites of the privatively modified property F is the property of not being an F, but also explains why it is so. Furthermore, the new definition also specifies what the modified property and the root property have in common. Privation deprives the root property of some *but not all* of its requisites. The more requisites of the root property F are preserved, the closer a relative the modified property is to F. Thus, we are able to keep track of the root property in the modified property, which in turn makes it possible to prove that, for instance, a demolished damaged house is not a demolished damaged bridge (see below for this example).

Example. The modifier *Wooden*: $((o\iota)_{\tau\omega}(o\iota)_{\tau\omega})$ is subsective with respect to the property of being a table, *Table*: $(o\iota)_{\tau\omega}$, but privative with respect to the property of being a horse, *Horse*: $(o\iota)_{\tau\omega}$. Of course, a wooden table is a table, but the essence of the property $[^0Wooden\,^0Table]$ is enriched by the property of being wooden. Being wooden is a requisite of the property of being a wooden table, but it is not a requisite of the property of being a table, because tables can be instead made of stone, iron, glass, etc.

$$[^0Ess\,^0Table] \subset [^0Ess\,[^0Wooden\,^0Table]]$$

But a wooden horse is not a horse. The modifier *Wooden*, the same modifier that just modified *Table*, deprives the essence of *Horse* of many requisites, for instance of the property of being a living thing, or having a bloodstream, or having kidneys, etc. Hence among the requisites of the property $[^0Wooden\,^0Horse]$ there are properties like *not being a living thing, not having a bloodstream*, etc., which are contradictory (not just contrary) to some of the requisites of the property *Horse*. On the other hand, the property $[^0Wooden\,^0Horse]$ shares many requisites with the property of being a horse, like the outline of the body, resemblance of a horse, etc., and has the additional requisite of being made of wood. Thus, we have (*LT*: $(o\iota)_{\tau\omega}$, the property of being a living thing, *HB*: $(o\iota)_{\tau\omega}$, the property of having blood):

$$[[^0Ess\,^0Horse] \cap [^0Ess\,[^0Wooden\,^0Horse]]] \neq \emptyset \land$$
$$[[[^0Ess\,^0Horse]\,^0LT] \land [[^0Ess\,[^0Wooden\,^0Horse]]\lambda w \lambda t\,\lambda x\,\neg[^0LT\,x]]] \lor$$
$$[[[^0Ess\,^0Horse]\,^0HB] \land [[^0Ess\,[^0Wooden\,^0Horse]]\lambda w \lambda t\,\lambda x\,\neg[^0HB\,x]]] \lor$$

etc.

At the outset of this paper we characterized the difference between subsective and privative modifiers by means of the rule of *right subsectivity*, which holds for subsective but not privative modifiers: a skillful surgeon is a surgeon; a fake banknote fails to be a bank note.

When $M_s \to ((o\iota)_{\tau\omega}(o\iota)_{\tau\omega})$ is a construction of a modifier subsective with respect to the property v-constructed by $F \to (o\iota)_{\tau\omega}$, then necessarily and for all individuals x the following rule of right subsectivity (*RS*) is valid:

$$\frac{[[M_sF]_{wt}\,x]}{[F_{wt}\,x]}\quad RS$$

By Definition 6 it holds that $[^0Ess\,F] \subseteq [^0Ess\,[M_sF]]$. Hence each requisite of F is also a requisite of $[M_sF]$, but not vice versa, provided M_s is non-trivially subsective. By Definition 4 and Claim 1, since each property is a requisite of itself, it follows that F is a requisite of $[M_sF]$:

$$\forall w \forall t\, [\forall x[[^0True_{wt}\,\lambda w\lambda t[[M_sF]_{wt}\,x]] \supset [^0True_{wt}\,\lambda w\lambda t[F_{wt}\,x]]]]$$

which proves the rule of right subsectivity (RS).

For privatives, we already suggested replacing Boolean negation by *property negation*, denoted by '*non*', to specify the rule governing privatives. Let $M_p \rightarrow ((o\iota)_{\tau\omega}(o\iota)_{\tau\omega})$ be a construction of a modifier privative with respect to the property v-constructed by $F \rightarrow (o\iota)_{\tau\omega}$. Then:

$$\frac{[[M_pF]_{wt}\,x]}{[[non\,F]_{wt}\,x]}\quad Priv$$

Of course, it also holds that if x is an $[M_p\,F]$ then it is not the case that x is an F:

$$\frac{[[M_pF]_{wt}\,x]}{\neg[F_{wt}\,x]}\quad Single\ Privation$$

The reason for replacing Boolean negation by property negation is this. For each individual x and for each property F, it is either true that x is an F or it is not true. Yet there are many individuals that are neither an F nor a $[non\,F]$. For instance, each individual either is or is not a banknote. Yet most individuals are neither a banknote nor a fake banknote, because a fake banknote must still have something in common with a banknote. A well-forged banknote is almost a banknote, because the property of being a well-forged banknote is a 'close relative' of the property of being a banknote, sharing many requisites with this property. Hence the property $[non\,F]$ is not contradictory but only contrary to F. Due to the difference between contradictory and contrary properties, the *Priv* rule is indeterministic between the three forks with the third fork having a further measure of indeterminacy, whereas the standard rule of single privation is deterministic. Our strategy being that the *non*-based rule of privation ought to be extended to all instances of single privation, the discrepancy between indeterministic and deterministic rules will vanish, as both the rule of single and the rule of iterated privation will now be indeterministic.

We are now going to define the property negation *non* and prove that *Priv* is valid for privative modifiers.

3.2. Property negation

The philosophical source of inspiration is Aristotle's observations that:

The sentences "It is a not-white log" and "It is not a white log" do not imply one another's truth. For if "It is a not-white log" is true, it must be a log: but that which is not a white log need not be a log at all. (*Prior Analytics* I, 46, 1.)

That is, in modern parlance, a set of logs divides into those that are white and those that are non-white, whereas a set of non-(white logs) divides into those elements that are non-white logs and those that are not even logs (though perhaps white). More specifically, this quotation has inspired us to adopt property negation. And directly relevant for our present purpose:

Iterated privation and positive predication

From the fact that John is not dishonest we cannot conclude that John is honest, but only that he is possibly so. ([26, p. 255])

The alternative is namely that John is neither dishonest, nor honest, so "John is not dishonest", if true, tells us what John *fails* to be and what the *alternatives* are: (i) being honest, (ii) neither being honest nor being dishonest. The contradictory property is that it is not the case that it is not the case that John is honest, which is logically equivalent to him being honest. More specifically, this quotation has inspired us to introduce the trifurcation of cases presented in the Introduction. This trifurcation is epistemic rather than ontological, as it bears on the (in-)validity of various inferences.

The definition of property negation must encapsulate the *contrariety clause* that the intensional negation of one of two conjuncts that are *mutually exclusive* does not entail the truth of the other conjunct.

Definition 7 *(Contrary properties).* Let $x \to \iota$; $F, G \to (o\iota)_{\tau\omega}$. Then the properties F, G are mutually *contrary* iff

$$\forall w \forall t \forall x \, [[F_{wt}\, x] \supset \neg[G_{wt}\, x]] \wedge \exists w \exists t \exists x \, [\neg[F_{wt}\, x] \wedge \neg[G_{wt}\, x]]$$

The definition states that it is not possible for x to co-instantiate F and G, and possibly x instantiates neither F, nor G. The left-hand conjunct,

$$\forall w \forall t \forall x \, [[F_{wt}\, x] \supset \neg[G_{wt}\, x]]$$

is the clause that F and G are *mutually exclusive*. The second conjunct,

$$\exists w \exists t \exists x \, [\neg[F_{wt}\, x] \wedge \neg[G_{wt}\, x]]$$

is the *contrariety* clause that the negation of one of the conjuncts $[F_{wt}\, x]$, $[G_{wt}\, x]$ does not entail the truth of the other one.

Next, we want to show that any property $[M_p F]$ formed from a property F by a modifier M_p privative with respect to F is a property contrary to F. First, we prove the left-hand conjunct:

$$\forall w \forall t \forall x \, [[[M_p F]_{wt}\, x] \supset \neg[F_{wt}\, x]]$$

To this end, we apply the second clause of the definition of privative modifiers (Definition 6): $\exists p \, [[[^0 Ess\, F]\, p] \wedge [[^0 Ess\, [M_p F]]\, \lambda w \lambda t \, [\lambda x \, \neg[p_{wt}\, x]]]]$. Hence the property $[M_p F]$ has among its requisites at least one property contradictory to a requisite of the property F. Let these properties be P and $\lambda w \lambda t \, [\lambda x \, \neg[P_{wt}\, x]]$, respectively. Then at no $\langle w, t \rangle$ is there an individual x that would satisfy both $[[M_p F]_{wt}\, x]$ and $[F_{wt}\, x]$; if there were such an x, then according to Definitions 4 and 5, x would also have to satisfy both $[P_{wt}\, x]$ and $\neg[P_{wt}\, x]$, which is logically impossible.

Remark. This proves that the previous definition found in [6, §4.4] and [28] is a corollary of the new Definition 6.

The contrariety clause $\exists w \exists t \exists x \, [\neg[[M_p F]_{wt}\, x] \wedge \neg[F_{wt}\, x]]$ holds due to the thesis of *individual anti-essentialism* which we subscribe to: no individual has any purely contingent property necessarily.

We should not forget, however, the limiting case where F is a *trivial*, non-contingent property with a constant extension, such as *being self-identical*. In this case, necessarily, when the type is (say) ι, F_{wt} is the entire type ι and $\lambda x \, \neg[F_{wt}\, x]$ is an empty ι-set, because at no $\langle w, t \rangle$ is there an individual that would be neither identical with itself nor non-identical with itself. Another example of a non-contingent property is the property *being identical to a or b*.[28] At all $\langle w,t \rangle$ the extension of this property is the set $\{a,b\}$, and at no $\langle w,t \rangle$ is there an individual that would be neither identical with a or b, nor non-identical with a or b, for both a and b are necessarily around to instantiate this property. The upshot is that non-contingent properties do not lend themselves to being modified by privative modifiers on pain of necessary falsehood. Hence, if *Tri* is such a trivial non-contingent property then the extension of $[M_p Tri]$ is necessarily the empty ι-set for any modifier privative with respect to *Tri*. Such a modifier turns *Tri* into an 'idle property' that has necessarily an empty extension.

Definition 8 *(General modifier privative with respect to a property f).* Let $=: (o((o\iota)_{\tau\omega}(o\iota)_{\tau\omega})((o\iota)_{\tau\omega}(o\iota)_{\tau\omega}))$ be the identity relation defined over first-order modifiers, $non \to ((o\iota)_{\tau\omega}(o\iota)_{\tau\omega})$ a variable ranging over first-order modifiers, $f \to (o\iota)_{\tau\omega}$, $Con : (o(o\iota)_{\tau\omega}(o\iota)_{\tau\omega})$ the relation of contrariety between properties. Then:

$$^0Non = \lambda f \lambda w \lambda t\, [\lambda x\, \exists non\, [[[non\, f]_{wt}\, x] \wedge [^0Con\, [non\, f]\, f]]]$$

is the *general modifier privative with respect to f*.

Remark. Any of the modifiers *non* meeting the condition specified by Definition 8 are privative with respect to the property F. Property negation takes a particular property F to an arbitrary property contrary to it, $[non\, F]$.[29]

Non is thus the unique general privative modifier, and it takes a property F to the general contrary property $[^0Non\, F]$. For instance, $[^0Non\, Banknote]$ is the general property contrary to the property of being a banknote. Necessarily, the extension of $[^0Non\, Banknote]_{wt}$ includes the extensions of the properties *forged banknote, banknote dissolved in acid, Monopoly banknote*, etc., some of the extensions possibly being empty. One might worry that it is too much to claim that, necessarily, the extension contains the full panoply of non-banknotes. But it follows from Definition 8 that the full panoply is indeed involved. At any $\langle w,t \rangle$, for any individual x and the property constructed by $F \to (o\iota)_{\tau\omega}$, this holds:

$$[[^0Non\, F]_{wt}\, x] = \exists non\, [[[non\, F]_{wt}\, x] \wedge [^0Con\, [non\, F]\, F]]$$

Hence, individual a has the property $[^0Non\, F]$ iff a has any property $[non\, F]$ for some *non* privative with respect to F. Thus, the set $[^0Non\, F]_{wt}$ is *almost* as large as the complement $\overline{F_{wt}}$ of the set F_{wt}. At *some*, but not all, $\langle w,t \rangle$ it is the case that $[^0Non\, F]_{wt} = \overline{F_{wt}}$. Or, when F_{wt} happens to be the entire type ι, then $[^0Non\, F]_{wt}$ must be the empty ι-set, i.e. the union of all empty sets $[^0Non\, F]_{wt}$. Definition 8 does not exclude such modifier functions as do not even have a name in our vernacular.

Contrariety provides the weaker form of negation that is suitable for privative modifiers as explained above. Definition 8 thus justifies the *elimination rule Priv* for modifiers M_p privative with respect to property F stated above:

$$[[M_p F]_{wt}\, x] \vdash [[^0Non\, F]_{wt}\, x]$$

The conclusion of *Priv* states that the predication of F eludes x: F does not get to be predicated of x. For instance, if the premise is that a is a *fake banknote* then the conclusion is that a is a *Non-banknote*, therefore the property banknote is not predicated of a. Or if b is a *wooden horse* then b is a *Non-horse*. But if c is

---

[28] TIL comes with a constant domain. See [6, 378–379].
[29] Martin [24, p. 449] says, "Semantically [infinite negation, e.g. *non-human*] converts a term into one that stands for its non-empty complement ...". Our property negation does not come with an ontological restriction such as non-emptiness. However, more importantly, our '*non-F*' does not denote a complement set, but a contrary *property*; what denotes a set is '*non-F_{wt}*'.

a *wooden bird* then it follows neither that c is a *Non-horse*, nor that c is a *horse*, because the properties *Non-horse* and *horse* necessarily have still something in common (at least one common requisite), unlike the properties *wooden bird* and *horse* or *Non-horse*.

Moreover, the partial order defined on sets of requisites makes it possible to compare how close the privatively modified property $[M_p F]$ is to F. Since $[M_p F]$ and F have some requisites in common, they are relatives. For instance, a fake banknote is not a fake passport or even a *Non*-passport; they are not relatives. Yet a fake banknote is a close relative of banknotes, closer than, for instance, a Monopoly banknote or a burnt banknote. From this point of view the most distant relative of the property F is thus the property $[^0 Non\, F]$.

Let us run a test case. Can a paradox be deduced from our theory? Consider this example:

(1) Individual a is a €10 banknote
(2) Whatever is a €10 banknote is a banknote

(3) a is a banknote

(a) a is a forged €100 banknote created by adding a '0' to '10' to form '100'
(b) Whatever is a forged banknote is a non-banknote

(c) a is a non-banknote

Contradiction: (3) and (c).

This does not follow, however. One fact is that a is a tampered-with €10 banknote. Yet having a zero add to '10' does not have to undermine a's property as a €10 banknote. Hence, a may remain a banknote, for the modifier *€10* is subsective with respect to the property of being a banknote. Another fact is that a is a forged €100 banknote. From this, however, it does not follow that a is no longer a banknote. It only follows that a is not a €100 banknote. The property that has been compromised by the attempted forgery is that of being a €100 banknote, not the property of being a banknote per se. The apparent paradox arises, because premise (b) fails to state that a is a forged €100 banknote and hence a non-€100 banknote. Therefore, premise (b) becomes irrelevant. Hence, a can be a €10 banknote (and thus a banknote) while being a non-€100 banknote.[30]

3.3. Double privation

We turn next to double privation, which has this form:

$$[M'_p [M_p F]]$$

Since M_p is privative with respect to $[M_p F]$, the intersection of the essences of $[M'_p [M_p F]]$ and $[M_p F]$ must be non-empty. And since M_p is privative with respect to F, the intersection of the essences of $[M_p F]$ and F must also be non-empty. One may then wonder whether the respective essences of $[M'_p [M_p F]]$ and F can be disjunctive. We think not. There must be an overlap of requisites, and not just of any old properties, but of carefully chosen ones.

Recall the earthquakes in central Italy in 2016. Many houses, bridges and other buildings and constructions were damaged, some beyond repair. A demolished damaged house is surely not a house, but debris: a particular object goes through the stages of being a house, then a damaged house and finally a demolished damaged house, which is in material terms nothing but debris. Yet a demolished damaged house is different

---

[30] We are indebted to Nikolaj Nottelmann and Lars Binderup for discussion of this example.

from a demolished damaged bridge. A demolished damaged house shares requisites with houses that it does not share with demolished damaged bridges.

It may so happen that the essence of $[M'_p [M_p F]]$ is a superset of the essence of F. In such a case, if x instantiates $[M'_p [M_p F]]$ then x also instantiates F. For instance, a repaired damaged house is again a house. To repair a damage is to undo the damage and in so doing returning the previously damaged artefact to its still earlier state of functioning properly; such is the semantics of the verb 'to repair' and the adjective 'repaired'. So here we have come full circle back to F. This particular instance of the modifier *repaired* is privative with respect to *damaged house*, because what is a non-house turns into a house. (We are presupposing, to get the example off the ground, that a damaged house is so damaged that it no longer qualifies as a house.) Being a repaired damaged house is one way of being a house. Formally:

$$[[^0Ess\,^0House] \subset [^0Ess\,[^0Repaired\,[^0Damaged\,^0House]]]]$$

Yet it may also so happen that the essence of $[M'_p [M_p F]]$ and the essence of F have a non-empty intersection, but neither is a subset of the other. For instance, a demolished damaged house is neither a damaged house, nor a house, but something altogether different, namely a pile of rubble. The modifier *demolished*, like *repaired* above, is privative with respect to *damaged house*, but the logical effect of applying it to *damaged house* is the opposite. The semantics of the verb 'to demolish' puts it in opposition to 'to repair' or 'to restore'. Nonetheless, a demolished damaged house must possess the requisite of having previously been a house.

As is seen, the property of being a demolished damaged house spans three states: first, being a house; second, being a damaged house; third, being a demolished damaged house. Formally:

$$[^0Ess\,[^0Demolished\,[^0Damaged\,^0House]]] \cap [^0Ess\,^0House] \neq \emptyset$$

Absent the requisite property of having been previously a house, there is nothing to block the inference that a demolished damaged house is (say) a demolished damaged bridge.

3.4. Three case studies

Here we revisit three examples that were broached above. For better readability of the following formulae, we will now abbreviate formulae for constructions of the form '$\lambda w \lambda t\, [\lambda x\, \neg[p_{wt}\, x]]$' as '*not-p*'.

3.4.1. First fork

Since *damaged* is privative with respect to *house*, we have (as per Definition 6):

$$[[^0Ess\,^0House] \cap [^0Ess\,[^0Damaged\,^0House]]] \neq \emptyset$$
$$\land\, \exists p\,[[[^0Ess\,^0House]\,p] \land [[^0Ess\,[^0Damaged\,^0House]]\,\textit{not-p}]]$$

Hence *damaged* has turned some of the requisites of *house* into their opposites. For instance, if one of the requisites of being a house is the property of being a place to live in, then *damaged* turns this property into the property of not being a place to live in. Since *repaired* is privative with respect to the property *damaged house*, we have:

$$[[^0Ess\,[^0Damaged\,^0House]] \cap [^0Ess\,[^0Repaired\,[^0Damaged\,^0House]]]] \neq \emptyset$$
$$\land\, \exists q\,[[[^0Ess\,[^0Damaged\,^0House]]\,q]$$
$$\land\, [[^0Ess\,[^0Repaired\,[^0Damaged\,^0House]]]\,\textit{not-q}]]$$

Now *repaired* cancels the effect of *damaged*; it must turn all those opposites *not-p* of *damaged house* back into the original requisites p of *House*. Thus, among those properties q that are contained in the essence of [$^0Damaged\,^0House$] and appear as *not-q* in the essence of [$^0Repaired\,[^0Damaged\,^0House]$] there must be all those properties p which are contained in the essence of *house* and their opposites *not-p* in the essence of [$^0Damaged\,^0House$]. As a result, among these properties q there are the properties $\lambda w \lambda t\,[\lambda x\,\neg\neg[p_{wt}\,x]]$, hence p. We obtain:

$$[[^0Ess\,^0House] \subset [^0Ess\,[^0Repaired\,[^0Damaged\,^0House]]]]$$

The property *repaired damaged house* has all the requisites of *house*, being again a place to live in.

3.4.2. Second fork

Contrast the above property with the property *demolished damaged house*. Whatever is a demolished damaged house cannot be a house, for the same reason that a demolished house cannot be a house. As soon as we understand the meaning of the predicate 'is a demolished damaged house', we are able to calculate which way it goes, and that we must land on the second fork. So, we know that a demolished damaged house is a non-house. But we know something positive about it, too: we know that it is now a pile of rubble. A demolished damaged house has been physically reduced to its raw matter (wood, steel, brick, etc.), just like a melted-down statue is reduced to its raw matter (bronze, clay, etc.). The internal link between being a demolished damaged house and being a pile of rubble is that that pile of rubble has a noble past as a damaged house and before that as a house.

3.4.3. Third fork

Consider again *former heir apparent*. This combination of privatives is doubly dynamic due to the backward-looking aspect of *former* and the forward-looking aspect of *apparent*, in the special sense of 'apparent' as 'designated to become'. Someone who is a designated F is currently not yet an F, though they are supposed to become one. We are deploying the strict interpretation of 'former' as a privative rather than a modal modifier to get the example of former heir apparent off the ground.[31] With that in place, someone who is a former heir apparent is not an heir, for one of two reasons: either the person succeeded in succeeding the previous monarch (promotion), or the person is no longer being even considered for the throne (demotion).

Accordingly, one requisite which *heir apparent* comes with is that any bearer must lack the property of being the successor (where it is understood which is the relevant royal position, e.g. the office of King of Denmark): this requisite property is due to the modification provided by *apparent*. Another requisite which *former heir apparent* comes with is that any bearer must lack the property of being any longer the prospective heir. The backward-looking aspect of *former* voids the forward-looking aspect of *apparent*, which brings us to the present time where the bearer of the property of being a former heir apparent may, or may not, be sitting on the throne.

3.4.4. Summary

To sum up these three case studies, which fork is the right one depends on the *semantics* of the modifiers involved. When faced with iterated privatives, the agents who operate within some interactive system for reasoning on the basis of natural-language texts can request additional information about particular modifiers.[32] The appropriate answer will be a refinement of the modifier in question. For instance, an appropriate refinement of *repaired* would be this:

---

[31] On the privative reading, from "a is a former F" it can be inferred that a is no longer an F, hence is not an F. On the modal reading, it cannot be excluded that a has been reinstated as an F.
[32] A particular such system is investigated in, e.g., [4] and [10].

$$\forall p \, [[[[^0Ess \, F] \, p] \wedge [[^0Ess[M_pF]] \, \textit{not-p}]] \supset [[^0Ess \, [^0Repaired \, [M_pF]]] \, p]]$$

Thus, we can infer that whatever x is a repaired $[M_pF]$ is also an F. Similarly, a supplementary piece of information about the semantics of *demolished* might be this:

$$\exists p \, [[[[^0Ess \, F] \, p] \wedge [[^0Ess[M_pF]] \, \textit{not-p}] \wedge [[^0Ess \, [^0Demolished \, [M_pF]]] \, \textit{not-p}]]$$

Then we can infer that a demolished $[M_pF]$ is not an F. If no such refinement can be supplied, then we cannot decide which of the first two forks an individual x lands on, and so we know that we are facing a case of the third fork.

4. Conclusion

The results obtained in this paper amount to an extension of the standard theory of property modification by adding a logic of iterated privation to it. We started out with the problem that the received rule of single privation is too crude, because it turns the root property into the contradictory property. To start solving the problem, we replaced Boolean negation by *property negation*, enabling us to operate on *contrary* rather than contradictory properties.

We then assigned so-called *requisites* to properties, and defined the *essence* of a property as the set of all its requisites. Also, properties formed by means of iterated privation are equipped with requisites. They underpin our *presuppositional* theory of *positive predication*, which is the predication of properties an object must have, as a matter of analytic necessity, if it has a particular privatively modified property.

The notion of requisite properties enabled us to show that properties formed from iterated privatives give rise to a *trifurcation* of cases between returning to the original root property or to a property contrary to it or being semantically undecidable for want of further information. We have thereby exceeded the general insight that pairs of privatives yield contraries rather than contradictories, because we are in a position to calculate which of the forks of the trifurcation we land on.

Acknowledgements

This research has been supported by a University of Padua project on *Disagreement*, PRAT UNIPD (Massimiliano Carrara), as well as by the Grant Agency of the Czech Republic Project No. GA15-13277S, *Hyperintensional Logic for Natural Language Analysis*, and Project SGS No. SP2017/133 of the internal grant agency of VŠB-TUO, *Knowledge Modelling and its Applications in Software Engineering III* (Marie Duží and Bjørn Jespersen). Various versions of this material have been presented by Bjørn Jespersen as invited lectures at the Heinrich Heine University Düsseldorf, 21 December 2017; at the *Network of Danish Philosophers Abroad*, University of Southern Denmark, 8–9 September 2017; conference *How To Say 'Yes' or 'No': Logical Approaches to Modes of Assertion and Denial*, Universitá del Salento, Lecce (21–22 January 2016); Ruhr-Universität Bochum (5 November 2013); Hong Kong University (8 May 2012); Hong Kong Polytechnic University (7 May 2012); as a tutorial at Technical University of Ostrava (26 February 2013); and, as solicited lectures at *LOGICA 2014*, Hejnice (17–20 June 2014) together with Massimiliano Carrara; *CLPS 13*, Ghent (16–18 September 2013). This research on iterated privation grew out of a project aimed at developing an intensional logic for reasoning about technical artefacts in general and technical malfunction in particular that Massimiliano Carrara and Bjørn Jespersen embarked upon in 2008 when the latter was affiliated with the then-Section of Philosophy, Delft University of Technology. The Section sponsored a one-month stay in Padua to initiate the project in cooperation with Massimiliano Carrara. Marie Duží later joined the sub-project on iterated privation. The present paper completes what we would occasionally refer to as 'the malfunction trilogy'. We wish to thank two anonymous reviewers for *Journal of Applied Logic* for very valuable comments and suggestions which improved the quality of the paper.

References

[1] K.R. Beesley, Evaluative adjectives as one-place predicates in Montague Grammar, J. Semant. 1 (1982) 195–249.
[2] M. Carrara, M. Soavi, Copies, replicas and counterfeits of artworks and artifacts, Monist 93 (2010) 417–435.
[3] S.S. Coulson, G. Fauconnier, Fake guns and stone lions: conceptual blending and privative adjectives, in: B. Fox, D. Jurafsky, L. Michaelis (Eds.), Cognition and Function in Language, CSLI, Palo Alto, CA, 1999.
[4] M. Číhalová, M. Duží, N. Ciprich, M. Menšík, 'Agents' reasoning using TIL-Script and Prolog', in: Information Modelling and Knowledge Bases XXI, in: Frontiers in Artificial Intelligence and Applications, vol. 206, 2010, pp. 135–154.
[5] L. Del Frate, Failure: Analysis of an Engineering Concept, PhD Thesis, Delft University of Technology, Delft, 2014.
[6] M. Duží, B. Jespersen, P. Materna, Procedural Semantics for Hyperintensional Logic, Springer, Dordrecht, 2010.
[7] M. Duží, How to unify Russellian and Strawsonian definite descriptions, in: R. Ciuni, H. Wansing, C. Willkommen (Eds.), Recent Trends in Philosophical Logic, vol. 41, 2014, pp. 85–101.
[8] M. Duží, Presuppositions and two kinds of negation, Log. Anal. 239 (2017) 245–263, special issue on *How to Say 'Yes' or 'No'*, D. Chiffi (ed.).
[9] M. Duží, M. Číhalová, Questions, answers and presuppositions, Comput. Sist. 19 (2015) 647–659.
[10] M. Duží, M. Číhalová, M. Menšík, Communication in a multi-agent system; questions and answers, in: 13th International Multidisciplinary Scientific GeoConference SGEM 2013, Albena, Bulgaria, 2013, pp. 11–22.
[11] M. Enç, Towards a referential analysis of temporal expressions, Linguist. Philos. 9 (1986) 405–426.
[12] L. Floridi, N. Fresco, G. Primiero, On malfunctioning software, Synthese 192 (2015) 1199–1220.
[13] L.R. Horn, A Natural History of Negation, University of Chicago Press, London, Chicago, 1989.
[14] L.R. Horn, Duplex negatio affirmat? On the economy of double negation, in: Papers from the Parasession on Negation, in: CSL, vol. 27, Chicago Linguistic Society, Chicago, 1991, pp. 80–106, pt. 2.
[15] **L.R. Horn, Lie-toe-tease: double negatives and unexcluded middles, Philos. Stud. (2017),** https://doi.org/10.1007/s11098-015-0509-y.
[16] Ł. Iwańska, Reasoning with intensional negative adjectivals: semantics, pragmatics, and context, Comput. Intell. 13 (1997) 348–390.
[17] B. Jespersen, Left subsectivity: how to infer that a round peg is round, Dialectica 70 (2016) 531–547.
[18] B. Jespersen, The phone booth puzzle, Organon F 13 (2006) 411–438.
[19] B. Jespersen, M. Carrara, A new logic of technical malfunction, Stud. Log. 101 (2013) 547–581.
[20] B. Jespersen, M. Carrara, Two conceptions of technical malfunction, Theoria 77 (2011) 117–138.
[21] B. Jespersen, P. Materna, Are wooden tables necessarily wooden?, Acta Anal. 17 (2002) 115–150.
[22] H. Kamp, Two theories about adjectives, in: E.L. Keenan (Ed.), Formal Semantics of Natural Language, Cambridge University Press, Cambridge, 1975, pp. 123–155.
[23] D.C. Makinson, Topics in Modern Logic, Methuen and Co., London, 1973.
[24] J.N. Martin, All brutes are subhuman: Aristotle and Ockham on private [*sic*]] negation, Synthese 134 (2003) 429–461.
[25] R. Montague, English as a formal language, in: B. Visentini (Ed.), Linguaggi nella società e nella tecnica, Edizioni di Communita, 1970, pp. 188–221.
[26] M. La Palme Reyes, et al., Models for non-Boolean negations in natural languages based on aspect analysis, in: D. Gabbay, H. Wansing (Eds.), What is Negation?, Springer, Dordrecht, 1999, pp. 239–260.
[27] B. Partee, Privative adjectives: subsective plus coercion, in: R. Bäuerle, et al. (Eds.), Presuppositions and Discourse, Elsevier, Amsterdam, 2001.
[28] G. Primiero, B. Jespersen, Alleged assassins: realist and constructivist semantics for modal modifiers, in: International Tbilisi Symposium on Logic, Language, and Computation, in: Lecture Notes in Computer Science, vol. 7758, 2013, pp. 94–114.
[29] M.E. Siegel, Capturing the Adjective, PhD Thesis, University of Massachusetts, Amherst, 1976.
[30] P. Tichý, Existence and god, J. Philos. 76 (1979) 403–420, reprinted in: in: V. Svoboda, B. Jespersen, C. Cheyne (Eds.), Collected Papers in Logic and Philosophy, University of Otago Press, Filosofia, Dunedin, Prague, 2004.

Further reading

[31] P. Tichý, in: V. Svoboda, B. Jespersen, C. Cheyne (Eds.), Collected Papers in Logic and Philosophy, University of Otago Press, Filosofia, Czech Academy of Sciences, Dunedin, Prague, 2004.

Left Subsectivity: How to Infer that a Round Peg is Round

Bjørn JESPERSEN

ABSTRACT

A property modifier is a function that takes a property to a property. For instance, the modifier *short* takes the property *being a Dutchman* to the property *being a short Dutchman*. Assume that *being a round peg* is a property obtained by means of modification, *round* being the modifier and *being a peg* the input property. Then how are we to infer that a round peg is a peg? By means of a rule of right subsectivity. How are we to infer that a round peg is round? By means of a rule of left subsectivity. This paper puts forward two rules (one general, the other special) of left subsectivity. The rules fill a gap in the prevalent theory of property modification. The paper also explains why the rules are philosophically relevant.

Introduction

Individual *a* before you is a round peg. Which rule do you invoke in order to infer that *a* is round? Conjunction elimination is your rule in case "*a* is a round peg" is elliptical for "*a* is round and *a* is a peg":

$$\frac{a \text{ is round} \wedge a \text{ is a peg}}{a \text{ is round}} \wedge E$$

But suppose we take the syntactic structure of "*a* is a round peg" at face value. Then the sentence is an instance of the predication of one *modified property*, (*round peg*), rather than of two unmodified properties, *round* and *peg*. Which rule will validate this inference?

$$\frac{a \text{ is a (round peg)}}{a \text{ is round}} \text{?}$$

The occurrence of 'round' in "*a* is a (round peg)" is in attributive position where it denotes a modifier. The occurrence of 'round' in "*a* is round" is in predicative position where it denotes a property. The grammar of the English sentence "A round peg is round" glosses over the semantic difference between when the adjective denotes a modifier and when a property. Other languages with a richer morphology than English will highlight the difference between attributive and predicative occurrences. For instance, German has "Ein runder Pflock ist rund".

This chapter originally appeared in Dialectica (2016), 70(4), pp. 531–547.

Left subsectivity: how to infer that a round peg is round

The major logical challenge the inference poses is how to somehow trade the property modifier denoted in the premise for the property denoted in the conclusion. The modifier cannot be simply detached from the context in which it modifies a property and be predicated of *a*. Modifiers cannot be predicated of anything: they are not true or false of anything and lack satisfaction classes.

Here is a case in point. (Heim and Kratzer 1998) introduces a rule dubbed 'PM', short for 'Predicate Modification'. PM is not accompanied by a type-shifting rule for replacing a modifier by a property (or a predicate, if the mode is formal and not material). PM allows that if x is a city in Texas then x is a city and x is in Texas (ibid., p. 65), without laying down how 'is a city in Texas' ('in Texas' denoting a modifier) may be factored out into 'is a city' and 'is in Texas' (both denoting a property). Formally, relative to Heim and Kratzer's framework, a type-shifting rule would have had to sustain swapping a term of the modifier type $\langle\langle e, t\rangle, \langle e, t\rangle\rangle$ for a term of the same shape of the property type $\langle e, t\rangle$. Both e and t are ground types, e being the type of (terms for) *entities* (individuals, particulars) and t the type of (terms for) truth-values, of which there are two, *true* and *false*. The derived functional type $\langle e, t\rangle$ types a functor (a term for a function) from entities to truth-values. This type is the type of the characteristic function of a set of entities: it is either true or else false that some entity is an element of the relevant set. The type $\langle\langle e, t\rangle, \langle e, t\rangle\rangle$ types a functor from sets to sets: for instance, given a set of strawberries, we are given its subset of ripe strawberries. It is characteristic of an extensionalist theory of properties and modifiers to assign the respective types $\langle e, t\rangle$ and $\langle\langle e, t\rangle, \langle e, t\rangle\rangle$. Heim and Kratzer are fully alert to the fact that some occurrences of, for instance, the adjective 'small' assign the type $\langle e, t\rangle$ to it while other occurrences assign the type $\langle\langle e, t\rangle, \langle e, t\rangle\rangle$. But their discussion of 'small' as it occurs in, e.g., "Jumbo is small" (ibid., p. 70, entry (18)) remains inconclusive.

The above lacuna is symptomatic of a general lacuna in the prevalent model-theoretic semantics of modifiers and properties (material mode) and adjectives (formal mode) as developed by Montague Grammar.[1] This theory lacks a rule to validate the inference that a round peg is round, that a city in Texas is in Texas, that a red house is red, and so on. The closest the framework comes is this equivalence:[2]

$$\exists P_{\langle e,t\rangle} \Box \forall Q_{\langle s,\langle e,t\rangle\rangle} \forall x_e \, [ADJ'\,(Q)(x) \leftrightarrow P(x) \wedge {}^{\vee}Q(x)]$$

---

[1] See, for instance, (Clark 1970), (Montague 1974), (Kamp and Partee 1995), (Partee 2001, 2007), (Abdullah and Frost 2005), (Amoia and Gardent 2007).

[2] See (Partee 2001, 3), formalizing what Montague says informally in (1974, 211). While Q is of the intensional type $\langle s, \langle e, t\rangle\rangle$ from world/time pairs to sets of entities, ${}^{\vee}Q$ is of the extensional type $\langle e, t\rangle$ due to extensionalization, which is the descent from an intension to one of its extensions, e.g. the descent from a property to a set or from a truth-condition to a truth-value, by applying a function (an intension) to an argument (a combined world/time pair). The type of the value of x is e, so the result of applying ${}^{\vee}Q$ to the value of x is of type t, and this result becomes in turn one of the two arguments for the truth-functional connective $\wedge$. Another thing, though, is that the result of applying ADJ' to Q, given Q's type assignment, must be of the same type as Q, hence ought to require extensionalization, for else $ADJ'\,(Q)$ cannot be predicated of the value of x. Yet the formula lacks the extensionalization ${}^{\vee}(ADJ'\,(Q))$. However, I will keep formalities to a minimum in the ensuing exposition, as they can be easily reconstructed. I will not flag the difference between sets and properties notationally, but mention it in prose whenever important.

Left subsectivity: how to infer that a round peg is round

The equivalence is to the effect *that* there is a set *P* as soon as there is a modifier *ADJ'*. What goes unexplained is *how* the equivalence is established. *Why* is it logically necessary that if something is in the set of individuals with the property (denoted by) *ADJ'* (*Q*) then it is also in the set *P*? The equivalence is on the right track, to be sure, for there must be such a *P*. But the equivalence underspecifies the logical transition from *x* belonging to *ADJ'* (*Q*) to *x* belonging to *P*.

The sort of rule we are looking for is a rule of *left subsectivity*.[3] This sort of rule is supposed to validate the following inference schema, *M* a property modifier and *F* a property, while *M** is a property obtained in a way still to be explained:

$$\frac{a \text{ is an } (MF)}{a \text{ is an } M^*} \text{ left subsectivity}$$

Contrast left with right subsectivity:

$$\frac{a \text{ is an } (MF)}{a \text{ is an } F} \text{ right subsectivity}$$

The latter inference obviously holds if (*MF*) is, say, the property (*round peg*) or (*skillful surgeon*), and obviously not in the case of, say, (*alleged assassin*) or (*fake banknote*). The former pair of modifiers are *subsectives*, of two different kinds: *round* is *intersective*; *skillful* is *purely subsective*. The intersectives form a proper subset of the subsectives. The latter pair are *non-subsectives*, again of two different kinds: *alleged* is *modal*; *fake* is *privative*. The pure subsectives are easy to describe formally: from *a* being a skillful surgeon, infer that *a* is a surgeon. The rule controlling pure subsectives is simply a rule of modifier elimination. The relevant rule is the one of right subsectivity. The logic, informally stated, is that a skillful surgeon must be a surgeon, while a surgeon may not be a skillful surgeon. The logic of intersectives is also easily stated informally. If *a* is a round peg then *a* must be round and *a* must be a peg, and if *a* is round and a peg then *a* must be a round peg. Intersectives are controlled by the combination of the rules of right and left subsectivity. As long as we lack a rule of left subsectivity, we cannot state any rule of inference for intersectives. The logic of modals can be stated informally: if *a* is an alleged assassin, then *a* may, or may not, be an assassin. Stating it formally is another matter.[4] I will not include modal modifiers in this paper. The logic of privatives, loosely stated, is that

---

[3] I have borrowed the term 'left subsectivity' from (Recanati 2011, 88). Recanati offers "A fake dollar is fake" (ibid., 89) as an example of left subsectivity, offering this formalization: "$AB \Rightarrow A$". It is not a matter of course that every theory of modification will need a rule of left subsectivity. For instance, in Primiero's extension of Martin-Löf's constructive type theory, "*a* is an (*MF*)" gets analyzed as $M(x)[x:F]$, which predicates *M* of *x*, provided *F* has been predicated of *x*. See (Jespersen and Primiero 2013). (Chatzikyriakidis and Luo 2013, 167), also coming from constructivist type theory, do something similar. When individual *a* is a red house, the propositional function *red* modifies individual *a* that has already been typed by *house*. Since *object* is a supertype of *house*, it follows that if *a* is a red house then *a* is a red object (a red something).

[4] Modals ostensibly do not validate much of logical interest: see (Partee 2007). (Jespersen and Primiero 2013) distils the logical essence of modal modifiers from a realist and a constructivist perspective, respectively.

if *a* is a fake banknote then *a* fails to be a banknote: no set of banknotes can be a subset of a set of fake banknotes. The logic of privatives can be stated formally once we have agreed upon whether to use boolean or property negation. I prefer the latter, but the standard boolean negation suffices for the points I wish to make in this paper.

The narrow scope of this paper is to put forward a rule of left subsectivity applicable to intersectives. This rule must justify that a round peg is round, a wooden house is wooden, and so on. The broader scope is to put forward a rule of left subsectivity that encompasses pure subsectives and privatives. As a by-product, this broader rule encompasses intersectives as well.

The broader rule, which I shall call *the general rule of left subsectivity*, is weaker than the narrow rule applicable to intersectives only, which I shall call *the special rule of left subsectivity*.[5] The difference hinges on whether the specification of the property that is predicated in the respective conclusions is absolute (i.e. unqualified) or relative (i.e. qualified by means of modification). The general rule does not allow inferring that a skillful surgeon is skillful *absoluter*, that a fake banknote is fake *simpliciter*, or that, nonsensically, a main station is main. The rule has been designed specifically to steer clear of the fallacy *secundum quid ad simpliciter*.[6] This fallacy trades a relative predication for an absolute one. The crux is to preserve the relativization from premise to conclusion.

We need the special rule for a number of reasons. I mentioned already that the rule of inference controlling intersectives requires both a rule of right subsectivity and a rule of left subsectivity. In addition to that, the special rule is indispensable for acquiring inferential knowledge. Inferential knowledge is new explicit knowledge that has been extracted from existing explicit knowledge by means of a sound argument. Explicit knowledge is knowledge we are aware of having, and being aware of it is a prerequisite for our applying rules of inference to it. If we know that *a* is a round peg then we are in a position to know the additional snippet that *a* is round by invoking the special rule of left subsectivity. Another example of inferential knowledge would be this. If it is known that *a* is a round peg and that *a* is a wooden artefact then it can be inferred that *a* is a round wooden artefact. This is to say that *round* carries over to any other empirical property *a* also instantiates. If we generalize this feature of *round* to all other intersectives, it turns out that, for any modifier, if it is intersective with respective to *some* property instantiated by some object then it is also intersective with respect to *all* other properties also instantiated by that object. If nothing else, this one feature is what drives a wedge in between the two kinds of subsectives, the pure ones and the intersectives. If *a* is a spelunker and *a* is also a skillful surgeon then it does not follow that *a* is a skillful spelunker. The relevant feature, more formally, is that intersectives are invariant under complementation and pure subsectives are not.

Finally, making explicit the special rule of left subsectivity sheds light on what sort of modifiers the intersectives are. What exactly is the nexus between the modifier *round* in *a* being a round peg and the property *round* in *a* being round? I argue below that the search

---

[5] In (Duží et al. 2010, §4.4) I put forward a rule called *pseudo-detachment*, which was a rudimentary precursor of the general rule of left subsectivity. I have deployed pseudo-detachment in, e.g., (Jespersen 2015) and (Jespersen and Carrara 2013). However, the present essay is the first full investigation into left subsectivity, thus surpassing the previous presentations.
[6] See (Szabó 2003, 409, fn. 1).

Left subsectivity: how to infer that a round peg is round

for a special rule of left subsectivity reveals that intersectives, though typed as modifiers, are really little other than properties in modifier's clothing, as far as their left subsectivity goes. The right subsectivity of the intersectives makes them modifiers in the traditional sense that they qualify or 'colour' a property: when a is a round peg then a is not just any sort of peg, but a peg of the round sort. But a is also round, pure and simple, whereas a skillful surgeon is not skillful, pure and simple, but with regard to being a surgeon (and also is not just a surgeon, but a skillful one). I suspect that the absoluteness that left subsectivity demands of intersectives is rooted in the absoluteness of certain empirical properties, such as *being round*.

Amidst this conjecture, someone might point out that, strictly speaking, when a is a round peg then a is not round, pure and simple. For sure, a may be round *as far as pegs go*, but it could not possibly be perfectly round as measured against the far more exacting standards of geometry. No empirical property, the thought continues, is absolute for want of perfection. Therefore, if there are no absolute empirical properties, then there can be no intersective modifiers of empirical properties, either. Instead all subsectives would come out pure subsectives. This view is austere, of course, but the notion of absolute, or unqualified, empirical property is not exactly uncontroversial, so the view is not inherently unreasonable. For this reason I am not going to assume that the notion has instances. What I wish to establish is, strictly speaking, something conditional: *if* we are to explain the nature of intersective modification *then* we must explain right and left subsectivity, which includes pointing out the assumption that absolute empirical properties exist. The special rule flows forth from a definition of intersectives that posits exactly one absolute property which matches a given intersective modifier. This definition is a refinement of the above Montagovian meaning postulate for intersectives. The crucial additional bit is an explanation of where the postulate's P (now retyped as a property) comes from. This explanation undergirds the logical link between P in the conclusion/consequent and the intersectively modified property in the premise/antecedent.

The special rule of left subsectivity validates the inference that if a is a round peg then a is round. There is a property such as being round in an unqualified manner. Hence there is a set (extension of a property) of objects that are round. This set intersects with other sets to form the set of those things that have the two properties in question. The general rule of left subsectivity validates the inference that if a is a round peg then there is a property f such that a is a (*round f*). The latter rule immediately generalizes to the pure subsectives and the privatives.[7] If a is a skillful surgeon then there is a property f such that a is a (skillful f). If a is a fake banknote then there is a property f such that a is a (fake f). There is no property such as being fake, pure and simple, hence no set of objects that are fake, hence no intersection with another set. But there is a property such as *being a (fake f)* for some property f. Therefore we can go on to form a set and subsequently its intersection with other sets. Similarly for the pure subsectives.

Here are two sketches of how to apply the general rule. Two people talking about John's exploits and pursuits may wonder whether John is famous for anything. Is there a property with respect to which John is famous? In fact, there is. To anticipate an example presented

---

[7] And the modals too, for that matter: if a is an alleged assassin then there is a property f such that a is an (alleged f), or in natural prose: then there is a property that a is alleged to have, or allegedly has. Being alleged to have some property or other (i.e. *being an alleged f*) is not a property everybody has, so it is not a trivial property.

below, John happens to be a famous ichthyologist, so there is a property f such that John is a (*famous f*). The emphasis is not on the particular property of being a famous ichthyologist, but on the property of being a famous something or other. The operative word is 'famous', not 'ichthyologist'. The same two people may also raise the question whether there is anything at all Mary is skillful at, considering how awkward she tends to be. One of them replies that there is indeed something Mary is skillful at – being a surgeon, as it happens. Scalpel in hand, Mary is as skillful as the next surgeon.

The rest of the paper is organized as follows. Section 1 is devoted to the general rule, section 2 to pure subsectives, section 3 to the special rule and intersectives, and section 4 to privatives.

1. The general rule of left subsectivity

Let M be a modifier that is either intersective, purely subsective, or privative, let F be any empirical property, and let f range over such properties. Then the general rule is this ('*LS*' for 'left subsectivity'):

$$\frac{a \text{ is an } (MF)}{\exists f (a \text{ is an } (Mf))} LS$$

The argument is valid as soon as we allow quantification over properties. The rule of existential quantification simply makes explicit in the conclusion an ontological commitment incurred in the premise. The domain of properties such that a has property (Mf) is non-empty, and the premise reveals one such property. But the rule also makes good philosophical sense. When we say, colloquially, that a is skillful we do so with the understanding that a is skillful with respect to one or more properties. A relativization to a property is always implicitly present, and the quantification over properties simply makes this relativization explicit. Whereas the rule of right subsectivity is a rule of modifier elimination, the general rule of left subsectivity carries the modifier occurring in the premise through to the conclusion. The rule is one for substituting one modified property with another modified property.

I have taken my lead from Kamp's summary in (1975, 123) of Montague's theory of adjectives:

> Predicative uses of adjectives are explained as elliptic attributive uses.

Accordingly, "A skillful surgeon is skillful" turns out to be elliptic for something like "A skillful surgeon is a skillful entity". This explanation allows *skillful* to remain a modifier, and this renders superfluous an explanation of how to trade a modifier for a property. Where the Montagovian has the dummy property *entity*, I have an existentially bound variable ranging over properties.

Had I argued that there was a transformation from attributive to predicative position then I would have fallen into a trap (Bolinger 1967) warns against. He argues (ibid., p. 2) that "There are many attributive adjectives that are never predicative", offering 'a total stranger' / *"The stranger is total" as one of multiple examples. One may dispute individual examples, of course. Thus "The defeat was total" is an impeccable English sentence, so 'total' is not an example of an adjective that can occur in attributive, but never in predicative, position. But Bolinger's point is well taken. For instance, the two-way transformation from "The former president is asleep" to *"The asleep president is former" is neither here nor there.[8]

LS does not require the impossible, that *"The total stranger is total", *"The runaway horse is runaway", etc., must come out well-formed and meaningful. The rule merely requires that "The runaway horse is a (runaway f)", where f is existentially bound, must come out well-formed and meaningful. So *LS* is not challenged at the logical level. But examples such as Bolinger's do challenge the rule at the syntactic level, since the formal predicate 'is an (Mf)' will sometimes lack a counterpart in this or that natural language, apart from the fallback option 'is an (M something)' as in 'is a (former something)'. The lack of natural-language counterparts is not a problem, though, since *LS* is a logical and not syntactic rule: *LS* is about preserving validity rather than well-formedness. There cannot be a translation function in the vein of Montague Grammar between formal and natural terms in the case of *LS*.

Nor does *LS* license the following fallacy, which Geach (1956, 33) brings up in:

> a is a big flea, so a is a flea and a is big; b is a small elephant, so b is an elephant and b is small; so a is a big animal and b is a small animal.

The illicit move is to steal the property *being an animal* into the conclusion, thereby making a, b commensurate. Both fleas and elephants are animals, to be sure, but a's being big and b's being small follow from a's being a flea and b's being an elephant. *LS* mandates only the following two inferences, where the values of p, q are two distinct properties:

> There is a property p such that a is a (*big p*); there is a property q such that b is a (*small q*). And a (*big p*) may well be smaller than a (*small q*), depending on the respective values assigned to p, q.[9]

(Clark 1970, 334) brings up various inferences, all of which he objects to. In some cases Clark is being too careful, while I agree with the rest, provided he is objecting to drawing an inference from a relative to an absolute measure.

> We cannot ... infer that something is red from the fact that it is a large, red ball. We cannot infer that John is famous from the fact that John is a famous ichthyologist. This may seem an awkward consequence of [my] account. Nonetheless, it is, I think, the way things should be. What we can infer from the fact that this is a large, red ball is that it is a large ball, and that it is a red ball. We do not want it to follow from the fact that this is a large chigger, that this is large. So, too, I believe, we should not want it to follow that the fact that this is a very red chigger, that this is very red. A very red chigger need not be very red at all. Similarly, we cannot correctly infer that John is famous ... from the fact that John is a famous ichthyologist. A famous ichthyologist may be an unknown in the marketplace.

---

[8] See (Paoli 1999, 69).
[9] (Heim and Kratzer ibid., 71, entries (13), (14)) appears to be making more or less the same point. See (Byrne 2016) for the most recent discussion of gradable adjectives and the distinction between predicative and attributive adjectives, and (ibid., §3.1) specifically for Geach's example above.

Left subsectivity: how to infer that a round peg is round

It is rewarding to examine a couple of his examples. If the premise is that a is a large, red ball then this is one thing we can do:

$$\frac{(\textit{large } (\textit{red ball})) \, a}{(\textit{red ball}) \, a} \text{ right subsectivity}$$

$$\frac{}{\exists f ((\textit{red } f) \, a)} \text{ LS}$$

A similar inference takes a from being a large chigger to being a (*large g*).

John is famous in ichthyologist quarters; is John thereby also famous among the fishmongers in the marketplace? No, not when *famous* is purely subsective. But *LS* validates the conclusion that there is a property g such that John is a (*famous g*). John's fame is relative and not absolute the way Michael Jackson's might have been at his apex.

2. Pure subsectives and left subsectivity

The set theory of pure subsectives is straightforward: any object instantiating a purely subsectively modified property must also instantiate the input property. Therefore the rule governing pure subsectives enjoins us to eliminate the purely subsective modifier M_s to isolate the input property F and then predicate F. The rule is the rule of right subsectivity:

$$\frac{a \text{ is an } (M_s \, F)}{a \text{ is an } F} \text{ RS}$$

The general rule of left subsectivity for pure subsectives is this:

$$\frac{a \text{ is an } (M_s \, F)}{\exists f \, (a \text{ is an } (M_s \, f))} \text{ LS}_s$$

When a has the property (M_s F) then, by *RS*, a has the property F and, by *LS$_s$*, a has some purely subsectively modified property. Therefore we can form the intersection of their respective extensions at the empirical parameters chosen for evaluation, and a is going to be a member of that common set. This set may, for instance, be the set of those who are both surgeons and skillful at something. Does the fact that we can form this intersection reveal that a purely subsective modifier is actually intersective? No. First, *RS* exhausts what is unique to pure subsectives. Forming the above intersection exceeds the definition of pure subsectives, because *LS$_s$* is called upon to yield a property and derivatively a set. Second, although the combination of right and left subsectivity is exactly what defines intersectives, the rule of left subsectivity that goes into that definition is not the general but the special one.

3. Intersectives and two rules of left subsectivity

The set theory of intersectives demands that a be an element of the intersection of two sets. The problem is to state the identity of one of the two sets. Sets are introduced as the extensions of properties. So the real problem is to state the identity of one of the two properties that *a* must have whenever *a* has an intersectively modified property. It is obvious that one of the properties must be *F*. Where is the other property to come from? (Kamp ibid.) suggests a tack worth pursuing. The first group of adjectives Kamp studies are those he labels as predicative. Apart from the fact that predicative adjectives can have extensions, it is plain that this syntactic category maps onto the semantic category of intersective modifiers.[10] (Kamp ibid., 124) says:

> Predicative adjectives behave essentially as if they were independent predicates. […] Predicative adjectives are, roughly speaking, those whose extensions are not affected by the nouns with which they are combined. Typical examples are technical and scientific adjectives, such as *endochrine*, *differentiable*, *superconductive*, etc.

One could add 'square', 'transparent', 'European', 'five-meter high', 'green', 'acidic' and other adjectives describing shape, colour, location and other physical features, provided we are prepared to include dispositional properties such as colours among the physical properties.[11]

(Kamp ibid., 127) continues:

> Some adjectives […] possess a certain invariance property that makes them behave as predicates, which when combined with a noun phrase give a complex equivalent in meaning to the conjunction of the predicate represented by the adjective and that represented by the noun phrase.

The reference to invariance could be interpreted as implying that there is some internal relation between intersectives and certain properties. This is the tack I will pursue here. I suggest that whenever a modifier *M* is intersective with respect to property *F* then there is exactly one particular property *G* that matches *M*. The syntactic link between *G* and the intersective modifier M_i is likely to spring from the page in the case of a language like English, in which the same homonymous adjective, e.g. 'red' or 'round', can denote either of them. For instance, if the modified property is denoted by the predicate 'is a round peg' then we know which property *G* is, namely the property denoted by the predicate 'is round'. But what we are searching for is a logical rule that will identify *G*.[12]

---

[10] (Kamp ibid., 125-26) notes that if a modifier is *intersective* then it is *extensional*, speculating whether the converse also holds. This rule defines extensional modifiers: if *a* is an (M_e *F*) and the properties *F*, *G* are co-extensional then *a* is an (M_e *G*). The converse does not hold, I would argue, due at least to certain *trivial* modifiers, namely those that are extensional and purely subsective. An example of this sort of modifier would be *genuine*: there is no such thing as a set of genuine things, pure and simple. The modifier is trivial because there is no difference between a diamond and a genuine diamond, trivial modifiers leaving the modified property unmodified, as it were.
[11] A strictly Montagovian tack has no conceptual space for independence and invariance, as understood above. See (Paoli 1999, 69).
[12] *Idioms* are tricky. For instance, does it follow that a so-called *Spanish prisoner* is a (Spanish *f*)? Naïvely, it does, for the predicate 'is a Spanish prisoner' undeniably exemplifies modification at the syntactic level. And on its literal meaning, a Spanish prisoner is a prisoner and a Spaniard. But 'is a Spanish prisoner' also has an idiomatic meaning. When idiomatically understood as a particular kind of scam, a Spanish prisoner is neither a prisoner, nor a Spaniard or a (Spanish *f*).

Left subsectivity: how to infer that a round peg is round

I will proceed in a fairly forthright manner. The intersective modifier M_i will be defined in terms of the two properties F, G in such a way that G, and no other property, matches M_i. The *definition* is not logically complicated and can be stated in prose:

> M is an *intersective modifier* with respect to property F if, and only if, there is exactly one property g such that g is identical to property G and such that instantiating the property (MF) is necessarily equivalent to simultaneously instantiating properties F and G.

This definition is more precise than the Montagovian postulate above. The definition states that there is exactly one property matching the modifier rather than at least one, and that G is this unique property. The Montagovian equivalence fails to make this internal link between M_i and G explicit.

A *corollary* of the definition is this equivalence:

> Instantiating property $(M_i F)$ is necessarily equivalent to simultaneously instantiating properties F and G.

The corollary justifies this introduction rule for M_i:

$$\frac{a \text{ is a } G \wedge a \text{ is an } F}{a \text{ is an } (M_i F)} M_i I$$

$M_i I$ is valid, provided the two properties in the premise are the two particular properties that any individual with a given intersectively modified property must have by definition. I am not imposing any formal restrictions on inputting any pair of properties and outputting an intersectively modified property. It is just that most of the so modified properties are liable to go unnamed in natural language, basically because we do not need them and so do not need a name for them. A limiting case arises when a pairing of properties yields a contradictory property, such that its extension can be none other than the empty set of individuals. Consider the properties *being wooden* and *being a horse*. The intersective modifier *wooden$_i$* is defined in terms of simultaneously instantiating *being wooden* and *being a horse*. The contradiction arises as soon as we make the reasonable assumption that the property *being a horse* comes with the constraint that all of its instances must be animate while the property *being wooden* excludes the property *being animate*.[13]

The elimination rule for M_i is simply the inversion of $M_i I$:

$$\frac{a \text{ is an } (M_i F)}{a \text{ is a } G \wedge a \text{ is an } F} M_i E$$

The respective premise and conclusion of $M_i I$ and $M_i E$ are necessarily equivalent, so the rules infer a truth-condition from itself. This is exactly what we want, for M_i is just G in modifier's clothing. To be competent with the property *being an* $(M_i F)$ (or with the

---

[13] This sort of constraint is conceptualized as *requisites*. See (Duží et al. ibid., §§4.1-4.2) for the philosophy and logic of requisites and the intensional essentialism which it undergirds.

Left subsectivity: how to infer that a round peg is round

predicate 'is an $(M_i\,F)$', if one prefers the formal mode) is to know which property is G, what property F is, and that to have the modified property is to have these two properties.

M_iE earns its keep as an auxiliary to the special rule of left subsectivity. The logic of this rule consists in applying $\wedge E$ to the conclusion of M_iE so as to detach its left conjunct:

$$\frac{a \text{ is a } G \wedge a \text{ is an } F}{a \text{ is a } G} \wedge E$$

Therefore *the special rule of left subsectivity* can be stated thus:

$$\frac{a \text{ is an } (M_i\,F)}{a \text{ is a } G} LS_{spec}$$

The general rule of left subsectivity for intersectives is this:

$$\frac{a \text{ is an } (M_i\,F)}{\exists f\,(a \text{ is an } (M_i\,f))} LS_i$$

This rule states that if a instantiates a particular intersectively modified property then there is some intersectively modified property that a instantiates. For instance, if a is a round peg then there is some property such that a is a (*round something*). Recall Clark's example of being a large, red ball and being red. Assume that the property of being a large, red ball is defined such that in order to instantiate this property the two properties of being red and being a ball must be instantiated. Suppose we deploy LS_{spec} in lieu of LS_i. This yields this argument:

$$\frac{a \text{ is a } (large\,(red_i\,ball))}{a \text{ is a } (red_i\,ball)} RS$$
$$\frac{}{a \text{ is red}} LS_{spec}$$

The conclusion predicates the unqualified property of redness to a. Should someone balk at drawing this conclusion, it is an option to redefine *red* as a purely subsective rather than intersective modifier and then apply LS_i rather than LS_{spec} to obtain a more guarded conclusion. For instance, (Wheeler 1972, 331) analyzes "That lobster is red" in terms of "That lobster is red for a lobster", which allows a red lobster to be pink. We do not want to infer that a red lobster that is pink is red, so the premise needs to be that a is a (red_s *lobster*) and the conclusion that there is a property f such that a is a (red_s f). What red_s does is qualify which sort of lobster a is. If a deserves to be called a red lobster in the first place, despite being pink (where *being pink* is assumed to be an unqualified property), then the conclusion that a is a (red_s *something*) is compatible with a being pink.

4. Privatives and left subsectivity

Privatives are the most complicated among the modifiers, but the fundamental fact about them is that their set-theoretic counterpart is a complement set. For instance, a is necessarily an element of the complement of a given set of banknotes whenever a is a fake banknote. This set-theoretic fact is reflected by the use of boolean negation in the standard rule governing privatives:

$$\frac{a \text{ is an } (M_p\ F)}{a \text{ is not an } F} M_pE$$

The complement set is likely to be a very mixed bag of objects, for the only thing the elements have in common is that they are negatively defined as being deprived of the property of being a banknote. Yet a fake banknote is not just any old non-banknote: it is the particular kind of non-banknote that is a fake banknote. Once we have formed the complement of the set of banknotes we can make a second move. We can go on to form, within the complement, its subset of all and only fake banknotes. This second move turns privatives into a special kind of subsectives – special, because the complement set needs to be formed first.[14] Making this second move can be worth making, for it enables us to extract far more information from a being a fake banknote than just the fact that a lacks a certain property. The property *being a fake banknote* comes with a package of other properties that lay down (while leaving room for borderline cases) when an artefact qualifies as a fake banknote and when not. Intuitively speaking, a fake banknote is a closer approximation to being a banknote than is any other non-banknote, with the possible exception of obsolete banknotes.

My discontentment with M_pE is that it captures very little, if something very important, of what privative modification is all about.[15] Still there are cases where M_pE is all we need for a purpose at hand. If I am holding a stash of colourful slips of paper with numerals, portraits, signatures, etc. on them, but do not quite trust the person on the delivering end, then all I am interested in is sorting the slips into those that are banknotes and those that are not. In case I establish that a is a fake banknote then a goes into the pile of objects that are not banknotes.

There are also cases where even less information is all we need. This is where *the general rule of left subsectivity for privatives* enters:

$$\frac{a \text{ is an } (M_p\ F)}{\exists f\,(a \text{ is an } (M_p\ f))} LS_p$$

---

[14] (Partee 2001) suggests construing as many modifiers as possible as subsectives. I find the approach I just sketched above for the privatives more natural than the strained coercion Partee puts forward. (Del Pinal 2015, 24-28) provides a crisp summary of Partee's project. (Duží et al. 2010, 400, fn. 52) address Partee's question "Is this gun fake or real"?, which she intends to undergird her subsective proposal. Our basic objection is that the question pre-empts the answer rather than admit of two different non-trivial answers.

[15] M_pE is also problematic because it fails to generalize to *iterated* privatives, as expressed by 'is a former heir apparent', 'weighs almost half a ton', 'is an imaginary fake painting', etc.

Left subsectivity: how to infer that a round peg is round

The conclusion states that a has at least one privatively modified property. Loosely stated, if a is a fake banknote then there is at least one property with respect to which a is a fake: a has a blemished record, so to speak.

Suppose I am decluttering the attic. I have reasons to suspect that there are some fakes hiding among the valuable stuff. I am not interested in what sorts of fakes they might be – fake banknotes, fake watches (perhaps still watches, but not manufactured by the alleged manufacturer), fake paintings (still paintings, but not painted by the alleged painter) – all I am interested in is gathering the fakes in one big pile and getting rid of them. I establish that a is a fake thousand-franc banknote, b is a fake Breitling, and c is a fake Klee. I apply LS_p three times over, thus quantifying away the three specific input properties and inferring (via some obvious additional steps) the new knowledge that I have three fakes in the attic. I have used LS_p to induce a coarse-grained dichotomy over the set of artefacts found in my attic into those that are genuine and those that are fake. The relativization to properties remains important: a fake banknote is fake with respect to the property of being a banknote, but genuine with respect to the property of being a slip of paper.

Conclusion

Modification would be formally straightforward and philosophically not all too exciting if all modifiers were purely subsective. The one-size-fits-all rule would be the rule of right subsectivity, which eliminates the modifier and predicates the surviving property. But modifiers other than the pure subsectives abound. I brought up the intersectives and the privatives. The privatives replace one sort of negation (deprivation) by another sort of negation. I also suggested that they were a special case of subsectives in an indirect manner. The intersectives demand both a rule of right subsectivity and a rule of left subsectivity. The latter rule must account for the logical link between an intersective modifier and a particular property.

I put forward a general rule of left subsectivity, which applies to all three kinds of modifiers canvassed here, and a special rule of left subsectivity, which applies exclusively to the intersectives. The special rule eliminates the modifier and replaces it by a property. The general rule does not eliminate the modifier, but instead replaces its original argument property (a specific one) by another property (an arbitrary one). These two rules are the two novelties that this paper has presented. I have argued, both abstractly and by way of examples, why the rules are both philosophically and formally indispensable.[*]

---

[*] I am indebted to Marie Duží and Pavel Materna, as well as four anonymous referees for *dialectica*, for very valuable comments on previous drafts. Various versions of this paper were read at School of Philosophy, Anthropology and Social Inquiry, University of Melbourne, 2009; *LOGICA 2009*, Hejnice, 2009; *SOPHA 2009*, Geneva, 2009; *SPE3*, Paris, 2010; Department of Chinese and Bilingual Studies, Hong Kong Polytechnic University, 2012; Department of Philosophy, Hong Kong University, 2012. The research reported herein was supported by Marie Curie Fellowship FP-7-PEOPLE-2013-IEF 628170 USHP and GAČR Grant 15-13277S.

REFERENCES

ABDULLAH, N. and FROST, R.A. 2005, "Adjectives: A Uniform Semantic Approach", Lecture Notes in Artificial Intelligence 3501, p. 330-41.
AMOIA, M. and GARDENT, C. 2007, "A First Order Semantic Approach to Adjectival Inference", in: Proceedings of the Workshop on Textual Entailment and Paraphrasis, Prague: Association for Computational Linguistics, pp. 185-92.
BOLINGER, D. 1967, "Adjectives in English: Attribution and Predication", Lingua 18, pp. 1-34.
BYRNE, T. 2016, "Might Anything be Plain Good? ", Philosophical Studies, doi 10.1007/s11098-016-0673-8.
CHATZIKYRIAKIDIS, S. and LUO, Z. 2013, "Adjectives in a Modern Type-theoretical Setting", Lecture Notes in Computer Science 8036, pp. 159-74.
CLARK, R. 1970, "Concerning the Logic of Predicate Modifiers", Noûs 4, pp. 311-35.
DEL PINAL, G. 2015, "Dual Content Semantics, Privative Adjectives, and Dynamic Compositionality", Semantics & Pragmatics 8, pp. 1-53.
DUŽÍ, M., JESPERSEN, B. and MATERNA, P. 2010, *Procedural Semantics for Hyperintensional Logic. Foundations and Applications of Transparent Intensional Logic*, Dordrecht: Springer.
GEACH, P.T. 1956, "Good and Evil", Analysis 17, pp. 33-42.
GEACH, P.T. 1972, *Logic Matters*, Los Angeles: University of California Press.
HEIM, I. and Kratzer, A. 1998, Semantics in Generative Grammar, Oxford: Blackwell.
JESPERSEN, B. 2015, "Structured Lexical Concepts, Property Modifiers, and Transparent Intensional Logic", Philosophical Studies 172, pp. 321-45.
JESPERSEN, B . and CARRARA, M. 2013, "A New Logic of Technical Malfunction", Studia Logica 101, pp. 547-81.
JESPERSEN, B. and PRIMIERO, G. 2013, "Alleged Assassins: Realist and Constructivist Semantics for Modal Modifiers", Lecture Notes in Computer Science 7758, pp. 94-114.
KAMP, H. 1975, "Two Theories about Adjectives", in: E. L. Keenan, ed., *Formal Semantics of Natural Language*, Cambridge: Cambridge University Press, pp. 123-55.
KAMP, H. and PARTEE, B. 1995, "Prototype Theory and Compositionality", Cognition 57, pp. 129-91.
MONTAGUE, R. 1974, *Formal Philosophy*, R. H. Thomasson, ed., New Haven, London: Yale University Press.
PAOLI, F. 1999, "Comparative Logic as an Approach to Comparison in Natural Language", Journal of Semantics 16, pp. 67-96.
PARTEE, B. 2001, "Privative Adjectives: Subsective Plus Coercion", in: *Presuppositions and Discourse*, R. Bäuerle et al., eds., Amsterdam: Elsevier, available at *http://people.umass.edu/partee/docs/ParteeInPressKampFest.pdf*.
PARTEE, B. 2007, "Compositionality and Coercion in Semantics: The Dynamics of Adjective Meaning", in: *Cognitive Foundations of Interpretation*, G. Bouma et al., eds., Amsterdam: Royal Netherlands Academy of Arts and Sciences, pp. 145-61.
RECANATI, F. 2011, *Truth-conditional Pragmatics*, Oxford: Oxford University Press.
SZABÓ, Z.G. 2003, "On Qualification", Philosophical Perspectives 17, pp. 385-414.
WHEELER, S.C. III 1972, "Attributives and Their Modifiers", Nous 6, pp. 310-34.

Structured lexical concepts, property modifiers, and Transparent Intensional Logic

Bjørn Jespersen

Abstract In a 2010 paper Daley argues, *contra* Fodor, that several syntactically simple predicates express structured concepts. Daley develops his theory of structured concepts within Tichý's Transparent Intensional Logic (TIL). I rectify various misconceptions of Daley's concerning TIL. I then develop within TIL an improved theory of how structured concepts are structured and how syntactically simple predicates are related to structured concepts.

1 Introduction

Fodor famously and notoriously argues that syntactically simple predicates like 'bachelor', 'dog' and 'doorknob' ("Doorknobs, of all things!" 1998, p. 123) represent unstructured concepts:

> *Conceptual atomism*: most lexical concepts have no internal structure (*ibid.*, p. 121); [...] practically every (lexical) concept is primitive (*ibid.*, p. 122).

Daley (2010) argues, *contra* Fodor, that multiple syntactically simple predicates express structured concepts. This is the hybrid thesis that often *conceptual atomism*, and often also *conceptual structuralism*, holds for lexical concepts. Throughout this paper, a *lexical concept* so-called will be an *objective concept* (rather than a mental object), or *objective meaning*, of a *lexical term*. Whereas Fodor is happy crisscrossing the lines between the mental, the syntactic, and the semantic, I will maintain barriers between the three. The points I am making bear exclusively on semantics and syntax. This paper is intended for those semanticists and philosophers of language who embrace a non-mentalistic theory of concepts.

I was happy to see Daley deploy my favourite theory as the framework within which he sets out to develop his account of *structured lexical concepts*. The theory in question is Tichy's Transparent Intensional Logic (TIL). TIL is a natural choice, as the theory has a well-developed account of structured concepts. I was less happy, however, about Daley's use of TIL. The concept theory Daley develops is in some fundamental regards somewhat removed from the concept theory that is actually part of TIL. This need not in itself be a problem, of course, for TIL may conceivably lend itself to parallel concept theories. Unfortunately, Daley's theory turns out to be too far removed also from the foundations of TIL so as to qualify as a TIL-based concept theory. Again, this need not be a problem in itself, obviously. But there are both formal and philosophical problems with Daley's concept theory as expounded in (*ibid.*).

The central formal problem is that, since Daley attempts to spell out the foundations of his concept theory by means of TIL, but misunderstands some of the foundations, he misapplies TIL, which leaves him with obscure foundations. In particular, he is looking for structured entities in the wrong place, because he misunderstands the typed universe of TIL, thereby ignoring the contrast between simple and ramified types. Daley's theory as it stands is not primed for application.

The central philosophical problem is that Daley propounds what is in effect a dysfunctional analysis of non-intersective compound predicates such as 'alleged felon' (Daley's example). According to my diagnosis he does so because he entirely neglects property modifiers. TIL already has a worked-out theory of non-intersective property modifiers, which will be set out below.

One thing to understand about TIL is that all concepts, without exception, are structured. Hence the qualification 'structured' in 'structured lexical concept' is redundant. Since the notion of Fodor-style conceptual atomism has no place in TIL, the theory cannot accommodate the hybrid thesis, in the way just stated. Yet TIL draws a distinction between *simple concepts*, which have little structure to speak of, and *complex concepts*, which have a richer structure. This way TIL is still in a position to accommodate a revised variant of the hybrid thesis. The revised hybrid thesis would be that lots of lexical predicates stand for simple concepts and lots of lexical predicates stand for complex concepts. The former are the ones Daley would be primarily interested in. There is little philosophical point in further developing the hybrid thesis in either of its variants at this point, since what Daley wishes to establish is that there are (however minimally) structured concepts available to go with lexical predicates.

What Daley calls structured lexical concepts will, I suggest, translate into those simple concepts that are expressed by lexical terms. For instance, 'bachelor' will match a simple concept conceptualizing the property of being a bachelor. The coupling of lexical predicates and simple concepts actually sits perfectly with the current principle within TIL of matching, ideally, syntactic structures with isomorphic semantic structures. Accordingly, minimal syntactic structure should be, ideally, coupled with minimal semantic structure. A case of isomorphism is a case of *literal meaning*. This notion will be deployed and defined below.

The explanation of how simple and non-simple concepts connect ties in with one of the central points of Daley's. Daley (*ibid.*, pp. 359ff) argues that a non-simple concept, like *Unmarried Man*, *simplifies*, as he calls it, to a simple (lexical) concept. So far TIL did not have a notion of simplification; it does already have the converse, namely a mapping called *refinement*. I will show how simplification can be incorporated into TIL. If a simple concept has been assigned to 'bachelor', that concept can be refined to various degrees. The logical link between literal and refined meanings is one of equivalence rather than synonymy. This would appear to be in agreement with Daley, who aims for 'necessary biconditional entailment' between the two. In the final analysis, I recommend that the predicates 'bachelor' and 'unmarried man' be equivalent, but not synonymous. Hence I recommend against 'bachelor' being synonymous with 'unmarried man' in virtue of a meaning postulate. If they were synonymous, 'bachelor' would be a lexical predicate whose meaning was a complex concept, thus divorcing syntactic from semantic structure.

The rest of this paper is organized as follows. Section 2 offers an overview of Daley's problem cases and his misconstrual of TIL. Section 3 shows how to type concepts in the ramified type hierarchy of TIL. Section 4 shows how to analyze property modification in TIL. Section 5 integrates Daley's notion of simplification into TIL and compares the concepts assigned to 'bachelor' and 'unmarried man' as their respective literal meaning.

2 Background and overview

Daley recommends, quite reasonably, a notion of *compositionality* for concepts. The structure of a structured concept should be a function of its constituent parts and their arrangement. The sort of concept theory Daley aims at must comply with five constraints (*ibid.*, p. 351). The first two appear to be the fundamental ones. First, the theory must account for the interior make-up of structured concepts. Second, the theory must account for how concepts hook up with the objects they conceptualize. Daley introduces TIL as a theory that satisfies all five constraints and which solves his problem cases. He uses square brackets, '[,]', to indicate what he calls *concepts*. I will stick to Daley's notation until introducing the notation of TIL, which also deploys '[,]' for one of its specific operations. Daley is looking for an analysis of the respective structures of the concepts

- [bachelor]
- [unmarried man]
- [flies]
- [is a father]
- [brown cow]
- [alleged felon]
- [Ken is human]

Each of Daley's seven problem cases will be solved.

Unfortunately, what Daley says about TIL suffers from two major misconceptions, apart from the issue, discussed in the Introduction, about all concepts being structured. One misconception is that *concepts can be typed in the simple type theory* of TIL. The fact is that *concepts must be typed in the ramified type hierarchy*. Actually, the bulk of Daley's minor misconceptions about how TIL works can be traced back to this one misunderstanding.[1] The other major misconception is that Daley's analyses of his problem cases are couched in terms of (what Daley calls) *concepts* when they should be analyzed in terms of *properties,* i.e. *intensions*, that have been *conceptualized* in this or that manner.

Both misconceptions are indicative of a conflation of two of the three tiers that are the backbone of the logical ontology of TIL. The lowest tier is the extensional one where we find truth-values, sets, individuals, etc. The intermediate tier is the intensional one where we find modal intensions such as properties of individuals, empirical propositions, relations-in-intension, individuals-in-intension (roles occupiable by individuals), etc. The highest tier is the hyperintensional one where we find structured entities such as concepts. This tier contains infinitely many levels, since concepts belonging to a lower order are in turn conceptualized by concepts belonging to a higher order. Daley runs together the hyperintensional and the intensional tier. The overall result is an inoperative concept theory, characterized by inappropriate type assignments, that enjoins us to look for structure where none is to be found, namely among the first-order objects.

In TIL *structured* objects such as concepts can be typed only in the ramified type theory. The simple type theory types non-composite objects, which are invariably *mappings* (*functions-in-extension*) in the ontology of TIL. Important mappings include modal intensions (mappings from possible worlds) and their extensions, like sets (identified with their characteristic functions), individuals and truth-values, the latter two being construed formally as 0-ary functions. While Daley duly points out that TIL concepts are distinct from what they conceptualize, he nonetheless confuses the categories of concept and possible-world intension when claiming of the latter that they are TIL concepts. At (*ibid.*, pp. 363ff) he furthermore confuses second-*order* objects (concepts conceptualizing non-concepts, i.e. functions) and second-*degree* first-order objects (possible-world intensions whose extensions are themselves intensional entities).

Daley intends to analyze 'non-intersective concepts' and 'relative concepts', as he dubs them, in terms of propositional functions. First of all, though, the notion of propositional function is like a square peg in a round hole, in the light of how the type theory of TIL is set up.[2] Second, Daley says, "[alleged], when combined with [felon], yields a subset of the extension of [alleged]" (*ibid.*, p. 366), where [alleged] is unpacked as [alleged to be something] or [alleged to be—], with a slot for a concept of a property. The concepts [alleged], [tall] are claimed to be 'incomplete', requiring an additional concept for completion.

---

[1] Three of the four TIL sources Daley quotes—Duží (2004), Materna (1998), Tichý (1988)—apply the ramified type hierarchy.

[2] Jespersen (2008, pp. 489–491) explains why.

Daley's account of *Alleged* lands him in various kinds of trouble. He needs to have the complement of *Alleged* as it occurs in the context [alleged felon] change its type to fit *Alleged*. But *type-theoretic coercion* is not an option in TIL. The general policy of TIL is to proceed in a top-down manner in the interest of uniform treatment and non-contextualism.[3] Hence types remain fixed. Daley also finds himself treating *Alleged* as though it had a satisfaction class or extension.[4] It is true that, given an empirical index, there will be a class (perhaps empty) of those individuals who are alleged to have some property or other. But I cannot agree that 'alleged to be something' is elliptical for 'alleged'. One reason is that the adjective 'alleged' can easily be assigned a stand-alone semantics without recourse to ellipsis (see below). Another reason is that the property of being alleged to be something comes with existential quantification over properties and as such is parasitic on the prior property of being alleged to have a specific property. So the right order of analysis is to get the semantics of 'alleged' down, then the semantics of 'alleged felon', and finally the semantics of 'alleged to be something'. Daley moves in the opposite direction, beginning with the most elaborate expression, thus getting things back to front.

The root of Daley's trouble with 'alleged felon' and other compound noun phrases is that he completely neglects *property modification*.[5] On his bottom-up approach, *Small*, *Tall*, etc. amount to a set-to-set mapping, and the resulting set is indexed to a world: cf. (*ibid.*, p. 366). Daley's set-to-set-plus-world mappings are in effect tantamount to something like proto-modification. The general problem with this typing, though, is that it fails to generalize to the various sorts of non-intersective modifiers, which are the philosophically interesting ones, anyway. What is wanted is instead a relativization or qualification by means of *Alleged*, *Tall*, *Fake*, etc., by having them modify properties rather than sets. This way modification becomes impervious to particular populations of properties. TIL follows Montague in construing a property modifier as a property-to-property mapping.[6] Accordingly, the result of applying the property modifier *Tall* to the property *Woman* is the property *Tall Woman*. Thus, if 'tall' denotes a modifier and 'woman' a property, "*a* is a tall woman" predicates one modified property of *a*, rather than two unmodified properties.

My suggestion is that 'alleged' expresses a concept conceptualizing a property modifier and denotes the property modifier so conceptualized; that 'alleged felon' expresses a complex concept conceptualizing a property and denotes the property so conceptualized; and that 'alleged to be something' expresses a concept conceptualizing

---

[3] See Duží et al. (*ibid.*, §1.2.2, §1.4.2.3).

[4] Already Kamp (1975, pp. 153–154) singles out 'alleged' as an adjective it appears impossible to pair off with a property. Instead, it seems, 'alleged' must be paired off with a modifier.

[5] In Daley's defence, at the time of his (2010) no published material was available on how TIL handles modifiers. TIL has, however, since then acquired a full-fledged theory of modification. See Duží et al. (*ibid.*, §4.4), Jespersen and Carrara (2013), Jespersen and Primiero (2012), Primiero and Jespersen (2010).

[6] Strictly speaking, Montague construes the meanings of *adjectives* as property-to-property mappings. His *meaning postulates* serve to differentiate between logically different sorts of adjectives. See Montague (1970), Partee (2001, 2007, ms.). For critical discussion, see Kamp (1975), Beesley (1982).

the existential generalization of a property *p* modified by *Alleged*. Thus, if *a* is an alleged felon then it follows that there is a property *p* such that *a* is an alleged *p*.

TIL has the adjective 'alleged' denote a so-called *modal modifier*. In logical terms, if *a* is an alleged felon then it can be inferred neither that *a* is a felon, nor that *a* is not a felon. This reflects the fact that some alleged felons are indeed felons while the rest of them are not. In semantic terms, if *a* is an alleged felon at some pair of empirical parameters ⟨*world*, *time*⟩ then at some ⟨*w'*, *t'*⟩ *Alleged* will behave as a subsective modifier with respect to *Felon* (these alleged felons being felons) and at an alternative ⟨*w''*, *t''*⟩ as a privative modifier with respect to *Felon* (these alleged felons failing to be felons). The open empirical question, which cannot be settled by logical or semantic means, is whether the pair of evaluation ⟨*w*, *t*⟩ at which *a* is an alleged felon is like ⟨*w'*, *t'*⟩ or like ⟨*w''*, *t''*⟩. Which way it goes depends on whether the allegation that *a* is a felon is true or is false at ⟨*w*, *t*⟩. A taxonomy of and semantics for modifiers will be provided in Sect. 4.

Daley treats *Cow*, *Small*, *Alleged* as being on an equal footing, namely as three different concepts. In TIL a *concept* is one sort of thing (a higher-order object with a structure), and a *property* quite another (a first-order object without structure). Property *modifiers* are, in TIL, in the same league as properties, because they are also unstructured, first-order objects. The type-theoretic difference between properties and their modifiers is that properties are *intensional* entities (qua mappings from possible worlds) whereas modifiers are *extensional* entities (qua non-world-indexed mappings, between intensional entities).

The relationship between *concepts*, *properties*, and *modifiers* is that modifiers modify properties in order to form new properties and that concepts conceptualize both properties and modifiers in order for them to be presented. TIL adheres to the Fregean (and constructivist) tenet that an object cannot be provided 'in the raw', but must be provided through a mode of presentation of it. Thus there are TIL concepts conceptualizing *Cow*, *Small*, *Alleged*, but the first concept would conceptualize a property and the other two concepts would conceptualize property modifiers. These concepts can themselves be conceptualized, namely by concepts located one order higher up. The type hierarchy of TIL needs to be ramified precisely in order to be able to always go one order higher up, so that entities one order below can be conceptualized. In this paper, however, we need only concepts belonging to the lowest order, because we are conceptualizing only functions (or rather such functions as are not defined on higher-order objects).

3 Concepts in the ramified type hierarchy

The logical core of TIL is its notion of *construction* and its *type hierarchy*, whose ramified type theory includes the simple type theory. The notion of *concept* is defined in terms of the notion of construction, and emphatically not in terms of the notion of mapping: *a concept is a construction in normal form*, as will be explained below. The various ways in which concepts conceptualize objects is defined, in TIL, in terms of the various ways in which constructions construct objects (or in well-defined cases fail to construct an object). The inductive definition presented below enumerates the various kinds of construction.

Daley (*ibid.*, pp. 366–367) provides a list of six operations allegedly generating complex concepts in accordance with the TIL framework. However, most importantly of all, *TIL concepts are themselves operations* (or *logical* or *algorithmic procedures*). This is the gist of the *procedural* conception of concepts inherent to TIL.[7] Concepts do not emanate from some operations or procedures beyond them that would produce those concepts.

TIL is *ante rem* Platonism, and as such proceeds in a top-down manner, from concepts to objects. Intuitively, TIL is primarily a theory of conditions (and of properties of and relations between conditions) and only secondarily a theory of their satisfiers (if any). In the idiom of procedures and their products, TIL focuses mainly on procedures and only derivatively on their products (if any). TIL does not come with the requirement that 'empty' concepts must be assigned an arbitrary object, like 0 or the sun or the empty set or the concepts themselves. Such concepts are fully integrated into the concept theory of TIL rather than being relegated to its margins as an embarrassment. They are simply procedures without a product, or roads to nowhere, itineraries without a destination. So not every concept conceptualizes an object, but is no less a concept for it. Given a domain A of *concepts*, of order n, that conceptualize *objects* (perhaps themselves concepts of a lower order) of order $n - 1$ in range B, the mapping from A to B is a *partial* one, in that some concepts may conceptualize no object at all.

Co-conceptualization is the phenomenon that two or more concepts conceptualize the same object. Given a domain A' of concepts and a range B' of objects they conceptualize, the mapping from the restricted subset of defined elements of A' to B' is a *surjection*, since it may happen that two elements or more in the subset get mapped onto the same element in B'.

With the preceding philosophical exposition in place, the relevant *definitions* are as follows.

Definition 1 (*types of order 1*) Let B be a *base*, where a base is a collection of pair-wise disjoint, non-empty sets. Then:

(i) Every member of B is an elementary *type of order 1 over B*.
(ii) Let $\alpha, \beta_1, \ldots, \beta_m$ ($m > 0$) be types of order 1 over B. Then the collection $(\alpha\ \beta_1 \ldots \beta_m)$ of all m-ary partial mappings from $\beta_1 \times \cdots \times \beta_m$ into α is a functional *type of order 1 over B*.
(iii) Nothing else is a *type of order 1 over B*. □

Remark 1 For the purposes of natural-language analysis, we are currently assuming the following base of *ground types*, each of which is part of the ontological commitments of TIL:

---

[7] See Duží et al. (*ibid.*, §2.2).

o: the set of truth-values {**T, F**};
ι: the set of individuals (constant universe of discourse);
τ: the set of real numbers (doubling as temporal continuum);
ω: the set of logically possible worlds (logical space).

Definition 2 (*construction*)

(i) (*Variable*) Let valuation v assign object o to variable x. Then x *v-constructs* the object o.

(ii) (*Trivialization*) Let X be any object whatsoever (i.e. an extension, an intension, or a *construction*). Then ^0X is the *Trivialization* of X, which *constructs* X without any change of X.

(iii) (*Composition*) Let X *v-construct* a function f of type $(\alpha\ \beta_1...\beta_m)$, and let Y_1, ..., Y_m *v-construct* entities B_1, ..., B_m of types β_1, ..., β_m, respectively. Then the *Composition* $[X\ Y_1...Y_m]$ *v-constructs* the value (an entity, if any, of type α) of f on the tuple argument $\langle B_1, ..., B_m \rangle$. Otherwise the *Composition* $[X\ Y_1...Y_m]$ does not *v-construct* anything and so is *v-improper*.

(iv) (*Closure*) Let $x_1,..., x_m$ be pair-wise distinct variables *v-constructing* entities of types β_1, ..., β_m, and let Y be a *construction v-constructing* an α-entity. Then $[\lambda x_1 ... x_m\ Y]$ is the *construction* λ-*Closure* (or *Closure*). It *v-constructs* the following function f of type $(\alpha\beta_1...\beta_m)$. Let $v'(B_1/x_1,...,B_m/x_m)$ be a valuation identical with v at least up to assigning objects B_1/β_1, ..., B_m/β_m to variables x_1, ..., x_m. If Y is $v'(B_1/x_1,...,B_m/x_m)$-improper (see iii), then f is undefined on $\langle B_1, ..., B_m \rangle$. Otherwise the value of f on $\langle B_1, ..., B_m \rangle$ is the α-entity $v'(B_1/x_1,...,B_m/x_m)$-*constructed* by Y.

(v) (*Single Execution*) Let X *v-construct* object o. Then the *Single Execution* ^1X *v-constructs* o. Let X be either a non-*construction* or a *v*-improper *construction*. Then ^1X is *v-improper*.

(vi) (*Double Execution*) Let X *v-construct* a *construction* Y and let Y *v-construct* object Z (possibly itself a *construction*). Then the *Double Execution* ^2X *v-constructs* Z. Let X be a non-*construction* or a *construction* not *constructing* another *construction*, or a *construction constructing* a *v*-improper *construction*. Then ^2X is *v-improper*.

(vii) Nothing else is a *construction*. □

Here are some informal explications of each kind of construction. Bear in mind that the overarching idea behind the notion of construction is that, given some input objects, we can apply constructions to obtain some output objects (or none, in some instances of Composition, Single and Double Execution). A *variable* constructs an object by having that object as its value dependent on a valuation function v arranging variables and objects in a sequence. *Trivialization* is our objectual counterpart of a non-descriptive constant term, which simply harpoons a particular object. In programming jargon, Trivialization *calls* an object: no object can be operated on without first having been called, i.e. retrieved from a pool of objects. *Composition* is the procedure of functional application, rather than the functional value (if any) resulting from application.[8] *Closure* is the procedure of functional abstraction, rather than the resulting function. The *Single Execution* ^1X is the same construction as X, provided X is a construction at all: the default mode in which constructions occur is Single Execution. Single Execution serves basically to differentiate between *v*-proper constructions, which are the 'successful' constructions, and everything else, which are either *v*-improper ('failing') constructions or non-constructions, which are not susceptible to execution at all. *Double Execution* encodes the transitivity of construction.[9]

Variables and Trivializations are the one-step or primitive or *atomic* constructions of TIL, and they cannot be improper. In particular, what does not exist cannot be Trivialized. (Similarly, what does not exist cannot be named; but it can be described, as per 'the largest prime', 'the planet orbiting between Mercury and the Sun', or 'is a winged unicorn'.) Those instances of Single Execution where X is itself atomic are also atomic, and those instances are (im-) proper where X is (im-) proper. Composition, Closure, and Double Execution are the multiple-step or *composite* procedures. So are those instances of Single Execution where X is also composite. An *atomic* construction is a structured whole with but one proper part, namely the construction itself. Importantly, the proper part of ^0X is ^0X and not X, which is located beyond ^0X: the product of a procedure is no part of the procedure. A *composite* construction is a structured whole with more proper parts than just itself.

The definition of the ramified hierarchy of types divides into three parts; firstly, simple types of order 1, which were already defined by Definition 1; secondly, constructions of order n; thirdly, types of order $n + 1$.

Definition 3 (*ramified hierarchy of types*) $\mathbf{T_1}$ (*types of order* 1). See Def. 1.
$\mathbf{C_n}$ (*constructions of order n*)

(i) Let x be a variable ranging over a type of order n. Then x is a *construction of order n over B*.
(ii) Let X be a member of a type of order n. Then ^0X, ^1X, ^2X are *constructions of order n over B*.
(iii) Let $X, X_1,..., X_m$ ($m > 0$) be constructions of order n over B. Then $[X\ X_1... X_m]$ is a *construction of order n over B*.
(iv) Let $x_1,...x_m, X$ ($m > 0$) be constructions of order n over B. Then $[\lambda x_1...x_m\ X]$ is a *construction of order n over B*.
(v) Nothing is a *construction of order n over B* unless it so follows from $\mathbf{C_n}$ (i)–(iv).

$\mathbf{T_{n+1}}$ (*types of order n + 1*)
Let $*_n$ be the collection of all constructions of order n over B. Then

---

[8] Cf. Soames (2010, p. 114).
[9] Triple (Quadruple,…) Execution is a theoretical possibility, though one we have so far never had any use for. Rather than one instance of Triple Execution we would deploy one instance of Double and one instance of Single Execution.

(i) $*_n$ and every type of order n are *types of order* $n + 1$.
(ii) If $m > 0$ and $\alpha, \beta_1,...,\beta_m$ are types of order $n + 1$ over B, then $(\alpha\ \beta_1...\beta_m)$ (see T_1 ii)) is a *type of order* $n + 1$ *over B*.
(iii) Nothing else is a *type of order* $n + 1$ *over B*. □

Empirical languages incorporate an element of *contingency* that non-empirical ones lack. Empirical terms and expressions denote *empirical conditions* that may, or may not, be satisfied at some chosen empirical index of evaluation $\langle w, t \rangle$. Non-empirical languages have no need for an additional category of expressions for empirical conditions. We model these empirical conditions as *possible-world intensions*. Intensions are entities of type $(\beta\omega)$: mappings from possible worlds to an arbitrary type β. The type β is frequently the type of the *chronology* of α-objects, i.e. a mapping of type $(\alpha\tau)$. Thus α-intensions are frequently functions of type $((\alpha\tau)\omega)$, abbreviated as '$\alpha_{\tau\omega}$'. Typically, an index of evaluation is a world/time pair $\langle w, t \rangle$ to cover both the modal and temporal aspects of empirical conditions: what is actually the case might not have been so, and what is presently the case might later not be so, etc.

Examples of frequently used *intensions* include:

- *propositions* (i.e. empirical truth-conditions) of type $o_{\tau\omega}$ (e.g. *that the sun is shining*)
- *properties of individuals* of type $(o\iota)_{\tau\omega}$ (e.g. *being happy*)
- *individual roles/offices* of type $\iota_{\tau\omega}$ (e.g. *the first dog in space*)
- *attributes* of type $\iota\iota_{\tau\omega}$ (e.g. *the father of*)
- *binary relations-in-intension between individuals* of type $(o\iota\iota)_{\tau\omega}$ (e.g. *kicking*)
- *propositional attitudes* of type $(o\iota o_{\tau\omega})_{\tau\omega}$ (e.g. *knowing that a certain proposition is true*)
- *hyperpropositional attitudes* of type $(o\iota*_1)_{\tau\omega}$ (e.g. *knowing* that a certain propositional construction constructs a proposition that is true*).

Remark 2 TIL distinguishes between *order* and *degree* (cf. Sect. 2). What in mathematics typically goes by the name of a *function of order n* is what in TIL is known as a *function of degree n*, reserving the distinction between *orders* for constructions (concepts). First-order objects come in various degrees. Thus an intensional entity whose extensions are themselves intensional entities is at least of degree 2. An example would be *a dictator's most striking property*, whose type is $((o\iota)_{\tau\omega})_{\tau\omega}$: relative to the dual empirical index $\langle w, t \rangle$, at most one first-degree property, of type $(o\iota)_{\tau\omega}$, will be the extension of the second-degree property *a dictator's most striking property*, depending on what (if any) is the most striking property of the dictators (if any) found at $\langle w, t \rangle$, such as *sporting a moustache* or *being a genocidal maniac*.

Extensional entities are entities of a type α where $\alpha \neq (\beta\omega)$ for any type β, e.g. *truth-functions*: $\wedge, \vee, \supset$ are of type (ooo), and $\neg$ of type (oo). Extensional entities need not be first-order objects. For instance, a *set* of constructions of order $*_n$ is a mapping from $*_n$ to o, hence this set is a higher-order object.

Below all type indications will be provided outside the formulae in order not to clutter the notation. 'X/α' means that object X is of type α. '$X \to_v \alpha$' means that the type of the object that X is typed to v-construct is α. It is assumed throughout that $w \to_v \omega$ and $t \to_v \tau$. If $C \to_v \alpha_{\tau\omega}$ then the frequently used Composition $[[C\ w]\ t]$, which is the *extensionalization* of the α-intension v-constructed by C, will be encoded as 'C_{wt}'. TIL does not have a special operation earmarked for extensionalization.[10]

The method of *explicit intensionalization and temporalization* encodes constructions of possible-world intensions directly in the logical syntax. The following logical form essentially characterizes the logical syntax of any empirical language:

$$\lambda w \lambda t [\ldots w \ldots t \ldots]$$

where α is the type of the object v-constructed by the Composition $[\ldots w \ldots t \ldots]$, by abstracting over the values of variables w and t we construct a function from worlds to a partial function from times to α, i.e. a function of type $\alpha_{\tau\omega}$.

Some examples to fix ideas. Let ^0F be the Trivialization of property $F/(o\iota)_{\tau\omega}$ and ^0a the Trivialization of individual a/ι. Then

$$\lambda w \lambda t \left[{}^0F_{wt}\ {}^0a \right]$$

is a Closure constructing the proposition $P/o_{\tau\omega}$ that a is an F. This Closure is a *structured hyperproposition* whereas what it constructs is a possible-world proposition. That is to say that TIL has a double-barrelled notion of proposition: *hyperproposition* (structured and hyperintensionally individuated) and *possible-world proposition* (unstructured and individuated up to logical equivalence). P above is equivalent to the empirical truth-condition

$$a \in F_{wt}$$

This condition is satisfied by any world/time pair $\langle w, t \rangle$ at which a is an element in the extension of F. Recall Daley's second constraint in Sect. 2: the types assigned spell out how to exit the above Closure/$*_1$ and arrive at what it constructs, in casu an empirical truth-condition/$o_{\tau\omega}$.

Daley's example "Ken is human" (*ibid.*, p. 365) will receive exactly the analysis just given. Daley's own analysis is

$$\lambda w [H_w K]$$

Apart from the missing Trivializations of H, K, Daley's analysis is correct, provided we rewind to first-generation TIL: pre-1980 TIL is atemporal.[11]

---

[10] See Jespersen (2008) for further details on extensionalization as Composition and a comparison with Bealer's extensionalization operator.

[11] Tichý (1971) sums up first-generation TIL, which only had the simple type theory and lacked type τ. Tichý (1980a) marks the inception of temporalized TIL.

For an example of *partiality*, the following Composition is typed as a construction of the unique number that is a prime and larger than or equal to any other number (i.e. the largest prime). Where ν is the type of natural numbers, the involved types are: ι/(ν(oν)) ; x, y/*₁→ ν; Pr/(oν); ≥/(oνν):

$${}^0\iota\lambda x\ [{}^0\wedge\ [{}^0Pr\ x]\ [{}^0\forall\ \lambda y\ [{}^0\supset\ [{}^0Pr\ y]\ [{}^0\geq x\ y]]]]$$

Only the snag is that there is no number for this Composition to construct. Still the definite description 'the largest prime' is a meaningful term in TIL, and its meaning is the Composition above.

For an example of *surjection*, the two Compositions [[⁰Tri ⁰Lateral] ⁰Figure] and [[⁰Tri ⁰Angular] ⁰Figure], whatever the exact types may be, co-conceptualize the same set of geometric figures, though in two different manners, because ⁰Lateral, ⁰Angular are not co-conceptualizing Trivializations. Likewise the two Compositions [⁰Half ⁰Full], [⁰Half ⁰Empty] co-conceptualize the same empirical property, since necessarily, whatever is half-full is half-empty, and vice versa, though they do so in two different manners, because ⁰Full, ⁰Empty are not co-conceptualizing Trivializations.[12]

The *concept theory* of TIL was developed by Materna in the 1990s. The driving motivation was to obtain a slightly coarser individuation of linguistic meanings than that afforded by Tichy's constructions. Originally, Materna (1998) defined a concept as an equivalence class of constructions. Materna was soon to realize, however, that a concept should not be identified with a *set*, even though the elements of that set were not themselves set-theoretic entities. Materna's revised concept theory, summarized in Duží et al. (*ibid.*, §2.2), identifies a concept with a privileged member of an equivalence class of *constructions*. That is, concepts were originally typed as (o*ₙ) and subsequently as *ₙ.

An equivalence class is obtained by means of the definition of *procedural isomorphism*.[13] Procedural isomorphism is TILs notion of *co-hyperintensionality*. The definition of procedural isomorphism presupposes a few other definitions, namely of *closed construction*, *subconstruction* and *free and bound occurrences of variables*.[14] TIL has propounded various definitions of procedural isomorphism, all of which slot in somewhere between Church's Alternatives (A0) and (A1). In Duží and Jespersen (2013, Def. 2.5), (A¾) amounts to α-convertibility, β-convertibility *by name*, and η-convertibility. The latest definition, (A1″), is cast in terms of a more detailed definition of α-convertibility and β-convertibility *by value*, while lopping

---

[12] I rehearse this example in my (2010). Nolan (2013, §3) objects that my hyperintensional distinction between a half-full and a half-empty glass should not be restricted to the conceptual sphere ('of representations'), but ought to be extended to the empirical sphere ('the world'). Maybe so; but TIL is not the right theory for pursuing worldly hyperintensionality, or worldly structure, for that matter.

[13] Cf. Carnap's *intensional isomorphism* and Church's *synonymous isomorphism*.

[14] See Duží et al. (2010, Def. 1.3, p. 46; Def. 1.4, p. 47).

off η-conversion, because it does not always preserve equivalence in a partial logic such as TIL.[15]

Definition 4 (*α-conversion, β-conversion by value*).

(α) Let C, D be constructions. Then C, D are *α-equivalent*, denoted '$^0C \approx_\alpha {}^0D$', $\approx_\alpha/(o*_n *_n)$, if they v-construct the same entity or are both v-improper, and either C, D differ at most by using different λ-bound variables, or their β-expanded forms differ at most by using different λ-bound variables.

(β) Let $Y \to_v \alpha; x_1, D_1 \to_v \beta_1,..., x_n, D_n \to_v \beta_n, [\lambda x_1...x_n\, Y] \to_v (\alpha\beta_1...\beta_n)$. Let C be a construction of the form $[[\lambda x_1...x_n\, Y]\, D_1...D_n]$. Then the conversion from $[[\lambda x_1...x_n\, Y]\, D_1...D_n]$ to $^2[^0Sub\, [^0Tr\, D_1]\, ^0x_1 \,...\, [^0Sub\, [^0Tr\, D_n]\, ^0x_n\, ^0Y]]$ is *β-reduction by value*. The reverse conversion is *β-expansion by value*. Constructions C, D are *β-equivalent*, denoted '$^0C \approx_\beta {}^0D$', $\approx_\beta/(o*_n *_n)$, iff one arises from the other by β-reduction or β-expansion by value. □

Definition 5 (*procedurally isomorphic constructions*). Let C, D be constructions. Then C, D are *procedurally isomorphic* iff either C, D are identical or there are constructions $C_1,..., C_n$ ($n > 1$) such that $^0C = {}^0C_1$, $^0D = {}^0C_n$, and each C_i, C_{i+1} ($1 \leq i < n$) are either α- or β-equivalent. □

Remark 3 $[[\lambda x\, [^0Prime\, x]]\, ^05]$ and $[[\lambda y\, [^0Prime\, y]]\, ^05]$ are procedurally isomorphic. $[\lambda x\, [[^0Card\, \lambda y\, [^0Divide\, y\, x]] = {}^02]]\, ^05]$ and $[^0Prime\, ^05]$ are not procedurally isomorphic. All four are equivalent, in that they all construct **T**, but they do so in three non-isomorphic manners.[16]

The members of an equivalence class of procedurally isomorphic constructions all construct the same object (or all fail to construct an object of a particular type), though they do so in slightly different manners. When we are concerned with the object constructed, rather than this or that particular manner of constructing it, any one element of the set will do. However, we can privilege a particular member as being representative of all the members. Pick a construction C and generate the set of constructions procedurally isomorphic to C. Each equivalence class of constructions can be well-ordered: pick some well-ordering or other. The representative element will be the first construction occurring in the given ordering. This construction will be the unique *normal form* of all the elements of the equivalence class generated from C. The representative element is designated as a *concept*.

Definition 6 (*concept*). A *concept* is a normalized closed construction. □

We define next concepts with particular features. Since concepts are constructions, they inherit the latter's bifurcation between *atomic* and *composite* ones. A particular kind of atomic constructions are singled out as *simple concepts*.[17]

---

[15] See Duží and Jespersen (ms.).

[16] See Duží et al. (2010, Def. 1.5, p. 48).

[17] The definition of *simple concept* found in Duží et al. (*ibid.*, Def. 2.4, p. 155) has a second clause stating that $[\lambda x\, x]$ is a *simple concept* of the identity function of type $(\alpha\alpha)$. However, this second clause involves a Closure, which is a composite construction, and as such ill-fitting as a simple concept. (The original

Definition 7 (*simple concept*). Let X be either a construction or an intensional or an extensional entity. Then ^0X is the unique *simple concept* of X. □

The philosophical idea behind the definition of *simple concept* is that a simple concept is one that single-handedly conceptualizes an object, without drawing upon additional concepts. Simple concepts must be conceptual rock bottom. For instance, when 0 is defined to be a natural number and the successor of 0 is also defined to be a natural number then the underlying concept of 0 is a *simple* concept of 0. Peano's definition of *natural number* provides no conceptual handle on 0, by withholding any information about 0. Transposed into TIL, Peano's base clause simply posits ^{00}, presupposing that the audience possess some (extra-definitional) means or other of harpooning 0. For instance, any mathematician will know that 0 is the additive identity.

A simple concept is a direct, one-step conceptualization of an object, representing the bare bones of the notion of conceptualization. If the only concept of some object X you command is ^0X then you have no knowledge about X other than what the type of X is and the ability to single out X among any other objects. Hence, on the one hand, ^0X is a highly potent concept, identifying as it does X in one fell swoop, while on the other hand being imbued with precious little information about X. In the ontology of TIL every single object (i.e. anything for which there is a proper construction) has a Trivialization, so there is a bijection between all the objects of a given type and their unique, individual simple concepts. With all those simple concepts available, it requires philosophical prudence when deciding whether to assign ^0X to a term or expression denoting X as its meaning.[18]

For instance, the simple concept of Venus (the planet, not the goddess) is ^0Venus.[19] Venus *cannot* be conceptualized by means of $^0The\_Morning\_Star$ or $^0The\_Evening\_Star$. For if so, sheer knowledge of these three simple concepts (supposedly) co-conceptualizing Venus would suffice to establish, a priori, that the Morning Star is the Evening Star and that Venus is both the Morning and the Evening Star. This would leave nothing for astronomy to discover. Nonetheless, Daley claims that

> one might think about Venus via [the morning star], [the evening star], or [Venus]. (*Ibid.*, p. 364.)

One may not, with the obvious exception of Daley's [Venus], i.e. TILs ^0Venus. The way TIL is set up, the individual office whose simple concept is $^0The\_Morning\_Star$

Footnote 17 continued

motivation for including [λ*x x*] was that no proper subconstruction within it is a concept.) Furthermore, Def. 7 differs from the previous definition of simple concept in that the definition extends now to constructions as well: also simple concepts of constructions are now an option.

[18] Cf. Fodor's misgivings (*ibid.*, pp. 123ff) about *doorknob* being a non-composite concept.

[19] The particular choice of language, name and notation is without semantic and conceptual significance: ^{0}ხუცაშვილი and ^{0}Сталин are one and the same Trivialization, one and the same simple concept, of one and the same individual. Similarly for ^0Venus and ^0Venere.

and the different individual office whose distinct simple concept is $^0\textit{The\_Evening\_Star}$ contingently share the same extension at the actual world. Furthermore, Venus is, contingently, their co-occupant. What Daley does is run three levels together: (simple) concepts, individual offices (e.g. *the brightest non-lunar body in the morning/evening sky*), and individuals (in casu Venus).[20]

4 Property modification

Here I discuss four of Daley's examples of properties: *flies, is a father, is a brown cow, is an alleged felon*. Daley (*ibid.*, p. 365) analyzes 'flies', 'is a father' by means of the schematic Closure

$$[\lambda x[Fx]]$$

where $F/(o\iota)$. Apart from leaving out the Trivialization of F in the Composition $[Fx]$, Daley's analysis fails to bring out the empirical character of the properties of flying and being a father. Where $F'/(o\iota)_{\tau\omega}$, the full TIL analysis is the schematic Closure

$$\lambda w \lambda t [\lambda x [^0 F'_{wt} x]]$$

which η-reduces to the Trivialization $^0F'$ of F'. This Trivialization and that Closure are non-isomorphic, but equivalent, constructions of the same property.

Property modification would be an easy-to-handle phenomenon if modifiers were set-to-set functions, such that modification would reduce to subset formation (comprehension).[21] Where M' is a set-to-set modifier/$((o\iota)(o\iota))$ and F a property typed as a set/$(o\iota)$, as per Daley's typing, an individual with the modified property constructed by $[^0M'\ ^0F]$ would belong to a subset of a set of Fs, provided M' is a *subsective* modifier. Typing modifiers as set-to-set functions makes sense in mathematics. For instance, given a set of (natural) numbers, the modifier *Prime* extracts its subset of prime numbers. Furthermore, many (most?) modifiers of *natural* language are, indeed, subsective:

$$\frac{[^0M'_s\ ^0F]\ ^0a}{[^0F\ ^0a]}$$

For instance, if a is a proud father then a is a father: any set of proud fathers is invariably extracted from a set of fathers. With '⊆' in the more familiar infix notation and without Trivialization[22]:

$$\lambda x[[^0Proud\ ^0Father_{wt}]x] \subseteq \lambda x[^0Father_{wt}\ x]$$

The type of ⊆ is $(o((o\iota)(o\iota)))$: it is true or false that a certain set is a subset of another set. So it is an option to construe the modifier *Proud* as a mapping from one

---

[20] See also Duží et al. (*ibid.*, §3.3.1).

[21] My (2004) translates the comprehension schema into TIL, stressing the procedural dimension of obtaining one set from another.

[22] In standard notation: $\{x \mid (Proud\ Father)\ x\} \subseteq \{x \mid Father\ x\}$, where *Father* is a set.

set of individuals to another set of individuals: given a set of individuals with property *F*, extract those that are proud *F*s.

However, there are well-known, manifest exceptions to the set-to-set typing. A modern-day *locus classicus* is Montague (1970, p. 211), who observes that some modifiers are *non-intersective* and others are even *non-subsective*. An individual with the property of being a *short* Dutchman is a Dutchman, so *Short* is subsective, but a short Dutchman is not short, pure and simple. A short Dutchman is not an element of the intersection of the extensions of the property of being a Dutchman and the (presumed) property of being short; for there is no such property as being short in an unqualified manner. This is to say that *Short* is non-intersective. An individual with the property of being a *fake* banknote is not a banknote: no set of fake banknotes is extracted from a set of banknotes. An individual with the property of being an *alleged* felon is maybe a felon: some sets of alleged felons are extracted from a set of felons and the rest are not. So *Fake* and *Alleged* are deemed non-subsective. (This claim will be qualified below.) Montague famously generalizes to the hardest case, such that all modifiers get typed as property-to-property mappings. TIL agrees with this typing, in the interest of a uniform, top-down treatment. Hence:

Definition 8 (*property modifier*). A function is a *property modifier* iff it is of type $((o\iota)_{\tau\omega} (o\iota)_{\tau\omega})$, i.e. a function from ι-properties to ι-properties. As a notational convention, abbreviate '$((o\iota)_{\tau\omega} (o\iota)_{\tau\omega})$' as '$(\pi\pi)$'. □

Remark 4 For comparison, a *propositional modifier* is of type $(o_{\tau\omega} o_{\tau\omega})$. Thus, 'allegedly' as it occurs in "Allegedly, *a* is an assassin" or "*a* is allegedly an assassin" denotes a propositional modifier, taking one proposition to another, as achieved by this Composition: $[^0Allegedly\ [\lambda w\lambda t\ [^0Assassin_{wt}\ ^0a]]]$. A *modifier of property modifiers* is of type $((\pi\pi)(\pi\pi))$. Thus, 'very' as this adverb occurs in "*a* is a very short Dutchman" denotes a function taking *Short* to *Very Short*: $\lambda w\lambda t\ [[[^0Very\ ^0Short]\ Dutchman]_{wt}\ ^0a]$.[23]

Let now *M* be a modifier/$(\pi\pi)$ and *F* a property/π. To obtain a modified property, apply *M* to *F* as per $[^0M\ ^0F]$. To predicate this modified property of *a*, just extensionalize it as we extensionalized *F* above, and Compose the resulting mapping, of type $(o\iota)$, with *a*:

$$\lambda w\lambda t\left[\left[^0M\ ^0F\right]_{wt}\ ^0a\right]$$

It has become standard to distinguish between four kinds of modifiers, according to their logical behaviour. Here is how I suggest characterizing them, in terms of entailments between propositions[24]:

---

[23] Jespersen and Primiero (2012, §2.3) has the details, and also rectifies a claim made in Duží et al. (*ibid.*, p. 506).

[24] Jespersen and Carrara (2013, §2.5), Jespersen et al. (ms.) point out that whether a given modifier is subsective, etc., is a function of its argument property (or argument modifier, for higher-degree modifiers). It is not fixed for a given modifier that it is subsective, etc. In this paper I am suppressing this relativization of a modifier's status to its argument property (argument modifier).

- *Subsective.* $\lambda w \lambda t\ [[^0M_s\ ^0F]_{wt}\ ^0a]$ entails $\lambda w \lambda t\ [^0F_{wt}\ ^0a]$ (e.g. a *large* horse is a horse).
- *Privative.* $\lambda w \lambda t\ [[^0M_p\ ^0F]_{wt}\ ^0a]$ entails $\lambda w \lambda t\ [[^0Non\ ^0F]_{wt}\ ^0a]$ (e.g. a *fake* banknote is a *Non*-banknote).[25]
- *Modal.* $\lambda w \lambda t\ [[^0M_m\ ^0F]_{wt}\ ^0a]$ entails $\lambda w \lambda t\ [^0\exists \lambda w'\ [^0\exists \lambda t'\ [[[^0M_m\ ^0F]_{wt}\ a] \rightarrow [^0F_{w't'}\ ^0a]]] \wedge\ ^0\exists \lambda w''\ [^0\exists \lambda t''\ [[[^0M_m\ ^0F]_{wt}\ ^0a] \rightarrow [^0Non\ ^0F]_{w''t''}\ ^0a]]]]$ (e.g. an *alleged* assassin is maybe an assassin).[26]
- *Intersective.* $\lambda w \lambda t\ [[^0M_i\ ^0F]_{wt}\ ^0a]$ entails $\lambda w \lambda t\ [[^0M^*_{wt}\ ^0a] \wedge [^0F_{wt}\ ^0a]]$ (e.g. a *round* peg is round* and a peg).

Remark 5 The left-hand conjunct of the conclusion of the rule controlling intersective modifiers is validated by a rule of *left subsectivity*. Intersective modification is the conjunction of right and left subsectivity, the above rule of subsective modification being the rule of right subsectivity. Within the current framework, the modifier M_i denoted in the premise must be replaced by a property, M^*, in the conclusion. Otherwise it cannot be inferred that a round peg is round*, say. ^0M cannot be detached from the context $[^0M\ ^0F]$ and its product, M, be predicated of a, for a modifier is of the wrong type to be predicated of anything. Duží et al. (*ibid.*, §4.4) introduces *pseudo-detachment* as TIL's rule of left subsectivity. Pseudo-detachment applies to all four kinds of modifiers. The rule proceeds by quantifying over properties in order to obtain the property M^* from the modifier M. The conclusion $[^0M^*_{wt}\ a]$ can be read as "a is an M-something". For instance, if $M = Fake$ then in case a is a fake diamond it follows that a is a fake-something, or fake with respect to some property; and if $M = Presumed$ then in case b is presumed innocent it follows that b is presumed to be something. The proof of the rule of left subsectivity runs as follows:

1.	$[[^0M\ ^0F]_{wt}\ ^0a]$	∅
2.	$^0\exists \lambda p\ [[^0M\ p]_{wt}\ ^0a]$	1, EG
3.	$[\lambda x\ ^0\exists \lambda p\ [[^0M\ p]_{wt}\ x]\ ^0a]$	2, β-expansion
4.	$[[\lambda w' \lambda t'\ [\lambda x\ ^0\exists \lambda p\ [[^0M\ p]_{w't'}\ x]]]_{wt}\ ^0a]$	3, β-expansion
5.	$^0A^* = \lambda w' \lambda t'\ [\lambda x\ ^0\exists \lambda p\ [[^0M\ p]_{w't'}\ x]]$	definition
6.	$[^0A^*_{wt}\ ^0a]$	4, 5, Leibniz's Law

As it happens, Daley (*ibid.*, p. 367) invokes a rule of left subsectivity, without explicitly acknowledging it, when claiming correctly that

> it is possible to know that [x is an alleged something or other] by way of knowing nothing other than [x is an alleged felon] (…) [*The two square brackets are my summaries of what Daley claims. The author.*]

---

[25] Jespersen et al. (ms.) explains why the rule of privation replaces M_p by *Non* (property negation) rather than ¬ (boolean negation).

[26] Jespersen and Primiero (2012, §2) justifies this analysis.

Daley (*ibid.*, §4.4) pursues a somewhat different tack than TIL when analyzing complex predicates like 'is a tall mouse' and 'is an alleged felon'. He says,

> Concepts such as [tall] and [alleged] can be understood as 'incomplete' insofar as they require another concept (...) in order to form a propositional function (...). While a sentence such as 'he is tall' is coherent, it expresses a proposition that is more explicit than the corresponding surface grammar may suggest (...). (...), while [tall] when combined with [mouse], yields a subset of the extension of [mouse], [alleged], when combined with [felon], yields a subset of the extension of [alleged] and not a subset of the extension of [felon]. (*Ibid.*, p. 366).

First, propositional functions have no place in TIL (cf. Sect. 2).[27] Second, while "He is tall" counts as a sentence in natural-language grammar, it is logically speaking an open formula, hence it does not denote a proposition in the absence of an assignment to 'he'. In TIL, provided we allow 'tall' to denote a property instead of a modifier, "He is tall" is squared off with the *open* Closure $\lambda w \lambda t \, [^0 Tall_{wt} \, x]$ as its meaning, x ranging over individuals.[28] Only when a value is assigned to x does a proposition emerge, which may be expressed or denoted. For instance, $\lambda w \lambda t \, [^0 Tall_{wt} \, x]$ v-(a/x)-constructs the closed Closure $\lambda w \lambda t \, [^0 Tall_{wt} \, {}^0 a]$, which constructs the proposition that a is tall. This proposition is denoted by the closed formula (sentence) "a is tall".[29] Third, the result of combining what Daley calls the concepts [alleged] and [felon]—in TIL: $^0 Alleged$, $^0 Felon$—is, in TIL, the Composition $[^0 Alleged \, ^0 Felon]$, constructing the property of being an alleged felon. It makes little sense to say, as Daley does, that the result would be a subset of the (or an) extension of [alleged] (or $^0 Alleged$, for that matter). What is conceptualized by the concept $^0 Alleged$ is the modifier *Alleged*, and a modifier is a mapping between properties, not itself a property, and so not true or false of anything.

Daley's analysis of [alleged felon] has, as I argued above, got things back to front. He claims that

> [felon] within [alleged felon] combines with [alleged] by operating upon the value of [alleged] in a particular world, then abstracting from that world. (*Ibid.*)

First some comments from within Daley's framework. Daley does not admit, and does not seem to notice, that this typing requires the notation '[felon alleged]' rather than '[alleged felon]' in order for the functor to precede its argument term. He does admit that he needs to change the type of [felon] from (οι)ω to (οι)(οι)ω. Probably, though,

---

[27] Daley's type assignments, like (οι)(οι)ω or (οι)ω, leave it unclear how a *proposition*, minimally of type (οω), is to be obtained as functional value. I have not come across a type like ((οω)ι) in Daley, which would seem the most obvious type to assign to his propositional functions.

[28] See Duží et al. (*ibid.*, §§3.4ff), Duží and Jespersen (2013, §3).

[29] I much prefer having 'tall' denote a modifier, which in "He is tall" modifies a value of the free variable f ranging over properties. The correct open Closure becomes $\lambda w \lambda t \, [[^0 Tall \, f]_{wt} \, x]$. "He is tall" is elliptic for "He is a (tall f)". When an utterance of "He is tall" is felicitous, the audience knows who is denoted by 'he' and what property is the implicit modifie of *Tall*.

'$((o\iota)(o\iota))_\omega$' would symbolize better Daley's intentions (and intensions): relative to world w, one set is taken to another set. Still we are not home-free, for when Daley at (*ibid.*, p. 367) attempts to abstract over ω in [alleged felon], or [felon alleged], there is no w variable for λ to bind: 'λw [alleged felon]' has a vacuous occurrence of 'λw'. That is to say that the syntax and the semantics and the types are out of touch.

Then five comments from the viewpoint of TIL. First, type assignments are absolute in TIL and not context-dependent, leaving no room for coercion, as Sect. 2 pointed out. Second, it is conducive to opacity that what is typed as something like a property—the TIL type of *Felon* would be $(o\iota)_{\tau\omega}$—in one place is typed as something like a modifier in another place. For then it seems we are, in effect, studying two functions where we originally thought we were studying but one.

Third, the crux of Daley's predicament is that he lacks an account of non-intersective modifiers, in this case modal modifiers. Daley wants, of course, to block the inference from someone being an alleged felon to their being a felon. Accordingly, Daley cannot align [alleged] with [tall] and [small]; for his [alleged] would take sets of felons as arguments. This explains why he decides to turn things around. He posits a set of individuals with the (presumed) property of being alleged at w, and attempts to extract its subset of felons at w, to form the set of alleged felons at w.

Fourth, however, there is no such a thing as 'the value of [alleged] in a particular world', as was noted above. What there is, is the property of being an [^{0}*Alleged p*] where p is $\exists$-bound, but this property is parasitic on the property [^{0}*Alleged* ^0F] where F is a definite property: cf. Remark 5. Maybe Daley's [alleged] is his counterpart of my [^{0}*Alleged p*], constructing the property *Alleged** (read: 'is alleged to be something'); but above I objected to starting out with a property that can emerge only at the end.

Fifth, world-indexing the application of [felon] to [alleged], or of [alleged] to [felon], for that matter, has little going for it; similarly for world-indexing the application of [tall] to [mouse] or [brown] to [cow]. To appreciate this fifth point, suppose $\langle w, t\rangle$'s set of brown cows is $\{b, c, d\}$ and $\langle w', t'\rangle$'s set of brown cows is $\{a, c, d, e\}$. Then, as a result of world-indexing, the *condition* of being a brown cow will not be the same for the two different indices $\langle w, t\rangle$, $\langle w', t'\rangle$. Instead property instantiation will depend on their parochial populations of brown cows. That is, to be a brown cow at $\langle w', t'\rangle$ an individual needs to be one of the elements of $\{a, c, d, e\}$, whereas the condition for $\langle w, t\rangle$ is being an element of $\{b, c, d\}$. What is deplorably lost is the *contingency* of having/failing to have an empirical property. What is regrettably gained is the *necessity* of being/failing to be an element of some particular set defined by enumeration of its elements: i.e. property instantiation reduces to (world-indexed) set membership. Consequently, an intensional entity such as a property is bound to track the world-relative vicissitudes of who is a brown cow, an alleged felon, etc., at each particular world. This puts the cart before the horse, for whether a is a brown cow (etc.) at w (and t) will no longer be a matter of a satisfying an empirical condition applying indiscriminately across all worlds (and times), but of being an element of a particular set at w (and t).[30]

---

[30] Tichý makes this point in various places, e.g. (1980b).

Instead, what should be world-indexed (or world- and time-indexed) is the property obtained by modifying a property. First Trivialize M, F to obtain $^{0}M, ^{0}F$, then insert these two Trivializations into a Composition, $[^{0}M\ ^{0}F]$, and only then apply world-and-time-indexing to obtain a set, $[^{0}M\ ^{0}F]_{wt}$. This approach applies indiscriminately to all four kinds of modifiers and evades spurious sets like $Alleged'_{wt}$ (in TIL notation).

Let us move on to the last case. The analysis of 'is a brown cow' excludes modification altogether, in case "a is a brown cow" is taken to be elliptical for 'is brown and is a cow': cf. Daley (*ibid.*, p. 367). Where both *Brown* and *Cow* are properties/π, the TIL analysis of the latter predicate is the Closure

$$\lambda w \lambda t [\lambda x [^{0}\wedge [^{0}Brown_{wt}\ x]\ [^{0}Cow_{wt}\ x]]]$$

There is only one analysis that would be simpler, namely the Trivialization of the property of being a brown cow. But this Trivialization barely qualifies as an analysis, constructing as it does the property in one go. A much better alternative option is to analyze 'is a brown cow' by means of the Composition

$$[^{0}Brown'\ ^{0}Cow]$$

where $Brown'/(\pi\pi)$. This Composition analyses 'is a brown cow' at face value, as specifying a specific sort of cow, namely the brown ones.

Which of the three analyses just mentioned one favours is beyond logic and formal semantics to adjudicate, calling for philosophical discretion instead. An obvious concern would be whether brown cows are brown in the same sense in which brown cookies, say, are brown. By contrast, 'is a tall mouse' and 'is an alleged felon' *must* be analyzed in terms of modified properties (or, less transparently, by way of Trivialization or variables) and emphatically not in terms of pairs of properties. As soon as we wish to study the logic of the construction of semantically and logically delicate properties as denoted by 'is a tall mouse', 'is an alleged felon', etc., atomic constructions are out. Hence, the logical structure of the concepts conceptualizing properties such as *being a tall mouse* and *being an alleged felon* must be the schematic Composition

$$[mf]$$

and cannot be the schematic Closure

$$\lambda w \lambda t [\lambda x [^{0}\wedge [f_{wt}x][g_{wt}x]]]$$

$m/*_1$ ranging over $(\pi\pi)$ and $f, g/*_1$ ranging over π.

5 Literal meaning, refinement and simplification

A strong argument in favour of some lexical concepts being composite and defined on the basis of other concepts is this. It is reasonable to maintain that the concept of man subsumes the concept of bachelor, because being a bachelor is one way of being a man. If one disregards this point about upward monotonicity, it becomes logically impossible to validate an inference such as this:

$$\frac{\text{a } \textit{bachelor} \text{ walks in the park}}{\text{a } \textit{man} \text{ walks in the park}}$$

From a logical point of view, there is every reason why the conceptualization of an individual as a bachelor ought to use the property of being a man as a stepping-stone. Otherwise the implicit inferential potential of the premise cannot be made explicit.

TIL makes available a tool to render this implicit inferential potential explicit. The tool is called *refinement*.[31] The definition of *refinement* presupposes the definition of *ontological definition*. TIL distinguishes between verbal and ontological definitions, parallel to what is commonly also known as 'nominal' and 'real' definitions, respectively. A verbal definition assigns a concept, already assigned to an existing term or expression as its meaning, to a new term or expression being introduced. For instance, if 'two weeks' has already had a concept assigned to it, that same concept may be assigned to the new term 'fortnight', making 'fortnight' and 'two weeks' synonymous, i.e. notational variants. Verbal definitions are what underlie *meaning postulates* in TIL. By contrast, an ontological definition does not assign meaning to a term, but conceptualizes an object.

Definition 9 (*ontological definition*). Let C be a composite concept conceptualizing object o. Then C is an *ontological definition* of o. □

Recall that all TIL concepts are, without exception, *structured*. But some of them are *atomic* (of one proper part only, namely themselves) and the rest are *composite* (of multiple proper parts):

- (*atomic*) ^0X, ^1X (provided X is atomic)
- (*composite*) ^2X, $[X\ Y_1...Y_m]$, $[\lambda x_1 \ldots x_m\ Y]$, ^1X (provided X is composite)

Hence in Def. 9, C must be either a Double Execution, a Composition, a Closure, or a composite instance of Single Execution.

Definition 10 (*refinement of a construction*). Let C_1, C_2, C_3 be constructions. Let ^0X be a simple concept of X, and let ^0X occur as a subconstruction within C_1. If C_2 differs from C_1 only by containing in lieu of ^0X an ontological definition of X, then C_2 is a *refinement of* C_1. If C_3 is a *refinement* of C_2 and C_2 is a *refinement* of C_1, then C_3 is a *refinement of* C_1. □

Daley (*ibid.*, p. 369) proposes what is in effect the inverse notion of refinement, namely *simplification*. The new Def. 11 incorporates *simplification* into TIL:

Definition 11 (*simplification of a construction*). Let C_1, C_2, C_3 be constructions. Let ^0X be a simple concept of X, and let ^0X occur as a subconstruction of C_1. C_1 is a *simplification* of C_2 if C_1 contains ^0X as a subconstruction where C_2 contains an ontological definition of X. If C_1 is a *simplification* of C_2 and C_2 a *simplification* of C_3, then C_1 is a *simplification of* C_3. A *fully simplified* construction contains as subconstructions no ontological definitions, but only simple concepts. □

---

[31] See Duží et al. (*ibid.*, p. 524, Def. 5.5).

Let us be agreed that $^0Bachelor$ is our sample simple concept and that, necessarily, x is a bachelor iff x is an unmarried man. (We also assume *unmarried* and *man* to be crisp notions to sidestep complicating factors like vagueness and fuzziness.) Then there are multiple ways of assigning structure to the concept of bachelor. Two of the candidate concepts are so-called *literal meanings*[32]:

Definition 12 (*literal meaning*). Let E be a term or expression whose semantically simple sub-expressions are $S_1, ..., S_n$, and let $S_1, ..., S_n$ denote objects $X_1, ..., X_n$. Let C_E be a construction that is assigned to E as its meaning such that there is no closed sub-construction of C_E constructing an object that is not denoted by a sub-expression of E. Then C_E is the *literal meaning* of E iff $^0X_1, ..., ^0X_m$ are all closed sub-constructions of C_E constructing objects $X_1, ..., X_m$, respectively. □

Remark 6 The idea informing Def. 12 is that the objects being denoted by semantically *simple* sub-expressions of E are to be constructed by their respective Trivializations. If E is simple then the Trivialization of the object that E denotes is the literal meaning of E. If E is composite the Trivializations of the objects denoted by the simple sub-expressions of E are combined into a composite construction of the object denoted by E.

The *literal meaning* of the lexical predicate 'bachelor' is $^0Bachelor$. The interesting question is which concept is the literal meaning of the composite predicate 'unmarried man'. I suggest $[[^0Un\ ^0Married]\ ^0Man]$. The types are $Un/((\pi\pi)(\pi\pi))$; $Married/(\pi\pi)$; Man/π.[33] This analysis factors out the three proper parts *Un*, *Married*, *Man*, laying down how they are unified into a whole. $[[^0Un\ ^0Married]\ ^0Man]$ decomposes thus:

- execute ^0Un to conceptualize the second-degree modifier *Un*
- execute $^0Married$ to conceptualize the property modifier *Married*
- apply *Un* to *Married* to conceptualize the property modifier (*Un Married*)
- execute ^0Man to conceptualize the property *Man*
- apply (*Un Married*) to *Man* to conceptualize the property ((*Un Married*) *Man*).

My analysis of 'unmarried man' differs somewhat from Daley's. He says (*ibid.*, p. 360):

complex concepts can be decomposed into their 'parts' [*why the scare quotes? BJ*]. But this implies that [unmarried man] *entails* [unmarried] and [man] (i.e. [x is an unmarried man] → ([x is unmarried] & [x is a man])).

Daley's analysis in effect a bottom-up, extensionalist analysis of 'unmarried man', being pivoted on the *intersection* of the *sets* $Unmarried_{wt}$, Man_{wt}. Daley does not study how his two concepts [unmarried], [man] cooperate so as to generate a third

---

[32] See Duží et al. (*ibid.*, p. 105, Def. 1.10) and also (*ibid.*, §2.1.3).

[33] As for the logic of the negation *Un*, see Jespersen et al. (ms.) for the logic of the second-degree modifier *Non**.

concept, [unmarried man]. This is in line with Daley's general stance at (*ibid.*, p. 359) that

> to say that [*AB*] is a complex concept composed of the 'structured constituents' of [*C*] is to say: $\Box \forall x$ ([*x* is *C*] ↔ [*x* is *AB*].

Daley purports to explain what it means for a complex concept to have the parts it has, so what must be explained is how a *concept* is formed from other *concepts*. Yet what Daley does is give an account of what it means for an *individual* x to be conceptualized by two concepts structured in two different ways. And what that means is that whenever x is conceptualized by one concept x is also conceptualized by the other. Daley's account shifts at least one level down, from concepts to objects. Daley's account fails to explain *how* [*AB*] is composed from [*C*]. Daley addresses merely the *logical* problem of obtaining the right entailments and not also the *merelogical* one of how simple concepts compose into compound ones.

To return to our initial conundrum, how do we succeed in inferring that if a bachelor is walking in the park then a man is walking in the park? Answer: by replacing $^0Bachelor$ by [[^0Un $^0Married$] ^0Man] by means of refinement and applying the rule of inference governing subsective modifiers to the modifier constructed by [^0Un $^0Married$].[34]

$$\frac{\lambda w \lambda t [^0 \exists \lambda x [^0 \wedge [^0 Walk_{wt}\ x] [[[^0Un\ ^0Married]\ ^0Man]_{wt} x]]]}{\lambda w \lambda t [^0 \exists \lambda x [^0 \wedge [^0 Walk_{wt} x] [^0 Man_{wt} x]]]}$$

The underlying methodology I just deployed is this. If our analysandum is the simple predicate 'bachelor', first pair it off with its *literal* meaning and afterwards *refine* this meaning. A simple predicate may be paired off with a composite concept in virtue of refinement, rather than in virtue of synonymy. For note that $^0Bachelor$ and [[^0Un $^0Married$] ^0Man] are not procedurally isomorphic. Instead they are *equivalent*, in that they construct the same property.

There is an alternative route, and a faster one at that, to pairing simple predicates off with composite concepts. The accompanying methodology is to put forward [[^0Un $^0Married$] ^0Man] as the literal meaning of 'unmarried man' and afterwards deploy the verbal definition that 'bachelor' is the definiendum and 'unmarried man' its definiens. The result is the meaning postulate that 'bachelor' is a notational variant of, hence synonymous with, the compound predicate. One upshot, though, is that 'bachelor' no longer has a literal meaning. $^0Bachelor$ has been written out of the story, for the sense of 'bachelor' has been stipulated to be [[^0Un $^0Married$] ^0Man]. But nor is [[^0Un $^0Married$] ^0Man] its new literal meaning, for this Composition and 'is a bachelor' differ structurally.

From a formal point of view at least, it is questionable what semantic and inferential gain may be accrued from introducing a redundant predicate like 'bachelor', on its construal as a notational variant of 'unmarried man'. Nor is this

---

[34] I interpret 'an unmarried man' as 'some unmarried man'. It is controversial, to be sure, to interpret an indefinite description by way of an existential quantifier, but the interpretation does not affect the point I am making. The shortcut renders superfluous the introduction of the separate category of indefinite descriptions.

predicate required in order to satisfy Daley's thesis that there are structured concepts, like [[^{0}Un ^{0}Married$]$ ^{0}Man], available for lexical predicates to be associated with. For ^{0}Bachelor is already structured. And this simple concept is best paired off with 'bachelor' as its literal meaning, making 'bachelor' non-synonymous with 'unmarried man'. The conclusion is that TIL's *simple concepts* are the right match for Daley's *structured lexical predicates*.

6 Conclusion

I addressed and solved two problems. One was to find a suitable notion of structured concept to accompany lexical predicates like 'bachelor'. I argued in favour of TIL's *simple concepts*, typed qua concepts in the ramified type hierarchy. The other was how to find a suitable semantics for non-intersective predicates like 'alleged felon'. I recommended *property modifiers*, typed qua functions in the simple type hierarchy. Finally I showed how to integrate Daley's notion of simplification into TIL, as the converse of the existing notion of refinement.

Acknowledgments A version of this paper was read as an invited tutorial at Department of Computer Science, TU Ostrava, as part of the *TIL Summer School*, 26–30 August 2013. The research reported herein forms part of the project *Unity of Structured Hyperpropositions*, Marie Curie Fellowship No. 628170, FP7-PEOPLE-2013-IEF. The research has also been supported by TU Ostrava Grant No. SP2014/157, *Knowledge Modelling, Process Simulation and Design*. I wish to thank Jakub Macek, Pavel Materna and, especially, Marie Duží for valuable comments.

References

Beesley, K. R. (1982). Evaluative adjectives as one-place predicates in Montague Grammar. *Journal of Semantics, 1*, 195–249.
Daley, K. (2010). The structure of lexical concepts. *Philosophical Studies, 150*, 349–372.
Duží, M. (2004). Concepts, language, and ontologies (from the logical point of view). In Y. Kiyoki, H. Kangassalo, & E. Kawaguchi (Eds.), *Information modelling and knowledge bases XV* (pp. 193–209). Amsterdam: IOS Press.
Duží, M., & Jespersen, B. (2013). Procedural isomorphism, analytic information and β-conversion by value. *Logic Journal of the IGPL, 21*, 291–308.
Duží, M., & Jespersen, B. (ms.). Transparent quantification into hyperintensional objectual attitudes (in revision).
Duží, M., Jespersen, B., & Materna, P. (2010). *Procedural semantics for hyperintensional logic*, Vol. 17 of *LEUS*. Dordrecht: Springer.
Fodor, J. A. (1998). *Concepts: Where cognitive science went wrong*. Oxford: Oxford University Press.
Jespersen, B. (2004). Aussonderung as procedure. In L. Běhounek (Ed.), *The logica yearbook 2003* (pp. 133–144). Prague: Filozofia.
Jespersen, B. (2008). Predication and extensionalization. *Journal of Philosophical Logic, 37*, 479–499.
Jespersen, B. (2010). How hyper are hyperpropositions? *Language and Linguistics Compass, 4*, 96–106.
Jespersen, B., & Carrara, M. (2013). A new logic of technical malfunction. *Studia Logica, 101*, 547–581.
Jespersen, B., Carrara, M., & Duží, M. (ms.). Double privation and multiply modified artefact properties (in submission).
Jespersen, B., & Primiero, G. (2012). Alleged assassins: Realist and constructivist semantics for modal modifiers. *Lecture Notes in Computer Science, 7758*, 94–114.
Kamp, H. (1975). Two theories of adjectives. In E. Keenan (Ed.), *Formal semantics of natural language* (pp. 123–155). Cambridge: Cambridge University Press.

Materna, P. (1998). *Concepts and objects*, Vol. 63 of *Acta Philosophica Fennica*. Helsinki: Philosophical Society of Finland.

Montague, R. (1970). English as a formal language. In B. Visentini, et al. (Eds.), *Linguaggi nella societá e nella tecnica* (pp. 189–224). Milan: Edizioni di Comunità.

Nolan, D. (2013). Hyperintensional metaphysics. *Philosophical Studies*. doi:10.1007/s11098-013-0251-2.

Partee, B. (2001). Privative adjectives: Subsective plus coercion. In R. Bäuerle, et al. (Eds.), *Presuppositions and discourse*. Amsterdam: Elsevier.

Partee, B. (2007). Compositionality and coercion in semantics. In G. Bouma, et al. (Eds.), *Cognitive foundations of interpretation* (pp. 145–161). Amsterdam: Royal Netherlands Academy of Arts and Sciences.

Partee, B. (ms.). Are there privative adjectives? Retrievable from http://people.umass.edu/partee/docs/ParteeInPressKampFest.pdf.

Primiero, G., & Jespersen, B. (2010). Two kinds of procedural semantics for privative modification. *Lecture Notes in Artificial Intelligence, 6284*, 252–271.

Soames, S. (2010). *What is meaning?* Princeton: Princeton University Press.

Tichý, P. (1971). An approach to intensional analysis. *Nous, 5*, 273–297. (Reprinted in V. Svoboda, B. Jespersen, & C. Cheyne (Eds.), *Collected Papers in Logic and Philosophy*. Prague/Dunedin: Filosofia, Czech Academy of Sciences/University of Otago Press.)

Tichý, P. (1980a). The logic of temporal discourse. *Linguistics and Philosophy, 3*, 343–369. (Reprinted in V. Svoboda, B. Jespersen, & C. Cheyne (Eds.), *Collected Papers in Logic and Philosophy*. Prague/Dunedin: Filosofia, Czech Academy of Sciences/University of Otago Press.)

Tichý, P. (1980b). Merrill on what a sentence says. *Philosophical Studies, 37*, 197–200. (Reprinted in V. Svoboda, B. Jespersen, & C. Cheyne (Eds.), *Collected Papers in Logic and Philosophy*. Prague/Dunedin: Filosofia, Czech Academy of Sciences/University of Otago Press.)

Tichý, P. (1988).*The Foundations of Frege's Logic*.Berlin: de Gruyter.

A New Logic of Technical Malfunction

BJØRN JESPERSEN
MASSIMILIANO CARRARA

Abstract. Aim of the paper is to present a new logic of technical malfunction. The need for this logic is motivated by a simple-sounding philosophical question: Is a malfunctioning corkscrew, which fails to uncork bottles, nonetheless a corkscrew? Or in general terms, is a malfunctioning F, which fails to do what Fs do, nonetheless an F? We argue that 'malfunctioning' denotes the modifier *Malfunctioning* rather than a property, and that the answer depends on whether *Malfunctioning* is *subsective* or *privative*. If subsective, a malfunctioning F is an F; if privative, a malfunctioning F is not an F. An *intensional* logic is required to raise and answer the question, because modifiers operate directly on *properties* and not on sets or individuals. This new logic provides the formal tools to reason about technical malfunction by means of a logical analysis of the sentence "a is a malfunctioning F".

0. Introduction

This paper presents a new logic for reasoning about *malfunction* in technological artefacts. The need for this logic is motivated by a simple-sounding philosophical question:

> Is a malfunctioning corkscrew, which fails to uncork bottles, nonetheless a corkscrew?

Or in general terms, is a malfunctioning F, which fails to do what Fs do, nonetheless an F? The key entities of the new logic are *properties* and property *modifiers*. Central is the distinction between a *subsective* and a *privative* interpretation of the property modifier *Malfunctioning*. The answer to the above question depends on whether this modifier is construed as being subsective or as being privative.

Our main argument for couching our analysis of malfunction in terms of modifiers is this. Consider the sentence "a is a malfunctioning corkscrew". It does not factor out into the conjunction "a is malfunctioning and a is a

---

Presented by **Jacek Malinowski;** *Received* May 19, 2011

This chapter originally appeared in Studia Logica (2013), 101, pp. 547–581.

corkscrew". The conjunctive analysis would require that a would be malfunctioning, pure and simple, without qualifying with respect to what a would be malfunctioning. This upshot would be analogous to factoring "b is a big elephant" out into "b is big and b is an elephant". Nothing is big, though, in disregard of a scale to distinguish between individuals that are big, medium-sized and small. The inference from b being a big elephant to b being big would be an invalid transition from a weaker to a stronger proposition: the premise attributes relative bigness to b (bigness, as far as elephants go); the conclusion attributes absolute bigness to b. This is the fallacy known as *secundum quid ad simpliciter*. Analogously, nothing malfunctions, pure and simple, but only with respect to a technical-artefact property. The assertion that a is malfunctioning will be incomplete without specifying with respect to what property a is malfunctioning. Thus the correct response to the claim "a is malfunctioning" is "a is a malfunctioning *what?*". Similarly with "b is big" and "b is a big *what?*"

The obvious alternative to the conjunctive analysis is to construe the adjectives 'big' and 'malfunctioning' as denoting modifiers rather than properties. Thus "b is a big elephant" and "a is a malfunctioning corkscrew" are instances of predication of one modified property rather than of two unmodified properties. This way it is no longer an option to infer from "a is malfunctioning corkscrew", by conjunction elimination, that a is a corkscrew. This is how it is avoided that the question as to whether a malfunctioning corkscrew is a corkscrew would be pre-empted by the analysis.

By having 'big' and 'malfunctioning' denote modifiers for the reason just given, there is a property that the modifiers *Big, Malfunctioning* cannot have: they cannot be *intersective*. Non-intersective modifiers are those that do not allow a modifier occurring in the premise to be substituted by a property in the conclusion so as to predicate that property of the individual. While it can be inferred from b being a big elephant that b is an elephant, it cannot be inferred that b is big (in an absolute sense).[1] The first of the two inferences goes through because *Big* is subsective: big elephants are elephants. As for a malfunctioning corkscrew being a corkscrew, the logical status of *Malfunctioning* – subsective or privative – needs to be settled before raising the question whether a malfunctioning corkscrew is a corkscrew. Once the logical status has been settled, the answer has already been implicitly given

---

[1] What can be inferred is that there is a property p such that b is a big p. Similarly, what can be inferred is that there is a property q such that a is a malfunctioning q. The rule of *pseudo-detachment*, or a similar rule of *left subsectivity*, is required for those two inferences. See §2.2.

to the question whether a malfunctioning corkscrew is a corkscrew. So the substantial question concerns the status of *Malfunctioning*.

In our logic a property modifier is (modelled as) a mapping from properties to properties, such that the result of the application of a modifier to a property is another property.[2] A property is (modelled as) a mapping from a logical space of possible worlds to a mapping from times to sets of individuals. A set of individuals is in turn a characteristic function from individuals to truth-values. So for an individual to instantiate a property, whether modified or not, is to be an element of its extension at a world/time pair.

In general, a modifier operates on intensional entities, such as properties or propositions. Our new logic of malfunction needs to be an intensional one in order to directly operate on intensions. A modifier is not itself an intensional entity. Instead it is a function not defined on possible worlds and, therefore, an extensional entity, in compliance with how possible-world semantics distinguishes between extensional and intensional entities. We are adopting this distinction in this paper.

In our logic the property of being a malfunctioning F is formed by means of *functional application* (symbolized by '$[XY]$', X a function, Y a functional argument) of the modifier *Malfunctioning* (abbreviated '*Malf*') to the property F. Functional application provides also the logic of *predication*, such that when predicating the property $[Malf\ F]$ of a, the result of applying a property to an individual is a truth-value. (This claim will be qualified below.)

The philosophical question as to whether a malfunctioning F is an F translates into the logical question as to whether the following argument is valid (in slightly simplified notation to begin):

$$\frac{[[MalfF]a]}{[Fa]}$$

The answer, of course, must be twofold, according as *Malf* is subsective or privative. If $[[Malf\ F]\ a]$ is true then on the subsective reading of *Malf* it follows that a is an F, while on the privative reading it follows that a is

---

[2]See Montague [29, p. 211]. We note in passing that if the modifier is *Genuine*, say, we get the limiting case where the result of the application is not a new property, since the modifier in question is the identity function on properties: $[Genuine\ F]$ and F are one and the same property. Hence there is no semantic or logical reason to apply a *trivial* modifier such as *Genuine* to F. A trivial modifier returns the modified property unmodified, as it were. We note that our adoption of the category of trivial modification is at variance with Kamp and Partee's *non-vacuity principle* [25, p. 161].

not an *F*. Equivalently, on the subsective reading, the properties of being a malfunctioning *F* and being an *F* are such that the latter subsumes the former (i.e. possibly some, though not necessarily all, *F*s are malfunctioning *F*s), whereas on the privative reading those two properties are necessarily mutually exclusive.

The logical task we address and solve in this paper consists in devising a framework of intensional logic in which to rigorously raise and qualify the answers to the question of the validity of the argument above, relative to whether *Malf* is a subsective or a privative modifier. This paper, therefore, brings together philosophical logic, formal semantics, philosophy of language, and philosophy of technology.

The property [*Malf F*] is formed via a logical operation (functional application) involving a property modifier and a property. It would be insufficient to merely manipulate sets (extensions of properties) and individuals (bearers of properties). The discussion in [13, p. 72] of *Former*, as it occurs in *Former lover of Bill's* and *Former tenant of 13 Green St* (to use their example), goes to show that modifiers should not be functions from *sets* to *sets*.[3] In this example, it so happens that the class of busy Bill's former lovers and the class of former tenants at 13 Green St are the same class. But the properties of being a former lover of Bill's and being a former tenant of 13 Green St ought to have the same satisfaction class only contingently, whereas the Montagovian typing $\langle\langle e,t\rangle,\langle e,t\rangle\rangle$ predicts that they must, of necessity, have the same satisfaction class. Heim and Kratzer point out that since *Former* has a temporal, or dynamic, dimension (calling for more than one temporal parameter), this modifier demands an intensional semantics. The authors, however, as they themselves acknowledge, leave the topic of intensional semantics underdeveloped. A more general insight, though, can be extracted from Heim and Kratzer's discussion of *Forme*r, namely that no modifier should map sets onto sets, but instead properties onto properties to accommodate both temporal and modal variability. This tack would also be in keeping with the methodologically sound strategy of generalizing from the hardest case to all cases in the interest of uniform treatment. Thus what

---

[3]Modifiers are functions from *sets* to *sets* in the *constructivist* theory of modifiers presented in [35], Jespersen and Primiero (forthcoming). But the point is that those sets are sets of proof-objects, and a (constructive) set of proof-objects is identical to a (constructive) *proposition*. Therefore, this constructive theory of modification still has a modifier take one *intensional* entity to another *intensional* entity. Jespersen and Primiero (forthcoming) shows why constructive property modification reduces, in the final analysis, to propositional modification: e.g. "*a* is an alleged assassin" ultimately gets analyzed as "Allegedly, *a* is an assassin".

is wanted are empirical parameters such as worlds and times at which the relevant set of Bill's former lovers does not invariably get mapped onto the set of former tenants of 13 Green St at the same set of parameters, or *vice versa*.

All in all, our intensional logic comes with a formal ontology of *individuals*, *sets of individuals*, *properties of individuals*, *sets of properties of individuals*, *relations-in-extension between properties of individuals*, *propositions*, and *property modifiers*. These extensional and intensional entities are organized in a *simple type theory* spanning four ground types: possible worlds, instants of time, individuals, and truth-values. Functional types, including those of possible-world intensions, are defined over those ground types in the standard manner.

The logical operations we need are *predication*, *intensionalization* (formation of intensional entities), *extensionalization* (descent from intension to extension at empirical parameters), *λ-introduction*, and *λ-elimination*. We are also going to need the propositional property of being *true* (a 'truth predicate') due to our adoption of *partial* functions.

Our logic of malfunction is developed within Tichý's *Transparent Intensional Logic (TIL)*. Formally, TIL is a *hyperintensional, partial, typed λ-calculus* equipped with a *procedural* or operational (as opposed to denotational or model-theoretic) *semantics*. Its type theory is a *ramified type hierarchy* including both first-order and higher-order types. Intensional and extensional entities are typed within its simple, or first-order, fragment (with provisos for sets with domain in higher-order objects). Hyperintensional entities are typed within its higher-order fragment. The simple type theory suffices for the entities listed in the ontology above. Below we motivate our choice of TIL as background theory, and we set out its relevant fragments.

We noted already that our logic of malfunction is an intensional logic. This is not to suggest that it would flout any or all of the laws of extensional logic (like substitution of equivalents, quantifying-in, etc.). Rather it means that it makes feasible the manipulation of intensional entities such as properties. What recommends TIL for the task at hand is not least the fact that it is an extensional logic of intensions and hyperintensions. The rules that are valid in one sort of context are also valid in any other sort of context. Thus Leibniz's Law, for instance, is valid throughout TIL, whether applied within an extensional, intensional or hyperintensional context. What changes, relative to context, is how permissive or how restrictive the Law is: the Law validates the fewest substitutions in hyperintensional contexts like "a knows that $7 + 5 = 12$, yet a does not know that $\sqrt{144} = 12$" because the identity criteria are stricter, and conversely for extensional contexts like

"7 + 5 = 12".[4] TIL, however, is not a fully *classical* logic, since it is not a total, but partial, logic in virtue of embracing partially defined functions. TIL allows truth-value gaps: some propositions fail to return a truth-value and instead return nothing, leaving a gap instead. Hence the law of excluded middle will have counterexamples. Thus TIL adopts weak bivalence (the thesis that the truth-values are exactly two in number) and rejects strong bivalence (the thesis that every truth-bearer takes a truth-value). Partiality is not particularly pressing for our present topoi. But we have a couple of reasons for explicitly wrapping our theory of properties around it. First, partiality is a key feature of TIL, for which reason we would not be faithful to our background theory without including partiality. Second, we intend later to apply the fragment of TIL set out below to other topics in philosophy of technology as well (and invite others to do the same), for which reason we want to be on the safe side by having already prepared our *general* intensional logic of technical artefacts to handle partial functions.

Our general intensional logic of technical artefacts is proved below to be adequate to reproduce the two key inferences of this paper: if *Malf* is subsective, then a malfunctioning F is an F, and if *Malf* is privative, then a malfunctioning F is not an F. It also provides a framework for additional applications within philosophy of technology. Some examples would be *malfunctioning fake*, *fake malfunctioning*, and *fake fake* artefacts, i.e. cases of iterated first-order or higher-order modification involving intricate interplay between subsective and privative (and perhaps other) modifiers.[5] Another example would be the formalization of technical functions in engineering design.[6]

The remainder of this paper is divided into two portions. The first, shorter, portion (Section 1) briefly summarizes the two conceptions of malfunction and the two conceptions of function introduced and discussed at

---

[4]See Tichý [42] regarding Leibniz's Law and intensional contexts, Tichý [43, Ch. 12] for the general program of a logic that is both intensional and transparent (i.e. not contextualist like Frege's or Montague's), and Duží and Jespersen (forthcoming; submitted) concerning Leibniz's Law and hyperintensional contexts.

[5]See Carrara and Jespersen (submitted).

[6]See Carrara and Vermaas [2]. An application outside of philosophy of technology might bear on *incapacitated Fs*, *impaired Gs*, *disabled Hs*, and other examples of agents who cannot fulfill a certain institutional role properly or at all. For instance, is an incapacitated pilot a pilot? *Incapacitated*, *Impaired*, *Disabled*, etc. may fruitfully be construed as modifiers lending themselves to either a subsective or a privative interpretation. Much of the discussion above concerning *Malfunctioning* would arguably carry over to *Incapacitated* and the rest.

length in our [21]. The second portion (Section 2 consisting of eight subsections) provides the logic. It first presents the overarching framework of formal semantics in which the subsective and the privative interpretations of *Malf* are explored and afterwards explains the details of both interpretations.

1. Function and Malfunction

The *subsective* conception of *Malf* (the subscript 's' abbreviating 'subsective') is defined by this rule of inference (leaving out the outermost parentheses and using slightly simplified notation for now), already broached in the Introduction:

$$\frac{[Malf_s\, F]\, a}{F a}$$

The *privative* conception of *Malf* (the subscript 'p' abbreviating 'privative') is defined by this rule of inference:

$$\frac{[Malf_p\, F]\, a}{\neg F a}$$

We come out in favour of neither conception of malfunction. We are charting the assumptions and consequences of two conceptions rather than advocating one over the other.

On a methodological note, a theory pertaining to a certain area of inquiry must be able to account not only for the success stories, but also for the fail tales. Thus a theory of linguistic sense must be able to account also for nonsense; a theory of possibility, for impossibility; a theory of truth, for falsehood; a theory of knowledge, for ignorance; etc. Hence a theory of technical function must include an account of technical malfunction. Which notions of *function* are compatible with, or appropriate for, which notion of *malfunction*? In [21] we distinguish between the *use* view and the *design* view of function.[7] The design view holds that what defines an artefact a as an F is that a is a token of the designed artefact type F. Hence a designed F remains an F, whether it be a functioning or a malfunctioning F ("once an F, always an F"). A malfunctioning F retains its *proper function* as an F, but forfeits its capacity to function as an F. What makes an artefact an F is not its capacity to function as an F, but its origin in a design and manufacturing process aimed at creating Fs. It must have the right sort of

---

[7]The design view squares roughly with the etiological, or proper-function, theories of function, and the use view with the causal-role theories. See, e.g., [5–7, 12, 27, 28, 32, 34, 36].

pedigree to be a corkscrew, say, whereas it is neither necessary nor sufficient to be an artefact that happens to function as a corkscrewing device. An artefact's origin anchors it to a particular artefact kind that makes the artefact impervious to failure to function in the way it was designed to.[8]

The use view, by contrast, holds that what defines an artefact a as an F is that a is being, or could be, used as an F, irrespective of whether a was designed as an F in the first place. Thus the distinction between proper and improper use does not apply. This is not to say that the notion of intention must be ruled out; far from it. Only the notion of intention cannot be one stemming from design.[9] The ability to be a malfunctioning F must have a different foundation than design, namely this: a is a malfunctioning F if a previously functioned, or could have functioned, as an F and currently fails to function as an F. The boundary of what a could have functioned as is something we take to be fixed, ultimately, by the actual laws of nature, i.e. by what is actually nomologically possible.[10] It would trivialize the notion of what a could have functioned as if the modal perimeter were solely logical possibility. This would include all the nomologically deviant worlds that are logically possible. No two artefacts would differ with respect to their nomological potential to function as an F. A noteworthy consequence (worthy of further exploration elsewhere) is that the use view is imbued with a *dynamic* dimension absent from the design view. The fact that a is *currently* a malfunctioning F presupposes (and not just entails), on the use view, that *a previously* functioned as an F, or equivalently, *previously* was a functioning F.

---

[8]Does the pure design view of function exclude *success criteria*? No, but it does not include them, either. There is conceptual space to include them, but they are not an integral part of the package. For instance, was British Petroleum in possession of undersea well-cappers when *Deepwater Horizon* polluted the Mexican Gulf in 2010? BP did have undersea well-cappers, even if all of them malfunctioned — on the combination of the design view with subsective *Malf*. The use view of function has a rather robust criterion of success: function as an F, or fail to be an F! The pure design view of function does not have success criteria beyond the initial point of having been designed as an F. This view may be too pure to be of much practical interest, but we are identifying the extremes in order to identify the perimeter of the conceptual space.

[9]For instance, if someone intends to slide down a snow-clad slope but has not got a ready-made snowboard then they may decide instead to select the most suitable snowboard-surrogate from among a pile of planks. As long as the agent is sliding down the slope on the plank, the plank *is* a snowboard because it functions as one. The agent *intended* the selected plank to function as a snowboard, and it does function as one, but the plank was *not designed* as one.

[10]If another world is considered as actual, then the laws of nature of that world would fix what counts as being actually nomologically possible.

As it turns out, the privative view of malfunction accommodates two variants of the use view of function. According to the *amodal* variant, an artefact is an F if, and only if, it functions as an F; according to the *modal* variant, an artefact is an F if, and only if, it has the structural and/or material capacity to function as an F, regardless of the actual realization of this capacity. It is the use (amodal variant) or usability (modal variant) of an artefact as an F that qualifies it as an F. Since we can infer *ab esse ad posse*, the modal variant subsumes the amodal variant.

One way of summarizing the distinction between the design view and the use view is in terms of a shift of perspective from *designer* to *user*, respectively. Roughly, on the design view it is the designer that makes a an F, whereas on the use view it is the (current) user that makes a an F. Another way of summarizing the difference between the design view and at least the amodal version of the use view might be cast (lightly) as the difference between an *aristocratic* and a *meritocratic* view: a is an F solely in virtue of its pedigree regardless of its own performance, whereas a is an F solely in virtue of its own performance regardless of its pedigree.

Since we are operating with two conceptions of malfunction and two conceptions of function, four combinations are mathematically possible. But one of them is logically impossible, because inconsistent. With '*Des*' abbreviating 'the design view' and '*Use*' 'the use view', and $Malf_s$, $Malf_p$ as above, the combinations individually amount to the following:

[1] $Des + Malf_s$. An artefact a was designed as an F, which is why a remains an F, even when a is a malfunctioning F.

[2] $Des + Malf_p$. An artefact a was designed as an F, but is not an F, because no malfunctioning F is an F. (It is left open whether a was ever a functioning F.)

[3] $Use + Malf_s$. This combination is logically impossible. If a is a malfunctioning F then a is an F; and if a is a malfunctioning F then a fails to function as an F and is, therefore, not an F. So, if a is a malfunctioning F then a both is, and is not, an F.[11]

[4] $Use + Malf_p$. An artefact a is a malfunctioning F, hence a was previously an F and no longer is one. (That a was previously an F also follows from a previously functioning as an F.)

---

[11]For clarification, on the modal variant, if a is a malfunctioning F then a lacks the structural and/or material capacity to function as an F and is, therefore, not an F. Any set of artefacts lacking that capacity has a (possibly empty) subset of malfunctioning Fs. Hence both the modal and the amodal variant are incompatible with subsective *Malf*.

The combination of $Malf_s$ with the design view is restrictive with respect to the property F (it is demanding for an artefact to qualify as an F because the artefact must have a pedigree as an F) and permissive with respect to $[Malf_s F]$ (no 'extra effort' is required of a malfunctioning F to remain an F). The combination of $Malf_p$ with the use view is permissive with respect to F (because also what the design view would deem successful *im*proper use of a as an F makes a an F) and restrictive with respect to $[Malf_p F]$ (the current incapacity to be used, or usable, as an F disqualifies a as an F).

Since, as entries [2] and [4] show, $Malf_p$ is compatible both with the design view and the use view, $Malf_p$ does not logically presuppose the design view of function. A noteworthy philosophical difference, however, between combining $Malf_p$ with the design view or the use view is that on the latter the notion of design is not sufficient to preserve a's status as an F. According to this combination, a designed F that fails to function as an F is a malfunctioning F and, therefore, not an F. But, it is far from clear why it would be philosophically rewarding to go with [2]. For as far as $Malf_p$ goes, the notion of design is rendered idle. This explains why [1], [4] are the two combinations we are concentrating on both in our [21] and in this paper.[12]

The property *functioning as an F* is indispensable for defining the twofold conceptions of function and of malfunction. Therefore we introduce the modifier *Functioning_as*, which is needed to generate, together with property F, the property *functioning as an F*.

The exact details of what it means for something to *function as an F* (while perhaps not being an F) are irrelevant for our present purposes. Our present concern is instead to carve out a niche for that property in our overall conceptual edifice of malfunction. The underlying idea, though, would be the following. For each technical-artefact property like *being a corkscrew* there exists the set of properties defining what the property amounts to; in this case, what *being a corkscrew* amounts to. We are making here the assumption that there is a set of properties that defines the property of being a corkscrew.[13] Each member of this set will be called a *requisite*.[14]

---

[12] See Kroes [26, Ch. 1] for a general discussion of what amounts in effect to the design and the use view of function and the subsective and the privative conception of *Malfunctioning*. (Ibid., p. 26, n. 22) places our formal framework of function and malfunction in a wider conceptual context.

[13] This assumption is substantiated in our [21].

[14] See [41] and [22].

A new logic of technical malfunction

A property F and its requisite properties $G_1, \ldots, G_n$ are organized in relations-in-extension, such that having any G_i is necessary for having F and having all G_i is sufficient for having F.

We are assuming that each set of requisites defining a technical-artefact property F will contain an element (a property) that lays down what Fs are for. That sort of 'what-for' property was already appealed to at the outset when raising the question whether a malfunctioning F, which fails to do what Fs do, is still an F. The bare claim that there is a property laying down what corkscrews are for is neutral between the design view and the use view. On the design view, the 'what-for' of corkscrews is to uncork bottles, *because* they are designed to do so. So this biconditional sums up the design view: something is an F iff it is designed as an F. On the use view, the 'what-for' of corkscrews is to uncork bottles, *because* they are, or can be, used to do that. So this biconditional sums up the two variants of the use view: something is a corkscrew iff it could be, or is, used to uncork bottles. Since the use view identifies the properties *being a corkscrew* and *being a bottle-uncorking device*, there is (as already noted) no room for the distinction between proper and improper use of an F, as there is in the design view. On the use view every use is, trivially, proper use.

There is an important difference, however, to be noted between the design view and the use view.[15] Since the design view adheres to the slogan "once an F, always an F", the design view entails that a token of F, *qua* instance of the artefact property F, cannot forfeit its *essence* as an F. This does not exclude that an F-token may be used, or may function, as a non-F-object – only this will constitute *improper* use of the F-token. The use view is flexible where the design view is rigid. On one occasion a user uses a round metal object to open a beer bottle. This use turns that round metal object into a beer-bottle opener; the property *being a beer-bottle opener* has a requisite property fixing what beer-bottle openers are for; therefore, that round metal object will have that requisite property. It may never have had that property prior to being used as, hence being, a beer-bottle opener. On a later occasion a user uses that same round metal object to pay for a bottle of beer. This use turns that object into a coin; the property *being a coin* has a requisite property fixing what coins are for (*making cash payments*, say); therefore, that object will have that requisite property. It may never have had that property prior to being used as, hence being, a coin (in case it is fresh out

---

[15]This difference is noted and discussed in [21, p. 130], from where the example of the bottle-opener/coin is taken.

of the mint, say). The design view anchors individual artefacts to one particular artefact property, and thereby to one particular what-for property. The use view does not. What does happen is that the use view entails that if an individual assumes, on a particular occasion of use, a certain artefact property then that individual *ipso facto* assumes the what-for property of that artefact property.

Here is another example to fix ideas.[16] Consider the use of a designed shoe as a weapon. *Being a weapon* is not a requisite property (hence cannot be the what-for property) of *being a shoe*. This is where the pure use view we are describing shows itself to be exceptionally pragmatic. On that very occasion of use, the object being used as a weapon *is* a weapon and *is not* a shoe, for it is not being used as a shoe. The use view would not describe this scenario in terms of using a *shoe* as a weapon, for the property of being a shoe is out of place here. (The modal variant of usability introduces complications we will not go into here.) So the what-for property that that object has, on that particular occasion of use, is the what-for property assigned to *being a weapon*, e.g. *being for inflicting damage upon an opponent*. When that object is no longer being wielded as a weapon, but worn as a shoe, it has stopped being a weapon and has become a shoe.

This wraps up our summary of the two conceptions of function (the design view and the use view) and the two conceptions of malfunction (the subsective and the privative one).

2. A Logic of Technical Malfunction

Our intensional logic of technical malfunction is a logic of properties, necessary relations between properties (in the form of requisites), and property modifiers. The logic will be developed within the first-order fragment of TIL, which encompasses intensional and extensional entities. The rest of Section 2 is devoted to what is central to our logic: a taxonomy of modifiers, a simple type theory, intensional essentialism, the property *functioning as an F*, and, finally, two formal derivations to check that the respective conclusions that an artefact that is a $[Malf_s\,F]$ is an F while an artefact that is a $[Malf_p\,F]$ is not an F follow as desired.

---

[16]We owe the shoe/weapon example to a referee, who put it forward as a challenge to the comprehensibility of the use view in its pure form.

2.1. Explicit Intensionalization and Temporalization

Tichý's TIL was conceived simultaneously with Montague's Intensional Logic (IL) in the mid-1960s onward.[17] Tichý's and Montague's respective intensional logics share the important feature that *mapping* (function-in-extension), rather than *set* or *relation*, say, is a basic concept.[18] This is important, because property modification is an operation defined over mappings rather than sets or relations. Hence no need for a detour around sets or relations to arrive at mappings.

TIL differs from IL in a number of respects, *inter alia*, by being thoroughly referentially transparent, hence the qualification 'transparent'.[19] TIL offers the advantage over IL of directly manipulating intensional entities such as properties thanks to the fact that it contains variables ranging over times and possible worlds, respectively. Montague's s is not a type in its own right and occurs only together with regular types like e and t, as in $\langle s, e \rangle$ or $\langle s, t \rangle$, which count as intensional types in IL. No variables can range over s. Therefore IL cannot use λ-abstraction to define terms denoting intensions. Nor can IL use application to define extensionalization of intensions to obtain extensions. Instead Montague introduces his well-known cap ˆ and cup ˇ. [40] shows why ˆ fails to be a function at all (because there is more than one 'backward path' from an extension to an intension having it as value) and why knowledge of which function is the function ˇ amounts to empirical omniscience.[20]

Because TIL abstracts over separate world and time variables, intensional entities turn out to have the following general form characteristic of *explicit intensionalization and temporalization*:[21]

---

[17] The three earliest TIL papers would be [37–39].

[18] Of course, the difference between *mappings, sets* and *relations* is a relative one, in that both sets and relations are themselves (modelled as) mappings in Montague and Tichý. Thus sets are characteristic functions from entities to truth-values, while two-place relations are mappings from $A \times B$ to truth-values (indexed to worlds and times, if a relation-in-intension). What we mean by contrasting mappings with sets and relations is that properties are not construed as either sets or relations (i.e. one-place relations), but as mappings straightaway, which are entities *sui generis*.

[19] See Tichý [40], [43, p. 133] for a crisp comparison between TIL and IL concerning opacity and transparency. See also Muskens [30] for objections to IL, e.g. the fact that IL fails to validate the Church-Rosser 'diamond' of λ-reduction.

[20] See Jespersen [14] for objections to 'omniscience functions'.

[21] Saying that *intensions* have this general form marks a departure from Tichý. He holds, correctly, that since intensions, as per the possible-world paradigm, are mappings they lack form, if by 'form' is intended parts organized into a structure (and not merely, say, the syntactic form of the terms and expressions standing for intensions). However,

$$\lambda w \lambda t\,[\ldots w \ldots t \ldots]$$

Just to be clear, we are not implying, in defiance of the known facts, that Montague would be incapable of modelling modification. What we are claiming is that Tichý offers a direct route to intensional entities thanks to explicit intensionalization and temporalization. What also recommends TIL over IL, apart from elegance and simplicity, is a substantial philosophical difference. TIL comes with a theory of *essence*, something wholly absent from IL.[22] Tichý's intensional essentialism – properties rather than individuals being the bearers of essential properties – was hinted at in Section 1 when the notion of *requisite* was broached. According to the notion of intensional essentialism invoked below, an *essence* is the set of requisites of a given property F. The notion of essence is a prerequisite for the property *functioning as an F*, formed by applying the modifier *functioning as* to the property F, because one element, W, of the essence of F lays down what Fs are for. To function as an F is to instantiate property W.

2.2. A Taxonomy of Property Modifiers

We begin by putting forward a *taxonomy of modifiers* to place subsective and privative modification in context.[23] In the interest of using standard notation at first, let $\|$ form extensions from intensional entities, *in casu* properties. Then *subsective*, *privative*, *intersective*, and *modal modifiers* are defined preliminarily as follows (see Section 2.4 for exact definitions).

Subsective. "If a is a *square box* then a is a *box*."

$$\frac{[M_s F]\,a}{F a}$$

Footnote 21 continued
imputing form to intensions saves a detour around Tichý's category of *construction*. Constructions are hyperintensional, structured, higher-order logical objects organized in the *ramified* type hierarchy of TIL. Strictly speaking, we ought to say that

$$\lambda w \lambda t\,[\ldots w \ldots t \ldots]$$

is the form of constructions yielding (non-constant) intensions. But in this paper we need not ascend into the ramified hierarchy, as the simple type theory will suffice, so we are making this shortcut to avoid a conceptually heavy detour. For *construction*, the single most important concept of TIL, see Tichý [43, esp. Ch. 5].

[22] See Tichý [41] and Jespersen and Materna [22] for a nominal essentialism based around requisites.

[23] See [4,24,25,33], and [19].

This rule, the most straightforward of the four, is valid thanks to upward monotonicity:

$$\text{Necessarily, } \|M_s F\| \subseteq \|F\|$$

Privative. "If a is a *forged banknote* then a is *not a banknote*."

$$\frac{[M_p F]\, a}{\neg F a}$$

Valid because

$$\text{Necessarily, } \|M_p F\| \cap \|F\| = \varnothing$$

or equivalently,

$$\text{Necessarily, } \|M_p F\| \subset \|\textit{non-}F\|$$

That is, $\|M_p F\|$ is a proper subset of the complement of $\|F\|$.[24]

Intersective. "If a is a *square box* then a is *square* and a is a *box*."

$$\frac{[M_i F]\, a}{M^* a \wedge F a}$$

This rule of inference is valid because, necessarily, an element of the set $\|M_i F\|$ is an element of the intersection of $\|M^*\|$ and $\|F\|$:

$$\text{Necessarily, } \|M_i F\| = \|M^*\| \cap \|F\|$$

Notice that M is a property *modifier*, while M^* is a *property*. Therefore, M cannot be detached from $[M_i F]$ and predicated of a on pain of attempting to make a modifier behave as though it were a property: such an attempt would constitute a blatant type-theoretic error.[25] To steer clear of this error, the *rule of pseudo-detachment* needs to be applied to trade the modifier M for the property M^*.[26] In general, whichever kind of modifier M may be,

---

[24] For further discussion of the relevant proper subset of the complement, see [3,21] and [35].

[25] For good measure, here is the relevant derivation pertaining to intersective modification:

$$\frac{\frac{[M_i F]a}{M^* a}\textit{pseudo-detachment} \quad \frac{[M_i F]a}{Fa}\textit{subsection}}{M^* a \wedge F a} \wedge I$$

For additional discussion and comparison of the various modifiers, see [19]. For privative modification in particular, see [35] and [3] for nested privative modifiers.

[26] The rule of pseudo-detachment was first introduced, in print, in [16]. [19] offers more by way of philosophical motivation and applications. The latter paper also argues why this meaning postulate, presented in [33, p. 3], to regulate intersective adjectives is insufficient:

the rule of pseudo-detachment validates the inference (schema)
$$\frac{[MF]\,a}{M^*a}$$
The proof of the validity of the inference is found in Section 2.4. The idea behind pseudo-detachment, however, is straightforward. While it is not trivial that somebody is a wise man, say, it follows trivially from this (provided we allow ourselves to quantify over properties) that there is a property with respect to which that person is wise. The property *wise** is the property of being wise with respect to some property (in this case the property of being a man). So pseudo-detachment works by quantifying away the original modified property, replacing it by a variable and having the original modifier modify the value of the variable instead.

This is how M is pseudo-detached from the context $[MF]$ and replaced by M^* in the conclusion above. Where p ranges over properties, 'M^*' is short for '$[Mp]$'. For another example, if a is a typical hammer then there is a property with respect to which a is typical*; the conclusion is not that a is typical, period, which would be nonsensical, just like inferring from b being a main station that b is main, period. The correct conclusions are that there is a property p such that a is a (typical p) and that there is a property q such that b is a (main q).[27] Or if c is a big hammer then the correct conclusion is that there is a property r such that c is a (big r). The inference does not extend from relative bigness (bigness, as far as hammers go) to absolute bigness, but preserves the relativization to a scale, as provided by r.[28]

Notice that there *is* such a property as being malfunctioning. This property, however, is literally derivative: a needs to be a $[Malf_s\,F]$ or a $[Malf_p\,F]$

Footnote 26 continued

For each intersective meaning ADJ' it holds that
$$\exists P_{\langle e,t\rangle}\forall Q_{\langle s,\langle e,t\rangle\rangle}[ADJ'(Q)(x)\equiv P(x)\wedge \check{Q}(x)].$$

The meaning postulate gets the truth-condition right, for sure, but fails to account for the logic of the transition from ADJ' to P, in the absence of a rule of left subsectivity such as pseudo-detachment.

[27] Already [1] warns against inferring from b being a main station to b being main, period. Bolinger observes that "There are many attributive adjectives that are never predicative" (*ibid.*, p. 2), citing, e.g., 'a total stranger'/*"The stranger is total" as another of several examples. [19] demonstrates why examples such as *"The total stranger is total" and *"The main station is main" do not constitute a counterexample to the validity of the rule of pseudo-detachment. The reason is because 'total' and 'main', when occurring in predicative position, should be logically analyzed as 'total*' and 'main*'.

[28] This point is analyzed at length in [19] in connection with the discussion of non-intersective modifiers, including scalar ones.

first before a can become $malfunctioning_s*$, i.e. $[Malf_s\,p]$, or $malfunctioning_p*$, $[Malf_p\,p]$.

The exact logical properties of the last kind of modifier, the *modal* one, are still disputed in the literature. In particular, it remains an open question how to provide a positive definition of modal modifiers. The unique feature, however, that modal modifiers have is that they oscillate between being subsective and being privative. So if the premise is that a is an *alleged terrorist*, say, then it is logically possible that a be a terrorist and it is logically possible that a not be a terrorist. The premise is not strong enough to either cancel out or rule in either possibility. For any given instance of $[M_m F]b$, it is an open question whether M_m is subsective or is privative, so it is an open question which side of $Fb, \neg Fb$ truth comes down on. We construe logical possibility as existential quantification over worlds w_i and times t_i. Therefore, the rule defining modal modification is this:

Modal. "If b is an *alleged terrorist* at $\langle w, t \rangle$, then there is a world/time pair $\langle w', t' \rangle$ at which b is a *terrorist* and there is another $\langle w'', t'' \rangle$ at which b is *not a terrorist*."

$$\frac{[M_m F]_{wt}\, b}{\exists w' t'\, [F_{w't'} b] \wedge \exists w'' t''\, \neg [F_{w''t''} b]}$$

Thus, formally put, the open question is whether the $\langle w, t \rangle$ at which b is an alleged terrorist is identical to $\langle w', t' \rangle$, where b is a terrorist, or to $\langle w'', t'' \rangle$, where b is not a terrorist. Whereas the set-theoretic counterparts of subsective and privative modification are subsection and complement, respectively, the set-theoretic counterpart of modal modification is the union of two disjoint sets. In the example of *alleged terrorist*, the relevant union is the union of the set of terrorists at $\langle w', t' \rangle$ and the set of non-terrorists at $\langle w'', t'' \rangle$. It is trivial that an alleged terrorist, just like any other individual, is a member of that union, but it is not trivial which of its two subsets a given alleged terrorist, or any other individual, belongs to. We are including modal modification for completeness, but are not going to make further use of it below.[29]

---

[29] See Jespersen and Primiero (forthcoming) for two definitions of modal modifiers, one based on alethic possibility as above, the other based on epistemic possibility. In that paper the above *elimination rule* for M_m falls out of a *definition* of M_m couched in terms of requisites. Note that modal modifiers should not be identified with so-called *intensional* (or *non-extensional*) ones, for the former are an instance of the latter. A modifier M is intensional if it fails to validate this argument (adapted from [24], p. 125):

$$\frac{F_{wt}x \leftrightarrow G_{wt}x}{[MF]_{wt}x \leftrightarrow [MG]_{wt}x}$$

2.3. Simple Type Theory

Here we introduce the *simple type theory* that fixes the perimeter of our formal ontology. It spans four basic types:

$o = \{1, 0\}$

$\iota = individuals$ ('universe')

$\tau = times$

$\omega = possible\ worlds$ ('logical space')

Functional types are then defined inductively over those basic types in the standard way. Formally, an *intensional entity* is a mapping whose domain is in ω; an *extensional entity* is a mapping whose domain is not in ω, including 0-adic mappings. Thus, as usual, truth-values, sets and individuals, for instance, are extensions, while properties and propositions, say, are intensions. A property of individuals is a mapping of the logical type

$$(worlds \rightarrow (times \rightarrow (sets\ of\ individuals)))$$

A proposition is a mapping of the logical type[30]

$$(worlds \rightarrow (times \rightarrow (truth\text{-}values)))$$

Let α be any type. Then $\alpha_{\tau\omega}$ indicates the segment $(worlds \rightarrow (times \rightarrow \alpha))$. A binary relation-in-*extension* between two objects of the same type

---

Footnote 29 continued
For instance, even if it so happens that all and only kings are philosophers, it may not follow that all and only belligerent kings are belligerent philosophers. An individual who is both philosopher and king may be a belligerent king (waging war in his capacity as king) without being a belligerent philosopher (waging war in his capacity as philosopher). Hence *Belligerent* is intensional. It seems safe to assume that just about every logically and philosophically interesting modifier is going to be intensional. What makes it interesting is why it fails to distribute.

[30] In keeping with possible-world semantics, TIL reserves the name 'proposition' for functions from worlds to (functions from times to) truth-values (equivalently: sets of worlds, identifying a proposition with its satisfaction class). TIL, however, also has an additional notion of *hyperproposition*. A hyperproposition is a fine-grained, structured mode of presenting a possible-world proposition. Hyperpropositions cannot be typed in the simple type theory, but must be typed in that higher-order fragment of the ramified type hierarchy where those higher-order objects that present first-order objects are located. Jespersen [14] provides a multiple-step decomposition of a structured hyperproposition, identifying its constituent parts with sub-procedures and the whole hyperproposition with a procedure whose product is a possible-world proposition. See [17, 18, 20] for introductions to hyperintensional logic, procedural semantics, structured meaning, and how TIL fits into the big picture. See also [31].

α is of type (oαα), i.e. a mapping from two α-objects to a truth-value, according as the relation obtains *a priori* between them or not. A binary such relation-in-*intension* is of type $(o\alpha\alpha)_{\tau\omega}$: a mapping from worlds to a mapping from times to a relation-in-extension. The functional value is 1 if the two α-objects are in the relation relative to the values assigned to the $\langle w, t \rangle$ pair of evaluation.

As announced in the Introduction, we need the following mappings, which receive the following types:

$(o\iota)$ = *set of individuals*

$(o\iota)_{\tau\omega}$ = *property of individuals*

$(o(o\iota)_{\tau\omega})$ = *set of properties of individuals*

$(o((o\iota)_{\tau\omega}(o\iota)_{\tau\omega}))$ = *binary relation-in-extension between properties of individuals*

$((o\iota)_{\tau\omega}(o\iota)_{\tau\omega})$ = *property modifier*

$o_{\tau\omega}$ = *proposition*

The *basic logical operations* we need are *functional abstraction* and *functional application*. Application is denoted as '[XY]', as explained in the Introduction.[31] Abstraction is denoted by '$[\lambda x_1 \ldots x_n Z]$', $x_1 \ldots x_n$ functional arguments, Z a functional value.[32]

Application is the logic of predication, modification, and extensionalization, the last being the descent from an intension to its extension at a given $\langle w, t \rangle$ of evaluation. Abstraction is the logic of explicit intensionalization, which is abstraction over possible worlds, and of explicit temporalization, which is abstraction over times.

Since we are inside a λ-calculus, all variable-binding is done by λ. Thus '∃x' abbreviates '[∃[λx A]]', where ∃ is a mapping from the set [λx A] to a truth-value, according as the set of x satisfying the condition A is non-empty. 'ιy' abbreviates '[ι[λy A]]', where ι is a mapping taking singletons to their unique members and being undefined on all other sets.

---

[31][XY] will do for now, since one-argument application is all we need.

[32]We are departing again from Tichý, who construes application as the very *procedure* of applying a function to an argument (rather than the result of the application, i.e. the value) and abstraction as the very *procedure* of forming a function (rather than the result of the abstraction, i.e. the mapping). See [43, §15, pp. 63–65]. Again, the simplification is an innocuous one here, because we are not studying the logic of constructions, but of what they construct, namely intensions.

As a notational convention, let 'π' abbreviate '$(o\iota)_{\tau\omega}$'. Accordingly, '$(o\pi\pi)$' will abbreviate '$(o((o\iota)_{\tau\omega}(o\iota)_{\tau\omega}))$'. Further, let '$\iota$-property' abbreviate 'property applicable to individuals', i.e. a ι-property is of type π. Finally, where a is an arbitrary entity and α an arbitrary type, 'a/α' means that a is an α-object.

First-order modification, which is all what we need in this paper, takes the already familiar form

$$[MF]$$

where M is of type $(\pi\pi)$ and F of type π. *Higher-order modification*, for comparison, takes the form

$$[[M'M]F]$$

an example of which would be *being a very large elephant*, where M is *large* and M' is *very*. Where F is of type π and M of type $(\pi\pi)$, M' needs to be of type $((\pi\pi)(\pi\pi))$ in order to modify M. The result of applying the higher-order modifier M' to the first-order modifier M is itself a first-order modifier (in this case *very large*), which is applicable to F.[33]

The *predication* of a property of an individual has the form

$$\lambda w \lambda t\, [F_{wt}\, a]$$

F_{wt} is an extensionalized property, i.e. a set. Sets being characteristic functions, $[F_{wt}\, a]$ is the result of applying an entity of type $(o\iota)$ to a ι-entity, namely a truth-value, of type o. The truth-value is 1 iff a is an element of the extension of F at the values of the elements of $\langle w, t \rangle$, and otherwise 0. We leave room for *truth-value gaps*, however, namely in case there is an individual a of which it is neither true nor false that it belongs to the extension of F at $\langle w, t \rangle$. (See below.)

The predication of a modified property of an individual has the form

$$\lambda w \lambda t\, [[MF]_{wt}\, a]$$

Again for comparison, if higher-order modification is involved, then predication has the form

$$\lambda w \lambda t [[[M'M]F]_{wt}\, a]$$

Why must $[MF]$ and $[[M'M]F]$ undergo extensionalization, as *per* $[MF]_{wt}$ and $[[M'M]F]_{wt}$? Because $[MF]$ and $[[M'M]F]$ are of type π, and a property

---

[33] See Carrara and Jespersen (submitted) for philosophical applications of higher-order modification.

cannot be directly predicated of an individual: $[[MF]\,a]$ is type-theoretically unacceptable, for an entity of type π is inapplicable to an entity of type ι. So a set, of type $(o\iota)$, must be obtained from $[MF]$ by means of extensionalization. $[MF]_{wt}$ is an extensionalized property, of type $(o\iota)$, and so applicable to a. Hence the reason why $[MF]$ needs to be extensionalized for predication is exactly the same as for F.[34]

The formulae we presented at the outset were slight simplifications. Thus, for instance, the proper formula for intersective modification would be this one, with extensionalization having been made explicit and outermost parentheses added on:

$$\frac{[[M_i F]_{wt}\,a]}{[[M^*_{wt}a] \wedge [F_{wt}a]]}$$

The philosophical, as opposed to type-theoretic, reason why predication consists in the application of extensionalized properties to individuals is that (non-constant, non-trivial) properties are always predicated of individuals relative to modal and temporal parameters (worlds and times): it is merely contingent whether a given individual has a given property. Only by reflecting the relativization to worlds and times in the logical analysis can the contingency of the predication of empirical properties be made logically perspicuous.[35] The truth-value resulting from application is abstracted over to obtain the proposition that a has property $[MF]$. This proposition induces a dichotomy over the set of $\langle w, t \rangle$ pairs: a given $\langle w, t \rangle$ pair is such as to make it true that a has the property $[MF]$, or it is not. This is in accordance with the possible-world conception of propositions as sets of worlds (and times, in its sophisticated version) or, equivalently, subsets of logical space.

2.4. Intensional Essentialism

In this subsection the relevant portions of the logic and semantics of *intensional essentialism* are presented. Its key notion is *requisite*. Let *Req* be the *requisite* relation-in-extension holding between two ι-properties, i.e. intensional objects of type π. Then *Req* is of type $(o\pi\pi)$. When *Req* obtains between two properties, one is a requisite of the other. We define the set of requisites of a given property as its *nominal* (as opposed to real) *essence*. A requisite of a property X is any property Y such that, for any $\langle w, t \rangle$, if

---

[34] See [15] for further discussion and technical details concerning extensionalization and predication. That paper also explains why TIL does not have a special operation earmarked for predication or a special operation earmarked for extensionalization.

[35] See [14,39].

individual x exemplifies X at $\langle w, t \rangle$ then x exemplifies Y at $\langle w, t \rangle$. Whereas a requisite of a property is part of what it takes for something to exemplify the property, the essence is all it takes. Hence a property can be fully defined by specifying its essence. We are assuming here that it be given for any empirical property X what its essence is.

Our intensional essentialism is not coupled with an extensional essentialism to the effect that one or more empirical properties (including relational ones, like *being the offspring of individual b*) would be necessarily instantiated by x. Thus, for us it is not necessary that x should exemplify X or any other particular empirical property at $\langle w, t \rangle$. (We are leaving it open whether x must exemplify some empirical property or other at $\langle w, t \rangle$ or may be 'bare' at $\langle w, t \rangle$.) If it had been necessary that x should exemplify some particular property X at $\langle w, t \rangle$ then X would have been (part of) the *real* essence of individual x. Our nominal essentialism is instead summarized in the conditional that *if x contingently exemplifies X at $\langle w, t \rangle$ then* it is necessary that x should also exemplify Y at $\langle w, t \rangle$. For instance, if a happens to be a whale at $\langle w, t \rangle$ then it is necessary that a should also be a mammal at $\langle w, t \rangle$. We do not have, and do not want, the conceptual resources to express that it is necessary or essential that a should be a mammal at $\langle w, t \rangle$. The essence of X is a *nominal* one, because the necessity of exemplification is rooted in a necessary relation between two properties and not in a necessary relation between an individual and a property. Phrased in an alternative vernacular, essential properties are *de dicto* only and never *de re*.[36]

Intensional essentialism is a welcome enrichment of our logic of modified properties. For instance, if it so happens that a has property X at $\langle w, t \rangle$ then, provided property Y is a requisite of X, we can infer that a also has Y at $\langle w, t \rangle$. Thus, if a has this or that particular modified property X at $\langle w, t \rangle$ it becomes inferable that a also has Y at $\langle w, t \rangle$, for any Y in the essence of that modified property. In particular, if Y is a requisite of $[Malf_s\, F]$ then if a has $[Malf_s\, F]$ at $\langle w, t \rangle$ it follows that a also has Y at $\langle w, t \rangle$. Thanks to requisites, the property $[Malf_s\, F]$ can be embedded within a network of other properties for a better understanding of $[Malf_s\, F]$; analogously for $[Malf_p\, F]$.

With this philosophical elucidation in place, we proceed to definitions.

---

[36] Our view is different from Fine's conception of essence in [10]: he defends the thesis that essential properties are *de re*, which is not an option for us. (We thank a referee for alerting us to [10]).

DEFINITION 1. (*Requisite relation over ι-properties*).
Let X, Y be intensions of type π, and let x range over ι. Then
$[Req\, Y\, X] = \forall w \forall t [\forall x [[True_{wt} \lambda w' \lambda t'\, [X_{w't'} x]] \supset [True_{wt} \lambda w' \lambda t'\, [Y_{w't'} x]]]]$

∎

REMARK 1. Gloss *definiendum* as, "Y is a requisite of X", and *definiens* as, "Necessarily, any x instantiating X at any $\langle w, t \rangle$ also instantiates Y at $\langle w, t \rangle$."

REMARK 2. The propositional property *True* will be explained in this subsection.

We define the requisite relation as a *quasi-order* (a.k.a. *pre-order*) over the set of ι-properties, of type (οπ), that can be strengthened to a *weak partial ordering*, by replacing *Req* by *Req'* (see below). However, it cannot be strengthened to a *strict ordering* on pain of paradox, since it would then both be reflexive and irreflexive. We wish to retain reflexivity, such that any intension will count itself among its requisites. Otherwise there would be world/time pairs at which a property Y was instantiated and $\neg[[Y_{wt} x] \supset [Y_{wt} x]]$ was true. This seems plain wrong, for surely it is necessary (understood *de dicto*) that if something is a corkscrew then it is a corkscrew.

CLAIM 1. *Req is a quasi-order over the set of ι-properties*.

PROOF 1. Let X, Y be of type π. Then *Req* belongs to the class of *quasi-orders* over π, of type (οππ).

Reflexivity. $[Req\, X\, X] = \forall w \forall t [\forall x [[True_{wt} \lambda w' \lambda t'\, [X_{w't'} x]] \supset [True_{wt} \lambda w' \lambda t'\, [X_{w't'} x]]]]$.

Transitivity. $[[[Req\, Y\, X] \wedge [Req\, Z\, Y]] \supset [Req\, Z\, X]] = [\forall w \forall t [\forall x [[True_{wt} \lambda w' \lambda t'[X_{w't'} x]] \supset [True_{wt} \lambda w' \lambda t'[Y_{w't'} x]]] \wedge [[True_{wt} \lambda w' \lambda t'\, [Y_{w't'} x]] \supset [True_{wt} \lambda w' \lambda t'\, [Z_{w't'} x]]]] \supset [[True_{wt} \lambda w' \lambda t'\, [X_{w't'} x]] \supset [True_{wt} \lambda w' \lambda t'\, [Z_{w't'} x]]]]]$ ∎

In order that *Req* be a weak partial order, it would have to be also antisymmetric. *Req* is, however, *not anti-symmetric*. If the properties X, Y are mutually in the *Req* relation (i.e. if $[[Req\, Y X] \wedge [Req\, X Y]]$) then at every $\langle w, t \rangle$ the two properties are going to be *true* of exactly the same individuals. This does not entail, however, that X, Y are *co-intensional*, hence *identical*. Why? Because there possibly is an individual x such that $[X_{wt}\, x]$ is *false* whereas $[Y_{wt}\, x]$ is *gappy*. For instance, let the truth-value distribution induced by the extensions of X, Y differ only for those individuals who never smoked. The property *having stopped smoking* presupposes that any individual exemplifying the property previously smoked. That a stopped smoking can be true or false only if a was once a smoker. If a was never a smoker, then it is neither true nor false of a that he or she stopped smoking. Similarly, that b is a $[Malf_p\, F]$ can be true or false only if b previously functioned, or could have functioned, as an F. If b never functioned, or could have functioned, as an F then it is neither true nor false of b that it is a $[Malf_p\, F]$.

Formally, the rift between the truth-value 0 and truth-value gaps arises because the extensions of properties are isomorphic to characteristic functions, whereby the latter mappings become susceptible to truth-value gaps, as soon as partiality is allowed in. That is, whereas X yields truth-value *gaps* on individuals who never smoked, Y is *false* of them:

$$X = \lambda w \lambda t[\lambda x\,[Stop\_smoke_{wt}x]]$$
$$Y = \lambda w \lambda t[\lambda x[True_{wt}\lambda w \lambda t\,[Stop\_smoke_{wt}x]]]$$

In order to do away with what is here an insignificant difference between X and Y, we introduce the equivalence relation $Eq/(o\pi\pi)$ over π. Eq, for its part, requires the propositional property *being true at* $\langle w, t\rangle$: $True/(o\, o_{\tau\omega})_{\tau\omega}$. Given a proposition P, $[True_{wt}P]$ is the truth-value 1 if $\langle w,t\rangle$ satisfies P; otherwise (i.e. if P is either false or undefined at $\langle w,t\rangle$) the truth-value is 0. Thus the rule of *True introduction* is

$$P_{wt} \vdash [True_{wt}P]$$

and the rule of *True elimination*,

$$[True_{wt}P] \vdash P_{wt}$$

The introduction and elimination rules, *True*I and *True*E, will be invoked in Section 2.7.

We next define

DEFINITION 2. (*equivalence relation over ι-properties*).

Let p, q range over π, and let $= /(ooo)$. Then:

$$Eq = \lambda pq[\forall x[[True_{wt}\lambda w' \lambda t'\,[p_{w't'}x]]] = True_{wt}\lambda w'\lambda t'\,[q_{w't'}x]]]] \qquad \blacksquare$$

Eq is an extensional entity of type $(o\pi\pi)$. So is Req', which we define next. The Req' relation is defined over the factor set of π as follows. Let $[p]_{eq} = \lambda q[Eq\,p\,q]$ and $[Req'[p]_{eq}\,[q]_{eq}] = [Req\,p\,q]$. Then

CLAIM 2. *Req' is a weak partial order over the factor set of π with respect to Eq.*

A new logic of technical malfunction

PROOF 2. It is sufficient to prove that Req' is well-defined. Let p', q' be ι-properties such that $[Eq\ pp']$, $[Eq\ qq']$. Then

$[Req'\ [p]_{eq}\ q]_{eq}] = [Req\ p\ q]$
$= \forall w \forall t [\forall x [[True_{wt} \lambda w' \lambda t'\ [p_{w't'} x]] \supset [True_{wt} \lambda w' \lambda t'\ [q_{w't'} x]]]]$
$= \forall w \forall t [\forall x [[True_{wt} \lambda w' \lambda t'\ [p'_{w't'} x]] \supset [True_{wt} \lambda w' \lambda t' [q'_{w't'} x]]]]$
$= [Req'\ ]p']_{eq}[q']_{eq}]$ ∎

Obviously, $[[Req'[p]_{eq}[q]_{eq}] \wedge [Req'[q]_{eq}[p]_{eq}]] \supset [[p]_{eq} = [q]_{eq}]$.

Henceforth, let the requisite relation be Req'. An effect of Req' being anti-symmetric is that the properties X, Y share, at any given $\langle w, t \rangle$ of evaluation, the same satisfaction class: they are *true* of the same set of individuals. But they are still *two* properties, despite the fact that necessarily co-extensional properties are identified, in accordance with possible-world semantics. For X, Y do not agree over the sets of individuals of which they are *not true*.

The requisite relation defined, we can now define the *essence* of an arbitrary property X:

DEFINITION 3. (*essence*). Let p, X range over π. Then:

$$[Essence\ X] = \lambda p[Req'\ p\ X]$$ ∎

That is, $\lambda p[Req'\ pX]$ is the set of ι-properties that are the requisites of X, making $\lambda p[Req'pX]$ the essence of X. *Essence*, then, is a mapping from a ι-property to a set of ι-properties, hence of type $((o\pi)\pi)$.

2.5. Modifiers Defined by Means of Requisites

We are now in a position to revisit the subsective, privative and intersective modifiers defined preliminarily in Section 2.2, and define them rigorously, by means of requisites. We are not making the naïve assumption that every modifier is only intersective, only privative, etc. For instance, a *false friend* is not a friend, whereas a *false proposition* is still a proposition. Or a *North Korean US 100-dollar bill* is not a US 100-dollar bill (but a counterfeit), whereas a *North Korean missile* is very much a missile. Similarly for *Nordic gold* not being gold (but a copper alloy) and a *Nordic salmon* being a salmon. So the logical status of the modifiers *False*, *North Korean*, and *Nordic* is a function of their relevant arguments.[37] Therefore we define the *sets* of modifiers that are, respectively, subsective, privative, and intersective.

---

[37] One referee suggested that 'false' (etc.) is actually a case of *two* different, yet *homonymous* adjectives. Then there would namely be no sensitivity to context. We did

E.g. the definition of *privative modifier* is a definition of the set of modifiers that are privative with respect to the argument property F. The type of a set of property modifiers is $(o(\pi\pi))$.

DEFINITION 4. (*Subsective, privative, intersective modifier*).

Let g, g', g'' range over $(\pi\pi)$; let g^* range over π; let x range over ι; let F/π. Then:

Subsective w.r.t. F: $\lambda g\,[Req'F[gF]]$

Privative w.r.t. F: $\lambda g'\,[Req'[\lambda w\lambda t\lambda x[\neg[F_{wt}x]]][g'F]]$

Intersective w.r.t. F: $\lambda g''\,[Req'\,[\lambda w\lambda t\lambda x[[g''^*_{wt}x] \wedge [F_{wt}x]]]\,[g''F]]$. ∎

Next, we prove the validity of the rule of pseudo-detachment. Just to be clear, pseudo-detachment is not a new modifier. Instead it is a rule that applies, without exception, to both intersective (hence subsective), privative and modal modifiers, since the relevant modified property, whichever way it may be modified, can always be quantified away. A skillful surgeon is skillful at something; a presumed killer is presumed to be something; a forged banknote is a forged something.

Let p range over π and let x range over ι; let $F, G^*/\pi, G/(\pi\pi), \exists/(o(o\pi))$. Then the *proof* of the rule of pseudo-detachment is this:

1. $[[GF]_{wt}\, a]$ ∅
2. $\exists p\,[[Gp]_{wt}\, a]$ 1, EG
3. $[\lambda x\, \exists p\,[[Gp]_{wt}\, x]\, a]$ $2, \beta$ − expansion
4. $[[\lambda w'\lambda t'\,[\lambda x\, \exists p\,[[Gp]_{w't'}\, x]]\,]_{wt} a]$ $3, \beta$ − expansion
5. $G^* = \lambda w'\lambda t'\,[\lambda x\exists p\,[[Gp]_{w't'}\, x]]$ definition
6. $[G^*_{wt} a]$ 4, 5, Leibniz's Law

Any valuation of the free occurrences of the variables w, t that makes the first premise true will also make the second, third and fourth steps true. The fifth premise is introduced as valid by definition. Hence any valuation of w, t that makes the first premise true will, together with step five, make the conclusion true. The above proof explains how pseudo-detachment enables the inference (sketched in §2.2) that if a is has the property $[Malf_s\, F]$ or the

---

Footnote 37 continued

consider that option already. We decided not to pursue it, though, since we are not prepared to decree homonymy where there may be none. It seems a safer route to us to allow that some modifiers are such that it does depend on the property occurring as argument on a particular occasion which kind the modifier is. Thus when the adjectives 'false' and 'North Korean' denote a modifier, it will depend on the argument property F whether *False* or *North Korean* is this or that kind of modifier.

property $[Malf_p\,F]$ at $\langle w, t\rangle$ then a also has the property $malfunctioning_s{*}$, i.e. $[Malf_s\,p]$, or the property $malfunctioning_p{*}$, i.e. $[Malf_p\,p]$, at $\langle w, t\rangle$.

2.6. Functioning as an F

Next up is an outline of the logic of *functioning as an F*. This property is needed, because it figures in the respective definitions of $Malf_s$ and $Malf_p$ in Section 2.7. We have already nearly everything it takes to make explicit the various logical steps that go into forming the property *functioning as an F* from the property F. We are making the assumptions that F has an essence, in accordance with the notion of intensional essence defined in Section 2.4, and that one of the elements of its essence is a property specifying what Fs are for. Thus, if F is *being a gun*, then that property would reasonably be something along the lines of *firing_bullets*.

When saying that guns are for firing bullets, we are in effect citing as *explanans* a functional property in the vein of *bottle-opener, doorstop, screwdriver*, etc., which specifies what a particular kind of artefact is for without necessarily also specifying how it goes about achieving that goal.[38] Citing an artefact property like *gun* as *explanans* of what some artefact is for would not be enlightening, until and unless we had extracted its what-for property. We suggest that an instance or token of a functional property is one that is deployed with a view to bringing about a transition in an object from one state to another. E.g. a corkscrew is applied to a cork fixed in a bottle, the corkscrew is operated, and on a good day the cork pops out. The cork has changed its state from being inside the bottle to being outside the bottle. This state transition triggers a state transition in the bottle as well, from closed to open. The purpose behind changing the state of the cork is to obtain a change of state in the bottle.[39]

In this section we show how to infer that if a is an F (in whichever manner a has acquired that property) then a is a W, where W is the what-for property of F. Let a have technical-artefact property F (either in virtue of a's design or use). Then it follows that a has requisite properties $F_1 \ldots F_n$.

---

[38] Cf. [45, p. 89] who says that "[a pen is] any rigid ink-applying writing implement, [and a clock] any time-keeping device [...] [C]locks, for instance, may be made of a variety of different kinds of material and may function by radically different kinds of mechanisms [and] are collected up not by reference to a theoretically hypothesized inner constitution but under functional descriptions that have to be indifferent to specific constitutions and particular modes of interaction with the environment."

[39] A first attempt to analyze corkscrews and other 'state-transforming tools' as the *instrument* belonging to an *instrumental system*, which also includes a *user* and an *object* whose state is to be transformed, has been made in [11].

Therefore, a has the what-for property W, W being identical to requisite property F_i. As the discussion in Section 1 showed, the design view identifies the artefact property of an individual artefact by looking at its origin, while the use view identifies the property by looking at the actual use (usability) of the artefact. Either way, an artefact property F is identified, and F is assumed to have a what-for property among its requisites.

Further, if a is a *functional* (i.e. non-malfunctioning) F then a is a *functional* W. For instance, if a is a functional gun then a is a functional bullet-firing device: a can perform its what-for property. If a is a *malfunctioning* F then there is a bifurcation of cases. If a is a malfunctioning$_s F$ then a is an F and a fails to function as an F, i.e. a is not a functional W. If a is a *malfunctioning$_p F$* then a is not an F and a fails to function as an F, i.e. a is not a functional W. As expected, on the design view an F may, or may not, function as an F, while on the use view an F must function as an F.

To revisit an example broached in Section 1, if a designed shoe is used, or functions, as a weapon then that artefact *is*, on that occasion, a weapon and not a shoe. So how could such an artefact, simultaneously, both be a weapon and a malfunctioning$_p$ weapon, hence not a weapon? It cannot, of course. Just as use is, trivially, proper use, so Fs are, trivially, functional Fs. The use view, recall, comes with a dynamic dimension that the design view lacks. It was explained in Section 1 that to have property $[Malf_p\ F]$ presupposes having had the property F, which amounts to having functioned (or having been capable of functioning) as an F. A *currently* malfunctioning$_p$ F was *previously* an F, i.e. a functional F. Therefore, this sentence makes good sense: "My shoe is currently a malfunctioning$_p$ weapon". The sentence expresses a truth if the speaker is currently using their designed shoe as a shoe after having previously used it as a weapon, *and* the designed shoe could, currently, not function as a weapon.[40]

To define the property of functioning as an F, we need the modifier *Func_as* (for '*Functioning_as*') as well as two mappings. The first mapping we need is of type $(\pi(o\pi))$: given the essence of F as argument, it extracts the property that specifies what Fs are for. So this mapping takes an artefact property to its what-for property. We dub this mapping '*What-for*'.[41]

---

[40]This truth-condition encompasses all the constraints available to the use view in its pure form. Much would need to be added by way of sufficiency conditions to generate a more realistic combination of the use view with $Malf_p$. Such an enterprise falls outside the purview of this paper, though.

[41]*Multiple-functional* artefacts appear to pose no extra theoretical challenges. In [21, pp. 128–129] we discuss the example of the *bi-functional claw hammer*. The property *being a claw hammer* has as its essence the union of the set of requisites of *being a claw* and the

Conversely, though, W may not be unique to F, for two distinct artefact properties F_1, F_2 may share the same what-for property (though obviously differing with respect to other requisite properties).

The second mapping we need is one we encountered in Section 2.4, namely *Essence*, of type $((o\pi)\pi)$. Given F as argument, *Essence* returns the essence of F; so *Essence* is the 'essence-extracting' mapping. Given F as argument, *Func_as*, of type $(\pi\pi)$, yields as value the property of functioning as an F.[42] The property *functioning as an F* is then formed thus:

$$[Func\_as[What\_for[Essence\ F]]]$$

If F is *being a gun*, as above, then $[Essence\ F]$ is the essence of *being a gun*, $[What\_for\ [Essence\ F]]$ is the property *firing_bullets*, and $[Func\_as\ [What\_for\ [Essence\ F]]]$ is the property *functioning as a gun*. This property may be phrased in different equivalent ways, e.g. 'functioning as a bullet-firing device' or 'performing the function of firing bullets'. The *predication* of that property of a then looks like this (gloss: "a functions as an F"):

$$\lambda w \lambda t [[Func\_as[What\_for[Essence\ F]]]_{wt}a]$$

What we have done here is merely spell out the bare logical bones of how to form the property *functioning as an F*. This is not an *ad hoc* solution, however, but more of a schema of what any logical analysis of that property would have to look like, given the two assumptions mentioned above: the assumption of nominal essence (in terms of requisites) and of a what-for property.

2.7. Subsective and Privative Malfunction Defined

With $[Func\_as[What\_for[Essence\ F]]]$ in place, we can now define the modifiers $Malf_s$, $Malf_p$. We need to define two mappings from π to π. The functional argument is in both cases property F. The respective functional values are $[Malf_s\ F]$, $[Malf_p\ F]$. The property *not functioning as an F* is a

---

set of requisites of *being a hammer*. Either set has a what-for property among its members. So a claw hammer has two what-for properties (*prying nails, pounding nails*, say), as expected. Obviously, a designer wants to make sure that the what-for properties of a designed, but not yet manufactured, multiple-functional artefact are, at the very least, logically and nomologically compatible. Given knowledge of the relevant laws of nature, it can be *calculated* whether all the what-for properties of a designed multiple-functional artefact property are nomologically compatible. Constructing a *prototype* to empirically test for compatibility would then be a matter of expedience rather than principle.

[42]It is a topic for further research to distinguish between modal (dispositional) and amodal conceptions of *Func_as*. Only then can the two variants of privative malfunction be accommodated within a theory of formal semantics.

requisite of these two functional values. F is a requisite of $[Malf_s\ F]$, while *not being an* F is a requisite of $[Malf_p\ F]$.

DEFINITION 5. ($Malf_s$). Let p, q range over π; let $Req'/(o\pi\pi)$. Then the *subsective modifier* $Malf_s/(\pi\pi)$ is the mapping

$$\lambda p\, \iota q[[Req'\ p\ q] \wedge$$
$$[Req'\lambda w \lambda t \lambda x \neg [[Func\_as[What\_for[Essence\ p]]]_{wt}\, x]\, q]]\qquad\blacksquare$$

COROLLARY 1. The set $\{[Malf_s\ F], F\}$ is a subset of the essence of the property $[Malf_s\ F]$.

DEFINITION 6. ($Malf_p$).

Let the types be as in Definition 5. Then the *privative modifier* $Malf_p/(\pi\pi)$ is the mapping

$$\lambda p\, \iota q[[Req'\lambda w \lambda t \lambda x \neg [p_{wt} x]\, q]$$
$$\wedge [Req'\lambda w \lambda t \lambda x \neg [[Func\_as[What\_for[Essence\ p]]]_{wt} x]]\, q]] \qquad\blacksquare$$

COROLLARY 2. The set $\{[Malf_p\ F], \lambda w \lambda t \lambda x \neg [F_{wt}\, x]\}$ is a subset of the essence of the property $[Malf_p\ F]$.

2.8. Two Derivations

Finally, we prove that our intensional logic of technical malfunction has the resources to validate the fact that if a has property $[Malf_s\ F]$ at $\langle w, t \rangle$ then a has also property F at $\langle w, t \rangle$, and that if a has property $[Malf_p\ F]$ at $\langle w, t \rangle$ then a lacks property F at $\langle w, t \rangle$.[43]

---

[43] We are not saying, "If a has property $[Malf_p\ F]$ at $\langle w, t \rangle$ then a has property *non-F* at $\langle w, t \rangle$". The reason is because we have not introduced term, or internal, or property, or predicate, negation in this paper, nor see any reason to. We very much see a reason, however, to introduce this weaker form of negation in [3] in order to handle *pairs of privative modifiers*. The rule of *single privation* says that the privative modifier is to be replaced by external, or propositional, or sentential negation. If this rule is applied twice over to pairs of privative modifiers we obtain, via double negation elimination, the conclusion that the doubly modified property is restored. Thus, if a is, say, a $[Fake[Malf_p F]]$ at $\langle w, t \rangle$ then a emerges as an F at $\langle w, t \rangle$. To bar this far too strong conclusion, our alternative rule of privation, which holds both for single and multiple privation, says that privative modifiers, whether first-order or higher-order, are to be replaced by internal negation. This is intuitive, anyway, since both first-order modifiers and internal negation operate on properties. The result of our alternative rule of privation is that a pair of privative modifiers is equivalent to a modal modifier. See (ibid.) for the proof.

A new logic of technical malfunction

First follows the derivation that a malfunctioning$_s$ F is still an F. We are to prove that the argument

$$\frac{[[Malf_s \, F]_{wt} \, a]}{[F_{wt} \, a]}$$

is valid. From the definition of a valid argument, it follows that we are to prove that for any $\langle w, t \rangle$ at which $[[Malf_s \, F]_{wt} \, a]$ is 1, $[F_{wt} \, a]$ is also 1. *Proof.*

(1)	$[[Malf_s \, F]_{wt} a]$		$\varnothing$
(2)	$[True_{wt} \lambda w \lambda t [[Malf_s \, F]_{wt} a]]$		1, $True$I
(3)	$[ReqF[Malf_s \, F]]$		Corollary 1
(4)	$\forall w' \forall t' \forall x [[True_{w't'} \lambda w \lambda t [[Malf_s \, F]_{wt} x]] \supset$		
	$[True_{w't'} \lambda w \lambda t [F_{wt} x]]]$		Def. 1
(5)	$[[True_{wt} \lambda w \lambda t [[Malf_s \, F]_{wt} a]] \supset$		
	$[True_{wt} \lambda w \lambda t [F_{wt} a]]]$		4, $\forall$E, $a/x, w/w'$
(6)	$[True_{wt} \lambda w \lambda t [F_{wt} a]]$		2, 5, MPP
(7)	$[F_{wt} \, a]$		6, $True$E

Next up is the derivation that an individual with property $[Malf_p \, F]$ lacks property F. We are to prove that

$$\frac{[[Malf_p \, F]_{wt} \, a]}{\neg [F_{wt} \, a]}$$

is valid. Proof.

(1')	$[[Malf_p \, F]_{wt} a]$		$\varnothing$
(2')	$[True_{wt} \lambda w \lambda t [[Malf_s \, F]_{wt} a]]$		1', $True$I
(3')	$[Req[\lambda w \lambda t [\lambda x \neg [F_{wt} \, x]]][Malf_p \, F]]$		Corollary 2
(4')	$\forall w' \forall t' \forall x [[True_{w't'} \lambda w \lambda t [[Malf_p \, F]_{wt} x]] \supset$		
	$[True_{w't'} \lambda w \lambda t \neg [F_{wt} \, x]]]$		Def. 1
(5')	$[[True_{wt} \lambda w \lambda t [[Malf_s \, F]_{wt} a]] \supset$		
	$[True_{wt} \lambda w \lambda t \neg [F_{wt} \, a]]]$		4', $\forall$E, $a/x, w/w'$
(6')	$[True_{wt} \lambda w \lambda t \neg [F_{wt} \, a]]$		2', 5', MPP
(7')	$\neg [F_{wt} \, a]$		6', $True$E

This completes the exposition of our logic of technical malfunction.

3. Conclusion

The logic of technical malfunction presented above offers three novelties.

First, our logic is an *intensional logic* encompassing the notions of property, property modification, and nominal essence by means of which to systematize and reason about the notion of technical malfunction.

Second, our logic distinguishes between two conceptions of technical malfunction, couched in terms of whether the modifier *Malfunctioning* should be given a *subsective* or a *privative* interpretation.

Third, we have sketched the essentials of the logic of the property *functioning as an F*. That property was required for the comparison of the design view and the use view of function, and its logical analysis was required for the respective definitions of the modifiers $Malf_s, Malf_p$.

As with $Malf_s, Malf_p$, the modifier *Functioning_as* can be formally accommodated only within an *intensional logic* enabling us to form and operate on properties. Thus, apart from the individual insights we have presented here, the overall morale is that some intensional logic or other can be not only fruitfully applied to, but is indispensable for, certain portions of analytic philosophy of technology. This paper has presented one such intensional logic.

Acknowledgements. The research reported herein was supported by Grant Agency of the Czech Republic Project 401/10/0792 *Temporal Aspects of Knowledge and Information* (Bjørn Jespersen), and *Sulla categorizzazione degli artefatti: semantica e cognizione (Progetto di ricerca di ateneo Bando 2008), University of Padua* (Massimiliano Carrara). The foundations of this paper were laid when Bjørn Jespersen was staying as a Visiting Researcher at *Seminario di logica e filosofia analitica, Università degli Studi di Padova*, in April and May of 2008. This research stay was made financially possible by the Section of Philosophy, Delft University of Technology, which Bjørn Jespersen was affiliated with at the time. We are much indebted to two anonymous referees for *Studia Logica* for engaging so thoroughly with the originally submitted version, offering insightful objections and very helpful suggestions on how to improve the quality of the paper, including the exposition of our non-mainstream background theory.

References

[1] BOLINGER, D., Adjectives in English: attribution and predication, *Lingua* 18:1–34, 1967.

[2] CARRARA, M., and P. VERMAAS, The fine-grained metaphysics of artefactual and biological functional kinds, *Synthese* 169:125–143, 2009.
[3] CARRARA, M., and B. JESPERSEN (ms.), Double privation, in submission.
[4] CLARK, R., Concerning the logic of predicate modifiers, *Noûs* 4:311–335, 1970.
[5] CUMMINS, R., Functional analysis, *Journal of Philosophy* 72:741–765, 1975.
[6] DAVIES, P. S., The nature of natural norms: why selected functions are systemic capacity functions, *Noûs* 34:85–107, 2000.
[7] DIPERT, R. R., *Artifacts, Art Works, and Agency*, Temple University Press, Philadelphia, 1993.
[8] DUŽI, M., and B. JESPERSEN (ms. 1), Transparent quantification into hyperpropositional contexts *de re*, *Logique et Analyse*, forthcoming.
[9] DUŽI, M., and B. JESPERSEN (ms. 2), Transparent quantification into hyperpropositional contexts *de dicto*, in submission.
[10] FINE, K., Essence and modality, *Philosophical Perspectives* 8:1–16, 1994.
[11] FRANSSEN, M., and B. JESPERSEN, From nut-cracking to assisted driving: stratified instrumental systems and the modeling of complexity, in R. Robins (ed.), *Engineering Systems: Achievements and Challenges*, MIT Press, Cambridge, MA, 2009, pp. 1–11.
[12] GRIFFITHS, P.E., Functional analysis and proper functions, *British Journal for the Philosophy of Science* 44:409–422, 1993.
[13] HEIM, I., and A. KRATZER, *Semantics in Generative Grammar*, Blackwell, Oxford, 1998.
[14] JESPERSEN, B., Explicit intensionalization, anti-actualism, and why Smith's murderer might not have murdered Smith, *Dialectica* 59:285–314, 2005.
[15] JESPERSEN, B., Predication and extensionalization, *Journal of Philosophical Logic* 37:479–499, 2008.
[16] JESPERSEN, B., From $(AB)a$ infer A^*a, in M. Peliš (ed.), *The Logica Yearbook 2009*, College Publications, London, 2010, pp. 97–108.
[17] JESPERSEN, B., How hyper are hyperpropositions?, *Language and Linguistics Compass* 4:96–106, 2010a.
[18] JESPERSEN, B., Hyperintensions and procedural isomorphism: Alternative (1/2), in T. Czarnecki, K. Kijania-Placek, O. Poller, and J. Woleński (eds.), *The Analytical Way. Proceedings of the 6th European Congress of Analytic Philosophy*, College Publications, London, 2010b, pp. 299–320.
[19] JESPERSEN, B. (ms.1) Left subsectivity, in submission.
[20] JESPERSEN, B., Recent work on structured meaning and propositional unity, *Philosophy Compass*, forthcoming.
[21] JESPERSEN, B., and M. CARRARA, Two conceptions of technical malfunction, *Theoria* 77:117–138, 2011.
[22] JESPERSEN, B., and P. MATERNA, Are wooden tables necessarily wooden?, *Acta Analytica* 17:115–150, 2002.
[23] JESPERSEN, B., and G. PRIMIERO (ms.), *Lecture Notes in Computer Science*, forthcoming
[24] KAMP, H., Two theories about adjectives, in E. L. Keenan (ed.), *Formal Semantics of Natural Language*, Cambridge University Press, Cambridge, 1975, pp. 123–155.

[25] KAMP, H., and B. PARTEE, Prototype theory and compositionality, *Cognition* 57:129–191, 1995.
[26] KROES, P., *Technical Artefacts: Creations of Mind and Matter*, Springer, forthcoming.
[27] MILLIKAN, R., Wings, spoons, pills and quills: a pluralist theory of function, *Journal of Philosophy* 96:192–206, 1999.
[28] MCLAUGHLIN, P., *What Functions Explain: Functional Explanation and Self-Reproducing Systems*, Cambridge University Press, Cambridge, 2001.
[29] MONTAGUE, R., English as a formal language, in B. Visentini et al. (eds.), *Linguaggi nella societá e nella tecnica*, Milan, 1970, pp. 189–224. Reprinted in: R. H. Thomasson (ed.), *Formal Philosophy*, Yale University Press, New Haven, London, 1974.
[30] MUSKENS, R., *Meaning and Partiality*, CSLI and FOLLI, Stanford, 1995.
[31] MUSKENS, R., Sense and the computation of reference, *Linguistics and Philosophy* 28:473–504, 2005.
[32] NEANDER, K., Functions as selected effects: the conceptual analyst's defense, *Philosophy of Science* 58:168–184, 1991.
[33] PARTEE, B., Privative adjectives: subsective plus coercion, in R. Bäuerle, U. Reyle, and T. E. Zimmermann (eds.), *Presupposition and Discourse*, Elsevier, Amsterdam, 2001.
[34] PRESTON, B., Why is a wing like a spoon? A pluralist theory of function, *Journal of Philosophy* 95:215–254, 1998.
[35] PRIMIERO, G., and B. JESPERSEN, Two kinds of procedural semantics for privative modification, *Lecture Notes in Artificial Intelligence* 6284:252–271, 2010.
[36] SLOMAN, S. A., and B. C. MALT, Artifacts are not ascribed essences, nor are they treated as belonging to kinds, *Language and Cognitive Processes* 18:563–582, 2003.
[37] TICHÝ, P., Smysl a procedura, *Filosofický časopis* 16:222–232, 1968. Reprinted as *Sense and Procedure*, [44], pp. 79–92.
[38] TICHÝ, P., Intension in terms of Turing machines, *Studia Logica* 26:7–25, 1969. Reprinted in [44], pp. 95–109.
[39] TICHÝ, P., An approach to intensional analysis, *Noûs* 5:273–297, 1971. Reprinted in [44], pp. 113–137.
[40] TICHÝ, P., Two kinds of intensional logic, *Epistemologia* 1:143–164, 1978. Reprinted in [44], pp. 307–364.
[41] TICHÝ, P., Existence and God, *Journal of Philosophy* 76:403–420, 1979. Reprinted in [44], pp. 355–372.
[42] TICHÝ, P., Indiscernibility of identicals, *Studia Logica* 45:251–273, 1986. Reprinted in [44], pp. 649–671.
[43] TICHÝ, P., *The Foundations of Frege's Logic*, DeGruyter, Berlin, 1988.
[44] TICHÝ, P., in V. Svoboda, B. Jespersen, and C. Cheyne (eds.), *Collected Papers in Logic and Philosophy*, Filosofia, Czech Academy of Science/University of Otago Press, Prague/Dunedin, 2004.
[45] WIGGINS, D., *Sameness and Substance Renewed*, Cambridge University Press, Cambridge, 2001.

Questions, Answers, Obligations and Norms

Modelling dynamic behaviour of agents in a multiagent world: Logical analysis of Wh-questions and answers

MARTINA ČÍHALOVÁ

MARIE DUŽÍ

Abstract

In a multiagent and multi-cultural world, the fine-grained analysis of agents' dynamic behaviour, i.e. of their activities, is essential. Dynamic activities are actions that are characterized by an agent who executes the action and by other participants of the action. Wh-questions on the participants of the actions pose a difficult particular challenge because the variability of the types of possible answers to such questions is huge. To deal with the problem, we propose the analysis and classification of Wh-questions apt for agents' communication in a multiagent system (MAS). Our proposal of such a system consists of agents who communicate with their fellow agents by messaging so that each autonomous agent, though resource-bounded, can make less or more rational decisions to meet its own and collective goals. In addition, by communicating with other fellow agents and their environment, agents can *learn* new concepts and enrich their ontology so that their behaviour is dynamic. We aim to make a general proposal of the system so that the 'envelope' of agents' messages can be formalized in any MAS standard, be it The Foundation for Intelligent Physical Agents - Agent Communication Language (FIPA-ACL) or Knowledge Query and Manipulation Language (KQML). Yet, the *content* of messages is encoded in a formalized *natural language*. To this end, we apply Transparent Intensional Logic (TIL) with its procedural semantics which is particularly apt for a fine-grained analysis in which all the semantically salient features of natural language can be plausibly formalized. In this paper, we concentrate on analysing the content of query messages, particularly the content of those that encode Wh-questions and the answers to them. We also summarize TIL deduction system that makes it possible to answer such questions in an intelligent way. Linguists distinguish several subtypes of Wh-questions. Though the linguistic classification is helpful, it is not always suitable for agents' communication and reasoning. We need the classification based on a logical analysis of Wh-questions so that the agents can infer possible answers to such questions rather than only looking for them by keywords. This paper aims to apply an appropriate classification of the logical types of Wh-questions and the analysis of such questions; we concentrate in particular on questions concerning the participants of activities. The application of these results to the analysis of *processes* and *events* based on verb valency frames is another novelty of the paper.

Keywords: activity, communication of agents, ontology, Transparent Intensional Logic, Wh-questions and answers

1. Introduction

A multiagent system (MAS) is a distributed system of (less or more) intelligent agents who are *active* in their perceiving environment and acting to achieve their individual and collective goals. In this paper, we deal with such types of MAS where the agents are autonomous in the sense of not being controlled by a central dispatcher; the system is driven only by messaging.[1] To avoid

---

*E-mail: martina.cihalova@upol.cz
**E-mail: marie.duzi@vsb.cz
[1] See, for instance, Wooldridge [60].

মisunderstanding, by 'agent', we will understand both software and human agents. Our primary goal is to *logically* analyse different kinds of Wh-questions and plausible answers in a multiagent and multi-cultural world. The application of these results to the analysis of *processes* and *events* based on verb valency frames is another goal and novelty of this paper. We concentrate on the dynamic behaviour and rational reasoning of agents.

We are going to propose the analysis of messages, the content of which is encoded in a formalized natural language. While there is just one type of answer to a Yes-No question, the class of Wh-questions is much more abundant in types. In ordinary, natural language communication, we ask using different pronouns in interrogative sentences, which indicate the type of a possible answer. In this way, we can integrate both logical and linguistic views to classify Wh-questions into more detailed classes. For instance, by 'who', we ask for an entity with an agentive function; by 'where', we ask for a location or position; and by 'when', we ask for the time. Our starting point is the type of a possible direct answer, which determines the type of the corresponding Wh-question. Each specialized subtype of a Wh-question conveys specific information for an agent on how and where to seek the corresponding direct answer; in addition, by applying Transparent Intensional Logic (TIL) deduction system, the agents can infer even more detailed answers, if needed. Detailed classification of queries can thus improve agents' communication and intelligent behaviour. One of the most important applications of these ideas is the classification of Wh-questions on the participants of agents' *dynamic activities*. The fine-grained logical analysis of such activities is the main novelty of this paper. The agents need to know *who* is the actor of an activity, *when* the activity starts and ends, by *which* instruments is it performed, etc.

Another goal is to propose an 'intelligent' way of answering such questions, i.e. not just to provide direct answers extracted from natural language texts or agents' knowledge bases just by keywords; rather, we also want to derive logical consequences of such answers. Duží and Fait [17] introduce Gentzen's system of natural deduction adjusted for TIL and natural language processing. The system derives logical consequences of information recorded in the enormous amount of input text data. Thus, the system not only answers the questions by providing explicitly recorded knowledge sought by keywords. It also answers questions in an 'intelligent' way by computing inferable knowledge such that rational human agents would obtain if only it were not beyond their time and space capacities. The analysis of Wh-questions results into λ-terms with a free variable x ranging over entities of type α, which is the type of a possible direct answer. The system provides answers by suitable substitutions of the α-entities extracted from input sentences, the constituents of which match a given λ-term. The proposed more detailed classification of Wh-questions restricts the domain of a plausible answer to a subtype of the type α, which makes it easier for the agents to provide a rigorous answer. In addition, it also makes it possible to derive as an answer even more information by applying the semantic rules rooted in the rich semantics of a natural language. In particular, the agents can make use of the relations of requisites and pre-requisites between intensions or the rules valid for factive verbs like 'knowing', 'regretting' and so on.

Ordinary systems of erotetic logics specify axioms and rules that are special for questioning and answering Yes-No questions.[2] These systems are valuable, as they render many exciting features of Yes-No questions and answers. However, many other essential features of questions stem from their *presuppositions*. Yet, to our best knowledge, none of the systems of erotetic logic deals with Wh-questions and presuppositions of questions in a plausible way. This is unsatisfactory because

---

[2] See, for instance, Harrah [33], Wisniewski [58] or Peliš and Majer [49]. A special system can provide these axioms and rules, for instance, one based on relevant logic [50]. Comprehensive and extensive exposition on current intensional approaches to the semantics of questions can be found in Wisniewski [59].

Modelling dynamic behaviour of agents in a multiagent world: logical analysis of wh-questions and answers

they fail to consider *properly partial functions*, which lack a value at some of their arguments. For instance, propositions (in their capacity as truth-bearers) can have *truth-value gaps*. Moreover, we need question-answering systems that would be able to extract pieces of information from natural language texts and answer not only Yes-No questions but also Wh-questions, which is beyond the capacities of ordinary erotetic logics. Recently, questions are studied in dynamic epistemic logics and belief revision theories.[3] Yet, these systems are intensional, while we vote for a hyperintensional approach to natural language semantics and questions.

Many other systems are dealing with Wh-questions and answers. Maybe one of the typical representatives of such studies is the work of Groenendijk [29]. We do not jeopardize the quality and advantages of Groenendijk's logic, as its language and notation are elegant and easy to implement. We agree that assertions and interrogatives have the same logical structure, provided the interrogative sentence is a Yes-No question.[4] Another point of agreement is the structure of Wh-questions that contain free variables (or lambda-bound variables if one applies the λ-calculus) the valuations of which one would like to know.

Haida [31] applies dynamic type logic Ty3 to the logical analysis of questions. Says Haida:

Question words show striking similarities among the languages of the world: They are typically morphologically related to indefinites and they are typically, if not universally, focused. I consider the identity of indefinite and interrogative pronouns as the basic phenomenon. For an illustration of the indefinite-interrogative affinity, consider the example in (1), which is a string of Lakhota words. This string has two readings, a *yes/no*-question and a *wh*-question reading (see the paraphrases in (1a) and (b), respectively).

(1) šúka ki táku yaxtáka he
dog the something/what bite.
a. 'Did the dog bite something?'
b. 'What did the dog bite?'

Note that on the first reading, the pronoun *táku* functions as an indefinite, and on the second, as a question word. Observations like this suggest that interrogative pronouns have the same denotation as the corresponding indefinite pronouns. (ibid. pp. 376–377)

Haida proceeds from Kartunnen's approach [40] and agrees that the Wh-phrases denote existential generalized quantifiers.

In the abstract of Wiese [57], the author argues similarly: '[...] that Wh-pronouns are not "interrogative". Rather they are underspecified elements, and due to this underspecification, Wh-words can form a constitutive part not only of interrogative, but also of exclamative and declarative clauses.'

We do not deal with pragmatic issues, as logic cannot decide which reading is the intended one. If a sentence is ambiguous, we furnish it with two or more meaning constructions. Disambiguation is a matter of additional communication; an agent can ask, 'What do you mean, this or that?'. Moreover, we aim at a *literal* analysis of a sentence so that we are not willing to include an existential quantifier if there is none. And, we are convinced that for the purpose of natural language processing, the system based on the first-order logic principles is less than enough. A generally accepted opinion is that hyperintensional logic is needed, as we will demonstrate below.[5]

---

[3] See, e.g. van Benthem and Minicâ [1], Peliš and Majer [49] and Enqvist [25].

[4] Tichý [52] also demonstrates that the semantic core of an interrogative sentence is the same as that of its declarative counterpart.

[5] For arguments in favour of hyperintensionality, see Jespersen and Duží [39].

Modelling dynamic behaviour of agents in a multiagent world: logical analysis of wh-questions and answers

Karttunen [40] adopts with some modifications Hamblin's [32] semantics for questions, which in turn is based on Montague's logic and grammar. Yet, we vote for Tichý's TIL for the following reasons.[6] Though Tichý's TIL system might be familiar to those who are familiar with Montague style semantics, as it has some features in common, it nevertheless deviates in four relevant respects from the version of λ-calculus made popular by Montague's intensional logic.

First, and most importantly, *meanings* are not identified with (or modelled as) mappings from world/time pairs. Instead, Montague-like meanings (i.e. mappings) are the products of our meaning procedures (TIL constructions). We assent to the tenet of *structured meanings*, as procedures are algorithmically structured, unlike set-theoretical mappings; there is no trace of the meaning structure in such a mapping.[7] Thus, while Montague's system is an *intensional* logic operating on functions and their values, TIL is a *hyperintensional* logic operating on constructions of functions, functions and their values. As a result, in TIL, we deal with three kinds of context, to wit, hyperintensional level of constructions, intensional level of set-theoretic functions and extensional level of the functional values. This distinction is important for a correct typing and valid substitutions.[8] And, as mentioned above, hyperintensionality is necessary for a plausible analysis of natural language.

Second, in TIL, *variables* are not linguistic items. The term y encodes an atomic procedure as its meaning and picks out the entity that an assignment function has assigned to y as its value. This is important when analysing Wh-questions, as the answers to these questions are the entities picked out by these atomic procedures. Furthermore, our variables can make themselves occur as products of procedures placed higher up. It is essential in what follows, in particular for operations into hyperintensional contexts.

Third, we are convinced that the analysis of a piece of language does not amount to translating it from some natural language into an artificial language (say, the λ-calculus), which in turn receives an interpretation, which is transferred back to the natural-language sentence. Instead, our λ-calculus is an inherently interpreted formal language, which serves as a device to directly denote (talk about) meanings; TIL λ-terms denote TIL constructions, i.e. meaning procedures. Meaning procedures are studied through their structure and constituents as encoded in the λ-calculus of TIL in virtue of the isomorphism between formulae and the procedures. It should be also stressed that TIL constructions are not linguistic entities; they are higher-order abstract procedures.

Fourth, in TIL, we have *explicit intensionalization* and *temporalization*. Whereas Montague's IL combines worlds and times, TIL treats worlds and times as two distinct ground types, which enables separate variables ranging over these two different types. We need this feature because we need to differentiate between several degrees of necessity; again, we are going to demonstrate it below when defining nomic necessities.

Last but not least, we vote for TIL approach, as this research is a part of a broader project on natural language processing in which logicians and linguists work hand-in-hand under the TIL umbrella. In terms of practical applications, our theoretical results are being implemented as one of the most important components of an intelligent question-answering system over large corpora of natural language texts.[9] To this end, we are making use of the Normal Translation Algorithm (NTA)

---

[6] See Tichý [54, 55].

[7] For the arguments in favour of structured meanings of questions and answers, see Krifka [42].

[8] For details on operating into a hyperintensional context, see Duží and Jespersen [20, 21]. Substitution rules with respect to a context have been specified in Fait and Duží [27]. Finally, the algorithm of context recognition has been introduced in Duží *et al.* [18].

[9] For instance, we implemented the algorithm of context recognition and valid substitution with respect to the context, the algorithm of anaphora preprocessing and resolution within the communication of agents, or the algorithm of atomic concepts

that has been developed in the Natural Language Processing Centre at the Faculty of Informatics, Masaryk University, Brno. NTA is a method that integrates linguistic analysis of sentences with a logical approach to semantics. The result of NTA applications so far is a corpus of more than 7000 TIL-constructions obtained by the analysis of newspaper and web sentences. Yet, the NTA development is still a work in progress. Currently, the formalization of natural language sentences is a semi-automated process. We are not entirely content with the issue of automatic typing, and manual checking and corrections are often necessary.

Concerning implementation issues, TIL specification and communication language has been tested ten years ago in the Research Laboratory of Intelligent Systems (http://labis.vsb.cz/). The application for a MAS traffic system has been developed here in which the authors (being inspired by Wooldridge [60]) voted for the FIPA ACL standards.[10] The content of messages has been specified in the TIL-Script language, which is the computational variant of TIL, while the 'envelopes' of messages follow FIPA ACL standards.[11]

Wooldridge in ([60], Ch.8) critically deals with speech act theory that treats communication as *action*. It is predicated on the assumption that speech actions are performed by agents just like other actions, in the furtherance of their intentions. Says Wooldridge: 'While the plan-based theory of speech acts was a major step forward, it was recognized that a theory of speech acts should be rooted in a more general theory of rational action. This observation led Cohen and Levesque to develop a theory in which speech acts were modelled as actions performed by rational agents in the furtherance of their intentions [9]. The foundation upon which they built this model of rational action was their theory of intention, described in [8].' (ibid. p. 167).

In early 1990s, the US-based DARPA-funded Knowledge Sharing Effort (KSE) was formed, with remit of developing protocols for the exchange of represented knowledge between autonomous information systems. The KSE generated two main deliverables as follows.

The *Knowledge Query and Manipulation Language* (KQML) is an 'outer' language for agent communication. It defines an 'envelope' format for messages, using which an agent can explicitly state the intended illocutionary force of a message. KQML is not concerned with the *content* part of messages.[12]

The *Knowledge Interchange Format* (SKIF; [34]). SKIF languages are syntactically compatible with LISP, i.e. the FOL syntax is extended with the possibility to mention properties and use variables ranging over properties. SKIF was explicitly intended to allow the representation of knowledge about some particular 'domain of discourse'. It was designed primarily (though not uniquely) to form the content parts of KQML messages.

KQML is a message-based language for agent communication. Thus, KQML defines a common format for messages. A KQML message may crudely be thought of as an object (in the sense of object-oriented programming); each message has a *performative* (which may be thought of as the class of the message) and a number of *parameters* (attribute/value pairs, which may be thought of as instance variable).

To summarize, Wooldridge ([60], p. 175) says this. Though the take-up of KQML by the MAS community was significant, and several KQML-based implementations were developed and

---

explication by applying supervised machine learning methods adjusted for natural language processing. For details, see Fait and Duží [27], Duží et al. [18] and Menšík et al. [45].

[10] See FIPA [28] Communicative Act Library Specification (2002).
[11] Details on the TIL-Script language can be found in [16].
[12] See Patil et al. [48].

distributed, KQML was subsequently criticized on several grounds as follows.
- The basic KQML performative set was rather fluid—it was never tightly constrained, and so different implementations of KQML were developed that could not, in fact, interoperate.
- Transport mechanisms for KQML messages (i.e. ways of getting a message from agent A to agent B) were never precisely defined, again making it hard for different KQML-talking agents to interoperate.
- The semantics of KQML were never rigorously defined in such a way that it was possible to tell whether two agents claiming to be talking KQML were, in fact, using the language 'properly'. The 'meaning' of KQML performatives was only defined using informal, English language descriptions, open to different interpretations.
- The language was missing an entire class of performatives—*commisives*, by which one agent makes a commitment to another. As Cohen and Levesque [8, 9] point out, it is difficult to see how many multiagent scenarios could be implemented without commisives, which appear to be important if agents are to *coordinate* their actions with one another.
- The performative set for KQML was overly large and, it could be argued, rather *ad hoc*.

These criticisms—among others—led to the development of a new but rather closely related language by the FIPA consortium.

Hence, though we might just refine the FIPA ACL performative Query-Ref by new subtypes, we decided to encode this information into the content of messages. The reason is that we aim at a general proposal of the system such that the 'envelope' of agents' messages can be formalized and implemented in any MAS standard, be it FIPA ACL or KQML. The content of messages is encoded in the *TIL-formalized natural language* for the reasons specified above.

The rest of the paper is organized as follows. Section 2 introduces the basic principles of TIL that serves as the specification language of agents' communication and reasoning. TIL logical analysis of Wh-questions, together with their new classification, is presented in Section 3. In Section 4, we illustrate the application of the proposed method by analysing examples of agents questioning and answering. Here, we concentrate mainly on analysing agents' *dynamic activities* and their *learning* by questioning and answering. Concluding remarks on further research can be found in Section 5.

2. Basic principles of TIL

Pavel Tichý, the founder of TIL, was inspired by Frege's semantic triangle.[13] However, while Frege did not define the sense of an expression but only characterized it as the 'mode of presentation', Tichý defined the sense of an expression, i.e. its *meaning*, as an abstract, algorithmically structured *procedure* that produces the object denoted by the expression, or in rigorously defined cases fails to produce a denotation if there is none.[14] Of course, there are non-denoting terms that have a perfect meaning, like 'the greatest prime number'. Mathematicians had obviously to understand the sense of the term first and only then could they prove that there is no such number. Hence, in TIL, the meaning of an expression is understood as a context invariant *procedure* encoded by a given expression. By context invariant, we mean this. The procedure encoded by an unambiguous expression is one and the same independently of the context in which the expression is used. If the expression is ambiguous, it is furnished with more than one procedure corresponding to its different meanings.

---

[13] See Tichý [54].
[14] A similar philosophy of meaning as a 'generalized algorithm' can be found in Moschovakis [46]; this conception has been further developed by Loukanova [44].

Modelling dynamic behaviour of agents in a multiagent world: logical analysis of wh-questions and answers

TIL is a hyperintensional, typed λ-calculus of *partial functions*. The λ-terms of the TIL language denote *constructions* (which could be approximated by Church's *functions-in-intension*) that produce set-theoretical mappings (functions-in-extension) or lower-order constructions.[15] Qua procedural objects, constructions can be *executed* so as to operate on input objects (of a lower-order type) and produce at most one object of the type they are typed to produce, while non-procedural objects (i.e. non-constructions, i.e. set-theoretical mappings) cannot be executed.

Tichý defined six kinds of meaning procedures and called them *constructions*. There are two kinds of *atomic* constructions that present input objects to be operated on by molecular constructions. They are *Trivialization* and *Variables*. Trivialization of an object X presents object X without the mediation of any other procedures. Using the terminology of programming languages, the Trivialization of X, denoted by '^0X', is just a *pointer* or *reference* to X. Trivialization can present an object of any type, even another construction C. Hence, if C is a construction, ^0C is said to *present* the construction C, whereby C occurs hyperintensionally, i.e. in the *non-executed* mode. Variables produce objects dependently on valuations; they are said to *v-construct*. The execution of a Trivialization or a variable never fails to produce an object. However, since TIL is a logic of partial functions, the execution of some of the molecular constructions can fail to present an object of the type they are typed to produce. When this happens, we say that a given construction is *v-improper*. This concerns in particular one of the molecular constructions, namely *Composition*, $[X\ X_1 \ldots X_n]$. It is the very *procedure of applying a function* f produced by X (if any) to the tuple argument $\langle a_1, \ldots, a_n \rangle$ (if any) produced by the procedures $X_1, \ldots, X_n$. A Composition is *v*-improper as soon as f is a *partial function* not defined at its tuple argument, or if one or more of its constituents $X, X_1, \ldots, X_n$ are *v*-improper. Another molecular construction is λ-*Closure*, $[\lambda x_1 \ldots x_n\ X]$. It is the very *procedure of producing a function* with the values *v*-produced by the procedure X, by abstracting over the values of the variables $x_1, \ldots, x_n$ to provide functional arguments. No Closure is *v*-improper for any valuation v, as a Closure always *v*-constructs a function (which may be, in an extreme case, a degenerate function undefined at all its arguments).

TIL being a *hyperintensional* system, each construction C can occur not only in execution mode designed to produce an object (if any) but also as an object in its own right on which other (higher-order) constructions operate. The Trivialization of C causes C to occur just presented as an argument, as mentioned above. Yet sometimes, we need to cancel the effect of Trivialization and trade the mode of C for execution mode. *Double Execution*, ^2C, does just that; it executes C twice over. If C *v*-constructs a construction D that in turn *v*-constructs an entity E, then ^2C *v*-constructs E. Otherwise, ^2C is *v*-improper. Hence, the following ^{20}-Elimination rule is valid; for any construction C, $^{20}C = C$.

DEFINITION 1
(*Construction*)

(i) *Variables* $x, y, \ldots$ are *constructions* that construct objects (i.e. elements of their respective ranges) dependently on a valuation function v; they *v*-construct.

(ii) Where X is an object whatsoever (even a *construction*), ^0X is the *construction Trivialization* that constructs X without any change.

---

[15]Church [3] broaches the question under which circumstances two functions can be considered the same. Function-in-extension corresponds to the modern notion of function as a mapping, while function-in-intension is given be the meaning of the rule of correspondence between arguments and values of the function. Hence, while functions-in-extension are extensionally individuated, two or more functions-in-intension can share the same set-theoretical mapping.

Modelling dynamic behaviour of agents in a multiagent world: logical analysis of wh-questions and answers

(iii) Let $X, Y_1, \ldots, Y_n$ be arbitrary *constructions*. Then the *Composition* $[X\ Y_1 \ldots Y_n]$ is the following *construction*. For any v, the Composition $[X\ Y_1 \ldots Y_n]$ is *v-improper* if one or more of $X, Y_1, \ldots, Y_n$ are v-improper, or if X does not v-construct a function that is defined at the n-tuple of objects v-constructed by $Y_1, \ldots, Y_n$. If X does v-construct a v-proper function, then $[X\ Y_1 \ldots Y_n]$ v-constructs the value of this function at the n-tuple.

(iv) (λ-) *Closure* $[\lambda x_1 \ldots x_m\ Y]$ is the following *construction*. Let $x_1, x_2, \ldots, x_m$ be pair-wise distinct variables and Y a *construction*. Then $[\lambda x_1 \ldots x_m\ Y]$ v-constructs the function f that takes any members $B_1, \ldots, B_m$ of the respective ranges of the variables $x_1, \ldots, x_m$ into the object (if any) that is $v(B_1/x_1, \ldots, B_m/x_m)$-constructed by Y, where $v(B_1/x_1, \ldots, B_m/x_m)$ is like v except for assigning B_1 to $x_1, \ldots, B_m$ to x_m.

(v) Where X is an object whatsoever, ^1X is the *construction Single Execution* that v-constructs what X v-constructs. Thus, if X is a v-improper construction or not a construction as all, ^1X is v-improper.

(vi) Where X is an object whatsoever, ^2X is the *construction Double Execution*. If X is not itself a *construction*, or if X does not v-construct a *construction*, or if X v-constructs a v-improper *construction*, then ^2X is v-improper. Otherwise, ^2X v-constructs what is v-constructed by the *construction* v-constructed by X.

(vii) Nothing is a *construction*, unless it so follows from (i) through (vi).

With constructions of constructions, constructions of functions, functions and functional values in TIL stratified ontology, we need to keep track of the traffic between multiple logical strata. The *ramified type hierarchy* discharges that task. The type of first-order objects includes all objects that are not constructions. Therefore, it not only includes the standard first-order objects of individuals and truth values but also sets, mappings and also functions defined on possible worlds (i.e. the *intensions* germane to possible-world semantics). The type of second-order objects includes constructions of first-order objects and functions that have such constructions in their domain or range. The type of third-order objects includes constructions of first- or second-order objects and functions that have such constructions in their domain or range; and so on ad infinitum.

DEFINITION 2
(*Ramified hierarchy of types*). Let B be a *base*, where a base is a collection of pair-wise disjoint, non-empty sets. Then:

T_1 (*types of order 1*)

i) Every member of B is an elementary *type of order 1 over B*.
ii) Let $\alpha, \beta_1, \ldots, \beta_m$ ($m > 0$) be types of order 1 over B. Then the collection $(\alpha\ \beta_1 \ldots \beta_m)$ of all m-ary partial mappings from $\beta_1 \times \ldots \times \beta_m$ into α is a functional *type of order 1 over B*.
iii) Nothing is a *type of order 1 over B* unless it so follows from (i) and (ii).

C_n (*constructions of order n*)

i) Let x be a variable ranging over a type of order n. Then x is a *construction of order n over B*.
ii) Let X be a member of a type of order n. Then $^0X, ^1X, ^2X$ are *constructions of order n over B*.
iii) Let $X, X_1, \ldots, X_m$ ($m > 0$) be constructions of order n over B. Then $[X\ X_1 \ldots X_m]$ is a *construction of order n over B*.

Modelling dynamic behaviour of agents in a multiagent world: logical analysis of wh-questions and answers

iv) Let $x_1, \ldots, x_m, X$ ($m > 0$) be constructions of order n over B. Then $[\lambda x_1 \ldots x_m\, X]$ is a *construction of order n over B*.

v) Nothing is a *construction of order n over B* unless it so follows from $\mathbf{C}_n$ (i)–(iv).

$\mathbf{T}_{n+1}$ (*types of order* $n+1$)
Let $*_n$ be the collection of all constructions of order n over B. Then:

i) $*_n$ and every type of order n are *types of order $n+1$*.
ii) If $m > 0$ and $\alpha, \beta_1, \ldots, \beta_m$ are types of order $n+1$ over B, then $(\alpha\, \beta_1 \ldots \beta_m)$ (see T_1 ii)) is a *type of order $n+1$ over B*.
iii) Nothing is a *type of order $n+1$ over B* unless it so follows from (i) and (ii).

For the purposes of natural language analysis, we are usually assuming the following base of ground types:[16]

o: the set of truth-values $\{\mathbf{T}, \mathbf{F}\}$;
ι: the set of individuals (the universe of discourse);[17]
τ: the set of real numbers (doubling as times);
ω: the set of logically possible worlds (the logical space).

Empirical expressions denote *empirical conditions*, which may or may not be satisfied at the world/time pair selected as points of evaluation. These empirical conditions are modelled as intensions. Intensions are entities of type $(\beta\omega)$: mappings from possible worlds to an arbitrary type β. The type β is frequently the type of the *chronology* of α-objects. These α-chronologies are, in turn, functions mapping time (of type τ) to the type α. Thus, α-intensions are frequently functions of type $((\alpha\tau)\omega)$, abbreviated as '$\alpha_{\tau\omega}$'. *Extensional entities* are entities of a type α where $\alpha \neq (\beta\omega)$ for any type β. Where w ranges over ω and t over τ, the following logical form essentially characterizes the logical syntax of empirical language: $\lambda w \lambda t\, [\ldots w \ldots t \ldots]$. Dealing with the two modal parameters, namely possible worlds and times, separately, is connected with many assets, to name at least analysis of physical entities or nomic laws of necessity.

Examples of frequently used α-intensions are: *propositions* of type $o_{\tau\omega}$, *properties of individuals* of type $(o\iota)_{\tau\omega}$, *binary relations-in-intension between individuals* of type $(o\iota\iota)_{\tau\omega}$ and *offices* or *roles* of type $\iota_{\tau\omega}$. Logical objects like *truth-functions* and *quantifiers* are extensional: $\wedge, \vee, \supset$ are of type (ooo), and $\neg$ of type (oo).

The *quantifiers* $\forall^\alpha, \exists^\alpha$ are type-theoretically polymorphic total functions of type $(o(o\alpha))$, for an arbitrary type α, defined as follows. The *universal quantifier* $\forall^\alpha$ is a function that associates a class A of α-elements with $\mathbf{T}$ if A contains all elements of the type α, otherwise with $\mathbf{F}$. The *existential quantifier* $\exists^\alpha$ is a function that associates a class A of α-elements with $\mathbf{T}$ if A is a non-empty class, otherwise with $\mathbf{F}$.

Notational conventions. Below, all type indications will be provided outside the formulae in order not to clutter the notation. Moreover, the outermost brackets of Closures will be omitted whenever no confusion can arise. Furthermore, 'X/α' means that an object X is (a member) of type α. '$X \to \alpha$' means that X is typed to v-construct an object of type α. Throughout, it holds that the variables $w \to \omega$ and $t \to \tau$. If $C \to \alpha_{\tau\omega}$ then the frequently used Composition $[[C\, w]\, t]$, which is the *extensionalization* of the α-intension v-constructed by C, will be encoded as 'C_{wt}'. When

---

[16] TIL is an open system, and the choice of base depends on the discourse and subject matter under scrutiny. For instance, for the purpose of mathematics, we might vote for another base consisting of $\{o, \eta\}$, where η is the type of natural numbers, as in mathematics possible worlds and times play no role.

[17] We assume that the universe of discourse ι is multivalued and consists of at least two elements, though we leave aside the cardinality of this basic type.

Modelling dynamic behaviour of agents in a multiagent world: logical analysis of wh-questions and answers

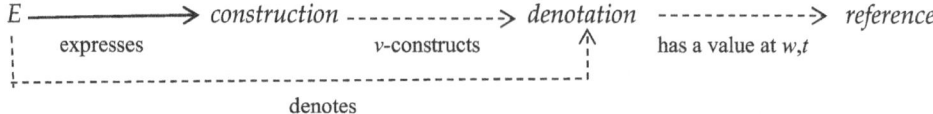

FIGURE 1. General semantic schema.

no confusion arises, we use the standard infix notation without Trivialization for the application of logical objects like truth-functions, equalities and quantifiers; thus, instead of '$[^0\forall \lambda x\, B]$', '$[^0\exists \lambda x\, B]$', we often write '$\forall x\, B$', '$\exists x\, B$' for any $B \to o$ to make quantified formulas easier to read. Arithmetic formulas will be also often written in the infix way, without Trivializing relations like $\leq, =, >$ or functions like $+$ or $\times$; for instance, instead of $[^0\leq x\, ^050]$, we write '$[x \leq {}^050]$', or instead of $[^0\neg [^0\exists \lambda x\, [^0= [^0+ x\, ^01]\, x]]]$, we can write '$\neg \exists x\, [[x + {}^01] = x]$'.

The *general semantic schema* involving the *meaning* (i.e. a construction) of an expression E, *denotation* (i.e. the object, if any, denoted by E) and *reference* (i.e. the value of an intension, if the denotation is an intension, in the actual world at the present time) is depicted by Figure 1.

In this schema, the assignment of the construction to an expression E is the essential semantic issue. Once the meaning construction of a term or expression has been given, it can be examined what is entailed by this construction. It can also be calculated what the construction produces (if anything), i.e. what the denotation of E is. Provided the denotation is not a trivial (i.e. constant) intension or a mathematical function, the reference cannot be calculated; instead, it must be established by extra-logical and extra-semantic means (i.e. empirical inquiry or mathematical calculation) what the reference, if any, is. TIL does not consider reference a semantic notion, so the semantic value of a term or expression cannot be its reference.

As mentioned above, TIL is a logic of partial *functions*. Therefore, sets and relations are modelled by their characteristic functions. For instance, $(o\tau)$ is the type of a set of numbers, while $(o\tau\tau)$ is the type of a binary relation-in-extension between numbers. That an element $a \to \iota$ belongs to the set $M \to (o\iota)$, which in set-theoretical notation is written as '$a \in M$', in TIL is recorded as an application of the function M to a: $[M\, a]$. For instance, having the set of prime numbers $Prime/(o\tau)$, the sentence '2 is a prime number' is furnished with this construction as its meaning: $[^0Prime\, {}^02]$.

Note that any non-procedural entities must be supplied to molecular constructions by Trivialization (or a variable, as the case may be). The reason is this. Constituents of procedures can be only their (sub)procedures. No non-procedural abstract or concrete object can be a constituent part of a procedure. The objects on which procedures operate are beyond them. Thus, while *Tom* is an individual that cannot be executed and thus cannot be a part of a procedure, ^0Tom is a procedure, albeit trivial.

Properties of individuals are intensions, objects of type $(o\iota)_{\tau\omega}$. In order to apply a property to an individual, a functional application is used. However, properties are not type-theoretically proper entities to be directly applied to an individual. They have to be extensionalized first. For instance, the sentence

'Tom is a student.'

ascribes the property of being a student to Tom. As any other non-procedural objects to be operated on, the individual Tom, as well as the property of being a student, are supplied by their Trivialization, ^0Tom, $^0Student$. Since the property is an intension of type $(((o\iota)\tau)\omega)$, or $(o\iota)_{\tau\omega}$ for short, the property must be applied to a possible world (type ω) first and then to time (type τ). To this end, we have variables $w \to \omega$ and $t \to \tau$; thus, we get $[[^0Student\, w]\, t]$, or $^0Student_{wt}$, for short. In this way, we obtain the population of students in the world w and time t in which we are going to evaluate the truth-value of the sentence. That Tom belongs to this population is expressed simply by the application of this population to Tom: $[^0Student_{wt}\ ^0Tom] \to$ o. Finally, we abstract over the values of the variables w and t to obtain the proposition that Tom is a student.

$$\lambda w \lambda t\, [^0Student_{wt}\ ^0Tom] \to o_{\tau\omega}$$

So much for the basic technicalities of TIL. Other ingredients that we need to illustrate communication of agents, their reasoning and learning by messaging are the notions of requisite, presupposition vs. entailment and refinement.

Duží et al. [19] (Ch. 4) introduce a logic of intensions that has been developed into an *intensional essentialism* which spells out how some intensions supervene on other intensions.[18] The key notion is that of *requisite*. Intuitively, a requisite of an intension A is a further intension B that must, as a matter of analytic necessity, be had by any entity that happens to be in the extension of A. For instance, the property of being a human being is a requisite for having the initial property of being a student. Formally, a requisite is a relation-in-extension between intensions of any type, though typically between individual properties or offices. For the sake of simplicity, here, we define the relation of requisite between individual properties of type $(o\iota)_{\tau\omega}$. Since TIL is a logic of partial function, to deal with partiality properly, we have to apply the property $True/(oo_{\tau\omega})_{\tau\omega}$ of propositions. The reason is this. Propositions can have truth-value gaps in some worlds and times; in such a case, the extensionalization of the proposition P, i.e. P_{wt}, fails to produce a truth-value, the Composition is v-improper. Partiality, as we all know very well, brings about technical complications. To manage them correctly, we define three properties of propositions *True*, *False* and *Undefined*, all of type $(oo_{\tau\omega})_{\tau\omega}$, as follows ($P \to o_{\tau\omega}$):

$[^0True_{wt}\ P]$ v-contructs **T** if P_{wt} v-contructs **T**, otherwise **F**;

$[^0False_{wt}\ P]$ v-contructs **T** if P_{wt} v-contructs **F**, otherwise **F**;

$[^0Undefined_{wt}\ P] = \neg[^0True_{wt}\ P] \wedge \neg[^0False_{wt}\ P]$.

DEFINITION 3

(*Requisite*). Let $f, g \to (o\iota)_{\tau\omega}$ be constructions v-constructing properties; $True/(oo_{\tau\omega})_{\tau\omega}$ the property of a proposition of being true at a given world and time; $x \to \iota$; and $Req/(o(o\iota)_{\tau\omega}(o\iota)_{\tau\omega})$. Then the property v-constructed by f is *a requisite of the property* v-constructed by g iff

$$[^0Req\,f\,g] = \forall w \forall t\, \forall x\, [[^0True_{wt}\ \lambda w\lambda t\,[g_{wt}\ x]] \supset [^0True_{wt}\ \lambda w\lambda t\,[f_{wt}\ x]]].$$

Remark. This definition applies the property *True* to a proposition because the relation obtains necessarily. If we carelessly defined the relation by way of $\forall w \forall t\, \forall x\, [[g_{wt}\ x] \supset [f_{wt}\ x]]$ the result would be a falsehood. The reason is that, at those worlds and times at which the Composition $[g_{wt}\ x]$ or $[f_{wt}\ x]$ is v-improper, the universal quantifiers would return the truth-value F.

The property of propositions *True* is also applied in the definition of the difference between a *presupposition* and *mere entailment*. To explain the difference informally, consider these examples. The property of being human is a requisite of the property of being a student. Hence, necessarily, in all worlds and times, if Tom happens to be a student, then Tom is a human being. In other words, the proposition that Tom is a student *entails* the proposition that Tom is a human being. Yet, it does

---

[18] Intensional essentialism obtains between intensions, unlike individual anti-essentialism that concerns bare individuals.

not presuppose it. If Tom is not a human being, it cannot be a student, of course. Tom can be a cat, or whatever. But in such a case, the proposition that Tom is a student is simply false. There is no reason for a truth-value gap. On the other hand, consider the sentence 'Tom stopped smoking.' It entails that Tom previously smoked. If he never smoked, he could not stop smoking, of course. But the sentence 'Tom did not stop smoking.' also entails that Tom previously smoked (and still smokes). Hence, if Tom never smoked, he could neither stop nor not stop smoking. Both the sentences have a truth-value gap. Therefore, the proposition that *Tom previously smoked* is a *presupposition* of both the sentences.

Thus, we define.

DEFINITION 4
(*Presupposition* vs. *mere entailment*)

Let P, Q be constructions of propositions. Then,

Q is entailed by P iff

$\forall w \forall t [[^0 True_{wt} P] \supset [^0 True_{wt} Q]];$

Q is a presupposition of P iff

$\forall w \forall t [[[^0 True_{wt} P] \vee [^0 False_{wt} P]] \supset [^0 True_{wt} Q]].$

As a *corollary*, we have the following:
Q is a presupposition of P iff $\forall w \forall t [\neg [^0 True_{wt} Q] \supset [^0 Undefined_{wt} P]]$. If a presupposition of proposition P is not true, then P has no truth value.

The relation of *refinement* obtains between *concepts*, i.e. closed constructions in their normal form.[19] Usually, we need to refine an atomic concept, i.e. Trivialization of an entity. For instance, the atomic concept of the property of being a bachelor is $^0 Bachelor$. Its refinement is an *ontological definition* of this property, where ontological definition is a molecular construction of the same property, like, e.g. $\lambda w \lambda t \lambda x [[^0 Unmarried\ ^0 Man]_{wt}\ x]$; $Unmarried/((o\iota)_{\tau\omega}(o\iota)_{\tau\omega})$: property modifier, $Man/(o\iota)_{\tau\omega}$.

DEFINITION 5 (*Refinement of a construction*) Let C_1, C_2, C_3 be constructions. Let $^0 X$ be an atomic concept of X, and let $^0 X$ occur as a constituent of C_1. If C_2 differs from C_1 only by containing in lieu of $^0 X$ an ontological definition of X, then C_2 is a *refinement of* C_1. If C_3 is a refinement of C_2 and C_2 is a refinement of C_1, then C_3 is a *refinement of* C_1.

For the needs of agents' communication, we introduce the function-in-intension $Refine/(*_n*_m)_{\tau\omega}$ assigning to a construction/concept its refinement; $[^0 Refine_{wt}\ ^0 C] = {^0 D}$ means that the concept D is a refinement of the concept C. Note that here we make use of the *hyperintensional* features of TIL. Constructions C and D do not occur in the execution mode; their products are irrelevant here. Rather, they are *presented* as arguments of the function *Refine*. Therefore, they must be supplied by Trivialization.

---

[19]Concept and the normal form of a construction are rigorously defined in [19] (Section 2.2.1). Briefly, the normal form of a construction C is the representant of the class of constructions that are procedurally isomorphic with C. It is defined as the alphabetically first, non-η-reducible construction. The relation of procedural isomorphism defined on constructions is rigorously explained in Duží [14]. See also Jespersen [37].

3. Wh-questions and answers

Linguistic classifications of Wh-questions are mostly based on the types of question pronouns, i.e. descriptors of interrogative sentences, e.g. why, where, how, etc.[20] Descriptors refer to objects of various types. In other words, Wh-questions can ask for time, reason, manner, individuals, the definition of something, etc. Hence, a significant amount of different types of queries belong under the umbrella of Wh-questions. Content information associated with persons, things and facts is usually sought using one set of Wh-words (frequently *who, what, whose, which*), while content information associated with time, place, reason and manner is usually sought using another set of Wh-words (*when, where, why, how*). However, there are many exceptions. We can ask, e.g., for a reason (which is mostly associated with *why*) via *what*-word: '*What* was the reason of that event?' or '*What* did you do that for?'. Likewise, *what* is not used merely for seeking information about things. For instance, in the question '*What* time did he come?', we ask about the *time* of somebody's arrival. So *time* is not strictly associated with the word '*when*'.

Though such linguistic classifications are inspiring, we need logical classification based on the types of possible answers, as the type of an object referred to by a descriptor conveys a helpful piece of information to the receiving agent where and how to look for the respective answer. For instance, if the sender wants to know the definition of something, the receiver should look for it in its ontology base among definitions. In order to answer the question about the distance between two places A and B, the receiver should look for this piece of information in the respective section of its base of facts. In addition, the agents can apply semantic rules if only they have them in their knowledge base.[21] For instance, they can apply the rule connecting a given intension with its requisites. Hence, a detailed classification of Wh-queries can significantly improve agents' intelligent behaviour.

From the logical point of view, *empirical questions* denote α-*intensions* that are functions with the domain of possible worlds. The direct answer to such a question is the value of type α of this intension in the actual world and time.[22] Hence, the type of possible answer dictates the type of empirical question. Recall that in TIL, we view α-intensions as functions mapping possible worlds (of type ω) to a type β, where β is frequently the type of a chronology of the elements of type α. Thus, α-intensions are usually mappings of type ($\omega \to (\tau \to \alpha)$), or in TIL notation $((\alpha\tau)\omega)$, $\alpha_{\tau\omega}$ for short.

Empirical Yes-No questions denote *propositions* of type $o_{\tau\omega}$, where o is the type of truth-values.[23] The inquirer wants to know the truth-value of the proposition in question in the world and time of evaluation. For instance, the answer to the question 'Is Tom a professor?' is Yes/No according as the proposition that Tom is a professor is true in the world and time of evaluation.

---

[20] See, for instance, Essberger [26] and Types of Wh-Questions [56].

[21] To avoid misunderstanding, we are going to use this terminology. *Knowledge base* will be used as a general term involving *ontology* and a *base of empirical facts*. While the former is a relatively stable part of the system that could also be called an intensional level of the system, the latter is its extensional level. In the intensional level, there are analytically necessary relations between concepts, relations of requisites and prerequisites between intensions, information on compatible and/or incompatible concepts, as well as inference rules that make it possible to deduce not only explicit but also implicit and computable knowledge.

[22] [15] distinguishes between *direct* and *complete* answer to an empirical question. *Direct* answer is an object X of type α i.e. the value (in the world and time of evaluation) of the α-intension asked for, while *complete answer* is the proposition that the value of the asked intension is the object X. The authors deal with presuppositions of questions. Their main thesis is this. If a presupposition of a given question is not true, then there is no direct answer. Instead, a plausible complete answer is the negated presupposition.

[23] For details on TIL analysis of questions and answers see ([19], §3.6.).

Modelling dynamic behaviour of agents in a multiagent world: logical analysis of wh-questions and answers

3.1. TIL analysis of Wh-questions and answers

As mentioned above, the variety of possible answers to Wh-questions is much greater depending on the type α of an α-intension the value of which is asked for. For instance, one can ask for the value of an *individual office* (or *role*) of type $\iota_{\tau\omega}$, like 'Which is the highest mountain of the Czech Republic?', 'Who is the mayor of the city Dunedin?' and 'Who is the No.1 player in ATP tennis singles?' A possible answer to such a question is a unique individual (an object of type ι) who happens to play a given role. For instance, the analysis of the question 'Who is the No.1 player in WTA tennis singles?' comes down to this construction.

$$\lambda w \lambda t \, [^0 I \, \lambda x \, [[^0 WTA\text{-}ranking_{wt} \, x] = \, ^0 1]] \to \iota_{\tau\omega}$$

Types: $I/(\iota(o\iota))$: the singularizer, i.e. the function that associates a set S of individuals with the only member of S provided S is a singleton, and otherwise (if S is an empty or a multi-valued set) the function I is undefined; $x \to \iota$: the variable ranging over individuals such that the direct answer would be provided by the valuation of this variable; $WTA\text{-}ranking/(\tau\iota)_{\tau\omega}$: an attribute, i.e. an empirical function that associates a given individual with a number that is its value in WTA ranking singles.

Another frequent type of intensions is the *property of individuals*, an object of type $(o\iota)_{\tau\omega}$. For instance, the direct answer to the question 'Which Czech ladies are among the first fifty players in WTA ranking singles?' should convey a set (of type $(o\iota)$) of individuals. Currently (written 10 October 2021), they are {Karolina Plíšková, Barbora Krejčíková, Petra Kvitová, Karolína Muchová, Marketa Vondroušová}. Hence, the question denotes a property of individuals, namely that of being a female Czech tennis player among the first fifty in WTA ranking singles. The analysis of the above question is this.

$$\lambda w \lambda t \, [\lambda y \, [[[^0 Female \, ^0 Czech]_{wt} \, y] \land [[^0 WTA\text{-}ranking \, y] \leq \, ^0 50]]] \to (o\iota)_{\tau\omega}$$

Types: $Female/((o\iota)_{\tau\omega}(o\iota)_{\tau\omega})$: the intersective property modifier that assigns to a property another modified property;[24] $Czech/(o\iota)_{\tau\omega}$; $y \to \iota$; the other types as above.

One can also ask for the value of an attribute at an argument like the salary of somebody. The possible answer to the question 'What is John's salary?' is some number of type τ. Hence, the question denotes a magnitude of type $\tau_{\tau\omega}$.

The temporal parameter τ can sometimes be superfluous or missing. As an example, consider the speed of light in vacuum; the *speed of* is an attribute, i.e. a function that dependently on possible worlds (type ω) associates an argument (here light in vacuum) with a number. Hence, the question 'What is the speed of light in vacuum?' denotes a τ_ω-object, where τ is the type of numbers. We omit the temporal parameter τ, for the speed of light in vacuum is a physical *constant*. According to Einstein's special theory of relativity, the speed of light in the vacuum is the upper limit for the speed at which matter and physical information can travel. However, the question denotes an *intension* because physics, unlike mathematics or logic, is an empirical science. The speed of light in vacuum *might* differ from its exact value in our actual world, which is defined as 299 792 458 m/s. It is correct because a metre is *defined* as the length of the path travelled by light in vacuum during a time interval of 1/299 792 458 seconds.

Duží and Fait [17] adjusted Gentzen's system of natural deduction for TIL so that the system can answer not only Yes-No questions by keywords searching but also Wh-questions by *inferring computable knowledge* from natural-language texts. Though the paper does not deal with the

---

[24] For details on property modifiers, see Jespersen *et al.* [38] or Duží [13].

classification of Wh-questions, a useful logical technique of their answering is described here. It consists of enriching the system of natural deduction with the special rules rooted in the rich semantics of a natural language. In addition, special technical rules are formulated to operate *into* hyperintensional contexts.

As illustrated above, Wh-questions transform into constructions with λ-bound variables corresponding to the meaning of descriptors, the value of which we ask for. The answers are then obtained by the technique of suitable substitution, i.e. unification known from the general resolution method.

For a simple example, assume that in an agent's knowledge base, there are these formalized sentences.

WTA ranking of Asheigh Barty is 1.
$\lambda w \lambda t \ [[^0 WTA\text{-}ranking_{wt} \ ^0 Barty] = \ ^0 1]$
WTA ranking of Aryna Sabalenka is 2.
$\lambda w \lambda t \ [[^0 WTA\text{-}ranking_{wt} \ ^0 Sabalenka] = \ ^0 2]$
WTA ranking of Karolina Pliskova is 3.
$\lambda w \lambda t \ [[^0 WTA\text{-}ranking_{wt} \ ^0 Pliskova] = \ ^0 3]$
WTA ranking of Iga Swiatek is 4.
$\lambda w \lambda t \ [[^0 WTA\text{-}ranking_{wt} \ ^0 Swiatek] = \ ^0 4]$
WTA ranking of Barbora Krejcikova is 5.
$\lambda w \lambda t \ [[^0 WTA\text{-}ranking_{wt} \ ^0 Krejcikova] = \ ^0 5]$
And so on ...
The answer to the question 'Who is the No.1 player in WTA tennis singles?', i.e.,
$\lambda w \lambda t \ [^0 I \ \lambda x \ [[^0 WTA\text{-}ranking_{wt} \ x] = \ ^0 1]] \to \iota_{\tau\omega}$
is derived like this.

(1) $[^0 I \ \lambda x \ [[^0 WTA\text{-}Ranking_{wt} \ x] = \ ^0 1]]$ Question
(2) $\lambda x \ [[^0 WTA\text{-}Ranking_{wt} \ x] = \ ^0 1]$ 1, I-E
(3) $[[^0 WTA\text{-}Ranking_{wt} \ ^0 Barty] = \ ^0 1]$ assumption
(4) $x = \ ^0 Barty$ 2, 3, β-reduction ($^0 Barty$/x, unification)

Comments. In the proof, we omitted the first proof steps that consist in the elimination of the left-most $\lambda w \lambda t$. It is the standard way of proving in TIL, which is justified due to this. As defined above, the relation of *entailment* obtains between constructions of propositions such that in all possible words and times whenever the propositions of assumptions are true, the proposition produced by the conclusion is true as well. Hence, in any world w_0 and time t_0 of evaluation, the derivation sequence must be truth-preserving from premises to the conclusion. Thus, the typical series of derivation steps is this. We have assumptions of the form $\lambda w \lambda t \ [\ldots w \ldots t \ldots] \to o_{\tau\omega}$, and we assume that the propositions produced by these constructions are true in the world w_0 at time t_0 of evaluation. Using the detailed notation, we have the Composition

$$[[[\lambda w \ [\lambda t \ [\ldots w \ldots t \ldots]]]w_0] \ t_0] \to o.$$

By applying restricted β-reduction twice,[25] we eliminate the left-most $\lambda w \lambda t$, thus obtaining [... w_0 ... t_0 ...] → o. Now, we proceed with derivation steps until the conclusion of the form [... w_0

---

[25]Restricted β-reduction consists just in substitution of variables for variables; hence, it is a 'safe' reduction that transforms the redex into an equivalent contractum. For more details on β-conversions in the logic of partial functions such as TIL, see Duží and Kosterec [22].

Modelling dynamic behaviour of agents in a multiagent world: logical analysis of wh-questions and answers

... t_0 ...] → o is derived. Since we are to derive a proposition, we finally abstract over the values of the variables w_0, t_0, thus introducing the left-most $\lambda w \lambda t$ back to construct a proposition:

$$\lambda w \lambda t \, [\ldots w \ldots t \ldots] \to o_{\tau\omega}.$$

A slightly more complicated example illustrates the application of the natural language semantic rules and dealing with a hyperintensional context.[26] The example deals with factive verbs like knowing or regretting. These verbs denote attitudes such that the attitudinal sentences come attached with a presupposition that the complement clause of the attitude is true.

For instance, both 'John regrets his coming late' and 'John doesn't regret his coming late' entail that John indeed came late. Thus, according to Def. 4, John's coming late is a presupposition of both sentences.

Assume that the input sentence is

'John regrets that Tom doesn't know that he (John) is sick.'

The analysis of the sentence comes down to this construction.

$\lambda w \lambda t \, [^0Regret_{wt} \, ^0John \, ^0[\lambda w \lambda t \, \neg [^0Know_{wt} \, ^0Tom \, [^0Sub \, [^0Tr \, ^0John] \, ^0he \, ^0[\lambda w \lambda t \, [^0Sick_{wt} \, he]]]]]]$

Types. *Regret*, *Know*/$(o\iota*_n)_{\tau\omega}$: hyperintensional factive attitudes, i.e. relations-in-intension of an individual to the construction of a proposition;[27] *John*, *Tom*/ι; *Sick*/$(o\iota)_{\tau\omega}$; *he* → ι: anaphoric variable.

The functions *Sub*/$(*_n*_n*_n*_n)$ and *Tr*/$(*_n\alpha)$ are two special vehicles to operate on constructions. They are defined as follows. Where C_1, C_2, C_3 → $*_{n+1}$ are constructions that v-construct constructions D_1, D_2, D_3 → $*_n$, D_2 being a variable, the Composition $[^0Sub \, C_1 \, C_2 \, C_3]$ v-constructs a construction D that results from D_3 by correctly substituting D_1 for D_2 into D_3. The function *Tr* associates and α-object with its Trivialization. Using these functions, we have developed a substitution method that serves for operating into hyperintensional contexts and also for dealing with anaphoric references, which is the case here.[28] Hence the Composition

$[^0Sub \, [^0Tr \, ^0John] \, ^0he \, ^0[\lambda w \lambda t \, [^0Sick_{wt} \, he]]]$

produces the adjusted Closure $[\lambda w \lambda t \, [^0Sick_{wt} \, ^0John]]$. Note that both occurrences of the variable *he* are in the scope of Trivialization; they are o-bound; the variable does not occur in the execution mode and its valuations are pointless; rather, the function *Sub* operates on this variable to substitute ^0John for it.

---

[26]This is a slightly adjusted example of Duží and Fait [17]. Here, we illustrate a top-down derivation from the hyperintensional level of the complements of regretting and not knowing to the extensional level of John's being sick by applying the rules for factive verbs and anaphora resolution. The rules for quantifying *into* hyperintensional contexts are proved in Duží and Jespersen [20].

[27]True, these attitudes could be analysed as relations-in-intension to a proposition. Yet, then we would face the problem of logical/mathematical omniscience. For this reason, we standardly analyse such propositional attitudes as hyperintensional, i.e. relations-in-intension to the construction of a proposition.

[28]The problem of anaphora resolution is a hard nut of linguistic analysis, of course, as anaphoric sentences are often ambiguous. Logic cannot decide any linguistic ambiguity; this is a pragmatic problem. Yet, logic such as TIL can contribute to disambiguation by proper typing. Anyway, if the sentence is ambiguous, we furnish the sentence with more than one meaning constructions. The algorithm of dealing with anaphoric references in TIL, and agents' communication using such sentences, has been introduced and implemented by Kotová [41]. In this example, the algorithm would first propose the substitution of Tom for *he* because Tom is the individual last mentioned in the discourse. Yet, if the user is not satisfied with this solution, the algorithm proposes the substitution of another individual, in this case John.

Modelling dynamic behaviour of agents in a multiagent world: logical analysis of wh-questions and answers

Now, we can ask questions like 'Who is sick?', 'How is John?' or 'What does Tom not know?'. Formalization of these questions comes down to

(Q1) $\lambda w \lambda t\ [^0 Sick_{wt}\ who]$

(Q2) $\lambda w \lambda t\ [how_{wt}\ ^0 John]$

(Q3) $\lambda w \lambda t\ \neg [^0 Know_{wt}\ ^0 Tom\ what]$

Additional types. $who \to \iota;\ how \to (o\iota)_{\tau\omega};\ what \to *_n$.

Note that the variables *who, how, what* that are asked for range over different types, which is given by the type structure of the whole construction.

Since regretting and knowing are factive verbs, we apply the rules for factiva that follow from the fact that the truth of the complement of such attitudes is a presupposition of such attitudinal sentences. Let $K/(o\iota*_n)_{\tau\omega}$ be a factive attitude, $a \to \iota,\ c \to *_n,\ ^2c \to o_{\tau\omega}$. Then,

(F1) $[^0 K_{wt}\ a\ c] \vdash\ ^2c_{wt}$

(F2) $\neg [^0 K_{wt}\ a\ c] \vdash\ ^2c_{wt}$

The derivation of the answers proceeds like this. (As explained above, for the sake of simplicity, we omit the elimination and reintroduction of the left-most $\lambda w \lambda t$.)

(1) $[^0 Regret_{wt}\ ^0 John\ ^0 [\lambda w \lambda t\ \neg [^0 Know_{wt}\ ^0 Tom\ [^0 Sub\ [^0 Tr\ ^0 John]\ ^0 he\ ^0 [\lambda w \lambda t\ [^0 Sick_{wt}\ he]]]]]]$

(2) $^{20}[\lambda w \lambda t\ \neg [^0 Know_{wt}\ ^0 Tom\ [^0 Sub\ [^0 Tr\ ^0 John]\ ^0 he\ ^0 [\lambda w \lambda t\ [^0 Sick_{wt}\ he]]]]]_{wt}$ 1, F1

(3) $[\lambda w \lambda t\ \neg [^0 Know_{wt}\ ^0 Tom\ [^0 Sub\ [^0 Tr\ ^0 John]\ ^0 he\ ^0 [\lambda w \lambda t\ [^0 Sick_{wt}\ he]]]]]_{wt}$ 2, ^{20}E

(4) $\neg [^0 Know_{wt}\ ^0 Tom\ [^0 Sub\ [^0 Tr\ ^0 John]\ ^0 he\ ^0 [\lambda w \lambda t\ [^0 Sick_{wt}\ he]]]]$ 3, β-red.

(5) $^2[^0 Sub\ [^0 Tr\ ^0 John]\ ^0 he\ ^0 [\lambda w \lambda t\ [^0 Sick_{wt}\ he]]]_{wt}$ 4, F2

(6) $^{20}[\lambda w \lambda t\ [^0 Sick_{wt}\ ^0 John]]_{wt}$ 5, *Sub, Tr*

(7) $[\lambda w \lambda t\ [^0 Sick_{wt}\ ^0 John]]_{wt}$ 6, ^{20}E

(8) $[^0 Sick_{wt}\ ^0 John]$ 7, β-red.

(9) $[^0 Sick_{wt}\ who]$ Q1

(10) $who =\ ^0 John$ 8,9 unif.

(11) $[how_{wt}\ ^0 John]$ Q2

(12) $how =\ ^0 Sick$ 8,11 unif.

(13) $\neg [^0 Know_{wt}\ ^0 Tom\ what]$ Q3

(14) $what = [^0 Sub\ [^0 Tr\ ^0 John]\ ^0 he\ ^0 [\lambda w \lambda t\ [^0 Sick_{wt}\ he]]]$ 4,13 unif.

(15) $what =\ ^0 [\lambda w \lambda t\ [^0 Sick_{wt}\ ^0 John]]$ 14, *Sub, Tr*

We derived the direct answers to the three questions as follows. 'Who is sick?', John; 'How is John?', sick; 'What does Tom not know?', that John is sick.

Note that if the input assumption were of the form

'John *believes* that Tom doesn't know that he is sick.'

we could not answer the questions (Q1), (Q2) and (Q3). Unlike knowing or regretting, believing is not a factivum. One can believe false or even impossible propositions.

From the point of view of dynamic behaviour of agents, Wh-questions on the participants of their activities are the most important. We are going to deal with them in Section 4.2.

3.2. Logical classification of Wh-questions

Číhalová and Štěpán [5] introduce the classification of Wh-questions according to the logical type of a possible answer. This classification is potentially infinite. We can ask for an object of any type of the infinite hierarchy of types. On the other hand, this classification is a bit too coarse-grained or perhaps non-plausibly oriented. For the needs of an intelligent communication of agents with their fellow agents, it might be helpful to classify questions in more detail. For instance, the type ι of individuals comprises human beings, animals, inanimate entities, etc., and the kind of a referential term can convey an additional useful piece of information.

Our starting point is distinguishing between relatively *static entities* like individuals with their properties and *dynamic entities* like activities that form processes. Sowa [51] defines process as 'an evolving sequence of states and events, in which one of the states or events is marked current at a context-dependent time called #now.' The sequence of states and events indicates a change that Sowa [51] formally specifies in the following way: 'a change occurs when certain facts that are true in a situation s_1 are no longer true in a later situation s_2.' The measure of the process's granularity depends on the aims of the application that the ontology serves. For instance, if we want to capture speed changes, we need to specify the process in more detail. For each speed change, we need to add accelerate and decelerate actions to the ontology. Generally, each process is composed of at least one event and two states. The process triggers are actions or passive events like 'turning pale', 'subsiding', etc., which are not intentional.

Both static and dynamic entities are characterized by their properties and attributes. In addition, dynamic entities (activities) are characterized by special relationships between activities and their participants. For instance, 'John is a student' is a relatively static entity. On the other hand, 'John is flying to Brussels' is a dynamic activity. Wh-questions then ask for the characteristics of entities, for instance, 'What is John?', or 'Who is flying to Brussels?'

3.2.1. Static entities Concerning the static entities, the properties assigned to them are usually denoted by a copular verb + predicative adjective or nominative. Typical copular verbs are *is, am, are, ..., appear, seem, look, sound, smell, taste, feel, become* and *get*. In the conceptual analysis of a given domain, it is useful to distinguish two basic classes of static objects' characteristics. The first are relatively stable relations between properties of objects, and the second are dynamic empirical facts about these objects. While the former are usually organized in agents' ontology into hierarchies of requisites and typical properties, also known as ISA hierarchies, the latter form agents' knowledge base of empirical facts.

Another distinction that we will make is between *substantive* and *accidental* properties of objects. For instance, consider horse racing as the domain of interest. Then the substantive property is that of being a horse with its subsumed substantive properties like a breed of horse, namely Thoroughbred, Standardbred, Arabian horse and Quarter horse. Concerning requisites, each horse is a mammal, namely an odd-toed ungulate mammal belonging to the taxonomic family Equidae. Accidental properties of an individual horse include, inter alia, the number of victories in races, the number of injuries, muscle structure, age, weight, temperament, etc. In addition, each substantive property is mostly associated with some accidental attributes of the individuals instantiating the given substantive property. For instance, the substantive property of being a horse can be associated with the above accidental properties.

Yet, from the logical point of view, we assent to the doctrine of individual *antiessentialism*. No bare individual has any non-trivial, i.e. non-constant property analytically necessarily unless it belongs to the essential core of the property.[29] Hence, to put the distinction between substantive and accidental properties on more solid ground, we must take into account that there are different degrees of necessity. Analytic necessity is the sort of necessity of the highest degree. It is defined as the validity in all possible worlds w and times t. So, the schema of analytic necessity is this: $[^0\forall\lambda w\ ^0\forall\lambda t\ \ldots]$. Weaker necessity is the 'nomic necessity' understood as the sort of necessity that pertains to laws of nature. Nomic necessity is logically contingent, so the source of universality is obtained by suspending temporal variability: $[\lambda w\ ^0\forall\lambda t\ \ldots]$. It means that it is true (false) at all instants of time that if so-and-so then so-and-so.[30] For instance, according to the laws of physics and biology, if an individual is born as a horse, then during its life span, it cannot become, say, a lion or a bridge. Hence, being a horse is a *substantive* property of such an individual. *Substantive properties* are those that individuals have nomically necessarily, while *accidental properties* are possessed by individuals purely contingently.

In summary, Wh-questions concerning static objects are the questions on

a) the substance of the object, i.e. on its substantive properties;
b) accidental properties of the object.

When analysing questions on properties of entities, we will explicitly specify only the case of asking for a substantive property. Questions on the other properties will be taken by default as asking for accidental properties.

3.2.2. Dynamic activities Our specification of *activities* is based on the linguistic theory of *verb valency frames*.[31] From the logical point of view, we deal with the verb phrases as denoting a *function* that is applied to its arguments. The number of arguments is controlled by the content verb *valency*. There are several types of valency. An *impersonal* (avalent) verb has no subject or a dummy subject. 'It rains.' is a typical example. Here, the grammatic subject 'it' is just a dummy subject because it does not refer to any concrete object. An *intransitive* (monovalent) verb has just one argument, the *subject* S; 'John (S) is singing.' A *transitive* (divalent) verb has two arguments, an agent (A) and a patient (P), as in 'John (A) kicked the ball (P).' A *ditransitive verb* has three arguments, an agent and two patients, for instance, in 'John (A) passed the ball (P) to Tom (P).' There are also a few verbs with more than three arguments (polyvalent, like tritransitive, ...), yet they mostly arise by valency increasing, where causatives or applicatives are typical valency increasing devices.[32]

Verb valency frames determine the obligatory and facultative arguments, i.e. thematic roles of a given verb, together with their types. Facultative arguments can be missing, of course. For instance, the verb 'buy' can occur in several sentences as denoting functions with a different number of arguments like 'Tom bought a book', 'Tom bought a book in Paris', 'On Friday, Tom bought a book', 'Tom bought a book for Jane in Paris', etc. In our analysis, we have to take these varieties into account. Linguists have created many classifications based on verb valency frames, for instance, VALLEX or Verba Lex.[33]

---

[29] For details on TIL individual anti-essentialism and intensional essentialism, see Duží *et al.* [19], (§1.4.2.1 and §4.2).
[30] For details on nomological necessity, see Duží *et al.* [19], §4.5.
[31] For the linguistic theory of verb valency frames, see [35] or [36]; in addition, [4] proposed ontology of events based on the theory of verb valency frames.
[32] For details, see Dixon [10].
[33] See, for instance, Lopatková *et al.* [43], Hlaváčková & Horák [35], Horák [36].

Modelling dynamic behaviour of agents in a multiagent world: logical analysis of wh-questions and answers

Sowa [51] proposed a specification tool for knowledge representation, where he adopted a linguistic approach to verbs. He developed the system of conceptual graphs in which Peirce's logic is combined with the semantic networks known from artificial intelligence. For the valency participants, Sowa uses the term *thematic roles* or *case relations*. His summary of all the thematic roles can be found in [51] (pp. 506–510). Thematic roles are represented by conceptual relations that link the concept of a verb to the concepts of the participants in the 'occurrent' expressed by the verb.[34] Here is an example. The linear form of the graph of the sentence 'Bob went to Danbury' is this [51] (p. 508):

$$[\text{Person: Bob}] \leftarrow (\text{Agnt}) \leftarrow [\text{Go}] \rightarrow (\text{Dest}) \rightarrow [\text{City: Danbury}].$$

In this linear form, square brackets [...] indicate concepts and parentheses (...) conceptual roles. Sowa distinguishes several types of thematic roles, for instance, Agent, Beneficiary, Destination, Duration, Effector, Experiencer, Instrument, Location, Matter, Patient and so on.[35] Thematic role or the type of participant expresses the role that a noun phrase plays with respect to the activity described by a governing verb. From the viewpoint of logic, it is the relation between two entities where one of them is an activity (expressed by the verb), and the other is a participant (expressed mostly by a noun, adverb or adjective). The number and the categories of participants depend on the respective domain of interest and the functions of the system of agents.

Being inspired by Sowa's ideas and verb valency dictionaries, we primarily use the following frequent kinds of participants:

Pat - object affected by the activity;
Ben - beneficient (somebody who has a benefit from the activity);
Manner - the manner of the activity execution (measure, speed, etc.);
Inst - instrument;
Time - when the activity takes place;
Time1 - when the activity starts;
Time2 - when the activity ends;
Loc - the place of activity;
Dir1 - the direction of activity—*from where*;
Dir2 - the direction of activity—*which way*;
Dir3 - the direction of activity—*where to*.

A large number of Wh-questions concern the participants of activities; we ask for their values in a world and time of evaluation. Hence, we can distinguish questions on the process itself (*what is going on?*) from Wh-questions on the primary agent and other participants of a given activity. For instance, assume we have the sentence 'John (the agent) is going (the activity) to London (Dir3) by car (Inst) at an average speed of 50 miles per hour (Man).' Then we can ask, 'What is John doing?', 'Who is going to London?', 'How quickly does John go to London?', etc. Our classification enables an agent to look for sentences that might provide a plausible answer at an appropriate component of the agent's knowledge base provided this piece of knowledge is there, or ask their fellow agents, or look for the answer in the huge amount of natural language texts available.

---

[34]'An occurrent is in a state of flux that prevents it from being recognized by a stable set of attributes. Instead, it can only be identified by its location in some region of space/time.' ([51], p. 71)
[35]For details, see Sowa [51].

3.2.3. Refinement and explication of concepts A particular category of questions concerns hyperintensional questions about a given *concept*. Our agents should be able to *learn* from experience through mutual communication with their fellow agents. In such a communication, it may happen that a receiving agent *b* does not 'know' a concept, i.e. a constituent of a sender's *a* message. By 'knowing a concept' *C*, we mean having the concept *C* in one's ontology. In such a situation, the receiving agent *b* can ask for the explication or a definition of the unknown concept.[36]

In TIL, we explicate *concepts as abstract procedures* that produce, or in well-defined cases fail to produce, functional objects. More precisely, *concepts* are defined as closed constructions in their normal form.[37] There are *atomic concepts* that do not have any other constituents but themselves and *molecular concepts* that consist of proper constituents. For instance, the atomic concept of prime numbers is the Trivialization of the set of primes, ^0Prime. This atomic concept does not convey much information about the set of primes, indeed. Mathematicians could hardly prove that there is no greatest prime number if they had only the atomic concept at their disposal. On the other hand, molecular concepts of this set convey much more information. There are many of them, like 'natural numbers with exactly two factors' or 'natural numbers greater than one divisible only by one and themselves'. Here are the corresponding constructions, i.e. molecular concepts of primes.

$$\lambda x\ [[^0Card\ \lambda y\ [^0Divisible\ x\ y]] = {}^02]$$

$$\lambda x\ [[^0{>}\ x\ {}^01] \wedge \neg \exists y\ [[^0Divisible\ x\ y] \wedge \neg[[y = {}^01] \vee [y = x]]]]$$

Types. $x, y \rightarrow \eta$ (the type of natural numbers); $Card/(\eta(o\eta))$: the number of elements of a set; $Divisible/(o\eta\eta)$: the relation of x being divisible by y; $1,2/\eta$.

For an example of empirical concepts, the atomic concept of a cat is the Trivialization of the property of being a cat, ^0Cat. The molecular concepts of a cat define this property. For instance, the biological definition could be 'The cat (Felix catus) is a domestic species of the carnivorous mammal in the family of Felidae'. The meaning of this definition comes down to

$$\lambda w \lambda t\ \lambda x\ [[[^0Domestic\ [^0Carnivorous\ {}^0Mammal]]_{wt}\ x] \wedge [^0Felidae_{wt}\ x]].$$

Types. $x \rightarrow \iota$; $Domestic, Carnivorous/((o\iota)_{\tau\omega}(o\iota)_{\tau\omega})$: property modifiers, i.e. functions that assign to a core property another, modified property; $Mammal, Felidae/(o\iota)_{\tau\omega}$.

When asking for the explication of the concept *C*, the agent does not 'talk about the object produced by *C*'. Rather, the concept, i.e. the procedure *C* itself, is a subject matter, i.e. asked for. Such a context where procedure *C* occurs just *presented* as an argument rather than *executed* to produce an object is *hyperintensional*. In [24], a special kind of a question is introduced, namely a question of type $Unrecognized/(o*_n)_{\tau\omega}$, the argument of which is an unknown concept *C*. The answer is then of type $Refine/(*_n*_n)_{\tau\omega}$, where the answer provides a concept C' which refines the unknown concept *C*. Thus, the schema of the content of messages asking for refinement is this.

$[^0Unrecognized_{wt}\ {}^{00}What]$; the atomic concept ^0What has not been recognized; a request for refinement. Note that *Unrecognized* is of type $(o*_n)_{\tau\omega}$, the property of *construction* (usually an atomic concept).

$[[^0Refine_{wt}\ {}^{00}What] = {}^0C]$; an answer to the message on unrecognized atomic concept. Construction *C* is the respective composed specification or explication of *What*.

---

[36] We have also successfully applied the adjusted method of supervised machine learning to extract explications and/or refinements of concepts from natural-language texts. For details, see, for instance, Menšík et al. [45].

[37] For details, see Duží et al. [19], §2.2.

For instance, the set of prime numbers can be defined as the set of numbers with two factors: $[[^0Refine_{wt}\ ^{00}Prime] = {^0}[\lambda x\ [^0Card\ \lambda y\ [^0Divisible\ x\ y] = {^0}2]]]$.

Refinement is defined above by Def. 5. To recall briefly, by refining an atomic concept of an object O, we mean discovering a molecular concept that produces the same object O. In mathematics, refining concerns definitions like 'a *group* is a set G equipped with a binary operation that combines any two elements of G to form another element of G in such a way that group axioms are satisfied, namely associativity, the existence of the neutral element in G and invertibility.' Here, the atomic concept to be refined is that of a 'group', i.e. ^0Group. The molecular concept refining ^0Group is encoded by the above definiens.

In the case of *empirical* concepts, it is more plausible to speak about *explication*. The reason is this. To say that a molecular concept C is a refinement of an atomic empirical concept D is risky. It would be a refinement only if the molecular concept C were *analytically equivalent* to the original concept D, which means that both are the concepts of the same object O, or both are improper, i.e. do not produce any object. However, in the most interesting cases of *empirical* concepts of PWS-*intensions*, we use a Carnapian *explication* rather than a definition proper. Then equivalence is undoubtedly not guaranteed, for one can hardly check the identity of the intensions produced by the two concepts. Rather, a new molecular concept C (explicatum) should define an intensional object O that is as close as possible to the object referred to by an inexact (prescientific) concept D (explicandum).

In *Meaning and Necessity* (1947), Carnap characterizes explication as follows:

> The task of making more exact a vague or not quite exact concept used in everyday life or in an earlier stage of scientific or logical development, or rather of replacing it by a newly constructed, more exact concept, belongs among the most important tasks of logical analysis and logical construction. We call this the task of explicating, or of giving an *explication* for, the earlier concept [...] ([2], pp. 7–8)

Keeping this difference in mind, we will use the term 'refinement' for both cases, including explication of empirical concepts because in most cases of explicating the concept unknown to an agent this simplification is harmless.

4. Questions, answers and reasoning in TIL

In this section, we illustrate agents' communication by messaging and their dynamic reasoning formalized in TIL. We concentrate on Wh-questions. As mentioned above, the analysis of empirical Wh-questions transforms in our TIL formalism into λ-terms denoting procedures that produce α-intensions where α is not a truth-value. The sought answer should provide an object of type α, which is the value of the α-intension asked for in the actual world at the current time.

4.1. Questions on properties of entities

When answering questions on properties of objects, the agents can exploit pieces of knowledge stored in their ontology to derive additional questions/answers. Most frequently, they apply the *requisite relation* provided their ontology contains those pieces of knowledge. For instance, necessarily, if X is a student or an employee, then X must be a human being. In addition, the agents can have more information in their ontology; in particular, they can have special attributes associated with a given property. For instance, if X is an employee, it makes sense to ask for his/her salary.

Modelling dynamic behaviour of agents in a multiagent world: logical analysis of wh-questions and answers

Here are a few examples. First, a few simple questions on the properties and attributes of an individual.

Q: What is (the substantive property of) John?

The content of the query message is this.

$$\lambda w \lambda t \, \lambda p \, [[p_{wt} \, {}^0 John] \wedge [{}^0 Subst_{wt} \, p]].$$

Types: $John/\iota$; $p \to (o\iota)_{\tau\omega}$; $Subst/(o(o\iota)_{\tau\omega})_{\tau\omega}$: the property of properties that are substantive for a given individual.
A possible answer can be $p = Man$.
Now the agent can deduce that John is a male human being, a mammal, etc.

Q: What is (the accidental property of) John?

Since now the agent is interested in the value of an accidental attribute of John, which is considered as default, we do not specify the type of the property, and the analysis of the question is simply this.

$$\lambda w \lambda t \, \lambda p \, [p_{wt} \, {}^0 John]$$

Now, assume that the answer is $p = Employee$. Then another question can be on John's salary.

Q: What is the salary of John?

$$\lambda w \lambda t \, \lambda x \, [x = [{}^0 Salary\text{-}of_{wt} \, {}^0 John]]$$

Types: $Salary\text{-}of/(\tau\iota)_{\tau\omega}$; $John/\iota$; $x \to \tau$; $=/(o\tau\tau)$: the identity of numbers.
Yet, John has no doubt more properties worth being asked for. Thus, another question can be this.

Q: What (else) is John?

$$\lambda w \lambda t \, \lambda p \, [p_{wt} \, {}^0 John]$$

Now, the agent should remember the previous answer to the same question and look for another John's accidental property. A possible answer can be $p = Surgeon$. If the agent has requisites of such property in his/her ontology, he/she deduces that John studied medicine. Another question can then be this.

Q: Which university did John graduate from?

$$\lambda w \lambda t \, \lambda y \, [[{}^0 Graduate_{wt} \, {}^0 John \, y] \wedge [{}^0 University_{wt} \, y]]$$

Types: $Graduate/(o\iota\iota)_{\tau\omega}$; $John/\iota$; $University/(o\iota)_{\tau\omega}$; $y \to \iota$.

4.2. Dynamic activities of agents

As mentioned at the outset, our primary goal and the novelty of this paper is the analysis of *processes* and *events*, which can improve agents' rational reasoning and dynamic behaviour.

Questions concerning *activities* or processes are a bit more complicated. The basic idea of their analysis is due to [53]. Its adjustment and simplification have been introduced in [6]. Tichý draws a distinction between *episodic* and *attributive* verbs. Attributive verbs ascribe properties to individuals. Their structure is usually a copula followed by an adjective or noun; for instance, 'is happy', 'is red', 'looks speedy' and 'is a student' are attributive verbs. On the other hand, episodic verbs express actions performed by entities. For instance, if John is getting up, it does not suffice to analyse this

Modelling dynamic behaviour of agents in a multiagent world: logical analysis of wh-questions and answers

activity by assigning the property of getting up to John. Instead, John is *doing* the activity of getting up, and one can ask, for instance, 'When does John get up?'.

For example, the sentence 'John is driving from Brussel to Paris at the average speed of 90 km/h.' should be analysed as describing a time-consuming *process* consisting of a series of *actions* and *events*. In [4], the basic idea of specifying event ontology by means of verb valency frames has been introduced. It consists in particular in refining the type of action executed within a given process. For instance, the specification of the activity *Charles is driving from Prague to München by train at the speed of 90 km/h* is determined by the sense of the verb 'to drive' together with its arguments (*who* is driving—the actor, *when* is (s)he driving, *from where*, *to where*, *by what kind of a vehicle*, in *which speed*, etc.).

From the logical point of view, an episodic verb denotes a relation-in-intension between an individual (the actor) and an activity. Each activity has several participants, and the valency of the verb determines the maximal number of the participants. Thus, each activity can be specified by a verb *Do*, and by *Who* (the actor), *What* (is being done), possibly with the attributes of the activity like objects to be operated on, resources, etc. The attributes/participants can be of various kinds like individuals, properties and quantities. Typical kinds of attributes have been specified above. To recall, they are

- *Pat* (the object affected by the activity),
- *Ben* (who has a benefit from the activity),
- *Manner* (manner of the activity execution),
- *Inst* (instrument),
- *Time* (time interval, when the activity takes place),
- *Time1* (the time when the activity started),
- *Time2* (the time when the activity ended),
- *Loc* (location of the activity),
- *Dir1* (direction of the event—from where),
- *Dir2* (direction of the event—where through),
- *Dir3* (direction of the event—where to).

If needed, other kinds of attributes can be specified; we only must keep the selected keywords fixed.

Using a general place holder π for the type of activity and $\alpha^{Kind\text{-}i}$ for an attribute/participant of a kind-i, the type of *Do* is $(o\iota\pi)_{\tau\omega}$, and the assignment of participants to the activity is then an entity *Asgn* of type $(o\pi\alpha^{Kind\text{-}i})_{\tau\omega}$. To simplify the notation and make the formulas easier to read, we will use '$^0X^{Kind\text{-}i}$' instead of '$[^0Kind\text{-}i\ ^0X]$' to signify that X belongs to the class of participants of a *Kind-i*. Thus, we obtain a general pattern for analysing an activity $P \to \pi$ with the actor A and participants $X_1^{Kind\text{-}1}, \ldots, X_n^{Kind\text{-}n}$.

$$\lambda w \lambda t\ [^0Do_{wt}\ A\ P] \wedge$$

$$[^0Asgn_{wt}\ P\ ^0X_1^{Kind\text{-}1}] \wedge [^0Asgn_{wt}\ P\ ^0X_2^{Kind\text{-}2}] \wedge \ldots \wedge [^0Asgn_{wt}\ P\ ^0X_n^{Kind\text{-}n}]$$

For instance, the analysis of the sentence 'John goes to Brussel by train' comes down to this construction.

$$\lambda w \lambda t\ [^0Do_{wt}\ ^0John\ ^0Go] \wedge$$

$$[^0Asgn_{wt}\ ^0Go\ ^0Train^{Inst}] \wedge [^0Asgn_{wt}\ ^0Go\ ^0Brussel^{Dir3}]$$

Modelling dynamic behaviour of agents in a multiagent world: logical analysis of wh-questions and answers

It may happen that in another time John would go to Brussel by plane. Then we have

$$\lambda w \lambda t \; [^0Do_{wt} \; ^0John \; ^0Go] \wedge$$
$$[^0Asgn_{wt} \; ^0Go \; ^0Plane^{Inst}] \wedge [^0Asgn_{wt} \; ^0Go \; ^0Brussel^{Dir3}]$$

For this reason, the relation *Asgn* between an activity and its participant is the relation-in-intension rather than in extension.

If there are two or more actors of the activity, we apply the relation-in-intension $Do/(o\iota \ldots \iota\pi)_{\tau\omega}$. For instance, the sentence 'John and Tom go to Brussel by plane on April 1.' is furnished with this analysis.

$$\lambda w \lambda t \; [^0Do_{wt} \; ^0John \; ^0Tom \; ^0Go] \wedge$$
$$[^0Asgn_{wt} \; ^0Go \; ^0Plain^{Inst}] \wedge [^0Asgn_{wt} \; ^0Go \; ^0Brussel^{Dir3}] \wedge [^0Asgn_{wt} \; ^0Go \; ^0April1^{Time}]$$

If an agent b has in his/her ontology the specification of all the possible participants of activity, and if b obtains an incomplete message concerning the activity, then b can ask his fellow agents for completing his/her pieces of knowledge. For instance, when receiving the first message about John's going to Brussel by train, the agent can send another query message asking from where does John go to Brussel. To this end, we again use a variable, the valuation of which would be the answer. The content of the query is then this.

$$\lambda w \lambda t \; \lambda d \; [^0Do_{wt} \; ^0John \; ^0Go] \wedge$$
$$[^0Asgn_{wt} \; ^0Go \; ^0Train^{Inst}] \wedge [^0Asgn_{wt} \; ^0Go \; d^{Dir1}] \wedge [^0Asgn_{wt} \; ^0Go \; ^0Brussel^{Dir3}]$$

A possible direct answer to agent b is $d = \, ^0Prague$. The complete answer would then be the message with this content.

$$\lambda w \lambda t \; [[^0Do_{wt} \; ^0John \; ^0Go] \wedge$$
$$[^0Asgn_{wt} \; ^0Go \; ^0Train^{Inst}] \wedge [^0Asgn_{wt} \; ^0Go \; ^0Prague^{Dir1}] \wedge [^0Asgn_{wt} \; ^0Go \; ^0Brussel^{Dir3}]]$$

Another advantage of this approach is this. Since in TIL we have two modal parameters, time and possible worlds, we can easily analyse the activities executed in *past* or *future* and model *dynamic behaviour* and reasoning of agents. For instance, the sentence 'John will go to Brussel by plane.' receives this analysis.

$$\lambda w \lambda t \; \exists t' \; [[^0Do_{wt'} \; ^0John \; ^0Go] \wedge [t' > t]] \wedge$$
$$[[^0Asgn_{wt} \; ^0Go \; ^0Plane^{Inst}] \wedge [^0Asgn_{wt} \; ^0Go \; ^0Brussel^{Dir3}]]$$

The situation gets more complicated if a sentence in past or future comes with a *time reference* T when this or that happened or will happen. In such a case, the sentence is associated with a *presupposition* that the current time t is in the proper relation with respect to the reference time T. Roughly, it means that for sentences in future t comes before the reference time T, while for sentences in past t comes after T; if it is not so, then the proposition has a truth-value gap. Moreover, the sentence can also convey information on the frequency of the activity to be executed in the reference time T like twice, always, all the time since, for the whole year. Duží [12] demonstrates the method of a fine-grained analysis of such sentences in past and future in TIL with a reference time interval T. In the paper, a general analytic schema for sentences that come associated with a presupposition is presented. To this end, the author utilizes a strict definition of the *If-then-else-fail* function that complies with the compositionality constraint.

For instance, the truth conditions of the sentence 'John will go to Brussel by plane in 2022.' presuppose that the current time t in which the truth conditions are being evaluated comes before the end of 2022. If it is not so, the sentence has *no truth value*. Thus, we have

$$\lambda w \lambda t \; [\textit{If } [t \leq_\tau {}^0 2022] \textit{ then}$$
$$\exists t' \; [[{}^0 Do_{wt'} \; {}^0 John \; {}^0 Go] \wedge [{}^0 2022 \; t']] \wedge$$
$$[{}^0 Asgn_{wt} \; {}^0 Go \; {}^0 Plain^{Inst}] \wedge [{}^0 Asgn_{wt} \; {}^0 Go \; {}^0 Brussel^{Dir3}] \wedge [{}^0 Asgn_{wt} \; {}^0 Go \; {}^0 2022^{Time}]$$
$$\textit{else fail}]$$

Additional types. $2022/(o\tau)$; $\leq_\tau / (o\tau(o\tau))$: $\leq_\tau$ stands for the relation between the evaluation time t and time interval of the year 2022 such that t comes before the end of the year 2022.[38] The path with the statement 'else fail' means that the denoted proposition evaluates to *no truth value*.

However, if an agent asks without time reference, 'When will John go to Brussel by plane?', then the test on presupposition validity is not applied, of course. Thus, we have $(c \to (o\tau))$

$$\lambda w \lambda t \; \lambda c \; \exists t' \; [[{}^0 Do_{wt'} \; {}^0 John \; {}^0 Go] \wedge [t' > t]] \wedge$$
$$[[{}^0 Asgn_{wt} \; {}^0 Go \; {}^0 Plane^{Inst}] \wedge [{}^0 Asgn_{wt} \; {}^0 Go \; {}^0 Brussel^{Dir3}] \wedge [{}^0 Asgn_{wt} \; {}^0 Go \; c^{Time}]]$$

By applying the above-described method of unification, the direct answer is ${}^0 2022$, provided the question is raised before the end of 2022. Otherwise, according to the above piece of agent's knowledge, there is no direct answer.

The method of analysis also takes into account the frequency of the activity to be executed in the reference time interval T. The general analytic schema for sentences S in future tenses is this.

$$\lambda w \lambda t \; [{}^0 Future_t \; [{}^0 Frequency_w \; S] \; {}^0 In\_Time] =$$
$$\lambda w \lambda t \; \textit{If } [{}^0 In\_Time >_\tau t] \textit{ then } [[{}^0 Frequency_w \; S] \; {}^0 In\_Time] \textit{ else fail}$$

Here, $>_\tau$ means that the reference interval $In\_Time/(o\tau)$ comes after time t, or, in general, in a proper relation with respect to time t. *Future* receives the same type as *Past* (which is applied for sentences in past tenses), i.e. $((o(o(o\tau))(o\tau))\tau)$; S is the proposition to be evaluated and *Frequency* of type $((o(o\tau))o_{\tau\omega})$ is the frequency of time intervals in which the proposition S takes the truth-value **T** in world w. The schema for sentences in past tenses is similar; it differs only by applying the constituent *Past* instead of *Future*.[39]

If John will go twice to Brussel by plane in 2022, then by applying the above schema, we obtain this construction.

$$\lambda w \lambda t \; [\textit{If } [t \leq_\tau {}^0 2022] \textit{ then } [[{}^0 Twice_w \; \lambda w \lambda t \; [[{}^0 Do_{wt} \; {}^0 John \; {}^0 Go] \wedge$$
$$[{}^0 Asgn_{wt} \; {}^0 Go \; {}^0 Plain^{Inst}] \wedge [{}^0 Asgn_{wt} \; {}^0 Go \; {}^0 Brussel^{Dir3}]] \; {}^0 2022]$$
$$\textit{else fail}]$$

The frequency modifier *Twice* denotes a world-dependent function that takes a proposition $p \to o_{\tau\omega}$ to the class of those intervals $d \to (o\tau)$ which are contained in the chronology of p (i.e. $p_w \to (o\tau)$). The class of those intervals d that have a non-empty intersection with a reference

---

[38] More on dealing with time and calendars can be found in [23].
[39] A detailed analysis of particular kinds of tenses can be found in [19] (Section 2.5.2).

interval T is of cardinality two. Thus, the application of *Twice* of type $((o(o\tau))o_{\tau\omega})_\omega$ to a proposition p and reference interval T comes down to this Composition:

$$[[^0Twice_w\, p]\, T] = [^0Card\, \lambda d\, [\forall t\, [[d\, t]\supset p_{wt}]\wedge \exists t\, [[d\, t]\wedge [T\, t]]] = {}^02]$$

In our case, the interval T is the year 2022 and the proposition p is $\lambda w\lambda t\, [[^0Do_{wt}\, {}^0John\, {}^0Go]$ $\wedge [^0Asgn_{wt}\, {}^0Go\, {}^0Plain^{Inst}] \wedge [^0Asgn_{wt}\, {}^0Go\, {}^0Brussel^{Dir3}]]$. As a result, we have

$$[[^0Twice_w\, \lambda w\lambda t\, [[^0Do_{wt}\, {}^0John\, {}^0Go]\wedge$$
$$[^0Asgn_{wt}\, {}^0Go\, {}^0Plain^{Inst}] \wedge [^0Asgn_{wt}\, {}^0Go\, {}^0Brussel^{Dir3}]]]\, {}^02022] =$$
$$[^0Card\, \lambda d\, [\forall t\, [[d\, t] \supset [[^0Do_{wt}\, {}^0John\, {}^0Go]\wedge$$
$$[^0Asgn_{wt}\, {}^0Go\, {}^0Plain^{Inst}] \wedge [^0Asgn_{wt}\, {}^0Go\, {}^0Brussel^{Dir3}]]] \wedge \exists t\, [[d\, t] \wedge [^02022\, t]]] = {}^02]$$

Having such a detailed analysis, the agents can ask, for instance, 'How frequently will John go to Brussel in 2022?'. The technique of answering is the same as described above.

4.3. Learning by experience

As mentioned above, our agents can *learn* by experience. They are 'born' with a minimal ontology of concepts, which is gradually extended during agents' lifespan. When an agent a receives a message from an agent b containing a concept C not contained in a's ontology, a does not 'understand' the message. In such a case, the agent a answers to b by sending a message asking for a *refinement* (i.e. a definition or explication by means of simpler concepts) of the unknown concept C. In this way, agents learn new concepts and share their knowledge.[40]

Imagine, for instance, that an agent a comes to Brussel by car, and he is looking for a car park with vacancies. When asking an agent b for information on car parks in Brussel, agent b does not have in its ontology the concept of a car park with vacancies. Then b may learn by asking his fellow agents that 'A car park with vacancies is a car park some of whose parking spaces nobody has occupied yet.' The content of a query message asking for the definition of 'car park with vacancies' is $[^0Unrecognized_{wt}\, {}^0[^0Vacant\, {}^0Car\text{-}Park]]$.

Types. *Unrecognized*/$(o*_n)_{\tau\omega}$; *Vacant*/$((o\iota)_{\tau\omega}(o\iota)_{\tau\omega})$: a property modifier; *Car-Park*/$(o\iota)_{\tau\omega}$.

The content of the reply is

$$[^0Refine_{wt}\, {}^0[^0Vacant\, {}^0Car\text{-}Park]] =$$
$${}^0[\lambda w\lambda t\, \lambda x\, [[^0Car\text{-}Park_{wt}\, x] \wedge \exists y\, [[^0Space\_of_{wt}\, y\, x] \wedge \neg[^0Occupied_{wt}\, y]]]]$$

Then the constructions

$$[^0Vacant\, {}^0Car\text{-}Park]$$
and
$$[\lambda w\lambda t\, \lambda x\, [[^0Car\_Park_{wt}\, x] \wedge \exists y\, [[^0Space\_of_{wt}\, y\, x] \wedge \neg[^0Occupied_{wt}\, y]]]]$$

are *ex definitione* equivalent by constructing one and the same property.

Note that here we utilize *hyperintensional* features of TIL. The very *concept*, i.e. the closed *construction* of the respective entity, is asked for. An agent who is asking for the refinement wants to obtain more detailed *instruction* so that he/she understands what to do. And this instruction, i.e. procedure, is an object to deal with here, rather than the product of the procedure.

---

[40] Similar method has been applied in [7].

5. Conclusion

In this paper, we dealt with logical analysis of Wh-questions and its utilization in intelligent communication and reasoning of agents in a multiagent world. First, after a brief introduction to the fundamentals of our background theory of TIL, we introduced logical analysis of Wh-questions in TIL and the way of their answering by applying Gentzen's natural deduction system adjusted to natural language processing in TIL. Second, we proposed a new classification of Wh-questions that matches the logical structure of agents' knowledge and the logical types of possible direct answers to Wh-questions. To this end, we distinguished questions on static entities, dynamic activities and their further characteristics. We can raise questions on activities, their participants, substantive properties of objects, accidental characteristics and, last but not the least, the agents can ask for explication of concepts themselves and thus learn new concepts and enrich their ontology. Finally, we dealt with the logical analysis of Wh-questions and answers in TIL with respect to dynamic aspects of agents' reasoning, including questions on participants of activities specified in different tenses with reference time and frequency when this or that activity happened or will happen. By way of examples, we illustrated the application of the general analytic schema that takes into account presuppositions of such questions.

In summary, there are two main novelties of the paper. They are a new detailed classification of Wh-questions in particular with respect to the analysis of dynamic activities of human and or software agents. This classification is apt for agents reasoning and communication, and it is utilized in the rigorous logical analysis of agents' dynamic activities, including queries on the participants of the activities.

Further research will concentrate on a more detailed analysis of messages in different grammatical tenses, presuppositions of such messages and the dynamic aspects of agents' activities. Here, we will also apply the results obtained in the area of the application of Gentzen's natural deduction adjusted for TIL, so that these methods could be integrated into one intelligent system. We will also investigate the semantics of negative polarity items like 'contribute a red cent' or 'bat an eye lash' concerning presuppositions of questions.[41] This is the field where semantics and pragmatics happen to meet each other, as it is also in the case of topic-focus ambiguity of questions that have been under scrutiny in Duží [11].

Acknowledgements

This research was supported by the University of Oxford project 'New Horizons for Science and Religion in Central and Eastern Europe' funded by the John Templeton Foundation. The opinions expressed in the publication are those of the author(s) and do not necessarily reflect the view of the John Templeton Foundation. In addition, this work was supported by the project 'JG_2020_005 Times, events, and logical specification' of Palacký University of Olomouc and by the grant of SGS no. SP2021/87, VŠB-Technical University of Ostrava, Czech Republic, 'Application of Formal Methods in Knowledge Modelling and Software Engineering IV'. A version of this paper has been presented by Marie Duží as an invited talk at the conference Logic and Algorithms in Computational Linguistics 2021 (LACompLing2021).

---

[41] See, for instance, Xiang [61] or Guerzoni [30].

References

[1] J. Benthem van and S. Minicâ. Toward a dynamic logic of questions. *Journal of Philosophical Logic*, **41**, 633–669, 2012.

[2] R. Carnap. *Meaning and Necessity*. Chicago University Press, Chicago, 1947.

[3] A. Church. *The Calculi of Lambda Conversion*. Annals of Mathematical Studies. Princeton University Press, Princeton, 1941.

[4] M. Číhalová. Event ontology specification based on the theory of valency frames. In *Frontiers in Artificial Intelligence and Applications, Information Modelling and Knowledge Bases XXVII*, T. Welzer, H. Jaakkola, B. Thalheim, Y. Kiyoki and N. Yoshida, eds, pp. 299–313. IOS Press, Amsterdam, 2016.

[5] M. Číhalová and J. Štěpán. Logical classification of queries for MAS. In *20th International Conference on Soft Computing MENDEL 2014*, R. Matoušek, ed, pp. 253–258. CNP MUNI, Brno, 2014.

[6] M. Číhalová, M. Duží, M. Menšík and L. Vích. Process ontology. In *RASLAN 2010*, P. Sojka, ed, pp. 77–88. CNP MUNI, Brno, 2011.

[7] M. Číhalová, M. Duží, N. Ciprich and M. Menšík. Agents' reasoning using TIL-Script and Prolog. In *Frontiers in Artificial Intelligence and Applications*, T. Welzer Družovec, H. Jaakkola, Y. Kiyoki, T. Tokuda and N. Yoshida, eds, pp. 135–154. IOS Press, Amsterdam, 2010.

[8] P. R. Cohen and H. J. Levesque. Intention is choice with commitment. *Artificial Intelligence*, **42**, pp. 213–261, 1990a.

[9] P. R. Cohen and H. J. Levesque. Rational interaction as the basis for communication. In *Intentions in Communication*, P. R. Cohen, J. Morgan and M. E. Pollack, eds, pp. 221–256. The MIT Press, Cambridge, MA, 1990b.

[10] R. M. W. Dixon. A typology of causatives: Form, syntax, and meaning. In *Changing Valency: Case Studies in Transitivity*, R. M. W. Dixon and A. Y. Aikhenvald, eds, pp. 30–41. Cambridge University Press, New York, NY, 2000.

[11] M. Duží. Topic-focus articulation from the semantic point of view. *Computational Linguistics and Intelligent Text Processing*, Lecture Notes in Computer Science, **5449**, 220–232, Springer, 2009.

[12] M. Duží. Tenses and truth-conditions: A plea for *if-then-else*. In *The Logica Yearbook 2009*, M. Peliš, ed, pp. 63–80. College Publications, London, 2010.

[13] M. Duží. Property modifiers and intensional essentialism. *Computación y Sistemas*, **21**, 601–613, 2018.

[14] M. Duží. If structured propositions are logical procedures then how are procedures individuated? *Synthese*, **196**, 1249–1283, 2019.

[15] M. Duží and M. Číhalová. Questions, answers and presuppositions. *Computación y Sistemas*, **19**, 647–659, 2015.

[16] M. Duží and M. Fait. Question answering system in the TIL-Script language. In *Frontiers in Artificial Intelligence and Applications, Information Modelling and Knowledge Bases XXXI*, A. Dahanayake, J. Huiskonen, Y. Kiyoki, B. Thalheim, H. Jaakkola and N. Yoshida, eds, pp. 501–518. IOS Press, Amsterdam, 2020.

[17] M. Duží and M. Fait. A hyperintensional theory of intelligent question answering in TIL. In *Natural Language Processing in Artificial Intelligence—NLPinAI 2020, Springer Series Studies in Computational Intelligence (SCI)*, R. Loukanova, ed., vol. 939, pp. 69–104. Springer, Cham, 2021.

[18] M. Duží, M. Fait and M. Menšík. Context recognition for a hyperintensional inference machine. In *AIP Proceeding of ICNAAM 2016: International Conference of Numerical Analysis and Applied Mathematics*, AIP Publishing, vol. 1863. Article No. 330004, 2017. https://doi.org/10.1063/1.4992145.
[19] M. Duží, B. Jespersen and P. Materna. *Procedural Semantics for Hyperintensional Logic: Foundations and Applications of Transparent Intensional Logic*, Series Logic, Epistemology, and the Unity of Science, vol. 17. Springer, Berlin, 2010.
[20] M. Duží and B. Jespersen. Transparent quantification into hyperintensional objectual attitudes. *Synthese*, **192**, 635–677, 2015.
[21] M. Duží and B. Jespersen. Transparent quantification into hyperpropositional contexts de dicto. *Linguistic and Philosophy*. https://doi.org/10.1007/s10988-021-09344-9.
[22] M. Duží and M. Kosterec. A valid rule of β-conversion for the logic of partial functions. *Organon F*, **24**, 10–36, 2017.
[23] M. Duží and J. Macek. Analysis of time references in natural language by means of Transparent Intensional Logic. *Organon F*, **25**, 21–40, 2018.
[24] M. Duží and P. Vojtáš. Multi-criterion search from the semantic point of view. In *Frontiers in Artificial Inteligence and Applications, Information Modelling and Knowledge Bases XIX*, H. Jaakkola, Y. Kiyoki and T. Tokuda, eds, pp. 21–39. IOS Press, Amsterdam, 2008.
[25] S. Enqvist. Interrogative belief revision based in modal logic. *Journal of Philosophical Logic*, **38**, 527–548, 2010.
[26] J. Essberger. WH-question words. English Club. http://www.englishclub.com/vocabulary/wh-question-words.htm (1 January 2021, date last accessed).
[27] M. Fait and M. Duží. Substitution rules with respect to a context. In *Lecture Notes in Electrical Engineering*, I. Zelinka, P. Brandstetter, T. T. Dao, V. H. Duy and S. B. Kim, eds, vol. 554, pp. 55–66, Springer 2020. AETA 2018—Recent Advances in Electrical Engineering and Related Sciences: Theory and Applications.
[28] FIPA Communicative act library specification, 2002. http://www.fipa.org/specs/fipa00037/SC00037J.html (1 October 2021, date last accessed).
[29] J. Groenendijk. Questions and answers: Semantics and logic. In *Proceedings of the 2nd CologNET-ElsET Symposium. Questions and Answers: Theoretical and Applied Perspectives*, pp. 16–23. OTS, Utretcht, 2003.
[30] E. Guerzoni. Even and minimizer NPIs in Wh-questions, 2002. MIT Institute. Online https://www.researchgate.net/publication/252543892_Even_and_Minimizer_NPIs_in_Wh-Questions.
[31] A. Haida. The indefiniteness and focusing of question words. *Proceedings of the Semantics and Linguistic Theory*, **18**, 376–393, 2008.
[32] C. L. Hamblin. Questions in Montague's English. In *Foundations of Language*, vol. 10, pp. 41–53. Springer, 1973.
[33] D. Harrah. The logic of questions. In *Handbook of Philosophical Logic*, D. M. Gabbay and F. Guenthner, eds, vol. **8**, pp. 1–60. Springer, Dordrecht, 2002.
[34] P. Hayes and C. Menzel. A semantics for the knowledge interchange format, IJCAI 2001 workshop, 2001. Available online (referred 13 December 2021): https://www.researchgate.net/publication/2373814_A_Semantics_for_the_Knowledge_Interchange_Format.
[35] D. Hlaváčková and A. Horák. VerbaLex—New comprehensive lexicon of verb valencies for Czech. In *Computer Treatment of Slavic and East European Languages*, pp. 107–115. Slovenský Národný Korpus, Bratislava, Slovakia, 2006.

[36] A. Horák. Verb valency and semantic classification of verbs. In *Proceedings of TSD'98*, pp. 61–66. Masaryk University, Brno (CR), 1998.
[37] B. Jespersen. First among equals; co-hyperintensionality for structured propositions. *Synthese*, **199**, pp. 4483–4497, 2021. https://doi.org/10.1007/s11229-020-02987-4.
[38] B. Jespersen, M. Carrara and M. Duží. Iterated privation and positive predication. *Journal of Applied Logic*, **25**, S48–S71, 2017.
[39] B. Jespersen and M. Duží. Introduction to the special issue on hyperintensionality. *Synthese*, **192**, 525–534, 2015.
[40] L. Karttunen. Syntax and semantics of questions. *Linguistics and Philosophy*, **1**, 3–44, 1977.
[41] I. Kotová. *Logika dynamického Diskursu*. Master Thesis. VSB-Technical University of Ostrava, 2018.
[42] M. Krifka. For a structured meaning account of questions and answers. https://amor.cms.hu-berlin.de/~h2816i3x/Publications/StructuredQuestions.pdf (23 October 2021, date last accessed).
[43] M. Lopatková, Z. Žabokrtský and V. Kettnerová. VALLEX 2.5.—Logical structure of the lexicon, 2006. http://ufal.mff.cuni.cz/vallex/2.5/doc/structure_en.html#sec:frame (1 October 2021, date last accessed).
[44] R. Loukanova. β-reduction and antecedent-anaphora relations in the language of acyclic recursion. In *IWANN 2009, Part I*, J. Cabestany et al., eds , pp. 496–503, 2009.Vol. 5517 of *Lecture Notes in Computer Science*
[45] M. Menšík, M. Duží, A. Albert, V. Patschka and M. Pajr. Refining concepts by machine learning. *Computación y Sistemas*, **23**, 943–958, 2019.
[46] Y. N. Moschovakis. A logical calculus of meaning and synonymy. *Linguistics and Philosophy*, **29**, 27–89, 2006.
[47] B. Nebel, C. Rich and W. R. Swartout, eds. *Principles of Knowledge Representation and Reasoning: Proceedings of the Third International Conference (KR '92)*. M. Kaufmann, 1992.
[48] R. S. Patil, R. E. Pikes, P. F. Patel-Schneider, D. McKay, T. Finin, T. Gruber and R. Neches. *The DARPA Knowledge Sharing Effort: Progress Report in [47]*, pp. 777–788, 1992.
[49] M. Peliš and O. Majer. Logic of questions and public announcements. In *Logic, Language, and Computation. TbiLLC 2009*, N. Bezhanishvili, S. Löbner, K. Schwabe and L. Spada, eds., vol. 6618 of *Lecture Notes in Computer Science*, Springer, Berlin, Heidelberg, 2011.
[50] V. Punčochář. A relevant logic of questions. *Journal of Philosophical Logic*, **49**, 905–939, 2020.
[51] J. F. Sowa. *Knowledge Representation (Logical, Philosophical, and Computational Foundations)*. Brooks Cole Publishing Co., Pacific Grove, CA, 2000.
[52] P. Tichý. Questions, answers and logic. *American Philosophical Quartely*, **15**, 275–284, 1978. Reprinted in (Tichý 2004: 293–304).
[53] P. Tichý. The semantics of episodic verbs. *Theoretical Linguistics*, **7**, 263–296, 1980. Reprinted in (Tichý 2004: 411–446).
[54] P. Tichý. *The Foundations of Frege's Logic*. De Gruyter, 1988.
[55] P. Tichý. *Collected Papers in Logic and Philosophy*, V. Svoboda, B. Jespersen and C. Cheyne, eds. Prague: Filosofia, Czech Academy of Sciences, and Dunedin: University of Otago Press, 2004.
[56] Types of Wh-questions, 2021 Rochester Institute of Technology. https://www.rit.edu/ntid/sea/processes/wh/grammatical/types (1 January 2021, date last accessed).
[57] H. Wiese. WH-words are not 'interrogative' pronouns: The derivation of interrogative interpretations for constituent questions, 2002. University of Berlin. https://core.ac.uk/download/pdf/14514062.pdf (1 October 2021, date last accessed).

[58] A. Wisniewski. *Questions, Inferences, and Scenarios (Studies in Logic)*. College Publications, 2013.
[59] A. Wisniewski. Semantics of questions. In *The Handbook of Contemporary Semantic Theory*, L. Shalom and C. Fox, eds, Ch. 9, 271–313. Wiley Online Library, 2015.
[60] M. Wooldridge. *An Introduction to Multi-Agent Systems*. John Wiley & Sons, London, 2009.
[61] Y. Xiang. ONLY: An NPI-licenser and NPI-unlicenser. *Journal of Semantics*, **34**, 447–481, 2017.

Δ-TIL and Normative Systems[1]

Daniela Glavaničová

ABSTRACT: According to a widespread view, deontic modalities are relative to normative systems. Four arguments in favour of this suggestion will be presented in this paper. Nevertheless, I have proposed and defended an analysis of deontic modalities in terms of Transparent Intensional Logic (TIL) that is non-relativistic (with respect to normative systems) and accommodates minimal semantics of TIL. This leads to a question whether one can do justice to arguments for deontic relativism and put forward a *relativistic* analysis of deontic modalities in TIL. The main aim of this paper is to amend the former analysis of deontic modalities in terms of TIL to incorporate both the standard (relativistic) view and the minimal semantics of TIL.

0. Introduction

Deontic operators such as "it is obligatory", "it is forbidden" and "it is permitted" are of a particular interest to descriptive deontic logic. These operators are sentential operators, i.e. as Dretske (1970, 1007) puts it, "when affixed to

---

[1] I would like to thank M. Zouhar for his brilliant criticism, useful remarks and interesting discussions. I am also indebted to L. Bielik, F. Gahér, I. Sedlár and the anonymous referees of *Organon F*.

a sentence or statement, they operate on it to generate another sentence or statement." The pre-theoretical meanings of these operators are called *deontic modalities*. I have proposed and defended an analysis of deontic modalities in terms of Transparent Intensional Logic (TIL);[2] see Glavaničová (2015a; 2015b). I will use the term "Δ-TIL" to refer to it. In sum, Δ-TIL makes a (semantically based) distinction between *implicit* and *explicit* deontic modalities. The former are analysed as properties of propositions and the latter as properties of propositional constructions. The distinction proves to be useful in resolving deontic paradoxes, but also in analysing strong and weak permissions.[3] These are the main motivations for employing Δ-TIL. The analysis is non-relativistic[4] and is in perfect line with the spirit of minimal semantics of TIL. On the other hand, there are substantial arguments in favour of deontic relativism. Deontic relativists argue that deontic expressions (and their meanings) are relative to various authorities (I will refer to them as "normative systems"). The main aim of this paper is to show that Δ-TIL can accommodate deontic relativism without violating its minimal semantics.

Section 1 presents four arguments in favour of deontic relativism. Section 2 contains a brief summary of Δ-TIL. Section 3 introduces the problem of implementing deontic relativism to Δ-TIL and section 4 suggests two possible solutions of this problem. Section 5 concludes the results and the final section examines some possible objections to the proposed analysis.

1. A case for deontic relativism

We can state deontic relativism as follows:

(DR) Normative systems enter into the truth-conditions of some descriptive deontic sentences.

---

[2] TIL was comprehensively introduced in Tichý (1988). See also recent works on TIL, most notably Raclavský (2009), Duží, Jespersen & Materna (2010) and Duží & Materna (2012). I will briefly explain some basic notions of TIL in Section 2 of this paper.

[3] Hansson (2013) argues for the usefulness of the distinction between implicit and explicit permissions in a similar vein.

[4] Whenever I refer to relativism in the present paper, I have in mind deontic relativism, i.e. relativism with respect to normative systems.

Without loss of generality, we may confine our attention to deontic sentences of the form $O\varphi$ (i.e. φ *is obligatory*), since parallel arguments can be made for descriptive deontic sentences of the form $F\varphi$ and $P\varphi$. Consequently, we may replace (DR) with:

(DRO) Normative systems enter into the truth-conditions of some $O\varphi$-sentences.

The first argument in favour of deontic relativism then goes as follows: Let us consider a situation, where we talk about $O\varphi$-sentences without mentioning any normative system. A person A asks a person B, whether some $O\varphi$-sentence is true or not. It may happen that (i) B assigns a truth-value to a given $O\varphi$-sentence with respect to *relevant* normative system or (ii) *B hesitates to answer* the question and asks for further information.

Let P represent the sentence "Some men have more than one wife at a time" and let us look at examples of cases (i) and (ii):

The case (i): Imagine that Mr. Fiable, an inhabitant of France, is in Saudi Arabia, asking one of its inhabitants, Mr. Amin, whether $O\neg P$ is true or not. Suppose that Mr. Amin is a reliable source of information about the legal system of Saudi Arabia. He supposes that Mr. Fiable's question concerns the legal system of Saudi Arabia and replies that $O\neg P$ is false. From now on, Mr. Fiable will (truly) think that the legal system of Saudi Arabia permits polygamy.

The case (ii): Imagine that case (i) has never happened. Mr. Amin and Mr. Fiable are visiting Tilburg. Neither of them knows the Dutch legal system. Again, Mr. Fiable asks Mr. Amin, whether $O\neg P$ is true or not. In this case, Mr. Amin is not likely to make similar supposition as in the case (i). He would hesitate and ask which normative system the question concerns.

However, in both cases, Mr. Amin was not able to assign a truth-value to $O\neg P$ without relativizing it to normative systems. Thus, both cases support (DRO).

The second argument in favour of deontic relativism has the following form: It is quite reasonable to demand that normative systems be internally consistent. The commonly employed system of deontic logic – *Standard Deontic Logic* (SDL), has an axiom that accommodates this requirement; cf. McNamara (2006, 207-208):

(A1) All tautologous wffs of the language.
(A2) $O(\varphi \to \psi) \to (O\varphi \to O\psi)$
(A3) $O\varphi \to \neg O\neg\varphi$
(R1) If $\vdash \varphi$ and $\vdash \varphi \to \psi$ then $\vdash \psi$
(R2) If $\vdash \varphi$ then $\vdash O\varphi$

In particular, it has an axiom A3, which tells us that if φ is obligatory, then its negation is not. As Goble (2000, 113) puts it, this principle "explicitly precludes conflicts of obligation". However, different normative systems can give rise to conflicts of obligations (sometimes called normative contradictions or moral dilemmas). The conflict of obligation is a statement of the form $O\varphi \land O\neg\varphi$. Besides entailing normative conflicts, different normative systems can be explicitly contradicting each other. This happens when one normative system permits some φ (i.e. $\neg O\neg\varphi$ holds for such system), whilst the other does not (i.e. $O\neg\varphi$ holds for such system).[5]

Let Q represent the sentence "Antigone buries her brother Polynices". Consider the following story:

The case of Antigone: Polynices is a (dead) traitor to the city. Creon is a king. The burial of Polynices is forbidden by Creon's proclamation. Therefore, it ought to be the case that $\neg Q$ (under *human law*). However, the soul of Polynices needs the proper burial of his body to proceed to the underworld. Polynices should go to the underworld, so the gods demand his burial. Antigone is the only one who is willing to bury Polynices. Therefore, it ought to be the case that Q (under *divine law*).

Therefore, we have both $O\neg Q$ and OQ. Consequently, we can derive a contradiction by deriving $\neg O\neg Q$ or $\neg OQ$ (by A3 and R1). SDL as it stands thus cannot consistently allow for conflicts of obligation even across different normative systems.

A possible solution is deontic relativism. Let $O_x A$ represent schematically the formula OA relativized to normative system x. We should amend A3 in such a way that if φ is obligatory (under a *certain* normative system x) then $\neg\varphi$ is not (under *that* normative system); schematically:

---

[5] Recall our first example concerning polygamy.

(A3*) $O_x\varphi \to \neg O_x\neg\varphi$

The reasonable requirement of internal consistency is preserved, whilst the unreasonable requirement of consistency across various systems is dismissed: "Each set of norms or regulations is presumed to be internally consistent, and conflicts only emerge as a result of rivalry between sets of norms" (Goble 2000, 117). Furthermore, remaining axioms and rules have to be decorated with subscripts too. Otherwise A3* would be useless in proofs.

The third argument is similar to the second one. It goes as follows: certain English text (namely well-known *Contrary-to-Duty Paradox*) is apparently consistent. However, its (most plausible) formalisation in SDL immediately leads to contradiction. Deontic relativism enables us to account for this problem in a simple and straightforward way.

Roderick Chisholm introduced so-called *contrary-to-duty (CTD)* imperatives as "imperatives telling us what we ought to do if we neglect certain of our duties" (Chisholm 1963, 33).[6] The problem with CTD obligations can be set forth as an argument of the following form:

(P1) Sophie shall not kill.
(P2) It ought to be that if Sophie does not kill, she is not punished for killing.
(P3) If Sophie kills, she ought to be punished for killing.
(P4) Sophie kills.

The text consisting of (P1)-(P4) is obviously consistent. However, its most plausible formalisation in SDL is inconsistent:

(P1') $O\neg A$
(P2') $O(\neg A \to \neg B)$
(P3') $A \to OB$
(P4') A

---

[6] Throughout this paper, I will ignore the difference between descriptive and declarative (modes of) deontic sentences. While the distinction constitutes an interesting and widely discussed problem for deontic logic, it does not affect my arguments.

1. OB R1, P3', P4'
2. $O(\neg A \rightarrow \neg B) \rightarrow (O\neg A \rightarrow O\neg B)$ A2
3. $O\neg A \rightarrow O\neg B$ R1, P2', 2
4. $O\neg B$ R1, P1', 3
5. $OB \rightarrow \neg O\neg B$ A3
6. $\neg O\neg B$ R1, 1, 5
7. $\bot$ A1, 4, 6

We can solve CTD problem via deontic relativism treating primary and secondary subsystems of certain normative systems as different normative systems. Subsequently, we acquire relativistic version of our argument:

(P1*) $O_n \neg A$

(P2*) $O_n(\neg A \rightarrow \neg B)$

(P3*) $A \rightarrow O_m B$

(P4*) A

1. $O_m B$ R1*, P3*, P4*
2. $O_n (\neg A \rightarrow \neg B) \rightarrow (O_n \neg A \rightarrow O_n \neg B)$ A2*
3. $O_n \neg A \rightarrow O_n \neg B$ R1*, P2*, 2.
4. $O_n \neg B$ R1*, P1*, 3.
5. $O_m B \rightarrow \neg O_m \neg B$ A3*
6. $\neg O_m \neg B$ R1*, 1., 5.
7. $O_n \neg B \rightarrow \neg O_n B$ A3*
8. $\neg O_n B$ R1*, 4., 7.

Inconsistency is thus avoided, for the set $\{O_n \neg B, \neg O_m \neg B, \neg O_n B, O_m B\}$ is consistent. Therefore, deontic relativism can solve the CTD paradox. However, this is clearly not the only possible solution to the CTD paradox (cf. Goble 2013). Nevertheless, it illustrates the usefulness of deontic relativism.

Finally, let us consider the fourth argument in favour of deontic relativism. This argument takes its inspiration from Lou Goble, though his aims are different from ours. Obviously, the opponent of deontic relativism can still reject the axiom scheme A3 $O\varphi \rightarrow \neg O\neg\varphi$. He can thus avoid the derivation of explicit contradiction from the conflict of obligation. Yet, he has another problem, namely *deontic explosion*: the formula $(O\varphi \land O\neg\varphi) \to O\psi$ is still valid. Therefore, as Goble (2000, 114) puts it, "if there is any conflict of obligation, then everything is obligatory." We can give an axiomatic proof of that proposition (in SDL):

1. $(\varphi \land \neg\varphi) \to \psi$ A1
2. $O((\varphi \land \neg\varphi) \to \psi)$ R2, 1
3. $O(\varphi \land \neg\varphi) \to O\psi$ A2, 2, R1
4. $\varphi \to (\neg\varphi \to (\varphi \land \neg\varphi))$ A1
5. $O(\varphi \to (\neg\varphi \to (\varphi \land \neg\varphi)))$ R2, 4
6. $O\varphi \to O(\neg\varphi \to (\varphi \land \neg\varphi))$ A2, R1, 5
7. $O(\neg\varphi \to (\varphi \land \neg\varphi)) \to (O\neg\varphi \to O(\varphi \land \neg\varphi))$ A2
8. $O\varphi \to (O\neg\varphi \to O(\varphi \land \neg\varphi))$ A1, R1, 6, 7
9. $(O\varphi \land O\neg\varphi) \to O(\varphi \land \neg\varphi)$ A1, R1, 8
10. $(O\varphi \land O\neg\varphi) \to O\psi$ A1, R1, 3, 9

Goble (2000, 113) claims that any logic, which contains all of

(a) $\vdash (\varphi \land \neg\varphi) \to \psi$,
(b) if $\vdash \varphi \to \psi$, then $\vdash O\varphi \to O\psi$ and
(c) $\vdash (O\varphi \land O\psi) \to O(\varphi \land \psi)$

will necessarily contain

(d) $(O\varphi \land O\neg\varphi) \to O\psi$.

Suppose that we are in a situation where a conflict of obligation comes to play: the case of Antigone, the CTD paradox or some real-world moral dilemma. Furthermore, suppose we reject deontic relativism as well as the axiom scheme A3. The derivation of explicit contradiction from conflict of obligation is thus avoided. Yet we derive $O\psi$ for any formula ψ whatsoever. This result is obviously counterintuitive and poses a problem for the opponent of deontic relativism. One possible solution is to repudiate one of (a)-(c). Another one is to adopt deontic relativism, since this does not pose a problem for deontic relativist: The theorem (d) is still valid. Yet we cannot use it, since all we have is a formula of the form $O_n\varphi \wedge O_m\neg\varphi$, which does not constitute a genuine conflict of obligation (i.e. it is not the formula of the form $O_x\varphi \wedge O_x\neg\varphi$).

2. Δ-TIL and its minimal semantics

Δ-TIL is a part of the system of TIL. For this reason, there is a need to introduce TIL briefly. Furthermore, there is a need to explain semantic minimalism of TIL.

The first comprehensive account of TIL was provided by Pavel Tichý in *The Foundations of Frege's Logic*. TIL is a hyperintensional partial lambda calculus with types. It is the logic of *constructions*. Construction is a hyperintensional, structured entity, a theoretical explicate of the notion of *meaning*. TIL employs six different kinds of constructions, most important among them are variables, trivialisation, composition, and closure. Tichý devised an objectual analysis of *variables* (so variables are understood as full-fledged objects). A variable is a construction that constructs an object with respect to some valuation; notation $w, t, x, y\ldots$ (possibly with subscripts). *Trivialisation* is a simple construction which picks out an object and returns the very same object; notation ^0X. *Composition* is a construction that applies a function to some arguments and returns the value of this function on the given arguments (if there is such a value); notation $[X\ Y_1\ldots Y_n]$. Composition has its syntactic surrogate in lambda calculus, namely application. *Closure* is a construction that construes a function by abstraction; notation $[\lambda x_1\ldots x_n\ Y]$. Closure has its syntactic surrogate in lambda calculus too, namely lambda abstraction.

It is quite common in TIL to use four basic types: o for two truth-values, ι for individuals, τ for moments of times (or real numbers), and ω for possible worlds. Constructions have higher order atomic types $*_n$ ($n \in \mathbb{N}$). These atomic types are the building blocks, and all mathematically possible functions are built upon them (as is quite common in lambda calculus). For instance, proposition is a function from world courses to truth-values, i.e. it has a type ((οτ)ω), in an abbreviated form o_τω; property of individuals has a type οι_τω; set of propositions has a type (o(o_τω)) and so on. Constructions of propositions (propositional constructions) are theoretical explicates of philosophically important notion of *structured proposition*.

The semantics of TIL is in accordance with semantic minimalism. According to semantic minimalism, as Borg (2009) puts it, "syntax provides the sole route to semantic content." Yet there are two characteristic versions of semantic minimalism (see Zouhar 2012, 708-713).[7] According to the first version of semantic minimalism, "[t]he semantic content of a sentence S is the content that all utterances of S share. It is the content that all the utterances of S express no matter how different their contexts of use are" (Cappelen & Lepore 2005, 143). According to the second version of semantic minimalism,

> literal meaning is held to be entirely context-invariant – a sentence, individuated in terms of its syntax, possesses the very same meaning no matter when, where, or by whom it is produced. (…) [A]s far as semantics is concerned, we should (…) concentrate just on the meaning of sentence-types as formal objects of study. (Borg 2004, 215)

This second version of semantic minimalism is closer to the semantics of TIL. However, these issues have not been extensively discussed yet. Sufficient examination of background syntactic theory of TIL is needed for a sufficient examination of minimal semantics of TIL. In any case, background syntactic theory of TIL needs to distinguish between surface structure and deep structure (or logical form) of expressions. This is so because the constructions of TIL involve modal and temporal variables, despite the fact that such variables are not present in surface structure of (empirical) expressions, but only in deep structure. It is this deep structure what constitutes the relevant basis for semantic analysis. Moreover, the semantic analysis is context invariant. Surely, one needs context to find the *intended* meaning, yet one does not need context to find the *literal* meaning. The apparent semantic function of context is explained away by *ambiguity*. Finally, since TIL has minimal semantics, Δ-TIL (as a part of TIL) has to adopt semantic minimalism too.

Let me now briefly introduce Δ-TIL. Deontic operators O, P and F stand for *implicit deontic modalities*. Implicit deontic modality is a function from world courses (i.e. a function from possible worlds to function from moments of time) to sets of propositions. Deontic operators O^*, P^* and F^* stand for *explicit deontic modalities*. Explicit deontic modality is a function from world courses to sets of constructions.

---

[7] For further discussion of semantic minimalism (and its competitors), cf. Zouhar (2011).

Δ-TIL and normative systems

Δ-TIL assumes that a sentence of the form "A is obligatory" is true *simpliciter*, as one can see from the truth-conditions stated below. Let ^0T constructs the truth-value True, ^0F constructs the truth-value False and let C be a construction of a proposition. We write $\alpha : \beta$ if and only if (iff) α construes the same object as β (with respect to some valuation).[8] The truth-conditions of formulas involving O and O^* are then as follows:[9]

$^0T : [^0O_{wt}\ C]$ iff $C \in O_{wt}$
$^0F : [^0O_{wt}\ C]$ otherwise.

$^0T : [^0O^*_{wt}\ ^0C]$ iff $^0C \in O^*_{wt}$
$^0F : [^0O^*_{wt}\ ^0C]$ otherwise.

Similarly, for P and P^*. The truth-conditions of formulas involving F and F^* are defined in the standard way via O and O^* (i.e., something is forbidden iff its negation is obligatory). The following schema represents the analysis of the expression "it is obligatory, that":

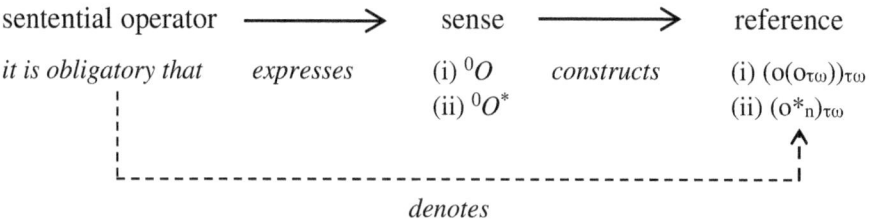

Note that when someone asserts that *It is obligatory that A*, it is ambiguous. The analysis (i), but also the analysis (ii) is correct. Surely, one can consequently ask which one is the *preferred* analysis. There is a way to answer such a question: namely, by answering additional question, whether the individual in question is talking about explicitly formulated obligations of about implicit consequences of some explicitly formulated obligations. Yet this is a step beyond the realm of semantics.

---

[8] This definition employs the notion of *match*, introduced by Pavel Tichý; see Tichý (1982, 64-65).

[9] We will use an arbitrary construction X with lower-case „wt" in a standard way as an abbreviation for $[[X\ w]\ t]$.

3. The problem

The problem can be stated this way: How to amend the analysis to be both in line with deontic relativism and semantic minimalism? There are at least two possible solutions:

> we might seek to complicate the syntax of natural language sentences, positing a range of 'hidden indexicals' which provide the syntactic triggers for the additional context-sensitivity (...) [or] introduce additional complexity into the way in which sentences map to truth-conditions, holding that the context-sensitivity (...) lies within the circumstances of evaluation, not in a truly indexical content for sentences. (Borg 2009, 424)

The former is characteristic of indexicalism. However, we want the analysis to accommodate semantic minimalism (recall that Δ-TIL is a part of TIL, so it should be consistent with TIL). Hence, we will consider *minimal indexicalism*[10] rather than mere indexicalism. What does it mean for Δ-TIL? A free variable ranging over normative systems would occur in deontic construction. Therefore, this construction would be open and we would need the process of completion (saturation – see Bach 1994) for obtaining a closed construction. Normative systems would thus belong to the *context of use*[11] and expressions denoting them would function just like indexicals. If normative systems belong to the context of use, one needs to specify them to determine *what has been said*.

The latter option is characteristic of (non-indexical) relativism. In this case, a lambda-bound variable ranging over normative systems would occur in deontic construction. Therefore, we gain closed construction, but it would not be a propositional construction anymore, since additional parameter for normative systems would be present in its type. Normative systems would thus belong to the *circumstances of evaluation* and would function just like possible worlds (and moments of time). If normative systems belong to the

---

[10] Minimal indexicalism was introduced by Marián Zouhar. For the most comprehensive account, see Zouhar (2011).

[11] The distinction between context of use and circumstances of evaluation was introduced in Kaplan (1989) (written already in 1977). For further discussion, see Zouhar (2013a).

circumstances of evaluation, one needs to specify them to determine *truth-values* of deontic sentences in question.

4. The two possible solutions

To begin with, let us look at a more detailed version of the previous analysis. The deontic sentence "C is obligatory" was supposed to represent either (i) the implicit deontic construction $[\lambda w \lambda t\ [^{0}O_{wt}\ C]]$ or (ii) the explicit deontic construction $[\lambda w \lambda t\ [^{0}O^{*}_{wt}\ {}^{0}C]]$. The construction $[\lambda w \lambda t\ [^{0}O_{wt}\ C]]$ is an abbreviation for $[\lambda w \lambda t\ [[[^{0}O\ w]\ t]\ C]]$; the construction $[\lambda w \lambda t\ [^{0}O^{*}_{wt}\ {}^{0}C]]$ abbreviates $[\lambda w \lambda t\ [[[^{0}O^{*}\ w]\ t]\ {}^{0}C]]$.

We need to add variables for normative systems. This leads to a problem: What is the proper type of normative systems? This remains, however, an open question. One option is to add a further atomic type to the basis. However, for the purposes of this paper, it will suffice to analyse them simply as individuals (note that even individual authorities such as parents, teachers, emperors etc. can be integrated into this framework). Therefore, variables for normative systems will be *individual variables*, so they will construe individuals, in technical notation $n \rightarrow_v \iota$ (we read this as "n v-construes an individual"). The operator O will represent a function from individuals to properties of propositions, in technical notation $O/(o o_{\tau\omega})_{\tau\omega\iota}$. The operator O^{*} will represent a function from individuals to properties of propositional constructions, in technical notation $O^{*}/(o^{*}_{n})_{\tau\omega\iota}$. Remaining types are $w \rightarrow_v \omega$ (w v-construes a possible world, i.e. w is a possible-world variable) and $t \rightarrow_v \tau$ (t v-construes a moment of time, i.e. t is a time-moment variable).

4.1. Minimal indexicalism

Δ-TIL combined with minimal indexicalism offers the first possible solution. The analysis of some $O\varphi$-sentence will be

(1.1)   implicit deontic construction $[\lambda w \lambda t\ [[[^{0}O\ n]\ w]\ t]\ C]]$ or

(1.2)   explicit deontic construction $[\lambda w \lambda t\ [[[^{0}O^{*}\ n]\ w]\ t]\ {}^{0}C]]$.

As we can see, the constructions in (1.1) and (1.2) are open, since they contain a free variable n. The evaluation (saturation) of this variable is needed to acquire a propositional construction.

4.2. Non-indexical relativism

Δ-TIL combined with non-indexical relativism offers the second possible solution. The analysis of some $O\varphi$-sentence will be

(2.1) implicit deontic construction $[\lambda n \lambda w \lambda t [[[^0 O\ n]\ w]\ t]\ C]]$ or

(2.2) explicit deontic construction $[\lambda n \lambda w \lambda t [[[^0 O* n]\ w]\ t]\ ^0C]]$.

As we can see, constructions in (2.1) and (2.2) are closed (because all variables are bound by lambda abstractors). Note that as a straightforward consequence of this analysis, constructions in (2.1) and (2.2) are no longer propositional constructions, and subsequently, deontic sentences do not denote propositions (in the standard sense) anymore.

5. Concluding remarks

Either way, the evaluation of n is needed for a truth-evaluation of certain $O\varphi$-sentence. Is it plausible? Let us recall our examples from the first section. We might (reasonably) hesitate to answer a question such as "Is φ obligatory?", since for a truth-evaluation of the sentence of the form $O\varphi$, we need to check the normative system in question. If no normative system is given at all, we do not know what to check. This result is in perfect accordance with the above presented analysis.

Finally, we may ask which of the competing options is better. Since in deontic sentences there is no explicit reference to normative systems (exactly as no explicit reference to possible worlds and moments of time), the second option seems more plausible. Yet the first option is feasible too. Further research is needed to examine them.

6. Response to possible objections

This section will anticipate some possible objections to the analysis and respond to them. To begin with, one can accept deontic relativism proposed in section 1 without thereby accepting the version of deontic relativism proposed in section 4. Certainly, there are alternative theories designed to account for the problems described in section 1: namely contextualism, ambiguity theory, subjectivism and objectivism; cf. MacFarlane (2014, 280-285).

To put it simply: Contextualists claim that there is just one word "obligatory", but since this word is context-sensitive, different contexts assign different meanings to this word. Ambiguity theory claims that there are many words "obligatory$_1$", "obligatory$_2$", …, with different meanings corresponding to them. Subjectivism claims that "obligatory" is relative to the normative system the speaker has in mind. Objectivism claims that "obligatory" is relative to the most general (common, important…) system of norms.

Yet none of them is able to explain disagreements.[12] Let M represent the sentence "The Maori children learn the names of their ancestors". Sophie asserts that OM is true, whilst Pavel asserts that OM is false. As regards the sentence OM, they are in a disagreement. How is it possible? Easily: Sophie thinks of the tribal laws Maoris have and Pavel thinks of the official law in New Zealand, however, they are talking about the same sentence with the same meaning. It is this sentence (and its meaning) what is the subject matter of their disagreement.

According to contextualism, they use the same word "obligatory", but contexts assign different meanings to this single word. They are both right, they assert the same sentence, but with different meanings. There is thus no disagreement. The same holds for subjectivism. According to ambiguity theory, they use different words (with different meanings). Again, they are both right. Yet they assert different sentences (with different meanings). Hence, there is again no disagreement. According to objectivism, they use the same word "obligatory", which is relative to the "universal law" (whatever it is). Yet, it is problematic to say what this so-called universal law is supposed to be.

Can deontic relativism solve the problem of disagreements? That is beyond doubt, since Sophie and Pavel are in a disagreement about a certain sentence with certain meaning. However, the meaning of this sentence needs evaluation (or saturation) of deontic variables for a truth-evaluation of the sentence. In our case, such evaluation (or saturation) will reveal the fact that Sophie and Pavel were thinking about different normative systems. Strictly speaking, they can be both right, because (free or lambda-bound) variables for normative systems will be evaluated differently. This does not necessarily mean the end of disagreement: Sophie and Pavel can still disagree about the preferred normative system.

---

[12] The argument takes its inspiration from MacFarlane (2014, 280-285) and Kratzer (1977, 338).

Moreover, there are further disadvantages of alternative theories. Firstly, contextualism is worse than minimal indexicalism for methodological reasons (see Zouhar 2013b). Secondly, ambiguity theory causes annoying profusion of "oughts"; (see Jackson 1991, 471; and MacFarlane 2014, 284). Similarly, contextualism causes annoying profusion of oughts. Finally, the objective sense of "obligatory" is too general. We usually use this word in talking about different legal systems, moral codes or tribal laws and so on. We can thus conclude that "obligatory" we are using in natural language is not the objective one.

Furthermore, one can accept deontic relativism without thereby accepting semantic minimalism. It is not the purpose of the present paper to criticize all the alternatives to semantic minimalism. Rather we outline some positive reasons, inspired by Cappelen & Lepore (2005, 151-154). Firstly, semantic minimalism does not end up requiring that semanticists do metaphysics. Fortunately, minimalism does not require of semantics to answer the question "What is obligation?" which is far beyond the borders of semantics. Secondly,

> [it] can account for how the same content can be expressed, claimed, asserted, questioned, investigated, etc. in radically different contexts. It is this content that enables audiences who find themselves in radically different contexts to understand each other, to agree or disagree, to question and debate with each other. (Cappelen & Lepore 2005, 152)

Moreover, it "can account for how Inter-Contextual Disquotational Indirect Reports can be true where the reporter and the reportee find themselves in radically different context..." (Cappelen & Lepore 2005, 152). Suppose the speaker S utters the sentence "A is obligatory". We can (truly) utter the sentence "S said that A is obligatory." Semantic minimalism can explain this fact, since it admits certain common content – in particular, the (minimal) semantic content of the sentence "A is obligatory".

Finally, one can accept deontic relativism without thereby accepting that deontic operator is relative to *a particular* (explicitly unspecified) normative system. We claim that a formula of the form $O\varphi$ means that φ is obligatory under *a particular* normative system. However, it seems that many other quantifiers can be employed. Let us discuss at least the applicability of existential and universal quantifiers. Hence, $O\varphi$ can mean (E) φ is obligatory under *some* normative systems or (A) φ is obligatory under *all* normative systems.

We can make use of the example discussed in section 1. Again, let P represent the sentence "Some men have more than one wife at a time". Consider the following situations:

The case of polygamous Saudi Arabia: Mr. Fiable, an inhabitant of France, is in Saudi Arabia, asking one of its inhabitants, Mr. Amin, whether $O\neg P$ is true or not. Mr. Amin is a reliable source of information about the legal system of Saudi Arabia. He supposes that Mr. Fiable's question concerns the legal system of Saudi Arabia and replies that $O\neg P$ is false. From now on, Mr. Fiable will (truly) think that the legal system of Saudi Arabia permits polygamy. However, the option (E) claims that $O\neg P$ is true because there is at least one normative system, which forbids P (e.g. the legal system of France). Yet it seems that Mr. Amin was right in claiming the opposite.

The case of monogamous France: Mr. Amin is in France, asking Mr. Fiable whether $O\neg P$ is true or not. Mr. Fiable is a reliable source of information about the French legal system. He supposes that Mr. Amin's question concerns the French legal system and replies that $O\neg P$ is true. From now on, Mr. Amin will (truly) think that the French legal system forbids polygamy. However, an option (A) claims that $O\neg P$ is false, because there is at least one normative system, which permits P (e.g. the legal system of Saudi Arabia). Yet it seems that Mr. Fiable was right in claiming the opposite.

The answer "$O\neg P$ is false" was expected in the case of polygamous Saudi Arabia. Yet according to (E), $O\neg P$ is true, since there is at least one normative system, which forbids P. Hence, the option (E) gives a wrong prediction. Moreover, the answer "$O\neg P$ is true" was expected in the case of monogamous France. Yet according to (A), $O\neg P$ is false, since there is at least one normative system, which permits P. Hence, the option (A) gives a wrong prediction.

Certainly the argument demonstrates only the *insufficiency* of analysing $O\varphi$-sentences in a fashion suggested by (E) or (A). This result is sufficient for the present purposes. Note, however, that it does not demonstrate their uselessness. We can employ such quantifiers when needed. For instance, we can use them to analyse sentences such as "It ought to be the case that φ under some system of norms" and "It ought to be the case that φ under any system of norms". Furthermore, we can use restricted quantifiers.

References

BACH, K. (1994): Conversational Impliciture. *Mind and Language* 9, No. 2, 124-162.
BORG, E. (2004): Formal Semantics and Intentional States. *Analysis* 64, 215-223.
BORG, E. (2009): Semantic Minimalism. In: Cummings, L. (ed.): *The Pragmatics Encyclopedia*. Routledge, 423-425.
CAPPELEN, H. & LEPORE, E. (2005): *Insensitive Semantics: A Defence of Semantic Minimalism and Speech Act Pluralism*. Oxford: Blackwell Publishing.
DUŽÍ, M., JESPERSEN, B. & MATERNA, P. (2010): *Procedural Semantics for Hyperintensional Logic. Foundations and Applications of Transparent Intensional Logic*. Berlin: Springer.
DUŽÍ, M. & MATERNA, P. (2012): *TIL jako procedurální logika (Průvodce zvídavého čtenáře Transparentní intensionální logikou)*. [*TIL as a Procedural Logic.*] Bratislava: aleph.
DRETSKE, F. (1970): Epistemic Operators. *Journal of Philosophy* 67, No. 24, 1007-1023.
GLAVANIČOVÁ, D. (2015a): K analýze deontických modalít v Transparentnej intenzionálnej logike. [On the Analysis of Deontic Modalities in Transparent Intensional Logic.] *Organon F* 22, No. 2, 211-228.
GLAVANIČOVÁ, D. (2015b): Implicitné a explicitné deontické modality. [Implicit and Explicit Deontic Modalities.] In: Brzobohatá, K. (ed.): *Logika pro právní praxi*. Brno: Masarykova univerzita, 36-45.
GOBLE, L. (2000): Multiplex Semantics for Deontic Logic. *Nordic Journal of Philosophical Logic 5*, No. 2, 113-134.
GOBLE, L. (2013): Prima Facie Norms, Normative Conflicts, and Dilemmas. In: Gabbay, D. M. et al. (eds.): *Handbook of Deontic Logic and Normative Systems*. College Publications.
CHISHOLM, R. M. (1963): Contrary-to-Duty Imperatives and Deontic Logic. *Analysis* 23, 33-36.
JACKSON, F. (1991): Decision-Theoretic Consequentialism and the Nearest and Dearest Objection. *Ethics* 101, No. 3, 461-482.
KAPLAN, D. (1989): Demonstratives. In: Almog, J., Perry, J. & Wettstein, H. (eds.): *Themes from Kaplan*. Oxford: Oxford University Press, 565-614.
KRATZER, A. (1977): What 'Must' and 'Can' Must and Can Mean. *Linguistics and Philosophy* 1, No. 3, 337-355.
MACFARLANE, J. (2014). *Assessment Sensitivity: Relative Truth and its Applications*. Oxford: Clarendon Press.
MCNAMARA, P. (2006): Deontic Logic. In: Gabbay, D. M. & Woods, J. (eds.): *Handbook of the History of Logic*: *Logic and the Modalities in the Twentieth Century*. Vol. 7. Amsterdam: Elsevier, 197-288.
RACLAVSKÝ, J. (2009): *Jména a deskripce: logicko-sémantická zkoumání*. [*Names and Descriptions: Logico-Semantical Investigations.*] Olomouc: Nakladatelství Olomouc.

TICHÝ, P. (1982): Foundations of Partial Type Theory. *Reports on Mathematical Logic* 14, 59-72.
TICHÝ, P. (1988): *The Foundations of Frege's Logic*. Berlin – New York: de Gruyter.
ZOUHAR, M. (2011): *Význam v kontexte*. [*Meaning in Context.*] Bratislava: aleph.
ZOUHAR, M. (2012): Indexikalizmus, sémantický minimalizmus a pravdivostný obsah. [Indexicalism, Semantic Minimalism, and Truth-Conditional Content.] *Filozofia* 67, No. 9, 705-717.
ZOUHAR, M. (2013a): Epistemický kontextualizmus a jeho motivácia. [Epistemic Contextualism and Its Motivation.] *Organon F* 20, Suppl. issue 2, 171-186.
ZOUHAR, M. (2013b): Sémanticky relevantné pragmatické procesy (2): Testy a metodologické aspekty. [Semantically Relevant Pragmatic Processes (2): Tests and Methodological Aspects.] *Filozofia* 68, No. 4, 296-308.

FICTION AND RELIGION

Rethinking Role Realism
Daniela Glavaničová

Role realism is a promising realist theory of fictional names. Different versions of this theory have been suggested by Gregory Currie, Peter Lamarque, Stein Haugom Olsen, and Nicholas Wolterstorff. The general idea behind the approach is that fictional characters are to be analysed in terms of roles, which in turn can be understood as sets of properties (or alternatively as kinds or functions from possible worlds to individuals). I will discuss several advantages and disadvantages of this approach. I will then propose a novel hyperintensional version of role realism (which I will call impossibilism), according to which fictional names are analysed in terms of individual concepts that cannot be matched by a reference (a full-blooded individual). I will argue that this account avoids the main disadvantages of standard role realism.

1. Introduction

Purely fictional names (henceforth fictional names)—in other words, expressions such as *Sherlock Holmes*, *Thérèse Raquin* and *Tengo Kawana*—constitute a challenge for semantic analysis. Fictional names can be tentatively defined as follows: 'an expression *N* is a fictional name if it is true in the fiction that *N* is a proper name but not true in the fiction of any existing person or thing that *N* is a name of that person or thing' (Currie, 1990, p. 128).[1] More often than not, it is supposed that fictional names are genuine proper names; as it often turns out, however, accounts that work rather well for standard proper names fail to do justice to fictional names. The challenge is that in the case of standard proper names, real, full-blooded referents are available. Such referents are not at our disposal in the case of fictional names, however—or at least not in a straightforward way. How might we devise a plausible semantics of fictional names in the face of an apparent lack of full-blooded referents combined with seemingly meaningful talk about fictional characters?

Numerous accounts have been proposed by those who have accepted this challenge. The general division of the proposed accounts is into realism and antirealism (see Kroon and Voltolini, 2018). The former encompasses accounts such as abstract artifactualism (Thomasson, 1999), possibilism (Lewis, 1978; Haraldsen, 2017), Meinongianism (Zalta, 1983; Berto, 2011), and role realism (Wolterstorff, 1980; Currie, 1988; Lamarque and Olsen, 1994). Gappy proposition theory (Adams, Fuller, and Stecker, 1997; Braun, 1993 and 2005) and various forms of fictionalism (Walton, 1990; Brock 2002 and 2016; Sainsbury, 2010; Everett, 2013; Armour-Garb and Woodbridge, 2015) can be subsumed under the latter heading (see also Friend, 2014 for a view employing mental files). However, it seems that neither pure realism nor pure antirealism is capable of accounting for the core data related to fictional names and fictional characters. The literature on fictional names (both realist and antirealist) supports this simple observation. For instance,

---

1 This definition is purposely neutral with respect to 'real names' (such as *London*) that appear in works of fiction.

Thomasson writes that 'no theory has won universal acceptance by giving us all we (pre-theoretically) wanted' (Thomasson, 2003, p. 205). Brock (2002, p. 14), in turn, considers it impossible to take the whole fictional discourse at face value. Braun (2005, p. 613) goes so far as to claim that 'most ordinary speakers' beliefs about fiction really are (deep down) inconsistent'. It seems, however, that speakers are not contradicting themselves and that realism gets one part of the picture right, and antirealism the remaining part. Because of this, a theory that combines features of realism with those of antirealism can fare well with respect to our pre-theoretical intuitions. Another motivation for the present paper is the fact that role realism is not currently getting the attention it deserves.[2]

This being said, role realism *will* be the centre of attention in this paper. Role realism is a realist account of fictional names, different versions of which have been suggested by Gregory Currie, Peter Lamarque and Stein Haugom Olsen, and Nicholas Wolterstorff. I will formulate an alternative role realist view that attempts to overcome the main problems of standard role realism. This view distinguishes between hyperintensional, intensional, and extensional occurrences of fictional names. Hyperintensional occurrences of fictional names are analysed in terms of individual concepts in the spirit of a careful hyperintensional and broadly Fregean form of realism about fictional characters (noting that the question of whether Frege himself was a realist or an antirealist remains highly controversial). Intensional occurrences of fictional names are analysed in terms of roles as functions from possible worlds to individuals. Extensional occurrences of fictional names are analysed in agreement with antirealism (full-blooded referents do not exist). Because of this, the account can be construed as a combination of realism with respect to the sense of fictional names and antirealism with respect to the reference of fictional names.

The structure of the paper is as follows: I provide a brief outline of the three most prominent versions of role realism (Section 2). The section focuses on highlighting the benefits of role realism. I then outline five difficult problems associated with role realism (Section 3). I consider whether they can be avoided and argue that a hyperintensional version of role realism can indeed deal with them, thus providing a promising alternative to existing role realist accounts (Sections 4–5). I then discuss three issues connected to fiction and hyperintensionality (Section 6). Finally, I summarize the paper's core results (Section 7).

2. Versions of Role Realism

Role realism is a bundle of realist theories of fictional names. The main idea behind this approach is that fictional characters are to be analysed in terms of roles. Roles, in turn, can be understood as sets of properties (which are essential to the given fictional character), or alternatively as kinds or as functions from possible worlds to individuals (functions which map a possible world to an individual that is the given fictional character in that world, provided there is such an individual). Three main versions of this approach have

---

2   A noteworthy exception is a recent paper by Stokke (2020). The author analyses fictional names in terms of individual concepts; unlike in the present paper, however, the latter are understood as functions from possible worlds to individuals (and thus intensionally, not hyperintensionally).

been proposed by Wolterstorff, Currie, and Lamarque and Olsen, respectively. I cannot describe these accounts in full detail here, so I will focus on features that are crucial, distinctive or particularly relevant to our purposes.

Wolterstorff (1980, p. 144) defends a Platonist variant of role realism, analysing fictional characters in terms of person-kinds ('not persons of a certain kind, but certain person-kinds'). Wolterstorff distinguishes kinds from sets and specifies kinds in terms of eleven definitions. For the present purposes, it is enough to say that kinds are abstract entities which can have examples. Kinds are not ontologically dependent on their examples, however, and their examples vary across possible worlds and times (Wolterstorff, 1980, p. 51). A person-kind is a kind such that to be an example of it, an entity must be a person. Kinds exist eternally. Creativity and authorial creation challenge this Platonist aspect of Wolterstorff's theory. In his account, fictional characters, understood as person-kinds, are not created (in the sense of being brought into existence) by authors of fiction: the originality lies in the selection, not in the creation. However, while kinds exist necessarily, they are not necessarily fictional characters.

Currie has formulated a complex possibilist version of role realism, thereby admitting that it is possible that Sherlock Holmes exists. The account offers different semantics of fictional names for different contexts (Currie, 1990, p. 181):

> The semantics of fictional names gets more complex the farther we move away from the fiction itself. In fiction itself these expressions serve merely to introduce bound variables. When we speak about the fiction they become disguised definite descriptions: expressions that have denotation in some worlds but not in others. When we move outside the world of the fiction and say things about the character that do not correspond to what is said in the fiction, they become names of functions from worlds to individuals. In these contexts, they denote superworldly, necessarily existing things.

Currie discusses three types of discourse that contain fictional names: *fictive* (occurrences within works of fiction), *metafictive* (statements about fiction) and *transfictive* (statements about characters that do not correspond to what is said in the fiction). The analysis of fictional names moves from bound variables (fictive discourse), through disguised definite descriptions (metafictive discourse), to names of functions from possible worlds to individuals (transfictive discourse). Prima facie, functions are not appropriate entities for being detectives (this problem will be discussed shortly as the *category mistake objection*).

Lamarque and Olsen propose a theory of fictional names which is clearly not Platonist in the sense of analysing fictional names (and fictional characters) in terms of necessarily existing abstract entities. This brings the account substantially closer to abstract artifactualism. Lamarque and Olsen (1994, pp. 42–43) propose that

> to speak of a fictional object (or character) is just a way of speaking of a certain kind of descriptive content; it does not involve reference to what does or does not exist in the world. A fictional object (or character) is an intensional object originating in a fictional description, such that the characteristics of the object are determined by the way it is described. What is important is origin not reference.

Lamarque further develops the theory, suggesting that fictional characters are initiated or indicated types. He employs Levinson's distinction between *types per se* (which can be understood as eternal abstract entities) and *initiated types* (which are not eternal and are ontologically dependent on authors). Fictional characters are grounded in acts of storytelling and have interest-relative and context-sensitive identity conditions (Lamarque, 2010, pp. 200–201).

The three accounts briefly sketched above share many positive features. They accommodate speaking and thinking about fictional characters, whether in lay discourse or in the serious discourse of literary criticism. They allow for the co-identification of fictional characters. In addition, they accommodate having attitudes towards fictional characters, such as admiring fictional characters or fearing them, even though some may doubt whether the entities provided by role realists are apt for being subjects of such attitudes. Furthermore, these accounts allow for quantification over fictional characters. While many of these advantages are shared with other realist accounts, they nevertheless make role realism a powerful alternative to antirealist accounts. Moreover, role realism proposes an analysis in terms of entities that are useful for the analysis of natural language beyond the domain of fiction, for instance in the analysis of definite descriptions. This feature makes role realism an attractive alternative to other realist accounts.

3. Five Problems for Role Realism

These benefits aside, this section focuses on five difficult problems faced by role realists. The first problem, which applies to all three versions of role realism, is Kripke's case against possibilism. The second problem is the problem of 'a rampant relativism of meaning', as voiced against Currie's proposal. The third problem is the category mistake objection, which again applies to all three versions. The fourth problem is the problem of authorial creation. This problem pertains mainly to Wolterstorff's and Currie's proposals. The final problem is the problem of negative existentials (or the problem of nonexistence claims). This problem applies (to some extent) to all realist theories of fictional names, even though Meinongian non-existents are perhaps better off.

Kripke's case against possibilism consists of two arguments. The first is that even if we were to find someone who instantiated all the properties ascribed to a fictional character in a given work of fiction, this individual could not plausibly be identified with that fictional character and could not be a semantic value of the given fictional name (under the supposition that this name is fictional). As Kripke (1980, p. 157) puts it: 'The mere discovery that there was indeed a detective with exploits like those of Sherlock Holmes would not show that Doyle was writing about this man'. Naturally, one may argue that we do not always know whether the author was writing about a real person or not (given that it is possible to write fiction about real people). Kripke admits that it is possible to find out that an expression is not a fictional name (the epistemic possibility that our supposition that *Sherlock Holmes* is a fictional name is mistaken). However, it is not metaphysically possible for a fictional name to refer accidentally to a real person (Kripke, 2013, pp. 41–42).

Kripke's second argument is that there are many equally suitable possible individuals, such that we cannot pick a unique possible individual who is Sherlock Holmes. As Kripke (1980, p. 158) puts it:

> Several distinct possible people, and even actual ones such as Darwin or Jack the Ripper, might have performed the exploits of Holmes, but there is none of whom we can say that he would have been Holmes had he performed these exploits. For if so, which one?

In sum, having performed the exploits of Holmes is not sufficient for being Holmes. One reason is that even if someone performed the exploits of Holmes, this would not show that Doyle was writing about that man, which seems to be a necessary condition for being identified with Holmes (the first argument). Another reason is that too many entities might have performed the exploits of Holmes (the second argument).

The second difficult problem was raised against Currie's version of role realism. Recall that Currie offered different analyses for different kinds of discourse (or different contexts). On the surface, Currie's proposal thus appears to be a combination of three different accounts, if not more. As Adams, Fuller, and Stecker (1997, p. 137) put it, 'Currie's account of the meaning of names changes depending upon the context. He's a direct reference theorist outside of fictive contexts and has various views ... when giving the meaning of fictive names'. Adams, Fuller and Stecker thus worry that in combination with meaning holism, what we arrive at is *a rampant relativism of meaning*.

The category mistake objection, the third difficult problem for the role realist, argues that entities suggested by role realists are incapable of being fictional characters because fictional characters are depicted as full-blooded people, not as abstract objects such as person-kinds, functions, sets or indicated types. As Brock (2002, p. 6) puts it, 'to claim that an abstract object is a woman, or lives at 221b Baker Street, would be to make a category mistake. Abstract objects are just not the kinds of things to have such properties'. Similarly, García-Carpintero (2016, p. 336) claims that 'neither of those entities can be straightforwardly taken to be the sort of thing capable of eating birds' inner organs'.

The fourth difficult problem, the problem of *authorial creation*, amounts to the following: while fictional characters are created, functions, sets and person-kinds are not. As Thomasson (2009, p. 14) puts it,

> whether fictional entities are taken to be unactualized possibilia, non-existent objects, or abstract kinds, it seems that in any of these cases the work of authors writing stories is completely irrelevant to whether or not there are these fictional entities: the relevant possibilia, non-existent objects, and abstract kinds were 'around' just as much before as after acts of authoring, and so we can't take seriously the idea that authors create fictional characters on any of these views.

As noted above, Wolterstorff bites the bullet and defends a version of Platonism. Lamarque (2010, p. 64) opposes the Platonic view, describing the creativity thus construed as 'a pale shadow of creativity'. He solves the problem in terms of a Levinson-inspired distinction between *types* (which are not created) and *indicated-types* (which are in a certain sense created), or between a character per se (which is not created) and *that* fictional character (which is created). In sum, the worry concerning authorial creation is that sentences such as (1) seem to be literally true:

(1) Sherlock Holmes was created by Conan Doyle.

However, the entities suggested by role realists are not particularly apt for things created by humans. Lamarque's version of role realism is a notable exception (see also Terrone, 2017).

The last difficult problem for role realists is the problem of *nonexistence claims* (or the problem of negative existentials). An example of a nonexistence claim runs as follows:

(2) Sherlock Holmes does not exist.

As Kripke (2013, p. 144) puts it, 'what can someone mean when he says that Sherlock Holmes does not exist? Is he talking of a definite thing, and saying of it that it doesn't exist?' In essence, the problem is that, on the one hand, sentences of this kind are most straightforwardly understood as true. On the other hand, however, Sherlock Holmes *does exist* according to role realists.

4. Hyperintensional Role Realism

In this section, I will formulate a role realist account of fictional names that is hyperintensional and able to overcome the five difficult problems discussed in the preceding section. This view distinguishes between hyperintensional, intensional, and extensional occurrences of fictional names (as I will argue later on, this three-way distinction is not affected by the objection to Currie's three-way distinction). I will present this view in terms of necessarily empty individual concepts expressed in a procedural semantics of *transparent intensional logic* (TIL), noting that several core notions can be specified in different ways.[3] The most important building block of TIL is the notion of constructions. Constructions are defined formally within TIL; for our purposes, it suffices to say that constructions are structured procedures (hyperintensions), which are the theoretical correlate of the notion of meaning (or sense). The source of their fine-grained structure is the way in which smaller semantic units are composed into larger semantic units. Let me now turn to the semantics of fictional names.

When a fictional name occurs extensionally, its semantic value is an individual. When a fictional name occurs intensionally, its semantic value is an individual role; in other words, a function from possible worlds to individuals. Finally, when a fictional name occurs hyperintensionally, its semantic value is an individual concept—in other words, a construction of an individual role that satisfies certain formal properties, such as being a

---

[3] TIL was introduced by Pavel Tichý (1988) and further developed by others. For recent theories of concepts in TIL, see, for instance, Duží, Jespersen, and Materna (2010) or Raclavský and Kuchyňka (2011).

closed construction.[4] The proposed view is broadly Fregean insofar as the level of sense (the hyperintensional level) can be distinguished from the level of reference (the extensional level). In addition, as Frege (1997, p. 178) claimed, 'for fiction the sense is enough'.[5] In a similar vein, while sense does exist according to the present account, the reference is always lacking.

As noted above, hyperintensional occurrence of a fictional name is analysed in terms of individual concepts, which produce a function from possible worlds to individuals. Taking Kripke's arguments seriously, these individual concepts are necessarily empty in the sense that they are never throughout logical space matched by a referent (a full-blooded Sherlock Holmes). Their emptiness concerns not the content but the extension of the concept.

Concepts are included in so-called *conceptual systems*. There are various ways to specify what conceptual systems are (Raclavský and Kuchyňka, 2011); the general idea, however, is that we start with simple concepts and generate complex concepts in terms of specified rules of generation. Unlike the standard TIL approach, however, these individual concepts are not to be understood as eternal. In one sense, of course, it is natural to think of all individual concepts as eternal. Given a conceptual system, the concept cannot cease to exist within it. This synchronic view of language surely makes sense (such a view considers the given language at a certain moment in time and does not take its historical development into account). When it comes to fiction and the arts in general, however, the element of creation and creativity is crucial. In order to make sense of creativity in fiction, we need to take a diachronic look at language and take the historical development of the given language into account. Because of this, I will not suppose that there is a single conceptual system that models how we speak and think about things. Instead, I will suppose that there are many such conceptual systems. When it comes to fiction, an author introduces a new fictional character by introducing a new individual concept. They standardly take the conceptual system we use in ordinary language as a starting point (after all, this is the system they use to conceptualise their initial thoughts) and amend it, thereby creating a new conceptual system (assuming that the identity of a conceptual system is a fragile issue, sensitive to the slightest change). This 'amending' can take several forms: removing or revising an 'old' concept, introducing a new concept, etc.

Furthermore, these individual concepts are associated with sets of (hyper)requisites.[6] The requisite set can be understood (with a grain of salt) as a set of essential properties. While it is probably more common to speak of essential properties of individuals, it makes perfect sense to speak of essential properties of intensional and hyperintensional entities.[7] For instance, *being a detective* is a requisite for being Sherlock Holmes, and *being an unhappily married woman* is a requisite for being Thérèse Raquin—in other words, occupying

---

4   For a discussion of views that are relevant to our purposes, see Raclavský and Kuchyňka (2011).
5   Note, however, that Frege offered no complete theory of fictional discourse; see Zouhar (2010).
6   To put it simply, requisites are appropriate for 'things' that are possible; hyperrequisites are needed for 'things' that are impossible. The latter is what we need for present purposes (for details, see Glavaničová, 2017, 2018; Duží, Jespersen and Glavaničová, 2020). For simplicity, I will use the expression 'requisite' to cover both requisites proper and hyperrequisites.
7   For a justification of this claim, see Kosterec (2018).

these two roles. Note that if the property of *being a detective* is a requisite for being Sherlock Holmes, the sentence *Sherlock Holmes is a detective* would be (on one, the *de dicto* reading) an analytic truth (another, *de re* reading construes the sentence as claiming that the individual that is Holmes is a detective). The analytic truth of the former reading is of course controversial. Nevertheless, if one wanted to find out whether Sherlock Holmes was a detective, it would be futile to conduct historical research into important detectives of the past; reading the relevant fictional story would suffice. Moreover, the analytic truth of this sentence sits well with the obvious possibility that Conan Doyle could have written a *different* story about a *different* fictional character named *Sherlock Holmes*—one who was a brilliant pipe-smoking *professor*, for instance.

An intensional occurrence of a fictional name is analysed in terms of roles as functions from possible worlds to individuals (recall Currie's version of role realism). However, since these individuals are necessarily lacking, the function in question is a partial function of a certain kind: a function from possible worlds to individuals that is never really mapped to any individual (note that there is only *one* such function, while there are many different fictional characters; this in turn motivates the introduction of the hyperintensional level). In this respect, fictional names resemble disguised definite descriptions, which, however, describe something impossible.

An extensional occurrence of a fictional name is analysed in agreement with antirealism. This is because corresponding full-blooded referents do not (and cannot) exist in the case of fictional names (more on this impossibility in the next section). In this respect, the account resembles antirealist theories, such as gappy proposition theory. Despite this, the account is arguably better off than gappy proposition theory insofar as even when we face an extensional occurrence of a fictional name, the gap we arrive at is not an undifferentiated gap (or a gap differentiated from other gaps solely in terms of syntax): it is a gap that is tied to the corresponding individual concept and the function it produces.[8]

Note also that this approach contains no reference shifts; what changes is the semantic value. If the semantic value is an extension (an individual), we are dealing with a *de re* reading; otherwise, we are dealing with *de dicto* readings. Since the reference is always lacking, the view sketched above can be entitled 'impossibilism' as opposed to possibilism.[9] In what follows, I will formulate a semi-formal analysis corresponding to an informal impossibilist account sketched above. For simplicity, I will ignore possible worlds and times in the analysis (supposing that we are evaluating sentences here and now). As already explained, the analysis distinguishes between hyperintensional, intensional and extensional occurrences of fictional names.

1. Hyperintensional occurrences: *Holmes^H* and *Watson^H* stand for hyperintensions: an individual concept of Sherlock Holmes and an individual concept of Dr Watson. Sample hyperintensional analyses (3*)–(5*) of sentences (3)–(5) are as follows:

   (3) Sherlock Holmes is a fictional character.
   (3*) *FictChar(Holmes^H)*

---

8   For an early criticism of Braun's gappy proposition theory, see Jespersen (2003).
9   A different variant of impossibilism was suggested by Vacek (2018).

(4) Dr Watson was created by Conan Doyle.
(4*) $CreatedBy(Watson^H, ConanDoyle)$
(5) Sherlock Holmes is a detective.
(5*) $Req^*(Detective, Holmes^H)$

Analysis (3*) says that the individual concept $Holmes^H$ has the property of being a fictional character; (4*) says that the individual concept $Watson^H$ was created by Conan Doyle; (5*) says that the individual concept $Holmes^H$ has the (hyper)requisite of being a detective.

2. Intensional occurrences: $Holmes^I$ stands for an intension: the individual role of Sherlock Holmes; a function from possible worlds (and times) to individuals. Sample intensional analyses (6*) and (7*) of sentences (6) and (7) are as follows:

(6) Sherlock Holmes does not exist.
(6*) $\neg Exist(Holmes^I)$
(7) Sherlock Holmes could not exist.
(7*) $\Box \neg Exist(Holmes^I)$

Analysis (6*) says that the individual role $Holmes^I$ is empty (there is *no such individual* who occupies the role). The idea here is that (non)existence is treated as a second-order property of individual roles: a role has the property of existence if it has an occupant; a role has the property of nonexistence if it lacks the occupant. Note that, analysed this way, we avoid the apparent paradox involved in saying that *there are things that do not exist*. Note also that this analysis is not to be confused with the claim that the role in question does not exist (this other claim could be expressed in our semi-formal analysis as $(\neg \exists r)$ $(r = Holmes^I)$). (7*) claims that the individual role $Holmes^I$ is necessarily empty.

3. Extensional occurrences: $Holmes^E$ and $Watson^E$ stand for extensions: individuals, were there such individuals. Yet there are no such individuals, so there are no extensions. As a result, the propositions will be gappy. Despite this, the corresponding sentences are meaningful: the sense is present even when the reference is missing. Sample extensional analyses (8*), (9*), (10*) and (11*) of sentences (8), (9), (10) and (11) are as follows:

(8) Holmes is a detective.
(8*) $Detective(Holmes^E)$
(9) Watson is a detective.
(9*) $Detective(Watson^E)$
(10) Watson admires Holmes.
(10*) $Admire(Watson^E, Holmes^E)$
(11) Holmes admires Holmes.
(11*) $Admire(Holmes^E, Holmes^E)$

Note that the extensional analysis is not particularly revealing. The semantic value delivered by the sense of (8) is the same as the semantic value delivered by the sense of (9), and similarly for the pair (10) and (11). But we should not be concerned, for this is how things are and should be. Fictional names are necessarily empty, so we have no extensions to work with. Still, any strategy that is open to antirealists is applicable here, if needed.

Such strategies are not needed, however, as hyperintensional (and intensional) analyses give us the granularity needed. Note also that the above sentences have other readings (see the hyperintensional analysis above). These readings serve to report the content of the story, and this job cannot (and need not) be done on the extensional level.

5. Five Problems Revisited

Let us now return to the five difficult problems outlined above: (1) Kripke's case against possibilism; (2) 'a rampant relativism of meaning'; (3) the category mistake objection; (4) the problem of authorial creation; and (5) the problem of negative existentials (or nonexistence claims). In this section, I will consider how the hyperintensional version of role realism proposed in the preceding section might deal with these concerns.

The impossibilist flavour of the account is the reason why Kripke's case against possibilism does not arise. This is so because a purely fictional name necessarily lacks a reference (a full-blooded individual), so a fictional name cannot accidentally pick out an individual. In other words, it cannot be that, unbeknownst to Conan Doyle, someone is (or rather, was) Sherlock Holmes. It also cannot be that we are forced either to say that there are several Sherlocks or to pick one arbitrarily (again, this is so because there is no full-blooded Sherlock Holmes).

It is one thing to show that, given that full-blooded fictional characters are impossible, Kripke's worry does not arise; it is another to explain what makes full-blooded fictional characters impossible. I have shown the former above—the latter task, however, would require a paper of its own. Below, I will list several reasons for the impossibility of full-blooded fictional characters.

To begin with, fictional characters are usually incompletely specified. How many moles does Sherlock Holmes have on his back? How many scars does he have? How many cousins? Many issues about fictional characters are not settled in the story. Another important reason is buried in Kripke's reasoning. If we were to find out that, accidentally and unbeknownst to Conan Doyle, there was someone who satisfied everything he said about Sherlock Holmes in the stories, this would not establish that Conan Doyle was writing about that person. Now *being the man whom Conan Doyle was writing about* is clearly a first-order property of individuals and thus fits into the requisite set very well. However, provided the name is fictional, Conan Doyle was not writing about anyone, and thus no one can satisfy this property (and because of this, no one can satisfy every property in the requisite set). Of course, there might be different ways to establish the impossibility result. Another alternative would be to explain impossibility in terms of fictionality; yet another option would be to employ authorial intention more directly. A clearly non-question-begging alternative would be to rebut the claim that Sherlock Holmes as an individual actually exists and to rebut the claim that Sherlock Holmes exists as a merely possible individual (this option requires a discussion of a fixed domain versus varying domains).

The problem of 'a rampant relativism of meaning' is addressed in the following way. In the present account, the semantic value of a fictional name can be of three different kinds: an individual concept (a hyperintensional occurrence), an individual role (an intensional occurrence), or an individual (an extensional occurrence). However, even if a fictional name appears extensionally, neither the corresponding hyperintension nor the corresponding intension disappears: we just do not speak about them in the present moment. The account is thus kept unified because the sense (hyperintension) is always the individual concept, the intension is always a function, and the reference is always lacking. The only thing that changes is what we are speaking about: hyperintension, intension, or extension.

When it comes to the category mistake objection, the extensional analysis is of the appropriate type (individuals), even though these individuals are never at our disposal in the case of fictional names, and thus no instantiation takes place. Despite this, the category mistake objection is avoided because the type of the occupant itself is appropriate (the type of the occupant is determined in terms of extensionalisation from the type of the role). Readings in terms of requisite properties (such as a *de dicto* reading of *Sherlock Holmes is a detective*) might appear more challenging because requisites are associated either with individual concepts or with individual roles. However, when we claim that anyone who is Sherlock Holmes is a detective, we are not claiming that the concept or the role is a detective, and so the problem is again avoided. When it comes to other properties such as *being a famous fictional character* (which are not individual properties), we again get a correct result insofar as these properties are ascribed not to putative individuals but to individual concepts that provide a model of fictional characters.

The solution to the worry concerning authorial creation is close in spirit—although different in detail—to Lamarque's suggestion sketched in Section 2. When Conan Doyle introduced the expression *Sherlock Holmes*, something that was a meaningless string of letters in the language spoken by Conan Doyle and his readers became a perfectly meaningful expression. By introducing a new fictional name (and a new fictional character), Doyle thus strictly speaking changed the conceptual system that he and the respective readers would subsequently use. Concepts are created in (and only in) the sense in which they are introduced. However, this sense is sufficient for granting the truth to relevant sentences.

Finally, nonexistence claims have been analysed in terms of second-order properties. According to the analysis, (non)existence is a property of certain functions (which are intensional objects). For instance, the claim that Sherlock Holmes does not exist is analysed in terms of the intension corresponding to Sherlock Holmes, which does not single out any individual. Importantly, the proposal is not *ad hoc*. This is because the nonexistence of objects that satisfy definite descriptions will be treated in the same way as the nonexistence of full-blooded fictional characters.

6. Fiction and Hyperintensionality

I will begin this section by comparing the present account with other hyperintensional theories of fictional characters, namely impossible world approaches. Furthermore, the account is open to future developments, and several directions for future research are worth mentioning. In this section, I will discuss two such directions related to fiction and hyperintensionality. The first is the idea of skipping the intensional level of the proposed analysis, thereby delegating tasks previously performed on the intensional level to the hyperintensional level. The second direction is to explore the connection between the hyperintensionality of fictional characters and the hyperintensionality of fiction (and thus the so-called *opacity of narrative*).

Impossible world accounts of fictional characters are hyperintensional, and because of this they can be viewed as the main competitors of (or, as I would like to say, as alternatives to) the present account. Two kinds of such accounts are worth mentioning. The first is the modal Meinongianism suggested by Francesco Berto (2011) and Graham Priest (2005); the second is the theory of property bundles suggested by Mark Jago (2014). An obvious difference is that my theory does not call for impossible world semantics because the fine-grained structure is due to structured, procedural meanings. Below, I will briefly describe both positions and discuss more subtle points of departure.

I will start with Berto's version of modal Meinongianism, which is probably the most advanced version of the approach. Berto employs the so-called *Qualified Comprehension Principle*, according to which, 'for any condition $A[x]$, with x free, some object satisfies $A[x]$ at some world' (Berto and Jago, 2019, p. 262). Importantly, the world in question need not be an actual world, and it need not be a possible world either. In addition, fictional characters are non-existents and as such cannot bear existence-entailing properties. A pressing worry for this theory is the problem of authorial creation. Berto and Jago describe this as a 'selection problem'—one without a satisfactory solution—noting that while the ordinary meaning of 'to create' involves bringing something into existence, this is not an option for Meinongian non-existents. By contrast, fictional characters as individual concepts are existing entities, and thus a similar worry does not arise for my theory. The crucial common feature shared by this account and my own is that both allow for the employment of impossible contents in the characterization of objects.

Let me now turn to Jago's view. According to Jago (2014, p. 156), 'fictional names are property-bundles, interpreted in the non-attributive, semantically rigid way. The worldmaking name h representing Holmes is a property-bundle {*is a detective, lives at 221b Baker Street, is a cocaine addict,* ...}.' Doyle associated the name *Sherlock Holmes* with h, but he did not create an abstract entity. Jago's account aligns with mine in some respects but not in others. As in my theory, there are no fictional characters, understood as extensional entities, but fictional names are nevertheless meaningful. In contrast to my account, Jago's theory does not take the problem of authorial creation seriously (in other words, it is not clear how we can truthfully say that Conan Doyle created Sherlock Holmes). In addition, Jago claims that in the sense in which Sherlock Holmes is a detective, he is inessentially so, while my theory treats this property as a requisite property (and thus as something akin to an essential property; see Berto and Jago, 2019, p. 256). Moreover, while my theory in principle allows for the identification of Clark Kent with Superman (the two names can be treated as expressing the same individual concept), Jago denies this possibility (note that I do not claim that we *should* identify them; I only claim that it is a theoretical possibility that should not be excluded from the outset).

Moving to the next issue, the need for an intensional level of analysis is an open question. It would be worth examining an alternative account that omits this layer. As a consequence, (non)existence would be treated as a property of individual concepts, not as an intensional property. An individual concept has the property of existence if it has an extension, that is, if it is a non-empty concept (and lacks it otherwise). The senses of fictional names would be akin to the senses of certain mathematical definite descriptions such as 'the largest prime'. This option might be problematic for some, but it may appear elegant to others (in particular, those who are sympathetic to the view that introducing a fictional character is akin to defining a new concept in a formal theory might find the idea of skipping the level of intensions plausible).

Zooming out, examining a broader picture that connects the hyperintensionality of fictional characters with the opacity of narrative could likewise be fruitful (Lamarque, 2014; McGregor, 2016). To put it simply, the opacity of narrative consists in the intimate relation between its content and the manner in which it is presented. In the case of literary fiction, the identity of fictional characters is essentially tied to descriptions that characterise them; similarly, the identity of a 'fictional world' is essentially tied to the manner in which it is presented (Lamarque, 2014, p. 3):

> Rather than supposing that narrative descriptions are a window through which an independently existing (fictional) world is observed, with the implication that the very same world might be presented (and thus observed) in other ways, from different perspectives, we must accept that there is no such transparent glass—only an opaque glass, painted, as it were, with figures seen not *through* it but *in* it.

The connection between the opacity of narrative and hyperintensionality draws attention to important parallels between the semantics, metaphysics, and logic underlying our discourse on works of fiction and the semantics, metaphysics, and logic behind our discourse on fictional characters. Namely, both (literary) works of fiction and fictional characters appear to have fine-grained identities, which in turn call for a hyperintensional treatment.

7. Concluding Remarks

In this paper I discussed three prominent versions of role realism and highlighted their advantages. I then explained five main problems confronting role realism and formulated an alternative view: a hyperintensional version of role realism. This view distinguishes between hyperintensional, intensional, and extensional occurrences of fictional names. The corresponding analyses are thus hyperintensional (an individual concept), intensional (a function from possible worlds to individuals), and extensional (an individual, which is always lacking in the case of fictional names).

Let me highlight the most important features of the proposed account. Naturally, one of the crucial features is the hyperintensional metaphysics of fictional characters (and the hyperintensional semantics of fictional names). Hyperintensionality is important for distinguishing between fictional characters and lines up well with the impossibility of full-blooded fictional characters. Because of this, I called this analysis *impossibilism*. The impossibilist flavour of the account makes this theory particularly apt for accounting for Kripke's case against possibilism. Furthermore, within the present account, individual concepts associated with fictional names are not understood as eternal. When an author introduces a new fictional name, what takes place is a change within (and strictly speaking, of) a conceptual system: a new individual concept is introduced by an author. This feature of the account brings it closer to the position known as abstract artifactualism and makes the theory apt for accounting for the problem of authorial creation. Finally, the combination of three layers of analysis makes the theory apt for accounting for the category mistake objection and for nonexistence claims without resulting in a 'rampant relativism of meaning'.

The potential for future research and a broader application in aesthetics (in connection with the opacity of narrative), along with the features discussed above, make the account a promising alternative both to standard role realism and to other realist and antirealist theories.[10]

References

Adams, F., Fuller, G., and Stecker, R. (1997). 'The Semantics of Fictional Names'. *Pacific Philosophical Quarterly*, 78, pp. 128–148.

Armour-Garb, B. and Woodbridge, J. A. (2015). *Pretense and Pathology*. Cambridge: Cambridge University Press.

Berto, F. (2011). 'Modal Meinongianism and Fiction: The Best of Three Worlds'. *Philosophical Studies*. 152, pp. 313–334.

Berto, F. and Jago, M. (2019). *Impossible Worlds*. Oxford: OUP.

Braun, D. (1993). 'Empty Names'. *Noûs*, 27, pp. 449–469.

Braun, D. (2005). 'Empty Names, Fictional Names, Mythical Names'. *Noûs*, 39, pp. 596–631.

Brock, S. (2002). 'Fictionalism about Fictional Characters'. *Noûs*, 36, pp. 1–21.

Brock, S. (2016). 'Fictionalism about Fictional Characters Revisited'. *Res Philosophica*, 93, pp. 377–403.

Currie, G. (1988). 'Fictional Names'. *Australasian Journal of Philosophy*. 66, pp. 471–488.

Currie, G. (1990). *The Nature of Fiction*. Cambridge: Cambridge University Press.

Duží, M., Jespersen, B., and Materna, P. (2010). *Procedural Semantics for Hyperintensional Logic: Foundations and Applications of Transparent Intensional Logic*. Berlin: Springer.

---

10   The work on this paper was supported by Vedecká grantová agentúra MŠVVaŠ SR a SAV (VEGA) grant no. 2/0117/19, Logic, Epistemology and Metaphysics of Fiction. I am grateful to Gregory Currie, Miloš Kosterec, Peter Lamarque, Matteo Pascucci, Mirco Sambrotta, Tom Stoneham, Martin Vacek, Dan Zeman, Marián Zouhar, and anonymous referees for extremely helpful comments on earlier versions of the paper. I am indebted to Carolyn Benson for proofreading.

Duží, M., Jespersen, B., and Glavaničová, D. (2020). 'Impossible Individuals as Necessarily Empty Individual Concepts', in Malinowski, J. and Giordani, A. (eds), *Logic in High Definition: Developing Fine-Grained Semantics, Studia Logica Series*, vol. 56, pp. 177-202, Berlin: Springer.

Everett, A. (2013). *The Nonexistent*. Oxford: OUP.

Frege, G. (1997). 'Comments on Sinn and Bedeutung', in Beaney, M. (ed.), *The Frege Reader*. Oxford: Blackwell, pp. 172–180.

Friend, S. (2014). 'Notions of Nothing', in García-Carpintero, M. and Martí, G. (eds), *Empty Representations*. Oxford: OUP, pp. 307–332.

García-Carpintero, M. (2016). 'Pretend Reference and Coreference', in Capone, A., Kiefer, F., and Lo Piparo, F. (eds), *Indirect Reports and Pragmatics*. Cham: Springer, pp. 333–358.

Glavaničová, D. (2017). 'Tichý and Fictional Names'. *Organon F*, 24, pp. 384–404.

Glavaničová, D. (2018). 'Fictional Names and Semantics: Towards a Hybrid View', in Stalmaszczyk, P. (ed.), *Objects of Inquiry in Philosophy of Language and Literature: Studies in Philosophy of Language and Linguistics*. Berlin: Peter Lang, pp. 59–73.

Haraldsen, F. (2017). 'The Truth about Sherlock Holmes'. *Organon F*, 24, pp. 339–365.

Jago, M. (2014) *The Impossible: An Essay on Hyperintensionality*. Oxford: OUP.

Jespersen, B. (2003). 'Why the Tuple Theory of Structured Propositions isn't a Theory of Structured Propositions'. *Philosophia*, 31, pp. 171–183.

Kosterec, M. (2018). 'On the Essence of Empty Properties'. *Synthese*. Available at: <https://doi.org/10.1007/s11229-018-02036-1> (Accessed: 28 September 2020).

Kripke, S. (1980). *Naming and Necessity*. Cambridge, MA: Harvard University Press.

Kripke, S. (2013). *Reference and Existence: John Locke Lectures*. New York: OUP.

Kroon, F. and Voltolini, A. (2018). 'Fictional Entities', in Zalta, E. N. (ed.), *Stanford Encyclopedia of Philosophy*. Available at: <https://plato.stanford.edu/archives/win2018/entries/fictional-entities/> (Accessed: 15 January 2020).

Lamarque, P. (2010). *Work and Object: Explorations in the Metaphysics of Art*. Oxford: OUP.

Lamarque, P. (2014). *The Opacity of Narrative*. London: Rowman & Littlefield.

Lamarque, P. and Olsen, S. H. (1994). *Truth, Fiction, and Literature: A Philosophical Perspective*. Oxford: Clarendon.

Lewis, D. (1978). 'Truth in Fiction'. *American Philosophical Quarterly*. 15, pp. 37–46.

McGregor, R. (2016). *The Value of Literature*. Lanham, MD: Rowman & Littlefield.

Priest, G. (2005). *Towards Non-Being*. Oxford: OUP.

Raclavský, J. and Kuchyňka, P. (2011). 'Conceptual and Derivation Systems'. *Logic and Logical Philosophy*, 20, pp. 159–174.

Sainsbury, R. M. (2010). *Fiction and Fictionalism*. London: Routledge.

Stokke, A. (2020). 'Fictional Names and Individual Concepts'. *Synthese*. Available at: <https://doi.org/10.1007/s11229-020-02550-1> (Accessed: 28 September 2020).

Terrone, E. (2017). 'On Fictional Characters as Types'. *BJA*, 57, pp. 161–176.

Thomasson, A. (1999). *Fiction and Metaphysics*. Cambridge: Cambridge University Press.

Thomasson, A. (2003). 'Speaking of Fictional Characters'. *Dialectica*, 57, pp. 205–223.

Thomasson, A. (2009). 'Fictional Entities'. in Kim, J., Sosa, E., and Rosenkrantz, G. (eds), *A Companion to Metaphysics*. Oxford: Blackwell, pp. 10–18.

Tichý, P. (1988). *The Foundations of Frege's Logic*. Berlin and New York: De Gruyter.

Vacek, M. (2018). 'Fiction: Impossible!'. *Axiomathes*, 28, pp. 247–252.

Walton, K. L. (1990). *Mimesis as Make-Believe*. Cambridge, MA: Harvard University Press.

Wolterstorff, N. (1980). *Works and Worlds of Art*. Oxford: Clarendon.

Zalta, E. (1983). *Abstract Objects*. Dordrecht: Reidel.

Zouhar, M. (2010). 'Frege on Fiction', in Koťátko, P., Pokorný, M., and Sabatés, M. (eds.), *Fictionality, Possibility, Reality*. Bratislava: Aleph, pp. 103–120.

Impossible individuals as necessarily empty individual concepts

Marie Duží, Bjørn Jespersen and Daniela Glavaničová

Abstract We talk about 'impossible objects' in many areas, ranging from empirical and non-empirical theories to the realm of fiction, myth and folklore: a mathematical pendulum, a perfect market, the set of all sets that are not members of themselves, Kafka's Gregor Samsa, Pegasus, The Puss in the Boots, and so forth. This paper proposes a hyperintensional account of a special case of impossible objects, so-called 'impossible individuals'. Our (broadly Fregean) proposal is to identify 'impossible individuals' with necessarily empty individual concepts. The main goal of the paper is to develop a method that enables us to discover inconsistencies in specifications of individual concepts and thus prove that such concepts could not possibly be matched by an extension (an individual). Furthermore, this approach allows for a fine-grained individuation of impossible individuals. Fine-graining will not be explored in the present paper, but its very possibility adds to the overall plausibility of the present account.

1 Introduction

We talk and think about *impossibilia* or impossible objects in various domains. One can start, for instance, with 'serious' areas of discourse such as empirical and non-empirical theories, and end with the realm of fiction, myth and folklore. Empirical theories discuss impossibilia of certain kinds in the form of substantially idealized notions such as: a mathematical pendulum swinging in a vacuum, a black body absorbing all the electro-magnetic radiation on its surface, or a perfect market populated by omniscient and fully rational agents. Non-empirical theories talk about impossibilia such as: the set of all sets that are not members of themselves, the largest cardinal number, the set of all ordinal numbers, a natural number between 0 and 1, or false tautologies. These impossibilities are often explicitly mentioned in indirect proofs for a *reductio* in order to establish that such a set or such a number could not possibly exist. The quickest runner who can never overtake the slowest runner is an example from philosophy; the man without properties, the fake banknote that is a banknote, and the wooden horse that is a horse are examples of semantical interest. In the realm of fiction, Kafka's Gregor Samsa is an excellent example of a human being who metamorphized into an insect: a fate that fortunately cannot befall real-world human beings; Vian's mouse begging the cat to end its life would be another example.[1] In mythology, examples abound: Pegasus and other winged horses, centaurs, harpies, sirens, and Phoenix. In folk tales and fairytales, examples likewise abound: the witty talking cat Puss in the Boots, Kisa the Cat, an enchanted princess cat turning into a princess in the end, or the heroic talking ant Ferda the Ant.

Assorted impossibilities of different kinds have been listed in the above paragraph, and it is not our present aim to say which witch is which.[2] Our aim rather is to propose a general hyperintensional account of a special case of impossible objects, so-called 'impossible individuals'. We begin with what the intensional logic of individuals-in-intension is custom-built to model, go on to point out where it runs out of steam, and proceed to spend the bulk of the paper putting forward a hyperintensional logic of individuals-in-hyperintension. Our broadly Fregean proposal suggests identifying 'impossible individuals' with necessarily empty individual concepts. The novelty of this paper consists in this particular logic. We develop a method that enables us to discover inconsistencies in specifications of individual concepts and thus prove that such concepts could not possibly be matched by an extension (such as an individual or a number). Furthermore, this approach makes possible a fine-grained individuation of impossible individuals. While we will not

---

[1] This is to suggest that some fictional characters, such as people changing into insects, or talking cats and mice, are impossible (given the biological definitions of humans, insects, cats and mice). A stronger thesis has been defended, namely, that all fictional characters are impossible; see [26] and [12], [13]. For present purposes, the weaker thesis that some fictional characters are impossible suffices.

[2] Moreover, it is an open question where *religious* discourse would slot in. Wherever it might end up on the spectrum, however, we subscribe to a methodology of parity to the effect that the semantics must be the same for 'Allah', 'God', 'Zeus', 'Odin', 'Hanuman', and any other names for any other deities in order not to pre-empt the question of the existence of a given deity (i.e., the term 'Greek mythology' pre-empts the question whether Zeus et al. exist). Our theory (TIL) does not come with a semantics for religious discourse per se, but in his [24] Tichý treats 'God' as a term for a contingently occupied office (though one typed to be occupied by other offices) in his reconstruction of Anselm's purported proof of the existence of the being superior to any other being.

explore the problem of individuation of impossible individuals here (i.e., we will not propose a criterion of sameness/difference for impossible individuals),[3] the very possibility of a fine-grained individuation of impossible individuals adds to the overall plausibility of the present proposal. It is also noteworthy that this possibility is an ontological free lunch, since contrary to object-based approaches we need not introduce any new objects to obtain fine-grained individuation of impossibilia. The logic is developed within an existing hyperintensional framework and while not requiring the introduction of novel entities, it does require the formulation of several new definitions. The benefits of this logic are that the logic underpins a formal semantics for definite descriptions like 'the fake banknote that is a banknote', assigning both a meaning and a denotation to them, as well as for predications like "The fake banknote that is a banknote is a banknote, and is not a banknote."

The modulation from intensional to hyperintensional logic is a case of 'new level, new devil', as the shift creates new problems. The key problem is how to obtain a *logic* in the first place, where a logic is understood to be a formal device that discriminates between valid and invalid inferences. The challenge hyperintensional logic poses is how to avoid both sterility (too little or nothing at all follows) and explosion (too much or even anything at all follows). In particular, if explosion is the outcome then we will be merely reinstating the problem that urged us to shift from intensional to hyperintensional logic in the first place. Therefore, the key definition put forward below is subject to a restriction that prevents explosion.

Here is the stage-setting. Contingently, there is no King of France: the actual world and the present time are among the world/time pairs that go without a unique King of France. But there might have been a unique King of France. A standard modal logic of intensions is eminently suited to handle cases of logically contingent absence from or presence in the actual world at the present time. However, the same standard modal logic is equally ill-suited to handle cases of necessary absence from any and all logically possible worlds and instants of time or intervals. It is equally ill-suited to handle necessary presence, for that matter.

Let us dwell on contingency and necessity for a moment. Modal logic handles contingency perfectly well. Formally, α and $\neg\alpha$ count as contingent as soon as they are satisfiable within the same model. Modal logic enables us to abstract from the actual by lining up possible alternatives to it, thus exploring the contrast between the actual and the merely possible, where the actual is one among several possibilities that has the unique feature of having been realized. Modal logic can also handle necessity well, as long as we are simply concerned with the preservation of necessity (e.g., as in the distribution of the K axiom where the necessity of an implication is carried through to both the antecedent and the consequent) and the interaction between the categories of the necessary, the merely possible, and the contingently actual. Modal logic cannot, however, handle necessity well at all when called upon to discriminate between two or more necessities within the same system. Trivially, modal logic can distinguish between, say, $S5$-necessity and T-necessity, because the box receives two different semantic interpretations. For sure, modal logic is de-

---

[3] See [8] for a sequence of rigorously defined criteria for fine-graining hyperpropositions, yielding different criteria of co-hyperintensionality.

signed to discriminate between the necessity defined on one frame (say, a serial one) and the necessity defined on another frame (say, a Euclidian one). But within a model based on a particular frame, there can be but one necessity, modelled as a function taking each world accessible within the model to the same extension. The logic of intensions as per modal logic is an extensional one in that necessary co-extensionality suffices for co-intensionality: $\forall w((f_w = g_w) \supset (f = g))$, where f, g range over intensional entities of the same type. As a corollary, there can be no two distinct necessary propositions, no two distinct necessary properties, and similarly for the other intensions. Since impossibility is just 'the dark side' of necessity, it follows that there can be no two impossible propositions, etc., within the same model.

The standard logic of intensions suffices for the purposes of *possibilia* or 'possible individuals', i.e. individuals-in-intension. The intensional fragment of our background theory—Tichý's Transparent Intensional Logic (TIL)–has gotten much mileage out of the contrast between individuals (-in-extension) and individuals-in-intension.[4] While the former are modelled formally as zero-place functions, the latter are identified formally with functions from worlds to partial functions from times to individuals, and are called *offices*. The designated *occupant* of an office is an individual. Relative to a particular world and time, a given office is *occupied* (has exactly one occupant) or else is *vacant*. If f, g are offices then $f = g$ as soon as they are occupied by the same individual or vacant in exactly the same worlds at exactly the same times. As a limiting case, if f, g go vacant at all worlds and times then $f = g$; this degenerate function is the *impossible individual-in-intension*, i.e. the *impossible office*.

Moreover, offices and properties can be joined by dint of a particular relation-in-extension such that a property supervenes on an office: as a matter of analytic necessity, if some individual occupies the office then the individual must instantiate the property. This a priori link between offices and properties is known as the *requisite* relation, the property being a requisite of the office. The problem with the impossible office is that since no individual could possibly occupy the impossible office, any property is one of its requisites. The challenge before us is how to extend, in a principled manner that prevents explosion of requisites, the twin notions of office and requisite from 'possible individuals', such as *the inventor of the zip*, to 'impossible individuals', such as the *King of France who is not a monarch*. The notions of requisite and *hyperrequisite* (to make up for the shortcomings of the former) will figure prominently below.

Having appreciated the core of the problem, as logicians, metaphysicians and semanticists we are facing a fork in the road here. The choice is between either expanding the notion of individual-in-extension in order to develop a theory of *impossible individuals* or expanding the notion of individual-in-intension in order to develop a theory of *impossible individuals-in-hyperintension*. Although a subspecies of hyperintensional theories, the former just broaden their extensional ontology, im-

---

[4] See, for instance, [23] and [9, §3.3, §4.3], the latter offering elaborate analyses of "Hesperus is Phosphorus" and "Clark Kent is Superman", on the assumption that each of these four grammatical proper names denotes a separate individual-in-intension (i.e., individual office).

possible individuals still being individuals. To use a pair of monikers, this approach qualifies as *Meinongian* and *object*-based. The latter batch of theories enrich their hyperintensional ontology, not by broadening it in virtue of adding new hyperintensions, but by defining new hyperintensional entities on the basis of existing ones. The approach we will be pursuing in this paper is pivoted on fine-graining by means of structured hyperintensions. Hence our approach is a *structure*-based one.[5]

Accordingly, the prong of the fork we will be following consists in developing a notion of individuals-in-hyperintension, which we will call *hyperoffices* (what we have been calling 'individual concepts' so far in the interest of a fairly neutral term).[6] A hyperoffice is a hyperintensional entity that presents an office. Importantly, it does not either present or represent an individual. Individuals do not factor into our account of hyperoffices at all. Offices, on the other hand, are a factor, but only insofar as they serve to distinguish between those hyperoffices that present the impossible office and those that do not. The latter sort of hyperoffices are those that present a particular office that is occupied by an individual at at least one possible world at at least one instant of time. To summarize, the thesis we are making a case for is this:

> **Thesis.** *An 'impossible individual' is explicated as an inconsistent hyperoffice presenting the impossible office.*

Our inquiry will be conducted exclusively at the hyperintensional level, which contrasts with the extensional level of individuals and the intensional level of offices. This is going to be critical to our logic of predication and to which inferences involving hyperoffices come out valid and which ones do not. The key questions, then, are these:

> **Predication.** *How to discriminate between which predications on the hyperintensional level with hyperoffices in subject position are true and which ones are either gappy or false?*
> **Inference.** *Which inferences can be validly drawn from the information inherent to a given hyperoffice?*
> **Inconsistency.** *How to develop a logic that will demonstrate why this or that hyperoffice is necessarily empty?*

The case for the thesis above will be developed with an amended version of TIL.[7] So will the answers to these three questions.

Formally speaking, TIL is a hyperintensional, typed λ-calculus of partial functions. These features make TIL eminently suited to offer philosophically principled and technically precise answers to these questions. TIL is a hyperintensional system in which hyperintensions are identified with abstract, structured, higher-order *procedures* producing lower-order intensional or extensional objects (or in some

---

[5] See [21] for the trifurcation of object-, structure-, and syntax-based theories of hyperintensionality

[6] See also [19, §3] for motivation.

[7] See [25, esp. chs. 1-4] and [9, ch.1] for foundations and motivation.

cases even lower-order procedures) as their product.[8] These procedures can in well-defined cases fail to produce an output, a feature which makes it possible to model gappy intensions such as impossible propositions or the impossible office, which trade each empirical index (such as worlds and times) for a gap. Gappiness is just fine for an intensional exploration of impossibility, a gap being a manifestation of the fact that nothing satisfies the condition associated with the intension at any possible world or instant of time. But more is expected of a hyperintensional exploration of impossibility, as it must discriminate between multiple manners of forming the impossible proposition, the impossible office, and any other impossible intension.

Furthermore, and importantly, the reorientation from intension to hyperintension affects the nature of the bearer of the property of being impossible. When we speak of an intension as being impossible, what we mean is that the intension is a logical object in its own right alongside all its fellow logical objects, though one with the quirky feature that it is a condition which could not possibly be satisfied. When we speak of a hyperintension as being impossible, what we mean is that the hyperintension is a logical object in its own right alongside all its fellow logical objects, though one with the quirky feature that it produces a condition which could not possibly be satisfied. In order to understand our Thesis as intended, it is important to appreciate the fact that TIL is radically anti-Meinongian. What some (neo-) Meinongian theories attempt to *procedural* approach, according to which some procedures (our hyperintensions) produce conditions necessarily devoid of satisfiers. Our procedural semantics of hyperintensions is an alternative to impossible-world semantics.[9]

We should probably stress in which regards our framework is presented as an alternative. The conundrum before us is what the formal semantics is of terms which, ostensibly, denote individuals (and other extensional entities, such as numbers) that could not possibly exist, and what are the logical properties of the meaning ascribed to such terms. The point of departure is that the existence of such terms is a fact of (primarily) natural language. The metaphysics involved is intended to track, or be a reflection of, the semantics and logic involved. We take this approach, putting semantics and logic before metaphysics, to be characteristic of analytic philosophy. That is, we are engaged in natural-language semantics rather than metaphysics pure and simple.[10] On our approach, the metaphysics characterizes and classifies the entities, their properties and the relations between them that our semantics requires in order to provide the account we are after (in our case, a top-down account that is heavy on the hyperintensions and light on the extensions). We assume that our fellow modal Meinongians on the other side of the fence are in the same business. Correspondingly, neither a bottom-up approach such as theirs nor a top-down approach such as ours attempts to make pronouncements about reality *an sich*, but rather

---

[8] See [16] and [8] for the procedural conception of structured hyperintensions.

[9] We share Fine's misgivings in [11] about impossible worlds as being a case of some sort of *reduplication* (whatever is impossible is relegated to impossible worlds). However, a comparison between TIL and the modal Meinongianism of Priest [20] and Berto [2] is for a later occasion.

[10] Cf. Bach [1]. We agree with the claim that "natural language is *very* intensional" (*ibid.*, 580), i.e. hyperintensional. We thank an anonymous referee for challenging us to clarify where we stand with respect to 'natural-language metaphysics' versus 'metaphysics'.

spells out the metaphysical implications of the chosen formal semantics and its adjacent logic. We want to know what it is we are talking about when talking about impossibilia, and we want to know what the implications are of talking in this way. The procedural hyperintensionalist and the impossible-world semanticist offer rival accounts of just that, and the respective adjacent metaphysical implications reflect these two alternative logico-semantic accounts. When we do object to 'impossible individuals on the ground' it is because such presumed entities seem to be entirely an artefact of a particular sort of theory that does not readily carry over to other theories, *a fortiori* not a theory like ours. What we can do is develop a counterpart within our theory (which is exactly what the notion of a hyperoffice generating the impossible office is intended as). We are more comfortable with this way of going about things, both for the theory-internal reason that we can build on our existing framework, and for the theory-external reason that we have little or no intuitive grasp on extensional impossibilia. Roughly, we understand the neo-Meinongian formal model, but we are not entirely sure exactly what is being modelled. Both theories, however, share a common pool of puzzles, hence our disagreement is substantial rather than merely verbal.

Our theory, prioritizing hyperintensions over intensions and intensions over extensions, might invite the objection that it gets the subjects of predication wrong. Surely, when predicating the property of being two metres tall of the man without properties, the property is not being predicated either of a procedure or a function. Somehow (the objection continues) a descent from a procedure or function to an individual has to be effected; yet, if our theory attempts to do that then it appears to be embracing impossible individuals, after all. Our response is that the objection is well-taken, but also that it gets no traction. We distinguish between *predication de re* and *de dicto*: the objection would have bite if our solution had to include predication de re, whereas it is toothless when we restrict ourselves to predication de dicto. The latter case involves only relations between hyperintensions or intensions, so no descent to extensions is required. The closest we get is when we say that any individual occupying the impossible office as presented in some particular manner would, as a matter of analytic necessity, have such-and-such properties. This sort of predication is handled by our type theory by specifying the type of the object the predication pertains to without actually descending to the realm of individuals.

The plan for the rest of the paper is as follows. Section 2 explains why intensional semantics does not suffice to capture the semantics and logic of 'impossible individuals', motivating the move to hyperintensional semantics. Section 3 offers a brief introduction into the fundamentals of TIL. Section 4 presents the core results. We define the novel notions of *hyperoffice* and *hyperrequisite*, the former being a hyperintensional counterpart of offices and the latter a hyperintensional counterpart of requisites. By means of some concrete examples, we demonstrate how to derive hyperrequisites of a hyperoffice and how to prove some of the hyperoffices impossible (because their hyperrequisites are inconsistent).

2 From offices to hyperoffices

Here we provide some background on the impossible office as viewed through the lens of general possible-world semantics. We wish to spell out exactly why intensionally individuated offices are insufficient to capture the logic of 'impossible individuals' in order to motivate the introduction of hyperoffices.

Necessity comes in basically two variants. There is the necessity that such-and-such is true, and there is the necessity that such-and-such is not true. Where α is a proposition, the contrast between the two variants is this:

$\Box \alpha$ (*necessarily, α is true*)
$\Box \neg \alpha$ (*necessarily, α is not true*)

We are using *wide-scope negation*, which adheres to the law of excluded middle: when untrue, a truth-bearer has the option of either being false or being gappy.[11] Instances of $\Box \alpha$ would be "Necessarily, e is a transcendental number" (where $\Box$ is interpreted as mathematical necessity) or "Necessarily, light travels faster than sound" (where $\Box$ is interpreted as nomological necessity).[12] Instances of $\Box \neg \alpha$ would be "Necessarily, zombies do not exist" (where $\Box$ is interpreted either as analytic or, again, as nomological necessity) or "Necessarily, no bachelor is married" (where $\Box$ is interpreted as analytic necessity). $\Box \neg \alpha$ expresses *impossibility*. When $\Box$ is interpreted as analytical necessity, then any impossible α is excluded from logical space, as soon as logical space is restricted to possible worlds. Therefore, impossibility is modelled as *vacuity* if *partially* defined intensions are embraced or else, if only *totally* defined intensions are allowed, by means of (random or designated) extensional entities as throwaway stopgaps. Here is an open-ended list of analytically impossible intensions:

a) *the impossible property (of objects of a particular type)*, i.e. the property that is necessarily uninstantiated: it takes all worlds and times to the empty set of objects;
b) *the impossible relation-in-intension of arity n (between objects of particular types)*, i.e. the relation-in-intension that is necessarily uninstantiated: it takes all worlds and times to the empty relation-in-intension of arity n, i.e. the empty set of n-tuples;
c) *the impossible proposition*, i.e. the proposition that is necessarily untrue: it takes all worlds and times to a truth-value gap or *falsum* if partiality is allowed, or to *falsum* only if partiality is disallowed;
d) *the impossible individual-in-intension*, i.e. the individual-in-intension that takes all possible worlds and times to a gap if partiality is allowed, or some either arbitrary or designated object if partiality is disallowed.

---

[11] See [7] on wide-scope and narrow-scope negation.
[12] *Nomological necessity* is whatever is the kind of necessity characteristic of the laws of nature. See [9, §4.5] for a sketch of how TIL conceptualizes nomological ('soft') necessity.

As is readily seen, (a) and (b) exemplify two different kinds of vacuity when $n > 1$: an empty (unordered) set of elements versus an empty set of n-tuples of elements; when $n = 1$, (a) and (b) both return an empty unordered set. The vacuity found in (c) is the empty set of possible worlds, whether the set be empty due to truth-value gaps or *falsum*. (d) deviates from the preceding three ones in that its kind of vacuity is invariably that of a gap, an absence, and a gap cannot be used to distinguish between whether what is absent is a truth-value or an individual. Still, gaps can be *typed* in TIL such that we have truth-value gaps, gaps of individuals, etc., where the typing serves to specify the type of the elements of the co-domain that a given intension is typed to take its arguments to. The standard alternative is to literally insert a stopgap in the form of a randomly selected individual, e.g. as per a selection function the way the ε-calculus does it.[13]

The above amounts to very coarse-grained discrimination of these four kinds of impossibilities. It is perfectly sufficient, however, as long as our only concern is to instill a dichotomy between what is impossible and its dual, i.e. what is at least merely possible. And these four kinds of impossible intensions are not equally coarse-grained, especially not if partiality is allowed. If partiality is allowed, there will be more than one impossible proposition, as any two impossible propositions will differ as for their distribution of gaps and *falsum* throughout logical space (impossibility equals here the absence of verum, leaving it open whether non-truth is *falsum* or a gap). If, on the other hand, an impossible proposition always returns *falsum* (as in a theory eschewing truth-value gaps) then there can be but one impossible proposition. The mix of gaps and *falsum* likewise spawns more than one impossible property and more than one impossible relation-in-intension (of a particular arity), as soon as sets (including empty sets) are identified with their characteristic functions. The outcome may be either *falsum* or a gap, and again there will be multiple distributions of gaps and *falsum*, as with impossible propositions.

The exception to this slight fine-graining of very coarse-grained individuation is (d) when partiality is allowed, because the only possible outcome is a gap, as we already noted. Hence, there can be but one impossible individual-in-intension. When gaps are not allowed, and an arbitrary or designated object is the outcome, there are two options. If the object is constant, we are again left with exactly one impossible individual-in-intension; if the object is a different one at different worlds and times then there will be more than one impossible individual-in-intension. Of course, one can attempt 'to Russell' a 'Frege-Church individual concept' along the lines of Kaplan [18], provided the individual concept (or office) is logically consistent, and the individual chosen does not offend Russell's self-declared 'robust sense of reality'. However, if one attempts to extend this extensionalist stance to unrealizable individual concepts, we are entering a new game defined by new rules. For the parallel extensionalist notion would be the one of impossible individual, which would be offensive to Russell's robust sense of reality. But the Meinongians, including the modal Meinongians invoking non-normal (i.e. impossible) worlds, offer to make sense of that notion. Roughly, an impossible individual is understood to be an

---

[13] See [22] for details on the issues and applications of the epsilon operator in linguistics and philosophy of language.

individual that is characterized by a characterization principle in some impossible world. There is a deep and wide chasm separating our top-down ('conceptualist') stance from the bottom-up ('objectualist') stance of modal Meinongianism. We do not need, and do not want, an individual 'on the ground' (as a member of the domain of some possible or impossible world) to serve as whoever or whatever is truthfully characterized by a characterization principle; we only need, and want, (our theoretical counterpart of) the characterization principle.[14]

The following will be our primary examples of an 'impossible individual', i.e. a hyperoffice producing the impossible office:

the fake banknote that is a banknote

The impossibility inherent to this hyperoffice is *analytical* in nature. The property modifier *fake* is privative when the property *being a banknote* occurs as its argument, hence a fake banknote fails to be a banknote.[15] Thus, we are confronted with an 'impossible individual' which both is, and fails to be, a banknote. TIL construes this 'impossible individual' as a hyperoffice that contains a pair of mutually exclusive hyperrequisites.

The other primary example is this:

the quickest runner who never overtakes the slowest runner,
if the former allows the latter a head start of $n > 0$ metres
and both run at a constant speed

This, of course, has been lifted from *Zeno's paradox*, that Achilles is unable to catch up with, not to mention overtake a tortoise. The quick runner Achilles is engaged in a race with a slow tortoise who has been granted a head start of 100 m. Though Achilles runs 10 times faster than the tortoise, Achilles will never overtake the tortoise if both run at a constant speed. While Achilles is covering the gap of 100 m between himself and the tortoise, the tortoise creates a new gap of 10 m. To Achilles's frustration, while he is covering this new gap, the tortoise is creating a new one of 1 m; and so on, ad infinitum. No matter how quickly Achilles closes each new gap, the slow but steady tortoise always opens a new one. Hence, Achilles can never catch up with or overtake the tortoise.

The impossibility inherent to this hyperoffice is part *mathematical* and part *physical* in nature. Consider this proposition:

Achilles is the quickest runner who never overtakes the slowest runner, if the former allows the latter a head start of $n > 0$ metres and both run at a constant speed

---

[14] These remarks serve only to indicate how we are positioned vis-á-vis modal Meinongianism and its ontology of impossible objects populating impossible worlds. There is, of course, also a Finnish school of impossible worlds due to Hintikka and Rantala, which is not Meinongian, but we cannot go into that here. Suffice it to say that the sort of sense TIL can make of the notion of impossible world is as a *condition* that no possible world could possibly satisfy. Therefore, impossible worlds are not worlds, according to TIL, just as impossible individuals are not individuals.

[15] Property modifiers will be explained in §3.2.

Which properties can be truth-fully predicated of Achilles on the basis of the information encapsulated in the above proposition? Section 4 provides the answer.

3 Foundations of Transparent Intensional Logic

The λ-terms of the TIL language denote abstract *procedures* (which could be approximated by Church's *functions-in-intension*) that produce set-theoretical mappings (functions-in-extension) or lower-order procedures. These procedures were originally introduced by Tichý under the moniker 'constructions', and we will stick to this original name here. Qua procedural objects, constructions can be *executed* so as to operate on input objects (of a lower-order type) and produce at most one object of the type they are typed to produce, while non-procedural objects (i.e. non-constructions, i.e. functions) cannot be executed.

There are two kinds of *atomic* constructions that present input objects to be operated on by molecular constructions. They are *Trivialization* and *Variable*. A Trivialization presents an object X without the mediation of any other procedures. Using the terminology of programming languages, the Trivialization of X, denoted by '^0X', is just a *pointer* or *reference* to X. Trivialization can present an object of any type, even another construction C. Hence, if C is a construction, ^0C is said to *display* the construction C, whereby C occurs hyperintensionally, i.e. *non-executed*. Variables produce objects dependently on valuations; they are said to *v-construct*. The execution of a Trivialization or a variable never fails to produce an object. However, the execution of some of the molecular constructions can fail to present an object of the type they are typed to produce. When this happens, we say that a given construction is *v-improper*.

There are two kinds of *molecular* constructions, which correspond to λ-*abstraction* and *application* in the λ-calculi, namely *Closure* and *Composition*. λ-*Closure*, $[\lambda x_1 \ldots x_n X]$, is the very procedure of producing a function with the values v-produced by the procedure X, by abstracting over the values of the variables $x_1,\ldots,x_n$ to provide functional arguments. No Closure is v-improper for any valuation v, as a Closure always v-constructs a function (which may be, for instance, a degenerate function undefined at all its arguments). *Composition*, $[X X_1 \ldots X_n]$, is the very procedure of applying a function f produced by X (if any) to the tuple argument $\langle a_1,\ldots,a_n \rangle$ (if any) produced by the procedures $X_1, \ldots, X_n$. A Composition is v-improper as soon as one or more of its constituents $X, X_1, \ldots, X_n$ are v-improper, or if f is a partial function not defined at its tuple argument. A third cause of improperness would be type-theoretical incoherence of the Composition, which causes the execution of the procedure to abort at the step where the mismatch occurs. A simple example would be the procedure prescribing the application of a function with domain in the natural numbers and range in the truth-values to an individual.

TIL being a *hyperintensional* system, each construction C can occur not only in execution mode so as to produce an object (if any), but also as an object in its own right on which other (higher-order) constructions operate. The Trivialization of C causes C to occur *displayed*, as mentioned above. Yet sometimes we need to cancel the effect of Trivialization and trade the displayed mode of C for execution mode. *Double Execution*, ^2C, will do that; it executes C twice over. Thus, if C v-constructs a construction D that in turn v-constructs an entity E then ^2C v-constructs E. Otherwise, ^2C is v-improper.

Definition 1. *Construction*

(i) *Variables* x, y, ... are *constructions* that construct objects (elements of their respective ranges) dependently on a valuation v; they v-construct.

(ii) Where X is an object whatsoever (even a construction), ^0X is the *construction Trivialization* that constructs X without any change.

(iii) Let X, $Y_1,...,Y_n$ be arbitrary constructions. Then the *Composition* $[X Y_1...Y_n]$ is the following *construction*. For any v, the Composition $[X Y_1...Y_n]$ is v-*improper* if some of the constructions X, $Y_1,...,Y_n$ is v-improper, or if X does not v-construct a function that is defined at the n-tuple of objects v-constructed by $Y_1,...,Y_n$. If X does v-construct such a function then $[X Y_1...Y_n]$ v-constructs the value of this function at the n-tuple.

(iv) (λ-)*Closure* $[\lambda x_1...x_m Y]$ is the following *construction*. Let x_1, x_2, ..., x_m be pair-wise distinct variables and Y a construction. Then $[\lambda x_1 ... x_m Y]$ v-*constructs* the function f that takes any members $B_1,...,B_m$ of the respective ranges of the variables $x_1,...,x_m$ into the object (if any) that is $v(B_1/x_1,...,B_m/x_m)$-constructed by Y, where $v(B_1/x_1,...,B_m/x_m)$ is like v except for assigning B_1 to x_1, ..., B_m to x_m.

(v) Where X is an object whatsoever, ^1X is the *construction Execution* that v-constructs what X v-constructs. Thus if X is a v-improper construction or not a construction as all, ^1X is v-improper.

(vi) Where X is an object whatsoever, ^2X is the *construction Double Execution*. If X is not itself a construction, or if X does not v-construct a construction, or if X v-constructs a v-improper construction, then ^2X is v-improper. Otherwise ^2X v-constructs what is v-constructed by the construction v-constructed by X.

(vii) Nothing is a *construction*, unless it so follows from (i) through (vi).

With constructions of constructions, constructions of functions, functions, and functional values in our stratified ontology, we need to keep track of the traffic between multiple logical strata. The *ramified type hierarchy* discharges that task. The type of first-order objects includes all objects that are not constructions. Therefore, it includes not only the standard objects of individuals and truth-values, but also sets, functions-in-extension and also functions defined on possible worlds (i.e., the *intensions* germane to possible-world semantics). The type of second-order objects includes constructions of first-order objects and functions that have such constructions in their domain or range. The type of third-order objects includes constructions of first- or second-order objects and functions that have such constructions in their domain or range; and so on ad infinitum.

Impossible individuals as necessarily empty individual concepts

Definition 2. *Ramified hierarchy of types.* Let B be a *base*, where a base is a collection of pair-wise disjoint, non-empty sets. Then:

T$_1$ *(types of order 1).*

i) Every member of B is an elementary *type of order 1 over B*.
ii) Let $\alpha, \beta_1, ..., \beta_m$ ($m > 0$) be types of order 1 over B. Then the collection $(\alpha \beta_1 ... \beta_m)$ of all m-ary partial mappings from $\beta_1 \times ... \times \beta_m$ into α is a functional *type of order 1 over B*.
iii) Nothing is a *type of order 1 over B* unless it so follows from (i) and (ii).

C$_n$ *(constructions of order n)*

i) Let x be a variable ranging over a type of order n. Then x is a *construction of order n over B*.
ii) Let X be a member of a type of order n. Then ^0X, ^1X, ^2X are *constructions of order n over B*.
iii) Let $X, X_1,..., X_m$ ($m > 0$) be constructions of order n over B. Then $[X X_1...X_m]$ is a *construction of order n over B*.
iv) Let $x_1, ..., x_m, X$ ($m > 0$) be constructions of order n over B. Then $[\lambda x_1...x_m X]$ is a *construction of order n over B*.
v) Nothing is a *construction of order n over B* unless it so follows from **C$_n$** (i)-(iv).

T$_{n+1}$ *(types of order n + 1)*
Let $*_n$ be the collection of all constructions of order n over B. Then

i) $*_n$ and every type of order n are *types of order n + 1*.
ii) If $\alpha, \beta_1,...,\beta_m$ ($m > 0$) are types of order $n + 1$ over B, then $(\alpha \beta_1 ... \beta_m)$ (see **T$_1$** (ii)) is a *type of order n + 1 over B*.
iii) Nothing is a *type of order n + 1 over B* unless it so follows from (i) and (ii).

For the purposes of natural-language analysis, we are usually assuming the following base of ground types:

> o: the set of truth-values **T, F**;
> ι: the set of individuals (the universe of discourse);
> τ: the set of real numbers (doubling as times);
> ω: the set of logically possible worlds (the logical space).

We assume that the universe of discourse ι is multivalued, though we leave aside the cardinality of this basic type. Sets and relations are modelled by (and in type-theoretic terms identified with) their characteristic functions. Thus, for instance, $(o\iota)$ is the type of a set of individuals, while $(o\iota\iota)$ is the type of a relation-in-extension between individuals. Empirical expressions denote *empirical conditions*, which may or may not be satisfied at the world/time pair selected as points of evaluation. These empirical conditions are modelled as (PWS-)*intensions*. Intensions are entities of type $(\beta\omega)$: mappings from possible worlds ω to an arbitrary type β. The type β is frequently the type of the *chronology* of α-objects, i.e., a mapping of type $(\alpha\tau)$. Thus α-intensions are frequently functions of type $((\alpha\tau)\omega)$ abbreviated as '$\alpha_{\tau\omega}$'.

Impossible individuals as necessarily empty individual concepts

Extensional entities are entities of a type α where $\alpha \neq (\beta \omega)$ for any type β. Where w ranges over ω and t over τ, the following logical form essentially characterizes the logical syntax of empirical language:

$$\lambda w \lambda t [...w...t...]$$

Examples of frequently used (PWS-)intensions are: *propositions* of type $o_{\tau\omega}$, *properties of individuals* of type $(o\iota)_{\tau\omega}$, *binary relations-in-intension between individuals* of type $(o\iota\iota)_{\tau\omega}$, and *individual offices* of type $\iota_{\tau\omega}$.

Logical objects like truth-functions and quantifiers are extensional; *truth-functions* $\land, \lor, \supset$ are of type (ooo), and $\neg$ of type (oo). The *quantifiers* $\forall^\alpha$, $\exists^\alpha$ are type-theoretically polymorphic total functions of type $(o(o\alpha))$, for an arbitrary type α, defined as follows. The *universal quantifier* $\forall^\alpha$ is a function that associates a class A of α-elements with **T** if A contains all elements of the type α, otherwise with **F**. The *existential quantifier* $\exists^\alpha$ is a function that associates a class α-elements with **T** if A is a non-empty class, otherwise with **F**.

Notational conventions. Below all type indications will be provided outside the formulae in order not to clutter the notation. Moreover, the outermost brackets of Closures will be omitted whenever no confusion can arise. Furthermore, 'X/α' means that an object X is (a member) of type α. '$X \to \alpha$' means that X is typed to v-construct an object of type α, regardless of whether X in fact v-constructs anything. Throughout, it holds that the variables $w \to \omega$ and $t \to \tau$. If $C \to \alpha_{\tau\omega}$ then the frequently used Composition $[[Cw]t]$, which is the intensional descent (i.e., extensionalization) of the α-intension v-constructed by C, will be encoded as 'C_{wt}'. When no confusion arises, we use the standard infix notation without Trivialization for the application of truth-functions and quantifiers. Moreover, instead of '$[^0\forall\lambda xB]$', '$[^0\exists\lambda xB]$' we often write '$\forall xB$', '$\exists xB$', for any $B \to o$, to make quantified formulas easier to read.

The *general semantic schema* involving the *meaning* (i.e., a construction) of an expression E, *denotation* (i.e., the object, if any, denoted by E) and *reference* (i.e., the value of an intension, if the denotation is an intension, in the actual world at the present time) is depicted by Fig. 1.

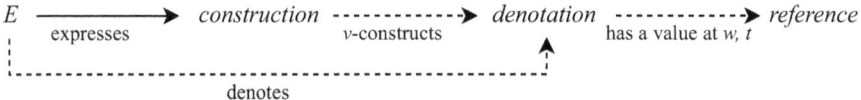

Fig. 1 General semantic schema

Once the meaning of a term or expression has been given, it can be calculated what its denotation is. Provided the denotation is not a trivial (i.e., constant) intension or a mathematical function, the reference cannot be calculated; instead it must be established by extra-logical and extra-semantic means (i.e., empirical inquiry or mathematical calculation) what the reference, if any, is. TIL does not consider reference a semantic notion, so the semantic value of a term or expression cannot be its reference. Nor can it, in all cases, be its denotation, because there are meaningful terms that do not denote any object, like 'the greatest prime'. However, the semantic value of an *empirical* term is invariably its denotation, i.e. an intension. Accordingly, an empirical term expresses a construction of an intension as its meaning and denotes this intension as its semantic value. Therefore, if E expresses as its meaning a construction of the impossible individual office then E denotes the impossible office. Any such E qualifies as an empirical term because its meaning constructs an intension of type $\iota_{\tau\omega}$.

3.1 Requisites

Duží et al. in [9, ch. 4] introduce a logic of intensions that has been developed into an *intensional essentialism* which spells out how some intensions supervene on other intensions. The key notion is that of *requisite*. Intuitively, a requisite is a further intension of a particular type that must, as a matter of analytic necessity, be had by any entity that has—by being (in) the extension of—some initial intension. For instance, the further property of being physically extended is a requisite for having the initial property of being coloured. Formally, a requisite is a relation-in-extension between intensions of any type, though typically (for philosophical purposes) between individual properties or offices. The type of requisite we need here is defined as follows.

Definition 3. *Property as a requisite of an office.* Let $p \to (o\iota)_{\tau\omega}$ and $q \to \iota_{\tau\omega}$ be constructions v-constructing a property and an office, respectively; $Occ/(o\iota_{\tau\omega})_{\tau\omega}$ the property of an office of being occupied at a given world and time; $True/(oo_{\tau\omega})_{\tau\omega}$ the property of a proposition of being true at a given world and time; and $Req/(o(o\iota)_{\tau\omega}\iota_{\tau\omega})$ the relation between a property and an office. Then the *property* v-constructed by p is a *requisite of the office* v-constructed by q iff

$$[^0Req\, p\, q] = [^0\forall \lambda w\, [^0\forall \lambda t\, [[^0Occ_{wt}\, q] \supset [^0True_{wt}\, \lambda w \lambda t\, [p_{wt}\, q_{wt}]]]]].$$

Remark. This definition applies the properties *Occ* and *True* to an office and a proposition, respectively, because the relation obtains necessarily. If we carelessly defined the relation by way of $[^0\forall \lambda w\, [^0\forall \lambda t\, [p_{wt}\, q_{wt}]]]$ the result would be a falsehood. The reason is that, at those worlds and times at which the office goes vacant, the Composition q_{wt} is v-improper, hence so would the Composition $[p_{wt}\, q_{wt}]$ be, hence the universal quantifiers would return the truth-value **F**.

Suppose now that the value of q is the impossible office. Then the antecedent Composition $[^0Occ_{wt}\, q]$ v-produces **F** for every valuation v, and thus the implication v-produces **T** for any valuation v and any value of p. The upshot is that *any property is a requisite of the impossible office*. This *explosion* of requisites is a straightforward corollary of Def. 3. One may wonder: does it matter? Narrowly speaking, it does not, for the explosion simply highlights the fact that the impossibility inherent to the impossible office fails to impose any sort of restriction on what must be true of the occupant. Since this extreme office will nowhere and never have an occupant, it is of no material or empirical import what the requisites of the office are. But – no restrictions, no logic.[16] There are basically two options. One is to develop a device to prevent explosion from arising in the first place. The other is to leave the explosion as is and instead develop an additional notion of office that brings explosion to a halt. We are pursuing the second option, so we need to restrict the proliferation of requisites to those that are, intuitively speaking, *conceptually relevant*, instead of alien, to a given construction that produces an impossible office. That is, we want to devise our logic in such a way that some, but certainly not all, properties can be inferred. What we will be doing is cap the explosion as soon as a witness of inconsistency has been identified.

3.2 Modifiers

Another notion we need to analyze due to our example of the fake banknote that is a banknote is that of *property modifier*.[17] This example involves a *privative* modifier, *fake*. TIL defines modifiers by way of requisites. First, property modifiers are extensional functions (relations-in-extension) of type $((o\iota)_{\tau\omega}(o\iota)_{\tau\omega})$, which trade the root property for the modified property. Second, we define the *essence* of a property.

Definition 4. *Essence of a property.* Let $f, g \to (o\iota)_{\tau\omega}$ be constructions of properties; let $Ess\ /\ (o\,(o\iota)_{\tau\omega}(o\iota)_{\tau\omega})$ be a function assigning to a given property f the set of its requisites defined thus:

$$^0Ess = \lambda f \lambda g\,[^0Req\,g\,f]$$

Then the *essence of a property* f is the set of its requisites:

$$[^0Ess f] = \lambda g\,[^0Req\,g\,f]$$

Now we are in a position to define a modifier privative with respect to a property h.

Definition 5. *Privative modifier.* Let the types be: $h \to (o\iota)_{\tau\omega}$; $M \to ((o\iota)_{\tau\omega}(o\iota)_{\tau\omega})$; $p \to (o\iota)_{\tau\omega}$; $x \to \iota$. Then a modifier M is *privative* with respect to a property h iff

$$[[^0Ess\,h] \cap [^0Ess\,[M\,h]]] \neq \emptyset \land$$
$$\exists p\,[[[^0Ess\,h]\,p] \land [[^0Ess\,[M\,h]]\,\lambda w \lambda t\,[\lambda x \neg[p_{wt}x]]]].$$

Hence a private modifier deprives the root property constructed by h of some, but not all, of its requisites by trading them for at least one contradictory property. As a

---

[16] Various versions of relevant / relevance logic have been put forward to address this sort of issue. See, for instance, [4].

[17] See [6] for the TIL treatment of modifiers and [17] for privative modifiers in particular.

result, the respective properties constructed by h and $[Mh]$ are contrary rather than contradictory. No individual can co-instantiate both properties; but many individuals instantiate neither of them.

4 Between explosion and sterility

We want to be able to infer that (colloquially speaking, at first) the fake banknote that is a banknote must be both a banknote and a fake banknote, and cannot be a zebra, a unicorn, a planet, a former smoker, ... The hyperoffice *subsumes* the properties of being a banknote and being a fake banknote, but it does not subsume being a zebra, etc. Since these two subsumed properties are contrary, hence logically mutually exclusive (because *fake* is privative with respect to *banknote*), this hyperoffice produces the impossible office.

4.1 Hyperrequisites of a hyperoffice

Above we defined the *essence* of an office $Off/\iota_{\tau\omega}$ as the set of *all* the requisite properties of the office. Next, we are going to show how to derive conceptually relevant hyperrequisites of a hyperoffice. Each hyperoffice $*Off/*_n \to \iota_{\tau\omega}$ produces an office $Off/\iota_{\tau\omega}$. The essence of Off being infinite, we cannot derive constructions of all the requisites belonging to the essence of Off. Yet this does not debar us from deriving those that are conceptually relevant. Therefore, the set of the properties produced by the conceptually relevant hyperrequisites of $*Off$ is a proper subset of the essence of Off.

The definition of *hyperrequisite* of a *hyperoffice* is the central definition being put forward in this paper. It must provide a solution to the problem of explosion of requisites of the impossible office, and the solution must not engender new problems of its own. In particular, it must not reinstate the problem of explosion, only now of hyperrequisites. This explains why we do not apply *ex falso quodlibet*. And this also explains why we define only *primary hyperrequisite of a hyperoffice*, where a primary hyperrequisite is defined negatively as one that does not demand *refinement* in order to be derived. Or, if defined positively, primary requisites are those constructions of properties that can be derived directly from the hyperoffice, i.e. that can be, as it were, 'read off of' the hyperoffice as it immediately presents itself.[18]

Definition 6. (*Primary hyperrequisite of a hyperoffice*). Let $*Off/*_n \to \iota_{\tau\omega}$; hyperrequisite $*Req/*_n \to (o(o\iota)_{\tau\omega}\iota_{\tau\omega})$. Then the *primary hyperrequisites* $*Req$ of the

---

[18] *Refinement* has been described and defined in [9, §5.4.4]. The idea behind refinement is that it takes us from an atomic construction (typically, a Trivialization) of a property F to a molecular construction of F. Refinement takes us, e.g., from *being a bachelor* to *being an unmarried adult male*. For applications, see [14, §5], which also defines *simplification*, the dual of refinement.

hyperoffice *Off are those property-producing constructions that are provably derivable from *Off without applying *ex falso quodlibet*.

Remark. In TIL we have developed several kinds of proof calculus. They include, inter alia, a general resolution method, the sequent calculus and natural deduction.[19] Hence by 'provably derivable' we intend the application of any of these methods.

Since our goal is to track down an inconsistency somewhere in a given definition of the impossible office, in case there is no explicit inconsistency among the primary hyperrequisites, we go on to derive *secondary* hyperrequisites of a given hyperoffice *Off. Secondary hyperrequisites of *Off are primary hyperrequisites of another hyperoffice *Off^r, where *Off^r is obtained by refining *Off. Since the refined construction is provably equivalent to the original one in the sense of producing the same office, in case the office in question is impossible we arrive after a finite number of steps at a pair of contradictory hyperrequisites, at which point we terminate the process.

Now we illustrate by way of an example the method of deriving hyperrequisites of a hyperoffice by natural deduction. Let the example be: '*the only bird that is red or blue*'. The meaning of this definite description is the hyperoffice identified with the following Closure:

$$\lambda w \lambda t \, [^0I \lambda x \, [[^0Bird_{wt}\, x] \wedge [[^0Red_{wt}\, x] \vee [^0Blue_{wt}\, x]]]]$$

Types. $I/(\iota(o\iota))$: singularizer, i.e., a function that associates a singleton S of individuals with its unique element and is otherwise undefined; Bird, Red, Blue/$(o\iota)_{\tau\omega}$; $x \to \iota$.

We want to derive the set *Req$_0$ of primary *hyperrequisites* of the above Closure (i.e., of the Closure itself rather than of its product of type $\iota_{\tau\omega}$). Here is how. Assume that in a world w and time t an individual a happens to be the only bird that is red or blue. Then:

1) $a = \lambda w \lambda t \, [^0I \lambda x \, [[^0Bird_{wt}\, x] \wedge [[^0Red_{wt}\, x] \vee [^0Blue_{wt}\, x]]]]_{wt}$ ∅
2) $a = [^0I \lambda x \, [[^0Bird_{wt}\, x] \wedge [[^0Red_{wt}\, x] \vee [^0Blue_{wt}\, x]]]]$ β-reduction, 1
3) $[[^0Bird_{wt}\, a] \wedge [[^0Red_{wt}\, a] \vee [^0Blue_{wt}\, a]]]$ IE, 2
4) $[^0Bird_{wt}\, a]$ $\wedge$E, 3
5) $[[^0Red_{wt}\, a] \vee [^0Blue_{wt}\, a]]$ $\wedge$E, 3
6) $[\lambda w \lambda t \lambda x \, [[^0Red_{wt}\, x] \vee [^0Blue_{wt}\, x]]_{wt}\, a]$ λI, 5

Remark. Line 3 employs a rule we call IE ('singularizer elimination'), and which can be stated formally thus:

$$[a = [^0I \lambda x H(x)]] \vdash H(a)$$

The rule dictates that if a is an entity equal to the only x such that $H(x)$ then it is derivable that $H(a)$. The types involved are these: $H(x)/*_n \to o$: construction

---

[19] For details, see, e.g. [3], [5], and [10].

with a free variable x; $\lambda x H(x)/*_n \to (o\alpha)$; $x/*_n \to \alpha$; $a/*_n \to \alpha$; $I/(\alpha(o\alpha))$. The *proof* of the rule follows immediately from the definition of *singularizer* as taking a singleton to its element and being undefined at empty or multi-element sets. If $[^0 I\lambda x H(x)]$ is proper then the set produced by $[\lambda x H(x)]$ is a singleton populated by a; therefore, $[a = [^0 I\lambda x H(x)]] = H(a)$. For the sake of simplicity, in the proofs that follow we will omit the first two steps and start directly at step (3), thus beginning at the condition that any individual a that would occupy the office would have to satisfy.

We just proved that any individual a that would be the only bird that is red or blue would have to have the properties of being a bird and being red or blue

(1) $^*Req_0 : \{^0 Bird, \lambda w \lambda t \lambda x [[^0 Red_{wt}\, x] \vee [^0 Blue_{wt}\, x]]\}$

where the constructions $^0 Bird \to (o\iota)_{\tau\omega}$, $\lambda w \lambda t \lambda x [[^0 Red_{wt}\, x] \vee [^0 Blue_{wt}\, x]] \to (o\iota)_{\tau\omega}$ are *provably derivable* from the hyperoffice of the only bird that is red or blue without refinement.

By iteration we keep deriving constructions of other properties from the constructions obtained at the previous step. If a given construction is of the form $^0 F$, i.e., the Trivialization of a property F, then we apply the method of *refinement*. It consists in using an equivalent, molecular construction defining the property F instead of $^0 F$. Hence, at step 2 we obtain the set $^*Req_1$ of constructions that are provably derivable from the refined elements of $^*Req_0$:

(2)   Derivation of $^*Req_1$

Since among $^*Req_0$ there is a Trivialization of the property of being a bird, we include a definition of this property instead of $^0 Bird$. We rely on the following definition:[20] a *bird* is an endothermic vertebrate of the class Aves, having a body covered with feathers, forelimbs modified into wings, scaly legs, a beak, and no teeth, and laying hard-shelled eggs. Formally, where the identity obtains between the property constructed by the Trivialization and the property constructed by the Closure:

$$^0 Bird = \lambda w \lambda t \lambda x [[[^0 Endothermic\, ^0 Vertebrate]_{wt}\, x] \wedge$$
$$[^0 Feather_{wt}\, x] \wedge$$
$$[^0 Wing_{wt}\, x] \wedge$$
$$[[^0 Toothless\, [^0 Beaked\, ^0 Jaw]]_{wt}\, x] \wedge$$
$$\forall y [[^0 Lay_{wt}\, x y] \supset [[^0 Hardshelled\, ^0 Egg]_{wt}\, y]] \wedge \ldots]$$

Hence, $^*Req_1$ are the constructions of properties that are provably derivable from this definition:

---

[20] See https://www.dictionary.com/browse/bird.

Impossible individuals as necessarily empty individual concepts

$^*Req_1: \{[^0Endothermic\,^0Vertebrate], {}^0Feather, {}^0Wing, [^0Toothless[^0Beaked\,^0Jaw]],$
$\lambda w \lambda t \lambda x \forall y [[^0Lay_{wt}\,xy] \supset [[^0Hardshelled\,^0Egg]_{wt}\,y]], \ldots\}$

Types: *Vertebrate, Feather, Wing, Jaw, Egg*/$(o\iota)_{\tau\omega}$; *Endothermic, Beaked, Toothless, Hardshelled*/$((o\iota)_{\tau\omega}(o\iota)_{\tau\omega})$: property modifiers; [$^0Endothermic\,^0Vertebrate$], [$^0Beaked\,^0Jaw$], [$^0Hardschelled\,^0Egg$] → $(o\iota)_{\tau\omega}$; [$^0Toothless\,[^0Beaked\,^0Jaw]]$ → $(o\iota)_{\tau\omega}$; *Lay*/$(o\iota\iota)_{\tau\omega}$; x, y → ι; …

– and so on. For instance, in step 3 we can derive from [$^0Endothermic\,^0Vertebrate$] the constructions of the properties of being a vertebrate and being endothermic, because *Endothermic* is an intersective modifier with respect to *Vertebrate*.[21] Similarly, we can derive constructions of the properties of having a beak, being toothless, etc. Note that we cannot derive constructions of the property *being red* or of the property *being blue*, which is as it should be. These are not among the hyperrequisites of our hyperoffice. Rather, the construction of the ('disjunctive') property *being red or blue* is one of its hyperrequisites. We can check that the set of properties produced by the hyperrequisites of the hyperoffice *the only bird who is red or blue* is a subset of the set of requisites of the office produced by this hyperoffice. For the sake of simplicity, let us denote the respective office as 'BRB'. Then, since we proved that if for any world w and time t the office of the only bird that is red or blue is occupied by an individual a then a is a bird and a is red or blue at $\langle w, t \rangle$, we can generalize to obtain this:

$$\forall w \forall t [[^0Occupied_{wt}\,^0BRB] \supset [^0True_{wt}\,\lambda w \lambda t\,[^0Bird_{wt}\,^0BRB_{wt}]]]$$
$$= [^0Req\,^0Bird\,^0BRB]$$

$$\forall w \forall t [[^0Occupied_{wt}\,^0BRB] \supset [^0True_{wt}\,\lambda w \lambda t\,[[^0Red_{wt}\,^0BRB_{wt}] \vee [^0Blue_{wt}\,^0BRB_{wt}]]]]$$
$$= [^0Req\,\lambda w \lambda t \lambda x\,[[^0Red_{wt}\,x] \vee [^0Blue_{wt}\,x]]\,^0BRB]$$

Anyway, since there is nothing inconsistent in the definition of the office of the only bird that is red or blue, we might derive still other hyperrequistes without arriving at a pair of contradictory properties.

Consider the impossible hyperoffice *the only fake banknote that is a banknote*. The office produced by this hyperoffice is necessarily vacant, because the properties of being a banknote and being a fake banknote are contrary. As explained above, this is due to the modifier *fake* being privative with respect to *banknote*. Thus, *fake* deprives the property of being a banknote of some—yet not all—of its requisites. For instance, a banknote must be issued by a bank and acceptable as tender, while a fake banknote is a fabrication that is parasitic on this institution, though it may in all other respects be both materially and conceptually indistinguishable from banknotes. Hence, though a fake banknote has much in common with a banknote, it is, and must be, a non-banknote.

---

[21] For a classification and description of three kinds of property modifiers, see [6], [17] and [15].

To forestall an explosion of requisites, we again apply our method of deriving conceptually relevant primary and secondary hyperrequisites of the hyperoffice, until we come across a witness of inconsistency. Thus, we prove that any x that might occupy the office produced by the hyperoffice would have to instantiate also the properties produced by the hyperrequisites. The hyperoffice is this Closure:

$$\lambda w \lambda t \, [{}^0I \lambda x \, [[{}^0Banknote_{wt}\, x] \wedge [[{}^0Fake\,{}^0Banknote]_{wt}\, x]]]$$

Step 1. Derivation of primary hyperrequisites $^*Req_0$: $\{{}^0Banknote, [{}^0Fake\,{}^0Banknote]\}$

1) $[[{}^0Banknote_{wt}\, x] \wedge [[{}^0Fake\,{}^0Banknote]_{wt}\, x]]$	$\varnothing$
2) $[{}^0Banknote_{wt}\, x]$	$\wedge$ E, 1
3) $[[{}^0Fake\,{}^0Banknote]_{wt}\, x]$	$\wedge$ E, 1

Step 2. First, refinement of ${}^0Banknote$. For now, this definition should do: "A banknote is a promissory note issued by a bank payable to the bearer on demand without interest and acceptable as money, a financial instrument to settle debt". Furthermore, we can apply the rule that no fake banknote is acceptable as money:

$$[[{}^0Fake\,{}^0Banknote]_{wt}\, x] \vdash \neg[{}^0Acceptable\text{-}as_{wt}\,{}^0Money\, x]$$

This gives us secondary hyperrequisites $^*Req_1$:

$$\{{}^0Promissory\text{-}note, \lambda w \lambda t \lambda x\, [{}^0Issued\text{-}by_{wt}\,{}^0Bank\, x],$$
$$\lambda w \lambda t \lambda x\, [{}^0Acceptable\text{-}as_{wt}\,{}^0Money\, x], \ldots,$$
$$\lambda w \lambda t \lambda x \neg[{}^0Acceptable\text{-}as_{wt}\,{}^0Money\, x], \ldots\}$$

We might proceed to steps 3, 4, and so on, ad infinitum. But then we would end up with the explosion of requisites that we wanted to prevent. However, since by deriving relevant hyperrequisites of a hyperoffice producing the impossible office we eventually discover some inconsistency that makes the office impossible, we finish at this point. Among the hyperrequisites in $^*Req_1$ there is a pair of contradictory hyperrequisites, namely:

$$\lambda w \lambda t \lambda x\, [{}^0Acceptable\text{-}as_{wt}\,{}^0Money\, x]$$

and

$$\lambda w \lambda t \lambda x \neg[{}^0Acceptable\text{-}as_{wt}\,{}^0Money\, x]$$

This is the main reason for introducing the notion of hyperrequisite of a hyperoffice. True, since the requisites of the impossible office are any and all properties whatsoever, they must include pairs such that they contradict each other. Only we do not know in advance whether a given hyperoffice under scrutiny produces the impossible office. Our method of deriving hyperrequisites of a hyperoffice makes it possible to eventually discover such conceptually relevant witnesses of impossibility. Hence, in no possible world at no time is there an individual that could hold the office, because this individual would have to be acceptable as money and at the same time not acceptable as money.

For another example, we want to derive that ^0Man is a hyperrequisite of the hyperoffice *the man without properties*, thus proving this hyperoffice to be inconsistent without also deriving just any property-producing procedure as yet another of its hyperrequisites. Here is the derivation:

1) $\lambda w \lambda t\, [^0I\lambda x\,[[^0Man_{wt}\,x] \wedge \forall p\, \neg [p_{wt}\,x]] = a]$ $\emptyset$
2) $[^0I\lambda x\,[[^0Man_{wt}\,x] \wedge \forall p\, \neg [p_{wt}\,x]] = a]$ λE, 1
3) $[[^0Man_{wt}\,a] \wedge \forall p\, \neg [p_{wt}\,a]]$ IE, 2
4) $[^0Man_{wt}\,a]$ $\wedge$E, 3
5) $\forall p\, \neg [p_{wt}\,a]$ $\wedge$E, 3
6) $\neg [^0Man_{wt}\,a]$ $\forall$E, $^0Man/p$, 5

In lines (4) and (6) we have derived a pair of contradictory hyperrequisites. So, our derivation terminates in keeping with Def. 6. Had our derivation not terminated, we could have gone on to derive that any property-producing procedure was a hyperrequisite of the hyperoffice in question, including a procedure producing the property of being a woman:

7) $\neg [^0Man_{wt}\,a] \vee [^0Woman_{wt}\,a]$ $\vee$I, 6
8) $[^0Woman_{wt}\,a]$ MTP, 4,7

If we were to allow the derivation that the man without properties is a woman we would be pulling the rug from under our key notion of hyperoffice and as a result could not carry out the advertised hyperintensional exploration of the realm of 'impossible individuals'. This goes to show why the ban on quodlibet is central to Def. 6 and far from being ad hoc.

For a more elaborate example, we turn to the example of the hyperoffice of *the quickest runner (a) who never overtakes the slowest runner (b), though a runs m times faster than b, provided a allows b a head start of n > 0 metres and both run at a constant speed.* Our task is to prove that this hyperoffice constructs the impossible office by demonstrating that there is an inconsistency buried in its definition.

Let us analyze the definition. We start out with *type assignments*: variables $x, y \rightarrow \iota$; $u, t \rightarrow \tau$; $Runner/(o\iota)_{\tau\omega}$; $Quickest, Slowest/(\iota_{\tau\omega}(o\iota_{\tau\omega}))$: a function taking a property to an office; (constant) $V(elocity\text{-}of)/(\tau\iota)_\omega$; $D/(\tau\iota)_{\tau\omega}$: the distance covered by an individual. The hyperoffice has this logical structure:

$$\lambda w \lambda t\, [^0I\lambda x \exists y\,[[x = [^0Quickest\,^0Runner]_{wt}]\quad [y = [^0Slowest\,^0Runner]_{wt}] \wedge$$
$$[[^0V_w\,x] = [m\,[^0V_w\,y]]] \wedge [[^0D_{wt}\,x] = {^0}0] \wedge [[^0D_{wt}\,y] = n] \wedge$$
$$\neg \exists u\,[[u > t] \wedge [[^0D_{wu}\,x] = [n + [^0D_{wu}\,y]]]]]]$$

Derivation:

a) $\lambda w \lambda t\, [^0I\lambda x \exists y\,[[x = [^0Quickest\,^0Runner]_{wt}]\quad [y = [^0Slowest\,^0Runner]_{wt}] \wedge$
$\quad [[^0V_w\,x] = [m\,[^0V_w\,y]]] \wedge [[^0D_{wt}\,x] = {^0}0] \wedge [[^0D_{wt}\,y] = n] \wedge$
$\quad \neg \exists u\,[[u > t] \wedge [[^0D_{wu}\,x] = [n + [^0D_{wu}\,y]]]]]]$ $\emptyset$

b) $[^0I\lambda x \exists y [[x = [^0Quickest \, ^0Runner]_{wt}] \wedge [y = [^0Slowest \, ^0Runner]_{wt}] \wedge$
   $[[^0V_w x] = [m [^0V_w y]]] \wedge [[^0D_{wt} x] = {^0}0] \wedge [[^0D_{wt} y] = n] \wedge$
   $\neg \exists u [[u > t] \wedge [[^0D_{wu} x] = [n + [^0D_{wu} y]]]]]$ $\lambda E, (a)$

c) $\lambda x \exists y [[x = [^0Quickest \, ^0Runner]_{wt}] \wedge [y = [^0Slowest \, ^0Runner]_{wt}] \wedge$
   $[[^0V_w x] = [m [^0V_w y]]] \wedge [[^0D_{wt} x] = {^0}0] \wedge [[^0D_{wt} y] = n] \wedge$
   $\neg \exists u [[u > t] \wedge [[^0D_{wu} x] = [n + [^0D_{wu} y]]]]]$ IE, (b)

d) $\exists y [[a = [^0Quickest \, ^0Runner]_{wt}] \wedge [y = [^0Slowest \, ^0Runner]_{wt}] \wedge$
   $[[^0V_w a] = [m [^0V_w y]]] \wedge [[^0D_{wt} a] = {^0}0] \wedge [[^0D_{wt} y] = n] \wedge$
   $\neg \exists u [[u > t] \wedge [[^0D_{wu} a] = [n + [^0D_{wu} y]]]]]$ $\lambda E, a/x, (c)$

e) $[[a = [^0Quickest \, ^0Runner]_{wt}] \wedge [b = [^0Slowest \, ^0Runner]_{wt}] \wedge$
   $[[^0V_w a] = [m [^0V_w b]]] \wedge [[^0D_{wt} a] = {^0}0] \wedge [[^0D_{wt} b] = n] \wedge$
   $\neg \exists u [[u > t] \wedge [[^0D_{wu} a] = [n + [^0D_{wu} b]]]]]$ $\exists E, b/y, (d)$

f) $[a = [^0Quickest \, ^0Runner]_{wt}]$ $\wedge E, (e)$
g) $[b = [^0Slowest \, ^0Runner]_{wt}]$ $\wedge E, (e)$
h) $[[^0V_w a] = [m [^0V_w b]]]$ $\wedge E, (e)$
i) $[[^0D_{wt} a] = {^0}0]$ $\wedge E, (e)$
j) $[[^0D_{wt} b] = n]$ $\wedge E, (e)$
k) $\neg \exists u [[u > t] \wedge [[^0D_{wu} a] = [n + [^0D_{wu} b]]]]$ $\wedge E, (e)$

In line (k) we have derived that there is no future moment u at which Achilles (a) has caught up with the tortoise (b). With a view to unearthing an inconsistency in this hyperoffice, we have to take physical laws on board, thereby stepping beyond pure logic. Physics tells us that $d = vt$, where d is distance, v velocity, and t time elapsed. At a constant velocity, the distance that something travels is equal to its velocity multiplied by the time spent. Since physical laws are empirical necessities, in TIL notation the law can be formulated like this.[22] Let $z \rightarrow \iota$; $t \rightarrow \tau$: the time spent moving. Then:

$$\lambda w \forall t \forall z [[^0D_w z] = [[^0V_w z] t]]$$

Let us calculate. The distance the quickest runner, Achilles (a), covers at time $u > t$ is m times larger than the distance the slowest runner, the tortoise (b), covers at the same time u, because the velocity of a is equal m times the velocity of b:

$$[[^0V_w a] = [m [^0V_w b]]] \Leftrightarrow [[[^0D_w u] a] = [m [[^0D_w u] b]]]$$

or "$[^0D_{wu} a] = [m [^0D_{wu} b]]$" for short. Achilles gives the tortoise a much-needed head start n,

$$[[^0D_{wt} a] = {^0}0] \wedge [[^0D_{wt} b] = n].$$

Should Achilles overtake the tortoise at some time $u > t$, he must catch up with it first. The distance Achilles must run at this time u is the head start n plus the distance the tortoise runs at the same time u:

---

[22] For the sake of simplicity, we use usual mathematical notation for arithmetic operations. For instance, we write '$[m [^0V_w b]]$', '$[[^0V_w a] t]$' for '$[^0Times \, m [^0V_w b]]$' and '$[^0Times [^0V_w a] t]$', respectively, where $Times/(\tau\tau\tau)$ is the multiplication function. Similarly for the other mathematical functions of addition (+), subtraction (-), and division (:).

$$[^0D_{wu}\,a] = [n + [^0D_{wu}\,b]]$$

Since $[^0D_{wu}\,a] = [m\,[^0D_{wu}\,b]]$, i.e. $[^0D_{wu}\,b] = [[^0D_{wu}\,a] : m]$, we have the simple algebraic equation: $[^0D_{wu}\,a] = [n + [[^0D_{wu}\,a] : m]]$. Yet this equation has a solution, namely:

$$[^0D_{wu}\,a] = [[n\,m] : [m-1]]$$

Since both n and m are given constant numbers, there is a time u at which Achilles catches up with the tortoise:

$$\exists u\,[[u > t] \wedge [[^0D_{wu}\,a] = [n + [^0D_{wu}\,b]]]]$$

which contradicts the construction at line (k). Thus, we have just proved that there is an inconsistency in the above hyperoffice; hence, there is no quickest runner (provided the laws of physics remain fixed); i.e., the hyperoffice constructs the impossible office.[23]

5 Conclusion

The problem we have addressed above is how to develop a hyperintensional notion of 'impossible individual' within Transparent Intensional Logic. The solution we put forward contains the novel concepts of hyperoffice and hyperrequisite. We identified 'impossible individuals' with a particular category of hyperoffices. The two novel concepts enabled us to calculate for a given hyperoffice whether or not it constructs the impossible office, which is necessarily vacant because any construction or definition of it is logically inconsistent. Our solution invokes no impossible individuals and only marginally intensions, namely the impossible office. Rather the focus is on structured hyperintensions—constructions as defined by Transparent Intensional Logic—some of which are typed to construct offices, including the impossible office.

Acknowledgements Marie Duží and Bjørn Jespersen were supported by the Grant Agency of the Czech Republic, project No. GA18-23891S, *Hyperintensional Reasoning over Natural Language Texts*. Daniela Glavaničová was supported by the Slovak Research and Development Agency under the contract no. APVV-17-0057 and by the VEGA grant No. 2/0117/19 *Logic, Epistemology and Metaphysics of Fiction*. We are grateful to members of the Department of Analytic Philosophy (Slovak Academy of Sciences) for comments on a previous version of this paper, in particular

---

[23] Note, however, that the condition of both runners maintaining a constant speed is critical here, because otherwise we could not apply the above physical law $d = vt$. If Achilles and the tortoise would get tired and keep slowing down in the right way, the series of gaps between them would not converge to zero. In Zeno's paradox the gaps are $n, \frac{n}{m}, \frac{n}{m^2}, \frac{n}{m^3}, \ldots$, which converge, because the series $\frac{1}{m} + \frac{1}{m^2} + \frac{1}{m^3} + \ldots$ converges to 1. But, for example, the series $\frac{1}{2} + \frac{1}{3} + \frac{1}{4} + \ldots$ which is ostensibly convergent is actually divergent. If Achilles had run the first part of the rate at $\frac{1}{2}$ km/h and the tortoise at $\frac{1}{2}$ km/h, then they would slow to $\frac{1}{3}$ km/h and $\frac{1}{4}$ km/h, respectively, and so on, thus the tortoise would always remain ahead.

to Miloš Kosterec, Martin Vacek and Marián Zouhar. Versions of this paper were presented by Daniela Glavaničová at *Trends in Logic*, Milan, 24- 27 September 2018; and Bjørn Jespersen at *OZSW 6th Conference*, University of Twente, 9-10 November 2018, and *Modal Metaphysics: Issues of the (Im)Possible VI*, Bratislava, 2-4 August 2018.

References

1. Bach, E. (1986). Natural language metaphysics. In *Logic, Methodology and Philosophy of Science VII*, ed. Barcan Marcus et al., 573–595. Elsevier.
2. Berto, F. (2017). Impossible worlds and the logic of imagination. *Erkenntnis* 82: 1277–1297
3. Číhalová, M., Duží, M., Ciprich, N., Menšík, M. (2010). Agents' reasoning using TIL-Script and Prolog. *Frontiers in Artificial Intelligence and Applications* 206: 135–154.
4. Dunn, J.M., Restall, G. (2002). Relevance logic. In *Handbook of Philosophical Logic 6*, eds. F. Guenthner and D. Gabbay, 1-136, Dordrecht: Kluwer.
5. Duží, M. (2012). Extensional logic of hyperintensions. *Lecture Notes in Computer Science* 7260: 268–290.
6. Duží, M. (2017). Property modifiers and intensional essentialism. *Computacin y Sistemas* 7260: 268–290.
7. Duží, M. (2018). Negation and presupposition, truth and falsity. *Studies in Logic, Grammar and Rhetoric* 54: 15–46.
8. Duží, M. (2019). If structured propositions are logical procedures then how are procedures individuated? *Synthese* 196: 1249–1283.
9. Duží, M., Jespersen, B., Materna, P. (2010). *Procedural Semantics for Hyperintensional Logic. Foundations and Applications of Transparent Intensional Logic*. Berlin: Springer.
10. Duží, M., Menšík, M. Inferring knowledge from textual data by natural deduction. *Computación y Sistemas*, forthcoming.
11. Fine, K. Constructing the impossible. In a forthcoming collection of papers for Dorothy Edgington.
12. Glavaničová, D. (2017). Tichý and fictional names. *Organon F* 24: 384-404.
13. Glavaničová, D. (2018). Fictional names and semantics: towards a hybrid view. In *Objects of Inquiry in Philosophy of Language and Literature. Studies in Philosophy of Language and Linguistics*, Berlin: Peter Lang, 59-73.
14. Jespersen, B. (2015). Structured lexical concepts, property modifiers, and Transparent Intensional Logic. *Philosophical Studies* 172: 321–345.
15. Jespersen, B. (2016). Left subsectivity: how to infer that a round peg is round. *dialectica* 70: 531–547.
16. Jespersen, B. (2019). Anatomy of a proposition. *Synthese* 196: 1285–1324.
17. Jespersen, B., Carrara, M., Duží, M. (2017). Iterated privation and positive predication. *Journal of Applied Logic* 25: 48-71.
18. Kaplan, D. (1975). How to Russell a Frege-Church. *Journal of Philosophy* 72: 716–729.
19. Kosterec, M. (2018). On the essence of empty properties. *Synthese*, https://doi.org/10.1007/s11229-018-02036-1
20. Priest, G. (2005). *Towards Non-Being*. Oxford: Oxford University Press.
21. Sedlár, I. (2019). Hyperintensional logic for everyone. *Synthese*, https://doi.org/10.1007/s11229-018-02076-7
22. Slater, B.H. (1994). The epsilon calculus' problematic, *Philosophical Papers* 23: 217–242.
23. Tichý, P. (1975). What do we talk about? *Philosophy of Science* 42: 80–93.
24. Tichý, P. (1979). Existence and God. *Journal of Philosophy* 76: 403–420.
25. Tichý, P. (1988). *The Foundations of Frege's Logic*. De Gruyter.
26. Vacek, M. (2017). Fiction: impossible! *Axiomathes* 28: 247-252.

St. Anselm's Ontological Arguments

Marie Duží

Abstract

In the paper I analyze Anselm's ontological arguments in favour of God's existence. The analysis is an explication and formalization of Pavel Tichý's study 'Existence and God', Journal of Philosophy, 1979. It is based on Transparent Intensional Logic with its bi-dimensional ontology of entities organized in the ramified hierarchy of types. The analysis goes as follows. First, necessary notions and principles are introduced. They are: (a) existence is not a (non-trivial) property of individuals but of individual *offices* to be occupied by an individual; (b) the notion of *requisite* is defined, which is a necessary relation between an office O and a property R: necessarily, if a happens to occupy O then a has the property R. (c) I demonstrate that an argument of the form "R is a requisite of O, hence the holder of O has the property R" is invalid. In order to be valid, it must be of the form "R is a requisite of O, the office O is *occupied*, hence the holder of O has the property R". Finally, (d) higher-order offices that can be occupied by individual offices are defined. Their requisites are properties of individual offices. Then the analysis of Anselm's arguments is presented. The expression 'God' denotes an individual office, a 'thing to be', rather than a particular individual. Thus the question whether God exists is a legitimate one. I analyze the expression 'that, than which nothing greater can be conceived'. Since 'greater than' is a relation-in-intension between individual offices here, the expression denotes a second-order office, and its requisites are properties of first-order offices such as necessary existence. The second Anselm's assumption is that individual office that has the property of necessary existence is greater than any other office lacking this property. From these it follows that the first-order holder of the office denoted by 'that, than which nothing greater can be conceived' (that is God) enjoys the property of necessary existence. Thus God exists necessarily, hence also actually. Anselm's argument is logically valid. If it were also sound, then an atheist would differ from a believer only by the former not believing whereas the latter believing in a tautology, which is absurd. Yet we may doubt the validity of Anselm's assumption that a necessary existence makes an office greater than any other office lacking this property.

This chapter originally appeared in Polish Journal of Philosophy (2011), 5(1), pp. 7–37, https://doi.org/10.5840/pjphil2011511.

1. Introduction

In this paper I am going to analyse St. Anselm's ontological arguments for the existence of God. There are two main sources which I wish to exploit. The first one is Dennis Jowers' (1999), a short study on Anselm's *Proslogion*, where the author says:

> Anselm's ontological argument for the existence of God is, in one sense, quite simple; God is that-than-which-no-greater-can-be-thought, and he must, therefore, exist, for otherwise he would not be that-than-which-no-greater-can-be-thought. Careful analysis of Anselm's Proslogion and his Reply to Gaunilo, however, will show that Anselm proposes not one, but six ontological arguments which, while relying on common premises about the nature of thought and the identity of God, differ in their contents, sometimes markedly. These six arguments may be conveniently divided into four classes: the arguments from God's perfection, the argument from His necessity, the argument from His eternity, and the arguments from His simplicity. As analysis of these arguments will show, Anselm proposes in the Proslogion and the Reply not merely a simple argument, but a whole method of reasoning about God fertile in its implications for His nature and existence.

The second principled source that I will thoroughly analyse is Pavel Tichý's excellent study 'Existence and God' published in the Journal of Philosophy, 1979. The explication of Tichý's study is the main goal of this paper. The analysis is based on Transparent Intensional Logic (TIL) with its bi-dimensional ontology of entities organized into a ramified hierarchy of types and it goes as follows. First, necessary notions and principles are introduced. They are: (a) existence is not a (non-trivial) property of individuals but of individual *offices* (Church's 'individual concepts') to be occupied by an individual; (b) the notion of *requisite* is defined, which is a necessary relation between an office O and a property R: necessarily, if a happens to occupy O then a has the property R. (c) it is shown that an argument of the form "R is a requisite of O, hence the holder of O has the property R" is invalid. In order to be valid, it must be of the form "R is a requisite of O, the office O is *occupied*, hence the holder of O has the property R". Finally, (d) higher-degree offices that are occupied by individual offices are defined. Their requisites are properties of individual offices like existence, significance, etc. Only then the analysis of Anselm's argument of Proslogion III can be detailed.

2. Four classes of arguments for the existence of God

Anselm's basic premises about God are four:[1]
   a) 'something greater than which cannot be thought' is God
   b) God can be thought
   c) God is thought
   d) God exists in the mind

Ad (a): The first premise, that the maximal being, or that-than-which-no-greater-can-be-thought, is identical to the Christian God, Anselm derives from Christian revelation.[2]

He derives his second and third premises, that God can be thought and that God is thought, from this same source. In addition he provides a three-fold philosophical defence of their plausibility. They are these:

---

[1] Portions of this section draw on material of Jowers (1999) and on Charlesworth (1965).
[2] See Charlesworth (1965, p. 169).

Ad (b): That God is a secret gives no legitimate grounds 'to the Fool' to deny that he can think about God at all. Denying this would be as foolish as saying that one cannot see daylight, because he cannot stare directly at the sun.

Ad (c): The *concept* of God as the *supremely good* resembles things *less good* insofar as they are both *good*. Thus one who knows things less good already knows something of the supreme good. Now he may augment his knowledge of the maximal being by thinking of better and better things until he reaches the limits of what he can think. That which *transcends* even these limits he knows is the *maximal being*. In addition, this maximal goodness is not only maximal but *the only one* supreme good. For, if there were two (or more) such maximal things, then each of them would be great due to something else. But then one could think of still a greater thing to be that is great due to both the criteria.

Ad (d): Even if the *concept* of God were entirely empty, that would not prevent one from thinking about it. This contention Anselm vindicates by distinguishing between the thing, that-than-which-no-greater-can-be-thought, and the concept which signifies the thing. Just as one can understand the concepts of the ineffable and the inconceivable, Anselm argues, without understanding the things they signify, so can one understand the concept, that-than-which-no-greater-can-be-thought, without understanding God Himself. Since his argument depends on the notion that human beings can think of the concept of the supreme good, and not that they can think of the being Himself, Anselm concludes that the concept of the maximal being would be adequate for his purposes even if it were purely empty. To complete the groundwork for his six ontological arguments, Anselm explains in the somewhat obscure passage that God exists in the mind:

> For, just as what is thought is thought by means of a thought, and what is thought by a thought is thus, as thought, in thought, so also, what is understood is understood by the mind, and what is understood by the mind is thus, as understood, in the mind. (Charlesworth 1965, pp. 173-75)

On these four premises, therefore, that the maximal being is the God of Christian revelation, that God can be thought, that God is thought, and that God is 'in the mind', Anselm proceeds to construct his arguments for the existence of God which may be divided into four classes:

I) the arguments from God's perfection

II) the argument from His necessity

III) the argument from His eternity

IV) the arguments from His simplicity.

The arguments from *God's perfection* are two. The first relies, in addition to the four premises stated above, on two premises:

I_1) if the maximal being exists in the mind, it can exist in reality as well

I_2) that being referred to in the second case is greater than the first.

It follows from these premises that God cannot exist merely in the mind. But we know from Anselm's fourth basic premise (d) that God does exist in the mind. God, therefore, exists also in reality.

The second argument from the perfection of God seems to be very simple. It relies on a single premise: it is greater to exist than not to exist. Since God is that than-which-no-greater-can-be-thought, he must, therefore, exist. This seemingly simple argument from Proslogion III is actually very sophisticated and an elegant one. It is a subject of Tichý's (1979) analysis and I will deal with it in details in Section 3.

The argument from *God's necessity* is perhaps the most complex of the six arguments Anselm proposes. There are two additional premises:

II$_1$) the maximal being, if he does exist, cannot not exist either actually or in the mind;

II$_2$) whatever can be thought to exist and does not exist could, if it were to exist, possibly not exist either in actuality or the mind.

Hence, since God can be thought (the premise (b)), it follows that God does, indeed, exist. For, otherwise, if the maximal being did exist only in mind and not in reality, then His existence would not be necessary, which is absurd.

The argument from *God's eternity* relies, similarly, on two additional premises:

III$_1$) the maximal being can only be thought of as without a beginning;

III$_2$) whatever can be thought of as existing, but does not actually exist, can be thought of as with a beginning.

From these and the introductory axiom (c) that God is actually thought it follows that He must exist, because, if He did not He could be thought of as having a beginning, which is self-contradictory.

The arguments from *God's simplicity* have precisely the same structure as the argument III).

IV$_1$) the maximal being cannot be thought of as not being whole or as having parts;

IV$_2$) whatever can be thought to exist yet does not exist, can be thought as other than a whole and as with parts.

The very fact that God is thought, therefore, proves that He exists, for He is thought in a way (i.e., as a whole and without parts) that is inconsistent with non-existence.

It seems that one could generate from the outline of Anselm's last three arguments II – IV as many arguments for the existence of God as there are known divine attributes, e.g. omnipotence, which are not shared with created things. Indeed, and in addition, it can be shown that applying the same structure of argumentation, one can 'prove' the existence of the greatest evil. Surprisingly, almost all the other ontological proofs and discussions on these arguments, beginning perhaps with Descartes' ontological proof and ending with Gödel's unpublished proof, concentrated on Anselm's Proslogion II to the exclusion of Proslogion III.[3]

So much for the arguments of Proslogion II. Now I am going to thoroughly explicate Tichý's (1979) analysis of Anselm's argument presented in Proslogion III using TIL.

3 Foundations of TIL

TIL with its bi-dimensional hierarchy of entities organized into a ramified hierarchy of types and procedural semantics is an overarching theory apt for any kind of discourse, whether colloquial, professional, logical or mathematical.[4] Procedural semantics contrasts with set-theoretical denotational semantics.[5] The prevailing denotational approach to semantics

---

[3] For details on Descartes' arguments, see, for instance, the entry in Stanford Encyclopedia, http://plato.stanford.edu/entries/descartes-ontological/. Detailed analysis of Gödel's proof can be found in particular in the articles of Petr Hájek, see, for instance, Hájek (1996), (2002). For a summary of contemporary discussion on ontological proofs, see http://www.formalontology.it/ontological-proof-contemporary.htm#godel
[4] Portions of this section draw on material published in Duží, Jespersen and Materna (2010).
[5] For discussion, see Johnson-Laird (1977).

conceives of the meaning of an expression E as the extra-linguistic entity denoted (or referred to) by E. Since the pioneering paper Frege (1892) the advocates of denotational semantics have striven to define so-called *structured meanings*.[6] Various adjustments of Frege's semantic schema have been proposed, shifting the entity named by an expression from the extensional level to the intensional level. Yet it has become increasingly clear since the 1970s that we need to individuate meanings more finely than in terms of what PWS intensions afford, and the need for *hyperintensional* semantics is now broadly recognised. My position is a plea for a hyperintensional semantics that takes expressions as encoding *algorithmically structured procedures* producing either extensional or intensional entities or lower-order procedures as their products. This approach — which could be characterized as being informed by an *algorithmic* or *computational turn* — has been advocated by, for instance, Moschovakis in (1994). Yet much earlier, in the early 1970s, Tichý introduced his notion of *construction* as the centrepiece of TIL.[7]

Constructions are based on a robust concept of semantic structure as an extra-linguistic, abstract procedure (a generalized algorithm). Because procedures are inherently structured, they consist of one or multiple constituent subprocedures that are to be executed in order to arrive at the product (if any) produced by the respective procedure. TIL agrees with Moschovakis's conception of Frege's sense as "an (abstract, idealized, not necessarily implementable) algorithm which computes the denotation of [a term]" (2006, p. 27).

To anticipate a common misapprehension, I wish to emphasize that the procedures I have in mind are not syntactic objects. They are objectual procedures consisting of sub-procedures. Thus an answer to Russell's question, "What binds the constituents of propositions together?" can be offered.[8] Propositional unity is established by the very procedure that generates a compound whole from its individual constituents. The meaning of an expression E is not a *list* of the meanings of the sub-expressions of E. Rather, it is the *procedure* detailing in what particular ways its sub-procedures are combined. A most important feature of TIL procedural semantics is that to exercise linguistic competence with respect to an expression is to know its sense, i.e. the procedure encoded by the expression, rather than the entity that this procedure produces. For instance, to master the empirical predicate 'is a bachelor' is neither to know what individuals or set of individuals it refers to, nor is it to know the property it denotes. (Empirical properties of individuals are construed as functions from logical space to chronologies of sets of individuals.) Rather it is to know a procedure which for any state of affairs enables the language-user to determine whether a given individual is a bachelor.[9] Moreover, some expressions do not denote anything, yet are anything but meaningless. For instance, mathematicians needed to understand the meaning of 'the greatest prime' prior to proving that there is no greatest prime. They had to master the procedure expressed by this expression in order to show that the procedure fails to produce a product.

TIL constructions are assigned to expressions as their algorithmically structured, context-invariant meanings. When claiming that constructions are algorithmically structured, I mean the following. The objects a construction operates on are not constituents of the construction. Just like the constituents of a computer program are its sub-programs, so the constituents of a construction are its sub-constructions. Thus on the lowest level of non-constructions, the objects that constructions work on have to be supplied by other (albeit trivial) constructions. This is in principle achieved by using atomic constructions. A construction C is atomic if it

---

[6] See, for instance, Cresswell (1985).
[7] See Tichý (1988, in particular Ch. Five) and (2004, pp. 873-885).
[8] See also King (2001).
[9] Fuzziness and vagueness aside.

does not contain any other constituent but C. There are two atomic constructions: *Variables* and *Trivializations*. They supply objects (of any type, including constructions) on which compound constructions operate. The constructions themselves may occur not only as constituents to be executed in order to arrive at the object, if any, they construct, but also as objects that still other constructions operate on. Thus when a construction C is Trivialized, it is not a constituent to be executed; rather, C itself is an object of predication. *Compound* constructions, which consist of other constituents than just themselves, are *Composition* and *Closure*. Composition is the procedure of applying a function f to an argument A to obtain the value (if any) of f at A. It is *improper* (i.e., does not construct anything) if f is not defined at A. Closure is the procedure of constructing a function by abstracting over variables in the ordinary manner of the λ-calculi.[10] The fundamental primitive objects of the ontology of TIL are functions rather than relations or sets. Thus the formal language in which TIL constructions are encoded is inspired by the (typed) λ-calculi. Yet *a function is not a procedure*. We view functions as set-theoretical mappings, and one and the same mapping can be produced by infinitely many procedures. Note that we strictly distinguish between procedures and their products, and between functions and their values.[11]

Constructions, as well as the entities they construct, all receive a type. The ontology of TIL is organized into an infinite, bi-dimensional hierarchy of types. One dimension, say horizontal, increases the molecular complexity of functions. The other dimension of the type hierarchy increases the order of constructions, which are higher-order entities constructing lower-order entities. Since in this paper I will not need the second dimension, I will confine myself to the simple hierarchy of types of order 1.

Definition 1 *(types of order 1)* Let B be a *base*, i.e., a finite collection of non-empty sets. Then
i) Every member of B is a *type of order 1*.
ii) Let α, $\beta_1,...,\beta_m$ be arbitrary *types of order 1*. Then the set $(\alpha\beta_1...\beta_m)$ of partial functions with values in α and arguments in $\beta_1,...,\beta_m$, respectively, is a *type of order 1*.
iii) *Nothing is a type of order 1 unless it so follows from* i) *and* ii). □

Definition 2 (*construction*)
i) *Variables* x, y, z, ...are *constructions* that construct objects of the respective types dependently on valuations v. Let a total valuation function v be given that associates variables $x_1, x_2, ..., x_n, ...$ with a sequence *Seq* of objects $a_0, a_1, ..., a_n, ...$ of a type α. Then the *variable* x_n *v(aluation)-constructs* the nth object a_n of *Seq* relative to v.
ii) *Trivialization*: Where X is an object whatsoever, ^0X is a *construction* called *Trivialization*. It constructs X without the mediation of other constructions and leaves X unchanged.
iii) The *Composition* $[X Y_1 ... Y_m]$ is this *construction*: If X v-constructs a function f of a type $(\alpha\ \beta_1...\beta_m)$, and $Y_1,...,Y_m$ v-construct entities $b_1,...,b_m$ of types $\beta_1,...,\beta_m$, respectively, then the *Composition* $[X Y_1 ... Y_m]$ v-constructs the value (an entity, if any, of type α) of the function f at the tuple argument $\langle b_1,...,b_m\rangle$. Otherwise the *Composition* $[X Y_1 ... Y_m]$ does not v-construct anything: it is v-*improper*.

---

[10] There are two other compound constructions, (single) *Execution* and *Double Execution*. Execution, ^1C, is the procedure of executing C in order to obtain the product, if any, of C. Thus, ^1C is the same procedure as C, because the default mode in which a construction occurs is its Execution. Higher-order constructions can be executed twice over, which is achieved by *Double Execution*, ^2C. However, in this paper we will not need Execution and Double Execution, and thus I omit these two constructions in the definitions below.

[11] The contrast between functions and constructions of functions is not unlike the contrast between functions-in-extension and functions-in-intension. But I am hesitant to push the parallel, since function-in-intension remains a poorly-understood notion. See Church (1941, pp. 2-3).

iv) *Closure*: Let $x_1, x_2, \ldots, x_m$ be pairwise distinct variables and Y a construction. Then $[\lambda x_1 \ldots x_m\, Y]$ is a *construction* called λ-*Closure* (or simply *Closure*). It v-*constructs* the following function f of type $(\alpha\, \beta_1 \ldots \beta_m)$. Let $v(b_1/x_1,\ldots,b_m/x_m)$ be a valuation identical with v at least up to assigning objects $b_1,\ldots,b_m$ of types $\beta_1,\ldots\beta_m$, respectively, to variables $x_1,\ldots,x_m$. If Y is $v(b_1/x_1,\ldots,b_m/x_m)$-improper (see iii), then f is undefined at $\langle b_1,\ldots,b_m\rangle$. Otherwise the value of f at $\langle b_1,\ldots,b_m\rangle$ is the object of type α $v(b_1/x_1,\ldots,b_m/x_m)$-constructed by Y.

v) Nothing is a *construction*, unless it so follows from (i) through (iv). □

Comment.
The *Trivialisation* ^0X of an object X simply constructs X without any change. One may wonder whether this construction is indispensable. Can't an object X construct itself? No, it cannot. As stated above, we strictly distinguish between procedures and their products, i.e., constructions and what they construct. Thus an object and its construction are different entities. TIL opts for homogeneity within constructions: the only possible constituents of a construction are constructions. Mont Blanc is as little a constituent of a construction as of a Fregean *Sinn*. What may be a constituent is a construction of Mont Blanc, for instance $^0Mont\_Blanc$, the simplest v-independent construction of this object.

To sum up, our neo-Fregean semantic schema is an adjusted version of Frege's semantic schema as visualized by the following figure.

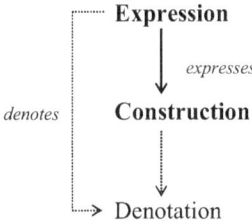

The most important relation in this schema is between an expression and its meaning, i.e., a construction. Once we have exactly defined *construction*, we can logically examine it; we can investigate what (if anything) the construction constructs, what is entailed by it, what is its analytic content, etc. Thus constructions are semantically primary, denotations secondary. Once a construction is explicitly given as a result of logical analysis, the entity (if any) it constructs is already implicitly given. As a limiting case, the logical analysis may reveal that the construction fails to construct anything by being improper. And if the construction is not improper, the denotation can be an object of any type of the TIL ontology.

The ontology of objects we can talk about within TIL is determined by the base of the type hierarchy. TIL is an open-ended system, with no one base being given once and for all. The choice of base depends on the domain(s) and language we happen to be investigating. When analyzing (fragments of) an ordinary natural language, we use the *epistemic base* $\{o, \iota, \tau, \omega\}$. It is the collection of four atomic, or ground, types:

$o = \{\mathbf{T}, \mathbf{F}\}$ (members: *truth-values*);
ι = the universe of discourse (members: *individuals*);
τ = the set of *real numbers* (doubling as *instants of time*);
ω = the logical space (members: *possible worlds*).

Since *function* is a basic notion, we model *sets* and *relations* by their characteristic functions. Thus, for example, the set of individuals is a function of type (οι) that associates any individual with **T** or **F**, according as the given individual belongs to the set. The binary relation > defined on numbers is a function of type (οττ) that associates any couple of numbers with **T** or **F**, according as the first number is greater than the second.

TIL operates with a single *procedural semantics*, as explained above. But within this one semantics TIL observes a strict demarcation between two kinds of subsidiary semantics: one for logical and mathematical languages and another for empirical languages, whether colloquial or scientific. The demarcation hinges not on formal vs. natural, but on empirical vs. non-empirical. The defining difference is that empirical languages incorporate an element of *contingency* that the non-empirical ones lack. Empirical expressions denote *empirical conditions* that may or may not be satisfied. For instance, the predicate 'is a student' does not denote each individual that happens to be a student, nor a class of individuals which happen to be students. Rather, it denotes a *property* of individuals, the 'populations' of which are particular sets of individuals depending on particular states-of-affairs. To master 'is a student' is not to know a particular set of individuals; rather, it is to know how, for any state-of-affairs, to determine whether a given individual satisfies the condition for being a student. We model these empirical conditions as possible-world (*PWS*) *intensions*.

PWS intensions are entities of type (βω): mappings from possible worlds to the arbitrary type β. The type β is frequently the type of the *chronology* of α-objects, i.e., a mapping of type (ατ). Thus α-intensions are frequently functions of type ((ατ)ω), abbreviated as '$α_{τω}$'. *Extensions* are entities of a type α where α ≠ (βω) for any type β.

As soon as we introduce an *epistemic base* for a given empirical language, the procedural semantics of the language operates in the same way as in the case of mathematical language. This is so because we apply *explicit intensionalization* and *temporalization*, that is, we insert terms for possible-world variables and times directly into the logical syntax. We can thus directly construct possible-world intensions. Where a variable *w* ranges over possible worlds, type ω, and *t* over times, type τ, the following form essentially characterizes the syntax of explicit intensionalization and temporalization:

$$λwλt\,[...w....t...].$$

In the parlance of TIL, this Closure is a construction constructing a possible-world intension. Alternative characterizations would be that the Closure is a hyperintensionally individuated, algorithmically structured mode of presentation of a function from logical space to a function from times to entities, or that it is a procedure whose product is a *condition* to be satisfied by world/time pairs.[12]

Examples of frequently used intensions are:

Propositions (denoted by declarative sentences) are of type ((οτ)ω), or '$ο_{τω}$' for short. For instance the proposition that the highest mountain is in Asia is currently true, but it might have been otherwise (hence the modal parameter ω), and it has not always been and presumably will not always be so (hence the temporal parameter τ).

Properties of individuals (usually denoted by nouns or intransitive verbs like 'is a student', 'walks') are of type (((οι)τ)ω), '$(οι)_{τω}$' for short; dependently on worlds ω and times τ they pick out the set of individuals that happen to have the property.

---

[12] For details see Jespersen (2005).

Binary *relations-in-intension* between individuals are of type $(((o\iota\iota)\tau)\omega)$, '$(o\iota\iota)_{\tau\omega}$' for short. For instance 'loves', 'is taller than' denote such relations-in-intension. That an individual a is taller than another individual b is only contingently so (modal parameter ω); and has not always been and will not always be so (temporal parameter τ).

Individual offices/roles (cf. Church's individual concepts) are of type $((\iota\tau)\omega)$, '$\iota_{\tau\omega}$' for short. For instance, 'the highest mountain', 'the Queen of Canada' denote individual offices. Again, that an individual a (currently Mt Everest) happens to be the highest mountain is only contingently so.

Sometimes it is said that the value of an intension in a possible world w and at a time t is an extension. As a general claim this is not true, however, because there are intensions of a *higher degree*. As an example of a higher-degree intension, consider, for instance, the expression 'Einstein's favourite proposition'. This definite description obviously does not *refer* rigidly: in some equivalence classes of worlds/times Einstein will favour one proposition, in another equivalence class he will favour another proposition, and in yet another equivalence class he will favour none at all. So the type of the *denotation* of 'Einstein's most favourite proposition' is $(o_{\tau\omega})_{\tau\omega}$: a 2nd-*degree proposition*, the type of whose values is $o_{\tau\omega}$.

Another example of a 2nd-*degree intension* would be *the highest US executive office*. This role is occupied by individual offices, currently by the office of US President, but it might be occupied by the US King or any other individual office. So the type of the intension denoted by 'The highest US executive office' is $(\iota_{\tau\omega})_{\tau\omega}$.

Quantifiers $\forall^\alpha$, $\exists^\alpha$ are extensions, *viz.* type-theoretically polymorphous functions of type $(o(o\alpha))$, for the arbitrary type α, defined as follows. The *universal quantifier* $\forall^\alpha$ is a function that associates a class A of α-elements with **T** if A contains all elements of the type α, otherwise with **F**. The *existential quantifier* $\exists^\alpha$ is a function that associates a class A of α-elements with **T** if A is a non-empty class, otherwise with **F**.

Notation and *abbreviations*.
- 'X/α' means that the object X is (a member) of type α;
- '$X \to_v \alpha$' means that the type of the object v-constructed by X is α. I use '$X \to \alpha$' if what is v-constructed does not depend on a valuation v.
- I will standardly use the variables $w \to_v \omega$ and $t \to_v \tau$.
- If $C \to_v ((\alpha\tau)\omega)$, i.e. $\alpha_{\tau\omega}$ for short, then the frequently used Composition $[[C\ w]\ t]$, which is the intensional descent (a.k.a. extensionalization) of the α-intension v-constructed by C, will be written as 'C_{wt}'.
- When using constructions of truth-value functions, namely $\wedge$ (conjunction), $\vee$ (disjunction) and $\supset$ (implication) of type (ooo), and $\neg$ (negation) of type (oo), I often omit Trivialisation and use infix notion to conform to standard notation in the interest of better readability. Also when using constructions of identities of α-entities, $=_\alpha/(o\alpha\alpha)$, I omit Trivialization, the type subscript, and use infix notion when no confusion arises.
 For instance, instead of '$[^0\supset [^0=_\iota a\ b]\ [^0=_{((o\tau)\omega)} \lambda w \lambda t\ [P_{wt}\ a]\ \lambda w \lambda t\ [P_{wt}\ b]]]$', where $=_\iota/(o\iota\iota)$ is the identity of individuals and $=_{(o\tau)\omega}/(oo_{\tau\omega}o_{\tau\omega})$ the identity of propositions; $a, b \to_v \iota$, $P \to_v (o\iota)_{\tau\omega}$, I will write '$[[a = b] \supset [\lambda w \lambda t\ [P_{wt}\ a] = \lambda w \lambda t\ [P_{wt}\ b]]]$'.
- I will use '$\forall x\ A$' and '$\exists x\ A$' instead of '$[^0\forall^\alpha \lambda x\ A]$' and '$[^0\exists^\alpha \lambda x\ A]$', respectively, when no confusion can arise.

When assigning constructions to expressions as their meanings as part of our semantic analysis, we use the following *method of semantic analysis*. The method consists in three

St. Anselm's ontological arguments

steps which are (a) type-theoretical analysis, (b) synthesis and (c) type-theoretical checking.[13] For illustration, here is an analysis of the well-known sentence "The King of France is bald".

(a) *Type-theoretical analysis*, i.e., assigning types to all the objects mentioned by various atoms and molecules of the analysed sentence. In our case we have:

King_of/$(\iota\iota)_{\tau\omega}$—an empirical function assigning to each individual another individual; *France*/ι; *KF*/$\iota_{\tau\omega}$—an individual office; *Bald*/$(o\iota)_{\tau\omega}$—property of individuals.

(b) *Synthesis*, i.e., using the *constructions* of the objects *ad* (a) in order to construct the proposition (of type $o_{\tau\omega}$) denoted by the whole sentence. Now we have to take into account the fact that the sentence does not talk about any particular individual. It talks about the individual office *KF* assigning to its holder (if any) the property of being bald. The office *KF* can be constructed by composing the empirical function *King_of* with *France*. Yet the empirical function is not a type-theoretically proper entity to be applied to an individual. It must be extensionalised first, i.e. applied to a particular possible world and time of evaluation: $[[^0King\_of\ w]\ t] \to_v (\iota\iota)$, or $^0King\_of_{wt}$ for short, and only then applied to *France* using the Composition $[^0King\_of_{wt}\ ^0France] \to_v \iota$. This Composition v-constructs an individual or is v-improper by constructing nothing according as there is an individual playing the role of the King of France at $\langle w, t\rangle$. Since in the actual world *W* at current time *T* there is no such individual, the Composition is $v(W/w, T/t)$-improper, the King of France does not exist. In other words, the office of the King is vacant. In order to construct the office *KF*, we have to abstract over the values of *w* and *t*:

$$\lambda w\lambda t\ [^0King\_of_{wt}\ ^0France] \to \iota_{\tau\omega}.$$

In order to assign the property of being bald to an individual that happens to occupy the office (if any), the property as well as the office must be again extensionalized first and then the former applied to the latter (if any):[14]

$$[^0Bald_{wt}\ [\lambda w\lambda t\ [^0King\_of_{wt}\ ^0France]_{wt}]] \to o$$

This Composition yields a truth-value or nothing, depending on whether at the given world and time the office is occupied and if so whether the individual that occupies the office has the property of being bald in a given $\langle w, t\rangle$-pair of evaluation.

Since the sentence "The King of France is bald" denotes a proposition rather than a truth-value, by abstracting over the values of *w* and *t*, we obtain the analysis of the sentence:

$$\lambda w\lambda t\ [^0Bald_{wt}\ [\lambda w\lambda t\ [^0King\_of_{wt}\ ^0France]_{wt}]].$$

(c) *Type-theoretical checking.*

In the interest of simplicity, I will draw a simplified type-theoretical tree. Thus, for instance, instead of the full tree on the left-hand side I will draw a shortened tree on the right-hand side:

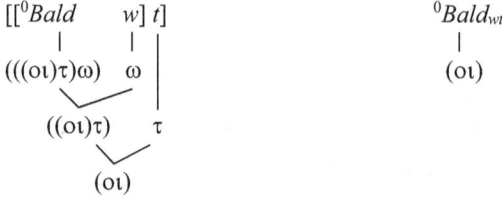

Thus the type-theoretical tree of our sentence is this:

---

[13] For details see Materna and Duží (2005) and also Duží et al (2010).
[14] For details on explicit intensionalization and temporalization, see Jespersen (2005).

St. Anselm's ontological arguments

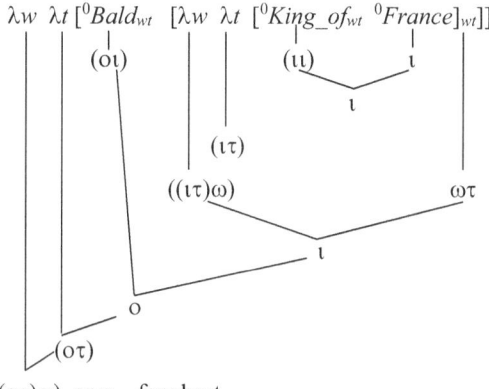

((οτ)ω), or ο_τω for short.

The type of the constructed object is ο_τω. So the sample sentence expresses as its meaning a construction constructing a proposition, which explains why the sentence denotes a proposition. Put differently, its meaning is a hyperproposition, which is a procedure producing a proposition.

3.1 Denotation and existence

In the previous section I explained the difference between *denotation* of an empirical expression, i.e. an intension, and a hyperintension, i.e. the construction assigned to the expression as its *meaning*. In case of mathematics there are meaningful expressions without denotation. However, empirical expressions always denote an object, namely an intension.

The above example of the analysis of the sentence "The King of France is bald" illustrated that even those expressions which do not refer to any object in a given ⟨w, t⟩ pair denote an intension. The sentence denotes a proposition (of type ο_τω) that the King of France is bald, and this proposition happens to have a value gap in the actual world now. This is due to the fact that the individual office denoted by the expression 'the King of France' is currently vacant. Hence the sentence does not talk about some "non-existing individual". Once the base has been chosen, the universe of discourse is fixed. We do not work with variant domains of individuals, and thus individuals exist trivially. They are *a priori*, pre-theoretically given. In other words, TIL does not work with *possibilia*. Instead we work with *partial* functions, i.e. mappings which assign *at most* one object to each argument. Properly partial functions have value gaps. In this way our procedural semantics operates smoothly with partiality and non-existence.

Now one can ask: *what kind of entity a non-trivial existence* is? As many philosophers observed, it cannot be a property of individuals, because individuals trivially exist. Some philosophers who have been involved in the contention on the nature of non-trivial existence are inclined to conclude that existence is simply not a property ascribable to things.[15]

Yet existence is often nontrivially ascribed and coherently denied. It is true and informative to say that the President of the USA exists whereas the King of France does not. However, as we explained in the previous section, these sentences do not mention any particular individual.

---

[15] For instance Aristotle in Analytica Posteriora, II, 7, 92b13, says "being is not a genus", Kant in Critique of Pure Reason "Being is ... not a real predicate", and according to Russell (Principia Mathematica, 2nd ed., p. 175) "... there is no reason to suppose that a meaning of existence could be found which would be applicable to immediately given subjects".

Instead, they mention individual *offices*, that is, intensions of type $\iota_{\tau\omega}$. In order to verify the existence of the President of the USA one does not take a particular individual and test whether this individual has the property of existence. If one has the individual at hand, the individual trivially exists and there is nothing to empirically verify. Instead, one examines the *condition* specified by the 'President of USA' and verifies whether there is an individual satisfying this condition in a given $\langle w, t \rangle$-pair of evaluation. In other words, one examines whether the American presidential office is occupied. Similarly, to verify that the King of France does not exist amounts for checking whether the office in question is vacant in a given $\langle w, t \rangle$-pair.

Hence TIL treats existence as a property of α-intensions of being occupied or instantiated, i.e. an object of type $(o\alpha_{\tau\omega})_{\tau\omega}$. Existence is a second-degree property of intensions: unicorns exist at $\langle w, t \rangle$ iff the intension *Unicorn* returns a non-empty set at $\langle w, t \rangle$; the Queen of Belgium exists at $\langle w, t \rangle$ iff the intension *The Queen of Belgium* returns exactly one individual at $\langle w, t \rangle$; etc.

The definition of existence (or occupancy) as a property of an individual office is this:

(E) $\qquad {}^0Exist = \lambda w \lambda t \, \lambda u \, [\exists x \, [u_{wt} = x]]$

Types: $Exist/(o\iota_{\tau\omega})_{\tau\omega}$; $u \to_v \iota_{\tau\omega}$; $x \to_v \iota$.

For instance, the analysis of the sentence

"The President of USA exists"

comes down to this Closure

$\lambda w \lambda t \, [{}^0Exist_{wt} \, \lambda w \lambda t \, [{}^0President\_of_{wt} \, {}^0USA]]$

that can be refined using the definition (E) and an equivalent β-reductions to

$\lambda w \lambda t \, [{}^0\exists x \, [\lambda w \lambda t \, [{}^0President\_of_{wt} \, {}^0USA]_{wt} = x]]$.

Additional types:
$President\_of/(\iota\iota)_{\tau\omega}$; USA/ι; $[{}^0President\_of_{wt} \, {}^0USA] \to_v \iota$; $\lambda w \lambda t \, [{}^0President\_of_{wt} \, {}^0USA] \to \iota_{\tau\omega}$.

Note that since *Exist* is a second degree intension the value of which is applicable to a first degree individual office, the Closure $\lambda w \lambda t \, [{}^0President\_of_{wt} \, {}^0USA]$ occurs *intensionally* in the Composition $[{}^0Exist_{wt} \, \lambda w \lambda t \, [{}^0President\_of_{wt} \, {}^0USA]]$. The whole office is an object of predication. Using medieval terminology, we also say that 'the President of USA' occurs with supposition *de dicto* in the sentence "The President of USA exists".

Compare the above analysis with the analysis of the sentence

"The President of USA is a Democrat".

Unlike *Exist*, the property of being a Democrat is a first degree intension of type $(o\iota)_{\tau\omega}$. Thus when being extensionalized, it is applicable to an individual. The analysis of the sentence comes down to

$\lambda w \lambda t \, [{}^0Democrat_{wt} \, \lambda w \lambda t \, [{}^0President\_of_{wt} \, {}^0USA]_{wt}]$.

Now the Closure $\lambda w \lambda t \, [{}^0President\_of_{wt} \, {}^0USA]$ occurs *extensionally* in the Composition $[{}^0Democrat_{wt} \, \lambda w \lambda t \, [{}^0President\_of_{wt} \, {}^0USA]_{wt}]$. Particular individual *v*-constructed by the Composition $\lambda w \lambda t \, [{}^0President\_of_{wt} \, {}^0USA]_{wt}$, i.e. the *value* (if any) of the individual office, is an object of predication. We also say that 'the President of USA' occurs with supposition *de re* in the sentence "The President of USA is a Democrat".

St. Anselm's ontological arguments

So much for the difference between first-degree properties of individuals like being a Democrat, being blue-eyed, and second-degree properties of individual offices like being occupied or vacant.

3.2 Requisites and intensional essentialism

In TIL we argue in favour of semantic anti-actualism: the actual world of all possible worlds should play no semantic role. A proposition is true in a set of possible worlds, and if it is actually true, then the actual world is an element of this set. The more we know, the more "powerful" propositions we are able to express. Only if we were empirically omniscient would we be competent to express a proposition true in a singleton containing just the actual world. However, this is the status belonging only to God.

In this section I am going to outline an essentialism that likewise accords no privileged status to the actual world by making the notion of essence independent of world and time and thus *a priori* instead. At the same time we adhere to ontological actualism, as outlined above. All the individuals at the actual world are all the individuals there are at all the other possible worlds as well. Hence there are no merely possible individuals, no *possibilia*.

Our essentialism is based on the idea that since no purely contingent intension can be essential of any individual, essences are borne by intensions rather than by individuals exemplifying intensions. That an intension has an essence means that a relation-in-extension obtains *a priori* between an intension and other intensions such that, necessarily, whenever an individual (a ι-entity) exemplifies the intension at some $\langle w, t \rangle$ then the same individual also exemplifies certain other intensions at the same $\langle w, t \rangle$. This relation is called the *requisite* relation. We base our essentialism on the requisite relation and call our position *intensional essentialism*, couching as it does essentialism in terms of interplay between intensions, regardless of who or what exemplifies a given intension.

Let the property of being a mammal be related by the requisite relation to the property of being a whale. Then by analytic necessity, that is in all worlds at all times, *if* the individual *a* is a whale at $\langle w, t \rangle$ *then a* is also a mammal at $\langle w, t \rangle$. It is an open question (epistemologically and ontologically speaking) *whether a* is a whale at $\langle w, t \rangle$. Establishing whether it is requires investigation *a posteriori*. On the other hand, establishing whether *a* must be a mammal in case *a* happens to be a whale is *a priori*, the requisite relation-in-extension and as such independent of what is true at any $\langle w, t \rangle$. Thus, there is a sense in which intensional essentialism qualifies as anti-essentialism; it is a theory which includes bare particulars and which claims that no purely contingent empirical property is essential of any individual.[16]

The requisite relations *Req* are a family of relations-in-extension between two intensions, hence of the polymorphous type $(o\alpha_{\tau\omega}\beta_{\tau\omega})$, where possibly $\alpha = \beta$. Infinitely many combinations of *Req* are possible, but the following ones are relevant for our purpose:

$Req_1/(o(o\iota)_{\tau\omega}\iota_{\tau\omega})$: an individual property is a requisite of an individual office.

$Req_2/(o(o\iota_{\tau\omega})_{\tau\omega}(\iota_{\tau\omega})_{\tau\omega})$: an individual-office property is a requisite of a second degree office.

The definitions of requisite relations must respect the fact that the requisite relation obtains between two intensions in all $\langle w, t \rangle$ pairs and thus a possible vacancy of an office in a given $\langle w, t \rangle$-pair is irrelevant. Partiality gives rise to the following complication when defining the requisite relation. If an office *X* has the requisite property *Y*, it is so no matter whether an office *X* is occupied or vacant at a given $\langle w, t \rangle$. For instance, even at those $\langle w, t \rangle$ where the

---

[16] For details see also Duží (2007).

office of King of France is vacant it is true that the property of being a king is a requisite of the office. Similarly, it is true at all $\langle w, t \rangle$ (including those where the office of President of USA is vacant) that the office of the Commander-in-Chief is a requisite of the office of President of USA. Therefore, it does not suffice to add the antecedent condition that X be occupied. For, at a $\langle w, t \rangle$ where X is vacant, the antecedent condition is False, and so the intensional descent of X to $\langle w, t \rangle$ picks up *no* individual. In other words, the Compositions X_{wt} and $[^0Y_{wt}\,^0X_{wt}]$ will be v-improper ($X/\iota_{\tau\omega}$; $Y/(o\iota)_{\tau\omega}$). The truth-functional connective of material implication ($\supset/(ooo)$) is such that when applied to a missing argument (a truth-value gap), the result is v-improper as well, making the Composition $[[^0Exist_{wt}\,^0X] \supset [^0Y_{wt}\,^0X_{wt}]]$ v-improper for $\langle w, t \rangle$. The whole *definiens* $\forall w \forall t\,[[^0Exist_{wt}\,^0X] \supset [^0Y_{wt}\,^0X_{wt}]]$ will, thus, construct False, because it is not true that the Composition $[[^0Exist_{wt}\,^0X] \supset [^0Y_{wt}\,^0X_{wt}]]$ v-constructs **T** for all $\langle w, t \rangle$ pairs ($Exist/(o\iota_{\tau\omega})_{\tau\omega}$ is the property of an individual office of being occupied.)

The solution is simple. We apply a property of propositions $True/(oo_{\tau\omega})_{\tau\omega}$ defined as follows (variable $p \rightarrow_v o_{\tau\omega}$):

$[^0True_{wt}\,p]$ v-constructs **T** iff p_{wt} v-constructs **T**, otherwise (that is if p_{wt} v-constructs **F** or p_{wt} is v-improper) **F**.

Now we are in a position to define the requisite relation between an α-property and an α-office.

Definition 3 (*requisites*) Let X, Y be intensional *constructions* such that $X/*_n \rightarrow \alpha_{\tau\omega}$, $Y/*_n \rightarrow (o\alpha)_{\tau\omega}$. Then

$[^0Req\ Y\,X] = \forall w \forall t\,[[^0Exist_{wt}\,X] \supset [^0True_{wt}\,\lambda w \lambda t\,[Y_{wt}\,X_{wt}]]]$.

Gloss *definiendum* as, "Y is a requisite of X", and *definiens* as, "Necessarily, if X is occupied at some $\langle w, t \rangle$ then it is true that whatever occupies X at $\langle w, t \rangle$ has the property Y at this $\langle w, t \rangle$."

Example. Requisites of the American presidential office are individual properties like to be a human being, to be properly elected, to be inaugurated, etc.

Remark. "The King of France is a king" is *ambiguous* between two readings — one necessarily true, the other contingently without a truth-value — as Tichý points out (1979, p. 408; 2004, p. 360). The former is the requisite (i.e., *de dicto*) reading:

$[^0Req\ ^0King\ \lambda w \lambda t\,[^0King\_of_{wt}\,^0France]]$.

Types: $King/(o\iota)_{\tau\omega}$; $King\_of/(\iota\iota)_{\tau\omega}$; $France/\iota$. If true, it is necessarily so, regardless of whether or not some $\langle w, t \rangle$ lacks an occupant of $\lambda w \lambda t\,[^0King\_of_{wt}\,^0France]$.

The other reading is the *de re* reading:

$\lambda w \lambda t\,[^0King_{wt}\,\lambda w \lambda t\,[^0King\_of_{wt}\,^0France]_{wt}]$.

If true, it is so only because somebody occupies the King's office constructed by $\lambda w \lambda t\,[^0King\_of_{wt}\,^0France]$ at $\langle w, t \rangle$ and its occupant is in the extension of *King* at $\langle w, t \rangle$.

Remark. When defining a requisite of an *office* X, the antecedent condition on X being occupied is required. Otherwise we shall have the following invalid argument on our hands (see Tichý, 1979, pp. 408ff; 2004, pp. 360ff):

(*)
$$\frac{P \text{ is a requisite of office } O}{\text{The occupant of } O \text{ instantiates } P.}$$

St. Anselm's ontological arguments

This inference pattern is fallacious,

> for the premise may be true even if O is vacant, in which case the conclusion, so far from being true, is vacuous (i.e., lacks a truth value). (*Ibid.*, p. 408, p. 360, resp.)

Applying this invalid inference pattern, we might easily "prove" the existence of the King of France. Here is how:

1)	The King of France is a king	
1*)	$[^0Req\ ^0King\ \lambda w\lambda t\ [^0King\_of_{wt}\ ^0France]]$	(necessarily true, *de dicto*)
2)	The current King of France is a king	(applying (*))
2*)	$\lambda w\lambda t\ [^0King_{wt}\ \lambda w\lambda t\ [^0King\_of_{wt}\ ^0France]_{wt}]$	(contingently true, *de re*)
3)	The King of France exists	(existential generalization)
3*)	$\lambda w\lambda t\ [^0Exist_{wt}\ \lambda w\lambda t\ [^0King\_of_{wt}\ ^0France]]$	

The step from (2) to (3) is valid, because in any world w at any time t, the step is truth-preserving. Here is the proof:

2a)	$[^0King_{wt}\ \lambda w\lambda t\ [^0King\_of_{wt}\ ^0France]_{wt}]$	assumption
2b)	$\lambda w\lambda t\ [^0King\_of_{wt}\ ^0France]_{wt}$	*v*-proper by Definition of Composition
2c)	$\lambda x\ [\lambda w\lambda t\ [^0King\_of_{wt}\ ^0France]_{wt} = x]$	constructs a *non-empty* class (from 2b)
2d)	$[^0\exists x\ [\lambda w\lambda t\ [^0King\_of_{wt}\ ^0France]_{wt} = x]]$	existential generalization
2e)	$[^0Exist_{wt}\ \lambda w\lambda t\ [^0King\_of_{wt}\ ^0France]]$	by Definition of *Exist*

However, the step from (1) to (2) is invalid, because it is the step from a *de dicto* reading to the *de re* reading. Whereas the *de re* reading not only entails, but also presupposes the existence of the King of France, the *de dicto* reading is necessarily true regardless whether the King exists.

A valid inference rule can be obtained by adding an extra premise to the effect that the relevant office is occupied:

(**)
$$\frac{P \text{ is a requisite of office } O \qquad \text{Office } O \text{ is occupied}}{\text{The occupant of } O \text{ instantiates } P.}$$

Proof: Let $P/*_n \to (o\alpha)_{\tau\omega}$; $O/*_m \to \beta_{\tau\omega}$.

i)	$[^0Req\ P\ O]$	assumption
ii)	$[^0Exist_{wt}\ O]$	assumption
iii)	$\forall w \forall t\ [[^0Exist_{wt}\ O] \supset [^0True_{wt}\ \lambda w\lambda t\ [P_{wt}\ O_{wt}]]]$	Definition 3
iv)	$[[^0Exist_{wt}\ O] \supset [^0True_{wt}\ \lambda w\lambda t\ [P_{wt}\ O_{wt}]]]$	$\forall E$
v)	$[^0True_{wt}\ \lambda w\lambda t\ [P_{wt}\ O_{wt}]]$	modus ponens ii), iv)

Now we turn to the definition of essence as a set of requisites. However, this drags type-theoretic complications along, since the requisites of an intension may well be of different types. In order to make the essence homogeneous, we define the essence of an intension as the set of properties that are necessary for an object to satisfy the condition specified by the intension. The reason why the definition of essence can be made homogeneous is because, given an arbitrary intension, there will always be a corresponding property. For instance, the

St. Anselm's ontological arguments

ι-office *the tallest woman* will correspond to the property *being an x such that x is identical to the tallest woman*. Again, for our purposes it is sufficient to define an essence of an office. The polymorphous type of such an *Essence* is $((o(o\alpha)_{\tau\omega})\beta_{\tau\omega})$: given an arbitrary β-office of type $\beta_{\tau\omega}$, *Essence* returns the set of α-properties that are the requisites of this office. Thus we define:

Definition 4 (*essence of an office*)
Let $Z \rightarrow_v \beta_{\tau\omega}$; $q \rightarrow_v (o\alpha)_{\tau\omega}$; $Req/((o(o\alpha)_{\tau\omega})\beta_{\tau\omega})$. Then $[^0Essence\ Z] = \lambda q\ [^0Req\ q\ Z]$.

Remark: It is beyond the capacities of human beings to know an intension such as an individual office or its essence. This would amount for knowing *actual infinity*, i.e. an uncountable infinite mapping. Yet we have capacities to know *potential infinity*. The meaning of an expression, such as 'the King of France' is the construction $\lambda w \lambda t\ [^0King\_of_{wt}\ ^0France]$. Its encoding in TIL language of constructions can be viewed as an instruction read as follows:

In *any* possible world (λw), at *any* time (λt) evaluate whether this or that individual satisfies the *condition* of being the King of France ($[^0King\_of_{wt}\ ^0France]$). Thus if one understands the meaning of 'King of France', it suffices to follow the instruction specified by this meaning; which *does not*, however, mean that one is always able to *execute* this instruction and thus to know the holder.

This will do as an outline of the philosophy of TIL, together with its basic definitions. Now I am going to apply the TIL formal apparatus to the explication of Anselm's argument in Proslogion III.

4 On Tichý's analysis of Proslogion III

Proslogion III is an earnest prayer rather than a proof. Yet it is a simple, crisp, entirely transparent and valid argument for the existence of God. Anselm's argument in Chapter III goes as follows:

> God cannot be conceived not to exist. – God is that, than which nothing greater can be conceived. – That which can be conceived not to exist is not God.
>
> AND it assuredly exists so truly, that it cannot be conceived not to exist. For, it is possible to conceive of a being which cannot be conceived not to exist; and this is greater than one which can be conceived not to exist. Hence, if that, than which nothing greater can be conceived, can be conceived not to exist, it is not that, than which nothing greater can be conceived. But this is an irreconcilable contradiction. There is, then, so truly a being than which nothing greater can be conceived to exist, that it cannot even be conceived not to exist; and this being you are, O Lord, our God.
>
> So truly, therefore, do you exist, O Lord, my God, that you can not be conceived not to exist; and rightly. For, if a mind could conceive of a being better than you, the creature would rise above the Creator; and this is most absurd. And, indeed, whatever else there is, except you alone, can be conceived not to exist. To you alone, therefore, it belongs to exist more truly than all other beings, and hence in a higher degree than all others. For, whatever else exists does not exist so truly, and hence in a less degree it belongs to it to exist. Why, then, has the fool said in his heart, there is no God (Psalms xiv. 1), since it is so evident, to a rational mind, that you do exist in the highest degree of all? Why, except that he is dull and a fool?

Now I am going to logically analyse the argument the core of which is the second paragraph of the above quotation. Tichý presents his analysis informally, only in prose. So much better for his paper. Yet, using the formal apparatus of Transparent Intensional Logic (TIL) makes it possible to clarify Tichý's ingenious analysis.

First, there is a question what does the expression 'God' mean or denote. If 'God' denoted an individual, then it would be purely contingent matter whether (s)he is omnipotent, omniscient, benevolent, etc., because any individual might have been malevolent, non-omniscient, non-omnipotent, etc. But the concept of a malevolent God is certainly not acceptable for a Christian. Thus the expression 'God' denotes an individual office, a 'thing to be', rather than a particular individual, and the question whether God exists is a legitimate one. We ask whether God-like *office* of type ι_τω is occupied.

Intermezzo on Descartes ontological proof.

In its very simple form, it is an argument from perfection that can be formulated as follows:

> The essence of God-office is formed by all positive perfections.
> Existence is a positive perfection.
> Hence, God exists.

What's wrong here? There are two problems, two flaws.

a) There is a confusion of the *intensional* and *extensional level* of abstraction: Existence is not a property of individuals. Rather, it is a property of the office itself. Thus existence cannot be a requisite of God-office, it is a second degree intension that is ascribable on the *intensional* level. However, requisites of an individual office are properties of individuals that are ascribable on the *extensional* level.

b) Descartes applies the invalid inference rule (*).

<u>Existence is a requisite of the office of God.</u>
Hence the holder of the office has the property of existence.

As we have seen above, there is a missing assumption on the occupancy of the office. Yet adding such an assumption makes the proof circular and thus futile.

End of intermezzo

In what follows I am going to show that Anselm's argument does not suffer any of these flaws, and is, indeed, valid. Thus the only question is whether it is also sound. Let us reformulate the argument in a concise form:

> It is *possible* to conceive of a being which cannot be conceived not to exist
> The being which cannot be conceived not to exist is *greater than* one which can be conceived not to exist.
> 'That, than which nothing greater can be conceived' cannot be conceived not to exist.
> ---
> 'That, than which nothing greater can be conceived' truly exists.

Descartes's and the other ontological arguments are objectionable also from a theological point of view. They assume that God's essence is known. In other words, they assume to know precisely *which* individual office is that of God. Yet God is a secret, and St. Anselm in Proslogion III is far from such arrogance. He addresses God by a modest 'That, than which nothing greater can be conceived'. All that Anselm here presumes to know is *something* about God's essence, namely that nothing can conceivably surpass it in greatness. Let us now analyse the expression 'That, than which nothing greater can be conceived'.

Greater_than/(οι_τωι_τω)_τω is a binary relation-in-intension between individual *offices*.

It is not a relation between bare individuals. If one says "Tom is greater than Peter", then this sentence is incomplete in its meaning, because the sentence lacks to provide a *criterion* according to which Tom and Peter are to be compared. For instance, Tom can be greater than

Peter as a musician whereas Peter can be greater than Tom as for his mathematical abilities. Tichý in (1979) adduces a nice example:

> Notice that the U.S. president is a strictly greater thing to be than the richest peanut farmer in Plains, Georgia, but that nothing of the sort can be said regarding the persons who happen to *be* those things, for they are one and the same. (ibid., p. 413, 2004, p. 365)

Moreover, it is a relation-in-*intension*, because it is a contingent fact that one office is greater than another one. For instance, the U.S. president is surely a greater office than that of the President of the Czech Republic in virtue of the comparative size and might of these countries. But this is clearly not a matter of logical necessity, it might have been otherwise.

Thus we can take it for granted that the set of individual offices is partially ordered. Some of the offices are incomparable, because they are great in virtue of incomparable criteria. Yet let us suppose that one of these offices is actually and currently the greatest one. Sure, in another possible world and time some other individual office may be the greatest thing. Thus *the greatest individual office* is not any particular office. Rather, it is something which this, that or other individual office can be. Hence, it is a second degree office—call this thing *H*— occupiable by individual offices.

Hence the expression 'that, than which nothing greater can be conceived' denotes $H/(\iota\tau\omega)\tau\omega$. Anselm's key assumption is that

(G) $\qquad\qquad$ *H* is occupied by *God-office*.

For an individual office to occupy *H*, no other office can conceivably be greater than it. But as we have seen in Section 3, one can be perfectly familiar with the *condition* what it amounts for an individual office to occupy *H*, without knowing *which* office satisfies this condition. Anselm presumes to know very well what it takes for an individual office to occupy *H*, that is to be the office of God; but since he does not know which particular individual office is the holder of *H*, he does not know exactly what it takes for an individual to be God.

Since existence is a property of individual offices, namely the property of being occupied, there is no category mistake in the assumption that existence is a part of the essence of *H*, i.e. a requisite of *H*. From a logical point of view it is a legitimate question to ask whether being occupied is one of the conditions that an individual office must satisfy in order to be the greatest conceivable individual office.

Similarly, *necessary existence*, conceived as a property of being occupied in *all* $\langle w, t\rangle$-pairs, can be a requisite of *H*. Note however, that necessarily occupied office cannot be vacant in any $\langle w, t\rangle$-pair. Thus there is a class $NE/(\omicron\iota\tau\omega)$ of necessarily occupied individual offices. Anselm's key assumption is the principle that necessary existence is a condition that overrides all others when it comes to grading individual offices as to greatness. In other words, he assumes that

(A) $\qquad$ An individual office that is necessarily occupied, i.e. that belongs to *NE*, is greater than any other that does not.

(A') $\qquad$ There is an individual office that enjoys necessary existence.[17]

From (A) and (A') it immediately follows that

(B) $\qquad$ Necessary existence is a requisite of *H*.

Here is the proof:

---

[17] Anselm himself seems to have considered this auxiliary fact too obvious to argue for.

St. Anselm's ontological arguments

i)	$\forall x\, [[H_{wt} \leq x] \supset [x = H_{wt}]]$	H is maximal greatness
ii)	$\forall z\, \forall y\, [[\neg[NE\ y] \wedge [NE\ z]] \supset [y \leq z]]$	assumption (A)
iii)	$\exists x\, [NE\ x]$	additional assumption (A')
iv)	$[NE\ g]$	$\exists$-elimination (g/x), iii)
v)	$\forall y\, [[\neg[NE\ y] \wedge [NE\ g]] \supset [y \leq g]]$	$\forall$-elimination (g/z), ii)
vi)	$\neg[NE\ H_{wt}]$	assumption of an indirect proof
vii)	$[\neg[NE\ H_{wt}] \wedge [NE\ g]]$	$\wedge$-introduction, iv) and vi)
viii)	$H_{wt} \leq g$	$\forall$-elimination (H_{wt}/y) + modus ponens, v)
ix)	$g = H_{wt}$	$\forall$-elimination (g/x), i)
x)	$[NE\ H_{wt}]$	substitution of identicals, iv), which contradicts vi), hence
xi)	$\neg\neg[NE\ H_{wt}] = [NE\ H_{wt}]$	

Types: $x, y, z \to \iota_{\tau\omega}$; $g/\iota_{\tau\omega}$; $H/(\iota_{\tau\omega})_{\tau\omega}$; $NE/(o\iota_{\tau\omega})$: the class of necessarily occupied individual offices.

To show that (A') is valid, Tichý defines a simple necessarily occupied individual office L in the following way. In every $\langle w, t\rangle$-pair there are offices that are occupied. One of them is the lowliest, the least great. (For instance, it may be the office of the only individual that instantiates only trivial properties like being identical with itself, being of the same mass as itself, etc.). We now stipulate that the individual that occupies the lowliest office in $\langle w, t\rangle$ is the holder of L.

From (B), however, it cannot be inferred that the occupant of H necessarily exists. We would have on our hands an instance of the invalid schema (*). We need to show that

(C) H is occupied.

Anselm is obviously aware of the importance of this assumption. In Chapter IV of his Monologion he offers a demonstration of the validity of (C). He does so in two steps. First he argues that some individual offices are surpassed by no others, they enjoy *maximal* greatness. In other words, he argues that there are maximal individual offices *transcendent* to all the others in their greatness. Second, he argues that there cannot be more than one such office. If there were two such maximally great offices, then they would be great in virtue of different criteria. But then one might conceive of still a greater thing-to-be that satisfies both the criteria. I am not going to question the conclusiveness of these two arguments, in particular the former. Anselm was undeniably aware that (C) is indispensable in his proof, and he evidently accepted the plausibility of (C).

Once we accept (B) and (C), the existence of God cannot be consistently denied, because the argument is of the valid form (**):

Necessary existence is a requisite of H.
H is occupied.
———————————————
The holder of H, i.e. God, necessarily exists.

Here is the formal proof:

St. Anselm's ontological arguments

i)	$[^0Req\ NE\ H]$	assumption
ii)	$[^0Exist_{wt}\ H]$	assumption
iii)	$\forall w \forall t\ [[^0Exist_{wt}\ H] \supset [^0True_{wt}\ \lambda w\lambda t\ [NE\ H_{wt}]]]$	Definition 3
iv)	$[[^0Exist_{wt}\ H] \supset [^0True_{wt}\ \lambda w\lambda t\ [NE\ H_{wt}]]]$	$\forall E$
v)	$[^0True_{wt}\ \lambda w\lambda t\ [NE\ H_{wt}]]$	modus ponens ii), iv)
vi)	$[NE\ H_{wt}]$	by definition of *True*

Since *NE* is the class of offices occupied in all $\langle w, t \rangle$-pairs, and since the holder of *H* is *God* according to Anselm's key assumption (G), we have proved that

$$\forall w \forall t\ [NE\ God].$$

Applying the definition of existence, we have proved that

$$\forall w \forall t\ \exists x\ [x = God_{wt}].$$

In other words, *God*'s existence is an *analytical fact*. God exists necessarily, hence also actually.

Remark. It is not clear whether Anselm should be understood as allowing trans-world comparisons between individual offices. Thus the question arises whether H_{wt} is supposed to be the individual office that surpasses all the other offices in the *actual-world* order, or rather the office whose greatness *in some possible world* surpasses all other offices in *any* world. David Lewis in (1970) argued that the validity of the Proslogion II argument depends on the correct answer to this question. It is readily seen, however, that the validity of the above Proslogion III argument is immune against these doubts.

Anselm's contemporary Gaunilo attempted to cast doubts on Anselm's proof in his famous "In Behalf of the Fool, and Anselm: Reply". In par. 6 he argues that by applying a completely parallel line of reasoning one can prove the existence of a perfect island. Again, the argument in Chapter III is immune to this objection. To see why, consider H^i, the second degree office occupiable by an *island*-office such that a greater *island*-office cannot be conceived. We have seen that in order to infer (B), i.e., that necessary existence is a requisite of *H*, from (A), the auxiliary assumption (A') is necessary. By analogy, in order to prove (B^i)—that necessary existence is a requisite of H^i—one must first prove that there is an *island*-office enjoying necessary existence. But there is *no* such *island*-office, because if there were a necessarily occupied island-office, then in every world *w* at any time *t* there would have to be at least one island. But this is untenable, for there is nothing impossible about a world that is at some time void of islands. Thus necessary existence is not a requisite of H^i.

The logic of St. Anselm's argument is impeccable. While one may quibble with his premises, Anselm combines them in such a way that he who admits their validity cannot but assent to Anselm's conclusions. Anselm has, therefore, overcome much of the gap between faith and understanding; for with the help of Anselm's techniques, one can defend that knowledge.

Anselm's argument is logically valid. Did Anselm prove the existence of God? The answer depends on whether the argument is also sound, i.e., whether his premises are plausible. There are two assumptions that might be impugnable.

First, one can doubt the argumentation in favour of the assumption (C). Is there really an upper bound in the order of 'things-to-be'? One can cast doubts at the assumption that there are *maximal* individual offices transcendent to all the others in their greatness and ask why we couldn't conceive always of a still greater office. Anselm obviously takes it for granted that though one *can* conceive of greater and greater things-to-be, there are maximal things transcendent in their greatness to any conceivable thing-to-be. Whether one is content with this is a matter of his/her philosophical datum.

Second, and perhaps more serious objection concerns the assumption (A). Is it plausible to assume that the office with necessary existence understood as occupancy in *all* possible worlds at *all* times is *eo ipso* greater than any other office? To this issue Tichý says:

> Excellence ... is *rare*. The greater an office, the more exacting it is to its occupants, hence the harder it is for individuals to become its occupants. (Tichý 1979, p. 418, 2004, p. 370)

For instance, the first man to run 100 meters in less than 9 seconds is greater office (from the athletics point of view) than the first man to run 100 meters in less than 10 seconds. For this reason the former is occupied *less frequently* than the latter. Recall the necessarily occupied lowliest office L. Tichý says

> Imagine that the office of the rottenest apple core in the Chicago rubbish dump is currently the lowliest of all actually occupied offices. Then the apple core that fills that office also fills L. Would anyone in his right mind insist that the apple core occupies an office that is greater than any office occupied by John Paul II?" (ibid.)

Tichý then shows that even a weaker variant of (A) that does not imply that necessary existence is *all by itself* sufficient to make an office superior to any office that is conceivably vacant, namely

(A'') For every office that does not instantiate necessary existence there is a greater one that enjoys necessary existence

does not solve the problem. Though (A'') and (C) are still strong enough to yield Anselm's conclusion, (A'') is no more plausible than (A) is. To show why, consider again the office of the first man to run 100 meters in less than 9 seconds. Call this office *Runner*. It is currently vacant. In order to utilize (A''), we should now increase its greatness by bestowing the attribute of necessary existence. Since the office is vacant, no individual has the capacities to hold the office. It is a *properly partial* function. In order to make this function total, we must stipulate its values in those $\langle w, t\rangle$-pairs where there are none. Let an individual a be the assigned value in a particular $\langle w, t\rangle$ at which *Runner* lacks a value. We obtain another office *Runner'*. But *Runner'* is not greater than *Runner*. Just opposite. Among the requisites of *Runner* there is a property of running 100 meters in less than 9 seconds. However, this property is not contained in the essence of *Runner'*. In the interest of necessary existence we lose greatness. Since there are no good candidates, *Runner'* is occupied by lower-quality individuals.

The essence of a necessarily occupied office is minimal, because necessary analytical existence works *against* greatness. The greater (more important) office, the more difficult for an individual it is to occupy it; thus an office that is occupied in all worlds and times must have a poor essence containing only trivial requisites. Take, for instance, omniscience. Since any individual is possibly ignorant of this or that fact, omniscience cannot be a requisite of an office occupied in all worlds and times. What makes the holder of the divine God-office so noteworthy is that the *office* he holds requires so much of its holders. But it is this very same fact that makes it conceivable that the office is actually vacant.

Propositions and truth show a closely analogous inverse dependence. The more commonly the proposition is true, that is the fewer possible worlds it excludes, the less informative it is. Necessary proposition that takes value true in all worlds and times says nothing informative about the world and is thus from this point of view worthless. Tichý concludes his paper by

> The analogy is, in fact, closer than it might seem. For an individual office has necessary existence if and only if the proposition that the office is occupied is true in all worlds at all times. Thus if God enjoyed necessary existence, then the proposition that God exists would be a tautology. It is hard to believe, and definitely unacceptable to those concerned, that the faithful should differ from an atheist in subscribing to a tautology. (1979, p. 420, 2004, p. 372)

When I say that analytically true sentences are uninformative, I do not mean that they do not convey any *analytic* information. In Duží (2010) I analyse the difference between *empirical* information about the word and analytic information. The classical theory of semantic information (ESI), as formulated by Bar-Hillel and Carnap in 1952, does not give a satisfactory account of the problem of what information, if any, analytically and/or logically true sentences have to offer. According to ESI, analytically true sentences lack informational content, and any two analytically equivalent sentences convey the same piece of information. This problem is connected with Cohen and Nagel's paradox of inference: Since the conclusion of a valid argument is contained in the premises, it fails to provide any novel information. Again, ESI does not give a satisfactory account of the paradox. I propose a solution based on the distinction between empirical information and analytic information. Declarative sentences are informative due to their meanings. I construe meanings as structured hyperintensions, modelled in Transparent Intensional Logic as constructions. As demonstrated in this paper, constructions are abstract, algorithmically structured procedures whose constituents are sub-procedures. My main thesis is that constructions are the vehicles of information. Hence, although analytically true sentences provide no empirical information about the state of the world, they convey analytic information, in the shape of constructions prescribing how to arrive at the truths in question. Moreover, even though analytically equivalent sentences have equal empirical content, their analytic content may be different. Finally, though the empirical content of the conclusion of a valid argument is contained in the premises, its analytic content may be different from the analytic content of the premises and thus convey a new piece of information.

Similarly, ascription of analytically necessary existence does not convey empirical information; it says nothing informative about the state of the world. However, its analytic content is, of course, valuable.

In order to avoid misconception, I wish to remark that this is not to say that the existence of such a perfect divine being is not *desirable*. And for a believer it is undeniably necessary existence. Only that God's necessary existence cannot be of *logico-analytical* character, that is occupancy in all possible worlds at all times. If 'metaphysical' has any sense then we might perhaps say that the existence of God is metaphysically necessary. Hence to say that "God exists in all possible universes", constrains the range of possible universes whereas the statement, "All bachelors are unmarried," does not. While the latter statement says nothing informative about the world, the former says something quite informative inasmuch as it excludes the possibility that the world is godless.

Acknowledgements This work has been supported by the Grant Agency of the Czech Republic, project No 401/10/0792, "Temporal aspects of knowledge and information". I am grateful to anonymous referees for their valuable comments that improved the quality of the paper.

References

St. Anselm: *Proslogium; Monologium.* Translated From The Latin By Sidney Norton Deane, B. A. Chicago: The Open Court Publishing Company, 1903, reprinted 1926.
   In Halsall, Paul (ed.), 'Internet Medieval Sourcebook', Fordham University Center for Medieval Studies, [http://www.fordham.edu/halsall/sbook.html], last modified December 2006.
   [http://www.fordham.edu/halsall/basis/anselm-proslogium.html]
Charlesworth, M.J. (1965): St. Anselm's Proslogion with 'A Reply on Behalf of the Fool' by Gaunilo and 'The Author's Reply to Gaunilo'. London: Oxford University Press.
Church, A. (1941): *The calculi of lambda conversion.* Annals of Mathematical Studies. Princeton: Princeton University Press.
Cresswell, M.J. (1985): *Structured meanings.* Cambridge: MIT Press.
Duží, M. (2007): Properties on the edge. In *The World of Language and the World Beyond Language: A Festschrift for Pavel Cmorej*, eds. T. Marvan, and M. Zouhar, 42-68. Bratislava: Department of Philosophy, Slovak Academy of Sciences.
Duží, M., Jespersen B., Materna P. (2010): *Procedural Semantics for Hyperintensional Logic; Foundations and Applications of Transparent Intensional Logic.* Series Logic, Epistemology and the Unity of Science. Berlin: Springer.
Duží, M. (2010): The paradox of inference and the non-triviality of analytic information. *Journal of Philosophical Logic*, 2010, vol. 39, No. 5, pp. 473-510.
Frege, G. (1892): Über Sinn und Bedeutung. *Zeitschrift für Philosophie und philosophische Kritik* 100: 25-50.
Hájek, P. (1996): Magari and others on Gödel's ontological proof. In *Logic and algebra.* Edited by Ursini Aldo and Agliani Paolo. New York: Dekker, pp. 125-136.
Hájek, P. (2002): A new small emendation of Gödel ontological proof. *Studia Logica* 71: 149-164.
Jespersen, B. 2005. Explicit intensionalisation, anti-actualism, and how Smith's murderer might not have murdered Smith. *Dialectica* 59: 285-314.
Johnson-Laird, P.N. 1977. Procedural semantics. *Cognition* 5: 189-214.
Jowers, D. (1999): Anselm's Proslogion: One Simple Proof? *Quodlibet Journal*, vol. 1, No. 4.
King, J.C. (2001): Structured propositions. http://plato.stanford.edu/entries/propositions-structured/, version as of 8 August 2001.
Lewis, D. (1970): Anselm and Actuality, *Noûs*, vol. 4, No. 2, pp. 175-188.
Materna, P. and M. Duží (2005): The Parmenides principle. *Philosophia* 32: 155-180.
Moschovakis, Y.N. (1994): Sense and denotation as algorithm and value. In *Lecture Notes in Logic*, eds. J. Väänänen and J. Oikkonen, vol. 2, 210-249. Berlin: Springer.
Moschovakis, Y.N. (2006): A logical calculus of meaning and synonymy. *Linguistics and Philosophy* 29: 27-89.
Tichý, P. (1979): Existence and God. *Journal of Philosophy* 76: 403-420. Reprinted in (Tichý 2004: 353-372).
Tichý, P. (1988): *The Foundations of Frege's Logic.* Berlin, New York: De Gruyter.
Tichý, P. (2004): *Collected Papers in Logic and Philosophy*, eds. V. Svoboda, B. Jespersen, C. Cheyne. Prague: Filosofia, Czech Academy of Sciences, and Dunedin: University of Otago Press.

Ambiguities in natural language and ontological proofs

Marie Duží

1. Introduction

In natural language we encounter many features of *ambiguity*, where one term/expression has more than one meaning. A logical analysis of such a piece of natural language should translate each of its unambiguous meanings into logically perfect notation. Frege's Begriffsschrift was the first major attempt in modern logic to create such a notation (though he primarily intended it for mathematical language).[1] There are various origins and various manifestations of ambiguity, not least cases bearing on quantifier scopes, like "Every boy dances with one girl". Another sort of example is "John loves his wife, and so does Peter", which is ambiguous between Peter loving John's wife and Peter loving his own wife, because it is ambiguous which property 'so' picks up.[2] A third, and perhaps less-noticed, sort of ambiguity is pivoted on *topic* and *focus* articulation of a sentence. For instance, "John only introduced Bill to Sue", to use Hajičová's example,[3] lends itself to two different kinds of construal: "John did not introduce other people to Sue except for Bill" and "The only person Bill was introduced to by John was Sue". There are two sentences whose semantics, logical properties and consequences only partially overlap. The fourth sort of ambiguity is pivoted on *de dicto* vs. *de re* way in which a constituent of a sentence is conceptualised. Put it in another way, this sort of ambiguity concerns *intensional* vs. *extensional* reading of a sentence. For instance, the sentence "God is omnipotent" can be read in two different ways. On its extensional reading, that is "God (whoever this being is) has the property of

---

[1] See (Frege, 1884).
[2] See (Neale, 2004), and also (Duží & Jespersen, to appear).
[3] See (Hajičová, 2008).

being omnipotent", the sentence presupposes that there be a unique God. If it is not so then the sentence has *no truth value*. Thus the extensional variant of the sentence is *empirical*. We cannot logically prove that there is God. The intensional variant is to be understood like this: "Omnipotence is among the requisites of God". On this reading the sentence is *analytically true*.

Topic-focus, *de dicto/de re* and intensional/extensional ambiguity have much in common, and in this paper I will deal with ambiguities of this kind. I am going to show that these ambiguities also crop up in the ontological proofs of the existence of God and I intend to illustrate how these proofs (with the exception of St. Anselm's arguments of Proslogion III)[4] are flawed by not respecting these ambiguities.

Based on an analysis of topic-focus articulation, in Duží (2009a) I proposed a solution to the almost hundred-year old dispute over Strawsonian vs. Russellian definite descriptions.[5] The point of departure of this solution is that sentences of the form "The F is a G" are ambiguous. Their ambiguity is not rooted in a shift of meaning of the definite description 'the F'. Rather, the ambiguity stems from different topic-focus articulations of such sentences. Russell and Strawson took themselves to be at loggerheads; whereas, in fact, they spoke at cross purposes. The received view still tends to be that there is room for at most one of the two positions, since they are deemed incompatible. And they are, of course, incompatible – *if* they must explain the same set of data. But they should not, in my view. One theory is excellent at explaining one set of data, but poor at explaining the data that the other theory is excellent at explaining; and *vice versa*. My novel contribution advances the research into definite descriptions by pointing out how progress has been hampered by a false dilemma and *how to move beyond that dilemma*. The point is this. If 'the F' is the topic phrase then this description occurs with *de re* supposition and Strawson's analysis appears to be what is wanted. On this reading the sentence *presupposes* the existence of the descriptum of 'the F'. The other option is 'G' occurring as topic and 'the F' as focus. This reading corresponds to Donnellan's *attributive* use of 'the F' and the description occurs with *de dicto*

---

[4] For the analysis of St. Anselm's arguments see Duží (2011).
[5] See, for instance, (Donnellan, 1966); (Fintel, 2004); (Neale 1990); (Russell, 1905, 1957); (Strawson 1950, 1964).

supposition. On this reading the Russellian analysis gets the truth-conditions of the sentence right. The existence of a unique *F* is merely entailed.

Ancillary to my analysis is a *general analytic schema* of sentences coming with a presupposition. This analysis makes use of a definition of the '*if-then-else*' connective known from programming languages. A broadly accepted view of the semantic nature of this connective is that it is a so-called non-strict function that does not comply with the principle of compositionality. However, the semantic nature of the connective is contested among computer scientists. I showed — and this is also a novel contribution of mine — that there is no cogent reason for embracing a non-strict definition and context-dependent meaning, *provided* a higher-order logic making it possible to operate on hyperintensions is applied. The framework of Tichý's Transparent Intensional Logic (TIL) possesses sufficient expressive power, and will figure as a background theory throughout my exposition in this paper.[6]

Tichý's TIL was developed simultaneously with Montague's Intensional Logic, IL.[7] The technical tools of disambiguation will be familiar from IL, with two exceptions. One is that we λ-bind separate variables $w, w_1, \ldots, w_n$ ranging over possible worlds and $t, t_1, \ldots, t_n$ ranging over times. This dual binding is tantamount to *explicit intensionalization and temporalization*. The other exception is that *functional application* is the logic both of extensionalization of intensions (functions from possible worlds) and of predication.[8] Application is symbolized by square brackets, '[...]'. Intensions are extensionalized by applying them to worlds and times, as in [[*Intension w*] *t*], abbreviated by subscripted terms for world and time variables: *Intension*$_{wt}$ is the extension of the generic intension *Intension* at $\langle w, t \rangle$. Thus, for instance, the extensionalization of a property yields a set (possibly an empty one), and the extensionalization of a proposition yields a truth-value (or no value at all). A general objection to Montague's IL is that it fails to accommodate *hyperintensionality*, as indeed any formal logic interpreted set-theoretically is bound to unless a domain of primitive hyperintensions is added to the frame. Any theory of natural-language analysis needs a hyperintensional (preferably procedural) semantics in order to crack the hard nuts of natural language semantics. In global terms,

---

[6] For details on TIL see, in particular, (Duží et al., 2010a); (Tichý, 1988, 2004).
[7] For a detailed critical comparison of TIL and Montague's IL, see (Duží et al., 2010a, § 2.4.3);
[8] For details, see (Jespersen, 2008).

without procedural semantics TIL is an anti-contextualist (i.e., transparent), explicitly intensional modification of IL. With procedural semantics, TIL rises above the model-theoretic paradigm and joins instead the paradigm of hyperintensional logic and structured meanings.

The structure of this chapter is as follows. Section 2 is an introduction to TIL. I introduce the semantic and logical foundations of TIL here. Sections 3 and 4 contain the main results of this study. In Section 3 I propose a solution to the dispute over Strawsonian vs. Russellian definite descriptions. Section 4 introduces the problem of ambiguities stemming from different topic-focus articulation and I present here a solution. Moreover I present generalization of the method of topic-focus disambiguation to sentences containing not only definite descriptions but also general terms occurring with different suppositions. To this end I make use of the strict analysis of the *if-then-else* function that is defined in paragraph 4.1. Section 5 presents a common fault that can be found in ontological proofs of God's existence, with the exception of Anselm's argument of Proslogion III, where St. Anselm carefully avoids this mistake. Finally, Section 6 summarizes the results.

2. Foundations of TIL

TIL is an overarching semantic theory for all sorts of discourse, whether colloquial, scientific, mathematical or logical. The theory is a *procedural* (as opposed to denotational) one, according to which sense is an abstract, extra-linguistic procedure detailing what operations to apply to what procedural constituents to arrive at the product (if any) of the procedure. Such procedures are rigorously defined as TIL *constructions*. The semantics is tailored to the hardest case, as constituted by hyperintensional contexts, and generalized from there to simpler intensional and extensional contexts. This entirely anti-contextual and compositional semantics is, to the best of my knowledge, the only one that deals with all kinds of context in a uniform way. Thus we can characterize TIL as an extensional logic of hyperintensions.[9] The sense of an empirical sentence is an algorithmically structured *construction* of the proposition denoted by the sentence. The denoted proposition is a flat, or unstructured, mapping with domain in a

---

[9] For the most recent application, see (Duží & Jespersen, fothcoming).

logical space of possible worlds. Our motive for working 'top-down' has to do with anti-contextualism: any given unambiguous term or expression (even one involving indexicals or anaphoric pronouns) expresses the same construction as its sense whatever sort of context the term or expression is embedded within. And the meaning of an expression determines the respective denoted entity (if any), but not vice versa. The denoted entities are (possibly 0-ary) functions understood as set-theoretical mappings. Thus we strictly distinguish between a procedure (construction) and its product (here, a constructed function), and between a function and its value. What makes TIL suitable for the job of disambiguation is the fact that the theory construes the semantic properties of the sense and denotation relations as remaining invariant across different sorts of linguistic contexts.[10] Thus logical analysis disambiguates ambiguous expressions in such a way that an ambiguous expression is furnished with more than one context-invariant meaning that is TIL construction. However, *logical* analysis cannot dictate *which* disambiguation is the intended one. It falls to *pragmatics* to select the intended one.

The context-invariant semantics of TIL is obtained by universalizing Frege's reference-shifting semantics custom-made for 'indirect' contexts.[11] The upshot is that it becomes trivially true that all contexts are transparent, in the sense that pairs of terms that are co-denoting outside an indirect context remain co-denoting inside an indirect context and vice versa. In particular, definite descriptions that only contingently describe the same individual never qualify as co-denoting.[12] Our term for the extra-semantic, factual relation of contingently describing the same entity is *'reference'*, whereas *'denotation'* stands for the intra-semantic, pre-factual relation between two words that pick out the same entity at the same world/time-pairs.

The syntax of TIL is Church's (higher-order) typed λ-calculus, but with the all-important difference that the syntax has been assigned a *procedural* (as opposed to denotational) semantics. Thus, abstraction transforms into the molecular procedure of forming a function, application into the molecular procedure of applying a function to an argument, and variables into atomic procedures for arriving at their values. Furthermore, TIL constructions

---

[10] *Indexicals* being the only exception: while the sense of an indexical remains constant, its denotation varies in keeping with its contextual embedding. See (Duží et al., 2010a, § 3.4).
[11] See (Frege, 1892).
[12] See Definition 7.

represent our interpretation of Frege's notion of *Sinn* (with the exception that constructions are not truth-bearers; instead some present either truth-values or truth-conditions) and are kindred to Church's notion of *concept*. Constructions are linguistic senses as well as modes of presentation of objects and are our hyperintensions. While the Frege-Church connection makes it obvious that constructions are not formulae, it is crucial to emphasize that constructions are not functions(-in-extension), either. They might be explicated as Church's 'functions-in-intension', but we do not use the term 'function-in-intension', because Church did no define it (he only characterized functions-in-intension as rules for presenting functions-in-extension). Rather, technically speaking, some constructions are modes of presentation of functions, including 0-place functions such as individuals and truth-values, and the rest are modes of presentation of other constructions. Thus, with constructions of constructions, constructions of functions, functions, and functional values in our stratified ontology, we need to keep track of the traffic between multiple logical strata. The ramified type hierarchy does just that. What is important about this traffic is, first of all, that constructions may themselves figure as functional arguments or values. Thus we consequently need constructions of one order higher in order to present those being arguments or values of functions. With both hyperintensions and possible-world intensions in its ontology, TIL has no trouble assigning either hyperintensions or intensions to variables as their values. However, the technical challenge of operating on constructions requires two (occasionally three) interrelated, non-standard devices. The first is *Trivialization*, which is an atomic construction, whose only constituent part is itself. The second is the function *Sub* (for 'substitution'). (The third is the function *Tr* (for 'Trivialization'), which takes an object to its Trivialization.) We say that Trivialization is *used* to *mention* other constructions.[13] The point of mentioning a construction is to make it, rather than what it presents, a functional argument. Hence for a construction to be mentioned is for it to be Trivialized; in this way the context is raised up to a hyperintensional level.

---

[13] The use/mention distinction normally applies only to *words*; in TIL it applies to the *meanings* of words (i.e., constructions). See (Duží, et al., 2010a, §2.6). In theory, a construction may be mentioned by another construction than Trivialization; but in this chapter we limit ourselves to Trivialization.

Our neo-Fregean semantic schema, which applies to all contexts, is this triangulation:

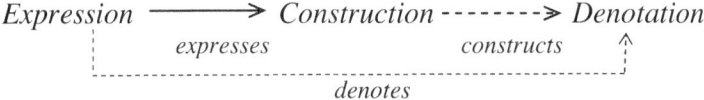

The most important relation in this schema is between an expression and its meaning, i.e., a construction. Once *constructions* have been defined, we can logically examine them; we can investigate *a priori* what (if anything) a construction constructs and what is entailed by it. Thus meanings (i.e. constructions) are semantically primary, denotations secondary, because an expression denotes an object (if any) *via* its meaning that is a construction *expressed* by the expression. Once a construction is explicitly given as a result of logical analysis, the entity (if any) it constructs is already implicitly given. As a limiting case, the logical analysis may reveal that the construction fails to construct anything by being *improper*.

In order to put our framework on a more solid ground, we now present particular definitions. First we set out the definitions of *first-order types* (regimented by a simple type theory), *constructions*, and *higher-order types* (regimented by a ramified type hierarchy), which taken together form the nucleus of TIL, accompanied by some auxiliary definitions.

The type of first-order objects includes all objects that are not constructions. Therefore, it includes not only the standard objects of individuals, truth-values, sets, etc., but also functions defined on possible worlds (i.e., the intensions germane to possible-world semantics). Sets, for their part, are always characteristic functions and insofar extensional entities. But the domain of a set may be typed over higher-order objects, in which case the relevant set is itself a higher-order object. Similarly for other functions, including relations, with domain or range in constructions. That is, whenever constructions are involved, we find ourselves in the ramified type hierarchy. The definition of the ramified hierarchy of types decomposes into three parts: firstly, simple types of order 1; secondly, constructions of order n; thirdly, types of order $n + 1$.

Definition 1 (*types of order 1*). Let B be a *base*, where a base is a collection of pair-wise disjoint, non-empty sets. Then:
(i) Every member of B is an elementary *type of order 1 over B*.
(ii) Let $\alpha, \beta_1, ..., \beta_m$ ($m > 0$) be types of order 1 over B. Then the collection $(\alpha \beta_1 ... \beta_m)$ of all m-ary partial mappings from $\beta_1 \times ... \times \beta_m$ into α is a functional *type of order 1 over B*.
(iii) Nothing is a *type of order 1 over B* unless it so follows from (i) and (ii).

Definition 2 (*construction*)
(i) The *Variable x* is a *construction* that constructs an object X of the respective type dependently on a valuation v; x v-constructs X.
(ii) *Trivialization*: Where X is an object whatsoever (an extension, an intension or a *construction*), ^0X is the *construction Trivialization*. It constructs X without any change.
(iii) The *Composition* $[X\ Y_1...Y_m]$ is the following *construction*. If X v-*constructs* a function f of a type $(\alpha\beta_1...\beta_m)$, and $Y_1, ..., Y_m$ v-*construct* entities $B_1, ..., B_m$ of types $\beta_1, ..., \beta_m$, respectively, then the *Composition* $[X\ Y_1...Y_m]$ v-*constructs* the value (an entity, if any, of type α) of f on the tuple-argument $\langle B_1, ..., B_m \rangle$. Otherwise the *Composition* $[X\ Y_1...Y_m]$ does not v-*construct* anything and so is v-*improper*.
(iv) The *Closure* $[\lambda x_1...x_m\ Y]$ is the following *construction*. Let $x_1, x_2, ..., x_m$ be pair-wise distinct variables v-constructing entities of types $\beta_1, ..., \beta_m$ and Y a construction v-constructing an α-entity. Then $[\lambda x_1 ... x_m\ Y]$ is the *construction* λ-*Closure* (or *Closure*). It v-*constructs* the following function f of the type $(\alpha\beta_1...\beta_m)$. Let $v(B_1/x_1,...,B_m/x_m)$ be a valuation identical with v at least up to assigning objects $B_1/\beta_1, ..., B_m/\beta_m$ to variables $x_1, ..., x_m$. If Y is $v(B_1/x_1,...,B_m/x_m)$-improper (see iii), then f is undefined on the argument $\langle B_1, ..., B_m \rangle$. Otherwise the value of f on $\langle B_1, ..., B_m \rangle$ is the α-entity $v(B_1/x_1,...,B_m/x_m)$-constructed by Y.
(v) The *Single Execution* ^1X is the *construction* that either v-constructs the entity v-constructed by X or, if X v-constructs nothing, is v-*improper* (yielding nothing relative to v).

(vi) The *Double Execution* ^2X is the following *construction*. Where X is any entity, the *Double Execution* ^2X is *v-improper* (yielding nothing relative to *v*) if X is not itself a construction, or if X does not *v*-construct a construction, or if X *v*-constructs a *v*-improper construction. Otherwise, let X *v*-construct a construction Y and Y *v*-construct an entity Z: then ^2X *v*-constructs Z.

(vii) Nothing is a *construction*, unless it so follows from (i) through (vi).

Definition 3 (*ramified hierarchy of types*)
T_1 (*types of order 1*). See Definition 1.
C_n (*constructions of order n*)
  i) Let *x* be a variable ranging over a type of order *n*. Then *x* is a *construction of order n over B*.
  ii) Let *X* be a member of a type of order *n*. Then ^0X, ^1X, ^2X are *constructions of order n over B*.
  iii) Let $X, X_1,..., X_m$ ($m > 0$) be constructions of order *n* over *B*. Then $[X X_1... X_m]$ is a *construction of order n over B*.
  iv) Let $x_1,...x_m$, X ($m > 0$) be constructions of order *n* over *B*. Then $[\lambda x_1...x_m X]$ is a *construction of order n over B*.
  v) Nothing is a *construction of order n over B* unless it so follows from C_n (i)-(iv).

T_{n+1} (*types of order n + 1*). Let $*_n$ be the collection of all constructions of order *n* over *B*. Then
  i) $*_n$ and every type of order *n* are *types of order n + 1*.
  ii) If $m > 0$ and $\alpha, \beta_1,...,\beta_m$ are types of order $n + 1$ over *B*, then $(\alpha\ \beta_1 ... \beta_m)$ (see T_1 ii)) is a *type of order n + 1 over B*.
  iii) Nothing is a *type of order n + 1 over B* unless it so follows from T_{n+1} (i) and (ii).

Remark. For the purposes of natural-language analysis, we are currently assuming the following base of ground types, which is part of the ontological commitments of TIL:
  ο: the set of truth-values {**T, F**};
  ι: the set of individuals (the universe of discourse);
  τ: the set of real numbers (doubling as discrete times);
  ω: the set of logically possible worlds (the logical space).

Empirical languages incorporate an element of *contingency*, because they denote *empirical conditions* that may or may not be satisfied at some world/time pair of evaluation. Non-empirical languages (in particular the language of mathematics) have no need for an additional category of expressions for empirical conditions. We model these empirical conditions as *possible-world intensions*. They are entities of type $(\beta\omega)$: mappings from possible worlds to an arbitrary type β. The type β is frequently the type of the *chronology* of α-objects, i.e., a mapping of type $(\alpha\tau)$. Thus α-intensions are frequently functions of type $((\alpha\tau)\omega)$, abbreviated as '$\alpha_{\tau\omega}$'. *Extensional entities* are entities of a type α where $\alpha \neq (\beta\omega)$ for any type β.

Examples of frequently used intensions are: *propositions* of type $o_{\tau\omega}$, *properties of individuals* of type $(o\iota)_{\tau\omega}$, binary *relations-in-intension* between individuals of type $(o\iota\iota)_{\tau\omega}$, *individual offices/roles* of type $\iota_{\tau\omega}$. Our *explicit intensionalization* and *temporalization* enables us to encode constructions of possible-world intensions, by means of terms for possible-world variables and times, directly in the logical syntax. Where variable w ranges over possible worlds (type ω) and t over times (type τ), the following logical form essentially characterizes the logical syntax of any empirical language: $\lambda w \lambda t [...w....t...]$. Where α is the type of the object v-constructed by $[...w....t...]$, by abstracting over the values of variables w and t we construct a function from worlds to a partial function from times to α, that is a function of type $((\alpha\tau)\omega)$, or '$\alpha_{\tau\omega}$' for short.

Logical objects like *truth-functions* and *quantifiers* are extensional: $\wedge$ (conjunction), $\vee$ (disjunction) and $\supset$ (implication) of type (ooo), and $\neg$ (negation) of type (oo). The *quantifiers* $\forall^{\alpha}$, $\exists^{\alpha}$ are type-theoretically polymorphous functions of type $(o(o\alpha))$, for an arbitrary type α, defined as follows. The *universal quantifier* $\forall^{\alpha}$ is a function that associates a class A of α-elements with **T** if A contains all elements of the type α, otherwise with **F**. The *existential quantifier* $\exists^{\alpha}$ is a function that associates a class A of α-elements with **T** if A is a non-empty class, otherwise with **F**. Another logical object we need is a *partial* polymorphic function *Singularizer* I^{α} of type $(\alpha(o\alpha))$. A singularizer is a function that associates a singleton S with the only member of S, and is otherwise (i.e. if S is an empty set or a multi-element set) undefined.

Below all type indications will be provided outside the formulae in order not to clutter the notation. Furthermore, 'X/α' means that an object X

is (a member) of type α. '$X \to_v \alpha$' means that the type of the object v-constructed by X is α. We write '$X \to \alpha$' if what is v-constructed does not depend on a valuation v. This holds throughout: $w \to_v \omega$ and $t \to_v \tau$. If $C \to_v \alpha_{\tau\omega}$ then the frequently used Composition $[[C\ w]\ t]$, which is the intensional descent (a.k.a. extensionalization) of the α-intension v-constructed by C, will be encoded as 'C_{wt}'. When using constructions of truth-functions, we often omit Trivialisation and use infix notation to conform to standard notation in the interest of better readability. Also when using constructions of identities of α-entities, $=_\alpha/(o\alpha\alpha)$, we omit Trivialization, the type subscript, and use infix notion when no confusion can arise. For instance, instead of

$$[^0 \supset [^0=_\iota a\ b]\ [^0=_{((o\tau)\omega)} \lambda w \lambda t\ [P_{wt}\ a]\ \lambda w \lambda t\ [P_{wt}\ b]]]$$

where $=_\iota/(o\iota\iota)$ is the identity of individuals and $=_{((o\tau)\omega)}/(oo_{\tau\omega}o_{\tau\omega})$ the identity of propositions; a, b constructing objects of type ι, P objects of type $(o\iota)_{\tau\omega}$, we write

$$[[a = b] \supset [\lambda w \lambda t\ [P_{wt}\ a] = \lambda w \lambda t\ [P_{wt}\ b]]]$$

We invariably furnish expressions with procedural structured meanings, which are explicated as TIL constructions. The analysis of an unambiguous sentence thus consists in discovering the logical construction encoded by a given sentence. The *TIL method of analysis* consists of three steps:

1. *Type-theoretical analysis*, i.e., assigning types to the objects that receive mention in the analysed sentence.
2. *Type-theoretical synthesis*, i.e., combining the constructions of the objects *ad* (1) in order to construct the proposition of type $o_{\tau\omega}$ denoted by the whole sentence.
3. *Type-theoretical checking*, i.e. checking whether the proposed analysans is type-theoretically coherent.

To illustrate the method, let us analyse the sentence

(A)   "The baptism site of Jesus is Bethany beyond the Jordan."

Ad 1. The sentence talks about the baptism site, Jesus and Bethany beyond the Jordan. Thus we have:

Baptism_site_of/$(\iota\iota)_{\tau\omega}$: an empirical function assigning to an individual another individual, viz. the baptism site; *Jesus*/ι; *Bethany(_beyond_the_ Jordan)*/ι.

Ad 2 and *3*. Now we have to compose the constructions of the objects *ad 1* so that to construct the proposition denoted by the whole sentence, and respect type-theoretical constraints. Here is how.

First, the definite description 'the baptism site of Jesus' does not denote a particular individual; rather, it denotes an individual role of type $\iota_{\tau\omega}$. Jesus could have been baptised anywhere else or nowhere. The only testimony that Jesus had been baptised is bible:

"Then Jesus came from Galilee to John at the Jordan to be baptised by him."
(Matthew 3:13)

Moreover, that at this very spot history was made was only recently discovered after becoming lost for centuries.

To construct this role, we first extensionalise the intension *Baptism_site_of* by composing it with w, $[^0 Baptism\_site\_of\ w] \to ((\iota\iota)\tau)$, and t, $[[^0 Baptism\_site\_of\ w]\ t] \to (\iota\iota)$, or $^0 Baptism\_site\_of_{wt} \to (\iota\iota)$ for short. Applying this function to *Jesus*/ι we obtain another individual: $[^0 Baptism\_site\_of_{wt}\ ^0 Jesus] \to \iota$. Finally by abstracting over the values of variables w and t we construct the role/office:

$$\lambda w \lambda t\ [^0 Baptism\_site\_of_{wt}\ ^0 Jesus] \to \iota_{\tau\omega}$$

Our sentence claims that this office is occupied by *Bethany*. Thus we must extensionalise the above office again to obtain an individual and apply the identity function to this individual and *Bethany*: $[[^0 Baptism\_site\_of_{wt}\ ^0 Jesus] = {}^0 Bethany]$. Since the sentence is empirical (it might have been otherwise), we again abstract over the values of w, t to obtain the proposition:

(A*) $\lambda w \lambda t\ [[^0 Baptism\_site\_of_{wt}\ ^0 Jesus] = {}^0 Bethany]$

Gloss: (A*) is the meaning expressed by the sentence (A). Hence the sentence encodes an instruction how in any possible world w at any time t to evaluate its truth-conditions. Read this instruction like this: in *any* possible world (λw), at *any* time (λt), apply the function *Baptism_site_of*$_{wt}$ to *Jesus* to obtain the particular site and check whether this spot is identical with Bethany. This is exactly what has happened as the letters of authentication testify: "The overwhelming biblical, archaeological, and historical evidence has led many religious leaders throughout the world to recognize this site as the authentic site of Jesus' baptism."[14]

---

[14] See http://www.baptismsite.com/index.php/authentication.html

3. Definite descriptions: Strawsonian or Russellian?

Now I am going to propose a solution to the well-known Strawson-Russell standoff. In other words, I am going to analyse the phenomena of presupposition and entailment connected with using definite descriptions with supposition *de dicto* or *de re*, and I will show how the topic-focus distinction determines which of the two cases applies.

Before presenting a summary of the *de dicto/de re* distinction, let me briefly introduce three kinds of context in which a construction can occur. They are characterized as follows:

i) *hyperintensional contexts*: the kind of context in which a construction is not used to *v*-construct an object; rather, it is itself *mentioned* as a functional argument (though a hyperintension of one order higher needs to be used to mention this lower-order construction);
ii) *intensional contexts*: this is a context generated by a construction that is *used* to present a *function* (mapping, possibly of 0-arity) without presenting a particular value of the function; moreover, the construction does not occur within another hyperintensional context, because a higher-order context is dominant over a lower one;
iii) *extensional contexts*: a construction is *used* to produce a particular *value* of the *v*-constructed function at a given argument; moreover, the construction does not occur within another intensional or hyperintensional context.

Using a construction of an intension either with de dicto or de re supposition is closely connected with the intensional or extensional occurrence of a constituent. Thus the *de dicto / de re* distinction can be briefly characterized like this. The distinction concerns constructions that construct intensions. The schema of such a construction is

$$\lambda w \lambda t\ [\ldots w \ldots t \ldots].$$

Now if a construction C occurs in the Composition $[\ldots w \ldots t \ldots]$ intensionally, then we say that C occurs with *de dicto* supposition, if C occurs in this Composition extensionally, then C occurs with *de re* supposition.

Examples. Consider, for instance,

(1) "The Pope is a German"

(2) "Joseph Ratzinger became the Pope on April 19, 2005".

Sentence (1) expresses the construction

(1') $\lambda w \lambda t \, [^0German_{wt} \, ^0Pope_{wt}]$

whereas (2) expresses

(2') $\lambda w \lambda t \, [^0Past_t \, \lambda c \, \exists t'[[c \, t'] \wedge [^0Become_{wt'} \, ^0Ratzinger \, ^0Pope]] \, ^0April19]$.

Types: $German/(o\iota)_{\tau\omega}$; $Pope/\iota_{\tau\omega}$; $Past/(o(o(o\tau))(o\tau))_\tau$; $Become/(o\iota_{\tau\omega})_{\tau\omega}$; $Ratzinger/\iota$; $April19/(o\tau)$; $c \rightarrow (o\tau)$; $t, t' \rightarrow \tau$.

The Trivialization $^0Pope \rightarrow \iota_{\tau\omega}$ occurs *extensionally* in $[^0German_{wt} \, ^0Pope_{wt}]$, because it is used to v-construct the value of an ι-office. Thus ^0Pope occurs with *de re* supposition in (1'), as only the value v-constructed by $[^0German_{wt} \, ^0Pope_{wt}]$ matters, the other values being irrelevant. On the other hand, in (2') ^0Pope occurs *intensionally*. The constituent ^0Pope is used to construct an ι-office rather than a particular value. The whole papal office matters in the truth-conditions of the proposition constructed by (2') rather than just a particular value. Thus ^0Pope occurs with *de dicto* supposition in (2'). Thus for (1) the two principles *de re* are valid. If Ratzinger is the Pope, then from (1) we may validly infer that Ratzinger is a German, whereas we cannot validly infer from (2) that Ratzinger became Ratzinger. Moreover, (1) not only implies but even presupposes that the Pope should exist, unlike (2).

3.1 Topic-focus ambiguity

When used in a communicative act, a sentence communicates something (the focus F) about something (the topic T). Thus the schematic structure of a sentence is $F(T)$. The topic T of a sentence S is often associated with a presupposition P of S such that P is entailed both by S and *non-S*. On the other hand, the clause in the focus usually occasions a mere entailment of some P by S. To give an example, consider the sentence "Our defeat was caused by John".[15] There are two possible readings of this sentence.

Taken one way, the sentence is about our defeat, conveying the snippet of information that it was caused by John. In such a situation the sentence is

---

[15] This and some other examples were taken from Hajičová (2008).

associated with the presupposition that we were defeated. Indeed, the negated form of the sentence, "Our defeat was not caused by John", also implies that we were defeated. Thus 'our defeat' is the topic and 'was caused by John' the focus clause.

Taken the other way, the sentence is about the topic John, ascribing to him the property that he caused our defeat (focus). Now the scenario of truly asserting the negated sentence can be, for instance, the following. Though it is true that John has a reputation for being rather a bad player, Paul was in excellent shape and so we won. Or, another scenario is thinkable. We were defeated, only not because of John but because the whole team performed badly. Hence, our being defeated is not presupposed by this reading, it is only entailed.

Schematically, if $\models$ is the relation of entailment, then the logical difference between a mere entailment and a presupposition is this:

P is a *presupposition* of *S*:   (*S* $\models$ *P*) and (*non-S* $\models$ *P*)

Corollary: If *P* is not true, then *neither S nor non-S* is true. Hence, *S* has no truth-value.

P is only *entailed* by *S*:

(*S* $\models$ *P*) and neither *(non-S $\models$ P)* nor *(non-S $\models$ non-P)*

Corollary: If *S* is not true, then we cannot deduce anything about the truth-value of *P*.

More precisely, the entailment relation obtains between hyper-propositions *P*, *S*; i.e., the *meaning* of *P* is analytically entailed or presupposed by the *meaning* of *S*. Thus

$\models/((o*_n*_n)$ is defined as follows. Let C^S, C^P be constructions assigned to sentences *S*, *P*, respectively, as their meanings. Then *S* entails *P*

$(C^S \models C^P)$ iff the following holds:[16]

$$\forall w \forall t \, [[^0 True_{wt} \, C^S] \supset [^0 True_{wt} \, C^P]]$$

Since we work with properly *partial* functions, we need to apply the propositional property $True/(o o_{\tau\omega})_{\tau\omega}$, which returns **T** for those $\langle w, t \rangle$-pairs at which the argument proposition is true, and **F** in all the remaining cases.

---

[16] For the general definition of entailment and the difference between analytical and logical entailment, see (Duží 2010).

There are two other propositional properties: *False* and *Undef*, both of type $(oo_{\tau\omega})_{\tau\omega}$. The three properties are defined as follows. Let P be a propositional construction ($P/*_n \to o_{\tau\omega}$). Then:

$[^0True_{wt}\, P]$ *v*-constructs the truth-value **T** iff
$\qquad P_{wt}$ *v*-constructs **T**, otherwise **F**.
$[^0False_{wt}\, P]$ *v*-constructs the truth-value **T** iff
$\qquad [\neg P_{wt}]$ *v*-constructs **T**, otherwise **F**.
$[^0Undef_{wt}\, P]$ *v*-constructs the truth-value **T** iff
$\qquad [\neg[^0True_{wt}\, P] \wedge \neg[^0False_{wt}\, P]]$ *v*-constructs **T**, otherwise **F**.

Thus we have:

$$\neg[^0Undef_{wt}\, P] = [[^0True_{wt}\, P] \vee [^0False_{wt}\, P]]$$
$$\neg[^0True_{wt}\, P] = [[^0False_{wt}\, P] \vee [^0Undef_{wt}\, P]]$$
$$\neg[^0False_{wt}\, P] = [[^0True_{wt}\, P] \vee [^0Undef_{wt}\, P]]$$

Hence, though we work with truth-value gaps, we do not work with a third truth-value, and our logic is in this weak sense bivalent.

3.2 The King of France revisited

To illustrate the topic-focus ambiguity, I will now briefly summarise my proposed solution of 100 years' dispute over Russellian vs. Strawsonian definite descriptions.[17] To this end I will use the notoriously known sentence "The King of France is bald".

On its perhaps most natural reading the sentence predicates the property of being bald (the focus) of the individual (if any) that is the present King of France (the topic). Yet there is another, albeit less natural reading of the sentence. Imagine that the sentence is uttered in a situation when we are talking about baldness, and somebody asks "Who is bald?" The answer might be "Well, among those who are bald there is the present King of France". If you got such an answer, you would most probably protest, "This cannot be true, for there is no King of France now". On such a reading the sentence is about baldness (topic) claiming that this property is instantiated, among others, by the King of France (focus).

---

[17] See Duží (2009a, and also 2012).

Since there are no rigorous grammatical rules in English to distinguish between the two variants, the input of our *logical* analysis is the result of a *linguistic* analysis, where the topic and focus of a sentence are made explicit.[18] Thus I will mark the topic clause in italics. The two readings of the above sentence are:

(S) *"The King of France* is bald"
(R) "The King of France is *bald*"

I am going to show that the two readings are not equivalent, because they have different truth-conditions. (S) is the variant with Strawsonian truth-conditions and (R) the variant that complies with Russellian truth-conditions.

The analysis of (S) is obtained in the very similar way as described in Section 2:

$$\lambda w \lambda t \, [^0Bald_{wt} \, \lambda w \lambda t \, [^0King\_of_{wt} \, ^0France]_{wt}]$$

Types: $Bald/(o\iota)_{\tau\omega}$; $King\_of/(\iota\iota)_{\tau\omega}$; $France/\iota$; $\lambda w \lambda t \, [^0King\_of_{wt} \, ^0France] \rightarrow \iota_{\tau\omega}$: the individual office of the King of France.

The meaning of 'the King of France', *viz.* $\lambda w \lambda t \, [^0King\_of_{wt} \, ^0France]$, occurs in (S) with *de re* supposition, because the object of predication is the unique *value* (in a $\langle w, t \rangle$-pair of evaluation) of the office rather than the office itself.[19] The following *two de re principles* are satisfied: the principle of *existential presupposition* and the principle of *substitution of co-referential* expressions. Thus the following arguments are valid (though not sound):

<u>*The King of France* is/is not bald</u>
The King of France exists

---

[18] For instance, the Prague linguistic school created The Prague Dependency Treebank for the Czech language, which contains a large amount of Czech texts with complex and interlink annotation on different levels. The tectogrammatical representation contains the semantic structure of sentences with topic-focus annotators. For details, see *http://ufal.mff.cuni.cz/pdt2.0/*.

[19] For details on *de dicto* vs. *de re* supposition, see (Duží et al., 2010a), esp. §§ 1.5.2 and 2.6.2, and also (Duží 2004).

The King of France is bald
The King of France is Louis XVI
Louis XVI is bald

Here are the proofs.
(a) *existential presupposition*:

First, existence is here a property of an individual *office* rather than of some non-existing individual (whatever it might mean for an individual not to exist). Thus we have $Exist/(o\iota_{\tau\omega})_{\tau\omega}$. To prove the validity of the first argument, we define $Exist/(o\iota_{\tau\omega})_{\tau\omega}$ as the property of an office's being occupied at a given world/time pair:

$$^0Exist =_{of} \lambda w \lambda t\, \lambda c\, [^0\exists \lambda x\, [x =_i c_{wt}]], \text{ i.e. } [^0Exist_{wt}\, c] =_o [^0\exists \lambda x\, [x =_i c_{wt}]]$$

Types: $\exists/(o(o\iota))$: the class of non-empty classes of individuals; $c \rightarrow_v \iota_{\tau\omega}$; $x \rightarrow_v \iota$; $=_o/(ooo)$: the identity of truth-values; $=_{of}/(o(o\iota_{\tau\omega})_{\tau\omega}(o\iota_{\tau\omega})_{\tau\omega})$: the identity of properties of individual offices; $=_i/(o\iota\iota)$: the identity of individuals, $x \rightarrow_v \iota$.

Now let $Empty/(o(o\iota))$ be the singleton containing the empty set of individuals, and $Improper/(o*_1)_{\tau\omega}$ the property of constructions of being *v*-improper at a given $\langle w, t\rangle$-pair, $Louis/\iota$, the other types as above. Then at any $\langle w, t\rangle$-pair the following proof steps are truth-preserving:

1) $(\neg)[^0Bald_{wt}\, \lambda w \lambda t\, [^0King\_of_{wt}\, ^0France]_{wt}]$ assumption
2) $\neg[^0Improper_{wt}\, ^0[\lambda w \lambda t\, [^0King\_of_{wt}\, ^0France]_{wt}]]$ by Def. 2, iii)
3) $\neg[^0Empty\, \lambda x\, [x =_i [\lambda w \lambda t\, [^0King\_of_{wt}\, ^0France]]_{wt}]]$ (2), by Def. 2, iv)
4) $[^0\exists \lambda x\, [x =_i [\lambda w \lambda t\, [^0King\_of_{wt}\, ^0France]]_{wt}]]$ EG
7) $[^0Exist_{wt}\, [\lambda w \lambda t\, [^0King\_of_{wt}\, ^0France]]]$ by def. of *Exist*.

(b) *substitution*:

1) $[^0Bald_{wt}\, \lambda w \lambda t\, [^0King\_of_{wt}\, ^0France]_{wt}]$ assumption
2) $[^0Louis =_i \lambda w \lambda t\, [^0King\_of_{wt}\, ^0France]_{wt}]$ assumption
3) $[^0Bald_{wt}\, ^0Louis]$ substitution of identicals

As explained above, the sentence (R) is not associated with the presupposition that the present King of France exist, because 'the King of France' occurs now in the focus clause. The truth-conditions of the Russellian "The King of France is *bald*" are these:
- True, if among those who are bald there is the King of France

- False, if among those who are bald there is no King of France (either because the present King of France does not exist or because the King of France is not bald).

Thus the two readings (S) and (R) have different truth-conditions, and they are not equivalent, albeit they are co-entailing. The reason is this. Trivially, a valid argument is *truth-preserving from premises to conclusion*. However, due to partiality, the entailment relation may fail to be *falsity-preserving from conclusion to premises*. As a consequence, if A, B are constructions of propositions such that $A \models B$ and $B \models A$, then A, B are not necessarily equivalent in the sense of constructing the same proposition. The propositions they construct may not be identical, though the propositions take the truth-value **T** at exactly the same world/times, because they may differ in such a way that at some $\langle w, t \rangle$-pair(s) one takes the value **F** while the other is undefined. The pair of meanings of (S) and (R) is an example of such co-entailing, yet non-equivalent hyperpropositions. If the value of the proposition constructed by the meaning of (S) is **T** then so is the value of the proposition constructed by the meaning of (R), and *vice versa*. But, for instance, in the actual world now the proposition constructed by (S) has *no truth-value* whereas the proposition constructed by (R) takes value **F**.

Russell argued for his theory in (1905, p. 3):
> The evidence for the above theory is derived from the difficulties which seem unavoidable if we regard denoting phrases as standing for genuine constituents of the propositions in whose verbal expressions they occur. Of the possible theories which admit such constituents the simplest is that of Meinong. This theory regards any grammatically correct denoting phrase as standing for an *object*. Thus 'the present King of France', 'the round square', etc., are supposed to be genuine objects. It is admitted that such objects do not *subsist*, but nevertheless they are supposed to be objects. This is in itself a difficult view; but the chief objection is that such objects, admittedly, are apt to infringe the law of contradiction. It is contended, for example, that the existent present King of France exists, and also does not exist; that the round square is round, and also not round, etc. But this is intolerable; and if any theory can be found to avoid this result, it is surely to be preferred.

We have such a theory at hand, *viz*. TIL. Moreover, TIL makes it possible to avoid the other objections against Russell's analysis as well. Russellian rephrasing of the sentence "The King of France is *bald*" is this:

"There is a unique individual such that he is the King of France and he is bald". This sentence expresses the construction

(R^*) $\lambda w \lambda t \, [^0 \exists \lambda x \, [x =_i [\lambda w \lambda t \, [^0 King\_of_{wt} \, ^0 France]_{wt}] \wedge [^0 Bald_{wt} \, x]]].$ [20]

TIL analysis of the 'Russellian rephrasing' does not deprive 'the King of France' of its meaning. The meaning is invariably, in all contexts, the Closure $\lambda w \lambda t \, [^0 King\_of_{wt} \, ^0 France]$. Thus the second objection to the Russellian analysis is not pertinent here. Moreover, even the third objection is irrelevant, because in (R^*) $\lambda w \lambda t \, [^0 King\_of_{wt} \, ^0 France]$ occurs intensionally unlike in the analysis of (S) where it occurs extensionally.[21] The existential quantifier ∃ applies to *sets* of individuals rather than a particular individual. The proposition constructed by (R^*) is true if the *set* of individuals who are bald contains the individual who occupies the office of King of France, otherwise it is simply false. The truth conditions specified by (R^*) are Russellian. Thus we might be content with (R^*) as an adequate analysis of the Russellian reading (R). Yet we should not be. The reason is this. Russell's analysis has another defect; it does not comply with *Carnap's principle of subject-matter*, which states, roughly, that only those entities that receive mention in a sentence can become constituents of its meaning.[22] In other words, (R^*) is not the literal analysis of the sentence "The King of France is *bald*", because existence and conjunction do not receive mention in the sentence. Russell did avoid the intolerable result that the King of France both does and does not exist, but the price he paid is too high, because his rephrasing of the sentence is too loose a reformulation of it. TIL, as a hyperintensional, typed *partial* λ-calculus, is in a much better position to solve the problem.

From the logical point of view, the two readings differ in the way their respective *negated* form is obtained. Whereas the Stawsonian negated form is "The *King of France* is *not* bald", which obviously lacks a truth-value if

---

[20] Note that in TIL we do not need the construction corresponding to $\forall y \, (Fy \supset x=y)$ specifying the uniqueness of the King of France, because it is inherent in the meaning of 'the King of France'. This holds also in languages like Czech or Polish, which lack grammatical articles. The meaning of descriptions 'the King of France', 'král Francie', 'Król Francji' is a construction of an individual office of type $\iota_{\tau\omega}$ occupied in each $\langle w, t \rangle$-pair by at most one individual.

[21] For the definition of extensional, intensional and hyperintensional occurrence of a construction, see (Duží et al., 2010a, § 2.6).

[22] See (Carnap 1947, §24.2, §26).

the King of France does not exist, the Russellian negated form is "It is not true that the King of France is bald", which is true at those ⟨w, t⟩-pairs where the office is not occupied. Thus in the Strawsonian case the property of not being bald is ascribed to the individual, if any, that occupies the royal office. The meaning of 'the King of France' occurs with *de re* supposition, as we have seen above. On the other hand, in the Russellian case the property of not being true is ascribed to the whole proposition that the King is bald, and thus (the same meaning of) the description 'the King of France' occurs with *de dicto* supposition. Hence we simply ascribe the property of being or not being true to the whole proposition. To this end we apply the propositional property $True/(oo_{\tau\omega})_{\tau\omega}$ defined above. Now the analysis of the sentence (R) is this construction:

(R') $\lambda w \lambda t \, [^0True_{wt} \, \lambda w \lambda t \, [^0Bald_{wt} \, \lambda w \lambda t \, [^0King\_of_{wt} \, ^0France]_{wt}]]$

Neither (R') nor its negation

(R'_neg) $\lambda w \lambda t \, \neg[^0True_{wt} \, \lambda w \lambda t \, [^0Bald_{wt} \, \lambda w \lambda t \, [^0King\_of_{wt} \, ^0France]_{wt}]]$

entail that the King of France exists, which is just as it should be. (R'_neg) constructs the proposition *non-P* that takes the truth-value **T** if the proposition that the King of France is bald takes the value **F** (because the King of France is not bald) or is undefined (because the King of France does not exist).

In summary, *Russell and Strawson* took themselves to be at loggerheads; whereas, in fact, they *spoke at cross purposes*. The received view still tends to be that there is room for at most one of the two positions, since they are *deemed incompatible*. And they are, of course, incompatible – *if* they must explain the same set of data. But *they should not*, in my view. One theory is excellent at explaining one set of data, but poor at explaining the data that the other theory is excellent at explaining; and *vice versa*.

My *novel contribution* advances the research into definite descriptions by pointing out how progress has been hampered by a false dilemma and *how to move beyond that dilemma*.

The sentence "The baptism site of Jesus is Bethany beyond the Jordan" is also ambiguous. We analysed this sentence in Section 2 as expressing the construction

$\lambda w \lambda t \, [\lambda w \lambda t \, [^0Baptism\_site\_of_{wt} \, ^0Jesus]_{wt} = {}^0Bethany]$

or (A*) for short. This analysis corresponds to Strawsonian reading

"*The baptism site of Jesus* is Bethany beyond the Jordan"

with 'the baptism site of Jesus' as the topic clause. On this reading the sentence *presupposes* that the Jesus' baptism site exists, and consequently that Jesus had been baptised.

The other variant is Russellian:

"The baptism site of Jesus is *Bethany beyond the Jordan*"

or in a bit more disambiguating way

"*Bethany beyond the Jordan* is the baptism site of Jesus"

This variant could be used for instance in such a situation when one asks "What is so interesting about the Bethany beyond the Jordan, why so many pilgrims come here"? The answer would be, "You don't know? This spot is the baptism site of Jesus!" But somebody might protest, "Oh no, it is not true, Jesus had not been baptised", or another objection might be "No, it is not true, Bethany is not the site of Jesus' baptism, it happened somewhere else".

Hence now the sentence *merely entails* that the site of Jesus' baptism exists. The sentence might be false either because there is no site of Jesus' baptism (that is that Jesus had not been baptised) or because the spot where Jesus had been baptised is located somewhere else (most probably at the river Jordan). The analysis of this second, Russellian variant is this:

(A**) $\lambda w \lambda t\ [^0 True_{wt}\ \lambda w \lambda t\ [^0 Bald_{wt}\ \lambda w \lambda t\ [^0 King\_of_{wt}\ ^0 France]_{wt}]]$

The negated sentence is then analysed as expressing the construction

(A**^{N}) $\lambda w \lambda t\ \neg [^0 True_{wt}\ \lambda w \lambda t\ [^0 Bald_{wt}\ \lambda w \lambda t\ [^0 King\_of_{wt}\ ^0 France]_{wt}]]$

4. Topic-focus ambivalence in general

The same topic-focus ambiguity crops up almost in all sentences, not only those containing desfinite description. Consider the sentence

(B)   "All Apostles of Jesus were Galilean Jews"

Up until now we have utilised the singularity of definite descriptions like 'the King of France', 'the baptism site of Jesus' that denote functions of type $\iota_{\tau\omega}$. If the King of France does not exist in some particular world W at some particular time T, the office is not occupied and the function does not have a value at $\langle W, T \rangle$. Due to the partiality of the office constructed by $\lambda w \lambda t$ [$^0 King\_of_{wt}$ $^0 France$] and the principle of compositionality, the respective analyses construct properly partial propositions associated with some presuppositions, as desired. Now I am going to generalize the topic-focus phenomenon to sentences containing general terms.

To get started, let us analyse the sentence

(B)   "All Apostles of Jesus were Galilean Jews"

There are (at least) two non-equivalent variants:

(B_1)   "*All Apostles of Jesus* were Galilean Jews"

(B_2)   "All Apostles of Jesus were *Galilean Jews*"

(B_1) is connected with the presupposition that there were some Apostles of Jesus and it only entails that Galilean Jews existed, because the negated sentence "*Some Apostles of Jesus* were not Galilean Jews" also entails that there were Apostles of Jesus. On the other hand, (B_2) presupposes that Galilean Jews existed and merely entails that Jesus had some Apostles.

Note however, a classical regimentation of (B_1) or (B_2) in the language of the first-order predicate logic (FOL) cannot distinguish the two variants, and moreover, in FOL we cannot get the truth-conditions of such a sentence that comes attached with a presupposition right. The FOL regimentation would be a formula like

$$\forall x \, [JA(x) \supset GJ(x)]\text{''},$$

with the intended interpretation assigning to the predicate *JA* the set of Jesus' Apostles and the set of Galilean Jews to *GJ*.[23] But this formula is true under every interpretation assigning an empty set of individuals to the predicate *JA* and false under interpretation assigning a non-empty set to *JA* and an empty set to *GJ*. In other words, FOL does not make it possible to render the truth-conditions of a sentence equipped with a presupposition, because FOL is a logic of *total* functions. We need to apply a richer logical system in order to express the instructions how to evaluate the truth-conditions of (B_1) and (B_2) in the above described way.

Let us start with (B_1). By reformulating the specification of the truth-conditions of (B_1) in a rather technical jargon of English, we get

---

[23] There is another flaw in this analysis, of course: *which* sets would it be?

"*If* Jesus had Apostles *then* check whether all of them were Galilean Jews, *else* fail to produce a truth-value."

We now analyse the particular constituents of this instruction. As always, we start with assigning types to the objects that receive mention in the sentence: $Apostle\_of/((o\iota)\iota)_{\tau\omega}$: an empirical function that dependently on states-of-affairs assigns to an individual a set of individuals, its aposteles; $Jesus/\iota$; $Galilean/((o\iota)_{\tau\omega}(o\iota)_{\tau\omega})$: a property modifiers, that is a function that assigns to a property of individual (here of being a Jew) another property of individuals (here being a Galilean Jew);[24] $\exists/(o(o\iota))$; $All/((o(o\iota))(o\iota))$: a restricted general quantifier that assigns to a given set the set of all its supersets; [$^0Galilean\ ^0Jew$] → $(o\iota)_{\tau\omega}$.

The presupposition that Jesus had Apostles receives the analysis[25]

$$\lambda w\lambda t\ [^0\exists\lambda x\ [[^0Apostle\_of_{wt}\ ^0Jesus]\ x]].$$

Now the literal analysis of the sentence "All Jesus's Apostles were Galilean Jews" on its *neutral* reading (that is, without existential presupposition), is best obtained by using the restricted quantifier *All*, because using a general quantifier $\forall$ would involve implication that does not receive mention in the sentence. Composing the quantifier with the set of Jesus's Apostles at the world/time pair of evaluation, [$^0All\ [^0Apostle\_of_{wt}\ ^0Jesus]$], we obtain the set of all supersets of Jesus' Apostles in w at t. The sentence claims that the population of those who are Galilean Jews, is one such superset:

$$\lambda w\lambda t\ [[^0All\ [^0Apostle\_of_{wt}\ ^0Jesus]]\ [^0Galilean\ ^0Jew]_{wt}].$$

The schematic analysis of sentence (B_1) on its topic-like reading that comes with the presupposition that Jesus had Apostles translates into this procedure:

(B^*_1) $\lambda w\lambda t$ [**If** $\exists x\ [[^0Apostle\_of_{wt}\ ^0Jesus]\ x]$ **then** $[[^0All\ [^0Apostle\_of_{wt}\ ^0Jesus]]\ [^0Galilean\ ^0Jew]_{wt}]$ **else Fail**.

The schema of analysis of (B_2) is obtained in a similar way:

---

[24] A detailed analysis of property modifiers can be found in Duží, et.al. (2010, §4.4).
[25] We now ignore the past tense. This simplification is irrelevant for the analysis of the problem of ambiguity. For details on the analysis of sentences in past, present and future tense, see, however, Duží, et.al. (2010, §2.5.2).

(B*₂) $\lambda w \lambda t$ [**If** $\exists x$ [[^{0}*Galilean* ^{0}*Jew*]$_{wt}$ x] **then** [[^{0}*All* [^{0}*Apostle_of*$_{wt}$ ^{0}*Jesus*]] [^{0}*Galilean* ^{0}*Jew*]$_{wt}$] **else Fail**.

To finish the analysis, we must define the *if-then-else-fail* function. This I am going to do in the next paragraph.

4.1 The *if-then-else* function

In a programming language the *if-then-else* conditional forces a program to perform different actions depending on whether the specified *condition* evaluates true or else false. This is always achieved by *selectively* altering the control flow based on the specified condition. However, an analysis in terms of material implication, ⊃, or even 'exclusive *or*' as known from propositional logic, is not adequate. The reason is this. Since propositional logic is strictly compositional, *both* the 'then clause' *and* the 'else clause' are always evaluated. For instance, it might seem that the instruction expressed by "The only number *n* such that if 5 = 5 then *n* equals 1, else *n* equals the result of 1 divided by 0" would receive the analysis

[^{0}I$^\tau$ λn [[[^{0}5=^{0}5] ⊃ [n=^{0}1]] ∧ [¬[^{0}5=^{0}5] ⊃ [n=[^{0}Div ^{0}1 ^{0}0]]]]]

Types: I$^\tau$/(τ($o\tau$)); $n \rightarrow_v \tau$; 0, 1, 5/τ; *Div*/($\tau\tau\tau$): the division function.

But the output of the above procedure should be the number 1 because the *else* clause is never executed. However, due to the strict principle of compositionality that TIL observes, the above analysis fails to produce anything, the construction being improper. For, the Composition [^{0}*Div* ^{0}1 ^{0}0] does not produce anything: it is improper because the division function takes no value at the argument ⟨1, 0⟩. Thus [n = [^{0}*Div* ^{0}1 ^{0}0]] is *v*-improper for any valuation *v*, because the identity relation = does not receive a second argument, and so any other Composition containing the improper Composition [^{0}*Div* ^{0}1 ^{0}0] as a constituent also comes out *v*-improper. The underlying principle is that partiality is being strictly propagated up. This is the reason why the *if-then-else* connective is often said to denote a *non-strict* function not complying with the principle of compositionality.

However, as I wish to argue, there is no cogent reason to settle for non-compositionality. I suggest applying a mechanism known in computer science as *lazy evaluation*. The *procedural* semantics of TIL operates smoothly even at the hyperintensional level of constructions. Thus it enables us to specify a definition of *if-then-else* that meets the compositionality constraint. The analysis of

"If P then C, else D"

reveals a procedure that decomposes into two phases. First, on the basis of the condition P, select one of C, D as the procedure to be executed. Second, execute the selected procedure. The first phase, *viz.* selection, is realized by the Composition

$$[^0I^* \lambda c \, [[P \supset [c = {}^0C]] \wedge [\neg P \supset [c = {}^0D]]]]$$

Types: $P \rightarrow_v o$ (the condition of the choice between the execution of C or of D); $C, D/*_n$; variable $c \rightarrow_v *_n$; $I^*/(*_n(o*_n))$: the singularizer.

The product of the Composition $[[P \supset [c={}^0C]] \wedge [\neg P \supset [c={}^0D]]]$ is v-constructed like this. If P v-constructs **T** then the variable c receives as its value the *construction C*, and if P v-constructs **F** then the variable c receives the *construction D* as its value. In either case the set v-constructed by $\lambda c \, [[P \supset [c={}^0C]] \wedge [\neg P \supset [c={}^0D]]]$ is a singleton whose element is a construction. Applying I^* to this set returns as its value the only member of the set, i.e. either C or D.[26]

Second, the chosen construction c is executed. To execute it we apply Double Execution; see Def. 2, vi). As a result, the schematic analysis of "If P then C, else D" turns out to be

(*) $\quad\quad\quad {}^2[^0I^* \lambda c \, [[P \supset [c={}^0C]] \wedge [\neg P \supset [c={}^0D]]]]$

Note that the evaluation of the first phase does not involve the execution of either of C or D. In this phase these constructions figure only as arguments of other functions. In other words, we operate at hyperintensional level. The second phase of execution turns the level down to intensional or extensional one. Thus we define:

Definition 4 (*If-then-else, if-then-else-fail*). Let $p/*_n \rightarrow_v o$; $c, d_1, d_2/*_{n+1} \rightarrow *_n$; ${}^2c, {}^2d_1, {}^2d_2 \rightarrow_v \alpha$. Then the polymorphic functions *if-then-else* and *if-then-else-fail* of types $(\alpha o *_n *_n)$, $(\alpha o *_n)$, respectively, are defined as follows:

^{0}*If-then-else* $= \lambda p \, d_1 \, d_2 \, {}^2[{}^0I^* \lambda c \, [[p \supset [c = d_1]] \wedge [\neg p \supset [c = d_2]]]]$

---

[26] In case P is v-improper the singleton is empty and *no* construction is selected to be executed so the execution aborts.

^{0}*If-then-else-fail* = $\lambda p\ d_1\ ^2[^0\text{I}^*\ \lambda c\ [p \wedge [c = d_1]]$

By the definition of *If-then-else* the product of this fiction is obtained as follows: If p v-constructs **T**, then the construction C is selected as the value of c. If p v-constructs **F**, then $[p \wedge [c=d_1]]$ v-constructs **F**, hence the class v-constructed by $\lambda c\ [p \wedge [c=d_1]]$ is empty. In this case the singularizer I^* is improper by not producing any value, just as it should be.

Now we are ready to specify the **general analytic schema of an (empirical) sentence S associated with a presupposition P.** In a technical jargon of English the evaluation instruction can be formulated as follows:

At any $\langle w, t \rangle$-pair do this:
if P_{wt} is true then evaluate S_{wt}, else *Fail* (to produce a truth-value).

Let $P/*_n \to o_{\tau\omega}$ be a construction of a presupposition, $S/*_n \to o_{\tau\omega}$ the meaning of the sentence S and $c/*_{n+1} \to_v *_n$ a variable. Then the corresponding TIL construction is this:

$\lambda w \lambda t\ [^0\textit{If-then-else-fail}\ P_{wt}\ ^0S_{wt}] = \lambda w \lambda t\ ^2[^0\text{I}^*\lambda c\ [P_{wt} \wedge [c = {}^0S_{wt}]]]$

Now we are in the position to refine the analyses of (B*$_1$) and (B*$_2$):

(B*$_1$) $\quad \lambda w \lambda t\ ^2[^0\text{I}^*\lambda c\ [\exists x\ [[^0\textit{Apostle\_of}_{wt}\ {}^0\textit{Jesus}]\ x] \supset$
$\qquad [c = {}^0[[^0\textit{All}\ [^0\textit{Apostle\_of}_{wt}\ {}^0\textit{Jesus}]]\ [^0\textit{Galilean}\ {}^0\textit{Jew}]_{wt}]]]]$

(B*$_2$) $\quad \lambda w \lambda t\ ^2[^0\text{I}^*\lambda c\ [\exists x\ [[^0\textit{Galilean}\ {}^0\textit{Jew}]_{wt}\ x] \supset$
$\qquad [c = {}^0[[^0\textit{All}\ [^0\textit{Apostle\_of}_{wt}\ {}^0\textit{Jesus}]]\ [^0\textit{Galilean}\ {}^0\textit{Jew}]_{wt}]]]]$

In the interest of better readability I will use a more standard notation. Hence instead of either "$\lambda w \lambda t\ [^0\textit{If-then-else-fail}\ P_{wt}\ {}^0S_{wt}]$" or "$\lambda w \lambda t\ ^2[^0\text{I}^*\lambda c\ [P_{wt} \supset [c = {}^0S_{wt}]]]$" I will simply write "$\lambda w \lambda t\ [\text{If } P_{wt} \text{ then } S_{wt} \text{ else Fail}]$".

5. A common fault in ontological proofs

At the outset of this paper I mentioned the ambiguity pivoted on *de dicto* and *de re* way in which a constituent of a sentence is conceptualised. We have seen that the topic clause occurs with *de re* supposition, whereas the focus clause with *de dicto* supposition. Put it in another way, this sort of ambiguity concerns *intensional* vs. *extensional* reading of a sentence.

For instance, the argument of Descartes' ontological proof, in its very simple form can be formulated as follows:

> The essence of God-office is formed by all positive perfections.
> Existence is a positive perfection.
> Hence, God exists.

What's wrong here? There are two problems, two flaws.

a) There is a confusion of the *intensional* and *extensional level* of abstraction: Existence is not a property of individuals. Rather, it is a property of the office itself. Thus existence cannot be a requisite of God-office, it is a second degree intension that is ascribable on the *intensional* level. However, requisites of an individual office are properties of individuals that are ascribable on the *extensional* level.

b) Descartes applies an invalid inference rule:

> Existence is a requisite of God's office.
> Hence God has the property of existence.

As we will see now, there is a missing assumption on the occupancy of the office. Yet adding such an assumption makes the proof circular and thus futile.

To explain the second flaw, we need to define and explicate some notions.

Definition 5 (*requisites*) Let X, Y be intensional *constructions* such that $X/*_n \to \alpha_{\tau\omega}$, $Y/*_n \to (o\alpha)_{\tau\omega}$. Then

$$[^0Req\ Y X] = \forall w \forall t\ [[^0Exist_{wt} X] \supset [^0True_{wt} \lambda w \lambda t\ [Y_{wt}\ X_{wt}]]].$$

Gloss *definiendum* as, "Y is a requisite of X", and *definiens* as, "Necessarily, if X is occupied at some $\langle w, t \rangle$ then it is true that whatever occupies X at $\langle w, t \rangle$ has the property Y at this $\langle w, t \rangle$."

Example. Requisites of the American presidential office are individual properties like to be a human being, to be properly elected, to be inaugurated, etc.

The sentence "The King of France is a king" is *ambiguous* between two readings — one necessarily true, the other contingently without a truth-value — as Tichý points out (1979, p. 408; 2004, p. 360). The former is the requisite (i.e., *de dicto*) reading:

$$[^0Req \; ^0King \; \lambda w \lambda t \; [^0King\_of_{wt} \; ^0France]].$$

Types: $King/(o\iota)_{\tau\omega}$; $King\_of/(\iota\iota)_{\tau\omega}$; $France/\iota$. If true, it is necessarily so, regardless of whether or not some $\langle w, t \rangle$ lacks an occupant of $\lambda w \lambda t \; [^0King\_of_{wt} \; ^0France]$.

The other reading is the *de re* reading:

$$\lambda w \lambda t \; [^0King_{wt} \; \lambda w \lambda t \; [^0King\_of_{wt} \; ^0France]_{wt}].$$

If true, it is so only because somebody occupies the King's office constructed by $\lambda w \lambda t \; [^0King\_of_{wt} \; ^0France]$ at $\langle w, t \rangle$ and its occupant is in the extension of *King* at $\langle w, t \rangle$.

When defining a requisite of an *office X*, the antecedent condition on *X* being occupied is required. Otherwise we shall have the following invalid argument on our hands (see Tichý, 1979, pp. 408ff; 2004, pp. 360ff):

(*)
$$\frac{P \text{ is a requisite of office } O}{\text{The occupant of } O \text{ instantiates } P.}$$

This inference pattern is fallacious, for the premise may be true even if *O* is vacant, in which case the conclusion, so far from being true, is vacuous (i.e., lacks a truth value). (*Ibid.*, p. 408, p. 360, resp.)

Applying this invalid inference pattern, we might easily "prove" the existence of the King of France. Here is how:

1) The King of France is a king
1*) $[^0Req \; ^0King \; \lambda w \lambda t \; [^0King\_of_{wt} \; ^0France]]$ (necessarily true, *de dicto*)

2) The current King of France is a king (applying (*))
2*) $\lambda w \lambda t \; [^0King_{wt} \; \lambda w \lambda t \; [^0King\_of_{wt} \; ^0France]_{wt}]$ (contingently true, *de re*)

3) The King of France exists (existential generalization)
3*) $\lambda w \lambda t \; [^0Exist_{wt} \; \lambda w \lambda t \; [^0King\_of_{wt} \; ^0France]]$

The step from (2) to (3) is valid, because in any world w at any time t, the step is truth-preserving. Here is the proof:

2a) $[^0King_{wt} \; \lambda w\lambda t \; [^0King\_of_{wt} \; ^0France]_{wt}]$ assumption

2b) $\lambda w\lambda t \; [^0King\_of_{wt} \; ^0France]_{wt}$ v-proper by Definition of Composition

2c) $\lambda x \; [\lambda w\lambda t \; [^0King\_of_{wt} \; ^0France]_{wt} = x]$ constructs a *non-empty* class (from 2b)

2d) $[^0\exists \lambda x \; [\lambda w\lambda t \; [^0King\_of_{wt} \; ^0France]_{wt} = x]]$ existential generalization

2e) $[^0Exist_{wt} \; \lambda w\lambda t \; [^0King\_of_{wt} \; ^0France]]$ by Definition of *Exist*

However, the step from (1) to (2) is invalid, because it is the step from a *de dicto* reading to the *de re* reading. Whereas the *de re* reading not only entails, but also presupposes the existence of the King of France, the *de dicto* reading is necessarily true regardless whether the King exists.

A valid inference rule can be obtained by adding an extra premise to the effect that the relevant office is occupied:

(**)
$$\frac{P \text{ is a requisite of office } O \qquad \text{Office } O \text{ is occupied}}{\text{The occupant of } O \text{ instantiates } P.}$$

Proof: Let $P/*_n \to (o\alpha)_{\tau\omega}$; $O/*_m \to \beta_{\tau\omega}$.

i) $[^0Req \; P \; O]$ assumption
ii) $[^0Exist_{wt} \; O]$ assumption
iii) $\forall w \forall t \; [[^0Exist_{wt} \; O] \supset [^0True_{wt} \; \lambda w\lambda t \; [P_{wt} \; O_{wt}]]]$ Definition 5
iv) $[[^0Exist_{wt} \; O] \supset [^0True_{wt} \; \lambda w\lambda t \; [P_{wt} \; O_{wt}]]]$ $\forall E$
v) $[^0True_{wt} \; \lambda w\lambda t \; [P_{wt} \; O_{wt}]]$ modus ponens ii), iv)

Now we turn to the definition of essence as a set of requisites. However, this drags type-theoretic complications along, since the requisites of an intension may well be of different types. In order to make the essence homogeneous, we define the essence of an intension as the set of properties that are necessary for an object to satisfy the condition specified by the intension. The reason why the definition of essence can be made homogeneous is because, given an arbitrary intension, there will always be a corresponding property. For instance, the ι-office *the tallest woman* will correspond to the property *being an x such that x is identical to the tallest woman*. Again, for our purposes it is sufficient to define an essence of an office. The polymorphous type of such an *Essence* is $((o(o\alpha)_{\tau\omega})\beta_{\tau\omega})$: given an arbitrary β-office of type $\beta_{\tau\omega}$, *Essence* returns the set of α-properties that are the requisites of this office. Thus we define:

Definition 6 (*essence of an office*)
Let $Z \to_v \beta_{\tau\omega}$; $q \to_v (o\alpha)_{\tau\omega}$; $Req/((o(o\alpha)_{\tau\omega})\beta_{\tau\omega})$. Then
$[^0Essence\ Z] = \lambda q\ [^0Req\ q\ Z]$.

Remark: It is beyond the capacities of human beings to know an intension such as an individual office or its essence. This would amount for knowing *actual infinity*, i.e. an uncountable infinite mapping. Yet we have capacities to know *potential infinity*. The meaning of an expression, such as 'the King of France' is the construction $\lambda w \lambda t\ [^0King\_of_{wt}\ ^0France]$. Its encoding in TIL language of constructions can be viewed as an instruction read as follows:

In *any* possible world (λw), at *any* time (λt) evaluate whether this or that individual satisfies the *condition* of being the King of France ($[^0King\_of_{wt}\ ^0France]$). Thus if one understands the meaning of 'King of France', it suffices to follow the instruction specified by this meaning; which *does not*, however, mean that one is always able to *execute* this instruction and thus to know the holder.

Application of the invalid inference rule (*) is a typical fault that can be found in almost all ontological proofs with the exception of St Anslem's argument presented in Proslogion III. For details and analysis of this argument see Duží (2011).

6. Conclusion

In this paper I brought out the *semantic*, as opposed to pragmatic, character of the ambivalences stemming from topic-focus articulation, pivoted on *de dicto* vs. *de re* supposition and confusing intensional and extensional level of abstraction. I showed that these ambiguities have much in common. In particular, ignoring the intensional vs. extensional context yields many problems.

The procedural semantics of TIL provided rigorous analyses such that sentences differing only in their topic-focus articulation were assigned different constructions producing different propositions (truth-conditions) and having different consequences. I showed that a definite description occurring in the topic of a sentence with *de re* supposition corresponds to the Strawsonian analysis of definite descriptions, while a definite description occurring in the focus with *de dicto* supposition corresponds to the Russellian analysis. While the clause standing in topic position triggers a presupposition, a focus clause usually entails rather than presupposes another proposition. Thus both opponents and proponents of Russell's quantificational analysis of definite descriptions are partly right and partly wrong.

Moreover, the proposed analysis of the Russellian reading does not deprive definite descriptions of their meaning. Just the opposite; 'the F' receives a context-invariant meaning. What is dependent on context is the way this (one and the same) meaning is used. Thus I also demonstrated that Donnellan-style referential and attributive uses of an occurrence of 'the F' do not bring about a shift of meaning of 'the F'. Instead, one and the same context-invariant meaning is a constituent of different procedures that behave in different ways.

The proposed analysis of topic-focus ambivalence was then generalized to sentences containing not only singular clauses like 'the F' but also general clauses like 'John's children', 'all students' in the topic or focus of a sentence. As a result, I proposed a general analytic schema for sentences equipped with a presupposition. This analysis makes use of the definition of the *if-then-else* function that complies with the desirable principle of compositionality. This is also my novel contribution to the old problem of the semantic character of the specification of the *if-then-else* function.

Finally, I illustrated the flaw that can be found in ontological proofs. This flaw is drawn by ignoring the difference between intensional and extensional reading of a sentence.

The moral to be drawn from my contribution is this. Logical analysis disambiguates ambiguous expressions, but cannot dictate *which* disambiguation is the intended one (leaving room for pragmatics here). Yet, our fine-grained method of analysis contributes to language disambiguation by making its hidden features *explicit* and *logically tractable*. In case there are more senses of a sentence we furnish the sentence with different TIL logical forms. Having a formal, fine-grained encoding of linguistic senses at our disposal, we are in a position to automatically infer the relevant consequences.

Acknowledgments

This research was funded by Grant Agency of the Czech Republic Project 401/10/0792 *Temporal Aspects of Knowledge and Information*. Versions of this study were read by the author as an invited talk at the University of Western Australia, Perth, Australia, March 4th, 2011. Portions of this chapter elaborate substantially on points made in (Duží, 2009a, 2009b). I am indebted to Bjørn Jespersen for valuable comments that improved the quality of this study.

References

Carnap, R. (1947). *Meaning and Necessity*, Chicago: Chicago University Press.
Donnellan, K. S., (1966). Reference and definite descriptions, *Philosophical Review*, vol. 77, 281-304.
Duží, M. (2003). Notional Attitudes (On wishing, seeking and finding). *Organon F*, vol. X, No. 3, pp. 237-260, ISSN 1335-0668
Duží, M. (2004). Intensional Logic and the Irreducible Contrast between *de dicto* and *de re*. *ProFil*, vol. 5, No. 1, pp. 1-34, ISSN 1212-9097
Duží, M. (2009a). Strawsonian vs. Russellian definite descriptions. *Organon F*, vol. XVI, No. 4, pp. 587-614, ISSN 1335-0668
Duží, M. (2009b). Topic-focus articulation from the semantic point of view. In: *Computational Linguistics and Intelligent Text Processing*, A. Gelbukh (Ed.), Berlin, Heidelberg: Springer-Verlag LNCS, vol. 5449, 220-232.
Duží, M. (2010). The paradox of inference and the non-triviality of analytic information. *Journal of Philosophical Logic*, vol. 39, No. 5, pp. 473-510. ISSN 0022-3611
Duží M. (2011). St. Anselm's Ontological Arguments. *Polish Journal of Philosophy*, vol. V, No. 1, Spring 2011, pp. 7-37.
Duží, M. (2012): *Resolving Topic-Focus Ambiguities in Natural Language*. In Semantics in Action – Applications and Scenarios. Ed. Muhammad Tanvir Afzal, Croatia: InTech Europe, 2012, pp. 239-266, ISBN 978-953-51-0536-7.
Duží, M & Jespersen, B. (forthcoming). 'Transparent quantification into hyperpropositional contexts *de re*', *Logique et Analyse*, vol. 220, 2012.
Duží, M. & Jespersen, B. (to appear). Procedural isomorphism and restricted beta-reduction. *Logic Journal of the IGPL*.

Duží, M., Jespersen, B. & Materna, P. (2010a): *Procedural Semantics for Hyperintensional Logic*; *Foundations and Applications of Transparent Intensional Logic*. Berlin: Springer, series Logic, Epistemology, and the Unity of Science, vol. 17, 2010, ISBN 978-90-481-8811-6, 550 pp.

Duží, M., Jespersen, B. & Materna, P. (2010b). The *logos* of semantic structure. In: *Philosophy of Language and Linguistics*, vol. 1: The Formal Turn. P. Stalmaszczyk (ed.) Frankfurt: Ontos Verlag, ISBN 978-3-86838-070-5, pp. 85-102.

Fintel, Kai von (2004). Would you believe it? The King of France is Back! (Presuppositions and Truth-Value Intuitions). In: *Descriptions and Beyond*, Reimer, M., Bezuidenhout, A. (eds.), Oxford: Clarendon Press, ISBN 0-19-927051-1, pp. 315 – 341.

Frege, G. (1884). *Die Grundlagen der Arithmetik*, Breslau: W. Koebner.

Frege, G. (1892). Über Sinn und Bedeutung. *Zeitschrift für Philosophie und philosophische Kritik*, vol. 100, pp. 25-50.

Hajičová, E. (2008). What we are talking about and what we are saying about it. In: *Computational Linguistics and Intelligent Text Processing*, A. Gelbukh (Ed.), Berlin, Heidelberg: Springer-Verlag LNCS, vol. 4919, 241-262.

Jespersen, B. (2008). Predication and extensionalization. *Journal of Philosophical Logic*, vol. 37, pp. 479 – 499.

Neale, S., (1990). *Descriptions*. Cambridge: MIT Press Books.

Neale, S., (2004). This, that, and the other. In: *Descriptions and Beyond*, A. Bezuidenhout and M. Reimer (eds.), Oxford: Oxford University Press, pp. 68-182.

Russell, B. (1905). On denoting. *Mind* vol. 14, pp. 479-493.

Russell, B., (1957). Mr. Strawson on referring, *Mind* vol. 66, pp. 385-389.

Strawson, P. F. (1950). On referring, *Mind* vol. 59, pp. 320-334.

Strawson, P. F. (1952). *Introduction to Logical Theory*. London: Methuen.

Strawson, P.F., (1964). Identifying reference and truth-values, *Theoria* vol. 3, pp. 96-118.

Tichý, P. (1979). Existence and God. *Journal of Philosophy* 76: 403-420. Reprinted in (Tichý 2004: 353-372).

Tichý, P. (1988). *The Foundations of Frege's Logic*, Berlin, New York: De Gruyter.

Tichý, P. (2004). *Collected Papers in Logic and Philosophy*, V. Svoboda, B. Jespersen, C. Cheyne (eds.), Prague: Filosofia, Czech Academy of Sciences, and Dunedin: University of Otago Press.